CasebookConnect.com

REGISTER NOW to access the Study Center for:

- Hundreds of practice questions
- Selections from popular study aids
- Progress trackers to save you time
- Tutorial videos

Combine this wealth of resources with an **enhanced ebook** and **outlining tool** and you will **SUCCEED** in law school

Use this unique code to connect your casebook today

Access Code: MASC837793479213

Go to www.casebookconnect.com and redeem your access code to get started.

PLEASE NOTE: Each access code can only be used once. This access code will expire one year after the discontinuation of the corresponding print title and must be redeemed before then. CCH reserves the right to discontinue this program at any time for any business reason. For further details, please see the Casebook Connect End User License Agreement.

PIN9111149079

22064

American Constitutional Law:
Powers and Liberties

ASPEN CASEBOOK SERIES

American Constitutional Law: Powers and Liberties

Fifth Edition

Calvin Massey

Daniel Webster Distinguished Professor of Law
University of New Hampshire School of Law
Professor of Law, Emeritus
University of California
Hastings College of the Law

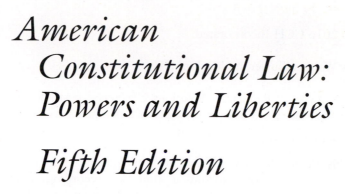 Wolters Kluwer

To contact Customer Service, e-mail customer.service@wolterskluwer.com, call 1-800-234-1660, fax 1-800-901-9075, or mail correspondence to:

Wolters Kluwer
Attn: Order Department
PO Box 990
Frederick, MD 21705

Printed in the United States of America.

2 3 4 5 6 7 8 9 0

ISBN 978-1-4548-6833-0

Library of Congress Cataloging-in-Publication Data

Names: Massey, Calvin R., author. | United States. Constitution.
Title: American constitutional law : powers and liberties / Calvin Massey.
Description: Fifth edition. | New York : Wolters Kluwer, [2016] | Series:
  Aspen casebook series | Includes index.
Identifiers: LCCN 2015041026 | ISBN 9781454868330
Subjects: LCSH: Constitutional law—United States—Cases. | LCGFT: Casebooks
Classification: LCC KF4550 .M269 2016 | DDC 342.73—dc23
LC record available at http://lccn.loc.gov/2015041026

About Wolters Kluwer Legal & Regulatory Solutions U.S.

Wolters Kluwer Legal & Regulatory Solutions U.S. delivers expert content and solutions in the areas of law, corporate compliance, health compliance, reimbursement, and legal education. Its practical solutions help customers successfully navigate the demands of a changing environment to drive their daily activities, enhance decision quality and inspire confident outcomes.

Serving customers worldwide, its legal and regulatory solutions portfolio includes products under the Aspen Publishers, CCH Incorporated, Kluwer Law International, ftwilliam.com and MediRegs names. They are regarded as exceptional and trusted resources for general legal and practice-specific knowledge, compliance and risk management, dynamic workflow solutions, and expert commentary.

For Martha, Ellen, and Seth

Calvin Massey passed away on September 23, 2015. Those who have taught from any of his earlier editions will surely recognize Calvin's thoughtful and diligent work in revising the Fifth Edition. We at Wolters Kluwer are deeply grateful for our long and fruitful collaboration.

Summary of Contents

Contents

1

THE ROLE OF THE COURTS IN CONSTITUTIONAL INTERPRETATION   1

1

Judicial Review and Constitutional Structure   3

2 ≣≣≣ *Doctrines Limiting the Scope of Judicial Review* — 51

II ENFORCING THE CONSTITUTIONAL ALLOCATION OF GOVERNMENT POWER   *127*

3

The Limits of Federal Legislative Power: Judicially or Politically Enforceable Federalism? 135

4 *Limiting the Scope of State Power over Interstate Commerce*   263

5 ≣ *Separation of Powers* — *351*

III ▬ INDIVIDUAL RIGHTS: LIMITS ON THE USE OF GOVERNMENTAL POWER — 451

6 ▬ Due Process — 455

≣ 9 ≣ Free Expression of Ideas 823

10 ═══ *The Religion Clauses* — *1119*

11 State Action and the Power to Enforce Constitutional Rights

12   *The Right to Keep and Bear Arms*   1265

Preface to the Fifth Edition

The tension between comprehensive coverage and concise presentation continues. I have pared down the space allotted to existing cases and removed some cases that have been eclipsed by events in order to make room for new material. I hope that this surgery has been successful. I have tried to allow the justices to speak for themselves, but I have attempted to limit their occasional tendency to engage in polemics. The structure of the book remains largely unchanged.

I am grateful to the many people who have made this edition possible. Thanks go to Lori Wood, the professors who reviewed the Fourth Edition and provided their useful comments, all the adopters of my casebook, and the students who have used my casebook. And thanks also to the justices of the United States Supreme Court, who provide much of the raw material for any Constitutional Law casebook. I have tried to let them speak. But not so much as to overwhelm the student of Constitutional Law, who has quite enough to assimilate and ponder as he or she plows through law school.

Calvin Massey

Deer Isle, Maine
August 2015

Preface to the Fourth Edition

In the interest of brevity I have eliminated some cases, edited others more tightly, and eliminated some extraneous notes and commentary. I have reorganized the materials on the interstate commerce power to provide a more chronological approach. I have also altered the presentation of the materials on free expression, mostly in an attempt to bring more clarity to the content-based categories that are outside of the First Amendment. Significant new principal cases include National Federation of Independent Business v. Sebelius, Snyder v. Phelps, United States v. Stevens, Brown v. Entertainment Merchants Association, and United States v. Alvarez. Other significant cases decided since the prior edition went to press are included as note cases, sometimes with extensive excerpts. This edition is current through October Term 2011.

I continue to be grateful to the many people who make this casebook possible. I thank everyone who wrote me about errors or suggestions for change. I am grateful to all the people at Aspen Publishers who have supported this casebook since its inception. Particular thanks go to Barbara Roth, Barbara Lasoff, and Paul Sobel, each of whom shepherded this edition through the publication process. As always, I appreciate the students who read this book and think about the issues raised in its pages, and I am grateful to the professors who use my book as the springboard for their teaching. I am especially in debt to my wife, Martha Massey, who never complains about the time I devote to this book, and who is a marvelously acute lay critic of Constitutional Law. Of course, I continue to have the utmost respect for those statesmen of the eighteenth century who brought into being the structure of government and charter of liberties we call the Constitution, and to all those who have come afterwards who have preserved our fundamental law for us and our descendants.

Calvin Massey

Concord, New Hampshire
November 2012

Preface to the Third Edition

It continues to be difficult to be concise without being superficial. I have tried to accommodate new cases and more problems by the judicious editing of existing materials. A few note cases have disappeared, and some interstitial commentary has been shortened.

I have reorganized the materials dealing with voting rights as an aspect of equal protection, mostly by separating denial and dilution of the right to vote. I have also reorganized some materials in the discussion of free expression, particularly by separating false statements of fact from such "civility torts" as intentional infliction of emotional distress. I have added a new, and short, Chapter 12—The Right to Keep and Bear Arms—which contains District of Columbia v. Heller and the many questions raised by that decision. This edition is current through the October 2007 term of the Supreme Court. I have included more problems and queries in this edition. I hope that these problems will prove useful to teachers and students, yet still leave plenty of opportunity for individual teachers of constitutional law to employ their own devices and strategies. As with the prior editions, I have attempted to avoid ideological bias in the presentation of constitutional law.

I continue to be grateful to the many people who make this casebook possible. First, I thank the fellow professors who provided suggestions for change or who found errors, especially Mark Weiner, Brannon Denning, and Robert Natelson. Second, I continue to appreciate the people at Aspen Publishers who have supported this casebook since its inception. Third, I appreciate the careful attention of Katy Thompson and the copy editors at Publication Services. Finally, I particularly value the students who read and think about the content of my book and the professors who choose it as the vehicle for their teaching.

Calvin Massey

San Francisco, California
February 2009

Preface to the Second Edition

The second edition of this casebook is intended to be concise, but achieving that goal gets harder as the reach of constitutional law grows ever larger. I have tried to pare materials even as I have included important new cases. This edition is current through the 2003-2004 term of the Supreme Court. I have included more problems and hypothetical issues, but I have continued to give short shrift to academic commentary. This is not so much because I think the academic literature unimportant; it stems from my overall philosophy that my casebook should focus on what actually gets discussed in the constitutional law classrooms of America.

I am grateful to many people for their assistance in connection with this edition. First, I am especially thankful to fellow professors who provided suggestions for change or found errors. Special thanks go to Mike Allen, Brannon Denning, Brian Landsberg, and Randy Lee. I am always delighted to receive comments from students and professors. Please let me know your thoughts. As always, I appreciate the people at Aspen Publishers who make it possible for this book to exist. Special thanks go to Kathy Yoon, Ruth Kwon, and Carol McGeehan. Finally, I particularly appreciate the students who read and think about my book and the professors who choose to use my book as the vehicle for their teaching. I have tried to make this book a teaching vehicle, and I have approached the task of its creation as if I were teaching on paper. I have tried to leave ample room for the individual approaches of constitutional law teachers and have tried to eschew any particular bias in the presentation of constitutional law. I hope I have succeeded.

Calvin Massey

Boston, Massachusetts
February 2005

Preface to the First Edition

This casebook is intended to be concise. Given the breathtaking scope of American constitutional law, this has been no easy task. I have tried to include the material that is actually covered in most survey courses of constitutional law taught in American law schools.

Constitutional law is a political subject, but it is not just politics. Learning constitutional law is a bit like learning a new language. New vocabulary, grammar, and syntax need to be learned in order to speak politics through the vernacular of the law. This is to suggest not that the making of constitutional law is some version of Orwellian "newspeak" but that constitutional law deals with political disagreement in a fashion of its own. A principal objective of this book is to enable the student to master, as thoroughly as is possible in an introductory course, the fundamentals of the language of constitutional law.

Like many legal subjects, constitutional law involves several levels of understanding. At its simplest, there is a prevailing doctrine to be learned. But learning doctrine alone is a superficial undertaking. One needs also to ask why the doctrine is the way it is, to determine whether it is justifiable in terms of the fundamental premises of constitutional law, and to propose alternative ways of expressing our constitutional principles. A survey course not only must ground students in doctrine but must simultaneously challenge them to evaluate doctrine critically. There is a constant tension between these two objectives—description and prescription—and that tension is reflected to some extent in this casebook. If I have emphasized one aspect of these objectives, it is probably doctrine, but that is because I place great faith in my fellow teachers of constitutional law to use their classrooms to spark the creative and critical thinking of their students. I hope that my text has at least planted the seed of critical thought in students; I have not tried to write a casebook that emphasizes theory above all.

The individual teachers will, of course, make their own determination of what materials they choose to cover. If this book is to be used for a single-semester survey course, teachers must decide which portions to omit. I have included as much free expression material as space would permit, but in a single-semester course substantial portions must be pared away. At the beginning of Chapter 9 I have included materials that capture the essential architecture of modern free expression law; beyond that it is for each instructor to choose. If this book is used in a year-long or two-semester survey course, virtually the entire book can be used, although teachers may wish to omit some materials and reorganize others. I have placed the subject of congressional power in the context of section 5 of the Fourteenth Amendment in Chapter 11, but this material could easily be assigned at the end of Chapter 3, which deals with the powers of Congress. I start discussion of the commerce power with United States v. Lopez, but teachers who prefer to teach the commerce clause chronologically could assign the remainder of that section to be read before the *Lopez* material. Other simple choices of reorganization can readily be made. Most of all, I have tried to create a good teaching tool for students and teachers alike.

I have edited cases to be faithful to the original text, but I have omitted internal citations in the cases, renumbered footnotes so that they appear in consecutive numerical order within each chapter of this book, and changed antiquated punctuation to conform to modern usage. Omitted material in cases is indicated by ellipses or brackets, and material added to cases is always within brackets.

Calvin Massey

Boston
January 2001

The Constitution of the United States

We the People of the United States, in Order to form a more perfect Union, establish Justice, insure domestic Tranquility, provide for the common defence, promote the general Welfare, and secure the Blessings of Liberty to ourselves and our Posterity, do ordain and establish this Constitution for the United States of America.

ARTICLE I

Section 1. All legislative Powers herein granted shall be vested in a Congress of the United States which shall consist of a Senate and House of Representatives.

Section 2. [1] The House of Representatives shall be composed of Members chosen every second Year by the People of the several States, and the Electors in each State shall have the Qualifications requisite for Electors of the most numerous Branch of the State Legislature.

[2] No Person shall be a Representative who shall not have attained to the Age of twenty five Years, and been seven Years a Citizen of the United States, and who shall not, when elected, be an Inhabitant of that State in which he shall be chosen.

[3] Representatives and direct Taxes shall be apportioned among the several States which may be included within this Union, according to their respective Numbers, which shall be determined by adding to the whole Number of free Persons, including those bound to Service for a Term of Years, and excluding Indians not taxed, three fifths of all other Persons. The actual Enumeration shall be made within three Years after the first meeting of the Congress of the United States, and within every subsequent Term of ten Years, in such Manner as they shall by Law direct. The Number of Representatives shall not exceed one for every thirty Thousand, but each State shall have at Least One Representative; and until such enumeration shall be made, the State of New

Hampshire shall be entitled to chuse three, Massachusetts eight, Rhode Island and Providence Plantations one, Connecticut five, New York six, New Jersey four, Pennsylvania eight, Delaware one, Maryland six, Virginia ten, North Carolina five, South Carolina five, and Georgia three.

[4] When vacancies happen in the Representation from any State, the Executive Authority thereof shall issue Writs of Election to fill such Vacancies.

[5] The House of Representatives shall chuse their Speaker and other Officers; and shall have the sole Power of Impeachment.

Section 3. [1] The Senate of the United States shall be composed of two Senators from each State, chosen by the Legislature thereof, for six Years; and each Senator shall have one Vote.

[2] Immediately after they shall be assembled in Consequence of the first Election, they shall be divided as equally as may be into three Classes. The Seats of the Senators of the first Class shall be vacated at the Expiration of the second Year, of the second Class at the Expiration of the fourth Year, and of the third Class at the Expiration of the sixth Year, so that one third may be chosen every second Year; and if Vacancies happen by Resignation, or otherwise, during the Recess of the Legislature of any State, the Executive thereof may make temporary Appointments until the next Meeting of the Legislature, which shall then fill such Vacancies.

[3] No Person shall be a Senator who shall not have attained to the Age of thirty Years, and been nine Years a Citizen of the United States, and who shall not, when elected, be an Inhabitant of that State for which he shall be chosen.

[4] The Vice President of the United States shall be President of the Senate, but shall have no Vote, unless they be equally divided.

[5] The Senate shall chuse their other Officers, and also a President pro tempore, in the absence of the Vice President, or when he shall exercise the Office of President of the United States.

[6] The Senate shall have the sole Power to try all Impeachments. When sitting for that Purpose, they shall be on Oath or Affirmation. When the President of the United States is tried, the Chief Justice shall preside: And no Person shall be convicted without the Concurrence of two thirds of the Members present.

[7] Judgment in Cases of Impeachment shall not extend further than to removal from Office, and disqualification to hold and enjoy any Office of honor, Trust or Profit under the United States: but the Party convicted shall nevertheless be liable and subject to Indictment, Trial, judgment and Punishment, according to Law.

Section 4. [1] The Times, Places and Manner of holding Elections for Senators and Representatives, shall be prescribed in each State by the Legislature thereof; but the Congress may at any time by Law make or alter such Regulations, except as to the Places of chusing Senators.

[2] The Congress shall assemble at least once in every Year, and such Meeting shall be on the first Monday in December, unless they shall by Law appoint a different Day.

Section 5. [1] Each House shall be the Judge of the Elections, Returns and Qualifications of its own members, and a Majority of each shall constitute a Quorum to do Business; but a smaller Number may adjourn from day to day, and may be authorized to compel the Attendance of absent members, in such Manner, and under such Penalties as each House may provide.

[2] Each House may determine the Rules of its Proceedings, punish its Members for disorderly Behavior, and, with the Concurrence of two thirds, expel a Member.

[3] Each House shall keep a Journal of its Proceedings, and from time to time publish the same, excepting such Parts as may in their Judgment require Secrecy; and the Yeas and Nays of the Members of either House on any question shall, at the Desire of one fifth of those Present, be entered on the Journal.

[4] Neither House, during the Session of Congress, shall, without the Consent of the other, adjourn for more than three days, nor to any other Place than that in which the two Houses shall be sitting.

Section 6. [1] The Senators and Representatives shall receive a Compensation for their Services, to be ascertained by Law, and paid out of the Treasury of the United States. They shall in all Cases, except Treason, Felony and Breach of the Peace, be privileged from Arrest during their Attendance at the Session of their respective Houses, and in going to and returning from the same; and for any Speech or Debate in either House, they shall not be questioned in any other Place.

[2] No Senator or Representative shall, during the Time for which he was elected, be appointed to any civil Office under the Authority of the United States, which shall have been created, or the Emoluments whereof shall have been encreased during such time; and no Person holding any office under the United States, shall be a Member of either House during his Continuance in Office.

Section 7. [1] All Bills for raising Revenue shall originate in the House of Representatives; but the Senate may propose or concur with Amendments as on other Bills.

[2] Every Bill which shall have passed the House of Representatives and the Senate, shall, before it becomes a Law, be presented to the President of the United States; If he approve he shall sign it, but if not he shall return it, with his Objections to the House in which it shall have originated, who shall enter the Objections at large on their Journal, and proceed to reconsider it. If after such Reconsideration two thirds of that House shall agree to pass the Bill, it shall be sent, together with the Objections, to the other House, by which it shall likewise be reconsidered, and if approved by two thirds of that House, it shall become a Law. But in all such Cases the Votes of both Houses shall be determined by yeas and Nays, and the Names of the Persons voting for and against the Bill shall be entered on the Journal of each House respectively. If any Bill shall not be returned by the President within ten Days (Sundays excepted) after it shall have been presented to him, the Same shall be a Law, in

like Manner as if he had signed it, unless the Congress by their Adjournment prevents its Return, in which Case it shall not be a Law.

[3] Every Order, Resolution, or Vote to which the Concurrence of the Senate and House of Representatives may be necessary (except on a question of Adjournment) shall be presented to the President of the United States; and before the Same shall take Effect, shall be approved by him, or being disapproved by him, shall be repassed by two thirds of the Senate and House of Representatives, according to the Rules and Limitations prescribed in the Case of a Bill.

Section 8. [1] The Congress shall have Power To lay and collect Taxes, Duties, Imposts and Excises, to pay the Debts and provide for the common Defence and general Welfare of the United States; but all Duties, Imposts and Excises shall be uniform throughout the United States;

[2] To borrow money on the credit of the United States;

[3] To regulate Commerce with foreign nations, and among the several States, and with the Indian Tribes;

[4] To establish an uniform Rule of Naturalization, and uniform Laws on the subject of Bankruptcies throughout the United States;

[5] To coin Money, regulate the value thereof, and of foreign Coin, and fix the Standard of Weights and Measures;

[6] To provide the Punishment of counterfeiting the Securities and current Coin of the United States;

[7] To establish Post Offices and post Roads;

[8] To promote the Progress of Science and useful Arts, by securing for limited Times to Authors and Inventors the exclusive Right to their respective Writings and Discoveries;

[9] To constitute Tribunals inferior to the supreme Court;

[10] To define and punish Piracies and Felonies committed on the high Seas, and Offenses against the Law of Nations;

[11] To declare War, grant Letters of Marque and Reprisal, and make Rules concerning Captures on Land and Water;

[12] To raise and support Armies, but no Appropriation of Money to that Use shall be for a longer Term than two Years;

[13] To provide and maintain a Navy;

[14] To make Rules for the Government and Regulation of the land and naval Forces;

[15] To provide for calling forth the Militia to execute the Laws of the Union, suppress Insurrections and repel Invasions;

[16] To provide for organizing, arming, and disciplining, the Militia, and for governing such Part of them as may be employed in the Service of the United States, reserving to the States respectively, the Appointment of the Officers, and the Authority of training the Militia according to the discipline prescribed by Congress;

[17] To exercise exclusive Legislation in all Cases whatsoever, over such District (not exceeding ten Miles square) as may, by Cession of particular States, and the Acceptance of Congress, become the Seat of the Government

of the United States, and to exercise like Authority over all Places purchased by the Consent of the Legislature of the State in which the Same shall be, for the Erection of Forts, Magazines, Arsenals, dock-Yards, and other needful Buildings;—And

[18] To make all Laws which shall be necessary and proper for carrying into Execution the foregoing Powers, and all other Powers vested by this Constitution in the Government of the United States, or in any Department or Officer thereof.

Section 9. [1] The Migration or Importation of such Persons as any of the States now existing shall think proper to admit, shall not be prohibited by the Congress prior to the Year one thousand eight hundred and eight, but a Tax or duty may be imposed on such Importation, not exceeding ten dollars for each Person.

[2] The privilege of the Writ of Habeas Corpus shall not be suspended, unless when in Cases of Rebellion or Invasion the public Safety may require it.

[3] No Bill of Attainder or ex post facto Law shall be passed.

[4] No Capitation, or other direct, Tax shall be laid, unless in Proportion to the Census or Enumeration herein before directed to be taken.

[5] No Tax or Duty shall be laid on Articles exported from any State.

[6] No Preference shall be given by any Regulation of Commerce or Revenue to the Ports of one State over those of another: nor shall Vessels bound to or from, one State, be obliged to enter, clear, or pay Duties in another.

[7] No Money shall be drawn from the Treasury, but in Consequence of Appropriations made by Law; and a regular Statement and Account of the Receipts and Expenditures of all public Money shall be published from time to time.

[8] No Title of Nobility shall be granted by the United States: And no Person holding any Office of Profit or Trust under them, shall, without the Consent of the Congress, accept of any present, Emolument, Office, or Title, of any kind whatever, from any King, Prince, or foreign State.

Section 10. [1] No State shall enter into any Treaty, Alliance, or Confederation; grant Letters of Marque and Reprisal; coin Money; emit Bills of Credit; make any Thing but gold and silver Coin a Tender in Payment of Debts; pass any Bill of Attainder, ex post facto Law, or Law impairing the Obligation of Contracts, or grant any Title of Nobility.

[2] No State shall, without the Consent of the Congress, lay any Imposts or Duties on Imports or Exports, except what may be absolutely necessary for executing its inspection Laws: and the net Produce of all Duties and Imposts, laid by any State on Imports or Exports, shall be for the Use of the Treasury of the United States; and all such Laws be subject to the Revision and Controul of the Congress.

[3] No State shall, without the Consent of Congress, lay any Duty of Tonnage, keep Troops, or Ships of War in time of Peace, enter into any Agreement or Compact with another State, or with a foreign Power, or engage in War, unless actually invaded, or in such imminent Danger as will not admit of delay.

ARTICLE II

Section 1. [1] The executive Power shall be vested in a President of the United States of America. He shall hold his Office during the Term of four Years, and, together with the Vice President, chosen for the same Term, be elected, as follows:

[2] Each State shall appoint, in such Manner as the Legislature thereof may direct, a Number of Electors, equal to the whole Number of Senators and Representatives to which the State may be entitled in the Congress: but no Senator or Representative, or Person holding an Office of Trust or Profit under the United States, shall be appointed an Elector.

[3] The Electors shall meet in their respective States, and vote by Ballot for two Persons, of whom one at least shall not be an Inhabitant of the same State with themselves. And they shall make a List of all the Persons voted for, and of the Number of Votes for each; which List they shall sign and certify, and transmit sealed to the Seat of the Government of the United States, directed to the President of the Senate. The President of the Senate shall, in the Presence of the Senate and House of Representatives, open all the Certificates, and the Votes shall then be counted. The Person having the greatest Number of Votes shall be the President, if such Number be a Majority of the whole Number of Electors appointed; and if there be more than one who have such Majority, and have an equal Number of Votes, then the House of Representatives shall immediately chuse by Ballot one of them for President; and if no Person have a Majority, then from the five highest on the List the said House shall in like Manner chuse the President. But in chusing the President, the Votes shall be taken by States, the Representation from each State having one Vote; a quorum for this Purpose shall consist of a Member or Members from two thirds of the States, and a Majority of all the States shall be necessary to a Choice. In every Case, after the Choice of the President, the Person having the greatest Number of Votes of the Electors shall be the Vice President. But if there should remain two or more who have equal Votes, the Senate shall chuse from them by Ballot the Vice President.

[4] The Congress may determine the Time of chusing the Electors, and the Day on which they shall give their Votes; which Day shall be the same throughout the United States.

[5] No person except a natural born Citizen, or a Citizen of the United States, at the time of the Adoption of this Constitution, shall be eligible to the Office of President; neither shall any Person be eligible to that Office who shall not have attained to the Age of thirty five Years, and been fourteen Years a Resident within the United States.

[6] In case of the removal of the President from Office, or of his Death, Resignation or Inability to discharge the Powers and Duties of the said Office, the Same shall devolve on the Vice President, and the Congress may by law provide for the Case of Removal, Death, Resignation or Inability, both of the President and Vice President, declaring what Officer shall then act as President, and such Officer shall act accordingly, until the Disability be removed, or a President shall be elected.

[7] The President shall, at stated Times, receive for his Services, a Compensation, which shall neither be increased nor diminished during the Period for which he shall have been elected, and he shall not receive within that Period any other Emolument from the United States, or any of them.

[8] Before he enter on the Execution of his Office, he shall take the following Oath or Affirmation: "I do solemnly swear (or affirm) that I will faithfully execute the Office of President of the United States, and will to the best of my Ability, preserve, protect and defend the Constitution of the United States."

Section 2. [1] The President shall be Commander in Chief of the Army and Navy of the United States, and of the Militia of the several States, when called into the actual Service of the United States; he may require the Opinion, in writing, of the principal Officer in each of the executive Departments, upon any subject relating to the Duties of their respective Offices, and he shall have Power to grant Reprieves and Pardons for Offenses against the United States, except in Cases of Impeachment.

[2] He shall have Power, by and with the Advice and Consent of the Senate, to make Treaties, provided two thirds of the Senators present concur; and he shall nominate, and by and with the Advice and Consent of the Senate, shall appoint Ambassadors, other public Ministers and Consuls, Judges of the supreme Court, and all other Officers of the United States, whose Appointments are not herein otherwise provided for, and which shall be established by Law: but the Congress may by Law vest the Appointment of such inferior Officers, as they think proper, in the President alone, in the Courts of Law, or in the Heads of Departments.

[3] The President shall have Power to fill up all Vacancies that may happen during the Recess of the Senate by granting Commissions which shall expire at the End of their next Session.

Section 3. He shall from time to time give to the Congress Information of the State of the Union, and recommend to their Consideration such Measures as he shall judge necessary and expedient; he may, on extraordinary Occasions, convene both Houses, or either of them, and in Case of Disagreement between them, with Respect to the Time of Adjournment, he may adjourn them to such Time as he shall think proper; he shall receive Ambassadors and other public Ministers; he shall take Care that the Laws be faithfully executed, and shall Commission all the Officers of the United States.

Section 4. The President, Vice President and all civil Officers of the United States, shall be removed from Office on Impeachment for, and Conviction of, Treason, Bribery, or other high Crimes and Misdemeanors.

ARTICLE III

Section 1. The judicial Power of the United States, shall be vested in one supreme Court, and in such inferior Courts as the Congress may from time to time ordain and establish. The Judges, both of the supreme and inferior

Courts, shall hold their Offices during good Behaviour, and shall, at stated Times, receive for their Services, a Compensation, which shall not be diminished during their Continuance in Office.

Section 2. [1] The Judicial Power shall extend to all Cases, in Law and Equity, arising under this Constitution, the Laws of the United States, and Treaties made, or which shall be made, under their Authority;—to all Cases affecting Ambassadors, other public Ministers and Consuls;—to all Cases of admiralty and maritime Jurisdiction;—to Controversies to which the United States shall be a Party;—to Controversies between two or more States;—between a State and Citizens of another State;—between Citizens of different States;—between Citizens of the same State claiming Lands under Grants of different States, and between a State, or the Citizens thereof, and foreign States, Citizens or Subjects.

[2] In all Cases affecting Ambassadors, other public Ministers and Consuls, and those in which a State shall be Party, the supreme Court shall have original Jurisdiction. In all the other Cases before mentioned, the supreme Court shall have appellate Jurisdiction, both as to Law and Fact, with such Exceptions, and under such Regulations as the Congress shall make.

[3] The Trial of all Crimes, except in Cases of Impeachment, shall be by Jury; and such Trial shall be held in the State where the said Crimes shall have been committed; but when not committed within any State, the Trial shall be at such Place or Places as the Congress may by Law have directed.

Section 3. [1] Treason against the United States, shall consist only in levying War against them, or in adhering to their Enemies, giving them Aid and Comfort. No person shall be convicted of Treason unless on the Testimony of two Witnesses to the same overt Act, or on Confession in open Court.

[2] The Congress shall have Power to declare the Punishment of Treason, but no Attainder of Treason shall work Corruption of Blood, or Forfeiture except during the Life of the Person attainted.

ARTICLE IV

Section 1. Full Faith and Credit shall be given in each State to the public Acts, Records, and judicial Proceedings of every other State. And the Congress may by general Laws prescribe the Manner in which such Acts, Records and Proceedings shall be proved, and the Effect thereof.

Section 2. [1] The Citizens of each State shall be entitled to all Privileges and Immunities of Citizens in the several States.

[2] A Person charged in any State with Treason, Felony, or other Crime, who shall flee from Justice, and be found in another State, shall on demand of the executive Authority of the State from which he fled, be delivered up, to be removed to the State having Jurisdiction of the Crime.

[3] No Person held to Service or Labour in one State, under the Laws thereof, escaping into another, shall, in Consequence of any Law or Regulation

therein, be discharged from such Service or Labour, but shall be delivered up on Claim of the Party to whom such Service or Labour may be due.

Section 3. [1] New States may be admitted by the Congress into this Union; but no new State shall be formed or erected within the Jurisdiction of any other State; nor any State be formed by the Junction of two or more States, or Parts of States, without the Consent of the Legislatures of the States concerned as well as of the Congress.

[2] The Congress shall have Power to dispose of and make all needful Rules and Regulations respecting the Territory or other Property belonging to the United States; and nothing in this Constitution shall be so construed as to Prejudice any Claims of the United States, or of any particular State.

Section 4. The United States shall guarantee to every State in this Union a Republican Form of Government, and shall protect each of them against Invasion; and on Application of the Legislature, or of the Executive (when the Legislature cannot be convened) against domestic Violence.

ARTICLE V

The Congress, whenever two thirds of both Houses shall deem it necessary, shall propose Amendments to this Constitution, or, on the Application of the Legislatures of two thirds of the several States, shall call a Convention for proposing Amendments, which, in either Case, shall be valid to all Intents and Purposes, as part of this Constitution, when ratified by the Legislatures of three fourths of the several States, or by Conventions in three fourths thereof, as the one or the other Mode of Ratification may be proposed by the Congress; Provided that no Amendment which may be made prior to the Year One thousand eight hundred and eight shall in any Manner affect the first and fourth Clauses in the Ninth Section of the first Article; and that no State, without its Consent, shall be deprived of its equal Suffrage in the Senate.

ARTICLE VI

[1] All Debts contracted and Engagements entered into, before the Adoption of this Constitution, shall be as valid against the United States under this Constitution, as under the Confederation.

[2] This Constitution, and the Laws of the United States which shall be made in Pursuance thereof; and all Treaties made, or which shall be made, under the Authority of the United States, shall be the supreme Law of the Land; and the Judges in every State shall be bound thereby, any Thing in the Constitution or Laws of any State to the Contrary notwithstanding.

[3] The Senators and Representatives before mentioned, and the Members of the several State Legislatures, and all executive and judicial Officers, both of the United States and of the several States, shall be bound by Oath or

Affirmation, to support this Constitution; but no religious Test shall ever be required as a Qualification to any Office or public Trust under the United States.

ARTICLE VII

The Ratification of the Conventions of nine States, shall be sufficient for the Establishment of this Constitution between the States so ratifying the Same.

Done in Convention by the Unanimous Consent of the States present the Seventeenth Day of September in the Year of our Lord one thousand seven hundred and Eighty seven and of the Independence of the United States of America the Twelfth.

ARTICLES IN ADDITION TO, AND AMENDMENT OF, THE CONSTITUTION OF THE UNITED STATES OF AMERICA, PROPOSED BY CONGRESS, AND RATIFIED BY THE LEGISLATURES OF THE SEVERAL STATES, PURSUANT TO THE FIFTH ARTICLE OF THE ORIGINAL CONSTITUTION.

AMENDMENT I [1791]

Congress shall make no law respecting an establishment of religion, or prohibiting the free exercise thereof; or abridging the freedom of speech, or of the press; or the right of the people peaceably to assemble, and to petition the Government for a redress of grievances.

AMENDMENT II [1791]

A well regulated Militia, being necessary to the security of a free State, the right of the people to keep and bear Arms, shall not be infringed.

AMENDMENT III [1791]

No Soldier shall, in time of peace be quartered in any house, without the consent of the Owner, nor in time of war, but in a manner to be prescribed by law.

AMENDMENT IV [1791]

The right of the people to be secure in their persons, houses, papers, and effects, against unreasonable searches and seizures, shall not be violated, and no Warrants shall issue, but upon probable cause, supported by Oath or affirmation, and particularly describing the place to be searched, and the persons or things to be seized.

Amendment V [1791]

No person shall be held to answer for a capital, or otherwise infamous crime, unless on a presentment or indictment of a Grand Jury, except in cases arising in the land or naval forces, or in the Militia, when in actual service in time of War or public danger; nor shall any person be subject for the same offence to be twice put in jeopardy of life or limb; nor shall be compelled in any criminal case to be a witness against himself, nor be deprived of life, liberty, or property, without due process of law; nor shall private property be taken for public use, without just compensation.

Amendment VI [1791]

In all criminal prosecutions, the accused shall enjoy the right to a speedy and public trial, by an impartial jury of the State and district wherein the crime shall have been committed; which district shall have been previously ascertained by law, and to be informed of the nature and cause of the accusation; to be confronted with the witnesses against him; to have compulsory process for obtaining witnesses in his favor, and to have the Assistance of Counsel for his defence.

Amendment VII [1791]

In Suits at common law, where the value in controversy shall exceed twenty dollars, the right of trial by jury shall be preserved, and no fact tried by a jury, shall be otherwise re-examined in any Court of the United States, than according to the rules of the common law.

Amendment VIII [1791]

Excessive bail shall not be required, nor excessive fines imposed, nor cruel and unusual punishments inflicted.

Amendment IX [1791]

The enumeration in the Constitution of certain rights, shall not be construed to deny or disparage others retained by the people.

Amendment X [1791]

The powers not delegated to the United States by the Constitution, nor prohibited by it to the States, are reserved to the States respectively, or to the people.

Amendment XI [1798]

The Judicial power of the United States shall not be construed to extend to any suit in law or equity, commenced or prosecuted against one of the United States by Citizens of another State, or by Citizens or Subjects of any Foreign State.

Amendment XII [1804]

The Electors shall meet in their respective states, and vote by ballot for President and Vice-President, one of whom, at least, shall not be an inhabitant of the same state with themselves; they shall name in their ballots the person voted for as President, and in distinct ballots the person voted for as Vice-President, and they shall make distinct lists of all persons voted for as President, and of all persons voted for as Vice-President, and of the number of votes for each, which lists they shall sign and certify, and transmit sealed to the seat of the government of the United States, directed to the President of the Senate;—The President of the Senate shall, in the presence of the Senate and House of Representatives, open all the certificates and the votes shall then be counted;—The person having the greatest number of votes for President, shall be the President, if such number be a majority of the whole number of Electors appointed; and if no person have such majority, then from the persons having the highest numbers not exceeding three on the list of those voted for as President, the House of Representatives shall choose immediately, by ballot, the President. But in choosing the President, the votes shall be taken by states, the representation from each state having one vote; a quorum for this purpose shall consist of a member or members from two-thirds of the states, and a majority of all the states shall be necessary to a choice. And if the House of Representatives shall not choose a President whenever the right of choice shall devolve upon them, before the fourth day of March next following, then the Vice President shall act as President, as in the case of the death or other constitutional disability of the President.—The person having the greatest number of votes as Vice-President, shall be the Vice-President, if such number be a majority of the whole number of Electors appointed, and if no person have a majority, then from the two highest numbers on the list, the Senate shall choose the Vice-President; a quorum for the purpose shall consist of two-thirds of the whole number of Senators, and a majority of the whole number shall be necessary to a choice. But no person constitutionally ineligible to the office of President shall be eligible to that of Vice-President of the United States.

AMENDMENT XIII [1865]

Section 1. Neither slavery nor involuntary servitude, except as a punishment for crime whereof the party shall have been duly convicted, shall exist within the United States, or any place subject to their jurisdiction.

Section 2. Congress shall have power to enforce this article by appropriate legislation.

AMENDMENT XIV [1868]

Section 1. All persons born or naturalized in the United States, and subject to the jurisdiction thereof, are citizens of the United States and of the State wherein they reside. No State shall make or enforce any law which shall abridge the privileges or immunities of citizens of the United States; nor shall any State deprive any person of life, liberty, or property, without due process of law; nor deny to any person within its jurisdiction the equal protection of the laws.

Section 2. Representatives shall be apportioned among the several States according to their respective numbers, counting the whole number of persons in each State, excluding Indians not taxed. But when the right to vote at any election for the choice of electors for President and Vice President of the United States, Representatives in Congress, the Executive and Judicial officers of a State, or the members of the Legislature thereof, is denied to any of the male inhabitants of such State, being twenty-one years of age, and citizens of the United States, or in any way abridged, except for participation in rebellion, or other crime, the basis of representation therein shall be reduced in the proportion which the number of such male citizens shall bear to the whole number of male citizens twenty-one years of age in such State.

Section 3. No person shall be a Senator or Representative in Congress, or elector of President and Vice President, or hold any office, civil or military, under the United States, or under any State, who, having previously taken an oath, as a member of Congress, or as an officer of the United States, or as a member of any State legislature, or as an executive or judicial officer of any State, to support the Constitution of the United States, shall have engaged in insurrection or rebellion against the same, or given aid or comfort to the enemies thereof. But Congress may by a vote of two-thirds of each House, remove such disability.

Section 4. The validity of the public debt of the United States, authorized by law, including debts incurred for payment of pensions and bounties for services in suppressing insurrection or rebellion, shall not be questioned. But neither the United States nor any State shall assume or pay any debt or obligation incurred in aid of insurrection or rebellion against the United States, or any claim for the loss or emancipation of any slave; but all such debts, obligations and claims shall be held illegal and void.

Section 5.   The Congress shall have power to enforce, by appropriate legislation, the provisions of this article.

AMENDMENT XV [1870]

Section 1.   The right of citizens of the United States to vote shall not be denied or abridged by the United States or by any State on account of race, color, or previous condition of servitude.

Section 2.   The Congress shall have power to enforce this article by appropriate legislation.

AMENDMENT XVI [1913]

The Congress shall have power to lay and collect taxes on incomes, from whatever source derived, without apportionment among the several States, and without regard to any census or enumeration.

AMENDMENT XVII [1913]

[1] The Senate of the United States shall be composed of two Senators from each State, elected by the people thereof, for six years, and each Senator shall have one vote. The electors in each State shall have the qualifications requisite for electors of the most numerous branch of the State legislatures.

[2] When vacancies happen in the representation of any State in the Senate, the executive authority of such State shall issue writs of election to fill such vacancies: *Provided,* That the legislature of any State may empower the executive thereof to make temporary appointments until the people fill the vacancies by election as the legislature may direct.

[3] This amendment shall not be so construed as to affect the election or term of any Senator chosen before it becomes valid as part of the Constitution.

AMENDMENT XVIII [1919]

Section 1.   After one year from the ratification of this article the manufacture, sale, or transportation of intoxicating liquors within, the importation thereof into, or the exportation thereof from the United States and all territory subject to the jurisdiction thereof for beverage purposes is hereby prohibited.

Section 2.   The Congress and the several States shall have concurrent power to enforce this article by appropriate legislation.

Section 3.   This article shall be inoperative unless it shall have been ratified as an amendment to the Constitution by the legislatures of the several States, as provided in the Constitution, within seven years from the date of the submission hereof to the States by the Congress.

AMENDMENT **XIX** [1920]

[1] The right of citizens of the United States to vote shall not be denied or abridged by the United States or by any State on account of sex.

[2] Congress shall have power to enforce this article by appropriate legislation.

AMENDMENT **XX** [1933]

Section 1.   The terms of the President and Vice President shall end at noon on the 20th day of January, and the terms of Senators and Representatives at noon on the 3d day of January, of the years in which such terms would have ended if this article had not been ratified; and the terms of their successors shall then begin.

Section 2.   The Congress shall assemble at least once in every year, and such meeting shall begin at noon on the 3d day of January, unless they shall by law appoint a different day.

Section 3.   If, at the time fixed for the beginning of the term of the President, the President elect shall have died, the Vice President elect shall become President. If a President shall not have been chosen before the time fixed for the beginning of his term, or if the President elect shall have failed to qualify, then the Vice President elect shall act as President until a President shall have qualified; and the Congress may by law provide for the case wherein neither a President elect nor a Vice President elect shall have qualified, declaring who shall then act as President, or the manner in which one who is to act shall be selected, and such person shall act accordingly until a President or Vice President shall have qualified.

Section 4.   The Congress may by law provide for the case of the death of any of the persons from whom the House of Representatives may choose a President whenever the right of choice shall have devolved upon them, and for the case of the death of any of the persons from whom the Senate may choose a Vice President whenever the right of choice shall have devolved upon them.

Section 5.   Sections 1 and 2 shall take effect on the 15th day of October following the ratification of this article.

Section 6. This article shall be inoperative unless it shall have been ratified as an amendment to the Constitution by the legislatures of three-fourths of the several States within seven years from the date of its submission.

AMENDMENT XXI [1933]

Section 1. The eighteenth article of amendment to the Constitution of the United States is hereby repealed.

Section 2. The transportation or importation into any State, Territory, or possession of the United States for delivery or use therein of intoxicating liquors, in violation of the laws thereof, is hereby prohibited.

Section 3. This article shall be inoperative unless it shall have been ratified as an amendment to the Constitution by conventions in the several States, as provided in the Constitution, within seven years from the date of the submission hereof to the States by the Congress.

AMENDMENT XXII [1951]

Section 1. No person shall be elected to the office of the President more than twice, and no person who has held the office of President, or acted as President, for more than two years of a term to which some other person was elected President shall be elected to the office of the President more than once. But this Article shall not apply to any person holding the office of President when this Article was proposed by the Congress, and shall not prevent any person who may be holding the office of President, or acting as President, during the term within which the Article becomes operative from holding the office of President or acting as President during the remainder of such term.

Section 2. This article shall be inoperative unless it shall have been ratified as an amendment to the Constitution by the legislatures of three-fourths of the several States within seven years from the date of its submission to the States by the Congress.

AMENDMENT XXIII [1961]

Section 1. The District constituting the seat of Government of the United States shall appoint in such manner as the Congress may direct:

A number of electors of President and Vice President equal to the whole number of Senators and Representatives in Congress to which the District would be entitled if it were a State, but in no event more than the least populous State; they shall be in addition to those appointed by the States, but they shall be considered, for the purposes of the election of President and

Vice President, to be electors appointed by a State; and they shall meet in the District and perform such duties as provided by the twelfth article of amendment.

Section 2.   The Congress shall have power to enforce this article by appropriate legislation.

Amendment XXIV [1964]

Section 1.   The right of citizens of the United States to vote in any primary or other election for President or Vice President, for electors for President or Vice President, or for Senator or Representative in Congress, shall not be denied or abridged by the United States or any State by reason of failure to pay any poll tax or other tax.

Section 2.   The Congress shall have power to enforce this article by appropriate legislation.

Amendment XXV [1967]

Section 1.   In case of the removal of the President from office or of his death or resignation, the Vice President shall become President.

Section 2.   Whenever there is a vacancy in the office of the Vice President, the President shall nominate a Vice President who shall take office upon confirmation by a majority vote of both Houses of Congress.

Section 3.   Whenever the President transmits to the President pro tempore of the Senate and the Speaker of the House of Representatives his written declaration that he is unable to discharge the powers and duties of his office, and until he transmits to them a written declaration to the contrary, such powers and duties shall be discharged by the Vice President as Acting President.

Section 4.   Whenever the Vice President and a majority of either the principal officers of the executive departments or of such other body as Congress may by law provide, transmit to the President pro tempore of the Senate and the Speaker of the House of Representatives their written declaration that the President is unable to discharge the powers and duties of his office, the Vice President shall immediately assume the powers and duties of the office as Acting President.

Thereafter, when the President transmits to the President pro tempore of the Senate and the Speaker of the House of Representatives his written declaration that no inability exists, he shall resume the powers and duties of his office unless the Vice President and a majority of either the principal officers of the executive department or of such other body as Congress may by law provide, transmit within four days to the President pro tempore of the Senate and the Speaker of the House of Representatives their written declaration that the President is unable to discharge the powers and duties of his office. Thereupon Congress shall decide the issue, assembling within forty-eight hours for that purpose if not in session. If the Congress, within twenty-one days after receipt of the latter written declaration, or, if Congress is not in session, within twenty-one days after Congress is required to assemble, determines by two-thirds vote of both Houses that the President is unable to discharge the powers and duties of his office, the Vice President shall continue to discharge the same as Acting President; otherwise, the President shall resume the powers and duties of his office.

AMENDMENT XXVI [1971]

Section 1.   The right of citizens of the United States, who are eighteen years of age or older, to vote shall not be denied or abridged by the United States or by any State on account of age.

Section 2.   The Congress shall have power to enforce this article by appropriate legislation.

AMENDMENT XXVII [1992]

No law, varying the compensation for the services of the Senators and Representatives, shall take effect, unless an election of Representatives shall have intervened.

I

THE ROLE OF THE COURTS IN CONSTITUTIONAL INTERPRETATION

The U.S. Constitution is not self-explanatory. It is uncommonly short. Brevity is accomplished in part by general expression of the powers of and limitations upon government and the corresponding liberties of the people (e.g., what power does Congress have by the Constitution's grant of authority to "regulate Commerce . . . among the several States"?). Over time, of course, these generalities have been applied to specific issues as they have arisen (e.g., may Congress use its "commerce power" to prohibit the interstate shipment of lottery tickets?). But the Constitution is silent on the question of *who* is given the authority to answer these questions of constitutional interpretation. As a fresh proposition, it is possible that the Constitution's meaning could be determined by the President, Congress, the federal courts, the state courts, the state governors, the state legislatures, law professors, or even every person for himself or herself. In one sense, every one of these actors determines constitutional meaning, but some interpretations are more authoritative than others.

Constitutional law is primarily the study of judicial interpretation of the U.S. Constitution. The Constitution and constitutional law are not the same thing, but as you can see from a brief perusal of this book, the strongest voice in constitutional interpretation is that of the U.S. Supreme Court. Part I explains how this came to be and explores the problems created by judicial assumption of the primary role in constitutional interpretation.

This is a casebook on *federal* constitutional law. Every state has its own constitution, and those constitutions serve to constrain state governments. State constitutions may prohibit state officials from actions that would be permitted under the federal Constitution, but state constitutions cannot empower state officials to act in a manner prohibited by the federal Constitution. Because of the supremacy of federal law, federal constitutional law is more important. However, do not forget the independent significance and importance of state constitutional law.

1
Judicial Review and Constitutional Structure

Judicial review is the process by which courts decide whether actions of government officials comply with the Constitution. The fundamental premise of a representative democracy is that the people, through our elected representatives, are free to decide social and political arrangements, but that freedom is constrained by the Constitution. Judicial review serves to ensure that governments act in accordance with the Constitution. But judges—especially federal judges, who enjoy life tenure during good behavior—are not elected or otherwise politically accountable. There is thus a continual tension in judicial review. Abuses of power by elected politicians are checked by unelected judges, especially the justices of the Supreme Court. But who can control the Supreme Court? As Justice Robert Jackson once put it, "We are not final because we are infallible; but we are infallible only because we are final." Brown v. Allen, 344 U.S. 443, 540 (1953). This combination of de facto finality and infallibility makes the Supreme Court a potential politburo of the Constitution. Fortunately, the Court has remained sensitive to this possibility. Aware of its inherently antidemocratic role, the Court has generally tried to exercise judicial review in a fashion that mediates rather than aggravates the tension between a judicially enforceable Constitution and our commitment to representative democracy.

This chapter explores the origins of judicial review and the extent to which the Supreme Court's constitutional interpretations bind other branches of the federal government and the state governments.

A. THE ORIGINS AND THEORY OF JUDICIAL REVIEW

For nearly 170 years American colonists were politically British but geographically Americans. They were loyal subjects of the Crown, but *American* colonists in Virginia or Massachusetts or Georgia. Each colony was governed in accordance with its royal charter, usually issued to a corporation or proprietor who wished to form a colony. While each charter was different, a colonial government typically consisted of an elected assembly, a council and governor appointed by the Crown, and a judiciary also appointed by the British king. In fact, power resided in the colonial governor and council, which often acted as the upper house of the legislature and as a court of appeals. But the limited recognition of self-government proved in the end to erode colonial submission to Parliament. When rebellion came in the 1770s, the colonists united for the common purpose of securing independence from Great Britain. With the Treaty of Paris in 1783, Great Britain recognized the independence of these allied former colonies.

The cooperation born in the struggle for independence produced the Articles of Confederation, the first American constitution. Adopted by the Continental Congress in 1777, the Articles were fully ratified by 1781. This constitution was more like a treaty, however, than a charter for a new nation. Under the Articles the "national" government consisted almost entirely of a Congress; there was no executive or judicial branch. Moreover, Congress lacked any authority to compel the various independent states to comply with its will. Congress was more like the present United Nations than a national legislature. Congress could enact laws but was forced to rely on the states' voluntary acquiescence to those laws, which was not often forthcoming, particularly in matters of taxation or economic regulation. Almost all power of the new state governments reposed in the legislature, including the power to appoint and remove judges at will and to choose each state's governor. This quickly proved to be a failure. State legislatures abused their power by enacting ex post facto laws, confiscating property, and enacting laws designed to strip property owners of many of the common law rights of property.

A decade later, in the 1780s, the states began to revise their constitutions to check legislative abuse by creating an independent judiciary and a stronger executive. This was done partly for pragmatic reasons, but it was also aided by the American realization that, because sovereignty resided with the people, they were free to allocate power to their legislative, executive, and judicial agents in whatever manner they desired. Not surprisingly, the Philadelphia Convention of 1787 followed this pattern in framing the Constitution.

The initial post-Revolution state governments were not rousing successes. Too many state officials were incompetent or corrupt. Even worse was the "beggar thy neighbor" attitude of the state governments. Interstate tariff barriers were legion. For example, states with ports, such as Pennsylvania and New York, exacted huge import and export fees for goods flowing to and from New Jersey, a state without port facilities. Further, the lack of a common national currency made interstate trade difficult. The inability of the "national" government to tax made it virtually impossible to repay large foreign debts incurred in the War for Independence. Some thought the solution to these problems was greater civic virtue: A perfected people would lead to perfected government. Skeptics doubted the efficacy of this approach and urged the creation of new institutional arrangements. The Philadelphia Convention of 1787 was the realization of this latter view.

The Philadelphia Convention produced a document with an eclectic intellectual pedigree. It drew upon American notions of popular sovereignty and Montesquieu's ideas of separated power to create three branches of government with overlapping and checking powers. It created a stronger central government, supreme within its sphere of power, and specifically disabled the states from exercising some aspects of sovereignty. But, most important, it reversed the usual presumption that governments possessed all powers except those specifically denied. Instead, the new federal government was given only a few specifically enumerated (but very important) powers. The presumption created was that unless the federal government could find authority for its acts in the Constitution, it had no authority to act. By contrast, states were presumed to have power to act unless denied by the Constitution, federal law, or the relevant state constitution.

The Constitution's structure was also designed to attract more virtuous citizens to public office. Representatives would be elected by larger geographic areas, thus reducing the risk of parochial legislators. Neither the President nor senators would be elected directly by the people. The Electoral College would select the President, and senators would be chosen by state legislatures. The hope was that the wisest and best of the society would rise to national prominence and authority.

In September 1787, the Constitution was submitted to the states for ratification. Opponents of the Constitution, termed Anti-Federalists, pointed out the lack of a bill of rights. They argued that the new government was all too powerful and would prove to be an engine for the destruction of personal liberty. The Federalists, as proponents of the Constitution, argued that the central government's powers were limited and defined, and that it might be dangerous to enumerate individual liberties for fear that it would be thought that those liberties were the only rights that existed. Anti-Federalists wanted public policy to be made primarily by majorities in the states; Federalists believed that a national majority, manifested in Congress and the President, should make public policy with respect to the matters given by the Constitution to the central government. While Anti-Federalists did not dispute the latter contention, they were worried that the Constitution might be interpreted to expand the scope of federal power so greatly as to deprive state majorities of power to make public policies vital to their interests. Anti-Federalists wanted some constitutional text to arrest this possibility; Federalists were content to rely on later interpretation of the existing text and, moreover, were less concerned about the displacement of state majorities by a national majority.

The Federalists prevailed. By June 1788, nine states had ratified the Constitution (although several included in their ratification a demand for a bill of rights), and the process of forming a national government began. In April 1789, the first Congress took office, and George Washington became President. By the following May, every state had ratified the Constitution. Washington appointed as the nation's first Chief Justice New Yorker John Jay, one of the authors of The Federalist, a significant series of newspaper essays urging ratification of the Constitution. The era of federal constitutional law had begun.

All was not lost for Anti-Federalists, however. Many of the state ratification conventions had called for a bill of rights to be added to the Constitution even as they ratified the Constitution that lacked that feature. Much of the work of the first Congress was devoted to drafting and submitting to the states for ratification the amendments that became the Bill of Rights.

For further background, see Wood, The Creation of the American Republic, 1776-1787 (1969); Farrand, The Records of the Federal Convention of 1787 (1911); Bailyn, The Ideological Origins of the American Revolution (1967); McDonald, *Novus Ordus Seclorum:* The Intellectual Origins of the Constitution (1985); Rakove, Original Meanings (1997).

1. Marbury v. Madison: The Establishment of Judicial Review

The political cleavage between Federalists and Anti-Federalists quickly manifested itself in the politics of the new nation. Federalists, committed to establishment of a strong national government, took steps under Presidents Washington and Adams to strengthen national authority in defense, finance, and trade. The Anti-Federalists, mostly agrarian and mostly Southern, became known as Democratic-Republicans, or simply Republicans (although their party persists today as the Democratic Party). Thomas Jefferson, who served as Washington's Secretary of State, became the leading Democratic-Republican and, for a variety of reasons, James Madison abandoned his Federalist allegiance and became Jefferson's principal lieutenant. Democratic-Republican victory finally occurred in 1800, with Jefferson's election to the presidency.

This passage of power from Federalist John Adams to Thomas Jefferson in the winter of 1800-1801 was a tense political moment. The intentions of Democratic-Republicans, victorious in Congress and the presidency, seemed all too clear to Federalists: The shining works of Federalism were to be destroyed—all of them. The mint, the Bank of the United States, the small standing army, the equally small but surprisingly effective navy, and the federal judiciary would all be swept away. The judiciary was perhaps the most pressing target. The Democratic-Republicans did not intend to abolish the federal courts; they merely wanted to control and confine them, to break them to the Democratic-Republican harness. President-elect Jefferson asserted that "the Federalists have retired into the judiciary as a stronghold . . . and from that battery all the works of republicanism are to be beaten down and erased."

This fear was not unfounded. A lame-duck Federalist Congress had enacted an entirely new 1801 Judiciary Act, which created 16 new federal appellate judges and reduced the size of the Supreme Court from 6 to 5 as soon as a vacancy occurred, thus depriving Jefferson of an appointment to the Court.

The new judges would constitute a new appeals court, to which appeals from the federal trial courts could be taken. Adams promptly appointed and the Senate confirmed 16 staunch Federalist circuit judges, promptly dubbed the "midnight judges." Adams hoped that these Federalist judges would check the Democratic-Republicans' "excessive democracy." He feared that the government would possess "neither justice nor stability" unless "some material parts of it" were made "independent of popular control."

Another lame-duck statute authorized Adams to appoint new justices of the peace for the District of Columbia. Among Adams's 42 appointees confirmed by the Senate was William Marbury. The appointments were sent over to Secretary of State John Marshall, appointed only a month before by President Adams as Chief Justice of the Supreme Court, for affixing of the seal and delivery. Unfortunately for Marbury, Marshall never got around to delivering the signed and sealed commission document before he left office.

Once in office the Democratic-Republicans repealed the law establishing the circuit courts and, to thwart the possibility that the Supreme Court might declare the repeal unconstitutional, eliminated the 1802 term of the Court. The congressional debate over repeal of the 1801 Judiciary Act had ultimately focused on whether courts had the power to invalidate laws, and the repeal of the 1801 Judiciary Act seemed to present that issue. But before the Court could decide the case challenging the repeal, Stuart v. Laird, 5 U.S. (1 Cranch) 299 (1803), the Court was called upon to decide whether William Marbury was entitled to his commission as a justice of the peace.

≡
≡ *Marbury v. Madison*
≡ *5 U.S. (1 Cranch) 137 (1803)*

[In December 1801, Marbury had filed suit against Madison, Jefferson's Secretary of State, in the Supreme Court, seeking a writ of mandamus to compel Madison to give Marbury his commission. The Court had ordered Madison to show cause why he should not deliver the commission but, because the Court's 1802 session had been canceled by Congress, it was not until the spring of 1803 that the Court was able to hear argument.]

CHIEF JUSTICE MARSHALL, for a unanimous Court.

At the last term . . . a rule was granted in this case, requiring the Secretary of State to show cause why a mandamus should not issue, directing him to deliver to William Marbury his commission as a justice of the peace. . . . No cause has been shown, and the present motion is for a mandamus. The peculiar delicacy of this case, the novelty of some of its circumstances, and the real difficulty attending the points which occur in it, require a complete exposition of the principles on which the opinion to be given by the court is founded.

In the order in which the court has viewed this subject, the following questions have been considered and decided.

1. Has the applicant a right to the commission he demands?
2. If he has a right, and that right has been violated, do the laws of his country afford him a remedy?
3. If they do afford him a remedy, is it a mandamus issuing from this court?

The first object of inquiry is, . . . [h]as the applicant a right to the commission he demands?

[A] commission for William Marbury as a justice of peace . . . was signed by John Adams, then president of the United States; after which the seal of the United States was affixed to it; but the commission has never reached the person for whom it was made out.

In order to determine whether he is entitled to this commission, it becomes necessary to inquire whether he has been appointed to the office. For if he has been appointed . . . he is entitled to the possession of those evidences of office, which, being completed, became his property.

It is . . . decidedly the opinion of the court, that when a commission has been signed by the president, the appointment is made; and that the commission is complete when the seal of the United States has been affixed to it by the Secretary of State.

To withhold the commission, therefore, is an act deemed by the court not warranted by law, but violative of a vested legal right.

This brings us to the second inquiry; which is, . . . [i]f he has a right, and that right has been violated, do the laws of his country afford him a remedy?

The very essence of civil liberty certainly consists in the right of every individual to claim the protection of the laws, whenever he receives an injury. One of the first duties of government is to afford that protection. Blackstone states . . . "that where there is a legal right, there is also a legal remedy by suit or action at law whenever that right is invaded." And [also,] "it is a settled and invariable principle in the laws of England, that every right, when withheld, must have a remedy, and every injury its proper redress." The government of the United States has been emphatically termed a government of laws, and not of men. It will certainly cease to deserve this high appellation, if the laws furnish no remedy for the violation of a vested legal right. If this obloquy is to be cast on the jurisprudence of our country, it must arise from the peculiar character of the case. It behooves us then to inquire whether there be in its composition any ingredient which shall exempt from legal investigation, or exclude the injured party from legal redress.

Is it in the nature of the transaction? Is the act of delivering or withholding a commission to be considered as a mere political act belonging to the executive department alone, for the performance of which entire confidence is placed by our constitution in the supreme executive; and for any misconduct respecting which, the injured individual has no remedy. That there may be such cases is not to be questioned; but that every act of duty to be performed in any of the great departments of government constitutes such a case, is not to be admitted.

[For example, federal law provides] that all patents shall be countersigned by the Secretary of State, and recorded in his office. If the Secretary of State should choose to withhold this patent; or the patent being lost, should refuse a copy of it; can it be imagined that the law furnishes to the injured person no remedy? It is not believed that any person whatever would attempt to maintain such a proposition.

It follows then that the question, whether the legality of an act of the head of a department be examinable in a court of justice or not, must always depend on the nature of that act.

By the constitution of the United States, the President is invested with certain important political powers, in the exercise of which he is to use his own discretion, and is accountable only to his country in his political character, and to his own conscience. To aid him in the performance of these duties, he is authorized to appoint certain officers, who act by his authority and in conformity with his orders. In such cases, their acts are his acts; and whatever opinion may be entertained of the manner in which executive discretion may be used, still there exists, and can exist, no power to control that discretion. The subjects are political. They respect the nation, not individual rights, and being entrusted to the executive, the decision of the executive is conclusive. The application of this remark will be perceived by adverting to the act of congress for establishing the department of foreign affairs. This officer, as his duties were prescribed by that act, is to conform precisely to the will of the president. He is the mere organ by whom that will is communicated. The acts of such an officer, as an officer, can never be examinable by the courts. But when the legislature proceeds to impose on that officer other duties; when he is directed peremptorily to perform certain acts; when the rights of individuals are dependent on the performance of those acts; he is so far the officer of the law; is amenable to the laws for his conduct; and cannot at his discretion sport away the vested rights of others.

The conclusion from this reasoning is, that where the heads of departments are the political or confidential agents of the executive, merely to execute the will of the president, or rather to act in cases in which the executive possesses a constitutional or legal discretion, nothing can be more perfectly clear than that their acts are only politically examinable. But where a specific duty is assigned by law, and individual rights depend upon the performance of that duty, it seems equally clear that the individual who considers himself injured has a right to resort to the laws of his country for a remedy.

If this be the rule, let us inquire how it applies to the case under the consideration of the court. The power[s] of [nomination and appointment of officers] are political powers, to be exercised by the President according to his own discretion. When he has made an appointment, he has exercised his whole power, and his discretion has been completely applied to the case. [Unless] the officer be removable at the will of the President . . . the rights he has acquired are protected by the law, and . . . cannot be extinguished by executive authority. . . .

It is then the opinion of the court, [that] Mr. Marbury . . . has a . . . right to the commission; a refusal to deliver which is a plain violation of that right, for which the laws of his country afford him a remedy.

It remains to be inquired whether . . . [h]e is entitled to the remedy for which he applies. This depends on . . . [1] [t]he nature of the writ applied for, and, [2] [t]he power of this court.

This writ, if awarded, would be directed to an officer of government, and its mandate to him would be, to use the words of Blackstone, "to do a particular thing therein specified, which appertains to his office and duty, and which the court has previously determined or at least supposes to be consonant to right and justice." Or, in the words of Lord Mansfield, the applicant, in this case, has a right to execute an office of public concern, and is kept out of possession of that right. These circumstances certainly concur in this case.

Still, to render the mandamus a proper remedy, the officer to whom it is to be directed, must be one to whom, on legal principles, such writ may be directed; and the person applying for it must be without any other specific and legal remedy.

The intimate political relation, subsisting between the president of the United States and the heads of departments, necessarily renders any legal investigation of the acts of one of those high officers peculiarly irksome, as well as delicate; and excites some hesitation with respect to the propriety of entering into such investigation. [In] such a case as this, the assertion, by an individual, of his legal claims in a court of justice, to which claims it is the duty of that court to attend, should at first view be considered by some, as an attempt to intrude into the cabinet, and to intermeddle with the prerogatives of the executive.

It is scarcely necessary for the court to disclaim all pretensions to such a jurisdiction. An extravagance, so absurd and excessive, could not have been entertained for a moment. The province of the court is, solely, to decide on the rights of individuals, not to inquire how the executive, or executive officers, perform duties in which they have a discretion. Questions, in their nature political, or which are, by the constitution and laws, submitted to the executive, can never be made in this court.

But, if this be not such a question; if so far from being an intrusion into the secrets of the cabinet, it respects a paper . . . a copy of which the law gives a right; . . . if it be no intermeddling with a subject, over which the executive can be considered as having exercised any control; what is there in the exalted station of the officer, which shall bar a citizen from asserting, in a court of justice, his legal rights, or shall forbid a court to listen to the claim; or to issue a mandamus, directing the performance of a duty, not depending on executive discretion, but on particular acts of congress and the general principles of law?

It is not by the office of the person to whom the writ is directed, but the nature of the thing to be done, that the propriety or impropriety of issuing a mandamus is to be determined. Where the head of a department . . . is directed by law to do a certain act affecting the absolute rights of individuals, . . . it is not perceived on what ground the courts of the country are further excused from the duty of giving judgment. This, then, is a plain case of a mandamus, either to deliver the commission, or a copy of it from the record; and it only remains to be inquired,

Whether it can issue from this court.

The act to establish the judicial courts of the United States authorizes the supreme court "to issue writs of mandamus, in cases warranted by the principles and usages of law, to any courts appointed, or persons holding office, under the authority of the United States."[1]

The Secretary of State, being a person, holding an office under the authority of the United States, is precisely within the letter of the description; and if this court is not authorized to issue a writ of mandamus to such an officer, it must be because the law is unconstitutional, and therefore absolutely incapable of conferring the authority, and assigning the duties which its words purport to confer and assign.

The constitution vests the whole judicial power of the United States in one supreme court, and such inferior courts as congress shall, from time to time, ordain and establish. This power is expressly extended to all cases arising under the laws of the United States; and consequently, in some form, may be exercised over the present case; because the right claimed is given by a law of the United States.

In the distribution of this power it is declared that "the supreme court shall have original jurisdiction in all cases affecting ambassadors, other public ministers and consuls, and those in which a state shall be a party. In all other cases, the supreme court shall have appellate jurisdiction."

It has been insisted at the bar, that as the original grant of jurisdiction to the supreme and inferior courts is general, and the clause, assigning original jurisdiction to the supreme court, contains no negative or restrictive words; the power remains to the legislature to assign original jurisdiction to that

---

1. Section 13 of the 1789 Judiciary Act, 1 Stat. 73, provided:

[T]he Supreme Court shall have exclusive jurisdiction of all controversies of a civil nature, where a state is a party, except between a state and its citizens; and except also between a state and citizens of other states, or aliens, in which latter case it shall have original but not exclusive jurisdiction. And shall have exclusively all such jurisdiction of suits or proceedings against ambassadors, or other public ministers, or their domestics, or domestic servants, as a court of law can have or exercise consistently with the law of nations; and original, but not exclusive jurisdiction of all suits brought by ambassadors, or other public ministers, or in which a consul, or vice consul, shall be a party. And the trial of issues of fact in the Supreme Court, in all actions at law against citizens of the United States, shall be by jury. *The Supreme Court shall also have appellate jurisdiction from the circuit courts and courts of the several states, in the cases herein after specially provided for; and shall have power to issue writs of prohibition to the district courts, when proceeding as courts of admiralty or maritime jurisdiction, and writs of mandamus, in cases warranted by the principles and usages of law, to any courts appointed, or persons holding office, under the authority of the United States.*

Emphasis added. — ED.

court in other cases than those specified in the article which has been recited; provided those cases belong to the judicial power of the United States.

If it had been intended to leave it in the discretion of the legislature to apportion the judicial power between the supreme and inferior courts according to the will of that body, it would certainly have been useless to have proceeded further than to have defined the judicial power, and the tribunals in which it should be vested. The subsequent part of the section is mere surplusage, is entirely without meaning, if such is to be the construction. If congress remains at liberty to give this court appellate jurisdiction, where the constitution has declared their jurisdiction shall be original; and original jurisdiction where the constitution has declared it shall be appellate; the distribution of jurisdiction made in the constitution, is form without substance.

Affirmative words are often, in their operation, negative of other objects than those affirmed; and in this case, a negative or exclusive sense must be given to them or they have no operation at all.

It cannot be presumed that any clause in the constitution is intended to be without effect; and therefore such construction is inadmissible, unless the words require it.

When an instrument organizing fundamentally a judicial system, divides it into one supreme, and so many inferior courts as the legislature may ordain and establish; then enumerates its powers, and proceeds so far to distribute them, as to define the jurisdiction of the supreme court by declaring the cases in which it shall take original jurisdiction, and that in others it shall take appellate jurisdiction, the plain import of the words seems to be, that in one class of cases its jurisdiction is original, and not appellate; in the other it is appellate, and not original. If any other construction would render the clause inoperative, that is an additional reason for rejecting such other construction, and for adhering to the obvious meaning.

To enable this court then to issue a mandamus, it must be shown to be an exercise of appellate jurisdiction, or to be necessary to enable them to exercise appellate jurisdiction. . . .

It is the essential criterion of appellate jurisdiction, that it revises and corrects the proceedings in a cause already instituted, and does not create that case. . . . [T]o issue [a writ of mandamus] to an officer for the delivery of a paper, is in effect the same as to sustain an original action for that paper, and therefore seems not to belong to appellate, but to original jurisdiction. Neither is it necessary in such a case as this, to enable the court to exercise its appellate jurisdiction.

The authority, therefore, given to the supreme court, by the act establishing the judicial courts of the United States, to issue writs of mandamus to public officers, appears not to be warranted by the constitution; and it becomes necessary to inquire whether a jurisdiction, so conferred, can be exercised.

The question, whether an act, repugnant to the constitution, can become the law of the land, is a question deeply interesting to the United States; but, happily, not of an intricacy proportioned to its interest. It seems only necessary to recognise certain principles, supposed to have been long and well established, to decide it.

That the people have an original right to establish, for their future government, such principles as, in their opinion, shall most conduce to their own happiness, is the basis on which the whole American fabric has been erected. The exercise of this original right is a very great exertion; nor can it nor ought it to be frequently repeated. The principles, therefore, so established are deemed fundamental. And as the authority, from which they proceed, is supreme, and can seldom act, they are designed to be permanent.

This original and supreme will organizes the government, and assigns to different departments their respective powers. It may either stop here; or establish certain limits not to be transcended by those departments. The government of the United States is of the latter description. The powers of the legislature are defined and limited; and that those limits may not be mistaken or forgotten, the constitution is written. To what purpose are powers limited, and to what purpose is that limitation committed to writing; if these limits may, at any time, be passed by those intended to be restrained? The distinction between a government with limited and unlimited powers is abolished, if those limits do not confine the persons on whom they are imposed, and if acts prohibited and acts allowed are of equal obligation. It is a proposition too plain to be contested, that the constitution controls any legislative act repugnant to it; or, that the legislature may alter the constitution by an ordinary act.

Between these alternatives there is no middle ground. The constitution is either a superior, paramount law, unchangeable by ordinary means, or it is on a level with ordinary legislative acts, and like other acts, is alterable when the legislature shall please to alter it.

If the former part of the alternative be true, then a legislative act contrary to the constitution is not law: if the latter part be true, then written constitutions are absurd attempts, on the part of the people, to limit a power in its own nature illimitable.

Certainly all those who have framed written constitutions contemplate them as forming the fundamental and paramount law of the nation, and consequently the theory of every such government must be, that an act of the legislature repugnant to the constitution is void. This theory is essentially attached to a written constitution, and is consequently to be considered by this court as one of the fundamental principles of our society. It is not therefore to be lost sight of in the further consideration of this subject.

If an act of the legislature, repugnant to the constitution, is void, does it, notwithstanding its invalidity, bind the courts and oblige them to give it effect? Or, in other words, though it be not law, does it constitute a rule as operative as if it was a law? This would be to overthrow in fact what was established in theory; and would seem, at first view, an absurdity too gross to be insisted on. It shall, however, receive a more attentive consideration.

It is emphatically the province and duty of the judicial department to say what the law is. Those who apply the rule to particular cases, must of necessity expound and interpret that rule. If two laws conflict with each other, the courts must decide on the operation of each.

So if a law be in opposition to the constitution: if both the law and the constitution apply to a particular case, so that the court must either decide that case conformably to the law, disregarding the constitution; or conformably to the constitution, disregarding the law: the court must determine which of these conflicting rules governs the case. This is of the very essence of judicial duty.

If, then, the courts are to regard the constitution; and the constitution is superior to any ordinary act of the legislature; the constitution, and not such ordinary act, must govern the case to which they both apply.

Those then who controvert the principle that the constitution is to be considered, in court, as a paramount law, are reduced to the necessity of maintaining that courts must close their eyes on the constitution, and see only the law. This doctrine would subvert the very foundation of all written constitutions. It would declare that an act, which, according to the principles and theory of our government, is entirely void, is yet, in practice, completely obligatory. It would declare, that if the legislature shall do what is expressly forbidden, such act, notwithstanding the express prohibition, is in reality effectual. It would be giving to the legislature a practical and real omnipotence with the same breath which professes to restrict their powers within narrow limits. It is prescribing limits, and declaring that those limits may be passed at pleasure.

That it thus reduces to nothing what we have deemed the greatest improvement on political institutions—a written constitution, would of itself be sufficient, in America where written constitutions have been viewed with so much reverence, for rejecting the construction. But the peculiar expressions of the constitution of the United States furnish additional arguments in favour of its rejection.

The judicial power of the United States is extended to all cases arising under the constitution. Could it be the intention of those who gave this power, to say that, in using it, the constitution should not be looked into? That a case arising under the constitution should be decided without examining the instrument under which it arises? This is too extravagant to be maintained.

In some cases then, the constitution must be looked into by the judges. And if they can open it at all, what part of it are they forbidden to read, or to obey?

There are many other parts of the constitution which serve to illustrate this subject. It is declared that "no tax or duty shall be laid on articles exported from any state." Suppose a duty on the export of cotton, of tobacco, or of flour; and a suit instituted to recover it. Ought judgment to be rendered in such a case? Ought the judges to close their eyes on the constitution, and only see the law?

The constitution declares that "no bill of attainder or ex post facto law shall be passed." If, however, such a bill should be passed and a person should be prosecuted under it, must the court condemn to death those victims whom the constitution endeavours to preserve? "No person," says the constitution, "shall be convicted of treason unless on the testimony of two witnesses to the same overt act, or on confession in open court." Here the language of the constitution is addressed especially to the courts. It prescribes, directly for them, a rule of evidence not to be departed from. If the legislature should change that rule, and declare *one* witness, or a confession *out* of court, sufficient for conviction, must the constitutional principle yield to the legislative act?

From these and many other selections which might be made, it is apparent, that the framers of the constitution contemplated that instrument as a rule for the government of *courts*, as well as of the legislature. Why otherwise does it direct the judges to take an oath to support it? This oath certainly applies, in an especial manner, to their conduct in their official character. How immoral to impose it on them, if they were to be used as the instruments, and the knowing instruments, for violating what they swear to support!

The oath of office, too, imposed by the legislature, is completely demonstrative of the legislative opinion on this subject. It is in these words: "I do solemnly swear that I will administer justice without respect to persons, and do equal right to the poor and to the rich; and that I will faithfully and impartially discharge all the duties incumbent on me as according to the best of my abilities and understanding, agreeably to *the constitution* and laws of the United States."

Why does a judge swear to discharge his duties agreeably to the constitution of the United States, if that constitution forms no rule for his government? If it is closed upon him and cannot be inspected by him? If such be the real state of things, this is worse than solemn mockery. To prescribe, or to take this oath, becomes equally a crime.

It is also not entirely unworthy of observation, that in declaring what shall be the *supreme law* of the land, the *constitution* itself is first mentioned; and not the laws of the United States generally, but those only which shall be made in *pursuance* of the constitution, have that rank. Thus, the particular phraseology of the constitution of the United States confirms and strengthens the principle, supposed to be essential to all written constitutions, that a law repugnant to the constitution is void, and that *courts*, as well as other departments, are bound by that instrument.

The rule must be discharged.

NOTES

1. The Meaning of Section 13 and the Scope of Article III.   In order to declare section 13 invalid the Court first had to interpret the section to give the Court original jurisdiction in all cases where a litigant seeks mandamus against a federal officer. Read the section carefully. Although the Court's jurisdiction over such mandamus cases appears in a sentence dealing with the Court's appellate jurisdiction, the Court construed the statute to give the Court original jurisdiction in such cases.

To appreciate the significance of this construction you must understand the scope of Article III, which defines the categories of cases the federal courts may hear. Marbury's suit was one "arising under . . . the Laws of the United States" because it involved Marbury's claim to a judicial commission under a federal law. Article III also specifies how the Supreme Court may exercise its power to hear the categories of cases open to federal courts. Article III divides the Supreme Court's authority into *original* cases—filed originally in the Supreme Court as a trial court—and *appellate* cases—those cases heard on appeal from the judgment of some lower court.

Article III gives the Supreme Court original jurisdiction over only a very few of the cases within the federal judicial power (cases involving foreign diplomats and cases in which a state is a party). All other cases within the federal judicial power may be heard by the Supreme Court only in its appellate capacity. But Article III also contains a clause that permits Congress to make "exceptions and regulations" to the appellate jurisdiction of the Supreme Court. Marbury argued that this clause permitted Congress to transfer cases from the appellate jurisdiction of the Supreme Court to its original jurisdiction but, as seen, the Court rejected this argument. Instead, the "exceptions and regulations" clause permits Congress to remove cases entirely from the Court's appellate jurisdiction (see Chapter 2, Section B.2) but not to transfer them from the Court's appellate to its original jurisdiction.

To the extent that Chief Justice Marshall implied that Article III creates mutually exclusive categories of original and appellate Supreme Court jurisdiction, he has been repudiated. While Congress may not add to the Court's original jurisdiction, it may confer jurisdiction upon inferior federal courts of cases coming within the Court's original jurisdiction, and the Court may hear those cases on appeal. See Bors v. Preston, 111 U.S. 252 (1884).

2. Marshall's Approach to the Issues: Political Guile?   The usual procedure is to decide first whether a court has jurisdiction. If not, the case is dismissed. Marbury lost in the end because the Supreme Court lacked jurisdiction—section 13, the only basis for the exercise of jurisdiction by the Court, was unconstitutional. Why didn't Marshall start with that issue? If he had done so, the Court would have ruled that acts of Congress were subject to judicial review but there would have been no occasion to consider whether executive action is similarly susceptible to judicial review. Instead, Marshall started with the question of whether Marbury had a right to his commission. In answering that he did, Marshall declared that Secretary of State Madison's refusal to deliver the commission was not lawful. Thus the Court asserted its power to review the validity of executive action. But by ruling that Congress had acted in violation of the Constitution in enacting section 13, thus depriving the Court of jurisdiction, Marshall asserted that the Court could review legislative acts as well and simultaneously avoided any confrontation with President Jefferson over enforceability of his conclusion that the Secretary of State had acted illegally. Jefferson won the battle but Marshall won the war.

3. Marshall's Justifications for Judicial Review.   Marshall offered four textual arguments and one structural argument in support of judicial review.

a. Structural implications from a written constitution.   Marshall's first argument was that a written constitution is meaningless if Congress could ignore it at its pleasure. The inference he drew is that the courts are empowered to enforce constitutional limits. Does that inference follow logically? Consider the possibility that there are two separate questions presented by a written constitution: (1) Is the Constitution binding on the federal and state governments? (2) If so, is the Supreme Court authorized to enforce the Constitution? It is possible to answer yes to the first question and no to the second: "It is the business of the judiciary to interpret the laws, not scan the authority of the lawgiver; and without the latter, it cannot take cognizance of a collision between a law and the constitution." Eakin v. Raub, 12 Serg. & Rawle 330, 347 (Pa. 1825) (Gibson, Chief Justice, dissenting). Moreover, if the Constitution binds the government, it must bind the Court just as much as Congress. What structural principle prevents Congress (or the President) from declaring that the Court's constitutional decisions are in violation of the Constitution? Is something more than the paramount status of the Constitution needed to vest a power of constitutional enforcement in the Court?

b. Article III's grant of judicial power over cases arising under the Constitution.   Marshall inferred the power of judicial review from Article III's grant to federal courts of the power to decide cases arising under the Constitution. Does the inference necessarily follow? A case does not "arise under the Constitution" unless the Constitution gives the courts the power of judicial review. And that is the question Marshall had to answer in *Marbury*. Suppose the Constitution specifically forbade federal courts from reviewing the constitutionality of congressional or presidential action. The Court would still have jurisdiction over those cases where the constitutionality of *state* actions is at issue. Is it possible that this was the intended meaning of the jurisdictional grant in Article III?

c. Constitutional provisions specially directed to courts.   Some constitutional provisions are specifically addressed to the courts, such as the requirement that convictions for treason must be founded on the testimony of at least two witnesses. Surely, argued Marshall, this "constitutional principle [must not] yield to the legislative act" of changing the rule. Does this argument provide a *general* defense for judicial review? Or does it merely contend that each branch of the federal government is responsible for interpreting the portions of the Constitution directed to it? By this reading, the President would have the last word on the meaning of his obligation to "take care that the laws be faithfully executed" and Congress would definitively interpret the scope of its power to "regulate commerce among the several states" or decide when it has made a law "abridging freedom of speech." *Marbury* fits within this narrow view of judicial review: The matter at issue was whether Congress could alter the Court's original jurisdiction, a matter addressed to the courts by Article III. But Marshall made a much more expansive claim than this argument supports. Is it convincing?

d. The supremacy clause. The supremacy clause, Article VI, clause 2, declares that state judges must apply the "Constitution and the laws of the United States which shall be made in pursuance thereof [as] the supreme Law of the Land." Marshall argued that since the Framers apparently expected state judges to decide if federal laws violated the Constitution they must also have expected the Supreme Court to exercise the same power in its appellate capacity. This argument rests on the assumption that the "in pursuance" phrase permits state judges to assess the substantive validity of federal laws rather than simply decide whether they were enacted in a procedurally correct manner. Did Marshall explain why the supremacy clause gives state judges the power to review the substantive validity of federal laws?

e. Judges' oath. Article VI requires judges to take an oath "to support this Constitution." Marshall argued that judges would violate this oath if they upheld unconstitutional laws. But suppose that the official duties of judicial office do not extend to inquiry into the validity of legislative or executive action. Would the oath then provide any support for Marshall's argument? Moreover, the Constitution requires members of Congress and executive officers to take the same oath, which presumably means that they are equally obliged to determine the constitutionality of their official actions. Thus, by passing legislation Congress vows that it is constitutional; by signing it into law the President vows that it is constitutional. Does this diminish the force of Marshall's oath argument?

4. Other Arguments for Judicial Review. Marshall might have made additional arguments in favor of judicial review.

a. Precedent. Colonists applied English law for their own purposes. As early as 1610, Lord Coke, the most influential English jurist of the seventeenth century, had ruled that "when an Act of Parliament is against common right and reason . . . the common law will controul it, and adjudge such Act to be void." Bonham's Case, 77 Eng. Rep. 646, 8 Coke's Rep. 113b (K.B. 1610). Historians have debated exactly what Coke meant by this cryptic declaration, as the British do not have constitutional judicial review, either then or now. American colonists, however, placed their own unique interpretation on Bonham's Case. In 1761 James Otis, Jr., relied on Bonham's Case to urge a colonial court to strike down the use of general search warrants authorized by act of Parliament. See Smith, The Writs of Assistance Case (1978). "[T]hen and there," said John Adams, "the child independence was born." 10 Adams, Life and Works 248 (Adams ed., 1850).

During the early 1780s, American state courts sporadically invoked state constitutions or unwritten conceptions of fundamental law to review and constrain state government conduct. These early uses of judicial review were controversial, but during the late 1780s and 1790s state courts began to use judicial review more frequently and with less controversy. See Charles Haines, The American Doctrine of Judicial Supremacy (1959).

Even more germane were a trio of Supreme Court precedents from the 1790s. In Ware v. Hylton, 3 U.S. (3 Dall.) 199 (1796), the Court voided a Virginia law as violative of a federal treaty. In Calder v. Bull, 3 U.S. (3 Dall.)

386 (1798), it rejected an ex post facto clause challenge to a Connecticut law but left no doubt of its view that it possessed the power to void the law. And in Hylton v. United States, 3 U.S. (3 Dall.) 171 (1796), the Court upheld the validity of a tax on carriages after explicitly considering whether the tax violated the constitutional provision against unapportioned direct taxes. Marshall did not mention these cases, perhaps because none of them explicitly discussed the judicial review question.

b. The Framers' intentions. The 1787 Constitutional Convention rejected a proposal that the Supreme Court join with the President to create a Council of Revision holding the veto power. Maryland's Luther Martin argued against the proposal on the ground that the justices would possess a "double negative" over laws, since they would already pass on the "[c]onstitutionality of laws . . . in their proper official capacity." Virginia's George Mason argued in favor on the ground that whereas the justices "could declare an unconstitutional law void," they would lack power to strike down laws as "unjust, oppressive, or pernicious" unless they were included in a Council of Revision. Perhaps the Framers assumed that judicial review was a sufficiently obvious attribute of courts that it was unnecessary to state it explicitly.

Another important source of the Framers' intentions is The Federalist, the series of newspaper essays that James Madison, Alexander Hamilton, and John Jay wrote under the pseudonym "Publius" in an effort to persuade the New York ratification convention to approve the Constitution. Federalist No. 78, authored by Hamilton, speaks most directly to the question of judicial review:

> [I]n a government in which [the] different departments of power [are] separated from each other, the judiciary, from the nature of its functions, will always be the least dangerous to the political rights of the constitution; because it will be least in a capacity to annoy or injure them. The judiciary can have no influence over either the sword or the purse, no direction either of the strength or wealth of the society, and can take no active resolution whatever. It may truly be said to have neither Force nor Will, but merely judgment. [Some] perplexity respecting the right of the courts to pronounce legislative acts void, because contrary to the constitution, has arisen from an imagination that the doctrine would imply a superiority of the judiciary to the legislative power. [There] is no position which depends on clearer principles, than that every act of a delegated authority, contrary to the tenor of the commission under which it is exercised, is void. No legislative act therefore contrary to the constitution can be valid. To deny this would be to affirm that [the] representatives of the people are superior to the people themselves; that men acting by virtue of powers may do not only what their powers do not authorise, but what they forbid.
>
> If it be said that the legislative body are themselves the constitutional judges of their own powers, and that the construction they put upon them is conclusive upon the other departments, it may be answered, that this cannot be the natural presumption, where it is not to be collected from any particular provisions in the constitution. [It] is far more rational to suppose that the courts were

designed to be an intermediate body between the people and the legislature, in order, among other things, to keep the latter within the limits assigned to their authority. The interpretation of the laws is the proper and peculiar province of the courts. A constitution is in fact, and must be, regarded by the judges as a fundamental law. It therefore belongs to them to ascertain its meaning as well as the meaning of any particular act proceeding from the legislative body. If there should happen to be an irreconcilable variance between the two, that which has the superior obligation and validity ought of course to be preferred; or in other words, the constitution ought to be preferred to the statute, the intention of the people to the intention of their agents.

Nor does this conclusion by any means suppose a superiority of the judicial to the legislative power. It only supposes that the power of the people is superior to both; and that where the will of the legislature declared in its statutes, stands in opposition to that of the people declared in the constitution, the judges ought to be governed by the latter, rather than the former. They ought to regulate their decisions by the fundamental laws, rather than by those which are not fundamental.

5. Is Judicial Review Obligatory or Discretionary? The fact that judicial review is an implied power leads to the issue of whether courts are *obliged* to exercise judicial review or whether it is a *discretionary* power. Some contend that the power to invalidate acts of Congress is an arguable violation of the principle of separation of powers and because judicial review is not expressly granted, courts ought to refrain from deciding constitutional issues whenever possible. Others assert that, despite its implied status, judicial review is grounded in the Constitution, and thus the courts must decide constitutional issues that are fairly presented for decision. Two eminent Supreme Court justices present the two sides of this issue.

a. Chief Justice John Marshall:

It is most true that this Court will not take jurisdiction if it should not: but it is equally true, that it must take jurisdiction if it should. The judiciary cannot, as the legislature may, avoid a measure because it approaches the confines of the constitution. We cannot pass it by because it is doubtful. With whatever doubts, with whatever difficulties, a case may be attended, we must decide it, if it be brought before us. We have no more right to decline the exercise of jurisdiction which is given, than to usurp that which is not given. The one or the other would be treason to the constitution.

Cohens v. Virginia, 19 U.S. (6 Wheat.) 264 (1821).

b. Justice Louis Brandeis:

The Court [has] developed, for its own governance in the cases confessedly within its jurisdiction, a series of rules under which it has avoided passing upon a large part of all the constitutional cases pressed upon it for decision. They are: [1] The Court will not pass upon the constitutionality of legislation in a friendly, non-adversary, proceeding. . . . "It never was the thought that, by means of a friendly suit, a party beaten in the legislature could transfer to the courts an inquiry as to the constitutionality of the legislative act." [2] The Court will not "anticipate a question of constitutional law in advance of the necessity of deciding it." [3] The Court will not "formulate a rule of constitutional law broader than is required by the precise facts to which it is to be applied." [4] The Court will not pass upon a constitutional question although properly presented by the record, if there is also present some other ground upon which the case may be disposed of. [Thus], if a case can be decided on either of two grounds, one involving a constitutional question, the other a question of statutory construction or general law, the Court will decide only the latter. [5] The Court will not pass upon the validity of a statute upon complaint of one who fails to show that he is injured by its operation. [6] The Court will not pass upon the constitutionality of a statute at the instance of one who has availed himself of its benefits. [7] "When the validity of an act of the Congress is drawn in question, and even if a serious doubt of constitutionality is raised, it is a cardinal principle that this Court will first ascertain whether a construction of the statute is fairly possible by which the question may be avoided."

Ashwander v. TVA, 297 U.S. 288, 346 (1936). Although Brandeis's comments came in a concurrence, they have been repeated verbatim by the Court in Rescue Army v. Municipal Court of Los Angeles, 331 U.S. 549 (1947). Did Marshall adhere to these principles in *Marbury*?

c. Resolution of Marshall v. Brandeis. The positions of Marshall and Brandeis are not necessarily irreconcilable. As we shall see in Chapter 2, the Court has limited judicial review by invoking the principle of separation of powers and the requirement of Article III that limits the judicial power to "cases or controversies." That process is entirely compatible with Marshall's view because it involves charting the constitutional boundaries of the judicial power. Nor is there any tension between the two points of view with respect to the wisdom of reading statutes, whenever possible, to avoid constitutional issues. The sharpest conflict emerges with respect to issues such as abstention, a doctrine with constitutional overtones that permits (and sometimes mandates) federal courts to refuse to exercise their jurisdiction in the interest of deferring to state courts.

2. Judicial Exclusivity in Constitutional Interpretation?

Are the courts the *exclusive* interpreters of the Constitution? May Congress or the President interpret the Constitution differently from the courts when they perform their official duties? Suppose the Court upholds the validity of a federal law that makes possession of marijuana a crime. The President may pardon those convicted under the law but may the President instruct the Justice Department not to prosecute people for possession of marijuana? Suppose the Court invalidated a federal law making marijuana possession a crime. May the President instruct the Justice Department to continue such prosecutions? In short, what is the *binding* scope of judicial review?

Everyone agrees that the Court's judgments bind the parties to the case. Everyone agrees that the President, Congress, and state officials have independent obligations of fidelity to the Constitution. Disagreement centers on the degree to which the politically accountable branches of the federal and state governments have room to differ with the Court on matters of constitutional interpretation.

≡ *Cooper v. Aaron*
358 U.S. 1 (1958)

[Following the ruling in Brown v. Board of Education, 347 U.S. 483 (1954), that official racial segregation in public schooling was unconstitutional, Little Rock, Arkansas, sought to integrate the public schools in accordance with a plan approved by a federal district court. Arkansas Governor Faubus called out the National Guard to prevent school integration and was then enjoined from this action. The schools were integrated under the protective umbrella of army paratroopers, but the following year the Little Rock schools sought to delay integration to avoid further "chaos, bedlam, and turmoil." The district court granted the delay, which was reversed by the Eighth Circuit. The Supreme Court affirmed. Governor Faubus and the Arkansas Legislature insisted that they were not bound by the Supreme Court's decision in *Brown* because they were not parties to the case. The Court, in the dicta following, addressed that collateral contention.]

CHIEF JUSTICE WARREN and JUSTICES BLACK, FRANKFURTER, DOUGLAS, BURTON, CLARK, HARLAN, BRENNAN, and WHITTAKER, for the Court.

[We] answer the [contention] of the Governor and Legislature that they are not bound by our holding in the *Brown* case.

[Article] VI of the Constitution makes the Constitution the "supreme Law of the Land." In 1803, Chief Justice Marshall, speaking for a unanimous Court, referring to the Constitution as "the fundamental and paramount law of the nation," declared in [*Marbury*] that "[i]t is emphatically the province and duty of the judicial department to say what the law is." This decision declared the basic principle that the federal judiciary is supreme in the exposition of the law of the Constitution, and that principle has ever since been respected by this Court and the Country as a permanent and indispensable feature of our constitutional system. It follows that the interpretation of the Fourteenth Amendment enunciated by this Court in the *Brown* case is the supreme law of the land, and Art. VI of the Constitution makes it of binding effect on the States "any Thing in the Constitution or Laws of any State to the Contrary notwithstanding." [Chief] Justice Marshall spoke for a unanimous Court in saying that: "If the legislatures of the several states may, at will, annul the judgments of the courts of the United States, and destroy the rights acquired under those judgments, the constitution itself becomes a solemn mockery." United States v. Peters, [9 U.S. (5 Cranch) 115 (1809)]. A Governor who asserts a power to nullify a federal court order is similarly restrained. If he had such power, said Chief Justice Hughes, in 1932, also for a unanimous Court, "it is manifest that the fiat of a state Governor, and not the Constitution of the United States, would be the supreme law of the land; that the restrictions of the Federal Constitution upon the exercise of state power would be but impotent phrases" Sterling v. Constantin, 287 U.S. 378, 397-398 [(1932)].

NOTE

Was the Cooper v. Aaron Court correct? Consider the following views.
   a. Justice Felix Frankfurter.   "The ultimate touchstone of constitutionality is the Constitution itself and not what we have said about it." Graves v. O'Keefe, 306 U.S. 466, 491-492 (1938) (Frankfurter, J., concurring). But is the meaning of the Constitution self-evident? Constant over time? Does Frankfurter mean to suggest that *stare decisis* has no role in constitutional adjudication?
   b. Constitutional scholars.   Thomas Cooley, the preeminent constitutional scholar of the late nineteenth century:

> [T]he judiciary is the final authority in the construction of the Constitution . . . , and its construction should be received and followed by the other departments [of government]. Their judgments become the law of the land on the points covered by them, and a disregard of them, whether by private citizens or by officers of the government, could only result in new controversy, to be finally determined by the judiciary in the same way.

Cooley, The General Principles of Constitutional Law 158 (1898). Two current constitutional scholars emphatically agree:

> The accepted wisdom is that *Cooper*'s statement of judicial supremacy was an overstatement, politically necessary in its context but indefensible as a general claim of judicial interpretive authority. To the contrary, we defend *Cooper* and its assertion of judicial primacy without qualification [because judicial primacy] provides the benefits of authoritative settlement [of constitutional disputes] as well as the related benefits of inducing socially beneficial cooperative behavior.

Alexander and Schauer, On Extrajudicial Constitutional Interpretation, 110 Harv. L. Rev. 1359, 1362, 1371 (1997). Is practicality an adequate reason for deference to the Court's constitutional interpretations as final?
   c. President Thomas Jefferson.   "[To grant] to the judges the right to decide what laws are constitutional, and what not, not only for themselves in their own sphere of action, but for the Legislature & Executive also, in their spheres, would make the judiciary a despotic branch." Letter to Abigail Adams, Sept. 11, 1804 (8 The Writings of Thomas Jefferson 310 (Ford ed., 1899)). Was Jefferson right? Is the judiciary despotic?

d. President Andrew Jackson.   The following is an excerpt from Jackson's 1832 veto message, when he vetoed the bill rechartering the Second Bank of the United States. Earlier, in McCulloch v. Maryland, 17 U.S. (4 Wheat.) 316 (1819), the Court had ruled that creation of the bank was a "necessary and proper" means employed by Congress to effectuate its expressly delegated powers.

> It is maintained by advocates of the bank that its constitutionality in all its features ought to be considered as settled [by] the decision of the Supreme Court [in *McCulloch*]. To this conclusion I cannot assent. . . . [The] opinion of the Supreme Court [ought] not to control the coordinate authorities of this Government. [It] is as much the duty of the House of Representatives, of the Senate, and of the President to decide upon the constitutionality of any bill [that] may be presented to them for passage [as] it is of the supreme judges when it may be brought before them for judicial decision. The opinion of the judges has no more authority over Congress than the opinion of Congress has over the judges, and on that point the President is independent of both. The authority of the Supreme Court must not, therefore, be permitted to control the Congress or the Executive when acting in their legislative capacities, but to have only such influence as the force of their reasoning may deserve.

2 Messages and Papers of the Presidents 576, 581-583 (Richardson ed., 1896). Would Jackson's reasoning be equally applicable if Congress had enacted the bank charter bill into law over his veto and Jackson had then refused to expend appropriated money to breathe life into the Second Bank?

e. President Abraham Lincoln.   In Scott v. Sandford (*Dred Scott*), 60 U.S. (19 How.) 393 (1857), the Supreme Court held that the right of whites to own black slaves was a constitutionally guaranteed property right and thus ruled that Congress could not bar the introduction of slavery into the territories, nor could blacks be citizens. Two days before the decision was announced, President James Buchanan in his inaugural address said that "the question of domestic slavery in the Territories [is] a judicial question which legitimately belongs to the Supreme Court, [and] will be speedily and finally settled." Recall Alexander and Schauer's comments on the "settlement function" of the Court, above.

In the wake of *Dred Scott*, the binding quality of the Court's decision became a political issue. In his first inaugural address, of March 4, 1861, Lincoln addressed this issue:

> I do not forget the position assumed by some that constitutional questions are to be decided by the Supreme Court, nor do I deny that such decisions must be binding in any case upon the parties to a suit as to the object of that suit, while they are also entitled to very high respect and consideration in all parallel cases by all other departments of the Government. [At] the same time, the candid citizen must confess that if the policy of the Government upon vital questions affecting the whole people is to be irrevocably fixed by decisions of the Supreme Court, the instant they are made in ordinary litigation between parties in personal actions, the people will have ceased to be their own rulers, having to that

extent practically resigned their Government into the hands of that eminent tribunal.

6 Messages and Papers of the Presidents 5, 9-10 (Richardson ed., 1897). The *Dred Scott* case decided the question of whether Scott was a slave or was free, and in doing so the Court declared its opinion that the federal government could not bar the introduction of slavery into the territories. Suppose that prior to secession and civil war, Lincoln had urged Congress to outlaw slavery in all federal territories and Congress had done so. Whose interpretation of the constitutionality of this action should be dispositive?

B. THE POWER TO REVIEW STATE COURT JUDGMENTS

The 1789 Judiciary Act, enacted by the First Congress, gave the Supreme Court power to review the final decisions of the highest state courts on matters of federal law.[2] Although this jurisdiction had been sporadically exercised by the Court from 1789 on, its validity was challenged by the Virginia Supreme Court of Appeals during Madison's presidency.

Lord Fairfax, a British subject, owned a vast tract of ground in Virginia's Northern Neck. During the Revolution Virginia seized property owned by loyal subjects of George III, including Fairfax's holdings. Later, Virginia delivered title to portions of the Fairfax estate to various Virginians, including Hunter. In 1781 Fairfax devised his seized estate to Denny Martin. In 1791, Hunter brought suit in the Virginia courts to eject Martin. Martin, represented by John Marshall, defended his title by relying on the 1783 Treaty of Paris, by which Britain recognized American independence, and Jay's Treaty of 1794, which settled some of the property

---

2. Section 25 of the 1789 Judiciary Act states:

That a final judgment or decree in any suit, in the highest court of law or equity of a State in which the decision in the suit could be had, where is drawn in question the validity of a treaty or statute of, or an authority exercised under the United States, and the decision is against their validity; or where is drawn in question the validity of a statute of, or an authority exercised under any State, on the ground of their being repugnant to the constitution, treaties, or laws of the United States, and the decision is in favour of their validity, or where is drawn in question the construction of any clause of the constitution, or of a treaty, or statute of, or commission held under the United States, and the decision is against the title, right, privilege or exemption specially set up or claimed by either party, under such clause of the said constitution, treaty, statute, or commission, may be re-examined and reversed or affirmed in the Supreme Court of the United States upon a writ of error. . . . [N]o other error shall be assigned or regarded as a ground of reversal in any such case as aforesaid, than such as appears on the face of the record, and immediately respects the before mentioned questions of validity or construction of the said constitution, treaties, statutes, commissions, or authorities in dispute.

claims Great Britain made against Americans in the wake of American independence. Martin claimed that the treaties prevented Virginia from seizing Fairfax's estate. Although Martin initially prevailed in the Virginia trial court, Virginia's highest court, the Supreme Court of Appeals, reversed and found for Hunter in Hunter v. Fairfax's Devisee, 15 Va. (1 Munf.) 218 (1810). The Virginia Supreme Court held that under Virginia law Martin, a nonresident alien, could not inherit Virginia realty; Virginia had perfected title before the treaties; and, in any case, Martin's claim was defeated by a 1796 Virginia Act of Compromise in which Martin had surrendered his claim to the land in question. These conclusions made the treaties irrelevant. Meanwhile, John Marshall and his brother had agreed to purchase a substantial portion of the Fairfax lands from Martin, and John Marshall had become Chief Justice. Thus, when the case came to the U.S. Supreme Court, Marshall recused himself. In Fairfax's Devisee v. Hunter's Lessee, 11 U.S. (7 Cranch) 603 (1813), the Court ruled in part that Virginia had not perfected title before the 1783 Peace Treaty and Jay's Treaty of 1794. The Court remanded the case to the Virginia courts with instructions to enter judgment for Martin.

The Virginia Supreme Court refused: "The appellate power of the Supreme Court of the United States, does not extend to this court, under a sound construction of the constitution of the United States;—that so much of the 25th section of the act of congress, to establish the judicial courts of the United States, as extends the appellate jurisdiction of the Supreme Court to this court, is not in pursuance of the constitution of the United States; . . . and that obedience to its mandate be declined by this court." Hunter v. Martin, 18 Va. (4 Munf.) 1, 58-59 (1813). Judge Cabell offered this justification: "The constitution of the United States . . . regards the *residuary* sovereignty of the states, as not less inviolable, than the *delegated* sovereignty of the United States. It must have been foreseen that controversies would sometimes arise as to the boundaries of the two jurisdictions. Yet the constitution has provided no umpire, has erected no tribunal by which they shall be settled. . . . [B]efore one Court can dictate to another . . . it must bear, to the other, the relation of an appellate Court. The term appellate, however, necessarily includes the idea of *superiority*. But one Court cannot be correctly said to be *superior* to another, unless both of them belong to the same sovereignty. It would be a misapplication of terms to say that a Court of Virginia is *superior* to a Court of Maryland, or *vice versa*. The Courts of the United States, therefore, belonging to one sovereignty, cannot be appellate Courts in relation to the State Courts, which belong to a different sovereignty—and of course, their commands or instructions impose no obligation." Id. at 9-10. The Virginia judges argued that Congress was free to create federal courts and to permit removal of "cases of federal cognizance" to the federal courts in order to ensure "uniformity of decision" in federal law and to avoid conflict with state interpretations of federal law. The Virginians never denied their obligation under the supremacy clause to apply federal law to the exclusion of contrary state law. They merely denied that Congress could constitutionally subject their decisions on matters of federal law to review by the United States Supreme Court.

The Court's response, which follows, is often considered one of the most important opinions of the Marshall Court. Justice Joseph Story, its author, was a Massachusetts Democratic-Republican appointed to the Court by Madison. His opinion was a great disappointment to the Democratic-Republicans of which Madison was a part.

Martin v. Hunter's Lessee
14 U.S. (1 Wheat.) 304 (1816)

JUSTICE STORY, for a unanimous Court.

This is a writ of error from the Court of Appeals of Virginia, founded upon the refusal of that court to obey the mandate of this Court, requiring the judgment rendered in this very cause, at February term, 1813, to be carried into due execution. [Let] us now proceed to the interpretation of the constitution. [Story first contended that the jurisdictional grant of Article III was] mandatory upon the legislature[, an issue reserved for discussion in Chapter 2, Section B.3. He then turned to the issue of whether Congress could give the Supreme Court power to review the judgments of state courts on issues of federal law, as section 25 of the 1789 Judiciary Act purported to do].

But, even admitting that the language of the constitution is not mandatory, and that congress may constitutionally omit to vest the judicial power in courts of the United States, it cannot be denied that when it is vested, it may be exercised to the utmost constitutional extent.

This leads us to the consideration of the great question as to the nature and extent of the appellate jurisdiction of the United States. [Appellate] jurisdiction [is] capable of embracing every case enumerated in the constitution, which is not exclusively to be decided by way of original jurisdiction. . . . [Thus], what is there to restrain its exercise over state tribunals in the enumerated cases?

The appellate power is not limited by the terms of the third article to any particular courts. The words are, "the judicial power (which includes appellate power) shall extend to *all* cases," &c., and "in all other cases before mentioned the supreme court shall have appellate jurisdiction." It is the *case*, then, and not the *court*, that gives the jurisdiction. If the judicial power extends to the case, it will be in vain to search in the letter of the constitution for any qualification as to the tribunal where it depends. . . . If the text be clear and distinct, no restriction upon its plain and obvious import ought to be admitted, unless the inference be irresistible.

If the constitution meant to limit the appellate jurisdiction to cases pending in the courts of the United States, it would necessarily follow that the jurisdiction of these courts would, in all the cases enumerated in the constitution, be exclusive of state tribunals. How otherwise could the jurisdiction extend to *all* cases arising under the constitution, laws, and treaties of the

United States, or to *all* cases of admiralty and maritime jurisdiction? If some of these cases might be entertained by state tribunals, and no appellate jurisdiction as to them should exist, then the appellate power would not extend to *all*, but to *some*, cases. [This] construction would abridge the jurisdiction of such court far more than has been ever contemplated in any act of congress.

[If] a discretion be vested in congress to establish, or not to establish, inferior courts at their own pleasure, and congress should not establish such courts, the appellate jurisdiction of the supreme Court would have nothing to act upon, unless it could act upon cases pending in the state courts. Under such circumstances it must be held that the appellate power would extend to state courts; for the constitution is peremptory that it shall extend to certain enumerated cases, which cases could exist in no other courts. . . .

But it is plain that the framers of the constitution did contemplate that cases within the judicial cognizance of the United States not only might but would arise in the state courts, in the exercise of their ordinary jurisdiction. With this view the sixth article [the supremacy clause] declares, that "this constitution, and the laws of the United States which shall be made in pursuance thereof, and all treaties made, or which shall be made, under the authority of the United States, shall be the supreme law of the land, and the judges in every state shall be bound thereby, any thing in the constitution or laws of any state to the contrary notwithstanding." It is obvious that this obligation is imperative upon the state judges in their official, and not merely in their private, capacities. From the very nature of their judicial duties they would be called upon to pronounce the law applicable to the case in judgment. They were not to decide merely according to the laws or constitution of the state, but according to the constitution, laws and treaties of the United States — "the supreme law of the land."

[Justice Story illustrated some ways in which federal constitutional issues might occur in cases in state courts, such as the assertion of a constitutional defense to a criminal prosecution.] It must [be] conceded that the constitution not only contemplated, but meant to provide for cases within the scope of the judicial power of the United States, which might yet depend before state tribunals. It was foreseen that in the exercise of their ordinary jurisdiction, state courts would incidentally take cognizance of cases arising under the constitution, the laws, and treaties of the United States. Yet to all these cases the judicial power, by the very terms of the constitution, is to extend. It cannot extend by original jurisdiction if that was already rightfully and exclusively attached in the state courts, which (as has been already shown) may occur; it must, therefore, extend by appellate jurisdiction, or not at all. It would seem to follow that the appellate power of the United States must, in such cases, extend to state tribunals; and if in such cases, there is no reason why it should not equally attach upon all others within the purview of the constitution.

It has been argued that such an appellate jurisdiction over state courts is inconsistent with the genius of our governments, and the spirit of the constitution. That the latter was never designed to act upon state sovereignties, but only upon the people, and that if the power exists, it will materially impair the sovereignty of the states, and the independence of their courts. We cannot yield to the force of this reasoning; it assumes principles which we cannot admit, and draws conclusions to which we do not yield our assent.

It is a mistake [to hold] that the constitution was not designed to operate upon states, in their corporate capacities. It is crowded with provisions which restrain or annul the sovereignty of the states in some of the highest branches of their prerogatives. The tenth section of the first article contains a long list of disabilities and prohibitions imposed upon the states. Surely, when such essential portions of state sovereignty are taken away, or prohibited to be exercised, it cannot be correctly asserted that the constitution does not act upon the states. The language of the constitution is also imperative upon the states as to the performance of many duties. It is imperative upon the state legislatures to make laws prescribing the time, places, and manner of holding elections for senators and representatives, and for electors of president and vice-president. And in these, as well as some other cases, congress have a right to revise, amend, or supercede the laws which may be passed by state legislatures. When, therefore, the states are stripped of some of the highest attributes of sovereignty, and the same are given to the United States; when the legislatures of the states are, in some respects, under the control of congress, and in every case are, under the constitution, bound by the paramount authority of the United States; it is certainly difficult to support the argument that the appellate power over the decisions of state courts is contrary to the genius of our institutions. The courts of the United States can, without question, revise the proceedings of the executive and legislative authorities of the states, and if they are found to be contrary to the constitution, may declare them to be of no legal validity. Surely the exercise of the same right over judicial tribunals is not a higher or more dangerous act of sovereign power.

Nor can such a right be deemed to impair the independence of state judges. It is assuming the very ground in controversy to assert that they possess an absolute independence of the United States. In respect to the powers granted to the United States, they are not independent; they are expressly bound to obedience by the letter of the constitution; and if they should unintentionally transcend their authority, or misconstrue the constitution, there is no more reason for giving their judgments an absolute and irresistible force, than for giving it to the acts of the other co-ordinate departments of state sovereignty.

The argument urged from the possibility of the abuse of the revising power, is equally unsatisfactory. It is always a doubtful course, to argue against the use or existence of a power, from the possibility of its abuse. It is still more difficult, by such an argument, to ingraft upon a general power a restriction which is not to be found in the terms in which it is given. From the very nature of things, the absolute right of decision, in the last resort, must rest somewhere—wherever it may be vested it is susceptible of abuse. In all questions of jurisdiction the inferior, or appellate court, must pronounce the final judgment; and common sense, as well as legal reasoning, has conferred it upon the latter. . . .

It is further argued, that no great public mischief can result from a construction which shall limit the appellate power of the United States to cases in their own courts: first, because state judges are bound by an oath to support the constitution of the United States, and must be presumed to be men of learning and integrity; and, secondly, because congress must have an unquestionable right to remove all cases within the scope of the judicial power from the state courts to the courts of the United States, at any time before final judgment, though not after final judgment. As to the first reason—admitting that the judges of the state courts are, and always will be, of as much learning, integrity, and wisdom, as those of the courts of the United States, (which we very cheerfully admit,) it does not aid the argument. It is manifest that the constitution has proceeded upon a theory of its own, and given or withheld powers according to the judgment of the American people, by whom it was adopted. We can only construe its powers, and cannot inquire into the policy or principles which induced the grant of them. The constitution has presumed (whether rightly or wrongly we do not inquire) that state attachments, state prejudices, state jealousies, and state interests, might some times obstruct, or control, or be supposed to obstruct or control, the regular administration of justice. Hence, in controversies between states; between citizens of different states; between citizens claiming grants under different states; between a state and its citizens, or foreigners, and between citizens and foreigners, it enables the parties, under the authority of congress, to have the controversies heard, tried, and determined before the national tribunals. No other reason than that which has been stated can be assigned, why some . . . of those cases should not have been left to the cognizance of the state courts. . . .

This is not all. A motive of another kind, perfectly compatible with the most sincere respect for state tribunals, might induce the grant of appellate power over their decisions. That motive is the importance, and even necessity of uniformity of decisions throughout the whole United States, upon all subjects within the purview of the constitution. Judges of equal learning and integrity, in different states, might differently interpret a statute, or a treaty of the United States, or even the constitution itself: If there were no revising authority to control these jarring and discordant judgments, and harmonize them into uniformity, the laws, the treaties, and the constitution of the United States would be different in different states, and might, perhaps, never have precisely the same construction, obligation, or efficacy, in any two states. The public mischiefs that would attend such a state of things would be truly deplorable; and it cannot be believed that they could have escaped the enlightened convention which formed the constitution. What, indeed, might then have been only prophecy, has now become fact; and the appellate jurisdiction must continue to be the only adequate remedy for such evils. . . .

On the whole, the court [is] of opinion, that the appellate power of the United States does extend to cases pending in the state courts; and that the 25th section of the judiciary act, which authorizes the exercise of this jurisdiction in the specified cases . . . is supported by the letter and spirit of the constitution. We find no clause in that instrument which limits this power; and we dare not interpose a limitation where the people have not been disposed to create one. Strong as this conclusion stands upon the general language of the constitution, it may still derive support from other sources. It is an historical fact, that this exposition of the constitution, extending its appellate power to state courts, was, previous to its adoption, uniformly and publicly avowed by its friends, and admitted by its enemies, as the basis of their respective reasonings, both in and out of the state conventions. It is an historical fact, that at the time when the judiciary act was submitted to the deliberations of the first congress, composed, as it was, not only of men of great learning and ability, but of men who had acted a principal part in framing, supporting, or opposing that constitution, the same exposition was explicitly declared and admitted by the friends and by the opponents of that system. It is an historical fact, that the supreme court of the United States have, from time to time, sustained this appellate jurisdiction in a great variety of cases, brought from the tribunals of many of the most important states in the union, and that no state tribunal has ever breathed a judicial doubt on the subject, or declined to obey the mandate of the supreme court, until the present occasion. This weight of contemporaneous exposition by all parties, this acquiescence of enlightened state courts, and these judicial decisions of the supreme court through so long a period, [place] the doctrine upon a foundation of authority which cannot be shaken, without delivering over the subject to perpetual and irremediable doubts. . . .

It is the opinion of the whole court, that the judgment of the court of appeals of Virginia, rendered on the mandate in this cause, be reversed.

NOTES

1. The Virginians' Arguments. The Virginia judges relied on two arguments.

a. Separate sovereignties. The United States and Virginia are separate sovereigns. While Virginia is a member of the United States, and its judges must apply federal law (including constitutional law) as superior to state law, the courts of the United States have no more power to correct errors made by the Virginia courts than they would have to correct errors of federal law made by a Canadian court applying American federal law to a case within its jurisdiction. The argument that because Article III extends federal judicial power to *all* cases arising under federal law the Court must have power to review those decided by state courts "proves too much, and what is utterly inadmissible. It would give appellate jurisdiction, as well over the courts of England or France, as over the state courts." 18 Va. (4 Munf.) at 4 (Cabell, J.). But Virginia's courts, unlike those of England or France, are subject to federal law.

b. Congressional obligation to secure uniformity of federal law. Uniformity of federal law is a virtue. In the absence of a single final authority, federal law would differ among the jurisdictions, producing dissonance, forum shopping, and apparent caprice. But, said the Virginians, this does not mean that the U.S. Supreme Court must have power to revise the judgments of state courts on matters of federal law. Instead, the burden is on Congress to create inferior federal courts endowed with jurisdiction as extensive as Article III permits, if desired, and to enable removal of cases within Article III from the state courts to the federal courts. The disagreement between Story and the Virginians was over how much of a burden Congress must assume. The Virginia position was that the burden is on Congress to create federal courts in which all issues of federal law may be heard and resolved. The Supreme Court can correct their errors, but if Congress fails to do so (and thus allows state courts to decide issues of federal law), it has chosen to permit a patchwork quilt of federal law because the decisions of state courts cannot be reviewed by the courts of another sovereign. Story asserted, by contrast, that Congress may achieve the end of uniformity more directly, by empowering the Supreme Court to review state court dispositions of federal law. Given today's extensive network of federal courts and the existence of removal jurisdiction, are the Virginians' arguments unworkable? The federal courts did not receive general "federal question" jurisdiction until 1875. If the Virginians had prevailed in *Martin*, would the federal courts have received that jurisdiction much earlier?

2. Story's Arguments. Justice Story relied on three principal arguments.

a. Article III. The Supreme Court can review state judgments on matters of federal law because Article III gives the federal courts jurisdiction over *all* cases arising under federal law. Some of those cases might be tried in state courts. If the Supreme Court could not review them, the federal courts would not have jurisdiction over *all* such cases. Note that for Story's argument to cohere, he must be seen to have implicitly contended that the universe of *all* cases arising under federal law extends only to such cases arising in U.S. courts, since the Supreme Court has no power to hear the (admittedly unlikely) case involving U.S. federal law that arises in the courts of a foreign nation.

Story's argument is on a better footing when he invokes a particular conception of federal union—that American federalism consists of a national government supreme within its constitutional authority and state governments that may not act contrary to federal law. By contrast, the Virginians assumed that federal union created coequal sovereigns with separate spheres of authority. Does Article III answer those competing conceptions? If not, where does (should) the answer come from? These differing views on the relative roles of the federal and state governments have permeated our national political and constitutional history.

b. The supremacy clause. State judges are obliged to apply federal law as superior to state law. Because state judges are bound by the U.S. Constitution, their constitutional interpretations ought to be subject to correction by the U.S. Supreme Court. Even so, is it "assuming the very ground in controversy" to assert that the Supreme Court is the organ of the United States endowed with the power to correct constitutional errors made by the state courts? It is surely possible, albeit unwieldy in the extreme, to imagine

Congress correcting state constitutional errors. More relevant, perhaps, is the question of why state judges ought not be presumed to be as faithful interpreters of the Constitution as are the justices of the Supreme Court. To this, Story had two answers: the possibility of undue state attachments and the need for uniformity in federal law. With respect to the former, the argument is commonly made that state judges are more politically accountable (and, hence, less independent) than federal judges. See Neuborne, The Myth of Parity, 90 Harv. L. Rev. 1105 (1977). If true, is this necessarily a virtue of the federal judiciary? Might the greater insulation of federal judges (especially Supreme Court justices) from the people cause them to devalue popular innovations or to become biased in favor of the exercise of their powerful veto? Is the answer to this likely to be colored by political expediency? Consider your own views, imagining the state judiciaries to be controlled by "liberals" and the federal courts captured by "conservatives," or the reverse.

c. The need for uniformity. Story emphasized the "importance, and even necessity of *uniformity* of decisions throughout the whole United States, upon all subjects within the purview of the constitution." But U.S. Supreme Court review of state decisions on federal law is not the only way to achieve this desirable objective. The Virginians' approach—extensive federal question jurisdiction in the federal courts coupled with extensive removal jurisdiction—would have accomplished the same thing by funneling most federal questions into the federal courts. Story might have responded to the Virginians (but did not) by noting that Congress possesses power to adopt measures that are "necessary and proper" to implement the powers delegated to the federal government under the Constitution. Consider this argument in light of McCulloch v. Maryland, Chapter 3, Section A.

Is uniformity a virtue? By interpreting their own constitutions, states may expand liberty beyond the guarantees of the federal Constitution, with the result that citizens of some states enjoy greater liberty than citizens of other states. Of course, Story was concerned about uniformity of *federal* law. If the U.S. Supreme Court could not review state court decisions about federal constitutional law, the meaning of the Constitution would vary from state to state. The only pressures on state judges to conform to the Supreme Court's reading of the Constitution would be their own sense of integrity and their political accountability.

3. Cohens v. Virginia. The jurisdictional issue did not die with the decision in Martin v. Hunter's Lessee. Five years later, in Cohens v. Virginia, 19 U.S. (6 Wheat.) 264 (1821), Virginia argued (again unsuccessfully) that section 25 of the 1789 Judiciary Act was void insofar as it gave the Court jurisdiction to review a final criminal conviction in the state courts. In the years after *Cohens* there were repeated, unsuccessful attempts in Congress to repeal section 25.

4. Review of State Law. *Martin* is understood to stand for the proposition that the Supreme Court has power under Article III to review the final decisions of the highest state courts on matters of *federal* law.

C. THE ADEQUATE AND INDEPENDENT STATE GROUNDS DOCTRINE

The U.S. Supreme Court may exercise only the jurisdiction given it under Article III and as validly limited by Congress. What happens when a state court has decided a case by applying state law only?

> This Court from the time of its foundation has adhered to the principle that it will not review judgments of state courts that rest on adequate and independent state grounds. [Our] only power over state judgments is to correct them to the extent that they incorrectly adjudge federal rights. And our power is to correct wrong judgments, not to revise opinions. We are not permitted to render an advisory opinion, and if the same judgment would be rendered by the state court after we corrected its views of federal laws, our review could amount to nothing more than an advisory opinion.

Herb v. Pitcairn, 324 U.S. 117, 125-126 (1945). On the constitutional prohibition upon federal courts rendering advisory opinions, see Chapter 2, Section C.1.

The adequate and independent state grounds doctrine requires assessment of the *adequacy* of the state basis for decision and its *independence* from federal law. The state basis must be *both* adequate and independent.

≡ *Michigan v. Long*
   463 U.S. 1032 (1983)

[After a routine traffic stop, sheriff's deputies searched Long's car and found a large quantity of marijuana. Following his conviction, Long claimed on appeal that the search violated the Fourth Amendment's ban on unreasonable searches and seizures and the Michigan Constitution's analogous provision. The Michigan Supreme Court agreed. "[T]he deputies' search of the vehicle was proscribed by the Fourth Amendment to the United States Constitution and art. 1, §11 of the Michigan Constitution." The Court granted certiorari and reversed.]

JUSTICE O'CONNOR, for the Court.

[We] must consider Long's argument that we are without jurisdiction to decide this case because the decision below rests on an adequate and independent state ground. The court below referred twice to the State Constitution in its opinion, but otherwise relied exclusively on federal law. Long argues that the Michigan courts have provided greater protection from searches and seizures under the State Constitution than is afforded under the Fourth Amendment, and the references to the State Constitution therefore establish an adequate and independent ground for the decision below.

It is, of course, "incumbent upon this Court [to] ascertain for itself [whether] the asserted non-federal ground independently and adequately supports the judgment." Respect for the independence of state courts, as well as avoidance of rendering advisory opinions, have been the cornerstones of this Court's refusal to decide cases where there is an adequate and independent state ground. [Accordingly], when, as in this case, a state court decision fairly appears to rest primarily on federal law, or to be interwoven with the federal law, and when the adequacy and independence of any possible state law ground is not clear from the face of the opinion, we will accept as the most reasonable explanation that the state court decided the case the way it did because it believed that federal law required it to do so. If a state court chooses merely to rely on federal precedents as it would on the precedents of all other jurisdictions, then it need only make clear by a plain statement in its judgment or opinion that the federal cases are being used only for the purpose of guidance, and do not themselves compel the result that the court has reached. [If] the state court decision indicates clearly and expressly that it is alternatively based on bona fide separate, adequate, and independent grounds, we, of course, will not undertake to review the decision.

This approach [will] provide state judges with a clearer opportunity to develop state jurisprudence unimpeded by federal interference, and yet will preserve the integrity of federal law. "It is fundamental that state courts be left free and unfettered by us in interpreting their state constitutions. But it is equally important that ambiguous or obscure adjudications by state courts do not stand as barriers to a determination by this Court of the validity under the federal constitution of state action."

NOTES

1. The Practical Significance of the Adequate and Independent State Grounds Doctrine.   The adequate and independent state grounds doctrine is of tremendous importance to the maintenance of two levels of constitutional scrutiny. Every state has its own constitution. If a given state law or practice is challenged as a violation of the U.S. Constitution, in theory it is necessary first to decide that the challenged law is valid under the state constitution. If it is not, and the state's highest court plainly says so, that should be sufficient to decide the case without reaching the federal constitutional issue at all. The U.S. Supreme Court would lack jurisdiction of such a decision because it would clearly be decided upon adequate and independent state grounds. Only if a state's highest court has concluded that the challenged state law or practice is *valid under the state constitution* would it be necessary to also decide the issue of its validity under the federal Constitution. This latter decision, of course, would be susceptible to review in the U.S. Supreme Court.

Thus a state may interpret its constitution to protect more individual liberties than is the case when the U.S. Supreme Court interprets the federal Constitution. Of course, by virtue of the supremacy clause, a state may not enforce state constitutional provisions that deny liberties protected by the federal Constitution. The result is that the federal Constitution provides a minimum floor for individual liberties but not a maximum ceiling. Challenges to the constitutional validity of state action should always be made by first contending that the action violates the state constitution and, second, that the action (if valid under state law) violates federal law.

2. A "Mechanical" Presumption.   *Long* created a presumption against the adequacy and independence of the state grounds used as the basis of decision by the state court. But this presumption is quite mechanical and easily overcome. All that a state court need do is insert a phrase somewhat like the following near the end of its opinion: "We have considered federal law only for its persuasive and informational value. Our decision is based entirely and exclusively upon state law. We express no opinion as to issues of federal law."

3. Constitutional or Statutory?   The Supreme Court has never squarely held that the adequate and independent state grounds doctrine is constitutionally required. In Murdock v. Memphis, 87 U.S. 590 (1874), the Court avoided the constitutional question by deciding that Congress had not statutorily given the Court authority to review state law. The Court's present rationale for the doctrine appears to be rooted in constitutional principles. "The reason [for the doctrine] is so obvious that it has rarely been thought to warrant statement. It is found in the partitioning of power between the state and federal judicial systems and in the limitations of our own jurisdiction." Herb v. Pitcairn, 324 U.S. at 125. The Constitution's structural principle of federalism suggests that federal courts have no power to decide issues of state law independently of state courts. Article III limits federal court jurisdiction to "cases or controversies," and advisory opinions are neither cases nor controversies. See Chapter 2, Section C.1. "[I]f the same judgment would be rendered by the state court after [the Supreme Court] corrected its views of federal laws, [Supreme Court] review could amount to nothing more than an advisory opinion." *Herb*, at 126.

D.   THE UTILITY OF JUDICIAL REVIEW

In *Marbury*, Marshall never made it clear whether the power of judicial review was merely an incidental attribute of the Supreme Court's function as a law court or whether judicial review was a special attribute of courts in a constitutional democracy. If it is only incidental to the prosaic work of deciding real disputes between litigants, constitutional interpretation is a necessary chore of the Court but one to be avoided whenever possible due to the inherently antidemocratic nature of judicial review. But if judicial review is the special calling of courts in a constitutional democracy, then courts ought to be far more willing to reach out to decide constitutional issues whenever they occur in a judicial context. These opposing conceptions of the role of courts in exercising judicial review influence resolution of many of the issues considered in Chapter 2—the doctrines limiting the scope of judicial review.

Your view of these conceptions is apt to be colored by your view of the utility of judicial review. Some of the arguments for and against its benefits are summarized in this section.

1. Counter-Majoritarian Role

The Court acts as a brake upon the politically accountable branches of government. This is argued to be both good and bad.

The argument in favor is that legislatures will manifest the will of the majority, which may (perhaps often) be intolerant of politically and socially unpopular minorities. Constitutional liberties extend to everyone, including unpopular minorities, so legislatures cannot be trusted. The Constitution reflects the judgment of a founding supermajority that certain actions are "off limits" to later majorities. The federal judiciary is relatively immune to majoritarian pressure, so it is better equipped to decide whether legislation is constitutional. See, for example, Bickel, The Least Dangerous Branch 26 (1962) (arguing that judges, being immune to political pressure, can follow the "ways of the scholar" in constitutional interpretation).

Note that this argument depends on the assumption that the Constitution has a meaning that exists apart from the transient and temporary majorities of the moment. (The question of how to figure out that meaning is deferred to the next section.) But if the Constitution has no relatively fixed meaning and is instead a "living" document that means whatever we want it to mean at any given time, it is not at all clear why we should defer to judges rather than to the politically accountable branches of government. Moreover, this argument assumes that judges are accurately translating these original limits of the Constitution into action today and are not just expressing their political preferences in the form of constitutional law.

A rebuttal to this rejoinder is that the Constitution deliberately used broad terms to limit and empower government in order to give subsequent generations the ability to calibrate the precise meaning of those terms to their peculiar circumstances. On this view it is the calling of judges to translate faithfully the enduring terms of constitutional text into a current vernacular. They do this by writing opinions that are constitutional sequels—fashioning constitutional law to make sense of today's issues while also making sense of that which has gone before. Judges, it is argued, are better able to do this without distortion from popular fashion because of their relatively greater insulation from popular accountability. Some argue that a proper counter-majoritarian role of the courts is to enforce a moral vision of the Constitution that may not be shared by the majority of the people.

The argument against judicial review is that it is carried out by unelected and politically unaccountable judges and is a repudiation of the fundamental principle of a representative democracy—rule by our elected representatives. Of course, to the extent judges are doing nothing more than enforcing the constitutional limits set by those earlier supermajorities, they are merely blocking what would otherwise be illegitimate action by the legislature or the executive. See, e.g., Ackerman, Discovering the Constitution, 93 Yale L.J. 1013 (1984). But because it is very difficult to correct constitutional decisions by the Supreme Court that are mere political preferences, there is an inherent risk that constitutional law will become partisan politics by another name.

2. Avoiding the Counter-Majoritarian Problem

Two common arguments are made to demonstrate that judicial review is not really antidemocratic after all. First, it is claimed that judicial review merely implements the majority will of earlier generations regarding fundamental limits on government. As noted above, this argument depends on faithful implementation of that departed majority's view. Second, it is claimed that judicial review is really pro-democratic to the extent that it is used to eliminate barriers to democratic participation. John Hart Ely's 1980 book, Democracy and Distrust, is a key defense of this theme.

Note that this argument depends on the assumption that judicial elimination of such impediments is the highest constitutional priority—to be preferred to other, perhaps conflicting, constitutional rules. For example, the Constitution leaves to the states discretion in establishing voter qualifications in state elections, except for sex, race, and certain age criteria. When the Court struck down a modest tax on voting in state elections, Harper v. Virginia State Board of Elections, 383 U.S. 663 (1966), it preferred a newly created and entirely nontextual right to the Constitution's grant of discretion to states to set voting standards. Which is more majoritarian—respecting the constitutional grant of discretion to states to set voting standards or removing state-imposed barriers to voting that strike the Court as imperfections in the democratic process? Whatever the answer, the process theory, or "representation reinforcement" as it is sometimes called, is influential. It is often invoked to justify a preferred position for free speech as a right essential to vindication of all other rights.

3. Stability

In favor of judicial review is the argument that unless some branch has the effective last word on constitutional interpretation, the Constitution would have no settled meaning. Note that this argument combines arguments favoring judicial review with a claim to judicial supremacy (if not exclusivity) in constitutional interpretation. The argument is pragmatic, perhaps best summarized by Judge Learned Hand's assertion that judicial review was justified by the need "to prevent the defeat of the venture at hand." Hand, The Bill of Rights 14 (1958). A variation on this theme is Justice Oliver Wendell Holmes's observation: "I do not think the United States would come to an end if we lost our power to declare an Act of Congress void. I do think the Union would be imperiled if we could not make that declaration as to the laws of the several States." Holmes, Collected Legal Papers 295-296 (1920). Did Holmes place too much faith in the constitutional fidelity of Congress? Too little in the constitutional faith of the states?

4. Entrenched Error

An argument against judicial review is that it makes it very difficult to correct mistaken interpretations of the Constitution. Neither Congress nor the President may ignore Court decisions with impunity. The only avenues for correction are (1) persuading the Court to change its mind (which often requires new justices), (2) impeachment and removal of justices, or (3) constitutional amendment. None of these is easy. Does judicial review mean that when the Court gets the Constitution wrong it stays wrong? This argument is an application of Bishop Hoadley's famous sermon delivered in 1717 before George I: "Whoever hath an absolute authority to interpret written or spoken laws; it is he who is truly the lawgiver to all intents and purposes and not the person who wrote or spoke them."

5. Erosion of Constitutional Responsibility by the Political Branches

It has been argued that frequent reliance on judicial review saps the will of the political branches to consider constitutional issues seriously. James Bradley Thayer, a great constitutional commentator at the turn of the twentieth century, identified dangers to both legislators and the people. Judicial review causes legislatures to "shed the consideration of constitutional restraints, [turning] that subject over to the courts; and, what is worse, they insensibly fall into the habit of assuming that whatever they can constitutionally do they may do,—as if honor and fair dealing and common honesty were not relevant to their inquiries." But judicial review also causes "the people [to] lose the political experience, and the moral education and stimulus that come from fighting the question out in the ordinary way, and correcting their own errors." The effect of judicial review is "to dwarf the political capacity of the people, and to deaden its sense of moral responsibility." Thayer, John Marshall, 104, 106-107 (1901). Was Thayer correct? Consider the following.

After the Supreme Court invalidated the National Industrial Recovery Act, a key piece of early New Deal legislation, President Franklin Roosevelt urged Congress to enact a nearly identical bill, suggesting that Congress put aside its doubts concerning the bill's constitutional validity: "[A]ll doubts should be resolved in favor of the bill, leaving to the courts, in an orderly fashion, the ultimate question of constitutionality. . . . [I hope Congress] will not permit doubts as to constitutionality, however reasonable, to block the suggested legislation." Letter from President Roosevelt to Representative Hill, July 6, 1935, 4 The Public Papers and Addresses of Franklin D. Roosevelt 297-298 (1938). Congress did Roosevelt's bidding, and the Court voided the resulting law. See Carter v. Carter Coal Co., 298 U.S. 238 (1936).

By the 1990s, Congress's sense of the constitutional limits on its power had so atrophied that it enacted the Gun-Free School Zones Act without ever considering the question of whether it had any constitutional authority to act. To Congress's surprise, the Court voided the law in a controversial opinion limiting the scope of congressional power to regulate interstate commerce. See United States v. Lopez, 514 U.S. 549 (1995), Chapter 3, Section B.1.

E. METHODS OF CONSTITUTIONAL INTERPRETATION

How do we know what the Constitution means? What *should* the Constitution mean? There is no agreement.

1. Interpretation or Imagination?

The first divide is the split between *noninterpretivists* and *interpretivists*. Expressing their position in its most extreme form, noninterpretivists claim that we should not even attempt to figure out what the text of the Constitution means; instead, we should make it a mirror of our present sense of fundamental justice. More commonly, noninterpretivists assert that courts are not *limited* to constitutional text, but may import wholly extraconstitutional norms as a source of constitutional decision. Interpretivists insist that the only legitimate form of judicial review is interpretation of the written text of the Constitution. This debate is not new.

≡
≡ ## *Calder v. Bull*
≡ *3 U.S. (3 Dall.) 386 (1798)*

[Connecticut's legislature set aside a probate court decision refusing to approve a will by enacting a law that required a new hearing. At the second hearing the will was approved. The heirs who would have taken the estate's assets had the will been ineffective challenged the Connecticut law as an ex post facto law. The Court rejected that claim, finding that the ex post facto clause applies only to criminal laws. In the years before John Marshall became Chief Justice, the justices wrote seriatim opinions. The following dicta in two of those opinions reflect the debate between interpretivism and noninterpretivism.]

JUSTICE CHASE: The purposes for which men enter into society will determine the nature and terms of the social compact: and as they are the foundation of the legislative power, they will decide what are the proper objects of it. [There] are certain vital principles in our free Republican governments, which will determine and over-rule an apparent and flagrant abuse of legislative power; as to authorize manifest injustice by positive law; or to take away that security for personal liberty, or private property, for the protection whereof the government was established. An Act of the Legislature (for I cannot call it a law) contrary to the great first principles of the social compact, cannot be considered a rightful exercise of legislative authority. . . . A few instances will suffice to explain what I mean. . . . [Imagine a] law that takes property from A and gives it to B: It is against all reason and justice, for a people to entrust a Legislature with *such* powers; and, therefore, it cannot be presumed that they have done it. The genius, the nature, and the spirit, of our State Governments, amount to a prohibition of such acts of legislation; and the general principles of law and reason forbid them. The Legislature [may not] change innocence into guilt; [or] violate the right of an antecedent lawful private contract; or the right of private property. To maintain that our Federal, or State, Legislature possesses such powers, if they had not been expressly restrained, would, in my opinion, be a political heresy, altogether inadmissible in our free republican governments.

JUSTICE IREDELL: [S]ome speculative jurists have held, that a legislative act against natural justice must, in itself, be void; but I cannot think that, [absent the limits imposed by a written constitution] any Court of Justice would possess a power to declare it so. Sir William Blackstone [states that] "there is no court that has power to defeat the intent of the Legislature." In order [to] guard against so great an evil, it has been the policy of [the] people of the United States, when they framed the Federal Constitution, to define with precision the objects of the legislative power, and to restrain its exercise within marked and settled boundaries. If any act of Congress, or of the Legislature of a state, violates those constitutional provisions, it is unquestionably [invalid]. If, on the other hand, the Legislature of the Union, or the Legislature of any member of the Union, shall pass a law, within the general scope of their constitutional power, the Court cannot pronounce it to be void, merely because it is, in their judgment, contrary to the principles of natural justice. The ideas of natural justice are regulated by no fixed standard: the ablest and the purest men have differed upon the subject; and all that the Court could properly say, in such an event, would be, that the Legislature (possessed of an equal right of opinion) had passed an act which, in the opinion of the judges, was inconsistent with the abstract principles of natural justice.

NOTES

1. The Role of Natural Law.   What role, if any, should natural law play in constitutional adjudication? To some extent, this may depend on what is meant by "natural law." Does natural law mean simply the natural outcome of a dominant opinion, in which case it is virtually indistinguishable from majority sentiment? Or does it mean divine command, a position that demands that its proponents prove adequately their accurate knowledge of divine will and that we are governed by this abstract divinity? Or does it mean a moral view that is shared by virtually everyone in society? In that case will there be many occasions for invoking natural law to void legislative judgments?

2. Some Difficulties with Noninterpretivism. Noninterpretivism poses a great many difficulties. Text-based judicial review may be counter-majoritarian, but is judicial review that is based on a judge's moral ideas or policy preferences authoritarian? Recall that one of Marshall's defenses of judicial review was that it followed from the concept of a *written* Constitution. If the written Constitution is discarded, how can the kernel of judicial review contained within it be retained? The result is that almost everyone today, barring extreme natural law theorists or "critical" thinkers who maintain that all text is hopelessly indeterminate or capable of infinite manipulation, is some form of interpretivist. Because the meaning of a great deal of constitutional text is not self-evident, however, almost all interpretivists admit that some sources outside of the text itself are permissible aids to interpretation. The debate then shifts to what nontextual sources are appropriate and how much weight to give them.

There are at least five methods commonly employed to decide the meaning of the Constitution. These methods are not mutually exclusive. Often they are combined in the same argument or opinion, but from case to case lawyers and judges may accentuate them differently. The best constitutional argument is one that can employ every one of these methods convincingly. Each will be briefly considered below.

2. The Textual Method

Because it is a *written* constitution it makes sense to start with its text. The textual argument "is drawn from a present sense of the words of the provision." Bobbitt, Constitutional Fate 7 (1982). Some contend that it is impossible to know authoritatively the meaning of any text. There may (or may not) be an authorial intention, which may (or may not) coincide with the reader's understanding. Granted that words are not crystals but the skins of living thoughts, to paraphrase Justice Holmes, it may still be possible to reach some common agreement on the meaning of ordinary thoughts residing within word skins. Fervent believers in the indeterminacy of language may contend that the Constitution's requirement that the President "shall . . . have attained to the Age of thirty five years" be read as a requirement of maturity, but less rarefied thinkers are probably content to treat this as a simple arithmetic calculation. On the other hand, the text of the Constitution may not be much help in deciphering the meaning of "cruel or unusual," "due process," or "equal protection of the laws." When text is inadequate, some other source of meaning is needed.

3.   Historical Argument

Historical argument may be broken down into two forms. One is commonly described as "originalism," which itself takes two forms: (1) determining the original intent of the drafters of the Constitution or (2) establishing the original meaning of its text. The other form of historical argument is less static and is an attempt to derive historical meaning from the "vectors" of history, the way in which constitutional understanding has changed over time.

a.   Original Intent

Determining original intent is an attempt to discover the authorial intent behind any constitutional provision. After all, these fundamental limits were intended to mean something, and if we do not try to ascertain that meaning we are essentially stating that the Constitution means whatever we would like it to mean today. Advocates of this method argue that focus on the original intent of the drafters prevents, or at least inhibits, the tendency of politically unaccountable judges to remake the Constitution to reflect their personal preferences. But there are significant obstacles to ascertaining intent. Whose intent counts? What about people excluded then but included now, like women and blacks? What is the best evidence of intent? What happens when the Framers disagree? Even if we resolve these considerable issues, does original intent matter when the application of the constitutional provision in question is to some problem utterly outside of the Framers' knowledge? See Powell, Rules for Originalists, 73 Va. L. Rev. 659 (1987). Because history is always an informed weighing of probabilities, there is considerable information (and hence value) to be gained from dispassionate examination of the thoughts left to us from the past. See also Robert G. Natelson, "The Founders' Hermeneutic: The Real Original Understanding of Original Intent," 68 Ohio State L.J. 1239 (2012).

b.   Original Meaning

Partly because the original intent of the authors of the constitutional text is so difficult to locate with certainty, many originalists focus instead on the original meaning of the text itself. As it is the text that binds, these originalists attempt to determine what the text meant at the time it was adopted. This can be more easily determined by reference to contemporary interpretations of that text. Of course, those interpretations are necessarily static, rooted in a single moment, the moment of adoption of the relevant constitutional text.

c.   The "Vectors" of History

History may be perceived as snapshots, faded sepia photographs in the national photo album, or it may be thought of as a video, continuously running and always recording new scenes. History as "original intentions" or "original meaning" is static; history as "vectors" is dynamic. Thus, in attaching meaning to "cruel or unusual punishment" one might wish to ascertain the contemporaneous definition of the term. The pillory was certainly not unusual in the late eighteenth century, but surely it is now.

In Poe v. Ullman, 367 U.S. 497 (1961), the Court decided that a challenge to a Connecticut law making contraceptive use a crime was not justiciable. Justice Harlan dissented and reached the merits, applying the due process clause of the Fourteenth Amendment.

> Due process has not been reduced to any formula. . . . The best that can be said is that [it] has represented the balance which our Nation, built upon postulates of respect for the liberty of the individual, has struck between that liberty and the demands of organized society. If the supplying of content to this Constitutional concept has of necessity been a rational process, it certainly has not been one where judges have felt free to roam where unguided speculation might take them. The balance of which I speak is the balance struck by this country, having regard to what history teaches are the traditions from which it developed as well as the traditions from which it broke. That tradition is a living thing. A decision of this Court which radically departs from it could not long survive, while a decision which builds on what has survived is likely to be sound. No formula could serve as a substitute, in this area, for judgment and restraint.

Of course, over-reliance on the vectors of history results in a methodology that is as much fortune-telling as constitutional interpretation. At some point, this method becomes indistinguishable from noninterpretivism. As Justice Harlan pointed out, constitutional interpretation devoid of good sense will fail.

A related issue is the level of generality at which we ought to consider historical practice. Michael H. v. Gerald D., 491 U.S. 110 (1989), was a case involving a claimed constitutional right of a natural father to establish a parental relationship with his child born into another's marriage as a result of an adulterous affair. Justice Scalia, for himself and Chief Justice Rehnquist, urged that historical traditions should be applied quite specifically:

> We refer to the most specific level at which a relevant tradition protecting, or denying protection to, the asserted right can be identified. If [there] were no societal tradition, either way, regarding the rights of the natural father of a child adulterously conceived, we would have to consult, and reason from, the traditions regarding natural fathers in general. But there is such a more specific tradition, and it unqualifiedly denies protection to such a parent. [G]eneral traditions provide imprecise guidance [and] permit judges to dictate rather than discern the society's views. [A] rule of law that binds neither by text nor by any particular, identifiable tradition, is no rule of law at all.

Justice Brennan replied that

[there were] good reasons for limiting the role of "tradition" in interpreting the Constitution's deliberately capacious language. [We] are not an assimilative, homogenous society, but a facilitative, pluralistic one, in which we must be willing to abide someone else's unfamiliar or even repellant practice because the same tolerant impulse protects our own idiosyncracies. "[L]iberty" must include the freedom not to conform. [Justice Scalia's approach] squashes this freedom by requiring specific approval from history. [Justice Scalia's] Constitution is a stagnant, archaic, hidebound document steeped in the prejudices and superstitions of a time long past.

In a later case Justice Scalia responded: "[The] difference between Justice Brennan [and me] has nothing to do with whether 'further progress [is] to be made' in the 'evolution of our legal system.' It has to do with whether changes are to be adopted as progressive by the American people or decreed as progressive by the Justices of this Court." Burnham v. Superior Court, 495 U.S. 604, 627 (1990).

4.   Structural Arguments

Structural arguments involve "claims that a particular principle or practical result is implicit in the structures of government and the relationships that are created by the Constitution among citizens and governments." Bobbitt, supra, at 7. Marshall's argument in *Marbury* that judicial review follows from the fact of a written Constitution is rooted in the claim that the structure of the Constitution implies an active role for the federal courts in deciding constitutional law. Structural arguments are postulates about the type of governance created by the Constitution. They are interpolations that compose an interstitial constitution—one that fills the gaps left by the government structures created by the Constitution. These types of arguments are particularly common when the underlying issue is federalism—the proper allocation of power between the federal and state governments—or separation of powers—the proper allocation of federal power among the three branches of the national government. See, e.g., Black, Structure and Relationship in Constitutional Law (1969).

5.   Doctrinal Arguments

Doctrinal argument "asserts principles derived from precedent" and sometimes "judicial or academic commentary on precedent." Bobbitt, supra, at 7. This is the familiar common law method. *Stare decisis,* or the rule of precedent, is a cornerstone of our common law method. Yet, as applied to constitutional law, the Court has repeatedly said that this doctrine is at its weakest—because of the extreme difficulty of correcting constitutional decisions of the Supreme Court. Even with a relatively weak principle of *stare decisis* in constitutional law, the Court adheres to past decisions with uncommon frequency. There is virtue in legal stability, for, as Justice Brandeis once put it, "in most matters it is more important that the applicable rule of law be settled than it be settled right." Burnet v. Coronado Oil & Gas Co., 285 U.S. 393, 406 (1932) (Brandeis, J., dissenting).

The Court does overturn precedent, however. In doing so,

> its judgment is customarily informed by a series of prudential and pragmatic considerations designed to test the consistency of overruling a prior decision with the ideal of the rule of law, and to gauge the respective costs of reaffirming and overruling a prior case. [W]e may ask whether the rule has proved to be intolerable simply in defying practical workability, whether the rule is subject to a kind of reliance that would lend a special hardship to the consequences of overruling and add inequity to the cost of repudiation, whether related principles of law have so far developed as to have left the old rule no more than a remnant of abandoned doctrine, or whether facts have so changed or come to be seen so differently, as to have robbed the old rule of significant application or justification.

Planned Parenthood v. Casey, 505 U.S. 833 (1992).

6.   Prudential Arguments

Prudential arguments boil down to "advancing particular doctrines according to the practical wisdom of using the courts in a particular way." Bobbitt, supra, at 7. In short, these arguments are the most removed from the more traditional sources of constitutional law. Nevertheless, they are important and at times so persuasive as to be dispositive. For example, the contention that courts should not review the grounds on which a President is impeached and convicted relies almost entirely on the powerful prudential argument that such judicial review would have a potentially catastrophic destabilizing effect on the national government. Many arguments surrounding the proper separation of powers are prudential arguments.

7.   Cultural Arguments

Cultural arguments are rooted in widely shared cultural norms, such nontextual sources as moral concepts of justice, theories of human autonomy, and cultural assumptions about fairness. By themselves, these arguments are not necessarily constitutional arguments, but when they are used in conjunction with other forms of constitutional argument, they can be of considerable persuasive force. To the extent a society has widely shared notions of justice, autonomy, and fairness, and those ideas are imperfectly reflected in more conventional constitutional arguments, cultural argument fills an important gap. As you study these materials, consider, for example, the role of cultural argument in such cases as Brown v. Board of Education (striking down official school segregation by race), Plyler v. Doe (voiding a Texas law denying free public education to children illegally present in the United States), or Obergefell v. Hodges (invalidating state laws limiting marriage to opposite-sex partners).

8. Constitutional Interpretation Versus Constitutional Implementation

It is possible to separate the *meaning* of the Constitution from the doctrinal devices that can be created to *implement* that meaning. Professor Keith Whittington contends that constitutional *interpretation* of the meaning of the Constitution is distinct from constitutional *construction* of that meaning. To illustrate, he asks you to imagine a constitutional provision that enjoins you to "buy a dog." Constitutional interpretation may focus on whether a wolf, coyote, fox, or hyena falls within the definition of "dog," or whether the provision should be limited to domesticated canines. The various modes of constitutional interpretation just discussed may be useful in making that distinction, but once we have settled on an interpretation, it is quite another matter to decide whether the constitutional command requires us to purchase a collie, a German shepherd, or a Boston terrier. The latter endeavor, argues Whittington, is a construction of meaning, an essentially political judgment, and thus ought to be left to the discretion of the politically accountable branches. Whittington, Constitutional Interpretation: Textual Meaning, Original Intent, and Judicial Review 5-14 (1999); Whittington, Constitutional Construction: Divided Powers and Constitutional Meaning (1999).

Another approach to the same problem is taken by Professor Mitch Berman, who argues that "constitutional doctrines that represent the judiciary's understanding of the proper meaning of a constitutional . . . provision are 'constitutional operative propositions' [but] doctrines that direct courts how to decide whether a constitutional operative proposition is satisfied [are] 'constitutional decision rules.'" Berman, Constitutional Decision Rules, 90 Va. L. Rev. 1, 9 (2004). While there may still be disagreement about how to interpret the Constitution to derive a "constitutional operative proposition," if the proposition can be stated with sufficient generality to garner consensus the constitutional adjudicator's task is to devise rules to determine whether the proposition has been satisfied. There are lots of possibilities. A judicial decision about which party has the burden of proof is one example, as is the evidentiary standard that must be met. Differing levels of judicial review are another device that courts use to implement the Constitution. As introduced below, a great deal of constitutional doctrine hinges on the levels of review that courts employ to decide whether or not governments have complied with the Constitution.

In studying constitutional law, you will not encounter much, if any, explicit acknowledgment of this divide. Interpretation and construction are conflated; constitutional operative propositions are fused with constitutional decision rules. Even if you can sift the decision rules from the Constitution's meaning, recognition of this distinction can be troubling, for it raises the question of whether the courts have the authority to fashion decision rules and, if so, which ones are legitimate and why that is so. Even so, some awareness of this theoretical distinction may help you to disentangle theory from doctrinal practice.

F. THE UNEVEN NATURE OF JUDICIAL REVIEW: TIERED REVIEW AND THE UNEQUAL STATUS OF CONSTITUTIONAL CLAIMS

Nothing in the Constitution states or even suggests that the Constitution's various limits on government should be treated differently by reviewing courts. Yet that is precisely what the courts do. As with animal rights in George Orwell's *Animal Farm* ("All animals are equal, but some animals are more equal than others"), so too with constitutional rights. Constitutional interpreters have devoted a great deal of their time and ingenuity to the explanation and justification of this curious state of affairs. These theoretical justifications will become apparent as the course progresses. For now, you should be aware of the basic outline of the constitutional doctrine that reflects these justifications.

Although it is a bit simplistic to describe them as such, courts use three levels, or tiers, of review, although not in every area of constitutional law. In some areas these levels of review are modified to respond to particular concerns, and in other areas (e.g., separation of powers) tiered review is nonexistent. Some justices, notably Thurgood Marshall and J.P. Stevens, have contended that tiered review is a misleading illusion, but the Court as a whole has never agreed with that view. So the basic, but not monolithic, theme is tiered review. A brief discussion of the three levels of scrutiny follows.

(1) Minimal Scrutiny: The Constitutional "Default" Level of Review

Courts begin with the presumption that statutes and other government actions are valid. Unless there is some reason to doubt that presumption, the challenger has the burden of proving that the law, regulation, or executive act is *not rationally related to a legitimate government objective*. This is a very weak basis for review, one that is very deferential to the political branches of government. So long as the government's reason for acting is legitimate—within the granted powers of the government in question and not violative of some constitutional restraint on the exercise of those powers—almost any means of achieving it will be accepted as "rationally related" to the objective. Legislation has to be truly bizarre to offend this prong of the standard. And the courts generally (but not always) accept any hypothetical objective as the government's goal, whether there is any evidence that the hypothesized objective was the actual objective. This level of review is frequently called "rational basis" or "rationality" review.

(2) Strict Scrutiny

At the opposite end of the spectrum is strict scrutiny. Some types of government action are presumptively invalid. The classic example, derived from the equal protection clause, is a statute that classifies by race. The use of race as a classifying device (e.g., "the entry fee to public parks is $2 for each white person, and $3 for each nonwhite person") is constitutionally suspect. In such cases, courts presume that the government action at issue is invalid. The defender of the government action has the burden of proving that the law or executive act is *necessary to accomplish a compelling government objective.* This is an extremely difficult standard to meet, but it is not impossible. The government's actual reason for using the presumptively invalid criterion (e.g., race) must be of paramount importance, and the use of the criterion must be essential to accomplish that very important goal. One of the few instances in which this standard has been met is the use of race to remedy official racial segregation. In order to achieve the compelling goal of dismantling unconstitutional state-mandated racial segregation in public education, it was necessary to use race for pupil and teacher assignments.

Strict scrutiny places a premium on identifying actions that are presumptively invalid. The conventional starting point is "famous footnote 4," authored by Chief Justice Harlan Stone in United States v. Carolene Products, 304 U.S. 144 (1938):

> There may be narrower scope for operation of the presumption of constitutionality when legislation appears on its face to be within a specific prohibition of the Constitution. [It] is unnecessary to consider now whether legislation which restricts those political processes which can ordinarily be expected to bring about repeal of undesirable legislation, is to be subjected to more exacting judicial scrutiny [than] are most other types of legislation. [Nor] need we enquire whether similar considerations enter into the review of statutes directed at particular religious, or national, or racial minorities; whether prejudice against discrete and insular minorities may be a special condition, which tends seriously to curtail the operation of those political processes ordinarily to be relied upon to protect minorities, and which may call for a correspondingly more searching judicial scrutiny.

Much of the modern law of equal protection and due process is traceable to this doctrinal acorn.

(3) Intermediate Scrutiny

Between the two extremes lies an intermediate level of review; which is triggered when the government action comes with some taint of presumptive invalidity but not quite enough to invoke strict scrutiny. The classic example is a statutory classification on the basis of sex. These "quasi-suspect" classifications, or other government actions with an odor of illegitimacy, are presumed to be invalid. The defender of the government action has the burden of proving that the *actual purpose* of the statute or action is *important* and that the statute or action is *substantially related to the accomplishment of that actual purpose.* This level of review is inherently subjective and, as a result, cases applying this standard (whether in free speech or equal protection) reflect a wide range of results.

As you study the substance of constitutional law, pay attention to the level of review the Court applies to alleged violations of various constitutional provisions. For example, the Court generally applies minimal scrutiny to questions of whether Congress has exceeded its granted powers; e.g., is an act of Congress a valid exercise of the power to regulate interstate commerce? The Court also applies a form of minimal scrutiny to claims that onerous government regulations have the effect of taking private property without just compensation, which would violate the takings clause of the Fifth Amendment, or to other claimed property protections under the due process or equal protection clause. Yet, also using the due process or equal protection clause, the Court applies strict scrutiny to government actions that interfere with some liberties unmentioned in the Constitution. On a purely doctrinal level, it is important to understand which rules apply to which claimed constitutional interests.

It is far more important, however, to understand the theory of this doctrine—why does the Court effectively police constitutional boundaries in a hierarchical fashion? What justifies deference to legislative majorities on some issues and not others? Why are some rights that are never mentioned in the Constitution treated more protectively than others explicitly set out in the text? The answers to these questions are not always obvious and will rest on different grounds for each issue that you confront. But awareness of this problem as you work through your course will increase the depth of your understanding.

2

Doctrines Limiting the Scope of Judicial Review

Judicial review, like Janus, has two faces. Judicial review may be a practical necessity to implementing the guarantees of a written constitution, but it also raises the possibility of government by an unelected judiciary. If judicial review is used to veto legislation as unconstitutional simply because it is not in accordance with the Supreme Court's view of sound public policy, the fundamental premise of representative self-governance is subverted. One way to avoid this problem is to rely on structural devices rather than the good faith of the justices. As James Madison said in Federalist 51: "If men were angels, no government would be necessary. If angels were to govern men, neither external nor internal controls on government would be necessary. In framing a government . . . you must . . . oblige [the government] to control itself."

This chapter examines some of the structural limitations on judicial review. Sections A and B are concerned with the devices available to the politically accountable branches to control the exercise of judicial review. Section C examines the "justiciability" doctrines, a congeries of rules designed to ensure that federal courts decide only cases presenting real, actual legal disputes that personally affect the litigants and that are capable of resolution by courts. Section D is a brief overview of the jurisdictional limits imposed on federal courts by the Eleventh Amendment.

A. DIRECT POLITICAL CONTROLS: AMENDMENT, APPOINTMENT, AND IMPEACHMENT

The direct political controls of the Supreme Court are difficult and uncertain. The Constitution may be amended to reverse constitutional decisions of the Court. New members of the Court may be appointed with the hope or expectation that they will vote to overrule specific past decisions. Any federal judge, including justices of the Court, may be impeached, convicted, and removed from office.

1. Amendment

The Constitution is not easily amended. Over 10,000 amendments have been introduced in or formally recommended to Congress, but only 33 have been adopted by Congress, and only 27 have actually been ratified. Of those, only four were intended to overrule some specific constitutional decision of the Supreme Court. Those four are the Eleventh Amendment, overturning Chisholm v. Georgia, 2 U.S. (2 Dall.) 419 (1793) (holding that Georgia was subject to suit by a private citizen in federal court without its consent); the Fourteenth Amendment, overturning Dred Scott v. Sandford, 60 U.S. (19 How.) 393 (1857) (holding in part that American blacks were not, and could not become, American citizens); the Sixteenth Amendment, overturning Pollock v. Farmers' Loan & Trust Co., 157 U.S. 429 (1895) (holding that an income tax was a direct tax and therefore subject to the constitutional rule of apportionment by population among the states); and the Twenty-sixth Amendment, overturning Oregon v. Mitchell, 400 U.S. 112 (1970) (holding in part that Congress lacked authority to require the states to permit those over 18 to vote in state elections). Rather than as a way to control the Court's use of judicial review, the amendment process is far more commonly used to address issues such as allocation of government power (e.g., the Fourteenth Amendment, which expressly enlarges the powers of the federal government and restricts those of the states), the operation of the electoral system (e.g., the Twelfth Amendment, which bundles electoral voting for the President and Vice President), or the Seventeenth Amendment, which provides that senators are to be elected by direct popular vote rather than by state legislatures. The amendment process has also created new constitutional rights (e.g., the Bill of Rights, or the Fifteenth and Nineteenth Amendments, prohibiting denial of suffrage on account of race or sex).

There are two basic modes of amendment specified in Article V. Amendments may be proposed either by a two-thirds vote of each House of Congress or by a constitutional convention called by Congress upon the application of two-thirds of the states. In either case a proposed amendment must be ratified by three-fourths of the state legislatures or state ratification conventions, whichever method of ratification Congress specifies. With one exception, the only method of amendment used has been proposal by Congress and ratification by three-fourths of the state legislatures. The Twenty-first Amendment, repealing prohibition of alcoholic beverages, was proposed by Congress and ratified by state ratification conventions.

a. Non-contemporaneous Ratification

Most amendments have been ratified shortly after their proposal, and most amendments proposed in the twentieth century have stipulated a time period (usually seven years) within which they must be ratified. The glaring exception is the Twenty-seventh Amendment, barring increases in congressional pay until a general election has first occurred, which was proposed in 1789 by the First Congress. Six states ratified it by 1791, Ohio ratified it in 1873, Wyoming in 1978, and 33 more states ratified it between 1983 and 1992. Article V contains no express requirement that ratification be a product of contemporaneous action, but the Court has hinted that such a requirement might be implied. In Dillon v. Gloss, 256 U.S. 368 (1921), the Court held that Congress could impose a reasonable time limit on ratification of a proposed amendment and offered the gratuitous observation that nothing in Article V "suggests that an amendment once proposed is to be open to ratification for all time, or that ratification in some of the states may be separated from that in others by many years and yet be effective." The Court added its obiter dictum opinion that the view that non-contemporaneous ratification could be effective "is quite untenable." So, is the Twenty-seventh Amendment an imposter?

The answer depends on who decides. If the issue of non-contemporaneous ratification is a non-justiciable political question, the validity of the Twenty-seventh Amendment would be left to Congress. In fact, once the legitimacy of the Twenty-seventh Amendment was placed in doubt Congress voted overwhelmingly to accept it. But if the issue is justiciable, Dillon v. Gloss casts some doubt on the legitimacy of the Twenty-seventh Amendment. Further exploration of this issue is best left for the political question doctrine.

b. Convention Calls

Although Article V contemplates the possibility of amendments proposed by a convention, we have never had two-thirds of the states unite in a call for such a convention. Among the unresolved issues surrounding such a convention are the following: Who decides when the convention call is constitutionally sufficient? What if Congress simply fails or refuses to call a convention? May Congress specify how the convention delegates are to be selected, or is that up to the states? May Congress (or the states) limit the subject matter jurisdiction of such a convention? What if the convention ignores those limits?

Given congressional acquiescence to non-contemporaneous ratification, does the same principle apply to calls for a convention? Suppose that 34 states have, at some point in the past, called for a convention and have never bothered to rescind the calls. Is Congress now obliged to summon a convention? See Paulsen, A General Theory of Article V: The Constitutional Lessons of the Twenty-seventh Amendment, 103 Yale L.J. 677 (1993) (arguing that this is indeed the case).

c. Rescission Before Ratification

May a state rescind its ratification of an amendment before the constitutional majority of three-fourths have ratified? Again, the answer depends on whether the issue is justiciable. In Coleman v. Miller, 307 U.S. 433 (1939), the Court established the principle that rescission is a political question not justiciable by courts. See Section C.4, infra. Congress ultimately decides whether to give effect to a purported rescission.

d. "Unconstitutional" Amendments?

Can there be such a thing as an unconstitutional amendment? There is one explicit limit on the substance of amendments. Article V forbids elimination of the states' equal representation in the Senate except by consent of an affected state. Taken literally, that might not prevent repeal of Article V's consent clause by ordinary amendment, followed by another amendment that reapportioned the Senate by population. But the substance of Article V would surely be offended by such a gambit. This leads to the general and more speculative issue of whether there is some implicit limit on the substance of amendments. The prevailing opinion is that there is not; any amendment, no matter how obnoxious to the existing spirit of the Constitution, is valid so long as it is adopted in the constitutionally prescribed fashion. Two-step Senate reapportionment might not be procedurally valid if the guarantee of equal state representation means that unanimity is required to eliminate the guarantee.

But what about an amendment that is procedurally valid but substantively inconsistent with the existing Constitution? Perhaps the best historical example is the Thirteenth Amendment, which abolished slavery, an institution recognized and given constitutional protection by at least nine other provisions of the then-existing Constitution. Everyone recognizes the validity of the Thirteenth Amendment, despite arguments made by its opponents that its substance was impliedly "unconstitutional." Nevertheless, some modern scholars argue that the Constitution should impliedly limit the subject matter of amendments. See, e.g., Murphy, An Ordering of Constitutional Values, 53 S. Cal. L. Rev. 703, 755-756 (1980) (contending that the Court could void amendments inconsistent with "human dignity"). But see Tribe, A Constitution We Are Amending: In Defense of a Restrained Judicial Role, 97 Harv. L. Rev. 433, 442 (1983) ("allowing the judiciary to pass on the merits of constitutional amendments would unequivocally subordinate the amendment process to the legal system it is intended to override and would thus gravely threaten the integrity of the entire structure"). An excellent source on the amending process is Bernstein, Amending America (1993).

2.   Appointment

Presidents frequently try to influence the Court's constitutional decisions by their power to appoint justices. All but three Presidents—William Henry Harrison, Andrew Johnson, and Jimmy Carter—have successfully appointed members of the Court. For several reasons the President's appointment power is an extremely uncertain method of altering the Court's view of the Constitution.

An appointment to the Court consists of a presidential nomination followed by senatorial confirmation of the appointment. Article II, section 2 of the Constitution stipulates that the President "shall nominate, and by and with the Advice and Consent of the Senate, shall appoint . . . Judges of the supreme Court." The Senate has not been shy about delivering its advice or withholding its consent. About one in every four nominees has failed to be confirmed. The most recent unsuccessful nominees were Robert Bork and Douglas Ginsburg, both in 1987, and Harriet Miers in 2005.

Sometimes this has been due to perceived ethical or other "nonpolitical" shortcomings, but mostly it has been the product of the Senate's ideological unhappiness with the nominee. Occasionally the Senate will informally propose nominees to the President. See generally Tribe, God Save This Honorable Court (1985).

When the Senate is not in session the President may make a "recess appointment" to judicial office. Such appointments, authorized under Article II, section 2 of the Constitution, expire at the end of the next session of the Senate unless the Senate confirms the nominee. The most recent recess appointee to the Supreme Court was William Brennan, appointed in 1956 and confirmed during the Senate's next session. John Rutledge, who served as Chief Justice in 1795 as a recess appointee by George Washington, was never confirmed. He holds the dubious distinction of being the only member of the Supreme Court who served as an unconfirmed recess appointee.

When Presidents make appointments to the Court with the intent of remaking constitutional law, they have existing law in mind. Thus, President Grant appointed Justices William Strong and Joseph Bradley in a successful bid to overturn Hepburn v. Griswold, 75 U.S. (8 Wall.) 603 (1870), which had held that Congress could not make paper money legal tender. See The Legal Tender Cases, 79 U.S. (12 How.) 457, 553 (1871). More recently, a succession of Presidents have sought by their appointments to overturn Roe v. Wade, 410 U.S. 113 (1973), with the result that Roe v. Wade was undercut, although not overruled, in Planned Parenthood v. Casey, 505 U.S. 833 (1992). But justices serve well beyond the time for resolution of an immediate issue, and their views on issues that are not even on the constitutional horizon when they are appointed cannot easily be known in advance.

Moreover, justices sometimes change their views once they begin to serve on the Court. As you read the cases in this book, consider the evolution of Harry Blackmun's views in the years following his appointment by President Nixon.

Presidents may also make mistakes. President Eisenhower is supposed to have said that his two biggest mistakes as President were in appointing Earl Warren and William Brennan. John Sununu, President George H.W. Bush's chief of staff, crowed that the appointment of David Souter was a "home run" for political conservatives, but Souter was regarded by most Court observers as a reliable member of the Court's "liberal" wing.

Finally, it takes a lot of vacancies to alter the Court's direction dramatically. Franklin Roosevelt served 12 years in office and appointed nine justices. The meaning of the Constitution changed radically during that time. On the other hand, Presidents Nixon, Ford, Reagan, and George H.W. Bush made 11 successive appointments without producing anything close to the constitutional convulsions of the Franklin Roosevelt era.

3.   Impeachment

Article II, section 4 provides that "all Civil Officers of the United States shall be removed from Office on Impeachment for, and Conviction of, Treason, Bribery, or other high Crimes and Misdemeanors." Article I, section 2 vests the House of Representatives with "the sole Power of Impeachment." Article I, section 3 gives the Senate the "sole Power to try all Impeachments" and stipulates that conviction and removal from office occurs if two-thirds of the senators present and voting concur in the House's articles of impeachment.

The meaning of the term "high crimes and misdemeanors" is not self-evident. President Gerald Ford declared, when he was minority leader of the House, that "an impeachable offense is whatever a majority of the House of Representatives considers it to be at a given moment in history." 116 Cong. Rec. H. 3113 (April 15, 1970). Thomas Cooley, an important late-nineteenth-century constitutional commentator, held the same view. Defenders of embattled officials facing impeachment typically contend that only an indictable offense qualifies as a "high crime [or] misdemeanor." This view can be traced back to Blackstone (an impeachment "is a prosecution of the already known and established law," 4 Blackstone *259) but is refuted by legal historian Raoul Berger, who has concluded that the term "high crimes and misdemeanors" is not limited to criminal acts. See Berger, Impeachment: The Constitutional Problems (1973). See also Black, Impeachment: A Handbook (1974). The practical reality of impeachment is that it is a device to remove a person from an office of public trust upon the occurrence of any behavior, criminal or not, that amounts to a serious abuse or breach of public trust. See House Judiciary Committee's Final Report on the Impeachment of Richard M. Nixon, H.R. Rep. No. 1035, 93d Cong. 2d Sess. By implication, perhaps some criminal behavior is not impeachable. But who is to decide? May courts review the substantive basis for impeachment? See Section C.4, infra.

As a practical matter, standards for impeachment may differ as applied to judges versus an executive official, such as the President. The President cannot serve longer than eight years. While that is certainly long enough to perform considerable mischief, the miscreant federal judge can wreak havoc for a lifetime. Only two Presidents, Andrew Johnson and Bill Clinton, have been impeached. Both survived a Senate trial, even though there was considerable partisan desire in both cases to remove the President. However, both Presidents Johnson and Clinton were weakened by the failed impeachment proceedings.

The unsuccessful impeachment of Justice Samuel Chase (the only Supreme Court justice ever to be impeached) is often cited for the proposition that political retribution is an inadequate basis for impeachment, at least in the context of judicial impeachments. When the Jeffersonian Democratic-Republicans took office in 1801 they vowed to sweep the judiciary clean of Federalist judges. To that end, arch-Federalist Samuel Chase was impeached for his partisan political rhetoric delivered in the course of instructing a jury and, more seriously, for his prejudiced administration of the trial of James Callender for seditious libel. The impeachment was openly political. Virginia Senator William Branch Giles candidly told Federalist John Quincy Adams that "[w]e want your offices, for the purposes of giving them to men who will fill them better." 2 Beveridge, The Life of John Marshall 157 (1919).

Chase's biased conduct in the Callender trial was "[b]y the standards of his own day [an] oppressive misuse of power; and it furnished grounds for impeachment under English law, to which the Founders looked for guidance." Berger, Impeachment, at 250. Following a dramatic trial the Senate narrowly acquitted Chase. President Jefferson bitterly commented that "impeachment is a farce that will not be tried again." 3 Beveridge, The Life of John Marshall 222. Even though Chase may have been a biased rascal deserving of ouster from the bench, his acquittal is generally regarded as having cemented the principle of an independent judiciary. It is politically unthinkable that a justice could be impeached and convicted for solely political reasons. But suppose it were to happen; would there be any remedy in the courts? See Section C.4, infra.

B. CONGRESSIONAL POWER TO CONTROL THE JURISDICTION OF THE FEDERAL COURTS

Article III gives Congress considerable, but not unlimited, discretion to control the jurisdiction of the federal courts. The scope of this power differs with respect to the Supreme Court and the inferior federal courts. Article III vests federal judicial power in one Supreme Court and "such inferior Courts as the Congress may from time to time ordain and establish." The scope of federal judicial power is limited to the heads of jurisdiction described in section 2, as modified by the Eleventh Amendment (e.g., federal question jurisdiction, diversity jurisdiction), and the jurisdiction of the Supreme Court is divided into original and appellate jurisdiction. The Court's original jurisdiction is limited to cases between states and those involving diplomats, but the Court is given appellate jurisdiction in all other cases within Article III "with such Exceptions, and under such Regulations as the Congress shall make."

1. Power to Establish Federal Courts

Because Article III assigns the "judicial power of the United States" to one Supreme Court and "such inferior Courts as the Congress may from time to time ordain and establish," Congress may (subject to the limits discussed in Section B.2, infra) curtail at its pleasure the jurisdiction of the inferior federal courts. See Sheldon v. Sill, 49 U.S. 441 (1850).

Congress probably may eliminate federal courts once they have been created. In 1801 the newly elected Jeffersonians eliminated the entire court of appeals created by the outgoing Federalist Congress. In Stuart v. Laird, 5 U.S. 299 (1803), the Supreme Court implicitly upheld the validity of this action. It is not entirely clear, however, whether Congress could eliminate the judgeships of terminated courts. Because Article III judges hold office for "good Behaviour" it may be that federal judges are entitled to their offices and their pay even when their duties and courtrooms are taken away.

2. Exceptions to and Regulations of Supreme Court Appellate Jurisdiction

Article III, section 2 endows the Supreme Court with appellate jurisdiction of all cases within the federal judicial power (other than those in which it has original jurisdiction) "with such Exceptions, and under such Regulations as the Congress shall make."

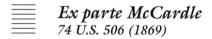

Ex parte McCardle
74 U.S. 506 (1869)

[William McCardle, a former Confederate Colonel, was a Vicksburg, Mississippi, newspaper editor who regularly used his newspaper to attack General Edward Ord, the military governor of Mississippi under the Reconstruction Acts. As a result, Ord invoked provisions of the Reconstruction Acts to arrest and imprison McCardle. Under an 1867 federal statute, McCardle sought his release by habeas corpus, charging that the Reconstruction Acts were unconstitutional. When he lost in federal circuit court, McCardle appealed to the Supreme Court under the same 1867 statute. The Court sustained jurisdiction over the government's objections, 73 U.S. (6 Wall.) 318 (1868), and set the case for argument.

The stakes were enormous and the drama was high. Disposition of the case turned on the validity of the Reconstruction Acts, an issue that opponents of the Acts had been attempting without success to get before the Court. A McCardle victory would doom the efforts of the Republicans in Congress to impose, over the objections of President Andrew Johnson, a radical new political and social order on the defeated South. Argument of the case before the Court in March of 1868 was interrupted by Chief Justice Chase's having to preside over the opening phase of the impeachment trial of President Johnson. After the *McCardle* case was taken under submission but before decision was rendered, Congress repealed the 1867 statute upon which McCardle asserted that the Supreme Court had jurisdiction. Despite the fact his impeachment trial was under way, President Johnson vetoed the repeal, but Congress quickly overrode his veto. The Court then ordered the *McCardle* case for re-argument during the next term, which produced the following opinion.]

CHIEF JUSTICE CHASE, for the Court.

The first question necessarily is that of jurisdiction; for, if the act of March, 1868, takes away the jurisdiction defined by the act of February, 1867, it is useless, if not improper, to enter into any discussion of other questions.

It is quite true, as was argued by the counsel for the petitioner, that the appellate jurisdiction of this court is not derived from acts of Congress. It is, strictly speaking, conferred by the Constitution. But it is conferred "with such exceptions and under such regulations as Congress shall make."

It is unnecessary to consider whether, if Congress had made no exceptions and no regulations, this court might not have exercised general appellate jurisdiction under rules prescribed by itself. For among the earliest acts of the first Congress, at its first session, was the act of September 24th, 1789, to establish the judicial courts of the United States. That act provided for the organization of this court, and prescribed regulations for the exercise of its jurisdiction.

The source of that jurisdiction, and the limitations of it by the Constitution and by statute, have been on several occasions subjects of consideration here. In the case of Durousseau v. The United States, [10 U.S. (6 Cranch) 312 (1810),] the court held, that while "the appellate powers of this court are not given by the judicial act, but are given by the Constitution," they are, nevertheless, "limited and regulated by that act, and by such other acts as have been passed on the subject." The court said, further, that the judicial act was an exercise of the power given by the Constitution to Congress "of making exceptions to the appellate jurisdiction of the Supreme Court." "They have described affirmatively," said the court, "its jurisdiction, and this affirmative description has been understood to imply a negation of the exercise of such appellate power as is not comprehended within it."

The principle that the affirmation of appellate jurisdiction implies the negation of all such jurisdiction not affirmed having been thus established, it was an almost necessary consequence that acts of Congress, providing for the exercise of jurisdiction, should come to be spoken of as acts granting jurisdiction, and not as acts making exceptions to the constitutional grant of it.

The exception to appellate jurisdiction in the case before us, however, is not an inference from the affirmation of other appellate jurisdiction. It is made in terms. The provision of the act of 1867, affirming the appellate jurisdiction of this court in cases of habeas corpus is expressly repealed. It is hardly possible to imagine a plainer instance of positive exception. We are not at liberty to inquire into the motives of the legislature. We can only examine into its power under the Constitution; and the power to make exceptions to the appellate jurisdiction of this court is given by express words. What, then, is the effect of the repealing act upon the case before us? We cannot doubt as to this. Without jurisdiction the court cannot proceed at all in any cause. Jurisdiction is power to declare the law, and when it ceases to exist, the only function remaining to the court is that of announcing the fact and dismissing the cause. And this is not less clear upon authority than upon principle.

[The] general rule [is], that "when an act of the legislature is repealed, it must be considered, except as to transactions past and closed, as if it never existed." And the [Court has] held that no judgment could be rendered in a suit after the repeal of the act under which it was brought and prosecuted. It is quite clear, therefore, that this court cannot proceed to pronounce judgment in this case, for it has no longer jurisdiction of the appeal; and judicial duty is not less fitly performed by declining ungranted jurisdiction than in exercising firmly that which the Constitution and the laws confer.

Counsel seem to have supposed, if effect be given to the repealing act in question, that the whole appellate power of the court, in cases of habeas corpus, is denied. But this is an error. The act of 1868 does not except from that jurisdiction any cases but appeals from Circuit Courts under the act of 1867. It does not affect the jurisdiction which was previously exercised.

The appeal of the petitioner in this case must be dismissed for want of jurisdiction.

NOTES

1. The Unofficial Dissent.   When in 1868 the Court postponed its decision to the following term, Justice Grier read from the bench a prepared statement that he then released to the press:

> This case was fully argued in the beginning of this month. It is a case that involves the liberty and rights not only of the appellant, but of millions of our fellow citizens. The country and the parties had a right to expect that it would receive the immediate and solemn attention of the Court. By the postponement of this case, we shall subject ourselves, whether justly or unjustly, to the imputation that we have evaded the performance of a duty imposed on us by the Constitution, and waited for Legislative interposition to supersede our action and relieve us from our responsibility. I am not willing to be a partaker of the eulogy or opprobrium that may follow; and can only say . . . I am ashamed that such opprobrium should be cast upon the Court, and that it cannot be refuted.

Justice Field agreed with Grier. The statements of Grier and Field are not part of the records of the Supreme Court and are not printed in the U.S. Reports, but were widely reported in newspapers of the day and in other accounts of the *McCardle* case. See Fairman, 6 Oliver Wendell Holmes Devise History of the Supreme Court of the United States: Reconstruction and Reunion, Part One: 1864-88, at 473-474 (1971); 3 Warren, The Supreme Court in United States History 204 (1922). Justice Field was of the opinion that had the case been decided on the merits, all but one of the justices would have ruled for McCardle. See Fairman, supra, at 467 n.143. For more on the historical background, see Van Alstyne, A Critical Guide to Ex parte McCardle, 15 Ariz. L. Rev. 229 (1973).

2. A Historic Epilogue. Another hot-headed Mississippi newspaper editor, Edward Yerger, killed the military mayor of Jackson, Mississippi, in a dispute over Yerger's unpaid taxes. Yerger was tried in a military court, and his lawyers sought his release in the Supreme Court by perfecting the convoluted procedure of habeas corpus aided by certiorari (see Note 3, infra). Once again the validity of the Reconstruction Acts was squarely at issue. Fearing a loss, since only Justices Miller and Swayne could be counted as supporters of the Reconstruction Acts, the federal government released Yerger to Mississippi officials for trial by a civil court. The Court dismissed Yerger's appeal. Ex parte Yerger, 75 U.S. (8 Wall.) 85 (1869). Yerger promptly escaped from prison. The validity of the Reconstruction Acts was never adjudicated.

3. The Penultimate Paragraph. The Court stated that the 1868 repeal legislation "does not except from [the Court's appellate] jurisdiction [over habeas corpus] any cases but appeals from Circuit Courts under the act of 1867. It does not affect the jurisdiction which was previously exercised." The Court's appellate jurisdiction previously exercised over habeas corpus was a cumbersome, byzantine process known as habeas corpus aided by certiorari. Although it was much harder via that process to obtain Supreme Court review of denial of petitions for habeas corpus, it was not impossible. See Ex parte Yerger, supra. Was this critical to the Court's decision?

In Felker v. Turpin, 518 U.S. 651 (1996), the Court avoided answering this question. Congress enacted the Antiterrorism and Effective Death Penalty Act, portions of which barred state prisoners from making two or more applications for federal habeas corpus unless a federal court of appeals had first given its permission, and denying to the Supreme Court any appellate review of these decisions by the courts of appeals. The Court upheld the Act, ruling that because a state prisoner could still seek habeas corpus relief in the Supreme Court in the old-fashioned method of "habeas corpus aided by certiorari," there was no need to consider whether Congress could completely strip the Court of all appellate jurisdiction over habeas corpus petitions.

Suppose that in *McCardle* Congress not only had repealed the 1867 statute but had flatly barred the Court from reviewing any denials of habeas corpus. On what basis might this absolute bar be attacked as unconstitutional? The following subsection explores the question of what limits, if any, the Constitution places on congressional power to restrict the appellate jurisdiction of the Supreme Court.

a. *"External" Limits on Congressional Power to Curtail the Supreme Court's Appellate Jurisdiction*

It is useful to think in terms of two types of limits on congressional power to restrict the jurisdiction of federal courts. Some limits on Congress may be implicit in the grant of judicial power contained in Article III. These limits are "internal limits" because they are implicit in, or fall inside of, the Article III grant of the federal judicial power to the federal courts. The other types of limits are those that are general constitutional limits on government action—such as the due process or equal protection guarantees. These limits have no specific connection to Article III and the judicial power—they are "external limits" because they are, in this sense, outside of Article III.

Some jurisdictional rules offend these "external limits." If the basis for denying jurisdiction, while consistent with Article III, offends other constitutional provisions, surely those "external limits" must apply to void the jurisdictional limit. Imagine jurisdiction limitations that apply to particular parties—for example, women, blacks, aliens, Republicans, Christians—in a fashion repugnant to the Constitution. A statute that eliminates all Supreme Court jurisdiction of cases in which the petitioner is a woman or is descended from African ancestors surely offends equal protection.

But jurisdictional limits that apply to entire categories of cases, rather than categories of litigants, are more debatable. Consider a statute that eliminates the Supreme Court's appellate jurisdiction over cases calling into question the validity of state regulations of abortion. Does this violate due process, because freedom from undue state burdens on abortion prior to fetal viability is a liberty protected by the substantive aspect of due process? Under the supremacy clause (Art. VI, cl. 2) state judges are obliged to strike down state laws that violate the Constitution, and federal judges are obliged to apply the Supreme Court's precedents. But if they fail to do so, the hypothesized statute would destroy any judicial means for correction of a mistaken (or rogue) state supreme court or federal appeals court.

Suppose instead that one state supreme court says a mandatory 48-hour waiting period before an abortion is an undue burden (and thus invalid) while another state says it is not (and upholds the law). Here are two differing views of the application of a federal constitutional principle. If the U.S. Supreme Court is muzzled, there is no certainty as to which is correct. So is the due process abortion right denied by the withdrawal of the Court's appellate jurisdiction? Or is it fully vindicated, with due process just having different meanings in different jurisdictions?

b. *"Internal" Limits on Congressional Power to Curtail the Supreme Court's Appellate Jurisdiction*

Are there any "internal limits"? Article III expressly gives Congress apparently unbounded discretion to make "exceptions" to and "regulations" of the

Court's appellate jurisdiction. In order to think about Article III's implicit "internal limits" on congressional withdrawal of jurisdiction, it is necessary to have some grasp of the principle of separation of powers, a topic covered extensively in Chapter 5. The three branches of the federal government are given specific, but sometimes overlapping, powers. When one branch exercises power properly belonging to another branch, or uses its power illegitimately to prevent another branch from performing its constitutionally assigned function, the separation of powers principle has been violated.

Is there anything illegitimate about Congress's excepting from the Court's appellate jurisdiction all cases of a particular category? Consider again a hypothetical withdrawal of Supreme Court appellate jurisdiction of cases that question the validity of state abortion regulations. In a famous article Professor Henry Hart, Jr., argued that the congressional "exceptions and regulations" power could not legitimately be used to impair the Court's "essential" function: "[T]he exceptions must not be such as will destroy the essential role of the Supreme Court in the constitutional plan." Hart, The Power of Congress to Limit the Jurisdiction of Federal Courts: An Exercise in Dialectic, 66 Harv. L. Rev. 1362, 1365 (1953).

But this simply raises the question, What is the Court's essential role? Professor Leonard Ratner argued that the Court's essential role is to (1) maintain the supremacy of federal law and (2) resolve conflicts as to federal law. See Ratner, Congressional Power Over the Appellate Jurisdiction of the Supreme Court, 109 U. Pa. L. Rev. 157 (1960); Majoritarian Constraints on Judicial Review: Congressional Control of Supreme Court Jurisdiction, 27 Vill. L. Rev. 929 (1982). A host of eminent scholars disagree. Professor Herbert Wechsler asserted that "the plan of the Constitution for the courts . . . was quite simply that the Congress would decide from time to time how far the federal [courts] should be used within the limits of the federal judicial power." Wechsler, The Courts and the Constitution, 65 Colum. L. Rev. 1001 (1965). See also Bator, Congressional Power over the Federal Courts, 27 Vill. L. Rev. 1032 (1982); Redish, Congressional Power to Regulate Supreme Court Appellate Jurisdiction Under the Exceptions Clause: An Internal and External Examination, 27 Vill. L. Rev. 900 (1982); Gunther, Congressional Power to Curtail Federal Court Jurisdiction: An Opinionated Guide to the Ongoing Debate, 36 Stan. L. Rev. 201 (1984). The argument over the Court's "essential role" depends in part on whether judicial review implies that the Court is the special caretaker of the Constitution or whether it merely obliges the Court to decide constitutional issues when they cannot be avoided. But there is nothing in the text of Article III that definitively answers this question. How should it be answered?

3.   Limitations on Congressional Control of the Jurisdiction of Inferior Federal Courts

The congressional power to establish (or eliminate) inferior federal courts implies power to limit the jurisdiction of the lower federal courts Congress chooses to create. Are there any limits on that power?

Consider a federal statute that withdraws jurisdiction from the lower federal courts of all constitutional issues. The state courts would interpret the Constitution subject to appellate review by the Supreme Court. Obviously, if such a law stripped the federal courts of jurisdiction by "singling out particular classes of *litigants* on the basis of their race or other 'suspect' classifications, or injuring them in the exercise of fundamental federal rights," the law would be presumptively void due to the "external limit" of equal protection. Gunther, supra. The hypothetical law, however, is simply a jurisdictional statute that distinguishes on the basis of *subject matter*.

> [T]here simply is no principle requiring all classes of federal question litigation to be handled in the same way. If one pays adequate heed to the Article III compromise giving Congress the power to make decisions about appropriate channeling of federal issues as between federal and state courts, assigning some cases to the state courts does not "discriminate against" or "burden" or "prejudice" the rights involved in those cases.

Id.

a. The Mandatory Federal Jurisdiction Position

Some scholars have seized upon Justice Joseph Story's dicta in Martin v. Hunter's Lessee to argue that Article III requires Congress to establish inferior federal courts endowed with the entirety of Article III jurisdiction, or at least to provide some possible federal court forum (whether trial or appellate) for cases arising under Article III. See, e.g., Akhil Amar, A Neo-Federalist View of Article III: Separating the Two Tiers of Federal Jurisdiction, 65 B.U. L. Rev. 205 (1985); The Two-Tiered Structure of the Judiciary Act of 1789, 138 U. Pa. L. Rev. 1499 (1990); Clinton, A Mandatory View of Federal Jurisdiction, 132 U. Pa. L. Rev. 741 (1984); Eisenberg, Congressional Authority to Restrict Lower Federal Court Jurisdiction, 83 Yale L.J. 498 (1974).

In Martin v. Hunter's Lessee, Justice Story grounded the actual decision on the assumption that Article III was not mandatory and that Congress need not vest the Article III judicial power in federal courts. But here are his obiter dictum thoughts on the possibility that Congress *must* vest Article III jurisdiction in federal courts:

> The language of [Article III] throughout is manifestly designed to be mandatory upon the legislature. Its obligatory force is so imperative, that congress could not, without a violation of its duty, have refused to carry it into operation. The judicial power of the United States *shall be vested* (not may be vested) in one supreme court, and in such inferior courts as congress may, from time to time, ordain and establish. . . .
>
> The same expression, "shall be vested," occurs in other parts of the constitution, in defining the powers of the other co-ordinate branches of the government. The first article declares that "all legislative powers herein granted shall

be vested in a congress of the United States." Will it be contended that the legislative power is not absolutely vested? That the words merely refer to some future act, and mean only that the legislative power may hereafter be vested? The second article declares that "the executive power shall be vested in a president of the United States of America." Could congress vest it in any other person; or, is it to await their good pleasure, whether it is to vest at all? It is apparent that such a construction, in either case, would be utterly inadmissible. Why, then, is it entitled to a better support in reference to the judicial department?

If, then, it is a duty of congress to vest the judicial power of the United States, it is a duty to vest the *whole judicial power*. The language, if imperative as to one part, is imperative as to all. If it were otherwise, this anomaly would exist, that congress might successively refuse to vest the jurisdiction in any one class of cases enumerated in the constitution, and thereby defeat the jurisdiction as to all; for the constitution has not singled out any class on which congress are bound to act in preference to others.

The next consideration is as to the courts in which the judicial power shall be vested. It is manifest that a supreme court must be established; but whether it be equally obligatory to establish inferior courts, is a question of some difficulty. If congress may lawfully omit to establish inferior courts, it might follow, that in some of the enumerated cases the judicial power could nowhere exist. The supreme court can have original jurisdiction in two classes of cases [only]. Congress cannot vest any portion of the judicial power of the United States, except in courts ordained and established by itself; and if in any of the cases enumerated in the constitution, the state courts did not then possess jurisdiction, the appellate jurisdiction of the supreme court (admitting that it could act on state courts) could not reach those cases, and, consequently, the injunction of the constitution, that the judicial power "*shall be vested,*" would be disobeyed. It would seem, therefore, to follow, that congress are bound to create some inferior courts, in which to vest all that jurisdiction which, under the constitution, is *exclusively* vested in the United States, and of which the supreme court cannot take original cognizance. [The] whole judicial power of the United States should be, at all times, vested either in an original or appellate form, in some courts created under its authority.

b.   *The Discretionary Position*

The argument that there are no "internal limits" on congressional discretion to create or limit the jurisdiction of the inferior federal courts is primarily rooted in precedent and history. Story's views of mandatory jurisdiction are contradicted by precedent and historical evidence. In Sheldon v. Sill, 49 U.S. (8 How.) 441 (1850), the Court rejected a contention that a portion of the 1789 Judiciary Act was unconstitutional because it barred jurisdiction by inferior federal courts of certain cases within Article III. The records of the 1787 federal convention clearly reveal a compromise by which inferior federal courts were to be authorized, but their existence and jurisdiction was to be left to congressional discretion. See 4 Kurland and Lerner eds., The Founders' Constitution 133-139 (excerpts from the record of the federal convention).

The congressional debates in the First Congress concerning the 1789 Judiciary Act, which established inferior federal courts and limited their jurisdiction, also reveal that the founding generation thought that Congress was free to limit the jurisdiction of the inferior federal courts. See 1 Annals of Congress 796-830. Thus,

> [i]f the Congress decides that a certain category of case arising under a federal law should be litigated in a state court, subject to Supreme Court review, neither the letter nor the spirit of the Constitution has been violated. What has happened is that Congress has taken up one of the precise options which the Constitutional Framers specifically envisaged.

Bator, Congressional Power over the Jurisdiction of the Federal Courts, 27 Vill. L. Rev. 1030 (1982).

c. *The Irrelevance of Motive*

Congress may withdraw jurisdiction because it dislikes the results the courts are reaching, so long as the withdrawal is not in substance a command to decide in a prescribed way. See United States v. Klein, infra. In 1932, Congress enacted the Norris-LaGuardia Act, which stripped federal courts of power to issue injunctions in labor disputes because Congress was irked by the propensity of federal trial judges to enjoin labor unions in labor disputes. The Court upheld the validity of the Act in Lauf v. E.G. Shinner & Co., 303 U.S. 323 (1938).

4. Limitations on Congressional Power to Curtail the Jurisdiction of All Federal Courts

Congressional power to limit the jurisdiction of all federal courts is a combination of (1) the power to make "exceptions and regulations" to the Supreme Court's appellate jurisdiction; and (2) the power to establish inferior federal courts, which implies authority to limit the jurisdiction of the lower federal courts. Taken together, do these powers suggest that Congress might be able to eliminate nearly all federal jurisdiction?

Consider the proposed Pledge Protection Act, which would deny jurisdiction to any federal court—lower courts and the Supreme Court—to decide "any question concerning the interpretation of, or the validity under the Constitution of," the Pledge of Allegiance (H.R. 699, 100th Cong., 2d Sess. (2007)). Some people argue that the phrase "under God" in the Pledge is an unconstitutional establishment of religion. Are there any "internal limits" upon this jurisdictional withdrawal? Should it make a difference that under the Pledge proposal *no* federal court could decide this constitutional issue?

Perhaps the implicit "plan of the Constitution" is, as Justice Story argued, that there must be the possibility that *some* Article III court can entertain a federal claim, whether originally or on appeal. This is the position taken by Professor Lawrence Sager, who reasons to this end from the structural guarantees of judicial independence in Article III (secure tenure and immunity from salary reduction). See Sager, Foreword: Constitutional Limitations on Congress' Authority to Regulate the Jurisdiction of the Federal Courts, 95 Harv. L. Rev. 17 (1981). Professor Martin Redish disagrees, arguing that Article III's structural guarantee of judicial independence implies nothing about the scope of the jurisdiction of the federal courts. See Redish, Constitutional Limitations on Congressional Power to Control Federal Jurisdiction: A Reaction to Professor Sager, 77 Nw. U. L. Rev. 143 (1982). We may never have a definitive answer, in part because Congress has never been inclined to curtail federal court jurisdiction in so draconian a fashion despite repeated proposals to do so. Perhaps Congress is reluctant because such proposals, if enacted, would "freeze in place" the constitutional decisions of the Supreme Court to which Congress objects. State courts, after all, are bound by the supremacy clause to follow the Constitution, and the Supreme Court's interpretations are, if not dispositive, extraordinarily powerful.

Congress might be tempted to withdraw jurisdiction from federal courts in a manner that compels decision of a case in a prescribed way.

United States v. Klein
80 U.S. (13 Wall.) 128 (1872)

[Klein, the administrator of Wilson's estate, had applied for compensation from the federal government for property seized by the federal government during the Civil War. Only those people who had remained loyal to the United States during the Civil War were entitled to compensation. Wilson had accepted President Johnson's general presidential amnesty and pardon following the war. Klein had proven Wilson's loyalty in the federal Court of Claims by relying upon United States v. Padelford, 76 U.S. (9 Wall.) 531 (1870), which held that amnesty recipients were conclusively deemed to be loyal despite any contrary facts. While the government's appeal of Klein's compensation award was pending, Congress enacted legislation that stripped the federal courts of jurisdiction over compensation cases where the claimant was basing eligibility for compensation upon receipt of amnesty. The act further provided that receipt of amnesty was "conclusive evidence" of disloyalty and directed that "on proof of such pardon and acceptance the jurisdiction of the court in the case shall cease, and the court shall forthwith dismiss the suit of such claimant." The intended effect, of course, was to deny compensation to claimants who had accepted amnesty.]

CHIEF JUSTICE CHASE, for the Court.

The Court of Claims [is] one of those inferior courts which Congress authorizes, and has jurisdiction of contracts between the government and the citizen, from which appeal regularly lies to this court. Undoubtedly [Congress] has complete control over the organization and existence of that court and may confer or withhold the right of appeal from its decisions. And if this act did nothing more, it would be our duty to give it effect. If it simply denied the right of appeal in a particular class of cases, there could be no doubt that it must be regarded as an exercise of the power of Congress to make "such exceptions from the appellate jurisdiction" as should seem to it expedient. But the [Act] shows plainly that it does not intend to withhold appellate jurisdiction except as a means to an end. Its great and controlling purpose is to deny to pardons granted by the President the effect which this court [in *Padelford*] had adjudged them to have. The [Act] declares that pardons shall not be considered by this court on appeal. We had already decided that it was our duty to consider them and give them effect, in cases like the present, as equivalent to proof of loyalty. It provides that whenever it shall appear that any judgment of the Court of Claims shall have been founded on such pardons, without other proof of loyalty, the Supreme Court shall have no further jurisdiction of the case and shall dismiss the same for want of jurisdiction. The [Act] further declares that every pardon granted to any suitor in the Court of Claims and reciting that the person pardoned has been guilty of any act of rebellion or disloyalty, shall [be] taken as conclusive evidence [of] the act recited; and on proof of pardon [the] jurisdiction of the court shall cease and the suit shall be forthwith dismissed.

It is evident from this statement that the denial of jurisdiction to this court, as well as to the Court of Claims, is founded solely on the application of a rule of decision, in causes pending, prescribed by Congress. The court has jurisdiction of the cause to a given point; but when it ascertains that a certain state of things exists, its jurisdiction is to cease and it is required to dismiss the cause for want of jurisdiction.

It seems to us that this is not an exercise of the acknowledged power of Congress to make exceptions and prescribe regulations to the appellate power. The court is required to ascertain the existence of certain facts and thereupon to declare that its jurisdiction on appeal has ceased, by dismissing the bill. What is this but to prescribe a rule for the decision of a cause in a particular way? . . .

Congress has inadvertently passed the limit which separates the legislative from the judicial power. [Congress] has already provided that the Supreme Court shall have jurisdiction of the judgments of the Court of Claims on appeal. Can it prescribe a rule in conformity with which the court must deny to itself the jurisdiction thus conferred, because and only because its decision, in accordance with settled law, must be adverse to the government and favorable to the suitor? This question seems to us to answer itself. . . .

NOTES

1. "Rule of Decision" or "Change in the Substantive Law"? Surely Congress may change the substance of the law to be enforced by federal courts and may even specify the rules of evidence or procedure to be followed by federal courts. But Congress may not direct the courts how to decide. How is this line to be drawn? Suppose that Congress denied jurisdiction to all federal courts to hear compensation claims when the claimant had received a pardon. Would that be a change in the substantive law or a forbidden directive to decide? Suppose instead that Congress amended the compensation statute to deny compensation to anyone who had received a pardon. Perhaps the vice in *Klein* was Congress's attempt to leave undisturbed the governing substantive and procedural law but to dictate to the courts what inference to draw from the evidence before them. Consider two cases:

In Robertson v. Seattle Audubon Society, 503 U.S. 429 (1992), environmentalists brought two suits challenging the legality of logging in old-growth forests in the Pacific Northwest. Congress responded with legislation that temporarily altered the rules governing logging in the Pacific Northwest and that "determine[d] and direct[ed]" that the logging challenged in the two suits, which were mentioned by name and docket number in the statute, was now legal. The Court upheld this law because it mandated a "change in law, not specific results under old law."

The other case is Plaut v. Spendthrift Farm, Inc., 514 U.S. 211 (1995). On June 18, 1991, the Supreme Court decided a case that established a uniform statute of limitations for certain securities fraud suits brought under the Securities and Exchange Act of 1934. As a result, many pending suits were dismissed as untimely. On December 19, 1991, Congress added a new section 27A to the Securities and Exchange Act of 1934 that created a new and different limitations period for the affected securities fraud suits. But new section 27A also provided that any such suit that had been dismissed on statute-of-limitations grounds from June 19, 1991 to December 19, 1991 could be "reinstate[d]." The Court voided the reinstatement provision of section 27A, noting that although section 27A "indisputably does set out substantive legal standards for the Judiciary to apply, and in that sense changes the law," it does so by interfering with the "expressed understanding that [Art. III] gives the Federal Judiciary the power, not merely to rule on cases, but to decide them, subject to review only by superior courts in the Article III hierarchy. [By] retroactively commanding the federal courts to reopen final judgments, Congress has violated this fundamental principle."

2. Questions.   Do any of the following hypothetical cases involve a forbidden directive by Congress to the courts as to how to decide the case?

a. Congress withdraws appellate jurisdiction from all federal courts of cases "in which a court of competent jurisdiction has determined that the treatment accorded to enemy combatants by the United States is lawful."

b. Congress denies to any federal court jurisdiction of any case "challenging the validity of any abortion regulation" and requires the Supreme Court to exercise its appellate jurisdiction to hear and decide "any final case from the state courts that has invalidated any abortion regulation."

c. Congress enacts a law that forbids any arm of the federal or state governments from regulating or prohibiting abortions, and that denies to any federal court jurisdiction of any case "challenging the validity" of the law.

d. Congress enacts a law specifying that its purpose in adding the phrase "under God" to the Pledge of Allegiance in 1954 was to achieve the secular end of distinguishing the United States from its Communist Cold War adversaries and declaring that the primary effect of the phrase is to promote patriotism. The same law denies to any federal court jurisdiction of any case in which a party contends that Congress's purpose was anything other than the specified secular purpose, or that the effect of the phrase is anything other than the promotion of patriotism.

C. JUSTICIABILITY: THE PROPER ROLE OF FEDERAL COURTS

The previous section examined the power of Congress to control the jurisdiction of the federal courts by legislation. This section examines the doctrines developed by the Court (mostly, but not entirely, rooted in the Constitution) to limit the kinds of cases the courts may decide.

Judicial review, said the Court in *Marbury*, is an unavoidable aspect of the courts' obligation to decide cases between adverse parties with real rights at stake when the resolution of such cases requires determination of the constitutional validity of legislation. By implication, it is not a power that can be exercised except as necessary to dispose of cases properly before the federal courts. Moreover, the jurisdiction of the federal courts is limited by Article III to "cases" or "controversies." The Court has sought to identify what constitutes a "case" or "controversy" that a federal court can hear and decide. In doing so, it has tried to define the proper role of the courts in the federal political system. It is an almost empty truism that Congress makes laws, the President enforces them, and the courts interpret them. But to the extent that courts decide "cases" that present no more than a disembodied policy issue, they risk poaching upon the legislative and executive domains. To map the frontier of justiciability, the Court has developed the doctrines considered in this section. Federal courts may not render advisory opinions. The standing requirement ensures that the federal courts are open only to litigants with real grievances that courts can resolve. The ripeness and mootness doctrines ensure that courts only decide cases when they need to be decided. The political question doctrine prevents courts from deciding issues that are not susceptible to judicial resolution.

In Flast v. Cohen, 392 U.S. 83 (1968), Chief Justice Warren made the following observations about justiciability:

> [T]he judicial power of federal courts is constitutionally restricted to "cases" and "controversies." [Those] two words have an iceberg quality, containing beneath their surface simplicity submerged complexities which go the very heart of our constitutional form of government. [In] part those words limit the business of federal courts to questions presented in an adversary context and in a form

historically viewed as capable of resolution through the judicial process. And in part those words define the role assigned to the judiciary [to] assure that the federal courts will not intrude into areas committed to the other branches of government. Justiciability is the term of art employed to give expression to this dual limitation placed upon federal [courts]. Federal judicial power is limited to those disputes which confine federal courts to a role consistent with a system of separated powers and which are traditionally thought to be capable of resolution through the judicial process. [Uncertainty] exists in the doctrine of justiciability because that doctrine has become a blend of constitutional requirements and policy considerations. And a policy limitation is "not always clearly distinguished from the constitutional limitation." For example, in his concurring opinion in Ashwander v. Tennessee Valley Authority, [Justice] Brandeis listed seven rules developed by this Court "for its own governance" to avoid passing prematurely on constitutional questions. [See Chapter 1, Section A.1.] Because the rules operate in "cases confessedly within [the Court's] jurisdiction," they find their source in policy, rather than purely constitutional, considerations. However, several of the cases cited by [Justice] Brandeis in illustrating the rules of self-governance articulated purely constitutional grounds for decision. The "many subtle pressures" which cause policy considerations to blend into the constitutional limitations of Article III make the justiciability doctrine one of uncertain and shifting contours.

Which of Justice Brandeis's seven *Ashwander* rules are constitutionally required and which are mere policy limitations? Which justiciability rules are constitutionally required and which are not? In general, justiciability rules that are designed to prevent decisions in matters that are neither cases nor controversies, or that are designed to keep the judiciary from invading the constitutionally assigned domain of the other two branches, are constitutionally compelled. Other justiciability rules are policy limitations, not constitutionally required. That line is easy to state; is it so easy to see in the following materials?

1. Advisory Opinions

From the earliest days of constitutional government the "case or controversy" requirement of Article III has been regarded as precluding federal courts from providing advisory opinions.

The Correspondence of Jefferson and the Justices
3 Correspondence and Public Papers of John Jay 633-635
(H. Johnston ed., 1893)

During George Washington's presidency, war erupted between France and Britain, thus raising a number of important issues of international law concerning American neutrality in that conflict. In July 1793, Secretary of State Thomas Jefferson, at Washington's request, wrote to the justices as follows:

The war which has taken place among the powers of Europe produces frequent transactions within our ports and limits, on which questions arise of considerable difficulty, and of greater importance to the peace of the United States. These questions depend for their solution on the construction of our treaties, on the laws of nature and nations, and on the law of the land, and are often presented under circumstances which do not give a cognizance of them to the tribunals of the country. Yet their decision is so little analogous to the ordinary functions of the Executive, as to occasion much embarrassment and difficulty. . . . The President would [be] much relieved if he found himself free to refer questions of this description to [the] Judges of the Supreme Court [whose] knowledge of the subject would secure us against errors dangerous to the peace of the United States, and their authority ensure the respect of all parties. He has therefore asked the attendance of such of the Judges as could be collected in time for the occasion, to know, in the first place, their opinion, whether the public may, with propriety, be availed of their advice on these questions. And if they may, to present, for their advice, the abstract questions which [have] already occurred, or may soon occur, from which they will themselves strike out such as any circumstances might, in their opinion, forbid them to pronounce upon.

Jefferson included in his letter 29 specific questions about treaties and international law, all pertaining to the maintenance of American neutrality. In August 1793, the justices replied:

We have considered the previous question stated [in Jefferson's July 1793 letter] regarding the lines of separation, drawn by the Constitution between the three departments of the government. These being in certain respects checks upon each other, and our being Judges of a Court in the last resort, are considerations which afford strong arguments against the propriety of our extrajudicially deciding the questions alluded to, especially as the power given by the Constitution to the President, of calling on the heads of departments for opinions, seems to have been *purposely* as well as expressly united to the *Executive* department. We exceedingly regret every event that may cause embarrassment to your Administration, but we derive consolation from the reflection that your judgment will discern what is right, and that your usual prudence, decision and firmness will surmount every obstacle to the preservation of the rights, peace, and dignity of the United States.

NOTES

1. Rationales. Ever since, it has been axiomatic that the Court lacks power to deliver advisory opinions. (Was the justices' reply to Jefferson an advisory opinion?)

When the federal judicial power is invoked to pass upon the validity of actions by the Legislative and Executive branches of the Government, the rule against advisory opinions implements the separation of powers prescribed by the Constitution and confines federal courts to the role assigned them by Article

III. [The] rule against advisory opinions also recognizes that such suits often "are not pressed before the Court with that clear concreteness provided when a question emerges precisely framed and necessary for decision from a clash of adversary argument exploring every aspect of a multifaceted situation embracing conflicting and demanding interests."

Flast v. Cohen, supra.

a. Separation of powers. The justices' reply to Jefferson suggests that separation of powers would be breached by "Judges of a Court in the last resort" rendering advisory opinions. This view — that judicial decisions must be final and not subject to alteration by the other branches — echoes an earlier decision. Federal law obliged the justices of the Supreme Court to certify persons as Revolutionary War veterans eligible for receipt of a pension. In Hayburn's Case, 2 U.S. 408 (1792), the justices, sitting on circuit, refused to do so because the statute assigned nonjudicial duties to the Court. The duties were nonjudicial in part because the Court's judgment was subject to modification by the Secretary of War. See also C. & S. Airlines v. Waterman Corp., 333 U.S. 103 (1948), in which the Court held that Congress had impermissibly demanded advisory opinions from the federal courts by requiring courts to review the award of international air routes, subject to presidential modification.

b. Policy limitations. The excerpt from Flast v. Cohen suggests that the ban on advisory opinions is also partly rooted in a belief that there is some danger in deciding abstract questions of law. The danger is thought to be (1) the lack of zealous advocacy for both sides of the question; and (2) the possibility of overbroad decision produced by the absence of a real-world application of the issue that narrows the conflict. Are these concerns realistic? Is the Court's skeptical view of such decisions rooted in the idea that an abstract controversy, even when ably argued and framed narrowly, is not a "case" or "controversy"? If so, the Court's view must be that the function of the courts is to decide individualized disputes, not to adjudicate points of law abstractly.

Other countries and some states permit their courts to render advisory opinions in limited circumstances, often at the request of the executive or the legislative branches of government.

2. Declaratory Judgments. Actions for declaratory relief, in which courts are asked to decide or declare the legal consequences of the litigants' conduct, are not advisory opinions if the controversy is sufficiently concrete to make the court's judgment a final disposition of the matter. In Nashville, C. & St. L. Ry. v. Wallace, 288 U.S. 249 (1933), the Court concluded that it was permissible to review a state court declaratory judgment concerning the constitutional validity of a state tax. The plaintiff railroad was about to become liable for the tax and contended that it was an invalid burden on interstate commerce. The declaratory judgment rendered by the state court was not advisory because the controversy was real, not hypothetical, presented sharply adverse positions, and the court's judgment was dispositive. Under these conditions, the form of the relief sought did not matter. The federal

Declaratory Judgment Act of 1934, which via 28 U.S.C. §2201(a) authorizes federal courts to grant declaratory judgment in a case within federal jurisdiction that poses an "actual controversy," was upheld in Aetna Life Insurance Co. v. Haworth, 300 U.S. 227 (1937).

2. Standing to Sue

Courts may not hear a case unless the plaintiff has "standing" to bring the claim. A person has standing if he or she has a sufficient stake in the controversy that he or she ought to be recognized as an appropriate party to assert the claim. Standing doctrine is an attempt to ensure that each lawsuit is brought by someone with a real and legally cognizable injury, rather than by an officious bystander lacking any personalized grievance. If your neighbor is struck by a speeding taxicab and injured, the tort claim that may result belongs to your neighbor. Absent some other connection to your neighbor, you lack standing to assert your neighbor's claim for personal injury. Standing rules for state courts are a matter of state law and are not considered here; this section concerns standing rules for federal courts.

The law of standing has a constitutional core and a cluster of peripheral doctrines that are not compelled by the Constitution but have been devised by the Court in the exercise of its prudential discretion. Rather than focusing upon the merits of the claim itself, standing law focuses upon the plaintiff and his or her connection to the claim: Is this litigant the proper party to raise these issues?

a. The Constitutional Core of Standing

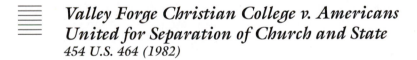

Valley Forge Christian College v. Americans United for Separation of Church and State
454 U.S. 464 (1982)

[A federal statute authorized the government to dispose of surplus property by conveying it to nonprofit tax-exempt educational institutions at a price reduced to reflect whatever public benefit would be received by the transfer. Using this authority, the Department of Health, Education, and Welfare (HEW) conveyed free of charge a surplus military hospital building to a religious college devoted to training students "for Christian service as either ministers or laymen." HEW had concluded that the transfer would produce a 100 percent public benefit. The Court held that the plaintiffs' status as taxpayers and citizens was insufficient to confer standing.]

JUSTICE REHNQUIST, for the Court.

Article III of the Constitution limits the "judicial power" of the United States to the resolution of "cases" and "controversies." [This] Court has always required that a litigant have "standing" to challenge the action sought to be adjudicated in the lawsuit. The term "standing" subsumes a blend of constitutional requirements and prudential considerations. [At] an irreducible minimum, Art. III requires the party who invokes the court's authority to "show that he personally has suffered some actual or threatened injury as a result of the putatively illegal conduct of the defendant," [that] the injury "fairly can be traced to the challenged action" and "is likely to be redressed by a favorable decision." In this manner does Art. III limit the federal judicial power "to those disputes which confine federal courts to a role consistent with a system of separated powers and which are traditionally thought to be capable of resolution through the judicial process."

The requirement of "actual injury redressable by the court" serves several of the "implicit policies embodied in Article III." It tends to assure that the legal questions presented to the court will be resolved, not in the rarified atmosphere of a debating society, but in a concrete factual context conducive to a realistic appreciation of the consequences of judicial action. The "standing" requirement serves other purposes. Because it assures an actual factual setting in which the litigant asserts a claim of injury in fact, a court may decide the case with some confidence that its decision will not pave the way for lawsuits which have some, but not all, of the facts of the case actually decided by the court.

The Article III aspect of standing also reflects a due regard for the autonomy of those persons likely to be most directly affected by a judicial order. The federal courts have abjured appeals to their authority which would convert the judicial process into "no more than a vehicle for the vindication of the value interests of concerned bystanders." Were the federal courts merely publicly funded forums for the ventilation of public grievances or the refinement of jurisprudential understanding, the concept of "standing" would be quite unnecessary. But the "cases and controversies" language of Art. III forecloses the conversion of courts of the United States into judicial versions of college debating forums. [The] exercise of judicial power, which can so profoundly affect the lives, liberty, and property of those to whom it extends, is therefore restricted to litigants who can show "injury in fact" resulting from the action which they seek to have the court adjudicate.

The exercise of the judicial power also affects relationships between the coequal arms of the National Government. The effect is, of course, most vivid when a federal court declares unconstitutional an act of the Legislative or Executive Branch. While the exercise of that "ultimate and supreme function" is a formidable means of vindicating individual rights, when employed unwisely or unnecessarily it is also the ultimate threat to the continued effectiveness of the federal courts in performing that role. While the propriety of such action by a federal court has been recognized since Marbury v. Madison it has been recognized as a tool of last resort on the part of the federal judiciary throughout its nearly 200 years of existence. . . .

Proper regard for the complex nature of our constitutional structure requires neither that the Judicial Branch shrink from a confrontation with the other two coequal branches of the Federal Government, nor that it hospitably accept for adjudication claims of constitutional violation by other branches of government where the claimant has not suffered cognizable injury. . . .

Beyond the constitutional requirements, the federal judiciary has also adhered to a set of prudential principles that bear on the question of standing. Thus, this Court has held that "the plaintiff generally must assert his own legal rights and interests, and cannot rest his claim to relief on the legal rights or interests of third parties." In addition, even when the plaintiff has alleged redressable injury sufficient to meet the requirements of Art. III, the Court has refrained from adjudicating "abstract questions of wide public significance" which amount to "generalized grievances," pervasively shared and most appropriately addressed in the representative branches. Finally, the Court has required that the plaintiff's complaint fall within "the zone of interests to be protected or regulated by the statute or constitutional guarantee in question."

[The Court then concluded that the plaintiffs lacked standing as taxpayers, since their claimed injury of a greater tax burden due to the alleged unconstitutional action was "'remote, fluctuating and uncertain.'" The plaintiffs also lacked standing as citizens, because their unadorned "interest in governmental observance of the Constitution" was insufficiently personal to constitute injury in fact.]

≡ *Lujan v. Defenders of Wildlife*
≡ *504 U.S. 555 (1992)*

JUSTICE SCALIA, for the Court with respect to Parts I, II, III.A, and IV, and, with respect to Part III.B, joined by CHIEF JUSTICE REHNQUIST and JUSTICES WHITE and THOMAS.

This case involves a challenge to a rule promulgated by the Secretary of the Interior interpreting §7 of the Endangered Species Act of 1973 (ESA) in such fashion as to render it applicable only to actions within the United States or on the high seas. The preliminary issue, and the only one we reach, is whether the respondents here, plaintiffs below, have standing to seek judicial review of the rule.

I. The ESA seeks to protect species of animals against threats to their continuing existence caused by man. The ESA instructs the Secretary of the Interior to promulgate by regulation a list of those species which are either endangered or threatened under enumerated criteria, and to define the critical habitat of these species. Section 7(a)(2) of the Act then provides, in pertinent part: "Each Federal agency shall, in consultation with and with the assistance of the Secretary [of the Interior], insure that any action authorized, funded, or carried out by such agency [is] not likely to jeopardize the continued existence of any endangered species or threatened species or result in the destruction or adverse modification of habitat of such species which is determined by the Secretary, after consultation as appropriate with affected States, to be critical." In 1978, the . . . Secretary of the Interior [issued a] regulation stating that the obligations imposed by §7(a)(2) extend to actions taken in foreign nations. . . . A revised . . . regulation, reinterpreting §7(a)(2) to require consultation only for actions taken in the United States or on the high seas, was . . . promulgated in 1986. Shortly thereafter, respondents, organizations dedicated to wildlife conservation and other environmental causes, filed this action against the Secretary of the Interior, seeking a declaratory judgment that the new regulation is in error as to the geographic scope of §7(a)(2), and an injunction requiring the Secretary to promulgate a new regulation restoring the initial interpretation. [The] Secretary moved for summary judgment on the standing issue, and respondents moved for summary judgment on the merits. The District Court denied the Secretary's motion, [granted] respondents' merits motion, and ordered the Secretary to publish a revised regulation. The Eighth Circuit affirmed. We granted certiorari.

II. [The] core component of standing is an essential and unchanging part of the case-or-controversy requirement of Article III. [The] irreducible constitutional minimum of standing contains three elements: First, the plaintiff must have suffered an "injury in fact"—an invasion of a legally-protected interest which is (a) concrete and particularized,[1] (b) "actual or imminent, not 'conjectural' or 'hypothetical.'" Second, there must be a causal connection between the injury and the conduct complained of—the injury has to be "fairly [traceable] to the challenged action of the defendant, and not [the] result [of] the independent action of some third party not before the court." Third, it must be "likely," as opposed to merely "speculative," that the injury will be "redressed by a favorable decision." The party invoking federal jurisdiction bears the burden of establishing these elements. [They] are not mere pleading requirements but rather an indispensable part of the plaintiff's case. . . .

III. Respondents [have] not made the requisite demonstration of (at least) injury and redressability.

A. Respondents' claim to injury is that the lack of consultation with respect to certain funded activities abroad "increas[es] the rate of extinction of endangered and threatened species." Of course, the desire to use or observe an animal species, even for purely aesthetic purposes, is undeniably a cognizable interest for purpose of standing. "But the 'injury in fact' test requires more than an injury to a cognizable interest. It requires that the party seeking review be himself among the injured." . . .

With respect to this aspect of the case, the Court of Appeals focused on the affidavits of two Defenders' members—Joyce Kelly and Amy Skilbred. Ms. Kelly stated that she traveled to Egypt in 1986 and "observed the traditional habitat of the endangered [N]ile crocodile there and intend[s] to do so again, and hope[s] to observe the crocodile directly," and that she "will suffer harm in fact as a result of [the American role] in overseeing the rehabilitation of the Aswan High Dam on the Nile [and in developing Egypt's]

---

1. By particularized, we mean that the injury must affect the plaintiff in a personal and individual way.

Master Water Plan." Ms. Skilbred averred that she traveled to Sri Lanka in 1981 and "observed th[e] habitat" of "endangered species such as the Asian elephant and the leopard" at what is now the site of the Mahaweli Project funded by the Agency for International Development (AID), although she "was unable to see any of the endangered species"; "this development project," she continued, "will seriously reduce endangered, threatened, and endemic species habitat including areas that I visited, [which] may severely shorten the future of these species"; that threat, she concluded, harmed her because she "intend[s] to return to Sri Lanka in the future and hope[s] to be more fortunate in spotting at least the endangered elephant and leopard." When Ms. Skilbred was asked at a subsequent deposition if and when she had any plans to return to Sri Lanka, she reiterated that "I intend to go back to Sri Lanka," but confessed that she had no current plans: "I don't know [when]. There is a civil war going on right now. I don't know. Not next year, I will say. In the future."

We shall assume for the sake of argument that these affidavits contain facts showing that certain agency-funded projects threaten listed species—though that is questionable. They plainly contain no facts, however, showing how damage to the species will produce "imminent" injury to Mss. Kelly and Skilbred. That the women "had visited" the areas of the projects before the projects commenced proves nothing. As we have said in a related context, "[p]ast exposure to illegal conduct does not in itself show a present case or controversy regarding injunctive relief [if] unaccompanied by any continuing, present adverse effects." And the affiants' profession of an "inten[t]" to return to the places they had visited before—where they will presumably, this time, be deprived of the opportunity to observe animals of the endangered species—is simply not enough. Such "some day" intentions—without any description of concrete plans, or indeed even any specification of when the some day will be—do not support a finding of the "actual or imminent" injury that our cases require. . . .

Standing is not "an ingenious academic exercise in the conceivable," [but] requires, at the summary judgment stage, a factual showing of perceptible harm. It is clear that the person who observes or works with a particular animal threatened by a federal decision is facing perceptible harm, since the very subject of his interest will no longer exist. It is even plausible—though it goes to the outermost limit of plausibility—to think that a person who observes or works with animals of a particular species in the very area of the world where that species is threatened by a federal decision is facing such harm, since some animals that might have been the subject of his interest will no longer exist. It goes beyond the limit, however, and into pure speculation and fantasy, to say that anyone who observes or works with an endangered species, anywhere in the world, is appreciably harmed by a single project affecting some portion of that species with which he has no more specific connection.

B. [Opinion of JUSTICE SCALIA, joined by CHIEF JUSTICE REHNQUIST and JUSTICES WHITE and THOMAS.] Besides failing to show injury, respondents failed to demonstrate redressability. [Because] the agencies funding the projects were not parties to the case, the District Court could accord relief only against the Secretary: He could be ordered to revise his regulation to require consultation for foreign projects. But this would not remedy respondents' alleged injury unless the funding agencies were bound by the Secretary's regulation, which is very much an open question. . . .

A further impediment to redressability is the fact that the agencies generally supply only a fraction of the funding for a foreign project. Respondents have produced nothing to indicate that the projects they have named will either be suspended, or do less harm to listed species, if that fraction is eliminated.

IV. The Court of Appeals found that respondents had standing for an additional reason: because they had suffered a "procedural injury." The so-called "citizen-suit" provision of the ESA provides, in pertinent part, that "any person may commence a civil suit on his own behalf (A) to enjoin any person, including the United States and any other governmental instrumentality or agency [who] is alleged to be in violation of any provision of this chapter." The court held that, because §7(a)(2) requires interagency consultation, the citizen-suit provision creates a "procedural righ[t]" to consultation in all "persons"—so that anyone can file suit in federal court to challenge the Secretary's (or presumably any other official's) failure to follow the assertedly correct consultative procedure, notwithstanding their inability to allege any discrete injury flowing from that failure. To understand the remarkable nature of this holding one must be clear about what it does not rest upon: This is not a case where plaintiffs are seeking to enforce a procedural requirement the disregard of which could impair a separate concrete interest of theirs (e.g., the procedural requirement for a hearing prior to denial of their license application, or the procedural requirement for an environmental impact statement before a federal facility is constructed next door to them). Nor is it simply a case where concrete injury has been suffered by many persons, as in mass fraud or mass tort situations. Nor, finally, is it the unusual case in which Congress has created a concrete private interest in the outcome of a suit against a private party for the government's benefit, by providing a cash bounty for the victorious plaintiff. Rather, the court held that the injury-in-fact requirement had been satisfied by congressional conferral upon all persons of an abstract, self-contained, noninstrumental "right" to have the Executive observe the procedures required by law. We reject this view.

We have consistently held that a plaintiff raising only a generally available grievance about government—claiming only harm to his and every citizen's interest in proper application of the Constitution and laws, and seeking relief that no more directly and tangibly benefits him than it does the public at large—does not state an Article III case or controversy. [Frothingham v. Mellon, United States v. Richardson, Schlesinger v. Reservists Committee to Stop the War.] To be sure, our generalized-grievance cases have typically involved Government violation of procedures assertedly ordained by the Constitution rather than the Congress. But there is absolutely no basis for making the Article III inquiry turn on the source of the asserted right. Whether the courts were to act on their own, or at the invitation of Congress, in ignoring the concrete injury requirement described in our cases, they would be discarding a principle fundamental to the separate and distinct constitutional role of the Third Branch—one of the essential elements that identifies those "Cases" and "Controversies" that are the business of the courts rather than of the political branches. "The province of the court," as Chief Justice Marshall said in Marbury v. Madison, "is, solely, to decide on the rights of individuals." Vindicating the public interest (including the public interest in government observance of the Constitution and laws) is the function of Congress and the Chief Executive. The question presented here is whether the public interest in proper administration of the laws (specifically, in agencies' observance of a particular, statutorily prescribed procedure) can be converted into an individual right by a statute that denominates it as such, and that permits all citizens (or, for that matter, a subclass of citizens who suffer no distinctive concrete harm) to sue. If the concrete injury requirement has the separation-of-powers significance we have always said, the answer must be obvious: To permit Congress to convert the undifferentiated public interest in executive officers' compliance with the law into an "individual right" vindicable in the courts is to permit Congress to transfer from the President to the courts the Chief Executive's most important constitutional duty, to "take Care that the Laws be faithfully executed." It would enable the courts, with the permission of Congress, "to assume a position of authority over the governmental acts of another and co-equal department," and to become "'virtually continuing monitors of the wisdom and soundness of Executive action.'" We have always rejected that vision of our role: "[U]nder Article III, Congress established courts to adjudicate cases and controversies as to claims of infringement of individual rights whether by unlawful action of private persons or by the exertion of unauthorized administrative power." "Individual rights," within the meaning of this passage, do not mean public rights that have been legislatively pronounced to belong to each individual who forms part of the public.

Nothing in this contradicts the principle that "[t]he . . . injury required by Art. III may exist solely by virtue of 'statutes creating legal rights, the invasion of which creates standing.'" "[Statutory] broadening [of] the categories of injury that may be alleged in support of standing is a different matter from abandoning the requirement that the party seeking review must himself have suffered an injury." [In] suits against the government, at least, the concrete injury requirement must remain. [We] hold that respondents lack standing to bring this action. [Reversed and remanded.]

JUSTICE KENNEDY, joined by JUSTICE SOUTER, concurring in part and concurring in the judgment.

Although I agree with the essential parts of the Court's analysis, I write separately to make several observations. . . .

[In] my view, Congress has the power to define injuries and articulate chains of causation that will give rise to a case or controversy where none existed before, and I do not read the Court's opinion to suggest a contrary view. In exercising this power, however, Congress must at the very least identify the injury it seeks to vindicate and relate the injury to the class of persons entitled to bring suit. The citizen-suit provision of the Endangered Species Act does not meet these minimal requirements, because while the statute purports to confer a right on "any person . . . to enjoin . . . the United States and any other governmental instrumentality or agency . . . who is alleged to be in violation of any provision of this chapter," it does not of its own force establish that there is an injury in "any person" by virtue of any "violation."

The Court's holding that there is an outer limit to the power of Congress to confer rights of action is a direct and necessary consequence of the case and controversy limitations found in Article III. I agree that it would exceed those limitations if, at the behest of Congress and in the absence of any showing of concrete injury, we were to entertain citizen-suits to vindicate the public's non-concrete interest in the proper administration of the laws. While it does not matter how many persons have been injured by the challenged action, the party bringing suit must show that the action injures him in a concrete and personal way. . . .

NOTES

1. The Contours of the Constitutional Core of Standing. Article III's "case or controversy" requirement and the principle of separation of powers combine to require a plaintiff to allege and prove (1) personal, actual, or imminent injury in fact (2) caused by or fairly traceable to the defendant's action complained of, which is (3) redressable by the courts.

a. Personal, actual, or imminent injury in fact. There must be injury to the plaintiff, but the constitutional conception of injury is quite catholic. Most injuries are economic or tangible; but aesthetic, emotional, and environmental injuries are sufficient to confer standing if the remaining elements of standing are present. In Sierra Club v. Morton, 405 U.S. 727 (1972), users of a national forest who alleged that a planned ski development would diminish their aesthetic and recreational pleasure and environmental well-being demonstrated injury in fact.

Injury must be actual or imminent. As *Lujan* demonstrates, if the injury has not already occurred, there must be a credible threat of its immediate occurrence. But even when indisputable injury has occurred, the presence or absence of "injury-in-fact" depends upon the remedy sought by the plaintiff. In Los Angeles v. Lyons, 461 U.S. 95 (1983), a motorist who suffered physical injury from an abusive "choke-hold" applied by police officers was held to lack standing to seek an *injunction* against choke-holds because there was no proof that he would again be choked without lawful reason. Of course, the motorist had standing to pursue damages for his personal injury.

The injury must be suffered personally. In Allen v. Wright, 468 U.S. 737 (1984), parents of black children attending Memphis public schools claimed that they were injured by the racial denigration inherent in the Internal

Revenue Service's alleged practice of failing to deny tax-exempt status to racially discriminatory private schools. The Court ruled that "the stigmatizing injury often caused by racial discrimination [is] sufficient to support standing" if the plaintiff has "suffered as a direct result of having personally been denied equal treatment." But the parents alleged only "*abstract* stigmatic injury"—they made no allegations of personal suffering—so the Court concluded they lacked personal injury.

If injury is personal, it does not matter how many other people suffer the same injury. For example, if through negligence a nuclear reactor explodes and emits radiation that poisons 100 million people, each one of those 100 million people has suffered personal injury. But some injuries are of such a nature that nobody can suffer "personalized injury." The paradigm of such injuries is the abstract and generalized interest everyone has in governmental observance of the law.

In Schlesinger v. Reservists Committee to Stop the War, 418 U.S. 208 (1974), the Court held that ordinary citizens lacked standing to pursue a claim that the "incompatibility clause" (Art. I, §6), which bars members of Congress from holding simultaneously any other federal office, prohibited members of Congress from holding commissions as reserve officers in the armed services. In United States v. Richardson, 418 U.S. 166 (1974), ordinary citizens were held to lack standing to challenge secret expenditures of the CIA as violative of the public accounting clause (Art. I, §9, cl. 7). In Fairchild v. Hughes, 258 U.S. 126 (1922), the Court, per Justice Brandeis, ruled that a citizen lacked standing to challenge the validity of the process by which the Nineteenth Amendment was ratified: "[This is] not a case within the meaning of . . . Article III. [Plaintiff] has asserted only the right, possessed by every citizen, to require that the Government be administered according to law. [This] general right does not entitle a private citizen to institute in the federal courts a suit." Accord, Ex parte Levitt, 302 U.S. 633 (1937) (citizen challenge to the validity of Justice Black's appointment); Whitmore v. Arkansas, 495 U.S. 149 (1990) (citizen challenge to the validity of the death penalty); Frothingham v. Mellon, infra.

In Susan B. Anthony List v. Driehaus, 134 S. Ct. 2334 (2014), the injury in fact requirement was held to be satisfied in a pre-enforcement challenge to an Ohio law that criminalizes false statements made in political campaigns. The plaintiff, a regular commentator on campaigns, proved that it intended to engage in arguably constitutionally protected speech that was illegal under the Ohio law. Because Ohio repeatedly instituted proceedings against speakers who alleged their speech was true, the threat of future prosecution was both credible and sufficiently imminent to support Article III injury in fact.

Questions: Is the critical difference between *Lujan* and *Driehaus* the difference between "someday intentions" and the next election cycle? Is it significant that the plaintiffs in *Driehaus* raised a constitutional claim and the plaintiffs in *Lujan* asserted a statutory claim? Is it vital that the *Driehaus* plaintiffs faced civil penalties while the *Lujan* plaintiffs had no such possible liability?

b. Causation.   Personalized injury-in-fact must be caused by, or be fairly traceable to, the defendant's conduct about which the plaintiff complains. What does the phrase "fairly traceable to" mean? Must the plaintiff show that the injury would not have occurred but for the defendant's action? Or will it suffice to prove that there is a substantial likelihood that the defendant's actions contributed significantly to the injury suffered?

In Allen v. Wright, parents of black children attending Memphis public schools lacked standing to enforce the Internal Revenue Service's obligation to deny tax-exempt status to racially discriminatory private schools because their injury-in-fact — "their children's diminished ability to receive an education in a racially integrated [Memphis public] school" — was not caused by the IRS. "[T]he injury to [the parents] is highly indirect and 'results from the independent action of some third party not before the court.'" There was neither claim nor proof that the alleged IRS practices were sufficiently pervasive to make a difference in the racial composition of the Memphis public schools. In part, this was because it was

> speculative [whether] withdrawal of a tax exemption from any particular school would lead the school to change its policies, [whether] any given parent of a child attending such a private school would decide to transfer the child to public school as a result of any changes in educational or financial policy made by the private school once it was threatened with loss of tax-exempt status, [and] whether, in a particular community, a large enough number of the numerous relevant school officials and parents would reach decisions that collectively would have a significant impact on the racial composition of the public schools. The links in the chain of causation between the challenged Government conduct and the asserted injury are far too weak for the chain as a whole to sustain [the parents'] standing.

In Warth v. Seldin, 422 U.S. 490 (1975), four separate sets of plaintiffs were held to lack standing to claim that the zoning laws of Penfield, New York, a relatively affluent suburb of Rochester, injured them by effectively preventing the construction of low-income housing. Plaintiffs consisted of (1) low-income people who claimed to have unsuccessfully sought housing in Penfield; (2) a civic group some of whose members lived in Penfield and who claimed to be injured by the lack of economic diversity within the community; (3) Rochester taxpayers who contended that the failure of Penfield to permit low-income housing caused Rochester taxes to be higher in order to construct such housing within Rochester; and (4) several real estate developers who asserted that they would have built low-income housing in Penfield if the zoning laws permitted. The low-income plaintiffs lacked standing because they had not alleged, and apparently could not prove, that even if the zoning restrictions were removed there was a "substantial probability" they would actually reside in Penfield. Without proof that a third party would build housing the claimants could afford and would desire, the requisite "substantial probability" was missing. The developers lacked standing because there was no specific project that had been prohibited by Penfield's zoning. The

Rochester taxpayers lacked standing because their taxes were a function of independent decisions made by Rochester. The civic group lacked standing because the asserted harm—the lack of economic diversity due to the exclusion of others—was treated as an injury to a third party. (See Section C.2.b.i, infra.)

In Simon v. Eastern Kentucky Welfare Rights Organization, 426 U.S. 26 (1976), welfare recipients and an organization representing them lacked standing to challenge an IRS ruling that granted charitable tax-exempt status to hospitals that provided only emergency services free of charge to indigents. There was no proof that the plaintiffs' injury—denial of free nonemergency medical services—was the result of the IRS ruling. But in Duke Power Co. v. Carolina Environmental Study Group, 438 U.S. 59 (1978), the Court permitted plaintiffs who resided near a nuclear power plant to challenge the validity of a federal statute limiting liability for nuclear accidents on the ground that the plaintiffs had demonstrated a "substantial likelihood" that the power plant near them would not have been constructed but for the liability limitations established by Congress.

Note the interdependence of the alleged injury and causation. If the injury in *Warth* had been stated to be the opportunity to "participat[e] in a housing market not fundamentally warped by unconstitutional zoning practices," causation might more readily be established. See Chayes, Public Law Litigation and the Burger Court, 96 Harv. L. Rev. 4, 18 (1982). Chayes asserts that "[t]here are only causal chains of different lengths" and the determination of when any chain is too long is dependent upon "the interests and sympathies of shifting configurations of five justices." Id. at 19. Causation may not be quite that indeterminate, because it must always be related to the claimed injury-in-fact. The asserted injury in *Warth*, as revised in the foregoing, might not be sufficiently personalized to constitute injury-in-fact. Perhaps the conclusion to draw is that a short causal chain tethered to a general injury is no more likely to produce standing than is a lengthy and attenuated chain connected to very personal injury. As a practical matter, the art of standing is to frame the injury no more generally than necessary to make the causal chain convincingly short. As with all arts, this is an exercise in judgment, an imperfect human faculty.

c. Redressability. Article III standing is lacking if the plaintiff's injury, even if caused by the defendant's conduct, cannot be redressed by some remedy within the court's power. In *Warth*, there was no evidence that even if Penfield's zoning law was enjoined, "such relief would benefit" the plaintiffs: "[T]heir inability to reside in Penfield is the consequence of the economics of the area housing market, rather than of [defendants'] assertedly illegal acts." In *Simon*, all the courts could do was order the IRS to stop granting tax-exempt status to hospitals that refused to provide free nonemergency services to indigents, but that change would not necessarily result in greater medical care to indigents. In *Lujan*, a court could order the Interior Secretary to interpret the Endangered Species Act differently, but there was no certainty that that would actually cure the injury complained of, because the American agencies supplying foreign aid were not defendants and the American aid supplied to the foreign developments was a minimal portion of their cost. Redressability is not just the ability of a court to issue some enforceable order; the court's order must assuage the injury of which the plaintiff complains.

In practice, causation and redressability are the Gemini twins of standing. They are so often linked that they are sometimes fused in discussion as a single "nexus" requirement.

2. The Rationale and Significance of the Constitutional Core of Standing. The Court says that the structural principle of separation of powers and the "case or controversy" requirement of Article III mandate the constitutional core to standing. The case or controversy requirement is often perceived as limiting judicial power to decisions concerning "atomized" conflicts—disputes between people with "real" injuries that the law recognizes and people who are allegedly legally responsible for those injuries, rather than fanciful, imaginary, or vaguely apprehended disputes. Separation of powers requires that courts refrain from adjudicating disembodied policy questions. If a litigant lacks the standing criteria, the courts are being asked to formulate public policy in the guise of a lawsuit. To do so would impermissibly infringe upon the powers of Congress and the President. The significance of the constitutional core to standing is that Congress may not confer standing upon a class of litigants who do not meet the core requirements simply by declaring that they have a right to sue in federal court. To confer standing on such litigants, Congress must change the substantive law in a way that enables those litigants to satisfy the core requirements.

a. The value of concrete disputes. What values are promoted by the requirement that a litigant have a personalized interest in an "atomistic" dispute? In *Valley Forge*, supra, the Court says that this ensures that legal issues will be decided in a "concrete factual context conducive to a realistic appreciation of the consequences of judicial action."

Suppose that a condemned prisoner facing an imminent execution date refuses to contest the constitutional validity of the state's intended mode of execution—beheading. Instead, a priest who actively opposes capital punishment asserts the claim, seeking to enjoin the impending execution. What, if anything, is insufficiently concrete to conduce "a realistic appreciation of the consequences of judicial action"? See Whitmore v. Arkansas, supra. Are the facts significantly more "concrete" if the plaintiff is the condemned prisoner's priest? The prisoner's spouse or child? Your answers to these questions may be colored by your view of whether the primary role of the courts is to use cases as a vehicle to resolve disputes about legal policy or to adjudicate individual rights and obligations.

b. Separation of powers. As you will see in Chapter 5, the boundaries between the branches of the federal government are hardly precise, but there are some core functions to each branch. Expressed generally, the judicial function is to decide cases or controversies within its jurisdiction. As John Marshall put it in *Marbury*, "[i]t is emphatically the province and duty of the judicial department to say what the law is." But this obligation inheres only when the question of law comes to the courts in the form of a case or controversy. Because the meaning of either "case" or "controversy" is not self-evident, the courts turn to the structural principles of separation of powers to help put substance into those terms.

The constitutional core of standing is a set of elements designed to close the courthouse doors to policy disputes masquerading as lawsuits presenting personal grievances. Separation of powers precludes professional litigants from using the courts to alter public policy rather than to vindicate a personal grievance. Congress and the executive branch are the proper fora for debate and resolution of the wisdom of differing public policies. The judicial branch encroaches upon that domain when it decides "cases" that do not resolve legally cognizable individual grievances. On this view, the judicial role is to "say what the law is" (and what the law is not) only in the course of adjudicating a legally cognizable claim of personalized injury.

c. Limits on congressional creation of standing. The constitutional core of standing prevents Congress from creating federal court jurisdiction over suits brought by people who lack the constitutional requirements for standing. In *Lujan*, the Court struck down the "citizen-suit" provision of the Endangered Species Act, which attempted to endow "any person" with the power to bring suit to enjoin anybody from violating the Act.

Suppose Congress amended the Act to provide that "any person with a professional interest in an endangered species whose ability to pursue that professional interest is diminished to any degree by government action or inaction" may bring suit to enjoin violations of the Act. Would this create standing? Consider Justice Kennedy's concurrence in *Lujan:*

> Congress has the power to define injuries and articulate chains of causation that will give rise to a case or controversy where none existed [before]. In exercising this power, however, Congress must at the very least identify the injury it seeks to vindicate and relate the injury to the class of persons entitled to bring suit.

Would standing be more clearly created if Congress instead provided that "any violation" of the Act that "diminished to any degree the ability of a person with a professional interest in an endangered species to pursue that interest" would render the violator liable to such person for an amount equal to $5,000 or treble the actual damages, whichever is greater? If there is a difference, perhaps it lies in the creation in the latter case of an entirely new substantive legal right—the right to receive damages for any wrongful diminution of professional ability to study an endangered species.

If Congress cannot endow citizens with standing to challenge unlawful government action that injures everyone abstractly, such actions can be stopped only through the political process. The message of separation of powers in this area seems to be that the federal courts are not available to stop government wrongdoing at the behest of any citizen who spots such unlawful activity and asks a federal court to intervene because he or she claims to be injured simply by knowledge of the wrongdoing.

Like private citizens, members of Congress must establish the constitutional core of standing in order to challenge the validity of federal legislation. In Raines v. Byrd, 521 U.S. 811 (1997), the Court ruled that six members of Congress who voted against the Line Item Veto Act lacked standing to challenge its validity. The claimed injury was a diminished "effectiveness of their votes." That was insufficient. The plaintiffs' votes "were given full effect. They simply lost that vote." The Court distinguished Coleman v. Miller, 307 U.S. 433 (1939) (see Section C.4, infra), where legislator standing was found because the votes of the legislator-plaintiffs in *Coleman* had been "completely nullified." The real injury in *Raines*, a relative transfer of power from Congress to the President, was inflicted upon the institution of Congress, not its individual members, and was thus wholly abstract and dispersed.

Problem: Suppose Congress enacted legislation declaring ex-Presidents to be U.S. senators "at large, for life, and with full voting power." Article I, Section 3 and the Seventeenth Amendment together stipulate that "[t]he Senate . . . shall be composed of two Senators from each State, elected by the people thereof, for six years." Who would have standing to challenge the validity of this legislation?

Consider Laird v. Tatum, 408 U.S. 1 (1972), and Federal Election Commission v. Akins, 524 U.S. 11 (1998). In *Laird*, the Supreme Court found to be nonjusticiable a claim that "the exercise of . . . First Amendment rights is being chilled by the mere existence, without more, of a governmental investigative and data-gathering activity that is alleged to be broader in scope than is reasonably necessary for the accomplishment of a valid governmental purpose. . . . Allegations of a subjective 'chill' are not an adequate substitute for a claim of specific present objective harm or a threat of specific future harm."

In *Akins*, a group of voters, united only by their opposition to the policies espoused by the American Israel Public Affairs Committee (AIPAC), sought review in federal court of a Federal Election Commission (FEC) determination that AIPAC was not a "political committee" required by the Federal Election Campaign Act (FECA) to make disclosures regarding its membership, contributions, and expenditures. FECA provides that "any person" who believes FECA has been violated may file a complaint with the FEC and that "any party aggrieved" by an FEC order dismissing such party's complaint may seek federal court review of the dismissal. The court ruled that the plaintiffs had suffered sufficient personal injury in fact to support standing: "The 'injury in fact' [they] have suffered consists of their inability to obtain information [that] the statute [arguably] requires that AIPAC make public. [A] plaintiff suffers an 'injury in fact' when the plaintiff fails to obtain information which must be publicly disclosed pursuant to a statute." See Public Citizen v. Department of Justice, 491 U.S. 440 (1989). Nor was the fact that the claim presented a generalized grievance a bar to standing. Citing *Schlesinger* and *Richardson*, the Court noted that "[w]hether styled as a constitutional or prudential limit on standing, the Court has sometimes determined that where large numbers of Americans suffer alike, the political process, rather than the judicial process, may provide the more appropriate remedy for a widely shared grievance." This rule, said the Court, applies mostly "where the harm at issue is not only widely shared, but is also of an abstract and indefinite nature." But "where a harm is concrete, though widely shared, the Court has found 'injury in fact.' [*Public Citizen*.] This conclusion seems particularly obvious where . . . large numbers of voters suffer interference with voting rights conferred by law. We conclude that similarly, the informational injury at issue here, directly related to voting, the most basic of political rights, is sufficiently concrete and specific such that the fact that it is widely shared does not deprive Congress of constitutional power to authorize its vindication in the federal courts."

Massachusetts v. Environmental Protection Agency
549 U.S. 497 (2007)

JUSTICE STEVENS delivered the opinion of the Court.

A . . . rise in global temperatures has coincided with a significant increase in the concentration of carbon dioxide in the atmosphere. Respected scientists believe the two trends are related. For when carbon dioxide is released into the atmosphere, it acts like the ceiling of a greenhouse, trapping solar energy and retarding the escape of reflected heat. It is therefore a species—the most important species—of a "greenhouse gas."

[A] group of States, local governments, and private organizations alleged in a petition for certiorari that the Environmental Protection Agency (EPA) has abdicated its responsibility under the Clean Air Act to regulate the emissions of four greenhouse gases, including carbon dioxide. Specifically, petitioners asked us to answer two questions concerning the meaning of §202(a)(1) of the Act: whether EPA has the statutory authority to regulate greenhouse gas emissions from new motor vehicles; and if so, whether its stated reasons for refusing to do so are consistent with the statute.

In response, EPA . . . correctly argued that we may not address those two questions unless at least one petitioner has standing to invoke our jurisdiction under Article III of the Constitution. . . .

I. Section 202(a)(1) of the Clean Air Act . . . provides [that the EPA Administrator "shall by regulation prescribe . . . standards applicable to the emission of any air pollutant from . . . new motor vehicles . . . , which in his judgment cause, or contribute to, air pollution which may reasonably be anticipated to endanger public health or welfare. . . ." The Act defines "air pollutant" to include "any . . . physical, chemical, biological, radioactive . . . substance or matter which is emitted into or otherwise enters the ambient air." "Welfare" is also defined broadly: among other things, it includes "effects on . . . weather . . . and climate." . . .

II. [In] 1999, a group of 19 private organizations filed a rulemaking petition asking EPA to regulate "greenhouse gas emissions from new motor vehicles under §202 of the Clean Air Act." Petitioners maintained that . . . carbon dioxide [and other] greenhouse gas emissions have significantly accelerated climate change; . . . that . . . "carbon dioxide remains the most important contributor to [man-made] forcing of climate change," [and] that climate change will have serious adverse effects on human health and the environment. . . . [In 2003,] the EPA denied the petition because the Clean Air Act does not authorize EPA to issue mandatory regulations to address global climate change. . . .

III. Petitioners, now joined by intervenor States and local governments, sought review of EPA's order in the United States Court of Appeals for the District of Columbia Circuit. [Because] "the EPA Administrator properly exercised his discretion under §202(a)(1) in denying the petition for rule making," [the D.C. Circuit] denied the petition for review. . . .

IV. . . . The parties' dispute turns on the proper construction of a congressional statute. . . . Congress has . . . authorized this type of challenge to EPA action.[2] [But we will not] "entertain citizen suits to vindicate the public's nonconcrete interest in the proper administration of the laws."

EPA maintains that because greenhouse gas emissions inflict widespread harm, the doctrine of standing presents an insuperable jurisdictional obstacle. We do not agree. . . .

Lujan holds that a litigant must demonstrate that it has suffered a concrete and particularized injury that is either actual or imminent, that the injury is fairly traceable to the defendant, and that it is likely that a favorable decision will redress that injury. However, a litigant to whom Congress has "accorded a procedural right to protect his concrete interests," — here, the right to challenge agency action unlawfully withheld — "can assert that right without meeting all the normal standards for redressability and immediacy." When a litigant is vested with a procedural right, that litigant has standing if there is some possibility that the requested relief will prompt the injury-causing party to reconsider the decision that allegedly harmed the litigant. . . . Only one of the petitioners needs to have standing to permit us to consider the petition for review. We stress here . . . the special position and interest of Massachusetts. It is of considerable relevance that the party seeking review here is a sovereign State and not, as it was in *Lujan*, a private individual. . . .

States are not normal litigants for the purposes of invoking federal jurisdiction. As Justice Holmes explained in Georgia v. Tennessee Copper Co., 206 U.S. 230, 237 (1907), a case in which Georgia sought to protect its citizens from air pollution originating outside its borders:

> The case has been argued largely as if it were one between two private parties; but it is not. . . . This is a suit by a State for an injury to it in its capacity of quasi-sovereign. In that capacity the State has an interest independent of and behind the titles of its citizens, in all the earth and air within its domain. It has the last word as to whether its mountains shall be stripped of their forests and its inhabitants shall breathe pure air.

2. 42 U.S.C. §7607(b)(1) provides, in part, "A petition for review of action of the [EPA] Administrator in promulgating . . . any standard under section 202, . . . or final action taken by the Administrator under this Act may be filed only in the United States Court of Appeals for the District of Columbia. . . ." [—Ed.]

Just as Georgia's "independent interest . . . in all the earth and air within its domain" supported federal jurisdiction a century ago, so too does Massachusetts' well-founded desire to preserve its sovereign territory today. . . . When a State enters the Union, it surrenders certain sovereign prerogatives. Massachusetts cannot invade Rhode Island to force reductions in greenhouse gas emissions, it cannot negotiate an emissions treaty with China or India, and in some circumstances the exercise of its police powers to reduce in-state motor-vehicle emissions might well be pre-empted. . . . These sovereign prerogatives are now lodged in the Federal Government, and Congress has ordered EPA to protect Massachusetts (among others) by prescribing standards applicable to [auto air pollutant emissions which, in the EPA Administrator's judgment, contribute to] "air pollution which may reasonably be anticipated to endanger public health or welfare." Congress has moreover recognized a concomitant procedural right to challenge the rejection of its rulemaking petition as arbitrary and capricious. Given that procedural right and Massachusetts' stake in protecting its quasi-sovereign interests, the Commonwealth is entitled to special solicitude in our standing analysis. . . . EPA's steadfast refusal to regulate greenhouse gas emissions presents a risk of harm to Massachusetts that is both "actual" and "imminent." There is, moreover, a "substantial likelihood that the judicial relief requested" will prompt EPA to take steps to reduce that risk.

The Injury

The harms associated with climate change are serious and well recognized[,] . . . Including "the global retreat of mountain glaciers, reduction in snow-cover extent, the earlier spring melting of rivers and lakes, [and] the accelerated rate of rise of sea levels during the 20th century relative to the past few thousand years. . . ."

That these climate-change risks are "widely shared" does not minimize Massachusetts' interest in the outcome of this litigation. According to petitioners' unchallenged affidavits, global sea levels rose somewhere between 10 and 20 centimeters over the 20th century as a result of global warming. These rising seas have already begun to swallow Massachusetts' coastal land. Because the Commonwealth "owns a substantial portion of the state's coastal property," it has alleged a particularized injury in its capacity as a landowner. The severity of that injury will only increase over the course of the next century: If sea levels continue to rise as predicted, one Massachusetts official believes that a significant fraction of coastal property will be "either permanently lost through inundation or temporarily lost through periodic storm surge and flooding events."

Causation

EPA does not dispute the existence of a causal connection between man-made greenhouse gas emissions and global warming. . . . EPA nevertheless maintains that its decision not to regulate greenhouse gas emissions from new motor vehicles contributes so insignificantly to petitioners' injuries that the agency cannot be haled into federal court to answer for them. For the same reason, EPA does not believe that any realistic possibility exists that the relief petitioners seek would mitigate global climate change and remedy their injuries. That is especially so because predicted increases in greenhouse gas emissions from developing nations, particularly China and India, are likely to offset any marginal domestic decrease.

But EPA overstates its case. Its argument rests on the erroneous assumption that a small incremental step, because it is incremental, can never be attacked in a federal judicial forum. . . . Agencies, like legislatures, do not generally resolve massive problems in one fell regulatory swoop. They instead whittle away at them over time, refining their preferred approach as circumstances change and as they develop a more-nuanced understanding of how best to proceed. That a first step might be tentative does not by itself support the notion that federal courts lack jurisdiction to determine whether that step conforms to law. [R]educing domestic automobile emissions is hardly a tentative step. Even leaving aside the other greenhouse gases, the United States transportation sector emits an enormous quantity of carbon dioxide into the atmosphere—. . . more than 1.7 billion metric tons in 1999 alone. That accounts for more than 6% of worldwide carbon dioxide emissions. To put this in perspective: Considering just emissions from the transportation sector, which represent less than one-third of this country's total carbon dioxide emissions, the United States would still rank as the third-largest emitter of carbon dioxide in the world, outpaced only by the European Union and China. Judged by any standard, U.S. motor-vehicle emissions make a meaningful contribution to greenhouse gas concentrations and hence, according to petitioners, to global warming.

The Remedy

While it may be true that regulating motor-vehicle emissions will not by itself reverse global warming, it by no means follows that we lack jurisdiction to decide whether EPA has a duty to take steps to *slow* or *reduce* it. Because of the enormity of the potential consequences associated with man-made climate change, the fact that the effectiveness of a remedy might be delayed during the (relatively short) time it takes for a new motor-vehicle fleet to replace an older one is essentially irrelevant. Nor is it dispositive that developing countries such as China and India are poised to increase greenhouse gas emissions substantially over the next century: A reduction in domestic emissions would slow the pace of global emissions increases, no matter what happens elsewhere. . . .

In sum—at least according to petitioners' uncontested affidavits—the rise in sea levels associated with global warming has already harmed and will continue to harm Massachusetts. The risk of catastrophic harm, though remote, is nevertheless real. That risk would be reduced to some extent if petitioners received the relief they seek. We therefore hold that petitioners have standing to challenge the EPA's denial of their rulemaking petition.

[On the merits, the Court concluded that, because greenhouse gases fit within the Clean Air Act's broad definition of "air pollutant," the EPA has statutory authority to regulate emission of such gases from new motor vehicles.] [Reversed and] remanded for further proceedings consistent with this opinion.

CHIEF JUSTICE ROBERTS, with whom JUSTICES SCALIA, THOMAS, and ALITO join, dissenting.

Global warming may be a "crisis," even "the most pressing environmental problem of our time." Indeed, it may ultimately affect nearly everyone on the planet in some potentially adverse way, and it may be that governments have done too little to address it. It is not a problem, however, that has escaped the attention of policymakers in the Executive and Legislative Branches of our Government, who continue to consider regulatory, legislative, and treaty-based means of addressing global climate change.

Apparently dissatisfied with the pace of progress on this issue in the elected branches, petitioners have come to the courts claiming broad-ranging injury, and attempting to tie that injury to the Government's alleged failure to comply with a rather narrow statutory provision. I would reject these challenges as nonjusticiable. Such a conclusion involves no judgment on whether global warming exists, what causes it, or the extent of the problem. Nor does it render petitioners without recourse. This Court's standing jurisprudence simply recognizes that redress of grievances of the sort at issue here "is the function of Congress and the Chief Executive," not the federal courts. [*Lujan.*]

I. . . . [P]etitioners bear the burden of alleging an injury that is fairly traceable to the Environmental Protection Agency's failure to promulgate new motor vehicle greenhouse gas emission standards, and that is likely to be redressed by the prospective issuance of such standards.

Before determining whether petitioners can meet this familiar test, however, the Court changes the rules. It asserts that "States are not normal litigants for the purposes of invoking federal jurisdiction," and that given "Massachusetts' stake in protecting its quasi-sovereign interests, the Commonwealth is entitled to *special solicitude* in our standing analysis." Relaxing Article III standing requirements because asserted injuries are pressed by a State, however, has no basis in our jurisprudence, and support for any such "special solicitude" is conspicuously absent from the Court's opinion. The general judicial review provision cited by the Court affords States no special rights or status. . . . Congress said [nothing] about the rights of States in this particular provision of the statute. Congress knows how to do that when it wants to,[3] but it has done nothing of the sort here. Under the law on which petitioners rely, Congress treated public and private litigants exactly the same.

Nor does the case law cited by the Court provide any support for the notion that Article III somehow implicitly treats public and private litigants differently. The Court has to go back a full century in an attempt to justify its novel standing rule, but even there it comes up short. The Court's analysis

---

3. Chief Justice Roberts cited 42 U.S.C. §7426(b), which affords states the right to petition EPA to regulate directly certain sources of pollution. — ED.

hinges on Georgia v. Tennessee Copper Co., 206 U.S. 230 (1907)—a case that did indeed draw a distinction between a State and private litigants, but solely with respect to available remedies. The case had nothing to do with Article III standing.

In *Tennessee Copper*, . . . Georgia sought to enjoin copper companies in neighboring Tennessee from discharging pollutants that were inflicting "a wholesale destruction of forests, orchards and crops" in bordering Georgia counties. Although the State owned very little of the territory allegedly affected, the Court reasoned that Georgia—in its capacity as a "*quasi-sovereign*"—"has an interest independent of and behind the titles of its citizens, in all the earth and air within its domain." The Court explained that while "the very elements that would be relied upon in a suit between fellow-citizens as a ground for equitable relief [were] wanting," a State "is not lightly to be required to give up *quasi*-sovereign rights for pay." Thus while a complaining private litigant would have to make do with a *legal* remedy—one "for pay"—the State was entitled to *equitable* relief.

In contrast to the present case, there was no question in *Tennessee Copper* about Article III injury. There was certainly no suggestion that the State could show standing where the private parties could not; there was no dispute, after all, that the private landowners had "an action at law." *Tennessee Copper* has since stood for nothing more than a State's right . . . to sue in a representative capacity as *parens patriae*. Nothing about a State's ability to sue in that capacity dilutes the bedrock requirement of showing injury, causation, and redressability to satisfy Article III.

A claim of *parens patriae* standing is distinct from an allegation of direct injury. Far from being a substitute for Article III injury, *parens patriae* actions raise an additional hurdle for a state litigant: the articulation of a "quasi-sovereign interest" "*apart* from the interests of particular private parties." Just as an association suing on behalf of its members must show not only that it represents the members but that at least one satisfies Article III requirements, so too a State asserting quasi-sovereign interests as *parens patriae* must still show that its citizens satisfy Article III. Focusing on Massachusetts's interests as quasi-sovereign makes the required showing here harder, not easier. The Court, in effect, takes what has always been regarded as a *necessary* condition for *parens patriae* standing—a quasi-sovereign interest—and converts it into a *sufficient* showing for purposes of Article III.

. . . The Court asserts that Massachusetts is entitled to "special solicitude" due to its "quasi-sovereign interests," but then applies our Article III standing test to the asserted injury of the State's loss of coastal property. In the context of *parens patriae* standing, however, we have characterized state ownership of land as a "nonsovereign interest" because a State "is likely to have the same interests as other similarly situated proprietors." [Alfred L. Snapp & Son, Inc. v. Puerto Rico ex rel. Barez, 458 U.S. 592, 601 (1982).]

On top of everything else, the Court overlooks the fact that our cases cast significant doubt on a State's standing to assert a quasi-sovereign interest—as opposed to a direct injury—against the Federal Government. As a general rule, we have held that while a State might assert a quasi-sovereign right as *parens patriae* "for the protection of its citizens, it is no part of its duty or power to enforce their rights in respect of their relations with the Federal Government. In that field it is the United States, and not the State, which represents them." Massachusetts v. Mellon, 262 U.S. 447, 485-486 (1923).

All of this presumably explains why petitioners never cited *Tennessee Copper* in their briefs before this Court or the D.C. Circuit. It presumably explains why not one of the legion of *amici* supporting petitioners ever cited the case. And it presumably explains why not one of the three judges writing below ever cited the case either. Given that one purpose of the standing requirement is "to assure that concrete adverseness which sharpens the presentation of issues upon which the court so largely depends for illumination," it is ironic that the Court today adopts a new theory of Article III standing for States without the benefit of briefing or argument on the point.

II. It is not at all clear how the Court's "special solicitude" for Massachusetts plays out in the standing analysis, except as an implicit concession that petitioners cannot establish standing on traditional terms. But the status of Massachusetts as a State cannot compensate for petitioners' failure to demonstrate injury in fact, causation, and redressability.

[The Court focuses] on the State's asserted loss of coastal land as the injury in fact. . . . That alleged injury must be "concrete and particularized" and "distinct and palpable." Central to this concept of "particularized" injury is the requirement that a plaintiff be affected in a "personal and individual way" and seek relief that "directly and tangibly benefits him" in a manner distinct from its impact on "the public at large." . . . The very concept of global warming seems inconsistent with this particularization requirement. Global warming is a phenomenon "harmful to humanity at large," and the redress petitioners seek is focused no more on them than on the public generally—it is literally to change the atmosphere around the world. If petitioners' particularized injury is loss of coastal land, it is also that injury that must be "actual or imminent, not conjectural or hypothetical," "real and immediate," and "certainly impending."

As to "actual" injury, the Court observes that "global sea levels rose somewhere between 10 and 20 centimeters over the 20th century as a result of global warming" and that "these rising seas have already begun to swallow Massachusetts' coastal land." But none of petitioners' declarations supports that connection. [A]side from a single conclusory statement, there is nothing in petitioners' 43 standing declarations and accompanying exhibits to support an inference of actual loss of Massachusetts coastal land from 20th century global sea level increases. It is pure conjecture.

The Court's attempts to identify "imminent" or "certainly impending" loss of Massachusetts coastal land fares no better. One of petitioners' declarants predicts global warming will cause sea level to rise by 20 to 70 centimeters *by the year 2100*. Another uses a computer modeling program to . . . calculate[] that the high-end estimate of sea level rise would result in the loss of significant state-owned coastal land. But the computer modeling program has a conceded average error [that may be so large that] it is difficult to put much stock in the predicted loss of land. But even placing that problem to the side, accepting a century-long time horizon and a series of compounded estimates renders requirements of imminence and immediacy utterly toothless.

III. Petitioners' reliance on Massachusetts's loss of coastal land as their injury in fact for standing purposes creates insurmountable problems for them with respect to causation and redressability. To establish standing, petitioners must show a causal connection between that specific injury and the lack of new motor vehicle greenhouse gas emission standards, and that the promulgation of such standards would likely redress that injury. As is often the case, the questions of causation and redressability overlap. [W]hen a party is challenging the Government's . . . lack of regulation of a third party, satisfying the causation and redressability requirements becomes "substantially more difficult."

Petitioners view the relationship between their injuries and EPA's failure to promulgate new motor vehicle greenhouse gas emission standards as simple and direct: Domestic motor vehicles emit carbon dioxide and other greenhouse gases. Worldwide emissions of greenhouse gases contribute to global warming and therefore also to petitioners' alleged injuries. Without the new vehicle standards, greenhouse gas emissions—and therefore global warming and its attendant harms—have been higher than they otherwise would have been; once EPA changes course, the trend will be reversed.

The Court [uses] the dire nature of global warming itself as a bootstrap for finding causation and redressability. . . . [It] is global emissions data that are relevant. . . . [D]omestic motor vehicles contribute about 6 percent of global carbon dioxide emissions and 4 percent of global greenhouse gas emissions. The amount of global emissions at issue here is smaller still; §202(a)(1) of the Clean Air Act covers only *new* motor vehicles and *new* motor vehicle engines, so petitioners' desired emission standards might reduce only a fraction of 4 percent of global emissions.

This gets us only to the relevant greenhouse gas emissions; linking them to global warming and ultimately to petitioners' alleged injuries next requires consideration of further complexities. As EPA explained in its denial of petitioners' request for rulemaking,

> predicting future climate change necessarily involves a complex web of economic and physical factors including: our ability to predict future global anthropogenic emissions of [greenhouse gases] and aerosols; the fate of these emissions once they enter the atmosphere (e.g., what percentage are absorbed by vegetation or are taken up by the oceans); the impact of those emissions that remain in the atmosphere on the radiative properties of the atmosphere; changes in critically important climate feedbacks (e.g., changes in cloud cover and ocean circulation); changes in temperature characteristics (e.g., average temperatures, shifts in daytime and evening temperatures); changes in other climatic parameters (e.g., shifts in precipitation, storms); and ultimately the impact of such changes on human health and welfare (e.g., increases or decreases in agricultural productivity, human health impacts).

Petitioners are never able to trace their alleged injuries back through this complex web to the fractional amount of global emissions that might have been limited with EPA standards. In light of the bit-part domestic new motor vehicle greenhouse gas emissions have played in what petitioners describe as a 150-year global phenomenon, and the myriad additional factors bearing on petitioners' alleged injury—the loss of Massachusetts coastal land—the connection is far too speculative to establish causation.

IV. Redressability is even more problematic. To the tenuous link between petitioners' alleged injury and the indeterminate fractional domestic emissions at issue here, add the fact that petitioners cannot meaningfully predict what will come of the 80 percent of global greenhouse gas emissions that originate outside the United States. As the Court acknowledges, . . . the domestic emissions at issue here may become an increasingly marginal portion of global emissions, and any decreases produced by petitioners' desired standards are likely to be overwhelmed many times over by emissions increases elsewhere in the world. . . .

No matter, the Court reasons, because *any* decrease in domestic emissions will "slow the pace of global emissions increases, no matter what happens elsewhere." Every little bit helps, so Massachusetts can sue over any little bit.

The Court's sleight-of-hand is in failing to link up the different elements of the three-part standing test. What must be *likely* to be redressed is the particular injury in fact. The injury the Court looks to is the asserted loss of land. The Court contends that regulating domestic motor vehicle emissions will reduce carbon dioxide in the atmosphere, *and therefore* redress Massachusetts's injury. But even if regulation *does* reduce emissions—to some indeterminate degree, given events elsewhere in the world—the Court never explains why that makes it *likely* that the injury in fact—the loss of land—will be redressed. . . . The realities make it pure conjecture to suppose that EPA regulation of new automobile emissions will *likely* prevent the loss of Massachusetts coastal land.

V. Petitioners' difficulty in demonstrating causation and redressability is not surprising given the evident mismatch between the source of their alleged injury—catastrophic global warming—and the narrow subject matter of the Clean Air Act provision at issue in this suit. The mismatch suggests that petitioners' true goal for this litigation may be more symbolic than anything else. The constitutional role of the courts, however, is to decide concrete cases—not to serve as a convenient forum for policy debates.

When dealing with legal doctrine phrased in terms of what is "fairly" traceable or "likely" to be redressed, it is perhaps not surprising that the matter is subject to some debate. But in considering how loosely or rigorously to define those adverbs, it is vital to keep in mind the purpose of the inquiry. The limitation of the judicial power to cases and controversies "is crucial in maintaining the tripartite allocation of power set forth in the Constitution." In my view, the Court today . . . fails to take this limitation seriously.

To be fair, it is not the first time the Court has done so. Today's decision recalls the previous high-water mark of diluted standing requirements, United

States v. Students Challenging Regulatory Agency Procedures (*SCRAP*), 412 U.S. 669 (1973). In *SCRAP*, the Court based an environmental group's standing to challenge a railroad freight rate surcharge on the group's allegation that increases in railroad rates would cause an increase in the use of non-recyclable goods, resulting in the increased need for natural resources to produce such goods. According to the group, some of these resources might be taken from the Washington area, resulting in increased refuse that might find its way into area parks, harming the group's members. Over time, *SCRAP* became emblematic not of the looseness of Article III standing requirements, but of how utterly manipulable they are if not taken seriously as a matter of judicial self-restraint. *SCRAP* made standing seem a lawyer's game, rather than a fundamental limitation ensuring that courts function as courts and not intrude on the politically accountable branches. Today's decision is *SCRAP* for a new generation.[4]

Perhaps the Court recognizes as much. How else to explain its need to devise a new doctrine of state standing to support its result? The good news is that the Court's "special solicitude" for Massachusetts limits the future applicability of the diluted standing requirements applied in this case. The bad news is that the Court's self-professed relaxation of those Article III requirements has caused us to transgress "the proper — and properly limited — role of the courts in a democratic society."

I respectfully dissent.

NOTES

1. State Standing as *Parens Patriae*. There are two ways in which a state may assert standing to litigate as *parens patriae* to protect its quasi-sovereign interests — those interests that concern the state as a whole, as distinct from the welfare of individual state citizens. First, a state may assert its *parens patriae* claim against a private party or another state. Second, a state may assert its *parens patriae* claim against the federal government. Only the second pattern was presented by Massachusetts v. EPA. Yet, the majority relied upon Georgia v. Tennessee Copper Company, 206 U.S. 230 (1907), which involved the first pattern, to support its contention that states enjoy specially relaxed standing requirements when they assert claims as *parens patriae*. In Massachusetts v. Mellon, 262 U.S. 447 (1923), the Court noted that

> [w]hile the State, under some circumstances, may sue [as *parens patriae*] for the protection of its citizens, it is no part of its duty or power to enforce their rights in respect of their relations with the Federal Government. In that field it

---

4. The difficulty with *SCRAP* . . . is the attenuated nature of the injury there. . . . Even in *SCRAP*, the Court noted that what was required was "something more than an ingenious academic exercise in the conceivable," and we have since understood the allegation there to have been "that the string of occurrences alleged would happen *immediately*," Whitmore v. Arkansas, 495 U.S. 149, 159 (1990) (emphasis added). That is hardly the case here. . . .

is the United States, and not the State, which represents them as *parens patriae*, when such representation becomes appropriate; and to the former, and not to the latter, they must look for such protective measures as flow from that status.

In Massachusetts v. EPA, the state argued that, as *parens patriae*, it was entitled to assert its citizens' claims that the EPA had failed to conform to its statutory obligations. According to *Mellon*, it is the United States, and not Massachusetts, that acts as *parens patriae* in such circumstances; the proper redress for aggrieved state citizens was said to be in the political processes of the nation as a whole. Did Massachusetts v. EPA repudiate *Mellon* without saying so? Or did the Court rely instead on Massachusetts's assertion of its own interests, as distinct from that of its citizens? The latter possibility is taken up in the following note.

2. State Standing as Proprietor. Massachusetts also asserted that it was injured by threatened loss of its state-owned land due to rising sea levels attributable to global warming, an injury no different from that suffered by private riparian landowners. In this capacity, Massachusetts was not acting as *parens patriae*, but for itself, as simply another injured landowner, although one clothed with a public trust. That threat, inundation—while real and, perhaps, inevitable—is hardly imminent. Nor was there a "substantial likelihood that the requested relief will remedy the alleged injury in fact." Vermont Agency of Natural Resources v. United States ex rel. Stevens, 529 U.S. 765, 771 (2000). Carbon dioxide emissions from new cars constitute a tiny fraction of global greenhouse gases. Does the majority opinion suggest that the Article III requirements have been altered for all litigants? Has *imminent* threatened injury been replaced by *inevitable* injury, or is inevitable injury a substitute for imminent injury? Has redressability been reduced from a requirement that a litigant prove a substantial likelihood that the relief he seeks will remedy his injury to a requirement that the requested relief will palliate the injury to some degree, however slight?

3. Two Tiers of Article III Standing? Another possibility is that the majority opinion created two tiers of Article III standing—one for states and the other for private litigants. Additional questions emerge if the majority altered the meaning of the Article III requirements just for states. What justifies two tiers of Article III jurisdiction? The Court makes a federalism-based argument to support the special solicitude it says states enjoy with respect to standing. Is that argument adequate when a state sues a private party in federal court? When the state sues the federal government, asserting an injury no different from that suffered by private citizens? When the state sues other states, asserting injury identical to that suffered by private litigants? Perhaps special solicitude applies only when the states sue as *parens patriae*, or when they assert an injury in a uniquely sovereign capacity. Even then, should special standing solicitude be shown to the states when they act as *parens patriae* with respect to federally created rights? *Mellon* said that the United States is the proper people's representative with respect to such rights.

Global warming threatens universal injury of some kind. Perhaps that is the critical fact. Should the majority opinion be read to suggest that the special solicitude afforded states is limited to instances in which states, as *parens patriae*, seek to remedy a diffuse injury, one suffered by everyone? On this reading, such cases as Whitmore v. Arkansas, 495 U.S. 149 (1990), Schlesinger v. Reservists Committee to Stop the War, 418 U.S. 208 (1974), United States v. Richardson, 418 U.S. 166 (1974), Ex parte Levitt, 302 U.S. 633 (1937), and Fairchild v. Hughes, 258 U.S. 126 (1922), are repudiated, at least to the extent those cases define a boundary that excludes universal injuries from Article III injury in fact. Does that open the door to states becoming a sort of civic ombudsman with respect to such claims? If not, what is the limiting principle?

4. The Narrow Case of "Taxpayer Standing." As with all federal court cases, a taxpayer's challenge to the validity of some federal expenditure is subject to the constitutional core of standing. Even so, taxpayer standing cases merit special mention. In Frothingham v. Mellon, 262 U.S. 447 (1923), a federal taxpayer alleged that federal expenditures to reduce maternal and infant mortality were beyond the enumerated powers of Congress. She claimed that her taxes would be increased by the expenditure and asserted that the increase was a taking of her property in violation of due process. The Court unanimously agreed that Frothingham lacked standing. Her financial interest in the expenditures was "shared with millions of others [and] is comparatively minute and indeterminable." The effect of the expenditures "upon future taxation [is] so remote, fluctuating, and uncertain" as to preclude standing. She lacked the requisite injury in fact—her injury was either too speculative or too universal to support standing. The same rule applies to suits premised on the plaintiff's status as a state or municipal taxpayer. Daimler Chrysler Corp. v. Cuno, 547 U.S. 332 (2006).

In Flast v. Cohen, 392 U.S. 83 (1968), federal taxpayers challenged the validity of federal financial aid to religious schools as a violation of the First Amendment's ban on government establishments of religion. The Court found standing to exist by reason of the plaintiff's taxpayer status whenever a taxpayer attacks a federal expenditure as a violation of some specific limit on congressional power (like the establishment clause) rather than because it is beyond Congress's enumerated powers.

This distinction did not endure. In *Valley Forge*, the Court found taxpayer standing inapplicable because the challenged government activity was not spending but a disposal of surplus property under the property clause. Although not overruled, *Flast* was left stranded, an isolated relic whose viability is in some doubt. It may well be confined to the special case of government spending that allegedly violates the constitutional clause prohibiting government "establishments of religion."

In Hein v. Freedom From Religion Foundation, 551 U.S. 587 (2007), the Court rejected another attempt to invoke *Flast*. Using funds that Congress had appropriated for the President's general discretionary expenditure, President George W. Bush established several executive offices to ensure that faith-based community groups were treated equally with secular groups in receiving federal financial support to deliver secular social services. Because the

President's initiative was a product of executive discretion rather than specific congressional mandate, a plurality found *Flast* to be inapplicable. The plurality rejected the idea that there was no real difference between executive discretion and congressional mandates: "[E]xtending the *Flast* exception to purely executive expenditures would effectively subject every federal action—be it a conference, proclamation or speech—to Establishment Clause challenge by any taxpayer in federal court. [This would] raise serious separation-of-powers concerns [as it] would enlist the federal courts to superintend, at the behest of any federal taxpayer, the speeches, statements, and myriad daily activities of the President, his staff, and other Executive Branch officials."

Justice Scalia and Justice Thomas concurred in the judgment, but would have overruled *Flast*. Justice Scalia noted that "whether the challenged government expenditure is expressly allocated by a specific congressional enactment *has absolutely no relevance* to the Article III criteria of injury in fact, traceability, and redressability." The fundamental problem with *Flast* is that it credits as Article III injury in fact the concept of "Psychic Injury—the taxpayer's *mental displeasure* that money extracted from him is being spent in an unlawful manner." Because the Court has "consistently held that a plaintiff raising only a generally available grievance about government—claiming only harm to his and every citizen's interest in proper application of the Constitution and laws, and seeking relief that no more directly and tangibly benefits him than it does the public at large—does not state an Article III case or controversy," there is no warrant for the continuation of *Flast*.

After Massachusetts v. EPA, could the claim rejected in *Hein* be brought by a state, acting as *parens patriae*?

In Arizona Christian School Tuition Organization v. Winn, 131 S. Ct. 1436 (2011), the Court found *Flast* inapplicable to a challenge by Arizona taxpayers to Arizona's provision of dollar-for-dollar tax credits for contributions to school tuition organizations (STOs), charitable entities that provide scholarships for students attending private schools that do not discriminate on the basis of race, handicap, national origin, or family status. Because some STOs provide scholarships to students attending religious schools the taxpayers contended that the credits violated the establishment clause. The Court ruled that the plaintiff taxpayers lacked standing under ordinary standing principles: "[E]ven if one assumes that [a] benefit depletes the government's coffers, [to] find injury, a court must speculate 'that elected officials will increase a taxpayer-plaintiff's tax bill to make up a deficit.' And to find redressability, a court must assume that, were the remedy the taxpayers seek to be allowed, 'legislators will pass along the supposed increased revenue in the form of tax reductions.' It would be 'pure speculation' to conclude that an injunction against a tax benefit 'would result in any actual tax relief' for a taxpayer-plaintiff." Nor was the *Flast* exception applicable:

> [Although] tax credits and governmental expenditures can have similar economic consequences, [they] do not both implicate individual taxpayers in sectarian activities. A dissenter whose tax dollars are "extracted and spent" knows

that he has in some small measure been made to contribute to an establishment in violation of conscience. In that instance the taxpayer's direct and particular connection with the establishment does not depend on economic speculation or political conjecture. The connection would exist even if the conscientious dissenter's tax liability were unaffected or reduced. When the government declines to impose a tax, by contrast, there is no such connection between dissenting taxpayer and alleged establishment. Any financial injury remains speculative. And awarding some citizens a tax credit allows other citizens to retain control over their own funds in accordance with their own consciences. . . .

Furthermore, respondents cannot satisfy the requirements of causation and redressability. When the government collects and spends taxpayer money, governmental choices are responsible for the transfer of wealth [and the] resulting subsidy of religious activity is . . . traceable to the government's expenditures. And an injunction against those expenditures would address the objections of conscience raised by taxpayer-plaintiffs. Here, by contrast, contributions result from the decisions of private taxpayers regarding their own funds. Private citizens create private STOs; STOs choose beneficiary schools; and taxpayers then contribute to STOs. While the State, at the outset, affords the opportunity to create and contribute to an STO, the tax credit system is implemented by private action and with no state intervention. Objecting taxpayers know that their fellow citizens, not the State, decide to contribute and in fact make the contribution. These considerations prevent any injury the objectors may suffer from being fairly traceable to the government. And while an injunction against application of the tax credit most likely would reduce contributions to STOs, that remedy would not affect non-contributing taxpayers or their tax payments. As a result, any injury suffered by respondents would not be remedied by an injunction limiting the tax credit's operation.

Justice Kagan, joined by Justices Ginsburg, Breyer, and Sotomayor, dissented:

Cash grants and targeted tax breaks are means of accomplishing the same government objective—to provide financial support to select individuals or organizations. Taxpayers who oppose state aid of religion have equal reason to protest whether that aid flows from the one form of subsidy or the other. Either way, the government has financed the religious activity. And so either way, taxpayers should be able to challenge the subsidy. . . . [A]ssume a State wishes to subsidize the ownership of crucifixes. It could purchase the religious symbols in bulk and distribute them to all takers. Or it could mail a reimbursement check to any individual who buys her own and submits a receipt for the purchase. Or it could authorize that person to claim a tax credit equal to the price she paid. Now, really—do taxpayers have less reason to complain if the State selects the last of these three options?

b. *"Prudential" or Non-constitutional Standing Rules*

Even if the constitutional core of standing has been satisfied, standing may be denied if a plaintiff fails to meet the Court's prudential requirements for standing. These rules are not compelled by the Constitution; the Court has created them because it believes these rules supply a prudent limitation upon the exercise of the federal judicial power.

i. Third-Party Standing

Generally, a person must assert his or her own rights, not someone else's rights. This rule is justified by (1) restraint—the desire to avoid unnecessary or premature decisions; (2) respect—the desire to respect the apparent decision of third parties not to assert their rights; and (3) autonomy—the belief that third parties can best represent themselves. See Brilmayer, The Jurisprudence of Article III: Perspectives on the "Case or Controversy" Requirement, 93 Harv. L. Rev. 297 (1979). Because the Court views third-party standing as a prudential, rather than constitutional, doctrine, the Court has created numerous exceptions, all of which may be "*sub silentio* recognitions of *first-party* rights—of the interests of the *litigant*." Tribe, American Constitutional Law 136 (2d ed. 1988). See also Monaghan, Third Party Standing, 84 Colum. L. Rev. 567 (1984).

For third-party standing to be present there must be (1) a substantial or special relationship between the claimant and the third party; (2) proof of the impossibility or impracticality of the third party asserting his or her own interest; and (3) a risk that the rights of the third party will be diluted or lost unless the claimant is allowed to assert the third party's claim. The "relationship" factor is satisfied if the claimant's rights are so inextricably connected to the third party's rights that vindication of one right will necessarily vindicate the other. The remaining elements are frequently fused together: Is the threatened impairment of the third party's rights so great that there is little likelihood of their preservation unless the claimant is permitted to assert the third party's rights? This can occur if (1) the plaintiff is legally obliged to take or refrain from action that prevents the third party from asserting his or her own rights; or (2) the third party has no practical ability to assert his or her own rights and the plaintiff's interest in the controversy is congruent with the third party's interest.

ii. The "Zone of Interests" Requirement

A "plaintiff's complaint [must] fall within the zone of interests protected by the law invoked." Allen v. Wright, supra. A plaintiff lacks standing unless the plaintiff's injury is of a type that the law invoked was meant to protect against. In Air Courier Conference v. APWU, 498 U.S. 517 (1991), U.S. Postal Service employees challenged the statutory validity of a Postal Service decision that the federal statute creating a postal monopoly did not prevent private couriers from depositing mail in foreign mail systems for delivery overseas. The Postal Service decision reduced mail volume, which threatened postal jobs, but the postal employees lacked standing because nothing in the language, history, or structure of the statute indicated "that Congress intended to protect [Postal Service] jobs."

c. Organizational Standing

Ordinary standing rules apply to organizations asserting their own rights, but when an organization (e.g., an unincorporated association) asserts the interests of people who they claim to represent (e.g., members) it must establish that (1) the members would have standing to sue independently; (2) the interests asserted are germane to the association's purpose; and (3) neither the claim asserted nor the relief requested requires the members' participation in the suit. In Hunt v. Washington State Apple Advertising Commission, 432 U.S. 333 (1977), the commission, a state agency created to promote and protect Washington's apple industry, had standing to challenge the constitutional validity of North Carolina's apple-marketing regulations. Washington apple growers and vendors had independent standing to sue, the asserted injuries to the growers (wrongful obstacles to the sale of apples in North Carolina) were germane to the commission's purpose, and neither the substance of the claim (the alleged unconstitutionality of the North Carolina regulations) nor the relief requested (an injunction) required the participation of the growers and vendors. In Summers v. Earth Island Institute, 555 U.S. 488 (2009), the Court reaffirmed the requirement that organizations must "make specific allegations establishing that at least one identified member had suffered or would suffer harm."

3. Ripeness and Mootness

Courts refuse to decide issues that are not ripe or that have become moot. An issue is not ripe if future events may render a decision unnecessary. An issue is moot if past events have made a decision unnecessary.

a. Ripeness

Legal conflicts often have a gestational period, somewhat like thunderstorms. A storm is brewing when cold and warm air masses converge, but it hasn't actually arrived until the masses collide. A person may take action that threatens to violate the legal rights of another, but a lawsuit is not ripe until the violation is certain. Ripeness is related to the advisory opinion doctrine; both doctrines seek to avoid decisions of abstract controversies. Ripeness involves "the fitness of the issues for judicial decision" and consideration of "the hardship to the parties of withholding court consideration."

To be ripe for decision, a plaintiff must (1) have already suffered harm; (2) be faced with a "specific present objective harm"; or (3) be under a "threat of specific future harm." In United Public Workers v. Mitchell, 330 U.S. 75 (1947), public employees sought a declaratory judgment that the federal Hatch Act, which barred public employees from "any active part in political management or in political campaigns," violated the free speech clause. All but one of the plaintiffs admitted that they had not violated the Act but asserted that they desired to do so. The controversy was not ripe because the plaintiffs' future intentions were vague, nonspecific, and general. The Court characterized their grievances as more of "an attack on the political expediency" of the Hatch Act than as an attempt to vindicate personal injuries. In Laird v. Tatum, 408 U.S. 1 (1972), the Court ruled that a suit attacking the validity of Army surveillance activities was unripe. The plaintiffs claimed that Army surveillance had a "present inhibiting effect" on their free speech rights. But this, said the Court, was really "fear of future, punitive action." The plaintiffs' "speculative apprehensi[on]" of future Army misuse of its surveillance information "in some way that would cause harm" to the plaintiffs was simply too vague to constitute either "specific present objective harm" or a "threat of specific future harm."

b. Mootness

A moot case need not be decided. A case is rendered moot if events occur after the case has begun that eliminate the plaintiff's stake in the controversy. Mootness is standing's cousin. It is "the doctrine of standing set in a time frame: The requisite personal interest that must exist at the commencement of the litigation (standing) must continue throughout its existence (mootness)." Monaghan, Constitutional Adjudication: The Who and When, 82 Yale L.J. 1363, 1384 (1973).

After Marco DeFunis, Jr., was denied admission to the University of Washington's law school, he brought suit, claiming that his rejection was due to racially discriminatory admission practices. A Washington trial court ordered his admission. The Washington Supreme Court reversed, but the U.S. Supreme Court granted certiorari and stayed the judgment of the Washington Supreme Court, allowing DeFunis to remain in school. When the Supreme Court heard the case, DeFunis was in his final quarter of study, and the school agreed that he would be allowed to complete his studies no matter what "view this Court might express on the merits." The Court, in DeFunis v. Odegaard, 416 U.S. 312 (1974), found the case moot; DeFunis no longer had any personal stake in the matter. "The controversy between the parties has clearly ceased to be 'definite and concrete' and no longer 'touch[es] the legal relations of parties having adverse legal interests.'"

Mootness is often said to be constitutionally required, an aspect of the "case or controversy" requirement. See, e.g., United States Parole Commission v. Geraghty, 445 U.S. 388, 395-397 (1980); Liner v. Jafco, Inc., 375 U.S. 301, 306 n.3 (1964). But the Court has fashioned so many exceptions to the doctrine that some commentators question whether the doctrine is really as constitutionally rooted as the Court says it is. See, e.g., Lee, Deconstitutionalizing Justiciability: The Example of Mootness, 105 Harv. L. Rev. 603 (1992).

The most important exception to mootness principles occurs when an issue is capable of repetition yet evades review. The exception, which originated in Southern Pacific Terminal Co. v. ICC, 219 U.S. 498 (1911), requires a showing that (1) the life of the controversy is too short to be fully litigated prior to its termination; and (2) that there is a reasonable expectation that the plaintiff will again be subjected to the same problem. The latter element has been broadened, particularly in class actions where the class representative may not face the same issue in the future but the similarly situated class members will. In Roe v. Wade, 410 U.S. 113 (1975), a pregnant woman challenged the constitutional validity of Texas's abortion prohibition, but by the time her case was heard by the Court she was no longer pregnant. The case, a class action, was not moot, given the relative speed of courts and human gestation. A constitutional challenge to abortion laws cannot be fully litigated through all stages of appellate review in nine months. Some members of the class of Texas women, if not the class plaintiff, would be pregnant again and desire abortions. In Sosna v. Iowa, 419 U.S. 393 (1975), the Court made it clear that to avoid mootness in class litigation it must be shown that the problem is "capable of repetition, yet evading review" as to the class. By contrast, DeFunis's challenge was for himself alone, not as a class representative.

4. Political Questions

The court has developed a doctrine that some issues are simply not susceptible to judicial resolution. Although this is called the "political question" doctrine, its aim is *not* to avoid deciding politically controversial issues. Rather, the objective is to identify those controversies that should be decided by the "political" branches of government—executive and legislative—either because the Constitution requires that disposition or because there are persuasive reasons of policy to leave the decision to the political branches. The political question doctrine is thus a mixture of rationales—some constitutional, some prudential.

The political question doctrine is not new. In Marbury v. Madison, Chief Justice Marshall disclaimed any power of the courts to review acts of the President within the President's "Constitutional or legal discretions. Questions, in their nature political, or which are, by the Constitution and laws, submitted to the executive can never be made in this court." While a member of the House of Representatives, Marshall gave a fuller expression of this point:

> By extending the judicial power to all cases in law and equity, the constitution had never been understood to confer on that department any political power whatever. To come within this department a question must assume a legal form for forensic litigation and judicial decision. There must be parties to come into

court, who can be reached by its process, and bound by its power; whose rights admit of ultimate decision by a tribunal to which they are bound to submit.

By this, Marshall meant that courts have power to act only through legal forms; whatever political effect they produce is a mere by-product of their resolution of lawsuits. The political question doctrine is firmly entrenched but, as will be seen, it is not capable of precise application.

The most important element of the political question doctrine, and the one that is most clearly constitutionally compelled, is the notion that courts will not decide cases where there is "a textually demonstrable constitutional commitment of the issue to a coordinate political department." The next most important strand is the idea that "a lack of judicially discoverable and manageable standards for resolving an issue" makes the issue a nonjusticiable political question. This aspect of political questions is a hybrid of constitutional requirements and prudential concerns. The final dimension of political questions is a related set of prudential principles that counsel against judicial decision of issues where judicial intervention would create institutional problems of great magnitude.

≡ *Baker v. Carr*
≡ *369 U.S. 186 (1962)*

[Tennessee's constitution required apportionment of the state legislature on the basis of population, but the legislature had not been reapportioned since 1901, with the result that the legislature was not apportioned by population. Tennessee voters alleged that this failure to reapportion as required under the Tennessee constitution was a denial of equal protection "by virtue of the debasement of their votes." The plaintiffs contended that there was no effective redress available in the Tennessee legislature because of its improperly apportioned character. Plaintiffs sought an injunction against further elections under the existing system, and a court order directing either elections at-large or reapportionment "by mathematical application of the Tennessee constitutional formulae to the most recent Federal Census figures." The lower federal court dismissed the claim as nonjusticiable.

In a prior decision, Colegrove v. Green, 328 U.S. 549 (1946), the Court had refused to hear a case challenging the constitutional validity of Illinois's congressional districts, which were not equal in populations. In *Colegrove*, the Court said, "the Constitution has conferred upon Congress exclusive authority to secure fair representation by the States in the [House of Representatives. Art. I, §4]. Courts ought not to enter this political thicket."]

JUSTICE BRENNAN, for the Court.

[We] hold that this challenge to an apportionment presents no nonjusticiable "political question." [The] mere fact that the suit seeks protection of a political right does not mean it presents a political question. Such an objection "is little more than a play upon words." Rather, it is argued that apportionment cases [can] involve no federal constitutional right except one resting on the guaranty of a republican form of government [Art. IV, §4], and that complaints based on that clause have been held to present political questions which are nonjusticiable. We hold that the claim pleaded here neither rests upon nor implicates the Guaranty Clause and that its justiciability is therefore not foreclosed by our decisions of cases involving that clause. To show why we reject the argument based on the Guaranty Clause, we must examine the authorities under it. But because there appears to be some uncertainty as to why those cases did present political questions [we] deem it necessary first to consider the contours of the "political question" doctrine.

Our discussion [requires] review of a number of political question cases, in order to expose the attributes of the doctrine—attributes which, in various settings, diverge, combine, appear, and disappear in seeming disorderliness. [That] review reveals that in the Guaranty Clause cases and in the other "political question" cases, it is the relationship between the judiciary and the coordinate branches of the Federal Government, and not the federal judiciary's relationship to the States, which gives rise to the "political question." [The] nonjusticiability of a political question is primarily a function of the separation of powers. . . . Deciding whether a matter has in any measure been committed by the Constitution to another branch of government, or whether the action of that branch exceeds whatever authority has been committed, is itself a delicate exercise in constitutional interpretation, and is a responsibility of this [Court].

Foreign relations: There are sweeping statements to the effect that all questions touching foreign relations are political questions. Not only does resolution of such issues frequently turn on standards that defy judicial application, or involve the exercise of a discretion demonstrably committed to the executive or legislature; but many such questions uniquely demand single-voiced statement of the Government's views. Yet it is error to suppose that every case or controversy which touches foreign relations lies beyond judicial cognizance. Our cases in this field seem invariably to show a discriminating analysis of the particular question posed, in terms of the history of its management by the political branches, of its susceptibility to judicial handling in the light of its nature and posture in the specific case, and of the possible consequences of judicial action. . . .

Validity of enactments: In Coleman v. Miller, [307 U.S. 433 (1939)], this Court held that the questions of how long a proposed amendment to the Federal Constitution remained open to ratification, and what effect a prior rejection had on a subsequent ratification, were committed to congressional resolution and involved criteria of decision that necessarily escaped the judicial grasp. Similar considerations apply to the enacting process: "The respect due to coequal and independent departments," and the need for finality and certainty about the status of a statute contribute to judicial reluctance to inquire whether, as passed, it complied with all requisite formalities. . . . Prominent on the surface of any case held to involve a political question is found a textually demonstrable constitutional commitment of the issue to a coordinate political department; or a lack of judicially discoverable and manageable standards for resolving it; or the impossibility of deciding without an initial policy determination of a kind clearly for nonjudicial discretion; or the impossibility of a court's undertaking independent resolution without expressing lack of the respect due coordinate branches of government; or an unusual need for unquestioning adherence to a political decision already made; or the potentiality of embarrassment from multifarious pronouncements by various departments on one question.

Unless one of these formulations is inextricable from the case at bar, there should be no dismissal for nonjusticiability on the ground of a political question's presence. The doctrine of which we treat is one of "political questions," not one of "political cases." . . .

[It] is argued that this case shares the characteristics of decisions that constitute a category not yet considered, cases concerning the Constitution's guaranty [of] a republican form of government. [Guaranty Clause] claims involve those elements which define a "political question," and for that reason and no other, they are nonjusticiable. [The] nonjusticiability of such claims has nothing to do with their touching upon matters of state governmental organization.

Republican form of government: Luther v. Borden, 7 How. [48 U.S.] 1 [1849], though in form simply an action for damages for trespass was, as Daniel Webster said in opening the argument for the defense, "an unusual case." The defendants, admitting an otherwise tortious breaking and entering, sought to justify their action on the ground that they were agents of the established lawful government of Rhode Island, which State was then under martial law to defend itself from active insurrection; that the plaintiff was engaged in that insurrection; and that they entered under orders to arrest the plaintiff. The case arose "out of the unfortunate political differences which agitated the people of Rhode Island in 1841 and 1842," and which had resulted in a situation wherein two groups laid competing claims to recognition as the lawful government. The plaintiff's right to recover depended upon which of the two groups was entitled to such recognition; but the lower court's refusal to receive evidence or hear argument on that issue, its charge to the jury that the earlier established or "charter" government was lawful, and the verdict for the defendants, were affirmed upon appeal to this Court. . . .

Chief Justice Taney's opinion for the Court reasoned as follows: (1) If a court were to hold the defendants' acts unjustified because the charter government had no legal existence during the period in question, it would follow that all of that government's actions—laws enacted, taxes collected, salaries paid, accounts settled, sentences passed—were of no effect; and that "the officers who carried their decisions into operation (were) answerable as trespassers, if not in some cases as criminals." [A] decision for the plaintiff would inevitably have produced some significant measure of chaos, a consequence to be avoided if it could be done without abnegation of the judicial duty to uphold the Constitution. (2) [The] courts of Rhode Island [had] held that "it rested with the political power to decide whether the charter government had been displaced or not," and that that department had acknowledged no change. (3) Since "[t]he question relates, altogether, to the constitution and laws of [the] State," the courts of the United States had to follow the state courts' decisions unless there was a federal constitutional ground for overturning them. (4) No provision of the Constitution could be or had been invoked for this purpose except Art. IV, §4, the Guaranty Clause. Having already noted the absence of standards whereby the choice between governments could be made by a court acting independently, Chief Justice Taney now found further textual and practical reasons for concluding that, if any department of the United States was empowered by the Guaranty Clause to resolve the issue, it was not the judiciary: "Under this article of the Constitution it rests with Congress to decide what government is the established one in a State. For as the United States guarantee to each State a republican government, Congress must necessarily decide what government is established in the State before it can determine whether it is republican or not. And when the senators and representatives of a State are admitted into the councils of the Union, the authority of the government under which they are appointed, as well as its republican character, is recognized by the proper constitutional authority. And its decision is binding on every other department of the government, and could not be questioned in a judicial tribunal. It is true that the contest in this case did not last long enough to bring the matter to this issue; [and] Congress was not called upon to decide the controversy. Yet the right to decide is placed there, and not in the courts." . . .

Clearly, several factors were thought by the Court in *Luther* to make the question there "political": the commitment to the other branches of the decision as to which is the lawful state government; the unambiguous action by the President, in recognizing the charter government as the lawful authority; the need for finality in the executive's decision; and the lack of criteria by which a court could determine which form of government was republican. But the only significance that *Luther* could have for our immediate purposes is in its holding that the Guaranty Clause is not a repository of judicially manageable standards which a court could utilize independently in order to identify a State's lawful government. The Court has since refused to resort to the Guaranty Clause — which alone had been invoked for the purpose — as the source of a constitutional standard for invalidating state action. [See] Pacific States Tel. & T. Co. v. Oregon, 223 U.S. 118 [1912], (claim that initiative and referendum negated republican government held nonjusticiable). . . . We come, finally, to the ultimate inquiry whether our precedents as to what constitutes a nonjusticiable "political question" bring the case before us under the umbrella of that doctrine. A natural beginning is to note whether any of the common characteristics which we have been able to identify and label descriptively are present. We find none: The question here is the consistency of state action with the Federal Constitution. We have no question decided, or to be decided, by a political branch of government coequal with this Court. Nor do we risk embarrassment of our government abroad, or grave disturbance at home if we take issue with Tennessee as to the constitutionality of her action here challenged.

Nor need the appellants, in order to succeed in this action, ask the Court to enter upon policy determinations for which judicially manageable standards are lacking. Judicial standards under the Equal Protection Clause are well developed and familiar, and it has been open to courts since the enactment of the Fourteenth Amendment to determine, if on the particular facts they must, that a discrimination reflects no policy, but simply arbitrary and capricious action. This case does, in one sense, involve the allocation of political power within a State, and the appellants might conceivably have added a claim under the Guaranty Clause. Of course, as we have seen, any reliance on that clause would be futile. But because any reliance on the Guaranty Clause could not have succeeded it does not follow that appellants may not be heard on the equal protection claim which in fact they tender. True, it must be clear that the Fourteenth Amendment claim is not so enmeshed with those political question elements which render Guaranty Clause claims nonjusticiable as actually to present a political question itself. But we have found that not to be the case here. . . .

We conclude that the complaint's allegations of a denial of equal protection present a justiciable constitutional cause of action upon which appellants are entitled to a trial and a decision. . . .

Reversed and remanded.

Justice Whittaker did not participate in the decision.

Justice Clark, concurring.

. . . I would not consider intervention by this Court into so delicate a field if there were any other relief available to the people of Tennessee. But the majority of the people of Tennessee have no "practical opportunities for exerting their political weight at the polls" to correct the existing "invidious discrimination." Tennessee has no initiative and referendum. I have searched diligently for other "practical opportunities" present under the law. I find none other than through the federal courts. The majority of the voters have been caught up in a legislative strait jacket. [Legislative] policy has riveted the present seats in the Assembly to their respective constituencies, and by the votes of their incumbents a reapportionment of any kind is prevented. The people have been rebuffed at the hands of the Assembly; they have tried the constitutional convention route, but since the call must originate in the Assembly it, too, has been fruitless. They have tried Tennessee courts with the same result, and Governors have fought the tide only to flounder. It is said that there is recourse in Congress and perhaps that may be, but from a practical standpoint this is without substance. To date Congress has never undertaken such a task in any State. We therefore must conclude that the people of Tennessee are stymied and without judicial intervention will be saddled with the present discrimination in the affairs of their state government.

Justice Frankfurter, joined by Justice Harlan, dissenting.

[From] its earliest opinions this Court has consistently recognized a class of controversies which do not lend themselves to judicial standards and judicial remedies. To classify the various instances as "political questions" is rather a form of stating this conclusion than revealing of analysis. [From some of the cases] emerge unifying considerations that are compelling.

1. The cases concerning war or foreign affairs, for example, are usually explained by the necessity of the country's speaking with one voice in such matters. While this concern alone undoubtedly accounts for many of the decisions, others do not fit the pattern. It would hardly embarrass the conduct of war were this Court to determine, in connection with private transactions between litigants, the date upon which war is to be deemed terminated. But the Court has refused to do so. [A] controlling factor in such cases is that, decision respecting these kinds of complex matters of policy being traditionally committed not to courts but to the political agencies of government for determination by criteria of political expediency, there exists no standard ascertainable by settled judicial experience or process by reference to which a political decision affecting the question at issue between the parties can be judged. . . .

2. The Court has been particularly unwilling to intervene in matters concerning the structure and organization of the political institutions of the States. . . .

3. The cases involving Negro disfranchisement are no exception to the principle of avoiding federal judicial intervention into matters of state government in the absence of an explicit and clear constitutional imperative. For here the controlling command of Supreme Law is plain and unequivocal. An end of discrimination against the Negro was the compelling motive of the Civil War Amendments. . . .

4. The Court has refused to exercise its jurisdiction to pass on "abstract questions of political power, of sovereignty, of government." [The] "political question" doctrine, in this aspect, reflects the policies underlying the requirement of "standing": that the litigant who would challenge official action must claim infringement of an interest particular and personal to himself, as distinguished from a cause of dissatisfaction with the general frame and functioning of government—a complaint that the political institutions are awry. [What] renders cases of this kind non-justiciable is not necessarily the nature of the parties to them . . . nor is it the nature of the legal question involved. . . . The crux of the matter is that courts are not fit instruments of decision where what is essentially at stake is the composition of those large contests of policy traditionally fought out in non-judicial forums, by which governments and the actions of governments are made and [unmade].

5. The influence of these converging considerations—the caution not to undertake decision where standards meet for judicial judgment are lacking, the reluctance to interfere with matters of state government in the absence of an unquestionable and effectively enforceable mandate, the unwillingness to make courts arbiters of the broad issues of political organization historically committed to other institutions and for whose adjustment the judicial process is ill-adapted—has been decisive of the settled line of cases, reaching back more than a century, which holds that Art. IV, §4, of the Constitution, guaranteeing to the States "a Republican Form of Government," is not enforceable through the courts. . . .

The present case involves all of the elements that have made the Guarantee Clause cases non-justiciable. It is, in effect, a Guarantee Clause claim masquerading under a different label. But it cannot make the case more fit for judicial action that appellants invoke the Fourteenth Amendment rather than Art. IV, §4, where, in fact, the gist of their complaint is the same—unless it can be found that the Fourteenth Amendment speaks with greater particularity to their situation. We have been admonished to avoid "the tyranny of labels." [Art. IV, §4] is not committed by express constitutional terms to Congress. It is the nature of the controversies arising under it, nothing else, which has made it judicially unenforceable. [Where] judicial competence is wanting, it cannot be created by invoking one clause of the Constitution rather than another. . . .

[Appellants'] complaint is that the basis of representation of the Tennessee Legislature hurts them. They assert that "a minority now rules in Tennessee," that the apportionment statute results in a "distortion constitutional system," that the General Assembly is no longer "a body representative of the people of the State of Tennessee," all "contrary to the basic principle of representative government. . . ." [Their] complaint is simply that the representatives are not sufficiently numerous or powerful—in short, that Tennessee has adopted a basis of representation with which they are dissatisfied. Talk of "debasement" or "dilution" is circular talk. One cannot speak of "debasement" or "dilution" of the value of a vote until there is first defined a standard of reference as to what a vote should be worth. What is actually asked of the Court in this case is to choose among competing bases of representation—ultimately, really, among competing theories of political philosophy—in order to establish an appropriate frame of government for the State of Tennessee and thereby for all the States of the Union. . . .

This is not a case in which a State [has] denied Negroes or Jews or red-headed persons a vote, or given them only a third or a sixth of a vote. [What] Tennessee illustrates is an old and still widespread method of representation—representation by local geographical division, only in part respective of population—in preference to [others]. Appellants contest this choice and . . . would make the Equal Protection Clause the charter of adjudication, asserting that the equality which it guarantees comports, if not the assurance of equal weight to every voter's vote, at least the basic conception that representation ought to be proportionate to population, a standard by reference to which the reasonableness of apportionment plans may be judged. . . . "[E]qual protection" is no more secure a foundation for judicial judgment of the permissibility of varying forms of representative government than is "Republican Form." Indeed since "equal protection of the laws" can only mean an equality of persons standing in the same relation to whatever governmental action is challenged, the determination whether treatment is equal presupposes a determination concerning the nature of the relationship. This, with respect to apportionment, means an inquiry into the theoretic base of representation in an acceptably republican state. For a court could not determine the equal-protection issue without in fact first determining the Republican-Form issue, simply because what is reasonable for equal-protection purposes will depend upon what frame of government, basically, is allowed. To divorce "equal protection" from "Republican Form" is to talk about half a question. . . .

Manifestly, the Equal Protection Clause supplies no clearer guide for judicial examination of apportionment methods than would the Guarantee Clause itself. Apportionment, by its character, is a subject of extraordinary complexity, involving — even after the fundamental theoretical issues concerning what is to be represented in a representative legislature have been fought out or compromised — considerations of geography, demography, electoral convenience, economic and social cohesions or divergencies among particular local groups, communications, the practical effects of political [institutions], ancient [traditions], respect for proven [incumbents], mathematical mechanics, [censuses], and a host of others. [These] are not factors that lend themselves to evaluations of a nature that are the staple of judicial determinations or for which judges are equipped to adjudicate by legal training or experience or native wit. [It] will add a virulent source of friction and tension in federal-state relations to embroil the federal judiciary in them.

[Concurring opinions by Justices Douglas and Clark, and a dissenting opinion by Justice Harlan, are omitted.]

NOTE

Baker v. Carr appeared to signal a diminished role for the political question doctrine. Thus the Court in Powell v. McCormack, 395 U.S. 486 (1969), declined to find a nonjusticiable political question in a challenge to the validity of the refusal by the House of Representatives to seat Representative Adam Clayton Powell, Jr., after a House committee found that he had "wrongfully diverted House funds" for his own use and had made "false reports" to the House. Powell contended that he met the age, citizenship, and residency requirements specified for House membership in Art. I, §2, cl. 2. McCormack, the Speaker of the House, replied that since Art. I, §5, cl. 1 makes "each House . . . the Judge of the . . . Qualifications of its own Members," the issue was plainly textually committed to the House for decision and thus not justiciable. Also, said McCormack's lawyers, a judicial resolution might produce a "potentially embarrassing confrontation between coordinate branches." The Court found the issue to be justiciable.

In his opinion Chief Justice Warren stated:

> In order to determine whether there has been a textual commitment to a co-ordinate department [we] must first determine what power the Constitution confers upon the House through Art. I, §5. . . . [In] order to determine the scope of any "textual commitment" under Art. I, §5, we necessarily must determine the meaning of the phrase "be the judge of the qualifications of its own members." Our [lengthy] examination of the relevant historical materials leads us to the conclusion that [the] Constitution leaves the House without authority to *exclude* any person, duly elected by his constituents, who meets all the requirements for membership expressly prescribed in [Art. I, §2, cl. 2 of] the

Constitution. [Art. I, §5] is at most a "textually demonstrable commitment" to Congress to judge only the qualifications expressly set forth in the Constitution. Therefore, the "textual commitment" formulation of the political question doctrine does not bar federal courts from adjudicating [Powell's] claims. . . .

[McCormack's] alternate contention is that the case presents a political question because judicial resolution . . . would produce a "potentially embarrassing confrontation between coordinate branches" of the Federal Government. [Our] system of government requires that federal courts on occasion interpret the Constitution in a manner at variance with the construction given the document by another branch. The alleged conflict that such an adjudication may cause cannot justify the courts' avoiding their constitutional responsibility. [The] case is justiciable.

Perhaps due to *Baker* and *Powell*, Professor Louis Henkin declared the political question chimerical:

[T]here may be no doctrine requiring abstention from judicial review of "political questions." The [supposed political question cases] called only for the ordinary respect by the courts for the political domain. Having reviewed, the Court refused to invalidate the challenged actions because they were within the constitutional authority of President or Congress rather than because they were nonjusticiable political questions.

See Henkin, Is There a "Political Question" Doctrine?, 85 Yale L.J. 597, 601 (1976). In Henkin's view, when the Court declares an issue to be a nonjusticiable political question it is really deciding, on the merits, that the challenged action is valid. Assuming Henkin is correct, why would the Court obfuscate matters? Perhaps it is a way of validating presidential or congressional actions without creating precedent on the merits, thus leaving the merits issue open. If so, is this principled adjudication?

But if the Court is truly committed to a political question doctrine, there must be some cases in which the challenged action is unconstitutional but nonjusticiable. The Court says that such cases theoretically exist: "[By] invoking the political question doctrine, a court acknowledges the possibility that a constitutional provision may not be judicially enforceable. Such a decision is of course very different from determining that specific congressional action does not violate the Constitution." United States Department of Commerce v. Montana, 503 U.S. 442 (1992), in which the Court found a challenge to the congressional method of apportioning House seats to be justiciable and upheld the method on the merits. Consider the following case.

≣≣≣ *Nixon v. United States*
≣≣≣ *506 U.S. 224 (1993)*

Chief Justice Rehnquist, for the Court.

Petitioner Walter L. Nixon, Jr., asks this court to decide whether Senate Rule XI, which allows a committee of Senators to hear evidence against an individual who has been impeached and to report that evidence to the full Senate, violates the Impeachment Trial Clause, Art. I, §3, cl. 6. That Clause provides that the "Senate shall have the sole Power to try all Impeachments." But before we reach the merits of such a claim, we must decide whether it is "justiciable," that is, whether it is a claim that may be resolved by the courts. We conclude that it is not.

Nixon, a former Chief Judge of the United States District Court for the Southern District of Mississippi, was convicted by a jury of two counts of making false statements before a federal grand jury and sentenced to prison. . . . Because Nixon refused to resign from his [judicial] office he continued to collect his judicial salary while serving out his prison sentence. On May 10, 1989, the House of Representatives adopted three articles of impeachment for high crimes and misdemeanors. After the House presented the articles to the Senate, the Senate voted to invoke its own Impeachment Rule XI, under which the presiding officer appoints a committee of Senators to "receive evidence and take testimony." The Senate committee held four days of hearings. [The] committee presented the full Senate with a complete transcript of the proceeding and a report stating the uncontested facts and summarizing the evidence on the contested facts. Nixon and the House impeachment managers submitted extensive final briefs to the full Senate and delivered arguments from the Senate floor during the three hours set aside for oral argument in front of that body. Nixon himself gave a personal appeal, and several Senators posed questions directly to both parties. The Senate voted by more than the constitutionally required two-thirds majority to convict Nixon. . . . The presiding officer then entered judgment removing Nixon from his [office]. Nixon thereafter commenced the present suit, arguing that Senate Rule XI violates the constitutional grant of authority to the Senate to "try" all impeachments because it prohibits the whole Senate from taking part in the evidentiary hearings. Nixon sought a declaratory judgment that his impeachment conviction was void and that his judicial salary and privileges should be reinstated. The District Court held that his claim was nonjusticiable, and the Court of Appeals [agreed].

A controversy is nonjusticiable—i.e., involves a political question—where there is "a textually demonstrable constitutional commitment of the issue to a coordinate political department; or a lack of judicially discoverable and manageable standards for resolving [it]." Baker v. Carr. But the courts must, in the first instance, interpret the text in question and determine whether and to what extent the issue is textually committed. Powell v. McCormack. As the discussion that follows makes clear, the concept of a textual commitment to a coordinate political department is not completely separate from the concept of a lack of judicially discoverable and manageable standards for resolving it; the lack of judicially manageable standards may strengthen the conclusion that there is a textually demonstrable commitment to a coordinate branch.

In this case, we must examine Art. I, §3, cl. 6, to determine the scope of authority conferred upon the Senate by the Framers regarding impeachment. It provides: "The Senate shall have the sole Power to try all Impeachments. . . ."

[Petitioner] argues that the word "try" . . . imposes by implication [a] requirement on the Senate in that the proceedings must be in the nature of a judicial trial. From there petitioner goes on to argue that this limitation precludes the Senate from delegating to a select committee the task of hearing the testimony of witnesses[:] "'[T]ry' means more than simply 'vote on' or 'review' or 'judge.' In 1787 and today, trying a case means hearing the evidence, not scanning a cold record." Petitioner concludes from this that courts may review whether or not the Senate "tried" him before convicting him.

There are several difficulties with this position which lead us ultimately to reject it. The word "try," both in 1787 and later, has considerably broader meanings than those to which petitioner would limit it. [Based] on the variety of [historical] definitions, however, we cannot say that the Framers used the word "try" as an implied limitation on the method by which the Senate might proceed in trying impeachments. [The] conclusion that [the] word "try" in the first sentence of the Impeachment Trial Clause lacks sufficient precision to afford any judicially manageable standard of review of the Senate's actions is fortified by the existence of the three very specific requirements that the Constitution does impose on the Senate when trying impeachments: the members must be under oath, a two-thirds vote is required to convict, and the Chief Justice presides when the President is tried. These limitations are quite precise, and their nature suggests that the Framers did not intend to impose additional limitations on the form of the Senate proceedings by the use of the word "try" in the first sentence.

[The first sentence in Art. I, §3, cl. 6] provides that "[t]he Senate shall have the sole Power to try all Impeachments." We think that the word "sole" is of considerable significance. . . . The common sense meaning of the word "sole" is that the Senate alone shall have authority to determine whether an individual should be acquitted or convicted. The dictionary definition bears this out. . . .

The history and contemporary understanding of the impeachment provisions support our reading of the constitutional language. The parties do not offer evidence of a single word in the history of the Constitutional Convention or in contemporary commentary that even alludes to the possibility of judicial review in the context of the impeachment powers. This silence is quite meaningful in light of the several explicit references to the availability of judicial review as a check on the Legislature's power with respect to bills of attainder, ex post facto laws, and statutes. See The Federalist No. 78.

The Framers labored over the question of where the impeachment power should lie. Significantly, in at least two considered scenarios [the Virginia Plan and the New Jersey Plan] the power was placed with the Federal Judiciary. Indeed, Madison and the Committee of Detail proposed that the Supreme Court should have the power to determine impeachments. Despite these proposals, the Convention ultimately decided that the Senate would have "the sole Power to Try all Impeachments." According to Alexander Hamilton, the Senate was the "most fit depositary of this important trust" because its members are representatives of the people. See The Federalist No. 65. . . .

There are two additional reasons why the Judiciary, and the Supreme Court in particular, were not chosen to have any role in impeachments. First, the Framers recognized that most likely there would be two sets of proceedings for individuals who commit impeachable offenses—the impeachment trial and a separate criminal trial. In fact, the Constitution explicitly provides for two separate proceedings. See Art. I, §3, cl. 7. The Framers deliberately separated the two forums to avoid raising the specter of bias and to ensure independent judgments. [Judicial] review of the Senate's "trial" would introduce the same risk of bias as would participation in the trial itself. Second, judicial review would be inconsistent with the Framers' insistence that our system be one of checks and balances. In our constitutional system, impeachment was designed to be the only check on the Judicial Branch by the Legislature. [Judicial] involvement in impeachment proceedings, even if only for purposes of judicial review, [would] eviscerate the "important constitutional check" placed on the Judiciary by the Framers. Nixon's argument would place final reviewing authority with respect to impeachments in the hands of the same body that the impeachment process is meant to regulate. [Nevertheless], Nixon argues that judicial review is necessary in order to place a check on the Legislature. Nixon fears that if the Senate is given unreviewable authority to interpret the Impeachment Trial Clause, there is a grave risk that the Senate will usurp judicial power. The Framers anticipated this objection and created two constitutional safeguards to keep the Senate in check. The first safeguard is that the whole of the impeachment power is divided between the two legislative bodies, with the House given the right to accuse and the Senate given the right to judge. [The] second safeguard is the two-thirds supermajority vote requirement. . . .

In addition to the textual commitment argument, we are persuaded that the lack of finality and the difficulty of fashioning relief counsel against justiciability. [Judicial] review [of] the procedures used by the Senate in trying impeachments would "expose the political life of the country to months, or perhaps years, of chaos." This lack of finality would manifest itself most dramatically if the President were impeached. The legitimacy of any successor, and hence his effectiveness, would be impaired severely, not merely while the judicial process was running its course, but during any retrial that a differently constituted Senate might conduct if its first judgment of conviction were invalidated. Equally uncertain is the question of what relief a court may give other than simply setting aside the judgment of conviction. Could it order the reinstatement of a convicted federal judge, or order Congress to create an additional judgeship if the seat had been filled in the interim?

Petitioner finally contends that a holding of nonjusticiability cannot be reconciled with our opinion in Powell v. McCormack. [Our] conclusion in *Powell* was based on the fixed meaning of "[q]ualifications" set forth in Art. I, §2. [The] decision as to whether a member satisfied these qualifications was placed with the House, but the decision as to what these qualifications consisted of was not. . . . We agree with Nixon that courts possess power to review either legislative or executive action that transgresses identifiable textual limits. [But] we conclude [that] the word "try" in the Impeachment Clause does not provide an identifiable textual limit on the authority which is committed to the Senate. . . .

Affirmed.

JUSTICE STEVENS, concurring.

For me, the debate about the strength of the inferences to be drawn from the use of the words "sole" and "try" is far less significant than the central fact that the Framers decided to assign the impeachment power to the Legislative Branch. . . .

JUSTICE WHITE, joined by JUSTICE BLACKMUN, concurring in the judgment.

. . . [I would] reach the merits of the claim. I concur in the judgment because the Senate fulfilled its constitutional obligation to "try" petitioner.

I. [As] a practical matter, it will likely make little difference whether the Court's or my view controls this case. This is so because the Senate has very wide discretion in specifying impeachment trial procedures and because it is extremely unlikely that the Senate would abuse its discretion and insist on a procedure that could not be deemed a trial by reasonable judges. Even taking a wholly practical approach, I would prefer not to announce an unreviewable discretion in the Senate to ignore completely the constitutional direction to "try" impeachment cases. [I] would not issue an invitation to the Senate to find an excuse, in the name of other pressing business, to be dismissive of its critical role in the impeachment process. . . .

II. [The] issue in the political question doctrine is not whether the Constitutional text commits exclusive responsibility for a particular governmental function to one of the political branches. . . . Rather, the issue is whether the Constitution has given one of the political branches final responsibility for interpreting the scope and nature of such a power. . . .

The majority finds a clear textual commitment in the Constitution's use of the word "sole" in the phrase "the Senate shall have the sole Power to try all impeachments." [The] significance of the Constitution's use of the term "sole" lies not in the infrequency with which the term appears, but in the fact that it appears exactly twice, in parallel provisions concerning impeachment. That the word "sole" is found only in the House and Senate Impeachment Clauses demonstrates that its purpose is to emphasize the distinct role of each in the impeachment process. [While] the majority is thus right to interpret the term "sole" to indicate that the Senate ought to " 'functio[n] independently and without assistance or interference,' " it wrongly identifies the judiciary, rather than the House, as the source of potential interference with which the Framers were concerned when they employed the term "sole." . . .

The majority also claims support in the history and early interpretations of the Impeachment [Clauses]. The majority's review of the historical record thus explains why the power to try impeachments properly resides with the Senate. It does not explain, however, the sweeping statement that the judiciary was "not chosen to have any role in impeachments." Not a single word in the historical materials cited by the majority addresses judicial review of the Impeachment Trial Clause. . . .

What the relevant history mainly reveals is deep ambivalence among many of the Framers over the very institution of impeachment, which, by its nature, is not easily reconciled with our system of checks and balances. As they clearly recognized, the branch of the Federal Government which is possessed of the authority to try impeachments, by having final say over the membership of each branch, holds a potentially unanswerable power over the others. [The] historical evidence reveals above all else that the Framers were deeply concerned about placing in any branch the "awful discretion, which a court of impeachments must necessarily have." The Federalist No. 65. Viewed against this history, the discord between the majority's position and the basic principles of checks and balances underlying the Constitution's separation of powers is clear. In essence, the majority suggests that the Framers conferred upon Congress a potential tool of legislative dominance yet at the same time rendered Congress'[s] exercise of that power one of the very few areas of legislative authority immune from any judicial review. While the majority rejects petitioner's justiciability argument as espousing a view "inconsistent with the Framers' insistence that our system be one of checks and balances," it is the Court's finding of nonjusticiability that truly upsets the Framers' careful design. In a truly balanced system, impeachments tried by the Senate would serve as a means of controlling the largely unaccountable judiciary, even as judicial review would ensure that the Senate adhered to a minimal set of procedural standards in conducting impeachment trials.

The majority also contends that the term "try" does not present a judicially manageable standard. [The] majority finds [that] the term "try" does not provide an "identifiable textual limit on the authority which is committed to the Senate." This argument comes in two variants. The first, which asserts that one simply cannot ascertain the sense of "try" which the Framers employed and hence cannot undertake judicial review, is clearly untenable. To begin with, one would intuitively expect that, in defining the power of a political body to conduct an inquiry into official wrongdoing, the Framers used "try" in its legal sense. That intuition is borne out by reflection on the alternatives. [The power to "try" impeachments] cannot seriously be read to mean that the Senate shall "attempt" or "experiment with" impeachments. It is equally implausible to say that the Senate is charged with "investigating" impeachments given that this description would substantially overlap with the House of Representatives' "sole" power to draw up articles of [impeachment]. The other variant of the majority position focuses not on which sense of "try" is employed in the Impeachment Trial Clause, but on whether the legal sense of that term creates a judicially manageable standard. The majority concludes that the term provides no "identifiable textual limit." Yet, [the] term "try" is hardly so elusive as the majority would have it. Were the Senate, for example, to adopt the practice of automatically entering a judgment of conviction whenever articles of impeachment were delivered from the House, it is quite clear that the Senate will have failed to "try" impeachments. Indeed in this respect, "try" presents no greater, and perhaps fewer, interpretive difficulties than some other constitutional standards that have been found amenable to familiar techniques of judicial construction, including, for example, "Commerce . . . among the several States," and "due process of law." . . .

III. The majority's conclusion that "try" is incapable of meaningful judicial construction is not without irony. One might think that if any class of concepts would fall within the definitional abilities of the judiciary, it would be that class having to do with procedural justice. . . .

JUSTICE SOUTER, concurring in the judgment.

I agree with the Court that this case presents a nonjusticiable political question. [A]pplication of the doctrine ultimately turns, as Learned Hand put it, on "how importunately the occasion demands an answer." L. Hand, The Bill of Rights 15 (1958). This occasion does not demand an answer. [It] seems fair to conclude that the Clause contemplates that the Senate may determine, within broad boundaries, such subsidiary issues as the procedures for receipt and consideration of evidence necessary to satisfy its duty to "try" impeachments. . . . One can, nevertheless, envision different and unusual circumstances that might justify a more searching review of impeachment proceedings. If the Senate were to act in a manner seriously threatening the integrity of its results, convicting, say, upon a coin-toss, or upon a summary determination that an officer of the United States was simply "a bad guy," judicial interference might well be appropriate. In such circumstances, the Senate's action might be so far beyond the scope of its constitutional authority, and the consequent impact on the Republic so great, as to merit a judicial response despite the prudential concerns that would ordinarily counsel silence. . . .

NOTES

1. The Strands of the Doctrine

a. "Textual commitment."   As the foregoing cases suggest, there are not many issues that are clearly textually committed for resolution by President or Congress. The Court decides whether the Constitution makes that "textual commitment" with respect to any given issue. A broad reading of "textual commitment" expands the scope of political questions; a narrow reading constricts it. *Powell* supplied a narrow reading to the Constitution's grant of power to each "House [to] judge the qualifications of its members." Suppose that the House decided not to seat the middle-aged Powell after concluding that he did not meet the Constitution's requirement that representatives be at least 25 years of age. Would Powell's challenge to this blatant dishonesty be justiciable? Suppose that two-thirds of the House had voted to expel Powell after the courts ordered him seated. Under Article I, section 5, clause 2, "[e]ach House may, . . . with the Concurrence of two thirds, expel a Member." Would a challenge to Powell's expulsion have been justiciable?

b. "Lack of judicially discoverable and manageable standards." This strand is often woven so tightly into the "textual commitment" strand that it is difficult to separate the two.

In Coleman v. Miller, a plurality of the Court concluded that two questions pertaining to the validity of a state's ratification of a proposed constitutional amendment were nonjusticiable political questions. The Kansas legislature had rejected a proposed constitutional amendment banning child labor, then had reversed itself in a vote in which the state's lieutenant governor, as the presiding officer of the state senate, had cast the tie-breaking vote in favor of ratification. Kansas legislators sued to establish the invalidity of the ratification, contending that the legislature could not undo its previous rejection of the proposed amendment. Alternatively, the plaintiffs contended that, because the lieutenant governor was not a member of the legislature, the proposed amendment had not been ratified by the legislature, as Article V of the Constitution requires. Chief Justice Hughes wrote:

> [T]he question of efficacy of ratifications by state legislatures, in the light of previous rejection or attempted withdrawal, should be regarded as a political [question], with the ultimate authority in the Congress. [We] find no basis in either Constitution or statute [for] judicial action [because] Article V, speaking solely of ratification, contains no provision as to [rejection].

If this was "textual commitment," it was commitment by omission.

Coleman may have been mostly about a lack of judicially cognizable standards for decision. The question of whether a proposed amendment becomes null if not ratified within a reasonable time was also raised. On this point, Hughes wondered "[w]here are to be found the criteria for such a judicial determination?" The answers, declared Hughes, were not to be found in the Constitution, but only in "political, social, and economic [factors outside] the appropriate range of evidence receivable in a court." This objection could as easily be made with respect to the question of ratification after rejection. As there was no answer fairly derivable from constitutional sources, the issue was not susceptible to judicial resolution. The *Coleman* Court by implication rejected the idea of constitutional "interpretation" built entirely upon sources extrinsic to constitutional text, history, structure, and precedent. For the view that issues concerning the procedure of constitutional amendment are justiciable, see Dellinger, The Legitimacy of Constitutional Change: Rethinking the Amendment Process, 97 Harv. L. Rev. 386 (1983).

In Davis v. Bandemer, 478 U.S. 109 (1986), the Court concluded that there were judicially discoverable and manageable standards by which to evaluate whether a political gerrymander of a state's congressional districts violated the equal protection clause. A plurality of the Court divined in the equal protection clause the standard of whether "the electoral system is arranged in a manner that will consistently degrade a voter's or a group of voters' influence on the political process as a whole." Justice O'Connor, dissenting, charged that this standard will over time either prove unmanageable and arbitrary or else evolve towards some loose form of [proportionality]. Federal courts will have no alternative but to attempt to recreate the complex process of legislative apportionment in the context of adversary litigation in order to reconcile the competing claims of political, religious, ethnic, racial, occupational, and socioeconomic groups [with] no clear stopping point to prevent the gradual evolution of a requirement of roughly proportional representation for every cohesive political group. [The] Equal Protection Clause does not supply judicially manageable standards for resolving purely political gerrymandering claims, and no group right to an equal share of political power was ever intended by the Framers of the Fourteenth Amendment.

Consider the possibility that the presence or absence of "judicially discoverable and manageable standards" for decision is inextricably linked to the merits. Assume that Justice O'Connor is correct that the equal protection clause does not mandate proportional representation for every conceivable affinity group. In that case, would judges lack manageable standards for decision, or would they simply decide that equal protection is not violated by political gerrymanders?

In Vieth v. Jubelirer, 541 U.S. 267 (2004), a plurality of four justices would have overturned *Bandemer* and declared the question of the validity of political gerrymanders to be a nonjusticiable political question. Justice Scalia, joined by Chief Justice Rehnquist and Justices O'Connor and Thomas, concluded that there are "no judicially discernible and manageable standards for adjudicating political gerrymandering claims."

First, the plurality concluded that *Bandemer*'s standard was neither discernible nor manageable. Although "intentional discrimination against an identifiable political group" is easy enough to prove, the plurality thought that judicial assessment of proof of "an actual discriminatory effect on that group" was well-nigh impossible. The plurality noted that "the legacy of [this] test is one long record of puzzlement and consternation." Second, the plurality rejected a proposed test focusing on "predominant intent" and specific effect. The problem with the "predominant intent" prong of the test was the near impossibility of proving that "partisan advantage was the predominant motivation" for the district boundaries. The "effects prong" of the proposed test would have required proof of (1) systematic "packing"[5] and "cracking"[6] of "the rival party's voters"; and (2) a totality of circumstances that establishes that the gerrymander "'thwart[s] the plaintiffs' ability to translate a majority of votes into a majority of seats.'" The plurality thought this prong was neither discernible nor manageable. First, because "[p]olitical affiliation is not an immutable characteristic, [it is] impossible to assess the effects of partisan

---

5. "Packing" is the practice of drawing district boundaries to include supermajorities of a given party's voters.

6. "Cracking" is the practice of drawing district boundaries to split a party's voters among a number of districts, in order to leave that party's voters in the minority in all the districts to which they have been distributed.

gerrymandering, to fashion a standard for evaluating a violation, and finally to craft a remedy."[7] Second, the proposed effects standard was not "judicially discernible in the sense of being relevant to some constitutional violation" because it "rests upon the principle that [political] groups have a right to proportional representation, [and] the Constitution contains no such principle." Finally, the proposed standard was "not judicially manageable" because it is virtually impossible to "identify a majority party" with certainty,[8] and even more difficult to ensure that the "majority" party wins a majority of seats, if only because voters remain maddeningly independent of party affiliation when it comes time to cast ballots.

c. The prudential reasons. The last four *Baker* factors—impossibility of deciding without an initial and judicially inappropriate policy decision, expression of a lack of respect due the coordinate branches, an unusual need to adhere to a political fait accompli, or the risk of national embarrassment resulting from multiple inconsistent resolutions—are all rooted in a policy of avoiding high costs. Institutional instability, enforcement problems, and risks to national security are just some of the underlying factors. These types of political questions do not often come purely in their prudential form; they are usually hybridized with the other strands.

In Goldwater v. Carter, 444 U.S. 996 (1979), a plurality of four justices found nonjusticiable the question of whether President Carter was constitutionally entitled unilaterally to abrogate a defense treaty with Taiwan. Citing *Coleman* with approval, Justice Rehnquist stated:

> [W]hile the Constitution is express as to the manner in which the Senate shall participate in the ratification of a Treaty, it is silent as to that body's participation in the abrogation of a Treaty. [In] light of the absence of any constitutional provision governing the termination of a Treaty, and the fact that different termination procedures may be appropriate for different treaties, the [issue is not justiciable]. I think that the justifications for concluding the question here is political in nature are even more compelling than in *Coleman* because it involves foreign relations.

Justice Powell concurred in the judgment on the grounds that the issue was "not ripe for judicial review," but thought it was justiciable because the

---

7. The plurality cited, as a "delicious illustration" of its conclusion, a case in which a trial judge had concluded that North Carolina's system of electing judges "had resulted in Republican candidates experiencing a consistent and pervasive lack of success and exclusion from the electoral process as a whole and that these effects were likely to continue unabated into the future." Five days later, every Republican candidate for superior court judge in North Carolina was victorious.

8. In Pennsylvania, in 2000, Democratic candidates received more votes for President and auditor general and Republicans garnered more votes for U.S. senator, attorney general, and treasurer. Or consider Massachusetts, in which a succession of Republican governors have presided alongside a solidly Democratic legislature and monolithically Democratic congressional delegation.

"case involves neither review of the President's activities as Commander-in-Chief nor impermissible interference in the field of foreign affairs."

Justice Brennan dissented:

[T]he political question doctrine restrains courts from reviewing an exercise of foreign policy judgment by the coordinate political branch to which authority to make that judgment has been "constitutional[ly] commit[ted]." [T]he doctrine does not pertain when a court is faced with the *antecedent* question whether a particular branch has been constitutionally designated as the repository of political decisionmaking power. The issue of decisionmaking authority must be resolved as a matter of constitutional law, not political discretion; accordingly it falls within the competence of the courts.

On the merits, Justice Brennan would have upheld the President's abrogation of the defense treaty because it was "a necessary incident to Executive recognition of the Peking government, [and] the Constitution commits to the President alone the power to recognize, and withdraw recognition from, foreign regimes."

As in *Coleman*, any "textual commitment" of the issue to a political branch was by omission. Consider, however, the institutional costs of judicial review. What effect on U.S. foreign policy might have been produced by judicial review, coupled with invalidation of the President's abrogation? Was Goldwater v. Carter really a case involving an unusual need to adhere to the decision already made by the President, or was it a case posing a grave risk of national embarrassment if the Court had ruled against the President on the merits? If you think Justice Brennan was correct on the justiciability issue, would your view change if you were certain that the President's action would be ruled void on the merits? Is it "unprincipled" or "prudential" to consider the impact of possible rulings on the merits when deciding the threshold issue of justiciability?

2. The Art of Application of the Political Question Doctrine. The political question doctrine may be summarized in six neat factors, as Justice Brennan did in Baker v. Carr, but the application of those factors to any particular case is a distinct art form. Consider the following:

In December 1998, the House impeached President Clinton for perjury and obstruction of justice. Although President Clinton was ultimately acquitted, suppose the Senate had convicted, and President Clinton then sought judicial review of the question of whether the charge constituted a high crime or misdemeanor. Is determination of the meaning of "high Crimes and Misdemeanors" textually committed to Congress? If so, what makes the impeachment process different from qualification to sit in Congress, considered in the *Powell* case? Is it the fact that the Constitution specifies the "qualifications" of members of Congress, and it does not specify what constitutes a high crime or misdemeanor?

There is a large body of historical evidence bearing on what the Framers might have had in mind by using this phrase. Should this negate any contention that there are no judicially discoverable standards for decision? Would the prudential considerations nevertheless be sufficient to conclude that this issue is a political question? So long as the hypothesized litigation lasted, there would be doubts about the validity of all executive action, doubts that might disable the presidency.

The Constitution gives Congress the power to declare war. The Vietnam War was fought without any declaration of war, although Congress did pass the Gulf of Tonkin Resolution and repeatedly appropriated billions of dollars to finance the war. Soldiers ordered to serve in Vietnam sometimes brought suit to contest the validity of their orders, arguing that the war was unconstitutional because of the failure of Congress to declare war. The Court routinely denied certiorari, so we do not know if the issue was justiciable. In Mora v. McNamara, 389 U.S. 934 (1967), two justices dissented from denial of certiorari, noting the "large and deeply troubling questions" presented, including justiciability, that "the Court should squarely face." Assess the justiciability of the soldiers' claims.

ENFORCING THE CONSTITUTIONAL ALLOCATION OF GOVERNMENT POWER

Much of the Constitution—particularly the document that emerged from Independence Hall in September 1787—is a charter of government. It defines the powers of government, allocates those powers between the state governments and the federal government, and distributes the powers of the federal government among its three branches. The Constitution creates a federal system of government—a national government with power to act upon the people of the entire nation, and state governments with power to act only upon the people of each state. Federalism is the name given to issues concerning the proper allocation of power between these two forms of government.

One of the most innovative features of the Constitution is the idea that the national government has *only those powers given to it in the Constitution.* By contrast, state governments possess inherent power to act for the perceived good of the state's citizenry so long as those actions comply with (1) the state constitution; (2) valid federal statutory law; and (3) the federal Constitution. The result of this arrangement is that questions arise about the outer limits of federal power. Congress may legislate only within the limits of its constitutionally specified sources of authority. The President may take only actions that are authorized by the Constitution or valid federal legislation. The federal courts may exercise only the judicial power granted by the Constitution and valid enabling legislation.

The allocation of governmental powers between the nation and the states can take several forms. First, both the national and state governments can be prohibited from acting. No government may establish a state religion because the Constitution, as interpreted by the Court, forbids that practice. Second, the national government may be given *exclusive* power over a subject. The Constitution provides that only the federal government may enter into treaties with foreign nations or coin money. Third, the state governments may be given *exclusive* power over a subject, but it may be difficult to identify any subjects over which the Constitution has given the states exclusive authority. Finally, the national and state governments may enjoy *concurrent* power over

127

a subject, as is the case with some aspects of interstate commerce. When powers are concurrent, the supremacy clause (Art. VI, ¶2) ensures that federal law prevails over any conflicting state law. This area is ripe for controversy: When does conflict exist? If Congress has not acted, are there some limits on state action implicit in the Constitution? Chapter 4 explores these issues in detail.

There are several major bones of contention about federalism: Who should decide whether a given federal or state initiative is a constitutionally appropriate exercise of power? What standards should govern the answer to that question? What is the purpose (or what is the value) of federalism? Your answer to the latter question may influence your view toward the former questions.

A.   WHO SHOULD DECIDE FEDERALISM ISSUES?

The Constitution does not specify which organ of government is to determine the permissible limits of federal authority. There are two competing points of view. One holds that, like other issues of constitutional law, this should be resolved by the courts and, ultimately, the Supreme Court. The other view is that the issue ought to be left to Congress, the President and, ultimately, the voters. Neither view is monolithic; advocates of judicial review of federalism issues may concede that some federalism issues are nonjusticiable, and advocates of a political control of federalism may concede that some federalism issues are subject to judicial review.

Because it is firmly established, it may appear that judicial review is the most obvious solution. The Constitution, which is the fundamental law, specifies the limits of federal authority, and "it is emphatically the province and duty of the judicial department to say what the law is." Marbury v. Madison. For most of our history the Court has indeed been the final arbiter of the limits of federal power. Federalism was judicially enforceable. But like the Cheshire Cat, whose grin lingered long after the rest of him had disappeared, the role of judicial review in federalism issues has atrophied.

The competing view of how the limits of federal power should be determined perceives federalism as politically enforceable. Several reasons are given in support of this perspective. Although the Constitution grants only limited powers to the federal government, these grants are generally phrased quite broadly. Long ago, this led the Anti-Federalists to argue against ratification of the Constitution on the ground that the federal government had been vested with virtually unlimited power. Anti-Federalists argued that the national government's powers were granted "in general and indefinite terms" that would require interpretation by the Supreme Court; thus the justices could "mould the government into almost any shape they please." Robert Yates, writing as *Brutus,* N.Y. Journal, Jan. 31 and Feb. 7, 1788. By contrast, James Madison, writing in Federalist No. 46, argued that the "ultimate authority" on federalism issues resides in the people alone. [If the] people should in [the] future become more partial to the federal than to the State governments, the change can only result from such manifest and irresistible proofs of a better administration as will overcome all their antecedent propensities. And in that case, the people ought not surely to be precluded from giving most of their confidence where they may discover it to be due.

More modern arguments have centered on the idea that the states have such a significant role in the structure of the federal government—both in the composition of Congress and in the selection of the President—that "the national political process in the United States [is] intrinsically well adapted to retarding or restraining new intrusions by the center on the domain of the states." Wechsler, The Political Safeguards of Federalism, 54 Colum. L. Rev. 543 (1954). Is Wechsler's claim still correct as of the second decade of the twenty-first century?

Another modern justification for diminished judicial review is that federalism issues are arguments about practicality rather than principle and are thus suited for resolution by the political process. This argument also contends that judicial review should be used only "in cases of individual constitutional liberties." Jesse Choper, Judicial Review and the National Political Process (1980). Is it so clear that federalism issues have no impact on individual constitutional liberties?

Yet another contemporary argument is the notion that judicial review is most effectively employed to eliminate distortions of the democratic process. In this view, the outcomes of a fair and open process should not be judicially invalidated, at least with respect to the issue of allocation of government power between state and federal governments. John Ely, Democracy and Distrust (1980).

These contending points of view underlie much of the material that follows, although the justices often do not directly say so.

B.   WHAT IS THE PURPOSE OR VALUE OF FEDERALISM?

Some of the values implicit in considering the appropriate allocation of power between states and the central government argue for decentralized government; others point toward greater power for the federal government. Which values are controlling? Which ones should be?

1.   The Liberty of Individual Choice

Policy choices made at the national level apply uniformly throughout the nation. But tastes may vary markedly from region to region. Liberty of individual choice may be frustrated by a national rule. To illustrate, assume the nation has two states, Urbania and Rustica, of equal population. Urbania's residents are concentrated in dense cities but the state encompasses much rural area. Rustica's residents are widely dispersed in a vast rural tract. In Urbania, 90 percent favor a ban on hunting; in Rustica, only 20 percent favor the ban. If the decision is made at the national level by simple aggregation of preferences, a ban will be enacted, pleasing 55 percent of the people of the country. If the decision is made at the state level, Urbania will ban hunting and Rustica will not, thus pleasing 85 percent of the people. See McConnell, Federalism: Evaluating the Founders' Design, 54 U. Chi. L. Rev. 1484 (1987).

This illustration is subject to two important objections related to the issue of who should decide federalism issues: (1) Is it likely that Rustica's congressional delegation (especially its senators) would vote for a ban? (2) Is hunting a constitutionally fundamental right? Of course not, but substitute "religious worship" for "hunting," and you can readily understand that local choice must necessarily be subordinated to the national liberties guaranteed by the Constitution.

Nonetheless, within these limits, it is quite likely that local decisions will in fact please more people than national decisions. National minorities may be local majorities. Local minorities may migrate to more congenial jurisdictions. Will avid hunters in Urbania have an incentive to move to Rustica?

In any case, local decision-making is more apt to produce greater participation in government. If a larger number of decisions are made at local and regional levels, there will inevitably be more public participation in those decisions than if all of those decisions were made by Congress.

2. Experimental Laboratories

Justice Louis Brandeis once wrote:

> It is one of the happy incidents of the federal system that a single courageous State may, if its citizens choose, serve as a laboratory; and try novel social and economic experiments without risk to the rest of the country. This Court has the power to prevent an experiment. [In] the exercise of this high power, we must ever be on our guard, lest we erect our prejudices into legal principles.

New State Ice Co. v. Liebman, 285 U.S. 262 (1932) (Brandeis, J., dissenting).

3. Thwarting Tyranny

Preserving substantial government authority in the states may frustrate the ambitions of a well-organized minority interest bent on authoritarian dominance of the nation through control of the federal government.

[T]he most influential protection that the states offer against tyranny is the protection against the special interest of the government itself. [If] the federal government [is] ever captured by an authoritarian movement [the] resulting oppression would almost certainly be much more severe and durable than that of which any state would be capable. [P]recisely because the states are governmental bodies that break the national authorities' monopoly on coercion [they] constitute the most fundamental bastion against a successful conversion of the federal government into a vehicle of the worst kind of oppression.

Rapaczynski, From Sovereignty to Process: The Jurisprudence of Federalism After *Garcia,* 1985 Sup. Ct. Rev. 341.

4.   Controlling Negative Externalities

Even if it is generally preferable to defer to local decisions, there are some arguments in favor of centralized decision-making. Some decisions by states may seek to capture benefits locally by imposing their costs externally. Consider a state law that taxes property owned by nonresidents of the state at a rate ten times that imposed on property owned by residents. Some paramount authority would be necessary to prevent this. That authority is the federal government. The same might be said of state actions that pollute an ecosystem extending beyond state boundaries.

This view of federalism raises some difficult issues. Which state initiatives impose negative externalities? An easy case is a state law imposing a toll only on nonresidents using the state's highways. The state is imposing costs that are external to its polity, and those outsiders have no ability to influence the imposition of the cost. But what of a California state law banning smoking? Suppose that the effect of this ban is to diminish tobacco production in North Carolina and thus depress economic activity in North Carolina. Does this involve a negative externality that ought to be controlled by the central government? If so, why?

5.   Fidelity to the Constitution's Design

One reason to insist upon some measure of state legislative autonomy is that the Constitution presupposes that the federal government's powers are defined and finite and that the residuum of government power is vested in the states. The rejoinder to this argument is usually to admit this and then argue that it should be up to the political process to determine the actual boundaries between the federal government's finite powers and the remainder left for the states. Thus this question will often be resolved into a debate as to whether the Founders' design specified judicial or political resolution of issues concerning allocation of government power between the states and the federal government. Whatever the outcome of that debate, at least its participants would agree that the Founders' design was for a central government of specified, limited powers.

6.   The Practical Value of Uniformity

In an economy that is enormous, globally important, and tremendously dependent upon interrelated activities throughout the country, to say nothing of the world, there is some practical value to establishing uniform rules of commercial conduct. Indeed, one major pressure group urging federal action to establish such uniform rules has been nationwide business interests. From a business perspective, if regulations must exist, it is more efficient for them to be uniform throughout the country rather than vary from state to state. Thus, for example, the auto industry prefers federal safety and pollution standards to state-by-state regulations. Note that this argument does not answer the question of the scope of federal regulatory power; it merely suggests a good reason for exercising federal power to the extent it is authorized by the Constitution. Nor does this argument have anything to say about the question of which entity—Court or Congress—should have the primary role in charting the limits of federal power.

C.   FEDERALISM AND FUNDAMENTAL CONSTITUTIONAL RIGHTS

Any discussion of the merits of federalism or the process by which it is to be enforced must be tempered by the preemptive effect of fundamental constitutional rights. The individual liberties guaranteed by the Constitution are, in effect, "trump cards" that, when asserted, cancel the validity of otherwise lawful government action. Originally, these liberties, embodied mostly in the Bill of Rights, were effective only against action by the federal government, but the Civil War and Reconstruction amendments, particularly the Fourteenth Amendment, changed that situation dramatically. Today, primarily via the Fourteenth Amendment's equal protection and due process clauses, virtually all constitutional liberties may be asserted to block either state or federal government action.

The effect on federalism is that constitutional liberties negate the preferences of local (or, for that matter, national) majorities. Perhaps the most important and dramatic example of that effect is the relatively recent constitutional history of racial discrimination by governments. From 1896 until 1954, the Supreme Court considered it no denial of equal protection for a state to discriminate on the basis of race in its official actions so long as each race was treated equally. This "separate but equal" doctrine permitted local majorities in many states (mostly, but not entirely, in the South) to require segregation of the races in public schools and public accommodations. But with Brown v. Board of Education, racial discrimination by governments became presumptively unconstitutional. Federalism issues became irrelevant. It did not matter that a local majority might prefer official racial segregation, because that practice was presumptively forbidden by the Constitution. Thus federalism issues exist only with respect to government actions that do not offend fundamental constitutional liberties. Wherever constitutionally guaranteed individual liberties reach, they cancel contrary government action.

3

The Limits of Federal Legislative Power: Judicially or Politically Enforceable Federalism?

A. IMPLEMENTING ENUMERATED POWERS AND "DEFAULT" RULES

The federal government is granted only the powers enumerated in the Constitution, but these powers cannot be exercised abstractly. The concrete exercise of federal power—whether through legislation, executive action, or judicial decision—focuses debate on the legitimate scope of federal power. That debate poses at least two questions: (1) Is the objective of the challenged action within an enumerated power? (2) Are the means chosen to achieve that objective constitutionally permissible? Subsection 1 examines both questions, but principally the latter question, while Subsection 2 examines a related issue: If the Constitution says nothing about whether a given power is delegated to the federal government or prohibited to the states, what sort of "default" rules apply to deal with that lacuna?

The remaining sections in this chapter examine the scope of the more important enumerated powers. As you work through those sections, note how difficult it is for the Court to separate neatly the scope of the enumerated power—the objective—from the means chosen by Congress to accomplish that objective.

1. Implementing Enumerated Powers: The "Necessary and Proper Clause"

Consider how much freedom the Constitution gives to Congress to decide upon the means to achieve its legislative objectives.

McCulloch v. Maryland
17 U.S. (4 Wheat.) 316 (1819)

[The Second Bank of the United States, the nation's second attempt to establish a central bank, met with determined opposition from local interests fearful of the effects of more centralized control of the nation's money supply. The attack was double-barreled. From a legal perspective, opponents contended that Congress lacked any constitutional authority to charter a national bank. The Second Bank of the United States was attacked politically in many ways, ultimately leading to President Jackson's successful veto of a bill to extend the bank's charter. In this case, the political vehicle of attack was Maryland's legislation providing that all nationally chartered banks doing business in Maryland either pay an annual tax of $15,000 or purchase stamped paper from the state for use in issuing its bank notes. There was only one such bank—the Bank of the United States. McCulloch, the treasurer of the Baltimore branch of the Bank, refused to pay the tax and was prosecuted in the Maryland courts. McCulloch was convicted on an agreed set of facts. The Maryland Court of Appeals affirmed. On appeal, the Supreme Court concluded that (1) Congress had the power to charter the Bank of the United States; and (2) Maryland's tax levied on the bank was an unconstitutional attempt to tax an instrumentality of the United States. Only the first issue is considered here. The Court's opinion with respect to the second issue is considered in the next subsection.]

CHIEF JUSTICE MARSHALL, for the Court.

In the case now to be determined, the defendant, a sovereign state, denies the obligation of a law enacted by the legislature of the Union, and the plaintiff, on his part, contests the validity of an act which has been passed by the legislature of that state. The constitution of our country, in its most interesting and vital parts, is to be considered; the conflicting powers of the government of the Union and of its members, as marked in that constitution, are to be discussed; and an opinion given, which may essentially influence the great operations of the government. No tribunal can approach such a question without a deep sense of its importance, and of the awful responsibility involved in its decision. But it must be decided peacefully, or remain a source of hostile legislation, perhaps, of hostility of a still more serious nature; and if it is to be so decided, by this tribunal alone can the decision be made. On the supreme court of the United States has the constitution of our country devolved this important duty.

The first question made in the cause is—has congress power to incorporate a bank? [T]his can scarcely be considered as an open question, entirely unprejudiced by the former proceedings of the nation respecting it. The principle now contested was introduced at a very early period of our history, has been recognised by many successive legislatures, and has been acted upon by the judicial department, in cases of peculiar delicacy, as a law of undoubted obligation. . . .

The power now contested was exercised by the first congress elected under the present constitution. The bill for incorporating the Bank of the

United States did not steal upon an unsuspecting legislature, and pass unobserved. Its principle was completely understood, and was opposed with equal zeal and ability. After being resisted, first, in the fair and open field of debate, and afterwards, in the executive cabinet, with as much persevering talent as any measure has ever experienced, and being supported by arguments which convinced minds as pure and as intelligent as this country can boast, it became a law. The original act [creating the First Bank of the United States] was permitted to expire; but a short experience of the embarrassments to which the refusal to revive it exposed the government, convinced those who were most prejudiced against the measure of its necessity, and induced the passage of the present law [establishing the Second Bank of the United States]. It would require no ordinary share of intrepidity to assert that a measure adopted under these circumstances was a bold and plain usurpation to which the constitution gave no countenance.

[Counsel] for the state of Maryland have deemed it of some importance, in the construction of the constitution, to consider that instrument not as emanating from the people but as the act of sovereign and independent states. The powers of the general government, it has been said, are delegated by the states, who alone are truly sovereign; and must be exercised in subordination to the states, who alone possess supreme dominion. It would be difficult to sustain this proposition. The convention which framed the constitution was indeed elected by the state legislatures. But the instrument, when it came from their hands, was a mere [proposal]. It was reported to the then existing congress of the United States, with a request that it might "be submitted to a convention of delegates, chosen in each state by the people thereof, under the recommendation of its legislature, for their assent and ratification." This mode of proceeding was adopted; and by the convention, by congress, and by the state legislatures, the instrument was submitted to the people. They acted upon it in the only manner in which they can act safely, effectively and wisely on such a subject, by assembling in convention. It is true, they assembled in their several states—and where else should they have assembled? No political dreamer was ever wild enough to think of breaking down the lines which separate the states, and of compounding the American people into one common mass. Of consequence, when they act, they act in their states. But the measures they adopt do not, on that account, cease to be the measures of the people themselves, or become the measures of the state governments.

From these conventions, the constitution derives its whole authority. The government proceeds directly from the people; is "ordained and established" in the name of the people; and is declared to be ordained "in order to form a more perfect union, establish justice, insure domestic tranquillity, and secure the blessings of liberty to themselves and to their posterity." The assent of the states, in their sovereign capacity, is implied, in calling a convention, and thus submitting that instrument to the people. But the people were at perfect liberty to accept or reject it; and their act was final. It required not the affirmance, and could not be negatived, by the state governments. The constitution, when thus adopted, was of complete obligation, and bound the state sovereignties. . . .

To the formation of a league, such as was the confederation, the state sovereignties were certainly competent. But when, "in order to form a more perfect union," it was deemed necessary to change this alliance into an effective government, possessing great and sovereign powers, and acting directly on the people, the necessity of referring it to the people, and of deriving its powers directly from them, was felt and acknowledged by all. The government of the Union [is], emphatically and truly, a government of the people. In form, and in substance, it emanates from them. Its powers are granted by them, and are to be exercised directly on them, and for their benefit.

This government [is] one of enumerated powers. The principle, that it can exercise only the powers granted to it, [is] now universally admitted. But the question respecting the extent of the powers actually granted is perpetually arising, and will probably continue to arise, so long as our system shall exist. [The] government of the Union, though limited in its powers, is supreme within its sphere of action. This would seem to result, necessarily, from its nature. It is the government of all; its powers are delegated by all; it represents all and acts for all. [The] government of the United States, then, though limited in its powers, is supreme; and its laws, when made in pursuance of the constitution, form the supreme law of the land, "anything in the constitution or laws of any state to the contrary notwithstanding." [Art. VI, §2.]

Among the enumerated powers, we do not find that of establishing a bank or creating a corporation. But there is no phrase in the instrument which, like the articles of confederation, excludes incidental or implied powers and which requires that everything granted shall be expressly and minutely described. Even the 10th amendment, which was framed for the purpose of quieting the excessive jealousies which had been excited, omits the word "expressly," and declares only that the powers "not delegated to the United States, nor prohibited to the states, are reserved to the states or to the people"; thus leaving the question, whether the particular power which may become the subject of contest, has been delegated to the one government, or prohibited to the other, to depend on a fair construction of the whole instrument. The men who drew and adopted this amendment had experienced the embarrassments resulting from the insertion of this word in the articles of confederation, and probably omitted it, to avoid those embarrassments. A constitution, to contain an accurate detail of all the subdivisions of which its great powers will admit, and of all the means by which they may be carried into execution, would partake of the prolixity of a legal code, and could scarcely be embraced by the human mind. It would, probably, never be understood by the public. Its nature, therefore, requires that only its great outlines should be marked, its important objects designated, and the minor ingredients which compose those objects be deduced from the nature of the objects themselves. [In] considering this question, then, we must never forget that it is a constitution we are expounding.

Although, among the enumerated powers of government, we do not find the word "bank" or "incorporation," we find the great powers[:] to lay and collect taxes; to borrow money; to regulate commerce; to declare and conduct a war; and to raise and support armies and navies. The sword and the purse, all the external relations, and no inconsiderable portion of the industry of the nation, are intrusted to its government. It can never be pretended, that these vast powers draw after them others of inferior importance merely because they are inferior. Such an idea can never be advanced. But it may with great reason be contended that a government intrusted with such ample powers, on the due execution of which the happiness and prosperity of the nation so vitally depends, must also be intrusted with ample means for their execution. The power being given, it is the interest of the nation to facilitate its execution. It can never be their interest, and cannot be presumed to have been their intention, to clog and embarrass its execution by withholding the most appropriate means. Throughout this vast republic, from the St. Croix to the Gulf of Mexico, from the Atlantic to the Pacific, revenue is to be collected and expended, armies are to be marched and supported. The exigencies of the nation may require that the treasure raised in the north should be transported to the south, that raised in the east conveyed to the west, or that this order should be reversed. Is that construction of the constitution to be preferred which would render these operations difficult, hazardous and expensive? Can we adopt that construction (unless the words imperiously require it), which would impute to the framers of that instrument, when granting these powers for the public good, the intention of impeding their exercise by withholding a choice of means? If, indeed, such be the mandate of the constitution, we have only to obey; but that instrument does not profess to enumerate the means by which the powers it confers may be executed; nor does it prohibit the creation of a corporation, if the existence of such a being be essential, to the beneficial exercise of those powers. It is, then, the subject of fair inquiry how far such means may be employed.

It is not denied that the powers given to the government imply the ordinary means of execution. [But] it is denied that the government has its choice of [means]. The power of creating a corporation [is] not, like the power of making war, or levying taxes, or of regulating commerce, a great substantive and independent [power]. It is never the end for which other powers are exercised, but a means by which other objects are accomplished. [The] power of creating a corporation is never used for its own sake, but for the purpose of effecting something else. No sufficient reason is, therefore, perceived, why it may not pass as incidental to those powers which are expressly given, if it be a direct mode of executing them.

But the constitution of the United States has not left the right of congress to employ the necessary means for the execution of the powers conferred on the government to general reasoning. To its enumeration of powers is added that of making "all laws which shall be necessary and proper for carrying into execution the foregoing powers, and all other powers vested by this constitution in the government of the United States, or in any department thereof." The counsel for the state of Maryland have urged various arguments to prove that this clause, though in terms a grant of power, is not so in effect but is really restrictive of the general right, which might otherwise be implied, of selecting means for executing the enumerated powers. [The] argument on which most reliance is placed is drawn from that peculiar language of this clause. Congress is not empowered by it to make all laws, which may have relation to the powers conferred on the government, but such only as may be "necessary and proper" for carrying them into execution. The word "necessary" is considered as controlling the whole sentence, and as limiting the right to pass laws for the execution of the granted powers, to such as are indispensable, and without which the power would be nugatory. That it excludes the choice of means, and leaves to congress, in each case, that only which is most direct and simple.

[Is] this the sense in which the word "necessary" is always used? Does it always import an absolute physical necessity so strong that one thing to which another may be termed necessary cannot exist without that other? We think it does not. [We] find that it frequently imports no more than that one thing is convenient, or useful, or essential to another. To employ the means necessary to an end is generally understood as employing any means calculated to produce the end, and not as being confined to those single means, without which the end would be entirely unattainable. [The] word "necessary" [has] not a fixed character peculiar to itself. It admits of all degrees of comparison and is often connected with other words, which increase or diminish the impression the mind receives of the urgency it imports. A thing may be necessary, very necessary, absolutely or indispensably necessary. To no mind would the same idea be conveyed by these several phrases. [It] is, we think, impossible to compare the sentence [in Art. I, §10] which prohibits a state from laying "imposts, or duties on imports or exports, except what may be absolutely necessary for executing its inspection laws," with that which authorizes congress "to make all laws which shall be necessary and proper for carrying into execution" the powers of the general government without feeling a conviction that the convention understood itself to change materially the meaning of the word "necessary," by prefixing the word "absolutely." This word, then, like others, is used in various senses; and, in its construction, the subject, the context, the intention of the person using them, are all to be taken into view.

Let this be done in the case under consideration. The subject is the execution of those great powers on which the welfare of a nation essentially depends. It must have been the intention of those who gave these powers to insure, so far as human prudence could insure, their beneficial execution. This could not be done by confiding the choice of means to such narrow limits as not to leave it in the power of congress to adopt any which might be appropriate, and which were conducive to the end. This provision is made in a constitution intended to endure for ages to come, and consequently to be adapted to the various crises of human affairs. To have prescribed the means by which government should, in all future time, execute its powers would have been to change, entirely, the character of the instrument, and give it the properties of a legal code. It would have been an unwise attempt to provide, by immutable rules, for exigencies which, if foreseen at all, must have been seen dimly, and which can be best provided for as they occur. To have declared that the best means shall not be used, but those alone, without which the power given would be nugatory, would have been to deprive the legislature of the capacity to avail itself of experience, to exercise its reason, and to accommodate its legislation to circumstances.

If we apply this principle of construction to any of the powers of the government, we shall find it so pernicious in its operation that we shall be compelled to discard it. [Take], for example, the power "to establish post-offices and post-roads." This power is executed, by the single act of making the establishment. But from this has been inferred the power and duty of carrying the mail along the post-road, from one post-office to another. And from this implied power has again been inferred the right to punish those who steal letters from the post-office, or rob the mail. It may be said, with some plausibility, that the right to carry the mail, and to punish those who rob it, is not indispensably necessary to the establishment of a post-office and post-road. This right is indeed essential to the beneficial exercise of the power, but not indispensably necessary to its existence. So, of the punishment of the crimes of stealing or falsifying a record or process of a court of the United States, or of perjury in such court. To punish these offences is certainly conducive to the due administration of justice. But courts may exist, and may decide the causes brought before them, though such crimes escape punishment. The baneful influence of this narrow construction on all the operations of the government, and the absolute impracticability of maintaining it without rendering the government incompetent to its great objects might be illustrated by numerous examples drawn from the constitution, and from our laws. . . .

But the argument which most conclusively demonstrates the error of the construction contended for by the counsel [for] Maryland is founded on the intention of the convention, as manifested in the whole clause. To waste time and argument in proving that, without it, congress might carry its powers into execution, would be not much less idle than to hold a lighted taper to the sun. As little can it be required to prove that in the absence of this clause, congress would have some choice of means. That it might employ those which, in its judgment, would most advantageously effect the object to be accomplished. That any means adapted to the end, any means which tended directly to the execution of the constitutional powers of the government were in themselves constitutional. This clause, as construed by the state of Maryland, would abridge, and almost annihilate, this useful and necessary right of the legislature to select its means. That this could not be intended, is, we should think, had it not been already controverted, too apparent for controversy.

We think so for the following reasons: 1st. The clause is placed among the powers of congress, not among the limitations on those powers. 2d. Its terms purport to enlarge, not to diminish the powers vested in the government. It purports to be an additional power, not a restriction on those already granted. No reason has been or can be assigned for thus concealing an intention to narrow the discretion of the national legislature, under words which purport to enlarge it. If [the Framers'] intention had been, by this clause, to restrain the free use of means which might otherwise have been implied, that intention would have been inserted in another place, and would have been expressed in terms resembling these. "In carrying into execution the foregoing powers, and all others," &c., "no laws shall be passed but such as are necessary and proper." Had the intention been to make this clause restrictive, it would unquestionably have been so in form as well as in effect.

The result of the most careful and attentive consideration bestowed upon this clause is, that if it does not enlarge, it cannot be construed to restrain the powers of congress, or to impair the right of the legislature to exercise its best judgment in the selection of measures to carry into execution the constitutional powers of the government. If no other motive for its insertion can be suggested, a sufficient one is found in the desire to remove all doubts respecting the right to legislate on that vast mass of incidental powers which must be involved in the constitution, if that instrument be not a splendid bauble.

We admit, as all must admit, that the powers of the government are limited, and that its limits are not to be transcended. But we think the sound construction of the constitution must allow to the national legislature that discretion, with respect to the means by which the powers it confers are to be carried into execution, which will enable that body to perform the high duties assigned to it in the manner most beneficial to the people. Let the end be legitimate, let it be within the scope of the constitution, and all means which are appropriate, which are plainly adapted to that end, which are not prohibited, but consist with the letter and spirit of the constitution, are constitutional.

That a corporation must be considered as a means not less usual, not of higher dignity, not more requiring a particular specification than other means, has been sufficiently proved. [If] a corporation may be employed, indiscriminately with other means, to carry into execution the powers of the government, no particular reason can be assigned for excluding the use of a bank if required for its fiscal operations. [That] it is a convenient, a useful, and essential instrument in the prosecution of its fiscal operations is not now a subject of controversy.

[Should] congress, in the execution of its powers, adopt measures which are prohibited by the constitution; or should congress, under the pretext of executing its powers, pass laws for the accomplishment of objects not intrusted to the government; it would become the painful duty of this tribunal, should a case requiring such a decision come before it, to say that such an act was not the law of the land. But where the law is not prohibited, and [is] calculated to effect [the] objects intrusted to the government, to undertake here to inquire into the degree of its necessity would be to pass the line which circumscribes the judicial department, and to tread on legislative ground. This court disclaims all pretensions to such a power.

After the most deliberate consideration, it is the unanimous and decided opinion of this court that the act to incorporate the Bank of the United States is a law made in pursuance of the constitution, and is a part of the supreme law of the land.

[The remainder of the opinion, dealing with the validity of Maryland's law imposing a tax on the bank, is omitted here. It is presented in the next subsection.]

NOTES

1. Conceptions of Sovereignty.   Marshall expresses his disagreement with the view that the Constitution was a compact among sovereign states. In antebellum America the nature of the federal union was a significant matter of political and legal dispute. The southern "agrarians," including such adept political theorists as John Calhoun, John Taylor of Caroline, and Abel Upshur, took the position (advanced by Maryland's lawyers in *McCulloch*) that the federal government was created by the states, not by the people composing the states. The logical and ultimate corollary to this position was that states were free to leave the union unilaterally. This theory was implicitly rejected as a matter of constitutional law by Marshall, but it took the Civil War to cement the political conclusion that, as the Court put it in Texas v. White, 74 U.S. (7 Wall.) 700 (1869), "[t]he Constitution . . . looks to an indestructible Union, composed of indestructible States." Marshall did not need to address this point to decide *McCulloch*, so his comments are dicta. This debate is not entirely stale. Consider the Court's division over the validity of state-imposed term limits on the state's congressional delegation, in U.S. Term Limits, Inc. v. Thornton, 514 U.S. 779 (1995), discussed in the next section.

2. Necessary and Proper: Means to Legitimate Ends.   The Court disclaimed the idea that the "necessary and proper" clause might be an *independent* source of federal legislative authority. All that the clause does is give Congress broad discretion to select the means it will employ to achieve one of the legislative objectives permitted it, or to realize some other federal power independently granted in the Constitution. After *McCulloch*, how much judicial review of congressional choices of means remains? The modern formulation of the standard of review is that the congressional choice must be rationally related to the accomplishment of a legitimate, constitutionally authorized objective. If there is any minimally plausible connection between the legitimate objective of legislation and the chosen means, that is rational enough.

In Sabri v. United States, 541 U.S. 600 (2004), Justice Thomas, concurring in the judgment, noted that *McCulloch* described the scope of the implementing power under the necessary and proper clause as consisting of all lawful "means which are appropriate [and] which are plainly adapted" to the accomplishment of constitutionally legitimate ends. He thought that "plainly adapted" means "obvious" or "clear." Thus, a "statute can have a 'rational' connection to an enumerated power without being obviously or clearly tied to that enumerated power. To show that a statute is 'plainly adapted' to a legitimate end . . . it would seem necessary to show some obvious, simple, and direct relation between the statute and the enumerated power."

An application of Justice Thomas's approach to the scope of the necessary and proper clause may be found in his dissent in Gonzales v. Raich, 545 U.S. 1 (2005). Justice Thomas thought that federal prohibition of medicinal marijuana was not "plainly adapted" to the legitimate end of regulating interstate commerce, and thus not "necessary," because state regulations governing the use of medicinal marijuana were adequate to prevent its leakage into the illicit interstate commercial market for marijuana, and the evidence suggested that the number of medicinal marijuana users was tiny in comparison with the vast population of recreational users of marijuana. Nor did Justice Thomas think that the federal ban was "proper":

> Congress may not use its incidental authority to subvert basic principles of federalism and dual sovereignty. Here, Congress has encroached on States' traditional police powers to define the criminal law and to protect the health, safety, and welfare of their citizens. Further, the Government's rationale — that it may regulate the production or possession of any commodity for which there is an interstate market — threatens to remove the remaining vestiges of States' traditional police powers. This would convert the Necessary and Proper Clause into precisely what Chief Justice Marshall did not envision, a "pretext . . . for the accomplishment of objects not intrusted to the government." *McCulloch.*

3. The "Pretext" Qualifier.   Marshall stated that if Congress, "under the pretext of executing its powers, [should] pass laws for the accomplishment of objects not intrusted to the government," such laws would be struck down. In essence, Marshall said that Congress may pick its means without much judicial oversight, but the Court will separately scrutinize the purported objectives of legislation. There was no occasion in *McCulloch* for the Court to consider how it would review these purported objectives. That problem is the subject of the remaining sections in this chapter.

Consider the following possibilities. Did Marshall concede to Congress control over legislative *means* partly because he believed that the Court would retain vigorous review of legislative *objectives*? Or was Marshall also prepared to cede to Congress unfettered control of the scope of legislative objectives? If so, why would Marshall have inserted the "pretext" qualifier? If the former possibility is more likely, how can (or should) the Court determine the objectives of Congress? These questions are at the center of the materials in Sections B through G.

4. A Contemporary Application: *Comstock*.   At issue in United States v. Comstock, 560 U.S. 186 (2010), was a federal law, 18 U.S.C. §4248, that permits a district court to order the civil commitment of federal prisoners, even after they have completed their prison sentence, if the government proves by clear and convincing evidence that they have "engaged or attempted to engage in sexually violent conduct or child molestation," currently "suffer[] from a serious mental illness, abnormality, or disorder," and are "sexually dangerous to others." The Court assumed that such civil commitment comported with the due process guarantee and concluded that section 4248 was a necessary and proper means to execute the government's enumerated powers:

> *First*, the Necessary and Proper Clause grants Congress . . . the legislative authority to enact a particular federal statute [if] the statute constitutes a means that is rationally related to the implementation of a constitutionally enumerated power. [The] relevant inquiry is simply "whether the means chosen are 'reasonably adapted' to the attainment of a legitimate end. . . ." [The] Constitution . . . "leaves to Congress a large discretion as to the means that may be employed in executing a given power."
>
> Congress routinely exercises its authority to enact criminal laws in furtherance of . . . its enumerated powers to regulate interstate and foreign commerce, to enforce civil rights, to spend funds for the general welfare, to establish federal courts, to establish post offices, to regulate bankruptcy, to regulate naturalization, and so forth. . . . Congress, in order to help ensure the enforcement of federal criminal laws enacted in furtherance of its enumerated powers, "can cause a prison to be erected at any place within the jurisdiction of the United States, and direct that all persons sentenced to imprisonment under the laws of the United States shall be confined there." Moreover, Congress, having established a prison system, can enact laws that seek to ensure that system's safe and responsible administration . . . and can also ensure the safety of the prisoners, prison workers and visitors, and those in surrounding communities by, for example, creating further criminal laws governing entry, exit, and smuggling, and by employing prison guards to ensure discipline and security. . . . Neither Congress'[s] power to criminalize conduct, nor its power to imprison individuals who engage in that conduct, nor its power to enact laws governing prisons and prisoners, is explicitly mentioned in the Constitution. But Congress nonetheless possesses broad authority to do each of those things in the course of "carrying into Execution" the enumerated powers "vested by" the "Constitution in the Government of the United States"—authority granted by the Necessary and Proper Clause.
>
> *Second*, the civil-commitment statute . . . constitutes a modest addition to a set of federal prison-related mental-health statutes that have existed for many decades. [Though] a longstanding history of related federal action does not demonstrate a statute's constitutionality [it helps to establish] the reasonableness of the relation between the new statute and pre-existing federal interests.
>
> *Third*, [because] the Federal Government is the custodian of its prisoners, . . . it has the constitutional power to act in order to protect nearby (and other) communities from the danger federal prisoners may pose. . . .
>
> *Fourth*, the statute [does not] improperly limit the scope of "powers that remain with the States" [but] requires *accommodation* of state interests: The Attorney General must inform the State in which the federal prisoner "is domiciled or was tried" that he is detaining someone with respect to whom those States may wish to assert their authority, and he must encourage those States to assume custody of the individual. He must also immediately "release" that person "to the appropriate official of" either State "if such State will assume [such] responsibility."
>
> *Fifth*, the links between §4248 and an enumerated Article I power are not too attenuated. [We reject the] argument that the Necessary and Proper Clause permits no more than a single step between an enumerated power and an Act of Congress. . . .

Justice Kennedy concurred in the judgment:

> When the inquiry is whether a federal law has sufficient links to an enumerated power to be within the scope of federal authority, the analysis depends not on the number of links in the congressional-power chain but on the strength of the chain. [But this] is merely the beginning, not the end, of the constitutional inquiry. The inferences must be controlled by some limitations lest, as Thomas Jefferson warned, congressional powers become completely unbounded by linking one power to another *ad infinitum* in a veritable game of " 'this is the house that Jack built.' " Letter from Thomas Jefferson to Edward Livingston (Apr. 30, 1800), 31 The Papers of Thomas Jefferson 547 (B. Oberg ed. 2004). . . . [There must be] a tangible link to [the enumerated power], not a mere conceivable rational relation. . . . [There must be] a demonstrated link in fact, based on empirical demonstration.

Justice Thomas, joined by Justice Scalia, dissented:

> Unless the end itself is "legitimate," the fit between means and end is irrelevant. In other words, no matter how "necessary" or "proper" an Act of Congress may be to its objective, Congress lacks authority to legislate if the objective is anything other than "carrying into Execution" one or more of the Federal Government's enumerated powers. . . . No enumerated power . . . delegates to Congress [or any other branch of the Federal Government] the power to enact a civil-commitment regime for sexually dangerous persons. . . .
>
> [Because] §4248 permits the term of federal civil commitment to continue beyond the date on which a convicted prisoner's sentence expires . . . [it] authorizes federal custody over a person at a time when the Government would lack jurisdiction to detain him for violating a criminal law that executes an enumerated power. . . . [Once] the Federal Government's criminal jurisdiction over a prisoner ends, so does any "special relation[ship]" between the Government and the former prisoner. . . .
>
> [T]oday's opinion . . . endorses the precise abuse of power Article I is designed to prevent—the use of a limited grant of authority as a "pretext . . . for the accomplishment of objects not intrusted to the government."

5. The Individual Mandate of Health Insurance. In National Federation of Independent Business v. Sebelius, 132 S. Ct. 2566 (2012), five justices agreed (but not in an opinion for the Court) that the requirement contained in the Patient Protection and Affordable Care Act (ACA) that all Americans have specified health insurance was beyond Congress's power to regulate interstate commerce and was not authorized by the Necessary and Proper Clause:

> [T]he Clause . . . does not license the exercise of any "great substantive and independent power[s]" beyond those specifically enumerated. . . . Even if the individual mandate is "necessary" to the Act's insurance reforms, such an expansion of federal power is not a "proper" means for making those reforms effective. . . ." Just as the individual mandate cannot be sustained as a law regulating

the substantial effects of the failure to purchase health insurance, neither can it be upheld as a "necessary and proper" component of the insurance reforms.

See also the excerpt of *Sebelius* in Section B.3, infra.

2. Implying "Default" Rules for Federal and State Power

When the Constitution fails to speak to the issue of whether the federal government has exclusive power over a subject or whether the states are prohibited from acting with respect to the subject, courts are forced to read into the Constitution some sort of "default" rules. There are several possibilities. In the absence of both a constitutional grant of exclusive authority over an issue to the federal government and denial to the states of power to act on that issue, one could presume that (1) states have power to act on the issue; or (2) only the federal government can act; or (3) both governments may act but the federal action prevails in case of conflict. The third possibility is in fact what happens when the federal government and the states both act on a subject that is shared concurrently. The cases discussed here raise a different issue: When a state government acts on an issue and the Constitution is silent on the question of whether that issue exclusively belongs to the federal government or is off-limits to the states, should the states be presumed to have the power to act? The answer to this question may vary depending on the nature of the issue on which a state acts. Pay careful attention to how this question is actually answered in the next two cases.

☰ *McCulloch v. Maryland*
17 U.S. (4 Wheat.) 316 (1819)

[In the prior portion of this opinion, the Court ruled that Congress had power to charter the Second Bank of the United States. At issue in this part of the opinion was the validity of Maryland's tax on banknotes issued by the Bank of the United States.]

CHIEF JUSTICE MARSHALL, for the Court.

. . . It being the opinion of the court, that the act incorporating the [Bank of the United States] is constitutional and that the power of establishing a branch in the state of Maryland might be properly exercised by the bank itself, we proceed to inquire [whether] Maryland may, without violating the constitution, tax that branch? That the power of taxation [is] retained by the states; that it is not abridged by the grant of a similar power to the government of the Union; that it is to be concurrently exercised by the two governments—are truths which have never been denied. But such is the paramount character of the constitution that its capacity to withdraw any subject from the action of even this power is admitted. [This] paramount character [restrains] a state from [such] exercise of [the taxing] power as is in its nature incompatible with, and repugnant to, the constitutional laws of the Union.

[On] this ground, [the] bank [claims] to be exempted from the power of a state to tax its operations. There is no express [provision], but the claim [is] sustained on [the] great principle [that] the constitution and the laws made in pursuance thereof are supreme; that they control the constitution and laws of the respective states, and cannot be controlled by them. From this, which may be almost termed an axiom, other propositions are deduced as [corollaries]. These are, 1st. That a power to create implies a power to preserve: 2d. That a power to destroy, if wielded by a different hand, is hostile to and incompatible with these powers to create and to preserve: 3d. That where this repugnancy exists, that authority which is supreme must control, not yield to that over which it is supreme.

[That] the power of taxing [the Bank of the United States] by the states may be exercised so as to destroy it is too obvious to be denied. But taxation is said to be an absolute power, which acknowledges no other limits than those expressly prescribed in the [Constitution]. But the very terms of this argument admit that the sovereignty of the state, in the article of taxation itself, is subordinate to and may be controlled by the constitution of the United States.

[Maryland contends] that [it] may exercise [its] acknowledged powers upon [the federal government], and that the constitution leaves [it] this right. [The] power of taxing the people and their property is essential to the very existence of government, and may be legitimately exercised on the objects to which it is applicable, to the utmost extent to which the government may choose to carry it. The only security against the abuse of this power is found in the structure of the government itself. In imposing a tax the legislature acts upon its constituents. This is, in general, a sufficient security against erroneous and oppressive taxation. The people of a state [give] to their government a right of taxing themselves and their property, and as the exigencies of government cannot be limited, they prescribe no limits to the exercise of this right, resting confidently on the interest of the legislator, and on the influence of the constituent over their representative, to guard them against its abuse. But the means employed by the government of the Union have no such security, nor is the right of a state to tax them sustained by the same theory. Those means are not given by the people of a particular state, not given by the constituents of the legislature, which claim the right to tax them, but by the people of all the states. They are given by all, for the benefit of all—and upon theory, should be subjected to that government only which belongs to all.

[Taxation] is an incident of sovereignty, and is co-extensive with that to which it is an incident. All subjects over which the sovereign power of a state extends are objects of taxation; but those over which it does not extend, are, upon the soundest principles, exempt from taxation. [Does state sovereignty] extend to those means which are employed by congress to carry into execution powers conferred on that body by the people of the United States? We think [it] does not. Those powers are not given by the people of a single state. They are given by the people of the United States to a government whose laws, made in pursuance of the constitution, are declared to be supreme.

Consequently, the people of a single state cannot confer a sovereignty which will extend over them. If we measure the power of taxation residing in a state by the extent of sovereignty which the people of a single state possess and can confer on its government, we have an intelligible standard, [a] principle which leaves the power of taxing the people and property of a state unimpaired; which leaves to a state the command of all its resources, and which places beyond its reach all those powers which are conferred by the people of the United States on the government of the Union, and all those means which are given for the purpose of carrying those powers into execution.

[It cannot be denied that] the power to tax involves the power to destroy; that the power to destroy may defeat and render useless the power to create; that there is a plain repugnance in conferring on [state governments] a power to control the constitutional measures of [the federal government when such federal measures are] declared [by the Constitution] to be supreme. [Taxation], it is said, does not necessarily and unavoidably destroy. To carry it to the excess of destruction would be an abuse, to presume which would banish that confidence which is essential to all government. But is this a case of confidence? Would the people of any one state trust those of another with a power to control the most insignificant operations of their state government? We know they would not. Why, then, should we suppose that the people of any one state should be willing to trust those of another with a power to control the operations of a government to which they have confided their most important and most valuable interests? In the legislature of the Union alone are all represented. The legislature of the Union alone, therefore, can be trusted by the people with the power of controlling measures which concern all, in the confidence that it will not be abused.

[If] we apply the principle for which the state of Maryland contends, to the constitution, generally, we shall find it capable of changing totally the character of that instrument. We shall find it capable of arresting all the measures of the government, and of prostrating it at the foot of the states. The American people have declared their constitution and the laws made in pursuance thereof to be supreme; but this principle would transfer the supremacy, in fact, to the states. If the states may tax one instrument employed by the government in the execution of its powers, they may tax any and every other instrument. They may tax the mail; they may tax the mint; they may tax patent-rights; they may tax the papers of the custom-house; they may tax judicial process; they may tax all the means employed by the government to an excess which would defeat all the ends of government. This was not intended by the American people. They did not design to make their government dependent on the states.

[If] the controlling power of the states be established; if their supremacy as to taxation be acknowledged; what is to restrain their exercising control in any shape they may please to give it? Their sovereignty is not confined to taxation; that is not the only mode in which it might be displayed. The question is, in truth, a question of supremacy; and if the right of the states to tax the means employed by the general government be conceded, the declaration that the constitution, and the laws made in pursuance thereof, shall be the supreme law of the land, is empty and unmeaning declamation. . . .

It has also been insisted, that, as the power of taxation in the general and state governments is acknowledged to be concurrent, every argument which would sustain the right of the general government to tax banks chartered by the states will equally sustain the right of the states to tax banks chartered by the general government. But the two cases are not on the same reason. The people of all the states have created the general government, and have conferred upon it the general power of taxation. The people of all the states, and the states themselves, are represented in congress, and, by their representatives, exercise this power. When they tax the chartered institutions of the states, they tax their constituents; and these taxes must be uniform. But when a state taxes the operations of the government of the United States, it acts upon institutions created not by their own constituents but by people over whom they claim no control. It acts upon the measures of a government created by others as well as themselves, for the benefit of others in common with themselves. The difference [is] between the action of the whole on a part, and the action of a part on the whole—between the laws of a government declared to be supreme, and those of a government which, when in opposition to those laws, is not supreme.

[The] states have no power, by taxation or otherwise, to retard, impede, burden, or in any manner control, the operations of the constitutional laws enacted by congress to carry into execution the powers vested in the general government. This is, we think, the unavoidable consequence of that supremacy which the constitution has declared. We are unanimously of [the] opinion that the [Maryland law] imposing a tax on the Bank of the United States is unconstitutional and void.

This opinion does not deprive the states of any resources which they originally possessed. It does not extend to a tax paid by the real property of the bank, in common with the other real property within the state, nor to a tax imposed on the interest which the citizens of Maryland may hold in this institution, in common with other property of the same description throughout the state. But this is a tax on the operations of the bank, and is, consequently, a tax on the operation of an instrument employed by the government of the Union to carry its powers into execution. Such a tax must be unconstitutional.

NOTES

1. The Source of the Implied Barrier to State Action. Marshall's textual anchor is the supremacy clause, but the real heart of his argument is structural. When a state taxes its own citizens, the right of those citizens to vote for the legislators who impose the tax is "a sufficient security against erroneous and oppressive taxation." But when a state taxes outsiders, that check is wholly absent. Human nature being what it is, the temptation is to tax outsiders (who can't vote) to reap benefits for insiders (who can and do vote). The federal government and its instrumentalities are outsiders for this purpose—a tax on the Bank of the United States is paid by national revenues, mostly collected from out-of-state sources, and the benefits of the tax are reaped entirely by insiders. Only Marylanders were represented in the Maryland legislature, but the Bank of the United States was a creature of national action, and most Americans were not represented in Maryland's legislature.

This may be true, but does it warrant *judicial* intervention? Why couldn't Congress have barred the states from taxing the bank—or all instrumentalities of the federal government? If Congress could have acted but simply chose not to, why was judicial intervention appropriate?

Marshall's explanation continues to resonate in the modern "representation-reinforcement" or "process" theories of constitutional law—the idea that a principal objective of constitutional judicial review is to identify and invalidate laws and government practices that block the full and fair functioning of the democratic process of representative government. See, e.g., John Hart Ely, Democracy and Distrust (1980). This theory will arise repeatedly as you study the remainder of constitutional law.

2. Regulatory Immunities. The federal government and its instrumentalities are generally free from state regulation. In Johnson v. Maryland, 254 U.S. 51 (1920), the Court reversed Maryland's conviction of a federal postal worker for driving his delivery truck without a license. Justice Holmes declared for the Court that

> the immunity of the instruments of the United States from state control in the performance of their duties extends to a requirement that they desist from performance until they satisfy a state officer upon examination that they are competent for a necessary part of [those federal duties]. Of course an employee of the United States does not secure a general immunity from state law while acting in the course of his employment. [When] the United States has not spoken [federal employees may be subject] to local law [consisting of] general rules that might affect incidentally the mode of carrying out the employment—as, for instance, a [law] regulating the mode of turning at [street corners].

More recently, in Hancock v. Train, 426 U.S. 167 (1976), the Court ruled that states could not require federal government air pollution sources to obtain a state permit. "[W]here Congress does not affirmatively declare its instrumentalities or property subject to regulation, the federal function must be left free of [state] regulation."

In North Dakota v. United States, 495 U.S. 423, 435 (1990), the Court declared that a state or local law is void "only if it regulates the United States directly or discriminates against the Federal Government or those with whom it deals." In United States v. City of Arcata, 629 F.3d 986 (2010), the Ninth Circuit applied these principles to invalidate two city ordinances that made it a civil offense for the federal government and its employees to "recruit, initiate contact with for the purpose of recruiting, or promote the future enlistment of any person under the age of eighteen into any branch of the United States Armed Forces." The ordinances exempted "individuals who are not employed by or agents of the U.S. government" from "encouraging people under the age of eighteen to join the military." The ordinances were intended to and did in fact regulate the federal government directly and, because of the exemption, also discriminated against the federal government.

Problem: San Francisco law provides: "No department, agency, commission, officer or employee of the City and County of San Francisco shall use any City funds or resources to assist in the enforcement of federal immigration law. . . ." Is this valid? Would it be valid if San Francisco barred "any person" from assisting in the enforcement of federal immigration law?

≡≡≡ ## U.S. Term Limits, Inc. v. Thornton
514 U.S. 779 (1995)

JUSTICE STEVENS delivered the opinion of the Court.

[Arkansas voters amended the Arkansas constitution to prohibit] the name of an otherwise-eligible candidate for Congress from appearing on the general election ballot if that candidate has already served three terms in the House of Representatives or two terms in the Senate. The Arkansas Supreme Court held that the amendment violates the Federal Constitution. We agree. [Such] a state-imposed restriction is contrary to the "fundamental principle of our representative democracy" [that] "the people should choose whom they please to govern them." Powell v. McCormack. Allowing individual States to adopt their own qualifications for congressional service would be inconsistent with the Framers' vision of a uniform National Legislature representing the people of the United States. If the qualifications set forth in the text of the Constitution [at Art. I, §§2 and 3, specifying age, residency, and citizenship requirements for membership in the House and Senate] are to be changed, that text must be amended.

[The] constitutionality of Amendment 73 depends [on] the resolution of two distinct issues[:] whether the Constitution forbids States from adding to or altering the qualifications specifically enumerated in the Constitution, [and] if the Constitution does so forbid, whether the fact that Amendment 73 is formulated as a ballot access restriction rather than as an outright disqualification is of constitutional significance.

[Powell v. McCormack] does not necessarily resolve [this case, because] petitioners argue that [the] historical and textual materials discussed in *Powell* do not support the conclusion that the Constitution prohibits additional qualifications imposed by States. In the absence of such a constitutional prohibition, petitioners argue, the Tenth Amendment and the principle of reserved powers require that States be allowed to add such qualifications. . . . We disagree for two independent reasons. First, we conclude that the power to add qualifications is not within the "original powers" of the States, and thus is not reserved to the States by the Tenth Amendment. Second, even if States possessed some original power in this area, we conclude that the Framers intended the Constitution to be the exclusive source of qualifications for members of Congress, and that the Framers thereby "divested" States of any power to add qualifications.

The [Constitution] draws a basic distinction between the powers of the newly created Federal Government and the powers retained by the preexisting sovereign States. As Chief Justice Marshall explained, "it was neither necessary nor proper to define the powers retained by the States. These powers proceed, not from the people of America, but from the people of the several States; and remain, after the adoption of the constitution, what they were before, except so far as they may be abridged by that instrument." Sturges v. Crowninshield, 17 U.S. 122 (1819). [The] text of the Tenth Amendment unambiguously confirms this principle: "The powers not delegated to the United States by the Constitution, nor prohibited by it to the States, are reserved to the States respectively, or to the people." [The] "States unquestionably do retain a significant measure of sovereign authority, [but] only to the extent that the Constitution has not divested them of their original powers and transferred those powers to the Federal Government."

Contrary to petitioners' assertions, the power to add qualifications is not part of the original powers of sovereignty that the Tenth Amendment reserved to the States. [That] Amendment could only "reserve" that which existed before. As Justice Story recognized, "the states can exercise no powers whatsoever, which exclusively spring out of the existence of the national government, which the constitution does not delegate to them. [No] state can say, that it has reserved, what it never possessed." . . . [With] respect to setting qualifications for service in Congress, no such right existed before the Constitution was ratified. [In] adopting [the Constitution] the Framers envisioned a uniform national system, rejecting the notion that the Nation was a collection of States, and instead creating a direct link between the National Government and the people of the United States. [In] that National Government, representatives owe primary allegiance not to the people of a State, but to the people of the Nation. As Justice Story observed, [representatives and senators] are as much officers of the entire union as is the President. States thus "have just as much right, and no more, to prescribe new qualifications for a representative, as they have for a president. [It] is no original prerogative of state power to appoint a representative, a senator, or president for the union."

We believe that the Constitution reflects the Framers' general agreement with the approach later articulated by Justice Story. For example, . . . the provisions governing elections reveal the Framers' understanding that powers over the election of federal officers had to be delegated to, rather than reserved by, the States, [because] the Constitution expressly requires [the] States [to prescribe] "the Times, Places and Manner of holding Elections for Senators and Representatives" [and] to "appoint [presidential] Electors."

[In short], electing representatives to the National Legislature was a new right, arising from the Constitution itself. The Tenth Amendment thus provides no basis for concluding that the States possess reserved power to add qualifications to those that are fixed in the Constitution. Instead, any state power to set the qualifications for membership in Congress must derive not from the reserved powers of state sovereignty, but rather from the delegated powers of national sovereignty. In the absence of any constitutional delegation to the States of power to add qualifications to those enumerated in the Constitution, such a power does not exist.

[Permitting] individual States to formulate diverse qualifications for their representatives would result in a patchwork of state qualifications, undermining the uniformity and the national character that the Framers envisioned and sought to ensure. [Such] a patchwork would also sever the direct link that the Framers found so critical between the National Government and the people of the United States.

[Petitioners] argue that, even if States may not add qualifications, Amendment 73 is constitutional because it is not such a qualification, [but only a ballot access measure that] is a permissible exercise of state power to regulate the "Times, Places and Manner of Holding Elections." We reject these contentions. [In] our view, Amendment 73 is an indirect attempt to accomplish what the Constitution prohibits Arkansas from accomplishing directly. . . .

The merits of term limits, or "rotation," have been the subject of debate since the formation of our Constitution, when the Framers unanimously rejected a proposal to add such limits to the Constitution. The cogent arguments on both sides of the question that were articulated during the process of ratification largely retain their force today. . . . It is not our province to resolve this longstanding debate. We are, however, firmly convinced that allowing the several States to adopt term limits for congressional service would effect a fundamental change in the constitutional framework. Any such change must come not by legislation adopted either by Congress or by an individual State, but [rather] through the Amendment procedures set forth in Article V.

[Affirmed.]

JUSTICE THOMAS, joined by CHIEF JUSTICE REHNQUIST and JUSTICES O'CONNOR and SCALIA, dissenting.

It is ironic that the Court bases today's decision on the right of the people to "choose whom they please to govern them." Under our Constitution, there is only one State whose people have the right to "choose whom they please" to represent Arkansas in Congress. [Nothing] in the Constitution deprives the people of each State of the power to prescribe eligibility requirements for the candidates who seek to represent them in Congress. The Constitution is simply silent on this question. And where the Constitution is silent, it raises no bar to action by the States or the people.

[The] majority fundamentally misunderstands the notion of "reserved" [powers]. Contrary to the majority's suggestion, the people of the States need not point to any affirmative grant of power in the Constitution in order to prescribe qualifications for their representatives in Congress, or to authorize their elected state legislators to do so.

Our system of government rests on one overriding principle: all power stems from the consent of the people. [The] ultimate source of the Constitution's authority is the consent of the people of each individual State, not the consent of the undifferentiated people of the Nation as a whole. [When] they adopted the Federal Constitution, of course, the people of each State surrendered some of their authority to the United States (and hence to entities accountable to the people of other States as well as to themselves). They affirmatively deprived their States of certain powers, [e.g., Art. I, §10,] and they affirmatively conferred certain powers upon the Federal Government [e.g., Art. I, §8]. Because the people of the several States are the only true source of power, however, the Federal Government enjoys no authority beyond what the Constitution confers: the Federal Government's powers are limited and enumerated.

In each State, the remainder of the people's powers—"the powers not delegated to the United States by the Constitution, nor prohibited by it to the States," Amdt. 10—are either delegated to the state government or retained by the people. The Federal Constitution does not specify which of these two possibilities obtains; it is up to the various state constitutions to declare which powers the people of each State have delegated to their state government. As far as the Federal Constitution is concerned, then, the States can exercise all powers that the Constitution does not withhold from them. The Federal Government and the States thus face different default rules: where the Constitution is silent about the exercise of a particular power—that is, where the Constitution does not speak either expressly or by necessary implication—the Federal Government lacks that power and the States enjoy it.

These basic principles are enshrined in the Tenth Amendment, which declares that all powers neither delegated to the Federal Government nor prohibited to the States "are reserved to the States respectively, or to the people." With this careful last phrase, the Amendment avoids taking any position on the division of power between the state governments and the people of the States: it is up to the people of each State to determine which "reserved" powers their state government may exercise. But the Amendment does make clear that powers reside at the state level except where the Constitution removes them from that level. All powers that the Constitution neither delegates to the Federal Government nor prohibits to the States are controlled by the people of each State.

[If] we are to invalidate Arkansas' Amendment 73, we must point to something in the Federal Constitution that deprives the people of Arkansas of the power to enact such measures. The majority disagrees that it bears this burden. But its arguments are unpersuasive.

The majority begins by announcing an enormous and untenable limitation on the principle expressed by the Tenth Amendment. . . . From the fact that the States had not previously enjoyed any powers over the particular institutions of the Federal Government established by the Constitution, the majority derives a rule precisely opposite to the one that the Amendment actually prescribes. . . . The majority's essential logic is that the state governments could not "reserve" any powers that they did not control at the time the Constitution was drafted. But it was not the state governments that were doing the reserving. The Constitution derives its authority instead from the consent of the people of the States. Given the fundamental principle that all governmental powers stem from the people of the States, it would simply be incoherent to assert that the people of the States could not reserve any powers that they had not previously controlled. [If] someone says that the power to use a particular facility is reserved to some group, he is not saying anything about whether that group has previously used the facility. He is merely saying that the people who control the facility have designated that group as the entity with authority to use it. The Tenth Amendment is similar: the people of the States, from whom all governmental powers stem, have specified that all powers not prohibited to the States by the Federal Constitution are reserved "to the States respectively, or to the people." The majority is therefore quite wrong to conclude that the people of the States cannot authorize their state governments to exercise any powers that were unknown to the States when the Federal Constitution was drafted.

[The] only true support for [the majority's view] of the Tenth Amendment comes from Joseph Story's 1833 treatise on constitutional law. Justice Story was a brilliant and accomplished man, and one cannot casually dismiss his views. On the other hand, he was not a member of the Founding generation, and his Commentaries on the Constitution were written a half century after the framing. Rather than representing the original understanding of the Constitution, they represent only his own understanding.

The majority also [suggests] that it would be inconsistent with the notion of "national sovereignty" for the States or the people of the States to have any reserved powers over the selection of Members of Congress. . . .

[But from] the framing to the present [the] selection of the Representatives and Senators from each State has been left entirely to the people of that State or to their state legislature. See Art. I, §2, cl. 1 (providing that members of the House of Representatives are chosen "by the People of the several States"); Art. I, §3, cl. 1 (originally providing that the Senators from each State are "chosen by the Legislature thereof"); Amdt. 17 (amending §3 to provide that the Senators from each State are "elected by the people thereof"). [The] selection of representatives in Congress is indisputably an act of the people of each State, not some abstract people of the Nation as a whole.

[The] Constitution does not call for Members of Congress to be elected by differentiated national citizenry; indeed, it does not recognize any mechanism at all (such as a national referendum) for action by the undifferentiated people of the Nation as a whole. Even at the level of national politics, then, there always remains a meaningful distinction between someone who is a citizen of the United States and of Georgia and someone who is a citizen of the United States and of Massachusetts. The Georgia citizen who is unaware of this distinction will have it pointed out to him as soon as he tries to vote in a Massachusetts congressional election.

[In] a final effort to deny that the people of the States enjoy "reserved" powers over the selection of their representatives in Congress, the majority suggests that the Constitution expressly delegates to the States certain powers over congressional elections. Such delegations of power, the majority argues, would be superfluous if the people of the States enjoyed reserved powers in this area. [But the] the Times, Places and Manner Clause of Article I, §4 [does] not delegate any authority to the States. Instead, it simply imposes a duty upon them. [Constitutional] provisions that impose affirmative duties on the States are hardly inconsistent with the notion of reserved powers. [If] the Clause did not exist at all, the States would still be able to prescribe the times, places, and manner of holding congressional elections; the deletion of the provision would simply deprive Congress of the power to override these state regulations.

[The] people of Arkansas do enjoy "reserved" powers over the selection of their representatives in Congress. Purporting to exercise those reserved powers, they have agreed among themselves that the candidates covered by §3 of Amendment 73—those whom they have already elected to three or more terms in the House of Representatives or to two or more terms in the Senate—should not be eligible to appear on the ballot for reelection, but should nonetheless be returned to Congress if enough voters are sufficiently enthusiastic about their candidacy to write in their names. Whatever one might think of the wisdom of this arrangement, we may not override the decision of the people of Arkansas unless something in the Federal Constitution deprives them of the power to enact such measures.

The majority settles on "the Qualifications Clauses" as the constitutional provisions that Amendment 73 violates. [I] do not read those provisions to impose any unstated prohibitions on the States. [The] Qualifications Clauses are merely straightforward recitations of the minimum eligibility requirements that the Framers thought it essential for every Member of Congress to meet. They restrict state power only in that they prevent the States from abolishing all eligibility requirements for membership in Congress. . . .

[On] their face [the] Qualifications Clauses do nothing to prohibit the people of a State from establishing additional eligibility requirements for their own representatives. . . . [Because] Congress wields power over all the States, the people of each State need some guarantee that the legislators elected by the people of other States will meet minimum standards of competence. The Qualifications Clauses provide that guarantee: they list the requirements that the Framers considered essential to protect the competence of the National Legislature. [If] the people of a State decide that they would like their representatives to possess additional qualifications, however, they have done nothing to frustrate the policy behind the Qualifications Clauses. Anyone who possesses all of the constitutional qualifications, plus some qualifications required by state law, still has all of the federal qualifications. Accordingly, the fact that the Constitution specifies certain qualifications that the Framers deemed necessary to protect the competence of the National Legislature does not imply that it strips the people of the individual States of the power to protect their own interests by adding other requirements for their own representatives.

The people of other States could legitimately complain if the people of Arkansas decide, in a particular election, to send a 6-year-old to Congress. But the Constitution gives the people of other States no basis to complain if the people of Arkansas elect a freshman representative in preference to a long-term incumbent. That being the case, it is hard to see why the rights of the people of other States have been violated when the people of Arkansas decide to enact a more general disqualification of long-term incumbents.

[Although] the Qualifications Clauses neither state nor imply the prohibition that it finds in them, the majority infers from the Framers' "democratic principles" that the Clauses must have been generally understood to preclude the people of the States and their state legislatures from prescribing any additional qualifications for their representatives in Congress. But the majority's evidence on this point establishes only two more modest propositions: (1) the Framers did not want the Federal Constitution itself to impose a broad set of disqualifications for congressional office; and (2) the Framers did not want the Federal Congress to be able to supplement the few disqualifications that the Constitution does set forth. The logical conclusion is simply that the Framers did not want the people of the States and their state legislatures to be constrained by too many qualifications imposed at the national level. The evidence does not support the majority's more sweeping conclusion that the Framers intended to bar the people of the States and their state legislatures from adopting additional eligibility requirements to help narrow their own choices.

I agree with the majority that Congress has no power to prescribe qualifications for its own Members. This fact, however, does not show that the Qualifications Clauses contain a hidden exclusivity provision. The reason for Congress'[s] incapacity is not that the Qualifications Clauses deprive Congress of the authority to set qualifications, but rather that nothing in the Constitution grants Congress this power. In the absence of such a grant, Congress may not act.

[Justice Thomas then examined in great detail a wide range of historical practices in the early republic that supported his claim that states actually imposed additional qualifications for election to Congress and that Congress acquiesced in those practices.]

[Today's] decision also means that no State may disqualify congressional candidates whom a court has found to be mentally incompetent [as does Florida], who are currently in prison [as does Illinois], or who have past vote-fraud convictions [as does Georgia]. Likewise, after today's decision, the people of each State must leave open the possibility that they will trust someone with their vote in Congress even though they do not trust him with a vote in the election for Congress. See, e.g., [Rhode Island's restriction of candidacy to people "qualified to vote"].

[Today's] decision reads the Qualifications Clauses to impose substantial implicit prohibitions on the States and the people of the States. [I] would read the Qualifications Clauses to do no more than what they say. I respectfully dissent.

NOTE

Which "Default" Rule? Of course, the federal government possesses only delegated powers and the states possess all residual powers, except to the extent that the Constitution prohibits them. The position taken by Marshall in *McCulloch* and Stevens in *Thornton* is essentially structural—a ban on state authority is implied from the structure of the Constitution. The position taken by Thomas in *Thornton* is essentially textual: Unless the Constitution gives a power to the federal government, or bars its exercise by the states, it belongs to the states. As you study the remainder of this chapter and Chapter 4, consider the implications of this debate. Does Thomas's position imply a restrictive view of the scope of the enumerated powers of the federal government? Chapter 4 deals with judicially implied limits on state power to regulate interstate commerce in the absence of federal exercise of the commerce power. Does the Thomas position deny any basis for imposing such judicially implied limits on state power?

B. COMMERCE

Although we often speak of the "commerce power," the Constitution does not give Congress power to regulate all commerce. Instead, in Article I, section 8, clause 3, it confers upon Congress power to regulate three different types of commerce: "Commerce with foreign Nations, [commerce] among the several States, and [commerce] with the Indian Tribes." The scope of foreign commerce is very broad, including "transactions which either immediately, or at some stage of their progress, must be extraterritorial." Veazie v. Moor, 55 U.S. 568, 573 (1852). The power to regulate commerce with Indian tribes has been substantially augmented by judicial decisions expanding other sources of federal authority over Indians. See, e.g., United States v. Kagama, 118 U.S. 375 (1886), in which the Court concluded that the federal government had an inherent and implied power to govern Indian affairs.

The interstate commerce power is of central importance to the federal government. It is the source of authority for a great many federal statutes. In this section we will consider the scope of that authority. Our particular focus will be on determining two things: (1) How deferential are the courts to congressional judgments of the scope of that power? (2) What standard of review do the courts employ in reviewing congressional actions? The answers to these questions will describe the constitutional law on this subject, but you should also think about what the Court *should* do, and formulate reasons to support your conclusions.

1. Origins, Development, and the New Deal "Revolution"

Gibbons v. Ogden
22 U.S. 1 (1824)

[In order to stimulate the development of the steamboat, New York granted to Livingston and Fulton the exclusive right to operate steamboats in New York waters. Livingston and Fulton licensed Ogden to operate a steamboat between New York and New Jersey. Gibbons, Ogden's former partner, obtained a license under a 1793 federal law that permitted him to operate his steamboat in the "coasting trade," and thus to compete with Ogden. At Ogden's request, the New York courts enjoined Gibbons from further operation of his steamboat in New York waters. Gibbons appealed to the Supreme Court, arguing that Congress had the power to enact the 1793 law regulating vessels in the coasting trade, and that the federal law preempted the contrary New York monopoly law due to the supremacy clause (Art. VI, cl. 2).]

CHIEF JUSTICE MARSHALL delivered the opinion of the Court:

[Gibbons] contends that [the New York injunction] is erroneous, because the [New York] laws which purport to give the exclusive privilege it sustains, are repugnant to . . . that clause in the constitution which authorizes Congress to regulate commerce. . . . The words are, "Congress shall have power to regulate commerce with foreign nations, and among the several States, and with the Indian tribes." The subject to be regulated is commerce. . . . [To] ascertain the extent of the power, it becomes necessary to settle the meaning of the word. The counsel for [Ogden] would limit it to traffic, to buying and selling, or the interchange of commodities, and do not admit that it comprehends navigation. . . . Commerce, undoubtedly, is traffic, but it is something more: it is intercourse. It describes the commercial intercourse between nations, and parts of nations, in all its branches, and is regulated by prescribing rules for carrying on that intercourse. The mind can scarcely conceive a system for regulating commerce between nations, which shall exclude all laws concerning navigation, which shall be silent on the admission of the vessels of the one nation into the ports of the other, and be confined to prescribing rules for the conduct of individuals, in the actual employment of buying and selling, or of barter.

If commerce does not include navigation, the government of the Union has no direct power over that subject. . . . Yet this power has been exercised from the commencement of the government, has been exercised with the consent of all, and has been understood by all to be a commercial regulation. All America understands, and has uniformly understood, the word "commerce," to comprehend navigation. It was so understood, and must have been so understood, when the constitution was framed. The power over commerce, including navigation, was one of the primary objects for which the people of America adopted their government, and must have been contemplated in forming it. The convention must have used the word in that sense, because all have understood it in that sense; and the attempt to restrict it comes too late. . . .

The subject to which the power is next applied, is to commerce "among the several States." The word "among" means intermingled with. A thing which is among others, is intermingled with them. Commerce among the States, cannot stop at the external boundary line of each State, but may be introduced into the interior. It is not intended to say that these words comprehend that commerce, which is completely internal, which is carried on between man and man in a State, or between different parts of the same State, and which does not extend to or affect other States. Such a power would be inconvenient, and is certainly unnecessary.

Comprehensive as the word "among" is, it may very properly be restricted to that commerce which concerns more States than one. The phrase is not one which would probably have been selected to indicate the completely interior traffic of a State, because it is not an apt phrase for that purpose; and the enumeration of the particular classes of commerce, to which the power was to be extended, would not have been made, had the intention been to extend the power to every description. The enumeration presupposes something not enumerated; and that something, if we regard the language or the subject of the sentence, must be the exclusively internal commerce of a State. The genius and character of the whole government seem to be, that its action is to be applied to all the external concerns of the nation, and to those internal concerns which affect the States generally; but not to those which are completely within a particular State, which do not affect other States, and with which it is not necessary to interfere, for the purpose of executing some of the general powers of the government. The completely internal commerce of a State, then, may be considered as reserved for the State itself. . . .

We are now arrived at the inquiry—What is this power? It is the power to regulate; that is, to prescribe the rule by which commerce is to be governed. This power, like all others vested in Congress, is complete in itself, may be exercised to its utmost extent, and acknowledges no limitations, other than are prescribed in the constitution. . . . If, as has always been understood, the sovereignty of Congress, though limited to specified objects, is plenary as to those objects, the power over commerce with foreign nations, and among the several States, is vested in Congress as absolutely as it would be in a single government, having in its constitution the same restrictions on the exercise of the power as are found in the constitution of the United States. The wisdom and the discretion of Congress, their identity with the people, and the influence which their constituents possess at elections, are, in this, as in many other instances, as that, for example, of declaring war, the sole restraints on which they have relied, to secure them from its abuse. They are the restraints on which the people must often rely solely, in all representative governments. . . .

But it has been urged . . . that, although the power of Congress to regulate commerce with foreign nations, and among the several States, be co-extensive with the subject itself, and have no other limits than are prescribed in the constitution, yet the States may severally exercise the same power, within their respective jurisdictions. . . . [Gibbons] contends that full power to regulate a particular subject, implies the whole power, and leaves no residuum; that a grant of the whole is incompatible with the existence of a right in another to any part of it. . . .

[The question of] whether this power is still in the States, [or] is surrendered by the mere grant to Congress, or is retained until Congress shall exercise the power, [may be dismissed] because it has been exercised, and the regulations which Congress deemed it proper to make, are now in full operation. The sole question is, can a State regulate commerce with foreign nations and among the States, while Congress is regulating it? . . . It has been contended by the counsel for the appellant, that, as the word "to regulate" implies in its nature, full power over the thing to be regulated, it excludes, necessarily, the action of all others that would perform the same operation on the same thing. That regulation is designed for the entire result, applying to those parts which remain as they were, as well as to those which are altered. It produces a uniform whole, which is as much disturbed and deranged by changing what the regulating power designs to leave untouched, as that on which it has operated. There is great force in this argument, and the Court is not satisfied that it has been refuted.

[But when] States . . . enact laws [that are] contrary to an act of Congress passed in pursuance of the constitution, the Court will enter upon the inquiry, whether the laws of New-York, as expounded by the highest tribunal of that State, have . . . come into collision with an act of Congress, and deprived a citizen of a right to which that act entitles him. Should this collision exist, it will be immaterial whether those laws were passed in virtue of a concurrent power "to regulate commerce with foreign nations and among the several States," or, in virtue of a power to regulate their domestic trade and police. In one case and the other, the acts of New-York must yield to the law of Congress; and the decision sustaining the privilege they confer, against a right given by a law of the Union, must be erroneous. . . . To the Court it seems very clear, that the whole act on the subject of the coasting trade . . . implies, unequivocally, an authority to licensed vessels to carry on the coasting trade. . . . The coasting trade is a term well understood. The law has defined it; and all know its meaning perfectly. The act describes, with great minuteness, the various operations of a vessel engaged in it; and it cannot, we think, be doubted, that a voyage from New-Jersey to New-York, is one of those operations. . . . [The] act of a State inhibiting the use of . . . any vessel having a license under the act of Congress, comes, we think, in direct collision with that act. [Reversed.]

NOTES

1. From *Gibbons* to the New Deal. Much of the Court's nineteenth-century involvement with the commerce clause centered on the knotty problem of whether the clause implied some limits on state power to regulate interstate commerce and, if so, what those limits might be. That question—the scope of the dormant, or negative, commerce clause—is explored in Chapter 4. With expansion of federal regulation of the national economy in the late nineteenth century the Court began to consider challenges to the scope of the affirmative powers of Congress to regulate interstate commerce. The Court employed a variety of approaches.

a. Categorization. In United States v. E.C. Knight Co., 156 U.S. 1 (1895), the Court ruled that the Sherman Act's prohibition of restraints on "trade or commerce among the several states" did not apply to a manufacturing monopoly. Although

> the power to control the manufacture of a given thing involves . . . the control of its disposition, . . . this is a secondary and not the primary [effect]; and although the exercise of that power may result in bringing the operation of commerce into play, it does not control it, and affects it only incidentally and indirectly. Commerce succeeds to manufacture, and is not a part of it.

In Standard Oil Co. of New Jersey v. United States, 221 U.S. 1 (1911), the Court disavowed *E.C. Knight*'s reliance on the distinction between manufacturing and commerce, declaring that approach "unsound." However, the Court continued to focus on the "directness" of the connection between the activity regulated by Congress and interstate commerce.

b. Direct and indirect effects. Along with the categorization approach, the Court focused on whether the activity regulated, if not part of interstate commerce, "directly affected" interstate commerce. Perhaps the apex of this approach was Carter v. Carter Coal Co., 298 U.S. 238 (1936). The Bituminous Coal Conservation Act authorized coal producers and coal miners to establish a code setting maximum hours and minimum wages for coal miners. A tax was imposed on all producers who failed to abide by the code. *Carter* was a shareholder's suit to restrain the company from complying with the code because it was allegedly beyond Congress's power to authorize. The Supreme Court agreed, striking down the Act. Writing for a majority, Justice George Sutherland noted that

> the powers which the [federal] government may exercise are only those specifically enumerated in the Constitution, and such implied powers as are necessary and proper to carry into effect the enumerated powers. Whether the end sought to be attained by an act of Congress is legitimate is wholly a matter of constitutional power and not at all of legislative discretion. [While] the powers are rigidly limited to the enumeration of the Constitution, the means which may be employed to carry the powers into effect are not restricted, save that they must be appropriate, plainly adapted to the end, and not prohibited by, but consistent with, the letter and spirit of the Constitution. Thus, it may be said that to a constitutional end many ways are open; but to an end not within the terms of the Constitution, all ways are closed. The proposition, often advanced and as often discredited, that the power of the federal government inherently extends to purposes affecting the Nation as a whole with which the states severally [cannot] adequately deal, and the related notion that Congress, entirely apart from

those powers delegated by the Constitution, may enact laws to promote the general welfare, have never been accepted but always definitely rejected by this court. [Mining] brings the subject-matter of commerce into existence. Commerce disposes of it. [The] effect of the labor provisions of the [Act] primarily falls upon production and not upon commerce. [Production] is a purely local activity. [That] the production of every commodity intended for interstate sale and transportation has some effect on interstate commerce may freely [be] granted; and we are brought to the final and decisive inquiry, whether here that effect is direct [or] indirect.

Whether the effect of a given activity [is] direct or indirect is not always easy to determine. The word "direct" implies that the activity or condition invoked or blamed shall operate proximately—not mediately, remotely, or collaterally—to produce the effect. It connotes the absence of an efficient intervening agency or condition. And the extent of the effect bears no logical relation to its character. The distinction between a direct and an indirect effect turns, not upon the magnitude of either the cause or the effect, but entirely upon the manner in which the effect has been brought about. [The] matter of degree has no bearing upon the question here, since that question is not—What is the *extent* of the local activity or condition, or the *extent* of the effect produced upon interstate commerce? but—What is the *relation* between the activity or condition and the effect?

Much stress is put upon the evils which come from the struggle between employers and employees over the matter of wages, working conditions, the right of collective bargaining, etc., and the resulting strikes, curtailment, and irregularity of production and effect on prices; and it is insisted that interstate commerce is greatly affected thereby. [The] conclusive answer is that the evils are all local evils over which the federal government has no legislative control. [Such] effect as they may have upon commerce, however extensive it may be, is secondary and indirect. An increase in the greatness of the effect adds to its importance. It does not alter its character.

Justices Cardozo, Brandeis, and Stone dissented, contending that the terms "'direct' and 'indirect' must not be read too narrowly [but require] suppleness of adaptation and flexibility of meaning. The [interstate commerce] power is as broad as the need that invokes it."

c. The protective principle. The essence of the protective principle is that *intrastate* commerce can be regulated when necessary to protect instrumentalities of interstate commerce. In Houston, East & West Texas Railway Co. v. United States (the *Shreveport Rate Case*), 234 U.S. 342 (1914), the Court upheld an Interstate Commerce Commission (ICC) order requiring the affected railroads to charge the same rate for interstate shipments as for intrastate shipments. Prior to the order Texas railroads charged less per mile for intrastate shipments than for interstate shipments. After concluding that this rate structure discriminated in favor of intrastate commerce and against interstate commerce, the ICC ordered the wholly intrastate rates increased to match the interstate rates. The railroads argued that Congress had no power to authorize the ICC to "control the intrastate charges of an interstate carrier."

The Court disagreed, with Justice (later, Chief Justice) Hughes explaining why:

> Interstate trade was not left to be destroyed or impeded by the rivalries of local government. The purpose was to . . . provide the necessary basis of national unity by insuring "uniformity of regulation against conflicting and discriminating state legislation." [Congressional] authority, extending to these interstate carriers as instruments of interstate commerce, necessarily embraces the right to control their operations in all matters having such a close and substantial relation to interstate traffic that the control is essential or appropriate to the security of that traffic, to the efficiency of the interstate service, and to the maintenance of conditions under which interstate commerce may be conducted upon fair terms and without molestation or hindrance. As it is competent for Congress to legislate to these ends, unquestionably it may seek their attainment by requiring that the agencies of interstate commerce shall not be used in such manner as to cripple, retard, or destroy it. The fact that carriers are instruments of intrastate commerce, as well as of interstate commerce, does not derogate from the complete and paramount authority of Congress over the latter, or preclude the Federal power from being exerted to prevent the intrastate operations of such carriers from being made a means of injury to that which has been confided to Federal care. Wherever the interstate and intrastate transactions of carriers are so related that the government of the one involves the control of the other, it is Congress, and not the state, that is entitled to prescribe the final and dominant rule, for otherwise Congress would be denied the exercise of its constitutional authority, and the state, and not the nation, would be supreme within the national field. [Congress], in the exercise of its paramount power, may prevent the common instrumentalities of interstate and intrastate commercial intercourse from being used in their intrastate operations to the injury of interstate commerce. This is not to say that Congress possesses the authority to regulate the internal commerce of a state . . . but that it does possess the power to foster and protect interstate commerce, and to take all measures necessary or appropriate to that end, although intrastate transactions of interstate carriers may thereby be controlled.

The *Shreveport Rate Case* was but one of a series of cases employing this principle to permit federal regulation of intrastate aspects of the instrumentalities of interstate commerce. In Southern Railway Co. v. United States, 222 U.S. 20 (1911), the Court sustained the validity of the Federal Safety Appliance Act, which required all rail cars "used on any railroad engaged in interstate commerce" to be equipped with certain safety features. The Court upheld application of the Act to railcars used exclusively for intrastate commerce because the railway employing them was "a highway of interstate commerce."

d. Metaphorical streams of commerce. In Swift & Co. v. United States, 196 U.S. 375 (1905), the Court upheld application of the Sherman Act's price-fixing provisions to local meat dealers. Justice Holmes, writing for the Court, explained that

> [w]hen cattle are sent for sale from [one] State [to another], with only the interruption necessary to find a purchaser at the stockyard, and when this is a typical,

constantly recurring course, the current thus existing is a current of commerce among the States, and the purchase of the cattle is a part and incident of such commerce.

In Stafford v. Wallace, 258 U.S. 495 (1922), the Court upheld regulations governing sales transactions in stockyards after livestock had arrived in interstate shipments and before they left in interstate shipments. Chief Justice Taft declared for the Court that the "stockyards are but a throat through which the current flows, and the transactions which occur therein are only incident to this current from the West to the East, and from one State to another." The regulated practices and transactions were "essential" to this current. When does the stream of commerce begin and when does it end?

e. Regulating interstate movement.   While Congress may regulate the interstate movement of articles of commerce, this technique became controversial when Congress employed it to regulate activities unrelated to interstate commerce. Champion v. Ames (*The Lottery Case*), 188 U.S. 321 (1903), is a classic example. Federal law prohibited the interstate shipment of lottery tickets. Champion was indicted for shipping a box of Paraguayan lottery tickets from Texas to California and sought dismissal of the indictment on the ground of the Act's unconstitutionality. The Court, 5-4, upheld the law.

Justice Harlan, for the majority, concluded (1) that lottery tickets were articles of commerce and (2) that the power to regulate interstate commerce includes the power to prohibit interstate commerce. Harlan invoked an earlier Supreme Court decision for the proposition that "the suppression of nuisances injurious to public health or morality is among the most important duties of government," and continued:

[As] a state may, for the purpose of guarding the morals of its own people, forbid all sales of lottery tickets within its limits, so Congress, for the purpose of guarding the people of the United States against the "widespread pestilence of lotteries" and to protect the commerce which concerns all the states, may prohibit the carrying of lottery tickets from one state to another. In legislating upon the subject of the traffic in lottery tickets, as carried on through interstate commerce, Congress only supplemented the action of those states—perhaps all of them—which, for the protection of the public morals, prohibit the drawing of lotteries, as well as the sale or circulation of lottery tickets, within their respective limits. It said, in effect, that it would not permit the declared policy of the states, which sought to protect their people against the mischiefs of the lottery business, to be overthrown or disregarded by the agency of interstate commerce. We should hesitate long before adjudging that an evil of such appalling character, carried on through interstate commerce, cannot be met and crushed by the only power competent to that end.

It is said [that] if, in order to suppress lotteries carried on through interstate commerce, Congress may exclude lottery tickets from such commerce, that principle leads necessarily to the conclusion that Congress may arbitrarily exclude from commerce among the states any article, commodity, or thing, of whatever kind or nature, or however useful or valuable, which it may choose, no matter with what motive, to declare shall not be carried from one state to another. It will be time enough to consider the constitutionality of such legislation when we must do so. [The] possible abuse of a power is not an argument against its existence. [If] what is done by Congress is manifestly in excess of the powers granted to it, then upon the courts will rest the duty of adjudging that its action is neither legal nor binding upon the people. But if what Congress does is within the limits of its power, and is simply unwise or injurious, the remedy is that suggested by Chief Justice Marshall in [*Gibbons*] when he said [that "the wisdom and the discretion of Congress, their identity with the people, and the influence which their constituents possess at elections" are the "sole restraints" upon congressional abuse.]

Chief Justice Fuller, joined by Justices Brewer, Shiras, and Peckham, dissented:

[An] act prohibiting the carriage of lottery matter would be necessary and proper to the execution of a power to suppress lotteries; but that power belongs to the states and not to Congress. To hold that Congress has general police power would be to hold that it may accomplish objects not intrusted to the general government. . . . [This] act cannot be brought within the power to regulate commerce among the several states, unless lottery tickets are articles of commerce and, therefore, when carried across state lines, of interstate commerce; or unless the power to regulate interstate commerce includes the absolute and exclusive power to prohibit the transportation of anything or anybody from one state to another. . . .

[A] lottery ticket is not an article of commerce, [so] how can it become so when placed in an envelope . . . and transported by an express company? To say that the mere carrying of an article which is not an article of commerce [turns it into] such the moment it is to be transported from one state to another is to transform a non-commercial article into a commercial one simply because it is transported. [It] would be to say that everything is an article of commerce the moment it is taken to be transported from place to place, and of interstate commerce if from state to state. An invitation to dine, or to take a drive, or a note of introduction, all become articles of commerce under the ruling in this case, by being deposited with an express company for transportation. This . . . is a long step in the direction of wiping out all traces of state lines, and the creation of a centralized government.

After Champion v. Ames, Congress enacted a variety of laws to protect public health or morals by prohibiting the interstate movement of goods or persons. For example, Congress banned the interstate shipment of meat that had not been inspected by federal health inspectors. The Pure Food and Drugs Act of 1906 prohibited the interstate movement of food or drugs that did not comply with the Act's standards. In Hipolite Egg Co. v. United States, 220 U.S. 45 (1911), the Court invoked the means enabling power of the "necessary and proper" clause to upheld seizure under that Act of a quantity of noncomplying preserved eggs.

[A]rticles which are outlaws of commerce may be seized wherever found. [This] is certainly appropriate to the right to bar them from interstate commerce, and completes its purpose, which is not to prevent merely the physical movement of adulterated articles, but . . . to prevent trade in them between the States by denying to them the facilities of interstate commerce. [An] appropriate means to that [legitimate] end [is] the seizure and condemnation of the articles at their point of destination.

See also Hoke v. United States, 227 U.S. 308 (1913), and Caminetti v. United States, 242 U.S. 470 (1917). *Hoke* sustained the validity of the Mann Act, which prohibited the interstate transportation of women in interstate commerce for immoral purposes, as applied to commercial prostitution; *Caminetti* upheld the Act as applied to an adulterous tryst crossing state lines.

When Congress enacted the Child Labor Act of 1916, which banned the interstate shipment of goods produced by child laborers, it had little doubt that it was authorized by the commerce clause to do so, but in Hammer v. Dagenhart, 247 U.S. 251 (1918), the Court (5-4) voided the Act. Justice Day wrote for the majority:

[I]t is insisted that adjudged cases in this court establish the doctrine that the power to regulate [interstate commerce] given to Congress incidentally includes the authority to prohibit the movement of ordinary commodities. [The] cases demonstrate the contrary. They rest upon the character of the particular subjects dealt with. [In] each of [*Champion, Hipolite Egg, Hoke,* and *Caminetti*] the use of interstate transportation was necessary to the accomplishment of harmful results. [This] element is wanting in the present case. [The] act in its effect does not regulate transportation among the states, but aims to standardize the ages at which children may be employed in mining and manufacturing within the states. The goods shipped are of themselves harmless. [When] offered for shipment, and before transportation begins, the labor of their production is over, and the mere fact that they were intended for interstate commerce transportation does not make their production subject to federal control under the commerce power. [Over] interstate transportation, or its incidents, the regulatory power of Congress is ample, but the production of articles, intended for interstate commerce, is a matter of local regulation. [If] it were otherwise, all manufacture intended for interstate shipment would be brought under federal control to the practical exclusion of the authority of the States.

[It] is further contended that the authority of Congress may be exerted to control interstate commerce in the shipment of child-made goods because of the effect of the circulation of such goods in other States where the evil of this class of labor has been recognized by local legislation, and the right to thus employ child labor has been more rigorously restrained than in the State of production. In other words, that the unfair competition, thus engendered, may be controlled by closing the channels of interstate commerce to manufacturers in those States where the local laws do not meet what Congress deems to be the more just standard of other States. There is no power vested in Congress to require the States to exercise their police power so as to prevent possible unfair competition. Many causes may cooperate to give one State, by reason of local laws or conditions, an economic advantage over others. The Commerce Clause was not intended to give to Congress a general authority to equalize such conditions.

[The] maintenance of the authority of the States over matters purely local is as essential to the preservation of our institutions as is the conservation of the supremacy of the federal power in all matters entrusted to the nation by the federal Constitution. In interpreting the Constitution it must never be forgotten that the nation is made up of States to which are entrusted the powers of local government. [To] sustain this statute [would] sanction an invasion by the federal power of the control of a matter purely local in its character, and over which no authority has been delegated to Congress in conferring the power to regulate commerce among the States. [In] our view the necessary effect of this act [is] to regulate the hours of labor of children in factories and mines within the States, a purely state authority. [The act] not only transcends the authority delegated to Congress over commerce but also exerts a power as to a purely local matter to which the federal authority does not extend. [If] Congress can thus regulate matters entrusted to local authority by prohibition of the movement of commodities in interstate commerce, all freedom of commerce will be at an end, and the power of the States over local matters may be eliminated, and thus our system of government be practically destroyed.

Justice Holmes, joined by Justices McKenna, Brandeis, and Clarke, dissented:

[I]f an act is within the powers specifically conferred upon Congress, it seems to me that it is not made any less constitutional because of the indirect effects that it may have, however obvious it may be that it will have those effects. [The] first step in my argument is to make plain what no one is likely to dispute—that the statute in question is within the power expressly given to Congress if considered only as to its immediate effects and that if invalid it is so only upon some collateral ground. The statute confines itself to prohibiting the carriage of certain goods in interstate or foreign commerce. Congress is given power to regulate such commerce in unqualified terms. [The] power to regulate [includes] the power to prohibit. [Champion v. Ames.] The question then is narrowed to whether the exercise of its otherwise constitutional power by Congress can be pronounced unconstitutional because of its possible reaction upon the conduct of the States in a matter upon which I have admitted that they are free from direct control. [I] should have thought that the most conspicuous decisions of this Court had made it clear that the power to regulate commerce [could] not be cut down or qualified by the fact that it might interfere with the carrying out of the domestic policy of any State. . . .

The Act does not meddle with anything belonging to the States. They may regulate their internal affairs and their domestic commerce as they like. But when they seek to send their products across the State line they are no longer within their rights. If there were no Constitution and no Congress their power to cross the line would depend upon their neighbors. Under the Constitution such commerce belongs not to the States but to Congress to regulate. It may carry out its views of public policy whatever indirect effect they may have upon the activities of the States. Instead of being encountered by a prohibitive tariff at her boundaries the State encounters the public policy of the United States which it is for Congress to express. The public policy of the United States is shaped with a view to the benefit of the nation as a whole. The national welfare as understood by Congress may require a different attitude within its sphere from that of some self-seeking State. It seems to me entirely constitutional for Congress to enforce its understanding by all the means at its command.

In United States v. Darby, 312 U.S. 100 (1941), the Court overturned *Dagenhart*. The federal Fair Labor Standards Act (FLSA) specified maximum hours and minimum wages for workers engaged in producing goods for interstate commerce and prohibited the interstate shipment of goods produced other than in conformity with the FLSA's wage and hour provisions. In an opinion by Justice Stone, the Court upheld the FLSA.

[While] manufacture is not of itself interstate commerce the shipment of manufactured goods interstate is such commerce and the prohibition of such shipment by Congress is indubitably a regulation of the commerce. . . . But it is said that [while] the present prohibition . . . is nominally a regulation of the commerce its motive or purpose is regulation of wages and hours of persons engaged in manufacture, the control of which has been reserved to the states. . . . The motive and purpose of the present regulation are plainly to make effective the Congressional conception of public policy that interstate commerce should not be made the instrument of competition in the distribution of goods produced under substandard labor conditions, which competition is injurious to the commerce and to the states from and to which the commerce flows. The motive and purpose of a regulation of interstate commerce are matters for the legislative judgment upon the exercise of which the Constitution places no restriction and over which the courts are given no control. Whatever their motive and purpose, regulations of commerce which do not infringe some constitutional prohibition are within the plenary power conferred on Congress by the Commerce Clause. Subject only to that limitation [we] conclude that the prohibition of the shipment interstate of goods produced under the forbidden substandard labor conditions is within the constitutional authority of Congress. . . . [*Dagenhart*] was a departure from the principles which have prevailed in the interpretation of the commerce clause both before and since the [decision]. It should be and now is overruled.

[The] validity of the [minimum wage/maximum hour provisions] turns on the question whether the employment, under other than the prescribed labor standards, of employees engaged in the production of goods for interstate commerce is so related to the commerce and so affects it as to be within the reach of the power of Congress to regulate it. . . . Congress may [by] appropriate legislation regulate intrastate activities where they have a substantial effect on interstate commerce [or] the exercise of the Congressional power over it. [Congress], having by the present Act adopted the policy of excluding from interstate commerce all goods produced for the commerce which do not conform to the specified labor standards, . . . may choose the means reasonably adapted to the attainment of permitted end, even though they involve control of intrastate activities. . . . We think also that [the wage and hour provisions are] sustainable independently of [the prohibition on] shipment or transportation of the proscribed goods. [The] evils aimed at by the Act are the spread of substandard labor conditions through the use of the facilities of interstate commerce for competition by the goods so produced with those produced under the prescribed or better labor conditions; and the consequent dislocation of the commerce itself caused by the impairment or destruction of local businesses by competition made effective through interstate commerce. The Act is thus directed at the suppression of a method or kind of competition in interstate commerce which it has in effect condemned as [unfair]. The means adopted by [the FLSA] for the protection of interstate commerce[—the wage and hour provisions—are] so related to [interstate] commerce and so affects it as to be within the reach of the commerce power. . . . [Our] conclusion is unaffected by the Tenth Amendment which provides: "The powers not delegated to the United States by the Constitution, nor prohibited by it to the States, are reserved to the States respectively, or to the people." The amendment states but a truism that all is retained which has not been surrendered. . . .

By overruling Hammer v. Dagenhart, the Court freed the commerce-prohibiting technique to serve any purpose desired by Congress. Note that in the portion of the opinion dealing with the validity of the wage and hour requirements the Court relied on two alternative rationales. One was the conclusion that the conditions of local employment had a substantial effect on interstate commerce. The alternative was to treat the wage and hour provisions as *means* reasonably related to the *end* of banning the interstate shipment of goods manufactured under nonconforming labor conditions. This gambit does *not* rely on an adequate connection between the regulated activity and interstate commerce; rather, it relies on a connection between the regulated activity and a different regulation of interstate commerce (the shipment ban). Because Congress can ban the interstate shipment of goods for any reason it chooses, may it then regulate wholly local activities that have no substantial effect on interstate commerce because that regulation is reasonably calculated to effectuate the interstate shipment ban?

2. The New Deal "Revolution." Beginning in 1933, the Franklin Roosevelt Administration began to address the nation's economic depression by a variety of laws regulating aspects of economic behavior that had largely been unregulated. Some of those measures, such as the act at issue in *Carter Coal*, were struck down. But by 1937 the Court's view of the scope of the interstate commerce power had changed, if not its apparent doctrinal tests for evaluating the limits of that power.

The source of this changed understanding is the subject of much debate. Some allege that it was the product of President Roosevelt's proposed bill to permit him to enlarge the Court to 15 members and appoint six new justices. After his electoral landslide of 1936, and armed with large Democratic majorities in Congress, Roosevelt proposed that one new justice be appointed for each sitting justice over the age of 70 who failed to retire, up to a maximum of 15 justices. The plan was abandoned after Congress and the nation turned against it. Most people saw the "Court-packing" plan for what it was—a device to overturn the Court's rulings that struck down key parts of the New Deal legislative program as unconstitutional.

In Railroad Retirement Board v. Alton, 295 U.S. 330 (1935), for example, the Court had voided a federal law creating a pension program for railroad workers as "not in purpose or effect a regulation of interstate commerce," but "really and essentially related solely to the social welfare of the worker, and therefore remote from any regulation of commerce." In A.L.A. Schechter Poultry Corp. v. United States, 295 U.S. 495 (1935), the Court had struck down the National Industrial Recovery Act, an elaborate program that enabled the President to promulgate "codes of fair conduct" binding on all businesses within an industry. The codes fixed minimum wages and prices and maximum hours, prohibited some business practices, and ensured collective bargaining. The Court concluded that the Act both unconstitutionally delegated legislative power (see Chapter 5) and, as applied to the intrastate actions of a wholesale poultry dealer, lacked a sufficiently direct connection to interstate commerce. By reversing itself, it was said that the Court capitulated to the institutional threat posed by Roosevelt's Court-packing proposal. However, another explanation is that the government began to introduce evidence demonstrating a strong relationship between the activity Congress sought to regulate and interstate commerce.

≡ *NLRB v. Jones & Laughlin Steel Corp.*
≡ *301 U.S. 1 (1937)*

[The Court upheld the National Labor Relations Act, which (among other things) defined the discharge of employees for union activities as an "unfair labor practice" and prohibited unfair labor practices "affecting [interstate] commerce."]

CHIEF JUSTICE HUGHES delivered the opinion of the Court.

[The NLRB found that Jones & Laughlin, a Pennsylvania corporation with its headquarters in Pittsburgh,] is engaged in the business of manufacturing iron and steel in plants situated in Pittsburgh and nearby Aliquippa, Pa. It manufactures and distributes a widely diversified line of steel and pig iron, being the fourth largest producer of steel in the United States. With its subsidiaries—nineteen in number—it is a completely integrated enterprise, owning and operating ore, coal and limestone properties, lake and river transportation facilities and terminal railroads located at its manufacturing plants. It owns or controls mines in Michigan and Minnesota. It operates four ore steamships on the Great Lakes, used in the transportation of ore to its factories. It owns coal mines in Pennsylvania. It operates towboats and steam barges used in carrying coal to its factories. It owns limestone properties in various places in Pennsylvania and West Virginia. It owns the Monongahela connecting railroad which connects the plants of the Pittsburgh works and forms an interconnection with the Pennsylvania, New York Central and Baltimore & Ohio Railroad systems. It owns [another railroad] which connects the Aliquippa works with [the] New York Central system. Much of its product is shipped to its warehouses in Chicago, Detroit, Cincinnati and Memphis,—to the last two places by means of its own barges and transportation equipment. [In] New York and in New Orleans it operates structural steel fabricating shops in connection with the warehousing of semifinished materials sent from its works. Through one of its wholly-owned subsidiaries it owns, leases, and operates stores, warehouses, and yards for the distribution of equipment and supplies for drilling and operating oil and gas wells and for pipe lines, refineries and pumping stations. It has sales offices in twenty cities in the United States and a wholly-owned subsidiary which is devoted exclusively to distributing its product in Canada. Approximately 75 per cent. of its product is shipped out of Pennsylvania. . . .

To carry on the activities of the entire steel industry, 33,000 men mine ore, 44,000 men mine coal, 4,000 men quarry limestone, 16,000 men manufacture coke, 343,000 men manufacture steel, and 83,000 men transport its product. Respondent has about 10,000 employees in its Aliquippa plant, which is located in a community of about 30,000 persons. . . .

The act is challenged in its entirety as an attempt to regulate all industry, thus invading the reserved powers of the States over their local concerns. It is asserted that the [NLRA] is not a true regulation of such commerce or of matters which directly affect it, but on the contrary has the fundamental object of placing under the compulsory supervision of the federal government all industrial labor relations within the nation. [We] think it clear that the [NLRA] may be construed so as to operate within the sphere of constitutional authority. [Section 10(a) of the NLRA empowers the NLRB] "to prevent any person from engaging in any unfair labor practice . . . affecting commerce." The critical words [are] "affecting commerce." The act specifically defines the "commerce" to which it refers [to mean] "trade, traffic, commerce, transportation, or communication among the several States [or] between points in the same State but through any other State or [any] foreign country." [The] commerce [is] interstate and foreign commerce in the constitutional sense. The [NLRA] also defines the term "affecting commerce" [to mean] "in commerce, or burdening or obstructing commerce or the free flow of commerce, or having led or tending to lead to a labor dispute burdening or obstructing commerce or the free flow of commerce."

[The NLRA] purports to reach only what may be deemed to burden or obstruct that commerce and, thus qualified, it must be construed as contemplating the exercise of control within constitutional bounds. It is a familiar principle that acts which directly burden or obstruct interstate or foreign commerce, or its free flow, are within the reach of the congressional power. Acts having that effect are not rendered immune because they grow out of labor disputes. It is the effect upon commerce, not the source of the injury, which is the criterion. Whether or not particular action does affect commerce in such a close and intimate fashion as to be subject to federal control [is] left by the statute to be determined as individual cases arise. We are thus to inquire whether in the instant case the constitutional boundary has been passed.

[Jones & Laughlin] says that, whatever may be said of employees engaged in interstate commerce, the industrial relations and activities in the manufacturing department of [its] enterprise are not subject to federal regulation. The argument rests upon the proposition that manufacturing in itself is not commerce. The government [argues] that these activities constitute a "stream" or "flow" of commerce, of which the Aliquippa manufacturing plant is the focal point, and that industrial strife at that point would cripple the entire movement. [J&L] contends that [the] raw materials which are brought to the plant are delayed for long periods and, after being subjected to manufacturing processes "are changed substantially as to character, utility and value." [We] do not find it necessary to determine whether these features of defendant's business dispose of the asserted analogy to the "stream of commerce" cases. [Congressional] authority to protect interstate commerce from burdens and obstructions is not limited to transactions which can be deemed to be an essential part of a "flow" of interstate or foreign commerce. Burdens and obstructions may be due to injurious action springing from other sources. The fundamental principle is that the power to regulate commerce is the power to enact "all appropriate legislation" for its "protection or advancement"; to adopt measures "to promote its growth and insure its safety"; [and] "to foster, protect, control, and restrain." That power is plenary and may be exerted to protect interstate commerce "no matter what the source of the dangers which threaten it." Although activities may be intrastate in character when separately considered, if they have such a close and substantial relation to interstate commerce that their control is essential or appropriate to protect that commerce from burdens and obstructions, Congress cannot be denied the power to exercise that control. Undoubtedly the scope of this power must be considered in the light of our dual system of government and may not be extended so as to embrace effects upon interstate commerce so indirect and remote that to embrace [them] would effectually obliterate the distinction between what is national and what is local and create a completely centralized government. The question is necessarily one of degree. [That] intrastate activities, by reason of close and intimate relation to interstate commerce, may fall within federal control is demonstrated in the case of carriers who are engaged in both interstate and intrastate transportation. [*Shreveport Rate Case* and other protective power cases.] . . .

[The] fact that the employees here concerned were engaged in production is not determinative. The question remains as to the effect upon interstate commerce of the labor practice involved. [Work] stoppage [in J&L's] operations [would] have a most serious effect upon interstate commerce. [It] is idle to say that the effect would be indirect or remote. It is obvious that it would be immediate and might be catastrophic. We are asked to shut our eyes to the plainest facts of our national life and to deal with the question of direct and indirect effects in an intellectual vacuum. [When] industries organize themselves on a national scale, making their relation to interstate commerce the dominant factor in their activities, how can it be maintained that their industrial labor relations constitute a forbidden field into which Congress may not enter when it is necessary to protect interstate commerce from the paralyzing consequences of industrial war? We have often said that interstate commerce itself is a practical conception. It is equally true that interferences with that commerce must be appraised by a judgment that does not ignore actual experience.

JUSTICES MCREYNOLDS, VAN DEVANTER, SUTHERLAND, and BUTLER, dissenting.

Any effect on interstate commerce by the discharge of employees shown here would be indirect and remote in the highest degree. . . . The immediate effect in the factory may be to create discontent among all those employed and a strike may follow, which, in turn, may result in reducing production, which ultimately may reduce the volume of goods moving in interstate commerce. By this chain of indirect and progressively remote events we finally reach the evil with which it is said the legislation under consideration undertakes to deal. A more remote and indirect interference with interstate commerce or a more definite invasion of the powers reserved to the states is difficult, if not impossible, to imagine. [Whatever] effect any cause of [worker] discontent may ultimately have upon commerce is far too indirect to justify congressional regulation. Almost anything—marriage, birth, death—may in some fashion affect commerce. . . .

Congress has power by appropriate means, not prohibited by the Constitution, to prevent direct and material interference with the conduct of interstate [commerce]. But the interference struck at must be direct and material, not some mere possibility contingent on wholly uncertain events.

NOTES

1. What Changed?   Was *Jones & Laughlin* a great change in the application of doctrine, or in the doctrine itself? Did the majority determine the "directness" of the effect on interstate commerce of the regulated activity by looking at actual facts rather than some logical "proximate" link between the two?

2. The Function of the "Means-Enabling" Power.   Note that in *Jones & Laughlin* and prior cases there are always two questions: (1) Is the end of the regulation at issue within the scope of congressional power to regulate interstate commerce? and (2) Is the specific regulation—the means chosen by Congress—an appropriate way to accomplish Congress's legitimate regulatory objective? The Court is not always transparent about separating those two inquiries, but the answer must be yes to each in order for an ostensible regulation of interstate commerce to be valid.

≣ *Wickard v. Filburn*
≣ *317 U.S. 111 (1942)*

[The Court sustained the validity of the Agricultural Adjustment Act's penalty provisions as applied to Filburn, an Ohio farmer. Under the Act, farmers were given maximum quotas for wheat production. Filburn's 1941 quota was 223 bushels. He grew an extra 239 bushels. In prior years Filburn had used his wheat crop to feed his livestock, as a seedstock for the next crop, for flour for home use, and to sell. The record did not reveal Filburn's use of his 1941 crop. Filburn was penalized $117 for growing the excess wheat. He contested the penalty, claiming that its imposition was beyond the interstate commerce power. The Court ruled that the penalty was valid by creating the "aggregation" or "cumulative effects" principle.]

JUSTICE JACKSON delivered the opinion of the Court.

[This] Act extends federal regulation to production not intended in any part for [interstate] commerce but wholly for consumption on the farm. [Filburn says that] regulation of production and consumption of wheat [is] beyond the reach of Congressional power under the Commerce Clause, since they are local in character, and their effects upon interstate commerce are at most "indirect." In answer the Government argues that the statute regulates neither production nor consumption, but only marketing; and, in the alternative, that if the Act does go beyond the regulation of marketing it is sustainable as a "necessary and proper" implementation of the power of Congress over interstate commerce. [Questions] of the power of Congress are not to be decided by reference to any formula which would give controlling force to nomenclature such as "production" and "indirect" and foreclose consideration of the actual effects of the activity in question upon interstate commerce. . . .

[The Court has recognized] the relevance [of] economic effects in the application of the [commerce clause]. Once an economic measure of the reach of the [interstate commerce power] is accepted, questions of federal power cannot be decided simply by finding the activity in question to be "production" nor can consideration of its economic effects be foreclosed by calling them "indirect." [Even] if [Filburn's] activity be local and though it may not be regarded as commerce, it may still, whatever its nature, be reached by Congress if it exerts a substantial economic effect on interstate commerce and this irrespective of whether such effect is what might at some earlier time have been defined as "direct" or "indirect."

The parties have stipulated a summary of the economics of the wheat industry. Commerce among the states in wheat is large and important. [The] decline in the export trade has left a large surplus in production which in connection with an abnormally large supply of wheat and other grains in recent years caused congestion in a number of markets; tied up railroad cars; and caused elevators in some instances to turn away grains, and railroads to institute embargoes to prevent further congestion. [In] the absence of regulation the price of wheat in the United States would be much affected by world conditions. During 1941 producers who cooperated with the Agricultural Adjustment program received an average price on the farm of about $1.16 a bushel as compared with the world market price of 40 cents a bushel. [The] effect of consumption of homegrown wheat on interstate commerce is due to the fact that it constitutes the most variable factor in the disappearance of the wheat crop. Consumption on the farm where grown appears to vary in an amount greater than 20 per cent of average production. The maintenance by government regulation of a price for wheat undoubtedly can be accomplished as effectively by sustaining or increasing the demand as by limiting the supply. The effect of the statute before us is to restrict the amount which may be produced for market and the extent as well to which one may forestall resort to the market by producing to meet his own needs. That [Filburn's] own contribution to the demand for wheat may be trivial by itself is not enough to remove him from the scope of federal regulation where, as here, his contribution, taken together with that of many others similarly situated, is far from trivial.

[One] of the primary purposes of the Act [was] to increase the market price of wheat and to that end to limit the volume thereof that could affect the market. It can hardly be denied that a factor of such volume and variability as home-consumed wheat would have a substantial influence on price and market conditions. This may arise because being in marketable condition such wheat overhangs the market and if induced by rising prices tends to flow into the market and check price increases. But if we assume that it is never marketed, it supplies a need of the man who grew it which would otherwise be reflected by purchases in the open market. Home-grown wheat in this sense competes with wheat in commerce. The stimulation of commerce is a use of the regulatory function quite as definitely as prohibitions or restrictions thereon. This record leaves us in no doubt that Congress may properly have considered that wheat consumed on the farm where grown if wholly outside the scheme of regulation would have a substantial effect in defeating and obstructing its purpose to stimulate trade therein at increased prices. . . .

NOTES

1. The Limits of *Wickard*. In Perez v. United States, 402 U.S. 146 (1971), the Court restated the aggregation principle. Federal law prohibited extortionate credit transactions — the practice of lending money at usurious rates of interest and enforcing the illegal interest rate by resort to violence. The Court upheld the law, concluding that "[e]ven where extortionate credit transactions are purely intrastate in character, they nevertheless directly affect interstate and foreign commerce." Congress may use its commerce power to regulate a "*class of activities* [without] proof that the particular intrastate activity" has an effect on interstate commerce. So long as the regulated activity (considered as a class and taken as a whole) has a substantial effect on interstate commerce, and the affected person is "*a member of the class*" that is regulated, the regulation is a valid use of the interstate commerce power.

In Maryland v. Wirtz, 392 U.S. 183 (1968), the Court stated:

> Neither here nor in *Wickard* has the Court declared that Congress may use a relatively trivial impact on [interstate] commerce as an excuse for broad general regulation of state or private activities. The Court has said only that where a general regulatory statute bears a substantial relation to [interstate] commerce, the de minimis character of individual instances arising under that statute is of no consequence.

2. Queries. Does the *Wickard* principle mean that Congress may cast a very broad regulatory net to control as much behavior as possible—behavior that could not be reached by a very specific statute?

Suppose Congress enacts the Omnibus Pollution Control Act, which prohibits any person from committing any act that contributes in any degree to environmental degradation. This covers such a multitude of actions that the regulated class of activities surely has a substantial effect on interstate commerce. Included in the class would be the actions of a ten-year-old Girl Scout who kindles a tiny fire, emitting a wisp of smoke, by rubbing two sticks together. Does the aggregation principle apply, or must there be some proportionality between the broad class regulated by the statute and the actions included within the class? Note that in *Wickard* the statute regulated the growing of wheat and the included action at issue was wheat grown on the farm for home consumption. In *Perez*, the statute reached all "extortionate credit transactions," and the actions at issue were those of a strictly neighborhood loan shark. Should a proportionality principle limit the scope of *Wickard*? See Justice Thomas's concurrence in United States v. Lopez, infra. See also Nagle, The Commerce Clause Meets the Delhi Sands Flower-Loving Fly, 97 Mich. L. Rev. 174, 192-204 (1998).

3. Civil Rights and the Commerce Power. Title II of the 1964 Civil Rights Act is the federal law that prohibits racial discrimination by private persons in public accommodations. In Heart of Atlanta Motel v. United States, 379 U.S. 241 (1964), the Court upheld the law:

> [In] framing [Title II] Congress was [dealing] with what it considered a moral problem. But that fact does not detract from the overwhelming evidence of the disruptive effect that racial discrimination has had on commercial intercourse. It was this burden which empowered Congress to enact appropriate [legislation]. Congress was not restricted by the fact that the particular obstruction to interstate commerce with which it was dealing was also deemed a moral and social wrong. It is said that the operation of the motel here is of a purely local character. [The] power of Congress to promote interstate commerce also includes the power to regulate [local activities] which might have a substantial and harmful effect upon that commerce.

2. The "Counter-Revolution"

≣≣≣ *United States v. Lopez*
514 U.S. 549 (1995)

CHIEF JUSTICE REHNQUIST, for the Court.

In the Gun-Free School Zones Act of 1990, Congress made it a federal offense "for any individual knowingly to possess a firearm at a place that the individual knows, or has reasonable cause to believe, is a school zone." 18

U.S.C. §922(q)(1)(A). The Act neither regulates a commercial activity nor contains a requirement that the possession be connected in any way to inter-state commerce. We hold that the Act exceeds the authority of Congress "to regulate Commerce . . . among the several States."

[Lopez], who was then a 12th-grade student, arrived at Edison High School in San Antonio, Texas, carrying a concealed .38 caliber handgun and five bullets. [Lopez] admitted that he was carrying the weapon. He was arrested and charged under Texas law with firearm possession on school premises. The next day, the state charges were dismissed after federal agents charged [him] with violating the Gun-Free School Zones Act of 1990.[1] . . .

[Lopez was indicted, tried, convicted, and sentenced] to six months' imprisonment and two years' supervised release. On appeal, [Lopez] chal-lenged his conviction based on his claim that §922(q) exceeded Congress'[s] power to legislate under the Commerce Clause. The Court of Appeals for the Fifth Circuit agreed and reversed respondent's conviction. [We] now affirm.

We start with first principles. The Constitution creates a Federal Government of enumerated powers. See U.S. Const., Art. I, §8. As James Madison wrote, "the powers delegated by the proposed Constitution to the federal government are few and defined. Those which are to remain in the State governments are numerous and indefinite." The Federalist No. 45. This constitutionally mandated division of authority "was adopted by the Framers to ensure protection of our fundamental liberties." Gregory v. Ashcroft, 501 U.S. 452 (1991). "Just as the separation and independence of the coordinate branches of the Federal Government serves to prevent the accumulation of excessive power in any one branch, a healthy balance of power between the States and the Federal Government will reduce the risk of tyranny and abuse from either front." Ibid. . . .

Jones & Laughlin Steel, Darby, and *Wickard* ushered in an era of Commerce Clause jurisprudence that greatly expanded the previously defined authority of Congress under that Clause. In part, this was a recognition of the great changes that had occurred in the way business was carried on in this country. Enterprises that had once been local or at most regional in nature had become national in scope. But the doctrinal change also reflected a view that earlier Commerce Clause cases artificially had constrained the authority of Congress to regulate interstate commerce.

But even these modern-era precedents . . . confirm that this power is subject to outer limits. In *Jones & Laughlin Steel*, the Court warned that the scope of the interstate commerce power "must be considered in the light of our dual system of government and may not be extended so as to embrace effects upon interstate commerce so indirect and remote that to embrace them, in view of our complex society, would effectually obliterate

---

1. The term "school zone" is defined as "in, or on the grounds of, a public, parochial or private school" or "within a distance of 1,000 feet from the grounds of a public, parochial or private school." §921(a)(25).

the distinction between what is national and what is local and create a completely centralized government." . . .

In Maryland v. Wirtz, 392 U.S. 183 (1968), the Court reaffirmed that . . . [n]either here nor in *Wickard* has the Court declared that Congress may use a relatively trivial impact on commerce as an excuse for broad general regulation of state or private activities." Rather, "the Court has said only that where a general regulatory statute bears a substantial relation to commerce, the de minimis character of individual instances arising under that statute is of no consequence."

Consistent with this structure, we have identified three broad categories of activity that Congress may regulate under its commerce power. First, Congress may regulate the use of the channels of interstate commerce. See, e.g., *Darby, Heart of Atlanta Motel.* Second, Congress is empowered to regulate and protect the instrumentalities of interstate commerce, or persons or things in interstate commerce, even though the threat may come only from intrastate activities. See, e.g., *Shreveport Rate Cases*, Southern R. Co. v. United States, 222 U.S. 20 (1911). Finally, Congress'[s] commerce authority includes the power to regulate those activities having a substantial relation to interstate commerce, *Jones & Laughlin Steel*, i.e., those activities that substantially affect interstate commerce.

Within this final category . . . our case law has not been clear whether an activity must "affect" or "substantially affect" interstate commerce in order to be within Congress'[s] power to regulate it under the Commerce Clause. We conclude, consistent with the great weight of our case law, that the proper test requires an analysis of whether the regulated activity "substantially affects" interstate commerce.

We now turn to consider the power of Congress, in the light of this framework, to enact §922(q). The first two categories of authority may be quickly disposed of: §922(q) is not a regulation of the use of the channels of interstate commerce, nor is it an attempt to prohibit the interstate transportation of a commodity through the channels of commerce; nor can §922(q) be justified as a regulation by which Congress has sought to protect an instrumentality of interstate commerce or a thing in interstate commerce. . . .

[We] have upheld a wide variety of congressional Acts regulating intrastate economic activity where we have concluded that the activity substantially affected interstate commerce. [The] pattern is clear. Where economic activity substantially affects interstate commerce, legislation regulating that activity will be sustained. . . .

Section 922(q) is a criminal statute that by its terms has nothing to do with "commerce" or any sort of economic enterprise, however broadly one might define those terms. Section 922(q) is not an essential part of a larger regulation of economic activity, in which the regulatory scheme could be undercut unless the intrastate activity were regulated. It cannot, therefore, be sustained under our cases upholding regulations of activities that arise out of or are connected with a commercial transaction, which viewed in the aggregate, substantially affects interstate commerce.

Second, §922(q) contains no jurisdictional element which would ensure, through case-by-case inquiry, that the firearm possession in question affects interstate commerce. [Section] 922(q) has no express jurisdictional element which might limit its reach to a discrete set of firearm possessions that have an explicit connection with or effect on interstate commerce.

Although as part of our independent evaluation of constitutionality under the Commerce Clause we of course consider legislative findings, and indeed even congressional committee findings, regarding effect on interstate commerce, the Government concedes that "neither the statute nor its legislative history contains express congressional findings regarding the effects upon interstate commerce of gun possession in a school zone." We agree with the Government that Congress normally is not required to make formal findings as to the substantial burdens that an activity has on interstate commerce. But to the extent that congressional findings would enable us to evaluate the legislative judgment that the activity in question substantially affected interstate commerce, even though no such substantial effect was visible to the naked eye, they are lacking here. . . .

The Government's essential contention is that we may determine here that §922(q) is valid because possession of a firearm in a local school zone does indeed substantially affect interstate commerce. The Government argues that possession of a firearm in a school zone may result in violent crime and that violent crime can be expected to affect the functioning of the national economy in two ways. First, the costs of violent crime are substantial, and, through the mechanism of insurance, those costs are spread throughout the population. Second, violent crime reduces the willingness of individuals to travel to areas within the country that are perceived to be unsafe. The Government also argues that the presence of guns in schools poses a substantial threat to the educational process by threatening the learning environment. A handicapped educational process, in turn, will result in a less productive citizenry. That, in turn, would have an adverse effect on the Nation's economic well-being. As a result, the Government argues that Congress could rationally have concluded that §922(q) substantially affects interstate commerce.

The Government admits, under its "costs of crime" reasoning, that Congress could regulate not only all violent crime, but all activities that might lead to violent crime, regardless of how tenuously they relate to interstate commerce. Similarly, under the Government's "national productivity" reasoning, Congress could regulate any activity that it found was related to the economic productivity of individual citizens: family law (including marriage, divorce, and child custody), for example. Under the theories that the Government presents [it] is difficult to perceive any limitation on federal power, even in areas such as criminal law enforcement or education where States historically have been sovereign. [If] we were to accept the Government's arguments, we are hard-pressed to posit any activity by an individual that Congress is without power to regulate. . . .

Admittedly, a determination whether an intrastate activity is commercial or noncommercial may in some cases result in legal uncertainty. But, so long as Congress'[s] authority is limited to those powers enumerated in the Constitution, and so long as those enumerated powers are interpreted as having judicially enforceable outer limits, congressional legislation under the Commerce Clause always will engender "legal uncertainty." . . . The Constitution mandates this uncertainty by withholding from Congress a plenary police power that would authorize enactment of every type of legislation. [In] *Jones & Laughlin Steel*, we held that the question of congressional power under the Commerce Clause "is necessarily one of degree." . . .

These are not precise formulations, and in the nature of things they cannot be. But we think they point the way to a correct decision of this case. The possession of a gun in a local school zone is in no sense an economic activity that might, through repetition elsewhere, substantially affect any sort of interstate commerce. . . .

To uphold the Government's contentions here, we would have to pile inference upon inference in a manner that would bid fair to convert congressional authority under the Commerce Clause to a general police power of the sort retained by the States. . . .

For the foregoing reasons the judgment of the Court of Appeals is [a]ffirmed.

JUSTICE THOMAS, concurring.

Although I join the majority, I write separately to observe that our case law has drifted far from the original understanding of the Commerce Clause. In a future case, we ought to temper our Commerce Clause jurisprudence in a manner that both makes sense of our more recent case law and is more faithful to the original understanding of that Clause.

We have said that Congress may regulate not only "Commerce . . . among the several states" but also anything that has a "substantial effect" on such commerce. This test, if taken to its logical extreme, would give Congress a "police power" over all aspects of American life. Unfortunately, we have never come to grips with this implication of our substantial effects formula. . . . [In] an appropriate case, I believe that we must further reconsider our "substantial effects" test with an eye toward constructing a standard that reflects the text and history of the Commerce Clause without totally rejecting our more recent Commerce Clause jurisprudence. . . .

I. At the time the original Constitution was ratified, "commerce" consisted of selling, buying, and bartering, as well as transporting for these purposes. [The] term "commerce" was used in contradistinction to productive activities such as manufacturing and agriculture. [The] Constitution not only uses the word "commerce" in a narrower sense than our case law might suggest, it also does not support the proposition that Congress has authority over all activities that "substantially affect" interstate commerce. The Commerce Clause does not state that Congress may "regulate matters that substantially affect commerce with foreign Nations, and among the several States, and with the Indian Tribes." [After] all, if Congress may regulate all matters that substantially affect commerce, there is no need for the Constitution to specify that

Congress may enact bankruptcy laws, cl. 4, or coin money and fix the standard of weights and measures, cl. 5, or punish counterfeiters of United States coin and securities, cl. 6. Likewise, Congress would not need the separate authority to establish post offices and post roads, cl. 7, or to grant patents and copyrights, cl. 8, or to "punish Piracies and Felonies committed on the high Seas," cl. 10. . . . Indeed, if Congress could regulate matters that substantially affect interstate commerce, there would have been no need to specify that Congress can regulate international trade and commerce with the Indians. As the Framers surely understood, these other branches of trade substantially affect interstate commerce. Put simply, much if not all of Art. I, §8 (including portions of the Commerce Clause itself) would be surplusage if Congress had been given authority over matters that substantially affect interstate commerce. An interpretation of cl. 3 that makes the rest of §8 superfluous simply cannot be correct. Yet this Court's Commerce Clause jurisprudence has endorsed just such an interpretation. . . .

IV. Apart from its recent vintage and its corresponding lack of any grounding in the original understanding of the Constitution, the substantial effects test suffers from the further flaw that it appears to grant Congress a police power over the Nation. When asked at oral argument if there were any limits to the Commerce Clause, the Government was at a loss for words. Likewise, the principal dissent insists that there are limits, but it cannot muster even one example. . . . The substantial effects test suffers from this flaw, in part, because of its "aggregation principle." [Congress] can regulate whole categories of activities that are not themselves either "interstate" or "commerce." In applying the effects test, we ask whether the class of activities as a whole substantially affects interstate commerce, not whether any specific activity within the class has such effects when considered in isolation. The aggregation principle is clever, but has no stopping point. . . . [One] always can draw the circle broadly enough to cover an activity that, when taken in isolation, would not have substantial effects on commerce. Under our jurisprudence, if Congress passed an omnibus "substantially affects interstate commerce" statute, purporting to regulate every aspect of human existence, the Act apparently would be constitutional. Even though particular sections may govern only trivial activities, the statute in the aggregate regulates matters that substantially affect commerce.

V. . . . If we wish to be true to a Constitution that does not cede a police power to the Federal Government, . . . I think we must modify our Commerce Clause jurisprudence. . . .

JUSTICE SOUTER, dissenting.

In reviewing congressional legislation under the Commerce Clause, we defer to what is often a merely implicit congressional judgment that its regulation addresses a subject substantially affecting interstate commerce "if there is any rational basis for such a finding." Hodel v. Virginia Surface Mining & Reclamation Assn., Inc., 452 U.S. 264 (1981). [The] practice of deferring to rationally based legislative judgments reflects our respect for the institutional competence of the Congress on a subject expressly assigned to it by the Constitution and our appreciation of the legitimacy that comes from Congress's political accountability in dealing with matters open to a wide range of possible choices. . . .

[Because] Justice Breyer's opinion demonstrates beyond any doubt that the Act in question passes the rationality review that the Court continues to espouse, today's decision may be seen as only a misstep, [but] hardly an epochal case. [But not] every epochal case has come in epochal trappings. *Jones & Laughlin* did not reject the direct-indirect standard in so many words; it just said the relation of the regulated subject matter to commerce was direct enough. But we know what happened.

JUSTICE BREYER, joined by JUSTICES STEVENS, SOUTER, and GINSBURG, dissenting.

[Section 922(q)] falls well within the scope of the commerce power as this Court has understood that power over the last half-century. . . . [T]he specific question before us . . . is not whether the "regulated activity sufficiently affected interstate commerce," but, rather, whether Congress could have had "a rational basis" for so concluding. . . . II. Applying these principles to the case at hand, we must ask whether Congress could have had a rational basis for finding a significant (or substantial) connection between gun-related school violence and interstate commerce. [The] answer to this question must be yes. Numerous reports and studies make clear that Congress could reasonably have found the empirical connection that its law, implicitly or explicitly, asserts. [Justice Breyer then referred to a voluminous bibliography of studies on education, school violence, and economic competitiveness.] [These] reports, hearings, and other readily available literature make clear that the problem of guns in and around schools is widespread and extremely serious, [reporting], for example, that four percent of American high school students (and six percent of inner-city high school students) carry a gun to school at least occasionally; that 12 percent of urban high school students have had guns fired at them; that 20 percent of those students have been threatened with guns; and that, in any 6-month period, several hundred thousand schoolchildren are victims of violent crimes in or near their schools. [They] report that this widespread violence in schools throughout the Nation significantly interferes with the quality of education in those schools. Based on [these] reports, Congress obviously could have thought that guns and learning are mutually exclusive. And, Congress could therefore have found a substantial educational problem—teachers unable to teach, students unable to learn—and concluded that guns near schools contribute substantially to the size and scope of that problem.

[Congress] could also have found, given the effect of education upon interstate and foreign commerce, that gun-related violence in and around schools is a commercial, as well as a human, problem. Education, although far more than a matter of economics, has long been inextricably intertwined with the Nation's economy. [In] recent years the link between secondary education and business has strengthened, becoming both more direct and more important. Scholars on the subject report that technological changes and innovations in management techniques have altered the nature of the workplace so that more jobs now demand greater educational skills. . . .

The economic links I have just sketched seem fairly obvious. Why then is it not equally obvious, in light of those links, that a widespread, serious, and substantial physical threat to teaching and learning also substantially threatens the commerce to which that teaching and learning is inextricably tied? [G]uns in the hands of six percent of inner-city high school students and gun-related violence throughout a city's schools must threaten the trade and commerce that those schools support. The only question, then, is whether the latter threat is . . . "substantial." [At] the very least, Congress could rationally have concluded that the links are "substantial." Specifically, Congress could have found that gun-related violence near the classroom poses a serious economic threat (1) to consequently inadequately educated workers who must endure low-paying jobs, and (2) to communities and businesses that [might] otherwise gain, from a well-educated work force, an important commercial advantage, of a kind that location near a railhead or harbor provided in the past. . . . [The] violence-related facts, the educational facts, and the economic facts, taken together, make [it] rational [to conclude] that "the occurrence of violent crime in school zones" has brought about a "decline in the quality of education" that "has an adverse impact on interstate commerce and the foreign commerce of the United States." . . .

NOTES

1. The Doctrine. In general, the judiciary says it will defer to the judgment of Congress about the scope of its interstate commerce power so long as Congress rationally has determined that the activity it seeks to regulate is (1) a part of interstate commerce (in the "channels" of interstate commerce); *or* (2) an instrumentality of interstate commerce; *or* (3) substantially affects interstate commerce. Of course, as with every exercise of an enumerated power, the means chosen by Congress must be reasonably adapted to the legitimate end. The burden of proof is on the challenger to prove that one or more of these elements of validity is lacking.

This test is extremely deferential to Congress. Before *Lopez*, it was thought that judicial review of the scope of the interstate commerce power was limited to the question of whether Congress had made a rational judgment that the activity it regulated had the requisite connection to interstate commerce. After *Lopez*, the scope of judicial review is increased. How much? In what way? The following notes explore facets of these questions.

2. The Dissenting Argument for Deference to Congress. The dissenters contend that judicial deference to Congress on the scope of the commerce power is, perhaps, constitutionally required. Justice Breyer states that the "Constitution requires" the Court to defer to Congress "because the

Constitution delegates the commerce power directly to Congress." Justice Souter added that deference "reflects our respect for the institutional competence of the Congress on a subject expressly assigned to it by the Constitution." Does this simply beg the question? The Constitution gives Congress control over three specified types of commerce, one of which is interstate commerce. The scope of the term "interstate commerce" is not self-evident, and the structure of the Constitution indicates that congressional power over "commerce" is not unlimited. The problem is this: Within the scope of the "commerce power," Congress may act at its discretion (so long as the means it uses are rationally connected to the end of regulating the commerce it has power to regulate), but the question of the *scope* of the commerce power is logically antecedent. Who decides the scope? The dissenters argue that Congress should decide; the majority insists that, whereas some deference to the congressional judgment of scope is appropriate, the decision is ultimately the Court's. Who is right? Why?

3. Activities "Affecting" Interstate Commerce.   Prior to *Lopez*, there was ambiguity about whether Congress could regulate activities that had a less-than-substantial effect on interstate commerce. The *Lopez* Court makes plain that an activity that neither involves a "channel" of interstate commerce (e.g., the interstate shipment of goods) nor an "instrumentality" of interstate commerce (e.g., a railroad) must *substantially affect* interstate commerce to be within congressional power to regulate it. But what is substantial and who decides? Consider the following notes.

4. The Standard of Review.   Ordinarily the Court will defer to rational congressional judgments about the scope of the interstate commerce power. Yet, in *Lopez*, the Court refused to defer to the implicit congressional judgment that guns in or near schools had a substantial effect on interstate commerce. What was critical to this decision? Was it the *noncommercial* nature of the activity regulated—possession of guns in or near schools? Was it the wholly *intrastate* nature of the activity regulated? Was it a combination of the intrastate and noncommercial nature of the regulated activity? Or was it the *lack of any congressional determination* about the effect on interstate commerce of the regulated activity? Or did the Court conclude that Congress could not have *rationally* determined that the possession of guns in or near schools has a substantial effect on interstate commerce? Another possibility is that the Court thought that the statute was a pretextual means to achieve an ultra vires end—the regulation of gun possession in or near schools.

Query: Suppose Congress prohibits marriage by anyone under the age of 21 years and makes no findings of fact concerning the connection between this activity and interstate commerce. Will the Court defer to Congress or examine on its own whether the connection is substantial? Would your view change if Congress makes a showing that marital age and interstate commerce are substantially related? Should it make any difference if the congressional determination is one of "pil[ing] inference upon inference" to connect a minimum marital age and interstate commerce?

5. Post-*Lopez* Developments: *Morrison*. In United States v. Morrison, 529 U.S. 598 (2000), the Court ruled 5-4 (with the same voting alignment as in *Lopez*) that the commerce power did not authorize Congress to enact the civil remedy provision of the Violence Against Women Act, 42 U.S.C. §13981, which created a civil cause of action against "a person who commits a crime of violence motivated by gender." Congress had explicitly determined that gender-motivated violence affected interstate commerce "by deterring potential victims from traveling interstate, from engaging in employment in interstate business, and from transacting with business, and in places involved in interstate commerce; by diminishing national productivity, increasing medical and other costs, and decreasing the supply and demand for interstate products." But the Court did not defer to these findings by asking simply whether they were rational. Instead, the Court declared that these "findings are substantially weakened by the fact that they rely so heavily on a method of reasoning that we have already rejected as unworkable if we are to maintain the Constitution's enumeration of powers." The inherent weakness was the length of the causal chain—from the violent crime to "every attenuated effect upon interstate commerce." The Court rejected the idea that Congress could

> regulate any crime as long as the nationwide, aggregated impact of that crime has substantial effects on employment, production, transit, or consumption. Indeed, if Congress may regulate gender-motivated violence, it would be able to regulate . . . any other type of violence since gender-motivated violence, as a subset of all violent crime, is certain to have lesser economic impacts [*sic*] than the larger class of which it is a part.

In short, Congress may not "use the Commerce Clause to completely obliterate the distinction between national and local authority. [The] Constitution requires a distinction between what is truly national and truly local."

The Court also noted that the act struck down in *Lopez* had "nothing to do with 'commerce' or any sort of economic enterprise, however broadly one might define those terms." Indeed,

> *Lopez*'s review of Commerce Clause case law demonstrates that in those cases where we have sustained federal regulation of intrastate activity based on the activity's substantial effects on interstate commerce, the activity in question has been some sort of economic endeavor. . . . Gender-motivated crimes of violence are not, in any sense of the phrase, economic activity. While we need not adopt a categorical rule against aggregating the effects of any non-economic activity in order to decide [this case], thus far in our nation's history our cases have upheld Commerce Clause regulation of intrastate activity only where that activity is economic in nature.

In his dissent, Justice Souter charged that under the Court's prior commerce cases,

Congress has the power to legislate with regard to an activity that, in the aggregate, has a substantial effect on interstate commerce. The fact of such a substantial effect is not an issue for the courts in the first instance, but for the Congress. [The] business of the courts is to review the Congressional assessment . . . simply for the rationality of concluding that a jurisdictional basis exists in fact. [The Court has supplanted] rational basis scrutiny with a new criterion of review.

What is the "new criterion of review"? Does the old level of review—rational basis review—apply when Congress regulates an intrastate *economic* activity that, in the aggregate, exerts a substantial impact on interstate commerce? Does a new level of less (or no) deference apply when Congress concludes that the aggregate impact of an intrastate *noneconomic* activity has a substantial effect on interstate commerce, or when Congress fails to make findings of fact about the effect on interstate commerce of an intrastate economic activity?

Suppose that Congress had made explicit findings that gender-motivated violence is frequently designed to produce economic benefits to the aggressor? Would (should) that have made a difference? After *Morrison*, could Congress regulate emissions from a residential fireplace? Would it make any difference that Congress had concluded that the aggregate emissions from home fireplaces produce substantial adverse economic effects on the national economy?

The Child Support and Recovery Act, 18 U.S.C. §228, makes it a crime to "willfully fail to pay a past due support obligation *with respect to a child who resides in another State.*" Is the italicized phrase essential to the constitutional validity of the provision? Suppose that the italicized phrase were omitted and Congress made findings of fact that the failure to pay support obligations has a substantial effect on interstate commerce.

6. Implications of *Lopez* and *Morrison*.   There are several ways to assess the significance of *Lopez* and *Morrison*. Consider the following.

a. Portent of a zone of exclusive state authority. Does the majority rationale in both cases rest on the idea that some matters are exclusively within the domain of state authority? If so, which ones? Neither crime nor education is exclusively reserved for state authority, so what might be the basis of this view? Is it the structural principle that Congress only has enumerated powers? The argument that follows from that principle is that the power to regulate interstate commerce must be bounded to prevent it from becoming a plenary grant of power to Congress to legislate on anything it feels might be in the general welfare of the nation. But does this argument help in identifying the activities, if any, that might be reserved exclusively for the *states*?

b. Insignificant anomaly.   *Lopez* and *Morrison* are aberrational and anomalous. They are easily circumvented by better draftsmanship or reliance on other federal powers. Note that, after *Lopez*, Congress amended 18 U.S.C. §922(q): "It shall be unlawful for any individual knowingly to possess a firearm that *has moved in or that otherwise* affects interstate commerce at a place that the individual knows, or has reasonable cause to believe, is a school zone." Might Congress avoid the impact of *Lopez* and *Morrison* by regulating a sphere of activity so broadly defined that the cumulative effect of individual acts has an undeniably substantial effect on commerce? Congress could also react to *Lopez* by conditioning the receipt of federal money for education purposes on state enactment of a statute identical to the original version of 18 U.S.C. §922(q), or to *Morrison* by conditioning receipt of federal money for law enforcement on state enactment of a statute identical to 42 U.S.C. §13981. These approaches are considered in Section D.1, infra.

7. Interpreting Statutes to Avoid Constitutional Issues. Recall that, in Ashwander v. T.V.A., Justice Brandeis summarized "a series of rules" the Court uses to avoid the necessity of constitutional decisions. One of those rules was that "if a case can be decided on either of two grounds, one involving a constitutional question, the other a question of statutory construction or general law, the Court will decide only the latter." More recently, the Court has stated that "where a statute is susceptible of two constructions, by one of which grave and doubtful constitutional questions arise and by the other of which such questions are avoided, our duty is to adopt the latter." Jones v. United States, 529 U.S. 848, 857 (2000). This principle has been vigorously applied of late to sidestep difficult issues posed by the scope of the commerce power.

In *Jones*, the Court applied this canon to overturn a conviction under the federal arson statute, 18 U.S.C. §844(i), as applied to the arson of an owner-occupied private residence. The statute made criminal arson of "any building . . . used in interstate or foreign commerce or *in any activity affecting* interstate or *foreign commerce*." Because the Court was of the view that a reading of the arson statute that included within its coverage any arson that merely "affected interstate commerce" would raise a significant question of the validity of the statute, it interpreted the statutory language to include only arson of buildings actually used in a commercial manner. A related version of this canon is the requirement, associated with United States v. Bass, 404 U.S. 336, 349 (1971), that "unless Congress conveys its purpose clearly, it will not be deemed to have significantly changed the federal-state balance in the prosecution of crimes."

≡ *Gonzales v. Raich*
≡ *545 U.S. 1 (2005)*

[California's Compassionate Use Act permits marijuana to be used for medicinal purposes. The federal Controlled Substances Act (CSA) prohibits the production, distribution, or possession of controlled substances, including marijuana. After federal law enforcement officials enforced the CSA by seizing and destroying medicinal marijuana belonging to respondent Monson, a seriously ill Californian who uses marijuana to relieve her pain, she and the remaining respondents brought suit in federal court. They sought to enjoin enforcement of the CSA, to the extent it prevents them from possessing, obtaining, or manufacturing marijuana for their personal medical use, on the ground that Congress had no constitutional authority to regulate the intrastate, noncommercial cultivation and possession of marijuana for personal medical purposes as recommended by a patient's physician pursuant to California's Compassionate Use Act. The district court denied a preliminary injunction, but the Ninth Circuit reversed.]

JUSTICE STEVENS delivered the opinion of the Court.

California is one of at least nine States that authorize the use of marijuana for medicinal purposes. The question presented in this case is whether the [interstate commerce] power . . . includes the power to prohibit the local cultivation and use of marijuana in compliance with California law.

I. . . . Respondents Angel Raich and Diane Monson are California residents who . . . have been using marijuana as a medication for several years pursuant to their doctors' recommendation, and both rely heavily on cannabis to function on a daily basis. Indeed, Raich's physician believes that forgoing cannabis treatments would certainly cause Raich excruciating pain and could very well prove fatal. . . .

II. [The CSA was intended] to conquer drug abuse and to control the legitimate and illegitimate traffic in controlled substances. Congress was particularly concerned with the need to prevent the diversion of drugs from legitimate to illicit channels. . . . In enacting the CSA, Congress classified marijuana as a Schedule I drug, [one with a] high potential for abuse, lack of any accepted medical use, and absence of any accepted safety for use in medically supervised treatment. . . .

III. Respondents . . . argue that the CSA's categorical prohibition of the manufacture and possession of marijuana as applied to the intrastate manufacture and possession of marijuana for medical purposes pursuant to California law exceeds Congress'[s] authority under the Commerce Clause. . . .

Our case law firmly establishes Congress'[s] power to regulate purely local activities that are part of an economic "class of activities" that have a substantial effect on interstate commerce. . . . We have never required Congress to legislate with scientific exactitude. When Congress decides that the "'total incidence'" of a practice poses a threat to a national market, it may regulate the entire class. . . .

[*Wickard*] establishes that Congress can regulate purely intrastate activity that is not itself "commercial," in that it is not produced for sale, if it concludes that failure to regulate that class of activity would undercut the regulation of the interstate market in that commodity. . . . Like the farmer in *Wickard*, respondents are cultivating, for home consumption, a fungible commodity for which there is an established, albeit illegal, interstate market. . . . In *Wickard*, we had no difficulty concluding that Congress had a rational basis for believing that, when viewed in the aggregate, leaving home-consumed wheat outside the regulatory scheme would have a substantial influence on price and market conditions. Here too, Congress had a rational basis for concluding that leaving home-consumed marijuana outside federal control would similarly affect price and market conditions. . . . In both cases, the regulation is squarely within Congress'[s] commerce power because production of the commodity meant for home consumption, be it wheat or marijuana, has a substantial effect on supply and demand in the national market for that commodity. . . .

In assessing the scope of Congress'[s] authority under the Commerce Clause, we stress that the task before us is a modest one. We need not determine whether respondents' activities, taken in the aggregate, substantially affect interstate commerce in fact, but only whether a "rational basis" exists for so concluding. . . . Given the enforcement difficulties that attend distinguishing between marijuana cultivated locally and marijuana grown elsewhere, and concerns about diversion into illicit channels, we have no difficulty concluding that Congress had a rational basis for believing that failure to regulate the intrastate manufacture and possession of marijuana would leave a gaping hole in the CSA. . . . That the regulation ensnares some purely intrastate activity is of no moment. . . .

IV. To support their contrary submission, respondents rely heavily on [*Lopez* and *Morrison*]. Here, respondents ask us to excise individual applications of a concededly valid statutory scheme. In contrast, in both *Lopez* and *Morrison*, the parties asserted that a particular statute or provision fell outside Congress'[s] commerce power in its entirety. This distinction is pivotal for we have often reiterated that "where the class of activities is regulated and that class is within the reach of federal power, the courts have no power 'to excise, as trivial, individual instances' of the class." [Perez v. United States, 402 U.S. 146, 154 (1971) (emphasis deleted), quoting Maryland v. Wirtz, 392 U.S. 183, 193 (1968).]

Unlike those at issue in *Lopez* and *Morrison*, the activities regulated by the CSA are quintessentially economic. "Economics" refers to "the production, distribution, and consumption of commodities." Webster's Third New International Dictionary 720 (1966). The CSA is a statute that regulates the production, distribution, and consumption of commodities for which there is an established, and lucrative, interstate market. . . .

We have no difficulty concluding that Congress acted rationally in determining that . . . the subdivided class of activities defined by the Court of Appeals was an essential part of the larger regulatory scheme.

First, the fact that marijuana is used "for personal medical purposes on the advice of a physician" cannot itself serve as a distinguishing factor. . . . [If] . . . the personal cultivation, possession, and use of marijuana for medicinal purposes is beyond the " 'outer limits' of Congress'[s] Commerce Clause authority," it must also be true that such personal use of marijuana (or any other homegrown drug) for recreational purposes is also beyond those " 'outer limits.' " . . . One need not have a degree in economics to understand why a nationwide exemption for the vast quantity of marijuana (or other drugs) locally cultivated for personal use (which presumably would include use by friends, neighbors, and family members) may have a substantial impact on the interstate market for this extraordinarily popular substance. The congressional judgment that an exemption for such a significant segment of the total market would undermine the orderly enforcement of the entire regulatory scheme is entitled to a strong presumption of validity. . . .

Second, limiting the activity to marijuana possession and cultivation "in accordance with state law" cannot serve to place respondents' activities beyond congressional reach [because the] Supremacy Clause unambiguously provides that if there is any conflict between federal and state law, federal law shall prevail. . . . Respondents . . . contend that their activities were not "an essential part of a larger regulatory scheme" because they had been "isolated by the State of California, and [are] policed by the State of California," and thus remain "entirely separated from the market." . . . The notion that California law has surgically excised a discrete activity that is hermetically sealed off from the larger interstate marijuana market is a dubious proposition, and, more importantly, one that Congress could have rationally rejected. Indeed, that the California exemptions will have a significant impact on both the supply and demand sides of the market for marijuana is . . . readily apparent. . . .

V. Respondents also raise a substantive due process claim [which was] not reached by the Court of Appeals. We therefore do not address the question. . . . [The] judgment of the Court of Appeals must be vacated. The case is remanded for further proceedings consistent with this opinion.

JUSTICE SCALIA, concurring in the judgment.
. . . In the CSA, Congress has undertaken to extinguish the interstate market in Schedule I controlled substances, including marijuana. The Commerce Clause unquestionably permits this. . . . Congress has prohibited almost all intrastate activities related to Schedule I substances—both economic activities (manufacture, distribution, possession with the intent to distribute) and noneconomic activities (simple possession). That simple possession is a noneconomic activity is immaterial to whether it can be prohibited as a necessary part of a larger regulation. Rather, Congress's authority to enact all of these prohibitions of intrastate controlled-substance activities depends only upon whether they are appropriate means of achieving the legitimate end of eradicating Schedule I substances from interstate commerce. [The] regulation must be sustained. Not only is it impossible to distinguish "controlled substances manufactured and distributed intrastate" from "controlled substances manufactured and distributed interstate," but it hardly makes sense to speak in such terms. Drugs like marijuana are fungible commodities. . . .

JUSTICE O'CONNOR, joined by CHIEF JUSTICE REHNQUIST and JUSTICE THOMAS, dissenting.
We enforce the "outer limits" of Congress'[s] Commerce Clause authority not for their own sake, but to protect historic spheres of state sovereignty from excessive federal encroachment and thereby to maintain the distribution of power fundamental to our federalist system of government. . . . The States' core police powers have always included authority to define criminal law and to protect the health, safety, and welfare of their citizens. Exercising those powers, California . . . has come to its own conclusion about the difficult and

sensitive question of whether marijuana should be available to relieve severe pain and suffering. Today the Court sanctions an application of the [CSA] that extinguishes that experiment, without any proof that the personal cultivation, possession, and use of marijuana for medicinal purposes, if economic activity in the first place, has a substantial effect on interstate commerce and is therefore an appropriate subject of federal regulation. In so doing, the Court announces a rule that gives Congress a perverse incentive to legislate broadly pursuant to the Commerce Clause—nestling questionable assertions of its authority into comprehensive regulatory schemes—rather than with precision. That rule and the result it produces in this case are irreconcilable with our decisions in *Lopez* [and *Morrison*]. Accordingly I dissent.

. . . Today's decision suggests that the federal regulation of local activity is immune to Commerce Clause challenge because Congress chose to act with an ambitious, all-encompassing statute, rather than piecemeal. [This] is tantamount to removing meaningful limits on the Commerce Clause. . . . Today's decision allows Congress to regulate intrastate activity without check, so long as there is some implication by legislative design that regulating intrastate activity is essential . . . to the interstate regulatory scheme. . . . If the Court is right, then *Lopez* stands for nothing more than a drafting guide: Congress should have described the relevant crime as "transfer or possession of a firearm anywhere in the nation"—thus including commercial and noncommercial activity, and clearly encompassing some activity with assuredly substantial effect on interstate commerce. . . . I cannot agree that our decision in *Lopez* contemplated such evasive or overbroad legislative strategies with approval. . . . *Lopez* and *Morrison* did not indicate that the constitutionality of federal regulation depends on superficial and formalistic distinctions. . . . If the Court always defers to Congress as it does today, little may be left to the notion of enumerated powers.

The hard work for courts . . . is to identify objective markers for confining the analysis in Commerce Clause cases. . . . I agree . . . that we must look beyond respondents' own activities. Otherwise, individual litigants could always exempt themselves from Commerce Clause regulation merely by pointing to the obvious—that their personal activities do not have a substantial effect on interstate commerce. The task is to identify a mode of analysis that allows Congress to regulate more than nothing (by declining to reduce each case to its litigants) and less than everything (by declining to let Congress set the terms of analysis). The analysis may not be the same in every case, for it depends on the regulatory scheme at issue and the federalism concerns implicated.

A number of objective markers are available to confine the scope of constitutional review here. Both federal and state legislation—including the CSA itself, the California Compassionate Use Act, and other state medical marijuana legislation—recognize that medical and nonmedical (i.e., recreational) uses of drugs are realistically distinct and can be segregated, and regulate them differently. Moreover, because fundamental structural concerns about dual sovereignty animate our Commerce Clause cases, it is relevant that this case involves the interplay of federal and state regulation in areas of criminal law and social policy, where "States lay claim by right of history and expertise." California, like other States, has drawn on its reserved powers to distinguish the regulation of medicinal marijuana. To ascertain whether Congress'[s] encroachment is constitutionally justified . . . , I would focus here on the personal cultivation, possession, and use of marijuana for medicinal purposes.

Having thus defined the relevant conduct, we must determine whether, under our precedents, the conduct is economic and, in the aggregate, substantially affects interstate commerce. Even if intrastate cultivation and possession of marijuana for one's own medicinal use can properly be characterized as economic, and I question whether it can, it has not been shown that such activity substantially affects interstate commerce. Similarly, it is neither self-evident nor demonstrated that regulating such activity is necessary to the interstate drug control scheme.

The Court's definition of economic activity is breathtaking. It defines as economic any activity involving the production, distribution, and consumption of commodities. And it appears to reason that when an interstate market for a commodity exists, regulating the intrastate manufacture or possession of that commodity is constitutional either because that intrastate activity is itself economic, or because regulating it is a rational part of regulating its market. [The] Court's definition of economic activity for purposes of Commerce Clause jurisprudence threatens to sweep all of productive human activity into federal regulatory reach. . . .

It will not do to say that Congress may regulate noncommercial activity simply because it may have an effect on the demand for commercial goods, or because the noncommercial endeavor can, in some sense, substitute for commercial activity. Most commercial goods or services have some sort of privately producible analogue. Home care substitutes for daycare. Charades games substitute for movie tickets. Backyard or windowsill gardening substitutes for going to the supermarket. To draw the line wherever private activity affects the demand for market goods is to draw no line at all, and to declare everything economic. We have already rejected the result that would follow—a federal police power. *Lopez.*

The homegrown cultivation and personal possession and use of marijuana for medicinal purposes has no apparent commercial character. . . . (Marijuana is highly unusual among the substances subject to the CSA in that it can be cultivated without any materials that have traveled in interstate commerce.) *Lopez* makes clear that possession is not itself commercial activity. And respondents have not come into possession by means of any commercial transaction; they have simply grown, in their own homes, marijuana for their own use, without acquiring, buying, selling, or bartering a thing of value.

The Court suggests that *Wickard* . . . established federal regulatory power over any home consumption of a commodity for which a national market exists. I disagree. . . . *Wickard* . . . did not extend Commerce Clause authority to something as modest as the home cook's herb garden. . . . *Wickard* did not hold or imply that small-scale production of commodities is always economic, and automatically within Congress'[s] reach.

Even assuming that economic activity is at issue in this case, the Government has made no showing in fact that the possession and use of homegrown marijuana for medical purposes . . . has a substantial effect on interstate commerce. Similarly, the Government has not shown that regulating such activity is necessary to an interstate regulatory scheme. Whatever the specific theory of "substantial effects" at issue (i.e., whether the activity substantially affects interstate commerce, whether its regulation is necessary to an interstate regulatory scheme, or both), a concern for dual sovereignty requires that Congress'[s] excursion into the traditional domain of States be justified. . . .

The Government has not overcome empirical doubt that . . . personal cultivation, possession, and use of medical marijuana . . . is enough to threaten the federal regime. Nor has it shown that Compassionate Use Act marijuana users have been or are realistically likely to be responsible for the drug's seeping into the market in a significant way. . . . Piling assertion upon assertion does not, in my view, satisfy the substantiality test of *Lopez* and *Morrison*. . . .

JUSTICE THOMAS, dissenting.

. . . If Congress can regulate this under the Commerce Clause, then it can regulate virtually anything—and the Federal Government is no longer one of limited and enumerated powers. . . . [The] Court abandons any attempt to enforce the Constitution's limits on federal power. . . .

In the early days of the Republic, it would have been unthinkable that Congress could prohibit the local cultivation, possession, and consumption of marijuana. [The CSA] regulates a great deal of marijuana trafficking that is interstate and commercial in character [but, because] it bans the entire market—intrastate or interstate, noncommercial or commercial—for marijuana [respondents] are correct that the CSA exceeds Congress'[s] commerce power as applied to their conduct, which is purely intrastate and noncommercial.

[Nor is the CSA] a valid exercise of Congress'[s] power to enact laws that are "necessary and proper for carrying into Execution" its power to regulate interstate commerce. The Necessary and Proper Clause is not a warrant to Congress to enact any law that bears some conceivable connection to the exercise of an enumerated power. [In] order to be "necessary," the intrastate ban must be more than "a reasonable means [of] effectuating the regulation of interstate commerce." It must be "plainly adapted" to regulating interstate marijuana trafficking—in other words, there must be an "obvious, simple, and direct relation" between the intrastate ban and the regulation of interstate commerce. Even assuming the CSA's ban on locally cultivated and consumed marijuana is "necessary," that does not mean it is also "proper." The means selected by Congress to regulate interstate commerce cannot be "prohibited" by, or inconsistent with the "letter and spirit" of, the Constitution. *McCulloch*. [Allowing] Congress to regulate intrastate, noncommercial activity under the Commerce Clause would confer on Congress a general "police power" over the Nation. This is no less the case if Congress ties its power to the Necessary and Proper Clause rather than the Commerce Clause. . . .

Even if Congress may regulate purely intrastate activity when essential to exercising some enumerated power, Congress may not use its incidental authority to subvert basic principles of federalism and dual sovereignty. Here, Congress has encroached on States' traditional police powers to define the criminal law and to protect the health, safety, and welfare of their citizens. Further, the Government's rationale—that it may regulate the production or possession of any commodity for which there is an interstate market—threatens to remove the remaining vestiges of States' traditional police powers. This would convert the Necessary and Proper Clause into precisely what Chief Justice Marshall did not envision, a "pretext . . . for the accomplishment of objects not intrusted to the government." *McCulloch.*

. . . The majority holds that Congress may regulate intrastate cultivation and possession of medical marijuana under the Commerce Clause, because such conduct arguably has a substantial effect on interstate commerce. [This] is further proof that the "substantial effects" test is a "rootless and malleable standard" at odds with the constitutional design. *Morrison* (Thomas, J., concurring).

The . . . substantial effects test is rootless[] because it is not tethered to either the Commerce Clause or the Necessary and Proper Clause. Under the Commerce Clause, Congress may regulate interstate commerce, not activities that substantially affect interstate commerce. . . . Whatever additional latitude the Necessary and Proper Clause affords, the question is whether Congress'[s] legislation is essential to the regulation of interstate commerce itself—not whether the legislation extends only to economic activities that substantially affect interstate commerce.

The . . . substantial effects test is malleable[] because the majority expands the relevant conduct [by] defining the class at a high level of generality. . . . The substantial effects test is easily manipulated for another reason. This Court has never held that Congress can regulate noneconomic activity that substantially affects interstate commerce. To evade even that modest restriction on federal power, the majority defines economic activity in the broadest possible terms, [thus subjecting] a vast swath of activities . . . to federal regulation. If the majority is to be taken seriously, the Federal Government may now regulate quilting bees, clothes drives, and potluck suppers throughout the 50 States. This makes a mockery of Madison's assurance . . . that the "powers delegated" to the Federal Government are "few and defined," while those of the States are "numerous and indefinite." The Federalist No. 45 . . . (J. Madison).

Moreover, . . . Congress is authorized to regulate "Commerce," and respondents' conduct does not qualify under any definition of that term. The majority's opinion only illustrates the steady drift away from the text of the Commerce Clause. There is an inexorable expansion from "commerce," to "commercial" and "economic" activity, and finally to all "production, distribution, and consumption" of goods or services for which there is an "established . . . interstate market." Federal power expands, but never contracts, with each new locution. The majority is not interpreting the Commerce Clause, but rewriting it. . . .

One searches the Court's opinion in vain for any hint of what aspect of American life is reserved to the States. Yet this Court knows that "'the Constitution created a Federal Government of limited powers.'" . . .

I respectfully dissent.

NOTES AND PROBLEMS

1. The Scope of *Raich*: The "Substantial Effects" Test.   Does *Raich* mean that Congress can regulate intrastate noncommercial activities only when the regulation of such activities is essential to the accomplishment of a broader, and independently valid, regulatory scheme of interstate commercial activity? The Court concluded that it was rational for Congress to include the narrow class of intrastate noncommercial medicinal marijuana cultivation and consumption within its regulation of interstate trade and use of marijuana because inclusion of the former class was essential to the latter regulatory end. Or does *Raich* mean that Congress can regulate any intrastate noncommercial activity so long as Congress has made a rational judgment that the activity has a substantial effect on interstate commerce? The Court said that the "modest" task before it was simply to determine whether it was rational for Congress to have determined that the cumulative effects of respondent's local, noncommercial activities substantially affected interstate commerce.

2. The Scope of *Raich*: The "Aggregation" Principle.   When *Wickard* created the aggregation principle it did so in the context of federal regulation that extended to intrastate commercial activity. The cumulative effect of that local economic activity on interstate commerce was what was important. The *Raich* majority asserted that *Wickard* applies to any economic activity and defined "economics" to mean the production, distribution, or consumption of any commodity. What is a "commodity"? Justice Stevens, writing for the majority, did not say. Is a commodity limited to things that are exchanged for value? The dictionary, which Stevens relied on to define "economics," defines a commodity as "anything that is bought and sold" or an "article of trade or commerce." But the marijuana at issue in *Raich* was neither bought, sold, nor bartered. Does that suggest that the Court's conception of a commodity is anything that is *capable* of exchange? Is there anything that is not *capable* of exchange? If so, are the dissenters correct that *Raich* eviscerates any limits on the scope of the commerce power and transforms it into a federal police power? If the broad view of a commodity—as anything capable of exchange—is what the Court had in mind, was it necessary to reach the issue of whether regulation of intrastate noncommercial medical marijuana was "essential" to the success of the larger regulatory scheme? If the broad view of a commodity underlies *Raich*, does this mean that *Wickard*'s cumulative effects doctrine applies whenever Congress regulates an economic activity, and that it also sweeps within that regulation all noneconomic activities that might substitute for the economic activity? At oral argument, the counsel for Raich argued that while *Wickard* might permit Congress to regulate wholly local prostitution, because it is an economic activity the cumulative effects of which might have a substantial effect on interstate commerce, *Wickard* does not permit Congress to regulate marital sexual activity, even though such sexual intercourse might substitute for the blatantly commercial variety. Did *Raich* reject this argument or simply find that medical marijuana use is commercial in a way that marital sex is not?

3. The Standard of Review. Under the "substantial effects" prong of modern Commerce Clause doctrine, the regulated activity must have a substantial effect on interstate commerce for Congress to be able validly to regulate the activity. Who has the burden of establishing the existence or nonexistence of this effect? *Lopez* and *Morrison* suggested that, at least when Congress seeks to regulate a wholly local and noncommercial activity, the burden falls on the government to prove the requisite substantial effect. What does *Raich* do to this understanding? The Court said its job was only to determine whether Congress had a "rational basis" for concluding that the local, noncommercial cultivation, distribution, and consumption of medical marijuana had a substantial effect on interstate commerce. The Court repeatedly stressed the rationality of the congressional judgment to regulate medical marijuana. Does this suggest that the challenger now bears the burden of proving the utter irrationality of Congress's belief that the regulated activity exerts a substantial effect on interstate commerce? If so, what is left of *Lopez* and *Morrison*? *Raich* does not purport to overturn either case, but does it do so silently?

4. "Objective Markers." Justice O'Connor claimed that the "hard task" for courts is to "identify objective markers for confining the analysis in Commerce Clause cases." She asserted that "federal and state legislation" could be one such marker, as well as "fundamental structural concerns about dual sovereignty," and whether the regulated activity lies within traditional areas of state regulation (such as "criminal law and social policy"). How would such markers work in practice? Are they so malleable that they would function as an articulation of judicial whim? Would reference to state legislation deliver a "reverse pre-emption" power to the states? According to Justice Thomas, "Congress has encroached on States' traditional police powers to define the criminal law and to protect the health, safety, and welfare of their citizens." Would reliance on these "traditional police powers" of the states as an "objective marker" be an effective way to limit the "substantial effects" prong of the commerce power, at least when Congress seeks to apply that prong to local, noncommercial activity?

5. Problems.

a. Homemade firearms. In United States v. Stewart, 545 U.S. 1112 (2005), the Court vacated the judgment of the Ninth Circuit and remanded for further consideration in light of *Raich*. The Ninth Circuit had overturned Stewart's conviction for possessing machine guns because Stewart had fabricated them himself. [Though] entirely homemade, . . . some of the machine-gun parts did move in interstate commerce. [O]f course, everything we own is composed of something that once traveled in commerce. . . . Some components of Stewart's machineguns had crossed state lines, but these components did not add up to a gun. Not even close. . . . This is quite different than if Stewart had ordered a disassembled gun and simply put the parts together, the way one might assemble a chair from IKEA. These machineguns were a "unique type of firearm," with legal parts mixed and matched from various origins; they required more than a simple turn of a screwdriver or a hit of a hammer to become machineguns. We therefore cannot say that the machineguns themselves—in any recognizable form—traveled in interstate commerce. Because these firearms were genuinely homemade, we find that Stewart did not obtain his machineguns by "using the channels of interstate commerce." [Nor can we] agree that simple possession of machineguns—particularly possession of homemade machineguns—has a substantial effect on interstate commerce. . . . Possession of a machinegun is not, without more, economic in nature. . . . [W]ithout some evidence that it will be sold or transferred—and there is none here—its relationship to interstate commerce is highly attenuated. Moreover, the regulation itself does not have an economic purpose: whereas the statute in *Wickard* was enacted primarily to control the market price of wheat, there is no evidence that [this law] was enacted to regulate commercial aspects of the machinegun business. More likely, [the law] was intended to keep machineguns out of the hands of criminals—an admirable goal, but not a commercial one. . . .

Assess what the Ninth Circuit should do on remand. Then see United States v. Stewart, 451 F.3d 1071 (9th Cir. 2006).

b. Foreign sexual tourism and the commerce power. In an attempt to stem the sordid practice of sexual tourism, particularly travel to foreign countries for sex with children, Congress enacted 18 U.S.C. §2423(b), which subjects any "person who travels in interstate commerce or travels into the United States, or a United States citizen or an alien admitted for permanent residence in the United States who travels in foreign commerce, for the purpose of engaging in any illicit sexual conduct with another person" to fine or imprisonment for up to 30 years. 18 U.S.C. §2423(c) subjects any American citizen or permanent resident alien "who travels in foreign commerce and engages in any illicit sexual conduct with another person" to the same penalty. Does 18 U.S.C. §2423(b) or (c) exceed the scope of Congress's commerce power? Construct the arguments for and against this claim.

c. Social host tort shield. Suppose that Congress enacts the following law: "A social host who serves alcoholic beverages to guests shall not be liable under the law of any State or political subdivision thereof for harm to persons or property that results from the consumption of such beverages." Suppose further that a person injured by a drunken driver sues the driver's social host in state court, alleging negligence on the part of the social host. The suit is dismissed because of the quoted federal law, which preempts contrary state law. On appeal the injured plaintiff claims that the Congress lacked authority to enact the federal law. What should be the result? Cf. Garcia v. Vanguard Car

Rental USA Inc., 540 F.3d 1242 (11th Cir. 2008); New York City v. Beretta USA Corp., 524 F.3d 384 (2d Cir. 2008).

    d. Personal appearance and interstate travel. Suppose Congress were to enact a law banning male facial hair and female unshaven legs, but that applies only to persons who have "used an instrumentality of interstate commerce, or who have traveled interstate." Assume for the moment that the presence or absence of male facial hair and unshaven female legs does not have a substantial effect on interstate commerce. Is the law valid because it applies only to people with an indisputable connection to interstate commerce? If so, is it correct to say that Congress may regulate any personal activity so long as the persons regulated have a substantial relationship to interstate commerce? Alternatively, would the law be valid because the practice of shaving versus abstention from shaving, in the aggregate, has a substantial effect on interstate commerce? Cf. Katzenbach v. McClung, 379 U.S. 294 (1964).

National Federation of Independent Business v. Sebelius
132 S. Ct. 2566 (2012)

[The Patient Protection and Affordable Care Act (ACA) required all Americans to have health insurance. Those who failed to comply were subject to a penalty, codified in the Internal Revenue Code, and paid to the Internal Revenue Service as part of one's income taxes. This individual mandate was challenged as beyond the congressional power to regulate interstate commerce. Chief Justice Roberts delivered an opinion in which he concluded that Congress lacked authority under the commerce clause to enact the mandate. Justices Ginsburg, Breyer, Sotomayor, and Kagan joined Roberts in ruling that the penalty was really a tax, and thus a valid exercise of the power to tax. Justices Scalia, Kennedy, Thomas, and Alito, dissenting, nevertheless agreed that the mandate was not within the interstate commerce power.]

    CHIEF JUSTICE ROBERTS.

    The Government's first argument is that the individual mandate is a valid exercise of Congress's power under the Commerce Clause and the Necessary and Proper Clause. According to the Government, the health care market is characterized by a significant cost-shifting problem. Everyone will eventually need health care at a time and to an extent they cannot predict, but if they do not have insurance, they often will not be able to pay for it. Because state and federal laws nonetheless require hospitals to provide a certain degree of care to individuals without regard to their ability to pay, hospitals end up receiving compensation for only a portion of the services they provide. To recoup the losses, hospitals pass on the cost to insurers through higher rates, and insurers, in turn, pass on the cost to policy holders in the form of higher premiums.

    [Congress also prohibited] insurance companies from denying coverage to those with [preexisting] conditions or charging unhealthy individuals higher premiums than healthy individuals, [but these provisions did not] address the issue of healthy individuals who choose not to purchase insurance to cover potential health care needs. In fact, the reforms sharply exacerbate that problem, by providing an incentive for individuals to delay purchasing health insurance until they become sick, relying on the promise of guaranteed and affordable coverage. The reforms also threaten to impose massive new costs on insurers, who are required to accept unhealthy individuals but prohibited from charging them rates necessary to pay for their coverage. This will lead insurers to significantly increase premiums on everyone.

The individual mandate was Congress's solution to these problems. By requiring that individuals purchase health insurance, the mandate prevents cost-shifting by those who would otherwise go without it. In addition, the mandate forces into the insurance risk pool more healthy individuals, whose premiums on average will be higher than their health care expenses. This allows insurers to subsidize the costs of covering the unhealthy individuals the reforms require them to accept. . . .

The Government contends that the individual mandate is within Congress's power because the failure to purchase insurance "has a substantial and deleterious effect on interstate commerce" by creating the cost-shifting problem. . . . Given its expansive scope, it is no surprise that Congress has employed the commerce power in a wide variety of ways to address the pressing needs of the time. But Congress has never attempted to rely on that power to compel individuals not engaged in commerce to purchase an unwanted product. . . .

The Constitution grants Congress the power to "*regulate* Commerce." The power to *regulate* commerce presupposes the existence of commercial activity to be regulated. If the power to "regulate" something included the power to create it, many of the provisions in the Constitution would be superfluous. For example, the Constitution gives Congress the power to "coin Money," in addition to the power to "regulate the Value thereof." And it gives Congress the power to "raise and support Armies" and to "provide and maintain a Navy," in addition to the power to "make Rules for the Government and Regulation of the land and naval Forces." If the power to regulate the armed forces or the value of money included the power to bring the subject of the regulation into existence, the specific grant of such powers would have been unnecessary. The language of the Constitution reflects the natural understanding that the power to regulate assumes there is already something to be regulated. . . .

Our precedent also reflects this understanding. . . . They uniformly describe the power as reaching "activity." It is nearly impossible to avoid the word when quoting them. . . . The individual mandate, however, does not regulate existing commercial activity. It instead compels individuals to *become* active in commerce by purchasing a product, on the ground that their failure to do so affects interstate commerce. Construing the Commerce Clause to permit Congress to regulate individuals precisely *because* they are doing nothing would open a new and potentially vast domain to congressional authority. Every day individuals do not do an infinite number of things. In some cases they decide not to do something; in others they simply fail to do it. Allowing Congress to justify federal regulation by pointing to the effect of inaction on commerce would bring countless decisions an individual could *potentially* make within the scope of federal regulation, and—under the Government's theory—empower Congress to make those decisions for him. . . .

[The] Government's logic would justify a mandatory purchase to solve almost any problem. . . . [M]any Americans do not eat a balanced diet. That group makes up a larger percentage of the total population than those without health insurance. The failure of that group to have a healthy diet increases health care costs, to a greater extent than the failure of the uninsured to purchase insurance. Those increased costs are borne in part by other Americans who must pay more, just as the uninsured shift costs to the insured. . . . Under the Government's theory, Congress could address the diet problem by ordering everyone to buy vegetables. People, for reasons of their own, often fail to do things that would be good for them or good for society. Those failures—joined with the similar failures of others—can readily have a substantial effect on interstate commerce. Under the Government's logic, that authorizes Congress to use its commerce power to compel citizens to act as the Government would have them act.

That is not the country the Framers of our Constitution envisioned. . . . The Government's theory would [permit] Congress to reach beyond the natural extent of its authority, "everywhere extending the sphere of its activity and drawing all power into its impetuous vortex." The Federalist No. 48, at 309 (J. Madison). Congress already enjoys vast power to regulate much of what we do. Accepting the Government's theory would give Congress the same license to regulate what we do not do, fundamentally changing the relation between the citizen and the Federal Government.

To an economist, perhaps, there is no difference between activity and inactivity; both have measurable economic effects on commerce. But the distinction between doing something and doing nothing would not have been lost on the Framers, who were "practical statesmen," not metaphysical philosophers. . . . The Framers gave Congress the power to *regulate* commerce, not to *compel* it, and for over 200 years both our decisions and Congress's actions have reflected this understanding. There is no reason to depart from that understanding now. . . .

Our precedents recognize Congress's power to regulate "class[es] of *activities*," not classes of *individuals*, apart from any activity in which they are engaged. The individual mandate's regulation of the uninsured as a class is, in fact, particularly divorced from any link to existing commercial activity. . . . If the individual mandate is targeted at a class, it is a class whose commercial inactivity rather than activity is its defining feature.

The Government . . . claims that this does not matter [because] almost all those who are uninsured will, at some unknown point in the future, engage in a health care transaction. [The] Government argues that because "[e]veryone subject to this regulation is in or will be in the health care market," they can be "regulated in advance." The proposition that Congress may dictate the conduct of an individual today because of prophesied future activity finds no support in our precedent. We have said that Congress can anticipate the *effects* on commerce of an economic activity, . . . [but] we have never permitted Congress to anticipate that activity itself in order to regulate individuals not currently engaged in commerce. . . . The Commerce Clause is not a general license to regulate an individual from cradle to grave, simply because he will predictably engage in particular transactions. Any police power to regulate individuals as such, as opposed to their activities, remains vested in the States. . . . The individual mandate forces individuals into commerce precisely because they elected to refrain from commercial activity. Such a law cannot be sustained under a clause authorizing Congress to "regulate Commerce."

The Government next contends that Congress has the power under the Necessary and Proper Clause to enact the individual mandate because the mandate is an "integral part of a comprehensive scheme of economic regulation"—the guaranteed-issue and community-rating insurance reforms.

[We] have been very deferential to Congress's determination that a regulation is "necessary," [but] we have also carried out our responsibility to declare unconstitutional those laws that undermine the structure of government established by the Constitution. Such laws, which are not "consist[ent] with the letter and spirit of the constitution," are not "*proper* [means] for carrying into Execution" Congress's enumerated powers. Rather, they are, "in the words of The Federalist, 'merely acts of usurpation' which 'deserve to be treated as such.'"

Applying these principles, the individual mandate cannot be sustained under the Necessary and Proper Clause as an essential component of the insurance reforms. Each of our prior cases upholding laws under that Clause involved exercises of authority derivative of, and in service to, a granted power. The individual mandate, by contrast, vests Congress with the extraordinary ability to create the necessary predicate to the exercise of an enumerated power. This is in no way an authority that is "narrow in scope" or "incidental" to the exercise of the commerce power. . . . Just as the individual mandate cannot be sustained as a law regulating the substantial effects of the failure to purchase health insurance, neither can it be upheld as a "necessary and proper" component of the insurance reforms. The commerce power thus does not authorize the mandate. . . . Accord, joint opinion of [Justices] Scalia, Kennedy, Thomas, and Alito, dissenting.

JUSTICES SCALIA, KENNEDY, THOMAS, and ALITO delivered a joint dissent.
. . . If [the individual mandate] "regulates" anything, it is the *failure* to maintain minimum essential coverage. One might argue that it regulates that failure by requiring it to be accompanied by payment of a penalty. But that failure—that abstention from commerce—is not "Commerce." To be sure, *purchasing* insurance *is* "Commerce"; but one does not regulate commerce that does not exist by compelling its existence. . . .

[In regulating the health-care industry] Congress has impressed into service third parties, healthy individuals who could be but are not customers of the . . . industry, to offset the undesirable consequences of the regulation. Congress'[s] desire to force these individuals to purchase insurance is motivated by the fact that they are further removed from the market than unhealthy individuals with pre-existing conditions, because they are less likely to need extensive care in the near future. If Congress can reach out and command even those furthest removed from an interstate market to participate in the market, then the Commerce Clause becomes a font of unlimited power, or in Hamilton's words, "the hideous monster whose devouring jaws . . . spare neither sex nor age, nor high nor low, nor sacred nor profane." The Federalist No. 33, p. 202 (C. Rossiter ed. 1961). . . .

3. Limits Imposed by Principles of State Autonomy

There are many external limits on the commerce power—free speech, due process, equal protection, and the religious liberty clauses of the Constitution, to name just a few. These limits are "external" in the sense that they form no part of the commerce clause (and thus are outside the clause) but are nevertheless constitutional limits upon federal power. The external limits considered in this section are of a different sort; indeed, they are arguably not external at all.

In this section, we consider whether Congress can use its commerce power to regulate *states* (as distinguished from ordinary people). The structure of the Constitution implies that states enjoy a fair amount of autonomy in governing themselves. States possess a general "police power"—the power to act for the general welfare of their residents—that is bounded only by the national Constitution, valid federal law, or the state's own constitution. The federal government has no analogous power. An important implication flowing from this is that, subject to the legitimate constraints of federal law, states are free to govern themselves however they choose. But the scope of this autonomous governance principle is debatable. It could be taken to mean that states enjoy a *substantive* immunity from federal regulation—that states may not be regulated as to certain substantive functions they perform. Or the autonomous governance principle could mean that states enjoy a *procedural* immunity from federal regulation—that the federal government may not employ certain procedures to regulate states.

a. *Substantive Immunity*

In National League of Cities v. Usery, 426 U.S. 833 (1976), the Court adopted the *substantive* immunity approach. Congress amended the Fair Labor Standards Act to extend its maximum hour and minimum wage provisions to all employees of state governments or their political subdivisions. The FLSA amendment was struck down as exceeding Congress's power under the interstate commerce clause. Justice Rehnquist, writing for the Court, concluded that Congress could not use the commerce power to regulate the "States qua States" in order "directly [to] displace the States' freedom to structure integral operations in areas of traditional governmental functions." In short, Congress could not use the commerce power to impinge upon a state's policy choices in matters that are traditionally regarded as governmental. Justice Rehnquist suggested a few such areas: "fire prevention, police protection, sanitation, public health, and parks and recreation." By contrast, Congress impliedly remained free to use the commerce power to regulate states in their capacity as proprietors of business enterprises, such as a state government-owned oil refinery. Justice Blackmun concurred, noting his belief that the majority's test would permit federal regulation of states "in areas such as environmental protection, where the federal interest is demonstrably greater and where [state] compliance with imposed federal standards would be essential."

Five years later, in Hodel v. Virginia Surface Mining & Reclamation Association, 452 U.S. 264 (1981), the Court restated the *National League of Cities* test of substantive immunity to require a challenger to prove four elements:

> First, there must be a showing that the challenged statute regulates the "States as States." Second, the federal regulation must address matters that are indisputably "attributes of state sovereignty." [Third], it must be apparent that the States' compliance with the federal law would directly impair their ability "to structure integral operations in areas of traditional government functions."

In a footnote, the Court added the fourth element: apparently successful challenges fail if "the federal interest advanced [by the challenged law] justifies state submission."

After *National League of Cities*, the courts struggled with the question of which activities were traditionally governmental and whether federal regulations as applied to states touched upon essential attributes of state sovereignty. For example, in United Transportation Union v. Long Island Railroad Co., 455 U.S. 678 (1982), the Court ruled that Congress could regulate the state-owned Long Island Railroad because rail service was not a traditional government function. And in Equal Employment Opportunities Commission v. Wyoming, 460 U.S. 226 (1983), the Court ruled that Congress could bar states from setting mandatory retirement ages for most of their employees because the law had little direct impact on government policy choices. But *National League of Cities* was overruled in 1985.

There remain, however, a few pockets of substantive immunity from federal regulation enjoyed by states. First, the Eleventh Amendment bars states from being subjected to most damage suits in federal court, although suits against state officials seeking injunctive relief are permitted. Congress is also forbidden from abrogating this immunity by exercise of most of its Article I, section 8 powers. See Seminole Tribe v. Florida, 517 U.S. 44 (1996).

But Congress can use its Art. I, §8 power over bankruptcy to abrogate state immunity. Central Virginia Community College v. Katz, 546 U.S. 356 (2006). Second, the so-called equal footing doctrine provides that Congress may not impose conditions on the admission of new states that place the newly admitted states "upon a plane of inequality with its sister States in the Union." Coyle v. Smith, 221 U.S. 559 (1911) (holding that Congress could not impose on Oklahoma, as a condition of admission, a requirement that Oklahoma not move its capital). Third, apart from its obligation to guarantee each state a republican form of government, the federal government may not dictate the terms of state governance. Thus, for example, Congress surely has no power to require that a state adopt a unicameral parliamentary system of government or to require that a state's judges enjoy life tenure, or to restrict state governors to a single term of service.

b. Procedural Immunity

Justice Blackmun, who had supplied the fifth vote for the majority in *National League of Cities*, eventually changed his mind. In 1985, he wrote the majority opinion in another 5-4 decision overruling *National League of Cities*.

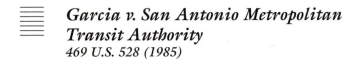

Garcia v. San Antonio Metropolitan Transit Authority
469 U.S. 528 (1985)

JUSTICE BLACKMUN delivered the opinion of the Court.

We revisit in these cases an issue raised in National League of Cities v. Usery, [in which] this Court [ruled] that the Commerce Clause does not empower Congress to enforce the minimum-wage and overtime provisions of the Fair Labor Standards Act (FLSA) against the States "in areas of traditional governmental functions." [*National League of Cities*] did not offer a general explanation of how a "traditional" function is to be distinguished from a "nontraditional" one. [Our] examination of this "function" standard [as] applied [over] the last eight years now persuades us that the attempt to draw the boundaries of state regulatory immunity in terms of "traditional governmental function" is not only unworkable but is also inconsistent with established principles of federalism. [*National League of Cities*,] accordingly, is overruled. . . . We therefore now reject, as unsound in principle and unworkable in practice, a rule of state immunity from federal regulation that turns on a judicial appraisal of whether a particular governmental function is "integral" or "traditional."

The [States] occupy a special position in our constitutional system [and] the scope of Congress'[s] authority under the Commerce Clause must reflect that position. [What] has proved problematic is not the perception that the Constitution's federal structure imposes limitations on the Commerce Clause, but rather the nature and content of those limitations. [The substantive immunity] approach to defining the limits on Congress'[s] authority to regulate the States under the Commerce Clause is to identify certain underlying elements of political sovereignty that are deemed essential to the States' "separate and independent existence" to single out particular features of a State's internal governance that are deemed to be intrinsic parts of state sovereignty. We doubt that courts ultimately can identify principled constitutional limitations on the scope of Congress'[s] Commerce Clause powers over the States merely by relying on a priori definitions of state sovereignty. In part, this is because of the elusiveness of objective criteria for "fundamental" elements of state sovereignty. [Also], the sovereignty of the States is limited by the Constitution itself. A variety of sovereign powers, for example, are withdrawn from the States by Article I, §10. . . .

The States unquestionably do "retai[n] a significant measure of sovereign authority." [But] to say that the Constitution assumes the continued role of the States is to say little about the nature of that role. [The] fact that the States remain sovereign as to all powers not vested in Congress or denied them by the Constitution offers no guidance about where the frontier between state and federal power lies. In short, we have no license to employ freestanding conceptions of state sovereignty when measuring congressional authority under the Commerce Clause.

When we look for the States' "residuary and inviolable sovereignty," in the shape of the constitutional scheme rather than in predetermined notions of sovereign power, a different measure of state sovereignty emerges. Apart from the limitation on federal authority inherent in the delegated nature of Congress'[s] Article I powers, the principal means chosen by the Framers to ensure the role of the States in the federal system lies in the structure of the Federal Government itself. It is no novelty to observe that the composition of the Federal Government was designed in large part to protect the States from overreaching by Congress.[2] The Framers thus gave the States a

---

2. See, e.g., J. Choper, Judicial Review and the National Political Process 175-184 (1980); Wechsler, The Political Safeguards of Federalism: The Role of the States in the Composition and Selection of the National Government, 54 Colum. L. Rev. 543 (1954); La Pierre, The Political Safeguards of Federalism Redux: Intergovernmental Immunity and the States as Agents of the Nation, 60 Wash. U. L.Q. 779 (1982).

[Choper argued that the Court should not decide federalism issues, but leave them for decision by the political process because "[n]umerous structural aspects of the national political system serve to assure that states' rights will not be trampled." Wechsler argued that because Congress is composed of state representatives and the states select the President via the Electoral College

> the states are the strategic yardsticks for the measurement of interest and opinion, the special centers of political activity, the separate geographical determinants of national as well as local politics. [The] national political [process]—especially the role of the states in the composition and selection of the central government—is intrinsically well adapted to retarding or restraining new intrusions by the center on the domain of the states.]

—ED.

role in the selection both of the Executive and the Legislative Branches of the Federal Government. [State] sovereign interests [are] more properly protected by procedural safeguards inherent in the structure of the federal system than by judicially created limitations on federal power. [We] are convinced that the fundamental limitation that the constitutional scheme imposes on the Commerce Clause to protect the "States as States" is one of process rather than one of result. Any substantive restraint on the exercise of Commerce Clause powers must find its justification in the procedural nature of this basic limitation, and it must be tailored to compensate for possible failings in the national political process rather than to dictate a "sacred province of state autonomy."

JUSTICE POWELL, joined by CHIEF JUSTICE BURGER and JUSTICES REHNQUIST and O'CONNOR, dissenting.

Today's opinion does not explain how the States' role in the electoral process guarantees that particular exercises of the Commerce Clause power will not infringe on residual state sovereignty. Members of Congress are elected from the various States, but once in office they are Members of the Federal Government. Although the States participate in the Electoral College, this is hardly a reason to view the President as a representative of the States' interest against federal encroachment. We noted recently "[t]he hydraulic pressure inherent within each of the separate Branches to exceed the outer limits of its power." [The] Court offers no reason to think that this pressure will not operate when Congress seeks to invoke its powers under the Commerce Clause, notwithstanding the electoral role of the States. . . .

More troubling than the logical infirmities in the Court's reasoning is the result of its holding, i.e., that federal political officials, invoking the Commerce Clause, are the sole judges of the limits of their own power. This result is inconsistent with the fundamental principles of our constitutional system. See, e.g., The Federalist No. 78 (Hamilton). At least since Marbury v. Madison it has been the settled province of the federal judiciary "to say what the law is" with respect to the constitutionality of Acts of Congress.

[The] Framers had definite ideas about the nature of the Constitution's division of authority between the Federal and State Governments. In The Federalist No. 39, for example, Madison explained [that while] a national form of government would possess an "indefinite supremacy over all persons and things," the form of government contemplated by the Constitution instead consisted of "local or municipal authorities [which] form distinct and independent portions of the supremacy, no more subject within their respective spheres to the general authority, than the general authority is subject to them, within its own sphere." Under the Constitution, the sphere of the proposed government extended to jurisdiction of "certain enumerated objects only, [leaving] to the several States a residuary and inviolable sovereignty over all other objects."

[The] Court today propounds a view of federalism that pays only lip service to the role of the States. [The] Court looks myopically only to persons elected to positions in the Federal Government. It disregards entirely the far more effective role of democratic self-government at the state and local levels. One must compare realistically the operation of the state and local governments with that of the Federal Government. Federal legislation is drafted primarily by the staffs of the congressional committees. In view of the hundreds of bills introduced at each session of Congress and the complexity of many of them, it is virtually impossible for even the most conscientious legislators to be truly familiar with many of the statutes enacted. Federal departments and agencies customarily are authorized to write regulations. Often these are more important than the text of the statutes. As is true of the original legislation, these are drafted largely by staff personnel. The administration and enforcement of federal laws and regulations necessarily are largely in the hands of staff and civil service employees. These employees may have little or no knowledge of the States and localities that will be affected by the statutes and regulations for which they are responsible. In any case, they hardly are as accessible and responsive as those who occupy analogous positions in state and local governments. [Members] of the immense federal bureaucracy are not elected, know less about the services traditionally rendered by States and localities, and are inevitably less responsive to recipients of such services, than are state legislatures, city councils, boards of supervisors, and state and local commissions, boards, and agencies. It is at these state and local levels—not in Washington as the Court so mistakenly thinks—that "democratic self-government" is best exemplified. [Although] the Court's opinion purports to recognize that the States retain some sovereign power, it does not identify even a single aspect of state authority that would remain when the Commerce Clause is invoked to justify federal regulation.

JUSTICE O'CONNOR, joined by JUSTICES POWELL and REHNQUIST, dissenting.

In my view, federalism cannot be reduced to the weak "essence" distilled by the majority today. The true "essence" of federalism is that the States *as States* have legitimate interests which the National Government is bound to respect even though its laws are supreme. If federalism so conceived and so carefully cultivated by the Framers of our Constitution is to remain meaningful, this Court cannot abdicate its constitutional responsibility to oversee the Federal Government's compliance with its duty to respect the legitimate interests of the States.

[The Court today] washes its hands of all efforts to protect the States, [opining] that unwarranted federal encroachments on state authority are and will remain "horrible possibilities that never happen in the real world." There is ample reason to believe to the contrary. The last two decades have seen an unprecedented growth of federal regulatory activity. [In] 1954, one could still speak of a "burden of persuasion on those favoring national intervention" in asserting that "National action [has] always been regarded as exceptional in our polity, an intrusion to be justified by some necessity, the special rather than the ordinary case." Wechsler, The Political Safeguards of Federalism: The Role of the States in the Composition and Selection of the National

Government, 54 Colum. L. Rev. 543, 544-545 (1954). Today, as federal legislation and coercive grant programs have expanded to embrace innumerable activities that were once viewed as local, the burden of persuasion has surely shifted, and the extraordinary has become ordinary. [The] political process has not protected against these encroachments on state activities, even though they directly impinge on a State's ability to make and enforce its laws. With the abandonment of *National League of Cities*, all that stands between the remaining essentials of state sovereignty and Congress is the latter's underdeveloped capacity for self-restraint.

The problems of federalism in an integrated national economy are capable of more responsible resolution than holding that the States as States retain no status apart from that which Congress chooses to let them retain. The proper resolution, I suggest, lies in weighing state autonomy as a factor in the balance when interpreting the means by which Congress can exercise its authority on the States as States. It is insufficient, in assessing the validity of congressional regulation of a State pursuant to the commerce power, to ask only whether the same regulation would be valid if enforced against a private party. That reasoning, embodied in the majority opinion, is inconsistent with the spirit of our Constitution. It remains relevant that a *State* is being [regulated]. If state autonomy is ignored in assessing the means by which Congress regulates matters affecting commerce, then federalism becomes irrelevant simply because the set of activities remaining beyond the reach of such a commerce power "may well be negligible."

Justice Rehnquist, dissenting.

I do not think it incumbent on those of us in dissent to spell out further the fine points of a principle that will, I am confident, in time again command the support of a majority of this Court.

NOTES

1. The *Garcia* Vision of Procedural Immunity. The *Garcia* majority stated that the state autonomy limit upon the commerce power is "one of process rather than one of result. Any substantive restraint on the [commerce power] must find its justification in the procedural nature of this basic limitation, and it must be tailored to compensate for possible failings in the national political process." To the *Garcia* majority the states enjoy whatever immunity from the commerce power the political process confers. As the quoted passage indicates, the Court might intervene to correct "possible failings in the national political process."

In South Carolina v. Baker, 485 U.S. 505 (1988), the Court suggested what might constitute such failings. Congress amended federal tax law to subject interest paid on state bearer bonds to federal income tax. Ordinarily, interest on state bonds is tax-exempt. South Carolina, an issuer of bearer bonds, objected because it was effectively forced either to issue bonds registered in the name of the purchaser in order to make its bonds tax-exempt or to increase the rate of interest it paid on bearer bonds to offset the loss of tax-exempt status. For the Court, Justice Brennan rejected South Carolina's claim that the tax change was the product of a defective political process because

> South Carolina has not even alleged that it was deprived of any right to participate in the national political process or that it was singled out in a way that left it politically isolated and powerless. Rather, South Carolina argues that the political process failed here because [the tax change] was "imposed by a vote of an uninformed Congress relying upon incomplete information."

This was not a defective process, said Brennan, but simply a case where South Carolina's position was a political loser.

In Gregory v. Ashcroft, 501 U.S. 452 (1991), the Court revived the *National League of Cities* brand of federalism, but as a principle of statutory construction. The federal Age Discrimination in Employment Act (ADEA) bars private and public employers from adopting mandatory retirement ages but exempts states from that rule with respect to "policymaking" employees. The Court ruled that the ADEA did not apply to Missouri's mandatory retirement age for judges, concluding that federalism principles created a presumption against congressional interference with state decisions that are "fundamental [for] a sovereign," and stating that only a clear and unequivocal statement of congressional intent to invade the domain of state sovereignty could suffice to establish that the statute had such an effect.

In short, the *Garcia* view of procedural immunity is that Congress can use the commerce power to regulate the states in whatever manner it pleases, so long as the regulation is (1) a clear and unequivocal statement of congressional intent to regulate a state's sovereign functions and (2) not the product of a political process as dramatically defective as *Baker* suggests.

Problem: Physician-Assisted Suicide. Only Washington and Oregon expressly permit physician-assisted suicide. If Congress were to prohibit that practice (assuming it has authority under the commerce clause to do so), would the ban be valid?

2. The Seed of an Alternative Vision of Procedural Immunity. In *Hodel*, a case decided before *Garcia*, the Court upheld against a state autonomy challenge a federal law regulating strip mining. The law did not "commandeer[ ] the legislative processes of the States by directly compelling them to enact and enforce a federal regulatory program." This thread was continued by Justice O'Connor in her dissent in another pre-*Garcia* case, FERC v. Mississippi, 456 U.S. 742 (1982). The Court upheld the Public Utility Regulatory Policies Act of 1978 (PURPA), which required state utility regulators to "consider" federal standards for utility rates and regulation. In dissent, O'Connor argued that PURPA effectively commanded state officials to adhere to a federally mandated agenda in considering their options when regulating utilities. Congress does not have the power, she said, to "conscript state utility commissions into the national bureaucratic army." An influential commentator, Professor Andrzej Rapaczynski, argued immediately after the *Garcia* decision that the case for judicial intervention is strong when Congress uses its commerce power to regulate "state governmental functions [directly] related to the federalist concern with preventing tyranny." The primary example he offered was "federal interference with the agenda of the highest state legislative [and] executive organs." See Rapaczynski, From Sovereignty to Process: The Jurisprudence of Federalism After Garcia, 1985 Sup. Ct. Rev. 341.

This alternative vision of procedural immunity bore fruit in the following cases.

New York v. United States
505 U.S. 144 (1992)

JUSTICE O'CONNOR delivered the opinion of the Court.

This case implicates one of our Nation's newest problems of public policy and perhaps our oldest question of constitutional law. The public policy issue involves the disposal of radioactive waste: In this case, we address the constitutionality of three provisions of the Low-Level Radioactive Waste Policy Amendments Act of 1985. The constitutional question is as old as the Constitution: It consists of discerning the proper division of authority between the Federal Government and the States. We conclude that while Congress has substantial power under the Constitution to encourage the States to provide for the disposal of the radioactive waste generated within their borders, the Constitution does not confer upon Congress the ability simply to compel the States to do so. We therefore find that only two of the Act's three provisions at issue are [constitutionally valid].

[The law was enacted to assure adequate disposal facilities for low-level radioactive waste. In 1980, Congress enacted] the Low-Level Radioactive Waste Policy Act, [which] declared a federal policy of holding each State "responsible for providing for the availability of capacity either within or outside the State for the disposal of low-level radioactive waste generated within its borders." [The] 1980 Act authorized States to enter into regional compacts that, once ratified by Congress, would have the authority beginning in 1986 to restrict the use of their disposal facilities to waste generated within member States. . . . By 1985, only three approved regional compacts had operational disposal facilities; not surprisingly, these were the compacts formed around South Carolina, Nevada, and Washington, the three sited States. The following year, the 1980 Act would have given these three compacts the ability to exclude waste from nonmembers, and the remaining 31 States would have had no assured outlet for their low level radioactive waste. With this prospect looming, Congress [enacted] the legislation challenged here. . . .

The 1985 Act [embodies] a compromise among the sited and unsited States. The sited States agreed to extend for seven years the period in which they would accept low level radioactive waste from other States. In exchange, the unsited States agreed to end their reliance on the sited States by 1992. The mechanics of this compromise are intricate. [In brief, the Act imposed three escalating sets of incentives to states either to enter into interstate disposal compacts or to provide a disposal site within their own borders. The first set of incentives authorized sited states to impose a surcharge upon waste received from outsiders, a portion of that surcharge was taxed by the federal government, and the tax proceeds spent on grants to states that achieved specific deadlines in developing disposal sites. The second group of incentives permitted sited states ultimately to deny access altogether to waste coming from outside the sited state or compact. The third incentive provided that any state failing to provide a disposal site (either on its own or through a compact) by a specified date must "take title" to and possession of all the waste generated within its borders and become liable for all damages caused by the state's failure to take possession. New York and two New York counties sought a declaration that the three sets of incentives were invalid because Congress lacked authority to impose them. The lower courts dismissed the complaint.]

[T]he task of ascertaining the constitutional line between federal and state power [can] be viewed [as] whether an Act of Congress is authorized by one of the powers delegated to Congress in Article I of the Constitution [or as] whether an Act of Congress invades the province of state sovereignty reserved by the Tenth Amendment. In a case like this one . . . the two inquiries are mirror images of each other. If a power is delegated to Congress in the Constitution, the Tenth Amendment expressly disclaims any reservation of that power to the States; if a power is an attribute of state sovereignty reserved by the Tenth Amendment, it is necessarily a power the Constitution has not conferred on Congress. It is in this sense that the Tenth Amendment "states but a truism that all is retained which has not been surrendered." [Congress] exercises its conferred powers subject to the limitations contained in the Constitution. Thus, for example, under the Commerce Clause Congress may regulate publishers engaged in interstate commerce, but Congress is constrained in the exercise of that power by the First Amendment. The Tenth Amendment likewise restrains the power of Congress, but this limit is not derived from the text of the Tenth Amendment itself, which . . . is essentially a tautology. Instead, the Tenth Amendment confirms that the power of the Federal Government is subject to limits that may, in a given instance, reserve power to the States. The Tenth Amendment thus directs us to determine . . . whether an incident of state sovereignty is protected by a limitation on an Article I power. . . .

B. Petitioners do not contend that Congress lacks the power to regulate the disposal of low level radioactive waste. [Regulation of the] interstate market in waste disposal [is] well within Congress'[s] authority under the Commerce Clause. Petitioners likewise do not dispute that under the Supremacy Clause Congress could, if it wished, pre-empt state radioactive waste regulation. Petitioners contend only that the Tenth Amendment limits the power of Congress to regulate in the way it has chosen. Rather than addressing the problem of waste disposal by directly regulating the generators and disposers of waste, petitioners argue, Congress has impermissibly directed the States to regulate in this field.

[This] is not a case in which Congress has subjected a State to the same legislation applicable to private parties. This case instead concerns the circumstances under which Congress may use the States as implements of regulation; that is, whether Congress may direct or otherwise motivate the States to regulate in a particular field or a particular way. . . .

1. As an initial matter, Congress may not simply "commandee[r] the legislative processes of the States by directly compelling them to enact and enforce a federal regulatory program." [T]he Constitution has never been understood to confer upon Congress the ability to require the States to govern according to Congress'[s] instructions. [Indeed], the question whether the Constitution should permit Congress to employ state governments as regulatory agencies was a topic of lively debate among the Framers. [The Constitutional] Convention generated a great number of proposals for the structure of the new Government, but two quickly took center stage. Under the Virginia Plan [Congress] would exercise legislative authority directly upon individuals, without employing the States as intermediaries. Under the New Jersey Plan [Congress] would continue to require the approval of the States before legislating, [as] under the Articles of Confederation. [One] frequently expressed objection to the New Jersey Plan was that it might require the Federal Government to coerce the States into implementing legislation. [In] the end, the Convention opted for a Constitution in which Congress would exercise its legislative authority directly over individuals rather than over [States]. [E]ven where Congress has the authority under the Constitution to pass laws requiring or prohibiting certain acts, it lacks the power directly to compel the States to require or prohibit those acts. . . .

2. This is not to say that Congress lacks the ability to encourage a State to regulate in a particular way, or that Congress may not hold out incentives to the States as a method of influencing a State's policy choices. . . . First, under Congress'[s] spending power, "Congress may attach conditions on the receipt of federal funds." Such conditions must (among other requirements) bear some relationship to the purpose of the federal spending; otherwise, of course, the spending power could render academic the Constitution's other grants and limits of federal authority. Where the recipient of federal funds is a State, as is not unusual today, the conditions attached to the funds by Congress may influence a State's legislative choices. [Second], where Congress has the authority to regulate private activity under the Commerce Clause, we have recognized Congress'[s] power to offer States the choice of regulating that activity according to federal standards or having state law pre-empted by federal regulation. [By] either of these two methods [the] residents of the State retain the ultimate decision as to whether or not the State will comply. If a State's citizens view federal policy as sufficiently contrary to local interests, they may elect to decline a federal grant. If state residents would prefer their government to devote its attention and resources to problems other than those deemed important by Congress, they may choose to have the Federal

Government rather than the State bear the expense of a federally mandated regulatory program, and they may continue to supplement that program to the extent state law is not preempted. Where Congress encourages state regulation rather than compelling it, state governments remain responsive to the local electorate's preferences; state officials remain accountable to the people. By contrast, where the Federal Government compels States to regulate, the accountability of both state and federal officials is diminished. If the citizens of New York, for example, do not consider that making provision for the disposal of radioactive waste is in their best interest, they may elect state officials who share their view. That view can always be pre-empted under the Supremacy Clause if it is contrary to the national view, but in such a case it is the Federal Government that makes the decision in full view of the public, and it will be federal officials that suffer the consequences if the decision turns out to be detrimental or unpopular. But where the Federal Government directs the States to regulate, it may be state officials who will bear the brunt of public disapproval, while the federal officials who devised the regulatory program may remain insulated from the electoral ramifications of their decision. Accountability is thus diminished when, due to federal coercion, elected state officials cannot regulate in accordance with the views of the local electorate in matters not pre-empted by federal regulation. With these principles in mind, we turn to the three challenged provisions of the [law].

III. . . . A. [Congressional authorization of a state] surcharge on radioactive waste received from other States [is] an unexceptionable exercise of Congress'[s] power to authorize the States to burden interstate commerce. [See Chapter 4.] [The] Secretary of Energy['s] collection of a percentage of the surcharge, is no more than a [valid] federal tax on interstate commerce. . . . [Disbursement of] portions of this fund [to states who arrange for waste disposal in timely fashion] is a conditional exercise of Congress'[s] authority under the Spending Clause: Congress has placed conditions—the achievement of the milestones—on the receipt of federal funds. . . . [Because] the first set of incentives is supported by affirmative constitutional grants of power to Congress, it is not inconsistent with the Tenth Amendment.

B. In the second set of incentives, Congress has authorized States and regional compacts with disposal sites gradually to increase the cost of access to the sites, and then to deny access altogether, to radioactive waste generated in States that do not meet federal deadlines. As a simple regulation, this provision would be within the power of Congress to authorize the States to discriminate against interstate commerce. Where federal regulation of private activity is within the scope of the Commerce Clause, we have recognized the ability of Congress to offer states the choice of regulating that activity according to federal standards or having state law pre-empted by federal regulation. This is the choice presented to nonsited States by the Act's second set of incentives: States may either regulate the disposal of radioactive waste according to federal standards by attaining local or regional self-sufficiency, or their residents who produce radioactive waste will be subject to federal regulation authorizing sited States and regions to deny access to their disposal sites. The affected States are not compelled by Congress to regulate, because any burden caused by a State's refusal to regulate will fall on those who generate waste and find no outlet for its disposal, rather than on the State as a sovereign. A State whose citizens do not wish it to attain the Act's milestones may devote its attention and its resources to issues its citizens deem more worthy; the choice remains at all times with the residents of the State, not with Congress. The State need not expend any funds, or participate in any federal program, if local residents do not view such expenditures or participation as worthwhile. Nor must the State abandon the field if it does not accede to federal direction; the State may continue to regulate the generation and disposal of radioactive waste in any manner its citizens see fit. The Act's second set of incentives thus represents a conditional exercise of Congress'[s] commerce power, along the lines of those we have held to be within Congress'[s] authority. . . .

C. The take title provision is of a different character. This third so-called "incentive" offers States, as an alternative to regulating pursuant to Congress'[s] direction, the option of taking title to and possession of the low level radioactive waste generated within their borders and becoming liable for all damages waste generators suffer as a result of the States' failure to do so promptly. In this provision, Congress has crossed the line distinguishing encouragement from coercion. [The] take title provision offers state governments a "choice" of either accepting ownership of waste or regulating according to the instructions of Congress. [On] one hand, the Constitution would not permit Congress simply to transfer radioactive waste from generators to state governments. Such a forced transfer, standing alone, would in principle be no different than a congressionally compelled subsidy from state governments to radioactive waste producers. The same is true of the provision requiring the States to become liable for the generators' damages. Standing alone, this provision would be indistinguishable from an Act of Congress directing the States to assume the liabilities of certain state residents. Either type of federal action would "commandeer" state governments into the service of federal regulatory purposes, and would for this reason be inconsistent with the Constitution's division of authority between federal and state governments. On the other hand, the second alternative held out to state governments—regulating pursuant to Congress'[s] direction—would, standing alone, present a simple command to state governments to implement legislation enacted by Congress. [The] Constitution does not empower Congress to subject state governments to this type of instruction.

Because an instruction to state governments to take title to waste, standing alone, would be beyond the authority of Congress and because a direct order to regulate, standing alone, would also be beyond the authority of Congress, it follows that Congress lacks the power to offer the States a choice between the two. . . . A choice between two unconstitutionally coercive regulatory techniques is no choice at all. Either way, "the Act commandeers the legislative processes of the States by directly compelling them to enact and enforce a federal regulatory program," [*Hodel*], an outcome that has never been understood to lie within the authority conferred upon Congress by the

Constitution. . . . Whether one views the take title provision as lying outside Congress'[s] enumerated powers, or as infringing upon the core of state sovereignty reserved by the Tenth Amendment, the provision is inconsistent with the federal structure of our Government established by the Constitution.

IV. Respondents raise a number of objections to this understanding of the limits of Congress'[s] power.

A. . . . [T]he United States argues that the Constitution's prohibition of congressional directives to state governments can be overcome where the federal interest is sufficiently important to justify state submission. . . . No matter how powerful the federal interest involved, the Constitution simply does not give Congress the authority to require the States to regulate . . . . Where a federal interest is sufficiently strong to cause Congress to legislate, it must do so directly; it may not conscript state governments as its agents. . . .

B. The sited State respondents . . . note that the Act embodies a bargain among the sited and unsited States, a compromise to which New York was a willing participant and from which New York has reaped much benefit. . . . How can a federal statute be found an unconstitutional infringement of State sovereignty when state officials consented to the statute's enactment? The answer [is that the] Constitution does not protect the sovereignty of States for the benefit of the States or state governments as abstract political entities, or even for the benefit of the public officials governing the States. To the contrary, the Constitution divides authority between federal and state governments for the protection of individuals. State sovereignty is not just an end in itself: "Rather, federalism secures to citizens the liberties that derive from the diffusion of sovereign power." [Where] Congress exceeds its authority relative to the States, therefore, the departure from the constitutional plan cannot be ratified by the "consent" of state officials. . . . State officials thus cannot consent to the enlargement of the powers of Congress beyond those enumerated in the Constitution.

Indeed, the facts of this case raise the possibility that powerful incentives might lead both federal and state officials to view departures from the federal structure to be in their personal interests. Most citizens recognize the need for radioactive waste disposal sites, but few want sites near their homes. As a result, . . . it is likely to be in the political interest of each individual official to avoid being held accountable to the voters for the choice of location. If a federal official is faced with the alternatives of choosing a location or directing the States to do it, the official may well prefer the latter, as a means of shifting responsibility for the eventual decision. If a state official is faced with the same set of alternatives—choosing a location or having Congress direct the choice of a location—the state official may also prefer the latter, as it may permit the avoidance of personal responsibility. The interests of public officials thus may not coincide with the Constitution's intergovernmental allocation of authority. Where state officials purport to submit to the direction of Congress in this manner, federalism is hardly being advanced. . . .

VII. . . . Some truths are so basic that, like the air around us, they are easily overlooked. Much of the Constitution is concerned with setting forth the form of our government, and the courts have traditionally invalidated measures deviating from that form. The . . . Constitution divides power among sovereigns and among branches of government precisely so that we may resist the temptation to concentrate power in one location as an expedient solution to the crisis of the day. The shortage of disposal sites for radioactive waste is a pressing national problem, but a judiciary that licensed extra-constitutional government with each issue of comparable gravity would, in the long run, be far worse.

States are not mere political subdivisions of the United States. State governments are neither regional offices nor administrative agencies of the Federal Government. The positions occupied by state officials appear nowhere on the Federal Government's most detailed organizational chart. The Constitution instead "leaves to the several States a residuary and inviolable sovereignty," reserved explicitly to the States by the Tenth Amendment. Whatever the outer limits of that sovereignty may be, one thing is clear: The Federal Government may not compel the States to enact or administer a federal regulatory program. . . .

JUSTICE WHITE, joined by JUSTICES BLACKMUN and STEVENS, dissenting as to the holding that the take title provision was unconstitutional.

I. [The Act] resulted from the efforts of state leaders to achieve a state-based set of remedies to the waste problem. They sought not federal preemption or intervention, but rather congressional sanction of interstate compromises they had reached. . . . A movement . . . arose to achieve a compromise between the sited and the unsited States, in which the sited States agreed to continue accepting waste in exchange for the imposition of stronger measures to guarantee compliance with the unsited States' assurances that they would develop alternate disposal facilities. [This compromise was the 1985 Act, which] was very much the product of cooperative federalism, in which the States bargained among themselves to achieve compromises for Congress to sanction. [Unlike] legislation that directs action from the Federal Government to the States, the 1980 and 1985 Acts reflected hard-fought agreements among States as refereed by Congress. The distinction is key, and the Court's failure properly to characterize this legislation ultimately affects its analysis of the take title provision's constitutionality.

II. . . . A. In my view, New York's actions subsequent to enactment of the 1980 and 1985 Acts fairly indicate its approval of the interstate agreement process embodied in those laws within the meaning of Art. I, §10, cl. 3 [the interstate compact clause. These] statutes are best understood as the products of collective state action, rather than as impositions placed on States by the Federal Government. [New York] acted in compliance with the requisites of both statutes in key respects, thus signifying its assent to the agreement achieved among the States as codified in these laws. . . .

B. [Seen] as a term of an agreement entered into between the several States, this measure proves to be less constitutionally odious than the Court opines. First, the practical effect of New York's position is that because it is unwilling to honor its obligations to provide in-state storage facilities for its low-level radioactive waste, other States with such plants must accept New York's waste, whether they wish to or not. [The] Court's refusal to force New York to accept responsibility for its own problem inevitably means that some other State's sovereignty will be impinged by it being forced, for public health reasons, to accept New York's low-level radioactive waste. I do not understand the principle of federalism to impede the National Government from acting as referee among the States to prohibit one from bullying another.

III. The Court announces that it has no occasion to revisit [*Garcia*] because "this is not a case in which Congress has subjected a State to the same legislation applicable to private parties." . . . [An] incursion on state sovereignty hardly seems more constitutionally acceptable if the federal statute that "commands" specific action also applies to private parties. The alleged diminution in state authority over its own affairs is not any less because the federal mandate restricts the activities of private parties. . . .

IV. Though I disagree with the Court's conclusion that the take title provision is unconstitutional, I do not read its opinion to preclude Congress from adopting a similar measure through its powers under the Spending or Commerce Clauses. . . . Congress [could] condition the payment of funds on the State's willingness to take title if it has not already provided a waste disposal facility. [Similarly], should a State fail to establish a waste disposal facility by the appointed deadline [Congress] has the power pursuant to the Commerce Clause to regulate directly the producers of the waste. . . .

V. The ultimate irony of the decision today is that in its formalistically rigid obeisance to "federalism," the Court gives Congress fewer incentives to defer to the wishes of state officials in achieving local solutions to local problems. This legislation was a classic example of Congress acting as arbiter among the States in their attempts to accept responsibility for managing a problem of grave import.

NOTE

Note that the "anticommandeering" principle merely forecloses that mode of regulation and applies only when Congress uses the commerce power to act exclusively upon the states. As Justice White asserts, Congress remains free to use its conditional spending power to extract state compliance, or Congress might simply use its commerce power to regulate the field and thus preempt contrary state legislation. The immunity thus afforded states from federal regulation is distinctly procedural. In New York v. United States, the "anticommandeering" principle was applied to a congressional attempt to direct state legislatures as to how they must legislate. But, as the following case makes clear, this principle also applies to federal commands issued to state executive officers.

≡≡ *Printz v. United States*
≡≡ *521 U.S. 898 (1997)*

JUSTICE SCALIA delivered the opinion of the Court.

The question presented [is] whether certain interim provisions of the Brady Handgun Violence Prevention Act, [commanding] state and local law enforcement officers to conduct background checks on prospective handgun purchasers and to perform certain related tasks, violate the Constitution.

I. [The Brady Act restricts the sale of handguns by mandating a background check on prospective handgun purchasers. Firearms dealers are required to notify the local Chief Law Enforcement Officer (CLEO) of the prospective purchaser's identity at least five days before the purchase is completed. Under some circumstances,] CLEOs are required to "make a reasonable effort to ascertain within 5 business days whether receipt or possession would be in violation of the law, including research in whatever State and local recordkeeping systems are available and in a national system designated by the Attorney General." [If] the CLEO notifies a gun dealer that a prospective purchaser is ineligible to receive a handgun, he must, upon request, provide the would-be purchaser with a written statement of the reasons for that determination. If the CLEO does not discover any basis for objecting to the sale, he must destroy any records in his possession relating to the transfer. [Knowing violations of these provisions are punishable by fine and imprisonment.]

[Federal district courts struck down these provisions as unconstitutional in separate suits brought by] Jay Printz and Richard Mack, the CLEOs for Ravalli County, Montana, and Graham County, Arizona. [The] Ninth Circuit reversed. . . .

II. [The] Brady Act purports to direct state law enforcement officers to participate [in] the administration of a federally enacted regulatory scheme. [The] petitioners here object to being pressed into federal service, and contend that congressional action compelling state officers to execute federal laws is unconstitutional. Because there is no constitutional text speaking to this precise question, the answer to the CLEOs' challenge must be sought in historical understanding and practice, in the structure of the Constitution, and in the jurisprudence of this Court. We treat those three sources, in that order, in this and the next two sections of this opinion.

Petitioners contend that compelled enlistment of state executive officers for the administration of federal programs is, until very recent years at least, unprecedented. The Government contends . . . that "the earliest Congresses enacted statutes that required the participation of state officials in the implementation of federal laws." The Government's contention demands our careful consideration, since early congressional enactments "provide 'contemporaneous and weighty evidence' of the Constitution's meaning." Indeed, such "contemporaneous legislative exposition of the [Constitution], acquiesced in for a long term of years, fixes the construction to be given its provisions." Conversely [if] earlier Congresses avoided use of this highly attractive power, we would have reason to believe that the power was thought not to exist. . . .

[Not] only do the enactments of the early Congresses [contain] no evidence of an assumption that the Federal Government may command the States' executive power in the absence of a particularized constitutional authorization, they contain some indication of precisely the opposite assumption. [The] First Congress enacted a law aimed at obtaining state assistance of the most rudimentary and necessary sort for the enforcement of the new Government's laws: the holding of federal prisoners in state jails at federal expense. Significantly, the law issued not a command to the States' executive, but a recommendation to their legislatures. [Moreover], when Georgia refused to comply with the request Congress's only reaction was a law authorizing the marshal in any State that failed to comply with the Recommendation [to] rent a temporary jail until provision for a permanent one could be made.

In addition to early legislation, the Government also appeals [to] portions of The Federalist which [state] . . . that Congress will probably "make use of the State officers and State regulations, for collecting" federal taxes [The Federalist No. 36 (Hamilton),] . . . that "the eventual collection [of internal revenue] under the immediate authority of the Union, will generally be made by the officers, and according to the rules, appointed by the several States," [Federalist No. 45 (Madison)] that the Constitution would "enable the [national] government to employ the ordinary magistracy of each [State] in the execution of its laws," [Federalist No. 27 (Hamilton)], and that it was "extremely probable that in other instances, particularly in the organization of the judicial power, the officers of the States will be clothed in the correspondent authority of the Union" [Federalist No. 45 (Madison)]. But none of these statements necessarily implies—what is the critical point here—that Congress could impose these responsibilities without the consent of the States. They appear to rest on the natural assumption that the States would consent to allowing their officials to assist the Federal Government.

[To] complete the historical record, we must note that there is not only an absence of executive-commandeering statutes in the early Congresses, but there is an absence of them in our later history as well, at least until very recent years. . . . The Government points to a number of federal statutes enacted within the past few decades that require the participation of state or local officials in implementing federal regulatory schemes. . . . Even assuming they represent assertion of the very same congressional power challenged here, they are of such recent vintage that they are no more probative than the statute before us of a constitutional tradition that lends meaning to the text. Their persuasive force is far outweighed by almost two centuries of apparent congressional avoidance of the practice.

III. [We] turn next to consideration of the structure of the Constitution, to see if we can discern among its "essential postulates" a principle that controls the present cases.

A. It is incontestible that the Constitution established a system of "dual sovereignty." Although the States surrendered many of their powers to the new Federal Government, they retained "a residuary and inviolable sovereignty." This is reflected throughout the Constitution's text. . . . Residual state sovereignty was also implicit, of course, in the Constitution's conferral upon Congress of not all governmental powers, but only discrete, enumerated ones, which implication was rendered express by the Tenth Amendment's assertion that "the powers not delegated to the United States by the Constitution, nor prohibited by it to the States, are reserved to the States respectively, or to the people."

[The] Framers rejected the concept of a central government that would act upon and through the States, and instead designed a system in which the state and federal governments would exercise concurrent authority over the people—who were, in Hamilton's words, "the only proper objects of government." [Federalist No. 15.] . . . The Constitution thus contemplates that a State's government will represent and remain accountable to its own citizens. This separation of the two spheres is one of the Constitution's structural protections of liberty. . . .

B. We have thus far discussed the effect that federal control of state officers would have upon [the] division of power between State and Federal Governments. It would also have an effect upon [the] separation and equilibration of powers between the three branches of the Federal Government itself. The Constitution does not leave to speculation who is to administer the laws enacted by Congress; the President, it says, "shall take Care that the Laws be faithfully executed," Art. II, §3, personally and through officers whom he appoints. . . . The Brady Act effectively transfers this responsibility to thousands of CLEOs in the 50 States, who are left to implement the program without meaningful Presidential control (if indeed meaningful Presidential control is possible without the power to appoint and remove). The insistence of the Framers upon unity in the Federal Executive—to insure both vigor and accountability—is well known. That unity would be shattered, and the power of the President would be subject to reduction, if Congress could act as effectively without the President as with him, by simply requiring state officers to execute its laws.

C. The dissent . . . resorts to the last, best hope of those who defend ultra vires congressional action, the Necessary and Proper Clause. It reasons that the power to regulate the sale of handguns under the Commerce Clause, coupled with the power to "make all Laws which shall be necessary and proper for carrying into Execution the foregoing Powers," conclusively establishes the Brady Act's constitutional validity, because the Tenth Amendment imposes no limitations on the exercise of delegated powers but merely prohibits the exercise of powers "not delegated to the United States." What destroys [this] argument, however, is not the Tenth Amendment but the Necessary and Proper Clause itself. When a "Law [for] carrying into Execution" the Commerce Clause violates the principle of state sovereignty reflected in the various constitutional provisions we mentioned earlier it is not a "Law . . . proper for carrying into Execution the Commerce Clause," and is thus, in the words of The Federalist, "merely [an] act of usurpation" which "deserves to be treated as such" [Federalist No. 33 (Hamilton)]. See Lawson & Granger, The "Proper" Scope of Federal Power: A Jurisdictional Interpretation of the Sweeping Clause, 43 Duke L.J. 267, 297-326, 330-333 (1993). . . .

IV. Finally, and most conclusively in the present litigation, we turn to the prior jurisprudence of this Court. Federal commandeering of state governments is such a novel phenomenon that this Court's first experience with it did not occur until the 1970s, when the Environmental Protection Agency promulgated regulations requiring States to prescribe auto emissions testing, monitoring and retrofit programs, and to designate preferential bus and carpool lanes. . . . After we granted certiorari to review the statutory and constitutional validity of the regulations, the Government declined even to defend them, and instead rescinded some and conceded the invalidity of those that remained. [Later] opinions of ours have made clear that the Federal Government may not compel the States to implement, by legislation or executive action, federal regulatory programs. [When] we were at last confronted squarely with a federal statute that unambiguously required the States to enact or administer a federal regulatory program, our decision should have come as no surprise [New York v. United States]. "The Federal Government," we held, "may not compel the States to enact or administer a federal regulatory program."

The Government contends that *New York* is distinguishable [because] unlike the "take title" provisions invalidated there, the background-check provision of the Brady Act does not require state legislative or executive officials to make policy, but instead issues a final directive to state CLEOs. . . .

Executive action that has utterly no policymaking component is rare, particularly at an executive level as high as a jurisdiction's chief law-enforcement officer. Is it really true that there is no policymaking involved in deciding, for example, what "reasonable efforts" shall be expended to conduct a background check? Is [the] decision whether to devote maximum "reasonable efforts" or minimum "reasonable efforts" not preeminently a matter of policy? It is quite impossible, in short, to draw the Government's proposed line at "no policymaking," and we would have to fall back upon a line of "not too much policymaking." How much is too much is not likely to be answered precisely; and an imprecise barrier against federal intrusion upon state authority is not likely to be an effective one.

Even assuming, moreover, that the Brady Act leaves no "policymaking" discretion with the States, we fail to see how that improves rather than worsens the intrusion upon state sovereignty. Preservation of the States as independent and autonomous political entities is arguably less undermined by requiring them to make policy in certain fields than (as Judge Sneed aptly described it over two decades ago) by "reducing [them] to puppets of a ventriloquist Congress," Brown v. EPA, 521 F.2d at 839. It is an essential attribute of the States' retained sovereignty that they remain independent and autonomous within their proper sphere of authority. It is no more compatible with this independence and autonomy that their officers be "dragooned" into administering federal law, than it would be compatible with the independence and autonomy of the United States that its officers be impressed into service for the execution of state laws. . . .

The Government also maintains that requiring state officers to perform discrete, ministerial tasks specified by Congress . . . does not diminish the accountability of state or federal officials. This argument fails even on its own terms. By forcing state governments to absorb the financial burden of implementing a federal regulatory program, Members of Congress can take credit for "solving" problems without having to ask their constituents to pay for the solutions with higher federal taxes. And even when the States are not forced to absorb the costs of implementing a federal program, they are still put in the position of taking the blame for its burdensomeness and for its defects. Under the present law, for example, it will be the CLEO and not some federal official who stands between the gun purchaser and immediate possession of his gun. And it will likely be the CLEO, not some federal official, who will be blamed for any error (even one in the designated federal database) that causes a purchaser to be mistakenly rejected. . . .

Finally, the Government puts forward a cluster of arguments that can be grouped under the heading: "The Brady Act serves very important purposes, is most efficiently administered by CLEOs during the interim period, and places a minimal and only temporary burden upon state officers." There is considerable disagreement over the extent of the burden, but we need not pause over that detail. . . . But where, as here, it is the whole object of the law to direct the functioning of the state executive, and hence to compromise the structural framework of dual sovereignty, such a "balancing" analysis is inappropriate. It is the very principle of separate state sovereignty that such a law offends, and no comparative assessment of the various interests can overcome that fundamental defect. We expressly rejected such an approach in [*New York*]. We adhere to that principle today, and conclude categorically, as we concluded categorically in *New York*: "The Federal Government may not compel the States to enact or administer a federal regulatory program." The mandatory obligation imposed on CLEOs to perform background checks on prospective handgun purchasers plainly runs afoul of that rule.

V. [We] held in *New York* that Congress cannot compel the States to enact or enforce a federal regulatory program. Today we hold that Congress cannot circumvent that prohibition by conscripting the State's officers directly. The Federal Government may neither issue directives requiring the States to address particular problems, nor command the States' officers, or those of their political subdivisions, to administer or enforce a federal regulatory program. It matters not whether policymaking is involved, and no case-by-case weighing of the burdens or benefits is necessary; such commands are fundamentally incompatible with our constitutional system of dual sovereignty. Accordingly, the judgment of the Court of Appeals for the Ninth Circuit is reversed.

JUSTICE O'CONNOR, concurring.

[The] Court appropriately refrains from deciding whether other purely ministerial reporting requirements imposed by Congress on state and local authorities pursuant to its Commerce Clause powers are similarly invalid. See, e.g., 42 U.S.C. §5779(a) (requiring state and local law enforcement agencies to report cases of missing children to the Department of Justice). The provisions invalidated here, however, which directly compel state officials to administer a federal regulatory program, utterly fail to adhere to the design and structure of our constitutional scheme.

JUSTICE STEVENS, joined by JUSTICES SOUTER, GINSBURG, and BREYER, dissenting.

When Congress exercises the powers delegated to it by the Constitution, it may impose affirmative obligations on executive and judicial officers of state and local governments as well as ordinary citizens. This conclusion is firmly supported by the text of the Constitution, the early history of the Nation, decisions of this Court, and a correct understanding of the basic structure of the Federal Government.

I. [The Commerce Clause] adequately supports the regulation of commerce in handguns effected by the Brady Act. Moreover, the additional grant of [authority] "to make all Laws which shall be necessary and proper for carrying into Execution the foregoing Powers" is surely adequate to support the temporary enlistment of local police officers in the process of identifying persons who should not be entrusted with the possession of handguns.

II. . . . [The] historical materials strongly suggest that the Founders intended to enhance the capacity of the federal government by empowering it . . . to act through local officials. Hamilton made clear that the new Constitution, "by extending the authority of the federal head to the individual citizens of the several States, will enable the government to employ the ordinary magistracy of each, in the execution of its laws." [Federalist No. 27.] Hamilton's meaning was [that] the federal government was to have the power to demand that local officials implement national policy programs. . . .

[The] Court rests its [historical] conclusion on the claim that there is little evidence the National Government actually exercised such a power in the early years of the Republic. [But] the fact that Congress did elect to rely on state judges and the clerks of state courts to perform a variety of executive functions is surely evidence of a contemporary understanding that their status as state officials did not immunize them from federal service. . . . [We] are far truer to the historical record by applying a functional approach in assessing the role played by these early state officials. . . .

III. [The] fact that the Framers intended to preserve the sovereignty of the several States simply does not speak to the question whether individual state employees may be required to perform federal [obligations]. . . . Perversely, the majority's rule seems more likely to damage than to preserve the safeguards against tyranny provided by the existence of vital state governments. By limiting the ability of the Federal Government to enlist state officials in the implementation of its programs, the Court creates incentives for the National Government to aggrandize itself. In the name of State's rights, the majority would have the Federal Government create vast national bureaucracies to implement its policies. . . .

IV. [Finally, New York v. United States] did not decide the question presented here, whether state executive officials—as opposed to state legislators—may in appropriate circumstances be enlisted to implement federal policy. . . . The provision of the Brady Act that crosses the Court's newly defined constitutional threshold is more comparable to a statute requiring local police officers to report the identity of missing children to the Crime Control Center of the Department of Justice than to an offensive federal command to a sovereign state. If Congress believes that such a statute will benefit the people of the Nation, and serve the interests of cooperative federalism better than an enlarged federal bureaucracy, we should respect both its policy judgment and its appraisal of its constitutional power.

NOTES AND QUESTIONS

1. Sovereign Immunity as a Procedural Immunity: Alden v. Maine. In Seminole Tribe of Florida v. Florida, 517 U.S. 44 (1996), the Court held that Congress lacked authority under its Article I powers to abrogate a state's Eleventh Amendment immunity from private damages suits in federal court. Thereafter, employees of the state of Maine filed suit in a Maine court seeking damages for Maine's alleged violation of the federal Fair Labor Standards Act, but the claim was dismissed due to Maine's sovereign immunity. In Alden v. Maine, 527 U.S. 706 (1999), the Supreme Court relied on a structural principle of state sovereign immunity (except as explicitly surrendered in the Constitution) to hold that Congress lacked authority to compel states to entertain in their own courts private damages suits based on federal law. The Court noted that because "the Supremacy Clause enshrines as 'the supreme Law of the Land' only those federal Acts that accord with the constitutional design, [this] merely raises the question of whether a law is a valid exercise of the national power." The Court struck down the law because the principle of state immunity from suit without its consent was a preconstitutional attribute of sovereignty that was not waived by the states in the Constitution, either explicitly or by any implication from the grant to the federal government of its enumerated powers. This conclusion was based on several important structural principles of federalism, foremost of which was the interference with a state's autonomy—its "decisionmaking ability"—presented by a congressional edict that states must entertain private suits for damages:

> A power to press a State's own courts into federal service to coerce the other branches of the State . . . is the power first to turn the State against itself and ultimately to commandeer the entire political machinery of the State against its will and at the behest of individuals. . . . Private suits against nonconsenting States—especially suits for money damages—may threaten the financial integrity of the States. . . . A general federal power to authorize private suits would

place unwarranted strain on the States' ability to govern in accordance with the will of their citizens. [The] allocation of scarce resources among competing needs and interests lies at the heart of the political process. . . . If the principle of representative government is to be preserved to the States, the balance between competing interests must be reached after deliberation by the political process established by the citizens of the State, not by judicial decree mandated by the Federal Government and invoked by the private citizen.

[A contrary ruling would] strike[] at the heart of the political account-ability so essential to our liberty and republican form of government [because it would] blur not only the distinct responsibilities of the State and National Governments but also the separate duties of the judicial and political branches of the state government. . . . A State is entitled to order the processes of its own governance, assigning to the political branches, rather than the courts, the re-sponsibility for directing the payment of debts.

As in *New York* and *Printz*, the "structural postulate at work in *Alden* was the procedural immunity principle. Congress remained free to impose liability on the states for violations of the FLSA and to enforce the states' resulting duty by suit brought by the United States; what Congress could not do was to impose an enforcement mechanism that interfered with the internal gover-nance processes of the states." Massey, Federalism and the Rehnquist Court, 53 Hastings L.J. 431, 469 (2002).

2. Questions. After *Printz*, can Congress compel state officials to report to the U.S. Department of Justice hate crimes that occur within their jurisdiction? Could Congress create a national registry of missing children and require state officials to report to the federal registry all details concerning any missing children that come to the attention of state officials?

Could Congress effectively accomplish its regulatory goals by enacting legislation that preempts an activity that the states have hitherto regulated unless the states either enact or administer a federally prescribed program? For example, suppose Congress enacted a new Brady Act that forbade any gun sale until and unless the seller had obtained certification from the federal government that the purchaser had no criminal background, but waived this requirement in those states that chose to order its chief local law enforcement officers to conduct background checks. What, if anything, is constitutionally suspect about this "conditional preemption"?

C. TAXATION

"Congress shall have Power to lay and collect Taxes, Duties, Imposts and Excises." Art. I, §8. This power is independent of the other powers given to Congress under the Constitution, which means that Congress may tax things that it may not have the power to regulate. The power to tax is not unlimited, however. The Constitution imposes some explicit limits: Congress may not tax exports (Art. I, §9), indirect taxes (those levied on an *activity* rather than upon property) may not discriminate among the states (Art. I, §8), and direct taxes (levied on property) other than the income tax must be levied in such a way that each state's proportion of the total revenue produced by the tax is the same as each state's proportion of the total population of the nation (Art. I, §2, and the Sixteenth Amendment).

The Supreme Court has also established some implied limits, but they have mostly withered away from lack of use. The theoretical problem is that every tax is likely to have some regulatory effect. Human nature being what it is, people alter their behavior to avoid taxes. Thus any tax is likely to discourage the activity or thing taxed, and by this alteration of human behavior some regulation will be accomplished. Justice Robert Jackson summed up this effect when he observed that "[o]ne cannot formulate a revenue-raising plan that would not have economic and social consequences." United States v. Kahriger, 345 U.S. 22 (1953). These regulatory consequences are not necessarily forbidden. If Congress has a separate, independent source of power to regulate, the regulatory effect of a tax is irrelevant, but if Congress does not have a source of regulatory power independent of the taxing power, a nominal tax that is really a disguised regulation ought not be valid. This was the problem the Court confronted in the following case.

Bailey v. Drexel Furniture Co. (Child Labor Tax Case)
259 U.S. 20 (1922)

[Congress reacted to Hammer v. Dagenhart, the case that struck down regulation of child labor using the commerce power, by enacting the Child Labor Tax Law, which imposed on virtually every employer of a child under 14 years of age (and on certain employers of children aged 14 to 16) a federal excise tax of 10 percent of the annual net profits of the employer. Drexel Furniture paid the tax, then successfully sued for a refund in federal district court.]

CHIEF JUSTICE TAFT delivered the opinion of the Court:

This case presents the question of the constitutional validity of the Child Labor Tax Law. [The] law is attacked on the ground that it is a regulation of the employment of child labor in the states—an exclusively state function under the federal Constitution and within the reservations of the Tenth Amendment. It is defended on the ground that it is a mere excise tax levied by the Congress of the United States under its broad power of taxation. [We] must construe the law and interpret the intent and meaning of Congress from the language of the act. [Does] this law impose a tax with only that incidental restraint and regulation which a tax must inevitably involve? Or does it regulate by the use of the so-called tax as a penalty?

[This act] provides a heavy exaction for a departure from a detailed and specified course of conduct in business. That course of business is that employers shall employ in mines and quarries, children of an age greater than

16 years; in mills and factories, children of an age greater than 14 years, and shall prevent children of less than 16 years in mills and factories from working more than 8 hours a day or 6 days in the week. If an employer departs from this prescribed course of business, he is to pay to the government one-tenth of his entire net income in the business for a full year. The amount is not to be proportioned in any degree to the extent or frequency of the departures, but is to be paid by the employer in full measure whether he employs 500 children for a year, or employs only one for a day. Moreover, if he does not know the child is within the named age limit, he is not to pay; [it] is only where he knowingly departs from the prescribed course that payment is to be exacted. Scienter is associated with penalties, not with taxes. The employer's factory is to be subject to inspection at any time not only by the taxing officers of the Treasury, the Department normally charged with the collection of taxes, but also by the Secretary of Labor and his subordinates, whose normal function is the advancement and protection of the welfare of the workers. In the light of these features of the act, a court must be blind not to see that the so-called tax is imposed to stop the employment of children within the age limits prescribed. Its prohibitory and regulatory effect and purpose are palpable. All others can see and understand this. How can we properly shut our minds to it?

[This] court has gone far to sustain taxing acts as such, even though there has been ground for suspecting, from the weight of the tax, it was intended to destroy its subject. But [the] presumption of validity cannot prevail [here], because the proof of the contrary is found on the very face of its provisions. Grant the validity of this law, and all that Congress would need to do [in] seeking to take over to its control any [subject] of public interest [reserved to the States] would be to enact a detailed measure of complete regulation of the subject and enforce it by a so-called tax upon departures from it. To give such magic to the word "tax" would be to break down all constitutional limitation of the powers of Congress and completely wipe out the sovereignty of the states. . . .

Where the sovereign enacting the law has power to impose both tax and penalty, the difference between revenue production and mere regulation may be immaterial, but not so when one sovereign can impose a tax only, and the power of regulation rests in another. Taxes are occasionally imposed in the discretion of the Legislature on proper subjects with the primary motive of obtaining revenue from them and with the incidental motive of discouraging them by making their continuance onerous. They do not lose their character as taxes because of the incidental motive. But there comes a time in the extension of the penalizing features of the so-called tax when it loses its character as such and becomes a mere penalty, with the characteristics of regulation and punishment. Such is the case in [this] law. . . .

But it is pressed upon us that this court has gone so far in sustaining taxing measures the effect and tendency of which was to accomplish purposes not directly within congressional power that we are bound by authority to maintain this law. [In] Veazie Bank v. Fenno, [75 U.S.] 8 Wall. 533 [1869], [a] law which increased a tax on the circulating notes of persons and state banks from one per centum to 10 per centum was upheld. [The] sole objection to the tax [was] its excessive character [but] the object of the excessive tax was [within] congressional authority, as [a] legitimate means taken by Congress to secure a national medium or [currency].

McCray v. United States, 195 U.S. 27 [1904], [upheld a] tax on white oleomargarine [of] one-quarter of a cent a pound, and on . . . yellow oleomargarine [of] 10 cents per pound. [As in *Veazie Bank*, the Court ruled that Congress], in selecting its subjects for taxation, might impose the burden where and as it would, and . . . a motive disclosed in its selection to discourage sale or manufacture of an article by a higher tax than on some other [does] not invalidate the tax.

United States v. Doremus, 249 U.S. 86 [1919], involved the validity of the Narcotic Drug Act, which imposed a special tax on the manufacture, importation and sale or gift of opium or coca leaves or their compounds or derivatives. It required every person subject to the special tax, to register with the collector of internal revenue his name and place of business and forbade him to sell except upon the written order of the person to whom the sale was made on a form prescribed by the Commissioner of Internal Revenue. [The] validity of a special tax in the nature of an excise tax on the manufacture, importation, and sale of such drugs was, of course, unquestioned. The provisions for subjecting the sale and distribution of the drugs to official supervision and inspection were held to have a reasonable relation to the enforcement of the tax and were therefore held valid. The court said that the act could not be declared invalid just because another motive than taxation, not shown on the face of the act, might have contributed to its passage. [But the Court in *Doremus*] made manifest its view that the provisions of the so-called taxing act must be naturally and reasonably adapted to the collection of the tax and not solely to the achievement of some other purpose plainly within state power. . . .

Affirmed.

NOTE

The Decline of the "Disguised Regulation" Approach.   The significance of Bailey v. Drexel Furniture Co. has declined for two reasons. First, the scope of the regulatory powers of Congress (especially the Commerce Clause) has increased so dramatically that there is much less likelihood that a tax will exert a regulatory effect that is not independently within congressional power. Second, the Court has progressively relaxed its standard of review of taxes as disguised regulations.

In Sonzinsky v. United States, 300 U.S. 506 (1937), the Court upheld an annual tax of $200 imposed on firearms dealers. The tax was

> productive of some revenue, [hence] we are not free to speculate as to the motives which moved Congress to impose it, or as to the extent to which it may

operate to restrict the activities taxed. As it is not attended by offensive regulation, and since it operates as a tax, it is within the national taxing power.

To similar effect was United States v. Sanchez, 340 U.S. 42 (1950), which upheld a tax on marijuana.

United States v. Kahriger
345 U.S. 22 (1953)

[After "sensationally exploited disclosures regarding gambling," Congress imposed a tax on bookies—professional gamblers in the business of accepting wagers. The tax law also required bookies to register with the Collector of Internal Revenue. Kahriger, in challenging the validity of the law, "said that Congress, under the pretense of exercising its power to tax has attempted to penalize illegal intrastate gambling through the regulatory features of the Act, and has thus infringed the police power which is reserved to the states." The Court rejected the challenge and upheld the law as a valid tax.]

JUSTICE REED delivered the opinion of the Court:

[Kahriger, the challenger,] would have us say that because there is legislative history indicating a congressional motive to suppress wagering, this tax is not a proper exercise of [the] taxing power. [The] intent to curtail and hinder, as well as tax, was also manifest in [*Veazie Bank, McCray, Doremus, Sonzinsky,* and *Sanchez,* and in each case the tax was upheld. A] federal excise tax does not cease to be valid merely because it discourages or deters the activities taxed. Nor is the tax invalid because the revenue obtained is negligible. [The] instant tax has a regulatory effect. [But] the wagering tax produces revenue. As such it surpasses both the narcotics and firearms taxes which we have found valid. [The] power of Congress to tax is extensive and sometimes falls with crushing effect on businesses deemed unessential or inimical to the public welfare. [The] remedy for excessive taxation is in the hands of Congress, not the courts. [Nor] do we find the registration requirements of the wagering tax offensive. [The] registration provisions make the tax simpler to collect.

JUSTICE FRANKFURTER, joined in substantial part by JUSTICE DOUGLAS, dissenting.

Congress may make an oblique use of the taxing power in relation to activities with which Congress may deal directly, as for instance, commerce between the States. [However], when oblique use is made of the taxing power as to matters which substantively are not within the powers delegated to Congress, the Court cannot shut its eyes to what is obviously, because designedly, an attempt to control conduct which the Constitution left to the responsibility of the States, merely because Congress wrapped the legislation in the verbal cellophane of a revenue measure. [What] is relevant to judgment here is that, even if the history of this legislation as it went through Congress did not give one the libretto to the song, the context of the circumstances which brought forth this [enactment] emphatically supports what was revealed on the floor of Congress, namely, that what was formally a means of raising revenue for the Federal Government was essentially an effort to check if not to stamp out professional gambling. A nominal taxing measure must be found an inadmissible intrusion into a domain of legislation reserved for the States not merely when Congress requires that such a measure is to be enforced through a detailed scheme of administration beyond the obvious fiscal needs, as in the Child Labor Tax Case. [Another] basis for deeming such a formal revenue measure inadmissible is presented by this case. In addition to the fact that Congress was concerned with activity beyond the authority of the Federal Government, the enforcing provision of this enactment is designed for the systematic confession of crimes with a view to prosecution for such crimes under State law.

NOTES

1. Not Quite Dead. CF & I Steel Corporation failed to make a $12.4 million contribution to its pension plans, as required by the Employee Retirement Income Security Act of 1974 (ERISA). Then it filed for bankruptcy protection. Because it had failed to make the required pension contribution, it became subject to a "tax" of 10 percent of any "accumulated funding deficiency," imposed by 26 U.S.C. §4971(a). The federal government sought priority for its claim in the bankruptcy proceeding, because it was founded on an unpaid tax liability of $1.24 million. The bankruptcy court ruled that the "tax" was actually a penalty not entitled to priority. In United States v. Reorganized CF & I Steel Fabricators of Utah, Inc., 518 U.S. 213 (1996), the Supreme Court affirmed:

> "A tax is an enforced contribution to provide for the support of government; a penalty . . . is an exaction imposed by statute as punishment for an unlawful act." United States v. La Franca, 282 U.S. 568, 572 (1931). We take *La Franca*'s statement of the distinction to be sufficient for the decision of this case; if the concept of penalty means anything, it means punishment for an unlawful act or omission, and a punishment for an unlawful omission is what this exaction is.

Id. at 224.

The penal character of the "tax" was demonstrated by the fact that failure to pay it promptly after notice that it was due subjected the entity to a further "tax" of 100 percent of the accumulated funding deficiency and a separate claim for 100 percent of that amount by the Pension Benefit Guaranty Corporation.

2. Judicially Enforceable Limits. Note that this near-total abandonment of judicially enforceable constitutional limits on the taxation power is confined to the problem of congressional use of the taxing power to accomplish regulatory ends beyond the federal legislative power. There is no doubt that the Court would enforce individual liberties guaranteed by the Constitution to curb the taxing power (e.g., an income tax of 10 percent on income earned by men and 20 percent on income earned by women).

National Federation of Independent Business v. Sebelius
132 S. Ct. 2566 (2012)

[In this portion of the case, the Court upheld the validity of the provisions in the Patient Protection and Affordable Care Act (ACA) that subjected all persons who fail to comply with the mandate that they have health insurance to a penalty, codified in the Internal Revenue Code, and paid to the Internal Revenue Service as part of one's income taxes. A threshold question was whether the Anti-Injunction Act, 26 U.S.C. §7421(a), precluded decision on this point. The Anti-Injunction Act forbids courts from adjudicating the validity of a tax until it has been imposed and collected, and the penalty provided in the ACA did not become effective until 2014.]

CHIEF JUSTICE ROBERTS, for the Court.

. . . The Anti-Injunction Act applies to suits "for the purpose of restraining the assessment or collection of any *tax*." §7421(a) (emphasis added). Congress, however, chose to describe the "[s]hared responsibility payment" imposed on those who forgo health insurance not as a "tax," but as a "penalty." There is no immediate reason to think that a statute applying to "any tax" would apply to a "penalty."

[It is argued] that even though Congress did not label the shared responsibility payment a tax, we should treat it as such under the Anti-Injunction Act because it functions like a tax. It is true that Congress cannot change whether an exaction is a tax or a penalty for *constitutional* purposes simply by describing it as one or the other. Congress may not, for example, expand its power under the Taxing Clause, or escape the Double Jeopardy Clause's constraint on criminal sanctions, by labeling a severe financial punishment a "tax." The Anti-Injunction Act and the Affordable Care Act, however, are creatures of Congress's own creation. How they relate to each other is up to Congress, and the best evidence of Congress's intent is the statutory text. . . . The Affordable Care Act does not require that the penalty for failing to comply with the individual mandate be treated as a tax for purposes of the Anti-Injunction Act. The Anti-Injunction Act therefore does not apply to this suit, and we may proceed to the merits. . . .

Because the Commerce Clause does not support the individual mandate, it is necessary to turn to the Government's second argument: that the mandate may be upheld as within Congress's enumerated power to "lay and collect Taxes." . . . The Government . . . asks us to read the mandate not as ordering individuals to buy insurance, but rather as imposing a tax on those who do not buy that product. . . .

The most straightforward reading of the mandate is that it commands individuals to purchase insurance. After all, it states that individuals "shall" maintain health insurance. . . . Under the mandate, if an individual does not maintain health insurance, the only consequence is that he must make an additional payment to the IRS when he pays his taxes. That, according to the Government, means the mandate can be regarded as establishing a condition—not owning health insurance—that triggers a tax—the required payment to the IRS. Under that theory, the mandate is not a legal command to buy insurance. Rather, it makes going without insurance just another thing the Government taxes, like buying gasoline or earning income. And if the mandate is in effect just a tax hike on certain taxpayers who do not have health insurance, it may be within Congress's constitutional power to tax. . . .

The exaction the Affordable Care Act imposes on those without health insurance looks like a tax in many respects. The "[s]hared responsibility payment," as the statute entitles it, is paid into the Treasury by "taxpayer[s] when they file their tax returns. It does not apply to individuals who do not pay federal income taxes because their household income is less than the filing threshold in the Internal Revenue Code. For taxpayers who do owe the payment, its amount is determined by such familiar factors as taxable income, number of dependents, and joint filing status. The requirement to pay is found in the Internal Revenue Code and enforced by the IRS, which . . . must assess and collect it "in the same manner as taxes." This process yields the essential feature of any tax: it produces at least some revenue for the Government. . . .

It is of course true that the Act describes the payment as a "penalty," not a "tax." But while that label is fatal to the application of the Anti-Injunction Act it does not determine whether the payment may be viewed as an exercise of Congress's taxing power. It is up to Congress whether to apply the Anti-Injunction Act to any particular statute, so it makes sense to be guided by Congress's choice of label on that question. That choice does not, however, control whether an exaction is within Congress's constitutional power to tax. . . .

We thus ask whether the shared responsibility payment falls within Congress's taxing power, "[d]isregarding the designation of the exaction, and viewing its substance and application." [This] functional approach . . . suggests that the shared responsibility payment may for constitutional purposes be considered a tax, not a penalty: First, for most Americans the amount due will be far less than the price of insurance. . . . It may often be a reasonable financial decision to make the payment rather than purchase insurance, unlike the "prohibitory" financial punishment in *Drexel Furniture*. Second, the individual mandate contains no scienter requirement. Third, the payment is collected solely by the IRS through the normal means of taxation—except that the Service is *not* allowed to use those means most suggestive of a punitive sanction, such as criminal prosecution. The reasons the Court in *Drexel Furniture* held that what was called a "tax" there was a penalty support the conclusion that what is called a "penalty" here may be viewed as a tax. . . .

In distinguishing penalties from taxes, this Court has explained that "if the concept of penalty means anything, it means punishment for an unlawful act or omission." While the individual mandate clearly aims to induce the purchase of health insurance, it need not be read to declare that failing to do so is unlawful. Neither the Act nor any other law attaches negative legal consequences to not buying health insurance, beyond requiring a payment to the IRS. . . .

If it is troubling to interpret the Commerce Clause as authorizing Congress to regulate those who abstain from commerce, perhaps it should be similarly troubling to permit Congress to impose a tax for not doing something. Three considerations allay this concern.

First, and most importantly, it is abundantly clear the Constitution does not guarantee that individuals may avoid taxation through inactivity. A capitation, after all, is a tax that everyone must pay simply for existing, and capitations are expressly contemplated by the Constitution. . . .

Second, [although] "'there comes a time in the extension of the penalizing features of the so-called tax when it loses its character as such and becomes a mere penalty with the characteristics of regulation and punishment,'" [we] have already explained that the shared responsibility payment's practical characteristics pass muster as a tax. . . . [We] need not here decide the precise point at which an exaction becomes so punitive that the taxing power does not authorize it. . . .

Third, although the breadth of Congress's power to tax is greater than its power to regulate commerce, the taxing power does not give Congress the same degree of control over individual behavior. Once we recognize that Congress may regulate a particular decision under the Commerce Clause, the Federal Government can bring its full weight to bear. Congress may simply command individuals to do as it directs. An individual who disobeys may be subjected to criminal sanctions, [which] can include not only fines and imprisonment, but all the attendant consequences of being branded a criminal: deprivation of otherwise protected civil rights, such as the right to bear arms or vote in elections; loss of employment opportunities; social stigma; and severe disabilities in other controversies, such as custody or immigration disputes. By contrast, Congress's authority under the taxing power is limited to requiring an individual to pay money into the Federal Treasury, no more. If a tax is properly paid, the Government has no power to compel or punish individuals subject to it. . . .

The Affordable Care Act's requirement that certain individuals pay a financial penalty for not obtaining health insurance may reasonably be characterized as a tax. Because the Constitution permits such a tax, it is not our role to forbid it, or to pass upon its wisdom or fairness. . . .

JUSTICES SCALIA, KENNEDY, THOMAS, and ALITO delivered a joint dissent.
. . . The provision challenged . . . is either a penalty or else a tax. . . . The two are mutually exclusive. . . . In this case, there is simply no way, "without doing violence to the fair meaning of the words used," to escape what

Congress enacted: a mandate that individuals maintain minimum essential coverage, enforced by a penalty. Our cases establish a clear line between a tax and a penalty: " '[A] tax is an enforced contribution to provide for the support of government; a penalty . . . is an exaction imposed by statute as punishment for an unlawful act.' " United States v. Reorganized CF&I Fabricators of Utah, Inc., 518 U.S. 213, 224 (1996) (quoting United States v. La Franca, 282 U.S. 568, 572 (1931)). In a few cases, this Court has held that a "tax" imposed upon private conduct was so onerous as to be in effect a penalty. But we have never held—*never*—that a penalty imposed for violation of the law was so trivial as to be in effect a tax. We have never held that *any* exaction imposed for violation of the law is an exercise of Congress'[s] taxing power—even when the statute *calls* it a tax, much less when (as here) the statute repeatedly calls it a penalty. When an act "adopt[s] the criteria of wrongdoing" and then imposes a monetary penalty as the "principal consequence on those who transgress its standard," it creates a regulatory penalty, not a tax.

So the question is, quite simply, whether the exaction here is imposed for violation of the law. It unquestionably is. The minimum-coverage provision . . . commands that every "applicable individual *shall* . . . ensure that the individual . . . is covered under minimum essential coverage." And the immediately following provision states that, "[i]f . . . an applicable individual . . . fails to meet the *requirement* of subsection (a) . . . there is hereby imposed . . . a *penalty*." And several of Congress'[s] legislative "findings" . . . confirm that it sets forth a legal requirement and constitutes the assertion of regulatory power, not mere taxing power. . . .

That the Government points out that "[t]he amount of the penalty will be calculated as a percentage of household income for federal income tax purposes," [but] varying a penalty according to ability to pay is an utterly familiar practice. . . .

The last of the feeble arguments . . . is the contention that what this statute repeatedly calls a penalty is in fact a tax because it contains no scienter requirement. The *presence* of such a requirement suggests a penalty . . . ; but the *absence* of such a requirement does not suggest a tax. Penalties for absolute-liability offenses are commonplace. . . .

And the nail in the coffin is that the mandate and penalty are located in Title I of the Act, its operative core, rather than where a tax would be found—in Title IX, containing the Act's "Revenue Provisions." In sum, "the terms of [the] act rende[r] it unavoidable" that Congress imposed a regulatory penalty, not a tax.

For all these reasons, to say that the Individual Mandate merely imposes a tax is not to interpret the statute but to rewrite it. Judicial tax-writing is particularly troubling. . . . [T]he Constitution requires tax increases to originate in the House of Representatives, . . . the legislative body most accountable to the people, where legislators must weigh the need for the tax against the terrible price they might pay at their next election, which is never more than two years off. . . . We have no doubt that Congress knew precisely what it was doing when it rejected an earlier version of this legislation that imposed a tax instead of a requirement-with-penalty. Imposing a tax through judicial legislation inverts the constitutional scheme, and places the power to tax in the branch of government least accountable to the citizenry. . . .

The Government [makes] the remarkable argument that [the penalty] is not a tax for purposes of the Anti-Injunction Act but is a tax for constitutional purposes. . . . What qualifies as a tax for purposes of the Anti-Injunction Act, unlike what qualifies as a tax for purposes of the Constitution, is entirely within the control of Congress. . . . Congress could have defined "tax" for purposes of [the ACA] in such fashion as to exclude some exactions that in fact are "taxes." It might have prescribed, for example, that a particular exercise of the taxing power "shall not be regarded as a tax for purposes of the Anti-Injunction Act." But there is no such prescription here. What the Government would have us believe in these cases is that the very same textual indications that show this is *not* a tax under the Anti-Injunction Act show that it *is* a tax under the Constitution. That carries verbal wizardry too far, deep into the forbidden land of the sophists. . . .

Note on State Immunity from Federal Taxation

As with the commerce power, there is a limited zone of state immunity from federal taxation, although its boundaries are configured differently. First, federal taxes may not discriminate against the states—they may not be levied on the states alone. Second, even if federal taxes are nondiscriminatory, a federal tax may not impair the sovereign functions of state government. The second principle, however, is subject to an important exception: A nondiscriminatory federal tax may impair state sovereign functions in order to recover from the states their "fair share" of the cost of a federal program that benefits the states.

Both principles were involved in New York v. United States, 326 U.S. 572 (1946), where a federal tax was imposed on all bottled mineral water. New York, which operated a commercial mineral water bottling plant, argued that it was immune from the tax. The Court upheld the tax because it concluded that it was not discriminatory, but in three separate opinions a majority of the Court concluded that Congress could not levy a tax solely upon a state, as opposed to a private person. Chief Justice Stone, writing for a plurality of four justices, asserted that nondiscriminatory federal taxes that impair the sovereign functions of a state are invalid. Justice Frankfurter thought that the unique functions of state government were immune from federal taxation. Justice Rutledge declared that state functions might be taxed so long as they were not "singled out for taxation when others performing them are not taxed or for special burdens when they are." Justices Douglas and Black dissented on the ground that state governments should enjoy an absolute immunity from federal taxation.

The exception permitting federal taxes to impair even the sovereign functions of state governments is rooted in Massachusetts v. United States, 435

U.S. 444 (1978), a case regarding a federal registration tax that was imposed on all civil aircraft in order to defray the expense of federally operated air navigational facilities and services. Massachusetts contended that it was immune from the tax as applied to its state police airplanes. The Court upheld the tax but could not agree on a common rationale. Four justices thought that state immunity should exist only to the extent

> necessary to protect the continued ability of the States to deliver traditional governmental services. [Where] the subject of a tax is a natural and traditional source of federal revenue and where it is inconceivable that such a revenue measure could ever operate to preclude traditional state activities, the tax is valid.

The plurality thought that this general conclusion was reinforced by the fact that the registration tax "defray[ed] the cost of a federal program by recovering a fair approximation of each beneficiary's share of the cost." Read most broadly, the plurality's view is that state immunity from federal taxation occurs only when the federal tax would conceivably preclude the performance of traditional state activities. Read most narrowly, the plurality's view is that states are immune from federal taxation of traditional state activities except when such taxation is necessary to recover the state's fair share of the cost of federal programs benefiting the state. Which statement of immunity better comports with the objective of preserving autonomous state governance?

D. SPENDING

Congress may "pay the Debts and provide for the common Defence and general Welfare of the United States." Art. I, §8. Congress may spend for anything it reasonably thinks will further the "general welfare" of the nation; it is not limited to spending in aid of its specific regulatory objectives. But this power is not unlimited. The *Butler* case, which follows, explores the problem of spending that is in purpose and effect entirely regulatory. Such "regulatory spending" is of no consequence when the ancillary regulation is within some independent regulatory power of Congress, such as the commerce power, but if spending is entirely regulatory and Congress has no source of regulatory authority, the spending initiative is invalid as an improper and pretextual means to attain an ultra vires end.

≡≡≡ **United States v. Butler**
≡≡≡ *297 U.S. 1 (1936)*

[The Agricultural Adjustment Act (AAA), one of Franklin Roosevelt's New Deal initiatives, was designed to limit production of farm commodities and thus increase prices of those commodities. To accomplish these objectives, the AAA authorized the Agriculture Department to enter into contracts with farmers requiring the farmers to limit their production in exchange for cash payments. The cash with which to make the payments was generated by a tax levied on the first processor of agricultural commodities. Butler, the receiver in insolvency of a processor of cotton on whom the tax was levied, challenged the entire taxing and spending apparatus of the AAA as an unconstitutional attempt by Congress to control agricultural production. The district court found the scheme to be valid. The court of appeals ruled that the Act was invalid. The Supreme Court agreed with the court of appeals, ruling that the spending under the Act was a void attempt to regulate a matter over which Congress had no constitutional regulatory authority.]

JUSTICE ROBERTS delivered the opinion of the Court.

The government [asks] us to separate [the] Act into two statutes, the one levying an excise on processors of certain commodities; the other appropriating the public moneys independently of the first. [The] legislation now before us is not susceptible of such separation and treatment.

The tax can only be sustained by ignoring the avowed purpose and operation of the [Act]. Beyond cavil the sole object of the legislation is to restore the purchasing power of agricultural [products]; to take money from the processor and bestow it upon farmers who will reduce their acreage for the accomplishment of the proposed [end]. The tax plays an indispensable part in the plan of regulation. [It] is "the heart of the law." [A] tax automatically goes into effect for a commodity when the Secretary of Agriculture determines [that] payments are to be made for reduction of production of that commodity. The tax is to cease [when] payments cease. The rate is fixed with the purpose of bringing about crop reduction and price raising. It is to equal the difference between the "current average farm price" and "fair exchange value." It may be altered to such amount as will prevent accumulation of surplus stocks. If the Secretary finds the policy of the act will not be promoted by the levy of the tax for a given commodity, he may exempt it. The whole revenue from the levy is appropriated in aid of crop control; none of it is made available for general governmental use. [It] is inaccurate and misleading to speak of the exaction from processors prescribed by the challenged act as a tax, or to say that as a tax it is subject to no infirmity. A tax, [as] used in the Constitution, signifies an exaction for the support of the government. The word has never been thought to connote the expropriation of money from one group for the benefit of another.

It does not follow that, as the act is not an exertion of the taxing power and the exaction not a true tax, the statute is void. . . . [The] government asserts that [the] Constitution authorizes the contemplated expenditure of the funds raised by the tax. This contention presents the great and the controlling question in the case. [The] government does not attempt to uphold the validity of the act on the basis of the commerce clause [but relies instead upon the spending clause]. It is not contended that [the spending clause] grants power to regulate agricultural production upon the theory that such legislation would promote the general welfare. The government concedes that the phrase "to provide for the general welfare" qualifies the power "to lay and collect taxes." The view that the clause grants power to provide for the general welfare, independently of the taxing power, has never been authoritatively accepted. . . . The true construction undoubtedly is that the only thing granted is the power to tax for the purpose of providing funds for payment of the nation's debts and making provision for the general welfare. Nevertheless, the government asserts . . . that Congress may appropriate and authorize the spending of moneys for the "general welfare"; that the phrase should be liberally construed to cover anything conducive to national welfare; that decision as to what will promote such welfare rests with Congress alone, and the courts may not review its determination; and, finally, that the appropriation under attack was in fact for the general welfare of the United States.

Since the foundation of the nation, sharp differences of opinion have persisted as to the true interpretation of the phrase. Madison asserted it amounted to no more than a reference to the other powers enumerated in the subsequent clauses of the same section; that, as the United States is a government of limited and enumerated powers, the grant of power to tax and spend for the general national welfare must be confined to the enumerated legislative fields committed to the Congress. [Hamilton], on the other hand, maintained the clause confers a power separate and distinct from those later enumerated, is not restricted in meaning by the grant of them, and Congress consequently has a substantive power to tax and to appropriate, limited only by the requirement that it shall be exercised to provide for the general welfare of the United States. [We] conclude that the reading advocated by [Hamilton] is the correct one. While [the] power to tax is not unlimited, its confines are set in the clause which confers it, and not in those of section 8 which bestow and define the legislative powers of the Congress. It results that the power of Congress to authorize expenditure of public moneys for public purposes is not limited by the direct grants of legislative power found in the Constitution.

But the adoption of the broader construction leaves the power to spend subject to limitations. [We] are not now required to ascertain the scope of the phrase "general welfare of the United States" or to determine whether an appropriation in aid of agriculture falls within it. Wholly apart from that question, another principle embedded in our Constitution prohibits the enforcement of the [Act]. The act invades the reserved rights of the states. It is a statutory plan to regulate and control agricultural production, a matter beyond the powers delegated to the federal government. The tax, the appropriation of the funds raised, and the direction for their disbursement, are but parts of the plan. They are but means to an unconstitutional end. [It] is an established principle that the attainment of a prohibited end may not be accomplished under the pretext of the exertion of powers which are granted. . . .

The government asserts that whatever might be said against the validity of the plan, if compulsory, it is constitutionally sound because the end is accomplished by voluntary co-operation. There are two sufficient answers to the contention. The regulation is not in fact voluntary. The farmer, of course, may refuse to comply, but the price of such refusal is the loss of benefits.

The amount offered is intended to be sufficient to exert pressure on him to agree to the proposed regulation. The power to confer or withhold unlimited benefits is the power to coerce or destroy. If the cotton grower elects not to accept the benefits, he will receive less for his [crops]. The result may [be] financial ruin. [This] is coercion by economic pressure. The asserted power of choice is illusory. . . .

But if the plan were one for purely voluntary co-operation it would stand no better so far as federal power is concerned. At best, it is a scheme for purchasing with federal funds submission to federal regulation of a subject reserved to the states. It is said that Congress has the undoubted right to appropriate money to executive officers for expenditure under contracts between the government and [individuals]. But appropriations and expenditures under contracts for proper governmental purposes cannot justify contracts which are not within federal power. And contracts for the reduction of acreage and the control of production are outside the range of that power. . . . The Congress cannot invade state jurisdiction to compel individual action; no more can it purchase such action. . . . There is an obvious difference between a statute stating the conditions upon which moneys shall be expended and one effective only upon assumption of a contractual obligation to submit to a regulation which otherwise could not be enforced. [It] is said that no one has doubted the power of Congress to stipulate the sort of education for which money shall be expended. But an appropriation to an educational institution which by its terms is to become available only if the beneficiary enters into a contract to teach doctrines subversive of the Constitution is clearly bad. An affirmance of the authority of Congress so to condition the expenditure of an appropriation would tend to nullify all constitutional limitations upon legislative power. [Because Congress] has no power to enforce its commands on the farmer to the ends sought by [the] Act . . . it may not indirectly accomplish those ends by taxing and spending to purchase compliance. . . .

JUSTICE STONE, joined by JUSTICES BRANDEIS and CARDOZO, dissenting.

[T]here is no basis for saying that the expenditure of public money in aid of farmers is not within the specifically granted power of Congress to levy taxes to "provide for the general welfare." The opinion of the Court does not declare otherwise. . . .

The suggestion of coercion finds no support in the record or in any data showing the actual operation of the act. Threat of loss, not hope of gain, is the essence of economic coercion. [It] is upon the contention that state power is infringed by purchased regulation of agricultural production that chief reliance is placed. [The] Constitution requires that public funds shall be spent for a defined purpose, the promotion of the general welfare. . . . The power of Congress to spend is inseparable from persuasion to action over which Congress has no legislative control. Congress may not command that the science of agriculture be taught in state universities. But if it would aid the teaching of that science by grants to state institutions, it is appropriate, if not necessary, that the grant be on the condition [that] it be used for the intended purpose. [It] makes no difference that there is a promise to do an act which the condition is calculated to induce. Condition and promise are alike valid since both are in furtherance of the national purpose for which the money is appropriated. [The] spending power of Congress is in addition to the legislative power and not subordinate to it. This independent grant of the power of the purse, [involving] in its exercise the duty to insure expenditure within the granted power, presuppose freedom of selection among divers ends and aims, and the capacity to impose such conditions as will render the choice effective. It is a contradiction in terms to say that there is power to spend for the national welfare, while rejecting any power to impose conditions reasonably adapted to the attainment of the end which alone would justify the expenditure.

The limitation now sanctioned must lead to absurd consequences. The government may give seeds to farmers, but may not condition the gift upon their being planted in places where they are most needed or even planted at all. The government may give money to the unemployed, but may not ask that those who get it shall give labor in return, or even use it to support their families. . . .

The action which Congress induces by payments of money to promote the general welfare, but which it does not command or coerce, is but an incident to a specifically granted power, but a permissible means to a legitimate end. If appropriation in aid of a program of curtailment of agricultural production is constitutional, and it is not denied that it is, payment to farmers on condition that they reduce their crop acreage is constitutional. It is not any the less so because the farmer at his own option promises to fulfill the condition. . . .

NOTE

The Erosion of *Butler*. The majority's approach reflected the view of earlier cases that agriculture was a subject reserved to the states. Though it said that the power to spend for the general welfare was not limited by the specific enumerated heads of federal authority, did it honor that principle in practice? Justice Stone's dissent concedes that conditional spending is inherently regulatory and asserts that regulation ancillary to spending is valid so long as it is reasonably related either to the general welfare of the nation or, perhaps, to the specific spending initiative.

A year later, the limits seen by the Court in *Butler* began to erode. Two companion cases, Steward Machine Co. v. Davis, 301 U.S. 548 (1937), and Helvering v. Davis, 301 U.S. 619 (1937), upheld the validity of the unemployment compensation and old-age pension aspects of the Social Security Act. In *Helvering*, the Court concluded that the payroll taxes assessed to fund old-age pensions and the pension spending itself were valid. Writing for the Court, Justice Cardozo declared:

> The discretion [as to what constitutes "general welfare"] belongs to Congress, unless the choice is clearly wrong, a display of arbitrary power, not an exercise

of judgment. [The problem of old-age pensions] is plainly national. [The] separate states cannot deal with it effectively. Congress, at least, had a basis for that belief. [When] money is spent to promote the general welfare, the concept of welfare or its opposite is shaped by Congress, not the states. [If] the concept be not arbitrary, the locality must yield.

This theme has been strongly echoed in later cases. In Buckley v. Valeo, 424 U.S. 1 (1976), the Court upheld federal spending to finance presidential campaigns, stating that "[i]t is for Congress to decide which expenditures will promote the general welfare."

Steward Machine involved a payroll tax levied on employers coupled with a credit against the tax for payments made by them into a state unemployment fund certified by a federal agency as complying with federal standards. The point of this arrangement was to pressure states into adopting unemployment compensation laws complying with federal standards. Despite this feature, the Court upheld the scheme, 5-4. Justice Cardozo, for the Court, insisted that the tax-and-credit feature was

> not void as involving the coercion of the States. [Before] Congress acted, unemployment compensation insurance was still [a] project and no more. [States] held back through alarm lest, in laying such a toll upon their industries, they would place themselves in a position of economic disadvantage. [The Social Security Act] is an attempt to find a method by which [all] may work together to a common end. [The challenger's] contention [confuses] motive with coercion. [Every] rebate from a tax when conditioned upon conduct is in some measure a temptation. But to hold that motive or temptation is equivalent to coercion is to plunge the law in endless difficulties. The outcome of such a doctrine is the acceptance of a philosophical determinism by which choice becomes impossible. Till now the law has been guided by a robust common sense which assumes the freedom of the will as a working hypothesis in the solution of its problems. [We] leave many questions open. We do not say that a tax is valid, when imposed by act of Congress, if it is laid upon the condition that a state may escape its operation through the adoption of a statute unrelated in subject matter to activities fairly within the scope of national policy and power. [It] is one thing to impose a tax dependent upon the conduct of taxpayers, or of the state in which they live, where the conduct to be stimulated or discouraged is unrelated to the fiscal needs, subserved by the tax in its normal operation, or to any other end legitimately national. [Bailey v. Drexel Furniture.] It is quite another thing to say that a tax will be abated upon the doing of an act that will satisfy the fiscal need, the tax and the alternative being approximate equivalents. In such [circumstances] inducement or persuasion does not go beyond the bounds of power. [The] statute does not call for a surrender by the states of powers essential to their quasisovereign existence.

State Autonomy Limits to the Spending Power

Given the development of state autonomy limits upon the commerce clause, one might expect a similar pattern with respect to the spending clause.

Indeed, Justice Cardozo hinted as much in *Steward Machine* when he focused on federal spending that coerced the states either to enact federally prescribed legislation outside the scope of federal power or to surrender power "essential" to sovereignty. Those suggested limits are similar in outline to the state autonomy doctrine with respect to the commerce clause. Yet, as revealed in the next case, the state autonomy limits on federal spending are in fact much weaker. Is there any good reason for this disparity? For an argument that state autonomy limits upon spending should be every bit as strong as those applicable to the commerce power, see Lewis Kaden, Politics, Money, and State Sovereignty: The Judicial Role, 79 Colum. L. Rev. 847 (1979).

South Dakota v. Dole
483 U.S. 203 (1987)

[Congress enacted 23 U.S.C. §158, directing the Secretary of Transportation to withhold 5 percent of the federal highway funds otherwise payable to a state from any state that fails to prohibit persons under 21 years of age from purchase or possession of alcoholic beverages. South Dakota permitted those age 19 or older to purchase and possess low-alcohol beer. The state sought a declaration that §158 violated state autonomy limits on the spending power as well as the Twenty-first Amendment, which gives states an ill-defined power to regulate the terms of consumption of alcoholic beverages. The lower federal courts rejected South Dakota's claims.]

CHIEF JUSTICE REHNQUIST delivered the opinion of the Court.

[We] need not decide [whether the Twenty-first Amendment] would prohibit an attempt by Congress to legislate directly a national minimum drinking age. Here, Congress has acted indirectly under its spending power to encourage uniformity in the States' drinking ages. [We] find this legislative effort within constitutional bounds even if Congress may not regulate drinking ages directly. [Incident to the spending] power, Congress may attach conditions on the receipt of federal funds, and has repeatedly employed the power "to further broad policy objectives by conditioning receipt of federal moneys upon compliance by the recipient with federal . . . directives." [*Butler*] determined that "the power of Congress to authorize expenditure of public moneys for public purposes is not limited by the direct grants of legislative power found in the Constitution." Thus, objectives not thought to be within Article I's "enumerated legislative fields" may nevertheless be attained through the use of the spending power and the conditional grant of federal funds. The spending power is of course not unlimited. [First], the exercise of the spending power must be in pursuit of "the general welfare." In considering whether a particular expenditure is intended to serve general public purposes, courts should defer substantially to the judgment of Congress. Second, [if] Congress desires to condition the States' receipt of federal funds, it "must do so unambiguously, [enabling] the States to exercise their choice knowingly, cognizant of the consequences of their participation." Third, our cases have suggested (without significant elaboration) that conditions on federal grants might be illegitimate if they are unrelated "to the federal interest in particular national projects or programs." Finally, we have noted that other constitutional provisions may provide an independent bar to the conditional grant of federal funds.

South Dakota does not seriously claim that §158 is inconsistent with any of the first three restrictions mentioned above. [The State] admits that it "has never contended that the congressional action [was] unrelated to a national concern in the absence of the Twenty-first Amendment." Indeed, the condition imposed by Congress is directly related to one of the main purposes for which highway funds are expended—safe interstate travel.[3] This goal of the interstate highway system had been frustrated by varying drinking ages among the States. A Presidential commission appointed to study alcohol-related accidents and fatalities on the Nation's highways concluded that the lack of uniformity in the States' drinking ages created "an incentive to drink and drive" because "young persons commut[e] to border States where the drinking age is lower." By enacting §158, Congress conditioned the receipt of federal funds in a way reasonably calculated to address this particular impediment to a purpose for which the funds are expended.

The remaining question about the validity of §158—and the basic point of disagreement between the parties—is whether the Twenty-first Amendment constitutes an "independent constitutional bar" to the conditional grant of federal funds. Petitioner, relying on its view that the Twenty-first Amendment prohibits *direct* regulation of drinking ages by Congress, asserts that "Congress may not use the spending power to regulate that which it is prohibited from regulating directly under the Twenty-first Amendment." But our cases show that this "independent constitutional bar" limitation on the spending power is not of the kind petitioner suggests. [*Butler*] established that the constitutional limitations on Congress when exercising its spending power are less exacting than those on its authority to regulate directly. We have also held that a perceived Tenth Amendment limitation on congressional regulation of state affairs did not concomitantly limit the range of conditions legitimately placed on federal grants . . . because the State could . . . adopt "the 'simple expedient' of not yielding to what she urges is federal coercion. The offer of benefits to a state by the United States dependent upon cooperation by the state with federal plans, assumedly for the general welfare, is not unusual."

---

3. Our cases have not required that we define the outer bounds of the "germaneness" or "relatedness" limitation on the imposition of conditions under the spending power. Amici urge that we take this occasion to establish that a condition on federal funds is legitimate only if it relates directly to the purpose of the expenditure to which it is attached. Because petitioner has not sought such a restriction, and because we find any such limitation on conditional federal grants satisfied in this case in any event, we do not address whether conditions less directly related to the particular purpose of the expenditure might be outside the bounds of the spending power.

[The] "independent constitutional bar" limitation on the spending power is not . . . a prohibition on the indirect achievement of objectives which Congress is not empowered to achieve directly. Instead, [the spending] power may not be used to induce the States to engage in activities that would themselves be unconstitutional. Thus, for example, a grant of federal funds conditioned on invidiously discriminatory state action or the infliction of cruel and unusual punishment would be an illegitimate exercise of the Congress'[s] broad spending power. But no such claim can be or is made here. [In] some circumstances the financial inducement offered by Congress might be so coercive as to pass the point at which "pressure turns into compulsion." [Here], however, Congress has directed only that a State desiring to establish a minimum drinking age lower than 21 lose a relatively small percentage of certain federal highway funds. Petitioner contends that the coercive nature of this program is evident from the degree of success it has achieved. We cannot conclude, however, that a conditional grant of federal money of this sort is unconstitutional simply by reason of its success in achieving the congressional objective. When we consider [that] all South Dakota would lose if she adheres to her chosen course as to a suitable minimum drinking age is 5% of the funds otherwise obtainable under specified highway grant programs, the argument as to coercion is shown to be more rhetoric than fact. [Congress] has offered relatively mild encouragement to the States to enact higher minimum drinking ages than they would otherwise choose. But the enactment of such laws remains the prerogative of the States not merely in theory but in fact. Even if Congress might lack the power to impose a national minimum drinking age directly, we conclude that encouragement to state action found in §158 is a valid use of the spending power. . . .

Affirmed.

Justice O'Connor, dissenting.

[Section] 158 is not a condition on spending reasonably related to the expenditure of federal funds and cannot be justified on that ground. Rather, it is an attempt to regulate the sale of liquor, an attempt that lies outside Congress'[s] power to regulate commerce because it falls within the ambit of §2 of the Twenty-first Amendment.

My disagreement with the Court is relatively narrow on the spending power issue: it is a disagreement about the application of a principle rather than a disagreement on the principle itself. [The] Court's application of the requirement that the condition imposed be reasonably related to the purpose for which the funds are expended is cursory and unconvincing. We have repeatedly said that Congress may condition grants under the spending power only in ways reasonably related to the purpose of the federal program. In my view, establishment of a minimum drinking age of 21 is not sufficiently related to interstate highway construction to justify so conditioning funds appropriated for that purpose. [The] Court reasons that Congress wishes that the roads it builds may be used safely, that drunken drivers threaten highway safety, and that young people are more likely to drive while under the influence of alcohol under existing law than would be the case if there were a uniform national drinking age of 21. It hardly needs saying, however, that if the purpose of §158 is to deter drunken driving, it is far too over and under-inclusive. It is over-inclusive because it stops teenagers from drinking even when they are not about to drive on interstate highways. It is under-inclusive because teenagers pose only a small part of the drunken driving problem in this Nation. . . .

When Congress appropriates money to build a highway, it is entitled to insist that the highway be a safe one. But it is not entitled to insist as a condition of the use of highway funds that the State impose or change regulations in other areas of the State's social and economic life because of an attenuated or tangential relationship to highway use or safety. Indeed, if the rule were otherwise, the Congress could effectively regulate almost any area of a State's social, political, or economic life on the theory that use of the interstate transportation system is somehow enhanced. If, for example, the United States were to condition highway moneys upon moving the state capital, I suppose it might argue that interstate transportation is facilitated by locating local governments in places easily accessible to interstate highways—or, conversely, that highways might become overburdened if they had to carry traffic to and from the state capital. In my mind, such a relationship is hardly more attenuated than the one which the Court finds supports §158.

There is a clear place at which the Court can draw the line between permissible and impermissible conditions on federal grants. It is the line identified in the Brief for the National Conference of State Legislatures et al. as Amici Curiae: "Congress has the power to *spend* for the general welfare, it has the power to *legislate* only for delegated purposes. [The] appropriate inquiry, then, is whether the spending requirement or prohibition is a condition on a grant or whether it is regulation. The difference turns on whether the requirement specifies in some way how the money should be spent, so that Congress'[s] intent in making the grant will be effectuated. Congress has no power under the Spending Clause to impose requirements on a grant that go beyond specifying how the money should be spent. A requirement that is not such a specification is not a condition, but a regulation, which is valid only if it falls within one of Congress'[s] delegated regulatory powers." This approach harks back to [*Butler*]. The *Butler* Court saw the Agricultural Adjustment Act for what it was—an exercise of regulatory, not spending, power. The error in *Butler* was not the Court's conclusion that the Act was essentially regulatory, but rather its crabbed view of the extent of Congress'[s] regulatory power under the Commerce Clause. The Agricultural Adjustment Act was regulatory but it was regulation that today would likely be considered within Congress'[s] commerce power. While *Butler*'s authority is questionable insofar as it assumes that Congress has no regulatory power over farm production, its discussion of the spending power and its description of both the power's breadth and its limitations remain sound. The Court's decision in *Butler* also properly recognizes the gravity of the task of appropriately limiting the spending power. If the spending power is to be limited only by Congress'[s] notion of the general welfare, the reality, given the vast financial resources of the Federal Government, is that the Spending Clause gives "power to the Congress to tear down the barriers, to invade the states' jurisdiction, and to become a parliament of the whole people, subject to no restrictions save such as are self-imposed." This, of course, as *Butler* held, was not the Framers' plan and it is not the meaning of the Spending Clause.

Our [post-*Butler*] cases are consistent with the notion that, under the spending power, the Congress may only condition grants in ways that can fairly be said to be related to the expenditure of federal funds. [As] discussed above, a condition that a State will raise its drinking age to 21 cannot fairly be said to be reasonably related to the expenditure of funds for highway construction. The only possible connection, highway safety, has nothing to do with how the funds Congress has appropriated are expended. Rather than a condition determining how federal highway money shall be expended, it is a regulation determining who shall be able to drink liquor. As such it is not justified by the spending power. Of the other possible sources of congressional authority for regulating the sale of liquor only the commerce power comes to mind. But in my view, the regulation of the age of the purchasers of liquor, just as the regulation of the price at which liquor may be sold, falls squarely within the scope of those powers reserved to the States by the Twenty-first Amendment. [Accordingly], Congress simply lacks power under the Commerce Clause to displace state regulation of this kind. The immense size and power of the Government of the United States ought not obscure its fundamental character. It remains a Government of enumerated powers. Because §158 cannot be justified as an exercise of any power delegated to the Congress, it is not authorized by the Constitution. . . .

NOTES

1. **Unconstitutional Conditions.** The problem of "unconstitutional conditions" pops up again and again throughout constitutional law. Governments need not provide many of the benefits they routinely provide. To what extent can a government condition receipt of such benefits upon relinquishing some constitutionally protected right? Most of the instances in which you will encounter this doctrine will involve conditions placed on receipt of individual benefits that require an individual to waive some constitutional liberty as the price of obtaining the benefit. These will be explored as they occur throughout Part III of this book. In *Dole*, the situation was slightly different. South Dakota, rather than an individual person, was alleging that its receipt of a benefit (100 percent of the federal highway funds that Congress had made available to it, although Congress need not have provided any highway funds to any state) was conditioned upon its surrender of its constitutionally recognized sovereign power to establish a minimum drinking age. In other contexts, such as the right of free speech, the "unconstitutional conditions" problem is resolved by separating denials of benefits that "penalize" speech

(unconstitutional conditions) from those that merely refrain from subsidizing speech (constitutionally valid conditions). See, e.g., Speiser v. Randall, 357 U.S. 513 (1958) (invalidating a California denial of a property tax exemption for veterans to any veteran who refused to declare that he did not advocate the forcible overthrow of government). Is the *Dole* test identical?

2. **"Directly Related."** In a footnote, Chief Justice Rehnquist noted that the Court was not deciding how much of a relationship between the condition and the purpose of the spending was necessary to establish that it was "directly related." In her dissent, Justice O'Connor answered that question—conditions may only "specif[y] in some way how the money should be spent." Under the majority opinion, could Congress condition a state's receipt of federal money for "all health and medical purposes" upon a state's banning the use of fetal tissue for medical research? Could Congress do so under Justice O'Connor's opinion? Would the answer be different if the condition applied only to federal money for "medical research"?

Suppose that Justice O'Connor's test had prevailed in *Dole* and that Congress had reacted by enacting legislation that required states receiving federal highway funds to spend the money only on highways from which are excluded all people under age 21 who have access under the state's law to alcoholic beverages. Would this condition violate Justice O'Connor's test? If not, is her test a practical limit on federal spending conditions?

3. **"Clear Statement" Required.** *Dole* states that if "Congress desires to condition the States' receipt of federal funds, it must do so unambiguously." Does this mean that every provision of a law enacted pursuant to the spending power must contain a clear statement of the condition attached to the federal funds, or only that the law, as a whole, must contain an unambiguous statement of the conditions attached to the spending?

Arlington Central School District Board of Education v. Murphy, 548 U.S. 291 (2006), involved a condition attached to federal funds to assist state and local agencies in educating children with disabilities. Receipt of the funds was contingent on state compliance with the obligation to provide private schooling if the public schools cannot adequately meet the educational needs of the disabled child. As part of that obligation, states are required to pay the "reasonable attorneys' fees" of parents who successfully sue to enforce a state's statutory duty. Because the attorneys' fees provision of the law did not specify whether expert witness fees were included in "attorneys' fees," the Court held that imposition of state liability for expert fees was an ambiguous condition, and thus invalid.

National Federation of Independent Business v. Sebelius
132 S. Ct. 2566 (2012)

[A part of the Patient Protection and Affordable Care Act (ACA) provided that the federal government would initially pay to the states the cost of expanded eligibility for Medicaid, a program operated by the states but funded in part by the federal government. However, if states did not agree to expand Medicaid eligibility as the ACA dictated, the Secretary of Health and Human Services was empowered to withhold all Medicaid funds from any state not in compliance.]

CHIEF JUSTICE ROBERTS delivered an opinion, in which JUSTICES BREYER and KAGAN joined.

. . . The States . . . contend that the Medicaid expansion exceeds Congress's authority under the Spending Clause. They claim that Congress is coercing the States to adopt the changes it wants by threatening to withhold all of a State's Medicaid grants, unless the State accepts the new expanded funding and complies with the conditions that come with it. This, they argue, violates the basic principle that the "Federal Government may not compel the States to enact or administer a federal regulatory program." *New York.*

There is no doubt that the Act dramatically increases state obligations under Medicaid. The current Medicaid program requires States to cover only certain discrete categories of needy individuals—pregnant women, children, needy families, the blind, the elderly, and the disabled. There is no mandatory coverage for most childless adults, and the States typically do not offer any such coverage. The States also enjoy considerable flexibility with respect to the coverage levels for parents of needy families. On average States cover only those unemployed parents who make less than 37 percent of the federal poverty level, and only those employed parents who make less than 63 percent of the poverty line. The Medicaid provisions of the Affordable Care Act, in contrast, require States to expand their Medicaid programs by 2014 to cover *all* individuals under the age of 65 with incomes below 133 percent of the federal poverty line. The Act also establishes a new "[e]ssential health benefits" package, which States must provide to all new Medicaid recipients—a level sufficient to satisfy a recipient's obligations under the individual mandate. The Affordable Care Act provides that the Federal Government will pay 100 percent of the costs of covering these newly eligible individuals through 2016. In the following years, the federal payment level gradually decreases, to a minimum of 90 percent. . . .

We have long recognized that Congress may use [the spending] power to grant federal funds to the States, and may condition such a grant upon the States' "taking certain actions that Congress could not require them to take." . . . At the same time, our cases have recognized limits on Congress's power under the Spending Clause to secure state compliance with federal objectives. . . . [That has] led us to scrutinize Spending Clause legislation to ensure that Congress is not using financial inducements to exert a "power akin to undue influence." Steward Machine Co. v. Davis. Congress may use its spending power to create incentives for States to act in accordance with federal policies. But when "pressure turns into compulsion," the legislation runs contrary to our system of federalism. "[T]he Constitution simply does not give Congress the authority to require the States to regulate." *New York.* That is true whether Congress directly commands a State to regulate or indirectly coerces a State to adopt a federal regulatory system as its own.

Permitting the Federal Government to force the States to implement a federal program would threaten the political accountability key to our federal system. . . . Spending Clause programs do not pose this danger when a State has a legitimate choice whether to accept the federal conditions in exchange for federal funds. In such a situation, state officials can fairly be held politically accountable for choosing to accept or refuse the federal offer. But when the State has no choice, the Federal Government can achieve its objectives without accountability, just as in *New York* and *Printz*. Indeed, this danger is heightened when Congress acts under the Spending Clause, because Congress can use that power to implement federal policy it could not impose directly under its enumerated powers. . . .

Congress may attach appropriate conditions to federal taxing and spending programs to preserve its control over the use of federal funds. In the typical case we look to the States to defend their prerogatives by adopting "the simple expedient of not yielding" to federal blandishments when they do not want to embrace the federal policies as their own. The States are separate and independent sovereigns. Sometimes they have to act like it.

The States . . . argue that the Medicaid expansion is far from the typical case. They object that Congress has "crossed the line distinguishing encouragement from coercion" in the way it has structured the funding: Instead of simply refusing to grant the new funds to States that will not accept the new conditions, Congress has also threatened to withhold those States' existing Medicaid funds. The States claim that this threat serves no purpose other than to force unwilling States to sign up for the dramatic expansion in health care coverage effected by the Act.

Given the nature of the threat and the programs at issue here, we must agree. We have upheld Congress's authority to condition the receipt of funds on the States' complying with restrictions on the use of those funds, because that is the means by which Congress ensures that the funds are spent according to its view of the "general Welfare." Conditions that do not here govern the use of the funds, however, cannot be justified on that basis. When . . . such conditions take the form of threats to terminate other significant independent grants, the conditions are properly viewed as a means of pressuring the States to accept policy changes. . . .

In South Dakota v. Dole, we . . . found that the inducement was not impermissibly coercive, because Congress was offering only "relatively mild encouragement to the States." . . . In this case, the financial "inducement" Congress has chosen is much more than "relatively mild encouragement"—it is a gun to the head. A State that opts out of the Affordable Care Act's expansion in health care coverage thus stands to lose not merely "a relatively small percentage" of its existing Medicaid funding, but *all* of it. Medicaid spending accounts for over 20 percent of the average State's total budget, with federal funds covering 50 to 83 percent of those costs. . . . The Federal Government estimates that it will pay out approximately $3.3 trillion between 2010 and 2019 in order to cover the costs of *pre*-expansion Medicaid. . . . It is easy to see how the *Dole* Court could conclude that the threatened loss of less than half of one percent of South Dakota's budget left that State with a "prerogative" to reject Congress's desired policy, "not merely in theory but in fact." The threatened loss of over 10 percent of a State's overall budget, in contrast, is economic dragooning that leaves the States with no real option but to acquiesce in the Medicaid expansion. . . .

The Court in *Steward Machine* did not attempt to "fix the outermost line" where persuasion gives way to coercion. . . . We have no need to fix a line either. It is enough for today that wherever that line may be, this statute is surely beyond it. Congress may not simply "conscript state [agencies] into the national bureaucratic army," and that is what it is attempting to do with the Medicaid expansion.

Nothing in our opinion precludes Congress from offering funds under the Affordable Care Act to expand the availability of health care, and requiring that States accepting such funds comply with the conditions on their use. What Congress is not free to do is to penalize States that choose not to participate in that new program by taking away their existing Medicaid funding. . . .

Congress has no authority to order the States to regulate according to its instructions. Congress may offer the States grants and require the States to comply with accompanying conditions, but the States must have a genuine choice whether to accept the offer. The States are given no such choice in this case: They must either accept a basic change in the nature of Medicaid, or risk losing all Medicaid funding. The remedy for that constitutional violation is to preclude the Federal Government from imposing such a sanction. . . .

JUSTICES GINSBURG and SOTOMAYOR concurred in the judgment.

E. TREATY IMPLEMENTATION

Article II, section 2 gives the President the power to make treaties, provided that two-thirds of the senators present and voting ratify the treaty. The supremacy clause (Art. VI, cl. 2) explicitly stipulates that "all Treaties made [under] the Authority of the United States shall be the supreme Law of the Land." Two questions of federal power are raised by treaties. First, does Congress have the power to implement treaties without regard to any other source of congressional power, or is Congress's implementation power no broader than the enumerated sources of regulatory authority granted Congress under the Constitution? Missouri v. Holland may answer this query. Second, if Congress is free to implement treaties without regard to some independent source of power, may Congress ignore all constitutional limits upon its power in implementing treaties? In Reid v. Covert, a plurality of the Court said no.

≣ *Missouri v. Holland*
≣ *252 U.S. 416 (1920)*

JUSTICE HOLMES delivered the opinion of the Court.

This is a bill in equity brought by the State of Missouri to prevent a game warden of the United States from attempting to enforce the [1918] Migratory Bird Treaty Act [on the] ground . . . that the statute is an unconstitutional interference with the rights reserved to the States by the Tenth Amendment. [A 1916] treaty between the United States and Great Britain [recited] that many species of birds in their annual migrations traversed many parts of the United States and of Canada, that they were of great value as a source of food and in destroying insects injurious to vegetation, but were in danger of extermination through lack of adequate protection. It therefore provided for specified closed seasons and protection in other forms, and agreed that the two powers would take or propose to their lawmaking bodies the necessary measures for carrying the treaty out. The [1918 Act] prohibited . . . killing, capturing or selling any of the migratory birds included in the terms of the treaty except as permitted by [federal] regulations compatible with those terms. [A federal district court upheld the validity of the 1918 Act. On appeal], the question raised is the general one whether the treaty and statute are void as an interference with the rights reserved to the States.

To answer this question it is not enough to refer to the Tenth Amendment [because] by Article [II], Section 2, the power to make treaties is delegated expressly, and by Article [VI] treaties made under the authority of the United States [are] declared the supreme law of the land. If the treaty is valid there can be no dispute about the validity of the statute under Article [I], Section 8, as a necessary and proper means to execute the powers of the Government. [It] is said that a treaty cannot be valid if it infringes the Constitution, that there are limits, therefore, to the treaty-making power, and that one such limit is that what an act of Congress could not do unaided, in derogation of the powers reserved to the States, a treaty cannot do. An earlier act of Congress that attempted by itself and not in pursuance of a treaty to regulate the killing of migratory birds within the States had been held bad [but that] cannot be accepted as a test of the treaty power. Acts of Congress are the supreme law of the land only when made in pursuance of the Constitution, while treaties are declared to be so when made under the authority of the United States. It is open to question whether the authority of the United States means more than the formal acts prescribed to make the convention. We do not mean to imply that there are no qualifications to the treaty-making power; but they must be ascertained in a different way. It is obvious that there may be matters of the sharpest exigency for the national well being that an act of Congress could not deal with but that a treaty followed by such an act could, and it is not lightly to be assumed that, in matters requiring national action, "a power which must belong to and somewhere reside in every civilized government" is not to be found. [In] dealing with words that also are a constituent act, like the Constitution [we] must realize that they have called into life a being the development of which could not have been foreseen completely by the most gifted of its begetters. It was enough for them to realize or to hope that they had created an organism; it has taken a century and has cost their successors much sweat and blood to prove that they created a nation. The case before us must be considered in the light of our whole experience and not merely in that of what was said a hundred years ago. The treaty in question does not contravene any prohibitory words to be found in the Constitution. The only question is whether it is forbidden by some invisible radiation from the general terms of the Tenth Amendment. We must consider what this country has become in deciding what that amendment has reserved. . . .

Here a national interest of very nearly the first magnitude is involved. It can be protected only by national action in concert with that of another power. The subject matter is only transitorily within the State and has no permanent habitat therein. But for the treaty and the statute there soon might be no birds for any powers to deal with. We see nothing in the Constitution that compels the Government to sit by while a food supply is cut off and the protectors of our forests and our crops are destroyed. It is not sufficient to rely upon the States. The reliance is vain, and were it otherwise, the question is whether the United States is forbidden to act. We are of [the] opinion that the treaty and statute must be upheld. [Affirmed.]

NOTES AND PROBLEMS

1. Scope of Congressional Power. By virtue of the Supremacy Clause, a valid treaty displaces any contrary state law. See, e.g., Ware v. Hylton, 3 U.S. 199 (1796). In *Holland*, the Court concluded that Congress is not confined to its Article I, §8 enumerated powers in implementing a treaty. Because that implementation will displace state law, the door is opened for broad federal preemption of state law. *Holland* does suggest that the treaty implementation power may be limited to subjects of "national concern," but that limit is implicit in the treaty power itself. An earlier case, De Geofroy v. Riggs, 133 U.S. 258 (1890), states that treaties may deal with issues "properly the subject of negotiation with a foreign country." If the President has negotiated a treaty with a foreign nation and the Senate has ratified it, is it appropriate for the Court to say that the subject is not a proper subject of negotiation with a foreign country? The importance of this broad power has declined as the scope of the enumerated powers (particularly the commerce power) has increased. Does the treaty power create the possibility of an obliteration of federalism through such treaties?

2. Bond v. United States. In Bond v. United States, 134 S. Ct. 2077 (2014), the Court dodged the question of whether *Holland* was correct. The United States became a party to the International Convention on Chemical Weapons, which obligates parties to outlaw chemical weapons. Congress implemented the Convention.by enacting the Chemical Weapons Convention Implementation Act of 1998. The Act makes it a federal crime for a person to use or possess any chemical weapon, and it punishes violators with severe penalties. Chemical weapon is defined as a toxic chemical. A toxic chemical is defined as "any chemical which through its chemical action on life processes can cause death, temporary incapacitation or permanent harm to humans or animals. The term includes all such chemicals, regardless of their origin or of their method of production, and regardless of whether they are produced in facilities, in munitions or elsewhere." Defined "peaceful purposes" of toxic chemicals are exempted. Carol Bond was convicted of violating the Act by her use of a toxic chemical to inflict minor, non-lasting harm on her husband's lover. The Court construed the statute to apply only to chemicals *"of the sort that an ordinary person would associate with instruments of chemical warfare."* The dissent derided this as a misreading of the law that rendered it unintelligible. The dissent insisted that Bond's act was criminal under the law and thus the constitutional validity of the statute was at issue. The dissent contended that Congress has the power to implement the *making* of treaties, but lacked power to implement the treaty itself without some additional source of legislative authority. Otherwise, "*Holland* places Congress only one treaty away from acquiring a general police power."

In a separate dissent Justice Thomas contended that the "Treaty Power is limited to matters of international intercourse. Even if a treaty *may* reach some local matters, it still *must* relate to intercourse with other nations. . . ."

3. Problems: *Domestic Violence Treaty.* In an effort to stem domestic violence worldwide, the United States and a number of European nations enter into a treaty obligating the parties to require successful completion of anger management classes as a condition of marriage. Congress enacts such a requirement. Is this valid under the treaty power? Under the commerce clause?

Convention on Children's Rights. A number of treaties have been negotiated (although not ratified by the U.S. Senate) that deal with the relationships of the Member States and their own citizens. An example is the Convention on the Rights of the Child (November 20, 1989), in which, among other things, nations are obliged to "[m]ake primary education compulsory and free to all" and to refrain from imposing "capital punishment [or] life imprisonment without possibility of release" upon a defendant convicted of a crime committed while a juvenile. In the absence of ratification of this treaty, could Congress validly enact federal laws implementing these requirements?

4. Limits on Congressional Power. May Congress ignore all constitutional limits when implementing the treaty power? After World War II, the United States entered into agreements with other nations that gave to U.S. military courts exclusive jurisdiction over offenses committed by U.S. military personnel or their dependents on foreign soil. Congress implemented the agreements with legislation giving military courts such exclusive jurisdiction. In Reid v. Covert, 354 U.S. 1 (1957), the wife of a U.S. military member was convicted of murder by a military court. She appealed, contending that Congress had no power to deprive her of a jury trial in a civilian court. The government invoked Missouri v. Holland, arguing that the statute was "necessary and proper to carry out the United States' obligations under the international agreements." A plurality of the Court struck down the law, noting that

> no agreement with a foreign nation can confer power on the Congress, or on any other branch of Government, which is free from the restraints of the Constitution. [It] would be manifestly contrary to the objectives of those who created the Constitution, as well as those who were responsible for the Bill of Rights—let alone alien to our entire constitutional history and tradition—to construe Article VI as permitting the United States to exercise power under an international agreement without observing constitutional provisions. [In *Holland*,] the Court carefully noted that the treaty involved was not inconsistent with any specific provision of the Constitution.

Justices Frankfurter and Harlan concurred on the ground that Congress's Art. I, §8 power to "make Rules for the Government and Regulation of the land and naval Forces" did not include the power to subject military dependents to court-martial in capital cases during peacetime.

5. More Problems: *Global Environment Treaty.* Suppose that the United States enters into a "Global Environmental Preservation" treaty that obligates all signatories to keep their national reproduction rate no higher than the rate that would maintain zero population growth. To implement the treaty Congress enacts legislation that requires any woman pregnant with a third child to abort the pregnancy. Is the legislation valid? Does it make any difference that reproductive rights are not specifically mentioned in the Constitution? Does it matter that the Court has never had occasion to deal with this precise issue?

Global Warming Treaty. Suppose that the President negotiates and the Senate ratifies a treaty that obligates Member States to reduce hydrocarbon emissions by specified amounts, and creates a Global Warming Commission vested with power to interpret the treaty, make those interpretations binding on all government organs of Member States, and impose sanctions on those Member States in violation. Suppose that the Global Warming Commission interprets the treaty in a fashion at odds with the interpretation given it by the U.S. Supreme Court and imposes sanctions on the United States. Would the interpretation of the treaty by the Global Warming Commission be binding on the U.S. Supreme Court?

F. POWER TO REGULATE IN AID OF WAR-MAKING

Congress may declare war; raise, support, and regulate the armed services; and tax and spend for national defense. Article I, §8. Through the necessary and proper clause, Congress has authority to enact reasonable measures to effectuate its power to provide the means for making war.

≡ ***Woods v. Cloyd W. Miller Co.***
≡ *333 U.S. 138 (1948)*

JUSTICE DOUGLAS delivered the opinion of the Court.

. . . Title II of the Housing and Rent Act of 1947 [imposed maximum rent controls]. The District Court was of the view that the authority of Congress to regulate rents by virtue of the war power ended with the Presidential Proclamation terminating hostilities on December 31, 1946, since that proclamation inaugurated "peace-in-fact" though it did not mark termination of the war. It also concluded that even if the war power continues, Congress did not act under it because it did not say [so]. We conclude [that] the war power sustains this legislation. The Court said in Hamilton v. Kentucky Distilleries and Warehouse Co., 251 U.S. 146 [1919], that the war power includes the power "to remedy the evils which have arisen from its rise and progress" and continues for the duration of that emergency. Whatever may be the consequences when war is officially terminated, the war power does not necessarily end with the cessation of hostilities. [Prohibition laws] enacted after the Armistice in World War I were sustained as exercises of the war power because they conserved manpower and increased efficiency of production in the critical days during the period of demobilization, and helped to husband the supply of grains and cereals depleted by the war effort. [Stewart v. Kahn, 78 U.S. (11 Wall.) 493 (1871)], held that Congress had the power to toll the statute of limitations of the States during the period when the process of their courts was not available to litigants due to the conditions obtaining in the Civil War. The constitutional validity of the present legislation follows a fortiori from those cases. The legislative history of the present Act makes abundantly clear that there has not yet been eliminated the deficit in housing which in considerable measure was caused by the heavy demobilization of veterans and by the cessation or reduction in residential construction during the period of hostilities due to the allocation of building materials to military projects. Since the war effort contributed heavily to that deficit, Congress has the power even after the cessation of hostilities to act to control the forces that a short supply of the needed article created. If that were not true, the Necessary and Proper Clause would be drastically limited in its application to the several war powers. [We] recognize the force of the argument that the effects of war under modern conditions may be felt in the economy for years and years, and that if the war power can be used in days of peace to treat all the wounds which war inflicts on our society, it may not only swallow up all other powers of Congress but largely obliterate the Ninth and the Tenth Amendments as well. There are no such implications in today's decision. We deal here with the consequences of a housing deficit greatly intensified during the period of hostilities by the war effort. Any power, of course, can be abused. But we cannot assume that Congress is not alert to its constitutional responsibilities. [The] question of the constitutionality of action taken by Congress does not depend on recitals of the power which it undertakes to exercise. Here it is plain from the legislative history that Congress was invoking its war power to cope with a current condition of which the war was a direct and immediate cause. . . . Reversed.

Justice Jackson, concurring.

I agree with the result in this case, but the arguments that have been addressed to us lead me to utter more explicit misgivings about war powers than the Court has done. The Government asserts no constitutional basis for this legislation other than this vague, undefined and undefinable "war power." No one will question that this power is the most dangerous one to free government in the whole catalogue of powers. It usually is invoked in haste and excitement when calm legislative consideration of constitutional limitation is difficult. It is executed in a time of patriotic fervor that makes moderation unpopular. And, worst of all, it is interpreted by the Judges under the influence of the same passions and pressures. Always, as in this case, the Government urges hasty decision to forestall some emergency or serve some purpose and pleads that paralysis will result if its claims to powers are denied or their confirmation delayed. Particularly when the war power is invoked to do things to the liberties of people, or to their property or economy that only indirectly affect conduct of the war and do not relate to the management of the war itself, the constitutional basis should be scrutinized with care.

I think we can hardly deny that the war power is as valid a ground for federal rent control now as it has been at any time. We still are technically in a state of war. I would not be willing to hold that war powers may be indefinitely prolonged merely by keeping legally alive a state of war that had in fact ended. I cannot accept the argument that war powers last as long as the effects and consequences of war for if so they are permanent—as permanent as the war debts. But I find no reason to conclude that we could find fairly that the present state of war is merely technical. We have armies abroad exercising our war power and have made no peace terms with our allies, not to mention our principal enemies. I think the conclusion that the war power has been applicable during the lifetime of this legislation is unavoidable.

PROBLEM

On September 14, 2001, Congress authorized the President to use military force against the "nations, organizations, or persons he determines planned, authorized, committed, or aided the terrorist attacks" of September 11, 2001. Could Congress validly invoke its regulatory power over war-making to ban the possession of guns or explosives in or near schools?

G. FOREIGN AFFAIRS

The Constitution does not explicitly vest in either Congress or the President a general power over foreign affairs. Some aspects of foreign affairs are entrusted to the President alone (e.g., diplomatic recognition of foreign governments); some are given to the President subject to Senate approval (e.g., treaties); some are given to Congress (e.g., the power to define and punish piracy, felonies on the high seas, and "offenses against the law of nations"). Nonetheless, however it is divided between the President and Congress, the Court has consistently declared that only the federal government has the power to conduct foreign affairs. This is partly the product of impeccable prudential logic, partly rooted in the historical intentions of the Founders, and partly inferred from constitutional structure, particularly the provisions of Article I, section 10, that disable states from making treaties, engaging in war, or entering into agreements with foreign nations without congressional consent.

In Perez v. Brownell, 356 U.S. 44, 57 (1958),[4] the Court upheld a federal law that stripped Americans of their citizenship if they voted in foreign elections:

> Although there is in the Constitution no specific grant to Congress of power to enact legislation for the . . . regulation of foreign affairs, there can be no doubt of the existence of this power in the law-making organ of the Nation. The States that joined together to form a single Nation and to create, through the Constitution, a Federal Government to conduct the affairs of that Nation must be held to have granted that Government the powers indispensable to its functioning effectively in the company of sovereign nations.

Although legislation that is rationally related to regulation of foreign affairs is valid, it is an open question whether the Court would actually conclude that Congress had not regulated foreign affairs when it said it was doing so.

Problem: Alcohol Prohibition. Suppose that, to improve relations with the Islamic world, Congress prohibits Americans from possessing or using alcoholic beverages while traveling abroad. Is this a valid exercise of the foreign relations power? Would it make any difference if the prohibition were limited to travel in predominantly Islamic countries?

Zschernig v. Miller and Exclusive Federal Power over Foreign Affairs

The effect of an *exclusive* federal power over foreign affairs is that it wholly disables the states from acting in that field. But what constitutes foreign affairs? In Zschernig v. Miller, 389 U.S. 429 (1968), the Court struck down an Oregon law barring inheritance by nonresident aliens of Oregon property if their countries would not permit Oregonians to inherit property sited in the foreign country. The Court said that the law touched upon "the

---

4. *Perez* was overruled on different grounds in Afroyim v. Rusk, 387 U.S. 253 (1967). In *Afroyim*, the Court held that the Fourteenth Amendment barred involuntary loss of citizenship, but did not disturb the conclusion in *Perez* that Congress holds an implied power to legislate in foreign affairs.

field of foreign affairs which the Constitution entrusts to the President and the Congress" by enabling state judicial inquiry into the "type of governments that obtain in particular foreign nations." By contrast, in Barclay's Bank v. Franchise Tax Board, 512 U.S. 298 (1994), the Court upheld California's method of assessing corporate income taxes by including income earned anywhere in the world.

Query: Is the difference between these two cases the fact that the Oregon law at issue in *Zschernig* effectively targeted foreign nations, and declared an Oregon policy toward the internal affairs of foreign nations, thus poaching upon the federal government's exclusive foreign affairs power, whereas the California law at issue in *Barclay's Bank* was not so targeted and was not a statement of California foreign policy?

In recent years, the Court has been more apt to strike down state laws touching upon foreign affairs on the ground that they conflict with federal action, rather than because they invade the exclusively federal field of foreign affairs. In Crosby v. National Foreign Trade Council, 530 U.S. 363 (2000), the Court ruled that a Massachusetts law barring state agencies from purchasing goods or services from companies doing business with Burma was impliedly preempted by federal law authorizing the President to impose similar economic sanctions against Burma and to lift those sanctions if (1) Burma should substantially improve its human rights practices and commitment to democratic governance or (2) if U.S. national security should so dictate. The Massachusetts law was an obstacle to the accomplishment of the intended purpose and natural effect of the federal law because it undermined presidential discretion to lift sanctions, interfered with the congressional decision to limit economic pressure against Burma to a specific range, and was at odds with the President's authority to speak for the nation in formulating an international strategy to deal with Burma.

Queries: In the absence of any federal legislation, could Massachusetts validly enact a law that bars the state from purchasing any item made in Burma? Enact a law that bars state officials from making official, state-funded visits to Burma?

In American Insurance Association v. Garamendi, 539 U.S. 396 (2003), the Supreme Court invalidated a California law, the Holocaust Victim Insurance Relief Act of 1999 (HVIRA), which required any insurer doing business in California to disclose information about all policies sold in Europe between 1920 and 1945 by the company or any related entity upon penalty of loss of its state business license. During the Nazi era, the government of Germany seized the proceeds of insurance policies owned by Jews; after the end of World War II, many insurers refused to pay on life insurance policies because of the absence of a death certificate or other proof of death. Acting in response to concerns raised by foreign governments and businesses about a spate of lawsuits in American courts against those governments and businesses, the United States entered into an executive agreement with Germany by which Germany established a fund to compensate Nazi era victims. The United States agreed to attempt to cause state and local governments to recognize the German fund as the sole remedy for such claims, and pledged to assert in any American court in which a German company was sued on a Nazi era claim a statement that it would be in the national interest of the United States to have the claim resolved exclusively by the fund. Similar executive agreements were reached between the United States and Austria, and the United States and France. All of the agreements dealt specifically with insurance claims by requiring the fund to coordinate its activities with the International Commission on Holocaust Era Insurance Claims (ICHEIC), a nongovernmental organization conceived to attempt to obtain from European insurers information about and settlement of outstanding insurance policies.

In *Garamendi*, the Court ruled that the HVIRA was preempted by the federal foreign affairs power.

Justice Souter wrote for the Court:

> . . . HVIRA interferes with foreign policy of the Executive Branch, as expressed principally in the executive agreements with Germany, Austria, and France. . . . There is . . . no question that at some point an exercise of state power that touches on foreign relations must yield to the National Government's policy. . . . Nor is there any question . . . that there is executive authority to decide what that policy should be. . . . [The] President has authority to make "executive agreements" with other countries, . . . [and] executive agreements to settle claims of American nationals against foreign governments is a particularly long-standing practice. [Valid] executive agreements . . . preempt state law, just as treaties [do, but because] the agreements include no preemption clause . . . their claim of preemption [rests] on asserted interference with the foreign policy those agreements embody. . . . Whereas the President [has chosen] flexibility in wielding "the coercive power of the national economy" as a tool of diplomacy, HVIRA [makes] exclusion from a large sector of the American insurance market the automatic sanction for noncompliance with the State's . . . policies on disclosure. . . . HVIRA threatens to frustrate the operation of the particular mechanism the President has chosen. . . . The basic fact is that California seeks to use an iron fist where the President has consistently chosen kid gloves.

Justice Ginsburg, joined by Justices Stevens, Scalia, and Thomas, dissented, arguing that the

> notion of "dormant foreign affairs preemption" with which *Zschernig* is associated resonates most audibly when a state action "reflects a state policy critical of foreign governments and involves 'sitting in judgment' on them." The HVIRA entails no such state action or policy. It takes no position on any contemporary foreign government and requires no assessment of any existing foreign regime. It is directed solely at private insurers doing business in California, and it requires them solely to disclose information in their or their affiliates' possession or control. I would not extend *Zschernig* into this dissimilar domain. . . .

See also Denning and Ramsey, American Insurance Association v. Garamendi and Executive Preemption in Foreign Affairs, 46 Wm. & Mary L. Rev. 825 (2004).

H. POWER TO ENFORCE THE RECONSTRUCTION AMENDMENTS

The Reconstruction Amendments—the Thirteenth, Fourteenth, and Fifteenth Amendments—greatly increased federal power over the states. Each of these amendments gives Congress power to enforce the substantive provisions of the amendment by "appropriate legislation." The Thirteenth Amendment prohibits slavery. The Fourteenth acts primarily to bar the states from denying to their residents either "equal protection of the laws" or "life, liberty or property without due process of law." The Fifteenth Amendment prohibits states from using race as a criterion for voting. The scope of the powers is very important, but because understanding their scope is aided by a solid grounding in the substance of equal protection, due process, and the First Amendment, consideration of these congressional powers is deferred until Chapter 11.

4

Limiting the Scope of State Power over Interstate Commerce

The Constitution limits state power both directly and by implication. Some of the more important direct limitations are found in Article I, §10; Article IV; the supremacy clause of Article VI; and the Thirteenth, Fourteenth, Fifteenth, Nineteenth, Twenty-fourth, and Twenty-sixth Amendments. The subject of this chapter is constitutional limits upon state regulation of interstate, foreign, and Indian commerce, which are also express and implied.

The express limitation upon state regulation of interstate commerce lies in the combination of the commerce power and the supremacy clause. If Congress uses its commerce power to legislate, the supremacy clause makes the federal legislation supreme, thus displacing any contrary state law. This is called "preemption." The concept of preemption is not limited to the commerce power—any valid federal law preempts contrary state law unless the federal law disclaims any such intent. Preemption occurs when Congress intends for it to occur, but because Congress does not always say what it intends, it is sometimes difficult to determine whether preemption has occurred. Preemption is always a potential issue when Congress has acted. These matters are explored more fully in Section C.

When Congress has *not* acted to regulate interstate commerce, a constitutional limit may still be implied from the commerce clause itself. Even though the power to regulate interstate commerce is not exclusively vested in Congress, the courts have concluded that certain forms of state regulation are inimical to the free trade principles embodied in the grant of authority to Congress to regulate interstate commerce. This is called the "dormant commerce clause" or the "negative commerce clause." Unfortunately, the line between permissible and impermissible state regulation of interstate commerce, in the absence of congressional action, is none too clear. Section A deals with the complexities of the doctrine that creates this uncertain and wavering line. Section D adds a short epilogue dealing with the specific problem of the dormant commerce clause as applied to state taxation of interstate commerce.

One of the peculiarities of the dormant commerce clause is that Congress can act to undo the constitutional judgments of the Court. When the Court decides a dormant commerce clause case it is deciding what the commerce clause implies as a limit on state power in the absence of any congressional exercise of the power. When Congress does exercise its power it is free to regulate interstate commerce however it pleases (provided, of course, it doesn't violate some other, independent constitutional limit in doing so). Thus Congress is free to consent to state regulation of interstate commerce that the Court has found to be impliedly unconstitutional. The logic and limit of this consent power are explored in Section C.

Finally, another constitutional provision, the "privileges and immunities" clause of Article IV, addresses some of the same concerns as the dormant commerce clause. The two clauses are by no means redundant, however. There are important differences in the scope of the two and in the judicial tests used to determine when a constitutional violation has occurred. Article IV's privileges and immunities clause is considered in Section B.

A. THE DORMANT COMMERCE CLAUSE

1. Introduction

a. *Theory*

The dormant aspect of the commerce clause occurs when two events coalesce: (1) a state regulates interstate commerce (or foreign or Indian commerce), and (2) Congress has not preempted the state regulation by federal legislation. In the absence of such congressional action the Court implies some limits upon state regulation of interstate commerce. But why? The text of the commerce clause does not indicate that Congress has exclusive power to regulate interstate commerce, and the Court has in fact rejected that interpretation. Indeed, the Court does not rely upon text; instead, it has relied on its reading of history to find that the grant of this congressional power implies some limits on the states' power, even when Congress has chosen not to exercise its commerce power.

Perhaps the best summation of the historical intentions surrounding the commerce clause and why those intentions support a negative implication upon state power to regulate commerce was given by Justice Robert Jackson in H.P. Hood & Sons v. DuMond, 336 U.S. 525 (1949):

> The Constitution "[was] framed upon the theory that the peoples of the several states must sink or swim together, and that in the long run prosperity and salvation are in union and not division." [When] victory relieved the Colonies from the pressure for solidarity that war had exerted, a drift toward anarchy and commercial warfare between states began. "[Each] state would legislate

according to its estimate of its own interests, the importance of its own products, and the local advantages or disadvantages of its position in a political or commercial view." This came "to threaten at once the peace and safety of the Union." The sole purpose for which Virginia initiated the movement which ultimately produced the Constitution was "to take into consideration the trade of the United States; to examine the relative situations and trade of the said states; to consider how far a uniform system in their commercial regulation may be necessary to their common interest and their permanent harmony." . . . The desire of the Forefathers to federalize regulation of foreign and interstate commerce stands in sharp contrast to their jealous preservation of power over their internal affairs. No other federal power was so universally assumed to be necessary, no other state power was so readily relinquished. There was no desire to authorize federal interference with social conditions or legal institutions of the states. Even the Bill of Rights amendments were framed only as a limitation upon the powers of Congress. The states were quite content with their several and diverse controls over most matters but, as Madison has indicated, "want of a general power over Commerce led to an exercise of this power separately, by the States, which not only proved abortive, but engendered rival, conflicting and angry regulations." The necessity of centralized regulation of commerce among the states was so obvious and so fully recognized that the few words of the Commerce Clause were little illuminated by debate. . . .

[The] material success that has come to inhabitants of the states which make up this federal free trade unit has been the most impressive in the history of commerce, but the established interdependence of the states only emphasizes the necessity of protecting interstate movement of goods against local burdens and repressions. We need only consider the consequences if each of the few states that produce copper, lead, high-grade iron ore, timber, cotton, oil or gas should decree that industries located in that state shall have priority. What fantastic rivalries and dislocations and reprisals would ensue if such practices were begun! Or suppose that the field of discrimination and retaliation be industry. May Michigan provide that automobiles cannot be taken out of that State until local dealers' demands are fully met? Would she not have every argument in the favor of such a statute that can be offered in support of New York's limiting sales of milk for out-of-state shipment to protect the economic interests of her competing dealers and local consumers? Could Ohio then pounce upon the rubber-tire industry, on which she has a substantial grip, to retaliate for Michigan's auto monopoly? Our system, fostered by the Commerce Clause, is that every farmer and every craftsman shall be encouraged to produce by the certainty that he will have free access to every market in the [Nation].

b. Doctrinal History

The Court's translation of theory into doctrine has evolved over time. In the first half of the nineteenth century, the Court, beginning with Gibbons v. Ogden, 22 U.S. (9 Wheat.) 1 (1824), avoided answering the question of whether the commerce power was exclusively federal or shared concurrently with the states. However, in *Gibbons*, Chief Justice Marshall, in dicta, recognized that states in the course of exercising their plenary reserved powers might regulate in a fashion that has an incidental effect on interstate commerce: State "inspection laws are . . . regulations of commerce," but are enacted under state authority to protect local health and welfare; yet they "may have a remote and considerable influence on commerce. . . ."

The New York steamboat monopoly statute at issue in *Gibbons* was hardly an inspection law, however, and the Court had no trouble concluding that the New York statute conflicted with the federal coastal navigation law and was thus preempted by virtue of the supremacy clause in Article VI. Only Justice William Johnson, in a concurring opinion, took the position that the commerce power was exclusively federal, leaving no room for any state regulation of interstate commerce, however incidental.[1]

Relying on the *Gibbons* dicta, the Court upheld state regulations that had an impact on interstate commerce, so long as the state regulations were fairly designed to improve the health, welfare, safety, or morals of the state polity. State laws implementing this plenary power of the states—the so-called police power—were treated as valid in the absence of some conflict with federal law. An example of this approach is Willson v. Black Bird Creek Marsh Co., 27 U.S. (2 Pet.) 245 (1829). Delaware authorized the company to dam a navigable tidal stream in order to drain a malarial swamp. Willson's vessel broke the dam and the company sued for damages. Delaware's courts rejected Willson's defense that the law authorizing construction of the dam violated the commerce clause. The Supreme Court, in an opinion by Chief Justice Marshall, agreed:

> [T]his is one of those many creeks, passing through a deep level marsh adjoining the Delaware, up which the tide flows for some distance. The value of the property on its banks must be enhanced by excluding the water from the marsh, and the health of the inhabitants probably improved. Measures calculated to produce these objects, provided they do not come into collision with the powers of the general government, are undoubtedly within those which are reserved to the states. . . . If congress had passed any act [in] execution of the power to regulate interstate commerce, the object of which was to control state legislation [over] small navigable creeks into which the tide flows [we] should feel not much difficulty in saying that a state law coming in conflict with such act would be void. But congress has passed no such act.

For the next two decades the justices argued about whether the commerce clause implied any limits on state regulation of interstate commerce and, if so, what the scope of those limits might be. Justice Joseph Story took the position that the commerce power was exclusively federal, thus precluding any state regulation of interstate commerce no matter what the state's purpose might have been. Chief Justice Taney, who served as Chief Justice from

---

1. It is one of the ironies of constitutional history that Johnson, Thomas Jefferson's first appointee to the Court, took a more nationalistic approach than Jefferson's arch-enemy, John Marshall.

1836 to 1864, thought that the commerce clause did not imply any limits on state regulation. To Taney, state regulations of interstate commerce were valid unless they conflicted with federal law regulating interstate commerce. The Court remained in disarray on this matter, with no single rationale commanding a majority, until Justice Benjamin Curtis, a brilliant Boston lawyer appointed by President Millard Fillmore, reconceived the subject in his first term on the Court, forming a majority around the view articulated in the following case.

≡ *Cooley v. Board of Wardens*
≡ *53 U.S. (12 How.) 299 (1851)*

[An 1803 Pennsylvania law required ships entering or leaving Philadelphia to hire a pilot familiar with local waters or to pay a penalty of half the pilotage fee. A 1789 federal law provided that "all pilots in [the] ports of the United States shall continue to be regulated in conformity with the existing laws of the states, [or] with such laws as the states may respectively hereafter enact for the purpose, until further legislative provision shall be made by Congress." The Pennsylvania courts found Cooley liable for the penalty.]

JUSTICE CURTIS delivered the opinion of the Court:

[T]he power to regulate commerce includes the regulation of navigation. [Regulations of pilots] constitute regulations of navigation, and consequently of [interstate] commerce. [It] becomes necessary, therefore, to consider whether this law of Pennsylvania, being a regulation of [interstate] commerce, is valid. [If the 1803] law of Pennsylvania [had] been in existence at the date of [the 1789 federal law], we might hold it to have been adopted by Congress, and thus made a law of the United States, and so valid. [What] effect then can be attributed to so much of the act of 1789, as declares that pilots shall continue to be regulated in conformity "with such laws as the States may respectively hereafter enact for the purpose, until further legislative provision shall be made by Congress"?

If the States were divested of the power to legislate on this subject by the grant of the commercial power to Congress, it is plain this act could not confer upon them power thus to legislate. If the Constitution excluded the States from making any law regulating commerce, certainly Congress cannot regrant, or in any manner reconvey to the States that power. And yet this act of 1789 gives its sanction only to laws enacted by the States. This necessarily implies a constitutional power [of the States] to legislate. [We] are brought directly and unavoidably to the consideration of the question, whether the grant of the commercial power to Congress did per se deprive the States of all power to regulate pilots. This question has never been decided by this [court].

The diversities of opinion [which] have existed on this subject have arisen from the different views taken of the nature of this power. But when [it] is said that the nature of the power requires that it should be exercised exclusively by Congress, it must be intended to refer to the subjects of that power, and to say they are of such a nature as to require exclusive legislation by Congress. Now the power to regulate commerce embraces a vast field, containing not only many but exceedingly various subjects, quite unlike in their nature; some imperatively demanding a single uniform rule, operating equally on the commerce of the United States in every port; and some, like the subject now in question, as imperatively demanding that diversity, which alone can meet the local necessities of navigation.

Either absolutely to affirm or deny that the nature of this power requires exclusive legislation by Congress is to lose sight of the nature of the subjects of this power, and to assert concerning all of them what is really applicable but to a part. Whatever subjects of this power are in their nature national, or admit only of one uniform system, or plan of regulation, may justly be said to be of such a nature as to require exclusive legislation by Congress. That this cannot be affirmed of laws for the regulation of pilots and pilotage is plain. The act of 1789 contains a clear and authoritative declaration by the first Congress that the nature of this subject is such that until Congress should find it necessary to exert its power, it should be left to the legislation of the States; that it is local and not national; that it is likely to be the best provided for, not by one system, or plan of regulations, but by as many as the legislative discretion of the several States should deem applicable to the local peculiarities of the ports within their limits.

Viewed in this light, so much of this act of 1789 as declares that pilots shall continue to be regulated "by such laws as the States may respectively hereafter enact for that purpose," instead of being held to be inoperative, as an attempt to confer on the States a power to legislate of which the Constitution had deprived them, [manifests] the understanding of Congress, at the outset of the government, that the nature of this subject is not such as to require its exclusive legislation. The practice of the States, and of the national government, has been in conformity with this declaration, from the origin of the national government to this time; and the nature of the subject when examined is such as to leave no doubt of the superior fitness and propriety [of] different systems of regulation, drawn from local knowledge and experience and conformed to local wants. How then can we say that by the mere grant of power to regulate commerce the states are deprived of all the power to legislate on this subject, because from the nature of the power the legislation of Congress must be exclusive. This would be to affirm that the nature of the power is in any case something different from the nature of the subject to which, in such case, the power extends, and that the nature of the power necessarily demands, in all cases, exclusive legislation by Congress, while the nature of one of the subjects of that power not only does not require such exclusive legislation, but may be best provided for by many different systems enacted by the States, in conformity with the circumstances of the ports within their limits. . . .

It is the opinion of a majority of the court that the mere grant to Congress of the power to regulate commerce did not deprive the States of power to regulate pilots, and that although Congress has legislated on this subject, its legislation manifests an intention [not] to regulate this subject, but to leave its regulation to the several States. To these precise questions, which are all we are called on to decide, this opinion must be understood to be confined. It does not extend to the question what other subjects, under the commercial power, are within the exclusive control of Congress, or may be regulated by the States in the absence of all congressional legislation; nor to the general question how far any regulation of a subject by Congress may be deemed to operate as an exclusion of all legislation by the States upon the same subject. . . .

We are of opinion that this State law was enacted by virtue of a power, residing in the State to legislate; that it is not in conflict with any law of Congress; that it does not interfere with any system which Congress has established by making regulations, or by intentionally leaving individuals to their own unrestricted action; that this law is therefore valid, and the judgment of the Supreme Court of Pennsylvania in each case must be affirmed.

NOTE

Cooley settled the question of whether Congress possessed exclusive authority to regulate interstate commerce by rejecting the "exclusively federal" position held by Story and William Johnson. But the Court also rejected Taney's position that the commerce clause had no limiting effect on state regulation of interstate commerce absent congressional exercise of the commerce power. Instead, *Cooley* introduced the question of whether the particular *subject* of regulation was inherently national (hence exclusively reserved to Congress) or inherently local (and thus subject to regulation by the states in the absence of conflicting federal law). Prior to *Cooley*, the states effectively had concurrent power to regulate commerce so long as their *purpose* was to regulate for local health, welfare, or safety benefits. After *Cooley*, the motives of the states were no longer of consequence; the issue became whether the *subject matter* of the legislation was national or local.

Cooley provided little guidance concerning the method of deciding whether any given subject was in fact national or local. The opinion does not tell us whether this characterization is to be made by examining legislative purpose, or effects, or something else. Nor does *Cooley* reveal whether, if a given subject is "local," there might still be implicit limits on state regulation.

Later cases sought to assess whether a regulatory subject was "national" or "local" by characterizing the effects of the regulation as imposing a "direct" or "indirect" burden on interstate commerce. See, for example, Di Santo v. Pennsylvania, 273 U.S. 34 (1927), in which the Court struck down a Pennsylvania licensing law for travel agents selling tickets for foreign travel as a "direct burden" on interstate commerce.

But sometimes the Court assessed the purpose of a state regulation in order to conclude that the burden it imposed was "direct." See, for example, Buck v. Kuykendall, 267 U.S. 307 (1925), holding that Washington's denial of a permit to operate a bus service between Seattle and Portland on the purported ground that the route was already adequately served was void because Washington's real purpose was to stifle competition.

Foreshadowing modern doctrine, the entire "direct/indirect" inquiry used as a proxy for determining "national/local" was criticized by Justices Stone, Holmes, and Brandeis in *Di Santo* as "too mechanical, too uncertain," and "too remote" from reality "to be of value." They argued instead for "a consideration of all the facts and circumstances"—"the nature of the regulation, its function, the character of the business involved and the actual effect on the flow of commerce"—in order to determine whether "the regulation concerns interests peculiarly local and does not infringe the national interest in maintaining the freedom of commerce across state lines."

While the "national/local" distinction drawn in *Cooley* continues to resonate in modern doctrine, albeit in altered form, another aspect of *Cooley* has been discarded. Justice Curtis rejected the idea that the 1789 federal law could authorize Pennsylvania to regulate pilotage if that subject was reserved for federal regulation: "If the Constitution excluded the States from making any law regulating commerce, certainly Congress cannot regrant or in any manner reconvey to the States that power." Curtis treated the federal law as evidence that pilotage was local. Today we understand the commerce power as vesting in Congress plenary authority to regulate interstate commerce however it chooses (consistent, of course, with other independent constitutional limits on the exercise of the commerce power). Thus, if Congress wishes to allow states to regulate interstate commerce in a fashion that might be implicitly forbidden by the commerce clause in the absence of congressional action, it is free to do so. This so-called consent power is explored further in Section C.

c. *Modern Doctrine*

Modern dormant commerce clause doctrine proceeds along two tracks. If a state regulation openly discriminates against interstate commerce, the regulation is presumed to be invalid. The regulation is valid only if the state can prove that it furthers a legitimate state interest that cannot be accomplished by any less discriminatory means. But if a state regulation is nondiscriminatory and has only incidental effects on interstate commerce, it is presumed valid. The regulation is void only if the challenger can prove that the burden imposed on interstate commerce is clearly excessive in relation to the putative local benefits of the regulation.

While these two differing standards of review are easy to state, they are harder to apply. Discrimination is evident when it is openly stated on the face of the state regulation, but the Court has more trouble with facially neutral regulations that are intended to be discriminatory or have a significantly discriminatory effect. If discriminatory purpose is unavoidably clear or the discriminatory effects of a regulation are especially large, the Court may treat the regulation as openly discriminatory and subject it to strict scrutiny. But not always. If the balancing test is applied, discriminatory purpose and effects are still relevant. A state regulation that is intended solely to protect local industries at the expense of outsiders serves an illegitimate purpose and will be voided. A facially neutral state regulation that is discriminatory in purpose or effect but that serves a legitimate objective may still impose burdens on interstate commerce that substantially outweigh its legitimate local benefits. In applying the balancing test, courts are essentially making *Cooley*'s "national" versus "local" distinction. They are asking, more or less, "Does this state regulation so interfere with the national interest in maintaining a free flow of interstate commerce that the local benefits of the regulation are comparatively slight?"

The modern balancing test has been sharply criticized. Justice Hugo Black called it the act of a "super-legislature" and asserted that such "balancing [is not] a matter for judicial determination, [but] for legislative" decision. Southern Pacific Co. v. Arizona, 325 U.S. 761 (1945). Justice Antonin Scalia has stated that "the scale analogy [of balancing] is not really appropriate, since the interests on both sides are incommensurate. It is more like judging whether a particular line is longer than a particular rock is heavy." Bendix Autolite Corp. v. Midwesco Enterprises, 486 U.S. 888 (1988). Like Black, Scalia urged that the courts should leave to Congress the "essentially legislative judgments" of weighing "the governmental interests of a State against the needs of interstate commerce."

It is important to realize that the loser of a dormant commerce clause case has recourse to Congress. Congress may use its commerce power to preempt otherwise valid state regulation of interstate commerce or to consent to otherwise invalid state regulation of such commerce. Thus, when the Court decides any dormant commerce clause case it is, in essence, deciding who—the state or the regulated person—will bear the burden of seeking congressional alteration of the Court's decision. If the Court decides that any given state regulation violates the dormant commerce clause, the burden falls on the state to obtain explicit congressional consent to the regulation. However, if the Court rules that any given state regulation is valid, the burden falls on the regulated entity to obtain congressional legislation that will preempt the state regulation. Obtaining congressional action may not be easy, so the Court's decision as to which party bears the burden of prodding Congress into action is of great practical significance.

2. Discrimination Against Interstate Commerce

When state regulations openly discriminate against interstate commerce, the regulations are strictly scrutinized. They are presumed invalid and are upheld only if the state can prove that they serve a legitimate purpose that cannot be achieved in any less discriminatory way.

Strict scrutiny is justified by one or more of three theories. First, the implicit commitment made by the commerce clause to an unfettered national market is most gravely attacked by state statutes that only serve protectionism. Like racial bias, this can never be a legitimate government objective.

Second, national free trade will in the long run provide more prosperity to the nation than balkanization of trade. States may be tempted to regulate in a manner that captures benefits for themselves and imposes the costs of those benefits mostly (or entirely) on outsiders. The openly discriminatory statute, while not always effective to capture benefits locally and impose costs outside the state, is sufficiently suspicious to trigger a presumption of invalidity. In short, the commerce clause demands a repudiation of economic "beggar thy neighbor" policies.

The third theory, related to the second, is that openly discriminatory state regulations of commerce are likely to be the product of a political system that undervalues (or completely ignores) the interests of out-of-staters. One might well reply that it is the job of state legislators to prefer their own constituents. Perhaps, but when they do so openly at the expense of outsiders, it is not realistic to expect the political process to correct the problem because outsiders are not represented in the state legislature.

These justifications also play a role when the state regulates in an apparently evenhanded fashion and courts employ the balancing test.

Philadelphia v. New Jersey
437 U.S. 617 (1978)

JUSTICE STEWART delivered the opinion of the Court.

A New Jersey law prohibits the importation of most "solid or liquid waste which originated or was collected outside the territorial limits of the State. . . ." In this case we are required to decide whether this statutory prohibition violates the Commerce Clause of the United States Constitution.

I. [Operators] of private landfills in New Jersey, and several cities in other States that had agreements with these operators for waste disposal [brought] suit against New Jersey [in] state court. [The] trial court declared the law unconstitutional because it discriminated against interstate commerce. The New Jersey Supreme Court [reversed, finding that the law] advanced vital health and environmental objectives with no economic discrimination against, and with little burden upon, interstate commerce.

[The] state law has not been pre-empted by federal legislation. The dispositive question, therefore, is whether the law is constitutionally permissible in light of the Commerce Clause of the Constitution.

II. [The Court concluded that] the interstate movement of those wastes banned by [the New Jersey law was] "commerce" . . . within the meaning of the Commerce Clause.

III. A. [The] opinions of the Court through the years have reflected an alertness to the evils of "economic isolation" and protectionism, while at the same time recognizing that incidental burdens on interstate commerce may be unavoidable when a State legislates to safeguard the health and safety of its people. Thus, where simple economic protectionism is effected by state legislation, a virtually per se rule of invalidity has been erected. The clearest example of such legislation is a law that overtly blocks the flow of interstate commerce at a State's borders. But where other legislative objectives are credibly advanced and there is no patent discrimination against interstate trade, the Court has adopted a much more flexible approach, the general contours of which were outlined in Pike v. Bruce Church, Inc., 397 U.S. 137 [(1970)]: "Where the statute regulates evenhandedly to effectuate a legitimate local public interest, and its effects on interstate commerce are only incidental, it will be upheld unless the burden imposed on such commerce is clearly excessive in relation to the putative local benefits. [If] a legitimate local purpose is found, then the question becomes one of degree. And the extent of the burden that will be tolerated will of course depend on the nature of the local interest involved, and on whether it could be promoted as well with a lesser impact on interstate activities." The crucial inquiry, therefore, must be directed to determining whether [the law] is basically a protectionist measure, or whether it can fairly be viewed as a law directed to legitimate local concerns, with effects upon interstate commerce that are only incidental.

B. [The] New Jersey Supreme Court [found] that New Jersey's existing landfill sites will be exhausted within a few years; that to go on using these sites or to develop new ones will take a heavy environmental toll, both from pollution and from loss of scarce open lands; that new techniques to divert waste from landfills to other methods of disposal and resource recovery processes are under development, but that these changes will require time; and finally, that "the extension of the lifespan of existing landfills, resulting from the exclusion of out-of-state waste, may be of crucial importance in preventing further virgin wetlands or other undeveloped lands from being devoted to landfill purposes." [The New Jersey] court concluded that [the law] was designed to protect, not the State's economy, but its environment, and that its substantial benefits outweigh its "slight" burden on interstate commerce.

The appellants strenuously contend that [the law], "while outwardly cloaked 'in the currently fashionable garb of environmental protection,' [is] actually no more than a legislative effort to suppress competition and stabilize the cost of solid waste disposal for New Jersey residents." [New Jersey denies that the law] was motivated by financial concerns or economic protectionism. [Noting] that New Jersey landfill operators are among the plaintiffs, [New Jersey's] brief argues that "[t]he complaint is not that New Jersey has forged an economic preference for its own commercial interests, but rather that it has denied a small group of its entrepreneurs an economic opportunity to traffic in waste in order to protect the health, safety and welfare of the citizenry at large."

This dispute about ultimate legislative purpose need not be resolved, because its resolution would not be relevant to the constitutional issue to be decided in this case. Contrary to the evident assumption of the state court and the parties, the evil of protectionism can reside in legislative means as well as legislative ends. Thus, it does not matter whether the ultimate aim of [the law] is to reduce the waste disposal costs of New Jersey residents or to save remaining open lands from pollution, for we assume New Jersey has every right to protect its residents' pocketbooks as well as their environment. And it may be assumed as well that New Jersey may pursue those ends by slowing the flow of *all* waste into the State's remaining landfills, even though interstate commerce may incidentally be affected. But whatever New Jersey's ultimate purpose, it may not be accomplished by discriminating against articles of commerce coming from outside the State unless there is some reason, apart from their origin, to treat them differently. Both on its face and in its plain effect, [the law] violates this principle of nondiscrimination.

The Court has consistently found parochial legislation of this kind to be constitutionally invalid, whether the ultimate aim of the legislation was to assure a steady supply of milk by erecting barriers to allegedly ruinous outside competition, Baldwin v. G. A. F. Seelig, Inc., 294 U.S. 511 [(1935)], or to create jobs by keeping industry within the State, Foster-Fountain Packing Co. v. Haydel, 278 U.S. 1 [(1928)], or to preserve the State's financial resources from depletion by fencing out indigent immigrants, Edwards v. California, 314 U.S. 160 [(1941)]. In each of these cases, a presumably legitimate goal was sought to be achieved by the illegitimate means of isolating the State from the national economy. Also relevant here are the Court's decisions holding that a State may not accord its own inhabitants a preferred right of access over consumers in other States to natural resources located within its borders. These cases stand for the basic principle that a "State is without power to prevent privately owned articles of trade from being shipped and sold in interstate commerce on the ground that they are required to satisfy local demands or because they are needed by the people of the State."

The New Jersey [law] falls squarely within the area that the Commerce Clause puts off limits to state regulation. On its face, it imposes on out-of-state commercial interests the full burden of conserving the State's remaining landfill space. It is true that in our previous cases the scarce natural resource was itself the article of commerce, whereas here the scarce resource and the article of commerce are distinct. But that difference is without consequence. In both instances, the State has overtly moved to slow or freeze the flow of commerce for protectionist reasons. It does not matter that the State has shut the article of commerce inside the State in one case and outside the State in the other. What is crucial is the attempt by one State to isolate itself from a problem common to many by erecting a barrier against the movement of interstate trade.

[New Jersey argues] that not all laws which facially discriminate against out-of-state commerce are forbidden protectionist regulations. In particular, [it points] to quarantine laws, which this Court has repeatedly upheld even though they appear to single out interstate commerce for special treatment. In [New Jersey's view, the law] is analogous to such health-protective measures, since it reduces the exposure of New Jersey residents to the allegedly harmful effects of landfill sites. It is true that certain quarantine laws have not been considered forbidden protectionist measures, even though they were directed against out-of-state commerce. But those quarantine laws banned the importation of articles such as diseased livestock that required destruction as soon as possible because their very movement risked contagion and other evils. Those laws thus did not discriminate against interstate commerce as such, but simply prevented traffic in noxious articles, whatever their origin.

The New Jersey statute is not such a quarantine law. There has been no claim here that the very movement of waste into or through New Jersey endangers health, or that waste must be disposed of as soon and as close to its point of generation as possible. The harms caused by waste are said to arise after its disposal in landfill sites, and at that point, as New Jersey concedes, there is no basis to distinguish out-of-state waste from domestic waste. If one is inherently harmful, so is the other. Yet New Jersey has banned the former while leaving its landfill sites open to the latter. The New Jersey law blocks the importation of waste in an obvious effort to saddle those outside the State with the entire burden of slowing the flow of refuse into New Jersey's remaining landfill sites. That legislative effort is clearly impermissible under the Commerce Clause. [Today], cities in Pennsylvania and New York find it expedient or necessary to send their waste into New Jersey for disposal, and New Jersey claims the right to close its borders to such traffic. Tomorrow, cities in New Jersey may find it expedient or necessary to send their waste into Pennsylvania or New York for disposal, and those States might then claim the right to close their borders. The Commerce Clause will protect New Jersey in the future, just as it protects her neighbors now, from efforts by one State to isolate itself in the stream of interstate commerce from a problem shared by all. [Reversed.]

JUSTICE REHNQUIST, joined by CHIEF JUSTICE BURGER, dissenting.

[According to the Court,] New Jersey must either prohibit all landfill operations, leaving itself to cast about for a presently nonexistent solution to the serious problem of disposing of the waste generated within its own borders, or it must accept waste from every portion of the United States, thereby multiplying the health and safety problems which would result if it dealt only with such wastes generated within the State. Because past precedents establish that the Commerce Clause does not present appellees with such a Hobson's choice, I dissent.

[In] my opinion, [the quarantine] cases are dispositive of the present one. Under them, New Jersey may require germ-infected rags or diseased meat to be disposed of as best as possible within the State, but at the same time prohibit the importation of such items for disposal at the facilities that are set up within New Jersey for disposal of such material generated within the State. The physical fact of life that New Jersey must somehow dispose of its own noxious items does not mean that it must serve as a depository for those of every other State. Similarly, New Jersey should be free under our past precedents to prohibit the importation of solid waste because of the health and safety problems that such waste poses to its citizens. The fact that New Jersey continues to, and indeed must continue to, dispose of its own solid waste does not mean that New Jersey may not prohibit the importation of even more solid waste into the State. I simply see no way to distinguish solid waste, on the record of this case, from germ-infected rags, diseased meat, and other noxious items. [I] do not see why a State may ban the importation of items whose movement risks contagion, but cannot ban the importation of items which, although they may be transported into the State without undue hazard, will then simply pile up in an ever increasing danger to the public's health and safety. The Commerce Clause was not drawn with a view to having the validity of state laws turn on such pointless distinctions. . . . I dissent.

NOTES

1. The Doctrinal Standard. The Court in Philadelphia v. New Jersey comes close to a rule of per se invalidity of discriminatory regulation, but says that discrimination against "articles of commerce coming from outside the State [is invalid] unless there is some reason, apart from their origin, to treat them differently." In later cases the Court elaborated on this theme and, in doing so, articulated the present standard. In Maine v. Taylor, 477 U.S. 131 (1986), the Court upheld Maine's absolute ban on the importation of bait fish. Maine argued that the ban was needed because its wild fish

> would be placed at risk by three types of parasites prevalent in out-of-state bait fish, but not common to wild fish in Maine [and] nonnative species inadvertently included in shipments of live bait fish could disturb Maine's aquatic ecology to an unpredictable extent by competing with native fish for food or habitat [or] by preying on native species.

Accepting the findings of the trial court that "there was no satisfactory way to inspect shipments of live baitfish for parasites or commingled species," the Court concluded "that Maine's ban on the importation of live bait fish serves legitimate local purposes that could not adequately be served by available nondiscriminatory alternatives."

By contrast, in Hughes v. Oklahoma, 441 U.S. 322 (1979), the Court voided Oklahoma's ban on the exportation of native minnows. Oklahoma's conservation objective was legitimate, but a flat export ban was the "most discriminatory means" for achieving that objective, "even though nondiscriminatory alternatives" were available and would have been equally or more effective in conserving Oklahoma's native minnow population.

2. Theoretical Concerns. One justification for strict scrutiny of open discrimination is the belief that such statutes are likely designed to reap local benefits at the expense of out-of-staters. But the Court in Philadelphia v. New Jersey made no attempt to assess this cost-benefit relationship. Losers under the New Jersey law include New Jersey landfill operators (less demand for their product, leading to lower revenues) and out-of-state waste generators (higher costs by reason of lost access to New Jersey dump sites). Winners include New Jersey waste generators (lower dumping costs due to increased relative space in New Jersey dumps) and out-of-state landfill operators (higher demand for their space leading to higher revenue). The failure of the Court to look at this picture may suggest (1) that the Court does not rely on this theoretical justification for striking down discriminatory regulations; or (2) that the Court views the proliferation of discriminatory regulations, rather than the effects in any given case, as pernicious to national economic welfare. If the latter suggestion is correct it is irrelevant what the actual distribution of costs and benefits may be; open discrimination reveals a deeply suspect motive.

Another justification for strict scrutiny of openly discriminatory statutes is the idea that disadvantaged out-of-staters are denied representation within the regulating state. But here the plaintiff New Jersey landfill operators would seem to be zealous advocates for the out-of-state waste generators whose business they want, and the out-of-staters can lobby in New Jersey or contribute heavily to New Jersey election campaigns. Does the Court's failure to comment on these points suggest that it does not believe that these are adequate proxies for representation?

In assessing a facially neutral law that produced some discriminatory effects, the Court has noted that "[t]he existence of major in-state interests adversely affected by the [challenged state regulation] is a powerful safeguard against legislative abuse." Minnesota v. Clover Leaf Creamery Co., 449 U.S. 456 (1981). Perhaps when discrimination against interstate commerce is on the face of the statute, the Court sees no need to examine whether the law effectively accomplishes its discriminatory intent, but such inquiry is germane when the question is whether a facially neutral law delivers sharply focused and discriminatory effects. See Section A.4, infra.

3. Discrimination That Isn't.   Overt discrimination that is intended to place insiders and outsiders on an equal footing and actually does so is not treated as discriminatory. The problem is almost entirely confined to "compensatory taxes." The clearest example is the compensating use tax. Most states impose sales taxes. To curb the revenue loss that occurs when residents avoid the sales tax by purchasing goods out-of-state, these states typically levy a "use" tax (equal in amount to the sales tax) on goods purchased out-of-state for use in-state. In Henneford v. Silas Mason Co., 300 U.S. 577 (1937), the Court upheld such a use tax. Washington imposed a 2 percent sales tax and a 2 percent use tax on goods purchased by Washingtonians out-of-state for use within Washington. The use tax was proportionately abated for sales taxes paid in other states of up to 2 percent, and was altogether inapplicable if a sales tax of 2 percent or more had been paid in another state.

A unanimous Court recognized that the scheme was designed to enable Washington retailers "to compete upon terms of equality with retail dealers in other states who are exempt from a sales tax." Imposition of the ostensibly discriminatory tax simply eliminated the incentive for Washingtonians to purchase goods in Oregon (a state with no sales tax) for use in Washington.

> Equality is the theme that runs through [the] statute. [The] stranger from afar is subject to no greater burdens [than] the dweller within the gates. [The] burden borne by the owner is balanced by an equal burden where the sale is strictly local. [Equality] and not preference is the end to be achieved. [Unlike a tariff, a compensatory] tax upon use is not a clog on the process of importation at all.

Compensatory taxes must be neatly fitted to come within the rule. In Fulton Corp. v. Faulkner, 516 U.S. 325 (1996), the Court struck down a North Carolina tax on corporate stock owned by North Carolinians that was inversely proportional to the amount of the corporation's income subject to North Carolina's income tax. The effect of the "intangibles tax" was that an owner of stock in a corporation 100 percent of whose income was subject to North Carolina's income tax would pay no intangibles tax, but an owner of stock in a corporation 5 percent of whose income was subject to North Carolina's income tax would pay a tax on 95 percent of the stock value. Because the proportion of corporate income subject to North Carolina income taxation was determined by the level of corporate activity in North Carolina relative to its activity elsewhere, the intangibles tax was facially discriminatory.

The Court identified the three elements that a state must prove to establish that a facially discriminatory tax is a valid compensatory tax. First, the state must identify the specific intrastate tax burden for which the discriminatory tax compensates, and show that the intrastate tax serves a purpose for which the state may legitimately burden interstate commerce. Second, the discriminatory tax must approximate but not exceed the tax imposed on intrastate commerce. Third, the discriminatory tax and the intrastate tax must fall on substantially equivalent events. North Carolina could not prove any of these elements.

See also Oregon Waste Systems, Inc. v. Department of Environmental Quality, 511 U.S. 93 (1994), in which the Court voided Oregon's imposition of a $2.25-per-ton fee on out-of-state solid waste deposited in Oregon while charging Oregon solid waste depositors $0.85 per ton. Oregon's argument that the differential was to recoup costs associated with solid waste disposal paid by Oregonians in the form of other, more general taxes was unsuccessful, as the discriminatory charge of $1.40 per ton and the intrastate general taxes were not levied on substantially similar events.

4. Intentional Discrimination and the Twenty-first Amendment. When national prohibition of alcoholic beverages ended with ratification of the Twenty-first Amendment, section 2 of that amendment prohibited the "transportation or importation into any State" of alcoholic beverages when doing so would violate the laws of the state. In Granholm v. Heald, 544 U.S. 460 (2005), the Supreme Court, 5-4, concluded that "§2 restored to the States the powers they had" prior to Prohibition. Thus, the Court concluded that the Twenty-first Amendment "did not give States the authority to pass nonuniform laws in order to discriminate against out-of-state goods, a privilege they had not enjoyed at any earlier time." In reaching this conclusion the Court relied on a train of cases that applied constitutional principles, ranging from the free speech and establishment clauses to the commerce clause, to state regulation of alcoholic beverages. Particularly relevant to this construction of the Twenty-first Amendment were Bacchus Imports, Ltd. v. Dias, 468 U.S. 263 (1984), Brown-Forman Distillers Corp. v. New York State Liquor Authority, 476 U.S. 573 (1986), and Healy v. Beer Institute, 491 U.S. 324 (1989), in each of which the Court had applied dormant commerce clause principles to strike down state liquor regulations. So construed, the Twenty-first Amendment afforded no immunity from dormant commerce clause scrutiny of Michigan and New York laws permitting mail-order sales of wine directly from winery to consumer if the winery was located in the state, but prohibiting such sales by out-of-state wineries. The justifications offered by Michigan and New York for this overt discrimination—"keeping alcohol out of the hands of minors and facilitating tax collection"—were found to be inadequate to meet the standard that discriminatory laws must "advance[] a legitimate local purpose that cannot be adequately served by reasonable non-discriminatory alternatives." There was no proof that there was a problem of minors purchasing alcohol by mail-order or Internet, much less that the supposed problem was peculiar to direct sales by out-of-state wineries; and even if such a problem existed it could be addressed by less discriminatory alternatives, such as requiring "an adult signature on delivery and a label so instructing on each package." The tax collection argument was similarly unavailing. Michigan relied on self-reporting by wineries of taxes due; thus, there was no showing that self-reporting by out-of-state direct sellers of wine would produce more tax evasion than self-reporting by those same out-of-state entities selling to Michigan wholesalers. New York could resort to less discriminatory alternatives, such as requiring out-of-state direct sellers to obtain a New York permit to enable New York to monitor such sales. A question left unanswered by *Granholm* is whether the Twenty-first Amendment affords any immunity from commerce clause scrutiny for state regulations concerning alcoholic beverages that are nondiscriminatory but impose incidental burdens on interstate commerce. After *Granholm*, there is no Twenty-first Amendment immunity for *discriminatory* liquor regulations, but does (should) such immunity exist for *nondiscriminatory* regulations? If not, such regulations would be subject to *Pike* balancing (discussed in the next section). See Durkin, What Does *Granholm v. Heald* Mean for the Future of the Twenty-first Amendment, the Three-Tier System, and Efficient Alcohol Distribution?, 63 Wash. & Lee L. Rev. 1095 (2006).

3.   Neutral Burdens on Interstate Commerce

State regulations that incidentally affect interstate commerce but that are not openly discriminatory toward interstate commerce are presumed to be valid. To invalidate such a law a challenger must prove that the burdens placed on interstate commerce by the law are *clearly excessive* in relation to the putative local benefits of the law. The classic statement of this balancing test occurred in Pike v. Bruce Church, Inc., 397 U.S. 137 (1970). Arizona required that Arizona-grown cantaloupes be identified as such on their shipping cartons. Bruce Church, an Arizona grower of superb cantaloupes, trucked his cantaloupes to California for packing in cartons that did not identify their Arizona origin. Arizona ordered Church to pack his cantaloupes in Arizona in crates identifying them as Arizona melons. To comply, Church would be required to spend $200,000 to build a packing facility for his annual crop, worth about $700,000.

A unanimous Court struck down the law. Justice Stewart thought that Arizona's interest in enhancing the reputation of Arizona cantaloupe growers was "legitimate" but "tenuous." The Court purported to apply the balancing test:

> Where the statute regulates even-handedly to effectuate a legitimate local public interest, and its effects on interstate commerce are only incidental, it will be upheld unless the burden imposed on such commerce is clearly excessive in relation to the putative local benefits. [If] a legitimate local purpose is found, then the question becomes one of degree. And the extent of the burden that will be tolerated [depends] on the nature of the local interest involved, and on whether it could be promoted as well with a lesser impact on interstate activities.

But the Arizona order was openly discriminatory, and the Court's opinion acknowledged as much:

> The nature of [Arizona's] burden [on Church] is, constitutionally, more significant than its extent. For the Court has viewed with particular suspicion state statutes requiring business operations to be performed in the home State that could more efficiently be performed elsewhere. Even where the State is pursuing a clearly legitimate local interest, this particular burden on commerce has been declared to be virtually per se illegal.

Although *Pike* may not have applied the balancing test, its formulation of balancing has remained the standard ever since. However, the origins of balancing predate *Pike*.

≡≡≡ ## *Southern Pacific Co. v. Arizona*
325 U.S. 761 (1945)

[Arizona's 1912 Train Limit Law barred passenger trains longer than 14 cars and freight trains longer than 70 cars. Southern Pacific's main rail line from Los Angeles eastward ran through Arizona, with the result that Southern Pacific was required to run 30 percent more trains through Arizona than it would have absent the law. This increased its annual operating costs by about $1 million. Because trains could not easily be assembled and broken up at the Arizona border, "the Arizona limitation govern[ed] the flow of traffic [from

Los Angeles] as far east as El Paso, Texas." Arizona sued Southern Pacific to recover penalties for its violation of the law. An Arizona trial court struck down the law on dormant commerce clause grounds. The Arizona Supreme Court reversed, ruling that because the law was designed to promote local safety it was valid. The Supreme Court reversed, finding that the law violated the dormant commerce clause.]

CHIEF JUSTICE STONE delivered the opinion of the Court.

[Ever] since Gibbons v. Ogden the states have not been deemed to have authority to impede substantially the free flow of commerce from state to state, or to regulate those phases of the national commerce which, because of the need of national uniformity, demand that their regulation, if any, be pre-scribed by a single authority.[2] [Some] enactments may be found to be plainly within and others plainly without state power. But between these extremes lies the infinite variety of cases in which regulation of local matters may also operate as a regulation of commerce, in which reconciliation of the conflicting claims of state and national power is to be attained only by some appraisal and accommodation of the competing demands of the state and national interests involved.

[The] commerce clause, without the aid of Congressional legislation, [affords] some protection from state legislation inimical to the national com-merce, and [in] such cases, where Congress has not acted, this Court, and not the state legislature, is under the commerce clause the final arbiter of the competing demands of state and national interests. Congress has undoubted power to redefine the distribution of power over interstate commerce. It may either permit the states to regulate the commerce in a manner which would otherwise not be permissible, or exclude state regulation even of matters of peculiarly local concern which nevertheless affect interstate commerce. But in general Congress has left it to the courts to formulate the [rules] interpreting the commerce clause [when Congress has not acted].

Hence the matters for ultimate determination here are the nature and extent of the burden which the state regulation of interstate trains, adopted as a safety measure, imposes on interstate commerce, and whether the rela-tive weights of the state and national interests involved are such as to make inapplicable the rule, generally observed, that the free flow of interstate com-merce and its freedom from local restraints in matters requiring uniformity of regulation are interests safeguarded by the commerce clause from state interference.

[The findings of the trial court] show that the operation of long trains [is] standard practice over the main lines of the railroads of the United States, and that, if the length of trains is to be regulated at all, national uniformity in the regulation adopted, such as only Congress can prescribe, is practically indispensable to the operation of an efficient and economical national railway

---

2. In applying this rule the Court has often recognized that, to the extent the burden of state regulation falls on interests outside the state, it is unlikely to be alleviated by the operation of those political restraints normally exerted when interests within the state are affected.

system. [The] unchallenged findings leave no doubt that the Arizona Train Limit Law imposes a serious burden [on] interstate commerce. [Enforcement] of the law in Arizona, while train lengths remain unregulated or are regulated by varying standards in other states, must inevitably result in an impairment of uniformity of efficient railroad operation because the railroads are subjected to regulation which is not uniform in its application. Compliance with a state statute limiting train lengths requires interstate trains of a length lawful in other states to be broken up and reconstituted as they enter each state according as it may impose varying limitations upon train lengths. The alternative is for the carrier to conform to the lowest train limit restriction of any of the states through which its trains pass, whose laws thus control the carriers' operations both within and without the regulating state. . . .

The trial court found that the Arizona law had no reasonable relation to safety, and made train operation more dangerous. [This] conclusion [rested] on facts [indicating] that such increased danger of accident and personal injury as may result from the greater length of trains is more than offset by the increase in the number of accidents resulting from the larger number of trains when train lengths are reduced. In considering the effect of the statute as a safety measure, therefore, the factor of controlling significance for present purposes is not whether there is basis for the conclusion of the Arizona Supreme Court that the increase in length of trains beyond the statutory maximum has an adverse effect upon safety of operation. The decisive question is whether in the circumstances the total effect of the law as a safety measure in reducing accidents and casualties is so slight or problematical as not to outweigh the national interest in keeping interstate commerce free from interferences which seriously impede it and subject it to local regulation which does not have a uniform effect on the interstate train journey which it interrupts.

The principal source of danger of accident from increased length of trains is the resulting increase of "slack action" of the train. Slack action is the amount of free movement of one car before it transmits its motion to an adjoining coupled car. [The] length of the train increases the slack since the slack action of a train is the total of the free movement between its several cars. [On] comparison of the number of slack action accidents in Arizona with those in Nevada, where the length of trains is now unregulated, the trial court found that with substantially the same amount of traffic in each state the number of accidents was relatively the same in long as in short train operations. [Reduction] of the length of trains also tends to increase the number of accidents because of the increase in the number of trains. [Accidents] due to grade crossing collisions between trains and motor vehicles and pedestrians, [which] are usually far more serious than those due to slack action, [in] general vary with the number of trains. [The] record lends support to the trial court's conclusion that the train length limitation increased rather than diminished the number of accidents.

[We] think, as the trial court found, that the Arizona Train Limit Law, viewed as a safety measure, affords at most slight and dubious advantage, if any, over unregulated train lengths, because it results in an increase in the number of trains and train operations and the consequent increase in train accidents of a character generally more severe than those due to slack action. Its undoubted effect on the commerce is the regulation, without securing uniformity, of the length of trains operated in interstate commerce, which lack is itself a primary cause of preventing the free flow of commerce by delaying it and by substantially increasing its cost and impairing its efficiency. In these respects the case differs from those where a state, by regulatory measures affecting the commerce, has removed or reduced safety hazards without substantial interference with the interstate movement of trains. Such are measures abolishing the car stove, requiring locomotives to be supplied with electric headlights, providing for full train crews, and for the equipment of freight trains with cabooses. The principle that, without controlling Congressional action, a state may not regulate interstate commerce so as substantially to affect its flow or deprive it of needed uniformity in its regulation is not to be avoided by "simply invoking the convenient apologetics of the police power." Here [the] state does go too far. Its regulation of train lengths, admittedly obstructive to interstate train operation, and having a seriously adverse effect on transportation efficiency and economy, passes beyond what is plainly essential for safety since it does not appear that it will lessen rather than increase the danger of accident.

[Reversed.]

JUSTICE BLACK, dissenting.

[The] state trial judge [heard] evidence over a period of 5½ months which appears in about 3000 pages of the printed record. . . . [This] new pattern of trial procedure makes it necessary for a judge to hear all the evidence offered as to why a legislature passed a law and to make findings of fact as to the validity of those reasons. [The trial court] acted, and this Court today is acting, as a "super-legislature." Even if this method of invalidating legislative acts is a correct one, [this record] leaves me with no doubt whatever that many employees have been seriously injured and killed in the past, and that many more are likely to be so in the future, because of "slack movement" in trains. [It] may be that offsetting dangers are possible in the operation of short trains. The balancing of these probabilities, however, is not in my judgment a matter for judicial determination, but one which calls for legislative consideration.

JUSTICE DOUGLAS, dissenting.

[My view is] that the courts should intervene only where the state legislation discriminate[s] against interstate commerce or [is] out of harmony with laws which Congress had enacted. . . .

≡ ### Kassel v. Consolidated Freightways Corp.
≡ *450 U.S. 662 (1981)*

JUSTICE POWELL announced the judgment of the Court and delivered an opinion, in which JUSTICES WHITE, BLACKMUN, and STEVENS joined.

The question is whether an Iowa statute that prohibits the use of certain large trucks within the State unconstitutionally burdens interstate commerce.

I. [Consolidated Freightways] is one of the largest common carriers in the country. [Consolidated] carries commodities through Iowa on Interstate 80, the principal east-west route linking New York, Chicago, and the West Coast, and on Interstate 35, a major north-south route. Consolidated mainly uses two kinds of trucks. One consists of a three-axle tractor pulling a 40-foot two-axle trailer. This unit, commonly called a single, or "semi," is 55 feet in length overall. Such trucks have long been used on the Nation's highways. Consolidated also uses a two-axle tractor pulling a single-axle trailer which, in turn, pulls a single-axle dolly and a second single-axle trailer. This combination, known as a double, or twin, is 65 feet long overall. Many trucking companies, including Consolidated, increasingly prefer to use doubles to ship certain kinds of commodities. Doubles have larger capacities, and the trailers can be detached and routed separately if necessary. Consolidated would like to use 65-foot doubles on many of its trips through Iowa.

[Unlike] all other States in the West and Midwest, Iowa generally prohibits the use of 65-foot doubles within its borders. Instead, most truck combinations are restricted to 55 feet in length. Doubles, mobile homes, trucks carrying vehicles such as tractors and other farm equipment, and singles hauling livestock, are permitted to be as long as 60 feet. [Iowa's] statute permits cities abutting the state line by local ordinance to adopt the length limitations of the adjoining State.[3] Iowa also provides for two other relevant exemptions. An Iowa truck manufacturer may obtain a permit to ship trucks that are as large as 70 feet. Permits also are available to move oversized mobile homes, provided that the unit is to be moved from a point within Iowa or delivered for an Iowa resident.[4]

Because of Iowa's statutory scheme, Consolidated cannot use its 65-foot doubles to move commodities through the State. Instead, the company must do one of four things: (i) use 55-foot singles; (ii) use 60-foot doubles; (iii) detach the trailers of a 65-foot double and shuttle each through the State separately;

---

3. The Iowa Legislature in 1974 passed House Bill 671, which would have permitted 65-foot doubles. But Iowa Governor Ray vetoed the bill, noting that it "would benefit only a few Iowa-based companies while providing a great advantage for out-of-state trucking firms and competitors at the expense of our Iowa citizens." The "border-cities exemption" was passed by the General Assembly and signed by the Governor shortly thereafter.

4. The parochial restrictions in the mobile home provision were enacted after Governor Ray vetoed a bill that would have permitted the interstate shipment of all mobile homes through Iowa. Governor Ray commented, in his veto message: "This bill . . . would make Iowa a bridge state as these oversized units are moved into Iowa after being manufactured in another state and sold in a third. None of this activity would be of particular economic benefit to Iowa."

or (iv) divert 65-foot doubles around Iowa. Dissatisfied with these options, Consolidated filed this suit in the District Court averring that Iowa's statutory scheme unconstitutionally burdens interstate commerce. Iowa defended the law as a reasonable safety measure enacted pursuant to its police power. The State asserted that 65-foot doubles are more dangerous than 55-foot singles and, in any event, that the law promotes safety and reduces road wear within the State by diverting much truck traffic to other States. [On] the question of safety, the District Court found that the "evidence clearly establishes that the twin is as safe as the semi." [The] District Court concluded that the state law impermissibly burdened interstate commerce: "[The] *total effect* of the law as a safety measure in reducing accidents and casualties is so slight and problematical that it does not outweigh the national interest in keeping interstate commerce free from interferences that seriously impede it." The Court of Appeals [accepted] the District Court's finding that 65-foot doubles were as safe as 55-foot singles. Thus, the only apparent safety benefit to Iowa was that resulting from forcing large trucks to detour around the State, thereby reducing overall truck traffic on Iowa's highways. The Court of Appeals noted that this was not a constitutionally permissible interest. It also commented that the several statutory exemptions identified above, such as those applicable to border cities and the shipment of livestock, suggested that the law in effect benefitted Iowa residents at the expense of interstate traffic. The combination of these exemptions weakened the presumption of validity normally accorded a state safety regulation. For these reasons, the Court of Appeals agreed with the District Court that the Iowa statute unconstitutionally burdened interstate commerce. [We] now affirm.

II. [A] State's power to regulate commerce is never greater than in matters traditionally of local concern. [Regulations] that touch upon safety—especially highway safety—are those that "the Court has been most reluctant to invalidate." Indeed, "if safety justifications are not illusory, the Court will not second-guess legislative judgment about their importance in comparison with related burdens on interstate commerce." [Raymond Motor Transportation, Inc. v. Rice, 434 U.S. 429 (1978).] Those who would challenge such bona fide safety regulations must overcome a "strong presumption of validity." But the incantation of a purpose to promote the public health or safety does not insulate a state law from Commerce Clause attack. Regulations designed for that salutary purpose nevertheless may further the purpose so marginally, and interfere with commerce so substantially, as to be invalid under the Commerce Clause. In [*Raymond*] we declined to "accept the State's contention that the inquiry under the Commerce Clause is ended without a weighing of the asserted safety purpose against the degree of interference with interstate commerce." This "weighing" by a court requires—and indeed the constitutionality of the state regulation depends on—"a sensitive consideration of the weight and nature of the state regulatory concern in light of the extent of the burden imposed on the course of interstate commerce."

III. Applying these general principles, we conclude that the Iowa truck-length limitations unconstitutionally burden interstate commerce. [Here], as in *Raymond*, the State failed to present any persuasive evidence that 65-foot doubles are less safe than 55-foot singles. Moreover, Iowa's law is now out of step with the laws of all other Midwestern and Western States. Iowa thus substantially burdens the interstate flow of goods by truck. In the absence of congressional action to set uniform standards, some burdens associated with state safety regulations must be tolerated. But where, as here, the State's safety interest has been found to be illusory, and its regulations impair significantly the federal interest in efficient and safe interstate transportation, the state law cannot be harmonized with the Commerce Clause.[5]

A. [The] District Court found that the "evidence clearly establishes that the twin is as safe as the semi." The record supports [the conclusion that] a 65-foot double was at least the equal of the 55-foot single in the ability to brake, turn, and maneuver. The double, because of its axle placement, produces less splash and spray in wet weather. And, because of its articulation in the middle, the double is less susceptible to dangerous "off-tracking,"[6] and to wind. None of these findings is seriously disputed by Iowa. [Statistical] studies supported the view that 65-foot doubles are at least as safe overall as 55-foot singles and 60-foot doubles. One such study . . . reviewed Consolidated's comparative accident experience in 1978 with its own singles and doubles. Each kind of truck was driven 56 million miles on identical routes. The singles were involved in 100 accidents resulting in 27 injuries and one fatality. The 65-foot doubles were involved in 106 accidents resulting in 17 injuries and one fatality. [A] study prepared by the Iowa Department of Transportation at the request of the state legislature concluded that "[s]ixty-five foot twin trailer combinations have not been shown by experiences in other states to be less safe than 60 foot twin trailer combinations or conventional [singles]."[7] . . .

B. Consolidated [demonstrated] that Iowa's law substantially burdens interstate commerce. Trucking companies that wish to continue to use 65-foot doubles must route them around Iowa or detach the trailers of the doubles and ship them through separately. Alternatively, trucking companies must use the smaller 55-foot singles or 60-foot doubles permitted under Iowa law. Each of these options engenders inefficiency and added expense. The record shows that Iowa's law added about $12.6 million each year to the costs of trucking companies. Consolidated alone incurred about $2 million per year

---

5. It is highly relevant that here, as in *Raymond*, the state statute contains exemptions that weaken the deference traditionally accorded to a state safety regulation.

6. "Off-tracking" refers to the extent to which the rear wheels of a truck deviate from the path of the front wheels while turning.

7. In suggesting that Iowa's law actually promotes safety, the dissenting opinion ignores the findings of the courts below and relies on largely discredited statistical evidence. The dissent implies that a statistical study identified doubles as more dangerous than singles. At trial, however, the author of that study—Iowa's own statistician—conceded that his calculations were statistically biased, and therefore "not very meaningful." The dissenting opinion also suggests that its conclusions are bolstered by the fact that the American Association of State Highway and Transportation Officials (AASHTO) recommends that States limit truck lengths. The dissent fails to point out, however, that AASHTO specifically recommends that States permit 65-foot doubles.

in increased costs. In addition to increasing the costs of the trucking companies (and, indirectly, of the service to consumers), Iowa's law may aggravate, rather than ameliorate, the problem of highway accidents. Fifty-five foot singles carry less freight than 65-foot doubles. Either more small trucks must be used to carry the same quantity of goods through Iowa, or the same number of larger trucks must drive longer distances to bypass Iowa. In either case, as the District Court noted, the restriction requires more highway miles to be driven to transport the same quantity of goods. Other things being equal, accidents are proportional to distance traveled. Thus, if 65-foot doubles are as safe as 55-foot singles, Iowa's law tends to *increase* the number of accidents, and to shift the incidence of them from Iowa to other States.

IV. Perhaps recognizing the weakness of the evidence supporting its safety argument, and the substantial burden on commerce that its regulations create, Iowa urges the Court simply to "defer" to the safety judgment of the State. [The] Court normally does accord "special deference" to state highway safety regulations. This traditional deference "derives in part from the assumption that where such regulations do not discriminate on their face against interstate commerce, their burden usually falls on local economic interests as well as other States' economic interests, thus insuring that a State's own political processes will serve as a check against unduly burdensome regulations." Less deference to the legislative judgment is due, however, where the local regulation bears disproportionately on out-of-state residents and businesses. Such a disproportionate burden is apparent here. Iowa's scheme, although generally banning large doubles from the State, nevertheless has several exemptions that secure to Iowans many of the benefits of large trucks while shunting to neighboring States many of the costs associated with their use.

[First], singles hauling livestock or farm vehicles were permitted to be as long as 60 feet. [This] provision undoubtedly was helpful to local interests. Second, cities abutting other States were permitted to enact local ordinances adopting the larger length limitation of the neighboring State. This exemption offered the benefits of longer trucks to individuals and businesses in important border cities without burdening Iowa's highways with interstate through traffic.[8]

The origin of the "border cities exemption" also suggests that Iowa's statute may not have been designed to ban dangerous trucks, but rather to discourage interstate truck traffic. In 1974, the legislature passed a bill that would have permitted 65-foot doubles in the State. Governor Ray vetoed the bill. He said: "[With] this bill, the Legislature has pursued a course that would benefit only a few Iowa-based companies while providing a great advantage for out-of-state trucking firms and competitors at the expense of our Iowa

---

8. [E]xemptions also are available to benefit Iowa truck makers and Iowa mobile home manufacturers or purchasers. Although these exemptions are not directly relevant to the controversy over the safety of 65-foot doubles, they do contribute to the pattern of parochialism apparent in Iowa's statute.

citizens." After the veto, the "border cities exemption" was immediately enacted and signed by the Governor.

It is thus far from clear that Iowa was motivated primarily by a judgment that 65-foot doubles are less safe than 55-foot singles. Rather, Iowa seems to have hoped to limit the use of its highways by deflecting some through traffic. In the [lower courts] the State explicitly attempted to justify the law by its claimed interest in keeping trucks out of Iowa. The Court of Appeals correctly concluded that a State cannot constitutionally promote its own parochial interests by requiring safe vehicles to detour around it.

V. In sum, the statutory exemptions, their history, and the arguments Iowa has advanced in support of its law in this litigation, all suggest that the deference traditionally accorded a State's safety judgment is not warranted. [Because] Iowa has imposed [a substantial] burden [on interstate commerce] without any significant countervailing safety interest,[9] its statute violates the Commerce Clause. . . .

JUSTICE BRENNAN, joined by JUSTICE MARSHALL, concurring in the judgment.

Iowa's truck-length regulation challenged in this case is nearly identical to the Wisconsin regulation struck down in [*Raymond* and the] same Commerce Clause restrictions that dictated that holding also require invalidation of Iowa's [regulation]. . . . For me, analysis of Commerce Clause challenges to state regulations must take into account three principles: (1) The courts are not empowered to second-guess the empirical judgments of lawmakers concerning the utility of legislation. (2) The burdens imposed on commerce must be balanced against the local benefits actually sought to be achieved by the State's lawmakers, and not against those suggested after the fact by counsel. (3) Protectionist legislation is unconstitutional under the Commerce Clause, even if the burdens and benefits are related to safety rather than economics.

I. [In] considering a Commerce Clause challenge to a state regulation, the judicial task is to balance the burden imposed on commerce against the local benefits sought to be achieved by the State's lawmakers. In determining those benefits, a court should focus ultimately on the regulatory purposes identified by the lawmakers and on the evidence before or available to them that might have supported their judgment. Since the court must confine its analysis to the purposes the lawmakers had for maintaining the regulation, the only relevant evidence concerns whether the lawmakers could rationally have believed that the challenged regulation would foster those purposes. It is not the function of the court to decide whether in fact the regulation promotes its intended purpose, so long as an examination of the evidence before or

9. Because the record fully supports the decision below [that Iowa's law unconstitutionally burdened interstate commerce], we need not consider whether the statute also operated to discriminate against that commerce. . . .

available to the lawmaker indicates that the regulation is not wholly irrational in light of its purposes.[10]

II. [Justices] Powell and Rehnquist make the mistake of disregarding the intention of Iowa's lawmakers and assuming that resolution of the case must hinge upon the argument offered by Iowa's attorneys: that 65-foot doubles are more dangerous than shorter trucks. [They] reach opposite conclusions as to whether the evidence adequately supports that empirical judgment. [Justices] Powell and Rehnquist have asked and answered the wrong question. For although Iowa's lawyers [have] defended the truck-length regulation on the basis of the safety advantages of 55-foot singles and 60-foot doubles over 65-foot doubles, Iowa's actual rationale for maintaining the regulation [was] to discourage interstate truck traffic on Iowa's highways. Thus, the safety advantages and disadvantages of the types and lengths of trucks involved in this case are irrelevant to the decision. . . .

III. Though [Justice] Powell recognizes that the State's actual purpose in maintaining the truck-length regulation was "to limit the use of its highways by deflecting some through traffic," he fails to recognize that this purpose, being *protectionist* in nature, is *impermissible* under the Commerce Clause. The Governor admitted that he blocked legislative efforts to raise the length of trucks because the change "would benefit only a few Iowa-based companies while providing a great advantage for out-of-state trucking firms and competitors at the expense of our Iowa citizens." [Kassel], Director of the Iowa Department of Transportation, while admitting that the greater 65-foot length standard would be *safer* overall, defended the more restrictive regulations because of their benefits *within Iowa*. [Iowa] may not shunt off its fair share of the burden of maintaining interstate truck routes, nor may it create increased hazards on the highways of neighboring States in order to decrease the hazards on Iowa highways. Such an attempt has all the hallmarks of the "simple . . . protectionism" this Court has condemned in the economic area. Philadelphia v. New Jersey. Just as a State's attempt to avoid interstate competition in economic goods may damage the prosperity of the Nation as a whole, so Iowa's attempt to deflect interstate truck traffic has been found to make the Nation's highways as a whole more hazardous. That attempt should therefore be subject to "a virtually per se rule of invalidity."

JUSTICE REHNQUIST, joined by CHIEF JUSTICE BURGER and JUSTICE STEWART, dissenting.

The result in this case suggests, to paraphrase Justice Jackson, that the only state truck-length limit "that is valid is one which this Court has not been able to get its hands on." Although the plurality opinion and the opinion concurring

---

10. I would emphasize that in the field of safety [once] the court has established that the intended safety benefit is not illusory, insubstantial, or nonexistent, it must defer to the State's lawmakers on the appropriate balance to be struck against other interests. I therefore disagree with my Brother Powell when he asserts that the degree of interference with interstate commerce may in the first instance be "weighed" against the State's safety interests. . . .

in the judgment strike down Iowa's law by different routes, I believe the analysis in both opinions oversteps our "limited authority to review state legislation under the commerce clause" and seriously intrudes upon the fundamental right of the States to pass laws to secure the safety of their citizens. . . .

I. [Every] State [regulates] the length of vehicles permitted to use the public roads. Nor is Iowa a renegade in [excluding] the 65-foot doubles favored by Consolidated. These trucks are prohibited [in] some 17 States and the District of Columbia, including all of New England and most of the Southeast. While pointing out that Consolidated carries commodities through Iowa on Interstate 80, "the principal east-west route linking New York, Chicago, and the west coast," the plurality neglects to note that both Pennsylvania and New Jersey, through which Interstate 80 runs before reaching New York, also ban 65-foot doubles. In short, the persistent effort in the plurality opinion to paint Iowa as an oddity standing alone to block commerce carried in 65-foot doubles is simply not supported by the facts.

II. [A] determination that a state law is a rational safety measure does not end the Commerce Clause inquiry. A "sensitive consideration" of the safety purpose in relation to the burden on commerce is required. . . . [The] purpose of the "sensitive consideration" [is] to determine if the asserted safety justification, although rational, is merely a pretext for discrimination against interstate commerce. We will conclude that it is if the safety benefits from the regulation are demonstrably trivial while the burden on commerce is great. [*Southern Pacific.*]

III. [There] can be no doubt that the challenged statute is a valid highway safety regulation and thus entitled to the strongest presumption of validity against Commerce Clause challenges. [All] 50 States regulate the length of trucks which may use their highways. . . . [The] particular limit chosen by Iowa—60 feet—is rationally related to Iowa's safety objective. [There] was sufficient evidence presented at trial to support the legislative determination that length is related to safety, and nothing in Consolidated's evidence undermines this conclusion.

The District Court approached the case as if the question were whether Consolidated's 65-foot trucks were as safe as others permitted on Iowa [highways]. The question, however, is whether the Iowa Legislature has acted rationally in regulating vehicle lengths and whether the safety benefits from this regulation are more than slight or problematical.[11] The answering of the

---

11. [Justice Brennan's opinion] mischaracterizes this dissent when it states that I assume "resolution of the case must hinge upon the argument offered by Iowa's attorneys: that 65-foot doubles are more dangerous than shorter trucks." I assume nothing of the sort. [The] State must simply prove, aided by a "strong presumption of validity," that the safety benefits of its law are not illusory. I review the evidence presented at trial simply to demonstrate that Iowa made such a showing in this case, not because the validity of Iowa's law depends on its proving [that] the excluded trucks are unsafe. [Iowa] must simply show a relation between vehicle length limits and safety, and that the benefits from its length limit are not illusory. [I] fully agree with Justice Brennan that the validity of Iowa's length limit does not turn on whether 65-foot trucks are less safe than 60-foot trucks.

relevant question is not appreciably advanced by comparing trucks slightly over the length limit with those at the length limit. It is emphatically not our task to balance any incremental safety benefits from prohibiting 65-foot doubles as opposed to 60-foot doubles against the burden on interstate commerce. Lines drawn for safety purposes will rarely pass muster if the question is whether a slight increment can be permitted without sacrificing safety. [The] question is rather whether it can be said that the benefits flowing to Iowa from a rational truck-length limitation are "slight or problematical." The particular line chosen by Iowa—60 feet—is relevant only to the question whether the limit is a rational one. Once a court determines that it is, it considers the overall safety benefits *from the regulation* against burdens on interstate commerce, and not any marginal benefits from the scheme the State established as opposed to that the plaintiffs desire. [*Southern Pacific.*] The difficulties with the contrary approach are patent. While it may be clear that there are substantial safety benefits from a 55-foot truck as compared to a 105-foot truck, these benefits may not be discernible in 5-foot jumps. Appellee's approach would permit what could not be accomplished in one lawsuit to be done in 10 separate suits, each challenging an additional five feet.

It must be emphasized that there is nothing in the laws of nature which make 65-foot doubles an obvious norm. Consolidated operates 65-foot doubles on many of its routes simply because that is the largest size permitted in many States through which Consolidated travels. Doubles can and do come in smaller [sizes]. Striking down Iowa's law because Consolidated has made a voluntary business decision to employ 65-foot doubles, a decision based on the actions of other state legislatures, would essentially be compelling Iowa to yield to the policy choices of neighboring States. Under our constitutional scheme, however, there is only one legislative body which can pre-empt the rational policy determination of the Iowa Legislature and that is Congress. . . .

[Justice] Brennan argues that the Court should consider only *the* purpose the Iowa legislators *actually* sought to achieve by the length limit, and not the purposes advanced by Iowa's lawyers in defense of the statute. This argument calls to mind what was said of the Roman Legions: that they may have lost battles, but they never lost a war, since they never let a war end until they had won it. The argument has been consistently rejected by the Court in other contexts [citing equal protection cases] and Justice Brennan can cite no authority for the proposition that possible legislative purposes suggested by a State's lawyers should not be considered in Commerce Clause cases. [Justice Brennan's view] assumes that individual legislators are motivated by one discernible "actual" purpose, and ignores the fact that different legislators may vote for a single piece of legislation for widely different reasons. How, for example, would a court adhering to [Justice Brennan's] views approach a statute, the legislative history of which indicated that 10 votes were based on safety considerations, 10 votes were based on protectionism, and the statute passed by a vote of 40-20? What would the *actual* purpose of the *legislature* have been in that case? . . .

Furthermore, the effort in both the plurality and the concurrence to portray the legislation involved here as protectionist is in error. Whenever a State enacts more stringent safety measures than its neighbors, in an area which affects commerce, the safety law will have the incidental effect of deflecting interstate commerce to the neighboring States. Indeed, the safety and protectionist motives cannot be separated: The whole purpose of safety regulation of vehicles is to *protect* the State from unsafe vehicles. If a neighboring State chooses *not* to protect its citizens from the danger discerned by the enacting State, that is its business, but the enacting State should not be penalized when the vehicles it considers unsafe travel through the neighboring State. The other States with truck-length limits that exclude Consolidated's 65-foot doubles would not at all be paranoid in assuming that they might be next on Consolidated's "hit list." The true problem with today's decision is that it gives no guidance whatsoever to these States as to whether their laws are valid or how to defend them. For that matter, the decision gives no guidance to Consolidated or other trucking firms either. Perhaps, after all is said and done, the Court today neither says nor does very much at all. We know only that Iowa's law is invalid and that the jurisprudence of the "negative side" of the Commerce Clause remains hopelessly confused.

NOTES

1. Balancing Benefits and Burdens: Incommensurate Values. The balancing test requires courts to compare the burdens on interstate commerce to the local benefits desired by the legislation. One problem with this comparison is that the two values may not easily be expressed in a common metric — a common measurement system. Burdens on commerce may be measured in dollars, but it is not so easy to measure safety, health, or moral values in dollars. If a common metric is not available, the comparison may be of apples to oranges — hence Justice Scalia's observation that this comparison is "more like judging whether a particular line is longer than a particular rock is heavy." Bendix Autolite Corp. v. Midwesco Enterprises, 486 U.S. 888 (1988). The doctrine requires this comparison, however, so we must consider how it can best be done. One way to ameliorate the problem is to assess the *quality* of the burdens and benefits as well as their *quantity*.

2. Assessing Burdens. The most obvious way to measure the impact of the state law on interstate commerce is in terms of the economic loss imposed. But noneconomic impact is important as well. The fact that a facially neutral law delivers discriminatory effects is, by itself, important. The same is true of disguised discriminatory purposes. Note the debate in *Kassel* between Powell, Brennan, and Rehnquist concerning the weight to be given to Governor Ray's veto message and the exemptions contained in the Iowa law. Both are evidence of a possible discriminatory motive underlying the law, but the Court fractures on the question of how to assess that evidence. Powell adds it in as another factor on the burden side of the scale, Brennan finds it dispositive, and Rehnquist treats it as irrelevant. This general topic—the neutral law that delivers discriminatory effects or that is the product of a suspected discriminatory motive—will be considered in greater detail in Section A.4, infra.

The burden imposed on interstate commerce by any given law is not assessed in isolation; it may depend on conditions outside the state, including the laws of the other states. The fact that the Iowa law at issue in *Kassel* was considered aberrant in relation to the truck length laws of its neighbors was certainly one factor influencing the Powell plurality's assessment of the burden imposed by Iowa's law. Consider Bibb v. Navajo Freight Lines, Inc., 359 U.S. 520 (1959). Illinois required trucks to have mud flaps contoured to the tire, while Arkansas prohibited contoured flaps and required straight ones. Virtually every other state required mud flaps but didn't care what kind were employed. Navajo Freight challenged the Illinois law, arguing that straight mud flaps were the industry norm and were permitted everywhere but Illinois. Traffic involving both Illinois and Arkansas was especially hampered. The Court voided the Illinois law:

> This case presents . . . the question whether one State could prescribe standards for interstate carriers that would conflict with the standards of another State, making it necessary, say, for an interstate carrier to shift its cargo to differently designed vehicles once another state line was reached. [The] Illinois statute seriously interferes with the "interline" operations of motor carriers [(the physical transfer of an entire trailer)]—between an originating carrier and another carrier when the latter serves an area not served by the former. [If] the originating carrier never operated in Illinois, it would not be expected to equip its trailers with contour mudguards. Yet if an interchanged trailer of that carrier were hauled to or through Illinois, the statute would require that it contain contour guards. Since carriers which operate in and through Illinois cannot compel the originating carriers to equip their trailers with contour guards, they may be forced to cease interlining with those who do not meet the Illinois requirements. [This is a] massive . . . burden on interstate commerce. . . . This is one of those cases—few in number—where local safety measures that are nondiscriminatory place an unconstitutional burden on interstate commerce.

3. Assessing Benefits.   The principal method courts use to assess the local benefits of a law is to determine how effectively the law actually accomplishes its purposes. It is up to the state legislature to decide the purposes of its laws—that is what public policy is about—but a law that poorly serves its purposes does not deliver much in the way of benefits. Assessing the effectiveness of the law is not an exercise in policy-making; it is more akin to grading the proficiency of the legislature. But even that form of legislative second-guessing would be improper if it were not for the fact that the means chosen by the legislature to accomplish local benefits—the law at issue—has an impact on interstate commerce.

Consider the Court's method in *Southern Pacific*. The Arizona train length law was enacted for the purpose of improving traffic safety at railroad grade crossings and reducing injuries to train workers. But the law didn't materially improve the safety of the train workers and actually reduced traffic safety at grade crossings by reason of the greater number and frequency of trains traveling through Arizona. In terms of its purposes the law was perverse—it actually produced the opposite of the intended effect. Because the benefits produced were less than zero, the burdens imposed on interstate commerce became very large by comparison.

In measuring the effectiveness of a law, the benefits, like the burdens, are not examined in isolation. Other laws of the state (or even of other jurisdictions) that undermine or reduce a law's purported benefits will be considered. In *Kassel*, for example, the fact that Iowa's truck length law was riddled with exemptions undermined the claimed safety benefits of the law.

In Edgar v. MITE Corp., 457 U.S. 624 (1982), Illinois adopted a "business takeover act" designed to regulate tender offers made to shareholders of corporations with certain specified contacts with Illinois. The benefits allegedly produced were protection of shareholders from coercive offers that might not be in their interest. The Court applied *Pike* balancing and concluded that, because federal securities laws supplied most of the benefits Illinois sought to obtain through methods similar to those employed by Illinois, the act placed "a substantial burden on interstate commerce which outweighs its putative local benefits." By contrast, in CTS Corp. v. Dynamics Corp. of America, 481 U.S. 69 (1987), the Court upheld an Indiana act that stripped an acquirer of control shares in an Indiana corporation of any voting rights with respect to the control shares until and unless a majority of the remaining shareholders restored those voting rights. Although the benefits sought were protection of shareholders from coercive tender offers, the method employed to deliver the benefits was uniquely within a state's legislative domain—regulating the governance rules of Indiana corporations—rather than duplicating the federal securities laws.

4. Balancing: Good or Bad Idea? To paraphrase T.R. Powell, a constitutional law professor of an earlier era equipped with a powerful intellect and savage wit, states may regulate interstate commerce so long as they don't regulate too much. The problem, of course, is deciding when there is too much state regulation. The answer is easy when states openly discriminate against interstate commerce, but when they don't—and balancing applies—the problem becomes amorphous. It is not clear that courts are competent to weigh national and state interests and assess the burdens and benefits of state regulation. Nor is it clear that the ultimate judgments based on this balancing are anything other than political judgments best left to Congress. Justice Scalia, for example, takes the position that the Court should exercise the dormant commerce clause power only when state laws discriminate against interstate commerce or "create an impermissible risk of inconsistent regulation by different States."

The balancing process is ill suited to the judicial function and should be under-taken rarely if at all. [I] do not know what qualifies us to make [the] ultimate (and most ineffable) judgment as to whether, given importance-level *x*, and effectiveness-level *y*, the worth of [a] statute is "outweighed" by impact-on-commerce *z*.

CTS Corp., supra (Scalia, J., dissenting).

Justice Scalia has since refined his position by stating that he would apply the dormant commerce clause when a state regulation "'facially discrimi-nates against interstate commerce' and . . . is 'indistinguishable from a type of law previously held unconstitutional by this Court.'" American Trucking Associations, Inc. v. Michigan Public Service Commission, 545 U.S. 429 (2005) (Scalia, J., concurring in the judgment), quoting West Lynn Creamery, Inc. v. Healy, 512 U.S. 186, 210 (1994) (Scalia, J., concurring in the judg-ment). Justice Thomas believes that "'the negative Commerce Clause has no basis in the text of the Constitution, makes little sense, and has proved vir-tually unworkable in application,' and, consequently, cannot serve as a basis for striking down a state statute." Hillside Dairy Inc. v. Lyons, 539 U.S. 59, 68 (2003) (Thomas, J., concurring in part and dissenting in part), quoting Camps Newfound Owatonna, Inc. v. Town of Harrison, 520 U.S. 564, 610 (1997) (Thomas, J., dissenting).

Before rejecting balancing as an arrogant exercise in futility, consider the consequences of dormant commerce clause cases. These cases always occur when Congress *could* act but has not done so. Thus, the Court is allocating the burden of overcoming congressional inaction because the loser, if an affected business, must go to Congress to seek uniform federal regulation of interstate commerce that will preempt the state law that was upheld. If a state law is struck down, the state must implore Congress to regulate interstate commerce by allowing the state to regulate in the fashion that the Court has voided.

Perhaps the Court has embraced balancing because it does not wish to place the burden of obtaining congressional action almost entirely on citizens affected by state regulations. But why? Is it because the Court simply distrusts state legislatures to strike an appropriate balance between the national inter-est in a common market and the states' interests, even when states regulate evenhandedly to obtain legitimate local benefits? What is the source of that distrust? Is it the Court's suspicion that some neutral regulations aiding legiti-mate local purposes are effectively discriminatory?

5. An Emerging "Public Function" Exemption. In United Haulers Association v. Oneida-Herkimer Solid Waste Management Authority, 550 U.S. 330 (2007), the Court considered a flow control ordinance that required all solid waste generated in the locality to be deposited in a public facility, which charged "tipping fees" that were substantially higher than those charged by previously available private facilities.

The laws at issue here require haulers to bring waste to facilities owned and operated by a state-created public benefit corporation [rather than a private facility]. We find this difference constitutionally significant. Disposing of trash has been a traditional government activity for years, and laws that favor the government in such areas—but treat every private business, whether in-state or out-of-state, exactly the same—do not discriminate against interstate commerce for purposes of the Commerce Clause. Applying [*Pike* balancing], we uphold these ordinances because any incidental burden they may have on interstate commerce does not outweigh the benefits they confer on the citizens of Oneida and Herkimer Counties.

The Court said that laws favoring "in-state business over out-of-state competition" deserve "rigorous scrutiny" because such laws are often protectionist, but laws "favoring local government, by contrast, may be directed toward any number of legitimate goals unrelated to protectionism." In *United Haulers*, the higher fees subsidized a public policy of extensive recycling of solid waste, and those costs were borne mostly "by the very people who voted for the laws," unlike *Kassel*, where the costs of Iowa's laws were borne by outsiders who could not vote on them. While Justice Scalia agreed that the ordinance did not discriminate against interstate commerce, he did not join in applying *Pike* balancing. On that issue, only a plurality of four justices (Roberts, C.J., and Souter, Ginsburg, and Breyer, JJ.) agreed. Justice Thomas concurred in the judgment, reiterating his view that "[t]he negative Commerce Clause has no basis in the Constitution and has proved unworkable in practice."

Justice Alito, joined by Justices Stevens and Kennedy, dissented. They argued that laws favoring local governments can be every bit as protectionist as those favoring local businesses. The flow control ordinance benefited "local residents who are employed at the facility, local businesses that supply the facility with goods and services, and local workers employed by such businesses," which demonstrated that such "discrimination amounts to economic protectionism in any realistic sense of the term." Second, the dissent contended that the Court's reliance on trash disposal as a traditional governmental function was inconsistent with such precedents as *Garcia* and, in any case, not factually accurate. Finally, the dissent rejected the Court's contention that the ordinance was nondiscriminatory because it treated in-state and out-of-state private businesses alike. Citing Dean Milk v. Madison, 340 U.S. 349 (1951), excerpted in Section A.4, infra, the dissent charged that the question "is whether the challenged legislation discriminates against interstate commerce," not whether it inflicts harm impartially upon in-state and out-of-state interests.

In Department of Revenue of Kentucky v. Davis, 553 U.S. 328 (2008), the Supreme Court upheld the validity of a Kentucky income tax provision that exempts from state income tax the interest earned on public debt issued by Kentucky and its political subdivisions, but fails to exempt interest earned on the public debt issued by other states. The Court thought that the *United Haulers*' "logic applies with even greater force to laws favoring a State's municipal bonds, given that the issuance of debt securities to pay for public projects is a quintessentially public function [that enables governments] to shoulder the cardinal civic responsibilities [of] protecting the health, safety, and welfare of citizens." Unlike *United Haulers*, the Court in *Davis* refused to apply *Pike* balancing, because it thought the judiciary was "not institutionally suited to draw reliable conclusions of the kind that would be necessary" to apply *Pike* balancing. The Court itemized a host of complex questions involved in assessing the burdens and benefits of the scheme and asserted that "the difficulty of answering them or the inevitable uncertainty of the predictions that might be made in trying to come up with answers" made the judicial process wholly unsuitable "for making whatever predictions and reaching whatever answers are possible at all. . . . The complexities of factual economic proof always present a certain potential for error, and courts have little familiarity with the process of evaluating . . . relative economic burden[s]."

In a concurrence, Justice Scalia argued that the

> problem is that courts are less well suited than Congress to perform this kind of balancing in every case. The burdens and the benefits are always incommensurate, and cannot be placed on the opposite balances of a scale without assigning a policy-based weight to each of them. It is a matter not of weighing apples against apples, but of deciding whether three apples are better than six tangerines. Here, on one end of the scale (the burden side) there rests a certain degree of suppression of interstate competition in borrowing; and on the other (the benefits side) a certain degree of facilitation of municipal borrowing. Of course you cannot decide which interest "outweighs" the other without deciding which interest is more important to you. And that will always be the case. I would abandon the *Pike*-balancing enterprise altogether and leave these quintessentially legislative judgments with the branch to which the Constitution assigns them.

Justices Kennedy and Alito dissented. They contended that even though the Kentucky law served to protect the public "health, safety, and welfare," this was "but a reformulation of the phrase 'police power.' . . . That a law has the police power label—as all laws do—does not exempt it from Commerce Clause analysis." The dissent charged that it was error to uphold the Kentucky law simply

> because bond issuance fulfills a governmental function: raising revenue for public projects. . . . The law . . . operates on those who hold the bonds and trade them, not those who issue them. The bonds are not issued with a covenant promising tax exemption or tax relief to the holder. . . . The security is issued as a formal obligation to repay. . . . [The] discrimination against out-of-state commerce [is] too plain and prejudicial to be sustained. . . . The challenged state activity is differential taxation, not bond issuance. The state tax provision at issue could be repealed tomorrow without altering or impairing a single obligation in the bonds. It is the tax that matters; and Kentucky gives favored tax treatment to some securities but not others depending solely upon the State of issuance, and it does so to disadvantage bonds from other States.

Queries: What is the principle that distinguishes government action that serves a public function (and is either exempt from commerce clause scrutiny or subject to *Pike* balancing) from government action that serves protectionist ends (and is subject to commerce clause scrutiny)? When does *Pike* balancing apply to government action that serves a public function?

4. Facially Neutral Regulations with Discriminatory Effects on Interstate Commerce

The problem of a facially neutral state regulation that serves legitimate local purposes but does so by effectively discriminating against interstate commerce has particularly vexed the Court. In theory, there are two ways the Court could have assimilated these cases to the present doctrine. On the one hand, it could treat state laws that discriminate in effect no differently from state laws that discriminate on their face, and subject both kinds of laws to strict scrutiny. Such laws would be presumed void, and the burden would be on the state to prove that there was no less discriminatory alternative that would accomplish the state's legitimate objective. On the other hand, because such state laws are facially evenhanded, the Court could examine them under the balancing test. While the state law would be presumed valid and the challenger would be required to prove that the burdens on interstate commerce grossly outweigh the local benefits of the law, the effective discrimination against interstate commerce would be powerful evidence of the heavy burden placed upon interstate commerce. The problem is that the Court uses both approaches without clear signals as to when a case is to be shunted onto one track or the other.

Consider the following possibilities as you read the cases that comprise this subsection: (1) When the discriminatory effect is particularly severe, strict scrutiny is triggered; (2) when the discriminatory effect is combined with some evidence of a discriminatory purpose, strict scrutiny is triggered; (3) all of the cases are really balancing cases, but discriminatory effects are so burdensome to commerce that they always "grossly outweigh" local benefits unless the benefits are only achievable with the discriminatory effect (apart from which party bears the burden of proof, is this any different from strict scrutiny?); and (4) the Court is incoherent in dealing with discriminatory effects (if you choose this explanation you must offer and defend an alternative approach).

≡≡≡ ### *Dean Milk Co. v. Madison*
≡≡ *340 U.S. 349 (1951)*

[Madison, Wisconsin, prohibited the sale of milk in that city "unless it has been processed and bottled at an approved pasteurization plant within a radius of five miles from the central square of Madison." Madison set this limit so that its health inspectors could easily and regularly inspect and certify the pasteurization plants and the dairy farms that supplied the plants with raw milk. Within the five-mile radius were five pasteurization plants, only three of which supplied Madison with pasteurized milk. Dean Milk was "an Illinois corporation engaged in distributing milk and milk products in Illinois and Wisconsin." It purchased milk from about "950 farms in northern Illinois and southern Wisconsin" and pasteurized it at two Illinois plants located at least 65 miles from Madison. Dean Milk "was denied a license to sell its products within Madison solely because its pasteurization plants were more than five miles away." Dean's milk was "supplied from farms and processed in plants licensed and inspected by public health authorities of Chicago, and is labeled 'Grade A' under the Chicago ordinance which adopts the rating standards recommended by the United States Public Health Service." Madison contended and the Court assumed that in some particulars its ordinance was more rigorous than that of Chicago. The Wisconsin Supreme Court upheld the five-mile limit. The Supreme Court reversed, concluding "that the ordinance imposes an undue burden on interstate commerce."]

JUSTICE CLARK delivered the opinion of the Court.

[There can be no] objection to the avowed purpose of this enactment. We assume that difficulties in sanitary regulation of milk and milk products originating in remote areas may present a situation in which "upon a consideration of all the relevant facts and circumstances it appears that the matter is one which may appropriately be regulated in the interest of the safety, health and well-being of local communities." [But] this regulation [in] practical effect excludes from distribution in Madison wholesome milk produced and pasteurized in Illinois. . . . In thus erecting an economic barrier protecting a major local industry against competition from without the State, Madison plainly discriminates against interstate commerce.[12] This it cannot do, even in the exercise of its unquestioned power to protect the health and safety of its people, if reasonable nondiscriminatory alternatives, adequate to conserve legitimate local interests, are available. A different view, that the ordinance is valid simply because it professes to be a health measure, would mean that the Commerce Clause of itself imposes no limitations on state action, [save] for the rare instance where a state artlessly discloses an avowed purpose to discriminate against interstate goods. Our issue then is whether the discrimination inherent in the Madison ordinance can be justified in view of the character of the local interests and the available methods of protecting them.

It appears that reasonable and adequate alternatives are available. If the City of Madison prefers to rely upon its own officials for inspection of distant milk sources, such inspection is readily open to it without hardship for it could charge the actual and reasonable cost of such inspection to the importing producers and processors. Moreover, appellee Health Commissioner of Madison

---

12. It is immaterial that Wisconsin milk from outside the Madison area is subjected to the same proscription as that moving in interstate commerce.

testified that as proponent of the local milk ordinance he had submitted the provisions here in controversy and an alternative proposal based [on] the Model Milk Ordinance recommended by the United States Public Health Service. The model provision imposes no geographical limitation on location of milk sources and processing plants but excludes from the municipality milk not produced and pasteurized conformably to standards as high as those enforced by the receiving city. [The] Commissioner testified that Madison consumers "would be safeguarded adequately" under either proposal and that he had expressed no preference.

[To] permit Madison to adopt a regulation not essential for the protection of local health interests and placing a discriminatory burden on interstate commerce would invite a multiplication of preferential trade areas destructive of the very purpose of the Commerce Clause. Under the circumstances here presented, the regulation must yield to the principle that "one state in its dealings with another may not place itself in a position of economic isolation."

[Reversed.]

JUSTICE BLACK, joined by JUSTICES DOUGLAS and MINTON, dissenting.

Today's holding invalidates [the Madison] ordinance on the following reasoning: (1) the section excludes wholesome milk coming from Illinois; (2) this imposes a discriminatory burden on interstate commerce; (3) such a burden cannot be imposed where, as here, there are reasonable, nondiscriminatory and adequate alternatives available. I disagree with the Court's premises, reasoning, and judgment.

(1) This ordinance does not exclude wholesome milk coming from Illinois or anywhere else. It does require that all milk sold in Madison must be pasteurized within five miles of the center of the city. But there was no [evidence that] Dean Milk Company is unable to have its milk pasteurized within the defined geographical area. As a practical matter, so far as the record shows, Dean can easily comply with the ordinance whenever it wants to. Therefore, Dean's personal preference to pasteurize in Illinois, not the ordinance, keeps Dean's milk out of Madison.

(2) Characterization of [the five-mile limit] as a "discriminatory burden" on interstate commerce is merely a statement of the Court's result, which I think incorrect. The [lower courts concluded that the ordinance] represents a good-faith attempt to safeguard public health by making adequate sanitation inspection possible. [The fact that the ordinance], like all health regulations, imposes some burden on trade, does not mean that it "discriminates" against interstate commerce.

(3) This health regulation should not be invalidated merely because the Court believes that alternative milk-inspection methods might insure the cleanliness and healthfulness of Dean's Illinois milk. [No] case is cited, and I have found none, in which a bona fide health law was struck down on the ground that some other method of safeguarding health would be as good as, or better than, the one the Court was called on to review. [If] the principle announced today is to be followed the Court should not strike down local

health regulations unless satisfied beyond a reasonable doubt that the substitutes it proposes would not lower health standards. [I] do not think that either of the alternatives suggested by the Court would assure the people of Madison as pure a supply of milk as they receive under their own ordinance. On this record I would uphold the Madison law. At the very least, however, I would not invalidate it without giving the parties a chance to present evidence and get findings on the ultimate issues the Court thinks crucial—namely, the relative merits of the Madison ordinance and the alternatives suggested by the Court today.

NOTES

1. The Standard of Review.   Does the Court apply strict scrutiny or balancing? Madison's ordinance was struck down because Madison had "reasonable nondiscriminatory alternatives" to accomplish its health objectives. The *Dean Milk* test thus appears to be identical to the standard employed in cases of overt discrimination: Discriminatory regulations are valid only when they advance "'a legitimate local purpose' [that] could not be served as well by available nondiscriminatory means." Maine v. Taylor, supra.

But why strict scrutiny? Justice Clark says that Madison "plainly discriminates" against interstate commerce, but Justice Black retorts that "Dean can easily comply with the ordinance whenever it wants to" and that it is only "Dean's personal preference to pasteurize in Illinois, not the ordinance, [that] keeps Dean's milk out of Madison." Justice Black is correct to the extent that the ordinance does not *on its face* exclude out-of-state milk. But Justice Clark is surely correct that the plain *effect* of the Madison ordinance is to exclude all but the most local Wisconsin milk. The practical effect is stark, excluding (as a practical matter) all out-of-state milk and almost all Wisconsin milk. Is it this easily visualized effective discrimination that causes the Court to treat this as a case of overt discrimination?

2. Intrastate Discrimination.   Justice Clark states that it is "immaterial" that Madison's ordinance effectively discriminates equally against out-of-state milk and non-Madison Wisconsin milk. Why? Isn't it possible that Wisconsin milk producers excluded from Madison would seek statewide legislation overturning the Madison ban? Should it matter that the affected intrastate businesses (non-Madison Wisconsin milk producers) have an incentive to correct the discrimination that also affects out-of-staters? But it is also possible that the correction sought and obtained by in-state interests would simply be similar local protection, with the result that every Wisconsin municipality would discriminate in favor of local milk. Wisconsin milk producers might find this an acceptable trade-off, but Illinois milk producers (such as Dean Milk) or Minnesota milk producers would still be effectively frozen out of the Wisconsin market. Finally, if interstate discrimination is ignored when coupled with intrastate discrimination, it is easy to avoid the pinch of strict scrutiny: Simply include some intrastate discrimination in the law.

a. Assessing Discriminatory Effects

It is easy enough to assert that the Court assimilates some cases of discriminatory effect into the doctrine governing overt discrimination, but it is quite another matter to state when those discriminatory effects are sufficiently pronounced to warrant strict scrutiny. Consider the following pair of cases.

Hunt v. Washington State Apple Advertising Commission
432 U.S. 333 (1977)

[North Carolina required the closed paperboard containers in which apples are shipped to display "no grade other than the applicable [USDA] grade or standard." Washington is the largest apple-producing state in the nation, shipping about half the apples that move in interstate commerce in closed containers. Washington developed its own grading standard for apples, standards that were superior to the USDA grades due to the stringent inspection program Washington imposed on Washington apples.]

CHIEF JUSTICE BURGER delivered the opinion for a unanimous Court.

North Carolina [adopted] an administrative regulation, unique in the 50 States, which in effect required all closed containers of apples shipped into or sold in the State to display either the applicable USDA grade or none at all. State grades were expressly prohibited. In addition to its obvious consequence prohibiting the display of Washington State apple grades on containers of apples shipped into North Carolina, the regulation presented the Washington apple industry with a marketing problem of potentially nationwide significance. Washington apple growers annually ship in commerce approximately 40 million closed containers of apples, nearly 500,000 of which eventually find their way into North Carolina, stamped with the applicable Washington State variety and grade. It is the industry's practice to purchase these containers preprinted with the various apple varieties and grades, prior to harvest. After these containers are filled with apples of the appropriate type and grade, a substantial portion of them are placed in cold-storage warehouses where the grade labels identify the product and facilitate its handling. These apples are then shipped as needed throughout the year; after February 1 of each year, they constitute approximately two-thirds of all apples sold in fresh markets in this country. Since the ultimate destination of these apples is unknown at the time they are placed in storage, compliance with North Carolina's unique regulation would have required Washington growers to obliterate the printed labels on containers shipped to North Carolina, thus giving their product a damaged appearance. Alternatively, they could have changed their marketing practices to accommodate the needs of the North Carolina market, i.e., repack apples to be shipped to North Carolina in containers bearing only the USDA grade, and/or store the estimated portion of the harvest destined for that market in such special containers. As a last resort, they could discontinue the use of the preprinted containers entirely. None of these costly and less efficient options was very attractive to the industry. Moreover, in the event a number of other States followed North Carolina's lead, the resultant inability to display the Washington grades could force the Washington growers to abandon the State's expensive inspection and grading system which their customers had come to know and rely on over the 60-odd years of its existence. . . .

[The trial court] found that the North Carolina statute, while neutral on its face, actually discriminated against Washington State growers and dealers in favor of their local counterparts. [North Carolina], unlike Washington, had never established a grading and inspection system. Hence, the statute had no effect on the existing practices of North Carolina producers; they were still free to use the USDA grade or none at all. Washington growers and dealers, on the other hand, were forced to alter their long-established procedures, at substantial cost, or abandon the North Carolina market. [The trial court concluded that this discrimination was not justified by the asserted local interest in eliminating deception and confusion in the apple market and so enjoined enforcement of the regulation.]

[A] finding that state legislation furthers matters of legitimate local concern, even in the health and consumer protection areas, does not end the inquiry. [Rather], when such state legislation comes into conflict with the Commerce Clause's overriding requirement of a national "common market," we are confronted with the task of effecting an accommodation of the competing national and local interests. [Pike v. Bruce Church.] [The] challenged statute has the practical effect of not only burdening interstate sales of Washington apples, but also discriminating against them. This discrimination takes various forms. The first, and most obvious, is the statute's consequence of raising the costs of doing business in the North Carolina market for Washington apple growers and dealers, while leaving those of their North Carolina counterparts unaffected. [This] disparate effect results from the fact that North Carolina apple producers, unlike their Washington competitors, were not forced to alter their marketing practices in order to comply with the statute. [Second], the statute has the effect of stripping away from the Washington apple industry the competitive and economic advantages it has earned for itself through its expensive inspection and grading system. The record demonstrates that the Washington apple-grading system has gained nationwide acceptance in the apple trade. [Third], the statute has a leveling effect which insidiously operates to the advantage of local apple producers. [Washington] apples which would otherwise qualify for and be sold under the superior Washington grades will now have to be marketed under their inferior USDA counterparts. Such "downgrading" offers the North Carolina apple industry the very sort of protection against competing out-of-state products that the Commerce Clause was designed to prohibit.

[Although there were indications that the law was motivated by a discriminatory purpose] we need not ascribe an economic protection motive to the North Carolina Legislature to resolve this case; we conclude that the challenged statute cannot stand insofar as it prohibits the display of Washington

State grades even if enacted for the declared purpose of protecting consumers from deception and fraud in the marketplace. When discrimination against [interstate commerce is] demonstrated, the burden falls on the State to justify it both in terms of the local benefits flowing from the statute and the unavailability of nondiscriminatory alternatives adequate to preserve the local interests at stake. North Carolina has failed to sustain that burden on both scores.

[The] challenged statute does remarkably little to [eliminate deception and confusion because it] permits the marketing of closed containers of apples under no grades at all. [Moreover], although the statute is ostensibly a consumer protection measure, it directs its primary efforts, not at the consuming public at large, but at apple wholesalers and brokers who are the principal purchasers of closed containers of apples. [Because] the statute does nothing at all to purify the flow of information at the retail level, it does little to protect consumers against the problems it was designed to eliminate.

In addition, it appears that nondiscriminatory alternatives to the outright ban of Washington State grades are readily available. For example, North Carolina could [permit] out-of-state growers to utilize state grades only if they also marked their shipments with the applicable USDA label.

Justice Rehnquist did not participate in the decision.

NOTE

Standard of Review. Chief Justice Burger first invokes *Pike* balancing but then states that "[w]hen discrimination against [interstate] commerce [is] demonstrated, the burden falls on the State to justify it both in terms of the local benefits flowing from the statute and the unavailability of nondiscriminatory alternatives adequate to preserve the local interests." Does this mean that when discrimination is established due to effects, the state must prove *more* than a legitimate local objective? If so, why should the state's burden be higher than in a facial discrimination case? Alternatively, did Chief Justice Burger mean to invoke a unique version of *Pike* balancing, one that reverses the burden of proof and also requires the state to prove the absence of less discriminatory alternatives? Or is this simply an artless rendition of the overt discrimination test?

≡≡≡ *Exxon Corp. v. Governor of Maryland*
≡≡≡ *437 U.S. 117 (1978)*

JUSTICE STEVENS delivered the opinion of the Court.

A Maryland statute provides that a producer or refiner of petroleum products [may] not operate any retail service station within the [State]. The

Court of Appeals of Maryland [upheld the statute against a dormant commerce clause challenge]. We affirm.

The Maryland statute is an outgrowth of the 1973 shortage of petroleum. [Gasoline] stations operated by producers or refiners [received] preferential treatment during the period of short supply. [No] petroleum products are produced or refined in Maryland, and the number of stations actually operated by a refiner [is] about 5% of the total number of Maryland [gasoline] retailers.

[Exxon argued that the law violated the commerce clause] by discriminating against interstate commerce [and] by unduly burdening interstate [commerce]. Plainly, the [law] does not discriminate against interstate goods, nor does it favor local producers and refiners. Since Maryland's entire gasoline supply flows in interstate commerce and since there are no local producers or refiners, such claims of disparate treatment between interstate and local commerce would be meritless. Appellants, however, focus on the retail market arguing that the effect of the statute is to protect in-state independent dealers from out-of-state competition. They [rely] on the fact that the [ownership ban] falls solely on interstate companies. But this fact does not lead, either logically or as a practical matter, to a conclusion that the State is discriminating against interstate commerce at the retail level. [There] are several major interstate marketers of petroleum that own and operate their own retail gasoline stations, compete directly [with] Maryland independent dealers, [and] are not affected by the Act because they do not refine or produce gasoline. In fact, the Act creates no barriers whatsoever against interstate independent dealers; it does not prohibit the flow of interstate goods, place added costs upon them, or distinguish between in-state and out-of-state companies in the retail market. The absence of any of these factors fully distinguishes this case from those in which a State has been found to have discriminated against interstate commerce. See, e.g., [*Hunt, Dean Milk*]. The fact that the burden of a state regulation falls on some interstate companies does not, by itself, establish a claim of discrimination against interstate commerce.[13]

Appellants argue [that] the Maryland statute impermissibly *burdens* interstate commerce [because some refiners may] stop selling in Maryland. [If so,] there is no reason to assume that their share of the entire supply will not be promptly replaced by other interstate refiners. The source of the consumers' supply may switch from company-operated stations to independent dealers, but interstate commerce is not subjected to an impermissible burden simply because an otherwise valid regulation causes some business to shift from one interstate supplier to another.

---

13. If the effect of a state regulation is to cause local goods to constitute a larger share, and goods with an out-of-state source to constitute a smaller share, of the total sales in the market—as in *Hunt* and *Dean Milk*—the regulation may have a discriminatory effect on interstate commerce. But the Maryland statute has no impact on the relative proportions of local and out-of-state goods sold in Maryland and, indeed, no demonstrable effect whatsoever on the interstate flow of goods.

[Exxon also argued that the law] interfered "with the natural functioning of the interstate market" [by] "chang[ing] the market structure by weakening the independent [refiners]." We cannot [accept Exxon's] underlying notion that the Commerce Clause protects the particular structure or methods of operation in a retail market. [The] Clause protects the interstate market, not particular interstate firms, from prohibitive or burdensome regulations. It may be true that the consuming public will be injured by the loss of the high-volume, low-priced stations operated by the independent refiners, but again that argument relates to the wisdom of the statute, not to its burden on commerce.

[Affirmed.]

JUSTICE BLACKMUN, dissenting on the commerce clause issue.

The Commerce Clause forbids discrimination against interstate [commerce]. The discrimination need not appear on the face of the state or local regulation. "[It] is our duty to determine whether the statute under attack [will] in its practical operation work discrimination against interstate commerce." The state or local authority need not intend to discriminate.

[It] is true that merely demonstrating a burden on some out-of-state actors does not prove unconstitutional discrimination. But when the burden is significant, when it falls on the most numerous and effective group of out-of-state competitors, when a similar burden does not fall on the class of protected in-state businessmen, and when the State cannot justify the resulting disparity by showing that its legislative interests cannot be vindicated by more evenhanded regulation, unconstitutional discrimination exists.

Justice Powell did not participate in the case.

NOTE

Reconciling Exxon and Hunt.   Did *Exxon* and *Hunt* turn on a perception of the relevant market? If the market in *Hunt* was "Washington graded apples," North Carolina excluded all interstate commerce in such apples. If the market was "apples," the North Carolina regulation had little effect. If the market in *Exxon* was gasoline (as the Court thought), the Maryland law excluded no gasoline. And even if the market was "major brand" gasoline, the Maryland law had little effect, for major brand gasoline would still be sold by independent franchisees. Only if the market was seen as "gasoline sold at retail by the refiner" would Maryland have discriminated against out-of-staters. Did the perception of discrimination differ because the national market for apples would be more seriously disrupted by a ban on display of Washington grades than the national market for gasoline would be by Maryland's ban on refiner-owned retail stations? If so, does this suggest that the Court measures the extent of the discriminatory effect in determining whether a given discriminatory effect is sufficient to constitute open discrimination and thus trigger strict scrutiny?

b. Assessing Discriminatory Purposes

If a state openly declares that the purpose of some law is to discriminate against interstate commerce, it is void per se—it lacks a legitimate objective. Only the most willful, stupid state legislature would enact such a law, so there are no cases on that point. But legislatures do enact laws that may well be motivated by such a purpose. There were hints of a discriminatory purpose in *Kassel, Hunt,* and *Exxon,* although the Court did not rely on discriminatory purpose in deciding any of those cases. What constitutes a discriminatory purpose? When is such a purpose adequately proven? What is the effect of a finding of discriminatory purpose?

≡ *West Lynn Creamery, Inc. v. Healy*
≡ *512 U.S. 186 (1994)*

Justice Stevens delivered the opinion of the Court.

A Massachusetts pricing order imposes an assessment on all fluid milk sold by dealers to Massachusetts retailers. About two-thirds of that milk is produced out of State. The entire assessment, however, is distributed to Massachusetts dairy farmers. The question presented is whether the pricing order unconstitutionally discriminates against interstate commerce. We hold that it does.

[After concluding that Massachusetts dairy farmers were in danger of extinction because their production costs exceeded the price of raw milk, the Massachusetts Department of Food and Agriculture declared a state of emergency and] issued the pricing order that is challenged in this proceeding.

[The] paradigmatic example of a law discriminating against interstate commerce is the protective tariff or customs duty, which taxes goods imported from other States, but does not tax similar products produced in State. A tariff is an attractive measure because it simultaneously raises revenue and benefits local producers by burdening their out-of-state competitors. Nevertheless, it violates the principle of the unitary national market by handicapping out-of-state competitors, thus artificially encouraging in-state production even when the same goods could be produced at lower cost in other States. Because of their distorting effects on the geography of production, tariffs have long been recognized as violative of the Commerce Clause. In fact, tariffs against the products of other States are so patently unconstitutional that our cases reveal not a single attempt by any State to enact one. Instead, the cases are filled with state laws that aspire to reap some of the benefits of tariffs by other means. In [*Seelig*], New York attempted to protect its dairy farmers from the adverse effects of Vermont competition by establishing a single minimum price for all milk, whether produced in New York or elsewhere. [Because] the minimum price regulation had the same effect as a tariff or customs duty—neutralizing the advantage possessed by lower cost out-of-state producers—it was held unconstitutional. Similarly, in Bacchus Imports, Ltd. v. Dias this Court invalidated a law which advantaged local production by granting a tax exemption to certain liquors produced in Hawaii. . . . Massachusetts' pricing order is clearly unconstitutional. Its avowed purpose and its undisputed effect are to enable higher cost Massachusetts dairy farmers to compete with lower cost dairy farmers in other States. The "premium payments" are effectively a tax which makes milk produced out of State more expensive. Although the tax also applies to milk produced in Massachusetts, its effect on Massachusetts producers is entirely (indeed more than) offset by the subsidy provided exclusively to Massachusetts dairy farmers. Like an ordinary tariff, the tax is thus effectively imposed only on out-of-state products. [The] Massachusetts pricing order thus will almost certainly "cause local goods to constitute a larger share, and goods with an out-of-state source to constitute a smaller share, of the total sales in the market." [*Exxon.*] In fact, this effect was the motive behind the promulgation of the pricing order. This effect renders the program unconstitutional, because it, like a tariff, "neutralizes advantages belonging to the place of origin." [*Seelig.*]

[The] Massachusetts pricing order is most similar to the law at issue in *Bacchus Imports.* Both involve a broad-based tax on a single kind of good and special provisions for in-state producers. *Bacchus* involved a 20% excise tax on all liquor sales, coupled with an exemption for fruit wine manufactured in Hawaii and for okolehao, a brandy distilled from the root of a shrub indigenous to Hawaii. The Court held that Hawaii's law was unconstitutional because it "had both the purpose and effect of discriminating in favor of local products." By granting a tax exemption for local products, Hawaii in effect created a protective tariff. Goods produced out of State were taxed, but those produced in State were subject to no net tax. It is obvious that the result in *Bacchus* would have been the same if instead of exempting certain Hawaiian liquors from tax, Hawaii had rebated the amount of tax collected from the sale of those liquors.

[Respondent argues that because] each component of the program — a local subsidy and a non-discriminatory tax — is valid, the combination of the two is equally [valid]. A pure subsidy funded out of general revenue ordinarily imposes no burden on interstate commerce, but merely assists local business. The pricing order in this case, however, is funded principally from taxes on the sale of milk produced in other States. By so funding the subsidy, respondent not only assists local farmers, but burdens interstate commerce. The pricing order thus violates the cardinal principle that a State may not "benefit in-state economic interests by burdening out-of-state competitors." More fundamentally, [by] conjoining a tax and a subsidy, Massachusetts has created a program more dangerous to interstate commerce than either part alone. [When] a nondiscriminatory tax is coupled with a subsidy to one of the groups hurt by the tax, a state's political processes can no longer be relied upon to prevent legislative abuse, because one of the in-state interests which would otherwise lobby against the tax has been mollified by the subsidy. So, in this case, one would ordinarily have expected at least three groups to lobby against the order premium, which, as a tax, raises the price (and hence lowers demand) for milk: dairy farmers, milk dealers, and consumers. But because the tax was coupled with a subsidy, one of the most powerful of these groups, Massachusetts dairy farmers, instead of exerting their influence against the tax, were in fact its primary supporters.

[Respondent] also argues that [the pricing order is not discriminatory because Massachusetts consumers bear the entire burden of the resulting price increases]. This argument, if accepted, would undermine almost every discriminatory tax case. State taxes are ordinarily paid by in-state businesses and consumers, yet if they discriminate against out-of-state products, they are unconstitutional. [The] cost of a tariff is also borne primarily by local consumers, yet a tariff is the paradigmatic Commerce Clause violation.

JUSTICE SCALIA, joined by JUSTICE THOMAS, concurring in the judgment.

"[The] historical record provides no grounds for reading the Commerce Clause to be other than what it says—an authorization for Congress to regulate commerce." Nonetheless, we formally adopted the doctrine of the negative Commerce Clause 121 years ago and since then have decided a vast number of negative-Commerce-Clause cases, engendering considerable reliance interests. As a result, I will, on stare decisis grounds, enforce a self-executing "negative" Commerce Clause in two situations: (1) against a state law that facially discriminates against interstate commerce, and (2) against a state law that is indistinguishable from a type of law previously held unconstitutional by this Court. Applying this approach—or at least the second part of it—is not always easy, since once one gets beyond facial discrimination our negative-Commerce-Clause jurisprudence becomes (and long has been) a "quagmire." The object should be, however, to produce a clear rule that honors the holdings of our past decisions but declines to extend the rationale that produced those decisions any further.

There are at least four possible devices that would enable a State to produce the economic effect that Massachusetts has produced here: (1) a discriminatory tax upon the industry, imposing a higher liability on out-of-state members than on their in-state competitors; (2) a tax upon the industry that is nondiscriminatory in its assessment, but that has an "exemption" or "credit" for in-state members; (3) a nondiscriminatory tax upon the industry, the revenues from which are placed into a segregated fund, which fund is disbursed as "rebates" or "subsidies" to in-state members of the industry (the situation at issue in this case); and (4) with or without nondiscriminatory taxation of the industry, a subsidy for the in-state members of the industry, funded from the State's general revenues. It is long settled that the first of these methodologies is unconstitutional under the negative Commerce Clause. The second of them, "exemption" from or "credit" against a "neutral" tax, is no different in principle from the first, and has likewise been held invalid. The fourth methodology, application of a state subsidy from general revenues, is so far removed from what we have hitherto held to be unconstitutional, that prohibiting it must be regarded as an extension of our negative-Commerce-Clause jurisprudence and therefore, to me, unacceptable.

The issue before us in the present case is whether the third of these methodologies must fall. Although the question is close, I conclude it would not be a principled point at which to disembark from the negative-Commerce-Clause train. The only difference between methodology (2) (discriminatory "exemption" from nondiscriminatory tax) and methodology (3) (discriminatory refund of nondiscriminatory tax) is that the money is taken and returned rather than simply left with the favored in-state taxpayer in the first place. The difference between (3) and (4), on the other hand, is the difference between assisting in-state industry through discriminatory taxation, and assisting in-state industry by other means.

I would therefore allow a State to subsidize its domestic industry so long as it does so from nondiscriminatory taxes that go into the State's general revenue fund. Perhaps, as some commentators contend, that line comports with an important economic reality: a State is less likely to maintain a subsidy when its citizens perceive that the money (in the general fund) is available for any number of competing, non-protectionist, purposes. That is not, however, the basis for my [position]. I draw the line where I do because it is a clear, rational line at the limits of our extant negative-Commerce-Clause jurisprudence.

CHIEF JUSTICE REHNQUIST, joined by JUSTICE BLACKMUN, dissenting.

The law [at issue] undoubtedly sought to aid struggling Massachusetts dairy farmers, beset by steady or declining prices and escalating costs. [The] value of agricultural land located near metropolitan areas is driven up by the demand for housing and similar urban uses; distressed farmers eventually sell out to developers. Not merely farm produce is lost, as is the milk production in this case, but, as the Massachusetts Special Commission whose report was the basis for the order in question here found: "Without the continued existence of dairy farmers, the Commonwealth will lose its supply of locally produced fresh milk, together with the open lands that are used as wildlife refuges, for recreation, hunting, fishing, tourism, and education."

Massachusetts has dealt with this problem by providing a subsidy to aid its beleaguered dairy farmers. [In] Milk Control Bd. v. Eisenberg Farm Products, 306 U.S. 346 (1939), the Court upheld a Pennsylvania statute establishing minimum prices to be paid to Pennsylvania dairy farmers against a Commerce Clause challenge by a Pennsylvania milk dealer which shipped all of its milk purchased in Pennsylvania to New York to be sold there. The Court observed that "the purpose of the statute [is] to reach a domestic situation in the interest of the welfare of the producers and consumers of milk in Pennsylvania." [The] Massachusetts subsidy [is similar] to the Pennsylvania statute described in *Eisenberg*. Massachusetts taxes all dealers of milk within its borders. The tax is even-handed[—]it affects all dealers regardless of the point of origin of the milk. [The] State[']s motives are purely local: "The premiums represent one of the costs of doing business in the Commonwealth, a cost all milk dealers must pay."

[But] the Court strikes down this method of state subsidization because the non-discriminatory tax levied against all milk dealers is coupled with a subsidy to milk producers. The Court does this because of its view that the method of imposing the tax and subsidy distorts the State's political process: the dairy farmers, who would otherwise lobby against the tax, have been mollified by the subsidy. [But] there are still at least two strong interest groups opposed to the milk order—consumers and milk dealers. More importantly, nothing in the dormant Commerce Clause suggests that the fate of state regulation should turn upon the particular lawful manner in which the state subsidy is enacted or promulgated. Analysis of interest group participation in the political process may serve many useful purposes, but serving as a basis for interpreting the dormant Commerce Clause is not one of them.

The Court [cites *Bacchus Imports* as an example] in which constitutional means were held to have unconstitutional effects on interstate commerce. [But] *Bacchus* [is] a far cry from this case. In *Bacchus*, the State of Hawaii [exempted] a local wine from the burdens of an excise tax levied on all other liquor sales. [I] agree with the Court's statement that *Bacchus* can be distinguished "by noting that the rebate in this case goes not to the entity which pays the tax (milk dealers) but to the dairy farmers themselves." This is not only a distinction, but a significant difference. No decided case supports the Court's conclusion that the negative Commerce Clause prohibits the State from using money that it has lawfully obtained through a neutral tax on milk dealers and distributing it as a subsidy to dairy farmers. Indeed, the case which comes closest to supporting the result the Court reaches is the ill-starred opinion in United States v. Butler, in which the Court held unconstitutional what would have been an otherwise valid tax on the processing of agricultural products because of the use to which the revenue raised by the tax was put. . . .

The wisdom of a messianic insistence on a grim sink-or-swim policy of laissez-faire economics would be debatable had Congress chosen to enact it; but Congress has done nothing of the kind. It is the Court which has imposed the policy under the dormant Commerce Clause, a policy which bodes ill for the values of federalism which have long animated our constitutional jurisprudence.

NOTES AND PROBLEMS

1. Discriminatory Purpose? Discriminatory Effects?   The purpose of the Massachusetts law was to keep Massachusetts dairy farmers in business. It did this by taxing Massachusetts milk consumers indirectly (through the dealer tax) and distributing the proceeds to Massachusetts farmers. Is this a discriminatory *purpose*, or is the case really about discriminatory *effects*? Or does the presence of discriminatory effects give rise to a presumption that the purpose is the impermissible one of local economic protection?

Does Bacchus Imports, Ltd. v. Dias, 468 U.S. 263 (1984), support the majority or the dissenters? Hawaii's liquor tax exemptions were intended to benefit uniquely Hawaiian products by exempting them from a tax that all outsiders must bear. The Massachusetts tax-and-subsidy scheme was intended to benefit Massachusetts dairy farmers by granting them a subsidy collected from a facially nondiscriminatory tax. Is this significantly different or merely illusory?

2. Problems. The City of San Francisco, like many other popular tourist sites, imposes a tax on hotel room charges. Although the tax is levied on all hotel guests, the hotel tax is paid almost entirely by visitors to San Francisco, most of whom are from out of state. The proceeds are used to subsidize a wide variety of local activities (e.g., the arts) that primarily (but not exclusively) benefit San Franciscans. After the *West Lynn Creamery* decision, is the hotel tax valid? Suppose San Francisco were to require that the hotel tax revenues be spent entirely on housing subsidies to poor San Franciscans. Would this version of the hotel tax be valid? In thinking about these questions, note that the subsidy to Massachusetts dairy farmers was designed to ensure a continued supply of milk that would not be drunk *exclusively* by Massachusetts residents.

Suppose that California, a state with no tobacco growers or processors, imposes a tax on all tobacco products sold in the state and simultaneously uses the tax proceeds to subsidize medical care of Californians afflicted with ailments produced by use of tobacco. Is this scheme valid after *West Lynn Creamery*? If so, is it because the purpose of the scheme is not economic protection?

3. Family Winemakers of California v. Jenkins: An Application. In 2006, Massachusetts enacted a law that permitted "small" wineries to use any of three distribution methods simultaneously: direct sales to consumers or retailers, or to use wholesalers to distribute their product. "Large" wineries were required to either sell only through wholesalers or apply for a license to sell directly to consumers, but were not to use both methods. In any case, "large" wineries could not sell directly to retailers. "Small" wineries were those producing annually 30,000 gallons of grape wine or less. Wineries producing fruit wine were treated as "small" wineries so long as their annual production of grape wine was less than 30,000 gallons, regardless of their total annual gallonage. In Family Winemakers of California v. Jenkins, 592 F.3d 1 (1st Cir. 2010), the court ruled that the law violated "the Commerce Clause because the effect of [the] gallonage cap is to change the competitive balance between in-state and out-of-state wineries in a way that benefits Massachusetts's wineries and significantly burdens out-of-state competitors. Massachusetts has used its 30,000 gallon grape wine cap to expand the distribution options available to 'small' wineries, including all Massachusetts wineries, but not to similarly situated 'large' wineries, all of which are outside Massachusetts. The advantages afforded to 'small' wineries by these expanded distribution options bear little relation to the market challenges caused by the relative sizes of the wineries. [The] statutory context, legislative history, and other factors also yield the unavoidable conclusion that this discrimination was purposeful. Nor does [the law] serve any legitimate local purpose that cannot be furthered by a non-discriminatory alternative."

"A state law is discriminatory in effect," said the court, "when, in practice, it affects similarly situated entities in a market by imposing disproportionate burdens on out-of-state interests and conferring advantages upon in-state interests." Quoting *Exxon*, the court declared that discrimination occurs when "the effect of a state regulation is to cause local goods to constitute a larger share, and goods with an out-of-state source to constitute a smaller share, of the total sales in the market." Citing *Hunt*, the court noted that "[s]tate laws that alter conditions of competition to favor in-state interests over out-of-state competitors in a market have long been subject to invalidation." The law delivered "a clear competitive advantage to 'small' wineries, which include all Massachusetts wineries, and creates a comparative disadvantage for 'large' wineries, none of which are in Massachusetts."

5. States as "Market Participants": An Exception to the Dormant Commerce Clause

When a state acts like an ordinary businessperson (as a participant in a market, rather than as a sovereign—as a regulator of market activity), it is exempt from scrutiny under the dormant commerce clause. The exemption is based on the premise that a state occupies a fundamentally different role when it buys or sells goods and services than it does when regulating transactions by others. Consider whether this is truly so as you read the following.

South-Central Timber Development, Inc. v. Wunnicke
467 U.S. 82 (1984)

[Alaska offered to sell about 49 million board-feet of standing timber it owned but made the sale conditional upon a requirement that "the successful bidder must partially process the timber prior to shipping it outside of the State." The processing requirement was applicable only to the state's timber that it was offering for sale and did "not limit the export of unprocessed timber not owned by the State." Alaska's "stated purpose of the requirement" was to "protect existing industries, [establish] new industries, [and] derive revenue." Alaska charged "a significantly lower price for the timber" with the processing requirement "than it otherwise would." South-Central, an Alaska corporation that purchases timber primarily for export to Japan (where it is milled into lumber), asserted that the Alaska processing requirement violated the dormant commerce clause. Alaska's principal defense was that it was a participant in the market, and thus the in-state processing requirement was immune from commerce clause scrutiny.]

JUSTICE WHITE delivered the opinion of the Court in Parts I and II.

I. We must first decide whether . . . Congress has authorized the challenged requirement. If Congress has not, we must [decide whether] Alaska's requirement is permissible because Alaska is acting as a market participant, rather than as a market regulator; and if [Alaska is not a market participant], whether the local-processing requirement is forbidden by the Commerce Clause.

II. [For] a state regulation to be removed from the reach of the dormant Commerce Clause, congressional intent must be unmistakably clear. . . . Unrepresented interests will often bear the brunt of regulations imposed by one State having a significant effect on persons or operations in other States. [But] when Congress acts, all segments of the country are represented and there is significantly less danger that one State will be in a position to exploit others. . . . A rule requiring a clear expression of approval by Congress ensures that there is, in fact, such a collective decision and reduces significantly the risk that unrepresented interests will be adversely affected by restraints on commerce. [The Court concluded that Congress had not authorized the in-state processing requirement.]

Justice White, joined by Justices Brennan, Blackmun, and Stevens, delivered a plurality opinion in Parts III and IV [the "market participant" and commerce clause issues].

III. We now turn [to] whether Alaska's restrictions on export of unprocessed timber from state-owned lands are exempt from Commerce Clause scrutiny under the "market-participant doctrine." Our cases make clear that if a State is acting as a market participant, rather than as a market regulator, the dormant Commerce Clause places no limitation on its activities. See White v. Massachusetts Council of Construction Employers, Inc., 460 U.S. 204 (1983); Reeves, Inc. v. Stake, 447 U.S. 429 (1980); Hughes v. Alexandria Scrap Corp., 426 U.S. 794 (1976). The precise contours of the market-participant doctrine have yet to be established, however, the doctrine having been applied in only three cases of this Court to date.

The first of the cases, [*Alexandria Scrap*], involved a Maryland program designed to reduce the number of junked automobiles in the State. A "bounty" was established on Maryland-licensed junk cars, and the State imposed more stringent documentation requirements on out-of-state scrap processors than on in-state ones. The Court rejected a Commerce Clause attack on the program, although it noted that under traditional Commerce Clause analysis the program might well be invalid because it had the effect of reducing the flow of goods in interstate commerce. The Court concluded that Maryland's action was not "the kind of action with which the Commerce Clause is concerned," because "[n]othing in the purposes animating the Commerce Clause prohibits a State, in the absence of congressional action, from participating in the market and exercising the right to favor its own citizens over others."

In [*Reeves*], the Court upheld a South Dakota policy of restricting the sale of cement from a state-owned plant to state residents, declaring that "[t]he basic distinction drawn in *Alexandria Scrap* between States as market participants and States as market regulators makes good sense and sound law." The Court relied upon "the long recognized right of trader or manufacturer, engaged in an entirely private business freely to exercise his own independent discretion as to parties with whom he will deal." In essence, the Court recognized the principle that the Commerce Clause places no limitations on a State's refusal to deal with particular parties when it is participating in the interstate market in goods.

The most recent of this Court's cases developing the market-participant doctrine is [*White*], in which the Court sustained against a Commerce Clause challenge an executive order of the Mayor of Boston that required all construction projects funded in whole or in part by city funds or city-administered funds to be performed by a work force of at least 50% city residents. The Court rejected the argument that the city was not entitled to the protection of the doctrine because the order had the effect of regulating employment contracts between public contractors and their employees. Recognizing that "there are some limits on a state or local government's ability to impose restrictions that reach beyond the immediate parties with which the government transacts business," the Court found it unnecessary to define those limits because "[e]veryone affected by the order [was], in a substantial if informal sense, 'working for the city.'" The fact that the employees were "working for the city" was "crucial" to the market-participant analysis in *White*.

The State of Alaska contends that its primary-manufacture requirement fits squarely within the market-participant doctrine, arguing that "Alaska's entry into the market may be viewed as precisely the same type of subsidy to local interests that the Court found unobjectionable in *Alexandria Scrap*." However, when Maryland became involved in the scrap market it was as a purchaser of scrap; Alaska, on the other hand, participates in the timber market, but imposes conditions downstream in the timber-processing market. Alaska is not merely subsidizing local timber processing in an amount "roughly equal to the difference between the price the timber would fetch in the absence of such a requirement and the amount the state actually receives." If the State directly subsidized the timber-processing industry by such an amount, the purchaser would retain the option of taking advantage of the subsidy by processing timber in the State or forgoing the benefits of the subsidy and exporting unprocessed timber. Under the Alaska requirement, however, the choice is made for him: if he buys timber from the State he is not free to take the timber out of state prior to processing.

The State also would have us find *Reeves* controlling. It states that "*Reeves* made it clear that the Commerce Clause imposes no limitation on Alaska's power to choose the terms on which it will sell its timber." Such an unrestrained reading of *Reeves* is unwarranted. Although the Court in *Reeves* did strongly endorse the right of a State to deal with whomever it chooses when it participates in the market, it did not—and did not purport to—sanction the imposition of any terms that the State might desire. For example, the Court expressly noted in *Reeves* that "Commerce Clause scrutiny may well be more rigorous when a restraint on foreign commerce is alleged"; that a natural resource "like coal, timber, wild game, or minerals," was not involved, but instead the cement was "the end product of a complex process whereby a costly physical plant and human labor act on raw materials"; and that South

Dakota did not bar resale of South Dakota cement to out-of-state purchasers. In this case, all three of the elements that were not present in *Reeves*—foreign commerce, a natural resource, and restrictions on resale—are present.

Finally, Alaska argues that since the Court in *White* upheld a requirement that reached beyond "the boundary of formal privity of contract," then, a fortiori, the primary-manufacture requirement is permissible, because the State is not regulating contracts for resale of timber or regulating the buying and selling of timber, but is instead "a seller of timber, pure and simple." Yet it is clear that the State is more than merely a seller of timber. In the commercial context, the seller usually has no say over, and no interest in, how the product is to be used after sale; in this case, however, payment for the timber does not end the obligations of the purchaser, for, despite the fact that the purchaser has taken delivery of the timber and has paid for it, he cannot do with it as he pleases. Instead, he is obligated to deal with a stranger to the contract after completion of the sale.

The market-participant doctrine permits a State to influence "a discrete, identifiable class of economic activity in which [it] is a major participant." [*White.*] Contrary to the State's contention, the doctrine is not carte blanche to impose any conditions that the State has the economic power to dictate, and does not validate any requirement merely because the State imposes it upon someone with whom it is in contractual privity.

The limit of the market-participant doctrine must be that it allows a State to impose burdens on commerce within the market in which it is a participant, but allows it to go no further. The State may not impose conditions, whether by statute, regulation, or contract, that have a substantial regulatory effect outside of that particular market.[14] Unless the "market" is relatively narrowly defined, the doctrine has the potential of swallowing up the rule that States may not impose substantial burdens on interstate commerce even if they act with the permissible state purpose of fostering local industry.

At the heart of the dispute in this case is disagreement over the definition of the market. Alaska contends that it is participating in the processed timber market, although it acknowledges that it participates in no way in the actual processing. South-Central argues, on the other hand, that although the State may be a participant in the timber market, it is using its leverage in that market to exert a regulatory effect in the processing market, in which it is not a participant. We agree with the latter position.

There are sound reasons for distinguishing between a State's preferring its own residents in the initial disposition of goods when it is a market participant and a State's attachment of restrictions on dispositions subsequent to the

---

14. The view of the market-participant doctrine expressed by Justice Rehnquist would validate under the Commerce Clause any contractual condition that the State had the economic power to impose, without regard to the relationship of the subject matter of the contract and the condition imposed. If that were the law, it would have been irrelevant that the employees in *White* were in effect "working for the city." If the only question were whether the condition is imposed by contract, a residency requirement could have been imposed with respect to the work force on all projects of any employer doing business with the city.

goods coming to rest in private hands. First, simply as a matter of intuition a State market participant has a greater interest as a "private trader" in the immediate transaction than it has in what its purchaser does with the goods after the State no longer has an interest in them. The common law recognized such a notion in the doctrine of restraints on alienation. Similarly, the antitrust laws place limits on vertical restraints. It is no defense in an action charging vertical trade restraints that the same end could be achieved through vertical integration; if it were, there would be virtually no antitrust scrutiny of vertical arrangements. We reject the contention that a State's action as a market regulator may be upheld against Commerce Clause challenge on the ground that the State could achieve the same end as a market participant. We therefore find it unimportant for present purposes that the State could support its processing industry by selling only to Alaska processors, by vertical integration, or by direct subsidy.

Second, downstream restrictions have a greater regulatory effect than do limitations on the immediate transaction. Instead of merely choosing its own trading partners, the State is attempting to govern the private, separate economic relationships of its trading partners; that is, it restricts the post-purchase activity of the purchaser, rather than merely the purchasing activity. In contrast to the situation in *White*, this restriction on private economic activity takes place after the completion of the parties' direct commercial obligations, rather than during the course of an ongoing commercial relationship in which the city retained a continuing proprietary interest in the subject of the contract.[15] In sum, the State may not avail itself of the market-participant doctrine to immunize its downstream regulation of the timber-processing market in which it is not a participant.

IV. Finally, the State argues that . . . the restriction does not substantially burden interstate or foreign commerce under ordinary Commerce Clause principles. We need not labor long over that contention.

Viewed as a naked restraint on export of unprocessed logs, there is little question that the processing requirement cannot survive scrutiny under the precedents of the Court. [Because] of the protectionist nature of Alaska's local-processing requirement and the burden on commerce resulting therefrom, we conclude that it falls within the rule of virtual per se invalidity of laws that "bloc[k] the flow of interstate commerce at a State's borders." [Philadelphia v. New Jersey.]

We are buttressed in our conclusion that the restriction is invalid by the fact that foreign commerce is burdened by the restriction. It is a well-accepted rule that state restrictions burdening foreign commerce are subjected to a more rigorous and searching scrutiny. It is crucial to the efficient execution of the Nation's foreign policy that "the Federal Government . . . speak with

---

15. This is not to say that the State could evade the reasoning of this opinion by merely including a provision in its contract that title does not pass until the processing is complete. It is the substance of the transaction, rather than the label attached to it, that governs Commerce Clause analysis.

one voice when regulating commercial relations with foreign governments." Michelin Tire Corp. v. Wages, 423 U.S. 276 (1976). In light of the substantial attention given by Congress to the subject of export restrictions on unprocessed timber, it would be peculiarly inappropriate to permit state regulation of the subject. [Reversed and remanded.]

Justice Marshall took no part in the decision of this case.

JUSTICE REHNQUIST, joined by JUSTICE O'CONNOR, dissenting.

In my view, the line of distinction drawn in the plurality opinion between the State as market participant and the State as market regulator is both artificial and unconvincing. The plurality draws this line "simply as a matter of intuition."[16]

[The] contractual term at issue here no more transforms Alaska's sale of timber into "regulation" of the processing industry than the resident-hiring preference imposed by the city of Boston in [*White*] constituted regulation of the construction industry. Alaska is merely paying the buyer of the timber indirectly, by means of a reduced price, to hire Alaska residents to process the timber. Under existing precedent, the State could accomplish that same result in any number of ways. For example, the State could choose to sell its timber only to those companies that maintain active primary-processing plants in Alaska. [*Reeves.*] Or the State could directly subsidize the primary-processing industry within the State. [*Alexandria Scrap.*] The State could even pay to have the logs processed and then enter the market only to sell processed logs. It seems to me unduly formalistic to conclude that the one path chosen by the State as best suited to promote its concerns is the path forbidden it by the Commerce Clause. For these reasons, I would affirm the judgment of the Court of Appeals.

NOTES

1. Proprietor or Sovereign? The case in which the market-participant doctrine originated, Hughes v. Alexandria Scrap, was decided on the same day that the Court decided National League of Cities v. Usery, the case ruling that the commerce power did not extend to regulation of the states in their sovereign capacities. *National League of Cities* was overruled in *Garcia*, partly because the Court concluded that the distinction between a state as proprietor

---

16. The plurality does offer one other reason for its demarcation of the boundary between these two concepts. "[D]ownstream restrictions have a greater regulatory effect than do limitations on the immediate transaction. Instead of merely choosing its own trading partners, the State is attempting to govern the private, separate economic relationships of its trading partners; that is, it restricts the post-purchase activity of the purchaser, rather than merely the purchasing activity." But, of course, this is not a "reason" at all, but merely a restatement of the conclusion. The line between participation and regulation is what we are trying to determine. To invoke that very distinction in support of the line drawn is merely to fall back again on intuition.

and a state as sovereign was unworkable. Why does the distinction remain alive here?

The answer may be that when states act as market participants they are making public investment choices. These choices create commerce rather than regulate other people's commerce. Public investment choices are less coercive than regulations because they are easier to avoid. Public investment choices are also far more expensive than regulations. Regulation offers states a cheap way to capture local benefits at the expense of outsiders, so discriminatory regulations are apt to proliferate. By contrast, the expense of public investment inherently limits this method of capturing local benefits at the expense of outsiders. Finally, some useful and desirable public investments would not be made if they could not be made on a discriminatory basis. For additional thoughts on this subject, see Coenen, Untangling the Market-Participant Exemption to the Dormant Commerce Clause, 88 Mich. L. Rev. 395 (1989); Regan, The Supreme Court and State Protectionism: Making Sense of the Dormant Commerce Clause, 84 Mich. L. Rev. 1091 (1986); Wells and Hellerstein, The Governmental-Proprietary Distinction in Constitutional Law, 66 Va. L. Rev. 1073 (1980).

2. In-State Subsidies. When states discriminate in favor of their residents and against outsiders they are conferring a benefit on their residents. There are at least six ways this can be done: (1) discriminatory regulations (e.g., Philadelphia v. New Jersey); (2) discriminatory taxation (e.g., Fulton Corp. v. Faulkner); (3) facially evenhanded taxation with exemptions targeted at residents (e.g., *Bacchus Imports*); (4) facially evenhanded taxation coupled with an in-state subsidy from the tax revenues (e.g., *West Lynn Creamery*); (5) discriminatory public investment choices by a state as market participant (e.g., *Reeves, White*); and (6) a subsidy to local interests from general tax revenues (assumed to be valid in *West Lynn Creamery*). Only the last two are valid under dormant commerce clause scrutiny. Why?

A favorite explanation of the commentators is that the last two involve highly visible public choices that constrain state actors: States are less likely to offer subsidies to their citizens (or some of them) from general funds, or to use such funds for discriminatory purchases, when their citizens perceive that their money is available for any number of alternative, nonprotectionist uses that may be deemed more socially beneficial. The same insight applies to discriminatory sales of state-owned or state-manufactured goods: Citizens may well perceive that discriminatory sales practices cost them money that could be used to fund other, more worthwhile activities. See, e.g., Coenen, Untangling the Market-Participant Exemption to the Dormant Commerce Clause, 88 Mich. L. Rev. 395, 479 (1989); Collins, Economic Union as a Constitutional Value, 63 N.Y.U. L. Rev. 43, 103 (1988); Gergen, The Selfish State and the Market, 66 Tex. L. Rev. 1097, 1138 (1988). But that explanation has been implicitly rejected by at least four members of the Court in *West Lynn Creamery*, where Chief Justice Rehnquist, joined by Justices Blackmun and (on this point) Justices Scalia and Thomas, observed that "analysis of interest group participation in the political process may serve many useful purposes, but serving as a basis for interpreting the dormant Commerce Clause is not one of them."

3. Monopoly or Competition? Some have argued that market actions of states ought to be exempt from the dormant commerce clause because market actions are less coercive than regulations. Regulations affect everybody, but the market acts of a state affect only those who deal with the state. Presumably, Nebraskans who cannot purchase cement from South Dakota's state-owned cement plant (Reeves v. Stake) have some other source of supply, even within South Dakota. Presumably, South-Central Timber can find other timber sources for export to Japan. By contrast, if South Dakota by law forbade the sale of cement by South Dakotans to outsiders, our hypothetical Nebraskan would be totally foreclosed from all South Dakota supply sources. And if Alaska enacted into law an in-state timber processing requirement, South-Central would be barred from shipping any unprocessed timber out of Alaska.

This explanation works fine so long as the market in which the state participates is reasonably competitive. Does it work when the state is a monopolist? Suppose that a state-employed scientist invents a drug that will cure AIDS and, pursuant to contract, the resulting patent falls under the ownership of the state. If the state refuses to sell the drug, via license or otherwise, to any out-of-state resident, is its refusal exempt from commerce clause scrutiny? Should it be exempt?

Consider C & A Carbone v. Clarkstown, 511 U.S. 383 (1994). Clarkstown, New York induced a private company to build a solid waste transfer facility and to sell it to the city after five years for $1. The inducement was a "flow control ordinance" that required all solid waste (other than recyclables and hazardous waste) generated in the town to be deposited in the facility and deposit fees paid. Carbone, a recycler that sorted waste in Clarkstown and would otherwise have shipped its nonrecyclable waste out of state to a lower-cost facility, challenged the law as a violation of the commerce clause. The Court agreed, ruling that the flow control ordinance discriminated against interstate commerce in a fashion similar to that in *Dean Milk*. What happens when the facility is transferred to Clarkstown in five years? Would the "flow control ordinance" still be invalid because it is in form a regulation? Or should it be treated as market participation?

In *Carbone* itself, Justice Souter dissented, arguing that the waste transfer facility, though nominally private, was "essentially a municipal facility." Justice Souter drew a distinction between "ordinances that restrict access to local markets for the benefit of local private firms" and laws that do so for the benefit of public enterprises.

> [P]rivate businesses [first] serve the private interests of their owners, and there is therefore only rarely a reason other than economic protectionism for favoring local businesses over their out-of-town competitors. [Local government] enters the market to serve the public interest of local [citizens]. Reasons other than economic protectionism are accordingly more likely to explain [an] ordinance

that favors a public facility. The facility [might] be one that private economic actors [would] not have built, but which the locality needs to abate [a] public nuisance. [A] law that favors [a] single [public] facility over all others is a law that favors the public sector over all private-sector processors, whether local or out of State. [While] a preference in favor of government may incidentally function as local favoritism as well, a more particularized enquiry is necessary before a court can say whether such a law does in fact smack too strongly of economic protectionism.

Justice Souter's view was adopted by the Court in United Haulers Association v. Oneida-Herkimer Solid Waste Management Authority, 550 U.S. 330 (2007), but the Court did not rely on the market participant doctrine to uphold a flow control ordinance that required all solid waste generated in the locality to be deposited in a public facility. In Department of Revenue of Kentucky v. Davis, 553 U.S. 328 (2008), a plurality composed of Justices Souter, Stevens, and Breyer argued that Kentucky's issuance of bonds coupled with its differential taxation scheme brought the scheme within the market participant doctrine. "[T]here is no ignoring the fact that imposing the differential tax scheme makes sense only because Kentucky is also a bond issuer. . . . States that regulated the price of milk [e.g., *West Lynn Creamery* and *Seelig*] did not keep herds of cows or compete against dairy producers for the dollars of milk drinkers. But when Kentucky exempts its bond interest, it is competing in the market for limited investment dollars, alongside private bond issuers and its sister States, and its tax structure is one of the tools of competition."

The plurality also characterized *United Haulers* as an unrecognized example of market participation:

Not only did the public authority . . . process trash, but its governmental superiors forbade trash haulers to deal with any other processors. . . . We upheld the government's decision to shut down the old market for trash processing only because it created a new one all by itself, and thereby became a participant in a market with just one supplier of a necessary service. If instead the government had created a monopoly in favor of a private hauler, we would have struck down the law just as we did in [*Carbone*]. *United Haulers* . . . turned on our decision to give paramount consideration to the public function in actively dealing in the trash market. . . .

On the other hand, the dissenters in *United Haulers* claimed that the market participant doctrine did not insulate the government from commerce clause scrutiny:

Respondents are doing exactly what the market participant doctrine says they cannot: While acting as market participants by operating a fee-for-service business enterprise in an area in which there is an established interstate market, respondents are also regulating that market in a discriminatory manner. . . . States cannot discriminate against interstate commerce unless they are acting solely as market participants. The Court suggests, contrary to its prior holdings, that

States can discriminate in favor of in-state interests while acting both as a market participant and as a market regulator.

Queries: According to the *Davis* plurality view, what should be the result in *Wunnicke*? Under what circumstances would (or should) the plurality uncouple government regulation from associated proprietary action by the government?

B. THE PRIVILEGES AND IMMUNITIES CLAUSE OF ARTICLE IV

Article IV, section 2 states: "The Citizens of each State shall be entitled to all Privileges and Immunities of Citizens in the several States." This privileges and immunities clause is quite different in content from the privileges or immunities clause in the Fourteenth Amendment. Don't confuse them. The Fourteenth Amendment prohibits states from making or enforcing laws that "abridge the privileges or immunities of citizens of the *United States.*" Although this clause may have been intended to prevent states from infringing upon the substantive liberties guaranteed by the Bill of Rights, the Court has rejected this reading. Instead, it has limited applicability of the Fourteenth Amendment's privileges or immunities clause to instances when states infringe some right that is peculiar to federal citizenship. The most noteworthy such right is the right of interstate travel and migration. For more discussion, see Chapter 6, Section B.1 and Chapter 8, Section F.5. Article IV, section 2 states a nondiscrimination principle—states may not discriminate against nonresidents; the privileges afforded insiders must also be available to outsiders. But, as we shall see, this is not an absolute rule.

There is a great deal of duplication between Article IV, section 2 and both the commerce clause and the equal protection clause of the Fourteenth Amendment, but the coverage is by no means coterminous. One aspect of equal protection is the presumptive invalidity of laws that penalize exercise of the implied constitutionally fundamental right of interstate migration—or right to travel. In Zobel v. Williams, 457 U.S. 55 (1982), the Court used this branch of equal protection to strike down an Alaska law that gave cash grants to Alaskans in amounts that varied by length of residency in Alaska. Justice O'Connor, concurring in the judgment, argued that "the plan denies non-Alaskans settling in the State the same privileges afforded longer-term residents" and urged that Article IV, section 2 analysis, rather than equal protection, should be used to assess the validity of this and other "'right to travel' claims."

There are at least five major differences between Article IV, section 2 and dormant commerce clause doctrine. (1) Corporations may bring commerce clause challenges but are not "citizens" for purposes of the privileges and immunities clause and thus are not protected by it. See Paul v. Virginia,

75 U.S. (8 Wall.) 168 (1869). (2) The privileges and immunities clause protects only certain rights that are "fundamental to the promotion of interstate harmony." By contrast, the dormant commerce clause applies to all interstate commercial activity. (3) There is no market participant exception to Article IV's privileges and immunities clause. (4) Congress cannot consent to state acts that violate the privileges and immunities clause, but it can consent to state regulation of interstate commerce that would otherwise violate the dormant commerce clause. Congress can no more waive the privileges and immunities clause than it can waive a state's violation of free speech or equal protection. However, because Congress has plenary power to regulate interstate commerce, it can permit states to regulate interstate commerce in ways they could not in the absence of congressional exercise of its commerce power. See Section C, infra. (5) The standard of review used in privileges and immunities cases is "intermediate" — more exacting than *Pike* balancing but not as stern as strict scrutiny.

United Building & Construction Trades Council v. City of Camden
465 U.S. 208 (1984)

JUSTICE REHNQUIST delivered the opinion of the Court.

A municipal ordinance of the city of Camden, New Jersey requires that at least 40% of the employees of contractors and subcontractors working on city construction projects be Camden residents. [Camden adopted the ordinance in 1980 pursuant to a New Jersey program setting hiring goals for racial minorities on public works projects.] Appellant, the United Building and Construction Trades Council of Camden and Vicinity (the Council), challenges that ordinance as a violation of the [Article IV, section 2] Privileges and Immunities Clause. [Council also argued that the hiring preference violated the commerce clause, but dropped that claim when the U.S. Supreme Court decided White v. Massachusetts Const. Council, in which the Court sustained a substantially identical hiring preference against a commerce clause attack. Because the Massachusetts Supreme Judicial Court in *White* had not decided the privileges and immunities issue, the Supreme Court also declined to decide that issue in *White*.] The [New Jersey] Supreme Court rejected [the] privileges and immunities attack on the ground that the ordinance discriminates on the basis of municipal, not state, residency. . . . We conclude that the challenged ordinance is properly subject to the strictures of the Clause. We therefore reverse [and] remand the case for a determination of the validity of the ordinance under the appropriate constitutional standard.

[We] first address the argument [that] the Clause does not even apply to a *municipal* ordinance such as this. Two separate contentions are advanced in support of this position: first, that the Clause only applies to laws passed by a *State* and, second, that the Clause only applies to laws that discriminate on the basis of *state* citizenship. The first argument can be quickly rejected.

[A] municipality is merely a political subdivision of the State from which its authority derives. It is as true of the Privileges and Immunities Clause as of the Equal Protection Clause that what would be unconstitutional if done directly by the State can no more readily be accomplished by a city deriving its authority from the State. Thus, even if the ordinance had been adopted solely by Camden, and not pursuant to a state program or with state approval, the hiring preference would still have to comport with the Privileges and Immunities Clause.

The second argument merits more consideration. The New Jersey Supreme Court concluded that the Privileges and Immunities Clause does not apply to an ordinance that discriminates solely on the basis of *municipal* residency. The Clause is phrased in terms of *state* citizenship and was designed "to place the citizens of each State upon the same footing with citizens of other States, so far as the advantages resulting from citizenship in those States are concerned." Paul v. Virginia, [75 U.S.] 8 Wall. 168 (1869). "The primary purpose of this clause, like the clauses between which it is located—those relating to full faith and credit and to interstate extradition of fugitives from justice—was to help fuse into one Nation a collection of independent, sovereign States. It was designed to insure to a citizen of State A who ventures into State B the same privileges which the citizens of State B enjoy. For protection of such equality the citizen of State A was not to be restricted to the uncertain remedies afforded by diplomatic processes and official retaliation." Toomer v. Witsell, 334 U.S. 385 (1948). Municipal residency classifications, it is argued, simply do not give rise to the same concerns.

We cannot accept this argument. We have never read the Clause so literally as to apply it only to distinctions based on state citizenship. [Despite] some initial uncertainty, it is now established that the terms "citizen" and "resident" are "essentially interchangeable" for purposes of analysis of most cases under the Privileges and Immunities Clause. A person who is not residing in a given State is ipso facto not residing in a city within that State. Thus, whether the exercise of a privilege is conditioned on state residency or on municipal residency he will just as surely be excluded.[17] . . .

---

17. The dissent suggests that New Jersey citizens not residing in Camden will adequately protect the interests of out-of-state residents and that the scope of the Privileges and Immunities Clause should be measured in light of this political reality. What the dissent fails to appreciate is that the Camden ordinance at issue in this case was adopted pursuant to a comprehensive, state-wide program applicable in all New Jersey cities. The Camden resident-preference ordinance has already received state sanction and approval, and every New Jersey city is free to adopt a similar protectionist measure. Some have already done so. Thus, it is hard to see how New Jersey residents living outside Camden will protect the interests of out-of-state citizens. More fundamentally, the dissent's proposed blanket exemption for all classifications that are less than state-wide would provide States with a simple means for evading the strictures of the Privileges and Immunities Clause. Suppose, for example, that California wanted to guarantee that all employees of contractors and subcontractors working on construction projects funded in whole or in part by state funds are state residents. Under the dissent's analysis, the California legislature need merely divide the State in half, providing one resident-hiring preference for Northern Californians on all such projects taking place in Northern California, and one for

Application of the Privileges and Immunities Clause to a particular instance of discrimination against out-of-state residents entails a two-step inquiry. As an initial matter, the court must decide whether the ordinance burdens one of those privileges and immunities protected by the Clause. Not all forms of discrimination against citizens of other States are constitutionally suspect. "Some distinctions between residents and nonresidents merely reflect the fact that this is a Nation composed of individual States, and are permitted; other distinctions are prohibited because they hinder the formation, the purpose, or the development of a single Union of those States. Only with respect to those 'privileges' and 'immunities' bearing upon the vitality of the Nation as a single entity must the State treat all citizens, resident and nonresident, equally." [Baldwin v. Montana Fish & Game Commission, 436 U.S. 371 (1978), in which the Court rejected a privileges and immunities attack on Montana's practice of charging nonresidents substantially higher elk-hunting license fees than Montanans because recreational "elk hunting by nonresidents in Montana is not" a fundamental privilege or immunity.] As a threshold matter, then, we must determine whether an out-of-state resident's interest in employment on public works contracts in another State is sufficiently "fundamental" to the promotion of interstate harmony so as to "fall within the purview of the Privileges and Immunities Clause." Id.

Certainly, the pursuit of a common calling is one of the most fundamental of those privileges protected by the Clause. . . . Public employment, however, is qualitatively different from employment in the private sector; it is a subspecies of the broader opportunity to pursue a common calling. We have held that there is no fundamental right to government employment for purposes of the Equal Protection Clause. Massachusetts v. Murgia, 427 U.S. 307 (1976). Cf. McCarthy v. Philadelphia Civil Service Comm'n, 424 U.S. 645 (1976) (rejecting equal protection challenge to municipal residency requirement for municipal workers). And in *White* we held that for purposes of the Commerce Clause everyone employed on a city public works project is, "in a substantial if informal sense, 'working for the city.'"

It can certainly be argued that for purposes of the Privileges and Immunities Clause everyone affected by the Camden ordinance is also "working for the city" and, therefore, has no grounds for complaint when the city favors its own residents. But we decline to transfer mechanically into this context an analysis fashioned to fit the Commerce Clause. Our decision in *White* turned on a distinction between the city acting as a market participant and the city acting as a market regulator. The question whether employees of contractors and subcontractors on public works projects were or were not, in some sense, working for the city was crucial to that analysis. [But] the

---

Southern Californians on all projects taking place in Southern California. State residents generally would benefit from the law at the expense of out-of-state residents; yet, the law would be immune from scrutiny under the Clause simply because it was not phrased in terms of *state* citizenship or residency. Such a formalistic construction would effectively write the Clause out of the Constitution.

distinction between market participant and market regulator relied upon in *White* to dispose of the Commerce Clause challenge is not dispositive in this context. The two Clauses have different aims and set different standards for state conduct.

The Commerce Clause acts as an implied restraint upon state regulatory powers. Such powers must give way before the superior authority of Congress to legislate on (or leave unregulated) matters involving interstate commerce. When the State acts solely as a market participant, no conflict between state regulation and federal regulatory authority can arise. The Privileges and Immunities Clause, on the other hand, imposes a direct restraint on state action in the interests of interstate harmony. Hicklin v. Orbeck, 437 U.S. 518 (1978).[18] This concern with comity cuts across the market regulator-market participant distinction that is crucial under the Commerce Clause. It is discrimination against out-of-state residents on matters of fundamental concern which triggers the Clause, not regulation affecting interstate commerce. Thus, the fact that Camden is merely setting conditions on its expenditures for goods and services in the marketplace does not preclude the possibility that those conditions violate the Privileges and Immunities Clause. [The] fact that Camden is expending its own funds or funds it administers in accordance with the terms of a grant is certainly a factor—perhaps the crucial factor—to be considered in evaluating whether the statute's discrimination violates the Privileges and Immunities Clause. But it does not remove the Camden ordinance completely from the purview of the Clause.

In sum, Camden may, without fear of violating the Commerce Clause, pressure private employers engaged in public works projects funded in whole or in part by the city to hire city residents. But that same exercise of power to bias the employment decisions of private contractors [against] out-of-state residents may be called to account under the Privileges and Immunities Clause. A determination of whether a privilege is "fundamental" for purposes of that Clause does not depend on whether the employees of private contractors [engaged] in public works projects can or cannot be said to be "working for the city." The opportunity to seek employment with such private employers is "sufficiently basic to the livelihood of the Nation" [*Baldwin*] as to fall within the purview of the Privileges and Immunities Clause even though the contractors [are] themselves engaged in projects funded in whole or part by the city.

The conclusion that Camden's ordinance discriminates against a protected privilege does not, of course, end the inquiry. We have stressed in prior cases that "[l]ike many other constitutional provisions, the privileges

---

18. In *Hicklin*, the Court voided Alaska's "Alaska Hire" law, which required that preference be given to Alaskans in hiring for certain oil industry jobs. This attempt to "bias [private] employment practices in favor of [Alaska] residents" violated the Privileges and Immunities clause because Alaska failed to prove "that nonresidents were 'a peculiar source of the evil' [the law addressed:] Alaska's 'uniquely high unemployment.'" In short, the discriminatory Alaska Hire law was not substantially related to a particular harm inflicted by nonresidents.—Ed.

and immunities clause is not an absolute." [Toomer v. Witsell.] It does not preclude discrimination against citizens of other States where there is a "substantial reason" for the difference in treatment. "[T]he inquiry in each case must be concerned with whether such reasons do exist and whether the degree of discrimination bears a close relation to them." Ibid. As part of any justification offered for the discriminatory law, nonresidents must somehow be shown to "constitute a peculiar source of the evil at which the statute is aimed." Id.

The city of Camden contends that its ordinance is necessary to counteract grave economic and social ills. Spiralling unemployment, a sharp decline in population, and a dramatic reduction in the number of businesses located in the city have eroded property values and depleted the city's tax base. The resident hiring preference is designed, the city contends, to increase the number of employed persons living in Camden and to arrest the "middle class flight" currently plaguing the city. The city also argues that all non-Camden residents employed on city public works projects, whether they reside in New Jersey or Pennsylvania, constitute a "source of the evil at which the statute is aimed." That is, they "live off" Camden without "living in" Camden. Camden contends that the scope of the discrimination practiced in the ordinance, with its municipal residency requirement, is carefully tailored to alleviate this evil without unreasonably harming nonresidents, who still have access to 60% of the available positions.

Every inquiry under the Privileges and Immunities Clause "must [be] conducted with due regard for the principle that the states should have considerable leeway in analyzing local evils and in prescribing appropriate cures." [*Toomer.*] This caution is particularly appropriate when a government body is merely setting conditions on the expenditure of funds it controls. The Alaska Hire statute at issue in Hicklin v. Orbeck swept within its strictures not only contractors [dealing] directly with the State's oil and gas; it also covered suppliers who provided goods and services to those [contractors]. We invalidated the Act as "an attempt to force virtually all businesses that benefit in some way from the economic ripple effect of Alaska's decision to develop its oil and gas resources to bias their employment practices in favor of the State's residents." No similar "ripple effect" appears to infect the Camden ordinance. It is limited in scope to employees working directly on city public works projects.

Nonetheless, we find it impossible to evaluate Camden's justification on the record as it now stands. No trial has ever been held in the case. No findings of fact have been made. The Supreme Court of New Jersey certified the case for direct appeal after the brief administrative proceedings that led to approval of the ordinance by the State Treasurer. It would not be appropriate for this Court either to make factual determinations as an initial matter or to take judicial notice of Camden's decay. We, therefore, deem it wise to remand the case to the New Jersey Supreme Court [to] decide, consistent with state procedures, on the best method for making the necessary findings.

. . . Reversed and Remanded.

NOTES AND PROBLEMS

1. Scope. The privileges and immunities clause prevents a state from treating citizens of other states differently from the way it treats its own citizens unless there is some very good reason for doing so. In Paul v. Virginia, 75 U.S. (8 Wall.) 168 (1869), Justice Stephen Field wrote for a unanimous Court:

[T]he object of the clause [was] to place the citizens of each State upon the same footing with citizens of other States, so far as the advantages resulting from citizenship in those States are concerned. It relieves them from the disabilities of alienage in other States; it inhibits discriminating legislation against them by other States; it gives them the right of free ingress into other States, and egress from them; it insures to them in other States the same freedom possessed by the citizens of those States in the acquisition and enjoyment of property and in the pursuit of happiness. [But] the privileges and immunities secured to citizens of each State in the several States [are] those privileges and immunities which are common to the citizens in the latter States under their constitution and laws by virtue of their being citizens. Special privileges enjoyed by citizens in their own States are not secured in other States by [the Clause]. It was not intended . . . to give to the laws of one State any operation in other States. [Special privileges] must, therefore, be enjoyed at home, unless the assent of other States to their enjoyment therein be given.

A similar observation was made by Justices Roberts and Black in Hague v. CIO, 307 U.S. 496, 511 (1939):

At one time it was thought that this section recognized a group [of] "natural rights"; and that the purpose of the section was to create rights of citizens of the United States by guaranteeing the citizens of every State the recognition of this group of rights by every other State. Such was the view of Justice Washington [in Corfield v. Coryell (see Note 2, infra)]. [But] it has come to be the settled view that Article IV, §2, does not [mean] that a citizen of one State carries with him into another fundamental privileges and immunities which come to him necessarily by the mere fact of his citizenship in the State first mentioned, but, on the contrary, that in any State every citizen of any other State is to have the same privileges and immunities which the citizens of that State enjoy. The section, in effect, prevents a State from discriminating against citizens of other States in favor of its own.

2. What's Fundamental? The Court often says that the privileges and immunities protected by Article IV are limited to certain "fundamental" rights. There is no unitary concept of "fundamental" rights in constitutional law. What is fundamental to a decent and good life (e.g., good health, education, an adequate income) is not necessarily fundamental as a matter of *constitutional right*. And what is fundamental for purposes of "substantive" due process (see Chapter 6) is not the same as what is fundamental for equal protection purposes (see Chapter 8). The fundamental rights protected as privileges and immunities by Article IV, section 2 differ from any of the foregoing. They consist of interests that are fundamental to the promotion of interstate harmony or to the maintenance and well-being of the nation. In practice, this boils down to the right to prevent a state from imposing unreasonable burdens on citizens of other states in (1) seeking a job, or, as the Court put it in Austin v. New Hampshire, 420 U.S. 656 (1975), "all the privileges of trade and commerce"; (2) the ownership and disposition of privately held property within the state (Blake v. McClung, 172 U.S. 239 (1898)); and (3) access to a state's courts (Canadian Northern Railway Co. v. Eggen, 252 U.S. 553 (1920)).

Privileges and immunities need not be so restricted. In Corfield v. Coryell, 6 Fed. Cas. 546 (No. 3230) (C.C.E.D. Pa. 1823), Justice Bushrod Washington (George Washington's nephew, appointed by John Adams), sitting as a circuit judge, declared that the privileges and immunities protected by Article IV include all rights that are

> *fundamental*, which belong of right to the citizens of all free [governments]. What these fundamental principles are, it would be more tedious than difficult to enumerate. They may all, however, be comprehended under the following general heads: protection by the government, with the right to acquire and possess property of every kind, and to pursue and obtain happiness and safety, subject, nevertheless, to such restraints as the government may prescribe for the general good of the whole.

This expansive view was rejected in Paul v. Virginia, insofar as it might have required a state to observe rights that were unique to some other state and unrecognized in the host state. But in Baldwin v. Montana Fish & Game Commission, 436 U.S. 371 (1978), the Court indicated that its precedents are best understood in light of Justice Bushrod Washington's approach to the problem:

> [Nothing convinces] us that we should completely reject the Court's earlier decisions. [In] *Coryell*, Mr. Justice Washington['s] list of situations in which [the] States would be obligated to treat each other's residents equally [included] only those where a nonresident sought to engage in an essential activity or exercise a basic right. [The] Court invoked the same principle in [*Paul* and later cases]. With respect to such basic and essential activities, interference with which would frustrate the purposes of the formation of the Union, the States must treat residents and nonresidents without unnecessary distinctions.

3. Citizenship and Residency: Truly Equivalent?   The Court says in *Camden* that "the terms 'citizen' and 'resident' are 'essentially interchangeable' for purposes of analysis" under the privileges and immunities clause of Article IV. Why should this be so? Citizenship and residency are surely not interchangeable for every purpose, as any lawful resident alien can tell you on election day. Does the interchangeability of the terms depend on the purposes behind Article IV's privileges and immunities clause?

4. The Standard of Review.   States may discriminate against outsiders if they can prove that there is a "substantial reason" for differential treatment. To do so, a state must prove (1) a substantial relationship between the discriminatory practice and the problem the law addresses, and (2) a lack of workable less discriminatory alternatives to achieve the state's goal.

The Court has described the first element as a requirement that non-residents must be shown to "constitute a peculiar source of the evil at which the statute is aimed." Toomer v. Witsell, 334 U.S. 385 (1948). For example, a state's refusal to let citizens of another state vote or hold elective office is defensible because outsider participation destroys the very idea of a discrete polity. In *Baldwin*, the Court noted that

> [suffrage] always has been understood to be tied to an individual's identification with a particular State. No one would suggest that the Privileges and Immunities Clause requires a State to open its polls to a person who declines to assert that the State is the only one where he claims a right to vote. The same is true as to qualification for an elective office of the State. Kanapaux v. Ellisor, 419 U.S. 891 (1974).

The remaining element is vividly illustrated by *Toomer*. South Carolina imposed a $25 license fee for commercial shrimp boats owned by South Carolinians and a $2,500 fee for commercial shrimp boats owned by non-residents. South Carolina argued that the differential was justified because it conserved shrimp and defrayed the cost of South Carolina's specific shrimp conservation measures attributable to outside fishing. The Court struck down the law, finding no evidence in the record "that non-residents use larger boats or different fishing methods than residents, or that any substantial amount of the State's general funds is devoted to shrimp conservation." South Carolina could have charged fees based on boat size or even a fee calculated to equalize the burden of conservation expenses between inside and outside users of the fishery.

5. Problems.   On remand, the *Camden* case settled. If it had not, could the city of Camden have adequately justified its hiring preference? Construct the argument.

Every state charges nonresidents higher public university tuition fees than residents are charged. Does this facially discriminatory practice violate the dormant commerce clause? Regardless of your answer to that question, does this practice violate Article IV, section 2's privileges and immunities clause? Construct the arguments for both sides of the issue.

C.   PREEMPTION AND CONSENT: CONGRESS HAS THE FINAL WORD

Recall that the dormant commerce clause applies only when Congress has not exercised its power to regulate interstate commerce by preempting state law or consenting to state regulation. When Congress so exercises its commerce power, the commerce clause is very much alive and awake. When Congress has not used its commerce power, state regulation of interstate commerce may be challenged under the *dormant* commerce clause. When Congress has affirmatively used its commerce power to preempt state law, state regulation of interstate commerce may be challenged on the ground that it has been *preempted* by the congressional regulation.

When an act of Congress displaces state authority, it preempts state law on the subject; the law imposes new limits on state power. Congress can also use its commerce power to remove preexisting limits on state regulatory power, limits that the courts find to be implied in the commerce clause. Subsection 1 examines preemption, and Subsection 2 examines the ability of Congress to remove the implied limits of the dormant commerce clause — in effect, to consent to state regulation of interstate commerce that in the absence of congressional action would be forbidden by the dormant commerce clause.

1. Preemption

The supremacy clause (Art. VI, cl. 2) makes valid federal law supreme, thus displacing or preempting contrary state law. The supremacy clause, however, does not specify the scope of preemption. Judicial doctrine has filled that gap.

It is extremely important to remember that preemption may apply *whenever Congress validly legislates.* Preemption is not a doctrine that is unique to the commerce power. Preemption is discussed in this section because it is particularly involved in questions of the dormant commerce clause. Don't make the mistake of thinking that preemption applies only when Congress uses its commerce power. It applies when any federal power is validly exercised.

Courts presume that when Congress acts it does not intend to preempt state law. Where it does manifest such intent, however, it does so either expressly or by implication. Express preemption requires explicit preemptive language in a federal law that defines the existence and scope of the preemption. Implied preemption can take either of two forms: "field preemption" or "conflict preemption."

Field preemption occurs when federal law leaves no doubt that Congress has intended by its legislation to occupy an entire field, such that even without a federal rule on some particular activity within the field, state regulation of that activity is preempted, leaving the activity unregulated by either state or federal law. This implied intent of Congress can be detected in several ways: (1) when federal regulation of a field is so pervasive as to make reasonable the inference that Congress intended to displace state regulatory authority; (2) when the federal law touches a field in which the federal interest is so dominant that the federal system is assumed to preclude enforcement of state laws on the same subject (e.g., immigration and nationality); or (3) when the object sought to be obtained by the federal law and the character of obligations imposed by it reveal a congressional intent fully to occupy the field. Courts are apt to construe the field that is occupied fairly narrowly to avoid the possibility of a regulatory vacuum: preclusion of state regulation but the absence of federal regulation.

An example of this in the context of pervasive regulation is PG&E v. State Energy Resources Conservation & Development Commission, 461 U.S. 190 (1983). The Court concluded that through the Atomic Energy Act Congress intended to occupy the field of the "safety aspects involved in the construction and operation of a nuclear plant." The Act's regulatory scheme was pervasive as to safety but regulated not at all as to the pricing of nuclear power. Thus California's refusal to license new nuclear plants until there existed a demonstrated nuclear waste disposal method was not preempted because the licensing requirement was a device to protect California utility rate payers from exposure to the open-ended costs of uncertain disposal methods.

Conflict preemption occurs in one of two ways. The first is when compliance with both state and federal law is literally impossible. In McDermott v. Wisconsin, 228 U.S. 115 (1913), the Court found implied "impossibility" conflict preemption in the Federal Food and Drugs Act of 1906 (which required specific labels on syrup) when Wisconsin law required labeling of syrup that would cause syrup sold in compliance with Wisconsin law to be misbranded under the federal law. The second form of implied conflict preemption is when a state law "stands as an obstacle to the accomplishment and execution of the full purposes and objectives of Congress." Hines v. Davidowitz, 312 U.S. 52 (1941).

If state law discourages behavior that federal law specifically encourages, "obstacle" conflict preemption is likely to be found. In Nash v. Florida Industrial Commission, 389 U.S. 235 (1967), the Court ruled that a Florida law refusing unemployment benefits to any person unemployed as a result of a labor dispute, as applied to a person fired because she had filed federal unfair labor practice charges, was preempted because the Florida law was an obstacle to the federal objectives of encouraging compliance with and ensuring enforcement of federal labor laws. But "obstacle" conflict preemption will not be found simply because state law is in "general tension with broad or abstract goals that may be attributed to various federal laws or programs." Laurence Tribe, American Constitutional Law 487 (2d ed. 1988). In Commonwealth Edison Co. v. Montana, 453 U.S. 609 (1981), the Court found no preemption of Montana's high severance tax on coal removed from the ground, even though the tax made coal more costly to the user and several federal laws expressed a general federal purpose to encourage coal use.

≡
Gade v. National Solid Wastes Management Association
505 U.S. 88 (1992)

JUSTICE O'CONNOR announced the judgment of the Court and delivered an opinion, Parts I, III, and IV of which represent the views of the Court, and Part II of which is joined by CHIEF JUSTICE REHNQUIST and JUSTICES WHITE and SCALIA.

In 1988, the Illinois General Assembly enacted [two licensing acts pertaining to workers involved in handling hazardous wastes]. The stated purpose of the acts is both "to promote job safety" and "to protect life, limb and property." [We] consider whether these "dual impact" statutes, which protect both workers and the general public, are pre-empted by the federal Occupational Safety and Health Act of 1970 (OSH Act), and the standards promulgated thereunder by the Occupational Safety and Health Administration (OSHA).

I. [OSHA] promulgated . . . detailed regulations on [hazardous waste] worker training requirements. [The] OSHA regulations require, among other things, that workers engaged in an activity that may expose them to hazardous wastes receive a minimum of 40 hours of instruction off the site, and a minimum of three days actual field experience under the supervision of a trained supervisor [and] eight hours of refresher training annually.

[In 1988] Illinois enacted the licensing acts at issue here. [Both] acts require a license applicant to provide a certified record of at least 40 hours of training under an approved program conducted within Illinois, to pass a written examination, and to complete an annual refresher course of at least eight hours of instruction. . . .

National Solid Wastes Management Association (the Association), [a] national trade association of businesses that remove, transport, dispose, and handle waste material, including hazardous waste, [sought] to enjoin [enforcement of] the Illinois licensing acts, claiming that the acts were preempted by the OSH Act and OSHA [regulations]. The District Court held that state laws that attempt to regulate workplace safety and health are not pre-empted by the OSH Act when the laws have a "legitimate and substantial purpose apart from promoting job safety." [The] Court of Appeals held that the OSH Act pre-empts all state law that "constitutes, in a direct, clear and substantial way, regulation of worker health and safety," unless the Secretary has explicitly approved the state law. [We] granted certiorari. . . . [The Court held that "dual impact" laws, designed to protect both worker and public health and safety, were preempted.]

II. [Opinion of JUSTICE O'CONNOR, joined by CHIEF JUSTICE REHNQUIST and JUSTICES WHITE and SCALIA] . . . "The question whether a certain state action is pre-empted by federal law is one of congressional intent. 'The purpose of Congress is the ultimate touchstone.'" Allis-Chalmers Corp. v. Lueck,

471 U.S. 202 (1985). "To discern Congress'[s] intent we examine the explicit statutory language and the structure and purpose of the statute." Ingersoll-Rand Co. v. McClendon, 498 U.S. 133 (1990).

In the OSH Act, Congress endeavored "to assure so far as possible every working man and woman in the Nation safe and healthful working conditions." To that end, Congress authorized the Secretary of Labor to set mandatory occupational safety and health standards applicable to all businesses affecting interstate commerce, and thereby brought the Federal Government into a field that traditionally had been occupied by the States. Federal regulation of the workplace was not intended to be all-encompassing, however. Section 18(a) [of the OSH Act] provides that the Act does not "prevent any State agency or court from asserting jurisdiction under State law over any occupational safety or health issue with respect to which no [federal] standard is in effect."

Congress not only reserved certain areas to state regulation, but it also, in §18(b) of the Act, gave the States the option of pre-empting federal regulation entirely [by creating an approved plan to establish and enforce occupational health and safety standards]. About half the States have received the Secretary's approval for their own state plans. . . . Illinois is not among them.

[The] Court of Appeals held that §18(b) "unquestionably" pre-empts any state law or regulation that establishes an occupational health and safety standard on an issue for which OSHA has already promulgated a standard, unless the State has obtained the Secretary's approval for its own plan. [We agree.]

Pre-emption may be either expressed or implied, and "is compelled whether Congress'[s] command is explicitly stated in the statute's language or implicitly contained in its structure and purpose." Jones v. Rath Packing Co., 430 U.S. 519 (1977). Absent explicit pre-emptive language, we have recognized at least two types of implied pre-emption: field pre-emption, where the scheme of federal regulation is "'so pervasive as to make reasonable the inference that Congress left no room for the States to supplement it,'" [Rice v. Santa Fe Elevator Corp., 331 U.S. 218 (1947)], and conflict pre-emption, where "compliance with both federal and state regulations is a physical impossibility," Florida Lime & Avocado Growers, Inc. v. Paul, 373 U.S. 132 (1963), or where state law "stands as an obstacle to the accomplishment and execution of the full purposes and objectives of Congress." Hines v. Davidowitz, 312 U.S. 52 (1941).

Our ultimate task in any pre-emption case is to determine whether state regulation is consistent with the structure and purpose of the statute as a whole. Looking to "the provisions of the whole law, and to its object and policy," we hold that nonapproved state regulation of occupational safety and health issues for which a federal standard is in effect is impliedly pre-empted as in conflict with the full purposes and objectives of the OSH Act. The design of the statute persuades us that Congress intended to subject employers and employees to only one set of regulations, be it federal or state, and that the only way a State may regulate an OSHA-regulated occupational safety and health issue is pursuant to an approved state plan that displaces the federal standards. The principal indication that Congress intended to pre-empt state law is §18(b)'s statement that a State "shall" submit a plan if it wishes to "assume responsibility" for "development and enforcement [of] occupational safety and health standards relating to any occupational safety or health issue with respect to which a Federal standard has been promulgated." The unavoidable implication of this provision is that a State may not enforce its own occupational safety and health standards without obtaining the Secretary's [approval]. Petitioner contends, however, that an approved plan is necessary only if the State wishes completely to replace the federal regulations, not merely to supplement them. She argues that the correct interpretation of §18(b) is that [a] State may either "oust" the federal standard by submitting a state plan to the Secretary for approval or "add to" the federal standard without seeking the Secretary's approval.

Petitioner's interpretation [is] not tenable in light of the OSH Act's surrounding provisions. [The] OSH Act as a whole evidences Congress'[s] intent to avoid subjecting workers and employers to duplicative regulation; a State may develop an occupational safety and health program tailored to its own needs, but only if it is willing completely to displace the applicable federal regulations.

Cutting against petitioner's interpretation of §18(b) is the language of §18(a), which saves from pre-emption any state law regulating an occupational safety and health issue with respect to which no federal standard is in effect. [Preservation] of state authority in the absence of a federal standard presupposes a background preemption of all state occupational safety and health standards whenever a federal standard governing the same issue is in effect. . . .

Our review of the Act persuades us that Congress sought to promote occupational safety and health while at the same time avoiding duplicative, and possibly counterproductive, regulation. It thus established a system of uniform federal occupational health and safety standards, but gave States the option of pre-empting federal regulations by developing their own occupational safety and health programs. [To] allow a State selectively to "supplement" certain federal regulations with ostensibly nonconflicting standards would be inconsistent with this federal scheme of establishing uniform federal standards, on the one hand, and encouraging States to assume full responsibility for development and enforcement of their own OSH programs, on the other.

We cannot accept petitioner's argument that the OSH Act does not pre-empt nonconflicting state laws because those laws, like the Act, are designed to promote worker safety. In determining whether state law "stands as an obstacle" to the full implementation of a federal law, "it is not enough to say that the ultimate goal of both federal and state law" is the same. "A state law also is pre-empted if it interferes with the methods by which the federal statute was designed to reach that goal." [International Paper Co. v. Ouellette, 479 U.S. 481 (1987).] The OSH Act does not foreclose a State from enacting its own laws to advance the goal of worker safety, but it does restrict the ways in which it can do so. If a State wishes to regulate an issue of worker safety for which a federal standard is in effect, its only option is to obtain the prior approval of the Secretary of Labor, as described in §18 of the Act.

III. [Opinion of the Court] Petitioner next argues that, even if Congress intended to pre-empt all nonapproved state occupational safety and health regulations whenever a federal standard is in effect, the OSH Act's pre-emptive effect should not be extended to state laws that address public safety as well as occupational safety concerns. [We] now consider whether a dual impact law can be an "occupational safety and health standard" subject to pre-emption under the Act.

The OSH Act defines an "occupational safety and health standard" as "a standard which requires conditions, or the adoption or use of one or more practices, means, methods, operations, or processes, reasonably necessary or appropriate to provide safe or healthful employment and places of employment." [Clearly], under this definition, a state law that expressly declares a legislative purpose of regulating occupational health and safety would, in the absence of an approved state plan, be pre-empted by an OSHA standard regulating the same subject matter. But petitioner asserts that if the state legislature articulates a purpose other than (or in addition to) workplace health and safety, then the OSH Act loses its pre-emptive force. We disagree.

Although "part of the pre-empted field is defined by reference to the purpose of the state law in question, [another] part of the field is defined by the state law's actual effect." [See, e.g., Pacific Gas & Electric Co. v. State Energy Resources Conservation and Development Commission, 461 U.S. 190 (1983).] In assessing the impact of a state law on the federal scheme, we have refused to rely solely on the legislature's professed purpose and have looked as well to the effects of the law. . . . "Any state legislation which frustrates the full effectiveness of federal law is rendered invalid by the Supremacy Clause." Perez v. Campbell, 402 U.S. 637 [(1971)].

[A] dual impact state regulation cannot avoid OSH Act pre-emption simply because the regulation serves several objectives rather than one. [Whatever] the purpose or purposes of the state law, pre-emption analysis cannot ignore the effect of the challenged state action on the pre-empted field. The key question is thus at what point the state regulation sufficiently interferes with federal regulation that it should be deemed pre-empted under the Act.

[The] Court of Appeals [held] that, in the absence of the approval of the Secretary, the OSH Act pre-empts all state law that "constitutes, in a direct, clear and substantial way, regulation of worker health and safety." We agree that this is the appropriate standard for determining OSH Act preemption. On the other hand, state laws of general applicability (such as laws regarding traffic safety or fire safety) that do not conflict with OSHA standards and that regulate the conduct of workers and non-workers alike would generally not be pre-empted. Although some laws of general applicability may have a "direct and substantial" effect on worker safety, they cannot fairly be characterized as "occupational" standards, because they regulate workers simply as members of the general public. In this case, we agree with the court below that a law directed at workplace safety is not saved from pre-emption simply because the State can demonstrate some additional effect outside of the workplace. . . .

[Affirmed.]

JUSTICE KENNEDY, concurring in part and concurring in the judgment.

[I] would find express pre-emption from the terms of the federal statute. I cannot agree that we should denominate this case as one of implied pre-emption. The contrary view of the plurality is based on an undue expansion of our implied pre-emption jurisprudence which [is] neither wise nor necessary. [Our] decisions establish that a high threshold must be met if a state law is to be pre-empted for conflicting with the purposes of a federal Act. Any conflict must be "irreconcilable; [the] existence of a hypothetical or potential conflict is insufficient to warrant the pre-emption of the state statute." Rice v. Norman Williams Co., 458 U.S. 654 (1982). In my view, this type of pre-emption should be limited to state laws which impose prohibitions or obligations which are in direct contradiction to Congress'[s] primary objectives, as conveyed with clarity in the federal legislation.

I do not believe that supplementary state regulation of an occupational safety and health issue can be said to create the sort of actual conflict required by our decisions. The purpose of state supplementary regulation, like the federal standards, is to protect worker safety and health. Any potential tension between a scheme of federal regulation of the workplace and a concurrent, supplementary state scheme would not, in my view, rise to the level of "actual conflict." [Absent] the express provisions of §18 [I] would not say that state supplementary regulation conflicts with the purposes of the OSH Act, or that it "interferes with the methods by which the federal statute was designed to reach [its] goal."

The plurality's broad view of actual conflict pre-emption is contrary to two basic principles of our pre-emption jurisprudence. First, we begin "with the assumption that the historic police powers of the States [are] not to be superseded [unless] that was the clear and manifest purpose of Congress." Rice v. Santa Fe Elevator Corp. Second, "'the purpose of Congress is the ultimate touchstone'" in all pre-emption cases. Malone v. White Motor Corp., 435 U.S. 497 (1978). A free-wheeling judicial inquiry into whether a state statute is in tension with federal objectives would undercut the principle that it is Congress rather than the courts that pre-empts state law.

[Preemption here] is mandated by the express terms of §18(b) of the OSH Act. It follows from this that the pre-emptive scope of the Act is also limited to the language of the statute. [A] finding of express pre-emption in this case is not contrary to our longstanding rule that we will not infer pre-emption of the States' historic police powers absent a clear statement of intent by Congress. Though most statutes creating express pre-emption contain an explicit statement to that effect, a statement admittedly lacking in §18(b), we have never required any particular magic words in our express pre-emption cases. Our task in all pre-emption cases is to enforce the "clear and manifest purpose of Congress." We have held, in express pre-emption cases, that Congress'[s] intent must be divined from the language, structure, and purposes of the statute as a whole. The language of the OSH statute sets forth a scheme in light of which the provisions of §18 must be interpreted, and from which the express pre-emption that displaces state law follows. [The] most reasonable inference from [the statutory] language is that when a State does not submit and secure approval of a state plan, it may not enforce occupational safety and health standards in that area. [Unartful] though the language of §18(b) may be, the structure and language of §18 leave little doubt that in the OSH statute Congress intended to pre-empt supplementary state regulation of an occupational safety and health issue with respect to which a federal standard exists. . . .

[The] necessary implication of finding express pre-emption in this case is that the pre-emptive scope of the OSH Act is defined by the language of §18(b). Because this provision requires federal approval of state occupational safety and health standards alone, only state laws fitting within that description are pre-empted. For that reason I agree with the Court that state laws of general applicability are not pre-empted. [So-called] "dual impact" state regulations which ["directly, substantially, and specifically" regulate occupational safety and health] are pre-empted by the OSH Act, regardless of any additional purpose the law may serve, or effect the law may have, outside the workplace. [I] therefore join all but Part II of the Court's opinion, and concur in the judgment of the Court.

JUSTICE SOUTER, joined by JUSTICES BLACKMUN, STEVENS, and THOMAS, dissenting.

[In] light of our rule that federal pre-emption of state law is only to be found in a clear congressional purpose to supplant exercises of the States' traditional police powers, the text of the Act fails to support the Court's conclusion.

I. [The] plurality today finds [conflict] pre-emption of [the] sort [that involves state law as an "obstacle to the accomplishment and execution of the full purposes and objectives of Congress"]. . . . As one commentator has observed, this kind of purpose-conflict pre-emption, which occurs when state law is held to "undermine a congressional decision in favor of national uniformity of standards," presents "a situation similar in practical effect to that of federal occupation of a field." L. Tribe, American Constitutional Law 486 (2d ed. 1988). Still, whether the pre-emption at issue is described as occupation of each narrow field in which a federal standard has been promulgated, as pre-emption of those regulations that conflict with the federal objective of single regulation, or, as [express] pre-emption, the key is congressional intent, and I find the language of the statute insufficient to demonstrate an intent to pre-empt state law in this way.

II. Analysis begins with the presumption that "Congress did not intend to displace state law." Maryland v. Louisiana, 451 U.S. 725 (1981). "Where [the] field which Congress is said to have pre-empted has been traditionally occupied by the States 'we start with the assumption that the historic police powers of the States were not to be superseded by the Federal Act unless that was the clear and manifest purpose of Congress.' [*Rice.*] This assumption provides assurance that the 'federal-state balance,' will not be disturbed unintentionally by Congress or unnecessarily by the courts. But when Congress has 'unmistakably . . . ordained,' that its enactments alone are to regulate a part of commerce, state laws regulating that aspect of commerce must fall." [Jones v. Rath Packing.] Subject to this principle, the enquiry into the possibly pre-emptive effect of federal legislation is an exercise of statutory construction. If the statute's terms can be read sensibly not to have a pre-emptive effect, the presumption controls and no pre-emption may be inferred.

III. . . . [S]ection 18(a) of the Act . . . simply rules out field pre-emption and is otherwise entirely compatible with the possibility that pre-emption will occur only when actual conflict between a federal regulation and a state rule renders compliance with both impossible. [Congress] intended no field pre-emption of the sphere of health and safety subject to regulation, but not necessarily regulated, under the Act. [The statute says that unlike] field pre-emption [absence] of a federal standard leaves a State free to do as it will on the issue. [The] provision is perfectly consistent with the conclusion that as long as compliance with both a federal standard and a state regulation is not physically impossible each standard shall be enforceable. [If] the presumption against pre-emption means anything, §18(a) must be read in just this way.

Respondent also relies on §18(b), [contending] that the necessary implication of this provision is clear: the only way that a state rule on a particular occupational safety and health issue may be enforced once a federal standard on the issue is also in place is by incorporating the state rule in a plan approved by the Secretary. [But] both the plurality and Justice Kennedy acknowledge [that] is not the necessary implication of §18(b). The subsection simply does not say that unless a plan is approved, state law on an issue is pre-empted by the promulgation of a federal standard. . . . [Nothing] in the provision's language speaks one way or the other to the question whether promulgation of a federal standard pre-empts state regulation, or whether, in the absence of a plan, consistent federal and state regulations may coexist. The provision thus makes perfect sense on the assumption that a dual regulatory scheme is permissible but subject to state pre-emption if the State wishes to shoulder enough of the federal mandate to gain approval of a plan.

Nor does the provision . . . indicate that a state regulation on an issue federally addressed is never enforceable unless incorporated in a plan so approved. [Respondent] argues, and the plurality concludes, that if state regulations were not pre-empted, [States] acting independently could enforce regulations [burdening] interstate commerce unduly. But this simply does not follow. . . . [It] is clearly a non sequitur to conclude . . . that pre-emption must have been intended to avoid the equally objectionable undue burden that independent state regulation might otherwise impose. Quite the contrary; the dormant Commerce Clause can take care of that, without any need to assume pre-emption. . . .

IV. In sum, our rule is that the traditional police powers of the State survive unless Congress has made a purpose to pre-empt them clear. The Act does not, in so many words, pre-empt all state regulation of issues on which federal standards have been promulgated. [Each statutory] provision can be read consistently with the others without any implication of pre-emptive intent. They are in fact just as consistent with a purpose and objective to permit overlapping state and federal regulation as with one to guarantee that employers and employees would be subjected to only one regulatory regime. Restriction to one such regime by precluding supplemental state regulation might or might not be desirable. But in the absence of any clear expression of congressional intent to pre-empt, I can only conclude that, as long as compliance with federally promulgated standards does not render obedience to Illinois' regulations impossible, the enforcement of the state law is not prohibited by the Supremacy Clause. I respectfully dissent.

NOTES

1. Preemption and the Commerce Clause. Preemption can occur when Congress uses any of its constitutional sources of legislative power, not just under the commerce power. Whereas preemption is always a matter of correctly ascertaining congressional intent, when Congress uses its commerce power and a preemption problem is raised, resolution of the problem involves, in theory, some of the same considerations that are present in dormant commerce clause cases. A finding of implied preemption forecloses the state regulation at issue, and places on the state the burden of obtaining legislation from Congress that permits the state regulation. A finding of field preemption is much like the old *Cooley* test of identifying those commercial activities that are "inherently national" and thus exclusively reserved for federal regulation. Activities outside the occupied field are analogous to the *Cooley* notion of activities that are "inherently local" and thus permissible for states to regulate. And a finding of "obstacle" conflict preemption is analogous to the *Pike* balancing process—a weighing of federal and local interests.

Recall that the Court presumes that preemption is not intended, at least with respect to subjects "traditionally" left to state control. This presumption in favor of state regulation is roughly akin to *Pike* balancing's presumption in favor of the validity of state regulation that is evenhanded and incidentally affects interstate commerce. However, to repeat, there is always a question of determining whether Congress intended preemption when it acted. The balancing concerns suggested here are not part of the doctrinal approach to preemption, but they exist nonetheless. Should the Court take these concerns into account explicitly when it grapples with implied preemption cases?

2. The Presumption Against Preemption: Observed in the Breach? The Court continues to recite that there is a presumption against preemption when Congress regulates an activity that has "traditionally" been a subject of state regulation. But observe what it has done in recent years.

Geier v. American Honda Motor Co., 529 U.S. 861 (2000), involved a claim by Geier, a Honda driver injured in an auto accident, that Honda was negligent in manufacturing an auto without an air bag. Honda claimed that its compliance with an interim Department of Transportation regulation that required it to equip some of its models (but not Geier's) with air bags insulated it from liability by reason of the regulation's preemption of state tort law. The Court agreed with Honda and applied obstacle-conflict preemption because the Department of Transportation had as its objective a gradual phasing in of air bags, an objective that would be frustrated by a state's imposition of tort liability on an auto manufacturer that complied with the standard by manufacturing a vehicle without an air bag.

Should it make any difference that the federal objective identified by the Court in *Geier* was an agency objective, not a congressional objective? Should an unequivocally clear statement of agency intent to preempt be required? Justice Stevens so argued in his dissent in *Geier*, noting that "[u]nlike Congress, administrative agencies are clearly not designed to represent the interests of States, yet with relative ease they can promulgate comprehensive and detailed regulations that have broad preemption ramifications for state law." Should preemption implied from an agency regulation be especially disfavored on the theory that agency administrators are politically unaccountable and concerned primarily about their narrow bailiwick, but members of Congress are politically accountable?

Finally, is there reason to wonder whether the entire category of "implied obstacle conflict preemption" is really warranted? See Nelson, Preemption, 86 Va. L. Rev. 225, 231-232 (2000): "[The Supremacy Clause supports preemption] if and only if state law contradicts a valid rule established by federal law, and the mere fact that the federal law serves certain purposes does not automatically mean that it contradicts everything that might get in the way of those purposes."

In a field preemption case, the entire inquiry is to decide whether what Congress has done is sufficiently pervasive to constitute an implicit declaration that no other regulation of the area is to be allowed. An important part of this inquiry is to identify the boundaries of the field. Should the presumption against preemption be retained as a device to hem in the field boundaries and prevent judges from deciding that the field is so vast as to be virtually limitless? Or is it appropriate to discard the presumption as soon as Congress embarks upon significant valid regulation, on the theory that Congress is occupying the field and the degree of that occupation should be resolved in favor of federal power? Note that field preemption can produce a regulatory vacuum when the federal scheme (which totally displaces state power to regulate in the field) fails to address some particular point that may be of concern to a state. Of course, Congress can correct that oversight, but it may be disinclined to do so if the vacuum is of consequence only to a tiny minority of states.

3. Wyeth v. Levine and Justice Thomas's View of Preemption. Diana Levine, a professional musician who played bass, guitar, and piano, entered a Vermont emergency room to receive Demerol, a pain-killer, to treat a severe migraine headache. Because Demerol also induced nausea in Levine, she also received Phenergan, an anti-nausea drug manufactured by Wyeth. Normally Phenergan was administered by injection, but Levine received Phenergan intravenously through the "IV-push" method. As a result Levine developed gangrene, and her forearm was amputated. A Vermont jury awarded Levine substantial damages after concluding that Wyeth had caused the injury by its failure to provide an adequate warning about the significant risks of administering Phenergan by the IV-push method. Wyeth contended that Levine's failure-to-warn claim was preempted by federal law because Phenergan's labeling had been approved by the federal Food and Drug Administration (FDA). In Wyeth v. Levine, 555 U.S. 555 (2009), the Supreme Court held that Levine's claim was not preempted. It was possible for Wyeth to comply with both Vermont's duty to warn and the FDA's labeling requirements because under federal law Wyeth retained the power to make unilateral changes to its label to strengthen its warnings. There was inadequate evidence that Congress intended to confer upon the FDA the power to exercise exclusive control of drug labeling because the only indication of such an intent was in a preamble to the operative statute.

Justice Thomas concurred in the judgment [but noted that] "I can no longer assent to a doctrine that pre-empts state laws merely because they 'stan[d] as an obstacle to the accomplishment and execution of the full purposes and objectives' of federal law as perceived by this Court."

A similar issue arose in Pliva, Inc. v. Mensing, 131 S. Ct. 2567 (2011). Long-term use of a generic drug, metoclopramide, has been linked to a severe neurological disorder. States began to require warning labels for the drug that were more stringent than those mandated by the Food and Drug Administration for Reglan, the brand-name version of metoclopramide. The FDA's rules limit the labeling of generic drugs to the same labels approved and required for the brand-name version. However, the FDA permits brand-name drug manufacturers to change the label for the brand-name drug in order to strengthen its warnings. It was this rule that caused the Court in *Wyeth* to conclude that the state laws at issue in that case were not preempted, because the manufacturer of a brand-name drug could comply with both federal and state law. However illogical it may be, the FDA does not permit manufacturers of generic drugs to deviate unilaterally from the approved brand-name label, thus creating a situation in which the manufacturer of Reglan could change its label to conform to state law but the manufacturers of metoclopramide, the generic version of Reglan, could not do so without FDA approval. Thus, the Court, in an opinion by Justice Thomas, ruled that the state laws were preempted because it was impossible to comply with both federal and state law. The Court noted that Congress and the FDA could correct this anomaly. In Mutual Insurance Company v. Bartlett, 133 S. Ct. 2466 (2013), the Court, 5-4, extended *Pliva* to find that state law claims of failure to warn of severe risks associated with a generic drug are preempted by the Food and Drug Act. Congress was again invited to change the law.

4. Preemption and Immigration. In Chamber of Commerce v. Whiting, 131 S. Ct. 1968 (2011), the Supreme Court upheld an Arizona law that revoked the business licenses of businesses that knowingly hire a person unlawfully present in the United States. The law also required Arizona employers to use the federal E-Verify system to determine if an applicant is lawfully present. Federal law prohibits employers from knowingly hiring persons unlawfully present in the country. The federal government made E-Verify available throughout the country for voluntary use by employers. The federal law that prohibits the knowing hire of illegal aliens expressly preempts "any State or local law imposing civil or criminal sanctions (other than through licensing and similar laws) upon those who employ . . . unauthorized aliens." The Court concluded that the Arizona law was within the exception and thus neither expressly or impliedly preempted. Although federal law forbids the federal government from mandating use of E-Verify it is silent on whether the states may do so. The Court found no implied preemption of Arizona's mandate that E-Verify be used because federal law is silent on the point and the federal government had authorized and promoted the use of E-Verify as a reliable means to determine an applicant's immigration status. There was no "impossibility" conflict with federal law and the Arizona law was in harmony with the federal government's objectives in creating E-Verify—to increase reliable determinations of immigration status.

Problem: California law permits persons who have attended a California high school for three years and who are unlawful residents of the United States to pay in-state tuition while denying those rates to lawful residents of the nation who are not California residents. Federal law prohibits a state from offering in-state tuition to unlawfully present aliens on the basis of their residence within the state unless the state permits non-residents of the state who are lawfully present in the United States the same benefit. In Martinez v. Regents of the University of California, 50 Cal. 4th 1277 (2010), the California Supreme Court upheld this law, reasoning that California did not offer the tuition benefit on the basis of *residence* within California. Is the California law preempted? The Supreme Court denied certiorari, 131 S. Ct. 2961 (2011).

2. Consent to State Regulation of Interstate Commerce

With respect to the commerce power, the obverse of preemption is congressional action that permits states to regulate interstate commerce in a fashion that would not be permitted but for the congressional consent. At first blush, this might appear to be a bit of a puzzle. When the Court decides a dormant commerce clause case it interprets the Constitution, so where is the source of congressional power to overturn by statute a constitutional judgment of the Court? The modern answer is that the commerce clause gives Congress complete authority to regulate interstate commerce, including (if it so desires) to consent to state regulation that the Court thinks is impliedly impermissible.

Congress, in this view, is simply exercising affirmatively its commerce power when it so consents. Of course, when it wishes to use its commerce power to consent to otherwise illegitimate state regulation, Congress must deliver its consent without ambiguity. The judicial presumption is that Congress does not consent to otherwise invalid state regulation; it is up to Congress to overcome that presumption by a clear statement of its intent.

A brief tour of relevant constitutional history will shed more light on the consent problem. Gibbons v. Ogden left open the question of whether the commerce power was exclusively federal, and Willson v. Black Bird Creek Marsh Co. recognized some concurrent power on the states' part to regulate interstate commerce. Antebellum jurists saw this as a problem of mutually exclusive categories. All possible commerce power could and *must* be divided into two separate categories: an exclusively federal domain and a concurrent domain. To the early-nineteenth-century Supreme Court, the task was to describe the line that divided these two subcategories of the commerce power. In Cooley v. Board of Wardens, the Court observed, in dicta, that to the extent "the Constitution exclude[s] the States from making [laws] regulating commerce, *certainly Congress cannot regrant, or in any manner reconvey to the States that power.*" (Emphasis added.) The Court in *Cooley* thus divided the molecule of commerce power into two atoms—an exclusively federal one, comprising all commercial acts that were inherently national, and a concurrent one, including all commercial activity that was inherently local.

Cooley exemplified the pre–Civil War understanding of the dormant commerce power: Whenever the dormant commerce clause operated to void a state regulation, there was no power in Congress to consent to such state regulation because the Court's decision had declared that subject to be exclusively federal. In this sense, the antebellum dormant commerce clause produced the same effect as field preemption does today: Both doctrines identify a zone of regulatory power that is exclusively federal.

This concept was undermined in the late nineteenth century. Congress enacted the Wilson Act, which provided that all alcoholic beverages shipped across state lines were subject to the laws of the importing state as though they had been produced there. In Wilkerson v. Rahrer, 149 U.S. 545 (1891), the Court upheld the Wilson Act as applied to a state's imposition of its prohibition laws on imported liquor in its original package: "Congress has not [delegated to the states] the power to regulate commerce, [or granted to the states] a power not possessed by [them but has provided] that certain designated subjects of interstate commerce shall be governed by a rule which divests them of that character at an earlier [time] than would otherwise be the case."

An entirely different justification for the consent power emerged in the mid-twentieth century. In United States v. South-Eastern Underwriters Association, 322 U.S. 533 (1944), the Court ruled that insurance companies were subject to the Sherman Anti-Trust Act. The following year Congress enacted the McCarran Act, which provided that taxation and regulation of insurance shall "be subject to the laws of the several States," and no federal law shall "invalidate, impair, or supersede" any state law on insurance unless the federal law "specifically" does so. In Prudential Insurance Co. v. Benjamin, 328 U.S. 408 (1946), the Court, relying on the McCarran Act, upheld a South Carolina tax on insurance premiums that openly discriminated against out-of-state insurers. Congress has power, said the Court, "to contradict the Court's previously expressed view that specific action taken by the states in Congress'[s] silence was forbidden by the commerce clause." The Court was less clear about why this was so. The best it could do was to conclude that congressional exercise of the commerce power

> is not restricted [by] any limitation which forbids it to discriminate against interstate commerce and in favor of local trade. [Congress] may exercise [this authority] alone [or] in conjunction with coordinated action by the states, in which case [constitutional] limitations imposed for the preservation of [congressional] powers become inoperative and only those [constitutional limits] designed to forbid action altogether by any power or combination of powers in our governmental system remain effective.

The meaning of this enigmatic passage from *Prudential Insurance* has been a subject of debate. Professor Noel Dowling, an influential constitutional law scholar of the time, had earlier suggested that "in the absence of affirmative consent a Congressional negative will be presumed [against state action unduly burdensome of interstate commerce], the presumption being rebuttable at the pleasure of Congress," but the Court did not expressly embrace his view. See Dowling, Interstate Commerce and State Power, 27 Va. L. Rev. 1 (1940).

Years later, Professor William Cohen argued that the Court's cryptic comment meant that Congress could consent to state laws otherwise repugnant to the Constitution only if the constitutional limitation on state power that Congress was removing "is not matched by a similar or identical limitation on federal power." Cohen, Congressional Power to Validate Unconstitutional State Laws: A Forgotten Solution to an Old Enigma, 35 Stan. L. Rev. 387 (1983). Thus, in Cohen's view Congress could not consent to a state law that violates, e.g., due process or equal protection, because Congress is also constrained by the due process or equal protection clauses; but Congress could consent to a state law that violates the dormant commerce clause because Congress is not subject to the dormant aspect of the commerce clause.

Consider the following explanation. The function of the dormant commerce clause is no longer to divide the commerce power into two mutually exclusive regulatory domains—one exclusively federal and the other shared by the states and Congress. Instead, the commerce power is entirely concurrent; but there are two separate zones of concurrent power, each characterized by a different mode in which state regulation occurs. The dormant commerce clause delineates the border between a "presumptively federal" domain (in which states may not regulate interstate commerce unless Congress consents) and the remaining territory of the commerce clause (in which the states may regulate unless Congress acts to preempt their regulations). The constitutional function of the dormant commerce clause, in this view, is simply to apportion the burden of persuading Congress to use its plenary commerce power affirmatively. When the Court uses the dormant commerce clause to invalidate state regulation, it finds that the state law is within the "presumptively federal" zone, and thus the Constitution impliedly compels the state to ask Congress for permission to regulate. When the Court upholds a state law against a dormant commerce clause challenge, it finds that the state law does not intrude upon the "presumptively federal" zone, and thus the Constitution impliedly compels the persons affected by the state's regulation to ask Congress to preempt the state's rule.

If this last explanation is correct, what implications might it have for the substance of the dormant commerce clause? Should the "presumptively federal" zone include only openly discriminatory state laws, or should it include some evenhanded laws that simply impose "undue" burdens on interstate commerce? In short, should the burden of displacing evenhanded but burdensome state laws through federal legislation be placed on the interests affected by state law, or should courts shift some of that burden by engaging in *Pike* balancing?

D. STATE TAXATION OF INTERSTATE COMMERCE

The dormant commerce clause also limits state power to tax interstate commerce.

Complete Auto Transit, Inc. v. Brady
430 U.S. 274 (1977)

JUSTICE BLACKMUN delivered the opinion of the Court.

[The] issue in this case is whether Mississippi runs afoul of the Commerce Clause when it applies the tax it imposes on "the privilege [of] doing business" within the State to appellant's activity in interstate commerce. [Mississippi imposed a tax of 5 percent of the gross revenue on appellant], a Michigan corporation engaged in the business of transporting motor vehicles by motor carrier for General Motors Corporation. General Motors assembles outside Mississippi vehicles that are destined for dealers within the State. The vehicles are then shipped by rail to [Mississippi, where] they are loaded onto appellant's trucks and transported by appellant to the Mississippi dealers. Appellant is paid on a contract basis for the transportation from the railhead to the dealers. Appellant paid the [tax] under protest and [sued for a refund in state court. The Mississippi Supreme Court unanimously upheld the validity of the tax.]

[Appellee] relies on decisions of this Court stating that "[i]t was not the purpose of the commerce clause to relieve those engaged in interstate commerce from their just share of state tax burden even though it increases the cost of doing the business." Western Live Stock v. Bureau of Revenue, 303 U.S. 250, 254 (1938). These decisions have considered [the] practical effect [of the tax] and have sustained a tax against Commerce Clause challenge when the tax is applied to an activity with a substantial nexus with the taxing State, is fairly apportioned, does not discriminate against interstate commerce, and is fairly related to the services provided by the State. . . .

[In] Northwestern Cement Co. v. Minnesota, 358 U.S. 450 (1959), the Court held that net income from the interstate operations of a foreign corporation may be subjected to state taxation, provided the levy is not discriminatory and is properly apportioned to local activities within the taxing State forming sufficient nexus to support the tax. . . . [Here, no] claim is made that the activity is not sufficiently connected to the State to justify a tax, or that the tax is not fairly related to benefits provided the taxpayer, or that the tax discriminates against interstate commerce, or that the tax is not fairly apportioned. . . . [The] judgment of the Supreme Court of Mississippi is affirmed.

NOTES

1. The Four Factors.   After the *Complete Auto* holding, a state tax violates the dormant commerce clause if the tax (1) applies to an activity that lacks a substantial nexus to the taxing state, or (2) is not fairly apportioned, or (3) discriminates against foreign or interstate commerce, or (4) is not fairly related to services supplied by the taxing state.

a. "Substantial nexus."   Only those activities that have a substantial connection to the taxing state may be taxed. In Quill Corp. v. North Dakota, 504 U.S. 298 (1992), the Court struck down North Dakota's requirement that mail-order vendors collect and remit the North Dakota use tax. As applied to Quill Corporation, a mail-order vendor whose only contact with North Dakota was the solicitation and filling of mail orders, there was no substantial nexus with North Dakota.

b. "Not fairly apportioned."   A state may tax only its fair share of an interstate business's activities. If the same activity (e.g., acquiring net income) can be taxed by more than one state, the taxing state must fairly apportion the taxed activity so that the *tax* minimizes the possibility of multiple taxation on the same event. To do so, states frequently use the average percentage of an interstate business's payroll, property, and sales within the taxing state as an apportionment factor.

c. "Discriminates against interstate commerce."   A tax that is openly discriminatory toward interstate commerce is void unless the taxing state can prove that there is a legitimate reason for the discrimination and there is no less discriminatory way to achieve that legitimate objective. Compare Bacchus Imports v. Dias, Henneford v. Silas Mason Co., Oregon Waste Systems v. Department of Environmental Quality, and Fulton Corp. v. Faulkner, all supra.

d. "Not fairly related."   The tax must be measured in such a way that it is "reasonably related to the extent of [the] activities or presence of the taxpayer in the State." In Commonwealth Edison Co. v. Montana, 453 U.S. 609 (1981), the Court upheld Montana's severance tax on coal, measured at 30 percent of the coal's value upon removal from the ground, because it was reasonably related to the taxpayer's activity in Montana. The taxpayer's activity in Montana increased as it mined more coal, and the tax (assessed on total value) was a reasonable measure of that activity. The Court explicitly rejected the idea that the tax must relate to the value of state services received by the taxpayer.

2. "Internal Consistency." *Comptroller of the Treasury of Maryland v. Wynne*, 2015 U.S. LEXIS 3404. Maryland levies a state income tax and a county income tax. The state income tax provides a credit against the Maryland state income tax liability for taxes paid to other states on income earned in those other states, but Maryland does not provide any such credit against the county tax. Maryland also imposes its state income tax on non-residents to the extent of their Maryland-source income. Because non-residents do not reside in a Maryland county, the county income tax does not apply to them but a special non-resident tax applies to Maryland source income, set at the lowest of the Maryland county tax rates.

The Wynnes, Maryland residents who received some income from out-of-state sources taxed in those states, challenged the state's denial of a credit against the county income tax. The Maryland Court of Appeals ruled in their favor, concluding that the Maryland scheme failed the fair apportionment and non-discrimination prongs of *Complete Auto Transit*. The Supreme Court, 5-4, affirmed. In three prior cases from the 1930s and 1940s, the Court had struck down state tax schemes that raised the risk of double taxation and discrimination against interstate commerce. Applying those cases, the Court conceded that although the "Due Process Clause allows a State to tax '*all* the income of its residents, even income earned outside the taxing jurisdiction,'" the dormant commerce clause forbids taxing schemes that discriminate against interstate commerce. The test, said the Court, "which helps courts identify tax schemes that discriminate against interstate commerce, 'looks to the structure of the tax at issue to see whether its identical application by every State in the Union would place interstate commerce at a disadvantage as compared with commerce intrastate.'" Maryland's tax failed this "internal consistency" test because its operation inherently discriminated against out-of-state income and in favor of in-state income. A Maryland resident with only Maryland income will pay the state income and county tax on that income. But a Maryland resident who earns her salary outside Maryland will pay Maryland's state income tax (albeit with a credit for out-state-income taxes paid) and the county tax. But that latter Maryland taxpayer will get no credit for the taxes paid to another state on income subject to the county tax. The facial specter of double taxation doomed the Maryland scheme. "The effect . . . is that some of the income earned by Maryland residents outside the state is taxed twice." Maryland created "an incentive for taxpayers to opt for intrastate rather than interstate economic activity."

Two of the dissenters—Scalia and Thomas—registered their disagreement with the dormant commerce clause generally. (A "judicial fraud," said Scalia, though he conceded that he would apply existing dormant commerce clause precedent solely as matter of *stare decisis*.) The remaining dissenters—Ginsburg and Kagan, joined by Scalia, thought "a taxpayer living in one state and working in another gains protection and benefits from both—and so can be called upon to share in the costs of both states' governments." Ultimately, the Ginsburg dissenters thought the case was "about policy choices: Should States prioritize ensuring that all who live or work within the State shoulder their fair share of the costs of government? Or must States prioritize avoidance of double taxation? . . . [S]tate legislatures and the Congress are constitutionally assigned and institutionally better equipped to balance such issues."

Queries: Given the special non-resident tax imposed in lieu of the county tax, aren't Maryland residents and non-residents treated equally? Was it the incentive Maryland created for its residents to prefer Maryland income to out-of-state income that was fatal? Or was the tax scheme doomed because of the specter of double taxation abounding if every state adopted some version of Maryland's tax system? Would Justice Ginsburg's observation that taxpayers with multi-state income derive multi-state benefits and should support the governments that provide those benefits be satisfied by a system of dollar-for-dollar credits for foreign taxes paid? Why or why not?

3. Taxation of Foreign Commerce. States may tax income derived from foreign trade and may also tax the property or services used in connection with foreign commerce.

a. Property or services. The four factors identified in *Complete Auto* apply to state taxation of property or services used in foreign commerce, but two additional factors are also relevant. First, the tax is void if there is *any* risk of multiple taxation of the same event, despite adequate apportionment under *Complete Auto.* Second, if a state tax impairs federal policy toward foreign trade, it is void even though otherwise valid. See, e.g., Japan Line, Ltd. v. County of Los Angeles, 441 U.S. 434 (1979).

b. Income. An income tax that taxes income from foreign commerce is generally valid if it complies with *Complete Auto.* Only if such a tax is certain to produce multiple taxation of the same event and the state has a reasonable and less burdensome alternative will the tax be voided. See, e.g., Barclay's Bank v. Franchise Tax Board, 512 U.S. 298 (1994); Container Corp. of America v. Franchise Tax Board, 463 U.S. 159 (1983).

5

Separation of Powers

A. THE REASONS FOR SEPARATED POWERS

The Constitution divides and separates government powers in order to enhance individual liberty by minimizing the possibility of concentrated government power. To that end, the Constitution allocates government authority in two dimensions: between the federal and state governments (federalism) and among the three branches of the federal government (separation of powers). The preceding chapters have examined federalism's allocation of power. This chapter examines the allocation of federal power accomplished by separation of powers. The two topics are related. The detailed procedures for lawmaking that the Constitution specifies, it is argued, also serve to safeguard federalism. See Clark, Separation of Powers as a Safeguard of Federalism, 79 Tex. L. Rev. 1321 (2001), and Symposium on Separation of Powers as a Safeguard of Federalism, 83 Notre Dame L. Rev. (May 2008).

The Constitution explicitly divides the powers of the national government into legislative, executive, and judicial powers. Article I endows Congress with the national legislative power. Article II gives all of the executive power to the President. Article III delivers the judicial power of the United States to the Supreme Court and such other federal courts that Congress may establish. The point of this arrangement was to inhibit the arbitrary tyranny that comes from concentrated power. Though divided power seems familiar to Americans, it is not universal. Even such ancient democracies as Britain do not separate legislative and executive power—the British Prime Minister (the chief executive) is the leader of the majority party in the House of Commons (the legislature).

This separation, however, is not hermetic. The Constitution itself contains a number of explicit "checks," devices by which one branch may frustrate the exercise of power by another branch. The President, for example, may veto legislation; the Senate may confirm or deny the President's appointment of his or her principal executive officers as well as federal judges; Congress, by exercising its impeachment power, may remove judges and executive officers, including the President. Some well-established checks are implied. Perhaps the most important implied check is the power of judicial review. The Constitution thus created, simultaneously, a neat division of legislative, executive, and judicial power and institutional devices by which each branch could be controlled to some degree by the others. The objectives of this scheme of separated powers are to prevent one branch from dominating the others and to prevent a fusion of executive, legislative, or judicial power into a common hand.

In Federalist No. 47 James Madison elaborated on this theme:

> The accumulation of all powers, legislative, executive, and judiciary, in the same hands . . . may justly be pronounced the very definition of tyranny. . . . Montesquieu, [who is generally credited with this claim,] did not mean that these departments ought to have no *partial agency* in, or no *control over*, the acts of each other. His meaning . . . can amount to no more than this, that where the *whole* power of one department is exercised by the same hands which possess the *whole* power of another department, the fundamental principles of a free constitution are subverted.

(Emphasis in original.) Madison continued in Federalist No. 51:

> But the great security against a gradual concentration of the several powers in the same department, consists in giving to those who administer each department the necessary constitutional means and personal motives to resist encroachment of the others. . . . If men were angels, no government would be necessary. If angels were to govern men, neither external nor internal controls on government would be necessary. In framing a government which is to be administered by men over men, the great difficulty lies in this: you must first enable the government to control the governed; and in the next place oblige it to control itself.

The boundaries between the branches thus are not distinct. A traveler moving from the arctic to the tropics will notice gradual changes in climate, terrain, and flora. Exactly where the arctic ends and the temperate zone begins may be debatable, but our traveler can declare with confidence that she is in the arctic when she is in northern Greenland, is in temperate North America when she is in Kentucky, and is in the tropics when she lands in Panama. Much the same phenomenon exists in trying to define the frontiers of legislative, executive, or judicial power. These muddled, ambiguous boundaries have produced conflict between the three branches, conflict not always resolved by the Supreme Court. There are few bright lines in constitutional law; there are almost none in separation of powers.

The sources of decision in separation of powers are more diverse than in any other area of constitutional law. The Court does not always decide, which leaves the resolution of certain issues to the political branches. Even when the Court does decide, its reasoning is eclectic. Historical precedent rooted in action and inaction of the President and Congress—what has been done and tolerated, what has been done and not tolerated, what has not been done—is important. So, too, are inferences from text and structure and, especially, intangible considerations of what is prudentially appropriate.

Section B examines the scope of executive power, especially when the President takes action without explicit authorization from Congress. Section C considers limits on congressional power to create new government devices that threaten the autonomy of each branch. Section D deals with the explicit and implicit constitutional immunities and privileges enjoyed by members of Congress and the President.

B.   EXECUTIVE ACTION

Article II assigns the national government's "executive Power" to "a President," but the Article provides only a vague description of the scope and extent of that power. Article II does assign to the President a number of specific powers (e.g., to appoint judges and principal executive officers, sign or veto legislation, negotiate treaties, grant reprieves and pardons, and extend and withdraw diplomatic recognition to other nations) but phrases the President's most important powers in general terms. The President is the Commander-in-Chief of the armed services, a power that is theoretically constrained by the Constitution's Article I provision that Congress has the sole power to declare war. The President is obliged to "take Care that the Laws be faithfully executed." This general power and duty is phrased in terms of the execution of the law, not its manufacture. What happens when the President takes action on his own without legislative authority to act?

At one extreme lies the position of Presidents Theodore Roosevelt and Taft, both of whom claimed that the President had the power and duty to do anything necessary for the good of the nation so long as his action did not violate the Constitution or a valid act of Congress. By this theory the President may act without any specific constitutional or legislative authority. Although Taft as Chief Justice endorsed this principle in dicta in Myers v. United States, 272 U.S. 52 (1926), it has never been accepted by a majority of the Court. Instead, the Court has treated the scope of the President's power to act unilaterally as depending on whether he is acting in foreign or domestic affairs. In the domestic sphere, the President's room for unilateral action is more restricted than when he is acting internationally.

1. In Domestic Affairs

Youngstown Sheet & Tube Co. v. Sawyer
(The Steel Seizure Case)
43 U.S. 579 (1952)

JUSTICE BLACK delivered the opinion of the Court.

We are asked to decide whether [President Truman] was acting within his constitutional power when he issued an order directing [Sawyer], the Secretary of Commerce, to take possession of and operate most of the Nation's steel mills. The mill owners argue that the President's order amounts to law-making, a legislative function which the Constitution has expressly confided to the Congress and not to the President. The Government's position is that the order was made on findings of the President that his action was necessary to avert a national catastrophe which would inevitably result from a stoppage of steel production, and that in meeting this grave emergency the President was acting within the aggregate of his constitutional powers as the Nation's Chief Executive and the Commander in Chief of the Armed Forces.

[At the height of the Korean War, a labor] dispute arose between the steel companies and their [unionized] employees. [The] United Steelworkers of America [gave] notice of an intention to strike . . . April 9. The indispensability of steel as a component of substantially all weapons and other war materials led the President to believe that the proposed work stoppage would immediately jeopardize our national defense and that governmental seizure of the steel mills was necessary in order to assure the continued availability of steel. Reciting these considerations for his action, the President, a few hours before the strike was to begin, issued Executive Order 10340, [which] directed the Secretary of Commerce to take possession of most of the steel mills and keep them running. The Secretary immediately issued his own possessory orders, calling upon the presidents of the various seized companies to serve as operating managers for the United States. [The] next morning the President sent a message to Congress reporting his action. [Congress] has taken no action.

Obeying the Secretary's orders under protest, the companies brought proceedings against him in the District Court. [On] April 30 [that court] issued a preliminary injunction restraining the Secretary from "continuing the seizure and possession of the plants [and] from acting under the purported authority of Executive Order No. 10340." On the same day the Court of Appeals stayed the District Court's injunction. Deeming it best that the issues raised be promptly decided by this Court, we granted certiorari on May 3 and set the cause for argument on May 12. [This decision was issued on June 2, 1952.]

The President's power, if any, to issue the order must stem either from an act of Congress or from the Constitution itself. There is no statute that expressly authorizes the President to take possession of property as he did here. Nor is there any act of Congress to which our attention has been directed from which such a power can fairly be implied. . . . Moreover, the use of the seizure technique to solve labor disputes in order to prevent work stoppages was not only unauthorized by any congressional enactment; prior to this controversy, Congress had refused to adopt that method of settling labor disputes. When the Taft-Hartley Act was under consideration in 1947, Congress rejected an amendment which would have authorized such governmental seizures in cases of emergency. [The] plan Congress adopted in that Act did not provide for seizure under any circumstances. Instead, the plan sought to bring about settlements by use of the customary devices of mediation, conciliation, [etc.]. All this failing, unions were left free to [strike].

It is clear that if the President had authority to issue the order he did, it must be found in some provision of the Constitution. And it is not claimed that express constitutional language grants this power to the President. The contention is that presidential power should be implied from the aggregate of his powers under the Constitution. Particular reliance is placed on provisions in Article II which say that "The executive Power shall be vested in a President"; that "he shall take Care that the Laws be faithfully executed"; and that he "shall be Commander in Chief of the Army and Navy of the United States."

The order cannot properly be sustained as an exercise of the President's military power as Commander in Chief of the Armed Forces. The Government attempts to do so by citing a number of cases upholding broad powers in military commanders engaged in day-to-day fighting in a theater of war. Such cases need not concern us here. Even though "theater of war" be an expanding concept, we cannot with faithfulness to our constitutional system hold that the Commander in Chief of the Armed Forces has the ultimate power as such to take possession of private property in order to keep labor disputes from stopping production. This is a job for the Nation's lawmakers, not for its military authorities.

Nor can the seizure order be sustained because of the several constitutional provisions that grant executive power to the President. In the framework of our Constitution, the President's power to see that the laws are faithfully executed refutes the idea that he is to be a lawmaker. The Constitution limits his functions in the lawmaking process to the recommending of laws he thinks wise and the vetoing of laws he thinks bad. And the Constitution is neither silent nor equivocal about who shall make laws which the President is to execute. [Article I] says that "All legislative Powers herein granted shall be vested in a Congress of the United States" [and] goes on to provide that Congress may "make all Laws which shall be necessary and proper for carrying into Execution [all] other Powers vested by this Constitution in the Government of the United States, or in any Department or Officer thereof."

The President's order does not direct that a congressional policy be executed in a manner prescribed by Congress—it directs that a presidential policy be executed in a manner prescribed by the President. The preamble of the order itself, like that of many statutes, sets out reasons why the President believes certain policies should be adopted, proclaims these policies as rules of conduct to be followed, and again, like a statute, authorizes a government official to promulgate [additional] regulations consistent with the policy proclaimed and needed to carry that policy into execution. The power of Congress to adopt such public policies as those proclaimed by the order is beyond question. It can authorize the taking of private property for public use. It can make laws regulating [labor] relationships [and] to settle labor disputes.

[It] is said that other Presidents without congressional authority have taken possession of private business enterprises in order to settle labor disputes. But even if this be true, Congress has not thereby lost its exclusive constitutional authority to make laws necessary and proper to carry out the powers vested by the Constitution "in the Government of the United States, or any Department or Officer thereof." The Founders of this Nation entrusted the lawmaking power to the Congress alone in both good and bad times. It would do no good to recall the historical events, the fears of power and the hopes for freedom that lay behind their choice. Such a review would but confirm our holding that this seizure order cannot stand.

The judgment of the District Court is [a]ffirmed.

JUSTICE FRANKFURTER, concurring.

[The] Founders of this Nation [rested] the structure of our central government [on] separation of powers. [These] long-headed statesmen had no illusion that our people enjoyed biological or psychological or sociological immunities from the hazards of concentrated power. It is absurd to see a dictator in a representative product of the sturdy democratic traditions of the Mississippi Valley. The accretion of dangerous power does not come in a day. It does come, however slowly, from the generative force of unchecked disregard of the restrictions that fence in even the most disinterested assertion of authority. [The] issue before us can be [met] without attempting to define the President's powers comprehensively. I shall not attempt to delineate what belongs to him by virtue of his office beyond the power even of Congress to contract; what authority belongs to him until Congress acts; what kind of problems may be dealt with either by the Congress or by the President or by both; what power must be exercised by the Congress and cannot be delegated to the President. . . .

Congress has frequently — at least 16 times since 1916 — specifically provided for executive seizure of [private property]. In every case it has qualified this grant of power with limitations and safeguards. [This] demonstrates that Congress deemed seizure so drastic a power as to require that it be carefully circumscribed whenever the President was vested with this extraordinary authority. [Congress] in 1947 was again called upon to consider whether governmental seizure should be used to avoid serious industrial shutdowns. [In adopting the Taft-Hartley Act,] Congress decided against conferring such [power]. A proposal that the President be given powers to seize plants to avert a shutdown where the "health or safety" of the Nation was endangered, was thoroughly canvassed by Congress and rejected.

[It] cannot be contended that the President would have had power to issue this order had Congress explicitly negated such authority in formal legislation. Congress has expressed its will to withhold this power from the President as though it had said so in so many words. [By the Taft-Hartley Act,] Congress said to the President, "You may not seize. Please report to us and ask for seizure power if you think it is needed in a specific situation." It is one thing to draw an intention of Congress from general language and to say that Congress would have explicitly written what is inferred, where Congress has not addressed itself to a specific situation. It is quite impossible, however, when Congress did specifically address itself to a problem, as Congress did to that of seizure, to find secreted in the interstices of legislation the very grant of power which Congress consciously withheld. To find authority so explicitly withheld is not merely to disregard in a particular instance the clear will of Congress. It is to disrespect the whole legislative process and the constitutional division of authority between President and Congress. . . .

Deeply embedded traditional ways of conducting government cannot supplant the Constitution or legislation, but they give meaning to the words of a text or supply them. It is an inadmissibly narrow conception of American constitutional law to confine it to the words of the Constitution and to disregard the gloss which life has written upon them. In short, a systematic, unbroken, executive practice, long pursued to the knowledge of the Congress and never before questioned, engaged in by Presidents who have also sworn to uphold the Constitution, making as it were such exercise of power part of the structure of our government, may be treated as a gloss on "executive Power" vested in the President.

[After examining historical instances of presidential seizures, summarized in a voluminous appendix to his opinion, Justice Frankfurter concluded that] the list of executive [seizures] in circumstances comparable to the present reduces to three in the six-month period from June to December of 1941. [These] three isolated instances do not add up, either in number, scope, duration or contemporaneous legal justification, to the kind of executive construction of the Constitution [that would support President Truman's seizure]. Nor do they come to us sanctioned by long-continued acquiescence of Congress giving decisive weight to a construction by the Executive of its powers.

A scheme of government like ours no doubt at times feels the lack of power to act with complete, all-embracing, swiftly moving authority. No doubt a government with distributed authority, subject to be challenged in the courts of law, at least long enough to consider and adjudicate the challenge, labors under restrictions from which other governments are free. [The] price was deemed not too high in view of the safeguards which these restrictions afford. I know no more impressive words on this subject than those of Mr. Justice Brandeis:

"The doctrine of the separation of powers was adopted by the Convention of 1787, not to promote efficiency but to preclude the exercise of arbitrary power. The purpose was, not to avoid friction, but, by means of the inevitable friction incident to the distribution of the governmental powers among three departments, to save the people from autocracy." Myers v. United States, 272 U.S. 52 [1926].

Justice Douglas, concurring.

There can be no doubt that the emergency which caused the President to seize these steel plants was one that bore heavily on the country. But the emergency did not create power; it merely marked an occasion when power should be exercised. And the fact that it was necessary that measures be taken to keep steel in production does not mean that the President, rather than the Congress, had the constitutional authority to act. [The] legislative nature of the action taken by the President seems to me to be clear. When the United States takes over an industrial plant to settle a labor controversy, it is condemning property. The seizure of the plant is a taking in the constitutional sense. [Though] the seizure is only for a week or a month, the condemnation is complete and the United States must pay compensation for the temporary possession. The power of the Federal Government to condemn property is well established. It can condemn for any public purpose. . . . But there is a duty to pay for all property taken by the Government. . . . The President has no power to raise revenues. That power is in the [Congress]. The President might seize and the Congress by subsequent action might ratify the seizure. But until and unless Congress acted, no condemnation would be lawful. The branch of government that has the power to pay compensation for a seizure is the only one able to authorize a seizure or make lawful one that the President has effected. . . .

Justice Jackson, concurring in the judgment and opinion of the Court.

[A] judge, like an executive adviser, may be surprised at the poverty of really useful and unambiguous authority applicable to concrete problems of executive power as they actually present themselves. Just what our forefathers did envision, or would have envisioned had they foreseen modern conditions, must be divined from materials almost as enigmatic as the dreams Joseph was called upon to interpret for Pharaoh. A century and a half of partisan debate and scholarly speculation yields no net result but only supplies more or less apt quotations from respected sources on each side of any question. They largely cancel each other. And court decisions are indecisive because of the judicial practice of dealing with the largest questions in the most narrow way. The actual art of governing under our Constitution does not and cannot conform to judicial definitions of the power of any of its branches based on isolated clauses or even single Articles torn from context. While the Constitution diffuses power the better to secure liberty, it also contemplates that practice will integrate the dispersed powers into a workable government. It enjoins upon its branches separateness but interdependence, autonomy but reciprocity. Presidential powers are not fixed but fluctuate, depending upon their disjunction or conjunction with those of Congress. We may well begin by a somewhat over-simplified grouping of practical situations in which a President may doubt, or others may challenge, his powers, and by distinguishing roughly the legal consequences of this factor of relativity.

1. When the President acts pursuant to an express or implied authorization of Congress, his authority is at its maximum, for it includes all that he possesses in his own right plus all that Congress can delegate. In these circumstances, and in these only, may he be said (for what it may be worth) to personify the federal sovereignty. If his act is held unconstitutional under these circumstances, it usually means that the Federal Government as an undivided whole lacks power. A seizure executed by the President pursuant to an Act of Congress would be supported by the strongest of presumptions and the widest latitude of judicial interpretation, and the burden of persuasion would rest heavily upon any who might attack it.

2. When the President acts in absence of either a congressional grant or denial of authority, he can only rely upon his own independent powers, but there is a zone of twilight in which he and Congress may have concurrent authority, or in which its distribution is uncertain. Therefore, congressional inertia, indifference or quiescence may sometimes, at least as a practical matter, enable, if not invite, measures on independent presidential responsibility. In this area, any actual test of power is likely to depend on the imperatives of events and contemporary imponderables rather than on abstract theories of law.

3. When the President takes measures incompatible with the expressed or implied will of Congress, his power is at its lowest ebb, for then he can rely only upon his own constitutional powers minus any constitutional powers of Congress over the matter. Courts can sustain exclusive presidential control in such a case only by disabling the Congress from acting upon the subject. Presidential claim to a power at once so conclusive and preclusive must be scrutinized with caution, for what is at stake is the equilibrium established by our constitutional system.

Into which of these classifications does this executive seizure of the steel industry fit? It is eliminated from the first by admission, for it is conceded that no congressional authorization exists for this seizure. [Can] it then be defended under flexible tests available to the second category? It seems clearly eliminated from that class because Congress has not left seizure of private property an open field but has covered it by three statutory policies inconsistent with this seizure. [This] leaves the current seizure to be justified only by the severe tests under the third grouping, where it can be supported only by any remainder of executive power after subtraction of such powers as Congress may have over the subject. In short, we can sustain the President only by holding that seizure of such strike-bound industries is within his domain and beyond control by Congress.

[The] Solicitor General seeks the power of seizure in three clauses of the Executive Article, the first reading, "The executive Power shall be vested in a President of the United States of America." Lest I be thought to exaggerate, I quote the interpretation which his brief puts upon it: "In our view, this clause constitutes a grant of all the executive powers of which the Government is capable." If that be true, it is difficult to see why the forefathers bothered to add several specific items, including some trifling ones. [I] cannot accept the view that this clause is a grant in bulk of all conceivable executive power but regard it as an allocation to the presidential office of the generic powers thereafter stated. The clause on which the Government next relies is that "The President shall be Commander in Chief of the Army and Navy of the United States." These cryptic [words] imply something more than an empty title [and] undoubtedly puts the Nation's armed forces under presidential command. Hence, this loose appellation is sometimes advanced as support for any presidential action, internal or external, involving use of force, the idea being that it vests power to do anything, anywhere, that can be done with an army or navy. That seems to be the logic of an argument tendered at our bar — that the President having, on his own responsibility, sent American troops abroad derives from that act "affirmative power" to seize the means of producing a supply of steel for them. [No] doctrine that the Court could promulgate would seem to me more sinister and alarming than that a President whose conduct of foreign affairs is so largely uncontrolled, and often even is unknown, can vastly enlarge his mastery over the internal affairs of the country by his own commitment of the Nation's armed forces to some foreign venture.

[Assuming] that we are in a war de facto, whether it is or is not a war de jure, does that empower the Commander in Chief to seize industries he thinks necessary to supply our army? The Constitution expressly places in Congress power "to raise and *support* Armies" and "to *provide* and *maintain* a Navy." (Emphasis supplied.) This certainly lays upon Congress primary responsibility for supplying the armed forces. Congress alone controls the raising of revenues and their appropriation and may determine in what manner and by what means they shall be spent for military and naval procurement. [There] are indications that the Constitution did not contemplate that the title Commander in Chief *of the Army and Navy* will constitute him also Commander in Chief of the country, its industries and its inhabitants. He has no monopoly of "war powers," whatever they are. While Congress cannot deprive the President of the command of the army and navy, only Congress can provide him an army or navy to command. [That] military powers of the Commander in Chief were not to supersede representative government of internal affairs seems obvious from the Constitution and from elementary American history. [The] purpose of lodging dual titles in one man was to insure that the civilian would control the military, not to enable the military to subordinate the presidential office. No penance would ever expiate the sin against free government of holding that a President can escape control of executive powers by law through assuming his military role. [The] third clause in which the Solicitor General finds seizure powers is that "he shall take Care that the Laws be faithfully executed." That authority must be matched against [the due process clause]. One gives a governmental authority that reaches so far as there is law, the other gives a private right that authority shall go no farther. These signify about all there is of the principle that ours is a government of laws, not of men, and that we submit ourselves to rulers only if under rules.

The Solicitor General lastly grounds support of the seizure upon nebulous, inherent powers never expressly granted but said to have accrued to the office from the customs and claims of preceding administrations. The plea is for a resulting power to deal with a crisis or an emergency according to the necessities of the case, the unarticulated assumption being that necessity knows no law. Loose and irresponsible use of adjectives colors all nonlegal and much legal discussion of presidential powers. "Inherent" powers, "implied" powers, "incidental" powers, "plenary" powers, "war" powers and "emergency" powers are used, often interchangeably and without fixed or ascertainable meanings. The vagueness and generality of the clauses that set forth presidential powers afford a plausible basis for pressures within and without an administration for presidential action beyond that supported by those whose responsibility it is to defend his actions in court. The claim of inherent and unrestricted presidential powers has long been a persuasive dialectical weapon in political controversy. While it is not surprising that counsel should grasp support from such unadjudicated claims of power, a judge cannot accept self-serving press statements of the attorney for one of the interested parties as authority in answering a constitutional question, even if the advocate was himself.

[To] declare the existence of inherent powers [necessary] to meet an emergency [would] do what many think would be wise, although it is something the forefathers omitted. They knew what emergencies were, [how] they afford a ready pretext for usurpation, [and] suspected that emergency powers would tend to kindle emergencies. . . .

[In] view of the ease, expedition and safety with which Congress can grant and has granted large emergency powers, certainly ample to embrace this crisis, I am quite unimpressed with the argument that we should affirm possession of them without statute. Such power either has no beginning or it has no end. If it exists, it need submit to no legal restraint. I am not alarmed that it would plunge us straightway into dictatorship, but it is at least a step in that wrong direction. As to whether there is imperative necessity for such powers, it is relevant to note the gap that exists between the President's paper powers and his real powers. The Constitution does not disclose the measure of the actual controls wielded by the modern presidential office. [Vast] accretions of federal power, eroded from that reserved by the States, have magnified the scope of presidential activity.

Executive power has the advantage of concentration in a single head in whose choice the whole Nation has a part, making him the focus of public hopes and expectations. [No] other personality in public life can begin to compete with him in access to the public mind through modern methods of communications. By his prestige as head of state and his influence upon public opinion he exerts a leverage upon those who are supposed to check and balance his power which often cancels their effectiveness. . . . [But] I have no illusion that any decision by this Court can keep power in the hands of Congress if it is not wise and timely in meeting its problems. A crisis that challenges the President equally, or perhaps primarily, challenges Congress. If not good law, there was worldly wisdom in the maxim attributed to Napoleon that "The tools belong to the man who can use them." We may say that power to legislate for emergencies belongs in the hands of Congress, but only Congress itself can prevent power from slipping through its fingers. [With] all its defects, delays and inconveniences, men have discovered no technique for long preserving free government except that the Executive be under the law, and that the law be made by parliamentary deliberations. Such institutions may be destined to pass away. But it is the duty of the Court to be last, not first, to give them up.

JUSTICE CLARK, concurring in the judgment of the Court.

[The] limits of presidential power are obscure. . . . In my view [the] Constitution does grant to the President extensive authority in times of grave and imperative national emergency. In fact, . . . such a grant may well be necessary to the very existence of the Constitution itself. [In] describing this authority I care not whether one calls it "residual," "inherent," "moral," "implied," "aggregate," "emergency," or otherwise. [I] conclude that where Congress has laid down specific procedures to deal with the type of crisis confronting the President, he must follow those procedures in meeting the crisis; but that in the absence of such action by Congress, the President's independent power to act depends upon the gravity of the situation confronting the nation. I cannot sustain the seizure in question because [here] Congress had prescribed methods to be followed by the President in meeting the emergency at hand. [Neither] the Defense Production Act nor Taft-Hartley authorized the seizure challenged here, and the Government made no effort to comply with the procedures established by the Selective Service Act of 1948, a statute which expressly authorizes seizures when producers fail to supply necessary defense materiel.

CHIEF JUSTICE VINSON, joined by JUSTICES REED and MINTON, dissenting.

[In] passing upon the question of Presidential powers in this case, we must first consider the context in which those powers were exercised. Those who suggest that this is a case involving extraordinary powers should be mindful that these are extraordinary times. A world not yet recovered from the devastation of World War II has been forced to face the threat of another and more terrifying global conflict. [Chief Justice Vinson then summarized extensive American commitments to the post–World War II global community, particularly focusing upon the U.N.-sponsored Korean War and the "large body of implementing legislation" Congress had enacted to support the Korean War.]

The President has the duty to execute the foregoing legislative programs. Their successful execution depends upon continued production of steel and stabilized prices for steel. Accordingly, when [a] strike shutting down the entire basic steel industry was threatened, the President acted to avert a complete shutdown of steel production. [The] uncontroverted affidavits in this record amply support the finding that "a work stoppage would immediately jeopardize and imperil our national defense." [Accordingly], if the President has any power under the Constitution to meet a critical situation in the absence of express statutory authorization, there is no basis whatever for criticizing the exercise of such power in this case. . . .

A review of executive action demonstrates that our Presidents have on many occasions exhibited the leadership contemplated by the Framers when they made the President Commander in Chief, and imposed upon him the trust to "take Care that the Laws be faithfully executed." . . .

The most striking action of President Lincoln was the Emancipation Proclamation, issued in aid of the successful prosecution of the War Between the States, but wholly without statutory authority. [In] an action furnishing a most apt precedent for this case, President Lincoln without statutory authority directed the seizure of rail and telegraph lines leading to Washington. [Congress later] recognized and confirmed the power of the President to seize railroads and telegraph lines [but] plainly rejected the view that the President's acts had been without legal sanction until ratified by [Congress]. Sponsors of the bill declared that its purpose was only to confirm the power which the President already possessed. Opponents insisted a statute authorizing seizure was unnecessary and might even be construed as limiting existing Presidential powers. . . .

Beginning with the Bank Holiday Proclamation and continuing through World War II, executive leadership and initiative were characteristic of President Franklin D. Roosevelt's administration. [Some] six months before Pearl Harbor, a dispute at a single aviation plant at Inglewood, California, interrupted a segment of the production of military aircraft. In spite of the comparative insignificance of this work stoppage to total defense production as contrasted with the complete paralysis now threatened by a shutdown of the entire basic steel industry, and even though our armed forces were not then engaged in combat, President Roosevelt ordered the seizure of the plant "pursuant to the powers vested in [him] by the Constitution and laws of the United States, as President [and] Commander in Chief." The Attorney General (Jackson) vigorously proclaimed that the President had the moral duty to keep this Nation's defense effort a "going concern." [In 1941 through 1943, six] additional industrial concerns were seized to avert interruption of needed production [and] the President directed seizure of the Nation's coal mines to remove an obstruction to the effective prosecution of the war. [This] is but a cursory summary of executive leadership. But it amply demonstrates that Presidents have taken prompt action to enforce the laws and protect the country whether or not Congress happened to provide in advance for the particular method of execution. [The] fact that Congress and the courts have consistently recognized and given their support to such executive action indicates that such a power of seizure has been accepted throughout our history. . . .

[There] is no statute prohibiting seizure as a method of enforcing legislative programs. [In] his Message to Congress immediately following the seizure, the President explained the necessity of his action [and] expressed his desire to cooperate with any legislative proposals approving, regulating or rejecting the seizure of the steel mills. Consequently, there is no evidence whatever of any Presidential purpose to defy Congress or act in any way inconsistent with the legislative will.

[The] broad executive power granted by Article II to an officer on duty 365 days a year cannot, it is said, be invoked to avert disaster. Instead, the President must confine himself to sending a message to Congress recommending action. Under this messenger-boy concept of the Office, the President cannot even act to preserve legislative programs from destruction so that Congress will have something left to act upon. [There] is no question that the [steel seizure] was other than temporary in character and subject to congressional direction—either approving, disapproving or regulating the manner in which the mills were to be administered and returned to the owners. [No] basis for claims of arbitrary action, unlimited powers or dictatorial usurpation of congressional power appears from the facts of this case. On the contrary, judicial, legislative and executive precedents throughout our history demonstrate that in this case the President acted in full conformity with his duties under the Constitution.

NOTES AND PROBLEM

1. Sources of Authority for Presidential Action. Justice Black made plain that the President's authority must be derived from an act of Congress or directly from the Constitution, but Black attached significance to the fact that Congress *failed to act* by rejecting a proposal to give the President seizure authority in labor disputes. How much significance should be attributed to congressional inaction? Should it make a difference that the inaction is relatively active—as in Congress's rejection of proposed seizure authority—or relatively passive—as when Congress acquiesces by doing nothing in the face of a presidential initiative of arguable validity? Justice Frankfurter attached great significance to such acquiescence, but only when it is sufficiently repetitive to create an historical pattern of constitutional understanding.

Does the presence of a national emergency alter the President's power to act unilaterally? If so, how? Is an emergency one of the "imperatives of events" and "contemporary imponderables" that inform Justice Jackson's "zone of twilight"? Should the presence of a national emergency enlarge presidential power to act unilaterally?

2. Methodology. Black's approach is categorical: Congress has either authorized the President to act or has not; the President's action was either executive or legislative. This approach emphasizes the Constitution's division of government power into three distinct categories and assumes that the only permissible shading of those boundaries is in accord with some textually specified "check," such as the President's power to veto legislation. The Frankfurter approach is highly colored by historical and prudential considerations. The Jackson approach emphasizes flexibility and prudential concerns in deciding the limits of unilateral presidential authority. You will see each of these methods in the cases to come, and it will not be entirely clear why the Court prefers a categorical, textual approach in one case and a flexible, prudential approach in another case. Keep in mind that the Court can be persuaded by either approach. Consider the possibility that the Court uses flexibility to establish some general tests for separation of powers and uses the categorical approach to deal with specific issues that are addressed by constitutional text.

3. Problem. In an effort to curb federal spending, President Nixon claimed he had authority to refuse to spend funds appropriated by Congress. The Supreme Court never decided the question of whether the President has power to impound appropriated funds. Instead, the controversy effectively ended when Congress enacted a statute prohibiting impoundment, the Impoundment Control Act of 1974, 31 U.S.C. §1301. Analyze the validity of presidential impoundment of appropriated funds under the various approaches taken by the justices in *Youngstown*.

a. *The Appointment Power*

The fact that Article II vests the nation's "executive Power" in the President alone does not mean that the President personally must wield all executive power. The Constitution contemplates the creation of a host of lesser executive officers to carry out the President's policies. Subject to Senate confirmation, Article II, section 2 gives the President the power to

> appoint Ambassadors, other public Ministers and Consuls, Judges of the supreme Court, and all other Officers of the United States, whose Appointments are not herein otherwise provided for, and which shall be established by Law: but the Congress may by Law vest the Appointment of such inferior Officers, as they think proper, in the President alone, in the Courts of Law, or in the Heads of Departments.

The "other Officers of the United States" consist of principal and inferior officers. The President has the sole power of appointment of principal officers, subject to Senate confirmation, but Congress may vest the appointment power of inferior officers in either the President, the courts, or the heads of the executive departments. Not all employees of the federal government are officers. An "officer of the United States," according to the Court in Buckley v. Valeo, 424 U.S. 1 (1976), is "any appointee exercising significant authority pursuant to the laws of the United States," but the Court has never precisely distinguished between principal and inferior officers.

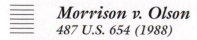

Morrison v. Olson
487 U.S. 654 (1988)

[The Court upheld the validity of the independent counsel provisions of the Ethics in Government Act of 1978. The Act created a mechanism for the

Attorney General to seek appointment of an independent counsel by a Special Division of the U.S. Court of Appeals for the D.C. Circuit whenever the Attorney General determines that there are "reasonable grounds to believe that further investigation and prosecution" of high-level executive officers specified in the Act "is warranted." The independent counsel's function is to investigate and prosecute alleged executive wrongdoing. To do so the independent counsel is given "full power and independent authority to exercise all investigative and prosecutorial functions and powers of the Department of Justice [and] the Attorney General." Moreover, under the Act the independent counsel is removable only by the Attorney General, not the President, and then only for "good cause." Olson contended (among other things) that Morrison's appointment as independent counsel violated the appointments clause. The Court disagreed.]

CHIEF JUSTICE REHNQUIST delivered the opinion of the Court.

The line between "inferior" and "principal" officers is one that is far from clear, and the Framers provided little guidance into where it should be drawn. [We] need not attempt here to decide exactly where the line falls between the two types of officers, because in our view appellant clearly falls on the "inferior officer" side of that line. Several factors lead to this conclusion.

First, appellant is subject to removal by a higher Executive Branch official. Although appellant may not be "subordinate" to the Attorney General (and the President) insofar as she possesses a degree of independent discretion to exercise the powers delegated to her under the Act, the fact that she can be removed by the Attorney General indicates that she is to some degree "inferior" in rank and authority. Second, appellant is empowered by the Act to perform only certain, limited duties: investigation [and] prosecution for certain federal crimes. Admittedly, the Act delegates to appellant "full power and independent authority to exercise all investigative and prosecutorial functions and powers of the Department of Justice," but this grant of authority does not include any authority to formulate policy for the Government or the Executive Branch, nor does it give appellant any administrative duties outside of those necessary to operate her office. [Third], appellant's office is limited in jurisdiction. Not only is the Act itself restricted in applicability to certain federal officials suspected of certain serious federal crimes, but an independent counsel can only act within the scope of the jurisdiction that has been granted by the Special Division pursuant to a request by the Attorney General. Finally, appellant's office is limited in tenure. There is concededly no time limit on the appointment of a particular counsel. Nonetheless, the office of independent counsel is "temporary" in the sense that an independent counsel is appointed essentially to accomplish a single task, and when that task is over the office is terminated, either by the counsel herself or by action of the Special Division. [These] factors relating to the "ideas of tenure, duration [and] duties" of the independent counsel are sufficient to establish that appellant is an "inferior" officer in the constitutional sense.

[This] does not, however, end our inquiry under the Appointments Clause. Appellees argue that even if appellant is an "inferior" officer, the Clause does not empower Congress to place the power to appoint such an officer outside the Executive Branch. They contend that the Clause does not contemplate congressional authorization of "interbranch appointments," in which an officer of one branch is appointed by officers of another branch. The relevant language of the Appointments Clause [admits] of no limitation on interbranch appointments. Indeed, the inclusion of "as they think proper" seems clearly to give Congress significant discretion to determine whether it is "proper" to vest the appointment of, for example, executive officials in the "courts of Law."

[We] do not mean to say that Congress'[s] power to provide for interbranch appointments of "inferior officers" is unlimited. In addition to separation-of-powers concerns, which would arise if such provisions for appointment had the potential to impair the constitutional functions assigned to one of the branches, [Congress's] decision to vest the appointment power in the courts would be improper if there was some "incongruity" between the functions normally performed by the courts and the performance of their duty to appoint. In this case, however, we do not think it impermissible for Congress to vest the power to appoint independent counsel in a specially created federal court. [We] have recognized that courts may appoint private attorneys to act as prosecutor for judicial contempt judgments, approved court appointment of United States commissioners who exercised certain limited prosecutorial powers, [and] indicated that judicial appointment of federal marshals, who are "executive officer[s]," would not be inappropriate. Lower courts have also upheld interim judicial appointments of United States Attorneys, and Congress itself has vested the power to make these interim appointments in the district courts. [In] the light of the Act's provision making the judges of the Special Division ineligible to participate in any matters relating to an independent counsel they have appointed we do not think that appointment of the independent counsel by the court runs afoul of the constitutional limitation on "incongruous" interbranch appointments.

JUSTICE SCALIA, dissenting.

Because appellant . . . was not appointed by the President with the advice and consent of the Senate, but rather by the Special Division of the United States Court of Appeals, her appointment is constitutional only if (1) she is an "inferior" officer within the meaning of the above Clause, and (2) Congress may vest her appointment in a court of law.

As to the first of these inquiries, the Court does not attempt to "decide exactly" what establishes the line between principal and "inferior" officers, but is confident that, whatever the line may be, appellant "clearly falls on the 'inferior officer' side" of it. The Court gives three reasons: First, she "is subject to removal by a higher Executive Branch official," namely, the Attorney General. Second, she is "empowered by the Act to perform only certain, limited duties." Third, her office is "limited in jurisdiction" and "limited in tenure."

The first of these lends no support to the view that appellant is an inferior officer. Appellant is removable only for "good cause" or physical or mental incapacity. By contrast, most (if not all) principal officers in the Executive

Branch may be removed by the President at will. I fail to see how the fact that appellant is more difficult to remove than most principal officers helps to establish that she is an inferior officer.

[The] second reason offered by the Court—that appellant performs only certain, limited duties—may be relevant to whether she is an inferior officer, but it mischaracterizes the extent of her powers. [In] addition to [the] general grant of ["full power and independent authority to exercise all investigative and prosecutorial functions and powers of the Department of Justice"] she is given a broad range of specifically enumerated powers, including a power not even the Attorney General possesses: to "contes[t] in court [any] claim of privilege or attempt to withhold evidence on grounds of national security." Once all of this is "admitted," it seems to me impossible to maintain that appellant's authority is so "limited" as to render her an inferior officer. The Court seeks to brush this away by asserting that the independent counsel's power does not include any authority to "formulate policy for the Government or the Executive Branch." But the same could be said for all officers of the Government, with the single exception of the President.

[The] final set of reasons given by the Court for why the independent counsel clearly is an inferior officer emphasizes the limited nature of her jurisdiction and tenure. [I] find nothing unusually limited about the independent counsel's tenure. To the contrary, unlike most high ranking Executive Branch officials, she continues to serve until she (or the Special Division) decides that her work is substantially completed. [Though] the scope of her jurisdiction [is] small, within it she exercises more than the full power of the Attorney General. The Ambassador to Luxembourg is not anything less than a principal officer, simply because Luxembourg is small.

[More] fundamentally, however, it is not clear from the Court's opinion why the factors it discusses—even if applied correctly to the facts of this case—are determinative of the question of inferior officer status. [The] text of the Constitution and the division of power that it establishes [demonstrate] that the independent counsel is not an inferior officer because she is not *subordinate* to any officer in the Executive Branch (indeed, not even to the President). . . . In a document dealing with the structure [of] a government . . . it would be unpardonably careless to use the word unless a relationship of subordination was intended. [At] the only other point in the Constitution at which the word "inferior" appears, it plainly connotes a relationship of subordination. . . .

[This] interpretation is, moreover, consistent with our admittedly sketchy precedent in this area. [While] it is not a sufficient condition for "inferior" officer status that one be subordinate to a principal officer, it is surely a necessary condition for inferior officer status that the officer be subordinate to another officer.

The independent counsel is not even subordinate to the President. The Court essentially admits as much, noting that "appellant may not be 'subordinate' to the Attorney General (and the President) insofar as she possesses a degree of independent discretion to exercise the powers delegated to her under the Act." In fact, there is no doubt about it. [Because] appellant is not subordinate to another officer, she is not an "inferior" officer and her appointment other than by the President with the advice and consent of the Senate is unconstitutional.

NOTES

1. Principal Officers.   After the holding in Morrison v. Olson, who are the principal officers of the United States? Cabinet secretaries and their equivalents? Anybody else?

2. Inferior Officers.   In Edmond v. United States, 520 U.S. 651 (1997), the Court held that judges of the Coast Guard Court of Criminal Appeals were inferior officers and thus could constitutionally be appointed by the Secretary of Transportation, a head of a department. The Court stated:

> Generally speaking, the term "inferior officer" connotes a relationship with some higher ranking officer or officers below the President: whether one is an "inferior" officer depends on whether he has a superior. It is not enough that other officers may be identified who formally maintain a higher rank, or possess responsibilities of a greater magnitude. If that were the intention, the Constitution might have used the phrase "lesser officer." Rather, in the context of a clause designed to preserve political accountability relative to important government assignments, we think it evident that "inferior officers" are officers whose work is directed and supervised at some level by others who were appointed by presidential nomination with the advice and consent of the Senate.

3. Scope of the Power to Appoint Inferior Officers.   While Congress has the power to decide whether the President alone, the law courts, or the heads of executive departments may appoint inferior officers, Congress may not itself appoint *any* executive officers. While Congress may specify qualifications for inferior officers so long as the qualifications are reasonably germane to the office, it may not actually appoint anyone who exercises any meaningful federal executive authority. See Shoemaker v. United States, 147 U.S. 282 (1893). However, Congress may appoint its own legislative subordinates—the aides, staff, and institutional officers who directly support the legislative function.

In the early 1970s, Congress created a Federal Election Commission to administer and enforce the Federal Election Campaign Act by rulemaking and civil prosecutions. Four of the six members of the Commission were appointed by the Speaker of the House and the President pro tempore of the Senate. In Buckley v. Valeo, supra, the Court found the Commission to be invalid because it wielded executive powers and Congress lacked authority to appoint executive officers.

> [N]either the Speaker of the House nor the President pro tempore of the Senate comes within [the] phrase "Heads of Departments." [The] Departments referred

to are themselves in the Executive Branch or at least have some connection with that branch. While the [Appointments] Clause expressly authorizes Congress to vest the appointment of certain officers in the "Courts of Law," the absence of similar language to include Congress must mean that neither Congress nor its officers were included within the language "Heads of Departments."

Following a series of spectacular accounting frauds involving public companies, Congress created the Public Company Accounting Oversight Board, an arm of government clothed with the power to investigate and discipline accounting firms that audit publicly held companies. The Board was composed of five members appointed by the commissioners of the Securities and Exchange Commission and subject to removal for good cause by the SEC commissioners. In Free Enterprise Fund v. Public Company Accounting Oversight Board, 561 U.S. 477 (2010), the Court upheld the validity of the appointment of the Board by the SEC commissioners. First, the Court invoked *Edmond* to conclude that the Board members were inferior officers because they have a superior and their work is subject to supervision or direction by the SEC commissioners. Next, the Court ruled that the SEC is a "department" for purposes of the appointments power because it is "a freestanding component of the Executive Branch, not subordinate to or contained within any other such component," a conclusion consistent with practice in the immediate aftermath of the Constitution's adoption. The SEC commissioners, as a body, were deemed to be the "head" of the department, rather than the Chairman of the SEC, because the SEC acts a body and the Chairman exercises no supervisory control over the actions of the SEC as a whole.

4. Recess Appointments. The President must obtain the advice and consent of the Senate for appointments of principal officers, but the Recess Appointments clause gives the President alone the power "to fill up all Vacancies that may happen during the Recess of the Senate, by granting Commissions which shall expire at the End of their next Session." Art. II, §2, cl. 3. In National Labor Relations Board v. Noel Canning, 134 S. Ct. 2550 (2014), the Supreme Court considered and decided three questions: 1) Is a recess only an inter-session recess or does it include intra-session recesses? 2) Are the "vacancies" that may be filled only those vacancies that occur during the recess or does it include vacancies that existed prior to the recess and continue to exist during the recess? 3) What length of Senate inactivity constitutes a recess? None of these issues had been decided by the Court in the prior history of the nation. President Obama made recess appointments to the NLRB while the Senate had risen but was holding *pro forma* sessions every three days. Noel Canning argued that an NLRB ruling made by the board that included the recess appointees was invalid because the appointments were invalid and, thus, a quorum of the NLRB did not exist. The Court ruled unanimously in favor of Noel Canning. A majority of five concluded that both intra-session and inter-session recesses constitute a recess, and that vacancies that occur before a recess but remain during the recess may be filled by a recess appointment. On the third question, the Court created a malleable rule. If the Senate says it is in session by stipulating that it hold *pro forma* sessions during a longer break, it is in session, provided that the interval between *pro forma* sessions is three days or less. But intervals of four to nine days are "presumptively" too short to constitute a recess, except for an "unusual circumstance" such as a "national catastrophe." Four justices concurred in the judgment but argued that historical practice amply supported the conclusion that only inter-session recesses count as recesses, that only vacancies that occur during the recess may be filled by recess appointments, and derided the Court's malleable rule as unstable and an invitation to Presidential experimentation.

b. The Removal Power

The Constitution explicitly provides for removal of federal executive officers by impeachment, but the Framers seem to have understood that impeachment was not the sole method of removal of executive officers other than the President and Vice President. Constitutional silence on the matter, however, spawned several questions of importance. Does the President have unilateral power to remove his own subordinates? May Congress restrict or even eliminate the President's removal power? May Congress unilaterally remove subordinate executive officers without impeachment?

The immediate reason for impeachment of President Andrew Johnson was Johnson's violation of the Tenure of Office Act, a statute that barred the President's removal of his cabinet secretaries without first obtaining Senate approval. Johnson fired Secretary of War Edwin Stanton, precipitating an impeachment trial in which Johnson escaped conviction by a single vote.

Years later, in Myers v. United States, 272 U.S. 52 (1926), the Court struck down a law providing that certain postmasters could not be removed by the President unless the Senate consented, thus implicitly finding the Tenure of Office Act to be unconstitutional. Former President and then Chief Justice Taft, writing for the Court, relied primarily on the historical record of the First Congress to conclude that the removal power is "incident to the power of appointment" and that "the President has the exclusive power of removing executive officers of the United States whom he has appointed" and the Senate has confirmed. This conclusion, said Taft, was also a "reasonable implication" from the President's duty to execute the laws. To discharge this duty he must be free to "select those [who] act for him under his direction." Since "his selection of administrative officers is essential to [the President's] execution of the laws, so must be his power of removing those for whom he can not continue to be responsible."

Myers has been eroded. Humphrey's Executor v. United States, 295 U.S. 602 (1935), involved the Federal Trade Commission, established by Congress as an executive agency "independent" of the President. Commissioners were appointed by the President for prescribed terms but could be removed by the President only for "inefficiency, neglect of duty, or malfeasance in office." The Court upheld the removal limits, reasoning that *Myers* recognized an "unrestrictable power of the President to remove purely executive officers." The

FTC, said the Court, was established as a "quasi-legislative or quasi-judicial agenc[y]" that was "require[d] to [act] independently of executive control." Thus, "as an appropriate incident" to the creation of such agencies, Congress could impose restrictions on presidential removal of such officials. The *Humphrey's Executor* principle was extended in Wiener v. United States, 357 U.S. 349 (1958), to "quasi-judicial" executive officers.

≣≣≣ **Morrison v. Olson**
≣≣≣ *487 U.S. 654 (1988)*

Chief Justice Rehnquist, for the Court.

[We] consider whether [the] provision of the [Ethics in Government] Act restricting the Attorney General's power to remove the independent counsel [only for] "good cause" [impermissibly] interferes with the President's exercise of his constitutionally appointed functions. [This] case does not involve an attempt by Congress itself to gain a role in the removal of executive officials other than [through] impeachment and conviction. The Act instead puts the removal power squarely in the hands of the Executive Branch; an independent counsel may be removed from office, "only by the personal action of the Attorney General, and only for good cause." There is no requirement of congressional approval of the Attorney General's removal decision, though the decision is subject to judicial review. In our view, [these] removal provisions [make] this case more analogous to [*Humphrey's Executor* and *Wiener*] than to *Myers* or *Bowsher*.

[Appellees] contend that *Humphrey's Executor* and *Wiener* are distinguishable from this case because they did not involve officials who performed a "core executive function." They argue that our decision in *Humphrey's Executor* rests on a distinction between "purely executive" officials and officials who exercise "quasi-legislative" and "quasi-judicial" powers. In their view, when a "purely executive" official is involved, the governing precedent is *Myers*, not *Humphrey's Executor*, [and,] under *Myers*, the President must have absolute discretion to discharge "purely" executive officials at will. We undoubtedly did rely on the terms "quasi-legislative" and "quasi-judicial" to distinguish the officials involved in *Humphrey's Executor* and *Wiener* from those in *Myers*, but our present considered view is that the determination of whether the Constitution allows Congress to impose a "good cause"–type restriction on the President's power to remove an official cannot be made to turn on whether or not that official is classified as "purely executive." The analysis contained in our removal cases is designed not to define rigid categories of those officials who may or may not be removed at will by the President, but to ensure that Congress does not interfere with the President's exercise of the "executive power" and his constitutionally appointed duty to "take care that the laws be faithfully executed" under Article II. *Myers* was undoubtedly correct in its holding, and in its broader suggestion that there are some "purely executive" officials who must be removable by the President at will if he is to be able to accomplish his constitutional role. [But] the characterization of the agencies in *Humphrey's Executor* and *Wiener* as "quasi-legislative" or "quasi-judicial" in large part reflected our judgment that it was not essential to the President's proper execution of his Article II powers that these agencies be headed up by individuals who were removable at will. We do not mean to suggest that an analysis of the functions served by the officials at issue is irrelevant. But the real question is whether the removal restrictions are of such a nature that they impede the President's ability to perform his constitutional duty, and the functions of the officials in question must be analyzed in that light.

[We] cannot say that the imposition of a "good cause" standard for removal by itself unduly trammels on executive authority. There is no real dispute that the functions performed by the independent counsel are "executive" in the sense that they are law enforcement functions that typically have been undertaken by officials within the Executive Branch. [But] the independent counsel is an inferior officer under the Appointments Clause, with limited jurisdiction and tenure and lacking policymaking or significant administrative authority. Although the counsel exercises no small amount of discretion and judgment in deciding how to carry out his or her duties under the Act, we simply do not see how the President's need to control the exercise of that discretion is so central to the functioning of the Executive Branch as to require as a matter of constitutional law that the counsel be terminable at will by the President.

Nor do we think that the "good cause" removal provision at issue here impermissibly burdens the President's power to control or supervise the independent counsel, as an executive official, in the execution of his or her duties under the Act. This is not a case in which the power to remove an executive official has been completely stripped from the President, thus providing no means for the President to ensure the "faithful execution" of the laws. Rather, because the independent counsel may be terminated for "good cause," the Executive, through the Attorney General, retains ample authority to assure that the counsel is competently performing his or her statutory responsibilities in a manner that comports with the provisions of the Act. [The] congressional determination to limit the removal power of the Attorney General was essential, in the view of Congress, to establish the necessary independence of the office. We do not think that this limitation as it presently stands sufficiently deprives the President of control over the independent counsel to interfere impermissibly with his constitutional obligation to ensure the faithful execution of the laws.

JUSTICE SCALIA, dissenting.

There is . . . no provision in the Constitution stating who may remove executive officers, except the provisions for removal by impeachment. Before the present decision it was established, however, (1) that the President's power to remove principal officers who exercise purely executive powers could not be restricted, and (2) that his power to remove inferior officers who exercise purely executive powers, and whose appointment Congress had removed from the usual procedure of Presidential appointment with Senate consent, could be restricted, at least where the appointment had been made by an officer of the Executive Branch.[1]

The Court could have resolved the removal power issue in this case by simply relying upon its erroneous conclusion that the independent counsel was an inferior officer, and then extending our holding that the removal of inferior officers appointed by the Executive can be restricted, to a new holding that even the removal of inferior officers appointed by the courts can be restricted. That would in my view be a considerable and unjustified extension, giving the Executive full discretion in neither the selection nor the removal of a purely executive officer. The course the Court has chosen, however, is even worse.

Since [*Humphrey's Executor*]—which was considered by many at the time the product of an activist, anti-New Deal Court bent on reducing the power of President Franklin Roosevelt—it has been established that the line of permissible restriction upon removal of principal officers lies at the point at which the powers exercised by those officers are no longer purely executive. [It] has often been observed, correctly in my view, that the line between "purely executive" functions and "quasi-legislative" or "quasi-judicial" functions is not a clear one or even a rational one. But at least it permitted the identification of certain officers, and certain agencies, whose functions were entirely within the control of the President. Congress had to be aware of that restriction in its legislation. Today, however, *Humphrey's Executor* is swept into the dustbin of repudiated constitutional principles. . . . What *Humphrey's Executor* (and presumably *Myers*) really means, we are now told, is not that there are any "rigid categories of those officials who may or may not be removed at will by the President," but simply that Congress cannot "interfere with the President's exercise of the 'executive power' and his constitutionally appointed duty to 'take care that the laws be faithfully executed.'"

One can hardly grieve for the shoddy treatment given today to *Humphrey's Executor*, which, after all, accorded the same indignity (with much less justification) to Chief Justice Taft's opinion 10 years earlier in *Myers*—gutting, in six quick pages devoid of textual or historical precedent for the novel principle it set forth, a carefully researched and reasoned 70-page opinion. It is in fact comforting to witness the reality that he who lives by the ipse dixit dies by the ipse dixit. But one must grieve for the Constitution. *Humphrey's Executor* at least had the decency formally to observe the constitutional principle that the President had to be the repository of all executive power, which, as *Myers* carefully explained, necessarily means that

---

1. [The] President must have control over all exercises of the executive power. That requires that he have plenary power to remove principal officers such as the independent counsel, but it does not require that he have plenary power to remove inferior officers. Since the latter [are] subordinate to, i.e., subject to the supervision of, principal officers who (being removable at will) have the President's complete confidence, it is enough—at least if they have been appointed by the President or by a principal officer—that they be removable for cause, which would include, of course, the failure to accept supervision. . . .

he must be able to discharge those who do not perform executive functions according to his liking. [Once] an officer is appointed " 'it is only the authority that can remove him, and not the authority that appointed him, that he must fear and, in the performance of his functions, obey.' " By contrast, "our present considered view" is simply that any executive officer's removal can be restricted, so long as the President remains "able to accomplish his constitutional role." There are now no lines. . . . This is an open invitation for Congress to experiment. What about a special Assistant Secretary of State, with responsibility for one very narrow area of foreign policy, who would not only have to be confirmed by the Senate but could also be removed only pursuant to certain carefully designed restrictions? Could this possibly render the President "[un]able to accomplish his constitutional role"? . . . The possibilities are endless, and the Court does not understand what the separation of powers, what "[a]mbition [counteracting] ambition," [Federalist No. 51 (Madison)], is all about, if it does not expect Congress to try them. As far as I can discern from the Court's opinion, it is now open season upon the President's removal power for all executive officers, with not even the superficially principled restriction of *Humphrey's Executor* as cover. . . .

NOTES

1. From Categories to Circumstances.   The progression of cases on removal—from *Myers* to *Morrison*—is a retreat from a categorical approach to a circumstantial one. In *Myers*, the Court reasoned that the President's obligation to execute the law required that he have control over his subordinates who carry out his policies, which meant that the President must have the power to remove his "purely executive" subordinates. After *Morrison*, the President's power to remove an executive subordinate may be severely limited so long as the limits do not impede the President's ability to perform his constitutional duty. That depends on the circumstances. Did President Clinton's inability to remove independent counsel Kenneth Starr impede his ability to perform his constitutional duties?

Suppose Congress creates a new executive office, an Ambassador for Peace, stipulating that the President may appoint the Peace Ambassador, subject to Senate confirmation, for a 14-year term, to be removable only for "good cause" by a majority vote among the Secretary of State, the Secretary of Defense, and the National Security Advisor. The Peace Ambassador is given "the complete power of the State Department to mediate conflicts of any kind in any part of the world." Imagine that the Peace Ambassador publicly declares that the United States should recognize Palestine and withdraw diplomatic recognition from Israel. The President demands that the Peace Ambassador be removed, but the Secretaries of State and Defense publicly disagree. Is the President's ability to perform his constitutional duties impeded? How can you tell?

2. Free Enterprise Fund: The Outer Boundaries of *Morrison*.   When Congress created the Public Company Accounting Oversight Board, it vested the power to remove Board members in the commissioners of the Securities and Exchange Commission, but only for "good cause shown." The SEC commissioners, in turn, are removable by the President only for "inefficiency, neglect of duty, or malfeasance in office." In Free Enterprise Fund v. Public Company Accounting Oversight Board, 561 U.S. 477 (2010), the Court invalidated this double-layered limitation on the President's removal power. Chief Justice Roberts wrote for a 5-4 majority:

May the President be restricted in his ability to remove a principal officer, who is in turn restricted in his ability to remove an inferior officer, even though that inferior officer determines the policy and enforces the laws of the United States? We hold that such multilevel protection from removal is contrary to Article II's vesting of the executive power in the President. The President cannot "take Care that the Laws be faithfully executed" if he cannot oversee the faithfulness of the officers who execute them. Here the President cannot remove an officer who enjoys more than one level of good-cause protection, even if the President determines that the officer is neglecting his duties or discharging them improperly. That judgment is instead committed to another officer, who may or may not agree with the President's determination, and whom the President cannot remove simply because that officer disagrees with him. This contravenes the President's "constitutional obligation to ensure the faithful execution of the laws."

[In prior cases] only one level of protected tenure separated the President from an officer exercising executive power. It was the President—or a subordinate he could remove at will—who decided whether the officer's conduct merited removal under the good-cause standard. The Act before us . . . not only protects Board members from removal except for good cause, but withdraws from the President any decision on whether that good cause exists. That decision is vested instead in other tenured officers—the Commissioners—none of whom is subject to the President's direct control. . . . Neither the President, nor anyone directly responsible to him, nor even an officer whose conduct he may review only for good cause, has full control over the Board. The President is stripped of the power our precedents have preserved, and his ability to execute the laws—by holding his subordinates accountable for their conduct—is impaired. That arrangement is contrary to Article II's vesting of the executive power in the President. Without the ability to oversee the Board, or to attribute the Board's failings to those whom he *can* oversee, the President is no longer the judge of the Board's conduct. . . . He can neither ensure that the laws are faithfully executed, nor be held responsible for a Board member's breach of faith. This violates the basic principle that the President "cannot delegate ultimate responsibility or the active obligation to supervise that goes with it," because Article II "makes a single President responsible for the actions of the Executive Branch."

Indeed, if allowed to stand, this dispersion of responsibility could be multiplied. If Congress can shelter the bureaucracy behind two layers of good-cause tenure, why not a third? At oral argument, the Government was unwilling to concede that even *five* layers between the President and the Board would be too many. The officers of such an agency—safely encased within a Matryoshka doll of tenure protections—would be immune from Presidential oversight, even as they exercised power in the people's name. The diffusion of power carries with it a diffusion of accountability. . . . Without a clear and effective chain of command, the public cannot "determine on whom the blame or the punishment of a pernicious measure, or series of pernicious measures ought really to fall." . . . By granting the Board executive power without the Executive's oversight, this Act subverts the President's ability to ensure that the laws are faithfully executed—as well as the public's ability to pass judgment on his efforts.

3. No Role for Congress in Removal.   In Bowsher v. Synar, 478 U.S. 714 (1986), the Court ruled that Congress by itself could not remove any executive officer except by impeachment. The Court struck down "the assignment by Congress to the Comptroller General [of] certain [executive] functions under the Balanced Budget and Emergency Deficit Control Act of 1985." The Act was designed to end protracted federal deficits by establishing federal spending ceilings and empowering the Comptroller General to exercise discretion in making program-by-program reductions in spending sufficient to comply with the spending ceilings. The Act required the President to implement the Comptroller General's spending reductions. The Comptroller General, appointed by the President and confirmed by the Senate, could be removed "only at the initiative of Congress [by] impeachment [or] by joint resolution of Congress 'at any time' for 'permanent disability, inefficiency, neglect of duty, malfeasance, or a felony or conduct involving moral turpitude.'" The Court concluded that this provision "brought [the Comptroller General] under the sole control of Congress." Because the functions performed by the Comptroller General under the Act were executive, "[b]y placing the responsibility for execution of the [Act] in the hands of an officer who is subject to removal only by itself, Congress in effect has retained control over the execution of the Act and has intruded into the executive function. The Constitution does not permit such intrusion."

The Court reasoned:

> The Constitution . . . explicitly provides for removal of [executive officers] by Congress only upon impeachment [and] conviction. [Congress] cannot reserve for itself the power of removal of an officer charged with the execution of the laws except by impeachment. To permit the execution of the laws to be vested in an officer answerable only to Congress would, in practical terms, reserve in Congress control over the execution of the laws. The structure of the Constitution does not permit Congress to execute the laws; it follows that Congress cannot grant to an officer under its control what it does not possess.

In dissent, Justice White argued that because a President could veto a joint declaration of removal of the Comptroller General, unilateral removal by Congress would require both houses of Congress to override the veto by a two-thirds margin, "a feat of bipartisanship more difficult than that required to impeach and convict." The "practical result of the removal provision" was that the Comptroller General was unlikely to be removed by Congress. In response, the Court asserted that separation of powers "cannot be permitted to turn on judicial assessment of whether an officer exercising executive power is on good terms with Congress."

2.   In Foreign Affairs

The President's unilateral power of action is greatest in the field of foreign affairs. Some aspects of this authority are rooted in the text of Article II (e.g., the President's power to "receive Ambassadors and other public Ministers" means that the President alone has authority to recognize foreign governments and to terminate such diplomatic relations), but other aspects are implicit in constitutional structure. Professor Louis Henkin, in Foreign Affairs and the Constitution (1972), asserts that

> [some foreign affairs] powers [belong] to the President, some to Congress, some to the President-and-Senate; some can be exercised by either the President or Congress, some require the joint authority of both. Irregular, uncertain division renders claims of usurpation more difficult to establish and the courts have not been available to adjudicate them.

Consider Henkin's assertion as you read the materials that follow.

a.   General Principles

≡ **United States v. Curtiss-Wright Export Corp.**
≡ *299 U.S. 304 (1936)*

JUSTICE SUTHERLAND delivered the opinion of the Court.

[An] indictment was returned in the court below [charging] that [appellees] conspired to sell in the United States certain arms of war, namely fifteen machine guns, to Bolivia, a country then engaged in armed conflict [with Paraguay] in the Chaco, in violation of [a] Joint Resolution of Congress, and the provisions of a proclamation issued on the same day by the President of the United States pursuant to authority conferred by §1 of the resolution. [The] Joint Resolution [provided in part:][2]

"That if the President finds that the prohibition of the sale of arms and munitions of war in the United States to those countries now engaged in

---

2. Only a year before the Court had ruled that Congress could not delegate to the President the power to promulgate elaborate industry-wide "codes of fair competition" drafted by labor and management representatives in each industry, the purpose of which was to stabilize wages and prices and stimulate economic activity in the midst of the Great Depression. See Panama Refining Co. v. Ryan, 293 U.S. 388 (1935); and Schechter Poultry Corp. v. United States, 295 U.S. 495 (1935). — ED.

armed conflict in the Chaco may contribute to the reestablishment of peace between those countries, and [if] he makes proclamation to that effect, it shall be unlawful to sell [any] arms or munitions of war in any place in the United States to the countries now engaged in that armed conflict [until] otherwise ordered by the President or by Congress."

[A federal district court dismissed the indictment because it concluded that the Joint Resolution was an invalid delegation of legislative power to the executive. A direct appeal was taken to the Supreme Court.]

Whether, if the Joint Resolution had related solely to internal affairs it would be open to the challenge that it constituted an unlawful delegation of legislative power to the Executive, we find it unnecessary to determine. The whole aim of the resolution is to affect a situation entirely external to the United States, and falling within the category of foreign affairs. [Assuming] (but not deciding) that the challenged delegation, if it were confined to internal affairs, would be invalid, may it nevertheless be sustained on the ground that its exclusive aim is to afford a remedy for a hurtful condition within foreign territory?

It will contribute to the elucidation of the question if we first consider the differences between the powers of the federal government in respect of foreign or external affairs and those in respect of domestic or internal affairs. [The] two classes of powers are different, both in respect of their origin and their nature. The broad statement that the federal government can exercise no powers except those specifically enumerated in the Constitution, and such implied powers as are necessary and proper to carry into effect the enumerated powers, is categorically true only in respect of our internal affairs. In that field, the primary purpose of the Constitution was to carve from the general mass of legislative powers *then possessed by the states* such portions as it was thought desirable to vest in the federal government, leaving those not included in the enumeration still in the states. . . . And since the states severally never possessed international powers, such powers could not have been carved from the mass of state powers but obviously were transmitted to the United States from some other source. During the colonial period, those powers were possessed exclusively by and were entirely under the control of the Crown. By the Declaration of Independence, "the Representatives of the United States of America" declared the United [not the several] Colonies to be free and independent states, and as such to have "full Power to levy War, conclude Peace, contract Alliances, establish Commerce and to do all other Acts and Things which Independent States may of right do." As a result of the separation from Great Britain by the colonies acting as a unit, the powers of external sovereignty passed from the Crown not to the colonies severally, but to the colonies in their collective and corporate capacity as the United States of America. [Thus,] the investment of the federal government with the powers of external sovereignty did not depend upon the affirmative grants of the Constitution. The powers to declare and wage war, to conclude peace, to make treaties, to maintain diplomatic relations with other sovereignties, if they had never been mentioned in the Constitution, would have vested in the federal government as necessary concomitants of nationality.

[Not] only . . . is the federal power over external affairs in origin and essential character different from that over internal affairs, but participation in the exercise of the power is significantly limited. In this vast external realm, with its important, complicated, delicate and manifold problems, the President alone has the power to speak or listen as a representative of the nation. He makes treaties with the advice and consent of the Senate; but he alone negotiates. Into the field of negotiation the Senate cannot intrude; and Congress itself is powerless to invade it. As [John] Marshall said [in] the House of Representatives, "The President is the sole organ of the nation in its external relations, and its sole representative with foreign nations."

[It] is important to bear in mind that we are here dealing not alone with an authority vested in the President by an exertion of legislative power, but with such an authority plus the very delicate, plenary and exclusive power of the President as the sole organ of the federal government in the field of international relations—a power which does not require as a basis for its exercise an act of [Congress]. It is quite apparent that if, in the maintenance of our international relations, embarrassment—perhaps serious embarrassment—is to be avoided and success for our aims achieved, congressional legislation [must] often accord to the President a degree of discretion and freedom from statutory restriction which would not be admissible were domestic affairs alone involved. Moreover, he, not Congress, has the better opportunity of knowing the conditions which prevail in foreign countries, and especially is this true in time of war. He has his confidential sources of information. He has his agents in the form of diplomatic, consular and other officials. Secrecy in respect of information gathered by them may be highly necessary, and the premature disclosure of it productive of harmful results.

[It] is evident that this court should not be in haste to apply a general rule which will have the effect of condemning legislation like that under review as constituting an unlawful delegation of legislative power. The principles which justify such legislation find overwhelming support in the unbroken legislative practice which has prevailed almost from the inception of the national government to the present day. An impressive array of legislation [enacted] by nearly every Congress from the beginning of our national existence to the present day must be given unusual [weight]. A legislative practice such as we have here, [marked] by the movement of a steady stream for a century and a half of time, goes a long way in [proving] unassailable ground for the constitutionality of the [practice]. Reversed.

NOTES

1. An Unenumerated Foreign Affairs Power. There is universal agreement that the foreign affairs power resides exclusively in the federal government, but Justice Sutherland's justification may not be the best case for that proposition. Sutherland made his historical claim that the United States acquired the incidents of sovereignty directly from the British Crown in order to argue that the federal government's foreign affairs powers are not limited to those enumerated in the Constitution. In Sutherland's view, the governmental powers enumerated in the Constitution serve to allocate to the states and the federal government the powers previously possessed by the states, but because the states never possessed any foreign affairs powers the totality of those powers (whether or not enumerated in the Constitution) are necessarily vested in the federal government. In short, the federal government has plenary authority over foreign affairs.

Sutherland's historical argument has been strongly attacked. See Lofgren, United States v. Curtiss-Wright Export Corporation: An Historical Reassessment, 83 Yale L.J. 1 (1973); Berger, The Presidential Monopoly of Foreign Relations, 71 Mich. L. Rev. 1 (1972); Levitan, The Foreign Relations Power: An Analysis of Mr. Justice Sutherland's Theory, 55 Yale L.J. 467 (1946); Goebel, Constitutional History and Constitutional Law, 38 Colum. L. Rev. 555 (1938). After all, when British sovereignty was wrested away by revolution, the "United States" consisted of discrete British colonies united in the common cause of treason against the Crown. There was no federal government as such. Who was available to receive sovereignty but the new states hatched from their colonial pupae?

There is, however, an overwhelming prudential argument that only the national government can exert the nation's sovereignty in dealing with other nations. Any other course is inconsistent with the idea of nationhood. But the conclusion that the federal government is the sole holder of the foreign affairs power says nothing about which branch of that government may wield power over foreign affairs.

2. The Scope of Presidential Authority. The precise issue in *Curtiss-Wright* was whether Congress was permitted to delegate to the President some "quasi-legislative" authority with respect to foreign affairs. The fact that Congress was recognized to have the authority to make broad delegations of power over foreign relations (apparently broader than with respect to domestic issues) does not mean that the President's power to act unilaterally is unlimited. To the extent that Congress shares control over foreign relations, it need not delegate power to the President. Indeed, Congress may limit the President's authority over matters that the Constitution assigns concurrently to Congress and the President. The hard question is to determine the scope of the President's unilateral authority over foreign affairs issues as to which the Constitution is silent on the question of presidential versus congressional authority.

On that point Sutherland argued that the President holds a "very delicate, plenary, and exclusive power [as] the sole organ of the federal government in the field of international relations—a power that does not require as a basis for its exercise an act of Congress." This dictum overstates the case. Perhaps Sutherland meant only that the Constitution presumes that the President has some measure of unilateral power over foreign affairs and that, because of this, Congress is permitted to authorize the President to act in foreign affairs without reference to any policies specified by Congress. But *Curtiss-Wright* is commonly relied on by enthusiastic advocates of unrestrained presidential power in foreign affairs to support the broader, and less tenable, position that the President can act independently of Congress on all matters of foreign relations save those over which the Constitution explicitly vests Congress with control.

≡ *Zivotofsky v. Kerry*
≡ *2015 U.S. LEXIS 3781*

[Since the Truman administration, it has been the policy of the President to regard Jerusalem as a city over which no nation-state has sovereignty. Accordingly, the State Department lists the place of birth on U.S. passports of American citizens born in Jerusalem as "Jerusalem." In 2002 Congress enacted a law that required the State Department, on request of a passport holder born in Jerusalem, to list "Israel" as the place of birth (the "Act"). The mother of Menachem Zivotofsky, born in 2002 in Jerusalem to American citizens, requested that Israel be listed as his place of birth on his passport. The State Department refused to do so and Zivotofsky brought suit to compel the State Department to act in accord with the law. A federal trial court dismissed the case as a non-justiciable political question and the D.C. Circuit affirmed, but the Supreme Court reversed, finding the issue to be justiciable and remanding for consideration on the merits. The D.C. Circuit found the Act unconstitutional and, after granting certiorari, the Supreme Court affirmed.]

JUSTICE KENNEDY delivered the opinion of the Court.

. . . The Court addresses two questions. . . . First, it must determine whether the President has the exclusive power to grant formal recognition to a foreign sovereign. Second, if he has that power, the Court must determine whether Congress can command the President and his Secretary of State to issue a formal statement that contradicts the earlier recognition. The statement in question here is a congressional mandate that allows a United States citizen born in Jerusalem to direct the President and Secretary of State, when issuing his passport, to state that his place of birth is "Israel."

[The Court summarized the long-standing position of the executive branch that the status of Jerusalem must be resolved by international agreement and is not a matter for unilateral assumption of sovereignty.] . . .

II. In considering claims of Presidential power this Court refers to Justice Jackson's familiar tripartite framework from Youngstown Sheet & Tube Co. v. Sawyer. [The third of Jackson's categories is] when "the President takes measures incompatible with the expressed or implied will of Congress . . . he can rely only upon his own constitutional powers minus any constitutional powers of Congress over the matter." To succeed in this third category, the President's asserted power must be both "exclusive" and "conclusive" on the issue. . . .

Because the President's refusal to implement [the Act] falls into Justice Jackson's third category, his claim must be "scrutinized with caution," and he may rely solely on powers the Constitution grants to him alone. To determine whether the President possesses the exclusive power of recognition the Court examines the Constitution's text and structure, as well as precedent and history bearing on the question. . . .

Recognition is a "formal acknowledgement" that a particular "entity possesses the qualifications for statehood" or "that a particular regime is the effective government of a state." . . . Despite the importance of the recognition power in foreign relations, the Constitution does not use the term "recognition." . . . The Secretary asserts that the President exercises the recognition power based on the Reception Clause, which directs that the President "shall receive Ambassadors and other public Ministers." Art. II, §3. At the time of the founding . . . prominent international scholars suggested that receiving an ambassador was tantamount to recognizing the sovereignty of the sending state. . . .

This in fact occurred early in the Nation's history when President Washington recognized the French Revolutionary Government by receiving its ambassador. . . .

The inference that the President exercises the recognition power is further supported by his additional Article II powers [to make treaties and appoint ambassadors, each with Senate consent]. As a matter of constitutional structure, these additional powers give the President control over recognition decisions. . . . The Constitution thus assigns the President means to effect recognition on his own initiative. Congress, by contrast, has no constitutional power that would enable it to initiate diplomatic relations with a foreign nation.

The text and structure of the Constitution grant the President the power to recognize foreign nations and governments. The question then becomes whether that power is exclusive. The various ways in which the President may unilaterally effect recognition—and the lack of any similar power vested in Congress—suggest that it is. So, too, do functional considerations. Put simply, the Nation must have a single policy regarding which governments are legitimate in the eyes of the United States and which are not. Foreign countries need to know, before entering into diplomatic relations or commerce with the United States, whether their ambassadors will be received; whether their officials will be immune from suit in federal court; and whether they may initiate lawsuits here to vindicate their rights. These assurances cannot be equivocal. Recognition is a topic on which the Nation must "speak . . . with one voice." . . . [T]he President since the founding has exercised this unilateral power to recognize new states—and the Court has endorsed the practice.

It remains true, of course, that many decisions affecting foreign relations—including decisions that may determine the course of our relations with recognized countries—require congressional action. Congress may "regulate Commerce with foreign Nations," "establish an uniform Rule of Naturalization," "define and punish Piracies and Felonies committed on the high Seas, and Offences against the Law of Nations," "declare War," "grant Letters of Marque and Reprisal," and "make Rules for the Government and Regulation of the land and naval Forces." In addition, the President cannot make a treaty or appoint an ambassador without the approval of the Senate. The President, furthermore, could not build an American Embassy abroad without congressional appropriation of the necessary funds. . . .

In practice, then, the President's recognition determination is just one part of a political process that may require Congress to make laws. The President's exclusive recognition power encompasses the authority to acknowledge, in a formal sense, the legitimacy of other states and governments, including their territorial bounds. . . .

No single precedent resolves the question whether the President has exclusive recognition authority and, if so, how far that power extends. . . . In the end, however, a fair reading of the cases shows that the President's role in the recognition process is both central and exclusive. . . . The Secretary . . . contends that under the Court's precedent the President has "exclusive authority to conduct diplomatic relations," along with "the bulk of foreign-affairs powers." In support . . . , the Secretary quotes United States v. Curtiss-Wright Export Corp., which described the President as "the sole organ of the federal government in the field of international relations." This Court declines to acknowledge that unbounded power. . . .

Curtiss-Wright . . . does not extend so far as the Secretary suggests. In *Curtiss-Wright*, the Court considered whether a congressional delegation of power to the President was constitutional. . . . The Court held that the delegation was constitutional, reasoning that Congress may grant the President substantial authority and discretion in the field of foreign affairs. . . . *Curtiss-Wright* did not hold that the President is free from Congress' lawmaking power in the field of international relations. The President does have a unique role in communicating with foreign governments, [but] whether the realm is foreign or domestic, it is still the Legislative Branch, not the Executive Branch, that makes the law. . . . The Executive is not free from the ordinary controls and checks of Congress merely because foreign affairs are at issue. . . . That said, judicial precedent and historical practice teach that it is for the President alone to make the specific decision of what foreign power he will recognize as legitimate, both for the Nation as a whole and for the purpose of making his own position clear within the context of recognition in discussions and negotiations with foreign nations. . . .

III. As the power to recognize foreign states resides in the President alone, the question becomes whether [the Act] infringes on the Executive's consistent decision to withhold recognition with respect to Jerusalem. . . . As a matter of United States policy, neither Israel nor any other country is acknowledged as having sovereignty over Jerusalem. In this way, [the Act] "directly contradicts" the "carefully calibrated and longstanding Executive branch policy of neutrality toward Jerusalem." . . . If the power over recognition is to mean anything, it must mean that the President not only makes the initial, formal recognition determination but also that he may maintain that determination in his and his agent's statements. This conclusion is a matter of both common sense and necessity. If Congress could command the President to state a recognition position inconsistent with his own, Congress could override the President's recognition determination. [W]hen a Presidential power is "exclusive," it "disabl[es] the Congress from acting upon the subject." Here, the subject is quite narrow: The Executive's exclusive power extends no further than his formal recognition determination. But as to that determination, Congress may not enact a law that directly contradicts it. This is not to say Congress may not express its disagreement with the President in myriad ways. For example, it may enact an embargo, decline to confirm an ambassador, or even declare war. But none of these acts would alter the President's recognition decision. If Congress may not pass a law, speaking in its own voice, that effects formal recognition, then it follows that it may not force the President himself to contradict his earlier statement. That congressional command would not only prevent the Nation from speaking with one voice but also prevent the Executive itself from doing so in conducting foreign relations.

Although the statement required by [the Act] would not itself constitute a formal act of recognition, it is a mandate that the Executive contradict his prior recognition determination in an official document issued by the Secretary of State. . . . As a result, it is unconstitutional. . . .

It is true . . . that Congress has substantial authority over passports. . . . The problem with [the Act], however, lies in how Congress exercised its authority over passports. It was an improper act for Congress to "aggrandiz[e] its power at the expense of another branch" by requiring the President to contradict an earlier recognition determination in an official document issued by the Executive Branch. To allow Congress to control the President's communication in the context of a formal recognition determination is to allow Congress to exercise that exclusive power itself. As a result, the statute is unconstitutional.

In holding [the Act] invalid the Court does not question the substantial powers of Congress over foreign affairs in general or passports in particular. This case is confined solely to the exclusive power of the President to control recognition determinations, including formal statements by the Executive Branch acknowledging the legitimacy of a state or government and its territorial bounds. Congress cannot command the President to contradict an earlier recognition determination in the issuance of passports.

JUSTICE BREYER, concurring.

I continue to believe that this case presents a political question inappropriate for judicial resolution. But because precedent precludes resolving this case on political question grounds I join the Court's opinion.

JUSTICE THOMAS, concurring in the judgment in part and dissenting in part.

. . . The statutory provision at issue implicates the President's residual foreign affairs power. . . . The President is not constitutionally compelled to implement [the Act] as it applies to passports because passport regulation falls squarely within his residual foreign affairs power and Zivotofsky has identified no source of congressional power to require the President to list Israel as the place of birth for a citizen born in Jerusalem on that citizen's passport. . . . Because the President has residual foreign affairs authority to regulate passports and because there appears to be no congressional power that justifies [the Act]'s application to passports, Zivotofsky's challenge to the Executive's designation of his place of birth on his passport must fail.

JUSTICE SCALIA, with whom THE CHIEF JUSTICE and JUSTICE ALITO join, dissenting.

. . . The Constitution contemplates that the political branches will make policy about the territorial claims of foreign nations the same way they make policy about other international matters: The President will exercise his powers on the basis of his views, Congress its powers on the basis of its views. That is just what has happened here.

The political branches of our Government agree on the real-world fact that Israel controls the city of Jerusalem. They disagree, however, about how official documents should record the birthplace of an American citizen born in Jerusalem. . . . No doubt congressional discretion in executing legislative powers has its limits; Congress's chosen approach must be not only "necessary" to carrying its powers into execution, but also "proper." Congress thus may not transcend boundaries upon legislative authority stated or implied elsewhere in the Constitution. But [the Act] does not transgress any such restriction.

. . . I agree that the Constitution *empowers* the President to extend recognition on behalf of the United States [but the Act] plainly does not concern recognition. Recognition is more than an announcement of a policy[;] it is a formal legal act with effects under international law. [But the Act] has nothing to do with recognition. [It] does not require the Secretary to make a formal declaration about Israel's sovereignty over Jerusalem. And nobody suggests that international custom infers acceptance of sovereignty from the birthplace designation on a passport or birth report, as it does from bilateral treaties or exchanges of ambassadors. [M]aking a notation in a passport or birth report does not encumber the Republic with any international obligations. . . .

[The Act] calls for nothing beyond a "geographic description"; it does not require the Executive even to assert, never mind formally recognize, that Jerusalem is a part of sovereign Israel. Since birthplace specifications in citizenship documents are matters within Congress's control, Congress may treat Jerusalem as a part of Israel when regulating the recording of birthplaces, even if the President does not do so when extending recognition. . . .

Even if the Constitution gives the President sole power to extend recognition, it does not give him sole power to make all decisions relating to foreign disputes over sovereignty. . . . Read naturally, power to "regulate Commerce with foreign Nations" includes power to regulate imports from Gibraltar as British goods or as Spanish goods. Read naturally, power to "regulate the Value . . . of foreign Coin" includes power to honor (or not) currency issued by Taiwan. And so on for the other enumerated powers. These are not airy hypotheticals. A trade statute from 1800, for example, provided that "the whole of the island of Hispaniola"—whose status was then in controversy—"shall for purposes of [the] act be considered as a dependency of the French Republic." . . .

The Constitution likewise does not give the President exclusive power to determine which claims to statehood and territory "are legitimate in the eyes of the United States." Congress may express its own views about these matters by declaring war, restricting trade, denying foreign aid, and much else besides. . . . [For example, Congress has expressed] "that . . . Tibet . . . is an occupied country under the established principles of international law" and that "Tibet's true representatives are the Dalai Lama and the Tibetan Government in exile." . . .

[The] Constitution may well deny Congress power to recognize. . . . But whatever else [the Act] may do, it plainly does not make (or require the President to make) a commitment accepting Israel's sovereignty over Jerusalem. . . .

In the end, the Court's decision does not rest on text or history or precedent. It instead comes down to "functional considerations"—principally the Court's perception that the Nation "must speak with one voice" about the status of Jerusalem. The vices of this mode of analysis go beyond mere lack of footing in the Constitution. Functionalism of the sort the Court practices today will *systematically* favor the unitary President over the plural Congress in disputes involving foreign affairs. It is possible that this approach will make for more effective foreign policy, perhaps as effective as that of a monarchy. It is certain that, in the long run, it will erode the structure of separated powers that the People established for the protection of their liberty.

NOTES AND QUESTIONS

1. One Voice.   The Court emphasized the importance of the nation speaking with one voice when it comes to diplomatic recognition. But whose voice? Is it so obvious that it is the President? Presidents change and policies change. The presidential voice may be the same but the message could be entirely different. Suppose President Obama extends diplomatic recognition to Cuba and a later President Rubio withdraws recognition. If Congress takes a clear position—e.g., denying the President the power to recognize Cuba—and that position is sustained over a veto, is it any less clear that the nation has spoken with one voice?

2. Why Now?   For 225 years the nation has managed to deal with diplomatic recognition without any resolution of the constitutional question of the locus of this authority. What was so pressing about *Zivotofsky* that required the Court to decide? Only Justice Breyer continued to insist that this issue should be treated as a non-justiciable political question. Would that have been a better outcome?

3. Scope of the Recognition Power.   *Zivotofsky* settled the question of whether the recognition power includes specification of the place of birth where sovereignty of the birthplace is contested, but how much further does the recognition power reach? Suppose as part of a nuclear arms deal President Obama extends diplomatic recognition to Iran and, in the course of doing so, pledges to refrain from military action against Iran should it breach the terms of the nuclear agreement. Iran breaches and Congress either declares war or authorizes the President to take military action against Iran. Are either (or both) of these congressional actions precluded by *Zivotofsky?*

Dames & Moore v. Regan
453 U.S. 654 (1981)

JUSTICE REHNQUIST delivered the opinion of the Court.

The questions presented by this case touch fundamentally upon the manner in which our Republic is to be governed. . . . [Our] decision today [is] confined to a resolution of the dispute presented to us. That dispute involves various Executive Orders and regulations by which the President nullified attachments and liens on Iranian assets in the United States, directed that these assets be transferred to Iran, and suspended claims against Iran that may be presented to an International Claims Tribunal. This action was taken in an effort to comply with an Executive Agreement between the United States and Iran. We granted certiorari before judgment in this case, and set an expedited briefing and argument schedule, because lower courts had reached conflicting conclusions on the validity of the President's actions and, as the Solicitor General informed us, unless the Government acted by July 19, 1981, Iran could consider the United States to be in breach of the Executive Agreement.

[We] stress that the expeditious treatment of the issues involved by all of the courts which have considered the President's actions makes us acutely aware of the necessity to rest decision on the narrowest possible ground capable of deciding the case. [We] attempt to lay down no general "guidelines" covering other situations not involved here, and attempt to confine the opinion only to the very questions necessary to decision of the case. . . .

[On] November 4, 1979, the American Embassy in Tehran was seized and our diplomatic personnel were captured and held hostage. In response to that crisis, President Carter, acting pursuant to the International Emergency Economic Powers Act [IEEPA], declared a national emergency [and] blocked the removal or transfer of "all property [of] the Government of Iran [that is] subject to the jurisdiction of the United States." [On] December 19, 1979, petitioner Dames & Moore filed suit in [federal district court] against the Government of Iran, the Atomic Energy Organization of Iran, and a number of Iranian banks, [alleging that the Iranian] Atomic Energy Organization [owed Dames & Moore] $3,436,694.30 plus interest for services performed under [an engineering consulting] contract prior to [its termination by the Iranian agency]. The District Court issued orders of attachment directed against property of the defendants, and the property of certain Iranian banks was then attached to secure any judgment that might be entered against them.

On January 20, 1981, the Americans held hostage were released by Iran pursuant to an [Executive] Agreement entered into the day before. [The] Agreement stated that "[it] is the purpose of [the United States and Iran] to terminate all litigation as between the Government of each party and the nationals of the other, and to bring about the settlement and termination of all such claims through binding arbitration." [The] Agreement called for the establishment of an Iran–United States Claims Tribunal which would arbitrate any claims not settled within six months. Awards of the Claims Tribunal are to be "final and binding" and "enforceable [in] the courts of any nation in accordance with its laws." Under the Agreement, the United States is obligated "to terminate all legal proceedings in United States courts involving claims of United States persons and institutions against Iran and its state enterprises, to nullify all attachments and judgments obtained therein, to prohibit all further litigation based on such claims, and to bring about the termination of such claims through binding arbitration." In addition, the United States must "act to bring about the transfer" by July 19, 1981, of all Iranian assets held in this country by American banks. One billion dollars of these assets will be deposited in a security account in the Bank of England, to the account of the Algerian Central Bank, and used to satisfy awards rendered against Iran by the Claims Tribunal. On January 19, 1981, President Carter issued a series of Executive Orders implementing the terms of the agreement, [including a provision that] "nullified" all non-Iranian interests in [Iranian assets]. On February 24, 1981, President Reagan issued an Executive Order in which he "ratified" the January 19th Executive Orders. Moreover, he "suspended" all "claims which may be presented to [the] Tribunal" and provided that such claims "shall have no legal effect in any action now pending in any court of the United States." The suspension of any particular claim terminates if the Claims Tribunal determines that it has no jurisdiction over that claim; claims are discharged for all purposes when the Claims Tribunal either awards some recovery and that amount is paid, or determines that no recovery is due.

[The federal district court vacated the attachments obtained by Dames & Moore and stayed further proceedings in its suit against various Iranian entities. Dames & Moore brought a new suit in federal district court against Regan, the Treasury Secretary, seeking a declaration that the executive orders were unconstitutional and an injunction restraining enforcement of the orders. The lower courts upheld the validity of the orders.]

The parties and the lower courts [have] all agreed that much relevant analysis is contained in [*Youngstown*]. Justice Black's opinion for the Court in that [case] recognized that "[the] President's power, if any, to issue the order must stem either from an act of Congress or from the Constitution itself." Justice Jackson's . . . classification of executive actions into three general categories [is] analytically useful [but] it is doubtless the case that executive action in any particular instance falls, not neatly in one of three pigeonholes, but rather at some point along a spectrum running from explicit congressional authorization to explicit congressional prohibition. This is particularly true as respects cases such as the one before us, involving responses to international crises the nature of which Congress can hardly have been expected to antici-pate in any detail.

The Government [has] principally relied on §203 of the IEEPA as authorization for these actions: "[T]he President [may] nullify, void, prevent or prohibit, any acquisition, holding, withholding, use, transfer, withdrawal, transportation, importation or exportation of, or dealing in, or exercising any right, power, or privilege with respect to, or transactions involving, any property in which any foreign country or a national thereof has any interest; by any person, or with respect to any property, subject to the jurisdiction of the United States." The Government contends that the acts of "nulli-fying" the attachments and ordering the "transfer" of the frozen assets are specifically authorized by the plain language of the above statute. Because the President's action in nullifying the attachments and ordering the trans-fer of the assets was taken pursuant to specific congressional authorization, it is "supported by the strongest of presumptions and the widest latitude of judicial interpretation, and the burden of persuasion would rest heavily upon any who might attack it." *Youngstown* (Jackson, J., concurring). Under the circumstances of this case, we cannot say that petitioner has sustained that heavy burden. A contrary ruling would mean that the Federal Government as a whole lacked the power exercised by the President, and that we are not prepared to say.

Although we have concluded that the IEEPA constitutes specific con-gressional authorization to the President to nullify the attachments and order the transfer of Iranian assets, there remains the question of the Presi-dent's authority to suspend claims pending in American courts. Such claims have, of course, an existence apart from the attachments which accompa-nied them. In terminating these claims [the] President purported to act under authority of both the IEEPA [and] the so-called "Hostage Act." We conclude [that] neither the IEEPA nor the Hostage Act constitutes spe-cific authorization of the President's action suspending claims. [But] both statutes [are] highly relevant in the looser sense of indicating congressional acceptance of a broad scope for executive action in circumstances such as those presented in this case. [The] IEEPA delegates broad authority to the President to act in times of national emergency with respect to property of a foreign country. The Hostage Act similarly indicates congressional willing-ness that the President have broad discretion when responding to the hostile acts of foreign sovereigns.

[We] cannot ignore the general tenor of Congress'[s] legislation in this area. . . . [Congress] cannot anticipate and legislate with regard to every pos-sible action the President may find it necessary to take or every possible situ-ation in which he might act. Such failure of Congress specifically to delegate authority does not, "especially [in] the areas of foreign policy and national security," imply "congressional disapproval" of action taken by the Execu-tive. On the contrary, the enactment of legislation closely related to the ques-tion of the President's authority in a particular case which evinces legislative intent to accord the President broad discretion may be considered to "invite" "measures on independent presidential responsibility," *Youngstown* (Jackson, J., concurring). At least this is so where there is no contrary indication of legislative intent and when, as here, there is a history of congressional acquiescence in conduct of the sort engaged in by the President. It is to that history which we now turn. . . .

[The] United States has repeatedly exercised its sovereign authority to settle the claims of its nationals against foreign countries. Though those settlements have sometimes been made by treaty, there has also been a long-standing practice of settling such claims by executive agreement without the advice and consent of the Senate. Under such agreements, the President has agreed to renounce or extinguish claims of United States nationals against foreign governments in return for lump-sum payments or the establishment of arbitration procedures. [Since] 1952, the President has entered into at least 10 [such] binding settlements with foreign [nations].

Crucial to our decision today is the conclusion that Congress has implicitly approved the practice of claim settlement by executive agreement. This is best demonstrated by Congress'[s] enactment of the International Claims Settlement Act of 1949, [which established] a procedure whereby funds resulting from [executive claims] settlements could be distributed [to American claimants]. By creating a procedure to implement future settlement agreements, Congress placed its stamp of approval on such agreements. [Over] the years Congress has frequently amended the International Claims Settlement Act to provide for particular problems arising out of settlement agreements, thus demonstrating Congress'[s] continuing acceptance of the President's claim settlement authority.

[In] light of all of the foregoing—the inferences to be drawn from the character of the legislation Congress has enacted in the area, such as the IEEPA and the Hostage Act, and from the history of acquiescence in executive claims settlement—we conclude that the President was authorized to suspend pending claims. [As] Justice Frankfurter pointed out in *Youngstown*, "a systematic, unbroken, executive practice, long pursued to the knowledge of the Congress and never before questioned [may] be treated as a gloss on 'Executive Power' vested in the President by §1 of Art. II." Past practice does not, by itself, create power, but "long-continued practice, known to and acquiesced in by Congress, would raise a presumption that the [action] had been [taken] in pursuance of its consent." United States v. Midwest Oil Co., 236 U.S. 459, 474 (1915).

[Our] conclusion is buttressed by the fact that the means chosen by the President to settle the claims of American nationals provided an alternative forum, the Claims Tribunal, which is capable of providing meaningful relief. [Just] as importantly, Congress has not disapproved of the action taken here. . . . Quite the contrary, the relevant Senate Committee has stated that the establishment of the Tribunal is "of vital importance to the United States." We are thus clearly not confronted with a situation in which Congress has in some way resisted the exercise of Presidential authority.

Finally, we re-emphasize the narrowness of our decision. We do not decide that the President possesses plenary power to settle claims, even as against foreign governmental entities. [But] where, as here, the settlement of claims has been determined to be a necessary incident to the resolution of a major foreign policy dispute between our country and another, and where, as here, we can conclude that Congress acquiesced in the President's action, we are not prepared to say that the President lacks the power to settle such claims.

[Affirmed.]

NOTE

Method and Result. Compare the Court's methodology with that of Justices Black, Frankfurter, and Jackson in *Youngstown*. Which *Youngstown* approach does the Court use in *Dames & Moore*?

Is there a significant difference between the legislative inaction in *Youngstown* (which led the Court to conclude that Congress had implicitly denied authority to the President) and that in *Dames & Moore* (which led the Court to conclude that Congress had implicitly granted authority to the President)? If so, what is that difference?

Consider the possibility that the Court erred by treating legislative inactivity as tacit approval. The events were unique; once the hostage accord had been executed and the hostages returned, the pressure to ratify the presidential deal in the courts was overpowering. But given that there was a six-month delay between the accord and the asset transfer, would it not have been preferable for the President to have asked Congress for explicit ratification of the accord? Almost surely Congress would have done so, and such ratification would have made it unnecessary for the Court to rely on congressional silence as approval. As it is, does legislative silence mean implicit disapproval with respect to domestic presidential action but implicit approval with respect to foreign initiatives of the President?

b. War

Congress has the power to "declare War." The President, as Commander-in-Chief, has the power to conduct war. But what about undeclared "wars," such as those in Korea, Vietnam, Iraq, and Afghanistan? Or that more modern phenomenon, the "surgical strike," exemplified by presidentially ordered attacks on Libya and Grenada (by Reagan), Panama (by George H.W. Bush), and Iraq and Sudan (by Clinton)?

≡ *The Prize Cases*
≡   *67 U.S. (2 Black) 635 (1863)*

[In April 1861, President Lincoln proclaimed a naval blockade of Southern ports and ordered the seizure of any ships carrying goods to or from the Confederate States. The Court, 5-4, upheld the validity of seizures pursuant to the blockade even though Congress had never declared war.]

JUSTICE GRIER delivered the opinion of the Court.

Congress alone has the power to declare a national or foreign war. It cannot declare war against a State, or any number of States, by virtue of any clause in the Constitution. [The President] has no power to initiate or declare a war either against a foreign nation or a domestic State. But by [Acts of Congress in 1795 and 1807] he is authorized to call out the militia and use the military and naval forces of the United States in case of invasion by foreign nations, and to suppress insurrection against the government of a State or of the United States.

If a war be made by invasion of a foreign nation, the President is not only authorized but bound to resist force, by force. He does not initiate the war, but is bound to accept the challenge without waiting for any special legislative authority. And whether the hostile party be a foreign invader, or States organized in rebellion, it is none the less a war, although the declaration of it be *"unilateral."* [The] President was bound to meet [the Civil War] in the shape it presented itself, without waiting for Congress to baptize it with a name. [If] it were necessary to the technical existence of a war that it should have a legislative sanction, we find it in almost every act passed at the extraordinary session of [Congress in] 1861, which was wholly employed in enacting laws to enable the Government to prosecute the war with vigor and efficiency. And finally, in 1861, we find [Congress] "approving, legalizing, and making valid all the acts, proclamations, and orders of the President [as] if they had been *issued and done under the previous express authority* and direction of the Congress." [Without] admitting that such an act was necessary under the circumstances, it is plain that if the President had in any manner assumed powers which it was necessary should have the authority or sanction of Congress, [this] ratification has operated to perfectly cure the defect.

JUSTICE NELSON, joined by CHIEF JUSTICE TANEY and JUSTICES CATRON and CLIFFORD, dissenting.

Before an insurrection against the established Government can be dealt with on the footing of a civil war, [it] must be recognized or declared by the war-making power of the Government. [There] is no difference in this respect between a civil or a public war. The Acts of 1795 and 1807 did not, and could not, under the Constitution, confer on the President the power of declaring war against a State of this Union, or of deciding that war existed, and upon that ground authorize the capture and confiscation of the property of every citizen of the State whenever it was found on the waters. The laws of [war] convert every citizen of the hostile State into a public enemy, and treat him accordingly, whatever may have been his previous conduct. This great power over the business and property of the citizen is reserved to the legislative department by the express words of the Constitution. It cannot be delegated or surrendered to the Executive. Congress alone can determine whether war exists or should be declared; and until they have acted, no citizen of the State can be punished in his person or property [as an enemy citizen]. The penalty of confiscation [cannot] lawfully be inflicted.

NOTE

Defensive Use of Armed Force. Justice Grier argued that Congress had exercised its Article I power to "provide for calling forth the Militia [to] suppress Insurrections and repel Invasions," and that President Lincoln acted pursuant to statutory authority. Justice Nelson asserted that Congress could not delegate its power to declare war but never responded to Grier's point that Article I implicitly provides for delegating to the President the power to suppress insurrections. Who has the better argument? Why?

Suppose that Congress had never acted to authorize the President to use force to suppress insurrections or repel invasions. Would Lincoln's action have been less justifiable? Without statutory authority to repel invasions, would it have been unconstitutional for Americans at Pearl Harbor to shoot back? In other words, does the President have inherent power to repel an invasion or rebellion? Grier did not have to reach that point. Note, however, that an early draft of the Constitution gave Congress power to "make war" but, on motion by James Madison and Elbridge Gerry in the 1787 Convention, the language was changed to "declare war" in order to "leav[e] to the Executive the power to repel sudden attacks."

≡≡≡ *The War Powers Resolution*
≡≡≡ *87 Stat. 555, 50 U.S.C. §§1541-1548*

[In 1973, in the wake of the Vietnam War (specifically, President Nixon's extension of the war into Laos and Cambodia), Congress enacted the War Powers Resolution over a veto by President Nixon. This unusual statute is often described as "quasi-constitutional" because it attempts to mandate a process for presidential use of armed force without a declaration of war.]

Purpose and Policy. Sec. 2. (a) It is the purpose of this joint resolution to fulfill the intent of the framers of the Constitution [and] insure that the collective judgment of both the Congress and the President will apply to the introduction of United States Armed Forces into hostilities, or into situations where imminent involvement in hostilities is clearly indicated by the circumstances, and to the continued use of such forces in hostilities or in such situations.

(b) Under [the] Constitution [Congress has] power to make all laws necessary and proper for carrying into execution, not only its own powers but also all other powers vested by the Constitution in the Government of the United States, or in any department or officer thereof.

(c) The constitutional powers of the President as Commander-in-Chief to introduce United States Armed Forces into hostilities, or into situations where imminent involvement in hostilities is clearly indicated by the circumstances, are exercised only pursuant to (1) a declaration of war, (2) specific statutory authorization, or (3) a national emergency created by attack upon the United States, its territories or possessions, or its armed forces.

Consultation. Sec. 3. The President in every possible instance shall consult with Congress before introducing United States Armed Forces into hostilities or into situations where imminent involvement in hostilities is clearly indicated by the circumstances, and after every such introduction shall consult regularly with the Congress until United States Armed Forces are no longer engaged in hostilities or have been removed from such situations.

Reporting. Sec. 4. (a) In the absence of a declaration of war, in any case in which United States Armed Forces are introduced —

(1) into hostilities or into situations where imminent involvement in hostilities is clearly indicated by the circumstances;

(2) into the territory, airspace or waters of a foreign nation, while equipped for combat, except for deployments which relate solely to supply, replacement, repair, or training of such forces; or

(3) in numbers which substantially enlarge United States Armed Forces equipped for combat already located in a foreign nation; the President shall submit within 48 hours to the Speaker of the House [and] to the President pro tempore of the Senate a report, in writing, setting forth [the facts and the legal authority relied on for introducing American armed forces, and] such other information as the Congress may request. . . .

Congressional Action. Sec. 5. . . . (b) Within sixty calendar days after a report is submitted or is required to be submitted pursuant to section 4(a)(1), whichever is earlier, the President shall terminate any use of [American] Armed Forces with respect to which such report was submitted (or required to be submitted), unless the Congress (1) has declared war or has enacted a specific authorization for such use of [American] Armed Forces, (2) has extended by law such sixty-day period, or (3) is physically unable to meet as a result of an armed attack upon the United States. Such sixty-day period shall be extended for not more than an additional thirty days if the President determines and certifies to the Congress in writing that unavoidable military necessity respecting the safety of [American] Armed Forces requires the continued use of such armed forces in the course of bringing about a prompt removal of such forces.

(c) Notwithstanding section (b), at any time that [American] Armed Forces are engaged in hostilities outside the territory of the [United States, without] a declaration of war or specific statutory authorization, such forces shall be removed by the President if the Congress so directs by concurrent resolution. . . .

Interpretation of Joint Resolution. Sec. 8. (a) Authority to introduce [American] Armed Forces into hostilities or into situations wherein involvement in hostilities is clearly indicated by the circumstances shall not be inferred —

(1) from any provision of law (whether or not in effect [before] enactment of this joint resolution), including any provision contained in any appropriation Act, unless such provision specifically authorizes the introduction of [American] Armed Forces into hostilities or into such situations and states that it is intended to constitute specific statutory authorization within the meaning of this joint resolution; or

(2) from any treaty heretofore or hereafter ratified unless such treaty is supplemented by legislation specifically authorizing the introduction of [American] Armed Forces into hostilities or into such situations and stating that it is intended to constitute specific statutory authorization within the meaning of this joint resolution. . . .

(d) Nothing in this joint resolution —

(1) is intended to alter the constitutional authority of the Congress or of the President, or the provisions of existing treaties; or

(2) shall be construed as granting any authority to the President with respect to the introduction of [American] Armed Forces into hostilities or into situations wherein involvement in hostilities is clearly indicated by the circumstances which authority he would not have had in the absence of this joint resolution. . . .

NOTES

1. Validity. Is the War Powers Resolution constitutionally valid? In his veto message, President Nixon objected particularly to section 5. He claimed that section 5(b), which requires the President to withdraw American armed forces within 60 to 90 days absent specific congressional authorization, "would terminate automatically, [without] overt congressional action, [certain] of the President's constitutional powers as Commander-in-Chief." Nixon characterized this congressional veto-by-inaction as irresponsible as well as unconstitutional. Section 5(c), which requires the President to withdraw American armed forces when both houses of Congress so demand, is an active legislative veto. INS v. Chadha, 462 U.S. 919 (1983), held that a single house of Congress could not veto executive action. Shortly after *Chadha*, the Court voided two-house legislative vetoes. After you have read *Chadha*, consider whether there is anything sufficiently different about war-making to render the two-house veto in section 5(c) an exception to the rule. Are the consultation and reporting requirements an impermissible encroachment on the President's authority as Commander-in-Chief?

2. Presidential War-Making After the War Powers Resolution. Presidents have contested the validity of the War Powers Resolution but have not entirely ignored it. One proposed version of the War Powers Resolution would have exempted from its coverage foreign incursions designed to rescue Americans abroad, but the exemption was ultimately deleted from the enacted resolution. President Ford used American forces to rescue Americans and South Vietnamese from Saigon at the close of the Vietnam War, although he first asked Congress for "clarification" of his authority to do so. President Carter used American armed forces in a totally secret and ultimately aborted mission in Iran to rescue the hostages held in Tehran. President Reagan invaded Grenada to rescue American students, who were said to be threatened by a Marxist regime. Did these actions violate the War Powers Resolution?

President Reagan committed American armed forces to combat (or its equivalent) in Nicaragua, El Salvador, Honduras, and Lebanon, all for purposes unrelated to the rescue of Americans. President Reagan also used American air power offensively in a raid on Libya designed to kill Colonel Gaddafi, the ruler of Libya. President George H.W. Bush used American armed forces in Panama to depose Manuel Noriega, Panama's ruler. President Clinton used American armed forces in Sudan, Afghanistan, and Iraq to retaliate against terrorism and to punish Iraq for its failure to abide by United Nations sanctions following the Persian Gulf War. Most of these ventures were concluded within the 60-day period stipulated by the War Powers Resolution.

President George H.W. Bush committed large numbers of American military personnel to the Persian Gulf in advance of the 1991 Gulf War. He relied on his powers as Commander-in-Chief and denied the validity of the War Powers Resolution. When he announced a further large commitment sufficient to achieve an "adequate offensive option," a constitutional debate ensued that ended when Congress voted to authorize the President to use force in aid of the United Nations resolution to expel Iraq from Kuwait.

Congress's authorization of President Bush to wage war in the Persian Gulf, though not styled a declaration of war, is one of a series of explicit acts of Congress conferring on the President authority to wage war in some limited sphere. Such actions date back to President Washington's naval "quasi-war" with France and include President Jefferson's expeditions against Tripoli in 1802, the Civil War, the Korean War, and the Vietnam War. By contrast, without prior congressional approval, President Clinton launched a sustained offensive air assault on Yugoslavia in an effort to compel that country to adhere to international standards of proper treatment for its ethnic minorities. Was that air assault constitutionally valid?

3. Problem.   In February 2011, the Libyan people began to protest the regime of Moammar Gaddafi, an uprising that quickly escalated into armed combat between protesters and the Libyan military loyal to Gaddafi. On March 19, 2011, after the United Nations had condemned the Gaddafi regime and imposed a "no-fly" zone over Libya, President Obama directed American armed forces to attack military targets in Libya to implement the United Nations resolutions. On March 31, 2011, the United States turned over full command and control of the military operations to a NATO coalition. By late May, the 60-day period prescribed in section 5 of the War Powers Resolution had expired. Even so, American armed forces provided about 70 percent of the military intelligence in the Libya campaign and a majority of the assets used in refueling of warplanes (including mid-air refueling), flew approximately 2,500 sorties in Libya (about 25 percent of all sorties) and a lesser proportion of air strikes against Libyan air defense targets, and sent numerous armed but unmanned "drone" aircraft to strike Libyan targets. The cost of American military involvement in the Libyan campaign from March through September 2011 is estimated to be about $1.1 billion.

On June 15, 2011, the President transmitted to Speaker John Boehner a report that summarized these matters and explained why the President believed that the War Powers Resolution was inapplicable:

> The President is of the view that the current U.S. military operations in Libya are consistent with the War Powers Resolution and do not under that law require further congressional authorization, because U.S military operations are distinct from the kind of "hostilities" contemplated by the Resolution's 60-day termination provision. . . . U.S. operations do not involve sustained fighting or active exchanges of fire with hostile forces, nor do they involve the presence of U.S. ground troops, U.S. casualties or a serious threat thereof, or any significant chance of escalation into a conflict characterized by those factors.

Within days of this report, ten members of Congress filed suit in the U.S. District Court for the District of Columbia, seeking a declaration that the Libyan conflict is a war and President Obama's commitment of U.S. military assets to the Libyan conflict was unconstitutional. The suit, Kucinich v. Obama, also sought an injunction to suspend further U.S. military operations in Libya absent a congressional declaration of war.

Did President Obama violate the War Powers Resolution? Would anyone have standing to assert that claim in court? See Kucinich v. Obama, 821 F. Supp. 2d 110 (D.D.C. 2011).

4. Utility of the War Powers Resolution. If Presidents don't bother to comply, has the War Powers Resolution accomplished anything? It may be that its very existence has caused Presidents to inform Congress of their war-making intentions, but if Presidents make war beyond their constitutional powers, is this of much significance? Perhaps it has placed a premium on short, less-than-60-day military adventures, but a great deal of damage can occur within 60 days. And, in any case, is there any provision in the Constitution authorizing the President to wage war at his sole discretion so long as its duration is less than 60 days?

Some scholars doubt the utility of the War Powers Resolution. The decision to commit the nation to war lies with Congress. "To do that requires understanding, . . . courage, . . . insight, [and] fortitude. For a Congress composed of such members, no War Powers Resolution would be necessary; for a Congress without them, no War Powers Resolution would be sufficient." Michael Glennon, Constitutional Diplomacy 123 (1990). For Congress to check a President determined to wage war unilaterally requires even more courage, no matter what the state of public opinion might be. Is the War Powers Resolution likely to be an efficacious vehicle to check such a President?

5. The War Against Terrorism After September 11, 2001. On September 11, 2001, four commercial airliners were hijacked and three were used as missiles to destroy New York's World Trade Center and to damage the Pentagon, with the loss of some 3,000 lives. The fourth airliner, apparently headed for the Capitol or the White House, crashed in Pennsylvania as a result of passenger resistance. Three days later, Congress enacted a joint resolution authorizing the President to use military force. The Authorization to Use Military Force (AUMF) recited that the "acts of treacherous violence . . . committed against the United States and its citizens . . . render it both necessary and appropriate that the United States exercise its rights to self-defense and to protect United States citizens both at home and abroad," declared that "such acts . . . pose an unusual and extraordinary threat to the national security and foreign policy of the United States," asserted that "the President has authority under the Constitution to take action to deter and prevent acts of international terrorism against the United States," and resolved that

> the President is authorized to use all necessary and appropriate force against those nations, organizations, or persons he determines planned, authorized, committed, or aided the terrorist attacks that occurred on September 11, 2001, or harbored such organizations or persons, in order to prevent any further acts of international terrorism against the United States by such nations, organizations or persons.

The AUMF also stated that "[c]onsistent with section 8(a)(1) of the War Powers Resolution, the Congress declares that [the AUMF] is intended to constitute specific statutory authorization within the meaning of section 5(b) of the War Powers Resolution" and further that "[n]othing in this resolution supercedes any requirement of the War Powers Resolution." H.J.R. 64, S.J.R. 23, Sept. 14, 2001.

Queries: Is this a declaration of war? If so, against what state? International law holds that war is between states. If this not a declaration of war, is the Joint Resolution constitutionally sufficient to permit the President to wage war in accordance with its terms? Is the AUMF an impermissible delegation to the President of the power to declare war? Consider *Curtiss-Wright* and *The Prize Cases*.

Consider these same queries in connection with the October 2002 congressional resolution that authorized the President to use American armed forces "as he determines to be necessary and appropriate in order to (1) defend the national security of the United States against the continuing threat posed by Iraq; and (2) enforce all relevant United Nations Security Council resolutions regarding Iraq," so long as the President determined these two objectives could not be attained by "further diplomatic or peaceful means" and that military action is "consistent" with the American response to the terrorist attacks of September 11, 2001. Is the Iraq War that commenced in March 2003 unconstitutional? If so, why? What remedy is available if you conclude that the Iraq War is unconstitutional?

Problem: In the winter of 2005-2006 it was revealed that the federal government had engaged in warrantless electronic surveillance in the United States of international communications of persons suspected of having ties to foreign terrorists and enemy combatants. This program was defended by the government as authorized by Congress under the Authorization to Use Military Force of September 14, 2001, and by virtue of the President's inherent powers as Commander-in-Chief. Under the Foreign Intelligence Surveillance Act, an order must be obtained from a special Foreign Intelligence Surveillance Court to engage in electronic surveillance in the United States for purposes of gathering intelligence related to foreign affairs. Does the President have the authority to engage in the actions just described?

6. Detention of Enemy Combatants. After the September 11 attacks, the United States and its allies invaded Afghanistan and overturned its fundamentalist Islamic Taliban government. In the process it captured a number of enemy combatants, some 600 of which were removed to and imprisoned in an American naval base at Guantanamo, Cuba. The United States asserted that all of the detainees are unlawful combatants under applicable international law because they wage war indiscriminately upon civilian and military targets and fail to identify themselves distinctively as armed combatants. The President took the position that, under the September 14, 2001 AUMF, he was authorized to detain these enemy combatants indefinitely. Two classes of suits developed. In one, non-citizen detainees challenged the validity of their detention and contended that they were entitled to bring a habeas corpus petition in federal court. In the other, detained American citizens made the same contentions.

These issues were not drawn on a clean slate. During the Civil War, President Lincoln suspended the writ of habeas corpus and Congress ratified his action by legislation. Toward the end of the war, the military seized Milligan, a civilian American citizen and resident of Indiana, tried him before a military tribunal on charges of aiding the Confederacy, and sentenced him to death. In *Ex parte Milligan*, 71 U.S. (4 Wall.) 2 (1866), the Court held that Lincoln's suspension of habeas corpus, though lawful, did not warrant the trial and conviction by a military tribunal of a civilian not engaged in actual warfare against the United States. Military tribunals, said the Court, "can never be applied to citizens in states which have upheld the authority of the government, and where the courts are open and their process unobstructed. . . . [No] usage of war could sanction a military trial there for any offence whatever of a citizen in civil life in nowise connected with military service."

During World War II, a group of German saboteurs landed on American soil and disguised themselves as civilians. Before they could carry out acts of sabotage they were arrested, subjected to a trial by military tribunal, sentenced to death, and executed. At least one of them was an American citizen. In *Ex parte Quirin*, 317 U.S. 1 (1942), the Court upheld the process by which they were tried and condemned. The Nazi saboteurs contended that the President lacked authority to subject them to a military tribunal and to deny them access to the civil courts and the constitutional protections afforded criminal defendants in the civil courts. Chief Justice Stone wrote for the Court:

> [It] is unnecessary . . . to determine to what extent the President as Commander in Chief has constitutional power to create military commissions without the support of congressional legislation. For here Congress has authorized trial of offenses against the law of war before such commissions. We are concerned

only with the question of whether it is within the constitutional power of the National Government to place petitioners upon trial before a military commission for the offenses with which they are charged. . . . [By] universal agreement and practice, the law of war draws a distinction between . . . lawful and unlawful combatants. Lawful combatants are subject to capture and detention as prisoners of war. . . . Unlawful combatants are likewise subject to capture and detention, but [also] are subject to trial and punishment by military tribunals for acts which render their belligerency unlawful. The spy . . . , or an enemy combatant who without uniform comes secretly . . . for the purpose of waging war by destruction of life and property, are familiar examples of [unlawful combatants] subject to trial and punishment by military tribunals. . . . [Ex parte Milligan is not applicable because Milligan] was not an enemy belligerent either entitled to the status of a prisoner of war or subject to the penalties imposed upon unlawful belligerents.

Rasul. In Rasul v. Bush, 542 U.S. 466 (2004), the Court faced "the narrow but important question of whether United States courts lack jurisdiction to consider challenges to the legality of the detention of foreign nationals captured abroad in connection with hostilities and incarcerated" by the United States "in a territory [such as Guantanamo] over which the United States exercises plenary and exclusive jurisdiction, but not 'ultimate sovereignty.'" Guantanamo occupies this unusual status because Cuba has leased it to the United States in perpetuity. The federal habeas corpus statute, 28 U.S.C. §2241, enables federal courts to hear challenges to the validity of imprisonment brought by persons within the jurisdiction of the federal courts. A prior decision, Johnson v. Eisentrager, 339 U.S. 763 (1950), held that "aliens detained outside the sovereign territory of the United States [may not] invoke a petition for a writ of habeas corpus." However, because under "the express terms of its agreements with Cuba, the United States exercises 'complete jurisdiction and control' over the Guantanamo Bay Naval Base, and may continue to exercise such control permanently if it so chooses," the Court thought that the habeas corpus statute included within its coverage all those detained at Guantanamo: "Aliens held at the base, no less than American citizens, are entitled to invoke the federal courts' authority under §2241." Because the case involved the scope of the federal habeas statute, the Court expressed no opinion on the separate question of whether the detainees were entitled to habeas corpus as a matter of constitutional law.

Three justices dissented, arguing that the text, history, and prior interpretation of the habeas corpus statute indicated that the statute applied only to persons within the territorial jurisdiction of the federal district court in which relief is sought. Because Guantanamo is not within the jurisdiction of any federal district court, the dissenters claimed the statute did not apply to non-citizen Guantanamo detainees. The dissent charged that the Court's treatment of the habeas corpus statute was "a wrenching departure from precedent" that

ought to be unthinkable when the departure has a potentially harmful effect upon the Nation's conduct of a war. . . . Congress is in session. If it wished to change federal . . . habeas jurisdiction . . . , it could have done so . . . by intelligent revision of the statute, instead of by today's clumsy, countertextual reinterpretation that confers upon wartime prisoners greater habeas rights than domestic detainees. The latter must challenge their present physical confinement in the district of their confinement, whereas under today's strange holding Guantanamo Bay detainees can petition in any of the 94 federal judicial districts. The fact that extraterritorially located detainees lack the district of detention that the statute requires has been converted from a factor that precludes their ability to bring a petition at all into a factor that frees them to petition wherever they wish — and, as a result, to forum shop. For this Court to create such a monstrous scheme in time of war, and in frustration of our military commanders' reliance upon clearly stated prior law, is judicial adventurism of the worst sort.

Hamdi. Among the Guantanamo detainees was an American citizen, Yaser Hamdi, who was later transferred to a naval brig in Charleston, South Carolina. Through his father, Hamdi brought a habeas corpus petition to challenge the validity of his imprisonment. The Fourth Circuit concluded that because it was "undisputed that Hamdi was captured in a zone of active combat in a foreign theater of conflict," he was not entitled to any "factual inquiry or evidentiary hearing."

In Hamdi v. Rumsfeld, 542 U.S. 507 (2004), the Supreme Court reversed. A four-justice plurality consisting of Justice O'Connor, joined by Chief Justice Rehnquist and Justices Kennedy and Breyer, first addressed the "threshold question [of] whether the Executive has the authority to detain citizens who qualify as 'enemy combatants.' . . ." The plurality concluded that Congress had authorized such detention in its AUMF of September 14, 2001.

> The capture and detention of lawful combatants and the capture, detention, and trial of unlawful combatants, by "universal agreement and practice," are "important incidents of war." [Ex parte Quirin.] The purpose of detention is to prevent captured individuals from returning to the field of battle and taking up arms once again. . . . There is no bar to this Nation's holding one of its own citizens as an enemy combatant. [*Quirin.*] . . . A citizen, no less than an alien, can be "part of or supporting forces hostile to the United States or coalition partners" and "engaged in an armed conflict against the United States"; such a citizen, if released, would pose the same threat of returning to the front during the ongoing conflict.

Ex parte Milligan did not apply because "*Milligan* turned in large part on the fact that Milligan was not a prisoner of war, but a resident of Indiana arrested while at home there. . . . Had Milligan been captured while he was assisting Confederate soldiers by carrying a rifle against Union troops on a Confederate battlefield, the holding of the Court might well have been different."

However, the plurality concluded that Hamdi was entitled to "receive notice of the factual basis for his classification [as an enemy combatant], and a fair opportunity to rebut the Government's factual assertions before a neutral decisionmaker."

Justices Scalia and Stevens dissented. They reasoned that because Congress had not suspended habeas corpus, Hamdi could not be detained indefinitely as an enemy combatant but could only be prosecuted under the federal criminal code in federal court. Justice Thomas also dissented, contending that the President's "*constitutional* authority to protect the national security" coupled with the September 14, 2001 AUMF vested in the President nonjusticiable "broad discretion" to determine whether Hamdi was in fact an enemy combatant.

Congress reacted to *Rasul* and *Hamdi* by enacting the Detainee Treatment Act of 2005 (DTA), which appeared to deny Guantanamo detainees any right to habeas corpus to contest the validity of their imprisonment. Instead, detainees were limited to trial by military commissions constituted by executive order. The military commissions were intended to determine whether each detainee was in fact an enemy combatant and, if necessary, to try such combatants for unspecified crimes.

Hamdan. In Hamdan v. Rumsfeld, 548 U.S. 557 (2006), the Supreme Court construed the DTA to preserve an alien detainee's right to seek habeas relief, and ruled that Congress had not authorized the creation of the military commissions, the President had no unilateral constitutional authority to create them, and the commissions violated various provisions of the Geneva Conventions.

> A four-justice plurality concluded that the military commissions were not authorized by the common law of war to try Hamdan with conspiracy to further the goals of Al Qaeda, because the crime of conspiracy is not recognized as a war crime under international treaties, conventions, or prior practice. A majority of the Court determined that Common Article 3 of the Geneva Conventions, which forbids "the passing of sentences and the carrying out of executions without previous judgment pronounced by a regularly constituted court affording all the judicial guarantees which are recognized as indispensable by civilized peoples," applied (because the United States has ratified that Convention, making it binding law) and that the military commissions were not a "regularly constituted court." . . .
>
> Justice Kennedy concurred, providing the fifth vote on the question of whether the military commissions were a "regularly constituted court." He applied Justice Jackson's three-part scheme from *Youngstown* and concluded that because Congress had enacted the Uniform Code of Military Justice, which limited the President's ability to create special military commissions, the case came within Jackson's third category. Given those limits, and the lack of a grant of constitutional authority to the President to act unilaterally, "the commission cannot be considered regularly constituted under United States law and thus does not satisfy Congress'[s] requirement that military commissions conform to the law of war. . . ."

Justice Thomas, joined by Justice Scalia, dissented:

[The] Founders conclude[d] that the "President has primary responsibility—along with the necessary power—to protect the national security and to conduct the Nation's foreign relations." [. . . This Court has observed that these provisions confer upon the President broad constitutional authority to protect the Nation's security in the manner he deems fit. . . . Congress, to be sure, has a substantial and essential role in both foreign affairs and national security. But "Congress cannot anticipate and legislate with regard to every possible action the President may find it necessary to take or every possible situation in which he might act," and "such failure of Congress . . . does not, 'especially . . . in the areas of foreign policy and national security,' imply 'congressional disapproval' of action taken by the Executive." *Dames & Moore.* Rather, in these domains, the fact that Congress has provided the President with broad authorities does not imply—and the Judicial Branch should not infer—that Congress intended to deprive him of particular powers not specifically enumerated. *Dames & Moore.* . . . Accordingly, in the very context that we address today, this Court has concluded that "the detention and trial of petitioners—ordered by the President in the declared exercise of his powers as Commander in Chief of the Army in time of war and of grave public danger—are not to be set aside by the courts without the clear conviction that they are in conflict with the Constitution or laws of Congress constitutionally enacted." *Ex parte Quirin,* 317 U.S. 1, 25 (1942).

Under this framework, the President's decision to try Hamdan before a military commission for his involvement with al Qaeda is entitled to a heavy measure of deference. . . . Military and foreign policy judgments " 'are . . . decisions of a kind for which the Judiciary has neither aptitude, facilities nor responsibility and which has long been held to belong in the domain of political power not subject to judicial intrusion or inquiry.' "

Justice Alito, joined by Justices Scalia and Thomas, also dissented:

[P]etitioner's commission is "a regularly constituted court." [A "regularly constituted" court is one that is] appointed or established in accordance with the appointing country's domestic law. . . . There is no reason why a court that differs in structure or composition from an ordinary military court must be viewed as having been improperly constituted. Tribunals that vary significantly in structure, composition, and procedures may all be "regularly" or "properly" constituted. . . .

Boumedienne. Congress reacted to *Hamdan* by enacting the Military Commissions Act, which amended the federal habeas statute to deny to aliens detained at Guantanamo the right to bring a habeas action. In Boumedienne v. Bush, 553 U.S. 723 (2008), the Supreme Court (5-4) ruled that Congress could not suspend habeas corpus relief for the detainees. The suspension clause, Art. I, §9, cl. 2, provides that "the Writ of Habeas Corpus shall not be suspended, unless when in cases of Rebellion or Invasion the public Safety may require it," but the threshold question was whether the constitutional right to habeas relief extends to aliens held by American armed forces outside the sovereign territory of the United States. Although Johnson v. Eisentrager, 339 U.S. 763 (1950), had held that that the Constitution does not guarantee habeas for aliens held by the United States in areas over which the United

States is not sovereign, the Court purported to extract from *Eisentrager* a malleable multi-factor test to determine when habeas has extraterritorial application: "(1) the citizenship and status of the detainee and the adequacy of the process through which that status determination was made; (2) the nature of the sites where apprehension and then detention took place; and (3) the practical obstacles inherent in resolving the prisoner's entitlement to the writ." The Court provided little guidance concerning the application of these factors, but concluded that the constitutional right of habeas extends to aliens detained at Guantanamo, "a territory that, while technically not part of the United States, is under the complete and total control of our Government." Thus, the suspension clause applied unless the Combatant Status Review Tribunal (CSRT) procedures created by Congress in the Detainee Treatment Act were an adequate substitute for habeas. The Court concluded that the procedures were inadequate due to "the constraints upon the detainee's ability to rebut the factual basis for the Government's assertion that he is an enemy combatant." In a CSRT, "the detainee has limited means to find or present evidence to challenge the Government's case against him, [lacks] the assistance of counsel and may not be aware of the most critical allegations that the Government relied upon to order his detention." While a "detainee can confront witnesses that testify during the CSRT proceedings[,] given that there are in effect no limits on the admission of hearsay evidence . . . the detainee's opportunity to question witnesses is likely to be more theoretical than real."

Four justices dissented, noting that the Court struck down "as inadequate the most generous set of procedural protections ever afforded aliens detained by this country as enemy combatants, . . . without bothering to say what due process rights the detainees possess, without explaining how the statute fails to vindicate those rights, and before a single petitioner has even attempted to avail himself of the law's operation. . . . The majority merely replaces a review system designed by the people's representatives with a set of shapeless procedures to be defined by federal courts at some future date. [T]his decision is not really about the detainees at all, but about control of federal policy regarding enemy combatants."

In a separate dissent, Justice Scalia, joined by Chief Justice Roberts and Justices Thomas and Alito, argued that *Eisentrager* positively controlled the question of the extraterritorial availability of habeas to aliens, and that the majority had effectively overruled *Eisentrager*:

> *Eisentrager* could not be clearer that the privilege of habeas corpus does not extend to aliens abroad. By blatantly distorting *Eisentrager*, the Court avoids the difficulty of explaining why it should be overruled. The rule that aliens abroad are not constitutionally entitled to habeas corpus has not proved unworkable in practice; if anything, it is the Court's "functional" test that does not (and never will) provide clear guidance for the future. *Eisentrager* forms a coherent whole with the accepted proposition that aliens abroad have no substantive rights under our Constitution. Since it was announced, no relevant factual premises have changed. It has engendered considerable reliance on the part of our military.

And, as the Court acknowledges, text and history do not clearly compel a contrary ruling. . . .

Queries: The United States detains aliens in American military custody in Iraq and Afghanistan. Under the *Boumedienne* rationale, are those detainees entitled to bring a habeas petition in federal court? If World War II had been conducted under *Boumedienne*'s principles, would a Nazi soldier taken prisoner by Patton's army in France be entitled to file a petition for writ of habeas corpus in a U.S. district court?

c. *Treaties and Executive Agreements*

Treaties may be negotiated by the President but must be ratified by a two-thirds vote of the Senate. Executive agreements are international agreements made by the President alone without Senate ratification. By reason of the supremacy clause, treaties and executive agreements preempt any contrary state law. While the precise dividing line between the two is murky at best, the President may enter into an executive agreement instead of a treaty if the subject of the agreement is within some enumerated power given to the President *alone*.

The principal examples are United States v. Pink, 315 U.S. 203 (1942), and United States v. Belmont, 301 U.S. 324 (1937). When President Franklin Roosevelt extended diplomatic recognition to the Soviet Union in 1933, the Soviet Union assigned to the United States its claims against Americans holding assets of Russians whose property had been seized by the Soviet government. The United States in turn agreed to prosecute these claims and remit the net proceeds to the Soviet Union. In reliance on this executive agreement (the so-called Litvinov Assignment), the United States then sued a New York bank to recover funds deposited by a Russian corporation. The lower courts dismissed the claim because New York public policy forbade assisting such naked government confiscation. In *Belmont*, the Court reversed, reasoning that diplomatic recognition was a power entrusted exclusively to the President, and that recognition and the executive agreement "were all parts of one transaction [within] the competence of the President, [who] had authority to speak as the sole organ" of the United States. More generally, said the Court, "an international compact [is] not always a treaty which requires the participation of the Senate. There are many such compacts, of which a protocol, a modus vivendi, a postal convention, and agreements like [the Litvinov Assignment] are illustrations." In *Pink*, which also involved the Litvinov Assignment, the Court reaffirmed its *Belmont* holding that, as an aspect of his sole power to extend or withdraw diplomatic recognition, the President "has the power to determine the policy [that shall] govern the question of recognition."

In recent years, two related phenomena have arisen: (1) executive agreements whose effectiveness is conditioned upon congressional approval, and (2) implementation by executive order of treaties negotiated but never ratified. International trade agreements such as NAFTA (the North American Free Trade Agreement) and GATT (the General Agreement on Trade and Tariffs) are examples of executive agreements conditioned on legislative ratification. Each agreement was negotiated by the President and became effective upon ratification by simple majorities in both houses of Congress. Under each agreement the United States agreed to conduct its domestic policies in ways that would not provide unfair subsidies to domestic industries, and resolution of claimed violations was committed to an international forum. Are NAFTA and GATT treaties (requiring Senate consent by a two-thirds majority) or executive agreements (whether or not conditioned on congressional approval)? Professor Henkin asserts that "[o]ne is compelled to conclude that there are agreements which the President can make on his sole authority and others which he can make only with the consent of the Senate, but neither Justice Sutherland [who wrote the Court's opinion in *Belmont*] nor any one else has told us which are which."

What is the source of the President's power to negotiate these agreements? If it is the treaty power, these "agreements" must be treaties. If it stems entirely from authorizing legislation but the result is a treaty (no matter what it is called), can Congress authorize the President to convert treaties into non-treaties, so long as both houses of Congress approve by simple majorities? If not, these "agreements" must be invalid.

If the President's power to enter into these agreements is rooted in an unenumerated federal power to enter into non-treaty international agreements, does the President hold this power exclusively or may it be shared with Congress? Critics of this method contend that the power to enter into non-treaty international agreements belongs entirely to the President. See, e.g., Tribe, Taking Text and Structure Seriously: Reflections on Free-Form Method in Constitutional Interpretation, 108 Harv. L. Rev. 1221, 1268-1269 (1995). But if the President wishes to condition the effectiveness of an executive agreement on congressional approval, why should he be prevented from doing so? The Constitution does not expressly forbid this course of action. Defenders contend that executive agreements conditioned on legislative approval are simply another way that "the nation can commit itself internationally." See Ackerman and Golove, Is NAFTA Constitutional?, 108 Harv. L. Rev. 799, 919-920 (1995).

The Kyoto global warming treaty raises the question of whether the President may implement a non-ratified treaty by executive order. Although the Senate had not ratified the treaty, the Clinton Administration sought to implement various aspects of it by executive order. Similarly, President Obama has ordered the U.S. Navy to conform to the unratified Law of the Sea treaty, and has ordered federal authorities to conform to an unratified treaty banning military use of space. Does the validity of this method hinge on the source of the President's authority to issue the implementing executive order? If the President has authority under some unrelated statute, should it matter that the specific use of that authority is designed to circumvent the necessity of Senate consideration and ratification?

For a general criticism of the extent to which executive agreements have been used to circumvent the treaty requirements and an argument that the scope of unilateral presidential power has been swollen in the interest of expediency, see Paul, The Geopolitical Constitution: Executive Expediency and Executive Agreements, 86 Cal. L. Rev. 671 (1998).

Note that treaties, like legislation, are declared by Article VI to be the supreme law of the land. Since treaties and federal statutes are of equal stature, in case of conflict the more recent act controls, so long as the treaty is self-executing. See Whitney v. Robertson, 124 U.S. 190 (1888). The effect of this rule is that a later statute can contravene a treaty, even though this may result in a breach of international law.

Note on Presidential Authority to Implement Treaties

Congress possesses broad authority to implement treaties that are not self-executing. To what extent does the President, in the exercise of his power over foreign affairs, possess unilateral authority to implement such treaties? In Medellin v. Texas, 552 U.S. 491 (2008), the Supreme Court provided an answer.

The United States is a party to the Vienna Convention on Consular Relations, Article 36 of which requires a country that has arrested a foreign national, upon request of the detainee, to notify the detainee's consulate of the detention and to inform the prisoner that he is entitled to request assistance from his consulate. The International Court of Justice, in Case Concerning Avena and Other Mexican Nationals (Mexico v. United States), 2004 I.C.J. 12 (*Avena*), concluded that the United States had violated this provision and ruled that 51 named Mexican citizens were entitled to review and reconsideration of their state court convictions and sentences in the United States, despite their failure to comply with generally applicable state rules governing challenges to criminal convictions. Later, in Sanchez-Llamas v. Oregon, 548 U.S. 331 (2006), the U.S. Supreme Court ruled that the Vienna Convention did not preclude the application of state default rules. In response, President George W. Bush issued an executive memorandum in which he "determined . . . that the United States will discharge its international obligations under [*Avena*], by having State courts give effect to the decision. . . ." Jose Medellin, a Mexican national named in *Avena* who had been convicted and sentenced in Texas state court for the brutal rape and murder of two teenage girls, sought review of his conviction via habeas corpus. The Texas courts denied the writ as untimely. In *Medellin*, the Supreme Court first determined that *Avena* is not binding on domestic courts because the U.N. Charter, the Statute of the International Court of Justice, and the optional protocol to the Vienna Convention, upon which *Avena* was founded, are not self-executing. Whereas self-executing treaties are automatically binding as domestic law, other treaties require legislation to be enforced domestically. The Supreme Court then rejected the contention that the President, in the exercise of his foreign affairs power, could unilaterally preempt state law in order to enforce the nation's international legal obligations. Chief Justice Roberts wrote for the Court:

> [The] President has an array of political and diplomatic means available to enforce international obligations, but unilaterally converting a non-self-executing treaty into a self-executing one is not among them. The responsibility for transforming an international obligation arising from a non-self-executing treaty into domestic law falls to Congress. [This] derives from the text of the Constitution, which divides the treaty-making power between the President and the Senate. . . . If the Executive determines that a treaty should have domestic effect of its own force, that determination may be implemented "in mak[ing]" the treaty, by ensuring that it contains language plainly providing for domestic enforceability. [Then] the Senate must consent to the treaty by the requisite two-thirds vote, consistent with all other constitutional restraints. Once a treaty is ratified without provisions clearly according it domestic effect, however, whether the treaty will ever have such effect is governed by the fundamental constitutional principle that "'[t]he power to make the necessary laws is in Congress; the power to execute is in the President.'" A non-self-executing treaty, by definition, is one that was ratified with the understanding that it is not to have domestic effect of its own force. That understanding precludes the assertion that Congress has implicitly authorized the President—acting on his own—to achieve precisely the same result. . . .

Despite the *Medellin* decision, the Vienna Convention remains a binding international law obligation of the United States. Compliance may be obtained by voluntary action of all the states and the federal government or by legislation that preempts contrary state law, but not by executive order. Yet in a footnote the majority noted that the dissent "finds it 'difficult to believe that in the exercise of his Article II powers pursuant to a ratified treaty, the President can *never* take action that would result in setting aside state law.' We agree."

Queries: Under what circumstances may the President unilaterally take action to set aside state law in order to enforce the nation's treaty obligations? Were *Dames & Moore, Pink,* and *Belmont* such occasions? If so, do they exhaust the circumstances under which the President may act unilaterally to set aside state law in order to implement treaty obligations?

C. LEGISLATIVE ACTION AND THE ADMINISTRATIVE STATE

1. General Themes

Congress sometimes employs its legislative powers in imaginative ways that raise serious questions of violation of separation of powers. Perhaps the most significant such use of legislative power has been the creation by Congress of a labyrinth of administrative agencies that compose what is occasionally referred to as a "headless fourth branch" of government. Some of these efforts run afoul of specific doctrines firmly rooted in constitutional text and structure: Congress may not delegate its legislative powers, or legislate without conforming to the constitutional procedures of bicameral action and presentment to the President, or entrust the execution of law to officials accountable only to Congress. But even if these specific doctrines are satisfied, the Court will void congressional action if it poses a danger of aggrandizement or encroachment. "Aggrandizement" occurs when Congress unreasonably enlarges a single branch's powers at the expense of the other two branches. "Encroachment" occurs when Congress enacts law that "undermine[s] the authority and independence" of any branch of the federal government.

Justice Powell, in INS v. Chadha, described these concerns as follows: "Functionally, [separation of powers] may be violated in two ways. One branch may interfere impermissibly with the other's performance of its constitutionally assigned function. Alternatively, the doctrine may be violated when one branch assumes a function that more properly is entrusted to another." These approaches are not neatly cabined; they can and do appear in any given case.

≣≣≣ ### *Mistretta v. United States*
488 U.S. 361 (1989)

JUSTICE BLACKMUN delivered the opinion of the Court.

[We] consider the constitutionality of the Sentencing Guidelines promulgated by the United States Sentencing Commission. The Commission is a body created under the Sentencing Reform Act of 1984 (Act). [Mistretta pleaded guilty to one count of conspiracy to distribute cocaine. A federal district court applied the Guidelines and found them to be constitutional. The Supreme Court granted certiorari before the Eighth Circuit considered Mistretta's appeal.]

I. For almost a century, the Federal Government employed in criminal cases a system of indeterminate sentencing. . . . [Under] the indeterminate-sentence system, Congress defined the maximum, the judge imposed a sentence within the statutory range . . . , and the Executive Branch's parole official eventually determined the actual duration of imprisonment. [Serious] disparities in sentences, however, were common. [Widespread] dissatisfaction with the uncertainties and the disparities [produced] the sweeping reforms that are at issue here.

[The Act] revises the old sentencing process in several ways: 1. It rejects imprisonment as a means of promoting rehabilitation and it states that punishment should serve retributive, educational, deterrent, and incapacitative goals. 2. It [creates] the United States Sentencing Commission, directing that Commission to devise guidelines to be used for [sentencing]. 3. It makes all sentences basically determinate. 4. It makes the Sentencing Commission's guidelines binding on the [courts]. 5. It authorizes limited appellate review of the [sentence].

The [Sentencing] Commission is established "as an independent commission in the judicial branch of the United States." It has seven voting [members] appointed by the President "by and with the advice and consent of the Senate." "At least three of the members shall be Federal judges selected after considering a list of six judges recommended to the President by the Judicial Conference of the United States." [The] members of the Commission are subject to removal by the President "only for neglect of duty or malfeasance in office or for other good cause shown." [The Commission must] promulgate determinative-sentence guidelines, [periodically] "review and revise" the guidelines, report to Congress "any amendments of the guidelines," [recommend] to Congress whether the grades or maximum penalties should be modified, issue "general policy statements" [regarding] application [of the guidelines,] "establish general policies [as] are necessary to carry out the purposes" of the legislation, [and perform various monitoring and training tasks]. . . .

IV. *Separation of Powers.* [Mistretta claims] that the Act violates the constitutional principle of separation of powers. [The] separation of governmental powers into three coordinate Branches is essential to the preservation of liberty. [We] have sought to give life to Madison's [view] that while our Constitution mandates that "each of the three general departments of government [must remain] entirely free from the control or coercive influence, direct or indirect, of either of the others," the Framers did not require—and indeed rejected—the notion that the three Branches must be entirely separate and distinct. . . . [Madison] recognized that our constitutional system imposes upon the Branches a degree of overlapping responsibility, a duty of interdependence as well as independence the absence of which "would preclude the establishment of a Nation capable of governing itself effectively."

[In] adopting this flexible understanding of separation of powers, we simply have recognized Madison's teaching that the greatest security against tyranny—the accumulation of excessive authority in a single Branch—lies not in a hermetic division among the Branches, but in a carefully crafted system of checked and balanced power within each Branch. "[T]he greatest security," wrote Madison, "against a gradual concentration of the several powers in the same department, consists in giving to those who administer each department, the necessary constitutional means, and personal motives, to resist encroachments of the others." The Federalist No. 51. [It] is this concern of encroachment and aggrandizement that has animated our separation-of-powers jurisprudence and aroused our vigilance against the "hydraulic pressure inherent within each of the separate Branches to exceed the outer limits of its power." Accordingly, we have not hesitated to strike down provisions of law that either accrete to a single Branch powers more appropriately diffused among separate Branches or that undermine the authority and independence of one or another coordinate Branch. . . . [We have] described our separation-of-powers inquiry as focusing "on the extent to which [a provision of law] prevents the Executive Branch from accomplishing its constitutionally assigned functions." In cases specifically involving the Judicial Branch, we have expressed our vigilance against two dangers: first, that the Judicial Branch neither be assigned nor allowed "tasks that are more properly accomplished by [other] branches," and, second, that no provision of law "impermissibly threatens the institutional integrity of the Judicial Branch."

Mistretta argues . . . that Congress [effected] an unconstitutional accumulation of power within the Judicial Branch while at the same time undermining the Judiciary's independence and integrity. [He] claims that in delegating to an independent agency within the Judicial Branch the power to promulgate sentencing guidelines, Congress unconstitutionally has required the [judiciary] to exercise not only judicial [but] legislative authority—the making of sentencing policy. [Such] rulemaking authority, petitioner contends, may be exercised by Congress, or delegated by Congress to the Executive, but may not be delegated to or exercised by the Judiciary. At the same time, petitioner asserts, Congress unconstitutionally eroded the integrity and independence of the Judiciary by requiring Article III judges to sit on the Commission, by requiring that those judges share their rulemaking authority with nonjudges, and by subjecting the Commission's members to appointment and removal by the President. [Although] the unique composition and responsibilities of the Sentencing Commission give rise to serious concerns about a disruption of the appropriate balance of governmental power among the coordinate Branches, we conclude [that these are] "more smoke than fire," and do not compel us to invalidate [the Sentencing Commission].

The Sentencing Commission unquestionably is a peculiar institution within the framework of our Government. [The] Commission is an "independent" body comprised of seven voting members including at least three federal judges, entrusted by Congress with the primary task of promulgating sentencing [guidelines]. Congress'[s] decision to create an independent rulemaking body to promulgate sentencing guidelines and to locate that body within the Judicial Branch is not unconstitutional unless Congress has vested in the Commission powers that are more appropriately performed by the other Branches or that undermine the integrity of the Judiciary.

. . . As a general [principle], " 'executive or administrative duties of a nonjudicial nature may not be imposed on judges holding office under Art. III of the Constitution.' " Nonetheless, we have recognized significant exceptions to this general rule and have approved the assumption of some nonadjudicatory activities by the Judicial Branch. . . . [We] specifically have held that Congress, in some circumstances, may confer rulemaking authority on the Judicial Branch. In Sibbach v. Wilson & Co., 312 U.S. 1 (1941), we upheld a challenge to certain rules promulgated under the Rules Enabling Act of 1934, which conferred upon the Judiciary the power to promulgate federal rules of civil procedure. . . . Congress expressly has authorized this Court to establish rules for the conduct of its own business and to prescribe rules of procedure for lower federal courts in bankruptcy cases, in other civil cases, and in criminal cases, and to revise the Federal Rules of Evidence. [By] established practice we have recognized Congress'[s] power to create the . . . Administrative Office of the United States Courts whose myriad responsibilities include the administration of the entire probation service. [In] light of this precedent and practice, we can discern no separation-of-powers impediment to the placement of the Sentencing Commission within the Judicial Branch.

[The] "practical consequences" of locating the Commission within the Judicial Branch pose no threat of undermining the integrity of the Judicial Branch or of expanding the powers of the Judiciary beyond constitutional bounds by uniting within the Branch the political or quasi-legislative power of the Commission with the judicial power of the courts.

First, [the Commission's] powers are not united with the powers of the Judiciary in a way that has meaning for separation-of-powers analysis. [It] is not a court, does not exercise judicial power, and is not controlled by or accountable to members of the Judicial Branch. The Commission, on which members of the Judiciary may be a minority, is an independent agency in every relevant sense. [The] Commission is fully accountable to Congress, which can revoke or amend any or all of the Guidelines as it sees [fit]. [The] Commission's members are subject to the President's limited powers of removal [and] its rulemaking is subject to the notice and comment requirements of the Administrative Procedure Act. . . .

Second, [the] placement of the Sentencing Commission in the Judicial Branch has not increased the Branch's authority. Prior to the passage of the Act, the Judicial Branch, as an aggregate, decided precisely the questions assigned to the Commission: what sentence is appropriate to what criminal conduct under what circumstances. It was the everyday business of judges, taken collectively, to evaluate and weigh the various aims of sentencing and to apply those aims to the individual cases that came before them. The Sentencing Commission does no more than this, [albeit] through the methodology of sentencing guidelines, rather than entirely individualized sentencing determinations. Accordingly, [Congress] cannot be said to have aggrandized the authority of [the Judicial] Branch or to have deprived the Executive Branch of a power it once possessed.

[What] Mistretta's argument comes down to [is that the Judicial] Branch is inevitably weakened by its participation in policymaking. We do not believe, however, that the placement within the Judicial Branch of an independent agency charged with the promulgation of sentencing guidelines can possibly be construed as preventing the Judicial Branch "from accomplishing its constitutionally assigned functions." [The] Commission is not incongruous or inappropriate to the Branch. [Nor] do the Guidelines, though substantive, involve a degree of political authority inappropriate for a nonpolitical Branch. [The] Guidelines [do] not bind or regulate the primary conduct of the public or vest in the Judicial Branch the legislative responsibility for establishing minimum and maximum penalties for every crime. They do no more than fetter the discretion [of] judges to do what they have done for generations—impose sentences within the broad limits established by Congress.

[We] now turn to petitioner's claim that [conscription of] individual federal judges for political service [undermines] the essential impartiality of the Judicial Branch. We find Congress'[s] requirement of judicial service somewhat troublesome, but we do not believe that the Act impermissibly interferes with the functioning of the Judiciary. The text of the Constitution contains no prohibition against the service of active federal judges on independent commissions such as that established by the Act. [Our] early history indicates that the Framers themselves did not read the Constitution as forbidding extrajudicial service by federal judges. The first Chief Justice, John Jay, served simultaneously as Chief Justice and as Ambassador to England, where he negotiated the treaty that bears his name. Oliver Ellsworth served simultaneously as Chief Justice and as Minister to France. While he was Chief Justice, John Marshall served briefly as Secretary of State and was a member of the Sinking Fund Commission with responsibility for refunding the Revolutionary War debt.[3] [In] 1877, five Justices served on the Election Commission that resolved the hotly contested [Hayes-Tilden] Presidential election of 1876. [Justice Owen] Roberts was a member of the commission organized to investigate the attack on Pearl Harbor. Justice Jackson was one of the prosecutors at the Nuremberg trials; and Chief Justice Warren presided over the commission investigating the assassination of President Kennedy. Such service has been no less a practice among lower court federal judges. [Our] 200-year tradition of extrajudicial service is additional evidence that the doctrine of separated powers does not prohibit judicial participation in certain extrajudicial activity.[4]

[In] light of the foregoing history and precedent, we conclude that the principle of separation of powers does not absolutely prohibit Article III judges from serving on commissions such as that created by the Act. The judges serve on the Sentencing Commission not pursuant to their status and

---

3. It would be naive history, however, to suggest that the Framers, including the Justices who accepted extrajudicial service, [believed] that such service was in all cases appropriate and constitutional. [Chief] Justice Marshall stepped down from his post as Secretary of State when appointed to the bench, agreeing to stay on only until a replacement could be found. Chief Justice Ellsworth accepted his posting to France with reluctance and his appointment was unsuccessfully opposed on constitutional grounds by Jefferson, Madison, and Pinckney. . . . [Relocated — ED.]

4. Perhaps the most interesting lament on the subject [of extrajudicial service] comes from Chief Justice Warren reflecting on his initial refusal to participate in the commission looking into President Kennedy's death:

> First, it is not in the spirit of constitutional separation of powers to have a member of the Supreme Court serve on a presidential commission; second, it would distract a Justice from the work of the Court, which had a heavy docket; and, third, it was impossible to foresee what litigation such a commission might spawn, with resulting disqualification of the Justice from sitting in such cases. I then told them that, historically, the acceptance of diplomatic posts by Chief Justices Jay and Ellsworth had not contributed to the welfare of the Court, that the service of five Justices on the Hayes-Tilden Commission had demeaned it, that the appointment of Justice Roberts as chairman to investigate the Pearl Harbor disaster had served no good purpose, and that the action of Justice Robert Jackson in leaving Court for a year to become chief prosecutor at Nürnberg after World War II had resulted in divisiveness and internal bitterness on the Court." E. Warren, The Memoirs of Earl Warren 356 (1977).

Despite his initial reservations, the Chief Justice served as Chairman of the commission and endured criticism for so doing.

authority as Article III judges, but solely because of their appointment by the President as the Act directs. Such power as these judges wield as Commissioners is not judicial power; it is administrative power derived from the enabling legislation. [The] Constitution, at least as a per se matter, does not forbid judges to wear two hats; it merely forbids them to wear both hats at the same time. This is not to suggest [that] every kind of extrajudicial service under every circumstance necessarily accords with the Constitution. [The] ultimate inquiry remains whether a particular extrajudicial assignment undermines the integrity of the Judicial Branch.

[We] do not believe that the President's appointment and removal powers over the Commission afford him influence over the functions of the Judicial Branch or undue sway over its members.[5] The notion that the President's power to appoint federal judges to the Commission somehow gives him influence over the Judicial Branch or prevents, even potentially, the Judicial Branch from performing its constitutionally assigned functions is fanciful. We have never considered it incompatible with the functioning of the Judicial Branch that the President has the power to elevate federal judges from one level to another or to tempt judges away from the bench with Executive Branch positions. [We] simply cannot imagine that federal judges will comport their actions to the wishes of the President for the purpose of receiving an appointment to the Sentencing Commission. The President's removal power over Commission members poses a similarly negligible threat to judicial independence. The Act does not, and could not under the Constitution, authorize the President to remove, or in any way diminish the status of Article III judges, as judges. [Also], the President's removal power under the Act is limited. . . .

[We] hold that the Act is constitutional. [Affirmed.]

JUSTICE SCALIA, dissenting.

While the products of the Sentencing Commission's labors have been given the modest name "Guidelines," they have the force and effect of laws. . . . A judge who disregards them will be reversed. I dissent [because] I can find no place within our constitutional system for an agency created by Congress to exercise no governmental power other than the making of laws. . . .

Today's decision may aptly be described as the *Humphrey's Executor* of the Judicial Branch, and I think we will live to regret it. Henceforth there may be agencies "within the Judicial Branch" (whatever that means), exercising governmental powers, that are neither courts nor controlled by courts, nor even controlled by judges. If an "independent agency" such as this can be given the power to fix sentences previously exercised by district courts, I must assume that a similar agency can be given the powers to adopt rules of

---

5. Petitioner does not raise the issue central to our most recent opinions discussing removal power, namely, whether Congress unconstitutionally has limited the President's authority to remove officials engaged in executive functions or has reserved for itself excessive removal power over such officials. See Morrison v. Olson; Bowsher v. Synar.

procedure and rules of evidence previously exercised by this Court. The bases for distinction would be thin indeed.

Today's decision follows the regrettable tendency of our recent separation-of-powers jurisprudence to treat the Constitution as though it were no more than a generalized prescription that the functions of the Branches should not be commingled too much—how much is too much to be determined, case-by-case, by this Court. The Constitution is not that. Rather, as its name suggests, it is a prescribed structure, a framework, for the conduct of government. In designing that structure, the Framers themselves considered how much commingling was, in the generality of things, acceptable, and set forth their conclusions in the document. That is the meaning of the statements concerning acceptable commingling made by Madison in defense of the proposed Constitution, and now routinely used as an excuse for disregarding it. When he said, as the Court correctly quotes, that separation of powers "'[does] not mean that these [three] departments ought to have no partial agency in, or no controul over the acts of each other,'" his point was that the commingling specifically provided for in the structure that he and his colleagues had designed—the Presidential veto over legislation, the Senate's confirmation of executive and judicial officers, the Senate's ratification of treaties, the Congress'[s] power to impeach and remove executive and judicial officers—did not violate a proper understanding of separation of powers. He would be aghast, I think, to hear those words used as justification for ignoring that carefully designed structure so long as, in the changing view of the Supreme Court from time to time, "too much commingling" does not occur. Consideration of the degree of commingling that a particular disposition produces may be appropriate at the margins, where the outline of the framework itself is not clear; but it seems to me far from a marginal question whether our constitutional structure allows for a body which is not the Congress, and yet exercises no governmental powers except the making of rules that have the effect of laws.

I think the Court errs [not] so much because it mistakes the degree of commingling, but because it fails to recognize that this case is not about commingling, but about the creation of a new Branch altogether, a sort of junior varsity Congress. It may well be that in some circumstances such a Branch would be desirable; perhaps the agency before us here will prove to be so. But there are many desirable dispositions that do not accord with the constitutional structure we live under. And in the long run the improvisation of a constitutional structure on the basis of currently perceived utility will be disastrous. . . .

≡ *Morrison v. Olson*
≡ *487 U.S. 654 (1988)*

[Portions of this opinion, in which the Court upheld the validity of the statute authorizing appointment of an independent counsel to investigate and, if necessary, prosecute criminal activity at the highest echelons of the executive branch, are found in Sections B.1.a and B.1.b, *supra*. This excerpt deals with the general separation-of-powers objections to the validity of the Act.]

CHIEF JUSTICE REHNQUIST, for the Court.

[We now] consider whether [the] Act, taken as a whole, violates the principle of separation of powers by unduly interfering with the role of the Executive Branch. [This] case does not involve an attempt by Congress to increase its own powers at the expense of the Executive Branch. [Apart from impeachment,] Congress retained for itself no powers of control or supervision over an independent counsel. [We] do not think that the Act works any judicial usurpation of properly executive functions. [The Special Division of the Court of Appeals] has no power to appoint an independent counsel [except] upon the specific request of the Attorney General, and the courts are specifically prevented from reviewing the Attorney General's decision not to seek appointment. [Nor does the Court have any] power to supervise or control the activities of the counsel. [The] Act does give a federal court the power to review the Attorney General's decision to remove an independent counsel, but in our view this is a function that is well within the traditional power of the Judiciary.

Finally, we do not think that the Act "impermissibly undermine[s]" the powers of the Executive Branch or "disrupts the proper balance between the coordinate branches [by] prevent[ing] the Executive Branch from accomplishing its constitutionally assigned functions." It is undeniable that the Act reduces the amount of control or supervision that the Attorney General and, through him, the President exercises over the investigation and prosecution of a certain class of alleged criminal activity. The Attorney General is not allowed to appoint the individual of his choice; he does not determine the counsel's jurisdiction; and his power to remove a counsel is limited. Nonetheless, [the] Attorney General retains the power to remove the counsel for "good cause," a power [that] provides the Executive with substantial ability to ensure that the laws are "faithfully executed" by an independent counsel. No independent counsel may be appointed without a specific request by the Attorney General, and the Attorney General's decision not to request appointment if he finds "no reasonable grounds to believe that further investigation is warranted" is committed to his unreviewable discretion. The Act thus gives the Executive a degree of control over the power to initiate an investigation by the independent counsel. In addition, the jurisdiction of the independent counsel is defined with reference to the facts submitted by the Attorney General. [In] our view these features of the Act give the Executive Branch sufficient control over the independent counsel to ensure that the President is able to perform his constitutionally assigned duties.

JUSTICE SCALIA, dissenting.

. . . If to describe this case is not to decide it, the concept of a government of separate and coordinate powers no longer has meaning. [The] Constitution provides: "The executive Power shall be vested in a President of the United States." [This] does not mean some of the executive power, but all of the executive power. [The] present statute must [invalidated] on fundamental separation-of-powers principles if the following two questions are answered affirmatively: (1) Is the conduct of a criminal prosecution (and of an investigation to decide whether to prosecute) the exercise of purely executive power? (2) Does the statute deprive the President of the United States of exclusive control over the exercise of that power? Surprising to say, the Court appears to concede an affirmative answer to both questions, but seeks to avoid the inevitable conclusion that since the statute vests some purely executive power in a person who is not the President of the United States it is void.

The Court concedes that ". . . the functions performed by the independent counsel are 'executive.'" [Governmental] investigation and prosecution of crimes is a quintessentially executive function. As for the second question, whether the statute before us deprives the President of exclusive control over that quintessentially executive activity: The Court does not, and could not possibly, assert that it does not. That is indeed the whole object of the statute. Instead, the Court points out that the President, through his Attorney General, has at least some control. . . . "Most importan[t]" among these controls, the Court asserts, is the Attorney General's "power to remove the counsel for 'good cause.'" This is somewhat like referring to shackles as an effective means of locomotion. . . .

[It] is ultimately irrelevant how *much* the statute reduces Presidential control. The case is over when the Court acknowledges, as it must, that "[i]t is undeniable that the Act reduces the amount of control or supervision that the Attorney General and, through him, the President exercises over the investigation and prosecution of a certain class of alleged criminal activity." . . . It is not for us to determine, and we have never presumed to determine, how much of the purely executive powers of government must be within the full control of the President. The Constitution prescribes that they all are.

The utter incompatibility of the Court's approach with our constitutional traditions can be made more clear, perhaps, by applying it to the powers of the other two branches. Is it conceivable that if Congress passed a statute depriving itself of less than full and entire control over some insignificant area of legislation, we would inquire whether the matter was "so central to the functioning of the Legislative Branch" as really to require complete control, or whether the statute gives Congress "sufficient control over the surrogate legislator to ensure that Congress is able to perform its constitutionally assigned duties"? Of course we would have none of that. Once we determined that a purely legislative power was at issue we would require it to be exercised, wholly and entirely, by Congress. Or to bring the point closer to home, consider a statute giving to non-Article III judges just a tiny bit of purely judicial power in a relatively insignificant field, with substantial control, though not total control, in the courts—perhaps "clear error" review, which would be a fair judicial equivalent of the Attorney General's "for cause" removal power here. Is there any doubt that we would not pause to inquire whether the matter was "so central to the functioning of the Judicial Branch" as really to require complete control, or whether we retained "sufficient control over the matters to be decided that we are able to perform our constitutionally assigned duties"? We would say that our "constitutionally assigned duties" include complete control over all exercises of the judicial power. [We] should say here that the President's constitutionally assigned duties include complete control over investigation and prosecution of violations of the law, and that the inexorable command of Article II is clear and definite: the executive power must be vested in the President of the United States. . . .

Is it unthinkable that the President should have such exclusive power, even when alleged crimes by him or his close associates are at issue? No more so than that Congress should have the exclusive power of legislation, even when what is at issue is its own exemption from the burdens of certain laws. No more so than that this Court should have the exclusive power to pronounce the final decision on justiciable cases and controversies, even those pertaining to the constitutionality of a statute reducing the salaries of the Justices. A system of separate and coordinate powers necessarily involves an acceptance of exclusive power that can theoretically be abused. . . .

[Worse] than what it has done, however, is the manner in which it has done it. A government of laws means a government of rules. Today's decision on the basic issue of fragmentation of executive power is ungoverned by rule, and hence ungoverned by law. . . .

NOTE

How Unitary Is the Unitary Executive?   The justices agree that the executive power is vested exclusively in a single President but differ sharply as to the consequences that flow from that fact. Everyone agrees that the executive power may be carried out though a host of executive subalterns, but must those subordinates be directly accountable to the President, or may they be given executive power while enjoying substantial independence from the President? Note that in *Morrison* the independent counsel, an executive officer vested with the important power of investigating and prosecuting crimes in the highest levels of the executive branch, was appointed by the courts (rather than by the President or any other executive officer) and removable by the Attorney General or the courts (but not by the President). Thus the Court upheld the validity of an executive officer's exercising an inherent, or core, executive power even though that officer was neither appointed nor removable by the President. Is executive power unitary under such circumstances? On these points the opinion of the Court of Appeals in *Morrison* is illuminating. See In re Sealed Case, 838 F.2d 476 (D.C. Cir. 1988). The successor to the independent counsel statute at issue in *Morrison* expired in 1999 and Congress failed to renew it.

2. Specific Limits

In this section we examine some of the specific limits, derived from the text and structure of the Constitution, on congressional action.

a. Nondelegation

≡ *Mistretta v. United States*
488 U.S. 361 (1989)

JUSTICE BLACKMUN delivered the opinion of the Court.

[We] consider the constitutionality of the Sentencing Guidelines promulgated by the United States Sentencing Commission. . . .

II. *Delegation of Power.* Petitioner argues that in delegating the power to promulgate sentencing guidelines for every federal criminal offense to an independent Sentencing Commission, Congress has granted the Commission excessive legislative discretion in violation of the constitutionally based nondelegation doctrine. We do not agree.

The nondelegation doctrine is rooted in the principle of separation of powers that underlies our tripartite system of Government. The Constitution provides that "[a]ll legislative Powers herein granted shall be vested in a Congress of the United States," and we long have insisted that "the integrity and maintenance of the system of government ordained by the Constitution" mandate that Congress generally cannot delegate its legislative power to another Branch. [However], the nondelegation doctrine [does] not prevent Congress from obtaining the assistance of its coordinate Branches. [So] long as Congress "shall lay down by legislative act an intelligible principle to which the person or body authorized to [exercise the delegated authority] is directed to conform, such legislative action is not a forbidden delegation of legislative power." [Hampton v. United States, 276 U.S. 394 (1928).]

Congress simply cannot do its job absent an ability to delegate power under broad general directives. [Accordingly], this Court has deemed it "constitutionally sufficient if Congress clearly delineates the general policy, the public agency which is to apply it, and the boundaries of this delegated authority." . . . [We] harbor no doubt that Congress'[s] delegation of authority to the Sentencing Commission is sufficiently specific and detailed to meet constitutional requirements. Congress charged the Commission with three goals: to "assure the meeting of the purposes of sentencing as set forth" in the Act; to "provide certainty and fairness in meeting the purposes of sentencing"; and to "reflect [knowledge] of human behavior as it relates to the criminal justice process." Congress further specified four "purposes" of sentencing that the Commission must pursue in carrying out its mandate: "to reflect the seriousness of the offense [and] promote respect for the law"; "to afford adequate deterrence to criminal conduct"; "to protect the public from further crimes of the defendant"; and "to provide the defendant with [needed] correctional treatment." In addition, [Congress] directed the Commission to develop a system of "sentencing ranges" applicable "for each category of offense involving each category of defendant," [so long as there were no] sentences in excess of the statutory maxima. Congress also required that for sentences of imprisonment, "the maximum of the range established for such a term shall not exceed the minimum of that range by more than the greater of 25 percent or 6 months, except that, if the minimum term of the range is 30 years or more, the maximum may be life imprisonment."

[Congress also directed the Commission] to consider seven factors [in creating offense categories and] set forth 11 factors for the Commission to consider in establishing categories of defendants. [Congress] provided even more detailed guidance to the Commission about [certain] categories of offenses [e.g., violent crimes and drug offenses] and offender characteristics [e.g., repeat offenders and major drug traffickers]. Congress also enumerated various aggravating and mitigating circumstances [to] be reflected in the guidelines. . . .

In Yakus v. United States, 321 U.S. 414 (1944), the Court . . . laid down the applicable principle: "Only [if] there is an absence of standards for the guidance of the Administrator's action, so that it would be impossible [to] ascertain whether the will of Congress has been obeyed, would we be justified in overriding its choice of means for effecting its declared purpose." Congress has met that standard [here].

Justice Scalia, dissenting.

. . . The whole theory of lawful congressional "delegation" is not that Congress is sometimes too busy or too divided and can therefore assign its responsibility of making law to someone else; but rather that a certain degree of discretion, and thus of lawmaking, inheres in most executive or judicial action, and it is up to Congress, by the relative specificity or generality of its statutory commands, to determine — up to a point — how small or how large that degree shall be. Thus, the courts could be given the power to say precisely what constitutes a "restraint of trade," see Standard Oil Co. of New Jersey v. United States, 221 U.S. 1 (1911), or to adopt rules of procedure, see Sibbach v. Wilson & Co., 312 U.S. 1, 22 (1941), . . . because that "lawmaking" was ancillary to their exercise of judicial powers. . . . [As] Justice Harlan wrote for the Court in Field v. Clark, 143 U.S. 649 (1892): "The true distinction [is] between the delegation of power to make the law, which necessarily involves a discretion as to what it shall be, and conferring authority or discretion as to its execution, to be exercised under and in pursuance of the law. The first cannot be done; to the latter no valid objection can be made." . . .

[A] pure delegation of legislative power is precisely what we have before us. It is irrelevant whether the standards are adequate, because they are not standards related to the exercise of executive or judicial powers; they are, plainly and simply, standards for further legislation.

The lawmaking function of the Sentencing Commission is completely divorced from any responsibility for execution of the law or adjudication of private rights under the law. It is divorced from responsibility for execution of the law [because] the Commission neither exercises any executive power on its own, nor is subject to the control of the President who does. The only functions it performs [are] prescribing the law, conducting the investigations useful and necessary for prescribing the law, and clarifying the intended application of the law that it prescribes. [And] the Commission's lawmaking is completely divorced from the exercise of judicial powers since, not being a court, it has no judicial powers itself, nor is it subject to the control of any other body with judicial powers. The power to make law at issue here, in other words, is not ancillary but quite naked. The situation is no different in principle from what would exist if Congress gave the same power of writing sentencing laws to a congressional agency such as the General Accounting Office, or to members of its staff. . . . The only governmental power the Commission possesses is the power to make law; and it is not the Congress.

NOTES

1. Intelligible Principles. The outer limit of the generality with which Congress may legislate is that Congress must declare a policy and define "the circumstances in which its command is to be effective." Opp Cotton Mills, Inc. v. Administrator, 312 U.S. 126 (1941). Legislation must at least set forth "an intelligible principle to which the person or body authorized to take action is directed to conform." J.W. Hampton, Jr. & Co. v. United States, 276 U.S. 394 (1928). But what does this mean?

When Congress enacted the Occupational Safety and Health Act it gave the Labor Secretary power to adopt those standards "reasonably necessary or appropriate to provide safe or healthful employment [which] most adequately assure[], to the extent feasible, on the basis of the best available evidence, that no employee will suffer material impairment of health." In Industrial Union v. American Petroleum Institute, 448 U.S. 607 (1980), the Court concluded that the directive was specific enough to comply with the nondelegation rule. In dissent, Justice Rehnquist argued that it was

> difficult to imagine a more obvious example of Congress simply avoiding a choice which was both fundamental for purposes of the statute and [too] politically divisive [to address with specificity]. It is the hard choices, not the filling in of the blanks, which must be made by the elected representatives of the people.

2. Policy Arguments. The nondelegation doctrine serves several functions in addition to preserving the constitutional assignment of all legislative power to Congress. First, it promotes accountability: Legislative policy choices must be made by elected representatives, not by unelected administrators who are accountable, if at all, to the President or some presidential appointee. Second, it increases predictability: If Congress makes specific policy choices, there is less likelihood that administrative rules will change with each political administration, as each administration interprets general legislative directions to suit its tastes. Third, it decreases the possibility that administrators will exercise discretion unfairly: Specific legislation gives administrators less room to impose their sometimes peculiar policy notions.

Whatever its benefits, the nondelegation doctrine is on the constitutional critical list. The Court has not encountered an impermissible delegation since 1935, when it decided *Panama Refining* and *Schechter Poultry*. A weaker version of the nondelegation doctrine occasionally surfaces in statutory construction cases, where the Court narrowly construes a statutory grant of administrative authority in order to avoid (or minimize) claims of an impermissible delegation. And it is likely that any attempt to give rulemaking power to a state agency or to a private group (as was true in *Schechter Poultry*) might violate the nondelegation doctrine.

Arguments can be made for breathing more life into the nondelegation doctrine. First, although the Court seems to assume that a congressional desire to retain power will curb delegation, in fact members of Congress derive significant political benefits from delegation. They can claim the benefits of legislation (e.g., clean air) while foisting onto bureaucrats the responsibility for the burdens (e.g., expensive and annoying auto emission checks, fireplace and wood stove bans, and higher fuel and electricity prices). When this occurs, electoral accountability is skewed. Second, the nondelegation doctrine is intended to ensure that Congress provides clear policy directions to administrators, but its current flaccidity permits Congress to escape even that duty. Thus administrators make more law than do members of Congress. Professor John Ely has wondered whether there is much "point in worrying about the distribution of the franchise and other personal political rights unless the important policy choices are being made by elected officials."

Defenders of the virtual demise of the nondelegation doctrine typically contend that regulation is so complex, and the legislative process so fraught with compromise between pressure groups, that Congress cannot be expected to reach "responsible decisions on questions of policy." Stewart, The Reformation of American Administrative Law, 88 Harv. L. Rev. 1667 (1975). It is said that "[d]etailed legislative specification of policy would require intensive and continuous investigation, decision, and revision of specialized and complex issues." Id. But Congress can call upon the expertise of experts in and outside government, and in the end all Congress needs to do is specify a clear policy; it need not write into law every facet of the implementation of the policy.

3. Query. Is it fair to say that in the absence of a meaningful nondelegation doctrine public policy comes not "from voter preferences or congressional enactments but from a process of tripartite bargaining between the specialized administrators, relevant members of Congress, and the representatives of self-interested organized interests"? Theodore Lowi, The End of Liberalism (2d ed. 1979).

b. Bicameralism and Presentment

Article I, sections 1 and 7 require that all legislation be bicameral—identical bills must pass both houses of Congress—and must be presented to the President for signature or veto. In recent years the Court has considered two devices that arguably violate these requirements. In each case, the Court found that bicameralism and presentment had not been satisfied.

INS v. Chadha
462 U.S. 919 (1983)

CHIEF JUSTICE BURGER delivered the opinion of the Court.

We [consider] a challenge to the constitutionality of the provision in §244(c)(2) of the Immigration and Nationality Act, authorizing one House of Congress, by resolution, to invalidate the decision of the Executive Branch, pursuant to authority delegated by Congress to the Attorney General of the United States, to allow a particular deportable alien to remain in the United States.

I. Chadha [was] lawfully admitted to the United States [on] a nonimmigrant student visa [that] expired on June 30, 1972. On October 11, 1973, the District Director of the Immigration and Naturalization Service ordered Chadha to show cause why he should not be deported for having "remained in the United States for a longer time than permitted." [After a hearing, an immigration judge ordered] that Chadha's deportation be suspended, [having] found that Chadha met the requirements of [the statute]: he had resided continuously in the United States for over seven years, was of good moral character, and would suffer "extreme hardship" if deported. Pursuant to [the statute], the Immigration Judge suspended Chadha's deportation and a report of the suspension was transmitted to Congress. [Immigration judges are INS employees, executive officers reportable to the Attorney General, so the immigration judge's decision suspending deportation was treated as a recommendation of the Attorney General.] Once the Attorney General's recommendation for suspension of Chadha's deportation was conveyed to Congress, Congress had the power under [the] Act to veto the Attorney General's determination that Chadha should not be deported.

[A year and a half later, and one week before Congress's statutory veto authority would have expired,] a resolution opposing "the granting of permanent residence in the United States to [six] aliens," including Chadha, . . . was passed without debate or recorded vote. Since the House action was pursuant to [the statutory veto provision,] the resolution was not treated as an Art. I legislative act; it was not submitted to the Senate or presented to the President for his action. After the House veto of the Attorney General's decision to allow Chadha to remain in the United States, [Chadha] was ordered deported pursuant to the House action. [After unsuccessful administrative appeals] Chadha [sought] review of the deportation order in the United States Court of Appeals for the Ninth Circuit, [which] held that the House was without constitutional authority to order Chadha's deportation. [We] now affirm. . . .

III. A. [The question is] whether action of one House of Congress under §244(c)(2) violates strictures of the Constitution. [The] fact that a given law or procedure is efficient, convenient, and useful in facilitating functions of government, standing alone, will not save it if it is contrary to the Constitution. Convenience and efficiency are not the primary objectives—or the hallmarks—of democratic government and our inquiry is sharpened rather than blunted by the fact that congressional veto provisions are appearing with increasing frequency in statutes which delegate authority to executive and independent [agencies]. . . .

Explicit and unambiguous provisions of the Constitution prescribe and define the respective functions of the Congress and of the Executive in the legislative process. [Article] I provides:

> All legislative Powers herein granted shall be vested in a Congress of the United States, which shall consist of a Senate *and* House of Representatives. Art. I, §1. (Emphasis added.)
>
> Every Bill which shall have passed the House of Representatives and the Senate, *shall*, before it becomes a law, be presented to the President of the United States. . . . Art. I, §7, cl. 2. (Emphasis added.)
>
> Every Order, Resolution, or Vote to which the Concurrence of the Senate and House of Representatives may be necessary (except on a question of Adjournment) *shall be* presented to the President of the United States; and before the Same shall take Effect, *shall be* approved by him, or being disapproved by him, *shall be* repassed by two thirds of the Senate and House of Representatives, according to the Rules and Limitations prescribed in the Case of a Bill. Art. I, §7, cl. 3. (Emphasis added.)

These provisions of Art. I are integral parts of the constitutional design for the separation of powers. [The] purposes underlying the Presentment Clauses and the bicameral requirement of Art. I, §1, and §7, cl. 2, guide our resolution of [this case].

B. *The Presentment Clauses.* The records of the Constitutional Convention reveal that the requirement that all legislation be presented to the President before becoming law was uniformly accepted by the Framers [and was] considered so imperative that the draftsmen took special pains to assure that [it] could not be circumvented. During the final debate on Art. I, §7, cl. 2, James Madison expressed concern that it might easily be evaded by the simple expedient of calling a proposed law a "resolution" or "vote" rather than a "bill." As a consequence, Art. I, §7, cl. 3, was added. The decision to provide the President with a limited and qualified power to nullify proposed legislation by veto was based on the profound conviction of the Framers that the powers conferred on Congress were the powers to be most carefully circumscribed. . . .

C. *Bicameralism.* The bicameral requirement of Art. I, §§1, 7, was of scarcely less concern to the Framers than was the Presidential veto and indeed the two concepts are interdependent. By providing that no law could take effect without the concurrence of the prescribed majority of the Members of both Houses, the Framers reemphasized their belief [that] legislation should not be enacted unless it has been carefully and fully considered by the Nation's elected officials. [T]he Framers were acutely conscious that the bicameral requirement and the Presentment Clauses would serve essential constitutional functions. The President's participation in the legislative process was to protect the Executive Branch from Congress and to protect the whole people from improvident laws. The division of the Congress into two distinctive bodies assures that the legislative power would be exercised only after opportunity for full study and debate in separate settings. The President's unilateral veto power, in turn, was limited by the power of two-thirds of both Houses of Congress to overrule a veto thereby precluding final arbitrary action of one person. [The] prescription for legislative action in Art. I, §§1, 7, represents the Framers' decision that the legislative power of the Federal Government be exercised in accord with a single, finely wrought and exhaustively considered, procedure.

IV. The Constitution sought to [assure] that each branch of government would confine itself to its assigned responsibility. The hydraulic pressure inherent within each of the separate Branches to exceed the outer limits of its power, even to accomplish desirable objectives, must be resisted. [Not] every action taken by either House is subject to the bicameralism and presentment requirements of Art. I. Whether actions taken by either House are, in law and fact, an exercise of legislative power depends not on their form but upon "whether they contain matter which is properly to be regarded as legislative in its character and effect." Examination of the action taken here by one House pursuant to §244(c)(2) reveals that it was essentially legislative in purpose and effect. In purporting to exercise power [to] "establish an uniform Rule of Naturalization," the House took action that had the purpose and effect of altering the legal rights, duties, and relations of persons, including the Attorney General, Executive Branch officials and Chadha, all outside the Legislative Branch. [The] one-House veto operated in [this case] to overrule the Attorney General and mandate Chadha's deportation; absent the House action, Chadha would remain in the United States. Congress has *acted* and its action has altered Chadha's status. The legislative character of the one-House veto in [this case] is confirmed by the character of the congressional action it supplants. Neither the House of Representatives nor the Senate contends that, absent the veto provision in §244(c)(2), either of them, or both of them acting together, could effectively require the Attorney General to deport an alien once the Attorney General, in the exercise of legislatively delegated authority, had determined the alien should remain in the United States. Without the challenged provision in §244(c)(2), this could have been achieved, if at all, only by legislation requiring deportation.

[The] nature of the decision implemented by the one-House veto in these cases further manifests its legislative character. After long experience with the clumsy, time-consuming private bill procedure, Congress made a deliberate choice to delegate to the Executive Branch, and specifically to the Attorney General, the authority to allow deportable aliens to remain in this country in certain specified circumstances. It is not disputed that this choice to delegate authority is precisely the kind of decision that can be implemented only in accordance with the procedures set out in Art. I. Disagreement with the Attorney General's decision on Chadha's deportation—that is, Congress'[s] decision to deport Chadha—no less than Congress'[s] original choice to delegate to the Attorney General the authority to make that decision, involves determinations of policy that Congress can implement in only one way; bicameral passage followed by presentment to the President. Congress must abide by its delegation of authority until that delegation is legislatively altered or revoked.

Finally, we see that when the Framers intended to authorize either House of Congress to act alone and outside of its prescribed bicameral legislative role, they narrowly and precisely defined the procedure for such action. There are four provisions in the Constitution, explicit and unambiguous, by which one House may act alone with the unreviewable force of law, not subject to the President's veto: [impeachment by the House, impeachment trials by the Senate, the Senate's power to deny or confirm presidential appointments, and the Senate's power to ratify treaties]. Since it is clear that the action by the House under §244(c)(2) was not within any of the express constitutional exceptions authorizing one House to act alone, and equally clear that it was an exercise of legislative power, that action was subject to the standards prescribed in Art. I[:] passage by a majority of both Houses and presentment to the President.

The veto authorized by §244(c)(2) doubtless has been in many respects a convenient shortcut; the "sharing" with the Executive by Congress of its authority over aliens in this manner is, on its face, an appealing compromise. [But] it is crystal clear [that] the Framers ranked other values higher than efficiency. [The] choices we discern as having been made in the Constitutional Convention impose burdens on governmental processes that often seem clumsy, inefficient, even unworkable, but those hard choices were consciously made by men who had lived under a form of government that permitted arbitrary governmental acts to go unchecked. There is no support in the Constitution or decisions of this Court for the proposition that the cumbersomeness and delays often encountered in complying with explicit constitutional standards may be avoided, either by the Congress or by the President. With all the obvious flaws of delay, untidiness, and potential for abuse, we have not yet found a better way to preserve freedom than by making the exercise of power subject to the carefully crafted restraints spelled out in the Constitution.

V. We hold that the congressional veto provision in §244(c)(2) [is] unconstitutional.

Justice Powell, concurring in the judgment.

[On] its face, the House's action appears clearly adjudicatory. The House did not enact a general rule; rather it made its own determination that six specific persons did not comply with certain statutory criteria. [Even] if the House did not make a de novo determination, but simply reviewed the Immigration and Naturalization Service's findings, it still assumed a function ordinarily entrusted to the federal courts. [The] impropriety of the House's assumption of this function is confirmed by the fact that its action raises the very danger the Framers sought to avoid—the exercise of unchecked power. In deciding whether Chadha deserves to be deported, Congress is not subject to any internal constraints that prevent it from arbitrarily depriving him of the right to remain in this country. Unlike the judiciary or an administrative agency, Congress is not bound by established substantive rules. Nor is it subject to the procedural safeguards, such as the right to counsel and a hearing before an impartial tribunal, that are present when a court or an agency adjudicates individual rights. The only effective constraint on Congress'[s] power is political, but Congress is most accountable politically when it prescribes rules of general applicability. When it decides rights of specific persons, those rights are subject to "the tyranny of a shifting majority." [In] my view, when Congress undertook to apply its rules to Chadha, it exceeded the scope of its constitutionally prescribed authority. I would not reach the broader question whether legislative vetoes are invalid under the Presentment Clauses.

JUSTICE WHITE, dissenting.

Today the Court not only invalidates §244(c)(2) [but] also sounds the death knell for nearly 200 other statutory provisions in which Congress has reserved a "legislative veto." . . . [The] legislative veto [has] become a central means by which Congress secures the accountability of executive and independent agencies. Without the legislative veto, Congress is faced with a Hobson's choice: either to refrain from delegating the necessary authority, leaving itself with a hopeless task of writing laws with the requisite specificity to cover endless special circumstances across the entire policy landscape, or in the alternative, to abdicate its law-making function to the Executive Branch and independent agencies. To choose the former leaves major national problems unresolved; to opt for the latter risks unaccountable policymaking by those not elected to fill that role. Accordingly, over the past five decades, the legislative veto has been placed in nearly 200 statutes. The device is known in every field of governmental concern: reorganization, budgets, foreign affairs, war powers, and regulation of trade, safety, energy, the environment, and the economy.

I. [The] legislative veto [is] an important if not indispensable political invention that allows the President and Congress to resolve major constitutional and policy differences, assures the accountability of independent regulatory agencies, and preserves Congress'[s] control over lawmaking. [The] history of the legislative veto also makes clear that it has not been a sword with which Congress has struck out to aggrandize itself at the expense of the other branches—the concerns of Madison and Hamilton. Rather, the veto has been a means of defense, a reservation of ultimate authority necessary if Congress is to fulfill its designated role under Art. I as the Nation's lawmaker. While the President has often objected to particular legislative vetoes, generally those left in the hands of congressional Committees, the Executive has more often agreed to legislative review as the price for a broad delegation of authority. To be sure, the President may have preferred unrestricted power, but that could be precisely why Congress thought it essential to retain a check on the exercise of delegated authority.

II. [The] constitutionality of the legislative veto is anything but clear-cut. [The] Constitution does not directly authorize or prohibit the legislative veto. Thus, our task should be to determine whether the legislative veto is consistent with the purposes of Art. I and the principles of separation of [powers]. We should not find the lack of a specific constitutional authorization for the legislative veto surprising, and I would not infer disapproval of the mechanism from its absence. From the summer of 1787 to the present the Government of the United States has become an endeavor far beyond the contemplation of the Framers. Only within the last half century has the complexity and size of the Federal Government's responsibilities grown so greatly that the Congress must rely on the legislative veto as the most effective if not the only means to insure its role as the Nation's lawmaker. But the wisdom of the Framers was to anticipate that the Nation would grow and new problems of governance would require different solutions. Accordingly, our Federal Government was intentionally chartered with the flexibility to respond to contemporary needs without losing sight of fundamental democratic principles. . . .

III. The [Court's reliance on the bicameralism and presentment requirements does not] answer the constitutional question before us. The power to exercise a legislative veto is not the power to write new law without bicameral approval or Presidential consideration. The veto must be authorized by statute and may only negative what an Executive department or independent agency has proposed. On its face, the legislative veto no more allows one House of Congress to make law than does the Presidential veto confer such power upon the President. . . .

The Court's holding today that all legislative-type action must be enacted through the lawmaking process ignores that legislative authority is routinely delegated to the Executive Branch, to the independent regulatory agencies, and to private individuals and groups. . . . In practice, however, restrictions on the scope of the power that could be delegated diminished and all but disappeared. [For] some time, the sheer amount of law—the substantive rules that regulate private conduct and direct the operation of government—made by the agencies has far outnumbered the lawmaking engaged in by Congress through the traditional process. There is no question but that agency rulemaking is lawmaking in any functional or realistic sense of the term.

[If] Congress may delegate lawmaking power to independent and Executive agencies, it is most difficult to understand Art. I as prohibiting Congress from also reserving a check on legislative power for itself. Absent the veto, the agencies receiving delegations of legislative or quasi-legislative power may issue regulations having the force of law without bicameral approval and without the President's signature. It is thus not apparent why the reservation of a veto over the exercise of that legislative power must be subject to a more exacting test. In both cases, it is enough that the initial statutory authorizations comply with the Art. I requirements. . . . [The] Court's decision today suggests that Congress may place a "veto" power over suspensions of deportation [in] the hands of an independent agency, but is forbidden to reserve such authority for itself. . . .

The Court also takes no account of perhaps the most relevant consideration: however resolutions of disapproval under §244(c)(2) are formally characterized, in reality, a departure from the status quo occurs only upon the concurrence of opinion among the House, Senate, and President. Reservations of legislative authority to be exercised by Congress should be upheld if the exercise of such reserved authority is consistent with the distribution of and limits upon legislative power that Art. I provides. [Section] 244(c)(2) withstands this analysis. [The] history of the Immigration and Nationality Act makes clear that §244(c)(2) did not alter the division of actual authority between Congress and the Executive. At all times, whether through private bills, or through affirmative concurrent resolutions, or through the present one-House veto, a permanent change in a deportable alien's status could be accomplished only with the agreement of the Attorney General, the House, and the Senate. The central concern of the presentment and bicameralism requirements of Art. I is that when a departure from the legal status quo is undertaken, it is done with the approval of the President and both Houses of Congress—or, in the event of a Presidential veto, a two-thirds majority in both Houses. This interest is fully satisfied by the operation of §244(c)(2). The President's approval is found in the Attorney General's action in recommending to Congress that the deportation order for a given alien be suspended. The House and the Senate indicate their approval of the Executive's action by not passing a resolution of disapproval within the statutory period. Thus, a change in the legal status quo—the deportability of the alien—is consummated only with the approval of each of the three relevant actors. The disagreement of any one of the three maintains the alien's pre-existing status: the Executive may choose not to recommend suspension; the House and Senate may each veto the recommendation. The effect [is] precisely the same as if a private bill were introduced but failed to receive the necessary approval. . . .

IV. [The] history of the separation-of-powers doctrine is also a history of accommodation and practicality. [The] Constitution does not contemplate total separation of the three branches of Government. [The] legislative veto provision does not "[prevent] the Executive Branch from accomplishing its constitutionally assigned functions." . . . [Nor] does §244 infringe on the judicial power, as Justice Powell would hold. Section 244 makes clear that Congress has reserved its own judgment as part of the statutory process. Congressional action does not substitute for judicial review of the Attorney General's decisions. [I] do not suggest that all legislative vetoes are necessarily consistent with separation-of-powers principles. A legislative check on an inherently executive function, for example, that of initiating prosecutions, poses an entirely different question. But the legislative veto device here—and in many other settings—is far from an instance of legislative tyranny over the

Executive. It is a necessary check on the unavoidably expanding power of the agencies, both Executive and independent, as they engage in exercising authority delegated by Congress. . . .

NOTES

1. The Scope of the Ruling. Does *Chadha* apply to all legislative vetoes, as Justice White charged, or is it confined to the relatively narrow category of one-house legislative vetoes of "adjudicatory" executive action affecting a single person or a tiny class of people? In Process Gas Consumers Group v. Consumers Energy Council of America, 463 U.S. 1216 (1983), and U.S. Senate v. FTC, 463 U.S. 1216 (1983), the Court summarily affirmed invalidation of a one-house legislative veto over administrative decisions on natural gas pricing (*Process Gas*) and a two-house veto over FTC rulemaking (*FTC*). Consider whether the two-house legislative veto provided for in the War Powers Resolution, supra, survives these decisions.

2. The Legislative Veto, Nondelegation, and the Administrative State. A key part of Justice White's defense of the legislative veto was his contention that the veto was well suited to preserving legislative control over public policy, given the virtually unbounded legislative powers exercised by executive administrators as a result of the demise of the nondelegation doctrine. Did the Court disagree or simply think his observation to be irrelevant? Is it irrelevant? Suppose that Justice White's observation is accurate. Given the outcome of *Chadha*, should the Court strengthen the nondelegation doctrine? If not, are there other controls that Congress may use to limit the exercise of executive discretion? Consider the following possibilities.

Hearings. Congressional committees could summon executive officials to appear and defend the discretionary choices they have made. Depending on how interested the public is in the issue, the resulting publicity might affect executive action.

Sunset authorization. Congress might limit the authority of executive agencies to specific terms, thus requiring new legislation to perpetuate the agencies' authority. Agency officials might be more sensitive to congressional desires in exercising their discretion, knowing that their continued tenure depends on the renewal of congressional approval.

Report-and-wait requirement. Congress might require that agencies report any proposed new rule to Congress and stipulate, in the authorizing legislation, that no such rule can become effective until after the elapse of a specified time period, during which Congress would be free to negate the proposed rule by enacting ordinary legislation. Would the effectiveness of this method of control be roughly inversely proportional to the number of rules that would be covered by the method?

Appropriations limits. Congress might specify in its appropriation of funds for an agency that no funds may be used to implement specified policies Congress finds undesirable. Or Congress could simply increase or decrease the total budget for an agency to facilitate or hamper the implementation of policies it likes or dislikes.

General limits on executive discretion. Congress might repeal agency authority to exercise wide discretion and instead limit the discretion that executive agencies are permitted to exercise. Of course, for this to be effective, Congress must specify in the authorizing legislation the particular policies and (possibly) implementing methods it desires. But Congress has given agencies enormous discretion precisely because it wished to avoid the necessity of making these difficult choices.

Conversion of agencies to advisory bodies. Congress might stipulate that no agency rule can become effective until after Congress has enacted it into law with the President's concurrence or over his veto. If this were the uniform practice with respect to all agencies, how do you think Congress would handle the torrent of proposed rules that flow out of administrative agencies? Would Congress act as a rubber stamp? Or would parties affected by proposed rules lobby Congress for approval or disapproval of such rules?

Suppose that, after *Chadha*, Congress amended the Immigration and Nationality Act to provide that the Attorney General's suspension of deportation of any deportable alien shall expire after one full session of Congress unless both houses of Congress have approved the suspension decision. Would this be valid in light of *Chadha*?

≡ Clinton v. City of New York
524 U.S. 417 (1998)

JUSTICE STEVENS delivered the opinion of the Court.

The Line Item Veto Act (Act) . . . became effective on January 1, 1997. [President Clinton invoked the Act to cancel two statutory provisions: (1) a portion of the 1997 Balanced Budget Act permitting New York to keep as much as $2.6 billion in Medicaid funds it would otherwise be required to return to the federal government, and (2) a provision of the Taxpayer Relief Act that permitted stockholders of food processing corporations to defer recognition of taxable gain on sales of their stock to farmers' cooperatives. New York City and various private entities challenged the validity of the first cancellation. The Snake River Potato Growers, a farmers' cooperative, challenged the validity of the second cancellation. The Court initially concluded that these plaintiffs had standing and that the claims were justiciable.]

The Line Item Veto Act gives the President the power to "cancel in whole" three types of provisions that have been signed into law: "(1) any dollar amount of discretionary budget authority; (2) any item of new direct spending; or (3) any limited tax benefit." It is undisputed that the New York case involves an "item of new direct spending" and that the Snake River case involves a "limited tax benefit" as those terms are defined in the Act. It is also undisputed that each of those provisions had been signed into law pursuant to Article I, §7 of the Constitution before it was canceled.

[In] identifying items for cancellation [the President] must determine [that each cancellation] will "(i) reduce the Federal budget deficit; (ii) not impair any essential Government functions; and (iii) not harm the national interest." Moreover, he must transmit a special message to Congress notifying it of each cancellation within five calendar days (excluding Sundays) after the enactment of the canceled provision. [A] cancellation takes effect upon receipt by Congress of the special message from the President. If, however, a "disapproval bill" pertaining to a special message is enacted into law, the cancellations set forth in that message become "null and void." [A] majority vote of both Houses is sufficient to enact a disapproval bill. The Act does not grant the President the authority to cancel a disapproval bill, but he does, of course, retain his constitutional authority to veto such a bill.

[In] both legal and practical effect, the President has amended two Acts of Congress by repealing a portion of each. "[R]epeal of statutes, no less than enactment, must conform with Art. I." INS v. Chadha. There is no provision in the Constitution that authorizes the President to enact, to amend, or to repeal statutes. [He] may initiate and influence legislative proposals [and], after a bill has passed both Houses of Congress, but "before it become[s] a Law," it must be presented to the President. If he approves it, "he shall sign it, but if not he shall return it, with his Objections to that House in which it shall have originated, who shall enter the Objections at large on their Journal, and proceed to reconsider it." Art. I, §7, cl. 2. His "return" of a bill, which is usually described as a "veto," is subject to being overridden by a two-thirds vote in each House.

There are important differences between the President's "return" of a bill pursuant to Article I, §7, and the exercise of the President's cancellation authority pursuant to the Line Item Veto Act. The constitutional return takes place before the bill becomes law; the statutory cancellation occurs after the bill becomes law. The constitutional return is of the entire bill; the statutory cancellation is of only a part. Although the Constitution expressly authorizes the President to play a role in the process of enacting statutes, it is silent on the subject of unilateral Presidential action that either repeals or amends parts of duly enacted statutes.

There are powerful reasons for construing constitutional silence on this profoundly important issue as equivalent to an express prohibition. The procedures governing the enactment of statutes set forth in the text of Article I were the product of the great debates and compromises that produced the Constitution itself. Familiar historical materials provide abundant support for the conclusion that the power to enact statutes may only "be exercised in accord with a single, finely wrought and exhaustively considered, procedure." *Chadha.* Our first President understood the text of the Presentment Clause as requiring that he either "approve all the parts of a Bill, or reject it in toto." What has emerged in these cases from the President's exercise of his statutory cancellation powers, however, are truncated versions of two bills that passed both Houses of Congress. They are not the product of the "finely wrought" procedure that the Framers designed.

The Government [contends that] cancellations do not amend or repeal properly enacted statutes in violation of the Presentment Clause [because] the cancellations were merely exercises of discretionary authority granted to the President by the Balanced Budget Act and the Taxpayer Relief Act read in light of the previously enacted Line Item Veto Act. [In] Field v. Clark, 143 U.S. 649 (1892), the Court upheld the constitutionality of the Tariff Act of 1890, [which directed the President to suspend a tariff exemption for certain commodities whenever] he should be satisfied that any country [imposed] duties on the agricultural products of the United States that he deemed to be "reciprocally unequal and unreasonable." [But Field v. Clark is inapposite.] First, the exercise of the suspension power was contingent upon a condition that did not exist when the Tariff Act was passed: the imposition of "reciprocally unequal and unreasonable" import duties by other countries. In contrast, the exercise of the cancellation power within five days after the enactment of the Balanced Budget and Tax Reform Acts necessarily was based on the same conditions that Congress evaluated when it passed those statutes. Second, under the Tariff Act, when the President determined that the contingency had arisen, he had a duty to suspend; in contrast, while it is true that the President was required by the Act to make three determinations before he canceled a provision, those determinations did not qualify his discretion to cancel or not to cancel. Finally, whenever the President suspended an exemption under the Tariff Act, he was executing the policy that Congress had embodied in the statute. In contrast, whenever the President cancels an item of new direct spending or a limited tax benefit he is rejecting the policy judgment made by Congress and relying on his own policy judgment. Thus, the conclusion in Field v. Clark that the suspensions mandated by the Tariff Act were not exercises of legislative power does not undermine our opinion that cancellations pursuant to the Line Item Veto Act are the functional equivalent of partial repeals of Acts of Congress that fail to satisfy Article I, §7.

[Neither] are we persuaded by the Government's contention that the President's authority to cancel new direct spending and tax benefit items is no greater than his traditional authority to decline to spend appropriated funds. The Government has reviewed in some detail the series of statutes in which Congress has given the Executive broad discretion over the expenditure of appropriated funds. . . . In those statutes . . . the President was given wide discretion with respect to both the amounts to be spent and how the money would be allocated among different functions. It is argued that the Line Item Veto Act merely confers comparable discretionary authority over the expenditure of appropriated funds. The critical difference between this statute and all of its predecessors, however, is that unlike any of them, this Act gives the President the unilateral power to change the text of duly enacted statutes. None of the Act's predecessors could even arguably have been construed to authorize such a change.

[We] express no opinion about the wisdom of the procedures authorized by the Line Item Veto Act. [Our] decision rests on the narrow ground that the procedures authorized by the Line Item Veto Act are not authorized by the Constitution. . . . If the Line Item Veto Act were valid, it would authorize the President to create a different law—one whose text was not voted on by either House of Congress or presented to the President for signature. . . . If there is to be a new procedure in which the President will play a different role in determining the final text of what may "become a law," such change must come not by legislation but through the amendment procedures set forth in Article V of the Constitution.

[A]ffirmed.

Justice Kennedy, concurring.

A nation cannot plunder its own treasury without putting its Constitution and its survival in peril. The statute before us, then, is of first importance, for it seems undeniable the Act will tend to restrain persistent excessive spending. Nevertheless, . . . the statute must be found invalid. Failure of political will does not justify unconstitutional remedies. . . . Liberty is always at stake when one or more of the branches seek to transgress the separation of powers. Separation of powers was designed to implement a fundamental insight: concentration of power in the hands of a single branch is a threat to liberty. . . . [The] citizen has a vital interest in the regularity of the exercise of governmental power. . . . [By] increasing the power of the President beyond what the Framers envisioned, the statute compromises the political liberty of our citizens, liberty which the separation of powers seeks to secure.

Justice Scalia, joined by Justice O'Connor, and as to Part III, Justice Breyer, concurring in part and dissenting in part.

[Unlike] the Court I find the President's cancellation of spending items to be [in] accord with the Constitution. . . .

III. . . . [Art. I, §7 does] not demand the result the Court reaches. It no more categorically prohibits the Executive reduction of congressional dispositions in the course of implementing statutes that authorize such reduction, than it categorically prohibits the Executive augmentation of congressional dispositions in the course of implementing statutes that authorize such augmentation—generally known as substantive rulemaking. There are, to be sure, limits upon the former just as there are limits upon the latter—and I am prepared to acknowledge that the limits upon the former may be much more severe. Those limits are established, however, not by some categorical prohibition of Art. I, §7, . . . but by what has come to be known as the doctrine of unconstitutional delegation of legislative authority: When authorized Executive reduction or augmentation is allowed to go too far, it usurps the nondelegable function of Congress and violates the separation of powers. It is this doctrine, and not the Presentment Clause, that was discussed in the *Field* opinion, and it is this doctrine, and not the Presentment Clause, that is the issue presented by the statute before us here. . . .

Insofar as the degree of political, "law-making" power conferred upon the Executive is concerned, there is not a dime's worth of difference between Congress's authorizing the President to cancel a spending item, and Congress's authorizing money to be spent on a particular item at the President's discretion. And the latter has been done since the Founding of the Nation. [The] constitutionality of such appropriations has never seriously been questioned. . . .

Certain Presidents [e.g., Grant, Franklin Roosevelt, and Truman] have claimed Executive authority to withhold appropriated funds even absent an express conferral of discretion to do so. [President] Nixon, the Mahatma Gandhi of all impounders, asserted at a press conference in 1973 that his "constitutional right" to impound appropriated funds was "absolutely clear." [Our] decision two years later in Train v. City of New York, 420 U.S. 35 (1975), proved him wrong, but it implicitly confirmed that Congress may confer discretion upon the executive to withhold appropriated funds, even funds appropriated for a specific purpose. [The] short of the matter is this: Had the Line Item Veto Act authorized the President to "decline to spend" any item of spending contained in the Balanced Budget Act of 1997, there is not the slightest doubt that authorization would have been constitutional. What the Line Item Veto Act does instead—authorizing the President to "cancel" an item of spending—is technically different. But the technical difference does not relate to the technicalities of the Presentment Clause, which have been fully complied with; and the doctrine of unconstitutional delegation, which is at issue here, is preeminently not a doctrine of technicalities. The title of the Line Item Veto Act, which was perhaps designed to simplify for public comprehension, or perhaps merely to comply with the terms of a campaign pledge, has succeeded in faking out the Supreme Court. The President's action it authorizes in fact is not a line-item veto and thus does not offend Art. I, §7; and insofar as the substance of that action is concerned, it is no different from what Congress has permitted the President to do since the formation of the Union.

JUSTICE BREYER, joined by JUSTICES O'CONNOR and SCALIA as to Part III, dissenting.

I. . . . In my view the Line Item Veto Act does not violate any specific textual constitutional command, nor does it violate any implicit Separation of Powers principle. . . .

II. . . . [The] Act represents a legislative effort to provide the President with the power to give effect to some, but not to all, of the expenditure and revenue-diminishing provisions contained in a single massive appropriations bill. And this objective is constitutionally proper. . . .

III. The Court believes that the Act violates the literal text of the Constitution. A simple syllogism captures its basic reasoning: Major Premise: The Constitution sets forth an exclusive method for enacting, repealing, or amending laws. Minor Premise: The Act authorizes the President to "repea[l] or amen[d]" laws in a different way, namely by announcing a cancellation of a portion of a previously enacted law. Conclusion: The Act is inconsistent with the Constitution. I find this syllogism unconvincing, however, because its Minor Premise is faulty. When the President "canceled" the two appropriation measures now before us, he did not repeal any law nor did he amend any law. He simply followed the law, leaving the statutes, as they are literally written, intact. [Imagine] that the canceled New York health care tax provision at issue here had instead [said] "that the President may prevent the just-mentioned provision from having legal force or effect if he determines x, y and z." [One] could not say that a President who "prevent[s]" the [law] from "having legal force or effect" has either repealed or amended [it]. Rather, the President [has] executed the law, not repealed it. It could make no significant difference to this linguistic point were [the] proviso to appear [at] the bottom of the statute page, say referenced by an asterisk, with a statement that it applies to every spending provision in the act next to which a similar asterisk appears. And that being so, it could make no difference if that proviso appeared, instead, in a different, earlier-enacted law, along with legal language that makes it applicable to every future spending provision picked out according to a specified formula. But, of course, this last-mentioned possibility is this very case. . . .

IV. Because I disagree with the Court's holding of literal violation, I must consider whether the Act nonetheless violates Separation of Powers [principles]. There are three relevant Separation of Powers questions here: (1) Has Congress given the President the wrong kind of power, i.e., "non-Executive" power? (2) Has Congress given the President the power to "encroach" upon Congress'[s] own constitutionally reserved territory? (3) Has Congress given the President too much power, violating the doctrine of "nondelegation"? [The] answer to all these questions is "no."

A. [The] Act [conveys] "executive" [power. It] closely resembles the kind of delegated authority—to spend or not to spend appropriations, to change or not to change tariff rates—that Congress has frequently granted the President, any differences being differences in degree, not kind. . . .

B. [One] cannot say that the Act "encroaches" upon Congress'[s] power, when Congress retained the power to insert [into] any [part of any] future appropriations bill [a] provision that says the Act will not apply. . . . [Nor] can one say the Act's grant of power "aggrandizes" the Presidential office. The grant is limited to the context of the budget. It is limited to the power to spend, or not to spend, particular appropriated items, and the power to permit, or not to permit, specific limited exemptions from generally applicable tax law from taking effect. These powers [resemble] those the President has exercised in the past on other occasions. . . .

C. . . . [This case] is limited to one area of government, the budget, and it seeks to give the President the power, in one portion of that budget, to tailor spending and special tax relief to what he concludes are the demands of fiscal responsibility. [The] broadly phrased limitations in the Act, together with its evident deficit reduction purpose, and a procedure that guarantees Presidential awareness of the reasons for including a particular provision in a budget [bill] guide the President's exercise of his discretionary powers. [Consequently,] I believe that the power the Act grants the President to prevent spending items from taking effect does not violate the "nondelegation" doctrine.

V. [T]he Act before us is novel. In a sense, it skirts a constitutional edge. But that edge has to do with means, not ends. The means chosen do not amount literally to the enactment, repeal, or amendment of a law [nor do they] violate any basic Separation of Powers principle. . . .

D.   IMMUNITIES AND PRIVILEGES

The Constitution explicitly creates two kinds of legislative immunities, but there are no parallel provisions creating either executive or judicial immunities. Nevertheless, to preserve the autonomy of each branch of government, implied executive and judicial immunities have been recognized. The first subsection deals briefly with the scope of the explicit legislative immunities. The second subsection examines the issue of the nature and scope of executive immunities. The last subsection explores the controversial topic of the existence and scope of an executive privilege to keep executive branch communications confidential.

1.   Legislative Immunities

Article I, section 6 confers on members of Congress two types of limited immunity from suit—via the "speech and debate" clause and the "privilege from arrest" clause. The "speech and debate" clause provides that members of Congress "shall not be questioned in any other Place [for] any Speech or Debate in either House." The purpose of such immunity is to foster uninhibited legislative debate and to protect legislators from the distraction of defending suits based on their performance of their duties. Members of Congress are absolutely immune from civil or criminal suits or even grand jury investigations premised upon their "legislative acts." This immunity also extends to legislative aides but only with respect to the "legislative acts" of the aides. See Gravel v. United States, 408 U.S. 606 (1972).

The term "legislative acts" includes everything that is integral to "the deliberative and communicative processes by which members participate" in the official business of Congress. This does not mean just the literal speeches and debates of Congress; it also includes voting, committee work, and Congress's other official business. It does not include constituent service, political campaigning, or even public announcements related to a member's policy views. For example, Senator William Proxmire, an ardent opponent of wasteful government spending, adopted the practice of publicly bestowing monthly a "Golden Fleece" award on some recipient of federal funds whose use of such funds was regarded by Senator Proxmire as particularly wasteful. By news conference and press release, with much attendant publicity and fanfare, Proxmire granted the Golden Fleece award to Ronald Hutchinson, a professor receiving a federal grant to pay for certain research into aggressive monkey behavior. The Court concluded that Proxmire was not immune from Hutchinson's defamation suit because his actions were not "legislative." Hutchinson v. Proxmire, 443 U.S. 111 (1979).

However, the "speech and debate" clause does not prevent prosecution for crimes that are related to legislative acts so long as the legislative act itself is not prosecuted or used as evidence. For example, a corrupt member of Congress may not be prosecuted for *voting in a particular manner* because he was bribed to do so, but he may be prosecuted for the nonlegislative act of *taking the bribe*. The resulting bribery prosecution may not, however, introduce evidence of legislative acts on the part of the member of Congress. See, e.g., United States v. Helstoski, 442 U.S. 477, 489 (1979); United States v. Brewster, 408 U.S. 501, 526 (1972); United States v. Johnson, 383 U.S. 169, 184-185 (1966).

The "privilege from arrest" clause of Article I, section 6 provides that, except for cases of "Treason, Felony and Breach of the Peace," members of Congress are "privileged from Arrest during their Attendance at the Session of their respective Houses, and in going to and returning from the same." In 1787, this effectively conferred an immunity from arrest for nonpayment of debt. The clause does not shield members of Congress from service of process, nor does it immunize members from arrest in a criminal matter.

2. Executive Immunities

In United States v. Nixon, 418 U.S. 683 (1974), the Court concluded that the President was not immune from judicial process and was required to produce certain recordings and documents in response to a subpoena duces tecum. In Nixon v. Fitzgerald, 457 U.S. 731 (1982), the Court ruled that the President was absolutely immune from civil liability for his official actions. Fitzgerald, a civilian employee of the Air Force, was discharged after he cast the Air Force in an unfavorable light in widely publicized testimony before a congressional committee. He brought a civil damage action against President Nixon and other government officials, claiming his free speech and certain statutory rights had been violated. Justice Powell wrote for the Court:

> [We] hold that [Richard Nixon], as a former President of the United States, is entitled to absolute immunity from damages liability predicated on his official acts. We consider this immunity a functionally mandated incident of the President's unique office, rooted in the constitutional tradition of the separation of powers and supported by our history. [Because] of the singular importance of the President's duties, diversion of his energies by concern with private lawsuits would raise unique risks to the effective functioning of government. As

is the case with prosecutors and judges—for whom absolute immunity now is established—a President must concern himself with matters likely to "arouse the most intense feelings." Yet [it] is in precisely such cases that there exists the greatest public interest in providing an official "the maximum ability to deal fearlessly and impartially with" the duties of his office. This concern is compelling where the officeholder must make the most sensitive and far-reaching decisions entrusted to any official under our constitutional system. Nor can the sheer prominence of the President's office be ignored. In view of the visibility of his office and the effect of his actions on countless people, the President would be an easily identifiable target for suits for civil damages. Cognizance of this personal vulnerability frequently could distract a President from his public duties, to the detriment of not only the President and his office but also the Nation that the Presidency was designed to serve.

[A] rule of absolute immunity for the President will not leave the Nation without sufficient protection against misconduct on the part of the Chief Executive. There remains the constitutional remedy of impeachment. In addition, there are formal and informal checks on Presidential action that do not apply with equal force to other executive officials. The President is subjected to constant scrutiny by the press. Vigilant oversight by Congress also may serve to deter Presidential abuses of office, as well as to make credible the threat of impeachment. Other incentives to avoid misconduct may include a desire to earn reelection, the need to maintain prestige as an element of Presidential influence, and a President's traditional concern for his historical stature. The existence of alternative remedies and deterrents establishes that absolute immunity will not place the President "above the law."

Justice White, joined by Justices Brennan, Marshall, and Blackmun, dissented:

Attaching absolute immunity to the Office of the President, rather than to particular activities that the President might perform, places the President above the law. It is a reversion to the old notion that the King can do no wrong. [Taken] at face value, the Court's position that as a matter of constitutional law the President is absolutely immune should mean that he is immune not only from damages actions but also from suits for injunctive relief, criminal prosecutions and, indeed, from any kind of judicial process. But [the] President is [not] immune from criminal prosecution, [at least after removal from office]. Neither can there be a serious claim that the separation-of-powers doctrine insulates Presidential action from judicial review, [or from the] judicial process, [or from] the courts' injunctive powers. [The] scope of immunity [should be] determined by function, not office. [The] only question that must be answered here is whether the dismissal of employees falls within a constitutionally assigned executive function, the performance of which would be substantially impaired by the possibility of a private action for damages. I believe it does not.

In a companion case, Harlow v. Fitzgerald, 457 U.S. 800 (1982), the Court declined to extend absolute presidential immunity to the President's chief of staff, although the Court did rule that such senior executive officers are entitled to the qualified immunity that attaches generally to executive officials.

Under the doctrine of qualified immunity, executive officials may not be held liable for their actions that were objectively reasonable under clearly established law at the time of the actions in question. When government officials are claimed to have violated constitutional rights, courts must determine whether the alleged conduct violated the right and whether the right was "clearly established" at the time of the alleged misconduct. In Pearson v. Callahan, 555 U.S. 223 (2009), the Court ruled that judges may first determine whether the claimed constitutional right was clearly established without determining whether the alleged misconduct violated the right. In any case, qualified immunity depends on the "objective legal reasonableness of the action, assessed in light of the legal rules that were clearly established at the time it was taken."

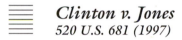

Clinton v. Jones
520 U.S. 681 (1997)

JUSTICE STEVENS delivered the opinion of the Court.

This case raises a constitutional and a prudential question concerning the Office of the President of the United States. Respondent, a private citizen, seeks to recover damages from the current occupant of that office based on actions allegedly taken before his term began. The President submits that in all but the most exceptional cases the Constitution requires federal courts to defer such litigation until his term ends and that, in any event, respect for the office warrants such a stay. [We] conclude that [the President's arguments] must be rejected.

Petitioner, William Jefferson Clinton, was elected to the Presidency in 1992, and re-elected in 1996. His term of office expires on January 20, 2001. In 1991 he was the Governor of the State of Arkansas. Respondent, Paula Corbin Jones, [commenced] this action in the United States District Court for the Eastern District of Arkansas [on May 6, 1994,] by filing a complaint naming petitioner [as a defendant]. As the case comes to us, we are required to assume the truth of the detailed [factual] allegations in the complaint.

Those allegations principally describe events that are said to have occurred on the afternoon of May 8, 1991, during an official conference held at the Excelsior Hotel in Little Rock, Arkansas. The Governor delivered a speech at the conference; respondent—working as a state employee—staffed the registration desk. She alleges that [a state policeman also named as a defendant] persuaded her to leave her desk and to visit the Governor in a business suite at the hotel, where he made "abhorrent" sexual advances that she vehemently rejected. She further claims that her superiors at work subsequently dealt with her in a hostile and rude manner, and changed her duties to punish her for rejecting those advances. Finally, she alleges that after petitioner was elected President, [various] persons authorized to speak for the President publicly branded her a liar by denying that the incident had occurred. Respondent seeks actual [and punitive] damages. Her complaint [alleges that she was deprived of her constitutional rights under color of state law, conspiracy to deprive her of those rights, intentional infliction of emotional distress, and defamation]. We assume, without deciding, that each [count] states a cause of action as a matter of law. With the exception of the [defamation] charge, which arguably may involve conduct within the outer perimeter of the President's official responsibilities, it is perfectly clear that the alleged misconduct of petitioner was unrelated to any of his official duties as President of the United States and, indeed, occurred before he was elected to that office.

[Petitioner filed] a motion to dismiss on grounds of Presidential immunity, and requested the court to defer all other pleadings and motions until after the immunity issue was resolved. [The] District Judge denied the motion to dismiss on immunity grounds and ruled that discovery in the case could go forward, but ordered any trial stayed until the end of petitioner's Presidency. [Both] parties appealed. [The] Court of Appeals affirmed the denial of the motion to dismiss, but because it regarded the order postponing the trial until the President leaves office as the "functional equivalent" of a grant of temporary immunity, it reversed that order.

[The President's] principal submission — that "in all but the most exceptional cases" the Constitution affords the President temporary immunity from civil damages litigation arising out of events that occurred before he took office — cannot be sustained on the basis of precedent. [The] principal rationale for affording certain public servants immunity from suits for money damages arising out of their official acts is inapplicable to unofficial conduct. . . . [I]mmunity serves the public interest in enabling [government] officials to perform their designated functions effectively without fear that a particular decision may give rise to personal liability. [That] rationale provided the principal basis for our holding that a former President of the United States was "entitled to absolute immunity from damages liability predicated on his official acts." [Nixon v. Fitzgerald.] Our central concern was to avoid rendering the President "unduly cautious in the discharge of his official duties." [Our] dominant concern [in *Fitzgerald*] was with the diversion of the President's attention during the decisionmaking process caused by needless worry as to the possibility of damages actions stemming from any particular official decision, [not] the possibility that a sitting President might be distracted by the need to participate in litigation during the pendency of his office.

This reasoning provides no support for an immunity for unofficial conduct. As we explained in *Fitzgerald*, "the sphere of protected action must be related closely to the immunity's justifying purposes." Because of the President's broad responsibilities, we recognized in that case an immunity from damages claims arising out of official acts extending to the "outer perimeter of his authority." But we have never suggested that the President, or any other official, has an immunity that extends beyond the scope of any action taken in an official capacity. [When] defining the scope of an immunity for acts clearly taken within an official capacity, we have applied a functional approach.

Hence, for example, a judge's absolute immunity does not extend to actions performed in a purely administrative capacity. [Immunities] are grounded in "the nature of the function performed, not the identity of the actor who performed it." . . .

[The President's] strongest argument supporting his immunity claim is . . . grounded in the character of the office that was created by Article II of the Constitution, and relies on separation of powers principles. [The President] contends that he occupies a unique office with powers and responsibilities so vast and important that the public interest demands that he devote his undivided time and attention to his public duties. He submits that—given the nature of the office—the doctrine of separation of powers places limits on the authority of the Federal Judiciary to interfere with the Executive Branch that would be transgressed by allowing this action to proceed.

We have no dispute with the initial premise of the argument. Former presidents, from George Washington to George Bush, have consistently endorsed petitioner's characterization of the office. . . . [It] does not follow, however, that separation of powers principles would be violated by allowing this action to proceed. [There] is no possibility that the decision will curtail the scope of the official powers of the Executive Branch. [Rather, the President] contends that—as a by-product of an otherwise traditional exercise of judicial power—burdens will be placed on the President that will hamper the performance of his official duties. . . . [In] the more than 200-year history of the Republic, only three sitting Presidents have been subjected to suits for their private actions.[6] If the past is any indicator, it seems unlikely that a deluge of such litigation will ever engulf the Presidency. [If this case is] properly managed by the District Court, it appears to us highly unlikely to occupy any substantial amount of petitioner's time.

[The] fact that a federal court's exercise of its traditional Article III jurisdiction may significantly burden the time and attention of the Chief Executive is not sufficient to establish a violation of the Constitution. [We] have long held that when the President takes official action, the Court has the authority to determine whether he has acted within the law. . . . [It] is also settled that the President is subject to judicial process in appropriate circumstances. Although Thomas Jefferson apparently thought otherwise, Chief Justice Marshall, when presiding in the treason trial of Aaron Burr, ruled that a subpoena duces tecum could be directed to the President. United States v. Burr, 25 F. Cas. 30 (No. 14,692d) (CC Va. 1807). We unequivocally and emphatically endorsed Marshall's position when we held that President Nixon was obligated to comply with a subpoena commanding him to produce certain tape recordings of his conversations with his aides. United States v. Nixon, 418 U.S. 683 (1974).

---

6. Suits pending against Theodore Roosevelt and Harry Truman were dismissed before they took office, and two suits against John Kennedy were settled shortly after he became President.—Ed.

Sitting Presidents have responded to court orders to provide testimony and other information with sufficient frequency that such interactions between the Judicial and Executive Branches can scarcely be thought a novelty.[7] [Moreover, Presidents Grant and Carter] voluntarily complied with judicial requests for testimony. [In] sum, "it is settled law that the separation-of-powers doctrine does not bar every exercise of jurisdiction over the President of the United States." *Fitzgerald*. If the Judiciary may severely burden the Executive Branch by reviewing the legality of the President's official conduct, and if it may direct appropriate process to the President himself, it must follow that the federal courts have power to determine the legality of his unofficial conduct. The burden on the President's time and energy that is a mere by-product of such review surely cannot be considered as onerous as the direct burden imposed by judicial review and the occasional invalidation of his official actions. We therefore hold that the doctrine of separation of powers does not require federal courts to stay all private actions against the President until he leaves office. . . .

[The] Federal District Court has jurisdiction to decide this case. Like every other citizen who properly invokes that jurisdiction, respondent has a right to an orderly disposition of her claims. [Affirmed.]

NOTE

The Aftermath of Clinton v. Jones.   After the Court's decision discovery resumed in Paula Jones's lawsuit, leading to a deposition of President Clinton in which he testified falsely about various aspects of a sexual relationship between himself and a young White House intern. The facts of the relationship soon became public, as did various actions of President Clinton that were consistent with the charge that he had obstructed justice by attempting to influence the intern to deny the existence of the sexual relationship and to cover up the facts. The President was subpoenaed to testify before a grand jury investigating the matter and in that forum gave misleading, if not false, testimony. As a result, the President was impeached by the House in December 1998 on charges that he committed perjury before the grand jury and obstructed justice. Following a trial in the Senate in January and February 1999, the vote for conviction was 45-55 on the perjury charge and 50-50 on the obstruction charge. His defenders contended that he was not guilty, that the charges did not amount to impeachable offenses, and that the entire matter was the product of a politically motivated investigation by a biased independent counsel. President Clinton's accusers noted that it was Clinton's decision to conduct a sexual affair with the intern, then to lie about it and induce others to lie about it, and that the falsehoods and cover-up were sufficient breaches of public trust to warrant removal from office. A few months later, the trial judge in Clinton v. Jones held President Clinton in contempt

----

7. In addition to Jefferson and Nixon, Justice Stevens cited Presidents Monroe, Ford, and Clinton. — ED.

of court for his false testimony in the civil deposition. Is a President immune from civil contempt sanctions?

3. Executive Privilege

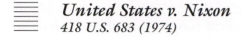

United States v. Nixon
418 U.S. 683 (1974)

[In the summer of 1972, the Democratic Party's headquarters in the Watergate office complex were burglarized by agents of President Nixon's reelection campaign. A Senate committee investigated and unearthed evidence that White House personnel may have been involved in the planning and cover-up of the burglary. President Nixon appointed a special prosecutor, Archibald Cox, whom he later fired. Cox's replacement, Leon Jaworski, obtained a subpoena directing President Nixon to produce certain recordings and documents that were relevant to the impending trial of seven Nixon aides for conspiracy to obstruct justice and other charges relating to the Watergate burglary. A grand jury indicted the "Watergate Seven" on March 1, 1974; the subpoena was issued on April 18; and the President issued edited transcripts of the recordings and moved to quash the subpoena on the grounds of "executive privilege." On May 20, the district judge denied the motion. The President appealed to the court of appeals, but on May 31 the Supreme Court granted certiorari prior to judgment, thus bypassing the court of appeals. Argument was heard on July 8, and this decision was rendered on July 24. President Nixon resigned on August 9, after the House Judiciary Committee approved three articles of impeachment.]

CHIEF JUSTICE BURGER delivered the opinion of the Court.

This litigation presents for review the denial of a motion, filed [on] behalf of the President [in] the case of United States v. Mitchell to quash a third-party subpoena duces tecum issued by [the] District Court. . . . The subpoena directed the President to produce certain tape recordings and documents relating to his conversations with aides and advisers. The court rejected the President's claims of absolute executive privilege. . . .

A. [We] turn to the claim that the subpoena should be quashed because it demands "confidential conversations between a President and his close advisors that it would be inconsistent with the public interest to produce." The first contention is a broad claim that the separation of powers doctrine precludes judicial review of a President's claim of privilege. The second contention is that if he does not prevail on the claim of absolute privilege, the court should hold as a matter of constitutional law that the privilege prevails over the subpoena. . . . The President's counsel [reads] the Constitution as providing an absolute privilege of confidentiality for all Presidential communications [that may not be reviewed by courts once asserted by the President]. Many decisions of this Court, however, have unequivocally reaffirmed the holding of Marbury v. Madison that "[it] is emphatically the province and duty of the judicial department to say what the law is." . . .

B. In support of his claim of absolute privilege, the President's counsel urges two grounds[:] the valid need for protection of communications between high Government officials and those who advise and assist them in the performance of their manifold duties [and separation of powers principles]. The importance [of] confidentiality is too plain to require further discussion. [The] President's counsel [invokes] the doctrine of separation of powers [to argue] that the independence of the Executive Branch within its own sphere insulates a President from a judicial subpoena in an ongoing criminal prosecution, and thereby protects confidential Presidential communications. However, neither the doctrine of separation of powers, nor the need for confidentiality of high-level communications, without more, can sustain an absolute, unqualified Presidential privilege of immunity from judicial process under all circumstances. The President's need for complete candor and objectivity from advisers calls for great deference from the courts. However, when the privilege depends solely on the broad, undifferentiated claim of public interest in the confidentiality of such conversations, a confrontation with other values arises. Absent a claim of need to protect military, diplomatic, or sensitive national security secrets, we find it difficult to accept the argument that even the very important interest in confidentiality of Presidential communications is significantly diminished by production of such material for in camera inspection with all the protection that a district court will be obliged to provide. The impediment that an absolute, unqualified privilege would place in the way of the primary constitutional duty of the Judicial Branch to do justice in criminal prosecutions would plainly conflict with the function of the courts under Art. III. . . . [To] read the Art. II powers of the President as providing an absolute privilege as against a subpoena essential to enforcement of criminal statutes on no more than a generalized claim of the public interest in confidentiality of nonmilitary and nondiplomatic discussions would upset the constitutional balance of "a workable government" and gravely impair the role of the courts under Art. III.

C. [A] President and those who assist him must be free to explore alternatives in the process of shaping policies and making decisions and to do so in a way many would be unwilling to express except privately. These are the considerations justifying a presumptive privilege for Presidential communications, [a] privilege [fundamental] to the operation of Government and inextricably rooted in the separation of [powers]. But this presumptive privilege must be considered in light of our historic commitment to the rule of law. This is nowhere more profoundly manifest than in our view that "the twofold aim [of criminal justice] is that guilt shall not escape or innocence suffer." [The] need to develop all relevant facts in the adversary system is both fundamental and comprehensive. [To] ensure that justice is done, it is imperative to the function of courts that compulsory process be available for the production of evidence needed either by the prosecution or by the defense. [Evidentiary privileges] are designed to protect weighty and legitimate competing interests [e.g., self-incrimination, confidentiality of communications to attorneys or priests. These] exceptions to the demand for every man's evidence are not lightly created nor expansively construed, for they are in derogation of the search for truth.

In this case the President challenges a subpoena served on him as a third party requiring the production of materials for use in a criminal prosecution; he does so on the claim that he has a privilege against disclosure of confidential communications. He does not place his claim of privilege on the ground they are military or diplomatic secrets. As to these areas of Art. II duties the courts have traditionally shown the utmost deference to Presidential responsibilities. [No] case of the Court, however, has extended this high degree of deference to a President's generalized interest in confidentiality. Nowhere in the Constitution [is] there any explicit reference to a privilege of confidentiality, yet to the extent this interest relates to the effective discharge of a President's powers, it is constitutionally based. The right to the production of all evidence at a criminal trial similarly has constitutional [roots in due process and the] Sixth Amendment [rights of a criminal defendant] "to be confronted with the witnesses against him" and "to have compulsory process for obtaining witnesses in his favor."

[In] this case we must weigh the importance of the general privilege of confidentiality of Presidential communications in performance of the President's responsibilities against the inroads of such a privilege on the fair administration of criminal justice. The interest in preserving confidentiality is weighty indeed and entitled to great respect. However, we cannot conclude that advisers will be moved to temper the candor of their remarks by the infrequent occasions of disclosure because of the possibility that such conversations will be called for in the context of a criminal prosecution. On the other hand, the allowance of the privilege to withhold evidence that is demonstrably relevant in a criminal trial would cut deeply into the guarantee of due process of law and gravely impair the basic function of the courts. A President's acknowledged need for confidentiality in the communications of his office is general in nature, whereas the constitutional need for production of relevant evidence in a criminal proceeding is specific and central to the fair adjudication of a particular criminal case in the administration of justice. [We] conclude that when the ground for asserting privilege as to subpoenaed materials sought for use in a criminal trial is based only on the generalized interest in confidentiality, it cannot prevail over the fundamental demands of due process of law in the fair administration of criminal justice. . . .

D. [If] a President concludes that compliance with a subpoena would be injurious to the public interest he may properly, as was done here, invoke a claim of privilege on the return of the subpoena. Upon receiving a claim of privilege from the Chief Executive, it became the further duty of the District Court to treat the subpoenaed material as presumptively privileged and to require the Special Prosecutor to demonstrate that the Presidential material was "essential to the justice of the [pending criminal] case." [We] affirm the order of the District Court that subpoenaed materials be transmitted to that court. We now turn to the important question of the District Court's responsibilities in conducting the in camera examination of Presidential materials or communications delivered under the compulsion of the subpoena duces tecum.

E. [To implement this decision a district court should isolate statements] that meet the test of admissibility and relevance; all other material must be excised. [The] District Court has a very heavy responsibility to see to it that Presidential conversations, which are either not relevant or not admissible, are accorded that high degree of respect due the President. [A] President's communications and activities encompass a vastly wider range of sensitive material than would be true of any "ordinary individual." It is therefore necessary in the public interest to afford Presidential confidentiality the greatest protection consistent with the fair administration of justice. The need for confidentiality even as to idle conversations with associates in which casual reference might be made concerning political leaders within the country or foreign statesmen is too obvious to call for further treatment. We have no doubt that the District Judge will at all times accord to Presidential records [a] high degree of deference [and] will discharge his responsibility to see to it that until released to the Special Prosecutor no in camera material is revealed to anyone.

Affirmed.

Justice Rehnquist took no part in the consideration or decision of these cases.

NOTE

Unanswered Questions.   The *Nixon* tapes case established for the first time the existence of any executive privilege, however qualified it may be. That in itself was a victory for the President. But a number of questions remain to be answered. Is the President the only person who can assert the privilege? Consider in this regard that it is an "executive" privilege and there is only one holder of executive power—the President. How is the presumptive privilege to be assessed when the President asserts a general need for confidentiality against a congressional subpoena of executive communications? Suppose that there is some evidence that the President may have committed a serious crime but no executive branch official will investigate. If a congressional committee investigates and demands that the President produce confidential executive branch documents bearing on the matter, is Congress's need to know greater than the President's need for confidentiality? How should these competing claims be assessed? See Senate Select Committee on Presidential Campaign Activities v. Nixon, 370 F. Supp. 521 (D.D.C. 1974), in which a district judge denied enforcement of a congressional subpoena seeking Nixon's Oval Office tapes in connection with its investigation of the Watergate burglary.

Queries: Congress has sought to compel testimony by officials in the administration of President George W. Bush concerning the replacement of various United States Attorneys on political grounds and the production of documents relating to that matter. Congress says it seeks to determine if these replacements involved any actions that would amount to criminal obstruction of justice. The President invokes executive privilege. How does this claim differ from that at issue in the *Nixon* tapes case? How should this claim be resolved?

After he left office, President Truman asserted executive privilege and refused to obey a congressional subpoena to testify before the House Un-American Activities Committee. His assertion of the privilege went unchallenged. President George W. Bush has indicated that he will assert executive privilege to block congressional demands for documents and testimony from his aides after he leaves office. Attorney General Holder asserted executive privilege to deny a Congressional demand for documents relating to a Justice Department program permitting weapons to be transferred to Mexican drug gangs. Are these claims valid?

III

INDIVIDUAL RIGHTS: LIMITS ON THE USE OF GOVERNMENTAL POWER

The Constitution that was adopted following the 1787 Philadelphia Convention did not include a bill of rights. This absence was regarded as a great failure by Anti-Federalist opponents of ratification. Federalists had argued that it was "not only unnecessary [but] would even be dangerous" to include a bill of rights because a listing of things the federal government could not do might lead to the inference that the government possessed implied powers. Federalist No. 84 (Alexander Hamilton). Hamilton argued that the nature of a bill of rights was to state

> various exceptions to powers that are not granted; and on this very account, would afford a colorable pretext to claim more than were granted. For why declare that things shall not be done that there is no power to do? Why for instance, should it be said, that the liberty of press shall not be restrained, when no power is given by which restrictions may be imposed?

The Federalist position, exemplified by Hamilton, suggests that the Founders regarded liberty as the absence of government power. Anti-Federalists agreed with that definition of liberty but thought that it was prudent to preclude the exertion of government power in two ways: (1) by confining the federal government's powers to those specified in the Constitution, and (2) by enumerating certain individual liberties with which the government had no power to interfere. With the adoption of the Bill of Rights, the Anti-Federalist position prevailed, at least as to the second point.

But this account has been altered by two centuries of constitutional interpretation. As you observed in Part II, the Court's willingness to enforce meaningful limits on the federal government's powers has waned to the point that judicial review of the scope of those powers is, in practice, vestigial. Part II might be styled a tale of continually shrinking judicial review, where in the end judicial oversight of the scope of federal legislative power is like the grin of the Cheshire Cat, existing in space long after the corporeal substance of the cat has faded away. Perhaps as a compensating consequence, at roughly the same time that judicial oversight of powers declined, the Court began to develop a robust brand of judicial review to enforce limitations on the exercise of government powers pertaining to individual rights. Part III explores the jurisprudence of individual rights, the textual foundation for which is mostly, but not exclusively, in the Bill of Rights and the Fourteenth Amendment. Part III is a tale of rapidly expanding judicial review, of the judiciary as bodybuilder, expanding legal muscle mass until the judicial robe is well-nigh bursting.

With almost no exceptions, the individual liberties guaranteed in the Constitution are enforceable only against governments. The free speech clause, for example, bars the state from punishing you for advocating socialism, but it does not apply if your private employer fires you because you are a socialist. Similarly, the equal protection clause forbids the government from denying you a driver's license because of your race, but it does not bar a private employer from firing you on account of your race. Of course, statutes—both state and federal—forbid private acts of racial discrimination in hiring and other areas of public life, but those statutes are not required by the Constitution. Much of what we regard as our fundamental civil rights is protected by statute, not by the Constitution. In short, the Constitution applies only to state action.

In most instances, the presence of state action will be obvious—the government has acted by statute or executive order. Sometimes, however, state action is not so obvious. The problem is to determine when a private person is exercising state power, thus turning nominally private action (to which the Constitution does not apply) into state action (to which the Constitution very much applies). That problem is examined in Chapter 11.

Chapter 6 deals with the two due process clauses. The chapter focuses particularly on the evolution of due process as a guarantee of certain substantive rights. The subject of Chapter 7 is the Constitution's explicit guarantee of certain economic rights, specifically the takings clause and the contracts clause. Chapter 8 examines equal protection of the laws, a right expressly guaranteed against state governments by the Fourteenth Amendment and made enforceable against the federal government via the Fifth Amendment's due process clause. Chapter 9 explores the complex body of law that has grown up to protect the free expression of ideas. Chapter 10 extends that inquiry to the specific guarantees of religious liberty embodied in the two religion clauses of the First Amendment. Chapter 11 focuses on the state action problem and congressional power to enforce important constitutional rights. Chapter 12 provides an opportunity to apply your accumulated skill in constitutional interpretation to a newly recognized individual right, the right to keep and bear arms.

In the course of this tour of the constitutional landmarks of individual liberty, you will quickly learn that the level of judicial review applied to claims of constitutional right varies widely. Government action is presumed to be valid unless there is some apparent reason to doubt that validity. Thus, most government actions will be subject to minimal scrutiny from courts. Under minimal scrutiny, government action is presumed valid and will be struck down only if the challenger can prove that the action is not rationally related to a legitimate state purpose. But if there is good reason to doubt the validity of government action, some form of heightened scrutiny will be applied. So-called strict scrutiny is the most stringent judicial review. Under strict scrutiny, the government action is presumed to be void; it will be upheld only if the government can prove that its action is necessary to achieve a compelling government objective.

There are also less exacting forms of heightened scrutiny, the most significant of which is so-called intermediate scrutiny. Under intermediate scrutiny, the government action is presumed to be void, and will be upheld only if the government can prove, generally, that its action is substantially related to the accomplishment of an important actual state interest.

This taxonomy of judicial review requires you to place claims of right in their proper pigeonholes, a task that is complicated by the fact that the Supreme Court has devised variations on these forms of scrutiny to address specific issues. Tiered review raises a number of thematic questions that pervade this area of constitutional law. What characteristics determine the level of judicial review used to examine the legitimacy of government action? What factors identify presumptively void government action? When government action is presumptively void, what determines whether strict or intermediate scrutiny applies? Is the entire structure of tiered review inappropriate or, perhaps, illusory?

Another feature of the constitutional landscape of individual liberty is that not all rights (and claims of rights) are treated equally. Government actions that infringe upon some constitutional liberties that are explicitly guaranteed (e.g., the prohibition on state government impairment of the obligations imposed by private contracts) are subject to a hybrid of minimal and intermediate scrutiny; but other government actions that infringe upon liberties that are unmentioned in the Constitution (e.g., the right to vote or the right to use contraceptives) are subject to strict scrutiny. This hodgepodge of preferred and not-so-preferred rights is not easy to explain or understand. Why are some rights elevated and others degraded? Are the principles used to accomplish this result consistent, plausible, and convincing? If not, why has this jurisprudence of differential status persevered? What, if anything, does a hierarchy of constitutional rights tell us about the process by which the courts make American constitutional law?

You should keep all of these major thematic questions somewhere in your consciousness as you explore the details of the doctrine that follows. Try to assess this area on two levels: What is the Court doing? Is the Court correct in what it is doing? To answer the second, and normative, question you must have answers to (or at least thoughts about) the serious thematic issues raised in this introduction to Part III.

6

Due Process

There are two due process clauses. The Fifth Amendment bars the federal government from depriving any person of "life, liberty, or property without due process of law." The Fourteenth Amendment applies the same prohibition to the states. The fact that the due process clauses protect a person's "life, liberty, or property" from government invasion unless the government has used "due *process* of law" suggests that this is a guarantee of certain procedures. It is that, but it is also far more. The more controversial aspect of due process is its role as a guarantee of certain substantive rights.

The requirements of procedural due process are pervasive, and they appear in the law school curriculum in Civil Procedure, Criminal Procedure, Conflicts of Law, Administrative Law, and, to some extent, nearly every other course that touches on public law. Section A of this chapter does not attempt to cover every facet of procedural due process; rather, it focuses on two particularly important problems: (1) What are the liberty and property interests protected by due process? (2) What sort of process is due?

Substantive due process is an oxymoron. "Due process" read literally refers to procedures that are suitable, fitting, or appropriate—the procedures that are minimally required for fairness. Procedures and processes do not guarantee substantive outcomes, though they may influence them. By and large, the quest of substantive due process is to identify certain liberties or rights that are not specifically mentioned in the Constitution and to raise a presumption that government interference with those rights is void. Substantive due process may be oxymoronic but it endures. Does it exist because it is necessary to preserve a domain of personal liberty from governments with swollen and nearly unbounded powers? Or is it an illegitimate construct of judicial policy preferences? Does the best explanation lie somewhere in between? Section B explores the rise and fall and modern revival of substantive due process. In the process, those questions will be addressed.

A. PROCEDURAL DUE PROCESS

At the very least, due process requires that before a person is deprived of life, liberty, or property he must be given "notice of the case against him and opportunity to meet it." Joint Anti-Fascist Refugee Commission v. McGrath, 341 U.S. 123 (1951) (Frankfurter, J., concurring). But this does not mean that due process includes a general right to procedural regularity. Constitutionally speaking, unless the government is depriving a person of a life, liberty, or property interest, it may use any procedure it wants, including arbitrary and capricious procedures. Professor William Van Alstyne has argued that while procedural regularity "is evidently not a free standing human interest [it] is plausible [to] treat freedom from arbitrary adjudicative procedures as a substantive element of one's liberty." Van Alstyne, Cracks in the New Property, 62 Cornell L. Rev. 445, 452, 487 (1977). Of course, if procedural regularity were regarded as a substantive entitlement, there would have been no need for the Founders to specify "life, liberty, and property" as the substantive interests to which procedural due process attaches.

Procedural due process involves two central issues: (1) What constitutes a "life," "liberty," or "property" interest that cannot be taken away by government without "due process of law"? (2) Once due process is required, what sort of notice and opportunity to be heard constitutes due process?

By contrast, substantive due process covers unenumerated substantive rights that are implicit in "liberty" and assesses the government's justification for their infringement. The focus of procedural due process is to identify substantive rights—life, liberty, or property—to assess whether the government's procedures for taking them away are constitutionally adequate.

1. Defining the Interests Protected by Due Process

In a great many instances there is no dispute that government seeks to deprive a person of life, liberty, or property. Accusations of crime are perhaps the clearest example. This section deals with the more difficult problem presented when a person asserts that his status as a government employee, licensee, or recipient of some government benefit may not be altered by the government without the provision of procedural due process. A court necessarily must first decide whether the status in question is a life, liberty, or property right to which due process attaches. If so, then the court must decide whether the pre-deprivation procedures are sufficient to constitute due process.

Over time, there have been three different approaches taken by the Court to defining liberty or property interests protected by procedural due process: (1) treating government benefits as privileges rather than rights; (2) treating government benefits as entitlements rather than privileges; and (3) deriving the content of property and (to a lesser extent) liberty from constitutionally external sources, such as contracts or statutes. The first approach has been abandoned; the second approach has been largely eclipsed by the third approach.

Under the benefits-as-privileges approach, the Court used the common law to define liberty or property interests. Because there was no common law property right in government employment or continued receipt of a government benefit, procedural due process was not applicable to deprivations of these interests. The essence of this view was expressed by Justice Holmes in McAuliffe v. Mayor of New Bedford, 155 Mass. 216 (1892), in which the Massachusetts Supreme Judicial Court upheld a rule barring police officers from soliciting money for political purposes: "[He] may have a constitutional right to talk politics, but he has no constitutional right to be a policeman." And you may have a right to due process if the government threatens to take away your car but not if the government threatens to fire you. See Bailey v. Richardson, 182 F.2d 46 (D.C. Cir. 1950), affirmed by an equally divided Court, 341 U.S. 918 (1951). In this view government employment and benefits were treated as "privileges" that the government could suspend at its pleasure, rather than individual rights that may be divested only after the individual has been afforded due process.

a. Property

As the social welfare state grew larger, making the social and economic significance of government employment and benefits ever more important, the "benefits as privileges" view came under attack. Yale Professor Charles Reich (who later enjoyed brief prominence as a counterculture seer with his best-selling 1970 book, The Greening of America) argued in The New Property, 73 Yale L.J. 733 (1963), that important statutory entitlements ought to be regarded as property interests to which procedural due process attaches.

Goldberg v. Kelly, 397 U.S. 254 (1970). The Court agreed with Reich and formulated a doctrine that held, at its high-water mark, that any government benefit that was extremely important to its recipient was a form of liberty or property to which due process attached. The importance of the interest was determined as a matter of constitutional law. The *Goldberg* Court held that a welfare recipient was entitled to "an evidentiary hearing before the termination of benefits" because the "benefits are a matter of statutory entitlement for persons qualified to receive them," and their continued receipt was of the utmost importance to the affected individual. Elimination of the welfare benefits would deprive the claimant "of the very means to live." The *Goldberg* principle was quickly extended to apply to claims made by government employees, licensees, students, prisoners, and debtors, to name a few. Emblematic of this approach was Bell v. Burson, 402 U.S. 535 (1971). Georgia law automatically suspended the vehicle registration and driver's license of any uninsured motorist who failed to post a security bond to cover the claimed damages in accidents to which he was a party. The Court invalidated the law because it failed to provide any form of pre-deprivation hearing. The Court said that due process attached because the licenses were "essential in the pursuit of a livelihood. Suspension [adjudicates] important interests of the licensees."

Goldberg's emphasis on the subjective importance of the right as the criterion of property did not last. Today, the "sufficiency of the claim of entitlement [to a protected property interest] must be decided by reference to state law." *Bishop v. Wood*, 426 U.S. 341 (1976). This property-is-defined-by-state-law approach began with a pair of cases decided on the same day in 1972.

Board of Regents v. Roth, 408 U.S. 564 (1972). Roth was hired by Wisconsin State University for a one-year term, with no right to continued employment. The university told Roth he would not be rehired, gave no explanation, and said its decision was final. The Court rejected Roth's claim that the university's failure to give him either an explanation or a chance to contest it at some hearing violated due process. Roth had no liberty or property interest at stake:

> [T]o determine whether due process requirements apply in the first place, we must look not to the "weight" but to the *nature* of the interest at stake. [To] have a property interest in a [government] benefit, [one] must have more than a unilateral expectation of it. He must [have] a legitimate claim of entitlement to [it]. Property interests [are] not created by the Constitution, [but] are created [and] defined by existing rules or understandings that stem from an independent source such as state law—rules or understandings that secure certain benefits and that support claims of entitlement to those benefits.

Perry v. Sindermann, 408 U.S. 593 (1972). Sindermann, a professor at Odessa Junior College, was not rehired when the fixed term of his contract expired. Sindermann claimed that the school had created a de facto tenure system by informing its faculty that the school "wishes each faculty member to feel that he has permanent tenure so long as his teaching services are satisfactory and as long as he displays a cooperative attitude." The Court concluded that Sindermann had raised a triable issue of fact regarding his claimed property interest in continuing employment. Sindermann's lack of a formal contract right to continuing employment was no barrier: "A teacher [who] has held his position for a number of years might be able to show from the circumstances of this service—and from other relevant facts—that he has a legitimate claim of entitlement to job tenure." The university's unilateral statement to its faculty was enough to create an issue of fact—whether that produced "a legitimate claim of entitlement to job tenure."

Cleveland Board of Education v. Loudermill
470 U.S. 532 (1984)

JUSTICE WHITE delivered the opinion of the Court.

[We] consider what pretermination process must be accorded a public employee who can be discharged only for cause.

In 1979 the Cleveland Board of Education [hired] respondent James Loudermill as a security guard. On his job application, Loudermill stated that he had never been convicted of a felony. Eleven months later, as part of a routine examination of his employment records, the Board discovered that in fact Loudermill had been convicted of grand larceny in 1968. By letter [the] Board's Business Manager informed Loudermill that he had been dismissed because of his dishonesty in filling out the employment application. Loudermill was not afforded an opportunity to respond to the charge of dishonesty or to challenge his dismissal. [Ten days later the Board officially approved] the discharge. Under Ohio law, Loudermill [could] be terminated only for cause and [could] obtain administrative review if discharged. [Loudermill pursued his administrative remedies, arguing] that he had thought that his 1968 larceny conviction was for a misdemeanor rather than a felony. [Although a hearing officer recommended reinstatement, the final administrative decision was to uphold the dismissal, and Loudermill was so advised by mail. In federal court Loudermill alleged that the administrative review provided] was unconstitutional on its face because it did not provide the employee an opportunity to respond to the charges against him prior to removal. [The] District Court dismissed [Loudermill's complaint] for failure to state a claim on which relief could be granted. It held that because the very statute that created the property right in continued employment also specified the procedures for discharge, and because those procedures were followed, Loudermill was, by definition, afforded all the process due. [The] Court of Appeals for the Sixth Circuit reversed. [We granted certiorari and] now affirm in all respects.

[Loudermill's] federal constitutional claim depends on [his] having had a property right in continued employment.[1] If [he] did, the State could not deprive [him] of this property without due process. Property interests are not created by the Constitution, "they are created and their dimensions are defined by existing rules or understandings that stem from an independent source such as state law." Board of Regents v. Roth. The Ohio statute plainly creates such an interest. [Under Ohio law Loudermill was] entitled to retain [his] position "during good behavior and efficient service," [and] could not be dismissed "except [for] misfeasance, malfeasance, or nonfeasance in office."

[The] Board argues, however, that the property right is defined by, and conditioned on, the legislature's choice of procedures for its deprivation. The Board stresses that in addition to specifying the grounds for termination, the statute sets out procedures by which termination may take place. The procedures were adhered to [and thus, according] to petitioner, "[to] require additional procedures would in effect expand the scope of the property interest itself." This argument [has] its genesis in the plurality opinion in Arnett v. Kennedy, 416 U.S. 134 (1974). *Arnett* involved a challenge by a former federal employee to the procedures by which he was dismissed. The plurality reasoned that where the legislation conferring the substantive right also sets

---

1. Of course, the Due Process Clause also protects interests of life and liberty. . . .

out the procedural mechanism for enforcing that right, the two cannot be separated:

> The employee's statutorily defined right is not a guarantee against removal without cause in the abstract, but such a guarantee as enforced by the procedures which Congress has designated for the determination of cause. [Where] the grant of a substantive right is inextricably intertwined with the limitations on the procedures which are to be employed in determining that right, a litigant . . . must take the bitter with the sweet.

This view garnered three votes in *Arnett*, but was specifically rejected by the other six Justices. [In] Vitek v. Jones, 445 U.S. 480, 491 (1980), we pointed out that "minimum [procedural] requirements [are] a matter of federal law, they are not diminished by the fact that the State may have specified its own procedures that it may deem adequate for determining the preconditions to adverse official action." In light of [*Vitek* and other cases], it is settled that the "bitter with the sweet" approach misconceives the constitutional guarantee. If a clearer holding is needed, we provide it today. [The] Due Process Clause provides that certain substantive rights—life, liberty, and property—cannot be deprived except pursuant to constitutionally adequate procedures. The categories of substance and procedure are distinct. Were the rule otherwise, the Clause would be reduced to a mere tautology. "Property" cannot be defined by the procedures provided for its deprivation any more than can life or liberty. The right to due process "is conferred, not by legislative grace, but by constitutional guarantee. While the legislature may elect not to confer a property interest in [public] employment, it may not constitutionally authorize the deprivation of such an interest, once conferred, without appropriate procedural safeguards." In short, once it is determined that the Due Process Clause applies, "the question remains what process is due." The answer to that question is not to be found in the Ohio statute.

JUSTICE REHNQUIST, dissenting.

[Here], the relevant Ohio statute [provides] that "[the] tenure of every officer or employee in the classified service [shall] be during good behavior and efficient service." [The] very next paragraph of [the statute sets forth precisely the procedures that were followed to terminate Loudermill for lack of good behavior]. In one legislative breath Ohio has conferred upon civil service employees [a] limited form of tenure during good behavior, and prescribed the procedures by which that tenure may be terminated. Here, as in *Arnett*, "[the] employee's statutorily defined right is not a guarantee against removal without cause in the abstract, but such a guarantee as enforced by the procedures which [the Ohio Legislature] has designated for the determination of cause." We stated in [*Roth* that property interests] "are created and their dimensions are defined by existing rules or understandings that stem from an independent source such as state law—rules or understandings that secure certain benefits and that support claims of entitlement to those benefits." We ought to recognize the totality of the State's definition of the property right in question, and not merely seize upon one of several paragraphs in a unitary statute to proclaim that in that paragraph the State has inexorably conferred upon a civil service employee something which it is powerless under [the] Constitution to qualify in the next paragraph of the statute. This practice ignores our duty under *Roth* to rely on state law as the source of property interests for purposes of [due process].

NOTES

1. Property as a Statutory Entitlement.   "Property" is defined by both statutory and common law sources. What are we to make of statutory entitlements that are not recognized as property under the common law? Under the *Roth/Loudermill* approach such statutory entitlements are property to which the protections of due process attach. But what is that property? If a statute specifies something that the government need not provide (e.g., public employment until there is "cause" for termination) and at the same time specifies how that thing is to be determined (e.g., each employee's supervisor decides whether "cause" exists, with no prior notice or hearing), what is the statutory entitlement? Is it "employment until cause for termination exists"? Or is it "employment until each employee's supervisor decides cause for termination exists"?

Can substance and procedure be neatly divorced? Is it true that any given procedure is "just a measure of how much the substantive entitlements are worth, of what we are willing to sacrifice to see a given goal attained," and, correspondingly, that any given substantive right is merely "a promised benefit coupled with a promised rate of mistake"? See Easterbrook, Substance and Due Process, 1982 Sup. Ct. Rev. 85. The essence of due process is notice and opportunity to be heard. The value of these rights inheres mostly in the possibility of reducing mistaken decisions and, to a lesser extent, in increasing the involvement of affected persons in the decision. Do mistakes of substance decrease as procedural protections increase?

If the substance of a property interest is to be determined from positive law without reference to the procedures that define eligibility for the property interest, is it really true that property interests "are created and their dimensions are defined by existing rules or understandings that stem from an independent source such as state law"? Or is it more correct to state that once a government has created a benefit, however limited, it cannot condition eligibility for its receipt upon procedures that offend constitutional principles of notice and opportunity and to be heard? If so, is Goldberg v. Kelly revived?

Query: Suppose that a city grants a reduction in property taxes to owners of so-called Green Residences, defined in the law as "homes using systems that conserve substantial amounts of energy and water." The next sentence of the law states that "the chief code enforcement officer shall determine annually whether a Green Residence conserves substantial amounts of energy and water, and the decision of that official shall be final." What right, if any, does a home owner have? Is the home owner entitled to a hearing on the question of whether his home conserves substantial amounts of energy and water? Should the answer be different if the law were missing the second quoted sentence? If the owner is entitled to a hearing, would that fact provide an incentive to the city to repeal the entire tax reduction?

2. Wholly Discretionary Entitlements. In Castle Rock v. Gonzalez, 545 U.S. 748 (2005), the Supreme Court ruled that "a benefit is not a protected entitlement if government officials may grant or deny it in their discretion." Jessica Gonzalez had obtained an order from a Colorado court restraining her estranged husband from contact with her three daughters, but Jessica's husband abducted the three daughters from their front lawn and murdered the girls. In a federal suit under 42 U.S.C. §1983, Jessica alleged that she had been deprived of due process because, in the words of the Tenth Circuit, the police had "never 'heard' nor seriously entertained her request to enforce and protect her interests in the restraining order."

The Supreme Court concluded that the police had discretion concerning how and when to enforce restraining orders; even if Colorado law mandated enforcement, the Court thought this did not mean that Colorado intended to confer a property or liberty entitlement on those protected by such orders, because the "serving of public rather than private ends is the normal course of the criminal law." Even if there was a personal entitlement, the Court thought it was "by no means clear that an individual entitlement to enforcement of a restraining order could constitute a 'property' interest for purposes of the Due Process Clause [because it] arises *incidentally*, not out of some new species of government benefit or service, but out of a function that government actors have always performed — to wit, arresting people who they have probable cause to believe have committed a criminal offense."

b. Liberty

A similar but not identical pattern affects the Court's approach to defining a person's liberty interests. Government actions that alter one's legal status under positive law implicate a liberty interest, but some government actions that may not do so are nevertheless such massive invasions of liberty that due process attaches.

The change-in-legal-status-equals-loss-of-liberty rule was developed in Paul v. Davis, 424 U.S. 693 (1976). After Davis was arrested for shoplifting, the Louisville, Kentucky, police placed his name on a list of "active shoplifters" circulated to local merchants. After the charges were dropped, Davis brought a federal civil rights claim against the police alleging that the circulation of his name had injured his reputation. Davis contended that before the police could validly deprive him of his "liberty" interest in his reputation they were required to afford him procedural due process. The Court rejected the claim. Acceptance of Davis's argument would "result in every legally cognizable injury which may have been inflicted by a state official acting under 'color of law' establishing a violation of the Fourteenth Amendment." That would produce a vast constitutionalization of tort law, at least with respect to tort claims against government officials, and the Court was unwilling so to expand the role of constitutional law. Thus, "reputation alone, apart from some more tangible interests such as employment, is [neither] 'liberty' [nor] 'property' by itself sufficient to invoke the procedural protection of the Due Process Clause."

The Court distinguished *Paul* from its prior ruling in Wisconsin v. Constantineau, 400 U.S. 433 (1971). Wisconsin law provided that whenever someone by "excessive drinking" exposes himself or his family "to want" or makes himself "dangerous to the peace," government officials could—without notice or hearing to the drinker—post the drinker's name in retail liquor outlets as a person to whom sales or gifts of liquor are forbidden for one year. Constantineau successfully challenged the posting of her name as not in compliance with procedural due process. In *Paul*, the Court noted that Constantineau had suffered more than injury to her reputation; Wisconsin had also deprived Constantineau "of a right previously held under state law—the right [to] obtain liquor in common with the rest of the citizenry." That added factor "significantly altered her status as a matter of state law. [It] was that alteration of legal status which, combined with the injury resulting from the defamation, justified the invocation of procedural safeguards."

In Meachum v. Fano, 427 U.S. 215 (1976), the Court ruled that no liberty interest was at stake when a state decided to shift a prisoner from a medium-security prison to a maximum-security facility:

> We reject [the] suggestion that *any* grievous loss visited upon a person by the State is sufficient to invoke [procedural due process. The] determining factor is the nature of the interest involved rather than its weight. [Once a] criminal defendant has been constitutionally deprived of his liberty [and] so long as the conditions of confinement do not otherwise violate the Constitution [the selection of a prison] is within the normal limits or range of custody which the conviction has authorized the State to impose. That life in one prison is much more disagreeable than in another does not in itself signify that a [constitutional] liberty interest is implicated.

But the breadth of this doctrine was undercut by Vitek v. Jones, 445 U.S. 480 (1980). Nebraska law provided that a prisoner may be transferred to a mental hospital upon a state physician's finding that the prisoner suffers from a "mental disease or defect" that cannot be treated adequately in prison. The Court ruled that before such a transfer a prisoner was entitled to procedural due process. First, Nebraska had created by statute and "official practice" an "'objective expectation' [that] a prisoner would not be transferred" except under the prescribed circumstances, thus creating "a liberty interest that entitled [the prisoner] to the benefits of appropriate procedures in connection with determining the conditions that warranted his transfer to a mental hospital." Second, "independently of [Nebraska law], the transfer of a prisoner from a prison to a mental hospital must be accompanied by appropriate procedural protections" because the prisoner's "residuum of liberty [would] be infringed by a transfer to a mental hospital." This loss of residual liberty was the result of the stigma of commitment to a mental hospital, the possibility of compelled drug and behavior modification treatment, and the lesser freedom permitted mental patients. Note that this second reason for finding a constitutional liberty interest was "independent" of state law. Does *Vitek* mean that constitutionally recognized liberty interests are either (1) the product of state alterations of legal status or (2) those that would be recognized as liberty interests for other constitutional purposes? Greenholtz v. Inmates, 442 U.S. 1 (1979), held that absent a clear statutory entitlement, no constitutional liberty interest is involved in a denial of parole. The Court said in dicta that *revocation* of parole implicated a constitutional liberty interest, indicating its view that the loss of a benefit already conferred is of greater moment than the refusal to exercise discretion to confer the benefit. Is there a significant difference? Additional clarification of the scope of the liberty interests of prison inmates was supplied in Wilkinson v. Austin, 545 U.S. 209 (2005). Ohio operates a so-called supermax prison, in which inmates are required to be in their constantly illuminated cells for 23 hours daily, take all meals in their cells, exercise alone for one hour per day, be afforded limited visits from outside, and be denied the ability to converse with other inmates, all with the result that "inmates are deprived of almost any environmental or sensory stimuli and of almost all human contact." Supermax inmates are confined indefinitely (but no longer than the duration of their sentence) and lose eligibility for parole while confined to the supermax facility. In a challenge to the sufficiency of the procedures by which Ohio prisoners are assigned to its supermax facility, the Court first concluded that the prisoners had asserted a constitutionally cognizable liberty interest:

> A liberty interest may arise from the Constitution itself, by reason of guarantees implicit in the word "liberty," or it may arise from an expectation or interest created by state laws or policies. [While] the Constitution itself does not give rise to a liberty interest in avoiding transfer to more adverse conditions of confinement, [in Sandin v. Conner, 515 U.S. 472 (1995), we noted that a prison inmate's liberty interest is implicated when a state] "imposes atypical and significant hardship on the inmate in relation to the ordinary incidents of prison life."

Although the Court declined to specify the baseline of the "ordinary incidents of prison life," it concluded "that assignment to [the supermax prison] imposes an atypical and significant hardship under any plausible baseline."

2. Determining the Process That Is Due

Once it has been determined that government action will deprive someone of a liberty or property interest, it is necessary to decide what procedures are required before that deprivation may occur. "The essence of due process is the requirement that 'a person in jeopardy of serious loss [be given] notice of the case against him and opportunity to meet it.'" Joint Anti-Fascist Refugee Commission v. McGrath, 341 U.S. 123, 171-172 (1951) (Frankfurter, J., concurring).

Mathews v. Eldridge
424 U.S. 319 (1976)

[Since 1968, Eldridge had received Social Security disability benefits for "chronic anxiety and back strain." The disability statute placed a continuing burden on the beneficiary to prove his eligibility for disability benefits and a continuing obligation on the government agency to investigate eligibility. In 1972, the agency sent Eldridge a questionnaire concerning his condition. Based on his answers, and on information provided by Eldridge's physician and psychiatric consultant, the agency tentatively concluded that Eldridge's disability had ceased. Eldridge was informed of this decision and the reasons for it by letter and invited to provide a written response and supply new evidence. He did so, disputing some of the agency's conclusions. The government nevertheless made a final determination that Eldridge's disability had ceased and terminated his benefits. Although he was entitled to seek reconsideration and to have an evidentiary hearing to contest the validity of the benefit termination (and to recover retroactive benefits if termination was found to be in error), Eldridge sued, contending that the pre-termination procedures were inadequate under the due process clause. The District Court and Court of Appeals agreed.]

JUSTICE POWELL delivered the opinion of the Court.

[The government] does not contend that procedural due process is inapplicable to terminations of Social Security disability benefits; [it recognizes that] the interest of an individual in continued receipt of these benefits is a statutorily created "property" interest protected by the Fifth Amendment. Rather, the [government] contends that the existing administrative procedures [provide] all the process that is constitutionally due before a recipient can be deprived of that interest.

This Court consistently has held that some form of hearing is required before an individual is finally deprived of a property interest. . . . The fundamental requirement of due process is the opportunity to be heard "at a meaningful time and in a meaningful manner." Eldridge agrees that the review procedures available to a claimant before the initial determination of ineligibility becomes final would be adequate if disability benefits were not terminated until after the evidentiary hearing stage of the administrative process. The dispute centers upon what process is due prior to the initial termination of benefits, pending review. . . .

"'Due process' [is] not a technical conception with a fixed content unrelated to time, place and circumstances [but] is flexible and calls for such procedural protections as the particular situation demands." Accordingly, res-olution of the issue whether the administrative procedures provided here are constitutionally sufficient requires analysis of the governmental and private interests that are affected. More precisely, identification of the specific dictates of due process generally requires consideration of three distinct factors: First, the private interest that will be affected by the official action; second, the risk of an erroneous deprivation of such interest through the procedures used, and the probable value, if any, of additional or substitute procedural safeguards; and finally, the Government's interest, including the function involved and the fiscal and administrative burdens that the additional or substitute proce-dural requirement would entail.

[Despite] the elaborate character of the administrative procedures pro-vided by the [government], the courts below held them to be constitutionally inadequate, concluding that due process requires an evidentiary hearing prior to termination. In light of the private and governmental interests at stake here and the nature of the existing procedures, we think this was error. Since a recipient whose benefits are terminated is awarded full retroactive relief if he ultimately prevails, his sole interest is in the uninterrupted receipt of this source of income pending final administrative decision on his claim. [Only] in *Goldberg* has the Court held that due process requires an evidentiary hearing prior to a temporary deprivation. It was emphasized there that welfare assis-tance is given to persons on the very margin of subsistence. [Eligibility] for disability benefits, in contrast, is not based upon financial need. Indeed, it is wholly unrelated to the worker's income or support from many other sources, such as earnings of other family members, workmen's compensation awards, tort claims awards, savings, private insurance, public or private pensions, vet-erans' benefits, food stamps, public assistance, or the "many other important programs, both public and private, which contain provisions for disability pay-ments." [As] *Goldberg* illustrates, the degree of potential deprivation that may be created by a particular decision is a factor to be considered in assessing the validity of any administrative decision-making process. . . . [To] remain eligi-ble for benefits a recipient must be "unable to engage in substantial gainful activity." Thus, [there] is little possibility that the terminated recipient will be able to find even temporary employment to ameliorate the interim loss. [And] "the possible length of wrongful deprivation [of benefits also] is an impor-tant factor in assessing the impact of official action on the private interests." [Here], the delay between the actual cutoff of benefits and final decision after a hearing exceeds one year.

In view of the torpidity of this administrative review process and the typ-ically modest resources of the family unit of the physically disabled worker, the hardship imposed upon the erroneously terminated disability recipient may be significant. Still, the disabled worker's need is likely to be less than that of a welfare recipient. In addition to the possibility of access to private resources, other forms of government assistance will become available where the termination of disability benefits places a worker or his family below the subsistence level. In view of these potential sources of temporary income, there is less reason here than in *Goldberg* to depart from the ordinary principle [that] something less than an evidentiary hearing is sufficient prior to adverse administrative action.

An additional factor to be considered here is the fairness and reliability of the existing pre-termination procedures, and the probable value, if any, of additional procedural safeguards. Central to the evaluation of any administrative process is the nature of the relevant inquiry. [Here,] a medical assessment of the worker's physical or mental condition is required. This is a more sharply focused and easily documented decision than the typical determination of welfare entitlement, [where] issues of witness credibility and veracity often are critical. [By] contrast, the decision whether to discontinue disability benefits will turn, in most cases, upon "routine, standard, and unbiased medical reports by physician specialists," concerning a subject whom they have personally examined. [Procedural] due process rules are shaped by the risk of error inherent in the truthfinding process as applied to the generality of cases, not the rare exceptions. The potential value of an evidentiary hearing, or even oral presentation to the decisionmaker, is substantially less in this context than in *Goldberg*. . . .

A further safeguard against mistake is the policy of allowing the disability recipient's representative full access to all information relied upon by the state agency. In addition, prior to the cutoff of benefits the agency informs the recipient of its tentative assessment, the reasons therefor, and provides a summary of the evidence that it considers most relevant. Opportunity is then afforded the recipient to submit additional evidence or arguments, enabling him to challenge directly the accuracy of information in his file as well as the correctness of the agency's tentative conclusions. . . .

In striking the appropriate due process balance the final factor to be assessed is the public interest. This includes the administrative burden and other societal costs that would be associated with requiring, as a matter of constitutional right, an evidentiary hearing upon demand in all cases prior to the termination of disability benefits. The most visible burden would be the incremental cost resulting from the increased number of hearings and the expense of providing benefits to ineligible recipients pending decision. No one can predict the extent of the increase, [but] experience with the constitutionalizing of government procedures suggests that the ultimate additional cost in terms of money and administrative burden would not be insubstantial.

Financial cost alone is not [controlling] in determining whether due process requires a particular procedural safeguard prior to some administrative decision. But the Government's interest, and hence that of the public, in conserving scarce fiscal and administrative resources is a factor that must be weighed. At some point the benefit of an additional safeguard to the individual affected by the administrative action and to society in terms of increased assurance that the action is just, may be outweighed by the cost. Significantly, the cost of protecting those whom the preliminary administrative process has identified as likely to be found undeserving may in the end come out of the pockets of the deserving since resources available for any particular program of social welfare are not unlimited. . . .

But more is implicated in cases of this type than ad hoc weighing of fiscal and administrative burdens against the interests of a particular category of claimants. The ultimate balance involves a determination as to when, under our constitutional system, judicial-type procedures must be imposed upon administrative action to assure fairness. . . . The essence of due process is the requirement that "a person in jeopardy of serious loss [be given] notice of the case against him and opportunity to meet it." All that is necessary is that the procedures be tailored, in light of the decision to be made, to "the capacities and circumstances of those who are to be heard," to insure that they are given a meaningful opportunity to present their case. In assessing what process is due in this case, substantial weight must be given to the good-faith judgments of the individuals charged by Congress with the administration of social welfare programs that the procedures they have provided assure fair consideration of the entitlement claims of individuals. . . .

We conclude that an evidentiary hearing is not required prior to the termination of disability benefits and that the present administrative procedures fully comport with due process. The judgment of the Court of Appeals is [r]eversed.

NOTES

1. Notice and Hearing. In some contexts, such as criminal charges or assertions of substantial civil liability, a formal trial is required. In others, as was true in *Goldberg*, a semiformal evidentiary hearing may be required. *Mathews* makes clear that, depending on the circumstances, evidentiary hearings are not indispensable. In Goss v. Lopez, 419 U.S. 565 (1975), the Court held that an informal conversation between a public school administrator and a student prior to the student's suspension from school for ten days was enough to satisfy due process, so long as the conversation included the charges, a summary of the evidence supporting the charges, and a chance for the student to tell his or her version of the events.

Does *Mathews* effectively scuttle *Goldberg*? Though *Mathews* distinguished *Goldberg* on the basis of the welfare recipient's greater need for continued benefits, Eldridge was in fact extremely dependent upon continued disability benefits. The dissenters in *Mathews* noted that because "disability benefits were terminated there was a foreclosure upon the Eldridge home, and the family's home was repossessed."

In Wilkinson v. Austin, 545 U.S. 209 (2005), the Court applied *Mathews* to uphold Ohio's procedures for determining which prison inmates should be confined in its "supermax" security prison. Despite the severity of the facility's restrictions, the Court concluded that the "private interest at stake here, while more than minimal, must be evaluated . . . within the context of the prison system and its attendant curtailment of liberties." The second

Mathews factor—the risk of error and the probable value to error reduction of other procedures—was adequately met by Ohio because it provided inmates notice of the reasons for their intended confinement in its supermax prison, afforded them an opportunity to rebut those reasons (though not to call witnesses), and provided multiple levels of review in which the inmate could rebut the state's reasons for proposed supermax confinement. The third *Mathews* factor—the government's interest—was the

> dominant consideration. . . . Prison security, imperiled by the brutal reality of prison gangs, provides the backdrop of the State's interest. [G]angs seek nothing less than to control prison life and to extend their power outside prison walls. . . . Testifying against, or otherwise informing on, gang activities can invite one's own death sentence. [For] prison gang members serving life sentences, some without the possibility of parole, the deterrent effects of ordinary criminal punishment may be substantially diminished. . . . Were Ohio to allow an inmate to call witnesses . . . before ordering transfer to [the supermax prison], both the State's immediate objective of controlling the prisoner and its greater objective of controlling the prison could be defeated. . . . The danger to witnesses, and the difficulty in obtaining their cooperation, make the probable value of an adversary-type hearing doubtful in comparison to its obvious costs.

2. Pre- or Post-Deprivation Hearing? Although due process generally requires the government to provide notice and opportunity to be heard *before* depriving someone of property or liberty, sometimes due process is satisfied by a post-deprivation hearing or other remedy. When governments deprive persons of property to prevent immediate public harm and provide adequate post-deprivation remedies, a pre-deprivation hearing is not necessarily required. See North American Cold Storage Co. v. Chicago, 211 U.S. 306 (1908), in which the Court ruled that no prior hearing was needed before the government destroyed tainted food, because the food was an immediate danger to public health and a later tort suit provided an adequate remedy. Mackey v. Montrym, 443 U.S. 1 (1979), upheld the suspension (without a hearing) of the driver's license of a motorist refusing to submit to tests for intoxication. Imminent threat to public safety coupled with the prospect of a timely post-deprivation hearing sufficed to satisfy due process. Post-deprivation remedies are adequate when the liberty or property interest at stake is relatively minor, and either the risk of erroneous deprivation is low or provision of pre-deprivation hearings is impractical. Ingraham v. Wright, 430 U.S. 651 (1977), involved a claim that a hearing was necessary before school officials could administer corporal punishment to students, as permitted under Florida law. The Court agreed that corporal punishment implicated a liberty interest sufficient to require due process but ruled that the due process clause was satisfied by the availability of a post-spanking right to bring suit seeking damages for excessive, unjustified infliction of physical harm.

To similar effect is a line of cases dealing with claims for property losses and personal injuries suffered by prisoners. Parratt v. Taylor, 451 U.S. 527 (1981), held that due process was satisfied by the availability of tort remedies for the negligent destruction of a prisoner's property. Hudson v. Palmer, 468 U.S. 517 (1984), extended this rule to intentional destruction of a prisoner's property. In both of these cases it was virtually impossible to provide a pre-deprivation hearing. But a pair of cases, Daniels v. Williams, 474 U.S 327 (1986), and Davidson v. Cannon, 474 U.S. 344 (1986), held that even when no post-deprivation tort remedy was available to recover damages caused by the negligence of government officials, due process was not offended. Due process, said the Court, is not a guarantee of due care on the part of state officials.

3. Megan's Laws: Registration and Public Disclosure of the Whereabouts of Sex Offenders. In Connecticut Department of Public Safety v. Doe, 538 U.S. 1 (2003), the Court upheld a Connecticut law that required convicted sex offenders to register and disclose publicly their whereabouts after release from custody. The Court reasoned that due process did not require a hearing prior to registration and disclosure because those obligations were imposed as a result of conviction, and the criminal trial resulting in conviction afforded ample due process protection. The Court expressed no opinion on whether the registration and disclosure requirements unconstitutionally infringed upon a fundamental liberty interest protected by substantive due process.

4. Detention of Citizens as Enemy Combatants. In Hamdi v. Rumsfeld, 542 U.S. 507 (2004), the Court concluded that an American citizen held as an enemy combatant was entitled to due process in his challenge of that status. Although he is entitled to "notice of the factual basis for his classification, and a fair opportunity to rebut the Government's factual assertions before a neutral decisionmaker, . . . the exigencies of the circumstances may demand that [such] proceedings may be tailored to alleviate their uncommon potential to burden the Executive at a time of ongoing military conflict. Hearsay, for example, may need to be accepted. . . . Likewise, the Constitution would not be offended by a presumption in favor of the Government's evidence, so long as that presumption remained a rebuttable one and fair opportunity for rebuttal were provided. . . ."

Queries: What constitutes a "neutral decisionmaker"? Is a military court sufficiently neutral? What procedures are necessary for a "fair opportunity"? Could a detainee be denied the ability to subpoena witnesses if the government asserted that either the witnesses or the government's efforts to combat terror strikes would be endangered by their testifying?

B. SUBSTANTIVE DUE PROCESS

Substantive due process is an elusive concept. The natural reading of "due process of law," as well as its historical root in Chapter 39 of Magna Charta, suggests that the phrase is all about *procedure* and has nothing to do with substantive outcomes. Critics have likened the union of "substantive procedure" (or "procedural substance") to "green pastel redness."[2] Yet, however awkward the phrase and the concept might be, from the beginning of American constitutional law there has been a doctrinal voice that insists there are unwritten individual rights that should be judicially protected against government invasion. Consider, for example, Justice Chase's opinion in Calder v. Bull.

The entire Court embraced judicially enforceable unwritten limits in Fletcher v. Peck, 10 U.S. (6 Cranch) 87 (1810). The Court ruled that Georgia could not validly repeal its conveyance of the "Yazoo" lands (most of present-day Mississippi and Alabama), even though the original grant had been obtained through mammoth bribery. The repeal was invalid, said Chief Justice Marshall for the Court, because it was inconsistent with "certain great principles of justice, whose authority is universally acknowledged" but that are not embedded in constitutional text. "It may well be doubted, whether the nature of society and of government does not prescribe some limits to the legislative power." Thus the Court was unanimous that "Georgia was restrained, either by general principles which are common to our free institutions, or by the particular provisions of the [C]onstitution" from revoking its grant. In his concurrence, Justice William Johnson declared that he would invalidate the repeal "on a general principle, on the reason and nature of things: a principle which will impose laws even on the Deity." C. Peter Magrath's Yazoo: Law and Politics in the New Republic (1966) is a thorough historical treatment of *Fletcher* and its background.

This frank reliance on natural reason and principle fell out of favor, but the desire to find limiting principles outside of constitutional text has remained. The result has been a search for unenumerated rights that are then grafted onto a textual root. However linguistically ill-suited they may be for the purpose, the due process clauses in their "substantive" dimension are the principal home of this doctrine. The concept is simple: Some liberties not mentioned in the Constitution but identified by the Court are considered so fundamental to the idea of liberty that their invasion by government is presumed to be void and can be sustained only if the government justifies the invasion. Substantive due process, then, is simply the major doctrinal part of a larger constitutional enterprise of judicial protection of fundamental but unwritten rights. The Court has extended constitutional protection, not always using due process, to such fundamental rights as the right to associate with others, the right to vote, the right to be accorded equal protection of the laws by the federal government, the right to be presumed innocent and to have that presumption overcome only by proof beyond a reasonable doubt, the right of interstate migration, the right to marry or not, the right to have children or not, and the right to enjoy a zone of personal privacy or autonomy into which government may not intrude.

Substantive due process has had two eras. The first was an era, now repudiated, in which economic regulations covering private property and contracts

2. John Ely, Democracy and Distrust 18 (1980).

were struck down as offensive to an unwritten liberty of contract. The second era, still continuing, is one in which some government regulations of intimate relationships or decisions have been invalidated. Substantive due process is and always has been highly controversial. At the heart of this controversy is disagreement over the proper scope of judicial review. Is the Court the best mechanism to ensure government observance of "fundamental" but constitutionally unexpressed rights? The answer may depend on your view of the legitimate scope of judicial review. Should such unwritten rights be left to legislative discretion? If no, because of fears about oppressive legislation produced by representatives responding to majority sentiment, does that suggest a heightened role for the Court to exercise judicial review to make the democratic process as fair as possible? If the Court is free to locate unwritten rights, assimilate them into the Constitution, and enforce them against governments, are the criteria by which the Court selects those unwritten rights sufficiently connected to the Constitution to fetter judicial whim in the selection process? Is it possible to phrase such criteria to confine judicial subjectivity? What makes substantive due process illegitimate when used to enforce unwritten economic liberties, but legitimate when used to enforce unwritten noneconomic liberties?

1. The Incorporation Doctrine

Perhaps the most enduring monument of substantive due process is the incorporation doctrine, by which most of the substantive guarantees of the Bill of Rights have been "incorporated" into the Fourteenth Amendment's due process clause and thus made applicable to the states. The debate over incorporation was not so much about whether the Fourteenth Amendment's due process clause made *any* of the Bill of Rights guarantees applicable to the states, but whether the due process clause incorporated those guarantees *in toto* and all at once or did so selectively. Although this debate is now over for all practical purposes, the nature of the debate, and the victory of those who championed selective incorporation, is instructive in understanding the larger project of substantive due process.

The first ten amendments, drafted by the First Congress and ratified in 1791, were created to alleviate fears that the Constitution would give the new federal government power to invade important individual liberties long cherished by Americans. State constitutions contained (and still contain) similar or identical rights guarantees enforceable against state government. Thus, while it was widely accepted that the Bill of Rights guarantees applied only to the federal government, the Court did not address that issue until 1833.

Barron v. Baltimore, 32 U.S. 243 (1833). To construct streets, Baltimore diverted streams, flushing silt and sand into the harbor, rendering Barron's wharf useless. Barron sued, claiming the city taken his property for public use without just compensation in violation of the Fifth Amendment. He argued that because the "takings" clause is "in favour of the liberty of the citizen, [it] ought to be so construed as to restrain the legislative power of a state, as well as that of the United States." For a unanimous court, Chief Justice Marshall wrote:

> The constitution was ordained and established by the people of the United States for themselves, for their own government, and not for the government of the individual states. Each state established a constitution for itself, and, in that constitution, provided such limitations and restrictions on the powers of its particular government as its judgment dictated. [The powers given to the federal] government were to be exercised by itself; and the limitations on power, if expressed in general terms, are naturally, and, we think, necessarily applicable to the government created by the instrument. . . . [The] fifth amendment must be understood as restraining the power of the general government, not as applicable to the states. . . .
>
>   [Article I, §9 restrains] the exercise of power by the [federal] government, and [Article I, §10 restrains] state legislation. . . . [If] the original constitution . . . draws this plain and marked line of discrimination between the limitations it imposes on the powers of the general government, and on those of the states . . . some strong reason must be assigned for departing from this safe and judicious course in framing the amendments, before that departure can be assumed. We search in vain for that reason. [Had] the people of the several states . . . required additional safeguards to liberty from the apprehended encroachments of their particular governments: the remedy was in their own hands, and would have been applied by themselves. [The] unwieldy and cumbrous machinery of procuring a recommendation from two-thirds of congress, and the assent of three-fourths of their sister states, could never have occurred to any human being as a mode of doing that which might be effected by the state itself. Had the framers of these amendments intended them to be limitations on the powers of the state governments, they would have imitated the framers of the original constitution, and have expressed that intention. . . .

Thirty-five years later, after the cyclone of the Civil War had blown through, the Fourteenth Amendment added three major limits on state power: (1) No state may "abridge the privileges or immunities of citizens of the United States"; nor (2) "deprive any person of life, liberty, or property, without due process of law"; nor (3) "deny to any person within its jurisdiction the equal protection of the laws." The idea that these provisions served to reverse Barron v. Baltimore was soon put to the test.

≡≡≡ *Slaughter-House Cases*
≡≡≡ *83 U.S. 36 (1873)*

[Ostensibly as a public health measure, Louisiana chartered the Crescent City Live-Stock Landing and Slaughter-House Company and gave it a 25-year monopoly over livestock slaughtering in and around New Orleans. Although other butchers were required to close, they were given the right to slaughter animals at the Crescent City Company's abattoir, upon payment of fees fixed by statute. The excluded butchers contended that the law deprived them of their right to exercise their trade, and that by so doing Louisiana had violated each of the Fourteenth Amendment's due process, equal protection, and privileges and immunities clauses. The Court rejected the butchers' arguments and sustained the validity of the law.]

JUSTICE MILLER delivered the opinion of the Court.

This court [is] called upon for the first time to give construction to [the Fourteenth Amendment]. The most cursory glance at [the Thirteenth, Fourteenth, and Fifteenth Amendments] discloses a unity of purpose, when taken in connection with the history of the times, which cannot fail to have an important bearing [on] their true meaning.

In [the Civil War] slavery . . . perished [as] a necessity of the bitterness and force of the conflict. [But] the war being over, those who had succeeded in re-establishing the authority of the Federal government were not content to [permit] emancipation to rest on the actual results of the contest. . . . Hence the [T]hirteenth [Amendment].

[But] notwithstanding the . . . abolition of slavery, [former Confederate States] imposed upon the colored race onerous disabilities and burdens, and curtailed their rights in the pursuit of life, liberty, and property to such an extent that their freedom was of little value. . . . These circumstances [motivated Congress to propose the] [F]ourteenth [A]mendment, and [to decline] to treat as restored to their full participation in the government of the Union the States which had been in insurrection, until they ratified that article by a formal vote of their legislative bodies.

[In] the light of [these] events, . . . the one pervading purpose found in [the Thirteenth, Fourteenth, and Fifteenth Amendments was to secure] the freedom of the slave race, the security and firm establishment of that freedom, and the protection of the newly-made freeman and citizen from the oppressions of those who had formerly exercised unlimited dominion over him. [We] do not say that no one else but the negro can share in this protection. Both the language and spirit of these articles are to have their fair and just weight in any question of construction. [But] what we do say [is] that in [construing] these amendments it is necessary to look to the purpose which [was] the pervading spirit of them all [and] the evil which they were designed to remedy.

[The] first section of the [F]ourteenth [Amendment] opens with a definition of citizenship—not only citizenship of the United States, but citizenship of the States. "All persons born or naturalized in the United States, and subject to the jurisdiction thereof, are citizens of the United States and of the State wherein they reside."

[This clause] declares that persons may be citizens of the United States without regard to their citizenship of a particular State, and it [makes] *all persons* born within the United States and subject to its jurisdiction citizens of the United States. That its main purpose was to establish the citizenship of the negro can admit of no doubt. [Also,] the distinction between citizenship of the United States and citizenship of a State is clearly recognized and established. [A man may] be a citizen of the United States without being a citizen of a [State]. He must reside within the State to make him a citizen of it, but it is only necessary that he should be born or naturalized in the United States to be a citizen of the Union. It is quite clear, then, that there is a citizenship of the United States, and a citizenship of a State, which are distinct from each other, and which depend upon different characteristics or circumstances in the individual.

[This] distinction and its explicit recognition in this amendment [is] of great weight in this argument, because the next paragraph of this same section, which is the one mainly relied on by the [appellants], speaks only of privileges and immunities of citizens of the United States, and does not speak of those of citizens of the several States. [The] language is, "No State shall make or enforce any law which shall abridge the privileges or immunities of citizens of the *United States.*" It is a little remarkable, if this clause was intended as a protection to the citizen of a State against the legislative power of his own State, that the word citizen of the State should be left out when it is so carefully used, and used in contradistinction to citizens of the United States, in the very sentence which precedes it. It is too clear for argument that the change in phraseology was adopted understandingly and with a purpose. . . . If, then, there is a difference between the privileges and immunities belonging to a citizen of the United States as such, and those belonging to the citizen of the State as such the latter must rest for their security and protection where they have heretofore rested; for they are not embraced by this paragraph of the amendment. . . .

Was it the purpose of the [F]ourteenth [A]mendment, by the simple declaration that no State should make or enforce any law which shall abridge the privileges and immunities of *citizens of the United States,* to transfer the security and protection of . . . civil rights from the States to the Federal government? And where it is declared that Congress shall have the power to enforce that article, was it intended to bring within the power of Congress the entire domain of civil rights heretofore belonging exclusively to the States?

All this and more must follow, if the proposition of the [appellants] be sound. For not only are these rights subject to the control of Congress whenever in its discretion any of them are supposed to be abridged by State legislation, but that body may also pass laws in advance, limiting and restricting the exercise of legislative power by the States. . . . [S]uch a construction [would] constitute this court a perpetual censor upon all legislation of the States, on the civil rights of their own citizens, with authority to nullify such as it did not approve as consistent with those rights, as they existed at the time of the adoption of this amendment. [T]hese consequences are so serious, so far-reaching and pervading, so great a departure from the structure and spirit of our institutions; [so] radically changes the whole theory of the relations of the State and Federal governments to each other and of both these governments to the people; [that we] are convinced that no such results were intended by the

Congress which proposed these amendments, nor by the legislatures of the States which ratified them.

[We] may hold ourselves excused from defining the privileges and immunities of citizens of the United States which no State can abridge, until some case involving those privileges may make it necessary to do so. But lest it should be said that no such privileges and immunities are to be found if those we have been considering are excluded, we venture to suggest some which owe their existence to the Federal government, its National character, its Constitution, or its laws. One of these is well described in the case of Crandall v. Nevada, [73 U.S. (6 Wall.) 35 (1867)]. It is said to be the right of the [U.S.] citizen, protected by implied guarantees of its Constitution, "to come to the seat of government to assert any claim he may have upon that government, to transact any business he may have with it, to seek its protection, to share its offices, to engage in administering its functions. He has the right of free access to its seaports, through which all operations of foreign commerce are conducted, to the subtreasuries, land offices, and courts of justice in the several States." [The] right to peaceably assemble and petition for redress of grievances, the privilege of the writ of habeas corpus, are rights of the citizen guaranteed by the Federal Constitution. The right to use the navigable waters of the United States, however they may penetrate the territory of the several States, all rights secured to our citizens by treaties with foreign nations, are dependent upon citizenship of the United States, and not citizenship of a State. [To] these may be added the rights secured by the thirteenth and fifteenth articles of amendment, and by the other clause[s] of the [F]ourteenth [Amendment]. But it is useless to pursue this branch of the inquiry, since we are of opinion that the rights claimed by [appellants] are not privileges and immunities of citizens of the United States within the meaning of the clause of the [F]ourteenth [A]mendment under consideration.

[The Court rejected appellants' arguments that the statute violated the due process and equal protection clauses of the Fourteenth Amendment. Due process was not implicated because the Court thought there was no deprivation of property. As to equal protection, the] existence of laws in the States where the newly emancipated negroes resided which discriminated with gross injustice and hardship against them as a class was the evil to be remedied by [equal protection], and by it such laws are forbidden. [We] doubt very much whether any action of a State not directed by way of discrimination against the negroes as a class, or on account of their race, will ever be held to come within the purview of this provision. It is so clearly a provision for that race and that emergency, that a strong case would be necessary for its application to any other. [The] judgments of the Supreme Court of Louisiana in these cases are affirmed.

JUSTICE FIELD, joined by CHIEF JUSTICE CHASE, and JUSTICES SWAYNE and BRADLEY, dissenting.

[If the privileges and immunities clause] only refers . . . to such privileges and immunities as were before its adoption specially designated in the

Constitution or necessarily implied as belonging to citizens of the United States, it was a vain and idle enactment, which accomplished nothing, and most unnecessarily excited Congress and the people on its passage. With privileges and immunities thus designated or implied no State could ever have interfered by its laws, and no new constitutional provision was required to inhibit such interference. The supremacy of the Constitution and the laws of the United States always controlled any State legislation of that character. But if the amendment refers to the natural and inalienable rights which belong to all citizens, the inhibition has a profound significance and consequence.

What, then, are the privileges and immunities which are secured against abridgment by State legislation? . . . The privileges and immunities designated are those *which of right belong to the citizens of all free governments.* Clearly among these [is] the right to pursue a lawful employment in a lawful manner, without other restraint than such as equally affects all persons. . . . [All] monopolies in any known trade or manufacture are an invasion of these privileges, for they encroach upon the liberty of citizens to acquire property and pursue [happiness].

[Equality] of right [in] the lawful pursuits of life, throughout the whole country, is the distinguishing privilege of citizens of the United States. To them, everywhere, all pursuits, all professions, all avocations are open without other restrictions than such as are imposed equally upon all others of the same age, sex, and condition. The State may prescribe such regulations for every pursuit and calling of life as will promote the public health, secure the good order and advance the general prosperity of society, but when once prescribed, the pursuit or calling must be free to be followed by every citizen who is within the conditions designated, and will conform to the regulations. This is the fundamental idea upon which our institutions rest [and which is] entirely rejected and trampled upon by the act of Louisiana. [It] is to me a matter of profound regret that its validity is recognized by a majority of this court, for by it the right of free labor, one of the most sacred and imprescriptible rights of man, is violated. "The property which every man has in his own labor," says Adam Smith, "as it is the original foundation of all other property, so it is the most sacred and inviolable. The patrimony of the poor man lies in the strength and dexterity of his own hands; and to hinder him from employing this strength and dexterity in what manner he thinks proper, without injury to his neighbor, is a plain violation of this most sacred property. It is a manifest encroachment upon the just liberty both of the workman and of those who might be disposed to employ him. As it hinders the one from working at what he thinks proper, so it hinders the others from employing whom they think proper." (Smith's Wealth of Nations, b. 1, ch. 10, part 2.) . . .

JUSTICE BRADLEY, dissenting.

The right of a State to regulate the conduct of its citizens is undoubtedly a very broad and extensive one, and not to be lightly restricted. But there are certain fundamental rights which this right of regulation cannot infringe. It may prescribe the manner of their exercise, but it cannot subvert the rights themselves. [In] this free country, the people of which inherited certain tradionary rights and privileges from their ancestors, citizenship [means] certain privileges and immunities [which] the government [cannot] take away or impair. . . .

The people of this country brought with them [the] rights of Englishmen; the rights which had been wrested from English sovereigns at various periods of the nation's history. . . . [Blackstone] classifies these fundamental rights [as] the right of personal security, the right of personal liberty, and the right of private property. [These] fundamental rights [can] only be interfered with [by] lawful regulations necessary or proper for the mutual good of all. [The] individual citizen [must] be left free to adopt such calling, profession, or trade as may seem to him most conducive to [his betterment]. This right to choose one's calling is an essential part of that liberty which it is the object of government to protect; and a calling, when chosen, is a man's property and right. [No privilege or immunity] is more essential and fundamental than the right to follow such profession or employment as each one may choose, subject only to uniform regulations equally applicable to all. . . .

The keeping of a slaughter-house is part of, and incidental to, the trade of a butcher—one of the ordinary occupations of human life. To compel a butcher [to] slaughter [his] cattle in another person's slaughter-house and pay him a toll therefor, is such a restriction upon the trade as materially to interfere with its prosecution. It is onerous, unreasonable, arbitrary, and unjust. It has none of the qualities of a police regulation. If it were really a police regulation, it would undoubtedly be within the power of the legislature. That portion of the act which requires all slaughter-houses to be located below the city and to be subject to inspection is clearly a police regulation. [But] the granting [of] exclusive privileges [is] an invasion of the right of others to choose a lawful calling, and an infringement of personal liberty. . . .

NOTES

1. The Range of Interpretations of the Slaughter-House Cases. The majority's interpretation makes sense against the antebellum background of reliance upon state constitutions to prevent state governments from intruding upon the liberties of its citizens. But the problem with the majority's interpretation is that the Fourteenth Amendment definitely was intended to create new federal limits upon the ability of states to invade the liberties of its residents. Reliance upon the difference in rights possessed by federal and state citizens made the "sole office" of the privileges and immunities clause the protection of "rights already given by some other federal law," thus rendering the clause redundant. Justice Miller thought this was necessary to avoid radical change to "the whole theory of the relations of the State and Federal governments to each other and of both these governments to the people," but that "quite arguably was precisely what the authors of the amendment had in mind." David Currie, The Constitution in the Supreme Court: The First Hundred Years 344-345 (1985).

The dissenters' view that all citizens of a free government had a right to engage in any lawful calling, subject only to valid police regulations, left two major issues unresolved. What determines the validity of a trade or occupation? Presumably the dissenters' answer was the common law, for it was Louisiana's statutory alteration of common law principles that offended the dissenters. Which regulations are valid police regulations and which are not? The dissenters recognized the validity of regulations requiring all slaughterhouses to be downriver from New Orleans, and of subjecting each abattoir to inspection, as there was a clear public health reason for such regulations. But the enforced monopoly was "onerous, unreasonable, arbitrary, and unjust," presumably because of the lack of any clear public benefit. Left unstated were the criteria by which judges could impartially filter clear public benefits from bogus ones. Three decades later, as the first era of substantive due process came into full flower, this problem would remain.

A third interpretation was provided much later by advocates of "total incorporation" of the Bill of Rights into the Fourteenth Amendment's due process clause. Justice Hugo Black canvassed the history of the adoption of the Fourteenth Amendment and asserted that "one of the chief objects that [the Fourteenth Amendment's privileges and immunities clause] was intended to accomplish was to make the Bill of Rights applicable to the states." Adamson v. California, 332 U.S. 46, 71-72 (1947) (Black, J., dissenting). To Black, the words of the privileges and immunities clause "seem [an] eminently reasonable way of expressing the idea that henceforth the Bill of Rights shall apply to the States. What more precious 'privilege' of American citizenship could there be than that privilege to claim the protection of our great Bill of Rights?" Duncan v. Louisiana, 391 U.S 145, 166 (1968) (Black, J., concurring).

One problem with Black's view was that it would make the due process clause mostly superfluous, because if the privileges and immunities clause incorporated the Bill of Rights (including the Fifth Amendment's due process clause), there was no need to add a new due process clause. Another problem is that Black's reading of the history of the Fourteenth Amendment's adoption may be wrong. After a careful examination, the eminent historian Charles Fairman concluded that nothing "in the practice of Congress, or the action of state legislatures, constitutional conventions or courts" suggested that the privileges and immunities clause was intended to incorporate the Bill of Rights. The Framers of the clause, states Fairman, never had a clear conception of their intentions. The best that can be said is that protection of those liberties that are "'implicit in the concept of ordered liberty' [is] as close as one can [come] to catching the vague aspirations that were hung upon the privileges and immunities clause." Fairman, Does the Fourteenth Amendment Incorporate the Bill of Rights? The Original Understanding, 2 Stan. L. Rev. 5, 139 (1949). Among those in disagreement with Fairman is Curtis, No State Shall Abridge: The Fourteenth Amendment and the Bill of Rights (1986), and Crosskey, Politics and the Constitution in the History of the United States (1953), who argue that the draftsmen of the Fourteenth Amendment's privileges and immunities clause did indeed have it in mind to use that clause to make the constitutional liberties secured to American citizens by the Bill of Rights enforceable against the states. See also Richard Aynes, Charles Fairman, Felix Frankfurter and the Fourteenth Amendment, 70 Chi.-Kent L. Rev. 1197 (1995).

Perhaps the lack of consensus among the Framers of the Fourteenth Amendment means that there was no clear single intent behind the privileges and immunities clause. Some drafters may have thought it provided constitutional protection only for legislation such as the 1866 Civil Rights Act protecting newly emancipated blacks. See Berger, Government by Judiciary 18-20 (1977). Others may have thought the clause incorporated the Bill of Rights. Representative John A. Bingham, chief Framer of the clause, stated as much. See Cong. Globe, 42d Cong., 1st Sess., app. 85 (1871). And other Framers, such as Senator Jacob Howard, thought the phrase encompassed the "fundamental rights lying at the basis of all society" and was willing to let the courts decide what those rights might be. See Cong. Globe, 39th Cong., 1st Sess. 2765-2766 (1866).

2. The Rights of Federal Citizenship: Not an Empty Category. Justice Miller argued that privileges and immunities of federal citizenship were not an empty category, pointing to the right of interstate travel or migration (among other rights) as incident to federal citizenship. Over the years, the Court has located the right of interstate migration in several different constitutional sources, including the commerce clause, Article IV, §2, and the constitutional structure as a whole.

In Saenz v. Roe, 526 U.S. 489 (1999), the Court invalidated a California law restricting the welfare benefits of new residents for the first year of their residency in California to the level provided by their former state of residence. In so doing, the Court ruled that one aspect of the right to travel—"the right of the newly arrived citizen to the same privileges and immunities enjoyed by other citizens of the same State[—]is protected not only by the new arrival's status as a state citizen, but also by her status as a citizen of the United States." In dissent, Justice Thomas, joined by Chief Justice Rehnquist, claimed that "the majority attributes a meaning to the Privileges or Immunities Clause that likely was unintended when the Fourteenth Amendment was enacted and ratified. . . . [At] the time the Fourteenth Amendment was adopted, people understood that 'privileges or immunities of citizens' were fundamental rights, rather than every public benefit established by positive law." For more, see Richard Aynes, On Misreading John Bingham and the Fourteenth Amendment, 103 Yale L.J. 57 (1993).

3. Incorporation: From Privileges and Immunities to Due Process. Once the Court had wrung most of the constitutional juice from the Fourteenth Amendment's privileges and immunities clause, thereby destroying that clause's potential to incorporate the Bill of Rights, the urge to apply the Bill of Rights to the states gravitated to the due process clause. In the process, the Court was required to formulate criteria for deciding which Bill of Rights guarantees were to be recognized as part of the substance guaranteed by the due process clause.

The first case to incorporate a guarantee contained in the Bill of Rights into the due process clause was Chicago, B. & Q. R.R. v. Chicago, 166 U.S. 226 (1897). Chicago had condemned a portion of the railroad's property to widen a street, paying the railroad $1 as compensation. The Supreme Court ruled that the takings clause of the Fifth Amendment was applicable to states and their political subdivisions as an aspect of the Fourteenth Amendment's guarantee of due process. The Court relied upon natural law notions to reach this conclusion, and also relied heavily on the idea that unjustly compensated interference with vested property rights was a denial of due process. In Twining v. New Jersey, 211 U.S. 78 (1908), however, the Court decided that New Jersey had not violated due process by instructing a jury that it could draw unfavorable inferences from a criminal defendant's failure to testify. The Court admitted that it was "possible that some of the personal rights safeguarded by [the Bill of Rights] against National action may also be safeguarded against state action, because a denial of them would be a denial of due process of law." But this was "not because those rights are enumerated in the [Constitution], but because they are of such a nature that they are included in the conception of due process of law." To the Court, the only such rights were those that constitute a "fundamental principle of liberty and justice which inheres in the very idea of free government and is the inalienable right of a citizen of such a government." The privilege against self-incrimination was not such a right because it was not to be found in "the great instruments in which we are accustomed to look for the declaration of fundamental rights [e.g., Magna Charta, the 1689 Declaration of Rights]," nor did the Framers of the Constitution regard it as part of due process because the Bill of Rights treated the two concepts "as exclusive of each other."[3]

In Palko v. Connecticut, 302 U.S. 319 (1937), the Court upheld Connecticut's practice of permitting the state to appeal criminal cases, although it assumed that the double jeopardy clause of the Fifth Amendment would bar the federal government from doing so. For the Court, Justice Cardozo stated that the Fourteenth Amendment's due process clause incorporated those parts of the Bill of Rights that are "the very essence of a scheme of ordered liberty," things " 'so rooted in the traditions and conscience of our people as to be ranked as fundamental,' " or rights such "that neither liberty nor justice would exist if they were sacrificed." But the "kind of double jeopardy to which [Connecticut subjected Palko was not] a hardship so acute and shocking that our polity [could] not endure it, [nor did] it violate those 'fundamental principles of liberty and justice which lie at the base of all our civil and political institutions.' "[4]

3. *Twining* was overturned by Malloy v. Hogan, 378 U.S. 1 (1964), and the self-incrimination privilege was thus incorporated into due process. Justice Brennan declared for the Court: "[T]he American system of criminal prosecution is accusatorial, not inquisitorial, and the [self-incrimination] privilege is its mainstay."

4. Benton v. Maryland, 395 U.S. 784 (1969), overturned *Palko* on this precise point, holding protection against double jeopardy to be so fundamental that it must be incorporated into due process.

The "selective incorporation" approach exemplified by *Palko* has always commanded a majority of the Court. Justice Black, joined by Justice Douglas, was the foremost advocate of "total incorporation"; his dissent in Adamson v. California, 332 U.S. 46 (1947), remains the clearest statement of "total incorporation." In *Adamson*, the Court upheld a conviction where the prosecutor had commented to the jury on the defendant's failure to testify. The Court acknowledged that the prosecutor's conduct would violate the self-incrimination privilege if it had occurred in federal court, but the Court reaffirmed *Twining*'s conclusion that the privilege against self-incrimination was not a part of due process. Justice Black dissented:

> This decision reasserts [*Twining*'s] constitutional theory [that] this Court is endowed by the Constitution with boundless power under "natural law" periodically to expand and contract constitutional standards to conform to the Court's conception of what at a particular time constitutes "civilized decency" and "fundamental liberty and justice." [I] think [*Twining*] and the "natural law" theory of the Constitution upon which it relies degrade the constitutional safeguards of the Bill of Rights and simultaneously appropriate for this Court broad power which we are not authorized by the Constitution to [exercise]. . . . [I] would follow what I believe was the original purpose of the Fourteenth Amendment—to extend to all the people of the nation the complete protection of the Bill of Rights.

Justice Black may have lost the battle over the mode of incorporation, but he largely won the war. Today, the only provisions of the first eight Amendments that have *not* been incorporated are the Third Amendment, the grand jury indictment clause of the Fifth Amendment, and the Seventh Amendment. In Duncan v. Louisiana, 391 U.S. 145 (1968), in which the Court held the Sixth Amendment jury trial right applicable to the states via the due process clause, the Court declared that the issue was not whether it was an abstract fundamental right but whether

> a particular procedure is fundamental—[necessary] to an Anglo-American regime of ordered liberty. [A] criminal process which was fair and equitable but used no juries is easy to imagine. It would make use of alternative guarantees and protections which would serve the purposes that the jury serves in the English and American systems. Yet no American State has undertaken to construct such a system. [The actual criminal processes of the States] have developed in connection with and reliance upon jury trial. [Because] we believe that trial by jury in criminal cases is fundamental to the American scheme of justice, we hold that the Fourteenth Amendment guarantees a right of jury trial in all criminal cases which—were they to be tried in a federal court—would come within the Sixth Amendment's guarantee.

The final chapter in incorporation was the Court's conclusion that the particular right incorporated into due process and made applicable to the states applied to the states in *precisely the same way* it would apply to the federal government. Prior to this so-called jot-for-jot approach to incorporation, an incorporated right might have one consequence when applied to the federal government and another when applied to the states. A good example is the exclusionary rule. Wolf v. Colorado, 338 U.S. 25 (1949), concluded that the "security of one's privacy against arbitrary intrusion by the police [was] basic to a free society," and thus the Fourth Amendment's search and seizure protections were "enforceable against the States through the Due Process Clause." But this did not mean that relevant evidence seized through unlawful searches must be excluded, as would be the case in the federal courts. It was not "a departure from basic standards" to leave victims of illegal searches with "the remedies of private action and such protection as the internal discipline of the police, under the eyes of an alert public opinion, may afford." Twelve years later, in Mapp v. Ohio, 367 U.S. 642 (1961), *Wolf* was overruled, and a uniform exclusionary rule was set in place for both federal and state courts. The notable exception to the principle of jot-for-jot incorporation is conviction of a criminal offense by less than unanimity of the jurors. Federal juries must reach criminal verdicts unanimously; state juries may convict a defendant by less than unanimity. Apodaca v. Oregon, 406 U.S. 404 (1972).

Incorporation, especially the jot-for-jot brand, produces national uniformity. Is that always desirable? Suppose that a state desires to replace the Anglo-American adversarial system of criminal prosecution and jury trial with a continental system of investigating magistrate and non-jury trial, coupled with appropriate safeguards imposed upon the magistrate. Although *Duncan* conceded that such a system could be "fair and equitable," the *Duncan* holding would preclude such state experimentation. Is this wise?

4. The Continuing Evolution of Incorporation.   In McDonald v. City of Chicago, 561 U.S. 742 (2010), the Supreme Court ruled that the Second Amendment right to possession of a firearm for purposes of self-defense was "fundamental to *our* scheme of ordered liberty" and thus applicable to the states by the Fourteenth Amendment. A four-justice plurality relied on past practices, state constitutions, and Reconstruction-era legislation to conclude that the right to bear arms for self-defense was deeply rooted in the nation's history and tradition. Justice Thomas concurred in the judgment, but argued that the Second Amendment right was a privilege of national citizenship encompassed in the Fourteenth Amendment's privileges or immunities clause. Reliance upon the due process clause to protect substantive liberties is "a legal fiction," said Justice Thomas. "The notion that a constitutional provision that guarantees only 'process' before a person is deprived of life, liberty, or property could define the substance of those rights strains credulity for even the most casual user of words."

2.   The Rise and Fall of Economic Rights as the Substance of Due Process

As demonstrated by such cases as Calder v. Bull and Fletcher v. Peck, the propensity to find in the Constitution unwritten rights began early in our constitutional history. The use of the due process clauses as an important assimilative device can be traced to Murray's Lessee v. Hoboken Land & Improvement Co., 59 U.S. (18 How.) 272 (1856), in which the Court observed that due process was "a restraint on the legislative as well as the executive and judicial powers of government." See Corwin, The Doctrine of Due Process Before the Civil War, 24 Harv. L. Rev. 366 (1911); Easterbrook, Substance and Due Process, 1982 Sup. Ct. Rev. 85, 95-100. A year later Chief Justice Taney asserted, in the infamous Scott v. Sandford (*Dred Scott*), 60 U.S. (19 How.) 393 (1857), that

> an act of Congress which deprives a citizen of the United States of his liberty or property, merely because he came himself or brought his property into a particular Territory of the United States, and who had committed no offence against the laws, could hardly be dignified with the name of due process of law.

The property in question, of course, was a man named Dred Scott, and the ruling was overturned in the bloodiest imaginable way.

Rulings and men may die, but words live on. In Hepburn v. Griswold, 75 U.S (8 Wall.) 603 (1870), the Court declared that Congress could not make paper money legal tender. As an alternative holding the Court reasoned that contracts were property; a requirement that creditors accept paper money instead of coin deprived them of property; and "whatever may be the operation of such an act, due process of law makes no part of it." The next term, however, with the introduction of two new justices, the Court overruled *Hepburn* in The Legal Tender Cases, 79 U.S. (12 Wall.) 457 (1870).

The Supreme Court was not alone in flirting with due process as a substantive limit on legislation interfering with vested property rights. The rights to acquire, use, possess, and dispose of property became increasingly important in the ever-expanding economy of the nineteenth century. Occasionally these common law property rights clashed with state regulation. Those clashes produced fitful resort to due process to protect vested property rights. Perhaps the earliest clear example is Wynehamer v. People, 13 N.Y. 378 (1856), in which the New York Court of Appeals relied on the New York constitution's due process clause to invalidate a liquor prohibition statute that made it a crime to possess liquor owned prior to the law's enactment. Since the "law annihilates the value of property," the owner of property "is deprived of it [within] the spirit of a constitutional provision intended expressly to shield private rights from the exercise of arbitrary power." The influential nineteenth-century constitutional treatise writer Thomas Cooley seized on *Wynehamer* to popularize his view that due process operated to assess the validity of government action by using "those principles of civil liberty and constitutional defence which have become established in our system of law, and not by any rules that pertain to forms of procedure only." Cooley, Constitutional Limitations 355-356 (1868).

While Cooley's enthusiasm for enveloping common law property rights in the cocoon of due process seems mirrored by the Slaughter-House Cases dissenters, the actual development of this phenomenon was far more measured.

As the industrialization of America reached its early maturity in the late nineteenth century, governments acted to remedy perceived abuses produced by the great disparity in economic power that resulted from industrialization. Simultaneously, economic theories supporting the inequalities of wealth produced by industrialization began to win favor among those benefited by industrialization. The doctrine developed by the Court mediated between these two opposing impulses.

In Munn v. Illinois, 94 U.S. 113 (1877), the Court upheld Illinois's regulation of grain storage rates, concluding that governments could regulate private property when it is "affected with a public interest," or "used in a manner to make it of public consequence, and affect[s] the community at large." The Court intimated that such regulations might be unreasonable and void, as violations of due process, when applied to "mere private contracts, relating to matters in which the public has no interest." Similarly, in Mugler v. Kansas, 123 U.S. 623 (1887), the Court upheld a Kansas law prohibiting alcoholic beverages against a challenge brought by Mugler, a brewer, who contended that the law deprived him of his property without due process. In dicta, the Court observed that laws having "no real or substantial relation" to a state's legitimate police powers, or which are "palpable invasion[s] of rights secured by the fundamental law" would be struck down.

These hints that the police powers of state governments might be bounded by due process bore fruit in Allgeyer v. Louisiana, 165 U.S. 578 (1897). Louisiana required that insurance contracts covering Louisiana property be made with an insurer licensed to do business in Louisiana. Allgeyer purchased marine insurance on his goods shipped from New Orleans from a New York insurer not licensed to do business in Louisiana. Allgeyer's conviction under the Louisiana law was unanimously reversed by the Court. The term "liberty" in the due process clause, said Justice Peckham for the Court,

> embrace[s] the right of the citizen to be free in the enjoyment of all his faculties; to be free to use them in all lawful ways; to live and work where he will; to earn his livelihood by any lawful calling; to pursue any livelihood or avocation, and for that purpose to enter into all contracts which may be proper, necessary and essential to his carrying out to a successful conclusion the purposes above mentioned.

This triumph of substantive due process was not limited to the property or liberty of natural persons. In Santa Clara County v. Southern Pacific Railroad, 118 U.S. 394 (1886), the Court intimated that corporations were persons for purposes of the Fourteenth Amendment, opening the door for corporate challenges to the constitutional validity of economic regulations. In Pembina Consolidated Silver Mining & Milling Co v. Pennsylvania, 125 U.S. 181 (1888), the Court so held. Though this ruling has been criticized from time to time,[5] its effect is to permit the constitutional claims of corporate

---

5. See, e.g., Conn. General Life Ins. Co. v. Johnson, 303 U.S 77, 85-90 (1938) (Black, J., dissenting); Wheeling Steel Corp. v. Glander, 337 U.S. 562, 576 (Douglas, J., dissenting).

owners—shareholders—to be asserted by the corporation (and thus adjudicated as a single claim) rather than via a multiplicity of claims by shareholders.

≡ *Lochner v. New York*
198 U.S. 45 (1905)

[New York law prohibited bakery workers from working more than 10 hours daily or 60 hours per week. The Court reversed Lochner's conviction under the statute on the ground that it violated due process.]

JUSTICE PECKHAM delivered the opinion of the Court.

The statute necessarily interferes with the right of contract between the employer and employees, concerning the number of hours in which the latter may labor in the bakery of the employer. The general right to make a contract in relation to his business is part of the liberty of the individual protected by the [due process clause of the] Fourteenth Amendment of the Federal Constitution. *Allgeyer*. . . . The right to purchase or to sell labor is part of the liberty protected by this amendment, unless there are circumstances which exclude the right. There are, however, certain powers existing in the sovereignty of each State, [somewhat] vaguely termed police powers, [that] relate to the safety, health, morals and general welfare of the public. Both property and liberty are held on such reasonable conditions as may be imposed by the governing power of the State in the exercise of those powers, and with such conditions the Fourteenth Amendment was not designed to interfere. *Mugler*. . . .

This court has recognized the existence and upheld the exercise of the police powers of the States in many [cases]. Among [them is] Holden v. Hardy, 169 U.S. 366 [(1898)]. A [Utah statute limited] the employment of workmen in all underground mines or workings [and ore smelters] to eight hours per day, "except in cases of emergency, where life or property is in imminent danger." [The] act was held to be a valid exercise of the police powers of the State. [It] was held that the kind of employment [and] the character of the employees [were] such as to make it reasonable and proper for the State to interfere to prevent the employees from being constrained by the rules laid down by the proprietors in regard to labor. [There] is nothing in Holden v. Hardy which covers the case now before us.

[Of course] there is a limit to the valid exercise of the police power by the State. There is no dispute concerning this general proposition. Otherwise the Fourteenth Amendment would have no efficacy and the legislatures of the States would have unbounded power, and it would be enough to say that any piece of legislation was enacted to conserve the morals, the health or the safety of the people; such legislation would be valid, no matter how absolutely without foundation the claim might be. [In] every case that comes before this court, therefore, where legislation of this character is concerned and where the protection of the Federal Constitution is sought, the question necessarily arises: Is this a fair, reasonable and appropriate exercise of the police power of the State, or is it an unreasonable, unnecessary and arbitrary interference with the right of the individual to his personal liberty or to enter into those contracts in relation to labor which may seem to him appropriate or necessary for the support of himself and his family? Of course the liberty of contract relating to labor includes both parties to it. The one has as much right to purchase as the other to sell labor.

This is not a question of substituting the judgment of the court for that of the legislature. If the act be within the power of the State it is valid, although the judgment of the court might be totally opposed to the enactment of such a law. But the question would still remain: Is it within the police power of the State? and that question must be answered by the court.

The question whether this act is valid as a labor law, pure and simple, may be dismissed in a few words. There is no reasonable ground for interfering with the liberty of person or the right of free contract, by determining the hours of labor, in the occupation of a baker. There is no contention that bakers as a class are not equal in intelligence and capacity to men in other trades or manual occupations, or that they are not able to assert their rights and care for themselves without the protecting arm of the State, interfering with their independence of judgment and of action. They are in no sense wards of the State. Viewed in the light of a purely labor law, with no reference whatever to the question of health, we think that a law like the one before us involves neither the safety, the morals nor the welfare of the public, and that the interest of the public is not in the slightest degree affected by such an act. The law must be upheld, if at all, as a law pertaining to the health of the individual engaged in the occupation of a baker. It does not affect any other portion of the public than those who are engaged in that occupation. Clean and wholesome bread does not depend upon whether the baker works but ten hours per day or only sixty hours a week. . . .

[The] mere assertion that the subject relates though but in a remote degree to the public health does not necessarily render the enactment valid. The act must have a more direct relation, as a means to an end, and the end itself must be appropriate and legitimate, before an act can be held to be valid which interferes with the general right of an individual to be free in his person and in his power to contract in relation to his own labor. . . .

We think the limit of the police power has been reached and passed in this case. There is, in our judgment, no reasonable foundation for holding this to be necessary or appropriate as a health law to safeguard the public health or the health of the individuals who are following the trade of a baker. If this statute be valid [there] would seem to be no length to which legislation of this nature might not go.

We think that there can be no fair doubt that the trade of a baker, in and of itself, is not an unhealthy one to that degree which would authorize the legislature to interfere with the right to labor, and with the right of free contract on the part of the individual, either as employer or employee. [It] might be safely affirmed that almost all occupations more or less affect the health. There must be more than the mere fact of the possible existence of some small amount of unhealthiness to warrant legislative interference with liberty. . . .

It is also urged [that] it is to the interest of the State that its population should be strong and robust, and therefore any legislation which may be said to tend to make people healthy must be valid as health laws, enacted under the police power. . . . Scarcely any law but might find shelter under such [assumptions]. Not only the hours of employees, but the hours of employers, could be regulated, and doctors, lawyers, scientists, all professional men, as well as athletes and artisans, could be forbidden to fatigue their brains and bodies by prolonged hours of exercise, lest the fighting strength of the State be impaired. We mention these extreme cases because the contention is extreme. [This] law, although passed in the assumed exercise of the police power, and as relating to the public health, or the health of the employees named, is not within that power, and is invalid. The act is not, within any fair meaning of the term, a health law, but is an illegal interference with the rights of individuals, both employers and employees, to make contracts regarding labor upon such terms as they may think best, or which they may agree upon with the other parties to such contracts. [Statutes] limiting the hours in which grown and intelligent men may labor to earn their living are mere meddlesome interferences with the rights of the individual, and they are not saved from condemnation by the claim that they are passed in the exercise of the police power and upon the subject of the health of the individual whose rights are interfered with, unless there be some fair ground, reasonable in and of itself, to say that there is material danger to the public health or to the health of the employees, if the hours of labor are not curtailed. [All that the state] could properly do [under its police power] has been done by it with regard to the conduct of bakeries [in] the other sections of the act, [which] provide for the inspection of the premises where the bakery is carried on, with regard to furnishing proper wash-rooms and water-closets, [providing] proper drainage, plumbing and painting, [ceiling heights, floor composition, and] other things of that [nature].

It was further urged [that] restricting the hours of labor in the case of bakers was valid because it tended to cleanliness on the part of the workers, [which would result in cleaner bread. In] our judgment it is not possible in fact to discover the connection between the number of hours a baker may work in the bakery and the healthful quality of the bread made by the workman. The connection, if any exists, is too shadowy and thin to build any argument for the interference of the legislature. . . .

It is manifest to us that the [New York statute] has no . . . direct relation to and no . . . substantial effect upon the health of the employee, as to justify us in regarding the section as really a health law. It seems to us that the real object and purpose were simply to regulate the hours of labor between the master and his employees . . . in a private business, not dangerous in any degree to morals or in any real and substantial degree, to the health of the employees. Under such circumstances the freedom of master and employee to contract with each other in relation to their employment, and in defining the same, cannot be prohibited or interfered with, without violating the Federal Constitution. . . .

Reversed.

JUSTICE HARLAN, joined by JUSTICES WHITE and DAY, dissenting.

[This] statute was enacted in order to protect the physical well-being of those who work in bakery and confectionery establishments. It may be that the statute had its origin . . . in the belief that employers and employees in such establishments were not upon an equal footing. [Be] this as it may, the statute must be taken as expressing the belief of the people of New York that . . . labor in excess of sixty hours during a week in such establishments may endanger the health of those who thus labor. Whether or not this be wise legislation it is not the province of the court to inquire. [In] determining the question of power to interfere with liberty of contract, the court may inquire whether the means devised by the State are germane to an end which may be lawfully accomplished and have a real or substantial relation to the protection of health [of bakery workers]. I find it impossible, in view of common experience, to say that there is here no real or substantial relation between the means employed by the State and the end sought to be accomplished by its legislation. . . .

There are many reasons of a weighty, substantial character, based upon the experience of mankind, in support of the theory that, all things considered, more than ten hours' steady work each day, from week to week, in a bakery or confectionery establishment, may endanger the health, and shorten the lives of the workmen, thereby diminishing their physical and mental capacity to serve the State, and to provide for those dependent upon them.

If such reasons exist that ought to be the end of this [case]. The judgment [should] be affirmed.

JUSTICE HOLMES, dissenting.

This case is decided upon an economic theory which a large part of the country does not entertain. If it were a question whether I agreed with that theory I should desire to study it further and long before making up my mind. But I do not conceive that to be my duty, because I strongly believe that my agreement or disagreement has nothing to do with the right of a majority to embody their opinions in law. [States] may regulate life in many ways which we as legislators might think as injudicious or if you like as tyrannical as this, and which equally with this interfere with the liberty to contract. Sunday laws and usury laws are ancient examples. A more modern one is the prohibition of lotteries. The liberty of the citizen to do as he likes so long as he does not interfere with the liberty of others to do the same, which has been a shibboleth for some well-known writers, is interfered with by school laws, by the Post Office, by every state or municipal institution which takes his money for purposes thought desirable, whether he likes it or not. The Fourteenth Amendment does not enact Mr. Herbert Spencer's Social Statics. . . . Some of these laws embody convictions or prejudices which judges are likely to share. Some may not. But a constitution is not intended to embody a particular economic theory, whether of paternalism and the organic relation of the citizen to the State or of laissez faire. It is made for people of fundamentally differing views, and the accident of our finding certain opinions natural and familiar or novel and even shocking ought not to conclude our judgment upon the question whether statutes embodying them conflict with the Constitution of the United States.

[Every] opinion tends to become a law. I think that the word liberty in the Fourteenth Amendment is perverted when it is held to prevent the natural outcome of a dominant opinion, unless it can be said that a rational and fair man necessarily would admit that the statute proposed would infringe fundamental principles as they have been understood by the traditions of our people and our law. [No] such sweeping condemnation can be passed upon the statute before us. A reasonable man might think it a proper measure on the score of health. . . .

NOTES

1. A Modern Paradox.   The *Lochner* version of substantive due process has been repudiated. The contemporary Court asserts that *Lochner* was wrong and that its view of substantive due process was illegitimate. Yet the modern Court has invoked substantive due process to protect other liberties, such as contraception, abortion, and certain familial choices. This paradox demands an explanation. What was wrong about *Lochner* that is not wrong about, e.g., Roe v. Wade, the original abortion case? Consider the following possible explanations.

2. Should Due Process Protect Unenumerated Rights?   The entire process of transforming Magna Charta's "law of the land" provision, from which the due process clauses are directly descended, into a guarantee of unstated liberties might be unjustified. Magna Charta provided in relevant part that no freeman's liberty or property was to be disturbed "except by the lawful judgment of his peers or by the law of the land." Lord Coke, the authoritative judge and commentator upon English law in the seventeenth century, said of this provision that by the time of Edward III (1312–1377) the meaning of due process was "that no man be taken, imprisoned, or put out of his freehold without due process of the Law, that is, by indictment or presentment, [or] by Writ original of the Common Law." 2 Coke, Institutes of the Laws of England 50 (1642). Coke was the legal gospel for early-eighteenth-century colonial Americans. See Corwin, The "Higher Law" Background of American Constitutional Law, 42 Harv. L. Rev. 149, 365 (1928). Blackstone, whose Commentaries were equally authoritative to late-eighteenth- and nineteenth-century Americans, treated the "absolute liberties" of Englishmen — life, liberty, and property — as always subject to limitation "by the laws of the land," which Blackstone regarded not as a substantive limit upon legislators but as a check "upon the arbitrary will of any judge." 1 Blackstone, Commentaries on the Laws of England *130-138 (1765). Thus, in the view of one modern commentator, the expansive reading of liberty in the *Slaughter-House* dissents and in *Allgeyer* was "not what was provided in Magna Charta" but was a "momentous and latitudinous interpretation" that amounted to "bald fiat."

Currie, The Constitution in the Supreme Court: The Second Century 45 (1990).

Does this cast doubt on the legitimacy of substantive due process? Does it make any difference whether the values protected by substantive due process serve economic or personal autonomy ends?

3. Are Economic Liberties Not Constitutionally Fundamental? Assuming that due process does impose limits on the substance of government action, should it protect only *constitutionally fundamental* liberties, a category that does not include economic liberties?

The text of the due process clause protects liberty—without qualification. Because there is no textual support for reading "constitutionally fundamental" into the document as a device to expand or limit constitutionally protected liberty, the argument must be grounded in some other source. History is not much help: The great legal historian Charles Warren argued persuasively that the English antecedents to the due process clause treated liberty as consisting only of freedom from physical restraint. See Warren, The New "Liberty" under the Fourteenth Amendment, 39 Harv. L. Rev. 431 (1926). Some other source must be relied upon to expand the concept of liberty. Perhaps that source is the recurring American idea of resort to some amorphous "higher law" as a restraint upon government action. The problem with this, of course, is that the scope of an unwritten higher law is potentially boundless. Legislators are the democratically elected representatives of the people; federal judges are not. If judges can veto legislation in the name of unwritten higher laws, the premise of representative democracy may no longer be viable.

Perhaps a way out of this dilemma is to treat the "liberty" protected by *Lochner* as property rather than liberty. Coppage v. Kansas, 236 U.S. 1 (1915), did so, concluding that the right of "personal property [includes] the right to make contracts." (The *Coppage* Court struck down a Kansas law prohibiting employment contracts that contained an employee promise not to join a labor union.) This gambit enables the modern version of substantive due process to protect personal liberties lacking property attributes (e.g., abortion) while rejecting like protection to property rights. But for this to be tenable there must be convincing reasons why property is the poor relation in the due process trinity.

Is property less significant or important than liberty? Acquisition of property is the key to economic security, a form of liberty much desired. Is there reason to think that popular majorities are less likely to oppress property than liberty? Consider wealth redistribution measures like graduated income and inheritance taxes, rent controls, or income tax rates of 100 percent. If legislatively mandated wealth redistribution is not "oppressive" to property, is legislatively prohibited abortion also not "oppressive" to liberty?

One reply might be that the concept of property is more socially contingent than that of liberty, and thus less deserving of special judicial protection from popular majorities. But consider the socially contingent relationship between liberty and a woman's control over her reproduction processes in the United States and in other cultures, particularly in the Islamic world and China. Perhaps the relevant comparison is within a culture, and in America the concept of property may be more contingent upon shifting societal perceptions than is liberty. But ponder the rapidly evolving attitudes in the United States to the claimed right of physician-assisted suicide or same-sex marriage.

Finally, what is to be made of the fact that the Constitution explicitly protects property by the takings clause[6] and the contracts clause?[7] Do these clauses mean that these are the only property rights to which the Constitution provides substantive protection, thus excluding unwritten property interests? If so, why is it legitimate to read unwritten liberties into the Constitution, even though the Constitution specifies protected liberties? Or do these clauses suggest that the Founders took property rights particularly seriously and intended that, as understood under the common law, property rights were to receive special constitutional protection?

4. Was the Court's Standard of Review Too Strict? Did the *Lochner* Court apply a standard of review that was too strict? First, was the Court's conception of the legitimate ends of government too narrow? Today we accept regulation of the conditions of employment—including hours and wages—as a permissible government objective. Second, even assuming that such labor regulation is illegitimate, should the Court have been more deferential to the state's choice of means to accomplish its legitimate objectives?

The first objection is related to the contention that property rights deserve less judicial protection than other forms of liberty. Perhaps the rationale for the New York legislation was that political power was needed to offset the inequality of power between employers (who would offer employment only on the condition that the employee work long hours) and employees (who might desire shorter working hours). But consider the possibility that the only legitimate goal of government is to increase and protect the good of the entire society, and that this occurs by protecting the individual rights of every member of the society. By this reckoning, redistributionist measures that are designed to benefit some people at the expense of others are never legitimate, because they are not directed toward enhancing the good of everyone. On the other hand, many people argue that such redistribution does in fact benefit everyone by reducing levels of social and economic tension that can rupture society. For example, the marginal utility of the last dollar of wealth to a billionaire is theoretically less than the marginal utility of that dollar delivered by forced transfer to an impoverished parent. Unhappily, there is no foolproof way to measure

6. U.S. Const. Amend. 5: "[N]or shall private property be taken for public use without just compensation."

7. U.S. Const. Art. I, §10, cl. 1: "No State shall . . . pass any . . . Law impairing the Obligation of Contracts."

marginal utility; thus, these arguments can be engaged only at the level of theory.

This debate is echoed in the modern theory of "public choice," which argues that many political outcomes are merely the product of superior organized power of special interest groups. For example, when benefits are concentrated and costs diffused, the putative beneficiaries will organize to capture the political process because there is little incentive for diffuse cost-bearers to organize opposition to the measure. Consider the possibility that the statute at issue in *Lochner* represented an organizational triumph of labor unions at the expense of bread consumers and unorganized immigrant laborers eager to take bakery jobs at long hours. But defenders of redistributionist measures would contend that, even so, this forced redistribution increased the overall good of society. Consider the possibility that all legislation is nothing more than a struggle between special interest groups, that there is no such thing as the "public interest" as separate from these contending special interests, and that Justice Holmes was correct in stating that due process cannot be used "to prevent the natural outcome of a dominant opinion." If Holmes was correct in *Lochner*, does the same hold true in the context of abortion regulation?

The second objection admits that property (and, presumably, liberty) may be regulated to achieve legitimate government objectives. The question is: What degree of deference should courts accord to legislative or executive judgments embodied in such regulation? The modern law of substantive due process has been preoccupied with this issue. Substantive infringements of constitutionally fundamental liberties (a category exclusively reserved for judicial definition) are presumptively void; the burden is on the government to prove that the infringement is necessary to achieve some compelling government objective. Substantive infringements of nonfundamental liberties (another category determined by judges and including most property rights) are presumptively valid; the burden is on the challenger to prove that the infringement is not rationally related to some legitimate government objective.

Thus, courts defer to legislative judgments about infringements of liberties that courts think are not fundamental but show no deference to legislative judgments about infringements of liberties that courts regard as constitutionally fundamental. These dramatically different levels of review invite the question of why courts should exhibit differing degrees of deference to legislative invasions of different types of personal liberty. This is a central question posed by modern substantive due process.

Note: The *Lochner* Era: Hardly a Monolithic Laissez-Faire Jurisprudence

Poorly informed constitutional lawyers sometimes suppose that the *Lochner* era—the six decades or so from roughly 1880 to 1940—was a period of implacable hostility to economic regulation. Yet, in the quarter century preceding *Lochner*, the Court upheld regulations with a legitimate public interest as their objective (e.g., Munn v. Illinois) while voiding those laws lacking such an objective (e.g., *Lochner*). This process continued after *Lochner*.

Adair v. United States, 208 U.S. 161 (1908), struck down a federal law that prohibited interstate railroads from enforcing contracts that required their employees, as a condition of employment, to promise not to join a labor union. Government intervention to assure workers unfettered ability to organize for collective bargaining purposes was perceived as a form of private benefit—a skewing of common law contractual freedom to benefit one side of the bargaining duo. Thus, in Coppage v. Kansas, 236 U.S. 1 (1915), the Court struck down a Kansas statute prohibiting all employers from using such contracts.[8]

Muller v. Oregon, 208 U.S. 412 (1908), however, upheld an Oregon law that limited women to no more than 10 hours of labor a day. Liberty of contract "is not absolute," said the Court. The Court justified a law that would be void as applied to men by citing the "inherent difference between the two sexes," the public interest in "healthy mothers," and the need to "protect women." In Bunting v. Oregon, 243 U.S. 426 (1917), the Court upheld an Oregon law that required overtime pay after 10 hours of labor in a day, and also barred *anyone* from working more than 13 hours in a day. Inexplicably, the Court did not mention *Lochner*. The cryptic opinion left many guessing whether *Lochner* had been silently overruled or whether there was an unarticulated public benefit in restricting labor to 13 hours daily that was not present in New York's 10-hour-day regulation.

However, in Adkins v. Children's Hospital, 261 U.S. 525 (1923), the Court struck down a D.C. law prescribing minimum wages for women. The Court seized on the Nineteenth Amendment as proof that women were now equal to men, and thus no longer warranted special legal treatment. A minimum wage, said the Court, was simply "a naked, arbitrary exercise" in political power designed to benefit some women at the expense of their employers and other women who would lose their jobs because their continued employment at the specified minimum wage was no longer economically viable.

The *Lochner* era came to an end with the Great Depression and Franklin Roosevelt's New Deal. The Court did not abandon its focus on the distinction between economic regulations of public benefit and those of only private benefit. Instead, the Court simply widened the scope of legitimate government objectives and employed a more deferential standard of review to measure the connection between legislative means and ends.

Nebbia v. New York, 291 U.S. 502 (1934), exemplifies this shift. New York sought to stabilize milk prices to preserve an adequate milk supply in the midst of a ruinous economic depression that threatened to drive many

8. *Adair* and *Coppage* were overturned by Phelps Dodge v. NLRB, 313 U.S. 177 (1941).

dairy farmers into extinction by setting nine cents as the retail price of a quart of milk. Nebbia, a retail grocer in Rochester convicted of selling milk for less than the fixed price, appealed on the ground that New York could not constitutionally fix milk prices. The Court, 5-4, upheld the regulation, reasoning that "the means selected [had] a real and substantial relation to the object sought to be attained." A state, said the Court, "is free to adopt whatever economic policy may reasonably be deemed to promote public welfare, and to enforce that policy by legislation adapted to its purpose." The Court did not so much reject *Lochner* as apply it in a far more deferential fashion. In Sunshine Coal Co. v. Adkins, 310 U.S. 381 (1940), the Court curtly rejected a due process challenge to a federal price-fix of coal: "Price control is one of the means available [to] protect and [promote] the welfare of the economy."

West Coast Hotel Co. v. Parrish, 300 U.S. 379 (1937), confirmed the shift in attitude. After Washington enacted a minimum-wage law for women, the West Coast Hotel owner contended that the law violated substantive due process because it infringed upon liberty of contract. Even though the Court had struck down an almost identical such law in Adkins v. Children's Hospital, the Court (5-4) upheld Washington's law and overruled Adkins v. Children's Hospital. The law was not "arbitrary or capricious" because Washington "was clearly entitled to consider the situation of women in employment, the fact that they are in the class receiving the least pay, that their bargaining power is relatively weak, and that they are the ready victims of those who would take advantage of their necessitous circumstances." Moreover, the law reasonably furthered a legitimate public purpose because "the denial of a living wage is not only detrimental to [worker] health and well being but casts a direct burden for their support upon the community." Thus, what had been seen as a redistributionist statute serving only private interests was reconceived as providing a public benefit.

The Court's position in *Nebbia* and *West Coast Hotel* proved to be transitional. Very quickly the Court moved toward a position of extreme deference to economic regulation. Perhaps this was inevitable once the Court began to see a public benefit in legislation designed to redistribute economic benefits from one segment of the polity to another. Emblematic of the new view was United States v. Carolene Products, 304 U.S. 144 (1938). Federal law banned the interstate shipment of "filled milk"—milk from which the butterfat has been removed and vegetable oils substituted. Congress had concluded that the substitution of vegetable oil for animal fat resulted in "undernourishment," although in fact the statute represented a triumph of the dairy industry over vegetable oil processors. Just as margarine is cheaper than butter, filled milk was cheaper, albeit perhaps less tasty. The Court upheld the law against a Fifth Amendment due process challenge. The congressional findings of fact were not necessary because "the existence of facts supporting the legislative judgment is to be presumed." More precisely, "regulatory legislation affecting ordinary commercial transactions" is constitutional unless the challenger proves that there is no rational basis for the legislation.

Today, laws that regulate commercial, economic, or business relations are upheld against due process challenges so long as there is some conceivable basis to conclude that the law bears a rational relationship to a constitutionally permissible objective of the government, and economic regulation by itself is a legitimate government objective. On this doctrinal evolution, see also Cushman, Rethinking the New Deal Court: The Structure of a Constitutional Revolution (1998); Cushman, Lost Fidelities, 41 Wm. & Mary L. Rev. 95 (1999).

By the early 1960s, substantive due process was so eroded that it was thought to be extinct. A classic expression of its death is contained in Ferguson v. Skrupa, 372 U.S. 726 (1963). Kansas made it unlawful for anyone except lawyers to carry on the business of debt adjusting. Skrupa, a nonlawyer debt adjuster, was thus barred from his business. The Court upheld the law: "There was a time when the Due Process Clause was used by this Court to strike down laws which were thought unreasonable, [unwise] or incompatible with some particular economic or social philosophy. [Substantive due process] has long since been discarded." Two years later, the Court would revive substantive due process in the name of personal privacy or autonomy.

3. The Modern Revival: "Privacy" Rights

Even though the Court has repudiated substantive due process as a device to protect unenumerated economic rights, it has displayed a willingness to use the due process clauses to strike down laws that impinge on what the Court thinks are fundamental unwritten noneconomic rights. The all-purpose rubric to describe these rights is "privacy," but that term is a bit of a misnomer. Rather, the Court uses the due process clauses to protect an ill-defined cluster of noneconomic personal interests that the Court thinks are critical to human autonomy.

The modern revival of substantive due process is not so much a resurrection as a resuscitation. In the heyday of the *Lochner* era, the Court did not hesitate to use due process to protect a variety of noneconomic liberties from government invasion. Two of those early cases, remnants of a discarded tradition, survive as foundation stones in the modern edifice of substantive due process. A third case, decided under the equal protection clause but invoking the logic of substantive due process, was also pivotal in the evolution of modern substantive due process.

Meyer v. Nebraska, 262 U.S. 390 (1923). Meyer was convicted of the crime of teaching German to children. The Court reversed his conviction, opining that the substantive "liberty" protected by due process included the right "to acquire useful knowledge, to marry, establish a home and bring up children, [and] generally to enjoy those privileges long recognized at common law as essential to the orderly pursuit of happiness by free men." Even so, the Court intimated that the law might have been upheld had Nebraska offered a convincing justification for its necessity.

Pierce v. Society of Sisters, 268 U.S. 510 (1925). Oregon enacted a law requiring all children to attend public schools. Parochial and private schools, together with students at such schools and their parents, challenged the validity of the law. A unanimous Court invalidated the law, finding that Oregon had shown no justification for its interference "with the liberty of parents and guardians to direct the upbringing and education of children under their control."

Skinner v. Oklahoma, 316 U.S. 535 (1942). Oklahoma mandated sterilization of people thrice convicted of felonies involving moral turpitude, which meant that repeat white-collar criminals were not subject to sterilization but recidivist chicken thieves such as Skinner were so subject. The Court emphasized that the law "involves one of the basic civil rights of man. Marriage and procreation are fundamental to the very existence and survival of the race." Application of the law would have "forever deprived [Skinner] of a basic liberty." The Court stated that these factors were not raised "to reexamine the scope of the police power," but merely "in emphasis" of the Court's application of strict scrutiny. Thus, the Court tried to avoid any taint of *Lochner* by denying that Skinner's fundamental liberty interest in procreation was a basis for curbing Oklahoma's police power, but simultaneously relied on this fundamental liberty to apply strict scrutiny. It is telling that later Courts invoke *Skinner* in support of the modern version of substantive due process.

Contemporary substantive due process proceeds on two tracks. Courts first determine whether a claimed right is a fundamental liberty. If so, a law infringing upon the right will be subjected to strict scrutiny; otherwise the law is subject only to minimal scrutiny. Under strict scrutiny, the law is presumed void: The government must prove that the infringement is necessary to achieve a compelling government objective. Under minimal scrutiny, the law is presumed valid: The challenger must prove that the law is not rationally related to a legitimate state interest. Thus, the level of judicial scrutiny turns on whether the right is fundamental, and the challenger of the law's validity has the burden of proving that the claimed right is fundamental. Although that is the doctrinal formula, pay attention to deviations from this script as you read the following cases. Why does the Court sometimes use less than strict scrutiny to assess the legitimacy of government interference with fundamental liberties? Is there a category of quasi-fundamental liberties? The Court does not say so. When you finish the chapter, ask yourself whether the doctrine is sound in its actual application. Is the Court doing something other than what it says it is doing? If so, what is it actually doing?

Recall that the issue of "fundamentality" was a central focus of selective incorporation. Incorporation of Bill of Rights guarantees into the due process clause of the Fourteenth Amendment is another form of substantive due process. Only those rights regarded as fundamental are entitled to be incorporated. The major difference between substantive due process as a whole and selective incorporation is that selective incorporation is more bounded. Only the Bill of Rights guarantees are eligible for inclusion into Fourteenth Amendment due process, while substantive due process writ large opens the door to judicial embrace of all manner of possible fundamental rights. In reading the following cases, be attentive to the devices the Court uses to identify which unwritten liberties are fundamental.

a. Origins: Contraceptive Use

≡≡≡ ### *Griswold v. Connecticut*
381 U.S. 479 (1965)

JUSTICE DOUGLAS delivered the opinion of the Court.

Griswold, [a Planned Parenthood official, and] Buxton, [a physician] gave information, instruction, and medical advice to *married persons* as to the means of preventing conception. [Connecticut made it a crime to "use any drug, medicinal article or instrument for the purpose of preventing conception" and imposed equal criminal penalties on "[a]ny person who assists, abets, counsels, causes, hires or commands another" to use a contraceptive device.] The appellants were found guilty as accessories and fined $100 each. [The Connecticut Supreme Court of Errors affirmed the convictions.]

We . . . are met with a wide range of questions that implicate the Due Process Clause of the Fourteenth Amendment. Overtones of some arguments suggest that Lochner v. New York should be our guide. But we decline that [invitation]. We do not sit as a super-legislature to determine the wisdom, need, and propriety of laws that touch economic problems, business affairs, or social conditions. This law, however, operates directly on an intimate relation of husband and wife and their physician's role in one aspect of that relation. The association of people is not mentioned in the Constitution nor in the Bill of Rights. The right to educate a child in a school of the parents' choice—whether public or private or parochial—is also not mentioned. Nor is the right to study any particular subject or any foreign language. Yet the First Amendment has been construed to include . . . those rights.

[The] right of freedom of speech and press includes not only the right to utter or to print, but the right to distribute, the right to receive, the right to read and freedom of inquiry, freedom of thought, and freedom to teach. . . . [Similarly, while association] is not expressly included in the First Amendment its existence is necessary in making the express guarantees fully meaningful. . . .

[S]pecific guarantees in the Bill of Rights have penumbras, formed by emanations from those guarantees that help give them life and substance. Various guarantees create zones of privacy. The right of association contained in the penumbra of the First Amendment is [one]. The Third Amendment in its prohibition against the quartering of soldiers "in any house" in time of peace without the consent of the owner is another facet of that privacy. The

Fourth Amendment explicitly affirms the "right of the people to be secure in their persons, houses, papers, and effects, against unreasonable searches and seizures." The Fifth Amendment in its Self-Incrimination Clause enables the citizen to create a zone of privacy which government may not force him to surrender to his detriment. The Ninth Amendment provides: "The enumeration in the Constitution, of certain rights, shall not be construed to deny or disparage others retained by the people." The Fourth and Fifth Amendments [protect] against all governmental invasions "of the sanctity of a man's home and the privacies of life." We recently referred [to] the Fourth Amendment as creating a "right to privacy, no less important than any other right carefully and particularly reserved to the people." . . .

The present case, then, concerns a relationship lying within the zone of privacy created by several fundamental constitutional guarantees. And it concerns a law which, in forbidding the *use* of contraceptives rather than regulating their manufacture or sale, seeks to achieve its goals by means having a maximum destructive impact upon that relationship. Such a law cannot stand in light of the familiar principle [that] a "governmental purpose to control or prevent activities constitutionally subject to state regulation may not be achieved by means which sweep unnecessarily broadly and thereby invade the area of protected freedoms." Would we allow the police to search the sacred precincts of marital bedrooms for telltale signs of the use of contraceptives? The very idea is repulsive to the notions of privacy surrounding the marriage relationship.

We deal with a right of privacy older than the Bill of Rights. . . . Marriage is . . . an association that promotes a way of life, not causes; a harmony in living, not political faiths; a bilateral loyalty, not commercial or social projects. . . . Reversed.

JUSTICE GOLDBERG, joined by CHIEF JUSTICE WARREN and JUSTICE BRENNAN, concurring.

[T]he concept of liberty protects those personal rights that are fundamental, and is not confined to the specific terms of the Bill of Rights. My conclusion that the concept of liberty [embraces] the right of marital privacy though that right is not mentioned explicitly in the Constitution is supported both by numerous decisions of this Court . . . and by the language and history of the Ninth Amendment, [which] reveal that the Framers of the Constitution believed that there are additional fundamental rights, protected from governmental infringement, which exist alongside those fundamental rights specifically mentioned in the first eight constitutional amendments.

The Ninth Amendment [was] proffered to quiet expressed fears that a bill of specifically enumerated rights could not be sufficiently broad to cover all essential rights and that the specific mention of certain rights would be interpreted as a denial that others were protected. [Statements] of Madison and [Justice] Story make clear that the Framers did not intend that the first eight amendments be construed to exhaust the basic and fundamental rights which the Constitution guaranteed to the people. While this Court has had little occasion to interpret the Ninth Amendment, "it cannot be presumed that any clause in the constitution is intended to be without effect." [To] hold that a right so basic and fundamental and so deep-rooted in our society as the right of privacy in marriage may be infringed because that right is not guaranteed in so many words by the first eight amendments to the Constitution is to ignore the Ninth Amendment and to give it no effect whatsoever. [I] do not mean to imply that the Ninth Amendment is applied against the States by the Fourteenth. Nor do I mean to state that the Ninth Amendment constitutes an independent source of rights protected from infringement by either the States or the Federal Government. Rather, the Ninth Amendment shows a belief of the Constitution's authors that fundamental rights exist that are not expressly enumerated in the first eight amendments and an intent that the list of rights included there not be deemed exhaustive. . . . [The] Ninth Amendment simply lends strong support to the view that the "liberty" protected by the Fifth and Fourteenth Amendments from infringement by the Federal Government or the States is not restricted to rights specifically mentioned in the first eight amendments.

In determining which rights are fundamental, judges . . . must look to the "traditions and [collective] conscience of our people" to determine whether a principle is "so rooted [there] as to be ranked as fundamental." . . . Although the Constitution does not speak in so many words of the right of privacy in marriage, I cannot believe that it offers these fundamental rights no protection. The fact that no particular provision of the Constitution explicitly forbids the State from disrupting the traditional relation of the family—a relation as old and as fundamental as our entire civilization—surely does not show that the Government was meant to have the power to do so. [A]bsent a showing of a compelling subordinating state interest, [the government] could not decree that all husbands and wives must be sterilized after two children have been born to them. Yet by [the dissenters'] reasoning such an invasion of marital privacy would not be subject to constitutional challenge because, while it might be "silly," no provision of the Constitution specifically prevents the Government from curtailing the marital right to bear children and raise a family. . . .

In a long series of cases this Court has held that where fundamental personal liberties are involved, they may not be abridged by the States simply on a showing that a regulatory statute has some rational relationship to the effectuation of a proper state purpose. "Where there is a significant encroachment upon personal liberty, the State may prevail only upon showing a subordinating interest which is compelling." The law must be shown "necessary, and not merely rationally related, to the accomplishment of a permissible state policy."

[Connecticut] argues that there is some rational relation between this statute and what is admittedly a legitimate subject of state concern—the discouraging of extra-marital relations. It says that preventing the use of birth-control devices by married persons helps prevent the indulgence by some in such extra-marital relations. The rationality of this justification is dubious, particularly in light of the admitted widespread availability to all persons [in] Connecticut, unmarried as well as married, of birth-control devices for the prevention of disease, as distinguished from the prevention of conception. But, in any event, it is clear that the state interest in safeguarding marital fidelity can be served by a [more] tailored statute, which does not, like the present one, sweep unnecessarily broadly, reaching far beyond the evil sought to be dealt with and intruding upon the privacy of all married couples. [Connecticut] does have statutes, the constitutionality of which is beyond doubt, which prohibit adultery and fornication. These statutes demonstrate that means for achieving the same basic purpose of protecting marital fidelity are available to Connecticut without the need to "invade the area of protected freedoms."

[T]he Court's holding today [in] no way interferes with a State's proper regulation of sexual promiscuity or misconduct. "Adultery, homosexuality and the like are sexual intimacies which the State forbids [but] the intimacy of husband and wife is necessarily an essential and accepted feature of the institution of marriage, an institution which the State not only must allow, but which always and in every age it has fostered and protected."

[The] right of privacy in the marital relation is fundamental and basic—a personal right "retained by the people" within the meaning of the Ninth Amendment. Connecticut cannot constitutionally abridge this fundamental right, which is protected by the Fourteenth Amendment from infringement by the States. . . .

JUSTICE HARLAN, concurring.

I fully agree with the judgment of reversal, but [I am] unable to join the Court's opinion [because it concludes that] the Due Process Clause of the Fourteenth Amendment does not touch this Connecticut statute unless [it] is found to violate some right assured by the letter or penumbra of the Bill of Rights. [In] my view, the proper constitutional inquiry in this case is whether this Connecticut statute infringes the Due Process Clause of the Fourteenth Amendment because [it] violates basic values "implicit in the concept of ordered liberty." For reasons stated at length in my dissenting opinion in Poe v. Ullman[, 367 U.S. 497 (1961)], I believe that it does. While the relevant inquiry may be aided by resort to one or more of the provisions of the Bill of Rights, it is not dependent on them or any of their radiations. The Due Process Clause of the Fourteenth Amendment stands, in my opinion, on its own bottom. . . .

Judicial self-restraint will be achieved in this area, as in other constitutional areas, only by continual insistence upon respect for the teachings of history, solid recognition of the basic values that underlie our society, and wise appreciation of the great roles that the doctrines of federalism and separation of powers have played in establishing and preserving American freedoms.

[In Poe v. Ullman, Justice Harlan dissented from the Court's dismissal of a challenge to the Connecticut statute at issue in *Griswold*. Justice Harlan reached the merits of the statute in his *Poe* dissent, excerpts from which follow.]

[A] statute making it a criminal offense for married couples to use contraceptives is an intolerable and unjustifiable invasion of privacy in the conduct of the most intimate concerns of an individual's personal life. [As this conclusion rests on] no explicit language of the Constitution [I] feel it desirable [to] state the framework of Constitutional principles in which I think the issue must be judged. [It] is not the particular enumeration of rights in the first eight Amendments which spells out the reach of Fourteenth Amendment due process, but rather [those] rights "which [are] *fundamental*; which belong [to] the citizens of all free governments."

Due process has not been reduced to any formula; its content cannot be determined by reference to any code. The best that can be said is that through the course of this Court's decisions it has represented the balance which our Nation, built upon postulates of respect for the liberty of the individual, has struck between that liberty and the demands of organized society. [That balance] is the balance struck by this country, having regard to what history teaches are the traditions from which it developed as well as the traditions from which it broke. That tradition is a living thing. A decision of this Court which radically departs from it could not long survive, while a decision which builds on what has survived is likely to be sound. No formula could serve as a substitute, in this area, for judgment and restraint. [The] "liberty" [protected by due process] is not a series of isolated points pricked out in terms of the [Bill of Rights]. It is a rational continuum which, broadly speaking, includes a freedom from all substantial arbitrary impositions and purposeless restraints, and which also recognizes . . . that certain interests require particularly careful scrutiny of the state needs asserted to justify their abridgment. . . .

The State [asserts] that it is acting to protect the moral welfare of its citizenry. [Society] is not limited in its objects only to the physical well-being of the community, but has traditionally concerned itself with the moral soundness of its people as well. . . . [The] State is asserting the right to enforce its moral judgment by intruding upon the most intimate details of the marital relation with the full power of the criminal law. [The] statute allows the State to enquire into, prove and punish married people for the private use of their marital intimacy. [This] enactment involves what, by common understanding throughout the English-speaking world, must be granted to be a most fundamental aspect of "liberty," the privacy of the home in its most basic sense, and it is this which requires that the statute be subjected to "strict scrutiny." [It] is difficult to imagine what is more private or more intimate than a husband and wife's marital relations. . . .

Of course, "the family [is] not beyond regulation," and it would be an absurdity to suggest either that offenses may not be committed in the bosom of the family or that the home can be made a sanctuary for crime. The right of privacy most manifestly is not an absolute. [I] would not suggest that adultery, homosexuality, fornication and incest are immune from criminal enquiry, however privately practiced. [But] the intimacy of husband and wife is necessarily an essential and accepted feature of the institution of marriage, an institution which the State not only must allow, but which always and in every age it has fostered and protected. It is one thing when the State exerts its power either to forbid extra-marital sexuality altogether, or to say who may marry, but it is quite another when, having acknowledged a marriage and the intimacies inherent in it, it undertakes to regulate by means of the criminal law the details of that intimacy.

[Since] the statute [abridges] important fundamental liberties protected by the Fourteenth Amendment, it will not do to urge in justification of that abridgment simply that the statute is rationally related to the effectuation of a proper state purpose. A closer scrutiny and stronger justification than that are required. Though the State has argued the Constitutional permissibility of the moral judgment underlying this statute, [it has not] even remotely suggest[ed] a justification for the obnoxiously intrusive means it has chosen to effectuate that policy. [The fact that] Connecticut has not [enforced] this [statute] conduces to the inference either that it does not consider the policy of the statute a very important one, or that it does not regard the means it has chosen for its effectuation as appropriate or necessary.

JUSTICE WHITE, concurring.

Surely the right invoked in this case, to be free of regulation of the intimacies of the marriage relationship, "come[s] to this Court with a momentum for respect lacking when appeal is made to liberties which derive merely from shifting economic arrangements."

[The] State claims but one justification for its anti-use statute: [to] serve the State's policy against all forms of promiscuous or illicit sexual relationships, be they premarital or extramarital, concededly a permissible and legitimate legislative goal. [I] wholly fail to see how the ban on the use of contraceptives by married couples in any way reinforces the State's ban on illicit sexual relationships. [Perhaps] the theory is that the flat ban on use prevents married people from possessing contraceptives and without the ready availability of such devices for use in the marital relationship, there will be no or less temptation to use them in extramarital ones. This reasoning rests on the premise that married people will comply with the ban in regard to their marital relationship, notwithstanding total nonenforcement in this context and apparent nonenforcibility, but will not comply with criminal statutes prohibiting extramarital affairs and the anti-use statute in respect to illicit sexual relationships, a premise whose validity has not been demonstrated and whose intrinsic validity is not very evident. [I] find nothing in this record justifying the sweeping scope of this statute, with its telling effect on the freedoms of married persons, and therefore conclude that it deprives such persons of liberty without due process of law.

JUSTICE BLACK, joined by JUSTICE STEWART, dissenting.

. . . I . . . add that the law is every bit as offensive to me as it is to my [Brethren]. . . . [I] get nowhere in this case by talk about a constitutional "right of privacy" as an emanation from one or more constitutional provisions. I like my privacy as well as the next one, but I am nevertheless compelled to admit that government has a right to invade it unless prohibited by some specific constitutional provision. . . .

I discuss the due process and Ninth Amendment arguments together because on analysis they turn out to be the same thing—merely using different words to claim for this Court and the federal judiciary power to invalidate any legislative act which the judges find irrational, unreasonable or offensive. [T]hese formulas based on "natural justice" . . . require judges to determine what is or is not constitutional on the basis of their own appraisal of what laws are unwise or unnecessary. The power to make such decisions is of course that of a legislative body. . . . [M]y Brothers White and Goldberg rely [on] the same natural law due process philosophy found in Lochner v. New York, [a] philosophy which many later opinions repudiated, and which I cannot accept. [My] Brother Goldberg has adopted the recent discovery that the Ninth Amendment as well as the Due Process Clause can be used by this Court as authority to strike down all state legislation which this Court thinks violates "fundamental principles of liberty and justice," or is contrary to the "traditions and [collective] conscience of our people." He also states [that] in making decisions on this basis judges will not consider "their personal and private notions." One may ask how they can avoid considering them.

[Many] good and able men have eloquently spoken and written [about] the duty of this Court to keep the Constitution in tune with the times. [I] reject that philosophy. The Constitution makers knew the need for change and provided for it [through the amendment process]. I cannot rely on the Due Process Clause or the Ninth Amendment or any mysterious and uncertain natural law concept as a reason for striking down this state law. . . .

Justice Stewart, joined by Justice Black, dissenting.

I think this is an uncommonly silly law. [But] we are not asked in this case to say whether we think this law is unwise, or even asinine. We are asked to hold that it violates the United States Constitution. And that I cannot do.

In the course of its opinion the Court refers to no less than six Amendments to the Constitution: the First, the Third, the Fourth, the Fifth, the Ninth, and the Fourteenth. But the Court does not say which of these Amendments, if any, it thinks is infringed by this Connecticut law. [As] to the First, Third, Fourth, and Fifth Amendments, I can find nothing in any of them to invalidate this Connecticut law, even assuming that all those Amendments are fully applicable against the States. [To] say that the Ninth Amendment has anything to do with this case is to turn somersaults with history. The Ninth Amendment, like its companion the Tenth, [was] framed by James Madison and adopted by the States simply to make clear that the adoption of the Bill of Rights did not alter the plan that the *Federal* Government was to be a government of express and limited [powers].

What provision of the Constitution, then, does make this state law invalid? The Court says it is the right of privacy "created by several fundamental constitutional guarantees." With all deference, I can find no such general right of privacy in the Bill of Rights, in any other part of the Constitution, or in any case ever before decided by this Court. [At] the oral argument [we] were told that the Connecticut law does not "conform to current community standards." But it is not the function of this Court to decide cases on the basis of community standards. It is the essence of judicial duty to subordinate our own personal views, our own ideas of what legislation is wise and what is not.

If, as I should surely hope, the law before us does not reflect the standards of the people of Connecticut, [they] can freely exercise [their] rights to persuade their elected representatives to repeal it. That is the constitutional way to take this law off the books.

NOTES

1. Sources of the "Privacy" Right. Where is the privacy right grounded? Consider the following possibilities.

a. Incorporated Bill of Rights guarantees. Justice Douglas's majority opinion invokes the metaphor of penumbral shadows cast by the Bill of Rights to connect the unwritten privacy right to specific constitutional text that had already been incorporated into the Fourteenth Amendment's due process clause. A problem with this reading is that some of the rights mentioned by Douglas have never been incorporated (e.g., the Third Amendment), and others had not been incorporated at the time *Griswold* was decided (e.g., the self-incrimination privilege). Perhaps Douglas's point was that the protection of a specific form of privacy against state invasion implied a general protection of privacy. But this argument cuts two ways. It may as easily be said that the Framers knew how to protect privacy and chose to protect only certain discrete and defined aspects of personal privacy.

b. Implied from tradition and history. Justice Douglas noted that the Court was "deal[ing] with a right of privacy older than the Bill of Rights." Did he mean to invoke the cultural tradition of marriage and the cultural presumption that consensual sexual relations within marriage were entirely private as sources of the privacy right protected in *Griswold*? If so, what part of constitutional text supports this claim? Are Justice Harlan's arguments, focusing on "the balance struck by this country, having regard to what history teaches are the traditions from which it developed as well as the traditions from which it broke," more persuasive? If cultural traditions provide substance to unwritten constitutional liberties, how are we to divine those traditions?

Consider in this regard the following colloquy between Justices Scalia and Brennan in Michael H. v. Gerald D., 491 U.S. 110 (1989). At issue was the validity of a California law providing that a child born to a married woman living with her husband is conclusively presumed to be a child of the marriage. Victoria was born to Carole and Gerald D., a married couple, but scientific tests established a better than 98 percent probability that Michael H., Carole's sometime lover, was Victoria's father. California courts rejected Michael's attempt to establish himself as Victoria's father, relying upon the statutory presumption to treat Michael as a legal stranger to Victoria. Michael claimed that the statute was an unjustified infringement upon his fundamental liberty to maintain a parental relationship with his natural child and thus violated the Fourteenth Amendment's due process clause. The Court rejected his claim, finding that an adulterous father has no fundamental liberty interest in creating or maintaining a parental relationship with a child born into another's marriage.

Writing for a four-justice plurality, Justice Scalia relied on a deeply rooted tradition that the "presumption of legitimacy was a fundamental principle of the common law." He noted an absence of authority "addressing specifically the power of the natural father to assert parental rights over a child born into a woman's existing marriage with another man," and observed that "[s]ince it is Michael's burden to establish that such a power [is] so deeply embedded within our traditions as to be a fundamental right, the lack of evidence alone might defeat his case. But the evidence shows that even in modern times [the] ability of a person in Michael's position to claim paternity has not been generally acknowledged." In a footnote, Justice Scalia replied to Justice Brennan's criticisms of his method of examining claims of fundamental rights:

> Justice Brennan criticizes our methodology in using historical traditions specifically relating to the rights of an adulterous natural father, rather than inquiring more generally "whether parenthood is an interest that historically has received our attention and protection." [We] do not understand why, having rejected our focus upon the societal tradition regarding the natural father's rights vis-à-vis a child whose mother is married to another man, Justice Brennan would choose to focus instead upon "parenthood." Why should the relevant category not be even more general—perhaps "family relationships"; or "personal relationships"; or even "emotional attachments in general"? Though the dissent has no basis for the level of generality it would select, we do: We refer to the most specific level at which a relevant tradition protecting, or denying protection to, the asserted right can be identified. If, for example, there were no societal tradition, either way, regarding the rights of the natural father of a child adulterously conceived, we would have to consult, and (if possible) reason from, the traditions regarding natural fathers in general. But there is such a more specific tradition, and it unqualifiedly denies protection to such a parent.

Justice Brennan charged that Justice Scalia's

> [plurality] ignores the kind of society in which our Constitution exists. We are not an assimilative, homogeneous society, but a facilitative, pluralistic one, in which we must be willing to abide someone else's unfamiliar or even repellant practice because the same tolerant impulse protects our own idiosyncracies. [Liberty] must include the freedom not to conform. [The plurality] squashes this freedom by requiring specific approval from history before protecting anything in the name of liberty. [This] is not the living charter that I have taken to be our Constitution; it is instead a stagnant, archaic, hidebound document steeped in the prejudices and superstitions of a time long past.

c. The Ninth Amendment. Justice Douglas mentioned the Ninth Amendment in passing, and Justice Goldberg's concurrence focused on it. Is it a more legitimate source of unwritten rights than due process? The Ninth Amendment was intended to prevent any inference that the federal government possessed powers other than those enumerated in the Constitution, but the Ninth Amendment was also intended to establish that the liberties enumerated in the Constitution are not an exhaustive list of human liberties. See, e.g., I, II The Rights Retained by the People (R. Barnett ed., 1989, 1993).

One way to accommodate both views is to argue, as has legal historian Raoul Berger, that the "rights retained by the people" exist in an area where "Government ought not to act," including judicial enforcement of such rights. By "'retaining' the unenumerated rights, the people reserved to themselves power to add to or subtract from the rights enumerated in the Constitution by the process of amendment." Berger, The Ninth Amendment, 66 Cornell L. Rev. 1 (1980). By this reckoning the Ninth Amendment did not transform unenumerated rights rooted in common law, state constitutional law, and state statutes into federal constitutional rights; it simply left those rights untouched "until modified or eliminated by state enactment, by federal preemption, or by a judicial determination of unconstitutionality." Caplan, The History and Meaning of the Ninth Amendment, 69 Va. L. Rev. 223 (1983).

Another way to accommodate both views of the Ninth Amendment is to argue that, because its intended function of blocking the creation of implied federal powers has failed, it should be read as a source of unwritten liberties that achieve much the same end. When the intended purpose of a charitable gift cannot be accomplished, courts apply the *cy pres* doctrine — they seek to accomplish the donor's intent as nearly as possible. Perhaps the Ninth Amendment should be read to perform a "constitutional *cy pres*" function by curbing federal power through the assertion of unwritten individual liberties rather than by restraining the growth of implied federal powers. See Massey, Silent Rights 97-115 (1995). A different view is expressed in Lash, The Lost History of the Ninth Amendment (2009). Lash argues that the Ninth Amendment requires courts to construe federal powers narrowly in order to preserve the retained rights of the people to govern themselves in their respective states.

2. Scope of the "Privacy" Right. What exactly was the privacy right protected by *Griswold*? The majority opinion and both concurring opinions in *Griswold* emphasize the fact that Connecticut's statute prohibited *married persons* from the *use* of contraceptives. After *Griswold*, could Connecticut ban the sale or distribution of contraceptives to all people, including married persons? Could Connecticut ban the *distribution* of contraceptives to unmarried persons? Could the state ban the *use* of contraceptives by unmarried persons?

In Eisenstadt v. Baird, 405 U.S. 438 (1972), the Court struck down on equal protection grounds a Massachusetts prohibition on the distribution of contraceptives to unmarried persons. The Court ruled that the law was not rationally connected to the legitimate objective of deterring premarital sexual intercourse because it "would [be] unreasonable to assume that Massachusetts has prescribed pregnancy and the birth of an unwanted child as punishment for fornication, [a] misdemeanor." The Court rejected the state's assertion that a "prohibition on contraception" was legitimate:

[W]hatever the rights of the individual to access to contraceptives may be, the rights must be the same for the unmarried and the married alike. . . . It is true that in *Griswold* the right of privacy in question inhered in the marital relationship. Yet the marital couple is not an independent entity with a mind and heart of its own, but an association of two individuals each with a separate intellectual and emotional makeup. If the right of privacy means anything, it is the right of the *individual*, married or single, to be free from unwarranted governmental intrusion into matters so fundamentally affecting a person as the decision whether to bear or beget a child.

See also Carey v. Population Services International, 431 U.S. 678 (1977), in which the Court voided a New York law prohibiting anyone but a licensed pharmacist from dispensing contraceptives.

b. Abortion

Roe v. Wade
410 U.S. 113 (1973)

Justice Blackmun delivered the opinion of the Court.

This [appeal presents] constitutional challenges to state criminal abortion legislation. The Texas statutes under attack [make procuring an abortion a crime except when performed upon medical advice to save the life of the pregnant woman]. Roe [claimed that] the Texas statutes . . . improperly invade [her] right [as a] pregnant woman to choose to terminate her pregnancy. Appellant would discover this right in the concept of personal "liberty" embodied in the Fourteenth Amendment's Due Process Clause; or in personal, marital, familial, and sexual privacy said to be protected by the Bill of Rights or its penumbras; or among those rights reserved to the people by the Ninth Amendment.

[The] restrictive criminal abortion laws in effect in a majority of States today are of relatively recent vintage, [enacted mostly] in the latter half of the 19th century. . . . [At] common law, abortion performed *before* "quickening" — the first recognizable movement of the fetus in utero . . . — was not an indictable offense. [C]ommon-law precedents [show] that even post-quickening abortion was never established as a common-law crime.

[The] law in effect in all but a few States until mid-19th century was the preexisting English common law. Connecticut, the first State to enact abortion legislation, adopted in 1821 [a law that prohibited abortion upon] a woman "quick with child." [At] common law, at the time of the adoption of our Constitution, and throughout the major portion of the 19th century, [a] woman enjoyed a substantially broader right to terminate a pregnancy than she does in most States today.

. . . When most criminal abortion laws were first enacted, the procedure was [hazardous]. Thus, it has been argued that a State's real concern in enacting a criminal abortion law was to protect the pregnant [woman]. Modern medical techniques have altered this situation. [Abortion prior] to the end of the first trimester [is] now relatively safe. [Of course, the] State has a legitimate interest in seeing to it that abortion, like any other medical procedure, is performed under circumstances that insure maximum safety for the patient [and has] a definite interest in protecting the woman's own health and safety when an abortion is proposed at a late stage of pregnancy. [Another] reason is the State's interest [in] protecting prenatal life. Some of the argument for this justification rests on the theory that a new human life is present from the moment of conception. [But] recognition may [also] be given to the less rigid claim that [since] *potential* life is involved the State may assert interests beyond the protection of the pregnant woman alone.

[The] Constitution does not explicitly mention any right of privacy [but] the Court has recognized that a . . . guarantee of certain areas or zones of privacy does exist under the Constitution. [O]nly personal rights that can be deemed "fundamental" or "implicit in the concept of ordered liberty" are included in this guarantee of personal privacy. [It is] clear that the right has some extension to activities relating to marriage, procreation, contraception, family relationships, and child rearing and education.

This right of privacy, whether it be founded in the Fourteenth Amendment's concept of personal [liberty], as we feel it is, [or] in the Ninth Amendment, is broad enough to encompass a woman's decision whether or not to terminate her pregnancy. . . . [Roe argues] that the woman's right is absolute and that she is entitled to terminate her pregnancy at whatever time, in whatever way, and for whatever reason she alone chooses. With this we do not agree. [Where] certain "fundamental rights" are involved, the Court has held that regulation limiting these rights may be justified only by a "compelling state interest," and that legislative enactments must be narrowly drawn to express only the legitimate state interests at stake.

[Texas] argues that the State's determination to recognize and protect prenatal life from and after conception constitutes a compelling state interest [because] the fetus is a "person" within the language and meaning of the Fourteenth Amendment. [If so, Roe's case] collapses, for the fetus's right to life would then be guaranteed specifically by the Amendment. [The] Constitution does not define "person" [and the Constitution's] use of the word is such that it has application only postnatally. [All] this, together with our observation [that] throughout the major portion of the 19th century prevailing legal abortion practices were far freer than they are today, persuades us that the word "person," as used in the Fourteenth Amendment, does not include the unborn. . . .

The pregnant woman . . . carries an embryo and, later, a [fetus]. [It] is reasonable [for] a State to decide that at some point in time another interest, that of health of the mother or that of potential human life, becomes significantly involved. . . .

Texas urges that, apart from the Fourteenth Amendment, life begins at conception and is present throughout pregnancy, and that, therefore, the

State has a compelling interest in protecting that life from and after conception. We need not resolve the difficult question of when life begins. . . . [W]e do not agree that, by adopting one theory of life, Texas may override the rights of the pregnant woman that are at stake. We repeat, however, that the State does have an important and legitimate interest in preserving and protecting the health of the pregnant woman [and] that it has still *another* important and legitimate interest in protecting the potentiality of human life. These interests are separate and distinct. Each grows in substantiality as the woman approaches term and, at a point during pregnancy, each becomes "compelling."

[The] State's important and legitimate interest in the health of the mother, the "compelling" point, in the light of present medical knowledge, is at approximately the end of the first trimester. This is so because . . . until the end of the first trimester mortality in abortion may be less than mortality in normal childbirth. It follows that, from and after this point, a State may regulate the abortion procedure to the extent that the regulation reasonably relates to the preservation and protection of maternal health. . . .

[The] State's important and legitimate interest in potential life, the "compelling" point is at viability. This is so because the fetus then presumably has the capability of meaningful life outside the mother's womb. State regulation protective of fetal life after viability thus has both logical and biological justifications. . . . Measured against these standards [the Texas criminal abortion statute] sweeps too broadly [and is unconstitutional].

To summarize and to repeat: . . .

(a) [P]rior to approximately the end of the first trimester the abortion decision and its effectuation must be left to the medical judgment of the pregnant woman's attending physician.

(b) [After] approximately the end of the first trimester, the State, [to promote] the health of the mother, [may] regulate [abortion] in [ways] reasonably related to maternal health.

(c) [S]ubsequent to viability, the State in promoting its interest in the potentiality of human life [may] regulate, and even proscribe, abortion except where it is necessary, in appropriate medical judgment, for the preservation of the life or health of the mother. . . .

JUSTICE STEWART, concurring.

In 1963, this Court, in Ferguson v. Skrupa, purported to sound the death knell for the doctrine of substantive due [process]. Barely two years later, in Griswold v. Connecticut, the Court held a Connecticut birth control law unconstitutional. [*Griswold*] can be rationally understood only as a holding that the Connecticut statute substantively invaded the "liberty" that is protected by the Due Process Clause of the Fourteenth Amendment.

[In *Eisenstadt*] we recognized "the right of the *individual* [to] be free from unwarranted governmental intrusion into matters so fundamentally affecting a person as the decision whether to bear or beget a child." That right necessarily includes the right of a woman to decide whether or not to terminate her pregnancy. [The] Texas abortion statute infringes that right directly. [The] question then becomes whether the state interests advanced to justify this abridgment can survive the "particularly careful scrutiny" that the Fourteenth Amendment here requires. The asserted state interests are protection of the health and safety of the pregnant woman, and protection of the potential future human life within her. These are legitimate objectives [but] the Court today has thoroughly demonstrated that these state interests cannot constitutionally support the broad abridgment of personal liberty worked by the existing Texas law.

JUSTICE WHITE, joined by JUSTICE REHNQUIST, dissenting.

[Nothing] in the language or history of the Constitution [supports] the Court's judgment. The Court simply fashions and announces a new constitutional right [and], with scarcely any reason or authority for its action, invests that right with sufficient substance to override most existing state abortion statutes. The upshot is that the people and the legislatures of the 50 States are constitutionally disentitled to weigh the relative importance of the continued existence and development of the fetus, on the one hand, against a spectrum of possible impacts on the mother, on the other hand. As an exercise of raw judicial power, the Court perhaps has authority to do what it does today; but in my view its judgment is an improvident and extravagant exercise of the power of judicial review. . . .

JUSTICE REHNQUIST, dissenting.

I have difficulty in concluding [that] the right of "privacy" is involved in this case. [The] performance of a medical abortion by a licensed physician on a plaintiff such as Roe [is] not "private" in the ordinary usage of that word. Nor is the "privacy" that the Court finds here even a distant relative of the freedom from searches and seizures protected by the Fourth [Amendment]. If the Court means by the term "privacy" no more than that the claim of a person to be free from unwanted state regulation of consensual transactions may be a form of "liberty" protected by the Fourteenth Amendment, there is no doubt that similar claims have been upheld in our earlier decisions on the basis of that liberty. [Liberty] is not guaranteed absolutely against [deprivation]. The test traditionally applied in the area of social and economic legislation is whether or not a law such as that challenged has a rational relation to a valid state objective. [If] the Texas statute were to prohibit an abortion even where the mother's life is in jeopardy, I have little doubt that such a statute would lack a rational relation to a valid state [objective]. But the Court's sweeping invalidation of any restrictions on abortion during the first trimester is impossible to justify under that standard, and the conscious weighing of competing factors that the Court's opinion apparently substitutes for the established test is far more appropriate to a legislative judgment than to a judicial one. [Adoption] of the compelling state interest standard will inevitably require this Court to examine the legislative policies and pass on the wisdom of these policies in the very process of deciding whether a particular state interest put forward may or may not be "compelling." The decision here to break pregnancy into three distinct terms and to outline the permissible restrictions the State may impose in each one, for example, partakes more of judicial legislation than it does of a determination of the intent of the drafters of the Fourteenth Amendment.

The fact that a majority of the States reflecting, after all, the majority sentiment in those States, have had restrictions on abortions for at least a century is a strong indication, it seems to me, that the asserted right to an abortion is not "so rooted in the traditions and conscience of our people as to be ranked as fundamental." . . .

NOTES

1. The Source of the Abortion Right. Does *Roe* follow ineluctably from *Griswold*? *Griswold*'s invalidation of a ban on the *use* of contraceptives, as distinguished from a distribution ban, was premised on the belief that enforcement of the use ban required invasion of "the sacred precincts of the marital bedroom." That premise is missing in *Roe*. Does this make *Roe* wrong? While there is very little that is "private"—in the *Griswold* sense of the term—in an abortion, prior to *Roe* the Court had protected a wide variety of interests as presumptively immune from government invasion, and many of those interests (e.g., the educational choice interests protected in *Meyer* and *Pierce*) had little if anything to do with conventional privacy. Moreover, *Eisenstadt* had extended *Griswold* beyond the marital community. Was *Roe* thus compelled (or at least permitted) by the totality of the precedents? If *Roe* was the product of precedent, why did Justice Blackmun canvass the history of abortion and abortion regulation so thoroughly? If *Roe* is not driven by precedent, what is its constitutional root? Consider the possibility that the "privacy" cases rest on the "moral fact" that a person belongs to herself, not to someone else or to the state. Abortion restrictions strip a woman of her "bodily self-possession." Pregnancy swells her uterus by up to 1,000 times, increases her pulse, and causes nausea, water retention, weight gain, back pain, and hemorrhoids, to say nothing of the excruciating labor of vaginal delivery or the risks attendant to invasive surgical delivery. Forcing a woman to carry her unwanted pregnancy to term "exert[s] far more profound intrusions into bodily integrity [than] stomach pumping [or] the surgical removal of a bullet from a shoulder," both of which the Court has voided. Estrich and Sullivan, Abortion Politics: Writing for an Audience of One, 138 U. Pa. L. Rev. 119, 125-127 (1989). But by this reckoning would not restrictions upon abortion in the latter part of pregnancy be even more objectionable than those applicable to the first trimester of pregnancy?

Perhaps the issue is more properly seen as one of sex discrimination. Only women need abortions because only women become pregnant. Laws against abortion compel women to carry a fetus to term, thus conscripting their bodies for the service of another. Men are not forced by law to give up their bodies for the service of another, as might be the case if a father was required by law to surrender organs needed by his children for their survival. The cases are not distinguishable by the fact that the sexual activity producing pregnancy might be voluntary, as fatherhood is equally voluntary. But do abortion laws discriminate by sex? The class of people barred from obtaining an abortion by a criminal abortion statute is composed of pregnant people (entirely female), but the class of people unaffected by the law is composed of nonpregnant people (all men and many women). This distinction (is it real?) has been adopted in another context by the Court. See Geduldig v. Aiello, 417 U.S. 484 (1974).

2. Persons and Fetuses. Did the Court refrain from deciding when life begins? Justice Blackmun declared that Texas could not override Jane Roe's liberties "by adopting one theory of life." Is it fair to say that the Court implicitly adopted a different theory of life in order to override the policy choices of the elected representatives of the citizens of Texas?

Justice Blackmun conceded that if fetuses are persons, "of course" Jane Roe's case collapses. Suppose fetuses are constitutional persons. To say that a person has a right to life is the merest beginning of analysis. The state may take someone's life if good cause exists. Moreover, it is not at all clear that a state is required by due process to prohibit private killings. In DeShaney v. Winnebago County Department of Social Services, 489 U.S. 189 (1989), the Court declared that "nothing in the language of the Due Process Clause [requires] the State to protect the life, liberty, and property of its citizens against invasion by private actors." But states do undertake to prohibit private killings, although every state permits self-defense as a complete defense to a criminal homicide charge. Thus, does the issue of abortion become a question of whether abortion is *justifiable*? If so, how is the justifiable nature of abortion to be determined?

The philosopher Judith Jarvis Thomson likens pregnancy to being physically linked for nine months to a famous violinist ill with a rare disease that will prove fatal if you are unhooked from the violinist. Is it unjust to unhook yourself? Perhaps not if you have been forced into the violinist's service. But suppose you go to concerts knowing that there is a risk that such medically needy violinists may attach themselves to your skin by means of invisible tendrils moving through the air of the concert hall. You guard against the possibility by wearing a hat, veil, gloves, and tight clothing. Alas, nonetheless you depart from an evening of Mozart concerti to find yourself firmly attached to the soloist. You could have avoided this plight by eschewing concerts. "But this won't do," says Thomson, in answer to a slightly different version of this scenario, "for by the same token anyone can avoid a pregnancy due to rape by having a hysterectomy, or anyway by never leaving home without a (reliable!) army." Thomson, A Defense of Abortion, 1 Phil. & Pub. Aff. 47 (1971).

3. Viability. Why does the state's interest in "potential life" become compelling at viability? If it is because the fetus can live outside the womb after viability, does this suggest that the abortion right is a right not to be pregnant, rather than a right not to become a mother?

There is nothing static about viability. Viability varies from fetus to fetus and is not easy to determine with precision. This raises legal issues of whether "viability" can be legislatively defined in a wholesale fashion (e.g., at the end of the twenty-fourth week of pregnancy), or if it must be determined in each case by the attending physician's medical judgment. Moreover, medical technology can push the viability date earlier into pregnancy. These issues confronted the Court repeatedly in the years following *Roe*.

Note: From *Roe* to *Casey*: Doctrinal Evolution

Roe v. Wade produced a variety of legislative initiatives, all designed to inhibit abortions. Some denied public funding for abortions while others sought to impose abortion regulations apparently permitted by *Roe*.

Consent Requirements. In Planned Parenthood v. Danforth, 428 U.S. 52 (1976), the Court invalidated a Missouri law requiring a married woman seeking an abortion to provide the prior written consent of her husband, except where abortion was necessary "to preserve the life of the mother." Missouri's objective of fostering marital communication was legitimate, but when husband and wife disagree on abortion the wife's view must prevail, because she "is the more directly and immediately affected." Does this conclusion flow inexorably from *Eisenstadt*'s recognition of an *individual* right to decide whether to "bear or beget a child"?

A state may condition abortion for an unemancipated minor upon either (1) the prior consent of one parent, or (2) a "judicial bypass" by which the minor may obtain judicial permission to abort her fetus upon a showing that either she is mature enough to decide for herself or it would be in her best interest to terminate her pregnancy. Bellotti v. Baird (*Bellotti II*), 443 U.S. 622 (1979), invalidated a Massachusetts requirement that a minor seeking an abortion must obtain either the consent of *both* her parents or a court order. In Planned Parenthood v. Ashcroft, 462 U.S. 476 (1983), the Court upheld a parental consent requirement that included an adequate judicial bypass.

Notice Requirements. Third-party notice requirements condition abortion upon prior *notice* to either a married woman's husband or, in the case of a minor, one or both of her parents. Planned Parenthood v. Casey, 505 U.S. 833 (1992), struck down a Pennsylvania spousal notice requirement, even though it excepted cases when the woman certified that (1) her husband was not the man who had impregnated her, (2) her husband could not be located, (3) the pregnancy resulted from a reported marital rape, or (4) she believed that notice would cause her husband or someone else to inflict bodily injury upon her. See also Hodgson v. Minnesota, 497 U.S. 417 (1990) (upholding a two-parent notification requirement coupled with an adequate judicial bypass); Ohio v. Akron Center for Reproductive Health, 497 U.S.

502 (1990) (upholding a one-parent notification requirement coupled with judicial bypass).

Hospitalization Requirements. In Akron v. Akron Center for Reproductive Health, 462 U.S. 416 (1983), the Court invalidated five provisions of an ordinance regulating abortions, including a requirement that all abortions after the first trimester be performed in hospitals. This was not "reasonably designed to further [the] state interest [in] health regulation," because the medical evidence showed that second-trimester outpatient abortions could be safely performed.

Note: Public Funding and Abortion

The question of whether governments may prohibit the use of public funds to facilitate abortions while permitting public funds to facilitate childbirth has produced several controversial decisions by the Court.

Maher v. Roe, 432 U.S. 464 (1977). Connecticut provided Medicaid benefits for childbirth but denied them for medically unnecessary abortions. The Court upheld the regulation against an equal protection challenge.

> The Constitution imposes no obligation on the States to pay the pregnancy-related medical expenses of indigent women, or indeed to pay any of the medical expenses of indigents. But when a State decides to alleviate some of the hardships of poverty by providing medical care, the manner in which it dispenses benefits is subject to constitutional limitations. . . . The central question in this case is whether the regulation "impinges upon a fundamental right explicitly or implicitly protected by the Constitution."
>
> [*Roe*] did not declare an unqualified "constitutional right to an abortion." [Rather], the right protects the woman from unduly burdensome interference with her freedom to decide whether to terminate her pregnancy. It implies no limitation on the authority of a State to make a value judgment favoring childbirth over abortion, and to implement that judgment by the allocation of public funds. . . . Connecticut . . . places no obstacles—absolute or otherwise—in the pregnant woman's path to an abortion. An indigent woman who desires an abortion suffers no disadvantage as a consequence of Connecticut's decision to fund childbirth; she continues as before to be dependent on private sources for the service she desires. The State may have made childbirth a more attractive alternative, thereby influencing the woman's decision, but it has imposed no restriction on access to abortions that was not already there. The indigency that may make it difficult—and in some cases, perhaps, impossible—for some women to have abortions is neither created nor in any way affected by the Connecticut regulation. We conclude that the Connecticut regulation does not impinge upon the fundamental right recognized in [*Roe*]. There is a basic difference between direct state interference with a protected activity and state encouragement of an alternative [activity]. Constitutional concerns are greatest when the State attempts to impose its will by force of law; the State's power to encourage actions deemed to be in the public interest is necessarily far broader.

[The] State unquestionably has a "strong and legitimate interest in encouraging normal childbirth." [The] Connecticut regulation rationally furthers that interest.

Justice Brennan, joined by Justices Marshall and Blackmun, dissented:

As a practical matter, many indigent women will feel they have no choice but to carry their pregnancies to term because the State will pay for the associated medical services, even though they would have chosen to have abortions if the State had also provided funds for that procedure. [This] operates to coerce indigent pregnant women to bear children they would not otherwise choose to have. [The] State has [thus] inhibited their fundamental right to make that choice free from state interference.

Harris v. McRae, 448 U.S. 297 (1980). Federal law barred the use of federal Medicaid funds for abortions except when the pregnancy resulted from rape or incest or when necessary to save the life of the pregnant woman, thus prohibiting some, but not all, medically necessary abortions. The Court upheld the law against a Fifth Amendment due process challenge.

[It] simply does not follow that a woman's freedom of choice [to terminate pregnancy] carries with it a constitutional entitlement to the financial resources to avail herself of the full range of protected choices. [Although] government may not place obstacles in the path of a woman's exercise of her freedom of choice, it need not remove those not of its own creation. Indigency falls in the latter category. [It] cannot be that because government may not prohibit the use of contraceptives, or prevent parents from sending their child to a private school, government therefore has an affirmative constitutional obligation to ensure that all persons have the financial resources to obtain contraceptives or send their children to private schools. [Nothing] in the Due Process Clause supports such an extraordinary result.

Justices Brennan, Marshall, and Blackmun dissented: "[It] is not simply the woman's indigency that interferes with her freedom of choice, but the combination of her own poverty and the Government's unequal subsidization of abortion and childbirth."

Webster v. Reproductive Health Services, 492 U.S. 490 (1989). The Court upheld a Missouri statute prohibiting "the use of public employees and facilities to perform or assist abortions not necessary to save the mother's life," reasoning that the law "leaves a pregnant woman with the same choices as if the State had chosen not to operate any public hospitals at all." The Court suggested the result might be different if a state had socialized medicine so that "all of its hospitals and physicians were publicly funded," or if the state barred a physician from public hospitals because he performed abortions privately.

Rust v. Sullivan, 500 U.S. 173 (1991). The Court upheld federal regulations that conditioned receipt of federal funds for family planning services on the recipient's agreement not to use the funds to "provide counseling concerning the use of abortion as a method of family planning or provide referral for abortion as a method of family planning, [or] encourage, promote or advocate abortion as a method of family planning." Recipients were required to physically and financially separate their government-funded activities from prohibited abortion activities. The Court said there is no right to receive any particular service from the government, even when "such aid may be necessary to secure life, liberty, or property interests of which the government itself may not deprive the individual." The gag rule was not an unconstitutional condition because "the government is not denying a benefit to anyone, but is instead simply insisting that public funds be spent for the purposes for which they were authorized." These cases, particularly *Maher* and *Harris*, raise the question of whether the selective funding constitutes an unconstitutional condition. The "unconstitutional conditions" doctrine holds that a government may not penalize the exercise of a constitutional right but may refrain from subsidizing the exercise of that right. *Maher, Harris, Webster*, and *Rust* all involve refusal to subsidize rather than imposition of a penalty. By contrast, if a state were to deny medical welfare benefits to anyone who had obtained an abortion, the state's action would be treated as a penalty imposed for exercising a constitutional right. In short, the government may not use its power to subsidize to induce people to forgo rights they might otherwise exercise using their own resources, but the government may simply decline to spend its money to support private choices with which it disagrees. The "unconstitutional conditions" doctrine can occur anywhere in constitutional law; indeed, one commentator claims that "[i]t roams about constitutional law like Banquo's ghost, invoked in some cases, but not in others." Richard Epstein, Bargaining with the State 9 (1993).

There is a large body of academic commentary on the unconstitutional conditions doctrine, much of it preoccupied with the question of determining the baseline from which to measure whether government has imposed a penalty or refused to provide a subsidy it need not provide. In addition to Epstein, see, e.g., Van Alstyne, The Demise of the Right-Privilege Distinction in Constitutional Law, 81 Harv. L. Rev. 1439 (1968); Kreimer, Allocational Sanctions: The Problem of Negative Rights in a Positive State, 132 U. Pa. L. Rev. 1293 (1984); Sullivan, Unconstitutional Conditions, 102 Harv. L. Rev. 1413 (1989); Sunstein, Why the Unconstitutional Conditions Doctrine Is an Anachronism, 70 B.U. L. Rev. 593 (1990).

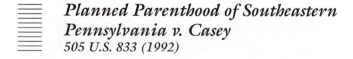

Planned Parenthood of Southeastern Pennsylvania v. Casey
505 U.S. 833 (1992)

JUSTICES O'CONNOR, KENNEDY, and SOUTER announced the judgment of the Court and delivered the opinion of the Court with respect to Parts I, II, III,

V-A, V-C, and VI, an opinion with respect to Part V-E, in which Justice Stevens joined, and an opinion with respect to Parts IV, V-B, and V-D.

I. [Opinion of the Court.]

. . . At issue [here] are five provisions of the Pennsylvania Abortion Control Act of 1982. The Act requires that a woman seeking an abortion give her informed consent prior to the abortion procedure, and specifies that she be provided with certain information at least 24 hours before the abortion is performed. For a minor to obtain an abortion, the Act requires the informed consent of one of her parents, but provides for a judicial bypass option if the minor does not wish to or cannot obtain a parent's consent. Another provision of the Act requires that, unless certain exceptions apply, a married woman seeking an abortion must sign a statement indicating that she has notified her husband of her intended abortion. The Act exempts compliance with these three requirements in the event of a "medical emergency." [The Act also] imposes certain reporting requirements on facilities that provide abortion services.

Before any of these provisions took effect [petitioners] brought this suit seeking declaratory and injunctive relief. Each provision was challenged as unconstitutional on its face. The District Court [held] all the provisions at issue here unconstitutional. [The] Court of Appeals [upheld] all of the regulations except for the husband notification requirement.

We [conclude that] the essential holding of [*Roe*] should be retained and . . . reaffirmed. [*Roe*'s] essential holding . . . has three parts. First is a recognition of the right of the woman to choose to have an abortion before viability and to obtain it without undue interference from the State. . . . Second is a confirmation of the State's power to restrict abortions after fetal viability, if the law contains exceptions for pregnancies which endanger a woman's life or health. And third is the principle that the State has legitimate interests from the outset of the pregnancy in protecting the health of the woman and the life of the fetus that may become a child. These principles do not contradict one another; and we adhere to each.

II. [Opinion of the Court.]

Constitutional protection of the woman's decision to terminate her pregnancy derives from the Due Process Clause. [The] controlling word [is] "liberty." . . . It is a promise of the Constitution that there is a realm of personal liberty which the government may not enter. [Neither] the Bill of Rights nor the specific practices of States at the time of the adoption of the Fourteenth Amendment marks the outer limits of the substantive sphere of liberty which the Fourteenth Amendment protects. See U.S. Const., Amend. 9. . . .

[Our] law affords constitutional protection to personal decisions relating to marriage, procreation, contraception, family relationships, child rearing, and education. These matters, involving the most intimate and personal choices a person may make in a lifetime, choices central to personal dignity and autonomy, are central to the liberty protected by the Fourteenth Amendment. At the heart of liberty is the right to define one's own concept of existence, of meaning, of the universe, and of the mystery of human life. Beliefs about these matters could not define the attributes of personhood were they formed under compulsion of the State.

These considerations begin our analysis of the woman's interest in terminating her pregnancy but cannot end it, for this reason: . . . Abortion is a unique act. It is an act fraught with consequences for others: for the woman who must live with the implications of her decision; for the persons who perform and assist in the procedure; for the spouse, family, and society which must confront the knowledge that these procedures exist, procedures some deem nothing short of an act of violence against innocent human life; and, depending on one's beliefs, for the life or potential life that is aborted. [But] it does not follow that the State is entitled to proscribe it in all instances. That is because the liberty of the woman is at stake in a sense unique to the human condition and so unique to the law.

III. [OPINION OF THE COURT.] A. [The] rule of stare decisis is not an "inexorable command," and certainly it is not such in every constitutional case. Rather, when this Court reexamines a prior holding, its judgment is customarily informed by a series of prudential and pragmatic considerations designed [to] gauge the respective costs of reaffirming and overruling a prior case. Thus, for example, we may ask whether the rule has proved to be intolerable simply in defying practical workability; whether the rule is subject to a kind of reliance that would lend a special hardship to the consequences of overruling and add inequity to the cost of repudiation; whether related principles of law have so far developed as to have left the old rule no more than a remnant of abandoned doctrine; or whether facts have so changed or come to be seen so differently, as to have robbed the old rule of significant application or justification. . . .

1. Although *Roe* has engendered opposition, it has in no sense proven "unworkable," representing as it does a simple limitation beyond which a state law is unenforceable. . . .

2. [F]or two decades [people] have organized intimate relationships and made choices that define their views of themselves and their places in society in reliance on the availability of abortion in the event that contraception should fail. . . .

3. No evolution of legal principle has left *Roe*'s doctrinal footings weaker than they were in 1973. [*Roe*] stands at an intersection of two lines of decisions, but in whichever doctrinal category one reads the case, the result for present purposes will be the same. *Roe* itself placed its holding in the recognized protection accorded to the liberty relating to intimate relationships, the family, and decisions about whether or not to beget or bear a child. [*Roe* may also be grounded in] personal autonomy and bodily integrity. . . .

4. [Time] has overtaken some of *Roe*'s factual assumptions: advances in maternal health care allow for abortions safe to the mother later in pregnancy than was true in 1973, and advances in neonatal care have advanced viability to a point somewhat earlier. But these facts go only to the scheme of time limits on the realization of competing interests and [have] no bearing on the validity of *Roe*'s central holding, that viability marks the earliest point at which

the State's interest in fetal life is constitutionally adequate to justify a legislative ban on nontherapeutic abortions. . . .

IV. [Opinion of JUSTICES O'CONNOR, KENNEDY, and SOUTER.]

[A] woman's liberty is not so unlimited [that] from the outset the State cannot show its concern for the life of the unborn, and at a later point in fetal development the State's interest in life has sufficient force so that the right of the woman to terminate the pregnancy can be restricted. [The] line should be drawn at viability, so that before that time the woman has a right to choose to terminate her pregnancy. We adhere to this principle for two reasons. First [is] stare decisis. [The] second reason is that the concept of viability [is] the time at which there is a realistic possibility of maintaining and nourishing a life outside the womb, so that the independent existence of the [fetus can] be the object of state protection that now overrides the rights of the woman. [In] some broad sense it might be said that a woman who fails to act before viability has consented to the State's intervention on behalf of the developing child. The woman's right to terminate her pregnancy before viability is the most central principle of [*Roe*].

On the other side of the equation is the interest of the State in the protection of potential life. [Though] the woman has a right to choose to terminate or continue her pregnancy before viability, it does not at all follow that the State is prohibited from taking steps to ensure that this choice is thoughtful and informed. Even in the earliest stages of pregnancy, the State may enact rules and regulations designed to encourage her to know that there are philosophic and social arguments of great weight that can be brought to bear in favor of continuing the pregnancy to full term and that there are procedures and institutions to allow adoption of unwanted children as well as a certain degree of state assistance if the mother chooses to raise the child herself.

We reject the trimester framework, which we do not consider to be part of the essential holding of *Roe*. [The] trimester framework suffers from these basic flaws: . . . it misconceives the nature of the pregnant woman's interest; and . . . it undervalues the State's interest in potential life. [Not] every law which makes a right more difficult to exercise is, ipso facto, an infringement of that right. . . . Only where state regulation imposes an undue burden on a woman's ability to make this decision does the power of the State reach into the heart of the liberty protected by the Due Process Clause.

[Not] all burdens on the right to decide whether to terminate a pregnancy will be undue. [A] finding of an undue burden is a shorthand for the conclusion that a state regulation has the purpose or effect of placing a substantial obstacle in the path of a woman seeking an abortion of a nonviable fetus. A statute with this purpose is invalid because the means chosen by the State to further the interest in potential life must be calculated to inform the woman's free choice, not hinder it. And a statute which [has] the effect of placing a substantial obstacle in the path of a woman's choice cannot be considered a permissible means of serving its legitimate ends. [An] undue burden is an unconstitutional burden. [A] law designed to further the State's interest in fetal life which imposes an undue burden on the woman's decision before fetal viability [is not] constitutional.

[Some] guiding principles should emerge. What is at stake is the woman's right to make the ultimate decision, not a right to be insulated from all others in doing so. Regulations which do no more than create a structural mechanism by which the State, or the parent or guardian of a minor, may express profound respect for the life of the unborn are permitted, if they are not a substantial obstacle to the woman's exercise of the right to choose. Unless it has that effect on her right of choice, a state measure designed to persuade her to choose childbirth over abortion will be upheld if reasonably related to that goal. Regulations designed to foster the health of a woman seeking an abortion are valid if they do not constitute an undue burden. [Our] adoption of the undue burden analysis does not disturb the central holding of [*Roe*] and we reaffirm that holding. [A] State may not prohibit any woman from making the ultimate decision to terminate her pregnancy before viability. [We] also reaffirm *Roe*'s holding that "subsequent to viability, the State in promoting its interest in the potentiality of human life may, if it chooses, regulate, and even proscribe, abortion except where it is necessary, in appropriate medical judgment, for the preservation of the life or health of the mother." [We] now turn to the issue of the validity of its challenged provisions.

V. A. [OPINION OF THE COURT.] Because . . . the Court of Appeals [read] "the medical emergency exception as intended by the Pennsylvania legislature to assure that compliance with its abortion regulations would not in any way pose a significant threat to the life or health of a woman" [we conclude that] the medical emergency definition imposes no undue burden on a woman's abortion right.

B. [Opinion of JUSTICES O'CONNOR, KENNEDY, and SOUTER.] We next consider the informed consent requirement. Except in a medical emergency, the statute requires that at least 24 hours before performing an abortion a physician inform the woman of the nature of the procedure, the health risks of the abortion and of childbirth, [the] "probable gestational age of the unborn child," [and] the availability of printed materials published by the State describing the fetus and providing information about medical assistance for childbirth, information about child support from the father, and a list of agencies which provide adoption and other services as alternatives to abortion. An abortion may not be performed unless the woman certifies in writing that she has been informed of the availability of these printed materials and has been provided them if she chooses to view them.

[As] with any medical procedure, the State may require a woman to give her written informed consent to an abortion. [To] the extent *Akron I* and *Thornburgh* [v. American College of Obstetricians and Gynecologists, 476 U.S. 747 (1986),] find a constitutional violation when the government requires . . . the giving of truthful, nonmisleading information about the nature of the procedure, the attendant health risks and those of childbirth, and the "probable gestational age" of the fetus, those cases go too far [and] are overruled. . . .

[Our] analysis of Pennsylvania's 24-hour waiting period between the provision of the information deemed necessary to informed consent and the performance of an abortion [requires] us to reconsider the premise behind the decision in *Akron I* invalidating a parallel requirement. [We] consider that conclusion to be wrong. The idea that important decisions will be more informed and deliberate if they follow some period of reflection does not strike us as unreasonable. [Whether] the mandatory 24-hour waiting period is nonetheless invalid because in practice it is a substantial obstacle to a woman's choice to terminate her pregnancy is a closer question. [Because] of the distances many women must travel to reach an abortion provider, the practical effect will often be a delay of much more than a day because the waiting period requires that a woman seeking an abortion make at least two visits to the doctor. [In] many instances this will increase the exposure of women seeking abortions to "the harassment and hostility of antiabortion protestors demonstrating outside a clinic." As a result, [for] those women who have the fewest financial resources, those who must travel long distances, and those who have difficulty explaining their whereabouts to husbands, employers, or others, the 24-hour waiting period will be "particularly burdensome." [But these findings] do not demonstrate that the waiting period constitutes an undue burden. [Under] the undue burden standard a State is permitted to enact persuasive measures which favor childbirth over abortion, even if those measures do not further a health interest. [Hence], in the context of this facial challenge we are not convinced that the 24-hour waiting period constitutes an undue burden. . . .

C. [OPINION OF THE COURT.] Pennsylvania's abortion law provides, except in cases of medical emergency, that no physician shall perform an abortion on a married woman without receiving a signed statement from the woman that she has notified her spouse that she is about to undergo an abortion [or has signed a] statement certifying that her husband is not the man who impregnated her; that her husband could not be located; that the pregnancy is the result of spousal sexual assault which she has reported; or that the woman believes that notifying her husband will cause him or someone else to inflict bodily injury upon her. . . .

The District Court [made] detailed findings of fact regarding the effect of this statute. "[Researchers] estimate that one of every two women will be battered at some time in their life. [Women] of all class levels, educational backgrounds, and racial, ethnic and religious groups are battered. [Married] women, victims of battering, have been killed in Pennsylvania and throughout the United States. [Battering] can often involve a substantial amount of sexual abuse, including marital rape and sexual mutilation. [In] a domestic abuse situation, it is common for the battering husband to also abuse the children in an attempt to coerce the wife. [Mere] notification of pregnancy is frequently a flashpoint for battering and violence within the family. [The] battering husband may deny parentage and use the pregnancy as an excuse for abuse. [Secrecy] typically shrouds abusive families. [Battering] husbands often threaten their wives or her children with further abuse if she tells an outsider of the violence and tells her that nobody will believe her. [Marital] rape is rarely discussed with others, reported [or] prosecuted. [It] is common for battered women to have sexual intercourse with their husbands to avoid being battered. [The] marital rape exception to [the notice requirement] cannot be claimed by women who are victims of coercive sexual behavior other than penetration."

These findings are supported by studies of domestic violence. . . . In well-functioning marriages, spouses discuss important intimate decisions such as whether to bear a child. But there are millions of women in this country who are the victims of regular physical and psychological abuse at the hands of their husbands. Should these women become pregnant, they may have very good reasons for not wishing to inform their husbands of their decision to obtain an abortion. The spousal notification requirement is thus likely to prevent a significant number of women from obtaining an abortion. It does not merely make abortions a little more difficult or expensive to obtain; for many women, it will impose a substantial obstacle. We must not blind ourselves to the fact that the significant number of women who fear for their safety and the safety of their children are likely to be deterred from procuring an abortion as surely as if [Pennsylvania] had outlawed abortion in all cases.

Respondents [argue that the notice requirement] imposes almost no burden at all for the vast majority of women seeking abortions. [Only] about 20 percent of the women who obtain abortions are married [and] of these women about 95 percent notify their husbands of their own volition. Thus, respondents argue, the effects of [the notice requirement] are felt by only one percent of the women who obtain abortions. [Because] some of these women will be able to notify their husbands without adverse consequences or will qualify for one of the exceptions, the statute affects fewer than one percent of women seeking abortions. [Thus,] it is asserted, the statute cannot be invalid on its face. We disagree. [Analysis] does not end with the one percent of women upon whom the statute operates; it begins there. Legislation is measured [by] its impact on those whose conduct it affects. [The] proper focus of constitutional inquiry is the group for whom the law is a restriction, not the group for whom the law is irrelevant. [In] a large fraction of the cases in which [the notice requirement] is relevant, it will operate as a substantial obstacle to a woman's choice to undergo an abortion. It is an undue burden, and therefore invalid.

[O]ur decisions upholding parental notification or consent requirements [are] based on the quite reasonable assumption that minors will benefit from consultation with their parents and that children will often not realize that their parents have their best interests at heart. We cannot adopt a parallel assumption about adult women.

[For] the great many women who are victims of abuse inflicted by their husbands, or whose children are the victims of such abuse, a spousal notice requirement enables the husband to wield an effective veto over his wife's decision. [A] husband has no enforceable right to require a wife to advise him before she exercises her personal choices. . . . A State may not give to a man the kind of dominion over his wife that parents exercise over their children. . . .

Women do not lose their constitutionally protected liberty when they marry. The Constitution protects all individuals, male or female, married or unmarried, from the abuse of governmental power, even where that power is employed for the supposed benefit of a member of the individual's family. . . .

D. [Opinion of JUSTICES O'CONNOR, KENNEDY, and SOUTER.] We next consider the parental consent provision. . . . [We reaffirm] that a State may require a minor seeking an abortion to obtain the consent of a parent or guardian, provided that there is an adequate judicial bypass procedure. . . .

E. [Opinion of JUSTICES O'CONNOR, KENNEDY, SOUTER, and STEVENS.] [Every] facility which performs abortions is required to file a report stating its name and address as well as the name and address of any related entity. . . . For each abortion performed, a report must be filed identifying [a wide variety of data, but excluding the identity of the woman]. [All] the provisions at issue here except that relating to spousal notice are constitutional. [The] collection of information with respect to actual patients is a vital element of medical research, and so it cannot be said that the requirements serve no purpose other than to make abortions more difficult. Nor do we find that the requirements impose a substantial obstacle to a woman's choice. At most they might increase the cost of some abortions by a slight amount. While at some point increased cost could become a substantial obstacle, there is no such showing on the record before us. . . .

JUSTICE STEVENS, concurring in part and dissenting in part.

The fact that the State's interest is legitimate does not tell us when, if ever, that interest outweighs the pregnant woman's interest in personal liberty. . . . First, [the] State's interest must be secular. . . . [The] state interest in potential human life is . . . an indirect interest supported by both humanitarian and pragmatic concerns.

In counterpoise is the woman's constitutional interest in liberty. . . . Decisional autonomy must limit the State's power to inject into a woman's most personal deliberations its own views of what is best. [The requirements that] a physician or counselor [provide] the woman with a range of materials clearly designed to persuade her to choose not to undergo the abortion [are unconstitutional]. While the State is free [to] produce and disseminate such material, the State may not inject such information into the woman's deliberations just as she is weighing such an important choice.

The 24-hour waiting period [raises] even more serious concerns. [There] is no evidence that the mandated delay benefits women or that it is necessary to enable the physician to convey any relevant information to the patient. The mandatory delay thus appears to rest on outmoded and unacceptable assumptions about the decisionmaking capacity of women. . . .

A burden may be "undue" either because the burden is too severe or because it lacks a legitimate, rational justification. The 24-hour delay requirement fails both parts of this test. [The] counseling provisions are similarly infirm. . . .

JUSTICE BLACKMUN, concurring in part, concurring in the judgment in part, and dissenting in part.

[Today], no less than yesterday, the Constitution [requires] that a State's abortion restrictions be subjected to the strictest of judicial scrutiny. [Limitations] on the right of privacy are permissible only if . . . the governmental entity imposing the restriction can demonstrate that the limitation is both necessary and narrowly tailored to serve a compelling governmental interest. *Roe* implemented these principles through [the trimester framework]. No majority of this Court has ever agreed upon an alternative approach. . . .

CHIEF JUSTICE REHNQUIST, joined by JUSTICES WHITE, SCALIA, and THOMAS, concurring in the judgment in part and dissenting in part.

The joint opinion [retains] the outer shell of [*Roe*] but beats a wholesale retreat from [its] substance. We believe that *Roe* was wrongly decided, and that it can and should be overruled consistently with our traditional approach to stare decisis in constitutional cases. We would adopt [minimal or rational basis scrutiny] and uphold the challenged provisions of the Pennsylvania statute in their entirety.

I. [The] Court in *Roe* read the earlier opinions upon which it based its decision much too broadly. Unlike marriage, procreation and contraception, abortion "involves the purposeful termination of potential life." . . . Nor do the historical traditions of the American people support the view that the right to terminate one's pregnancy is "fundamental." [It] can scarcely be said that any deeply rooted tradition of relatively unrestricted abortion in our history supported the classification of the right to abortion as "fundamental." . . .

II. . . . *Roe* decided that a woman had a fundamental right to an abortion. The joint opinion rejects that view. *Roe* decided that abortion regulations were to be subjected to "strict scrutiny." [The] joint opinion rejects that view. *Roe* analyzed abortion regulation under a rigid trimester framework. [The] joint opinion rejects that framework. [While] purporting to adhere to precedent, the joint opinion instead revises it. *Roe* continues to exist, but only in the way a storefront on a western movie set exists: a mere facade to give the illusion of reality. . . . [The strict scrutiny standard of *Roe*] at least had a recognized basis in constitutional law. . . . The same cannot be said for the "undue burden" standard, which is created largely out of whole cloth by the authors of the joint opinion. [Because] the undue burden standard is plucked from nowhere, the question of what is a "substantial obstacle" to abortion will [be resolved by resort to what are] quintessentially legislative [judgments]. We [believe] that the Constitution does not subject state abortion regulations to heightened scrutiny. [The] correct analysis is that [a] woman's interest in having an abortion is a form of liberty protected by the Due Process Clause, but States may regulate abortion procedures in ways rationally related to a legitimate state interest.

[Chief Justice Rehnquist then examined each of the challenged provisions and concluded that each one was rationally related to a legitimate state interest.]

JUSTICE SCALIA, joined by CHIEF JUSTICE REHNQUIST and JUSTICES WHITE and THOMAS, concurring in the judgment in part and dissenting in part.

[The] permissibility of abortion, and the limitations upon it, are to be resolved like most important questions in our democracy: by citizens trying to persuade one another and then voting. [A] State's choice between two positions on which reasonable people can disagree is constitutional even when (as is often the case) it intrudes upon a "liberty" in the absolute sense. [The] issue in this case [is] not whether the power of a woman to abort her unborn child is a "liberty" in the absolute sense; or even whether it is a liberty of great importance to many women. Of course it is both. The issue is whether it is a liberty protected by the Constitution of the United States. I am sure it is not. I reach that conclusion . . . because of two simple facts: (1) the Constitution says absolutely nothing about it, and (2) the longstanding traditions of American society have permitted it to be legally proscribed.[9] . . .

[Applying] the rational basis test, I would uphold the Pennsylvania statute in its entirety. . . .

NOTES

1. The Role of Precedent in Constitutional Cases. The joint authors of *Casey* refer to changed "facts, or an understanding of facts," as if they were interchangeable. Does a changed "understanding of facts" mean a change in values? Was the Court's repudiation of Plessy v. Ferguson (which upheld "separate but equal" racial segregation) in Brown v. Board of Education and of *Lochner* in *West Coast Hotel* more attributable to a change in cultural values than to newly discovered facts? If this is so, does this suggest that value sources are legitimate engines of constitutional interpretation? Does change in cultural values adequately explain why *Lochner* was wrong and the "essential holding" of *Roe* is correct?

2. Undue Burden. Will the undue-burden standard produce results that depend on the values of the judges deciding the cases? Or will that standard simply require challengers to prove underlying facts that clearly establish the practical obstacles to a pre-viability abortion produced by any given abortion regulation?

---

9. [The] suggestion that adherence to tradition would require us to uphold laws against interracial marriage is entirely wrong. Any tradition in that case was contradicted by a text—an Equal Protection Clause that explicitly establishes racial equality as a constitutional value. [The] enterprise launched in *Roe*, by contrast, sought to establish—in the teeth of a clear, contrary tradition—a value found nowhere in the constitutional text. . . .

Gonzales v. Carhart; Gonzales v. Planned Parenthood Federation of America
550 U.S. 124 (2007)

JUSTICE KENNEDY delivered the opinion of the Court.

These cases require us to consider the validity of the Partial-Birth Abortion Ban Act of 2003 (Act), a federal statute regulating abortion procedures. . . . We conclude the Act should be sustained against the objections lodged by the broad, facial attack brought against it. . . .

I. A. The Act proscribes a particular manner of ending fetal life, so it is necessary . . . to discuss abortion procedures in some detail. . . . Between 85 and 90 percent of the approximately 1.3 million abortions performed each year in the United States take place in the first three months of pregnancy, [or] the first trimester. The most common first-trimester abortion method is vacuum aspiration in which the physician vacuums out the embryonic tissue. Early in this trimester an alternative is to use medication, such as mifepristone (commonly known as RU.486), to terminate the pregnancy. The Act does not regulate these procedures. Of the remaining abortions that take place each year, most occur in the second trimester. The surgical procedure referred to as "dilation and evacuation" or "D&E" is the usual abortion method in this trimester. . . . A doctor must first dilate the cervix at least to the extent needed to insert surgical instruments into the uterus and to maneuver them to evacuate the fetus. . . . The woman is placed under general anesthesia or conscious sedation. The doctor, often guided by ultrasound, inserts grasping forceps through the woman's cervix and into the uterus to grab the fetus. The doctor grips a fetal part with the forceps and pulls it back through the cervix and vagina, continuing to pull even after meeting resistance from the cervix. The friction causes the fetus to tear apart. For example, a leg might be ripped off the fetus as it is pulled through the cervix and out of the woman. The process of evacuating the fetus piece by piece continues until it has been completely removed. A doctor may make 10 to 15 passes with the forceps to evacuate the fetus in its entirety, though sometimes removal is completed with fewer passes. Once the fetus has been evacuated, the placenta and any remaining fetal material are suctioned or scraped out of the uterus. The doctor examines the different parts to ensure the entire fetal body has been removed.

Some doctors, especially later in the second trimester, may kill the fetus a day or two before performing the surgical evacuation. They inject digoxin or potassium chloride into the fetus, the umbilical cord, or the amniotic fluid. Fetal demise may cause contractions and make greater dilation possible. Once dead, moreover, the fetus'[s] body will soften, and its removal will be easier. Other doctors refrain from injecting chemical agents, believing it adds risk with little or no medical benefit.

The abortion procedure that was the impetus for the numerous bans on "partial-birth abortion," including the Act, is a variation of this standard

D&E, [variously] referred to as "intact D&E," "dilation and extraction" (D&X), and "intact D&X." For discussion purposes this D&E variation will be referred to as intact D&E. The main difference between the two procedures is that in intact D&E a doctor extracts the fetus intact or largely intact with only a few passes. . . . In an intact D&E procedure the doctor extracts the fetus [by] pulling out its entire body, instead of ripping it apart. One doctor, for example, testified [that he attempts] "to have an intact delivery, if possible." . . .

Intact D&E gained public notoriety when, in 1992, Dr. Martin Haskell gave a presentation describing his method of performing the operation. In the usual intact D&E the fetus'[s] head lodges in the cervix, and dilation is insufficient to allow it to pass. Haskell explained the next step as follows:

> At this point, the . . . surgeon slides [his] fingers . . . along the back of the fetus and "hooks" the shoulders of the fetus. . . . While maintaining this tension, lifting the cervix and applying traction to the shoulders . . . , the surgeon takes a pair of blunt curved Metzenbaum scissors [and] carefully advances the tip, curved down, along the spine . . . until he feels it contact the base of the skull. . . . [T]he surgeon then forces the scissors into the base of the skull. . . . Having safely entered the skull, he spreads the scissors to enlarge the opening. The surgeon removes the scissors and introduces a suction catheter into this hole and evacuates the skull contents. With the catheter still in place, he applies traction to the fetus, removing it completely from the patient. H.R. Rep. No. 108-58, p.3 (2003).

This is an abortion doctor's clinical description. Here is another description from a nurse who witnessed the same method performed on a 26½-week fetus and who testified before the Senate Judiciary Committee:

> Dr. Haskell went in with forceps and grabbed the baby's legs and pulled them down into the birth canal. Then he delivered the baby's body and the arms—everything but the head. The doctor kept the head right inside the uterus. . . . The baby's little fingers were clasping and unclasping, and his little feet were kicking. Then the doctor stuck the scissors in the back of his head, and the baby's arms jerked out, like a startle reaction, like a flinch, like a baby does when he thinks he is going to fall. The doctor opened up the scissors, stuck a high-powered suction tube into the opening, and sucked the baby's brains out. Now the baby went completely limp. . . . He cut the umbilical cord and delivered the placenta. He threw the baby in a pan, along with the placenta and the instruments he had just used. *Ibid.*

. . . D&E and intact D&E are not the only second-trimester abortion methods. Doctors also may abort a fetus through medical induction, [in which labor is induced] and contractions occur to deliver the fetus. . . . Doctors turn to two other methods of second-trimester abortion, hysterotomy and hysterectomy, only in emergency situations because they carry increased risk of complications. In a hysterotomy, as in a cesarean section, the doctor removes the fetus by making an incision through the abdomen and uterine wall to gain access to the uterine cavity. A hysterectomy requires the removal of the entire uterus. . . .

B. . . . In 2003 Congress passed the Act at issue here. . . . First, Congress . . . found . . . that "[a] moral, medical, and ethical consensus exists that the practice of performing a partial-birth abortion . . . is a gruesome and inhumane procedure that is never medically necessary and should be prohibited." Second, . . . the [Act provides that anyone who] "in or affecting interstate or foreign commerce, knowingly performs a partial-birth abortion and thereby kills a human fetus shall be fined . . . or imprisoned not more than 2 years, or both." [The criminal prohibition, however,] "does not apply to a partial-birth abortion that is necessary to save the life of a mother. . . ." [The Act declared that a] "woman upon whom a partial-birth abortion is performed may not be prosecuted under" [the Act].

C. [The Eighth Circuit in *Carhart* invalidated the Act because] it lacked an exception allowing the procedure where necessary for the health of the mother.

D. [The Ninth Circuit in *Planned Parenthood* concluded that] the absence of a health exception rendered the Act unconstitutional. [The Ninth Circuit also concluded] that the Act placed an undue burden on a woman's ability to obtain a second-trimester abortion [and] found the Act void for vagueness [because it] did not offer physicians clear warning of its regulatory reach. . . .

II. . . . [We] must determine whether the Act furthers the legitimate interest of the Government in protecting the life of the fetus that may become a child. . . . We now apply [*Casey*'s] standard to the cases at bar.

III. . . . We conclude that the Act is not void for vagueness, does not impose an undue burden . . . , and is not invalid on its face.

A. The Act punishes "knowingly perform[ing]" a "partial-birth abortion." It defines the unlawful abortion in explicit terms.

First, the person performing the abortion must "vaginally delive[r] a living fetus." The Act does not restrict an abortion procedure involving the delivery of an expired fetus [or] abortions that do not involve vaginal delivery (for instance, hysterotomy or hysterectomy). The Act does apply both pre-viability and post-viability. . . .

Second, the Act's definition of partial-birth abortion requires the fetus to be delivered "until, in the case of a head-first presentation, the entire fetal head is outside the body of the mother, or, in the case of breech presentation, any part of the fetal trunk past the navel is outside the body of the mother." [If] an abortion procedure does not involve the delivery of a living fetus to one of these "anatomical landmarks" . . . the prohibitions of the Act do not apply.

Third, to fall within the Act, a doctor must perform an "overt act, other than completion of delivery, that kills the partially delivered living fetus." [The] overt act causing the fetus'[s] death must be separate from delivery. And the overt act must occur after the delivery to an anatomical landmark. . . .

Fourth, the Act contains scienter requirements concerning all the actions involved in the prohibited abortion. [The] physician must have "deliberately and intentionally" delivered the fetus to one of the Act's anatomical landmarks. If a living fetus is delivered past the critical point by accident or inadvertence, the Act is inapplicable. In addition, the fetus must have been delivered "for the purpose of performing an overt act that the [doctor] knows will kill [it]." If either intent is absent, no crime has occurred. . . .

B. . . . The Act provides doctors "of ordinary intelligence a reasonable opportunity to know what is prohibited." Indeed, it sets forth "relatively clear guidelines as to prohibited conduct" and provides "objective criteria" to evaluate whether a doctor has performed a prohibited procedure. . . . The Act is not vague.

C. . . . The Act prohibits a doctor from intentionally performing an intact D&E [because the elements] necessary for criminal liability correspond with the steps generally undertaken during this type of procedure. [T]he Act excludes most D&Es in which the fetus is removed in pieces, not intact, . . . because the doctor will not have delivered the living fetus to one of the anatomical landmarks or committed an additional overt act that kills the fetus after partial delivery. . . .

IV. [The Act] would be unconstitutional "if its purpose or effect is to place a substantial obstacle in the path of a woman seeking an abortion before the fetus attains viability." The abortions affected by the Act's regulations take place both pre-viability and post-viability. . . . The question is whether the Act . . . imposes a substantial obstacle to late-term, but pre-viability, abortions. The Act does not on its face impose a substantial obstacle, and we reject this further facial challenge to its validity.

A. . . . The Act proscribes a method of abortion in which a fetus is killed just inches before completion of the birth process. Congress stated [that implicit approval of] "such a brutal and inhumane procedure by choosing not to prohibit it will further coarsen society to the humanity of not only newborns, but all vulnerable and innocent human life, making it increasingly difficult to protect such life." The Act expresses respect for the dignity of human life.

Congress was [also] concerned . . . with the effects on the medical community and on its reputation caused by the practice of partial-birth abortion [because it] "confuses the medical, legal, and ethical duties of physicians to preserve and promote life. . . ." There can be no doubt the government "has an interest in protecting the integrity and ethics of the medical profession."

Casey reaffirmed [that] government may use its voice and its regulatory authority to show its profound respect for the life within the woman. . . . The third premise [of *Casey*], that the State, from the inception of the pregnancy, maintains its own regulatory interest in protecting the life of the fetus that may become a child, cannot be set at naught by interpreting *Casey*'s requirement of a health exception so it becomes tantamount to allowing a doctor to choose the abortion method he or she might prefer. Where it has a rational basis to act, and it does not impose an undue burden, the State may use its regulatory power to bar certain procedures and substitute others, all in furtherance of its legitimate interests in regulating the medical profession in order to promote respect for life, including life of the unborn.

The Act's ban on abortions that involve partial delivery of a living fetus furthers the Government's objectives. . . . Congress determined that the abortion methods it proscribed had a "disturbing similarity to the killing of a newborn infant," and thus it was concerned with "draw[ing] a bright line that clearly distinguishes abortion and infanticide." The Court has . . . confirmed the validity of drawing boundaries to prevent certain practices that extinguish life and are close to actions that are condemned. [Washington v. Glucksberg] found reasonable the State's "fear that permitting assisted suicide will start it down the path to voluntary and perhaps even involuntary euthanasia." . . .

In a decision so fraught with emotional consequence some doctors may prefer not to disclose precise details of the means that will be used, confining themselves to the required statement of risks the procedure entails. [Many] patients facing imminent surgical procedures would prefer not to hear all details, lest the usual anxiety preceding invasive medical procedures become the more intense. This is likely the case with the abortion procedures here in issue. It is, however, precisely this lack of information concerning the way in which the fetus will be killed that is of legitimate concern to the State. The State has an interest in ensuring so grave a choice is well informed. . . . It is objected that the standard D&E is in some respects as brutal, if not more, than the intact D&E, so that the legislation accomplishes little. [But it] was reasonable for Congress to think that partial-birth abortion, more than standard D&E, "undermines the public's perception of the appropriate role of a physician during the delivery process, and perverts a process during which life is brought into the world." . . .

B. [The] next question [is] whether the Act has the effect of imposing an unconstitutional burden on the abortion right because it does not allow use of the barred procedure where "necessary, in appropriate medical judgment, for [the] preservation of the . . . health of the mother." [Casey.] The . . . Act would be unconstitutional . . . if it "subject[ed] [women] to significant health risks." [Whether] the Act creates significant health risks for women has been a contested factual question. . . . Respondents presented evidence that intact D&E may be the safest method of abortion [because] that intact D&E decreases the risk of cervical laceration or uterine perforation[,] reduces the risks that fetal parts will remain in the uterus[,] and . . . takes less time to complete. . . . These contentions were contradicted by other doctors [who] concluded that the alleged health advantages were based on speculation without scientific studies to support them. They considered D&E always to be a safe alternative.

[When there] is documented medical disagreement whether the Act's prohibition would ever impose significant health risks on women [the] question becomes whether the Act can stand when this medical uncertainty persists. The Court's precedents instruct that the Act can survive this facial attack. The Court has given state and federal legislatures wide discretion to pass legislation in areas where there is medical and scientific uncertainty. . . . Alternatives are available to the prohibited procedure. [The] Act does not proscribe D&E. [Because] the Act's prohibition only applies to the delivery of "a living fetus," [if] the intact D&E procedure is truly necessary in some circumstances, it appears likely an injection that kills the fetus is an alternative under the Act that allows the doctor to perform the procedure. . . .

V. [These] facial attacks should not have been entertained in the first instance. [The] proper means to consider exceptions is by as-applied challenge. The Government has acknowledged that pre-enforcement, as-applied challenges to the Act can be maintained. This is the proper manner to protect the health of the woman if it can be shown that in discrete and well-defined instances a particular condition has or is likely to occur in which the procedure prohibited by the Act must be used. In an as-applied challenge the nature of the medical risk can be better quantified and balanced than in a facial attack. The latitude given facial challenges in the First Amendment context is inapplicable here. [Respondents] have not demonstrated that the Act would be unconstitutional in a large fraction of relevant cases. . . .

Respondents have not demonstrated that the Act, as a facial matter, is void for vagueness, or that it imposes an undue burden on a woman's right to abortion based on its overbreadth or lack of a health exception. [The] judgments of the Courts of Appeals for the Eighth and Ninth Circuits are reversed. . . .

JUSTICE THOMAS, with whom JUSTICE SCALIA joins, concurring.

I join the Court's opinion because it accurately applies [*Casey*]. I write separately to reiterate my view that the Court's abortion jurisprudence, including *Casey* and [*Roe*], has no basis in the Constitution. I also note that whether the Act constitutes a permissible exercise of Congress'[s] power under the Commerce Clause is not before the Court. . . .

JUSTICE GINSBURG, with whom JUSTICE STEVENS, JUSTICE SOUTER, and JUSTICE BREYER join, dissenting.

. . . Today's decision . . . refuses to take *Casey* . . . seriously. It tolerates, indeed applauds, federal intervention to ban nationwide a procedure found necessary and proper in certain cases by the American College of Obstetricians and Gynecologists. [For] the first time . . . the Court blesses a prohibition with no exception safeguarding a woman's health. . . .

I. A. [The] Court has consistently required that laws regulating abortion, at any stage of pregnancy and in all cases, safeguard a woman's health. . . . .

B. . . . The congressional findings on which the Partial-Birth Abortion Ban Act rests do not withstand inspection. . . . Many of the Act's recitations are incorrect. . . . Congress claimed there was a medical consensus that the banned procedure is never necessary [but, according to the trial courts,] the evidence "very clearly demonstrate[d] the opposite." . . . Similarly, Congress found that "[t]here is no credible medical evidence that partial-birth abortions are safe or are safer than other abortion procedures." . . . But the congressional record includes . . . statements from nine professional associations . . . attesting that intact D&E carries meaningful safety advantages over other methods. . . .

C. In contrast to Congress, the District Courts made findings after full trials. . . . During [those] trials, "numerous" "extraordinarily accomplished" and "very experienced" medical experts explained that, in certain circumstances and for certain women, intact D&E is safer than alternative procedures and necessary to protect women's health. [The] safety advantages of intact D&E are marked for women with . . . uterine scarring, bleeding disorders, heart disease, or compromised immune systems[, are significant] for women with certain pregnancy-related conditions, such as placenta previa and accreta, and for women carrying fetuses with certain abnormalities, such as severe hydrocephalus. . . .

Nevertheless, . . . the Court asserts that the Partial-Birth Abortion Ban Act can survive "when . . . medical uncertainty persists." This assertion is bewildering. Not only does it defy the Court's longstanding precedent affirming the necessity of a health exception, with no carve-out for circumstances of medical uncertainty, it gives short shrift to the records. . . .

II. A. . . . Today's ruling, the court declares, advances . . . the Government's "legitimate and substantial interest in preserving and promoting fetal life." But the Act scarcely furthers that interest: The law saves not a single fetus from destruction, for it targets only a *method* of performing abortion. [T]he Court upholds a law that, while doing nothing to "preserv[e] . . . fetal life," bars a woman from choosing intact D&E although her doctor "reasonably believes [that procedure] will best protect [her]." . . .

III. A. The Court further confuses our jurisprudence when it declares that facial attacks are not permissible . . . where medical uncertainty exists. . . . But *Casey* makes clear that . . . a provision restricting access to abortion "must be judged by reference to those [women] for whom it is an actual rather than an irrelevant restriction." Thus the absence of a health exception burdens all women for whom it is relevant. . . .

IV. . . . Though today's opinion does not . . . discard *Roe* or *Casey*, the Court . . . is hardly faithful to our earlier invocations of . . . "principles of *stare decisis*." [The] Act, and the Court's defense of it, cannot be understood as anything other than an effort to chip away at a right declared again and again by this Court—and with increasing comprehension of its centrality to women's lives. . . .

I dissent. . . .

NOTES

1. The Role of Moral Concerns. Writing for the majority, Justice Kennedy stated that so long as Congress does not impose an undue burden on access to abortions before fetal viability it "may use . . . its regulatory authority to show its profound respect for the life within the woman" and may forbid intact D&E because that procedure "implicates . . . ethical and moral concerns that justify a special prohibition." The joint opinion in *Casey*, of which Justice Kennedy was an author, noted that while abortion is "offensive to our most basic principles of morality, [our] obligation is to define the liberty of all, not to mandate our own moral code." In Lawrence v. Texas, Justice Kennedy, again writing for the majority, declared that governments may not enforce "profound and deep . . . moral principles . . . on the whole society through . . . the criminal law." Does *Carhart* repudiate these statements from *Casey* and *Lawrence*? If not, how may they be reconciled with the rationale of *Carhart*?

Justice Ginsburg charged that the moral concerns that justified the ban on intact D&E "could yield prohibitions on any abortion." Is she correct? Both the majority and the dissenters agree that D&E, whether intact or by fetal dismemberment, is the "usual" or "most frequently used" abortion method for second-trimester abortions, which constitute 10 to 15 percent of all abortions. If intact D&E is morally repugnant, surely fetal dismemberment is equally so. Would this be sufficient to justify a ban on all abortions by the D&E method?

2. Facial and As-Applied Challenges. The majority suggested that even though the partial-birth abortion ban was facially valid (because it was not shown that the ban "would be unconstitutional in a large fraction of relevant cases"), it could be challenged as applied, and hinted that such a challenge might be appropriate prior to enforcement of the ban. Consider the practical issues involved. The ban was facially valid, in part, because medical opinion was divided on the question of whether intact D&E is necessary to preserve the pregnant woman's health. Could a pre-enforcement challenge be successfully brought as applied to the class of pregnant women for whom, as Justice Ginsburg argued, "the safety advantages of intact D&E are marked" or for whom intact D&E is "significantly safer"? To succeed in such a challenge, would it be necessary to prove that intact D&E is safer for all such women? For most? For some? Or would such as-applied challenges be viable only when brought on behalf of a particular pregnant woman?

c. Family Relationships

Government interference with certain family relationships is subject to heightened constitutional scrutiny. This section introduces some of the family values protected by substantive due process. Other aspects of government involvement in familial relationships are considered in connection with equal protection and the First Amendment's speech and religion clauses. As was true with the preceding cases, these cases invite dispute concerning the relevant traditions to be drawn upon to determine which family interests are constitutionally fundamental liberty interests.

≡ *Moore v. City of East Cleveland*
≡ 431 U.S. 494 (1977)

JUSTICE POWELL announced the judgment of the Court, and delivered an opinion in which JUSTICES BRENNAN, MARSHALL, and BLACKMUN joined.

East Cleveland's housing ordinance [limits] occupancy of a dwelling unit to members of a single family, [and] recognizes as a "family" only a few categories of related individuals. Because her family, living together in her home, fits none of those categories, appellant stands convicted of a criminal offense. The question in this case is whether the ordinance violates the Due Process Clause of the Fourteenth Amendment. Appellant, Mrs. Inez Moore, lives in her East Cleveland home together with her son, Dale Moore, Sr., and her two grandsons, Dale, Jr., and John Moore, Jr. The two boys are first cousins rather than brothers; we are told that John came to live with his grandmother, [uncle, and cousin] after his mother's death. . . .

The city argues [that] Village of Belle Terre v. Boraas, 416 U.S. 1 (1974), requires us to sustain the ordinance attacked here. Belle Terre, like East Cleveland, imposed limits on the types of groups that could occupy a single dwelling unit; [we] sustained the Belle Terre ordinance on the ground that it bore a rational relationship to permissible state objectives. But [the] Belle Terre [ordinance] affected only unrelated individuals. It expressly allowed all who were related by "blood, adoption, or marriage" to live together, and in sustaining the ordinance we were careful to note that it promoted "family needs" and "family values." East Cleveland [has] chosen to regulate the occupancy of its housing by slicing deeply into the family itself. [When] a city undertakes such intrusive regulation of the family [the] usual judicial deference to the legislature is inappropriate. [We have] "long recognized that freedom of personal choice in matters of marriage and family life is one of the liberties protected by the Due Process Clause of the Fourteenth Amendment." [While] the family is not beyond regulation, [when] the government intrudes on choices concerning family living arrangements, this Court must examine carefully the importance of the governmental interests advanced and the extent to which they are served by the challenged regulation.

When thus examined, this ordinance cannot survive. The city seeks to justify it as a means of preventing overcrowding, minimizing traffic and parking congestion, and avoiding an undue financial burden on East Cleveland's school system. Although these are legitimate goals, the ordinance before us serves them marginally, at best. For example, the ordinance permits any family consisting only of husband, wife, and unmarried children to live together, even if the family contains a half dozen licensed drivers, each with his or her own car. At the same time it forbids an adult brother and sister to share a household, even if both faithfully use public transportation. The ordinance would permit a grandmother to live with a single dependent son and children, even if his school-age children number a dozen, yet it forces Mrs. Moore to find another dwelling for her grandson John, simply because of the presence of his uncle and cousin in the same household. We need not labor the point. . . .

The city [suggests] that any constitutional right to live together as a family extends only to the nuclear family—essentially a couple and their dependent children. [The line of cases beginning with *Meyer* and *Pierce*] did not expressly consider the family relationship presented here. They were immediately concerned with freedom of choice with respect to childbearing, or with the rights of parents to the custody and companionship of their own children, or with traditional parental authority in matters of child rearing and education. But unless we close our eyes to the basic reasons why certain rights associated with the family have been accorded shelter under the Fourteenth Amendment's Due Process Clause, we cannot avoid applying the force and rationale of these precedents to the family choice involved in this case. Understanding those reasons requires careful attention to this Court's function under the Due Process Clause [as described by Justice Harlan in his Poe v. Ullman dissent, reprinted in *Griswold*].

Substantive due process has at times been a treacherous field for this Court. There are risks when the judicial branch gives enhanced protection to certain substantive liberties without the guidance of the more specific provisions of the Bill of Rights. [T]here is reason for concern lest the only limits to such judicial intervention become the predilections of those who happen at the time to be Members of this Court. [While that] counsels caution and restraint, . . . it does not counsel abandonment, nor does it require what the city urges here: cutting off any protection of family rights at the first convenient, if arbitrary boundary—the boundary of the nuclear family. Appropriate limits on substantive due process come not from drawing arbitrary lines but rather from careful "respect for the teachings of history [and] solid recognition of the basic values that underlie our society." Our decisions establish that the Constitution protects the sanctity of the family precisely because the institution of the family is deeply rooted in this Nation's history and tradition. It is through the family that we inculcate and pass down many of our most cherished values, moral and cultural. Ours is by no means a tradition limited to respect for the bonds uniting the members of the nuclear family. The tradition of uncles, aunts, cousins, and especially grandparents sharing a household along with parents and children has roots equally venerable and equally deserving of constitutional recognition. Over the years millions of our citizens have grown up in just such an environment, and most, surely, have profited from it. Even if conditions of modern society have brought about a decline in extended family households, they have not erased the accumulated wisdom of civilization, gained over the centuries and honored throughout our history, that supports a larger conception of the family. Out of choice, necessity, or a sense of family responsibility, it has been common for close relatives to draw together and participate in the duties and the satisfactions of a common home. [In] times of adversity, such as the death of a spouse or economic need, the broader family has tended to come together for mutual sustenance and to maintain or rebuild a secure home life. This is apparently what happened here. Whether or not such a household is established because of personal tragedy, the choice of relatives in this degree of kinship to live together may not lightly be denied by the State. [The] Constitution prevents East Cleveland from standardizing its children—and its adults—by forcing all to live in certain narrowly defined family patterns.

Reversed.

JUSTICE STEVENS, concurring in the judgment.

[There] appears to be no precedent for an ordinance which excludes any of an owner's relatives from the group of persons who may occupy his residence on a permanent basis. . . . Since this ordinance has not been shown to have any "substantial relation to the public health, safety, morals, or general welfare" of the city of East Cleveland, and since it cuts so deeply into a fundamental right normally associated with the ownership of residential property—that of an owner to decide who may reside on his or her property—[East Cleveland's] unprecedented ordinance constitutes a taking of property without due process and without just compensation. . . .

JUSTICE STEWART, joined by JUSTICE REHNQUIST, dissenting.

[Appellant's interest] in permanently sharing a single kitchen and a suite of contiguous rooms with some of her relatives simply [is not "implicit in the concept of ordered liberty"]. To equate this interest with the fundamental decisions to marry and to bear and raise children is to extend the limited substantive contours of the Due Process Clause beyond recognition. . . .

JUSTICE WHITE, dissenting.

[W]e must always bear in mind that the substantive content of the [Due Process] Clause [is] nothing more than the accumulated product of [its] judicial interpretation. . . . This is not to suggest, at this point, that any of these cases should be overruled, or that the process by which they were decided was illegitimate or even unacceptable, but only to underline Mr. Justice Black's constant reminder to his colleagues that the Court has no license to invalidate legislation which it thinks merely arbitrary or unreasonable. [That] the Court has ample precedent for the creation of new constitutional rights should not lead it to repeat the process at will. [Under] our cases, the Due Process Clause extends substantial protection to various phases of family life, but none requires that the claim made here be sustained. . . . [The] present claim is hardly one of which it could be said that "neither liberty nor justice would exist if [it] were sacrificed." [Justice] Powell would apparently construe the Due Process Clause to protect from all but quite important state regulatory interests any right or privilege that in his estimate is deeply rooted in the country's traditions. For me, this suggests a far too expansive charter for this [Court]. What the deeply rooted traditions of the country are is arguable; which of them deserve the protection of the Due Process Clause is even more debatable. The suggested view would broaden enormously the horizons of the Clause; and, if the interest involved here is any measure of what the States would be forbidden to regulate, the courts would be substantively weighing and very likely invalidating a wide range of measures that Congress and state legislatures think appropriate to respond to a changing economic and social order. . . .

NOTES AND PROBLEMS

1. Who Is Family? Who constitutes the family—the functional, existing "family," regardless of genetic connections, or the genetic "family," without regard to its functionality? Which sort of family did *Moore* recognize? Consider again Michael H. v. Gerald D., supra, where the Court upheld a California statute that had the effect of denying parental rights to a natural father of a child born into an existing marriage to which he was not a party.

Suppose that at birth baby Elizabeth, born to Eve, was switched with baby Diana, born to Dolores. Eve takes home Diana and Dolores takes home Elizabeth. Twelve years later, Diana dies from a genetically transmitted condition. Eve learns the truth and demands custody of Elizabeth, a demand that Dolores and Elizabeth resist. Is any liberty interest of Eve violated if a court awards custody of Elizabeth to Dolores on the ground that that is in the best interest of Elizabeth? Would Dolores's or Elizabeth's liberty interest be violated if the court awarded custody of Elizabeth to Eve solely on the basis of the genetic link?

A related issue was presented to the Court in Troxel v. Granville, 530 U.S. 57 (2000). Washington law permitted "any person" to obtain visitation rights with a child whenever such "visitation may serve the best interests of the child." A Washington court granted the Troxels visitation rights with their granddaughters over the objection of Granville, the girls' mother, who was conceded to be a fit custodial parent. (The girls' father, who was the Troxels' son, was deceased.) A four-justice plurality of the Supreme Court ruled that the Washington law, as applied, violated Granville's due process right to make decisions concerning the care, custody, and control of her daughters, because the law permitted courts totally to disregard the desires of a fit custodial parent regarding visitation.

The plurality declined to decide whether state-imposed nonparental visitation would be justified upon a showing of harm or potential harm to the child without such visitation. Justice Thomas, concurring in the judgment, hinted that he regarded as unsettled the question of whether due process includes a substantive fundamental liberty interest in child-rearing but, in the absence of any direct challenge to the validity of the claim, explicitly adopted strict scrutiny as the appropriate standard of review. Justices Stevens and Kennedy, in separate dissents, thought that the "best interests" standard might be valid in some circumstances, and neither was convinced that a showing of harm or potential harm was necessary to support third-party visitation. Justice Scalia rejected the entire notion that there was any judicially enforceable liberty interest of parents in child-rearing.

2. Sources of Conflict.   When families are in conflict, there are three separate entities vying for primacy: parents, children, and the state. In Parham v. J.R., 442 U.S. 584 (1979), the Court upheld Georgia's practice of not requiring formal adversary hearings before parents commit their children to public mental institutions. The Court balanced the "individual, family, and social interests" at stake to conclude that the informal Georgia admissions procedure was valid, given "the parents' traditional interests in and responsibility for the upbringing of their child" and a longstanding societal tradition of recognizing "the family as a unit with broad parental authority over minor children."

Conflict also arises between biological and adoptive parents. Quilloin v. Walcott, 434 U.S. 246 (1978), is an example. Under Georgia law, if the biological father of a child born outside a marital relationship has not formally acknowledged his paternity, only the mother's consent is required for adoption. Quilloin had never formalized paternity of his 11-year-old son. The mother consented to the boy's adoption by her husband, with whom she and her son were living. Quilloin sought to block the adoption but did not seek custody or visitation rights. A trial court concluded that it was in the best interests of the child to grant the adoption, and a unanimous Court affirmed, rejecting Quilloin's contention that his status as the biological father conferred constitutionally fundamental rights that Georgia could not eliminate except by a narrowly drawn law to achieve compelling objectives. The Court readily agreed "that the relationship between parent and child is constitutionally protected," and opined that "the Due Process Clause would be offended '[if] a State were to attempt to force the breakup of a natural family, over the objection of the parents and their children, without some showing of unfitness and for the sole reason that to do so was thought to be in the children's best interests.'" But "adoption in this case [gives] full recognition to a family unit already in existence."

3. Nonmarital Families.   Stanley v. Illinois, 405 U.S. 645 (1972), reveals that the constitutional liberty interests of families is not confined to families blessed by the marital sacrament. Joan and Peter Stanley never married each other, but lived together off and on for 18 years and had three children together. After Joan Stanley's death Peter discovered that Illinois law automatically made children of deceased unwed mothers wards of the state. Peter maintained that Illinois deprived him of equal protection, because a married father in his situation could not be deprived of his children unless the state proved his parental unfitness. The court invoked the fundamental rights branch of equal protection (in which laws that impinge on "fundamental rights" are subjected to strict scrutiny) and struck down the Illinois conclusive presumption of parental unfitness on the part of unwed fathers. At least where the natural father could establish an existing functional relationship with his children, his interest "in the companionship, care, custody, and management of [his] children" warranted heightened judicial scrutiny. Illinois had insufficient justification for its conclusive presumption that, as applied, would break up Peter Stanley's family. Decision "by presumption is always cheaper and easier than individualized determination. But when, as here, the procedure risks running roughshod over the important interests of both parent and child [it] cannot stand."

But the claims of natural fatherhood are not always constitutionally fundamental. Consider *Quilloin* and *Michael H.*: Context, like timing in comedy, is everything.

4. Scope of the Liberty Interest. *Pierce* and *Meyer* recognized a protected liberty interest of parents and children in access to private schooling and foreign language instruction. In *Pierce*, the Court described this interest as "the liberty of parents and guardians to direct the upbringing and education of children under their control." Wisconsin v. Yoder, 406 U.S. 205 (1972), used the free exercise of religion clause as well as due process to void a compulsory education law as applied to the Old Order Amish, whose religious beliefs forbid education past the eighth grade. See Chapter 10, Section B.1. However, an earlier case, Prince v. Massachusetts, 321 U.S. 158 (1944), sustained the validity of child labor laws as applied to religious proselytizing activities. *Parham* deferred to the parents' judgment about whether their minor child should be committed to a mental institution. *Quilloin* preferred social to biological realities. *Stanley* protected a culturally abnormal parental arrangement. Which of the following statements is the best description of the Court's doctrine in this area? Which should be observed? Why?

a. Any parental choice with respect to child-rearing is a fundamental liberty. Though government infringement of those choices is subject to strict scrutiny, the government has many compelling reasons for limiting parental choices.

b. The only parental choices about child-rearing that are fundamental liberties are those with a long cultural tradition of being within the exclusive domain of parents. State interference with such parental choices is subject to strict scrutiny, but the state may regulate all other aspects of child-rearing subject only to minimal scrutiny.

c. Parental choices about child-rearing that impose no harm on the child or on the society are fundamental liberties with which the government may interfere only by overcoming strict scrutiny. All other parental choices may be regulated, subject only to minimal scrutiny of the regulation.

5. Problems. Assess the validity of each of the following scenarios.

a. A city adopts a curfew that prohibits children under the age of 18 from appearing in public after 10 P.M. on weeknights and after 11 P.M. on weekends, unless accompanied by one or both parents.

b. A city declares that children under the age of seven need 10 to 12 hours of sleep and thus prohibits any child under the age of seven from appearing in public after 8 P.M.

c. A state's supreme court rules that the state's statutory prohibition of child labor extends to household chores performed within and around the home, thus upholding a substantial fine levied against a parent who requires her child to weed the family vegetable garden.

d.   *The Right to Die*

The Court has never squarely held that there is a "right to die," though it has intimated its existence. In the cases raising this claim under due process, the specific claimed right has been rejected, but each case involved something more than the unvarnished claim of a mentally competent adult to kill himself unaided, whether by active means or by refusing unwanted lifesaving medical treatment.

Cruzan v. Director, Missouri Department of Health
497 U.S. 261 (1990)

[Nancy Cruzan, a 25-year-old single woman, suffered injuries in an auto accident that left her in "a persistent vegetative state, [exhibiting] some motor reflexes but no indications of significant cognitive functions." For seven years she lay insensate in a hospital bed, curled into a fetal position. She was kept alive only by means of a gastronomy tube in her stomach, through which she received necessary nutrition and fluid. When her parents decided that the gastronomy tube should be removed and Nancy be permitted to die, her medical caregivers were not willing to comply without a court order to that effect. The Cruzans obtained the order from a Missouri trial court, but on appeal the Missouri Supreme Court reversed because it was not persuaded that, as required by Missouri law, there was "clear and convincing" evidence that Nancy had expressed her desire, when competent, to refuse life-sustaining measures in her present condition. The Supreme Court upheld Missouri's proof requirement.]

CHIEF JUSTICE REHNQUIST delivered the opinion of the Court.

[The] common law doctrine of informed consent is viewed as generally encompassing the right of a competent individual to refuse medical treatment. . . . In this Court, the question is simply and starkly whether the Constitution prohibits Missouri from choosing the rule of decision which it did. [The] principle that a competent person has a constitutionally protected liberty interest in refusing unwanted medical treatment may be inferred from our prior decisions. [But] determining that a person has a "liberty interest" under the Due Process Clause does not end the inquiry; "whether respondent's constitutional rights have been violated must be determined by balancing his liberty interests against the relevant state interests." Petitioners insist that under the general holdings of our cases, the forced administration of life-sustaining medical treatment, and even of artificially delivered food and water essential to life, would implicate a competent person's liberty interest. Although we think the logic of the cases [would] embrace such a liberty interest, the dramatic consequences involved in refusal of such treatment would inform the inquiry as to whether the deprivation of that interest is constitutionally permissible. But for purposes of this case, we assume that the United States Constitution would grant a competent person a constitutionally protected right to refuse life-saving hydration and nutrition.

Petitioners go on to assert that an incompetent person should possess the same right in this respect as is possessed by a competent person. [This] begs the question: An incompetent person is not able to make an informed and voluntary choice to exercise a hypothetical right to refuse treatment or any other right. Such a "right" must be exercised for her, if at all, by some sort of surrogate. Here, Missouri has in effect recognized that under certain circumstances a surrogate may act for the patient in electing to have hydration and nutrition withdrawn in such a way as to cause death, but it has established a procedural safeguard to assure that the action of the surrogate conforms [to] the wishes expressed by the patient while competent. Missouri requires that evidence of the incompetent's wishes as to the withdrawal of treatment be proved by clear and convincing evidence. The question, then, is whether [the] Constitution forbids the establishment of this procedural requirement by the State. We hold that it does not.

Whether or not Missouri's clear and convincing evidence requirement comports with [the] Constitution depends in part on what interests the State may properly seek to protect in this situation. Missouri relies on its interest in the protection and preservation of human life, and there can be no gainsaying this interest. [We] do not think a State is required to remain neutral in the face of an informed and voluntary decision by a physically able adult to starve to death. But in the context presented here, a State has more particular interests at stake. The choice between life and death is a deeply personal decision of obvious and overwhelming finality. We believe Missouri may legitimately seek to safeguard the personal element of this choice through the imposition of heightened evidentiary requirements. [T]he Due Process Clause protects an interest in life as well as an interest in refusing life-sustaining medical treatment. Not all incompetent patients will have loved ones available to serve as surrogate decision-makers. And even where family members are present, "[there] will, of course, be some unfortunate situations in which family members will not act to protect a patient." A State is entitled to guard against potential abuses in such situations. [Finally], we think a State may properly decline to make judgments about the "quality" of life that a particular individual may enjoy, and simply assert an unqualified interest in the preservation of human life to be weighed against the constitutionally protected interests of the individual.

In our view, Missouri has permissibly sought to advance these interests through the adoption of a "clear and convincing" standard of proof to govern such proceedings. [The] more stringent the burden of proof a party must bear, the more that party bears the risk of an erroneous decision. We believe that Missouri may permissibly place an increased risk of an erroneous decision on those seeking to terminate an incompetent individual's life-sustaining treatment. An erroneous decision not to terminate results in a maintenance of the status quo; the possibility of subsequent developments such as advancements in medical science, the discovery of new evidence regarding the patient's intent, changes in the law, or simply the unexpected death of the patient despite the administration of life-sustaining treatment at least create the potential that a wrong decision will eventually be corrected or its impact mitigated. An erroneous decision to withdraw life-sustaining treatment, however, is not susceptible of correction. [In] sum, we conclude that a State may apply a clear and convincing evidence standard in proceedings where a guardian seeks to discontinue nutrition and hydration of a person diagnosed to be in a persistent vegetative state. . . .

Petitioners alternatively contend that Missouri must accept the "substituted judgment" of close family members even in the absence of substantial proof that their views reflect the views of the patient. [We] do not think the Due Process Clause requires the State to repose judgment on these matters with anyone but the patient herself. Close family members may have a strong feeling—a feeling not at all ignoble or unworthy, but not entirely disinterested, either—that they do not wish to witness the continuation of the life of a loved one which they regard as hopeless, meaningless, and even degrading. But there is no automatic assurance that the view of close family members will necessarily be the same as the patient's would have been had she been confronted with the prospect of her situation while competent. . . .

JUSTICE O'CONNOR, concurring.

I agree that a protected liberty interest in refusing unwanted medical treatment may be inferred from our prior decisions, and that the refusal of artificially delivered food and water is encompassed within that liberty interest. . . . [The] Court does not . . . decide . . . whether a State must also give effect to the decisions of a surrogate decisionmaker. In my view, such a duty may well be constitutionally required to protect the patient's liberty interest in refusing medical treatment. . . . [Today's decision does] not preclude a future determination that the Constitution requires the States to implement the decisions of a patient's duly appointed surrogate. . . .

JUSTICE SCALIA, concurring.

[This] case portray[s] quite clearly the difficult, indeed agonizing, questions that are presented by the constantly increasing power of science to keep the human body alive for longer than any reasonable person would want to inhabit it. The States have begun to grapple with these problems through legislation. I am concerned, from the tenor of today's opinions, that we are poised to confuse that enterprise as successfully as we have confused the enterprise of legislating concerning abortion—requiring it to be conducted against a background of federal constitutional imperatives that are unknown because they are being newly crafted from Term to Term. That would be a great misfortune. . . . I would have preferred that we announce, clearly and promptly, that the federal courts have no business in this field; that American law has always accorded the State the power to prevent, by force if necessary, suicide—including suicide by refusing to take appropriate measures necessary to preserve one's life; that the point at which life becomes "worthless," and the point at which the means necessary to preserve it become "extraordinary" or "inappropriate," are neither set forth in the Constitution nor known to the nine Justices of this Court any better than they are known to nine people picked at random from the Kansas City telephone directory; and hence, that even when it is demonstrated by clear and convincing evidence that a patient no longer wishes certain measures to be taken to preserve his or her life, it is up to the citizens of Missouri to decide, through their elected representatives, whether that wish will be honored. It is quite impossible (because the Constitution says nothing about the matter) that those citizens will decide upon a line less lawful than the one we would choose; and it is unlikely (because we know no more about "life and death" than they do) that they will decide upon a line less reasonable.

[No] "substantive due process" claim can be maintained unless the claimant demonstrates that the State has deprived him of a right historically and traditionally protected against state interference. That cannot possibly be established here. At common law [suicide] was criminally liable [and] at the time of the adoption of the Fourteenth [Amendment] assisting suicide was a criminal offense.

Petitioners rely on three distinctions to separate Nancy Cruzan's case from ordinary suicide: (1) that she is permanently incapacitated and in pain; (2) that she would bring on her death not by any affirmative act but by merely declining treatment that provides nourishment; and (3) that preventing her from effectuating her presumed wish to die requires violation of her bodily integrity. None of these suffices. Suicide was not excused even when committed "to avoid those ills which [persons] had not the fortitude to endure." [The] second asserted distinction [relies] on the dichotomy between action and inaction. [Starving] oneself to death is no different from putting a gun to one's temple as far as the common-law definition of suicide is [concerned]. The third asserted basis of distinction — that frustrating Nancy Cruzan's wish to die in the present case requires interference with her bodily integrity — is likewise inadequate, because such interference is impermissible only if one begs the question whether her refusal to undergo the treatment on her own is suicide. It has always been lawful not only for the State, but even for private citizens, to interfere with bodily integrity to prevent a felony. That general rule has of course been applied to suicide. . . .

JUSTICE BRENNAN, joined by JUSTICES MARSHALL and BLACKMUN, dissenting.

[The] right to be free from medical attention without consent, to determine what shall be done with one's own body, is deeply rooted in this Nation's traditions, as the majority acknowledges. [Nor] does the fact that Nancy Cruzan is now incompetent deprive her of her fundamental rights. [The] question is not whether an incompetent has constitutional rights, but how such rights may be exercised.

[The] State has no legitimate general interest in someone's life, completely abstracted from the interest of the person living that life, that could outweigh the person's choice to avoid medical treatment. [This] is not to say that the State has no legitimate interests to assert here. [Missouri has an] interest in providing Nancy Cruzan, now incompetent, with as accurate as possible a determination of how she would exercise her rights under these circumstances. [Until] Nancy's wishes have been determined, the only state interest that may be asserted is an interest in safeguarding the accuracy of that determination. [Missouri] may constitutionally impose only those procedural requirements that serve to enhance the accuracy of a determination of Nancy Cruzan's wishes or are at least consistent with an accurate determination. The Missouri "safeguard" that the Court upholds today does not meet that standard. [Missouri's] rule of decision imposes a markedly asymmetrical evidentiary burden. Only [clear and convincing] evidence of specific statements of treatment choice made by the patient when competent is admissible to support a finding that the patient, now in a persistent vegetative state, would wish to avoid further medical treatment. [No] proof is required to support a finding that the incompetent person would wish to continue treatment. . . .

JUSTICE STEVENS, dissenting.

[The] Constitution requires the State to care for Nancy Cruzan's life in a way that gives appropriate respect to her own best interests. [If, as the trial court found], Nancy Cruzan has no interest in continued treatment, and if she has a liberty interest in being free from unwanted treatment, and if the cessation of treatment would have no adverse impact on third parties, and if no reason exists to doubt the good faith of Nancy's parents, then what possible basis could the State have for insisting upon continued medical treatment? . . .

NOTES

1. Substituted Decisions by or for Competent Patients. Note that *Cruzan* suggests, but does not hold, that competent patients have a fundamental liberty to refuse invasive, life-prolonging medical care. This right, however, is of most value when it constitutionally disappears—the moment one becomes incompetent. Given the result in *Cruzan*, a prudent person while competent would execute a "living will" or durable power of attorney that provides explicit instructions about medical care in the case of incompetency, or appoints someone to make those decisions, or both. But what if the state prohibits such devices—are governments constitutionally obligated to observe living wills? The Court in *Cruzan* expressly avoided deciding this question. What should be the answer?

2. Assisted Suicide. If there is a fundamental liberty interest of competent adults to reject unwanted lifesaving techniques, does that mean that competent adults also possess a fundamental liberty interest to commit suicide? Justice Scalia's concurrence, though rejecting any constitutional protection for suicide, treated the termination of life-support measures as just another form of suicide. Did *Cruzan* implicitly recognize a liberty interest in suicide? A *fundamental* liberty interest? If so, does it include the power to obtain assistance from others in committing suicide?

Washington v. Glucksberg
521 U.S. 702 (1997)

CHIEF JUSTICE REHNQUIST delivered the opinion of the Court.

The question presented [is] whether Washington's prohibition against "causing" or "aiding" a suicide offends the Fourteenth Amendment to the United States Constitution. We hold that it does not.

It has always been a crime to assist a suicide [in] Washington. . . . Today, Washington law [imposes felony punishment upon a person who] "knowingly causes or aids another person to attempt suicide." [At] the same time, Washington's Natural Death Act, enacted in 1979, states that the "withholding or withdrawal of life-sustaining treatment" at a patient's direction "shall not, for any purpose, constitute a suicide." . . .

Respondents [are Washington] physicians [who] occasionally treat terminally ill, suffering patients, and declare that they would assist these patients in ending their lives if not for Washington's assisted-suicide ban. [These physicians], along with three gravely ill, pseudonymous plaintiffs who have since died and Compassion in Dying, a nonprofit organization that counsels people considering physician-assisted suicide, [sought] a declaration that [Washington's assisted suicide ban] is, on its face, unconstitutional. [The District Court declared the ban void, and the Court of Appeals, en banc,] concluded that "the Constitution encompasses a due process liberty interest in controlling the time and manner of one's death" [and] that the State's assisted-suicide ban was unconstitutional "as applied to terminally ill competent adults who wish to hasten their deaths with medication prescribed by their physicians." . . . [We] now reverse.

We begin, as we do in all [substantive] due-process cases, by examining our Nation's history, legal traditions, and practices. In almost every State—indeed, in almost every western democracy—it is a crime to assist a suicide. The States' assisted-suicide bans [are] longstanding expressions of the States' commitment to the protection and preservation of all human life. Indeed, opposition to and condemnation of suicide—and, therefore, of assisting suicide—are consistent and enduring themes of our philosophical, legal, and cultural heritages. [For] over 700 years, the Anglo-American common-law tradition has punished or otherwise disapproved of both suicide and assisting suicide. . . . In the 13th century, Henry de Bracton, one of the first legal-treatise writers, observed that "just as a man may commit felony by slaying another so may he do so by slaying himself." [Those guilty of suicide forfeited their property to the Crown.] Centuries later, [Blackstone] referred to suicide as "self-murder" [and] emphasized that "the law [has] ranked [suicide] among the highest crimes." . . .

For the most part, the early American colonies adopted the common-law approach [but, over time], abolished these harsh common-law penalties [of forfeiture]. The movement away from the common law's harsh sanctions did not represent an acceptance of suicide; rather, [this] change reflected the growing consensus that it was unfair to punish the suicide's family for his wrongdoing. [Colonial] and early state legislatures and courts did not retreat from prohibiting assisting suicide. And the prohibitions against assisting suicide never contained exceptions for those who were near death. [By] the time the Fourteenth Amendment was ratified, it was a crime in most States to assist a suicide. . . .

Though deeply rooted, the States' assisted-suicide bans have in recent years been reexamined and, generally, reaffirmed. [Public] concern and democratic action [are] sharply focused on how best to protect dignity and independence at the end of life, with the result that [many States] now permit "living wills," surrogate health-care decisionmaking, and the withdrawal or refusal of life-sustaining medical treatment. At the same time, however, voters and legislators continue for the most part to reaffirm their States' prohibitions on assisting suicide, [although] voters in Oregon enacted [a] "Death With Dignity Act," which legalized physician-assisted suicide for competent, terminally ill adults. [Federal law] prohibits the use of federal funds in support of physician-assisted suicide. [Attitudes] toward suicide itself have changed since Bracton, but our laws have consistently condemned, and continue to prohibit, assisting suicide. . . .

We have . . . "always been reluctant to expand the concept of substantive due process because guideposts for responsible decisionmaking in this unchartered area are scarce and open-ended." By extending constitutional protection to an asserted right or liberty interest, we, to a great extent, place the matter outside the arena of public debate and legislative action. We must therefore "exercise the utmost care whenever we are asked to break new ground in this field," lest the liberty protected by the Due Process Clause be subtly transformed into the policy preferences of the members of this Court.

Our established method of substantive-due-process analysis has two primary features: First, we have regularly observed that the Due Process Clause specially protects those fundamental rights and liberties which are, objectively, "deeply rooted in this Nation's history and tradition," and "implicit in the concept of ordered liberty," such that "neither liberty nor justice would exist if they were sacrificed." Second, we have required in substantive-due-process cases a "careful description" of the asserted fundamental liberty interest. Our Nation's history, legal traditions, and practices thus provide the crucial "guideposts for responsible decisionmaking," that direct and restrain our exposition of the Due Process Clause. . . .

[The asserted] right to commit suicide, [including] a right to assistance in doing so [is at odds] with a consistent and almost universal tradition that has long rejected the asserted right, and continues explicitly to reject it today, even for terminally ill, mentally competent adults. To hold for respondents, we would have to reverse centuries of legal doctrine and practice, and strike down the considered policy choice of almost every State. [The] right assumed in *Cruzan*, however, was not simply deduced from abstract concepts of personal autonomy. Given the common-law rule that forced medication was a battery, and the long legal tradition protecting the decision to refuse unwanted medical treatment, our assumption was entirely consistent with this Nation's history and constitutional traditions. The decision to commit suicide with the assistance of another may be just as personal and profound as the decision to refuse unwanted medical treatment, but it has never enjoyed similar legal protection. Indeed, the two acts are widely and reasonably regarded as quite distinct. . . . [The] asserted "right" to assistance in committing suicide is not a fundamental liberty interest protected by the Due Process Clause. The Constitution also requires, however, that Washington's assisted-suicide ban be rationally related to legitimate government interests. This requirement is unquestionably met here. . . .

First, Washington has an "unqualified interest in the preservation of human life."

[The] State also has an interest in protecting the integrity and ethics of the medical profession. [The] American Medical Association . . . has concluded that "physician-assisted suicide is fundamentally incompatible with the physician's role as healer." And physician-assisted suicide [could] undermine the trust that is essential to the doctor-patient relationship by blurring the time-honored line between healing and harming.

Next, the State has an interest in protecting vulnerable groups—including the poor, the elderly, and disabled persons—from abuse, neglect, and mistakes. [We recognize] the real risk of subtle coercion and undue influence in end-of-life situations. . . . [The] State's interest here goes beyond protecting the vulnerable from coercion; it extends to protecting disabled and terminally ill people from prejudice, negative and inaccurate stereotypes, and "societal indifference."

[Finally], the State may fear that permitting assisted suicide will start it down the path to voluntary and perhaps even involuntary euthanasia. [What] is couched as a limited right to "physician-assisted suicide" is likely, in effect, a much broader license, which could prove extremely difficult to police and contain. [This] concern is further supported by evidence about the practice of euthanasia in the Netherlands. The Dutch government's own study [reveals that] euthanasia in the Netherlands has not been limited to competent, terminally ill adults who are enduring physical suffering, and that regulation of the practice may not have prevented abuses in cases involving vulnerable persons, including severely disabled neonates and elderly persons suffering from dementia. [Washington] reasonably ensures against this risk by banning, rather than regulating, assisting suicide.

We need not weigh exactly the relative strengths of these various interests. They are unquestionably important and legitimate, and Washington's ban on assisted suicide is at least reasonably related to their promotion and protection. We therefore hold that [Washington's assisted suicide ban] does not violate the Fourteenth Amendment, either on its face or "as applied to competent, terminally ill adults who wish to hasten their deaths by obtaining medication prescribed by their doctors."

Throughout the Nation, Americans are engaged in an earnest and profound debate about the morality, legality, and practicality of physician-assisted suicide. Our holding permits this debate to continue, as it should in a democratic society. [Reversed.]

JUSTICE O'CONNOR, concurring.[10]

I join the Court's opinions because I agree that there is no generalized right to "commit suicide." [Respondents] urge us to address the narrower question whether a mentally competent person who is experiencing great suffering has a constitutionally cognizable interest in controlling the circumstances of his or her imminent death. I see no need to reach that question in the context of the facial challenges to the New York and Washington laws at issue here. [All] agree that in these States a patient who is suffering from a terminal illness and who is experiencing great pain has no legal barriers to obtaining medication, from qualified physicians, to alleviate that suffering, even to the point of causing unconsciousness and hastening death. . . .

JUSTICE STEVENS, concurring in the judgments.

[The Court's holding] does not foreclose the possibility that some applications of the statute might well be invalid. . . . [There] are situations in which an interest in hastening death is . . . entitled to constitutional protection. . . . Avoiding intolerable pain and the indignity of living one's final days incapacitated and in agony is certainly "at the heart of [the] liberty [to] define one's own concept of existence, of meaning, of the universe, and of the mystery of human life." *Casey*. [Although] there is no absolute right to physician-assisted suicide, *Cruzan* makes it clear that some individuals who no longer have the option of deciding whether to live or to die because they are already on the threshold of death have a constitutionally protected interest that may outweigh the State's interest in preserving life at all costs. The liberty interest at stake in a case like this [is] an interest in deciding how, rather than whether, a critical threshold shall be crossed. . . .

NOTES

1. Vacco v. Quill. In the companion case to *Glucksberg*, Vacco v. Quill, 521 U.S. 793 (1997), the Court rejected an equal protection challenge to New York's ban on assisted suicide that also permitted patients to refuse life-saving medical treatment. The Court of Appeals had concluded that the laws provided differential treatment because terminally ill patients on life support could direct caregivers to withdraw life support and thus hasten death while terminally ill patients not on life support could not hasten death by assisted suicide. Said the Supreme Court:

10. Justice Ginsburg concurs in the Court's judgments substantially for the reasons stated in this opinion. Justice Breyer joins this opinion except insofar as it joins the opinions of the Court. [The other judgment and opinion referred to is Vacco v. Quill, infra, a companion case upholding New York's assisted-suicide law against an equal protection challenge.—ED.]

This conclusion depends on the submission that ending or refusing lifesaving medical treatment "is nothing more nor less than assisted suicide." [But] we think the distinction between assisting suicide and withdrawing life-sustaining treatment, a distinction widely recognized and endorsed in the medical profession and in our legal traditions, is both important and logical; it is certainly rational. The distinction comports with fundamental legal principles of causation and intent. First, when a patient refuses life-sustaining medical treatment, he dies from an underlying fatal disease or pathology; but if a patient ingests lethal medication prescribed by a physician, he is killed by that medication. [Second,] a physician who withdraws, or honors a patient's refusal to begin, life-sustaining medical treatment purposefully intends [only] to respect his patient's wishes and "to cease doing useless and futile or degrading things to the patient when [the patient] no longer stands to benefit from them." The same is true when a doctor provides aggressive palliative care; in some cases, painkilling drugs may hasten a patient's death, but the physician's purpose and intent is, or may be, only to ease his patient's pain. A doctor who assists a suicide, however, "must, necessarily and indubitably, intend primarily that the patient be made dead." . . . The law has long used actors' intent or purpose to distinguish between two acts that may have the same result. . . .

By permitting everyone to refuse unwanted medical treatment while prohibiting anyone from assisting a suicide, New York law follows a longstanding and rational distinction. New York's [valid] and important public interests [(the same as in *Glucksberg*)] easily satisfy the constitutional requirement that a legislative classification bear a rational relation to some legitimate end.

2. What Is the Holding? Justice O'Connor's concurrence was the crucial fifth vote in both cases, but she refused to decide the critical issue of "whether a mentally competent person who is experiencing great suffering has a constitutionally cognizable interest in controlling the circumstances of his or her imminent death." Suppose a state prohibits physicians from prescribing painkillers in amounts that "may foreseeably hasten death." Is the state law unconstitutional?

3. Postscript: Assisted Suicide in Oregon. Oregon's Death With Dignity Act, Or. Rev. Stat. §§127.800 *et seq.* (2003), enacted by popular initiative in 1994, bars civil or criminal liability for physicians who, in compliance with the Act, dispense or prescribe a lethal dose of drugs upon the request of a terminally ill patient. Invoking his ostensible authority under the federal Controlled Substances Act, which governs various drugs, including those used to induce death, the United States Attorney General in 2001 issued a ruling having the force of law, declaring that the use, dispensation, or prescription of controlled substances to assist suicide is not a legitimate medical practice and is unlawful under the Controlled Substances Act. In Gonzales v. Oregon, 546 U.S. 243 (2006), the Supreme Court ruled that the Attorney General lacked the statutory authority to issue his ruling. As a result, while Oregon's experiment in assisted suicide survived, the Court had no occasion to decide any of the underlying constitutional issues.

e. *Consensual Sexual Choices*

Does an adult individual have the right to be free from unwarranted government interference in making private consensual sexual choices?

The Court first encountered this issue in Bowers v. Hardwick, 478 U.S. 186 (1986), in which it upheld the validity of Georgia's criminal sodomy law, which provided that "a person commits the offense of sodomy when he performs or submits to any sexual act involving the sex organs of one person and the mouth or anus of another." Hardwick, an adult male, was charged with violation of this law as a result of his consensual sexual activity with another adult male in the bedroom of Hardwick's home. The prosecution was dropped, but Hardwick brought suit in federal court, challenging the validity of the law. In a 5-4 decision, the Court concluded that Hardwick did not assert a fundamental liberty interest. Accordingly, the Court applied minimal scrutiny and upheld the law because it was rationally related to Georgia's legitimate interest of declaring homosexual sodomy

immoral and unacceptable. This is said to be an inadequate rationale to support the law. The law, however, is constantly based on notions of morality, and if all laws representing essentially moral choices are to [be] invalidated under the Due Process Clause, the courts will be very busy indeed. . . . [N]one of the rights announced in [*Pierce, Meyer, Skinner, Loving, Griswold, Eisenstadt,* or *Roe*] bears any resemblance to the claimed constitutional right of homosexuals to engage in acts of sodomy. . . . No connection between family, marriage, or procreation on the one hand and homosexual activity on the other has been demonstrated. Moreover, any claim that these cases nevertheless stand for the proposition that any kind of private sexual conduct between consenting adults is constitutionally insulated from state proscription is unsupportable. . . . [F]undamental liberties . . . are "implicit in the concept of ordered liberty," such that "neither liberty nor justice would exist if [they] were sacrificed," [or they are] those liberties that are "deeply rooted in this Nation's history and tradition." It is obvious to us that neither of these formulations would extend a fundamental right to homosexuals to engage in consensual sodomy. Proscriptions against that conduct have ancient roots. Sodomy was a criminal offense at common law and was forbidden by the laws of the original 13 States when they ratified the Bill of Rights. In 1868, when the Fourteenth Amendment was ratified, all but 5 of the 37 States in the Union had criminal sodomy laws. In fact, until 1961, all 50 States outlawed sodomy, and today, 24 States and the District of Columbia continue to provide criminal penalties for sodomy performed in private and between consenting adults. Against this background, to claim that a right to engage in such conduct is "deeply rooted in this Nation's history and tradition" or "implicit in the concept of ordered liberty" is, at best, facetious.

In a dissent joined by Justices Brennan, Marshall, and Stevens, Justice Blackmun contended that the Court ignores

"the basic reasons why certain rights associated with the family have been accorded shelter under [the] Due Process Clause." We protect those rights . . .

because they form so central a part of an individual's life. "[The] concept of privacy embodies the 'moral fact that a person belongs to himself and not others nor to society as a whole.'" Only the most willful blindness could obscure the fact that sexual intimacy is "a sensitive, key relationship of human existence, central to family life, community welfare, and the development of human personality." [The] right of an individual to conduct intimate relationships in the intimacy of his or her own home seems to me to be the heart of the Constitution's protection of privacy. . . .

In a separate dissent, Justice Stevens, joined by Justices Brennan and Marshall, argued that the Court's

prior cases . . . establish that a State may not prohibit sodomy within "the sacred precincts of marital bedrooms," or, indeed, between unmarried heterosexual adults. . . . [If this] is a protected . . . liberty for the vast majority of Georgia's citizens . . . the State must assume the burden of justifying a selective application of its law. Either the persons to whom Georgia seeks to apply its statute do not have the same interest in "liberty" that others have, or there must be a reason why the State may be permitted to apply a generally applicable law to certain persons that it does not apply to others. The first possibility is plainly unacceptable. [Every] free citizen has the same interest in "liberty" that the members of the majority share. . . . The second possibility is similarly unacceptable. A policy of selective application must be supported by a neutral and legitimate interest—something more substantial than a habitual dislike for, or ignorance about, the disfavored group. Neither the State nor the Court has identified any such interest in this case.

≡≡≡ *Lawrence v. Texas*
539 U.S. 558 (2003)

JUSTICE KENNEDY delivered the opinion of the Court.

Liberty protects the person from unwarranted government intrusions into a dwelling or other private places. In our tradition the State is not omnipresent in the home. And there are other spheres of our lives and existence, outside the home, where the State should not be a dominant presence. Freedom extends beyond spatial bounds. Liberty presumes an autonomy of self that includes freedom of thought, belief, expression, and certain intimate conduct. The instant case involves liberty of the person both in its spatial and more transcendent dimensions.

I. The question before the Court is the validity of a Texas statute making it a crime for two persons of the same sex to engage in certain intimate sexual conduct.

[Houston police officers] were dispatched to a private residence in response to a reported weapons disturbance. They entered an apartment where one of the petitioners, John Geddes Lawrence, resided. The right of the police to enter does not seem to have been questioned. The officers observed Lawrence and another man, Tyron Garner, engaging in a sexual act. The two petitioners were arrested, held in custody over night, and charged and convicted. . . .

The complaints described their crime as "deviate sexual intercourse, namely anal sex, with a member of the same sex (man)." The applicable state law is Tex. Penal Code Ann. §21.06(a) (2003). It provides: "A person commits an offense if he engages in deviate sexual intercourse with another individual of the same sex." The statute defines "deviate sexual intercourse" as "any contact between any part of the genitals of one person and the mouth or anus of another person; or . . . the penetration of the genitals or the anus of another person with an object." §21.01(1). . . . The [Texas] Court of Appeals . . . affirmed the convictions . . . [because it] considered our decision in Bowers v. Hardwick to be controlling on the federal due process aspect of the case. *Bowers* then being authoritative, this was proper. . . .

The petitioners were adults at the time of the alleged offense. Their conduct was in private and consensual.

II. We . . . deem it necessary to reconsider the Court's holding in *Bowers*. . . .

To say that the issue in *Bowers* was simply the right to engage in [homosexual sodomy] demeans the claim the individual put forward, just as it would demean a married couple were it to be said marriage is simply about the right to have sexual intercourse. The laws involved in *Bowers* and here are, to be sure, statutes that purport to do no more than prohibit a particular sexual act. Their penalties and purposes, though, have more far-reaching consequences, touching upon the most private human conduct, sexual behavior, and in the most private of places, the home. The statutes do seek to control a personal relationship that, whether or not entitled to formal recognition in the law, is within the liberty of persons to choose without being punished as criminals.

This, as a general rule, should counsel against attempts by the State, or a court, to define the meaning of the relationship or to set its boundaries absent injury to a person or abuse of an institution the law protects. . . . When sexuality finds overt expression in intimate conduct with another person, the conduct can be but one element in a personal bond that is more enduring. The liberty protected by the Constitution allows homosexual persons the right to make this choice.

[The *Bowers* Court asserted that proscriptions against sodomy "have ancient roots."] We need not . . . reach a definitive historical judgment, but . . . there is no longstanding history in this country of laws directed at homosexual conduct as a distinct matter. Beginning in colonial times there were prohibitions of sodomy derived from the English criminal laws passed in the first instance by the Reformation Parliament of 1533. The English prohibition was understood to include relations between men and women as well as relations between men and men. Nineteenth-century commentators similarly read American sodomy, buggery, and crime-against-nature statutes as criminalizing certain relations between men and women and between men and men. . . . Thus early American sodomy laws were not directed at homosexuals as such. . . . This does not suggest approval of homosexual conduct. It does tend to show that this particular form of conduct was not thought of as a separate category from like conduct between heterosexual persons.

. . . American laws targeting same-sex couples did not develop until the last third of the 20th century. . . . It was not until the 1970s that any State singled out same-sex relations for criminal prosecution, and only nine States have done so. Over the course of the last decades, States with same-sex prohibitions have moved toward abolishing them. In summary, the historical grounds relied upon in *Bowers* . . . , at the very least, are overstated.

[The] Court in *Bowers* was making the broader point that for centuries there have been powerful voices to condemn homosexual conduct as immoral. . . . For many persons these are not trivial concerns but profound and deep convictions accepted as ethical and moral principles. . . . These considerations do not answer the question before us, however. The issue is whether the majority may use the power of the State to enforce these views on the whole society through operation of the criminal law. "Our obligation is to define the liberty of all, not to mandate our own moral code." [*Casey*.]

. . . [We] think that our laws and traditions in the past half century are of most relevance here. These references show an emerging awareness that liberty gives substantial protection to adult persons in deciding how to conduct their private lives in matters pertaining to sex. . . . In 1955 the American Law Institute promulgated the Model Penal Code and made clear that it did not recommend or provide for "criminal penalties for consensual sexual relations conducted in private." [A]lmost five years before *Bowers* was decided the European Court of Human Rights . . . held that [Northern Ireland's laws proscribing homosexual] conduct were invalid under the European Convention on Human Rights. Dudgeon v. United Kingdom, 45 Eur. Ct. H.R. (1981) P52.

[The] deficiencies in *Bowers* became even more apparent in the years following its announcement. The 25 States with laws prohibiting the relevant conduct referenced in the *Bowers* decision are reduced now to 13, of which 4 enforce their laws only against homosexual conduct. In those States where sodomy is still proscribed, whether for same-sex or heterosexual conduct, there is a pattern of nonenforcement with respect to consenting adults acting in private. . . . The central holding of *Bowers* has been brought in question by this case, and it should be addressed. Its continuance as precedent demeans the lives of homosexual persons.

The stigma this criminal statute imposes, moreover, is not trivial. . . . We are advised that if Texas convicted an adult for private, consensual homosexual conduct under the statute here in question the convicted person would come within the [sex offender] registration laws of a least four States were he or she to be subject to their jurisdiction. . . . Furthermore, the Texas criminal conviction carries with it the other collateral consequences always following a conviction, such as notations on job application forms, to mention but one example. . . .

The rationale of *Bowers* does not withstand careful analysis. . . . *Bowers* was not correct when it was decided, and it is not correct today. . . . Bowers v. Hardwick should be and now is overruled.

The present case does not involve minors. It does not involve persons who might be injured or coerced or who are situated in relationships where consent might not easily be refused. It does not involve public conduct or prostitution. It does not involve whether the government must give formal recognition to any relationship that homosexual persons seek to enter. The case does involve two adults who, with full and mutual consent from each other, engaged in sexual practices common to a homosexual lifestyle. The petitioners are entitled to respect for their private lives. The State cannot demean their existence or control their destiny by making their private sexual conduct a crime. Their right to liberty under the Due Process Clause gives them the full right to engage in their conduct without intervention of the government. "It is a promise of the Constitution that there is a realm of personal liberty which the government may not enter." The Texas statute furthers no legitimate state interest which can justify its intrusion into the personal and private life of the individual. . . .

The judgment of the [Texas] Court of Appeals . . . is reversed, and the case is remanded for further proceedings not inconsistent with this opinion.

JUSTICE O'CONNOR, concurring in the judgment.

. . . I joined *Bowers*, and do not join the Court in overruling it. Nevertheless, I agree with the Court that Texas'[s] statute banning same-sex sodomy is unconstitutional. . . . I base my conclusion on the Fourteenth Amendment's Equal Protection Clause.

. . . The statute at issue here makes sodomy a crime only if a person "engages in deviate sexual intercourse with another individual of the same sex." Sodomy between opposite-sex partners, however, is not a crime in Texas. . . . The Texas statute makes homosexuals unequal in the eyes of the law by making particular conduct—and only that conduct—subject to criminal sanction. . . .

Texas attempts to justify its law . . . by arguing that the statute satisfies rational basis review because it furthers the legitimate governmental interest of the promotion of morality. [While in *Bowers* we pointed] to the government's interest in promoting morality, *Bowers* did not hold that moral disapproval of a group is a rational basis under the Equal Protection Clause to criminalize homosexual sodomy when heterosexual sodomy is not punished. This case raises a different issue than *Bowers:* whether, under the Equal Protection Clause, moral disapproval is a legitimate state interest to justify by itself a statute that bans homosexual sodomy, but not heterosexual sodomy. It is not. Moral disapproval of this group, like a bare desire to harm the group, is an interest that is insufficient to satisfy rational basis review under the Equal Protection Clause. Indeed, we have never held that moral disapproval, without any other asserted state interest, is a sufficient rationale under the Equal Protection Clause to justify a law that discriminates among groups of persons.

Moral disapproval of a group cannot be a legitimate governmental interest under the Equal Protection Clause because legal classifications must not be "drawn for the purpose of disadvantaging the group burdened by the law."

. . . [Because] Texas so rarely enforces its sodomy law as applied to private, consensual acts, the law serves more as a statement of dislike and disapproval against homosexuals than as a tool to stop criminal behavior. The Texas sodomy law "raises the inevitable inference that the disadvantage imposed is born of animosity toward the class of persons affected." . . . Whether a sodomy law that is neutral both in effect and application would violate the substantive component of the Due Process Clause is an issue that need not be decided today. . . .

A law branding one class of persons as criminal solely based on the State's moral disapproval of that class . . . runs contrary to the values of the Constitution and the Equal Protection Clause, under any standard of review. I therefore concur in the Court's judgment that Texas'[s] sodomy law banning "deviate sexual intercourse" between consenting adults of the same sex, but not between consenting adults of different sexes, is unconstitutional.

JUSTICE SCALIA, with whom CHIEF JUSTICE REHNQUIST and JUSTICE THOMAS join, dissenting.

Most of . . . today's opinion has no relevance to its actual holding—that the Texas statute "furthers no legitimate state interest which can justify" its application to petitioners under rational-basis review. Though there is discussion of "fundamental propositions" and "fundamental decisions," nowhere does the Court's opinion declare that homosexual sodomy is a "fundamental right" under the Due Process Clause; nor does it subject the Texas law to the standard of review that would be appropriate (strict scrutiny) if homosexual sodomy *were* a "fundamental right." . . .

I. . . . State laws against bigamy, same-sex marriage, adult incest, prostitution, masturbation, adultery, fornication, bestiality, and obscenity are likewise sustainable only in light of *Bowers*'[s] validation of laws based on moral choices. Every single one of these laws is called into question by today's decision; the Court makes no effort to cabin the scope of its decision to exclude them from its holding. The impossibility of distinguishing homosexuality from other traditional "morals" offenses is precisely why *Bowers* rejected the rational-basis challenge. "The law," it said, "is constantly based on notions of morality, and if all laws representing essentially moral choices are to be invalidated under the Due Process Clause, the courts will be very busy indeed." [*Bowers.*] . . .

II. Having decided that it need not adhere to *stare decisis*, the Court still must establish that *Bowers* was wrongly decided and that the Texas statute, as applied to petitioners, is unconstitutional. . . .

It is . . . entirely irrelevant whether the laws in our long national tradition criminalizing homosexual sodomy were "directed at homosexual conduct as a distinct matter." Whether homosexual sodomy was prohibited by a law targeted at same-sex sexual relations or by a more general law prohibiting both homosexual and heterosexual sodomy, the only relevant point is that it *was* criminalized—which suffices to establish that homosexual sodomy is not a right "deeply rooted in our Nation's history and tradition." . . .

[The Court states:] "We think that our laws and traditions in the past half century are of most relevance here. These references show *an emerging awareness* that liberty gives substantial protection to adult persons in deciding how to conduct their private lives *in matters pertaining to sex*" (emphasis added). Apart from the fact that such an "emerging awareness" does not establish a "fundamental right," the statement is factually false. States continue to prosecute all sorts of crimes by adults "in matters pertaining to sex": prostitution, adult incest, adultery, obscenity, and child pornography. . . . In any event, an "emerging awareness" is by definition not "deeply rooted in this Nation's history and traditions," as we have said "fundamental right" status requires. Constitutional entitlements do not spring into existence because some States choose to lessen or eliminate criminal sanctions on certain behavior. Much less do they spring into existence because *foreign nations* decriminalize conduct. . . .

IV. I turn now to the ground on which the Court squarely rests its holding: the contention that there is no rational basis for the law here under attack. . . .

The Texas statute undeniably seeks to further the belief of its citizens that certain forms of sexual behavior are "immoral and unacceptable"—the same interest furthered by criminal laws against fornication, bigamy, adultery, adult incest, bestiality, and obscenity. *Bowers* held that this *was* a legitimate state interest. The Court today reaches the opposite conclusion. . . . This effectively decrees the end of all morals legislation. If, as the Court asserts, the promotion of majoritarian sexual morality is not even a *legitimate* state interest, none of the above-mentioned laws can survive rational-basis review.

V. Finally, I turn to petitioners' equal-protection challenge, which no Member of the Court save Justice O'Connor embraces. . . . No purpose to discriminate against men or women as a class can be gleaned from the Texas law, so rational-basis review applies. That review is readily satisfied here by . . . society's belief that certain forms of sexual behavior are "immoral and unacceptable." This is the same justification that supports many other laws regulating sexual behavior that make a distinction based upon the identity of the partner—for example, laws against adultery, fornication, and adult incest, and laws refusing to recognize homosexual marriage. . . .

I dissent.

JUSTICE THOMAS, dissenting.

. . . I write separately to note that the law before the Court today "is . . . uncommonly silly." [*Griswold* (Stewart, J., dissenting).] If I were a member of the Texas Legislature, I would vote to repeal it. . . . [But] I "can find [neither in the Bill of Rights nor any other part of the Constitution a] general right of privacy," or as the Court terms it today, the "liberty of the person both in its spatial and more transcendent dimensions."

NOTES

1. Methodology: Due Process. Does *Lawrence* signal an extension of modern substantive due process, or does it reflect the subjective nature of substantive due process? *Lawrence* overruled *Bowers* but did not characterize the liberty interest at issue as a fundamental liberty. The Court in *Bowers* characterized the issue as whether the Constitution confers a fundamental right upon homosexuals to engage in sodomy, but in *Lawrence* the Court framed the issue differently: Whether laws that "seek to control a personal relationship . . . [offend] the liberty of persons to choose [to enter such relationships] without being punished as criminals" where there is no "injury to a person or abuse of an institution the law protects." Is this not a fundamental liberty because there is no deeply rooted tradition extending protection to such a liberty? Is it not a fundamental liberty interest because it is phrased at too high a level of generality? Recall that in *Glucksberg* the Court stated its requirement of a "careful description" of fundamental liberty interests. If a careful description of the right at issue in *Lawrence* is the right of adults to have consensual sex in private with persons of the same sex as part of a larger relationship, what disqualifies that right from fundamental status? Is it the lack of a deeply rooted tradition of protecting that right?

Perhaps *Lawrence* treated the liberty interest at issue as a "quasi-fundamental" right, one that does not trigger strict scrutiny but raises a form of minimal scrutiny that is not as deferential to governments as minimal scrutiny usually is. If that is so, how do we determine when a claimed liberty interest falls into this limbo category? How should we state the level of scrutiny that attaches to such quasi-fundamental liberty interests?

Some federal courts of appeals have read *Lawrence* to require heightened judicial scrutiny of classifications based on sexual orientation. See, e.g., Witt v. Department of the Air Force, 527 F.3d 806, 813 (9th Cir. 2008); Cook v. Gates, 528 F.3d 42, 53-56 (1st Cir. 2008).

2. Methodology: Equal Protection. Is equal protection a better lens through which to examine the issue presented in *Lawrence*? As you will see in Chapter 8, the first step in equal protection analysis is to decide if the statutory classification is sufficiently suspect to merit a presumption of invalidity or, alternatively, whether the classification materially infringes a fundamental right. If it does, the government bears the burden of justifying the classification. If it does not, the challenger bears the burden of proving that the classification is not rationally related to a legitimate state interest. You will learn that fundamental rights for equal protection are not the same as fundamental rights for purposes of due process. Assuming that *Lawrence* does not present a fundamental-for-equal-protection right, is Justice O'Connor's approach preferable to the majority approach? Note that Justice O'Connor treats as illegitimate Texas's interest in criminalizing homosexual sexual conduct only in a context where Texas chose to criminalize sexual behavior between persons of the same sex but not the identical behavior between opposite-sex partners. To O'Connor, this was sufficient evidence that the Texas law was designed simply to harm homosexuals, an illegitimate objective. These issues are explored further in Chapter 8, Section B.2.

3. Implications of *Lawrence*: Other Sexual Conduct.   *Lawrence* struck down the Texas law because the Court found that moral disapproval was an illegitimate objective. Is expression of moral disapproval never a legitimate objective of the state? If so, what justifies prohibitions of sexual activity outside marriage, such as fornication or adultery? What justifies bans on obscenity? What justifies bans on prostitution? To be sure, the Court in *Lawrence* was careful to note that the liberty interest affected was a part of a mutually consensual enduring relationship in which sexual activity was only one element. The Court intimated that the result might be different if the facts involved "public conduct or prostitution," minors, persons in relationships in which they are vulnerable or susceptible to coercion, threatened injury to persons, or "abuse of an institution the law protects." Do these caveats permit enforcement of laws against adult incest, bigamy, adultery, or fornication? If an enduring relationship is necessary, may Texas criminalize private, consensual, sexual conduct between two men who have decided to have one-time casual sex?

4. Implications of *Lawrence*: Obscenity.   In United States v. Extreme Associates, 352 F. Supp. 2d 578 (W.D. Pa. 2005), a federal district judge relied in part on *Lawrence* to dismiss an indictment for criminal distribution of obscenity: After *Lawrence*, said the judge, "the government can no longer rely on the advancement of a moral code, i.e., preventing consenting adults from entertaining lewd or lascivious thoughts, as a legitimate . . . state interest." The Third Circuit reversed, reasoning that the Supreme Court had implicitly rejected privacy claims to immunize the distribution of obscenity and, in any case, it was for the Supreme Court to decide if *Lawrence* has stripped the government of any legitimate interest in imposing criminal prohibitions on distribution of obscenity. United States v. Extreme Associates, 431 F.3d 150 (3d Cir. 2005).

f. Marriage

Loving v. Virginia, 388 U.S. 1 (1967). Virginia made interracial marriage a crime. The Lovings, a married couple consisting of a black woman and a white man, were convicted under the law. The Court upheld both their equal protection challenge and their substantive due process claim. Chief Justice Warren wrote for the Court:

> These statutes [deprive] the Lovings of liberty without due process of [law]. The freedom to marry has long been recognized as one of the vital personal rights essential to the orderly pursuit of happiness by free men. Marriage is one of the "basic civil rights of man," fundamental to our very existence and survival. To deny this fundamental freedom on so unsupportable a basis as [race] is surely to deprive all the State's citizens of liberty without due process of law.

[Under] our Constitution, the freedom to marry, or not marry, a person of another race resides with the individual and cannot be infringed by the State.

Because Virginia's interest in barring interracial marriage—preserving white supremacy—was illegitimate, the Court did not articulate precisely what standard of review might apply to more legitimate infringements upon marriage.

Zablocki v. Redhail, 434 U.S. 374 (1978). Wisconsin law prohibited marriage by anyone not in compliance with valid court-ordered child support obligations. The Court invalidated this law under the fundamental rights prong of equal protection, although Justice Stewart, concurring, called it "no more than substantive due process by another name." Justice Marshall wrote for the Court:

[O]ur past decisions make clear that the right to marry is of fundamental importance. Because the classification at issue here significantly interferes with the exercise of that right, we believe that "critical examination" of the state interests advanced in support of the classification is required. . . . [But not] every state regulation which relates in any way [to] marriage must be subjected to rigorous scrutiny.

To the contrary, reasonable regulations that do not significantly interfere with decisions to enter into the marital relationship may legitimately be imposed. [In] Califano v. Jobst [, 434 U.S. 47 (1977)], we upheld sections of the Social Security Act [terminating] a dependent child's benefits upon marriage to an individual not entitled to benefits under the Act. [The] rule terminating benefits upon marriage was not "an attempt to interfere with the individual's freedom to make a decision as important as marriage," [it] placed no direct legal obstacle in the path of persons desiring to get married, [and] there was no evidence that the laws significantly discouraged, let alone made "practically impossible," any marriages. The statutory classification at issue here, however, clearly does interfere directly and substantially with the right to marry. [It] cannot be upheld unless it is supported by sufficiently important state interests and is closely tailored to effectuate only those interests. [We accept that the state's interests in protecting children and counseling fathers as to the necessity of meeting child support obligations] are legitimate and substantial interests, but, since the means selected by the State for achieving these interests unnecessarily impinge on the right to marry, the statute cannot be sustained. [The] State already has numerous other means for exacting compliance with support obligations, [such as] wage assignments, civil contempt proceedings, and criminal penalties. [The] net result of preventing the marriage is simply more illegitimate children.

In a concurrence Justice Powell stated:

[The] majority's rationale sweeps too broadly in an area which traditionally has been subject to pervasive state regulation. [The Court would] subject all state regulation which "directly and substantially" interferes with the decision to marry [to] "critical examination" or "compelling state interest" analysis. [Because] state regulation in this area typically takes the form of a prerequisite or barrier to marriage or divorce, the degree of "direct" interference with the decision to marry or to divorce is unlikely to provide either guidance for state legislatures or a basis for judicial oversight. [The] marriage relation traditionally has been subject to [regulation]. The State, representing the collective expression of moral aspirations, has an undeniable interest in ensuring that its rules of domestic relations reflect the widely held values of its people. [State] regulation has included bans on incest, bigamy, and homosexuality, as well as various preconditions to marriage, such as [age or] blood tests. [A] "compelling state purpose" inquiry would cast doubt on the network of restrictions that the States have fashioned to govern marriage.

In Turner v. Safly, 482 U.S. 78 (1987), a unanimous Court relied on *Zablocki* to invalidate a prison regulation that permitted inmates to marry only when the prison warden found compelling reasons for the marriage. The regulation was a substantial interference with the right to marry and, although the state had legitimate security reasons to restrict inmate marriage, the regulation was far more incursive than necessary.

These decisions eventually led to the argument that prohibitions upon same-sex marriage are unjustified infringements upon the fundamental right to marry.

≡ **Obergefell v. Hodges**
≡ *2015 U.S. LEXIS 4250*

JUSTICE KENNEDY delivered the opinion of the Court.

The Constitution promises liberty to all within its reach, a liberty that includes certain specific rights that allow persons, within a lawful realm, to define and express their identity. The petitioners in these cases seek to find that liberty by marrying someone of the same sex and having their marriages deemed lawful on the same terms and conditions as marriages between persons of the opposite sex. . . .

Under the Due Process Clause of the Fourteenth Amendment, no State shall "deprive any person of life, liberty, or property, without due process of law." The fundamental liberties protected by this Clause . . . extend to certain personal choices central to individual dignity and autonomy, including intimate choices that define personal identity and beliefs. . . . The identification and protection of fundamental rights is an enduring part of the judicial duty to interpret the Constitution. That responsibility, however, "has not been reduced to any formula." Rather, it requires courts to exercise reasoned judgment in identifying interests of the person so fundamental that the State must accord them its respect. That process is guided by many of the same considerations relevant to analysis of other constitutional provisions that set forth broad principles rather than specific requirements. History and tradition guide and discipline this inquiry but do not set its outer boundaries. . . . [T]he Court has long held the right to marry is protected by the Constitution. . . . It cannot be denied that this Court's cases describing the right to marry presumed a relationship involving opposite-sex partners. The Court, like many institutions, has made assumptions defined by the world and time of which it is a part. . . . This Court's cases have expressed constitutional principles of broader reach. In defining the right to marry these cases have identified essential attributes of that right based in history, tradition, and other constitutional liberties inherent in this intimate bond. . . . This analysis compels the conclusion that same-sex couples may exercise the right to marry. The four principles and traditions to be discussed demonstrate that the reasons marriage is fundamental under the Constitution apply with equal force to same-sex couples.

A first premise of the Court's relevant precedents is that the right to personal choice regarding marriage is inherent in the concept of individual autonomy. . . . Choices about marriage shape an individual's destiny. . . . The nature of marriage is that, through its enduring bond, two persons together can find other freedoms, such as expression, intimacy, and spirituality. This is true for all persons, whatever their sexual orientation.

A second principle in this Court's jurisprudence is that the right to marry is fundamental because it supports a two-person union unlike any other in its importance to the committed individuals. . . .

A third basis for protecting the right to marry is that it safeguards children and families and thus draws meaning from related rights of childrearing, procreation, and education. . . . As all parties agree, many same-sex couples provide loving and nurturing homes to their children, whether biological or adopted. And hundreds of thousands of children are presently being raised by such couples. . . . Excluding same-sex couples from marriage thus conflicts with a central premise of the right to marry. Without the recognition, stability, and predictability marriage offers, their children suffer the stigma of knowing their families are somehow lesser. . . . That is not to say the right to marry is less meaningful for those who do not or cannot have children. An ability, desire, or promise to procreate is not and has not been a prerequisite for a valid marriage in any State. . . .

Fourth . . . , this Court's cases and the Nation's traditions make clear that marriage is a keystone of our social order. [J]ust as a couple vows to support each other, so does society pledge to support the couple, offering symbolic recognition and material benefits to protect and nourish the union. Indeed, while the States are in general free to vary the benefits they confer on all married couples, they have throughout our history made marriage the basis for an expanding list of governmental rights, benefits, and responsibilities. . . . There is no difference between same- and opposite-sex couples with respect to this principle. Yet by virtue of their exclusion from that institution, same-sex couples are denied the constellation of benefits that the States have linked to marriage. This harm results in more than just material burdens. Same-sex couples are consigned to an instability many opposite-sex couples would deem intolerable in their own lives.

. . . *Glucksberg* did insist that liberty under the Due Process Clause must be defined in a most circumscribed manner, with central reference to specific historical practices. Yet while that approach may have been appropriate for the asserted right there involved (physician-assisted suicide), it is inconsistent with the approach this Court has used in discussing other fundamental rights, including marriage and intimacy. . . .

The right to marry is fundamental as a matter of history and tradition, but rights come not from ancient sources alone. They rise, too, from a better informed understanding of how constitutional imperatives define a liberty that remains urgent in our own era. Many who deem same-sex marriage to be wrong reach that conclusion based on decent and honorable religious or philosophical premises, and neither they nor their beliefs are disparaged here. But when that sincere, personal opposition becomes enacted law and public policy, the necessary consequence is to put the imprimatur of the State itself on an exclusion that soon demeans or stigmatizes those whose own liberty is then denied. Under the Constitution, same-sex couples seek in marriage the same legal treatment as opposite-sex couples, and it would disparage their choices and diminish their personhood to deny them this right.

The right of same-sex couples to marry that is part of the liberty promised by the Fourteenth Amendment is derived, too, from that Amendment's guarantee of the equal protection of the laws. The Due Process Clause and the Equal Protection Clause are connected in a profound way, though they set forth independent principles. Rights implicit in liberty and rights secured by equal protection may rest on different precepts and are not always coextensive, yet in some instances each may be instructive as to the meaning and reach of the other. In any particular case one Clause may be thought to capture the essence of the right in a more accurate and comprehensive way, even as the two Clauses may converge in the identification and definition of the right. . . .

It is now clear that the challenged laws burden the liberty of same-sex couples, and it must be further acknowledged that they abridge central precepts of equality. Here the marriage laws enforced by the respondents are in essence unequal: same-sex couples are denied all the benefits afforded to opposite-sex couples and are barred from exercising a fundamental right. Especially against a long history of disapproval of their relationships, this denial to same-sex couples of the right to marry works a grave and continuing harm. The imposition of this disability on gays and lesbians serves to disrespect and subordinate them. And the Equal Protection Clause, like the Due Process Clause, prohibits this unjustified infringement of the fundamental right to marry. . . . These considerations lead to the conclusion that the right to marry is a fundamental right inherent in the liberty of the person, and under the Due Process and Equal Protection Clauses of the Fourteenth Amendment couples of the same-sex may not be deprived of that right and that liberty. The Court now holds that same-sex couples may exercise the fundamental right to marry. . . .

CHIEF JUSTICE ROBERTS, with whom JUSTICE SCALIA and JUSTICE THOMAS join, dissenting.

Petitioners make strong arguments rooted in social policy and considerations of fairness. They contend that same-sex couples should be allowed to affirm their love and commitment through marriage, just like opposite-sex couples. That position has undeniable appeal; over the past six years, voters and legislators in eleven States and the District of Columbia have revised their laws to allow marriage between two people of the same sex. But this Court is not a legislature. Whether same-sex marriage is a good idea should be of no concern to us. Under the Constitution, judges have power to say what the law is, not what it should be. The people who ratified the Constitution authorized courts to exercise "neither force nor will but merely judgment." The Federalist No. 78, p. 465 (C. Rossiter ed. 1961) (A. Hamilton). . . .

Although the policy arguments for extending marriage to same-sex couples may be compelling, the legal arguments for requiring such an extension are not. The fundamental right to marry does not include a right to make a State change its definition of marriage. And a State's decision to maintain the meaning of marriage that has persisted in every culture throughout human history can hardly be called irrational. In short, our Constitution does not enact any one theory of marriage. The people of a State are free to expand marriage to include same-sex couples, or to retain the historic definition. . . .

The majority's decision is an act of will, not legal judgment. The right it announces has no basis in the Constitution or this Court's precedent. The majority expressly disclaims judicial "caution" and omits even a pretense of humility, openly relying on its desire to remake society according to its own "new insight" into the "nature of injustice."

It can be tempting for judges to confuse our own preferences with the requirements of the law. But as this Court has been reminded throughout our history, the Constitution "is made for people of fundamentally differing views." Accordingly, "courts are not concerned with the wisdom or policy of legislation." The majority today neglects that restrained conception of the judicial role. It seizes for itself a question the Constitution leaves to the people, at a time when the people are engaged in a vibrant debate on that question. And it answers that question based not on neutral principles of constitutional law, but on its own "understanding of what freedom is and must become." I have no choice but to dissent.

Understand well what this dissent is about: It is not about whether, in my judgment, the institution of marriage should be changed to include same-sex couples. It is instead about whether, in our democratic republic, that decision should rest with the people acting through their elected representatives, or with five lawyers who happen to hold commissions authorizing them to resolve legal disputes according to law. The Constitution leaves no doubt about the answer. . . .

If you are among the many Americans—of whatever sexual orientation—who favor expanding same-sex marriage, by all means celebrate today's decision. Celebrate the achievement of a desired goal. Celebrate the opportunity for a new expression of commitment to a partner. Celebrate the availability of new benefits. But do not celebrate the Constitution. It had nothing to do with it.

JUSTICE SCALIA, with whom JUSTICE THOMAS joins, dissenting.

. . . These cases ask us to decide whether the *Fourteenth Amendment* contains a limitation that requires the States to license and recognize marriages between two people of the same sex. Does it remove *that* issue from the political process? Of course not. It would be surprising to find a prescription regarding marriage in the Federal Constitution since, as the author of today's opinion reminded us only two years ago (in an opinion joined by the same Justices who join him today): "[R]egulation of domestic relations is an area that has long been regarded as a virtually exclusive province of the States." "[T]he Federal Government, through our history, has deferred to state-law policy decisions with respect to domestic relations."

But we need not speculate. When the Fourteenth Amendment was ratified in 1868, every State limited marriage to one man and one woman, and no one doubted the constitutionality of doing so. That resolves these cases. When it comes to determining the meaning of a vague constitutional provision—such as "due process of law" or "equal protection of the laws"—it is unquestionable that the People who ratified that provision did not understand it to prohibit a practice that remained both universal and uncontroversial in the years after ratification. We have no basis for striking down a practice that is not expressly prohibited by the Fourteenth Amendment's text, and that bears the endorsement of a long tradition of open, widespread, and unchallenged use dating back to the Amendment's ratification. Since there is no doubt whatever that the People never decided to prohibit the limitation of marriage to opposite-sex couples, the public debate over same-sex marriage must be allowed to continue.

But the Court ends this debate, in an opinion lacking even a thin veneer of law. Buried beneath the mummeries and straining-to-be-memorable passages of the opinion is a candid and startling assertion: No matter *what* it was the People ratified, the Fourteenth Amendment protects those rights that the Judiciary, in its "reasoned judgment," thinks the Fourteenth Amendment ought to protect. That is so because "[t]he generations that wrote and ratified the Bill of Rights and the Fourteenth Amendment did not presume to know the extent of freedom in all of its dimensions. . . ." One would think that sentence would continue: ". . . and therefore they provided for a means by which the People could amend the Constitution," or perhaps ". . . and therefore they left the creation of additional liberties, such as the freedom to marry someone of the same sex, to the People, through the never-ending process of legislation." But no. What logically follows, in the majority's judge-empowering estimation, is: "and so they entrusted to future generations a charter protecting the right of all persons to enjoy liberty as we learn its meaning." The "we," needless to say, is the nine of us. "History and tradition guide and discipline [our] inquiry but do not set its outer boundaries." Thus, rather than focusing on *the People's* understanding of "liberty"—at the time of ratification or even today—the majority focuses on four "principles and traditions" that, *in the majority's view*, prohibit States from defining marriage as an institution consisting of one man and one woman. . . .

This is a naked judicial claim to legislative—indeed, *super*-legislative—power; a claim fundamentally at odds with our system of government. . . . Judges are selected precisely for their skill as lawyers; whether they reflect the policy views of a particular constituency is not (or should not be) relevant. Not surprisingly then, the Federal Judiciary is hardly a cross-section of America. Take, for example, this Court, which consists of only nine men and women, all of them successful lawyers who studied at Harvard or Yale Law School. Four of the nine are natives of New York City. Eight of them grew up in east- and west-coast States. Only one hails from the vast expanse in-between. Not a single Southwesterner or even, to tell the truth, a genuine Westerner (California does not count). Not a single evangelical Christian (a group that comprises about one quarter of Americans), or even a Protestant of any denomination. The strikingly unrepresentative character of the body voting on today's social upheaval would be irrelevant if they were functioning as *judges*, answering the legal question whether the American people had ever ratified a constitutional provision that was understood to proscribe the traditional definition of marriage. But of course the Justices in today's majority are not voting on that basis; *they say they are not.* And to allow the policy question of same-sex marriage to be considered and resolved by a select, patrician, highly unrepresentative panel of nine is to violate a principle even more fundamental than no taxation without representation: no social transformation without representation. . . .

But what really astounds is the hubris reflected in today's judicial Putsch. The five Justices who compose today's majority are entirely comfortable concluding that every State violated the Constitution for all of the 135 years between the Fourteenth Amendment's ratification and Massachusetts' permitting of same-sex marriages in 2003. They have discovered in the Fourteenth Amendment a "fundamental right" overlooked by every person alive at the time of ratification, and almost everyone else in the time since. They see what lesser legal minds—minds like Thomas Cooley, John Marshall Harlan, Oliver Wendell Holmes, Jr., Learned Hand, Louis Brandeis, William Howard Taft, Benjamin Cardozo, Hugo Black, Felix Frankfurter, Robert Jackson, and Henry Friendly—could not. They are certain that the People ratified the Fourteenth Amendment to bestow on them the power to remove questions from the democratic process when that is called for by their "reasoned judgment." These Justices *know* that limiting marriage to one man and one woman is contrary to reason; they *know* that an institution as old as government itself, and accepted by every nation in history until 15 years ago, cannot possibly be supported by anything other than ignorance or bigotry. And they are willing to say that any citizen who does not agree with that, who adheres to what was, until 15 years ago, the unanimous judgment of all generations and all societies, stands against the Constitution. . . .

NOTES AND QUESTIONS

1. Queries. Are prohibitions upon bigamous, polygamous, polyandrous, or incestuous marriages susceptible to attack under *Obergefell*? Suppose that a state required any prospective marital partner to be at least 25 years old, declaring its purpose to be to encourage mature reflection regarding the marital commitment. What level of scrutiny would apply? Would the law be valid?

2. Standard of Review. The Court says that marriage is a fundamental right. But that does not end the question. A government may, in theory, justify infringement of a fundamental right by overcoming strict scrutiny. Does *Obergefell* establish that there is no possible justification for infringing upon the right to marry, at least with respect to same-sex partners?

g.   *Other Asserted Privacy or Autonomy Interests*

A variety of privacy interests have been considered and rejected by the Court.

Personal appearance. In Kelley v. Johnson, 425 U.S. 238 (1976), the Court upheld police regulations that controlled hair length, style, mustaches, sideburns, and prohibited beards and goatees save for medical reasons. The Court assumed that "the citizenry at large has some sort of 'liberty' interest [in] matters of personal appearance," but concluded that regulation of the personal appearance of policemen posed no substantial interference with any fundamental liberty interest protected by the due process clause. The Court applied minimal scrutiny and upheld the regulations as rationally related to a hypothesized government objective of instilling *esprit de corps* in the police department or furthering public recognition of police officers.

The hypothesized liberty interest of the public in "matters of personal appearance" is, of course, not unlimited. At one extreme, laws banning public nudity almost surely do not violate this interest. Suppose a publicly owned restaurant informs its patrons "No Shirt, No Shoes, No Service." Is this constitutionally valid?

Personal anonymity: freedom from data collection. Perhaps the most obvious application of a right of "privacy" is freedom from government accumulation of personal data about individuals. But in Whalen v. Roe, 429 U.S. 589 (1977), the Court rejected such a claim. New York required physicians to report the details of all prescriptions written for specified legal drugs susceptible to abuse, particularly opiates and amphetamines. The state then stored this information, specifically including the names and addresses of the patients. Constitutionally speaking, said the Court, privacy involves either an interest in avoiding disclosure of personal matters or an interest in making certain important decisions affecting one's life. Neither interest was substantially implicated by the New York data collection and storage practice.

Query: Suppose a government-operated Web site automatically installs software into the computer of each visitor to the site, such that the government can then monitor future Web sites visited by the computer user. Would *Whalen* support the validity of this practice?

In Connecticut Department of Public Safety v. Doe, 538 U.S. 1 (2003), the Court declined to reach the question of whether any fundamental liberty interest was infringed by a Connecticut law that required convicted sex offenders to register and disclose publicly their whereabouts after release from custody. Does the *public* disclosure of the identities and residences of convicted sex offenders implicate a fundamental liberty interest? If so, how would you state that interest, bearing in mind the Court's admonition in *Glucksberg* that it is essential to make a "careful description" of claimed fundamental liberty interests? If not, do sex offender registration and disclosure laws nonetheless violate substantive due process under the rationale of *Lawrence*?

h.   The Methodology of Substantive Due Process: A Debate

Substantive due process is controversial in part because there is marked disagreement concerning the appropriate methodology to be employed in determining which rights may be constitutionally fundamental. Much of that controversy has been revealed in the cases you have studied in this chapter, but an explicit debate on the issue erupted between Justices Stevens and Scalia in the following case.

McDonald v. City of Chicago
561 U.S. 742 (2010)

[The Court held that the Second Amendment right to possess a firearm for purposes of self-defense was constitutionally fundamental and made applicable to the states through the Fourteenth Amendment. Four justices thought the right was incorporated into the due process guarantee; Justice Thomas, concurring in the judgment, thought the right was one of the privileges or immunities protected by the Fourteenth Amendment.]

JUSTICE STEVENS, dissenting: This is a substantive due process case. [S]everal important principles . . . ought to guide our resolution of this case. . . . The first, and most basic, principle . . . is that the rights protected by the Due Process Clause are not merely procedural in nature. . . . [S]ubstance and procedure are often deeply entwined. [The clause] can be read to "impos[e] nothing less than an obligation to give substantive content to the words 'liberty' and 'due process of law,'" lest superficially fair procedures be permitted to "destroy the enjoyment" of life, liberty, and property. . . . The second principle . . . is that substantive due process is fundamentally a matter of personal liberty. . . . Whether an asserted substantive due process interest is explicitly named in one of the first eight Amendments to the Constitution or is not mentioned, the underlying inquiry is the same: We must ask whether the interest is "comprised within the term liberty." . . .

How should a court go about the analysis, then? Our precedents have established, not an exact methodology, but rather a framework for decision-making. . . . [We] must ask whether the allegedly unlawful practice violates values "implicit in the concept of ordered liberty." [*Palko.*] [This] test undeniably requires judges to apply their own reasoned judgment. . . . Textual commitments laid down elsewhere in the Constitution, judicial precedents, English common law, legislative and social facts, scientific and professional developments, practices of other civilized societies, and, above all else, the "'traditions and conscience of our people'" are critical variables. . . .

[A] rigid historical methodology is unfaithful to the Constitution's command. For if it were really the case that the Fourteenth Amendment's guarantee of liberty embraces only those rights "so rooted in our history, tradition, and practice as to require special protection," then the guarantee would serve little function, save to ratify those rights that state actors have *already* been according the most extensive protection. That approach is unfaithful to the expansive principle Americans laid down when they ratified the Fourteenth Amendment and to the level of generality they chose when they crafted its language; it promises an objectivity it cannot deliver and masks the value judgments that pervade any analysis of what customs, defined in what manner, are sufficiently "'rooted'"; it countenances the most revolting injustices in the name of continuity . . . ; and it effaces this Court's distinctive role in saying what the law is, leaving the development and safekeeping of liberty to majoritarian political processes. It is judicial abdication in the guise of judicial modesty. . . .

[The] liberty safeguarded by the Fourteenth Amendment is not merely preservative in nature but rather is a "dynamic concept." . . . [H]ow are we to do justice to its . . . open texture—and to the grant of interpretive discretion [it] embodies—without injecting excessive subjectivity or unduly restricting the States "broad latitude in experimenting with possible solutions to problems of vital local concern"? . . .

[O]nly certain types of especially significant personal interests may qualify for especially heightened protection. . . . Government action that shocks the conscience, pointlessly infringes settled expectations, trespasses into sensitive private realms or life choices without adequate justification, perpetrates gross injustice, or simply lacks a rational basis will always be vulnerable to judicial invalidation. [The] strength of the individual's liberty interests and the State's regulatory interests must always be assessed and compared. No right is absolute. . . . Another key constraint on substantive due process analysis is respect for the democratic process. If a particular liberty interest is already being given careful consideration in, and subjected to ongoing calibration by, the States, judicial enforcement may not be appropriate. . . .

[S]ensitivity to the interaction between the intrinsic aspects of liberty and the practical realities of contemporary society provides an important tool for guiding judicial discretion. This sensitivity is an aspect of a deeper principle: the need to approach our work with humility and caution. . . .

First, firearms have a fundamentally ambivalent relationship to liberty. Just as they can help homeowners defend their families and property from intruders, they can help thugs and insurrectionists murder innocent victims. . . . *Your* interest in keeping and bearing a certain firearm may diminish *my* interest in being and feeling safe from armed violence. And while granting you the right to own a handgun might make you safer on any given day—assuming the handgun's marginal contribution to self-defense outweighs its marginal contribution to the risk of accident, suicide, and criminal mischief—it may make you and the community you live in less safe overall, owing to the increased number of handguns in circulation. It is at least reasonable for a democratically elected legislature to take such concerns into account in considering what sorts of regulations would best serve the public welfare. . . .

Second, the right to possess a firearm of one's choosing is different in kind from the liberty interests we have recognized under the Due Process Clause. . . . [The] ability to own a handgun, or any particular type of firearm, is [not] critical to leading a life of autonomy, dignity, or political equality. . . . The liberty interest asserted [here] is also dissimilar from those we have recognized in its capacity to undermine the security of others. . . .

Third, the experience of other advanced democracies, including those that share our British heritage, undercuts the notion that an expansive right to keep and bear arms is intrinsic to ordered liberty. . . .

Under the "historically focused" approach [Justice Scalia] advocates, numerous threshold questions arise before one ever gets to the history. At what level of generality should one frame the liberty interest in question? What does it mean for a right to be "deeply rooted in this Nation's history and tradition"? By what standard will that proposition be tested? Which types of sources will count, and how will those sources be weighed and aggregated? There is no objective, neutral answer to these questions. . . . It is hardly a novel insight that history is not an objective science, and that its use can therefore "point in any direction the judges favor. . . ." The historian must choose which pieces to credit and which to discount, and then must try to assemble them into a coherent whole. . . .

Justice Scalia's . . . method . . . is unsatisfying on its own terms. For a limitless number of subjective judgments may be smuggled into his historical analysis. Worse, they may be *buried* in the analysis. At least with my approach, the judge's cards are laid on the table for all to see, and to critique. The judge must exercise judgment, to be sure. When answering a constitutional question to which the text provides no clear answer, there is always some amount of discretion; our constitutional system has always depended on judges filling in the document's vast open spaces. But there is also transparency. . . .

[It] makes little sense to give history dispositive weight in every case. And it makes *especially* little sense to answer questions like whether the right to bear arms is "fundamental" by focusing only on the past, given that both the practical significance and the public understandings of such a right often change as society changes. . . . Not only can historical views be less than completely clear or informative, but they can also be wrong. Some notions that many Americans deeply believed to be true, at one time, turned out not to be true. Some practices that many Americans believed to be consistent with the Constitution's guarantees of liberty and equality, at one time, turned out to be inconsistent with them. . . .

JUSTICE SCALIA, concurring:

[M]uch of what Justice Stevens writes is a broad condemnation of the theory of interpretation which underlies the Court's opinion, a theory that makes the traditions of our people paramount. He proposes a different theory, which he claims is more "cautiou[s]" and respectful of proper limits on the judicial role. It is that claim I wish to address. . . .

Justice Stevens [urges] the theory of incorporation articulated in *Palko*. But in fact he does not favor application of that theory at all. . . . That Justice Stevens is not applying any version of *Palko* is clear from comparing, on the one hand, the rights he believes *are* covered, with, on the other hand, his conclusion that the right to keep and bear arms is *not* covered. Rights that pass his test include not just those "relating to marriage, procreation, contraception, family relationships, and child rearing and education," but also rights against "[g]overnment action that shocks the conscience, pointlessly infringes settled expectations, trespasses into sensitive private realms or life choices without adequate justification, [or] perpetrates gross injustice." Not *all* such rights are in, however, since only "*some* fundamental aspects of personhood, dignity, and the like" are protected. Exactly what is covered is not clear. But whatever else is in, he *knows* that the right to keep and bear arms is out, despite its being as "deeply rooted in this Nation's history and tradition" as a right can be. I can find no other explanation for such certitude except that Justice Stevens, despite his forswearing of "personal and private notions," deeply believes it should be out. . . .

The subjective nature of Justice Stevens'[s] standard is also apparent from his claim that it is the courts' prerogative—indeed their *duty*—to update the Due Process Clause so that it encompasses new freedoms the Framers were too narrow-minded to imagine. Courts, he proclaims, must "do justice to [the Clause's] urgent call and its open texture" by exercising the "interpretive discretion the latter embodies." (Why the *people* are not up to the task of deciding what new rights to protect, even though it is *they* who are authorized to make changes [by constitutional amendment] is never explained.) And it would be "judicial abdication" for a judge to [be] guided by what the American people throughout our history have thought. It is only we judges, exercising our "own reasoned judgment," who can be entrusted with deciding the Due Process Clause's scope—which rights serve the Amendment's "central values"—which basically means picking the rights we want to protect and discarding those we do not.

Justice Stevens resists this description, insisting that his approach provides plenty of "guideposts" and "constraints" to keep courts from "injecting excessive subjectivity" into the process. Plenty indeed—and that alone is a problem. The ability of omnidirectional guideposts to constrain is inversely proportional to their number. But even individually, each lodestar or limitation he lists either is incapable of restraining judicial whimsy or cannot be squared with the precedents he seeks to preserve. . . .

Justice Stevens moves on to the "most basic" constraint on subjectivity his theory offers: that he would "esche[w] attempts to provide any all-purpose, top-down, totalizing theory of 'liberty.'" The notion that the absence of a coherent theory of the Due Process Clause will somehow *curtail* judicial caprice is at war with reason. Indeterminacy means opportunity for courts to impose whatever rule they like; it is the problem, not the solution. The idea that interpretive pluralism would *reduce* courts' ability to impose their will on the ignorant masses is not merely naive, but absurd. If there are no right answers, there are no wrong answers either.

Justice Stevens also argues that requiring courts to show "respect for the democratic process" should serve as a constraint. That is true, but Justice Stevens would have them show respect in an extraordinary manner. In his view, if a right "is already being given careful consideration in, and subjected to ongoing calibration by, the States, judicial enforcement may not be appropriate." In other words, a right, such as the right to keep and bear arms, that has long been recognized but on which the States are considering restrictions, apparently deserves *less* protection, while a privilege the political branches (instruments of the democratic process) have withheld entirely and continue to withhold, deserves *more*. . . .

The next constraint Justice Stevens suggests is harder to evaluate. He describes as "an important tool for guiding judicial discretion" "sensitivity to the interaction between the intrinsic aspects of liberty and the practical realities of contemporary society." I cannot say whether that sensitivity will really guide judges because I have no idea what it is. Is it some sixth sense instilled in judges when they ascend to the bench? Or does it mean judges are more constrained when they agonize about the cosmic conflict between liberty and its potentially harmful consequences? Attempting to give the concept more precision, Justice Stevens explains that "sensitivity is an aspect of a deeper principle: the need to approach our work with humility and caution." Both traits are undeniably admirable, though what relation they bear to sensitivity is a mystery. . . .

If Justice Stevens'[s] account of the constraints of his approach did not demonstrate that they do not exist, his application of that approach to the case before us leaves no doubt. He offers several reasons for concluding that the Second Amendment right to keep and bear arms is not fundamental enough to be applied against the States. None is persuasive [and] each is either intrinsically indeterminate, would preclude incorporation of rights we have already held incorporated, or both. His approach therefore does nothing to stop a judge from arriving at any conclusion he sets out to reach. . . .

Justice Stevens begins with the odd assertion that "firearms have a fundamentally ambivalent relationship to liberty," since sometimes they are used to cause (or sometimes accidentally produce) injury to others. The source of the rule that only nonambivalent liberties deserve Due Process protection is never explained—proof that judges applying Justice Stevens'[s] approach can add new elements to the test as they see fit. The criterion, moreover, is inherently manipulable. Surely Justice Stevens does not mean that the Clause covers only rights that have *zero* harmful effect on *anyone*. Otherwise even the First Amendment is out. Maybe what he means is that the right to keep and bear arms imposes *too great* a risk to others' physical well-being. But . . . other rights we have already held incorporated pose similarly substantial risks to public safety. In all events, Justice Stevens supplies neither a standard for how severe the impairment on others' liberty must be for a right to be disqualified, nor (of course) any method of measuring the severity.

Justice Stevens next suggests that the Second Amendment right is not fundamental because it is "different in kind" from other rights we have recognized. In one respect, of course, the right to keep and bear arms *is* different from some other rights we have held the Clause protects and he would recognize: It is deeply grounded in our nation's history and tradition. But Justice Stevens has a different distinction in mind: Even though he does "not doubt for a moment that many Americans . . . see [firearms] as critical to their way of life as well as to their security," he pronounces that owning a handgun is not "critical to leading a life of autonomy, dignity, or political equality." Who says? Deciding what is essential to an enlightened, liberty-filled life is an inherently political, moral judgment—the antithesis of an objective approach that reaches conclusions by applying neutral rules to verifiable evidence. . . .

No determination of what rights the Constitution of the United States covers would be complete, of course, without a survey of what *other* countries do. When it comes to guns, Justice Stevens explains, our Nation is *already* an outlier among "advanced democracies." . . . Never mind that he explains neither which countries qualify as "advanced democracies" nor why others are irrelevant. For there is an even clearer indication that this criterion lets judges pick which rights States must respect and those they can ignore: [T]his follow-the-foreign-crowd requirement would foreclose rights that we have held (and Justice Stevens accepts) are incorporated, but that other "advanced" nations do not recognize—from the exclusionary rule to the Establishment Clause. A judge applying Justice Stevens'[s] approach must either throw all of those rights overboard or, . . . simply ignore foreign law when it undermines the desired conclusion. . . . .

Justice Stevens'[s] final reason for rejecting incorporation of the Second Amendment reveals, more clearly than any of the others, the game that is afoot. Assuming that there is a "plausible constitutional basis" for holding that the right to keep and bear arms is incorporated, he asserts that we ought not to do so *for prudential reasons*. Even if we had the authority to withhold rights that are within the Constitution's command (and we assuredly do not), two of the reasons Justice Stevens gives for abstention show just how much power he would hand to judges. The States' "right to experiment" with solutions to the problem of gun violence, he says, is at its apex here because "the best solution is far from clear." That is true of most serious social problems—whether, for example, "the best solution" for rampant crime is to admit confessions unless they are affirmatively shown to have been coerced. . . . The implication of Justice Stevens'[s] call for abstention is that if We The Court conclude that They The People's answers to a problem are silly, we are free to "interven[e]," but if we too are uncertain of the right answer, or merely think the States may be on to something, we can loosen the leash.

A second reason Justice Stevens says we should abstain is that the States have shown they are "capable" of protecting the right at issue, and if anything have protected it too much. That reflects an assumption that judges can distinguish between a *proper* democratic decision to leave things alone (which we should honor), and a case of democratic market failure (which we should step in to correct). I would not—and no judge should—presume to have that sort of omniscience, which seems to me far more "arrogant" than confining courts' focus to our own national heritage.

Justice Stevens . . . makes the usual rejoinder of "living Constitution" advocates to the criticism that it empowers judges to eliminate or expand what the people have prescribed: The traditional, historically focused method, he says, reposes discretion in judges as well. Historical analysis can be difficult; it sometimes requires resolving threshold questions, and making nuanced judgments about which evidence to consult and how to interpret it. I will stipulate to that. But the question to be decided is not whether the historically focused method is a *perfect means* of restraining aristocratic judicial Constitution-writing; but whether it is the *best means available* in an imperfect world. Or indeed, even more narrowly than that: whether it is demonstrably much better than what Justice Stevens proposes. I think it beyond all serious dispute that it is much less subjective, and intrudes much less upon the democratic process. It is less subjective because it depends upon a body of evidence susceptible of reasoned analysis rather than a variety of vague ethico-political First Principles whose combined conclusion can be found to point in any direction the judges favor. In the most controversial matters brought before this Court—for example, the constitutionality of prohibiting abortion, assisted suicide, or homosexual sodomy, or the constitutionality of the death penalty—*any* historical methodology, under *any* plausible standard of proof, would lead to the same conclusion. Moreover, the methodological differences that divide historians, and the varying interpretive assumptions they bring to their work, are nothing compared to the differences among the American people (though perhaps not among graduates of prestigious law schools) with regard to the moral judgments Justice Stevens would have courts pronounce. And whether or not special expertise is needed to answer historical questions, judges most certainly have no "comparative . . . advantage" in resolving moral disputes. What is more, his approach would not eliminate, but multiply, the hard questions courts must confront, since he would not *replace* history with moral philosophy, but would have courts consider *both*. . . .

7

Economic Rights: The Takings and Contracts Clauses

The Framers of the Constitution considered economic rights to be as much a part of constitutional liberty as noneconomic rights. The principal devices to protect economic rights were the Fifth Amendment's takings clause—which bars governments from taking private property for public use without payment—and the contracts clause of Article I, section 10—which bars states from impairing contractual obligations. By judicial construction, however, these barriers to government invasion of economic interests have been much reduced.

A. THE TAKINGS CLAUSE

The Fifth Amendment's takings clause provides that "private property [shall not] be taken for public use without just compensation." The takings clause applies to the states as well as the federal government, via incorporation into the Fourteenth Amendment's due process clause. See Chicago, Burlington & Quincy Railway v. Chicago, 166 U.S. 226 (1897). The "just compensation" requirement of the takings clause prevents forced redistribution of private property by ensuring that when government power is used to take private property the public pays for it. The "public use" requirement prevents even fully compensated takings if the purpose is to force a person to transfer his property to another entirely for the latter's private benefit. The public use requirement thus ensures that government compulsion is used only to secure public benefits.

Most takings are straightforward: The government admits it is taking private property, and the only issue is the amount of compensation. When a taking is acknowledged, the major constitutional issue presented is determining whether an acknowledged and fully compensated taking is for public use. Sometimes the government denies it has taken property, claiming it has merely regulated property. When that occurs, the constitutional issue is to determine when a regulation of property is so extensive that it amounts to a de facto taking of property.

The takings clause applies to all types of property—tangible or intangible—and applies to executive and legislative actions. See Horne v. Department of Agriculture, 2015 US LEXIS 4064; Ruckelshaus v. Monsanto Co., 467 U.S. 986 (1984) (forced disclosure of trade secrets constituted a taking). The degree to which the takings clause applies to judicial action is unsettled.

In Stop the Beach Renourishment, Inc. v. Florida Department of Environmental Conservation, 560 U.S. 702 (2010), the Supreme Court affirmed the Florida Supreme Court's ruling that a Florida statutory scheme that allegedly curtailed the common law rights of beachfront landowners in order to restore hurricane-eroded beaches was not a taking. In reaching that decision, four justices (Chief Justice Roberts and Justices Scalia, Thomas, and Alito) opined that

> [s]tates effect a taking if they recharacterize as public property what was previously private property. . . . The Takings Clause . . . is concerned simply with the act, and not with the governmental actor. . . . There is no textual justification for saying that the existence or the scope of a State's power to expropriate private property without just compensation varies according to the branch of government effecting the expropriation. Nor does common sense recommend such a principle. It would be absurd to allow a State to do by judicial decree what the Takings Clause forbids it to do by legislative fiat. Our precedents provide no support for the proposition that takings effected by the judicial branch are entitled to special treatment, and in fact suggest the contrary. [PruneYard Shopping Center v. Robins, 447 U.S. 74 (1980); Webb's Fabulous Pharmacies, Inc. v. Beckwith, 449 U.S. 155 (1980).] . . . If a legislature *or a court* declares that what was once an established right of private property no longer exists, it has taken that property, no less than if the State had physically appropriated it or destroyed its value by regulation. [emphasis in original]

Even so, the Court ruled that there was no taking because the Florida law did not eliminate any right of private property that was previously established in Florida law. Justice Kennedy, joined by Justice Sotomayor, concurred in the judgment. They suggested that the due process clauses, rather than the takings clause, might be the vehicle to address alleged judicial takings. See also Hughes v. Washington, 389 U.S. 290 (1967) (takings clause impliedly applicable to any government action); Thompson, Judicial Takings, 76 Va. L. Rev. 1449 (1990).

Recall that the first incarnation of substantive due process protected economic liberties. A major difference between that version of substantive due process and the takings clause is that substantive due process was far more wide-ranging: It permitted courts to void statutes because the statutory objectives were thought to be illegitimate. Regulatory takings jurisprudence, by contrast, does not concern itself with the legitimacy of the state's regulatory objectives; it merely examines the means by which those objectives are sought to be attained.

1. The Public Use Requirement

"Nor shall private property be taken for public use, without just compensation." U.S. Const., Amend. V.

Hawaii Housing Authority v. Midkiff
467 U.S. 229 (1984)

JUSTICE O'CONNOR delivered the opinion of the Court.

[Does] the Public Use [Clause], made applicable to the States through the Fourteenth Amendment, prohibit[] the State of Hawaii from taking, with just compensation, title in real property from lessors and transferring it to lessees in order to reduce the concentration of ownership of fees simple in the State[?] We conclude that it does not. . . .

[W]hile the State and Federal Governments owned almost 49% of [Hawaii's] land, another 47% was in the hands of only 72 private landowners. . . . [On] Oahu, the most urbanized of the islands, 22 landowners owned 72.5% of the fee simple titles. The legislature concluded that concentrated land ownership was responsible for skewing the State's residential fee simple market, inflating land prices, and injuring the public tranquility and welfare. To redress these problems, the legislature decided to compel the large landowners to break up their estates [and] enacted the Land Reform Act of 1967 (Act), which created a mechanism for condemning residential tracts and for transferring ownership of the condemned fees simple to existing lessees. [Under] the Act's condemnation scheme, tenants living on single-family residential lots within developmental tracts at least five acres in size are entitled to ask the Hawaii Housing Authority (HHA) to condemn the property on which they live. When [a minimum number of tenants have so asked, and the HHA has determined that the] public purposes [of the Act] will be served, it is authorized to [acquire,] at prices set either by condemnation trial or by negotiation between lessors and lessees, the former fee owners' full "right, title, and interest" in the land. After compensation has been set, HHA may sell the land titles to tenants who have applied for fee simple ownership. [In] practice, funds to satisfy the condemnation awards have been supplied entirely by lessees.

[Midkiff] filed suit . . . , asking that the Act be declared unconstitutional and that its enforcement be enjoined. The District Court [upheld the Act]. The Court of Appeals for the Ninth Circuit reversed, [finding that the taking] was simply "a naked attempt on the part of the state of Hawaii to take the private property of A and transfer it to B solely for B's private use and benefit." . . .

The starting point [of] analysis [is] Berman v. Parker, 348 U.S. 26 (1954). In *Berman*, the Court held constitutional the District of Columbia Redevelopment Act of 1945. That Act provided both for the comprehensive use of the eminent domain power to redevelop slum areas and for the possible sale or lease of the condemned lands to private interests. In discussing whether the takings authorized by that Act were for a "public use," the Court stated:

> [Subject] to specific constitutional limitations, when the legislature has spoken, the public interest has been declared in terms well-nigh conclusive. In such cases the legislature, not the judiciary, is the main guardian of the public needs to be served by social legislation. [This] principle admits of no exception merely because the power of eminent domain is involved. [The] power of eminent domain is merely the means to the end. [Once] the object is within the authority of Congress, the means by which it will be attained is also for Congress to determine. Here one of the means chosen is the use of private enterprise for redevelopment of the area. Appellants argue that this makes the project a taking from one businessman for the benefit of another businessman. But the means of executing the project are for Congress and Congress alone to determine, once the public purpose has been established.

The "public use" requirement is thus coterminous with the scope of a sovereign's police powers. [While there is] a role for courts to play in reviewing a legislature's judgment of what constitutes a public use, . . . it is "an extremely narrow" one. [In] short, the Court has made clear that it will not substitute its judgment for a legislature's judgment as to what constitutes a public use, "unless the use be palpably without reasonable foundation."

[The] Court's cases have repeatedly stated that "one person's property may not be taken for the benefit of another private person without a justifying public purpose, even though compensation be paid." [But] where the exercise of the eminent domain power is rationally related to a conceivable public purpose, the Court has never held a compensated taking to be proscribed by the Public Use Clause.

[We] have no trouble concluding that the Hawaii Act is constitutional. The people of Hawaii have attempted [to] reduce the perceived social and economic evils of a land oligopoly [that has] created artificial deterrents to the normal functioning of the State's residential land market and forced thousands of individual homeowners to lease, rather than buy, the land underneath their homes. Regulating oligopoly and the evils associated with it is a classic exercise of a State's police powers. We cannot disapprove of Hawaii's exercise of this power.

Nor can we condemn as irrational the Act's approach to correcting the land oligopoly problem. The Act presumes that when a sufficiently large number of persons declare that they are willing but unable to buy lots at fair prices the land market is malfunctioning. When such a malfunction is signalled, the Act authorizes HHA to condemn lots in the relevant tract. The Act limits the number of lots any one tenant can purchase and authorizes HHA to use public funds to ensure that the market dilution goals will be achieved. This is a comprehensive and rational approach to identifying and correcting market failure.

NOTES

1. The Meaning of "Public Use." Justice O'Connor stated that "[t]he 'public use' requirement [is] coterminous with the scope of a sovereign's police powers." The police power is an ill-defined concept. In state government, it is the state's inherent power to act for the health, safety, or general welfare of the people, bounded only by the state's constitution and federal constitutional or statutory law. In the federal government, it is the sum of the federal government's enumerated powers, bounded by the constitutional limits on the exercise of those powers. Thus the police power "mark[s] the line between *noncompensable* regulation and compensable takings of property. [Legitimately] exercised, the police power requires no compensation." Merrill, The Economics of Public Use, 72 Cornell L. Rev. 61, 70 (1986). Does *Midkiff* disturb this line, so that "a state could freely choose between compensation and noncompensation any time its actions served a 'public use' "? One possible alternative to the Court's conception of public use is a requirement that the general public must actually *use* the taken property. Cf. Rubenfeld, Usings, 102 Yale L.J. 1077 (1993), arguing that the public use requirement should serve to define the point at which compensation is due: "[W]hen government conscripts someone's property for state use, then it must pay." Would this enable governments to compel the transfer of someone's home to McDonald's for conversion to a fast-food outlet on the ground that the general public is invited to use the facility? Another possibility, advanced by Richard Epstein, Takings: Private Property and the Power of Eminent Domain 166-169 (1985), is that the public use requirement is not satisfied unless the government devotes the taken property to the provision of what an economist would call "public goods," or something very close to them. A pure "public good" is something from which nobody can be excluded and that remains available for consumption no matter how many people have consumed its benefits. National defense and a lighthouse beacon are typical examples of the genre. Recognizing that there are very few pure public goods, Epstein concedes that the public use requirement would be satisfied if the taken property were devoted to provision of public benefits that are close to pure public goods. Would Epstein's formula permit the government to condemn an entire neighborhood to be demolished and devoted to the construction of a General Motors factory that builds tanks for sale to the U.S. armed forces?

2. The *Poletown* Saga. In Poletown Neighborhood Council v. City of Detroit, 410 Mich. 616, 304 N.W.2d 455 (1981), the Michigan Supreme Court found the public use requirement satisfied when Detroit condemned an entire viable neighborhood for the purpose of razing the buildings and transferring the site to General Motors for construction of a new assembly plant. The Michigan court said that condemnation for a private use cannot be authorized whatever its incidental public benefit and condemnation for a public purpose cannot be forbidden whatever the incidental private gain. [Detroit] presented substantial evidence of [its] severe economic conditions . . . , the need for new industrial development to revitalize local industries, the economic boost the project would provide, and the lack of other adequate available sites to implement the project. . . . The power of eminent domain is to be used in this instance primarily to accomplish the essential public purpose of alleviating unemployment and revitalizing the economic base of the community. The benefit to a private interest is merely incidental.

Twenty-three years later, in County of Wayne v. Hathcock, 471 Mich. 445, 684 N.W.2d 765 (2004), the Michigan Supreme Court overruled *Poletown*. The Michigan court held that taking land to create a business and technology park was not for public use within the meaning of the Michigan Constitution's takings clause. When private property is condemned for transfer to another private owner, public use is satisfied, said the Michigan court, when any of three elements is present: (1) condemnation is necessary to obtain the public benefits; (2) management of the property remains, after transfer to the new private owner, accountable to the public; or (3) the purpose of the condemnation itself, as distinguished from the later transfer and new use, is to secure a public benefit independent of the benefits produced by the later transfer and new use.

None of these elements was satisfied. The project could be accomplished by voluntary transfers; there would be no public oversight once the land was transferred to the private businesses; and condemnation was not for an independent public benefit, such as improving public health and safety by eliminating a crime-ridden slum dotted with unsafe and unsanitary structures. The Michigan court held that a "generalized economic benefit" of the sort present in *Poletown* was insufficient to constitute a public use. "Every business . . . contribute[s] in some way to the commonweal. To justify the exercise of eminent domain solely on the basis of the fact that the use of that property by a private entity seeking its own profit might contribute to the economy's health is to render impotent our constitutional limitations on the government's power of eminent domain. *Poletown*'s 'economic benefit' rationale would validate practically *any* exercise of the power of eminent domain on behalf of a private entity."

≡≡≡ ### *Kelo v. City of New London*
545 U.S. 469 (2005)

JUSTICE STEVENS delivered the opinion of the Court.

In 2000, the city of New London approved a development plan that . . . was "projected to create in excess of 1,000 jobs, to increase tax and other revenues, and to revitalize an economically distressed city, including its downtown and waterfront areas." [The city] proposes to use the power of eminent domain to acquire . . . property from unwilling owners in exchange for just compensation. The question presented is whether the city's proposed disposition of this property qualifies as a "public use" within the meaning of the Takings Clause of the Fifth Amendment to the Constitution.

[New London, Connecticut, an economically depressed city of some 24,000 residents, concluded that the Fort Trumbull area, a 90-acre peninsula jutting into the Thames River consisting of some 115 privately owned properties and a 32-acre state park, was ideally suited for redevelopment. The occasion for this decision was pharmaceutical manufacturer Pfizer's decision to build a large research facility adjacent to the Fort Trumbull area. New London decided that Fort Trumbull should be converted into mixed uses, including a "waterfront conference hotel at the center of a 'small urban village' that will include restaurants and shopping," a pedestrian "riverwalk," recreational and commercial marinas, "approximately 80 new residences organized into an urban neighborhood," a parcel to "contain at least 90,000 square feet" of privately owned and occupied "research and development office space," a site reserved for future use "to support the adjacent state park, by providing parking or retail services for visitors, or to support the nearby marina," and other sites for privately owned "office and retail space, parking, and water-dependent commercial uses."] In addition to creating jobs, generating tax revenue, and helping to "build momentum for the revitalization of downtown New London," the plan was also designed to make the City more attractive and to create leisure and recreational opportunities on the waterfront and in the park. [The Connecticut Supreme Court upheld the plan, and the Supreme Court affirmed.]

Two polar propositions are perfectly clear. On the one hand, it has long been accepted that the sovereign may not take the property of *A* for the sole purpose of transferring it to another private party *B*, even though *A* is paid just compensation. On the other hand, it is equally clear that a State may transfer property from one private party to another if future "use by the public" is the purpose of the taking; the condemnation of land for a railroad with common-carrier duties is a familiar example. Neither of these propositions, however, determines the disposition of this case.

[The] City would no doubt be forbidden from taking petitioners' land for the purpose of conferring a private benefit on a particular private party. Nor would the City be allowed to take property under the mere pretext of a public purpose, when its actual purpose was to bestow a private benefit. [Here, there is] no evidence of an illegitimate purpose. . . . [The] City's development plan was not adopted "to benefit a particular class of identifiable individuals."

On the other hand, this is not a case in which the City is planning to open the condemned land—at least not in its entirety—to use by the general public. Nor will the private lessees of the land in any sense be required to operate like common carriers, making their services available to all comers. But . . . this "Court long ago rejected any literal requirement that condemned property be put into use for the general public." [*Midkiff*.] [We afford] legislatures broad latitude in determining what public needs justify the use of the takings power. [*Berman, Midkiff*.]

[The City's] determination that the area was sufficiently distressed to justify a program of economic rejuvenation is entitled to our deference. The City has carefully formulated an economic development plan that it believes will provide appreciable benefits to the community, including—but by no means limited to—new jobs and increased tax revenue. . . . Given the comprehensive character of the plan, the thorough deliberation that preceded its adoption, and the limited scope of our review, it is appropriate . . . to resolve the challenges of the individual owners, not on a piecemeal basis, but rather in light of the entire plan. [That] plan unquestionably serves a public purpose. . . .

To avoid this result, petitioners urge us to adopt a new bright-line rule that economic development does not qualify as a public use. . . . Promoting economic development is a traditional and long accepted function of government. There is, moreover, no principled way of distinguishing economic development from the other public purposes that we have recognized. In our cases upholding takings that facilitated agriculture and mining, for example, we emphasized the importance of those industries to the welfare of the States in question; in *Berman*, we endorsed the purpose of transforming a blighted area into a "well-balanced" community through redevelopment; [and] in *Midkiff*, we upheld the interest in breaking up a land oligopoly that "created artificial deterrents to the normal functioning of the State's residential land market. . . ."

[P]etitioners maintain that for takings of this kind we should require a "reasonable certainty" that the expected public benefits will actually accrue. . . . "When the legislature's purpose is legitimate and its means are not irrational, our cases make clear that empirical debates over the wisdom of takings . . . are not to be carried out in the federal courts." *Midkiff*. . . . A constitutional rule that required postponement of the judicial approval of every condemnation until the likelihood of success of the plan had been assured would unquestionably impose a significant impediment to the successful consummation of many [comprehensive redevelopment] plans. . . .

We emphasize that nothing in our opinion precludes any State from placing further restrictions on its exercise of the takings power. [While] the necessity and wisdom of using eminent domain to promote economic development are certainly matters of legitimate public debate, [this] Court's authority . . . extends only to determining whether the City's proposed condemnations are for a "public use." . . .

JUSTICE KENNEDY, concurring.

. . . [T]ransfers intended to confer benefits on particular, favored private entities, and with only incidental or pretextual public benefits, are forbidden by the Public Use Clause. A court applying rational-basis review under the Public Use Clause should strike down a taking that, by a clear showing, is intended to favor a particular private party, with only incidental or pretextual public benefits. . . . A court confronted with a plausible accusation of impermissible favoritism to private parties should . . . review the record to see if it has merit, though with the presumption that the government's actions were reasonable and intended to serve a public purpose. Here, the trial court conducted a careful and extensive inquiry [and] concluded that "there is nothing in the record to indicate that . . . [respondents] were motivated by a desire to aid . . . particular private entities." . . . This taking occurred in the context of a comprehensive development plan meant to address a serious city-wide depression, and the projected economic benefits of the project cannot be characterized as *de minimis*. The identit[ies] of most of the private beneficiaries were unknown at the time the city formulated its plans. The city complied with elaborate procedural requirements that facilitate review of the record and inquiry into the city's purposes. [W]hile . . . there may be categories of cases in which the transfers are so suspicious, or the procedures employed so prone to abuse, or the purported benefits are so trivial or implausible, that courts should presume an impermissible private purpose, no such circumstances are present in this case.

JUSTICE O'CONNOR, joined by CHIEF JUSTICE REHNQUIST and JUSTICES SCALIA and THOMAS, dissenting.

Over two centuries ago, just after the Bill of Rights was ratified, Justice Chase wrote that an "act of the legislature (for I cannot call it a law) . . . that takes property from A and gives it to B . . . is against all reason and justice." . . . Today the Court abandons this long-held, basic limitation on government power. Under the banner of economic development, all private property is now vulnerable to being taken and transferred to another private owner, so long as it might be upgraded—i.e., given to an owner who will use it in a way that the legislature deems more beneficial to the public—in the process. To reason, as the Court does, that the incidental public benefits resulting from the subsequent ordinary use of private property render economic development takings "for public use" is to wash out any distinction between private and public use of property—and thereby effectively to delete the words "for public use" from the Takings Clause of the Fifth Amendment. . . .

The public use requirement [means that] Government may compel an individual to forfeit her property for the *public's* use, but not for the benefit of another private person. This requirement promotes fairness as well as security. [While we] give considerable deference to legislatures' determinations about what governmental activities will advantage the public[,] were the political branches the sole arbiters of the public-private distinction, the Public Use Clause would amount to little more than hortatory fluff. . . .

This case . . . presents an issue of first impression: Are economic development takings constitutional? I would hold that they are not. We are guided by two precedents about the taking of real property by eminent domain. [*Berman* and *Midkiff*.] . . .

In . . . both [*Berman* and *Midkiff*] the . . . precondemnation use of the targeted property inflicted affirmative harm on society—in *Berman* through blight resulting from extreme poverty and in *Midkiff* through oligopoly resulting from extreme wealth. [A] public purpose was realized when the harmful use was eliminated. Because each taking *directly* achieved a public benefit, it did not matter that the property was turned over to private use. Here, in contrast, New London does not claim that Susette Kelo's and Wilhelmina Dery's well-maintained homes are the source of any social harm. Indeed, it could not so claim without adopting the absurd argument that any single-family home that might be razed to make way for an apartment building, or any church that might be replaced with a retail store, or any small business that might be more lucrative if it were instead part of a national franchise, is inherently harmful to society and thus within the government's power to condemn.

[The] Court today . . . holds that the sovereign may take private property currently put to ordinary private use, and give it over for new, ordinary private use, so long as the new use is predicted to generate some secondary benefit for the public—such as increased tax revenue, more jobs, maybe even aesthetic pleasure. But nearly any lawful use of real private property can be said to generate some incidental benefit to the public. Thus, . . . the words "for public use" do not realistically exclude *any* takings, and thus do not exert any constraint on the eminent domain power.

[While] we said in *Midkiff* that "the 'public use' requirement is coterminous with the scope of a sovereign's police powers," [this] case . . . demonstrates why, when deciding if a taking's purpose is constitutional, the police power and "public use" cannot always be equated. . . . The trouble with economic development takings is that private benefit and incidental public benefit are, by definition, merged and mutually reinforcing. In this case . . . any boon for Pfizer or the plan's developer is difficult to disaggregate from the promised public gains in taxes and jobs. . . . If it is true that incidental public benefits from new private use are enough to ensure the "public purpose" in a taking, why should it matter . . . what inspired the taking in the first place? How much the government does or does not desire to benefit a favored private party has no bearing on whether an economic development taking will or will not generate secondary benefit for the public. And . . . the effect is the same from the constitutional perspective—private property is forcibly relinquished to new private ownership. . . . The specter of condemnation hangs over all property. Nothing is to prevent the State from replacing any Motel 6 with a Ritz-Carlton, any home with a shopping mall, or any farm with a factory. . . .

Finally, in a coda, the Court suggests that property owners should turn to the States, who may or may not choose to impose appropriate limits on economic development takings. . . . States play many important functions in our system of dual sovereignty, but compensating for our refusal to enforce properly the Federal Constitution (and a provision meant to curtail state action, no less) is not among them. . . .

Any property may now be taken for the benefit of another private party, but the fallout from this decision will not be random. The beneficiaries are likely to be those citizens with disproportionate influence and power in the political process, including large corporations and development firms. As for the victims, the government now has license to transfer property from those with fewer resources to those with more. The Founders cannot have intended this perverse result. "That alone is a *just* government," wrote James Madison, "which *impartially* secures to every man, whatever is his *own*." For the National Gazette, Property (Mar. 29, 1792), reprinted in 14 Papers of James Madison 266 (R. Rutland et al. eds., 1983).

JUSTICE THOMAS, dissenting.

. . . Today's decision is simply the latest in a string of our cases construing the Public Use Clause to be a virtual nullity, without the slightest nod to its original meaning. . . . The most natural reading of the Clause is that it allows the government to take property only if the government owns, or the public has a legal right to use, the property, as opposed to taking it for any public purpose or necessity whatsoever. . . . The Constitution's text . . . suggests that the Takings Clause authorizes the taking of property only if the public has a right to employ it, not if the public realizes any conceivable benefit from the taking. . . .

There is no justification . . . for affording almost insurmountable deference to legislative conclusions that a use serves a "public use." . . . We would not defer to a legislature's determination of the various circumstances that establish . . . when a search of a home would be reasonable. . . . [It] is backwards to adopt a searching standard of constitutional review for nontraditional property interests, such as welfare benefits, while deferring to the legislature's determination as to what constitutes a public use when it exercises the power of eminent domain, and thereby invades individuals' traditional rights in real property. The Court has elsewhere recognized "the overriding respect for the sanctity of the home that has been embedded in our traditions since the origins of the Republic," when the issue is only whether the government may search a home. Yet today the Court tells us that we are not to "second-guess the City's considered judgments" when the issue is, instead, whether the government may take the infinitely more intrusive step of tearing down petitioners' homes. Something has gone seriously awry with this Court's interpretation of the Constitution. Though citizens are safe from the government in their homes, the homes themselves are not. . . .

Berman and *Midkiff* erred by equating the eminent domain power with the police power of States. Traditional uses of that regulatory power, such as the power to abate a nuisance, required no compensation whatsoever, in sharp contrast to the takings power, which has always required compensation. The question whether the State can take property using the power of eminent domain is therefore distinct from the question whether it can regulate property pursuant to the police power. . . . The consequences of today's decision are not difficult to predict, and promise to be harmful. Allowing the government to take property [for] any economically beneficial goal guarantees that these losses will fall disproportionately on poor communities. Those communities are not only systematically less likely to put their lands to the highest and best social use, but are also the least politically powerful. . . . Urban renewal projects have long been associated with the displacement of blacks; "in cities across the country, urban renewal came to be known as 'Negro removal.'" Pritchett, The "Public Menace" of Blight: Urban Renewal and the Private Uses of Eminent Domain, 21 Yale L. & Pol'y Rev. 1, 47 (2003). Over 97 percent of the individuals forcibly removed from their homes by the "slum-clearance" project upheld by this Court in *Berman* were black. Regrettably, the predictable consequence of the Court's decision will be to exacerbate these effects.

NOTES AND PROBLEMS

1. Legislative Reaction. In the wake of *Kelo*, virtually every state has considered changes to its limits on eminent domain. At least 27 states have adopted meaningful additional limits on the eminent domain power. Some of those changes are statutory; others are amendments to the state constitution. Some forbid most or all takings for economic development, others limit such takings to "blighted" properties, and still others impose more modest limits, such as requiring economic development takings to be authorized by the state legislature rather than municipalities.

2. Judicial Reactions. In Norwood v. Horney, 110 Ohio St. 3d 353 (2006), the Ohio Supreme Court relied on the Ohio Constitution to conclude that a taking for economic development purposes was invalid: "[A]lthough economic factors may be considered in determining whether private property may be appropriated, the fact that the appropriation would provide an economic benefit to the government and community, standing alone, does not satisfy the public-use requirement of . . . the Ohio Constitution. . . . [A]ny taking based solely on financial gain is void as a matter of law and the courts owe no deference to a legislative finding that the proposed taking will provide financial benefit to a community."

3. Problems: *Global Products.* Suppose that Global Products, Inc., proposes to relocate to your city, and bring with it the credible prospect of thousands of jobs, but will do so only if the city condemns your residence (providing you with just compensation) and then transfers title to the residence to the chief executive officer of Global Products, Inc., for use as his private residence. Public use?

Historic District. Suppose a city decides that a historic and architecturally distinguished waterfront district occupied by artists, art dealers, bookstores, architects, designers, and the occasional lawyer would deliver more economic benefits to the city if it were condemned and converted into a waterfront historic theme park, owned and operated by a private developer to be selected by a public bidding process. In that bidding process, the city council, by a 4-3 vote, selects Development Corporation, a private enterprise, instead of a well-funded imitator of the Colonial Williamsburg Foundation. Later, it is revealed that two of the four council members voting for Development purchased several thousand shares of Development common stock in ordinary market transactions immediately after the vote was made public. Public use?

Private/Public Partnership. Suppose a city agrees with a private company (Privaco) that Privaco will be the sole developer for a redevelopment project. After a public hearing, the city resolved that the public welfare warrants condemnation of the entire area. Baker, owner of a parcel that straddles the boundary of the redevelopment project, begins to negotiate with ABC, a pharmacy chain, to construct an ABC outlet on Baker's site. Privaco learns of this and demands from Baker $800,000 to avert condemnation of his property within the redevelopment district, and also a 50 percent ownership interest in Baker's ABC project. Baker refuses; two days later Baker's property within the redevelopment district is condemned. Public use?

4. Summing Up "Public Use." Consider the following formulations of the public use requirement. Which best captures the Supreme Court's view? Which should be the operational definition of public use, and why?

a. Public use is satisfied whenever there is a general public benefit that will conceivably result from the condemnation. It makes no difference whether the public benefit thus obtained is economic or not, or whether the public benefit is widely or uniformly dispersed to the public, or whether private entities will profit from the use of the condemnation power, so long as the government's action is the product of reasonable and thorough deliberation.

b. Public use is satisfied only when the government owns or controls the property after condemnation and the property is devoted to use by or for the general public. It makes no difference whether the public's use is conditioned upon payment of user fees, so long as the property is open to the public on equal terms.

c. Public use is satisfied only when the government condemns private property to deliver a public good or a quasi-public good. In applying this standard, it is essential to verify that the resulting use is unlikely to be one that would be provided to the public by private action.

d. Public use is satisfied when condemnation is indispensably necessary to deliver a general public benefit, or the public controls the subsequent use of the condemned property, or the condemnation produces immediate public benefits unrelated to general public benefits that are the product of subsequent transfer of the condemned property. It makes no difference that the property may or will be subsequently transferred to private owners, and that those owners may reap profits from their use of the property, so long as one or more of the stated conditions is met.

2. Regulatory Takings: When Does Regulation Become a Taking?

The principal constitutional problem of takings is defining the point at which government regulation of property is so extensive that it amounts to a de facto taking even though the government denies that it is taking the property. There is no general answer to this question.

The Court applies three categorical rules and several balancing tests to assess whether a regulation is a de facto taking. The categorical rules are as follows. (1) There is no taking, no matter what the economic impact of the regulation, if government regulation of property merely abates a common law nuisance. (2) A taking has occurred when government regulations produce a permanent physical occupation of private property, no matter how slight. (3) A taking has occurred when government regulations (other than nuisance abatement) leave the owner with no economically viable use of his or her property.

The general balancing test, applied when the categorical rules provide no answer, posits that regulations are takings when they are "functionally comparable to government appropriation or invasion of private property." Lingle v. Chevron USA, 544 U.S. 528 (2005). To make this comparison courts examine the magnitude and character of the burden imposed on property owners, as well as how that burden is distributed among owners. The underlying principle is to prevent the government "from forcing some people alone to bear burdens which, in all fairness and justice, should be borne by the public as a whole." Armstrong v. United States, 364 U.S. 40, 49 (1960).

Two specific balancing tests are used when governments attach conditions to the issuance of building or land use permits that would be takings if imposed alone. Such conditions are takings unless the government can prove each of the following: (1) The condition is substantially related to the state's otherwise valid reason for restricting land use at all, and (2) the nature and scope of the condition are roughly proportional to the public impact of the proposed land use.

a. Early Approaches

Pennsylvania Coal Co. v. Mahon
260 U.S. 393 (1922)

JUSTICE HOLMES delivered the opinion of the Court.

This is a bill in equity . . . to prevent the Pennsylvania Coal Company from mining under their property in such way as to remove the supports and cause a subsidence of the surface and of their house. [In 1878, the Coal Company conveyed] the surface, but in express terms reserve[d] the right to remove all the coal under the same, and the grantee [took] the premises with the risk, and waive[d] all claim for damages that may arise from mining out the coal. But [Mahon] say[s] that whatever may have been the Coal Company's rights, they were taken away by [Pennsylvania's] Kohler Act. . . .

The statute forbids the mining of anthracite coal in such way as to cause the subsidence [of] any structure used as a human habitation, [except] land where the surface is owned by the owner of the underlying coal and is distant more than one hundred and fifty feet from any improved property belonging to any other person. As applied to this case the statute is admitted to destroy previously existing rights of property and contract. The question is whether the police power can be stretched so far. [A state trial court had declared the Kohler Act unconstitutional, but the Pennsylvania Supreme Court reversed.]

Government hardly could go on if to some extent values incident to property could not be diminished without paying for every such change in the general law. [S]ome values are enjoyed under an implied limitation and must yield to the police power. But obviously the implied limitation must have its limits. . . . One fact for consideration in determining such limits is the extent of the diminution. When it reaches a certain magnitude, in most if not in all cases there must be an exercise of eminent domain and compensation to sustain the act. So the question depends upon the particular facts.

[The] act cannot be sustained as an exercise of the police power, so far as it affects the mining of coal under streets or cities in places where the right to mine such coal has been reserved. "[For] practical purposes, the right to coal consists in the right to mine it." What makes the right to mine coal valuable is that it can be exercised with profit. To make it commercially impracticable to mine certain coal has very nearly the same effect for constitutional purposes as appropriating or destroying it. This we think that we are warranted in assuming that the statute does. . . .

The general rule [is] that while property may be regulated to a certain extent, if regulation goes too far it will be recognized as a taking. It may be doubted how far exceptional cases, like the blowing up of a house to stop a conflagration, go—and if they go beyond the general rule, whether they do not stand as much upon tradition as upon principle. In general it is not plain that a man's misfortunes or necessities will justify his shifting the damages to his neighbor's shoulders. [A] strong public desire to improve the public condition is not enough to warrant achieving the desire by a shorter cut than the constitutional way of paying for the change. [Reversed.]

JUSTICE BRANDEIS, dissenting.

[Coal] in place is land; and the right of the owner to use his land is not absolute. He may not so use it as to create a public nuisance; and uses, once harmless, may, owing to changed conditions, seriously threaten the public welfare. Whenever they do, the legislature has power to prohibit such uses without paying compensation. . . . [Every] restriction upon the use of property imposed in the exercise of the police power deprives the owner of some right theretofore enjoyed, and is, in that sense, an abridgment by the State of rights in property without making compensation. But restriction imposed to protect the public health, safety or morals from dangers threatened is not a taking. The restriction here [is] merely the prohibition of a noxious use. The property so restricted remains in the possession of its owner. The State does not appropriate it or make any use of it [but] merely prevents the owner from making a use which interferes with paramount rights of the public. . . .

Restriction upon use does not become inappropriate as a means, merely because it deprives the owner of the only use to which the property can then be profitably put. [Nor] is a restriction imposed through exercise of the police power inappropriate as a means, merely because the same end might be effected through exercise of the power of eminent domain. [If] by mining anthracite coal the owner would necessarily unloose poisonous gasses, I suppose no one would doubt the power of the State to prevent the mining, without buying his coal fields. And why may not the State, likewise, without paying compensation, prohibit one from digging so deep or excavating so near the surface, as to expose the community to like dangers? In the latter case, as in the former, carrying on the business would be a public nuisance.

It is said that one fact for consideration in determining whether the limits of the police power have been exceeded is the extent of the resulting diminution in value; and that here the restriction destroys existing rights of property and contract. But values are relative. If we are to consider the value of the coal kept in place by the restriction, we should compare it with the value [of] the whole property. [For] aught that appears the value of the coal kept in place by the restriction may be negligible as compared with the value of the whole property, or even as compared with that part of it which is represented by the coal remaining in place and which may be extracted despite the statute.

[It] is said that [the Kohler Act] cannot be sustained as an exercise of the police power where the right to mine such coal has been reserved. The conclusion seems to rest upon the assumption that in order to justify such exercise of the police power there must be "an average reciprocity of advantage" as between the owner of the property restricted and the rest of the community; and that here such reciprocity is absent. [Where] the police power is exercised [to] protect the public from detriment and danger there [is] no room for considering reciprocity of advantage. There was no reciprocal advantage to the owner prohibited from using his [brickyard in Hadacheck v. Sebastian,] 239 U.S. 394 [1915,] unless it be the advantage of living and doing business in a civilized community. That reciprocal advantage is given by the act to the coal operators.

NOTES

1. Critical Factors. Did the Kohler Act go too far because the public benefit produced was less than the private injury inflicted? If so, how were costs and benefits measured? Or did the Act go too far because the private injury was simply too great? If so, did the Kohler Act deprive the coal company of all economic use of its coal left in place for support, or did it merely diminish the value of the underground coal as a whole? The latter problem is sometimes referred to as the "conceptual severance" problem. See Radin, The Liberal Conception of Property: Cross Currents in the Jurisprudence of Takings, 88 Colum. L. Rev. 1667, 1676 (1988). The problem is to identify the fraction of the affected property that is taken by the regulation. If the regulatory impact is the numerator, the property affected is the denominator. In Holmes's view the denominator was the coal required to be left in place to support the surface, a conclusion reinforced by the fact that Pennsylvania law regarded the "support estate" as a legally separate piece of property. That meant the regulatory impact and the affected property were equal, and that is a taking of *all* the affected property. To Brandeis, the denominator was the value of the "entire property," which meant the affected property—the value of the coal required to be left in place—should be compared with the value of the "entire property." Who is right? Why?

2. "Average Reciprocity of Advantage."   This concept suggests that affected property owners must receive some benefit from the regulation that burdens them. Richard Epstein proposes a modern version. Professor Epstein contends that redistributive regulations—those that impose costs and deliver benefits disproportionally—are takings, but he qualifies this conclusion by suggesting that many such regulations are fully compensated by "implicit in-kind compensation." See Epstein, Takings, at 195-215. An example of Epstein's implicit in-kind compensation, or Brandeis's average reciprocity of advantage, is a zoning ordinance that limits the use of all property in a given area to single-family residential use. In theory, the burden of limited use placed upon any given property owner is roughly offset by the advantage of having his neighbors similarly restrained. But Brandeis rejected the concept as irrelevant when governments do no more than exercise their police powers to protect the public from harm.

3. The Kohler Act Revisited?   In Keystone Bituminous Coal Association v. DeBenedictis, 480 U.S. 470 (1987), the Court upheld a modern version of the Kohler Act. Pennsylvania's 1966 Subsidence Act required sufficient coal to be left in place to support the surface. The Court distinguished the Subsidence Act from the Kohler Act on two grounds. First, the Subsidence Act was intended to "arrest [a] significant threat to the common welfare," while the Kohler Act was seen as a device to sacrifice the "private economic interests of coal companies" to benefit the "private interests of the surface owners." Perhaps, but wouldn't the effect of the statutes be identical? Second, the coal that the Subsidence Act forced miners to leave in place to support the surface did "not constitute a separate segment of property for takings law purposes" despite the fact that Pennsylvania law considered underground support of the surface a separate legal estate. The coal left in place was only a small fraction of the total amount of coal that could be removed; thus the miners had "not come close [to] proving that they have been denied the economically viable use of [their] property."

Miller v. Schoene
276 U.S. 272 (1928)

[Virginia law required the removal of all red cedar trees within two miles of an apple orchard whenever it was determined that the cedars hosted "cedar rust" fungus, a parasite that inflicts no damage whatever to the cedars but will ruin apple orchards located within two miles of cedars harboring the fungus. The owners of the cedars were compensated for the cost of cutting the trees and allowed to use the cedar logs, but were denied any compensation for the loss of their value as standing trees or resulting decrease in market value of the realty. An owner of cedars ordered destroyed under the law challenged the law as an uncompensated taking. The Virginia courts upheld the validity of the order, and a unanimous Supreme Court affirmed.]

JUSTICE STONE delivered the opinion of the Court.

[C]edar rust is an infectious plant disease [that] is destructive of the fruit and foliage of the apple, but without effect on the value of the cedar. . . . It is communicated by spores from one to the other over a radius of at least two miles. It appears not to be communicable between trees of the same species but only from one species to the other, and other plants seem not to be appreciably affected by it. The only practicable method of controlling the disease and protecting apple trees from its ravages is the destruction of all red cedar trees, subject to the infection, located within two miles of apple orchards.

The red cedar, aside from its ornamental use, has occasional use and value as lumber. [Its] value throughout the state is shown to be small as compared with that of the apple orchards of the state. Apple growing is one of the principal agricultural pursuits in Virginia.

[The] state was under the necessity of making a choice between the preservation of one class of property and that of the other wherever both existed in dangerous proximity. It would have been none the less a choice if, instead of enacting the present statute, the state, by doing nothing, had permitted serious injury to the apple orchards within its borders to go on unchecked. When forced to such a choice the state does not exceed its constitutional powers by deciding upon the destruction of one class of property in order to save another which, in the judgment of the legislature, is of greater value to the public. It will not do to say that the case is merely one of a conflict of two private interests and that the misfortune of apple growers may not be shifted to cedar owners by ordering the destruction of their property; for it is obvious that there may be, and that here there is, a preponderant public concern in the preservation of the one interest over the other. And where the public interest is involved preferment of that interest over the property interest of the individual, to the extent even of its destruction, is one of the distinguishing characteristics of every exercise of the police power which affects property.

We need not weigh with nicety the question whether the infected cedars constitute a nuisance according to the common law; or whether they may be so declared by statute. For where, as here, the choice is unavoidable, we cannot say that its exercise, controlled by considerations of social policy which are not unreasonable, involves any denial of due process.

QUESTIONS

Why didn't the Virginia law "go too far"? Was it because ownership of red cedar trees that harbor cedar rust was a noxious use? If so, why did the Court in *Mahon* not think that the act of mining coal sufficient to undermine the surface and threaten a collapse was a noxious use? Was the Virginia law valid because the public benefits of eliminating cedar rust substantially outweighed the burdens on affected property owners, and, by contrast, the public benefits of eliminating surface subsidence from underground coal mining did not outweigh the burdens on affected coal miners? How can we tell?

If it was acceptable for Virginia to decide which class of property owners—cedar tree owners or apple orchardists—should bear the misfortune of loss, why was it unacceptable for Pennsylvania to make the same decision via the Kohler Act? Should the loss of cedar trees in *Miller* have been treated as a burden "which, in all fairness and justice, should be borne by the public as a whole"? Armstrong v. United States, 364 U.S. 40, 49 (1960).

b.   The Categorical Approach

Lucas v. South Carolina Coastal Council
505 U.S. 1003 (1992)

JUSTICE SCALIA delivered the opinion of the Court.

[Lucas] paid $975,000 for two residential lots . . . on the Isle of Palms, [a barrier island east of Charleston,] on which he intended to build single-family homes. [Two years later,] the South Carolina Legislature enacted the Beachfront Management Act, which had the direct effect of barring petitioner from erecting any permanent habitable structures on his two parcels. A state trial court found that this prohibition rendered Lucas's parcels "valueless." This case requires us to decide whether the Act's dramatic effect on the economic value of Lucas's lots accomplished a taking of private property under the Fifth and Fourteenth Amendments requiring the payment of "just compensation."

[Under the Act the South Carolina Coastal] Council was directed to establish a "baseline" connecting the landwardmost "points of erosion [during] the past forty years" in the region of the Isle of Palms that includes Lucas's lots. [T]he Council fixed this baseline landward of Lucas's parcels. That was significant, for under the Act construction of occupiable improvements was flatly prohibited seaward of a line drawn 20 feet landward of, and parallel to, the baseline. The Act provided no exceptions.

[Lucas argued that the] construction bar effected a taking of his property without just compensation. Lucas did not take issue with the validity of the Act as a lawful exercise of South Carolina's police power, but contended that the Act's complete extinguishment of his property's value entitled him to compensation regardless of whether the legislature had acted in furtherance of legitimate police power objectives. [The trial] court agreed. [The] Supreme Court of South Carolina reversed, [ruling] that when a regulation respecting the use of property is designed "to prevent serious public harm" no compensation is owing under the Takings Clause regardless of the regulation's effect on the property's value.

Prior to . . . Pennsylvania Coal Co. v. Mahon, it was generally thought that the Takings Clause reached only a "direct appropriation" of property, or the functional equivalent of a "practical ouster of [the owner's] possession." Justice Holmes recognized in *Mahon*, however, that if the protection against physical appropriations of private property was to be meaningfully enforced, the government's power to redefine the range of interests included in the ownership of property was necessarily constrained by constitutional limits. [Thus,] "while property may be regulated to a certain extent, if regulation goes too far it will be recognized as a taking." [But] *Mahon* offered little insight into when, and under what circumstances, a given regulation would be seen as going "too far" for purposes of the Fifth Amendment. In 70-odd years of succeeding "regulatory takings" jurisprudence, we have generally eschewed any "set formula" for determining how far is too far, preferring to "engage [in] essentially ad hoc, factual inquiries," Penn Central Transportation Co. v. New York City, 438 U.S. 104, 124 (1978).

We have, however, described at least two discrete categories of regulatory action as compensable without case-specific inquiry into the public interest advanced in support of the restraint. The first encompasses regulations that compel the property owner to suffer a physical "invasion" of his property. In general (at least with regard to permanent invasions), no matter how minute the intrusion, and no matter how weighty the public purpose behind it, we have required compensation. For example, in Loretto v. Teleprompter Manhattan CATV Corp., 458 U.S. 419 (1982), we determined that New York's law requiring landlords to allow television cable companies to emplace cable facilities in their apartment buildings constituted a taking, even though the facilities occupied at most only 1 cubic feet of the landlords' property [and consisted of a few wires and junction boxes largely obscured from view].

The second situation in which we have found categorical treatment appropriate is where regulation denies all economically beneficial or productive use of land. As we have said on numerous occasions, the [takings clause] is violated when land-use regulation ". . . *denies an owner economically viable use of his land.*" [Agins v. Tiburon, 447 U.S. 255, 260 (1980) (emphasis added).[1]] . . .

---

1. Regrettably, the rhetorical force of our "deprivation of all economically feasible use" rule is greater than its precision, since the rule does not make clear the "property interest"

We have never set forth the justification for this rule. Perhaps it is simply [that] total deprivation of beneficial use is, from the landowner's point of view, the equivalent of a physical appropriation. Surely, at least, in the extraordinary circumstance when no productive or economically beneficial use of land is permitted, it is less realistic to indulge our usual assumption that the legislature is simply "adjusting the benefits and burdens of economic life," in a manner that secures an "average reciprocity of advantage" to everyone concerned. . . .

On the other side of the balance, affirmatively supporting a compensation requirement, is the fact that regulations that leave the owner of land without economically beneficial or productive options for its use—typically, as here, by requiring land to be left substantially in its natural state—carry with them a heightened risk that private property is being pressed into some form of public service under the guise of mitigating serious public harm. [The many state and federal] statutes [that] provide for the use of eminent domain to impose servitudes on private scenic lands preventing developmental uses, or to acquire such lands altogether, suggest the practical equivalence in this setting of negative regulation and appropriation. [In] short, [there] are good reasons [to conclude] that when the owner of real property has been called upon to sacrifice all economically beneficial uses in the name of the common good, that is, to leave his property economically idle, he has suffered a taking. . . .

The South Carolina Supreme Court [thought] the Beachfront Management Act [involved] an exercise of South Carolina's "police powers" to mitigate the harm to the public interest that petitioner's use of his land might occasion. . . .

It is correct that many of our prior opinions have suggested that "harmful or noxious uses" of property may be proscribed by government regulation without the requirement of compensation. [But] the South Carolina Supreme Court was too quick to conclude that that principle decides the

---

against which the loss of value is to be measured. When, for example, a regulation requires a developer to leave 90% of a rural tract in its natural state, it is unclear whether we would analyze the situation as one in which the owner has been deprived of all economically beneficial use of the burdened portion of the tract, or as one in which the owner has suffered a mere diminution in value of the tract as a whole. (For an extreme—and, we think, unsupportable—view of the relevant calculus, see Penn Central Transportation Co. v. New York City, 438 U.S. 104 (1978), where the state court examined the diminution in a particular parcel's value produced by a municipal ordinance in light of total value of the taking claimant's other holdings in the vicinity.) Unsurprisingly, this uncertainty regarding the composition of the denominator in our "deprivation" fraction has produced inconsistent pronouncements by the Court. Compare Pennsylvania Coal Co. v. Mahon with Keystone Bituminous Coal Assn. v. DeBenedictis, 480 U.S. 470 (1987). [The] answer to this difficult question may lie in how the owner's reasonable expectations have been shaped by the State's law of property—i.e., whether and to what degree the State's law has accorded legal recognition and protection to the particular interest in land with respect to which the takings claimant alleges a diminution in (or elimination of) value. In any event, we avoid this difficulty in the present case, since the "interest in land" that Lucas has pleaded (a fee simple interest) is an estate with a rich tradition of protection at common law, and since the South Carolina [trial court] found that the Beachfront Management Act left each of Lucas's beachfront lots without economic value.

present case. The "harmful or noxious uses" principle was the Court's early attempt to describe in theoretical terms why government may, consistent with the Takings Clause, affect property values by regulation without incurring an obligation to compensate. [The harmful use] "cases are better understood as resting not on any supposed noxious quality of the prohibited uses but rather on the ground that the restrictions were reasonably related to the implementation of a policy . . . expected to produce a widespread public benefit and applicable to all similarly situated property."

. . . The transition from our early focus on control of "noxious" uses to our contemporary understanding of the broad realm within which government may regulate without compensation was an easy one, since the distinction between "harm-preventing" and "benefit-conferring" regulation is often in the eye of the beholder. It is quite possible, for example, to describe in *either* fashion the ecological, economic, and aesthetic concerns that inspired the South Carolina legislature in the present case. One could say that imposing a servitude on Lucas's land is necessary in order to prevent his use of it from "harming" South Carolina's ecological resources; or, instead, in order to achieve the "benefits" of an ecological preserve. . . . A given restraint will be seen as mitigating "harm" to the adjacent parcels or securing a "benefit" for them, depending upon the observer's evaluation of the relative importance of the use that the restraint favors. See Sax, Takings and the Police Power, 74 Yale L.J. 36, 49 (1964) ("The problem [in this area] is not one of noxiousness or harm-creating activity at all; rather it is a problem of inconsistency between perfectly innocent and independently desirable uses"). Whether Lucas's construction of single-family residences on his parcels should be described as bringing "harm" to South Carolina's adjacent ecological resources thus depends principally upon whether the describer believes that the State's use interest in nurturing those resources is so important that any competing adjacent use must yield.

When it is understood that . . . the distinction between a regulation that "prevents harmful use" and that which "confers benefits" is difficult, if not impossible, to discern on an objective, value-free basis . . . it becomes self-evident that noxious-use logic cannot serve as a touchstone to distinguish regulatory "takings"—which require compensation—from regulatory deprivations that do not require compensation. *A fortiori* the legislature's recitation of a noxious-use justification cannot be the basis for departing from our categorical rule that total regulatory takings must be compensated. If it were, departure would virtually always be allowed.

[Where] the State seeks to sustain regulation that deprives land of all economically beneficial use, we think it may resist compensation only if the logically antecedent inquiry into the nature of the owner's estate shows that the proscribed use interests were not part of his title to begin with.[2] [O]ur

---

2. Drawing on our [free exercise of religion clause] jurisprudence, [Employment Division v. Smith, 494 U.S. 872 (1990); see Chapter 10, Section B.1,] Justice Stevens would "look to the generality of a regulation of property" to determine whether compensation is owing. The

"takings" jurisprudence . . . has traditionally been guided by the understandings of our citizens regarding the content of, and the State's power over, the "bundle of rights" that they acquire when they obtain title to property. [T]he property owner necessarily expects the uses of his property to be restricted, from time to time, by various measures newly enacted by the State in legitimate exercise of its police [powers]. And in the case of personal property, by reason of the State's traditionally high degree of control over commercial dealings, he ought to be aware of the possibility that new regulation might even render his property economically worthless (at least if the property's only economically productive use is sale or manufacture for sale). Andrus v. Allard, 444 U.S. 51 (1979) (prohibition on sale of eagle feathers). In the case of land, however, we think the notion . . . that title is somehow held subject to the "implied limitation" that the State may subsequently eliminate all economically valuable use is inconsistent with the historical compact recorded in the Takings Clause that has become part of our constitutional culture.[3]

Where "permanent physical occupation" of land is concerned, we have refused to allow the government to decree it anew (without compensation), no matter how weighty the asserted "public interests" involved—though we assuredly would permit the government to assert a permanent easement that was a pre-existing limitation upon the landowner's title. We believe similar treatment must be accorded confiscatory regulations, i.e., regulations that prohibit all economically beneficial use of land. Any limitation so severe cannot be newly legislated or decreed (without compensation), but must inhere in the title itself, in the restrictions that background principles of the State's law of property and nuisance already place upon land ownership. A law or decree with such an effect must [do] no more than duplicate the result that could have been achieved [by] adjacent landowners (or other uniquely affected persons) under the State's law of private nuisance, or by the State under its

---

Beachfront Management Act is general, in his view, because it "regulates the use of the coastline of the entire state." [But the] equivalent of a law of general application that inhibits the practice of religion without being aimed at religion is a law that destroys the value of land without being aimed at land. Perhaps such a law—the generally applicable criminal prohibition on the manufacturing of alcoholic beverages challenged in *Mugler* comes to mind—cannot constitute a compensable taking. But a regulation specifically directed to land use no more acquires immunity by plundering landowners generally than does a law specifically directed at religious practice acquire immunity by prohibiting all religions. . . .

3. [Justice Blackmun argues] that our description of the "understanding" of land ownership that informs the Takings Clause is not supported by early American experience. That is largely true, but entirely irrelevant. The practices of the States prior to incorporation of the [takings clause]—[which] occasionally included outright physical appropriation of land without compensation—were out of accord with any plausible interpretation of [the takings clause]. [And] the text of the Clause can be read to encompass regulatory as well as physical deprivations (in contrast to the text originally proposed by Madison[:] "No person shall [be] obliged to relinquish his property, where it may be necessary for public use, without a just compensation." . . .

complementary power to abate nuisances that affect the public generally, or otherwise.[4]

[On] this analysis, [the] corporate owner of a nuclear generating plant would not be entitled to compensation when it is directed to remove all improvements from its land upon discovery that the plant sits astride an earthquake fault. Such regulatory action may well have the effect of eliminating the land's only economically productive use, but it does not proscribe a productive use that was previously permissible under relevant property and nuisance principles. The use of these properties for what are now expressly prohibited purposes was always unlawful, and (subject to other constitutional limitations) it was open to the State at any point to make the implication of those background principles of nuisance and property law explicit. . . . When, however, a regulation that declares "off-limits" all economically productive or beneficial uses of land goes beyond what the relevant background principles would dictate, compensation must be paid to sustain it.[5]

The "total taking" inquiry we require today will ordinarily entail (as the application of state nuisance law ordinarily entails) analysis of, among other things, the degree of harm to public lands and resources, or adjacent private property, posed by the claimant's proposed activities, the social value of the claimant's activities and their suitability to the locality in question, and the relative ease with which the alleged harm can be avoided through measures taken by the claimant and the government (or adjacent private landowners) alike. The fact that a particular use has long been engaged in by similarly situated owners ordinarily imports a lack of any common-law prohibition (though changed circumstances or new knowledge may make what was previously permissible no longer so). So also does the fact that other landowners, similarly situated, are permitted to continue the use denied to the claimant.

It seems unlikely that common-law principles would have prevented the erection of any habitable or productive improvements on petitioner's land; they rarely support prohibition of the "essential use" of land. The question, however, is one of state law to be dealt with on remand. We emphasize that to win its case South Carolina must do more than proffer the legislature's declaration that the uses Lucas desires are inconsistent with the public interest, or the conclusory assertion that they violate a common-law maxim such as *sic utere tuo ut alienum non laedas* ["use your property so as not to injure another"]. [A] "State, by *ipse dixit*, may not transform private property into public property without [compensation]." Instead, as it would be required to do if it sought to restrain Lucas

---

4. The principal "otherwise" that we have in mind is litigation absolving the State (or private parties) of liability for the destruction of "real and personal property, in cases of actual necessity, to prevent the spreading of a fire" or to forestall other grave threats to the lives and property of others. Bowditch v. Boston, 101 U.S. 16 (1880).

5. Of course, the State may elect to rescind its regulation and thereby avoid having to pay compensation for a permanent deprivation. But "where the [regulation has] already worked a taking of all use of property, no subsequent action by the government can relieve it of the duty to provide compensation for the period during which the taking was effective." [First English Evangelical Lutheran Church v. County of Los Angeles, 482 U.S. 304, 321 (1987).]

in a common-law action for public nuisance, South Carolina must identify background principles of nuisance and property law that prohibit the uses he now intends in the circumstances in which the property is presently found. Only on this showing can the State fairly claim that, in proscribing all such beneficial uses, the Beachfront Management Act is taking nothing.[6] [Reversed and remanded.]

Justice Kennedy, concurring in the judgment.

[The] finding of no value must be considered under the Takings Clause by reference to the owner's reasonable, investment-backed expectations. [*Penn Central.*] . . . Where a taking is alleged from regulations which deprive the property of all value, the test must be whether the deprivation is contrary to reasonable, investment-backed expectations. . . . The common law of nuisance is too narrow a confine for the exercise of regulatory power in a complex and interdependent society. The State should not be prevented from enacting new regulatory initiatives in response to changing conditions, and courts must consider all reasonable expectations whatever their source. . . .

Justice Blackmun, dissenting.

[Until] today, the Court explicitly had rejected the contention that the government's power to act without paying compensation turns on whether the prohibited activity is a common-law nuisance. [In] *Miller*, the Court found it unnecessary to "weigh with nicety the question whether the infected cedars constitute a nuisance according to common law; or whether they may be so declared by statute." Instead the Court has relied in the past [on] legislative judgments of what constitutes a harm. . . .

[Whether] the owner has been deprived of all economic value of his property will depend on how "property" is defined. . . . In *Keystone*, the Court determined that the "support estate" was "merely a part of the entire bundle of rights possessed by the owner," [and so] concluded that the support estate's destruction merely eliminated one segment of the total property. The dissent, however, characterized the support estate as a distinct property interest that was wholly destroyed.

[Even] more perplexing, however, is the Court's reliance on common-law principles of nuisance. [In] determining what is a nuisance at common law, state courts make exactly the decision that the Court finds so troubling when made by the South Carolina General Assembly today: they determine whether the use is harmful. [If] judges can [do this], why not legislators? . . . Nor does history indicate any common-law limit on the State's power to regulate harmful uses even to the point of destroying all economic value. Nothing

---

6. Justice Blackmun decries our reliance on background nuisance principles at least in part because he believes those principles to be [manipulable]. There is no doubt some leeway in a court's interpretation of what existing state law permits—but not remotely as much, we think, as in a legislative crafting of the reasons for its confiscatory regulation. We stress [that] eliminating all economically beneficial uses may be defended only if an objectively reasonable application of relevant precedents would exclude those beneficial uses in the circumstances in which the land is presently found.

in the discussions in Congress concerning the Taking Clause indicates that the Clause was limited by the common-law nuisance doctrine.

JUSTICE STEVENS, dissenting.

. . . [The] categorical rule the Court establishes [is] unsound and unwise[, and] the Court's formulation of the exception to that rule is too rigid and too narrow.

The Categorical Rule. [The categorical] rule is wholly arbitrary. A landowner whose property is diminished in value 95% recovers nothing, while an owner whose property is diminished 100% recovers the land's full value. . . . The arbitrariness of such a rule is palpable.

[Because] of the elastic nature of property rights, the Court's new rule will also prove unsound in practice. In response to the rule, courts may define "property" broadly and only rarely find regulations to effect total takings. [It] could easily be said in this case [that] Lucas may put his land to "other uses"—fishing or camping, for example—or may sell his land to his neighbors as a buffer. In either event, his land is far from "valueless." [Developers] and investors may market specialized estates to take advantage of the Court's new rule. The smaller the estate, the more likely that a regulatory change will effect a total taking. Thus, an investor may, for example, purchase the right to build a multi-family home on a specific lot, with the result that a zoning regulation that allows only single-family homes would render the investor's property interest "valueless." In short, the categorical rule will likely have one of two effects: Either courts will alter the definition of the "denominator" in the takings "fraction," rendering the Court's categorical rule meaningless, or investors will manipulate the relevant property interests, giving the Court's rule sweeping effect. To my mind, neither of these results is desirable or [appropriate].

The Nuisance Exception. The exception . . . effectively freezes the State's common law, denying the legislature much of its traditional power to revise the law governing the rights and uses of property. [The] human condition is one of constant learning and evolution—both moral and practical. Legislatures implement that new learning; in doing so they must often revise the definition of property and the rights of property owners. [Of] course, some legislative redefinitions of property will effect a taking and must be compensated—but it certainly cannot be the case that every movement away from common law does so. [The] Court's categorical approach rule will, I fear, greatly hamper the efforts of local officials and planners who must deal with increasingly complex problems in land-use and environmental regulation. . . .

≡ ## *Horne v. Department of Agriculture*
2015 U.S. LEXIS 4064

CHIEF JUSTICE ROBERTS delivered the opinion of the Court.

Under the United States Department of Agriculture's California Raisin Marketing Order, a percentage of a grower's crop must be physically set aside in certain years for the account of the Government, free of charge. The Government then sells, allocates, or otherwise disposes of the raisins in ways it determines are best suited to maintaining an orderly market. The question is whether the Takings Clause of the Fifth Amendment bars the Government from imposing such a demand on the growers without just compensation.

. . . In 2002–2003, . . . raisin growers [were ordered] to turn over 47 percent of their crop. In 2003–2004, 30 percent. . . . Growers generally ship their raisins to a raisin "handler," who physically separates the raisins due the Government (called "reserve raisins"), pays the growers only for the remainder ("free-tonnage raisins"), and packs and sells the free-tonnage raisins. The [Government] acquires title to the reserve raisins . . . and decides how to dispose of them in its discretion. . . . Raisin growers retain an interest in any net proceeds from [these dispositions.] In the years at issue in this case, those proceeds were less than the cost of producing the crop one year, and nothing at all the next.

The Hornes . . . refused to set aside any raisins for the Government, believing they were not legally bound to do so. The Government sent trucks to the Hornes' facility . . . to pick up the raisins, but the Hornes refused entry. . . . The Government then assessed against the Hornes a fine equal to the market value of the missing raisins—some $480,000—as well as an additional civil penalty of just over $200,000 for disobeying the order to turn them over. When the Government sought to collect the fine, the Hornes turned to the courts, arguing that the reserve requirement was an unconstitutional taking of their property under the Fifth Amendment. [The Ninth Circuit concluded that there was no taking. It reasoned] that "the Takings Clause affords less protection to personal than to real property," [and] viewed the reserve requirement as a use restriction, similar to a government condition on the grant of a land use permit. As in such permit cases, the Court of Appeals explained, the Government here imposed a condition (the reserve requirement) in exchange for a Government benefit (an orderly raisin market). And just as a landowner was free to avoid the government condition by forgoing a permit, so too the Hornes could avoid the reserve requirement by "planting different crops." . . . We granted certiorari.

. . . The first question [is] "Whether the government's 'categorical duty' under the Fifth Amendment to pay just compensation when it 'physically takes possession of an interest in property,' applies only to real property and not to personal property." The answer is no. . . . [The] "classic taking [is one] in which the government directly appropriates private property for its own use." Nor is there any dispute that, in the case of real property, such an appropriation is a *per se* taking that requires just compensation. *Loretto.* Nothing in the text or history of the Takings Clause, or our precedents, suggests that the rule is any different when it comes to appropriation of personal property. The Government has a categorical duty to pay just compensation when it takes your car, just as when it takes your home. The Takings Clause . . . protects "private property" without any distinction between different types. [This principle] goes back at least 800 years to Magna Carta, which specifically protected agricultural crops from uncompensated takings. . . . The colonists brought the principles of Magna Carta with them to the New World, including that charter's protection against uncompensated takings of personal property. . . . The reserve requirement . . . is a clear physical taking. Actual raisins are transferred from the growers to the Government. . . . Raisin growers subject to the reserve requirement thus lose the entire "bundle" of property rights in the appropriated raisins—"the rights to possess, use and dispose of" them. . . .

[The dissent thinks it baffling that the Hornes] concede that "the government may prohibit the sale of raisins without effecting a per se taking." But that distinction flows naturally from the settled difference in our takings jurisprudence between appropriation and regulation. A physical taking of raisins and a regulatory limit on production may have the same economic impact on a grower. The Constitution, however, is concerned with means as well as ends. The Government has broad powers, but the means it uses to achieve its ends must be "consist[ent] with the letter and spirit of the constitution." *McCulloch*. . . .

The second question [is] "Whether the government may avoid the categorical duty to pay just compensation for a physical taking of property by reserving to the property owner a contingent interest in a portion of the value of the property, set at the government's discretion." The answer is no. . . . The Government contends that because growers are entitled to [the] net proceeds [of the reserve raisins] there is no taking in the first place. But when there has been a physical appropriation, "we do not ask . . . whether it deprives the owner of all economically valuable use" of the item taken. . . . "When the government physically takes possession of an interest in property . . . it has a categorical duty to compensate the former owner, regardless of whether the interest that is taken constitutes an entire parcel or merely a part thereof." . . . The fact that the growers retain a contingent interest of indeterminate value does not mean there has been no physical taking, particularly since the value of the interest depends on the discretion of the taker, and may be worthless, as it was for one of the two years at issue here. . . . The Government and dissent . . . confuse our inquiry concerning *per se* takings with our analysis for regulatory takings. A regulatory restriction on use that does not entirely deprive an owner of property rights may not be a taking under *Penn Central*. . . . But once there is a taking, as in the case of a physical appropriation, any payment from the Government in connection with that action goes, at most, to the question of just compensation. . . .

The third question [is] "Whether a governmental mandate to relinquish specific, identifiable property as a 'condition' on permission to engage in commerce effects a per se taking." The answer, at least in this case, is yes. The Government contends that the reserve requirement is not a taking because raisin growers voluntarily choose to participate in the raisin market. According to the Government, if raisin growers don't like it, they can "plant different crops," or "sell their raisin-variety grapes as table grapes or for use in juice or wine." [The] Government is wrong as a matter of law. In *Loretto*, we rejected the argument that the New York law was not a taking because a landlord could avoid the requirement by ceasing to be a landlord. . . . Selling produce in interstate commerce, although certainly subject to reasonable government regulation, is . . . not a special governmental benefit that the Government may hold hostage, to be ransomed by the waiver of constitutional protection. [This case is unlike Ruckelshaus v. Monsanto Co., 467 U.S. 986 (1984), where we upheld a government requirement that] companies manufacturing pesticides [must] disclose health, safety, and environmental information about their products as a condition to receiving a permit to sell those products. While such information included trade secrets in which pesticide manufacturers had a property interest, those manufacturers were not subjected to a taking because they received a "valuable Government benefit" in exchange—a license to sell dangerous chemicals. . . . Raisins are not dangerous pesticides; they are a healthy snack. [*Monsanto*] is hardly on point. . . .

[The Government argues that] we should remand for the Court of Appeals to calculate "what compensation would have been due if petitioners had complied with the reserve requirement." . . . The Government has already calculated the amount of just compensation in this case, when it fined the Hornes the fair market value of the raisins: $483,843.53. The Government cannot now disavow that valuation, and does not suggest that the marketing order affords the Hornes compensation in that amount. There is . . . no need for a remand; the Hornes should simply be relieved of the obligation to pay the fine and associated civil penalty they were assessed when they resisted the Government's effort to take their raisins. [Reversed.]

JUSTICE BREYER, joined by JUSTICE GINSBURG and JUSTICE KAGAN, concurred, but dissented with respect to the Court's decision not to remand.

[In] calculating just compensation [it is necessary to set] off from the value of the portion that was taken the value of any benefits conferred upon the remaining portion of the property. [Applied] to the marketing order's reserve requirement, "the benefit [to the free-tonnage raisins] may be set off against the value of the [reserve raisins] taken." The value of the raisins taken might exceed the value of the benefit conferred. In that case, the reserve requirement effects a taking without just compensation. . . . On the other hand, the benefit might equal or exceed the value of the raisins taken. In that case, the California Raisin Marketing Order does not effect a taking without just compensation. [The] Takings Clause requires compensation in an amount equal to the value of the reserve raisins adjusted to account for the benefits received. . . . I would remand the case, permitting the lower courts to consider argument on the question of just compensation.

JUSTICE SOTOMAYOR, dissenting.

. . . Because the Order does not deprive the Hornes of all of their property rights, it does not effect a *per se* taking. . . . *Loretto* . . . does not encompass the circumstances of this case because it only applies where all property rights have been destroyed by governmental action. Where some property right is retained by the owner, no *per se* taking under *Loretto* has occurred. . . . To qualify as a *per se* taking under *Loretto*, the governmental action must be so completely destructive to the property owner's rights—all of them—as to render the ordinary, generally applicable protections of the *Penn Central* framework either a foregone conclusion or unequal to the task. Simply put, the retention of even one property right that is not destroyed is sufficient to defeat a claim of a *per se* taking under *Loretto*. . . . The Hornes, however, retain at least one meaningful property interest in the reserve raisins: the right to receive some money for their disposition. . . . Granted, this equitable distribution may represent less income than what some or all of the reserve raisins could fetch if sold in an unregulated market. In some years, it may even turn out (and has turned out) to represent no net income. But whether and when that occurs turns on market forces for which the Government cannot be blamed and to which all commodities—indeed, all property—are subject.

NOTE

Categorical Rules. The *Lucas* Court summarized and reaffirmed the categorical (or per se) rules that apply in regulatory takings.

a. Permanent physical occupation. When a government causes a permanent physical occupation of all or a part of private property, whether by the government or by a third party authorized by the government, the government has taken that property. The burden of proving permanent physical occupation is on the property owner. This rule, with its long pedigree, was expressly adopted by the Court in Loretto v. Teleprompter Manhattan CATV Corp., 458 U.S. 419 (1982). New York mandated that landlords must permit cable television operators to install cable facilities on their property. Loretto, owner of an apartment house burdened by Teleprompter's cable installation, claimed that Teleprompter's installation pursuant to the New York law was an uncompensated taking of her property. The Court agreed, concluding that a "permanent physical occupation authorized by government is a taking without regard to the public interests that it may serve." Note that temporary physical occupations of private property do not trigger this per se takings rule; whether such occupations are takings depends on application of the balancing tests. As *Horne* makes clear, the physical possession rule applies to personal property as well. See also Webb's Fabulous Pharmacies v. Beckwith, 449 U.S. 155 (1980).

In rare cases, the Court will find government action to be a taking on the ground that it constitutes a constructive permanent physical occupation. In United States v. Causby, 328 U.S. 256 (1946), the Court found a taking due to continuous government aircraft flights over Causby's land. Since the landowner could not use his land for any purpose due to the frequency and altitude of government overflights, the resulting loss was "as complete as if the United States had entered upon the surface of the land and taken exclusive possession of it." However, in Yee v. City of Escondido, 503 U.S. 519 (1992), the Court rejected application of this principle to a rent control ordinance. The ordinance authorized a tenant to occupy the landlord's property at a price below what the landlord regarded as sufficient inducement to permit the tenant to do so. The Court held that the permanent physical occupation requirement was not implicated because the initial decision of a landlord to deliver occupation of the property to the tenant was not compelled by the state and the owner was free to evict tenants in order to devote his property to an entirely new purpose.

b. Destruction of all economically viable use.   The *Lucas* Court explicitly recognized as a categorical rule that regulations that destroy all economically viable use of private property and that are not abatements of public or private nuisances are takings per se. The property owner has the burden of proving that the regulations at issue destroy all economically viable use of the property. This rule makes the conceptual severance issue extremely important. Does Justice Scalia's hint that each separate fee title might be recognized as the denominator in the conceptual severance fraction implicitly overrule the Court's conclusion in *Keystone* that Pennsylvania's recognition of the support estate as a separate fee title was inconsequential to conceptual severance?

c. Nuisance abatement, not just regulation of "noxious" use.   *Lucas* made clear that regulations that do no more than abate common law nuisances are valid per se, no matter how economically destructive they may be. But regulations that aim to preclude property uses that are "noxious" but not actionable nuisances are not within this categorical rule of per se validity. Does the nuisance rule effectively transfer power from legislatures to courts, by depriving legislatures of the ability to identify property uses that pose new public harms? If so, is that a good or a bad idea? It has been argued that legislatures are better able to identify diffuse sources of harm, such as small individual acts of pollution that add up to urban smog. On the other hand, even if that is true, legislative control of minute, diffuse sources of public harm will almost never render property economically worthless, and thus there will never be an occasion to seek the protection of the per se nuisance abatement rule.

Consider the argument made by William Fischel, Regulatory Takings: Law, Economics, and Politics (1995). Fischel argues that the legislative process can be relied on to protect private property so long as it is acting democratically. Courts should intervene to make sure that political insiders are not abusing people who lack either a meaningful voice in the process or the ability to leave the jurisdiction. There is no exit option to a landowner because land obviously can't be moved. Particularly in small government units, argues Fischel, there is a great likelihood that the political process will respond to those in place (e.g., existing residents of a low-density suburb who want controls on growth and density) and ignore the interests of outsiders (e.g., developers, would-be residents, in-place residents who wish to develop their land more intensively to accommodate new residents). Is the nuisance abatement rule a rough proxy for Fischel's process theory, since it requires that extreme regulations that make land worthless must survive the more objective (and less politically accountable) scrutiny of the judiciary?

Finally, to what extent does state common law control the scope of the nuisance abatement rule? "Background principles" of common law nuisance control, says the Court, but Justice Scalia adds a cautionary reminder in a footnote that a state court's application of the nuisance abatement rule must comport with "objectively reasonable application of relevant precedents." This means that the Court might review a state court's determination of the status of its common law of nuisance. Thus, the question of whether any given regulation is within the nuisance abatement rule becomes an issue of federal constitutional law.

c. The Balancing Approach

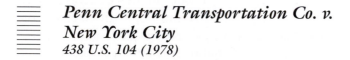

Penn Central Transportation Co. v. New York City
438 U.S. 104 (1978)

[New York City designated Penn Central's Grand Central Terminal an architectural landmark, thus subjecting any proposed architectural changes to advance approval by New York City's Landmarks Preservation Commission. Penn Central's proposal to build a 55-story slab-sided office tower above Grand Central Terminal was rejected by the Commission. Penn Central claimed that the Commission's refusal to permit the development constituted a taking. The New York courts ruled that the landmark regulations were not a taking. The Supreme Court affirmed.]

JUSTICE BRENNAN delivered the opinion of the Court.

[Landmark designation restricts] the property owner's [use] of the landmark site. [No alterations of] the exterior architectural features of the landmark [may be made without prior approval]. But landmark designation also enhances the economic position of the landmark owner [by permitting] owners of real property who have not developed their property to the full extent permitted [by] zoning laws [to] transfer development rights to contiguous parcels on the same city block.

[This Court] has been unable to develop any "set formula" for determining when "justice and fairness" require that economic injuries caused by public action be compensated by the government, rather than remain disproportionately concentrated on a few persons. Indeed, we have frequently observed that whether a particular restriction will be rendered invalid by the government's failure to pay for any losses proximately caused by it depends largely "upon the particular circumstances [in that] case." In engaging in these essentially ad hoc, factual inquiries, the Court [has] identified several factors that have particular significance. The economic impact of the regulation on the claimant and, particularly, the extent to which the regulation has interfered with distinct investment-backed expectations are, of course, relevant considerations. So, too, is the character of the governmental action. A "taking" may more readily be found when the interference with property can be characterized as a physical invasion by government than when interference arises from some public program adjusting the benefits and burdens of economic life to promote the common good.

[Appellants] observe that the airspace above the Terminal is a valuable property interest. [They] urge that the Landmarks Law has deprived them of any gainful use of their "air rights" above the Terminal and that, irrespective of the value of the remainder of their parcel, the city has "taken" their right to this . . . airspace, thus entitling them to "just compensation" measured by the fair market value of these air rights. "[Takings]" jurisprudence does not divide a single parcel into discrete segments and attempt to determine whether rights in a particular segment have been entirely abrogated. In deciding whether a particular governmental action has effected a taking, this Court focuses rather both on the character of the action and on the nature and extent of the interference with rights in the parcel as a [whole].

Next, appellants observe that New York City's law . . . does not impose identical or similar restrictions on all structures located in particular physical communities. It follows, they argue, that New York City's law is inherently incapable of producing the fair and equitable distribution of benefits and burdens of governmental action which is characteristic of zoning laws and historic-district legislation and which they maintain is a constitutional requirement if "just compensation" is not to be afforded. It is . . . true that the Landmarks Law has a more severe impact on some landowners than on others, but that in itself does not mean that the law effects a "taking." Legislation designed to promote the general welfare commonly burdens some more than others. . . . [Z]oning laws often affect some property owners more severely than others but have not been held to be invalid on that account. . . .

[We] now must consider whether the interference with appellants' property is of such a magnitude that "there must be an exercise of eminent domain and compensation to sustain [it]." That inquiry may be narrowed to the question of the severity of the impact of the law on appellants' parcel, and its resolution in turn requires a careful assessment of the impact of the regulation on the Terminal site. [The] New York City law does not interfere in any way with the present uses of the Terminal . . . : as a railroad terminal containing office space and concessions. So the law does not interfere with what must be regarded as Penn Central's primary expectation concerning the use of the parcel. More importantly, on this record, we must regard the New York City law as permitting Penn Central not only to profit from the Terminal but also to obtain a "reasonable return" on its investment.

[Moreover], to the extent appellants have been denied the right to build above the Terminal, [they have not] been denied all use of even those pre-existing air rights. Their ability to use these rights has not been abrogated; they are made transferable to at least eight parcels in the vicinity of the Terminal, one or two of which have been found suitable for the construction of new office buildings. [While] these rights may well not have constituted "just compensation" if a "taking" had occurred, the rights nevertheless undoubtedly mitigate whatever financial burdens the law has imposed on appellants and, for that reason, are to be taken into account in considering the impact of regulation. [Application] of New York City's Landmarks Law has not effected a "taking" of appellants' property. The restrictions imposed are substantially related to the promotion of the general welfare and not only permit reasonable beneficial use of the landmark site but also afford appellants opportunities further to enhance not only the Terminal site proper but also other properties. Affirmed.

JUSTICE REHNQUIST, joined by CHIEF JUSTICE BURGER and JUSTICE STEVENS, dissenting.

Of the over one million buildings and structures in the city of New York, appellees have singled out 400 for designation as official landmarks. The owner of a building might initially be pleased that his property has been chosen [for] such a singular distinction. But he may well discover [that] the landmark designation imposes upon him a substantial cost, with little or no offsetting benefit except for the honor of the designation. The question in this case is whether the cost associated with the city of New York's desire to preserve a limited number of "landmarks" within its borders must be borne by all of its taxpayers or whether it can instead be imposed entirely on the owners of the individual properties. . . .

Typical zoning restrictions [so] limit the prospective uses of a piece of property as to diminish the value of that property in the abstract because it may not be used for the forbidden purposes. But any such abstract decrease in value will more than likely be at least partially offset by an increase in value which flows from similar restrictions as to use on neighboring properties. All property owners in a designated area are placed under the same restrictions, not only for the benefit of the municipality as a whole but also for the common benefit of one another. . . . [T]here is "an average reciprocity of advantage." Where a relatively few individual buildings, all separated from one another, are singled out and treated differently from surrounding buildings, no such reciprocity exists. The cost to the property owner which results from the imposition of restrictions applicable only to his property and not that of his neighbors may be substantial—in this case, several million dollars—with no comparable reciprocal benefits. And the cost associated with landmark legislation is likely to be of a completely different order of magnitude than that which results from the imposition of normal zoning restrictions. Unlike the regime affected by the latter, the landowner is not simply prohibited from using his property for certain purposes, while allowed to use it for all other purposes. Under the historic-landmark preservation scheme adopted by New York, the property owner is under an affirmative duty to preserve his property as a landmark at his own expense. To suggest that because traditional zoning results in some limitation of use of the property zoned, the New York City landmark preservation scheme should likewise be upheld, represents the ultimate in treating as alike things which are different. [The takings clause] bars the "Government from forcing some people alone to bear public burdens which, in all fairness and justice, should be borne by the public as a whole." . . . [The transferable development rights are relevant only to the question of whether those rights] constitute a "full and perfect equivalent for the property taken."

NOTES

1. Balancing Public Benefits and Private Costs. The validity of the landmarks regulations turned on assessment of a variety of factors. Which were most important?

Unlike *Lucas*, the property owner was not stripped of all value by the regulations. Penn Central could still earn a "reasonable return" on its "investment-backed expectations." What were those expectations? In the early 1900s, when the terminal was planned, the goal was to put the tracks underground to facilitate development of the surface. But when the terminal was actually constructed, it was operated solely as a rail terminal. Which expectations matter? By the early 1950s, rail travel had so declined that the New York Central Railroad (Penn Central's predecessor) planned to demolish the terminal and build an office tower. It did construct a 59-story tower on the north side of the terminal. Do "investment-backed expectations" include the expectation that one's investment will assume different functions over time?

2. "Reasonable Return" on Investment. To calculate this one must determine the investment and then decide what annual rate of return on that investment is "reasonable." The initial cost of the terminal (in pre–World War I dollars) was about $80 million, but that amount, expressed in 2015 dollars, is somewhere between $2 to $3 billion. One can only speculate about replacement cost, given the architectural details that could not easily be duplicated. Even if you can settle on the size of the investment, a "reasonable" rate of return is debatable. In mid-2015, interest rates on U.S. government obligations run from near zero for short term instruments to 3 percent or so on long term obligations. In 1980, ten-year U.S. government bonds yielded about 16 percent. So what's a reasonable rate of return?

3. The Uneasy Line Between *Lucas* and *Penn Central*. The application of the *Lucas* rule turns on characterization of the property interest affected by the regulation. Does a property owner lack any reasonable expectation of investment return if he acquires property subject to existing regulations that would, if applied to him after acquisition of the property, constitute a taking? No, said the Court in Palazzolo v. Rhode Island, 533 U.S. 606 (2001). Such a rule would immunize extreme and unreasonable regulations against attack by future generations; it would be capricious, permitting older owners or those with the will and means to hold property for a long time to challenge regulations, but deny that ability to younger owners or those who have recently arrived in a locality and acquired property. It would also deprive owners of the ability to transfer to others the same title they had. In a concurrence, Justice O'Connor suggested that regulations in place at the time an owner acquires property are relevant to the *Penn Central* issue of the owner's reasonable investment-backed expectations.

Has a property owner lost all economically viable use of his property if regulations absolutely forbid any development or use for a protracted period of time, albeit not forever?

Tahoe-Sierra Preservation Council, Inc. v. Tahoe Regional Planning Agency
535 U.S. 302 (2002)

JUSTICE STEVENS delivered the opinion of the Court.

The question presented is whether a moratorium on development imposed during the process of devising a comprehensive land-use plan constitutes a *per se* taking of property requiring compensation. . . . [Tahoe Regional Planning Agency (TRPA) imposed two moratoria, totaling 32 months (or nearly six years, as the dissenters read the record), on development in the Lake Tahoe Basin while formulating a comprehensive land-use plan for the area designed to address the threat of pollution of Lake Tahoe from increasing residential development. Petitioners, real estate owners affected by the moratoria and an association representing such owners, filed parallel suits, later consolidated, claiming that TRPA's actions constituted a taking of their property without just compensation.]

I. The relevant facts are undisputed. . . . Lake Tahoe is "uniquely beautiful," [so much so] that Mark Twain aptly described the clarity of its waters as "not *merely* transparent, but dazzlingly, brilliantly so." [M. Twain, Roughing It 174-175 (1872), emphasis added by the Court.] Lake Tahoe's exceptional clarity is attributed to the absence of algae that obscures the waters of most other lakes. Historically, the lack of nitrogen and phosphorus, which nourish the growth of algae, has ensured the transparency of its waters. Unfortunately, the lake's pristine state has deteriorated rapidly over the past 40 years; increased land development in the Lake Tahoe Basin (Basin) has threatened the "noble sheet of blue water" beloved by Twain and countless others. "[D]ramatic decreases in clarity first began to be noted in the [1950s], shortly after development at the lake began in earnest." The lake's unsurpassed beauty, it seems, is the wellspring of its undoing. The upsurge of development in the area has caused "increased nutrient loading of the lake largely because of the increase in impervious coverage of land in the Basin resulting from that development," [a trend that, unless stopped, was predicted to cause the lake to] "lose its clarity and its trademark blue color, becoming green and opaque for eternity."

[The TRPA identified properties with steep slopes and] certain areas near streams or wetlands known as "Stream Environment Zones" (SEZs) [as] especially vulnerable to the impact of development because, in their natural state, they act as filters for much of the debris that runoff carries. [To implement an interstate compact concerning the Tahoe Basin, TRPA enacted two ordinances to suspend development until it adopted] the permanent plan required by the Compact. . . . In combination, [the two ordinances] effectively prohibited all construction on sensitive lands in California and on all SEZ lands in the entire Basin for 32 months, and on sensitive lands in Nevada (other than SEZ lands) for eight months. It is these two moratoria that are at issue in this case. . . .

II. . . . [The District Court ruled that the moratoria constituted a taking under *Lucas* because they temporarily deprived petitioners of all economically viable use of their land. On appeal, the Ninth Circuit reversed, concluding] that because the regulations had only a temporary impact on petitioners' fee interest in the properties, no categorical taking [under *Lucas*] had occurred. . . . [T]he moratoria involve only a "temporal 'slice,' " of the fee interest. [The Ninth Circuit noted that] "a property interest may include a physical dimension (which describes the size and shape of the property in question), a functional dimension (which describes the extent to which an owner may use or dispose of the property in question), and a temporal dimension (which describes the duration of the property interest)." [It rejected the argument] "that we should conceptually sever each plaintiff's fee interest into discrete segments in at least one of these dimensions—the temporal one—and treat each of those segments as separate and distinct property interests for purposes of takings analysis." . . . We now affirm.

III. Petitioners make only a facial attack on [the moratoria]. They contend that the mere enactment of a temporary regulation that, while in effect, denies a property owner all viable economic use of her property gives rise to an unqualified constitutional obligation to compensate her for the value of its use during that period. . . . [We] conclude that the circumstances in this case are best analyzed within the *Penn Central* framework.

IV. . . . When the government physically takes possession of an interest in property for some public purpose, it has a categorical duty to compensate the former owner, regardless of whether the interest that is taken constitutes an entire parcel or merely a part thereof. [*Loretto, Causby.*] But a government regulation that . . . bans certain private uses of a portion of an owner's property . . . does not constitute a categorical taking. [*Keystone Bituminous Coal, Penn Central.*] "The first category of cases requires courts to apply a clear rule; the second necessarily entails complex factual assessments of the purposes and economic effects of government actions." Yee v. Escondido, 503 U.S. 519, 523 (1992). . . .

[Petitioners] rely principally on [*Lucas*] to argue that the *Penn Central* framework is inapplicable here. [E]ven though multiple factors are relevant in the analysis of regulatory takings claims, in such cases we must focus on "the parcel as a whole." [*Penn Central.*] . . .

[In First English Evangelical Lutheran Church of Glendale v. County of Los Angeles, 482 U.S. 304 (1987), the Court adopted the principle that] "once a court finds that a police power regulation has effected a 'taking,' the government entity must pay just compensation for the period commencing on the date the regulation first effected the 'taking,' and ending on the date the government entity chooses to rescind or otherwise amend the regulation." [While] nothing that we say today qualifies [*First English*,] we did not address in that case the quite different and logically prior question whether the temporary regulation at issue had in fact constituted a taking. . . . Petitioners seek to bring this case under the rule announced in *Lucas* by arguing that we can effectively sever a 32-month segment from the remainder of each landowner's fee simple estate, and then ask whether that segment has been taken in its entirety by the moratoria. Of course, defining the property interest taken in terms of the very regulation being challenged is circular. . . . Petitioners' "conceptual severance" argument is unavailing because it ignores *Penn Central*'s admonition that in regulatory takings cases we must focus on "the parcel as a whole."

An interest in real property is defined by the metes and bounds that describe its geographic dimensions and the term of years that describes the temporal aspect of the owner's interest. Both dimensions must be considered if the interest is to be viewed in its entirety. Hence, a permanent deprivation of the owner's use of the entire area is a taking of "the parcel as a whole," whereas a temporary restriction that merely causes a diminution in value is not. Logically, a fee simple estate cannot be rendered valueless by a temporary prohibition on economic use, because the property will recover value as soon as the prohibition is lifted. . . . *Lucas* [and] *First English* . . . make clear that the categorical rule in *Lucas* was carved out for the "extraordinary case" in which a regulation permanently deprives property of all value; the default rule remains that, in the regulatory taking context, we require a more fact specific inquiry.

V. [An] extreme categorical rule that any deprivation of all economic use, no matter how brief, constitutes a compensable taking surely cannot be sustained, [for it] would apply to [such normal matters as] orders temporarily prohibiting access to crime scenes, businesses that violate health codes, fire-damaged buildings, or other [issues] that we cannot now foresee. . . . A rule that required compensation for every delay in the use of property would render routine government processes prohibitively expensive or encourage hasty decisionmaking. [W]e are persuaded that the better approach to claims that a regulation has effected a temporary taking "requires careful examination and weighing of all the relevant circumstances." . . . In rejecting petitioners' *per se* rule, we do not hold that the temporary nature of a land-use restriction precludes finding that it effects a taking; we simply recognize that it should not be given exclusive significance one way or the other.

[Moratoria] are used widely among land-use planners to preserve the status quo while formulating a more permanent development strategy [and] are an essential tool of successful development. Yet even the weak version of petitioners' categorical rule would treat these interim measures as takings regardless of the good faith of the planners, the reasonable expectations of the landowners, or the actual impact of the moratorium on property values.

[With] a temporary ban on development there is a lesser risk that individual landowners will be "singled out" to bear a special burden that should be shared by the public as a whole. At least with a moratorium there is a clear "reciprocity of advantage" because it protects the interests of all affected land-owners against immediate construction that might be inconsistent with the provisions of the plan that is ultimately adopted. . . . In fact, there is reason to believe property values often will continue to increase despite a moratorium. Such an increase makes sense in this context because property values throughout the Basin can be expected to reflect the added assurance that Lake Tahoe will remain in its pristine state. . . .

In our view, the duration of the restriction is [only] one of the important factors that a court must consider in the appraisal of a regulatory takings claim. . . . We conclude [that] "fairness and justice" will be best served by relying on the familiar *Penn Central* approach when deciding cases like this, rather than by attempting to craft a new categorical rule. [Affirmed.]

CHIEF JUSTICE REHNQUIST, with whom JUSTICE SCALIA and JUSTICE THOMAS join, dissenting.

For over half a decade petitioners were prohibited from building homes, or any other structures, on their land. Because the Takings Clause requires the government to pay compensation when it deprives owners of all economically viable use of their land, and because a ban on all development lasting almost six years does not resemble any traditional land-use planning device, I dissent.

I. [Although the Court] relies on the flawed determination of the Court of Appeals that the relevant time period lasted only from August 1981 until April 1984[, in fact, because] respondent caused petitioners' inability to use their land from 1981 through 1987, that is the appropriate period of time from which to consider their takings claim.

II. I now turn to determining whether a ban on all economic development lasting almost six years is a taking. . . . [The] Court refuses to apply *Lucas* on the ground that the deprivation was "temporary." Neither the Takings Clause nor our case law supports such a distinction. For one thing, a distinction between "temporary" and "permanent" prohibitions is tenuous. The "temporary" prohibition in this case that the Court finds is not a taking lasted almost six years. The "permanent" prohibition that the Court held to be a taking in *Lucas* lasted less than two years . . . because the law, as it often does, changed. Under the Court's decision today, the takings question turns entirely on the initial label given a regulation, a label that is often without much meaning. There is every incentive for government to simply label any prohibition on development "temporary," or to fix a set number of years. As in this case, this initial designation does not preclude the government from repeatedly extending the "temporary" prohibition into a long-term ban on all development. The Court now holds that such a designation by the government is conclusive even though in fact the moratorium greatly exceeds the time initially specified. . . .

More fundamentally, even if a practical distinction between temporary and permanent deprivations were plausible, to treat the two differently in terms of takings law would be at odds with the justification for the *Lucas* rule, [which is] that a "total deprivation of use is, from the landowner's point of view, the equivalent of a physical appropriation." The regulation in *Lucas* was the "practical equivalence" of a long-term physical appropriation. . . . The "practical equivalence," from the landowner's point of view, of a "temporary" ban on all economic use is a forced leasehold. . . . Surely that leasehold would require compensation. [What] happened in this case is no different than if the government had taken a 6-year lease of their property. . . .

Lucas is implicated when the government deprives a landowner of "all economically beneficial or productive use of land." The District Court found, and the Court agrees, that the moratorium "temporarily" deprived petitioners of "all economically viable use of their land." [The] "temporary" denial of all viable use of land for six years is a taking.

III. The Court worries that applying *Lucas* here compels finding that an array of traditional, short-term, land-use planning devices are takings. . . . When a regulation merely delays a final land use decision, we have recognized that there are other background principles of state property law that prevent the delay from being deemed a taking. We thus noted in *First English* that our discussion of temporary takings did not apply "in the case of normal delays in obtaining building permits, changes in zoning ordinances, variances, and the like." [The] short-term delays attendant to zoning and permit regimes are a longstanding feature of state property law and part of a landowner's reasonable investment-backed expectations. . . . But a moratorium prohibiting all economic use for a period of six years is not one of the longstanding, implied limitations of state property law. Moratoria [that] prohibit only certain categories of development, such as fast-food restaurants, or all commercial development, . . . do not implicate *Lucas* because they do not deprive landowners of all economically beneficial use of their land. As for moratoria that prohibit all development, these do not have the lineage of permit and zoning requirements and thus it is less certain that property is acquired under the "implied limitation" of a moratorium prohibiting all development. . . .

But this case does not require us to decide as a categorical matter whether moratoria prohibiting all economic use are an implied limitation of state property law, because the duration of this "moratorium" far exceeds that of ordinary moratoria. . . . Because the prohibition on development of nearly six years in this case cannot be said to resemble any "implied limitation" of state property law, it is a taking that requires compensation.

Lake Tahoe is a national treasure and I do not doubt that respondent's efforts at preventing further degradation of the lake were made in good faith in furtherance of the public interest. But, as is the case with most governmental action that furthers the public interest, the Constitution requires that the costs and burdens be borne by the public at large, not by a few targeted citizens.

JUSTICE THOMAS, with whom JUSTICE SCALIA joins, dissenting.

I write separately to address the majority's conclusion that the temporary moratorium at issue here was not a taking because it was not a "taking of 'the parcel as a whole.'" . . . *First English* put to rest the notion that the "relevant denominator" is land's infinite life. Consequently, a regulation effecting a total deprivation of the use of a so-called "temporal slice" of property is compensable under the Takings Clause unless background principles of state property law prevent it from being deemed a taking. . . .

A taking is exactly what occurred in this case. No one seriously doubts that the land use regulations at issue rendered petitioners' land unsusceptible of *any* economically beneficial use. This was true at the inception of the moratorium, and it remains true today. [The Court's] "logical" assurance that a "temporary restriction . . . merely causes a diminution in value" is cold comfort to the property owners in this case or any other. After all, "*in the long run* we are all dead." John Maynard Keynes, Monetary Reform 88 (1924).

I would hold that regulations prohibiting all productive uses of property are subject to *Lucas*'s *per se* rule, regardless of whether the property so burdened retains theoretical useful life and value if, and when, the "temporary" moratorium is lifted. To my mind, such potential future value bears on the amount of compensation due and has nothing to do with the question whether there was a taking in the first place.

NOTES AND PROBLEM

1. The End of Conceptual Severance? Conceptual severance, you will recall, is the idea that property affected by a regulation might be conceptually severed into two parcels, one of which bears the full impact of the regulation. Does *Tahoe-Sierra* bury conceptual severance, or does it cover only the narrower issue of applying conceptual severance to a temporal severance — the precise issue involved in the moratoria at issue in the case?

2. Problem. Suppose that in 1981, immediately prior to the date the Tahoe moratorium began, an owner had leased land that became subject to the moratorium for a 32-month period. Under the Court's analysis, would the moratorium constitute a taking of all viable economic use of the lessee's interest in the land?

3. The Meaning of Just Compensation. Washington required lawyers and escrow agents to deposit client funds into separate, individual interest-bearing trust accounts if the deposited funds would earn interest, net of transaction costs, and to pay the net interest to the principal owner, but required all other client funds to be deposited into a pooled interest-bearing trust account. Then it took the interest earned on the pooled account and used it to pay for legal services provided to indigents. In Phillips v. Washington Legal Foundation, 524 U.S. 156 (1998), the Court had held that the interest earned on the pooled account accounts was the property of the owner of the principal. At issue in Brown v. Legal Foundation of Washington, 538 U.S. 216 (2003), was whether Washington's practice denied just compensation to the clients whose funds earned the interest. The Court ruled that no compensation was due to the clients. The interest generated was in amounts so small that they would never be paid to the owners because the costs of computing and paying the interest to the owners would exceed the amount of earned interest. Thus, said the Court, no compensation was due to such depositors because their "pecuniary loss" was "zero." Just compensation, said the Court, must be measured by the property owner's "net loss rather than the value of the public's gain."

Justice Scalia, writing for the four dissenters, contended that there was no difference between "the value the owner has lost [and] the value the government has gained." They "have lost the interest that *Phillips* says rightfully belongs to them—which is precisely what the government has gained. . . . The State could satisfy its obligation to pay just compensation by simply returning [the property owners'] money to the . . . account from which it was seized, leaving others to incur the accounting costs in the event [the property owners] seek to extract their interest from the account." Justice Scalia noted that the Court in *Phillips* had illustrated its holding by observing that "[t]he government may not seize rents received by the owner of a building simply because it can prove that the costs incurred in collecting the rents exceed the amount collected."

4. The Scope of the Balancing Approach: Further Clarification. In response to the fact that the wholesale distribution of gasoline in Hawaii was highly concentrated in the hands of large oil companies, Hawaii enacted a law limiting the maximum rent payable by lessees of gasoline service stations owned by oil companies. Chevron attacked the rent cap as an uncompensated taking of its property, and the Ninth Circuit agreed, relying on Agins v. City of Tiburon, 447 U.S. 255, 260 (1980), in which the Supreme Court declared that government regulation of private property "effects a taking if [such regulation] does not substantially advance legitimate state interests. . . ." In Lingle v. Chevron U.S.A., 544 U.S. 528 (2005), the Supreme Court rejected that standard "as a freestanding takings test," declaring that "it has no proper place in our takings jurisprudence." The Court reiterated its commitment to the per se regulatory takings rules, but asserted that "[o]utside these . . . relatively narrow categories (and the special context of land-use exactions discussed [in *Nollan* and *Dolan*]), regulatory takings challenges are governed by the standards set forth in *Penn Central*. . . ."

Justice O'Connor, writing for the Court, explained that each of the per se rules and the *Penn Central* balancing approach "aims to identify regulatory actions that are functionally equivalent to the classic taking in which government directly appropriates private property or ousts the owner from his domain. Accordingly, each of these tests focuses directly upon the severity of the burden that government imposes upon private property rights." The Court noted that the " 'substantially advances' formula suggests a means-ends test: It asks . . . whether a regulation of private property is *effective* in achieving some legitimate public purpose." But this inquiry "reveals nothing about the *magnitude or character of the burden* a particular regulation imposes upon private property rights[, nor] does it [illuminate] how any regulatory burden is *distributed* among property owners." Accordingly, the "substantially advances" test "does not help to identify those regulations whose effects are functionally comparable to government appropriation or invasion of private property." Instead, this "inquiry probes the regulation's underlying validity," but that issue "is logically prior to and distinct from the question whether a regulation effects a taking, for the Takings Clause presupposes that the government has acted in pursuit of a valid public purpose." The Court emphasized that its holding "does not require us to disturb any of our prior holdings," thus leaving intact *Agins* itself and the doctrine crafted by *Nollan* and *Dolan* that deals with exactions in the context of land-use regulations.

3. Conditional Regulatory Takings

Conditional regulatory takings are another application of the unconstitutional conditions doctrine. Imagine a valid regulatory scheme that by itself is not a taking — for example, an ordinance that requires a property owner to obtain a building permit before beginning new construction. May the government condition issuance of a building permit upon the property owner's consent to what would otherwise be an uncompensated taking? Put differently, if the condition by itself would be a taking, is it saved by virtue of its attachment to an independently valid building permit? As applied here, the "unconstitutional conditions" doctrine means that a government may not require a person to surrender his property without compensation "in exchange for a discretionary benefit conferred by the government where the property sought has little or no relationship to the benefit." Dolan v. City of Tigard, 512 U.S. 374 (1994). That general standard consists of two components: (1) an "essential nexus" between the state's underlying legitimate regulatory interest and the condition imposed so that the condition advances the state's legitimate reason for regulating in the first place; and (2) "rough proportionality" between the condition imposed and the impact of the owner's proposed action upon the state's legitimate regulatory interest. The government has the burden of proving each of these elements.

Nollan v. California Coastal Commission
483 U.S. 825 (1987)

[Nollan wished to demolish his small, dilapidated beachfront cottage and replace it with a larger residence in keeping with the neighborhood. The California Coastal Commission refused to grant him a coastal development permit unless he recorded an easement permitting the public to cross his beachfront. Nollan contended the condition was a taking. The California courts held that there was no taking.]

JUSTICE SCALIA delivered the opinion of the Court.

Had California simply required the Nollans to make an easement across their beachfront available to the public on a permanent basis in order to increase public access to the beach, rather than conditioning their permit to rebuild their house on their agreeing to do so, we have no doubt there would have been a taking. To say that the appropriation of a public easement across a landowner's premises does not constitute the taking of a property interest but rather (as Justice Brennan contends) "a mere restriction on its use," is to use words in a manner that deprives them of all their ordinary meaning. Indeed, one of the principal uses of the eminent domain power is to assure that the government be able to require conveyance of just such interests, so long as it pays for them. Perhaps because the point is so obvious, we have never been confronted with a controversy that required us to rule upon it, but our cases' analysis of the effect of other governmental action leads to the same conclusion. [We] think a "permanent physical occupation" has occurred . . . where individuals are given a permanent and continuous right to pass to and fro, so that the real property may continuously be traversed, even though no particular individual is permitted to station himself permanently upon the premises.

[Given that] requiring uncompensated conveyance of the easement outright would violate the Fourteenth Amendment, the question becomes whether requiring it to be conveyed as a condition for issuing a land-use permit alters the outcome. We have long recognized that land-use regulation does not effect a taking if it "substantially advance[s] legitimate state interests" and does not "den[y] an owner economically viable use of his land." Our cases have made clear . . . that a broad range of governmental [purposes] satisfies these requirements. The Commission argues that among these permissible purposes are protecting the public's ability to see the beach, assisting the public in overcoming the "psychological barrier" to using the beach created by a developed shorefront, and preventing congestion on the public beaches. We assume, without deciding, that this is so—in which case the Commission unquestionably would be able to deny the Nollans their permit outright if their new house (alone, or by reason of the cumulative impact produced in conjunction with other construction) would substantially impede these purposes, unless the denial would interfere so drastically with the Nollans' use of their property as to constitute a taking.

The Commission argues that a permit condition that serves the same legitimate police-power purpose as a refusal to issue the permit should not be found to be a taking if the refusal to issue the permit would not constitute a taking. We agree. Thus, if the Commission attached to the permit some condition that would have protected the public's ability to see the beach notwithstanding construction of the new house—for example, a height limitation, a width restriction, or a ban on fences—so long as the Commission could have exercised its police power (as we have assumed it could) to forbid construction of the house altogether, imposition of the condition would also be constitutional. Moreover, [the] condition would be constitutional even if it consisted of the requirement that the Nollans provide a viewing spot on their property for passersby with whose sighting of the ocean their new house would interfere. Although such a requirement, constituting a permanent grant of continuous access to the property, would have to be considered a taking if it were not attached to a development permit, the Commission's assumed power to forbid construction of the house in order to protect the public's view of the beach must surely include the power to condition construction upon some concession by the owner, even a concession of property rights, that serves the same end. . . .

The evident constitutional propriety disappears, however, if the condition substituted for the prohibition utterly fails to further the end advanced as the justification for the prohibition. When that essential nexus is eliminated, the situation becomes the same as if California law forbade shouting fire in a crowded theater, but granted dispensations to those willing to contribute $100 to the state treasury. While a ban on shouting fire can be a core exercise of the State's police power to protect the public safety, and can thus meet even our stringent standards for regulation of speech, adding the unrelated condition alters the purpose to one which, while it may be legitimate, is inadequate to sustain the ban. Therefore, even though, in a sense, requiring a $100 tax contribution in order to shout fire is a lesser restriction on speech than an outright ban, it would not pass constitutional muster. Similarly here, the lack of nexus between the condition and the original purpose of the building restriction converts that purpose to something other than what it was. The purpose then becomes, quite simply, the obtaining of an easement to serve some valid governmental purpose, but without payment of compensation. Whatever may be the outer limits of "legitimate state interests" in the takings and land-use context, this is not one of them. [U]nless the permit condition serves the same governmental purpose as the development ban, the building restriction is not a valid regulation of land use but "an out-and-out plan of extortion." . . .

It is quite impossible to understand how a requirement that people already on the public beaches be able to walk across the Nollans' property reduces any obstacles to viewing the beach created by the new house. It is also impossible to understand how it lowers any "psychological barrier" to using the public beaches, or how it helps to remedy any additional congestion on them caused by construction of the Nollans' new house. We therefore find that the Commission's imposition of the permit condition cannot be treated as an exercise of its land-use power for any of these purposes.

[Our] cases describe the condition for abridgment of property rights through the police power as a "*substantial* advanc[ing]" of a legitimate state interest. We are inclined to be particularly careful about the adjective where the actual conveyance of property is made a condition to the lifting of a land-use restriction, since in that context there is heightened risk that the purpose is avoidance of the compensation requirement, rather than the stated police-power objective.

[The] Commission's [belief] that the public interest will be served by a continuous strip of publicly accessible beach along the coast . . . may well be

. . . a good idea, but that does not establish that the Nollans (and other coastal residents) alone can be compelled to contribute to its realization. California is free to advance its [objective] by using its power of eminent domain for this "public purpose," but if it wants an easement across the Nollans' property, it must pay for it.

Reversed.

≡ *Dolan v. City of Tigard*
≡ *512 U.S. 374 (1994)*

[Florence Dolan wished to expand her building supply store in Tigard, Oregon, a suburb of Portland. The city refused to grant her a building permit unless she donated about 10 percent of her property to the city for two purposes—enhanced flood control regarding the creek adjoining her property and construction of a pedestrian and bicycle pathway along the creek. Dolan contended that the conditions imposed constituted a taking. The Oregon Supreme Court ruled that the conditions were not a taking.]

CHIEF JUSTICE REHNQUIST delivered the opinion of the Court.

[We] must first determine whether the "essential nexus" [required by *Nollan*] exists between the "legitimate state interest" and the permit condition exacted by the city. If we find that a nexus exists, we must then decide the required degree of connection between the exactions and the projected impact of the proposed development. We were not required to reach this [latter] question in *Nollan*, because we concluded that the connection did not meet even the loosest standard. Here, however, we must decide this question.

[Unlike *Nollan*, no] gimmicks are associated with the permit conditions imposed by the city in this case. [T]he prevention of flooding along Fanno Creek and the reduction of traffic congestion in the Central Business District qualify [as] legitimate public purposes. It seems equally obvious that a nexus exists between preventing flooding along Fanno Creek and limiting development within the creek's 100-year floodplain. Petitioner proposes to double the size of her retail store and to pave her now-gravel parking lot, thereby expanding the impervious surface on the property and increasing the amount of stormwater runoff into Fanno Creek. The same may be said for the city's attempt to reduce traffic congestion by providing for alternative means of transportation. In theory, a pedestrian/bicycle pathway provides a useful alternative means of transportation for workers and shoppers.

The second part of our analysis requires us to determine whether the degree of the exactions demanded by the city's permit conditions bear the required relationship to the projected impact of petitioner's proposed development. [The] city required that petitioner dedicate "to the city as Greenway all portions of the site that fall within the existing 100-year floodplain [of Fanno Creek] and all property 15 feet above [the floodplain] boundary." [The] city relies on the Commission's rather tentative findings that increased stormwater flow from petitioner's property "can only add to the public need to manage the [floodplain] for drainage purposes" to support its conclusion that the "requirement of dedication of the floodplain area on the site is related to the applicant's plan to intensify development on the site." The city [found that] "the proposed expanded use of this site is anticipated to generate additional vehicular traffic thereby increasing [traffic congestion]. Creation of a convenient, safe pedestrian/bicycle pathway system as an alternative means of transportation [could] lessen the increase in traffic congestion."

The question for us is whether these findings are constitutionally sufficient to justify the conditions imposed by the city on petitioner's building permit. Since state courts have been dealing with this question a good deal longer than we have, we turn to representative decisions made by them. In some States, very generalized statements as to the necessary connection between the required dedication and the proposed development seem to suffice. We think this standard is too lax to adequately protect petitioner's right to just compensation if her property is taken for a public purpose. Other state courts require a very exacting correspondence, described as the "specific and uniquely attributable" test. [Under] this standard, if the local government cannot demonstrate that its exaction is directly proportional to the specifically created need, the exaction becomes "a veiled exercise of the power of eminent domain and a confiscation of private property behind the defense of police regulations." We do not think the Federal Constitution requires such exacting scrutiny, given the nature of the interests involved. A number of state courts have taken an intermediate position, requiring the municipality to show a "reasonable relationship" between the required dedication and the impact of the proposed development. Typical is the Supreme Court of Nebraska's opinion in Simpson v. North Platte, 206 Neb. 240, 245 (1980), where that court stated:

> The distinction [which] must be made between an appropriate exercise of the police power and an improper exercise of eminent domain is whether the requirement has some reasonable relationship [to] the use to which the property is being made or is merely being used as an excuse for taking property simply because at that particular moment the landowner is asking the city for some license or permit.

Thus, the court held that a city may not require a property owner to dedicate private property for some future public use as a condition of obtaining a building permit when such future use is not "occasioned by the construction sought to be permitted." Some form of the reasonable relationship test has been adopted in many other jurisdictions. . . .

We think the "reasonable relationship" test adopted by a majority of the state courts is closer to the federal constitutional norm than either of those previously discussed. But we do not adopt it as such, partly because the term "reasonable relationship" seems confusingly similar to the term "rational basis" which describes the minimal level of scrutiny under the Equal Protection Clause of the Fourteenth Amendment. We think a term such as

"rough proportionality" best encapsulates what we hold to be the requirement of the [takings clause]. No precise mathematical calculation is required,
but the city must make some sort of individualized determination that the
required dedication is related both in nature and extent to the impact of the
proposed development. . . .

We turn now to analysis of whether the findings relied upon by the city
here, first with respect to the floodplain easement, and second with respect to
the pedestrian/bicycle path, satisfied these requirements. It is axiomatic that
increasing the amount of impervious surface will increase the quantity and rate
of storm-water flow from petitioner's property. Therefore, keeping the floodplain open and free from development would likely confine the pressures on
Fanno Creek created by petitioner's development. [But] the city demanded
more—it not only wanted petitioner not to build in the floodplain, but it also
wanted petitioner's property along Fanno Creek for its Greenway system. The
city has never said why a public greenway, as opposed to a private one, was
required in the interest of flood control. The difference to petitioner, of course,
is the loss of her ability to exclude others. As we have noted, this right to exclude
others is "one of the most essential sticks in the bundle of rights that are commonly characterized as property." It is difficult to see why recreational visitors
trampling along petitioner's floodplain easement are sufficiently related to the
city's legitimate interest in reducing flooding problems along [the creek], and
the city has not attempted to make any individualized determination to support
this part of its request. [Imposition of] a permanent recreational easement upon
petitioner's property [would strip petitioner of] all rights to regulate the time in
which the public entered onto the Greenway, regardless of any interference it
might pose with her retail store. Her right to exclude would not be regulated;
it would be eviscerated. . . . We conclude that the findings upon which the city
relies do not show the required reasonable relationship between the floodplain
easement and the petitioner's proposed new building.

With respect to the pedestrian/bicycle pathway, we have no doubt that
the city was correct in finding that the larger retail sales facility proposed by
petitioner will increase traffic on the streets of the Central Business District.
[But] on the record before us, the city has not met its burden of demonstrating that the additional number of vehicle and bicycle trips generated by
the petitioner's development reasonably relate to the city's requirement for a
dedication of the pedestrian/bicycle pathway easement. The city simply found
that the creation of the pathway "could offset some of the traffic demand
[and] lessen the increase in traffic congestion." As Justice Peterson of the
[Oregon Supreme Court] explained in his dissenting opinion, "the findings of
fact that the bicycle pathway system '*could* offset some of the traffic demand'
is a far cry from a finding that the bicycle pathway system *will*, or is *likely
to*, offset some of the traffic demand." (Emphasis in original.) No precise
mathematical calculation is required, but the city must make some effort to
quantify its findings in support of the dedication for the pedestrian/bicycle
pathway beyond the conclusory statement that it could offset some of the
traffic demand generated. [Reversed and remanded.]

NOTES

1. Essential Nexus.   Prior to *Nollan*, governments were able to impose comprehensive but valid development regulations and then to insist on concessions of all kinds from the property owner as the price for relief from the regulations. *Nollan* limits these exactions to those that are substantially related to the purpose of the underlying regulation.

Problem: To ease demand for parking spaces on public streets, a city could require all new structures to offer off-street parking. Could the city waive those requirements if the owner agrees to contribute money to a mass transit development fund? What about a waiver conditioned on the owner's dedicating the off-street parking to the public? Or a waiver conditioned on the owner's donating a Rodin sculpture for the town square?

2. Rough Proportionality.   The rough proportionality test seeks to establish an adequate link between the condition imposed and the negative externalities of the owner's proposed activity. A development that imposes significant external costs may fairly be conditioned on the owner's taking action to absorb some of the external costs he is producing.

Problem: Consider again the city that requires new structures to provide off-street parking to ease congestion on public streets. Assuming that the essential nexus test is met by a waiver conditioned on a monetary contribution to the mass transit fund, how would you determine whether the monetary contribution is roughly proportional to the impact of the development on parking? Suppose the development is an apartment building (without parking) in which 60 people are likely to live. Would a monetary contribution in an amount sufficient to purchase, staff, and maintain one extra bus be roughly proportional to the impact?

3. Koontz v. St John's River Water Management District, 133 S. Ct. 2586 (2013).   Koontz acquired a 15 acre parcel of undeveloped land near Orlando, Florida. The state enacted legislation requiring an owner to obtain permits before any development that would affect water resources. Koontz applied for a development permit, offering to develop four acres and covenant not to develop the remainder. The District denied the permit and told Koontz he could either develop one acre and deed a conservation easement to the District on the remaining 14 acres or he could develop four acres, deed a conservation easement on the remainder of the land *and* make improvements, at his expense, on District-owned land some miles away. Koontz refused and brought suit, contending that the District's actions constituted a taking. The Florida Supreme Court found no taking was involved. The U.S. Supreme Court reversed:

> The principles that undergird our decisions in *Nollan* and *Dolan* do not change depending on whether the government *approves* a permit on the condition that the applicant turn over property or *denies* a permit because the applicant refuses to do so. . . . A contrary rule would be especially untenable in this case because it would enable the government to evade the limitations of *Nollan* and *Dolan*

simply by phrasing its demands for property as conditions precedent to permit approval. . . . Our unconstitutional conditions cases have long refused to
attach significance to the distinction between conditions precedent and conditions subsequent. . . . To do so here would effectively render *Nollan* and *Dolan*
a dead letter.

A Note on Takings Remedies

Several remedies apply once a regulation has been found to be a taking.
Future enforcement of the regulation may be enjoined; if the government
wishes to proceed with the regulatory scheme, it must openly exercise its
power of eminent domain and pay just compensation for its taking of property. Injunctive relief provides no redress for the time period during which
the regulation (which was a taking) was in place. For a long time, the Court
refused to provide a damages remedy for this "interim taking" of property,
but since First English Evangelical Lutheran Church of Glendale v. County
of Los Angeles, 482 U.S. 304 (1987), that is no longer the case. Temporary
takings are no different from permanent takings, said the Court, save in their
duration: "[W]here the government's activities have already worked a taking
of all use of property, no subsequent action by the government can relieve it
of the duty to provide compensation for the period during which the taking
was effective." The affected property owner is entitled to damages for the
loss of the use of his property during the period a regulatory taking was in
effect.

B.   THE CONTRACTS CLAUSE

The contracts clause provides that "[n]o State shall . . . pass any . . .
Law impairing the Obligation of Contracts." Art. I, §10. By virtue of judicial
interpretation, the contracts clause today should read: "No state may *unreasonably* impair the obligation of contracts." The contracts clause was intended
to prevent the states from altering the economic consequences produced by
private, voluntary contracts. Specifically, the clause was intended to prevent
states from enacting laws relieving debtors of their contractual obligations and
thereby depriving creditors of their contractual rights, as several states had
done in the decade prior to adoption of the Constitution.

During the first quarter of the nineteenth century the Court acted vigorously to protect vested contract rights. The first significant contracts clause
cases arose in connection with public contracts. In Fletcher v. Peck, 10 U.S.
87 (1810), the Court held that Georgia could not rescind its conveyance
of public lands even though the sales had been obtained by massive bribery of a thoroughly corrupt legislature. In Trustees of Dartmouth College

v. Woodward, 17 U.S. 518 (1819), the Court ruled that New Hampshire's revocation of Dartmouth College's royal charter, which would have transformed it from a private to a public institution, abrogated the public contract implicit in the charter, even though the Court offered its dictum opinion that the motive for the contracts clause was almost certainly to protect private contracts from state impairment. In Sturges v. Crowninshield, 17 U.S. 122 (1819), the Court held that a New York bankruptcy law violated the contracts clause because it permitted the debtor's preexisting contractual obligations to be erased completely. In Ogden v. Saunders, 25 U.S. 213 (1827), however, the Court upheld a New York bankruptcy law that applied to contracts made *after* its enactment, reasoning that the law in effect at the time a contract is formed is the "law of the contract." As *Ogden* suggests, the constitutional barrier to state regulation of private or public contracts is not impermeable. In his concurrence in *Dartmouth College*, Justice Story reminded legislators that if they wished to alter corporate charters granted by the state, they must reserve that power in the initial grant. Moreover, the Court's approach became ever more flexible. Charles River Bridge v. Warren Bridge, 36 U.S. 420 (1837), is an important example. In 1785 Massachusetts had granted to the Charles River Bridge Company the right to construct and operate a toll bridge across the Charles River. In 1828 Massachusetts chartered another company to construct a competing, toll-free bridge. The Court rejected the Charles River Bridge Company's contention that Massachusetts had impaired its charter. Massachusetts had never promised "not to establish a free bridge at the place where the Warren bridge is erected," nor had it promised an exclusive franchise to the Charles River Bridge Company. Massachusetts may have destroyed the economic value of the Charles River Bridge Company's charter, but it had not impaired the legal rights granted under it. Later the Court concluded that states, through public contracts, could not surrender their power to control matters bearing on public health or welfare. In Stone v. Mississippi, 101 U.S. 814 (1880), the Court upheld a statute outlawing lotteries even though a prior legislature had granted to a private party the right to run a lottery. The Court said that the "legislature cannot bargain away the police power."

By the end of the nineteenth century it was well established that the contracts clause did not bar "the legislature from enacting laws intended for the public good." Manigault v. Springs, 199 U.S. 473 (1905). But did this mean that the states merely retained the power to prohibit certain activities (and thus nullify contracts to perform those activities), or did it mean that the state could alter the terms of contracts for lawful purposes in order to achieve some perceived public good? For example, surely a state could prohibit the slaughter of horses for human consumption (and thus nullify a contract by which one party agrees to provide a butcher with horses for slaughter), but could a state leave human horse consumption unregulated and instead bar any remedies for breach of such contracts? That question (though involving mortgages, not horses) was considered in the next case.

≡ *Home Building & Loan Association v. Blaisdell*
≡ 290 U.S. 398 (1934)

[In 1933, during the Great Depression, Minnesota enacted a mortgage moratorium law that declared an economic emergency and for the period of the emergency (but not after May 1, 1935) authorized Minnesota courts to postpone mortgage sales, extended the post-sale redemption period so long as the mortgagor paid "all or a reasonable part" of the fair rental value of the property to the mortgagee, and barred actions for a deficiency judgment during the court-ordered extension. Blaisdell obtained a court order extending the redemption period on the condition that he pay Home Building & Loan $40 per month. Minnesota's Supreme Court upheld the mortgage moratorium law, relying on the economic emergency as adequate justification. At oral argument before the U.S. Supreme Court, Minnesota's Attorney General conceded "that in normal times and under normal conditions the . . . Law would be unconstitutional. But these are not normal times nor normal conditions. A great economic emergency has arisen in which the State has been compelled to invoke the police power to protect its people in the possession and ownership of their homes and farms and other real estate from the disastrous effects of the wholesale foreclosure of real estate mortgages which inevitably resulted from the present state-wide, nation-wide, and world-wide economic depression. General conditions resulting from this depression are well known."]

CHIEF JUSTICE HUGHES delivered the opinion of the Court.

[Home Building & Loan validly exercised its power of sale under the mortgage. The] period of redemption from the sale was one year, extended by the [Minnesota court for two more years] over the opposition of [Home. During] the period thus extended [Home] will be unable to obtain possession, or to obtain or convey title in fee, as [it] would have been able to do had the statute not been enacted. The statute does not impair the integrity of the mortgage indebtedness. The obligation for interest remains. The statute does not affect the validity of the sale or the right of a mortgagee-purchaser to title in fee, or his right to obtain a deficiency judgment, if the mortgagor fails to redeem within the prescribed period. Aside from the extension of time, the other conditions of redemption are unaltered. While the mortgagor remains in possession he must pay the [court-determined] rental value, [an amount that pays] taxes, insurance, and interest on the mortgage indebtedness.

[In] determining whether the provision for this temporary and conditional relief exceeds the power of the State by reason of the [contracts clause], we must consider the relation of emergency to constitutional power, the historical setting of the contract clause, the development of the jurisprudence of this Court in the construction of that clause, and the principles of construction which we may consider to be established.

Emergency does not create power. Emergency does not increase granted power or remove or diminish the restrictions imposed upon power granted or reserved. [While] emergency does not create power, emergency may furnish the occasion for the exercise of power. [Where] constitutional grants and limitations of power are set forth in general clauses, which afford a broad outline, the process of construction is essential to fill in the details. That is true of the contract clause. [The] reasons which led to the adoption of [the contracts clause] are not [in] doubt and have frequently been described. The widespread distress following the revolutionary period, and the plight of debtors, had called forth in the States an ignoble array of legislative schemes for the defeat of creditors and the invasion of contractual obligations. Legislative interferences had been so numerous and extreme that the confidence essential to prosperous trade had been undermined and the utter destruction of credit was threatened.

[But] full recognition of the occasion and general purpose of the clause does not suffice to fix its precise scope. [J]udicial decisions in its application . . . put it beyond question that the prohibition is not an absolute one and is not to be read with literal exactness like a mathematical formula. [The] inescapable problems of construction have been: What is a contract? What are the obligations of contracts? What constitutes impairment of these obligations? What [power remains] in the States [to] protect the vital interests of the community? [The] obligation of a contract is "the law which binds the parties to perform their agreement," [including] "its validity, construction, discharge and enforcement." [But] this broad language cannot be taken without qualification. "[Without] impairing the obligation of the contract, the remedy may certainly be modified as the wisdom of the nation shall direct, [provided] no substantial right secured by the contract is thereby impaired. [Every] case must be determined upon its own circumstances." [The] question is "one of reasonableness, and of that the legislature is primarily the judge."

The obligations of a contract are impaired by a law which renders them invalid, or releases or extinguishes them, [or which] derogate[s] from substantial contractual rights. [Not] only is the constitutional provision qualified by the measure of control which the State retains over remedial processes, but the State also continues to possess authority to safeguard the vital interests of its people. [The] reservation of essential attributes of sovereign power [is] read into contracts as a postulate of the legal order. The policy of protecting contracts against impairment presupposes the maintenance of a government by virtue of which contractual relations are worth[while]. This principle of harmonizing the constitutional prohibition with the necessary residuum of state power has had progressive recognition in the decisions of this Court. . . .

This principle precludes a construction which would permit the State to adopt as its policy the repudiation of debts or the destruction of contracts or the denial of means to enforce them. But it does not follow that conditions may not arise in which a temporary restraint of enforcement may be consistent with the spirit and purpose of the constitutional provision and thus be found to be within the range of the reserved power of the State to protect the vital interests of the community. [If] state power exists to give temporary relief from the enforcement of contracts in the presence of disasters due to physical causes such as fire, flood or earthquake, that power cannot be said to be nonexistent when the urgent public need demanding such relief is produced

[by] economic causes. [The] protective power of the State, its police power, may be exercised [in] directly preventing the immediate and literal enforcement of contractual obligations, by a temporary and conditional restraint, where vital public interests would otherwise [suffer]. It is manifest . . . that there has been a growing appreciation of public needs and of the necessity of finding ground for a rational compromise between individual rights and public welfare. [The] question is no longer merely that of one party to a contract as against another, but of the use of reasonable means to safeguard the economic structure upon which the good of all depends.

It is no answer to say that this public need was not apprehended a century ago, or to insist that what the provision of the Constitution meant to the vision of that day it must mean to the vision of our time. If by the statement that what the Constitution meant at the time of its adoption it means to-day, it is intended to say that the great clauses of the Constitution must be confined to the interpretation which the framers, with the conditions and outlook of their time, would have placed upon them, the statement carries its own refutation. It was to guard against such a narrow conception that Chief Justice Marshall uttered the memorable warning—"We must never forget that it is a *constitution* we are [expounding], a constitution intended to endure for ages to come, and consequently, to be adapted to the various crises of human affairs." [*McCulloch.*] [With] a growing recognition of public needs and the relation of individual right to public security, the court has sought to prevent the perversion of the clause through its use as an instrument to throttle the capacity of the States to protect their fundamental interests.

[W]e conclude: [An] emergency existed in Minnesota which furnished a proper occasion for the exercise of the reserved power of the State to protect the vital interests of the community. [The] legislation was not for the mere advantage of particular individuals but for the protection of a basic interest of society. [The] conditions upon which the period of redemption is extended do not appear to be unreasonable. [The] integrity of the mortgage indebtedness is not impaired; interest continues to run; the validity of the sale and the right [to] title or to obtain a deficiency judgment, if the mortgagor fails to redeem within the extended period, are maintained; and the conditions of redemption, if redemption there be, stand as they were under the prior law. The mortgagor during the extended period is not ousted from possession but he must pay the rental [value]. The mortgagee-purchaser [thus] is not left without compensation for the withholding of possession. [The] contract clause is not an absolute and utterly unqualified restriction of the State's protective power. [This] legislation is clearly so reasonable as to be within the legislative competency. [The] legislation is temporary in operation. It is limited to the exigency which called it forth. [The statute] could not validly outlast the emergency or be so extended as virtually to destroy the contracts. We are of the opinion that the Minnesota statute as here applied does not violate the [contracts clause]. [A]ffirmed.

JUSTICE SUTHERLAND, joined by JUSTICES VAN DEVANTER, MCREYNOLDS, and BUTLER, dissenting.

He simply closes his eyes to the necessary implications of the decision who fails to see in it the potentiality of future gradual but ever-advancing encroachments upon the sanctity of private and public contracts. [A] provision of the Constitution [does] not mean one thing at one time and an entirely different thing at another time. [The] whole aim of construction . . . of the Constitution is to discover the meaning, to ascertain and give effect to the intent, of its framers and the people who adopted it. [An] application of these principles to the question under review removes any doubt [that] the contract impairment clause denies to the [states] the power to mitigate hard consequences resulting to debtors from financial or economic exigencies by an impairment of the obligation of contracts of indebtedness. A candid consideration of the history and circumstances which led up to and accompanied the framing and adoption of [the contracts] clause will demonstrate conclusively that it was framed and adopted with the specific and studied purpose of preventing legislation designed to relieve debtors especially in time of financial distress. . . .

[A] statute which materially delays enforcement of the mortgagee's contractual right of ownership and possession does not modify the remedy merely; it destroys, for the period of delay, *all* remedy so far as the enforcement of that right is concerned. The phrase "obligation of a contract" in the constitutional sense imports a legal duty to perform the specified obligation of *that* contract, not to substitute and perform, against the will of one of the parties, a different, albeit equally valuable, obligation. And a state [has] no more power to accomplish such a substitution than has one of the parties to the contract against the will of the other. [If] it could, the efficacy of the constitutional restriction would, in large measure, be made to disappear. . . .

NOTE

"Reasonable and Appropriate" Exercise of the Police Power.   Was it the totality of the circumstances or one particular factor that led the Court to conclude that the mortgage moratorium law was a valid exercise of Minnesota's police power?

Emergency.   The Court said that "[e]mergency does not create [or increase] power," so what was the relevance of the economic emergency facing Minnesota? Did it lend special urgency to the "legitimate end" of the legislation? If there had been no emergency, would the legislation have had a legitimate end? If not, does that suggest that emergency did in fact create or at least increase the scope of Minnesota's police power?

Reasonable in scope.   The Court said the mortgage moratorium was a "reasonable and appropriate" way to achieve the state's objective. Was this because the moratorium was for the general "protection of a basic interest of society," not for the "mere advantage of particular individuals"? Or was it due to the "character [of] the relief afforded"—the fact that it suspended the finality of mortgage foreclosure but did not cancel the mortgage? Or was it because the moratorium was "temporary"—"limited to the exigency which called it forth"?

Total circumstances. If no particular factor was dispositive, does *Blaisdell* suggest that *all* of these factors are necessary to establish validity of contractual modifications? Or might other factors be equally efficacious in proving the reasonableness of contractual modifications? Should reasonableness depend on the severity of the modifications? Should reasonableness differ between public and private contracts? Should the level of judicial scrutiny vary with these factors? The next two subsections address these issues.

1. Public Contracts After *Blaisdell*

United States Trust Co. v. New Jersey
431 U.S. 1 (1977)

[In 1962, New York and New Jersey, acting together through the Port Authority, borrowed millions of dollars from the investing public on the strength of a statutory promise that the Port Authority would not use its revenues to subsidize rail transit. In 1974, New York and New Jersey decided that rail subsidies were needed to "discourag[e] automobile use and improv[e] mass transit." Each state enacted a law that repealed the promise. The repeal laws were challenged in separate suits in the New Jersey and New York courts. This suit originated in New Jersey, brought by an owner of Port Authority bonds and trustee for other bondholders. The New Jersey courts upheld the repeal as "a reasonable exercise of New Jersey's police power." The Supreme Court reversed.]

JUSTICE BLACKMUN delivered the opinion of the Court.

[We] first examine [the] claim that repeal of the 1962 covenant impaired the obligation of the States' contract with the bondholders. [The] Contract Clause limits the power of the States to modify their own contracts as well as to regulate those between private parties. Yet the Contract Clause does not prohibit the States from repealing or amending statutes generally, or from enacting legislation with retroactive effects. [But this] repeal has the effect of impairing a contractual obligation [because the] trial court found [and nobody denies] that the 1962 covenant constituted a contract between the two States and the [bondholders]. [A] statute is [treated] as a contract when the language and circumstances evince a legislative intent to create private rights of a contractual nature enforceable against the State. The intent to make a contract is clear from the statutory language, [the] purpose of the covenant was to invoke the constitutional protection of the Contract Clause as security against repeal, [and] the States received the benefit they bargained for: [enhanced] public marketability of Port Authority [bonds].

[A] finding that there has been a technical impairment is merely a preliminary step in resolving the more difficult question whether that impairment is [constitutionally permitted]. The States must possess broad power to adopt general regulatory measures without being concerned that private contracts will be impaired, or even destroyed, as a result. Otherwise, one would be able to obtain immunity from state regulation by making private contractual arrangements. [Yet] private contracts are not subject to unlimited modification under the police power. [Legislation] adjusting the rights and responsibilities of [private] contracting parties must be upon reasonable conditions and of a character appropriate to the public purpose justifying its adoption. As is customary in reviewing economic and social regulation, [courts] properly defer to legislative judgment as to the necessity and reasonableness of a particular measure.

When a State impairs the obligation of its own contract [the] initial inquiry concerns the ability of the State to enter into an agreement that limits its power to act in the future. [While] the Contract Clause does not require a State to adhere to a contract that surrenders an essential attribute of its sovereignty[, the] Court has regularly held that the States are bound by their debt contracts. [But the] Contract Clause is not an absolute bar to subsequent modification of a State's own financial obligations. As with laws impairing the obligations of private contracts, an impairment may be constitutional if it is reasonable and necessary to serve an important public purpose. In applying this standard, however, complete deference to a legislative assessment of reasonableness and necessity is not appropriate because the State's self-interest is at stake. [If] a State could reduce its financial obligations whenever it wanted to spend the money for what it regarded as an important public purpose, the Contract Clause would provide no protection at all.

[The] extent of impairment is certainly a relevant factor in determining its reasonableness. But we cannot sustain the repeal of the 1962 covenant simply because the bondholders' rights were not totally destroyed. [Mass] transportation, energy conservation, and environmental protection are goals that are important and of legitimate public concern. Appellees contend that these goals are so important that any harm to bondholders from repeal of the 1962 covenant is greatly outweighed by the public benefit. We do not accept this invitation to engage in a utilitarian comparison of public benefit and private loss. [A] State cannot refuse to meet its legitimate financial obligations simply because it would prefer to spend the money to promote the public good rather than the private welfare of its creditors. We can only sustain the repeal of the 1962 covenant if that impairment was both reasonable and necessary to serve the admittedly important purposes claimed by the State.

The more specific justification offered for the repeal of the 1962 covenant was the States' plan for encouraging users of private automobiles to shift to public transportation. The States intended to discourage private automobile use by raising bridge and tunnel tolls and to use the extra revenue from those tolls to subsidize improved commuter railroad service. Appellees contend that repeal of the 1962 covenant was necessary to implement this plan because the new mass transit facilities could not possibly be self-supporting and the covenant's "permitted deficits" level had already been exceeded. We reject this justification because the repeal was neither necessary to achievement of the plan nor reasonable in light of the circumstances.

The determination of necessity can be considered on two levels. First, it cannot be said that total repeal of the covenant was essential; a less drastic modification would have permitted the contemplated plan. . . . Second, without modifying the covenant at all, the States could have adopted alternative means of achieving their twin goals of discouraging automobile use and improving mass transit. [A] state is not free to impose a drastic impairment when an evident and more moderate course would serve its purposes equally well. [The] State has failed to demonstrate that repeal of the 1962 covenant was [necessary].

We also cannot conclude that repeal of the covenant was reasonable in light of the surrounding circumstances. [The repeal was not designed to deal with] unforeseen and unintended [effects. The] need for mass transportation in the New York metropolitan area was not a new development, and the likelihood that publicly owned commuter railroads would produce substantial deficits was well known. [During] the 12-year period between adoption of the covenant and its repeal, public perception of the importance of mass transit undoubtedly grew because of increased general concern with environmental protection and energy conservation. But these concerns were not unknown in 1962, and the subsequent changes were of degree and not of kind. We cannot say that these changes caused the covenant to have a substantially different impact in 1974 than when it was adopted in 1962. And we cannot conclude that the repeal was reasonable in the light of changed circumstances. [Reversed.]

JUSTICE BRENNAN, joined by JUSTICES WHITE and MARSHALL, dissenting.

Today's decision [remolds] the Contract Clause into a potent instrument for overseeing important policy determinations of the state legislature. [The 1962 covenant is an] effective barrier to the development of rapid transit in the [region and] squarely conflicts with the legitimate needs of the New York metropolitan [community]. It was in response to these societal demands that the New Jersey and New York Legislatures repealed the 1962 covenant. The trial court found [that expanded rail mass transit] "was not economically feasible under the terms of the 1962 covenant."

[Equally] unconvincing is the Court's contention that repeal of the 1962 covenant was unreasonable because the environmental and energy concerns that prompted such action "were not unknown in 1962, and the subsequent changes were of degree and not of kind." Nowhere are we told why a state policy, no matter how responsive to the general welfare of its citizens, can be reasonable only if it confronts issues that previously were absolutely unforeseen. . . . [Moreover, the] repeal of the 1962 covenant has occasioned only the most minimal damage [to bondholders. The] validity of [the bonds remains unimpaired]. No creditor complains [of failure to pay interest or to] redeem a bond that has matured. In fact, the Court does not even offer any reason whatever for fearing that, as a result of the covenant's repeal, the securities [are] jeopardized. [The] trial judge [found that] the security afforded bondholders had been substantially augmented by a vast increase in Authority revenues and [reserves]. [The Court's analysis] fundamentally misconceives the nature of the Contract Clause guarantee. One of the fundamental premises of our popular democracy is that each generation of representatives can and will remain responsive to the needs and desires of those whom they represent. Crucial to this end is the assurance that new legislators will not automatically be bound by the policies and undertakings of earlier days. [Thus], the Framers [conceived] of the Contract Clause primarily as protection for economic transactions entered into by purely private parties, rather than obligations involving the State itself. [As] a purely practical matter, an interference with state policy is no less intrusive because a contract prohibits the State from resorting to the most realistic and effective financial method of preserving its citizens' legitimate interests in healthy and safe transportation systems rather than directly proscribing the States from exercising their police powers in this area. . . . [There] is nothing sacrosanct about a contract. All property rights, no less than a contract, are rooted in certain "expectations" about the sanctity of one's right of ownership. . . . [The] Court . . . has granted wide latitude to "a valid exercise of [the States'] police powers," even if it results in severe violations of property rights. . . . [This] Court should have learned long ago that the Constitution—be it through the Contract or Due Process Clause—can actively intrude into such economic and policy matters only if [it is] prepared to bear enormous institutional and social costs. Because I consider the potential dangers of such judicial interference to be intolerable, I dissent.

NOTE

1. Self-Interest or Public Policy?   Should a public contract be subject to heightened scrutiny, as *U.S. Trust* holds, because a state is a party to such contract and thus infected with self-interest? Should public contracts be exempt from contract clause scrutiny (or subject to minimal scrutiny) because a state's interest is inseparable from that of its citizens, and thus it is always acting to promote public welfare?

2. Burdon of Proof.   Circuit courts divide on who has the burden of proving reasonableness and necessity (or lack of thereof). Compare Southern Cal. Gas Co. v. City of Santa Ana, 336 F.3d 855 (9th Cir. 2003), and Toledo Area AFL-CIO Council v. Pizza, 154 F.3d 367 (6th Cir. 1998) (state has burden), with United Auto., Aero., Agric. Implement Workers of America Int'l Union v. Fortuño, 633 F.3d 37 (1st Cir. 2011) (plaintiff has burden).

2. Private Contracts After *Blaisdell*

The Court has delivered a mixed message concerning the standard of review for state action impairing private contracts.

≡ *Allied Structural Steel Co. v. Spannaus*
≡ 438 U.S. 234 (1978)

[Minnesota enacted a "pension protection law" that required certain employers with pension plans who either terminate the plan or cease doing business in Minnesota to (1) provide pensions to all employees with at least ten years' service and (2) make a lump-sum payment to the state in an amount sufficient to provide the required pensions. Allied's pension plan stipulated that Allied could amend or terminate the plan at any time for any reason. Thus pensions were payable only to employees upon reaching age 65 *if* Allied was still in business *and* the pension plan still existed. Allied ceased doing business in Minnesota, and the state demanded $185,000 under its pension protection law. A federal district court upheld the law.]

JUSTICE STEWART delivered the opinion of the Court.

The Act substantially altered [Allied's contractual] relationships by superimposing pension obligations upon the company conspicuously beyond those that it had voluntarily agreed to undertake. [Though the] Contract Clause [is not as] unambiguously absolute [as it appears, it] is not a dead letter. [While] the Contract Clause does not operate to obliterate the police power of the States, [if it] is to retain any meaning at all [it] must be understood to impose some limits upon the power of a State to abridge existing contractual relationships, even in the exercise of its otherwise legitimate police power. . . .

[T]he first inquiry must be whether the state law has, in fact, operated as a substantial impairment of a contractual relationship. The severity of the impairment measures the height of the hurdle the state legislation must clear. Minimal alteration of contractual obligations may end the inquiry at its first stage. Severe impairment, on the other hand, will push the inquiry to a careful examination of the nature and purpose of the state legislation. The severity of an impairment of contractual obligations can be measured by the factors that reflect the high value the Framers placed on the protection of private contracts. Contracts enable individuals to order their personal and business affairs according to their particular needs and interests. Once arranged, those rights and obligations are binding under the law, and the parties are entitled to rely on them.

Here, [Allied] had no reason to anticipate that its employees' pension rights could become vested except in accordance with the terms of the plan. It relied heavily, and reasonably, on this legitimate contractual expectation in calculating its annual contributions to the pension fund. The effect of Minnesota's [Act] on this contractual obligation was severe. [A] basic term of the pension contract [was] substantially modified. The result was that, although the company's past contributions were adequate when made, they were not adequate when computed under the 10-year statutory vesting requirement. The Act thus forced a current recalculation of . . . past . . . contributions based on the new, unanticipated 10-year vesting requirement. [The statute] nullifies express terms of the company's contractual obligations and imposes a completely unexpected liability in potentially disabling amounts. [There] is no showing [that] this severe disruption of contractual expectations was necessary to meet an important general social problem. The presumption favoring "legislative judgment as to the necessity and reasonableness of a particular measure" simply cannot stand in this case.

[Whether] or not the legislation was aimed largely at a single employer, it clearly has an extremely narrow focus. It applies only to private employers who have at least 100 employees, at least one of whom works in Minnesota, and who have established voluntary private pension plans, qualified under §401 of the Internal Revenue Code. And it applies only when such an employer closes his Minnesota office or terminates his pension plan. Thus, this law can hardly be characterized, like the law [in *Blaisdell*], as one enacted to protect a broad societal interest rather than a narrow class.

Moreover, in at least one other important respect the Act does not resemble the mortgage moratorium legislation [upheld in] *Blaisdell*. This legislation, imposing a sudden, totally unanticipated, and substantial retroactive obligation upon the company to its employees, was not enacted to deal with a situation remotely approaching the broad and desperate emergency economic conditions of the early [1930s]. The law was not even purportedly enacted to deal with a broad, generalized economic or social problem. It did not operate in an area already subject to state regulation at the time the company's contractual obligations were originally undertaken, but invaded an area never before subject to regulation by the State. It did not effect simply a temporary alteration of the contractual relationships of those within its coverage, but worked a severe, permanent, and immediate change in those relationships—irrevocably and retroactively. And its narrow aim was leveled, not at every Minnesota employer, not even at every Minnesota employer who left the State, but only at those who had in the past been sufficiently enlightened as voluntarily to agree to establish pension plans for their employees. [Reversed.]

JUSTICE BRENNAN, joined by JUSTICES WHITE and MARSHALL, dissenting.

[The Minnesota Act] does not abrogate or dilute any obligation due a party to a private contract; rather, like all positive social legislation, the Act imposes new, additional obligations on a particular class of persons. In my view, any constitutional infirmity in the law must therefore derive, not from the Contract Clause, but from the Due Process Clause of the Fourteenth Amendment. I perceive nothing in the Act that works a denial of due process and therefore I dissent. . . .

▤ *Energy Reserves Group, Inc. v. Kansas*
Power & Light Co.
459 U.S. 400 (1983)

[Kansas Power agreed to purchase natural gas from Energy Reserves Group (ERG) under a contract providing that the price would be the highest permitted by any government regulation. Congress enacted the Natural Gas Policy Act of 1978, which regulated maximum gas prices by indexing such prices to inflation. Kansas then enacted the Kansas Natural Gas Price Protection Act (Kansas Act), which barred any price increases based on the federal law, thus preventing the price escalator clause in the Kansas Power/ERG contract from having further effect. The Kansas courts "found that the Kansas Act did not violate the Contract Clause, reasoning that Kansas has a legitimate interest in addressing and controlling the serious economic dislocations that the sudden increase in gas prices would cause, and that the Kansas Act reasonably furthered that interest." The Court upheld the Kansas law.]

JUSTICE BLACKMUN delivered the opinion of the Court.

The threshold inquiry is "whether the state law has, in fact, operated as a substantial impairment of a contractual relationship." [*Allied.*] Total destruction of contractual expectations is not necessary for a finding of substantial impairment. On the other hand, state regulation that restricts a party to gains it reasonably expected from the contract does not necessarily constitute a substantial impairment. [If] the state regulation constitutes a substantial impairment, the State, in justification, must have a significant and legitimate public purpose behind the regulation, such as the remedying of a broad and general social or economic problem. . . . One legitimate state interest is the elimination of unforeseen windfall profits. The requirement of a legitimate public purpose guarantees that the State is exercising its police power, rather than providing a benefit to special interests.

Once a legitimate public purpose has been identified, the next inquiry is whether the adjustment of "the rights and responsibilities of contracting parties [is based] upon reasonable conditions and [is] of a character appropriate to the public purpose justifying [the legislation's] adoption." [*U.S. Trust Co.*] Unless the State itself is a contracting [party,] "courts properly defer to legislative judgment as to the necessity and reasonableness of a particular measure."

[ERG] knew its contractual rights were subject to alteration by state price regulation. Price regulation existed and was foreseeable as the type of law that would alter contract obligations. [ERG's] reasonable expectations have not been impaired by the Kansas Act. [In any case,] the Kansas Act rests on, and is prompted by, significant and legitimate state interests. Kansas has exercised its police power to protect consumers from the escalation of natural gas prices caused by deregulation. The State reasonably could find that higher gas prices have caused and will cause hardship among those who use gas heat but must exist on limited fixed incomes. [Affirmed.]

NOTES AND PROBLEMS

1. Incidental Impairment.   In Exxon Corp. v. Eagerton, 462 U.S. 176 (1983), the Court applied the idea of "incidental impairment" to uphold an Alabama law barring increased severance taxes on oil and gas from being passed on to purchasers. Alabama increased its severance tax and prohibited the increase from being passed through to purchasers of oil and gas at the wellhead. Exxon contended that the law impaired its contractual right to pass through to the customer all such tax increases. The Court held that the effect of Alabama's law on Exxon's contracts was simply an incidental by-product of a law declaring "a generally applicable rule of conduct"; the law was not directed at contractual obligations. Because Exxon could not prove that the law had a strongly disproportionate effect on private contractual obligations and that the law did not advance a "broad societal interest," the Alabama law was not subject to contracts clause scrutiny.

2. The Standard of Review.   The *Allied* Court stated that the more severe the impairment, the more stringent the scrutiny. The *Energy Reserves* Court said the "threshold inquiry" is whether there has been a substantial impairment of contract obligations. In *Eagerton*, the contracts clause was not even implicated by a law that only incidentally impaired contracts. Are there three levels of contracts clause review: (1) no review of "incidental impairments," (2) minimal review of "substantial impairments," and (3) heightened review of "severe impairments"? If so, what are the component parts of (2) and (3)?

Consider the following synthesis. Substantial impairments (those reasonably foreseeable and not financially overwhelming) are valid if the state has a legitimate and significant public purpose for the impairment, the impairment is reasonable, and it is of a character appropriate to the public purpose. In applying this test, courts "defer to [the] legislative judgment as to the necessity and reasonableness of a particular measure." By contrast, severe impairments (those unforeseeable and financially overwhelming) are valid only if the state can prove that the impairment is temporary, reasonable in scope, and directly related to a compelling or emergency objective.

3. Problems: *Stock Options.*   Suppose a state concludes that the sudden increase in wealth attributable to exercise of stock options granted employees in computer technology companies has fueled destructive hyperinflation in the housing market, making it increasingly difficult for people of modest means to house their families. In 2007, the state enacts one of the following laws:

1. A law prohibiting the exercise of existing stock options.
2. A law limiting the quantity of existing stock options that can be exercised annually by any one person to no more than the quantity that would produce a profit of $100,000.
3. A law like that in (2) but that would expire in five years or when the NASDAQ stock index has declined by at least 50 percent from 2007 levels.

Heating Oil. Suppose that a state with very cold winters concludes that the inability of low-income residents to afford high heating oil prices is a danger to the life and health of such persons. Accordingly, the state enacts a law that requires fuel oil dealers to deliver fuel oil during the winter regardless of whether the recipient can pay for the fuel, and despite any preexisting contractual arrangements explicitly giving dealers the right to cease deliveries if the recipient has an unpaid balance for prior deliveries.

In each of these examples, what level of contract clause scrutiny should apply to these laws? Are any of them unconstitutional?

8

Equal Protection

A. OVERVIEW

The Fourteenth Amendment provides that no state may "deny to any person within its jurisdiction the equal protection of the laws." What does this simple statement mean? It cannot mean that everyone is treated identically for all purposes; the very nature of the law is to distinguish between cases. A law that permits only a person who has received a law degree to practice law divides people into two classifications, those with law degrees and those without; but the law does not deny equal protection. Why? One might say that the law treats all people the same — all people who possess a law degree may practice law and all people who lack a law degree may not practice law. But this merely restates the distinction and leads to ludicrous results. By this logic a law that permits only men (or whites) to practice law would not deny women (or blacks) equal protection. A better explanation is to note that the government's legitimate reason for its classification (its objective) is reasonably served by the classification. The objective is to limit law practice to those qualified by training to do so. The classification (persons who have law degrees or do not) makes sense in light of the objective. When race or sex is substituted for the law degree classification, however, the classification no longer makes sense in light of the objective. Of course, the race or sex classification would make sense if the government changed its objective (e.g., to keep women at home or to disadvantage racial minorities). The problem then is that these reconstituted objectives are not legitimate. But why not?

In the late nineteenth century, the Supreme Court saw no infirmity in a state's bar of married women from the practice of law because women lacked the contractual capacity to establish an attorney-client relationship. Bradwell v. State, 83 U.S. (16 Wall.) 130 (1873). Justice Bradley, concurring, thought the bar was justified because "the paramount destiny and mission of woman are to fulfill the noble and benign offices of wife and mother." Id.

at 141. In the infamous *Dred Scott* case, the Supreme Court declared that black Americans "had no rights which the white man was bound to respect." Scott v. Sandford, 60 U.S. (19 How.) 393 (1857). To say that "things have changed" is accurate but not helpful. Equal protection requires us not only to examine the relationship between government objectives and classifications but also to formulate a theory as to why some objectives are presumptively illegitimate and others are presumptively valid. It is not obvious from the text of the clause what that theory might be.

What substantive values might be protected by equal protection? One extreme is represented by the majority opinion in the *Slaughter-House Cases*, which suggested that equal protection might have no substantive application outside of government racial discrimination. That position is now rejected almost universally, although, as we shall see, a great deal of disagreement exists over how the equal protection clause should operate to ensure racial equality by governments. Once we move beyond race, however, the substantive vision of equality is quite contested. In one sense, equality is a empty concept; it acquires meaning only when one identifies the values with respect to which equality is required, and those values cannot be derived from equal protection itself, but must be found in other constitutional guarantees (e.g., free speech or substantive due process). See, e.g., Westen, The Empty Idea of Equality, 95 Harv. L. Rev. 537 (1982). Nevertheless, the Court has articulated a substantive vision of equality and has embodied that vision in its equal protection doctrine.

The equal protection clause applies to governments, not private actions. The Fourteenth Amendment explicitly obligates *states* to provide equal protection of the laws. In Bolling v. Sharpe, 347 U.S. 497 (1954), the Court concluded that the due process clause of the Fifth Amendment obliged the federal government to provide equal protection, and so struck down racially segregated public schools in the District of Columbia: "Segregation in public education is not reasonably related to any proper governmental objective. [In] view of our decision [in Brown v. Board of Education] that the Constitution prohibits the states from maintaining racially segregated public schools, it would be unthinkable that the same Constitution would impose a lesser duty on the Federal Government." Later Courts have declared that "[e]qual protection analysis in the Fifth Amendment area is the same as that under the Fourteenth Amendment." Buckley v. Valeo, 424 U.S. 1, 93 (1976) (per curiam), citing Weinberger v. Wiesenfeld, 420 U.S. 636, 638 n.2 (1975).

1. Levels of Judicial Scrutiny

At a minimum, a legislative classification must be rationally related to a legitimate government objective. This "minimal review" or "rational basis scrutiny" might be thought of as the default level of equal protection review. The plaintiff challenging the validity of a legislative classification must prove either (1) that the classification does not rationally advance a legitimate state objective or (2) that, no matter how well the classification serves the objective, the objective is not legitimate. There is considerable disagreement, however, concerning how the government's objectives should be determined. These issues are examined in Section B.

Some classifications are presumptively void, either because they employ suspect criteria (e.g., race) or because they impinge substantially on a constitutionally fundamental right. When such a classification is encountered, the burden is on the government to prove that the classification is necessary (or "narrowly tailored") to accomplish a compelling government objective. This is called "strict scrutiny." A threshold problem with strict scrutiny is determining which classifications are suspect, or which rights are constitutionally fundamental, and why. To complicate matters, the Court has devised an intermediate level of scrutiny to deal with classifications by sex or illegitimate birth. In essence, the Court views these classifications as "quasi-suspect," or somewhat suspect, and thus they are presumptively void. The government has the burden of proving that these classifications are substantially related to an important state interest. The government's objective need not be compelling, but it must be more than merely legitimate. The classification need not be necessary, or narrowly tailored, to the objective, but it must be more closely related to the objective than merely rational. This standard requires an explanation of why these classifications, if sufficiently suspicious to merit a presumption of invalidity, are not subjected to strict scrutiny. Even then, there remain the issues of what constitutes compliance with these criteria, and why.

There are several variations on this general theme. As we work through the application of these standards we will encounter some peculiar rules fashioned to meet specific problems, particularly when governments classify on the basis of citizenship, and also when governments employ legitimate classification devices in a manner that is highly suggestive of a government desire merely to harm some discrete (and usually vulnerable) segment of society.

2.   Classifications and Objectives

A law is enacted to achieve a legislative objective, but the classification employed by the law may not perfectly achieve that objective. A statutory classification necessarily divides people (or things) into two classes (e.g., only law school graduates may practice law). Think of that classification as the "statutory classification." There is, however, another division of people (or things) that is not necessarily accomplished by the statutory classification. Because the purpose of each statutory classification is to achieve some objective, there exists a hypothetical classification by which people (or things) would be classified in a manner that is precisely necessary to achieve the objective. Think of that perfect classification as the "optimal classification." A statutory classification may include (or exclude) more people or things than necessary to achieve the objective perfectly, and thus be *over-inclusive*. A statutory classification may also include (or exclude) fewer people or things than necessary to achieve the objective perfectly. If so, the statute is *under-inclusive*.

Some examples will clarify the point. Consider a juvenile curfew law requiring minors to be off the streets from midnight to 6 A.M., which has been enacted for the sole purpose of preventing nocturnal crime by minors. The classification is *over-inclusive*. Minors who are criminals (the optimal classification) are completely included in the group of people affected by the statutory classification (all minors), but many minors are not criminals. More people are included in the statutory classification than are necessary to accomplish its objective.

By contrast, suppose a city banned all sport utility vehicles from its streets in order to improve a driver's view in traffic and reduce air pollution. This law is *under-inclusive:* Sport utility vehicles (the statutory classification) impede a driver's view and produce air pollution but constitute only a small fraction of the vehicles and other objects that impede a driver's view and produce air pollution (the optimal classification). Fewer things are included in the statutory classification than are optimal to accomplish its objective.

A legislative classification may be simultaneously over-inclusive and under-inclusive. Consider a typical statute establishing age 16 as the minimum age to qualify for a driver's license. The law's objective is to limit driver eligibility to those equipped with sufficient maturity and judgment to drive safely. The law is under-inclusive because the class of immature people hobbled by poor judgment (the optimal classification) includes many people over the age of 16. The law is over-inclusive because the optimal classification surely would include within the class of eligible drivers those people under age 16 who are mature and possess good judgment.

It is rare, if not virtually impossible, for a statutory classification and an optimal classification to coincide perfectly. Assume that sugar maple trees are susceptible to a parasite that is not present in North America but is present in Australia (call it the "Southern beetle"). Assume that whenever a Southern beetle contacts a sugar maple, the sugar maple dies, and that the sugar maple is immune to all other parasites. A law prohibiting the importation of the Southern beetle to protect the sugar maple and the maple syrup industry creates a statutory classification (the Southern beetle) that is congruent with the optimal classification (parasites that will kill sugar maples). It is perfect—neither under-inclusive nor over-inclusive.

It is almost as rare for the statutory classification and the optimal classification to have no overlap at all. Suppose that a state bars the consumption of mineral water for the express purpose of limiting human consumption of animal fats. The optimal classification (foods containing animal fats) and the statutory classification (mineral water) have absolutely no overlap. The classification does *nothing* to achieve its objective.

Over-inclusion and under-inclusion by themselves are not enough to invalidate laws as violations of equal protection. They are simply helpful tools in applying equal protection doctrine. The classic treatment of over- and under-inclusion is Tussman and tenBroek, The Equal Protection of the Laws, 37 Cal. L. Rev. 341 (1949).

3. Categorizing Classifications

Legislative classifications are presumed to be valid unless there is some reason to be suspicious of the classifying device or its effect. Such a presumption of validity can be overcome only by proof that the government's objective is illegitimate or that the classification is utterly irrational in relation to legitimate objectives. Classifications that are "suspect" or "semi-suspect," or that infringe upon a constitutionally fundamental right, are presumed to be void and subject to some version of heightened scrutiny, whether strict or intermediate. The equal protection clause itself, however, says nothing about presumptions of invalidity or suspicious classifications. What is the justification for this tiered level of judicial review?

Justice Harlan Fiske Stone's canonical footnote 4 to his opinion for the Court in United States v. Carolene Products Co., 304 U.S. 144 (1938), is the Rosetta stone for this puzzle:

> There may be narrower scope for operation of the presumption of constitutionality when legislation appears on its face to be within a specific prohibition of the Constitution, such as those of the first ten amendments, which are deemed equally specific when held to be embraced within the Fourteenth. It is unnecessary to consider now whether legislation which restricts those political processes which can ordinarily be expected to bring about repeal of undesirable legislation, is to be subjected to more exacting judicial scrutiny under the general prohibitions of the Fourteenth Amendment than are most other types of legislation. [Prior cases employing heightened scrutiny involved] restrictions upon the right to vote, [restraints] upon the dissemination of information, [interferences] with political organizations, [and] prohibition of peaceable assembly. Nor need we enquire whether similar considerations enter into the review of statutes directed at particular religious, or national, or racial minorities; whether prejudice against discrete and insular minorities may be a special condition, which tends seriously to curtail the operation of those political processes ordinarily to be relied upon to protect minorities, and which may call for a correspondingly more searching judicial inquiry.

Justice Stone identified three types of legislative classifications that might be suitable for heightened scrutiny: (1) those that are in facial conflict with specific rights guaranteed by the Constitution; (2) those that inhibit the democratic process; and (3) those that classify on the basis of race, religion, or membership in any other "discrete and insular" minority. Much of the modern idea of heightened scrutiny can be linked to these three classifications.

The first type identified by Stone is fairly obvious. A law prohibiting speech critical of the government is surely a free speech violation, but it is also presumptively void as a matter of equal protection because the classification seriously impinges upon the specifically guaranteed free speech right.

The second type reflects the theme, first articulated in McCulloch v. Maryland, that the courts have a heightened role in protecting the democratic process from structural distortions. Perhaps the clearest legacy in equal protection of this theme is the development of the idea of voting as a constitutionally fundamental right. The Constitution leaves to the states a great deal of control over who may vote, but the Court has used the equal protection clause extensively to police state limits on voting, reasoning that the right to vote is an implicit constitutionally fundamental right, and thus state impingements upon that right distort the democratic process enough to warrant heightened scrutiny. This topic is explored more fully in Section F.2, infra.

The third type of classification is rooted in a union of concerns about democratic process, the historical reasons for equal protection, and the perception that such classifications are rarely germane to any legitimate government objective. To the extent that a minority is saddled with disadvantages created by legislative classifications that use the minority trait as the criterion for classification and that minority is blocked by prejudice from success in the democratic arena, the normal process of shifting political alliances is unlikely to occur.

This has been most clearly true with respect to racial minorities, but not every minority experiences such blockage. Consider the economic struggle of oleomargarine producers and the dairy industry. In the late nineteenth century dairymen reacted to the development of oleomargarine as a butter substitute by obtaining state laws prohibiting the sale of oleomargarine. Powell v. Pennsylvania, 127 U.S. 678 (1888), upheld such a law against a due process challenge. From an equal protection perspective one might contend that the oleomargarine producers were a minority blocked by prejudice from political success, but later cases have made it clear that an economic minority is not the type of minority that activates equal protection concern. Why? One answer is that one's racial status is immutable, while one's economic status is not. But not all immutable traits trigger heightened scrutiny. A person born blind is possessed of an immutable trait, but a law barring blind persons from driving automobiles is not likely to be subjected to strict scrutiny. Thus a more complete reply is that an immutable trait, coupled with widespread irrational prejudice about that trait, is likely to produce legislative classifications using that trait even though the immutable trait is not germane to any legitimate objective. The same irrational prejudice that produces such legislation is also likely permanently to block political redress. The combination of these factors justifies higher judicial scrutiny. Bixby, The Roosevelt Court, Democratic Ideology, and Minority Rights: Another Look at *United States v. Classic*, 90 Yale L.J. 741 (1981), argues that this prong of footnote 4 was motivated by fears of a tyrannical majority preying on vulnerable minorities, as was occurring in Nazi Germany.

B. MINIMAL SCRUTINY: THE DEFAULT LEVEL OF REVIEW

1. Means: What Is Not Rational?

Should extreme under-inclusion or over-inclusion be enough to establish that the classification is not rationally connected to its objective? Consider the following cases.

≡ *Railway Express Agency, Inc. v. New York*
   336 U.S. 106 (1949)

JUSTICE DOUGLAS delivered the opinion of the Court.

[A New York City traffic regulation] provides: "No person shall operate, or cause to be operated, in or upon any street an advertising vehicle; provided that nothing herein contained shall prevent the putting of business notices upon business delivery vehicles, so long as such vehicles are engaged in the usual business or regular work of the owner and not used merely or mainly for advertising."

Appellant is engaged in a nation-wide express business. It operates about 1,900 trucks in New York City and sells the space on the exterior sides of these trucks for advertising. That advertising is for the most part unconnected with its own business. It was convicted [and] fined. [The] conviction was [upheld by New York's Court of Appeals].

The [New York courts] concluded that advertising on vehicles using the streets of New York City constitutes a distraction to vehicle drivers and to pedestrians alike and therefore affects the safety of the public in the use of the streets. [The] question of equal protection [is pressed]. It is pointed out that the regulation draws the line between advertisements of products sold by the owner of the truck and general advertisements. It is argued that unequal treatment on the basis of such a distinction is not justified by the aim and purpose of the regulation. It is said, for example, that one of appellant's trucks carrying the advertisement of a commercial house would not cause any greater distraction of pedestrians and vehicle drivers than if the commercial house carried the same advertisement on its own truck. Yet the regulation allows the latter to do what the former is forbidden from doing. It is therefore contended that the classification which the regulation makes has no relation to the traffic problem since a violation turns not on what kind of advertisements are carried on trucks but on whose trucks they are carried.

[But the] local authorities may well have concluded that those who advertise their own wares on their trucks do not present the same traffic problem in view of the nature or extent of the advertising which they use. It would take a degree of omniscience which we lack to say that such is not the case. [The] advertising displays that are exempt [may] have less incidence on traffic than those of appellants.

We cannot say that that judgment is not an allowable one. [T]he classification has relation to the purpose for which it is made and does not contain the kind of discrimination against which the Equal Protection Clause affords protection. [T]he fact that New York City sees fit to eliminate from traffic this kind of distraction but does not touch what may be even greater ones in a different category, such as the vivid displays on Times Square, is immaterial. It is no requirement of equal protection that all evils of the same genus be eradicated or none at all. [Affirmed.]

JUSTICE JACKSON, concurring.

There are two clauses of the Fourteenth Amendment which this Court may invoke to invalidate ordinances by which municipal governments seek to solve their local problems: [due process and equal protection]. [The] burden should rest heavily upon one who would persuade us to use the due process clause to strike down a substantive law or ordinance [because its use] frequently disables all government—state, municipal and federal—from dealing with the conduct in [question]. Invalidation of a statute or an ordinance on due process grounds leaves ungoverned and ungovernable conduct which many people find objectionable.

Invocation of the equal protection clause, on the other hand, does not disable any governmental body from dealing with the subject at hand. It merely means that the prohibition or regulation must have a broader impact. [There] is no more effective practical guaranty against arbitrary and unreasonable government than to require that the principles of law which officials would impose upon a minority must be imposed generally. Conversely, nothing opens the door to arbitrary action so effectively as to allow those officials to pick and choose only a few to whom they will apply legislation and thus to escape the political retribution that might be visited upon them if larger numbers were affected. Courts can take no better measure to assure that laws will be just than to require that laws be equal in operation.

[If] the City of New York should assume that display of any advertising on vehicles [distracts] the attention of persons using the highways and [increases] the dangers of its traffic, I should think it fully within its constitutional powers to forbid it all. The same would be true if the City should undertake to eliminate or minimize the hazard by any generally applicable restraint, such as limiting the size, color, [or] shape [of] vehicular advertising. Instead of such general regulation of advertising, however, the City seeks to reduce the hazard only by saying that while some may, others may not exhibit such appeals. The same display, for example, advertising cigarettes, which this appellant is forbidden to carry on its trucks, may be carried on the trucks of a cigarette dealer and might on the trucks of this appellant if it dealt in cigarettes. And almost an identical advertisement, certainly one of equal size, shape, color and appearance, may be carried by this appellant if it proclaims its own offer to transport cigarettes. But it may not be carried so long as the message is not its own but a cigarette dealer's offer to sell the same cigarettes.

The City [argues] that, while [its regulation] does not eliminate vehicular advertising, it does eliminate such advertising for hire and to this extent cuts down the hazard sought to be controlled. [The] difference between carrying on any business for hire and engaging in the same activity on one's own is . . . invoked here to sustain a discrimination in a problem in which the two classes present identical dangers. . . . This Court has often announced the principle that the differentiation must have an appropriate relation to the object of the legislation or ordinance. . . .

Where individuals contribute to an evil or danger in the same way and to the same degree, may those who do so for hire be prohibited, while those who do so for their own commercial ends but not for hire be allowed to continue? I think the answer has to be that the hireling may be put in a class by himself and may be dealt with differently than those who act on their own. But this is not merely because such a discrimination will enable the lawmaker to diminish the evil. That might be done by many classifications, which I should think wholly unsustainable. It is rather because there is a real difference between doing in self-interest and doing for hire, so that it is one thing to tolerate action from those who act on their own and it is another thing to permit the same action to be promoted for a price. . . .

NOTES

1. Williamson v. Lee Optical Co.   Oklahoma barred opticians from making eyeglasses without a prescription from either an ophthalmologist or an optometrist. In Williamson v. Lee Optical Co., 348 U.S. 483 (1955), the Supreme Court reversed a federal trial judge's ruling that the ban was not "reasonably and rationally related [to] health and welfare." The Court, in an opinion by Justice Douglas, upheld the law against both due process and equal protection challenges. On the equal protection point, Justice Douglas wrote:

> [T]he District Court held that it violated [equal protection] to subject opticians to this regulatory system and to exempt [all] sellers of ready-to-wear glasses. [Evils] in the same field may be of different dimensions and proportions, requiring different remedies. Or so the legislature may think. Or the reform may take one step at a time, addressing itself to the phase of the problem which seems most acute to the legislative mind. The legislature may select one phase of one field and apply a remedy there, neglecting the others. The prohibition of [equal protection] goes no further than the invidious discrimination. We cannot say that that point has been reached here. For all this record shows, the ready-to-wear branch of this business may not loom large in Oklahoma or may present problems of regulation distinct from the other branch.

So long as there was "an evil at hand for correction," however modest it may be, the law must be upheld if "it might be thought that the [legislation] was a rational way to correct it." In essence, the Court ruled that if there was any conceivable basis to surmise that a law was rationally related to a legitimate state goal, the law would be upheld.

2. The Problems of Under-inclusion. Was Justice Jackson correct to note that under-inclusion raises the possibility that someone is being "picked upon" unfairly? Should we care if the reason someone is being singled out has nothing to do with traits that will block that individual from access to the political process? Oklahoma opticians and Railway Express were losers in the political process, but next time they might be winners. Or should we say that when the classification does little to foster any real and demonstrable public purpose but is instead likely to be the product of a naked preference for one private interest at the expense of another, the government ought to be required to justify the classification? On this reading, the presence of significant under-inclusion is strong evidence of a naked preference. See Sunstein, Naked Preferences and the Constitution, 84 Colum. L. Rev. 1689 (1984).

Until you read the last paragraph of his concurrence, you might think Jackson was writing a dissent. He concurs only because he thought "the hireling may be put in a class by himself." What difference exists between the "self-interest" of one who advertises his own wares and the "self-interest" of one who, for a price, advertises another's wares?

3. The Problem of Over-inclusion. Over-inclusive classifications burden more people than necessary to accomplish the classification's legitimate objective. That virtually eliminates the possibility that the classification is designed to pick on the weak, but it raises the question of whether laws imposing such "unfair" or "inefficient" burdens ought to be scrutinized carefully.

In an effort to ensure job and passenger safety, New York City's Transit Authority refused to hire any methadone user, because methadone is used to help break addiction to opiates. The regulation was attacked as a violation of equal protection—it was severely over-inclusive because about 75 percent of the people who have used methadone for a year or more are no longer illicit drug addicts. In New York City Transit Authority v. Beazer, 440 U.S. 568 (1979), the Court applied minimal scrutiny and upheld the law: The "'no drugs' policy . . . is supported by the legitimate inference that so long as a treatment program (or other drug use) continues, a degree of uncertainty persists."

In order to ensure a physically fit and vigorous cadre of police officers, Massachusetts required all uniformed state police officers retire at age 50. In Massachusetts Board of Retirement v. Murgia, 427 U.S. 307 (1976), the Court upheld the regulation. The Court said there was no fundamental right to public employment and rejected the notion that classifications by age ought to be treated as suspect. Thus, minimal scrutiny applied. Even though some (possibly many) officers over age 50 are fit and vigorous and some under 50 are not, the Court regarded the retirement age as rational:

Perfection in making [classifications] is neither possible nor necessary. [That] the State chooses not to determine fitness more precisely after age 50 is not to say that the objective of assuring physical fitness is not rationally furthered by a maximum age limitation. It is only to say [that] the State perhaps has not chosen the best means to accomplish this purpose. But where rationality is the test, a State "does not violate [equal protection] merely because the classifications made by its laws are imperfect."

4. Determining Legislative Objectives Under Minimal Scrutiny. There are several ways courts can determine legislative objectives. Courts can rely on the legislature's *stated* purpose—if there is one—or on the *actual* purpose, or on any *conceivable* purpose, which includes anything that *might have been* a legislative purpose. If the actual purpose is critical, should it be determined by the legislation itself, by legislative history, or by some other method? Consider these questions in the following case.

United States Railroad Retirement Board v. Fritz
449 U.S. 166 (1980)

[Until 1974, retirees who had worked for both a railroad and a non-railroad employer received retirement benefits under Social Security and a separate railroad retirement plan. In 1974, Congress eliminated these dual retirement benefits for some, but not all, railroad workers. The 1974 legislation denied dual benefits to nonretired persons vested in both retirement plans unless they either (1) had worked in or had a "current connection" with the railroad industry in 1974, or (2) had completed 25 years of railroad service by 1974. Nonretired people not currently working in the railroad industry but with 10 to 25 years of past service and presently vested retirement benefits were stripped of their railroad retirement pension benefits, while current railroad workers with vested benefits and nonretired workers working elsewhere but with 25 years of railroad service received their benefits. The benefit losers contended that the statutory distinction violated equal protection.]

JUSTICE REHNQUIST delivered the opinion of the Court.

The District Court [found] that a differentiation based solely on whether an employee was "active" in the railroad business as of 1974 was not "rationally related" to the congressional purposes of insuring the solvency of the railroad retirement system and protecting vested benefits. We disagree and reverse.

The initial issue presented by this case is the appropriate standard of judicial review to be applied when social and economic legislation enacted by Congress is challenged as being violative of [equal protection]. In F. S. Royster Guano Co. v. Virginia, 253 U.S. 412 (1920), the Court said that for a classification to be valid under [equal protection] it "must rest upon some ground of difference having a fair and substantial relation to the object of the legislation," [but in recent] cases involving social and economic benefits [the Court] has consistently refused to invalidate on equal protection grounds legislation which it simply deemed unwise or unartfully drawn.

[The] plain language of [the statute] marks the beginning and end of our inquiry. . . . Because Congress could have eliminated windfall benefits for all classes of employees, it is not constitutionally impermissible for Congress to have drawn lines between groups of employees for the purpose of phasing out those benefits. The only remaining question is whether Congress achieved its purpose in a patently arbitrary or irrational way. . . .

Congress could properly conclude that persons who had actually acquired statutory entitlement to windfall benefits while still employed in the railroad industry had a greater equitable claim to those benefits than the members of appellee's class who were no longer in railroad employment when they became eligible for dual benefits. [Congress] could assume that those who had a current connection with the railroad industry when the Act was passed in 1974, or who returned to the industry before their retirement, were more likely than those who had left the industry prior to 1974 and who never returned, to be among the class of persons who pursue careers in the railroad industry, the class for whom the Railroad Retirement Act was designed. [Where], as here, there are plausible reasons for Congress'[s] action, our inquiry is at an end. It is, of course, "constitutionally irrelevant whether this reasoning in fact underlay the legislative decision," because this Court has never insisted that a legislative body articulate its reasons for enacting a statute.

[Finally], we disagree with the District Court's conclusion that Congress was unaware of what it accomplished or that it was misled by the groups that appeared before it. If this test were applied literally to every member of any legislature that ever voted on a law, there would be very few laws which would survive it. The language of the statute is clear, and we have historically assumed that Congress intended what it enacted. To be sure, appellee lost a political battle in which he had a strong interest, but this is neither the first nor the last time that such a result will occur in the legislative forum. [Reversed.]

JUSTICE STEVENS, concurring in the judgment.

. . . [When] Congress deprives a small class of persons of vested rights that are protected [for] others who are in a similar though not identical position, I believe the Constitution requires something more than merely a "conceivable" or a "plausible" explanation for the unequal treatment. I do not, however, share Justice Brennan's conclusion that every statutory classification must further an objective that can be confidently identified as the "actual purpose" of the legislature. Actual purpose is sometimes unknown. . . . I therefore believe that we must discover a correlation between the classification and either the actual purpose of the statute or a legitimate purpose that we may reasonably presume to have motivated an impartial legislature. If the adverse impact on the disfavored class is an apparent aim of the legislature, its impartiality would be suspect. If, however, the adverse impact may reasonably be viewed as an acceptable cost of achieving a larger goal, an impartial lawmaker could rationally decide that that cost should be incurred. . . .

[Congress's broad objective was to protect] the solvency of the entire railroad retirement program. Two purposes that conflicted somewhat with this broad objective were the purposes of preserving those benefits that had already vested and of increasing the level of payments to beneficiaries whose rights were not otherwise to be changed. [Congress] originally intended to protect all vested benefits, but it ultimately sacrificed some benefits in the interest of achieving other objectives. [The] congressional purpose to eliminate dual benefits is unquestionably legitimate. [Any] distinction it chose within the class of vested beneficiaries would involve a difference of degree rather than a difference in entitlement. I am satisfied that a distinction based upon currency of railroad employment represents an impartial method of identifying that sort of difference.

JUSTICE BRENNAN, joined by JUSTICE MARSHALL, dissenting.

[The] legal standard applicable to this case is the "rational basis" test. [The] Court today purports to apply this standard, but . . . I suggest that the mode of analysis employed by the Court in this case virtually immunizes social and economic legislative classifications from judicial review.

I. A legislative classification may be upheld only if it bears a rational relationship to a legitimate state purpose. [The] burden rests on those challenging a legislative classification to demonstrate that it does not bear the "fair and substantial relation to the object of the legislation" required under the Constitution. Nonetheless, the rational-basis standard "is not a toothless one" and will not be satisfied by flimsy or implausible justifications for the legislative classification, proffered after the fact by Government attorneys. When faced with a challenge to a legislative classification under the rational-basis test, the court should ask, first, what the purposes of the statute are, and, second, whether the classification is rationally related to achievement of those purposes.

II. [A] "principal purpose" of the Railroad Retirement Act of 1974, as explicitly stated by Congress, was to preserve the vested earned benefits of retirees who had already qualified for them. The classification at issue here, which deprives some retirees of vested dual benefits that they had earned prior to 1974, directly conflicts with Congress'[s] stated purpose. As such, the classification is not only rationally unrelated to the congressional purpose; it is inimical to it.

III. The Court today avoids the conclusion that [the statute] must be invalidated. . . . First, the Court adopts a tautological approach to statutory [purpose]. Second, it disregards the actual stated purpose of Congress in favor of a justification which was never suggested by [anyone in Congress], and which in fact conflicts with the stated congressional purpose. Third, it upholds the classification without any analysis of its rational relationship to the identified purpose.

A. The Court states that "the plain language of [the statute] marks the beginning and end of our inquiry" [but] the "plain language" of the statute can tell us only what the classification is; it can tell us nothing about the purpose of the classification, let alone the relationship between the classification and that purpose. . . . [By] presuming purpose from result, the Court reduces analysis to tautology. It may always be said that Congress intended to do what it in fact did. If that were the extent of our analysis, we would find every statute [perfectly] tailored to achieve its purpose. But equal protection scrutiny under the rational-basis test requires the courts first to deduce the independent objectives of the statute . . . and second to analyze whether the challenged classification rationally furthers achievement of those objectives. The Court's tautological approach will not suffice.

B. The Court analyzes the rationality of [the statute] in terms of a justification suggested by Government attorneys, but never adopted by Congress. The Court states that it is " 'constitutionally irrelevant whether this reasoning in fact underlay the legislative decision.' " [Where] Congress has articulated a legitimate governmental objective, and the challenged classification rationally furthers that objective, we must sustain the provision. In other cases, however, the courts must probe more deeply. Where Congress has expressly stated the purpose of a piece of legislation, but where the challenged classification is either irrelevant to or counter to that purpose, we must view any post hoc justifications proffered by Government attorneys with skepticism. A challenged classification may be sustained only if it is rationally related to achievement of an *actual* legitimate governmental purpose.

The Court argues that Congress chose to discriminate against appellee for reasons of equity, [but] Congress expressed the view that it would be inequitable to deprive any retirees of any portion of the benefits they had been promised and that they had earned under prior law. The Court is unable to cite even one statement in the legislative history . . . that makes the equitable judgment it imputes to Congress. [The] only persons to state that the equities justified eliminating appellee's earned dual benefits were representatives of railroad management and labor, whose self-serving interest in bringing about this result destroys any basis for attaching weight to their statements. [Congress] asked railroad management and labor representatives to negotiate and submit a bill to restructure the Railroad Retirement [system]. The members of this Joint Labor-Management Negotiating Committee were not appointed by public officials, nor did they represent the interests of the appellee class, who were no longer active railroaders or union members. [The] Joint Committee [initially] devised a means whereby the system deficit could be completely eliminated without depriving retirees of vested earned benefits. However, labor representatives demanded that benefits be increased for their current members, the cost to be offset by divesting the appellee class of a portion of the benefits they had earned under prior law. [The] Joint Committee negotiators and Railroad Retirement Board members who testified at congressional hearings perpetuated the inaccurate impression that all retirees with earned vested dual benefits under prior law would retain their benefits unchanged. [Misstatements] by witnesses before Congress would not ordinarily lead us to conclude that Congress misapprehended what it was doing. In this instance, however, where complex legislation was drafted by outside parties and Congress relied on them to explain it, where the misstatements are frequent and unrebutted, and where no Member of Congress can be found to have stated the effect of the classification correctly, we are entitled to suspect that Congress may have been misled. [Therefore], I do not think that this classification was rationally related to an *actual* governmental purpose.

NOTE

The majority's very deferential version of minimal scrutiny assumes that, at least with respect to economic legislation, there is no reason to interfere with the outcomes produced by the tug-of-war of politics. The "actual purpose" version proposed by Justice Brennan assumes that the political process cannot be trusted always to be free of defects.

Query: Suppose Congress had declared that its actual purpose was to favor current union members at the expense of other workers. Would (or should) Justice Brennan have upheld the law? If so, what is the point of "actual purpose" review? If not, what would justify judicial intervention here but not in *Railway Express* or *Lee Optical*?

2.   Ends: What Purposes Are Not Legitimate?

The Court often declares that in applying minimal scrutiny it will not strike down legislation because its purpose is unwise. How can courts separate the merely unwise from the illegitimate?

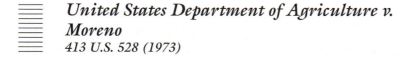

United States Department of Agriculture v. Moreno
413 U.S. 528 (1973)

JUSTICE BRENNAN delivered the opinion of the Court.

This case requires us to consider the constitutionality of §3(e) of the Food Stamp Act of 1964, which [excludes] from participation in the food stamp program any household containing an individual who is unrelated to any other member of the household. [The] federal food stamp program was established in 1964 in an effort to alleviate hunger and malnutrition among the more needy segments of our society. Eligibility for participation in the program is determined on a household rather than an individual basis. An eligible household purchases sufficient food stamps to provide that household with a nutritionally adequate diet. The household pays for the stamps at a reduced rate based upon its size and cumulative income. The food stamps are then used to purchase food at retail stores, and the Government redeems the stamps at face value, thereby paying the difference between the actual cost of the food and the amount paid by the household for the stamps. As initially enacted, §3(e) defined a "household" as "a group of related or non-related individuals, who are not residents of an institution or boarding house, but are living as one economic unit sharing common cooking facilities and for whom food is customarily purchased in common." In January 1971, however, Congress redefined the term "household" so as to include only groups of related individuals. Appellees [consist] of several groups of individuals who allege that, although they satisfy the income eligibility requirements for federal food assistance, they have nevertheless been excluded from the program solely because the persons in each group are not "all related to each other." [Appellees] contend, and the District Court held, that the "unrelated person" provision of §3(e) creates an irrational classification in violation of the equal protection component of the Due Process Clause of the Fifth Amendment. We agree.

[The] challenged statutory classification [is] clearly irrelevant to the stated purposes of the Act, [which are to alleviate hunger and malnutrition and "strengthen our agricultural economy"]. Thus, if it is to be sustained, the challenged classification must rationally further some legitimate governmental interest other than [the stated purposes. The legislative history] of the 1971 amendment of §3(e) . . . indicates that [it] was intended to prevent so-called "hippies" and "hippie communes" from participating in the food stamp program. The challenged classification clearly cannot be sustained by reference to this congressional purpose. For if the constitutional conception of "equal protection of the laws" means anything, it must at the very least mean that a bare congressional desire to harm a politically unpopular group cannot constitute a legitimate governmental interest. As a result, "[a] purpose to discriminate against hippies cannot, in and of itself and without reference to [some independent] considerations in the public interest, justify the 1971 amendment."

[The] Government maintains that the challenged classification should nevertheless be upheld as rationally related to the clearly legitimate governmental interest in minimizing fraud in the administration of the food stamp program. [The] Government contends [that] Congress might rationally have thought (1) that households with one or more unrelated members are more likely than "fully related" households to contain individuals who abuse the program by fraudulently failing to report sources of income or by voluntarily remaining poor; and (2) that such households are "relatively unstable," thereby increasing the difficulty of detecting such abuses. [The] Food Stamp Act itself contains provisions, wholly independent of §3(e), aimed specifically at the problems of fraud and of the voluntarily poor. [Moreover], the challenged classification simply does not operate so as rationally to further the prevention of fraud. [Section] 3(e) defines an eligible "household" as "a group of related [individuals] [1] living as one economic unit [2] sharing common cooking facilities [and 3] for whom food is customarily purchased in common." Thus, two unrelated persons living together and meeting all three of these conditions would constitute a single household ineligible for assistance. If financially feasible, however, these same two individuals can legally avoid the "unrelated person" exclusion simply by altering their living arrangements so as to eliminate any one of the three conditions. By so doing, they effectively create two separate "households," both of which are eligible for assistance. [Thus], in practical operation, the 1971 amendment excludes from participation in the food stamp program, not those persons who are "likely to abuse the program" but, rather, only those persons who are so desperately in need of aid that they cannot even afford to alter their living arrangements so as to retain their eligibility. [The] classification here in issue is not only "imprecise," it is wholly without any rational basis.

Affirmed.

JUSTICE REHNQUIST, joined by CHIEF JUSTICE BURGER, dissenting.

[I] do not think it is unreasonable for Congress to conclude that the basic unit which it was willing to support with federal funding through food stamps is some variation on the family as we know it—a household consisting of related individuals. This unit provides a guarantee which is not provided by households containing unrelated individuals that the household exists for some purpose other than to collect federal food stamps. . . . Since the food stamp program is not intended to be a subsidy for every individual who desires low-cost food, this was a permissible congressional decision quite consistent with the underlying policy of the Act. The fact that the limitation will have unfortunate and perhaps unintended consequences beyond this does not make it unconstitutional.

≡ **Romer v. Evans**
≡ *517 U.S. 620 (1996)*

JUSTICE KENNEDY delivered the opinion of the Court.

I. [Amendment 2,] an amendment to the [Colorado Constitution], adopted in a 1992 statewide referendum, [was prompted by] ordinances that had been passed in various Colorado municipalities, [banning discrimination on the basis of sexual orientation] in many transactions and activities, including housing, employment, education, public accommodations, and health and welfare services. [Amendment 2] prohibits all legislative, executive or judicial action at any level of state or local government designed to protect the named class, a class we shall refer to as homosexual persons or gays and lesbians. The amendment reads:

> No Protected Status Based on Homosexual, Lesbian, or Bisexual Orientation. Neither the State of Colorado, through any of its branches or departments, nor any of its agencies, political subdivisions, municipalities or school districts, shall enact, adopt or enforce any statute, regulation, ordinance or policy whereby homosexual, lesbian or bisexual orientation, conduct, practices or relationships shall constitute or otherwise be the basis of or entitle any person or class of persons to have or claim any minority status, quota preferences, protected status or claim of discrimination. This Section of the Constitution shall be in all respects self-executing. . . .

[The Colorado] Supreme Court held that Amendment 2 was subject to strict scrutiny under the Fourteenth Amendment because it infringed the fundamental right of gays and lesbians to participate in the political process. . . . We [now] affirm, [but] on a rationale different from that adopted by the State Supreme Court.

II. The State's principal argument in defense of Amendment 2 is that it puts gays and lesbians in the same position as all other persons. [T]he State says the measure does no more than deny homosexuals special rights. This reading of the amendment's language is implausible. . . . Sweeping and comprehensive is the change in legal status effected by this law. [Homosexuals] are put in a solitary class with respect to transactions and relations in both the private and governmental spheres. The amendment withdraws from homosexuals, but no others, specific legal protection from the injuries caused by discrimination, and it forbids reinstatement of these laws and policies [except by constitutional amendment.] . . .

[We] cannot accept the view that Amendment 2's prohibition on specific legal protections does no more than deprive homosexuals of special rights. To the contrary, the amendment imposes a special disability upon those persons alone. Homosexuals are forbidden the safeguards that others enjoy or may seek without constraint. They can obtain specific protection against discrimination only by enlisting the citizenry of Colorado to amend the state constitution. . . . We find nothing special in the protections Amendment 2 withholds. These are protections taken for granted by most people either because they already have them or do not need them; these are protections against exclusion from an almost limitless number of transactions and endeavors that constitute ordinary civic life in a free society.

III. . . . We have [stated] that, if a law neither burdens a fundamental right nor targets a suspect class, we will uphold the legislative classification so long as it bears a rational relation to some legitimate end. Amendment 2 fails, indeed defies, even this conventional inquiry. First, the amendment has the peculiar property of imposing a broad and undifferentiated disability on a single named group, an exceptional and, as we shall explain, invalid form of legislation. Second, its sheer breadth is so discontinuous with the reasons offered for it that the amendment seems inexplicable by anything but animus toward the class that it affects; it lacks a rational relationship to legitimate state interests.

. . . By requiring that the classification bear a rational relationship to an independent and legitimate legislative end, we ensure that classifications are not drawn for the purpose of disadvantaging the group burdened by the law. Amendment 2 [is] at once too narrow and too broad. It identifies persons by a single trait and then denies them protection across the board. The resulting disqualification of a class of persons from the right to seek specific protection from the law is unprecedented in our jurisprudence. . . . Central . . . to the . . . Constitution's guarantee of equal protection is the principle that government and each of its parts remain open on impartial terms to all who seek its assistance. [Respect] for this principle explains why laws singling out a certain class of citizens for disfavored legal status or general hardships are rare. A law declaring that in general it shall be more difficult for one group of citizens than for all others to seek aid from the government is itself a denial of equal protection of the laws in the most literal sense. [Also,] laws of the kind now before us raise the inevitable inference that the disadvantage imposed is born of animosity toward the class of persons affected. "If the constitutional conception of 'equal protection of the laws' means anything, it must at the very least mean that a [bare] desire to harm a politically unpopular group cannot constitute a legitimate governmental interest." [*Moreno.*] [In] making a general announcement that gays and lesbians shall not have any particular protections from the law, [Amendment 2] inflicts on them immediate, continuing, and real injuries that outrun and belie any legitimate justifications that may be claimed for it. [A] law must bear a rational relationship to a legitimate governmental purpose and Amendment 2 does not.

The primary rationale the State offers for Amendment 2 is respect for other citizens' freedom of association, and in particular the liberties of landlords or employers who have personal or religious objections to homosexuality. Colorado also cites its interest in conserving resources to fight discrimination against other groups. The breadth of the Amendment is so far removed from these particular justifications that we find it impossible to credit them. We cannot say that Amendment 2 is directed to any identifiable legitimate purpose or discrete objective. It is a status-based enactment divorced from any factual context from which we could discern a relationship to legitimate state interests. . . . [We] must conclude that Amendment 2 classifies homosexuals not to further a proper legislative end but to make them unequal to everyone else. This Colorado cannot do. A State cannot so deem a class of persons a stranger to its laws. Amendment 2 violates the Equal Protection Clause, and the judgment of the Supreme Court of Colorado is affirmed.

JUSTICE SCALIA, joined by CHIEF JUSTICE REHNQUIST and JUSTICE THOMAS, dissenting.

. . . [Amendment 2] is not the manifestation of a " 'bare [desire] to harm' " homosexuals, but is rather a modest attempt [to] preserve traditional sexual mores against the efforts of a politically powerful minority to revise those mores through use of the laws. . . . In holding that homosexuality cannot be singled out for disfavorable treatment, the Court . . . places the prestige of this institution behind the proposition that opposition to homosexuality is as reprehensible as racial or religious bias. Whether it is or not is *precisely* the cultural debate that gave rise to the Colorado constitutional amendment (and to the preferential laws against which the amendment was directed). Since the Constitution of the United States says nothing about this subject, it is left to be resolved by normal democratic means, including the democratic adoption of provisions in state constitutions. . . . I vigorously dissent.

I. . . . The amendment prohibits special treatment of homosexuals, and nothing more. It would not affect, for example, a requirement of state law that pensions be paid to all retiring state employees with a certain length of service; homosexual employees, as well as others, would be entitled to that benefit. But it would prevent the State or any municipality from making death-benefit payments to the "life partner" of a homosexual when it does not make such payments to the longtime roommate of a non-homosexual employee. . . . The only denial of equal treatment it contends homosexuals have suffered is this: They may not obtain *preferential* treatment without amending the state constitution. That is to say, the principle underlying the Court's opinion is that one who is accorded equal treatment under the laws, but cannot as readily as others obtain *preferential* treatment under the laws, has been denied equal [protection]. If merely stating this alleged "equal protection" violation does not suffice to refute it, our constitutional jurisprudence has achieved terminal silliness. . . .

III. [What Colorado] has done is not only unprohibited, but eminently reasonable. [The] Court's opinion contains grim, disapproving hints that Coloradans have been guilty of "animus" or "animosity" toward homosexuality, [but] I had thought that one could consider certain conduct reprehensible — murder, for example, or polygamy, or cruelty to animals — and could exhibit even "animus" toward such conduct. Surely that is the only sort of "animus" at issue here: moral disapproval of homosexual conduct. . . .

[Three] Colorado cities — Aspen, Boulder, and Denver — had enacted ordinances that listed "sexual orientation" as an impermissible ground for discrimination, equating the moral disapproval of homosexual conduct with racial and religious bigotry. [The] Governor [had] signed an executive order . . . directing state agency-heads to "ensure non-discrimination" in hiring and promotion based [on] "sexual orientation." I do not mean to be critical of these legislative successes; homosexuals are as entitled to use the legal system for reinforcement of their moral sentiments as are the rest of society. But they are subject to being countered by lawful, democratic countermeasures as well.

That is where Amendment 2 came in. It put directly, to all the citizens of the State, the question: Should homosexuality be given special protection? They answered no. The Court today asserts that this most democratic of procedures is unconstitutional. Lacking any cases to establish that facially absurd proposition, it simply asserts that it must be unconstitutional, because it has never happened before. [What] the Court says is even demonstrably false at the constitutional level. The Eighteenth Amendment to the Federal Constitution, for example, deprived those who drank alcohol not only of the power to alter the policy of prohibition locally or through state legislation, but even of the power to alter it through state constitutional amendment or federal legislation. The Establishment Clause of the First Amendment prevents theocrats from having their way by converting their fellow citizens at the local, state, or federal statutory level; as does the Republican Form of Government Clause prevent monarchists. . . .

IV. . . . [To suggest that] this constitutional amendment springs from nothing more than " 'a [bare] desire to harm a politically unpopular group' " is nothing short of insulting. (It is also nothing short of preposterous to call "politically unpopular" a group which enjoys enormous influence in American media and politics, and which, as the trial court here noted, though composing no more than 4% of the population had the support of 46% of the voters on

Amendment 2.) . . . Today's opinion has no foundation in American constitutional law, and barely pretends to. The people of Colorado have adopted an entirely reasonable provision which does not even disfavor homosexuals in any substantive sense, but merely denies them preferential treatment. . . . Striking it down is an act, not of judicial judgment but of political will. I dissent.

NOTES

1. Identifying Illegitimate Purposes.   In *Moreno*, the Court's alternative conclusion that the objective was illegitimate was based partly on indiscreet statements of legislators and partly on the perceived inutility of the classification to achieve the asserted objectives. In *Romer*, the Court's conclusion that the objective was illegitimate was based mostly on the fact that homosexuals were required by Amendment 2 to amend Colorado's constitution to achieve their political objectives. From that, the Court concluded that the amendment's extreme under-inclusion and over-inclusion in relation to its asserted objectives—associational freedom and conservation of government resources to combat invidious discrimination—were enough to impeach the authenticity of those objectives.

Both cases, however, were decided under a minimal scrutiny standard. Do these cases suggest that the Court will not always accept uncritically *any conceivable objective* as adequate? If so, the majority position in *Fritz* needs to be qualified. Under some circumstances, the Court appears to ignore a conceivable (if hypothetical) legitimate objective and instead finds that the actual objective is not legitimate. What factors prompt the Court to do this?

Does *Romer* forbid a state from repealing a law forbidding private discrimination in housing, employment, and public accommodations on the basis of sexual orientation?

2. Morality as a Legislative Objective.   Recall that in Lawrence v. Texas, 539 U.S. 558 (2003), the Court struck down a Texas law that made it a crime for persons of the same sex to engage in sexual intimacies but imposed no sanctions on the same conduct when engaged in by persons of the opposite sex. In applying minimal scrutiny under substantive due process, the majority thought that Texas's objective of expressing its moral disapproval was illegitimate. Justice O'Connor concurred in the judgment but thought that the Texas law violated equal protection: "Moral disapproval of a group cannot be a legitimate governmental interest under the Equal Protection Clause because legal classifications must not be 'drawn for the purpose of disadvantaging the group burdened by the law.' "

Are laws prohibiting bigamy, adultery, or fornication invalid because they express moral disapproval or valid because they seek to protect the institution of marriage? What about laws limiting marriage to opposite sex partners? If utilitarian reasons are necessary to support these laws, what might they be? Bear in mind that the Court treats classifications by sexual orientation as presumptively valid and subject to minimal scrutiny.

3. Other Illegitimate Objectives. Whenever a statute uses a classification only to achieve a constitutionally forbidden objective, that statute violates the equal protection clause. Two lines of cases illustrate the principle.

Discrimination against newcomers and out-of-staters. A state objective to discriminate purposefully against out-of-staters and newcomers is not legitimate, either (1) because the classification is void under the commerce clause or Article IV's privileges and immunities clause, or (2) because it amounts to a forbidden penalty upon exercise of the constitutionally fundamental right of interstate migration. In the latter instance, equal protection is violated. Zobel v. Williams, 457 U.S. 55 (1982), voided an Alaska law granting to each Alaskan a cash rebate from the state's fiscal surplus that varied with one's length of residence in Alaska. The Court thought that rewarding longevity of citizenship was "not a legitimate state purpose," because it interfered with the fundamental right of interstate mobility. Justice O'Connor concurred, but thought that the law should have been struck down as an unjustified interference with the privileges and immunities protected by Article IV, section 2.

This theme was given more forceful shape in Hooper v. Bernalillo County Assessor, 472 U.S. 612 (1985), in which the Court voided a New Mexico special tax exemption to Vietnam War veterans who were New Mexico residents as of a certain date, thus denying the exemption to Vietnam War veterans who later became New Mexico residents. The law created illegitimate " 'fixed, permanent distinctions between [classes] of concededly bona fide residents' based on when they arrived in the State."

Irrational and arbitrary legislation. Statutes that classify in an arbitrary manner, or perversely in relation to the objective, fail minimal scrutiny. Is the objective illegitimate, or is the classification simply irrational in relation to the objective? Consider the following cases.

Logan v. Zimmerman Brush Co., 455 U.S. 422 (1982). The Court voided, as applied to Logan's claim, an Illinois regulation that required an administrative fact-finding hearing within 120 days of filing a claim of unlawful handicap discrimination and extinguished the claim if a timely hearing was not held. Through the state's negligence, a timely hearing on Logan's claim was not held. Noting that the purpose of the timely hearing rule was to expedite dispute resolution, the Court called the section "patently irrational"—terminating a claim because the state acted negligently is not "a rational way of expediting the resolution of disputes."

Allegheny Pittsburgh Coal Co. v. County Commission, 488 U.S. 336 (1989). The Court invalidated a county tax assessor's practice of assessing newly purchased property at market value but not altering old valuations of long-held property. The Court concluded that the county assessor's practice was not rationally related to the objective specified by the West Virginia constitution: "[T]axation shall be equal and uniform throughout the State, and all property [shall] be taxed in proportion to its value."

Nordlinger v. Hahn, 505 U.S. 1 (1992). The Court upheld a California constitutional provision requiring that real property be assessed for taxation on the basis of its purchase price and sharply limiting later increases in such assessments. Longtime owners of real property had much lower assessments and taxes than new purchasers of nearly identical property. The Court applied minimal scrutiny and upheld the law because it was rationally related to California's objective of preserving neighborhood stability and protecting the expectations of existing owners. Can *Nordlinger* and *Allegheny Pittsburgh* be explained by the different objectives of the states?

3. "Enhanced" Minimal Scrutiny: Is the Problem Means, Ends, or Both?

In some cases the Court purports to apply minimal scrutiny but in fact seems to be applying a different test. Some say that the Court is really employing "heightened" scrutiny—something more than minimal scrutiny—which the Court will often deny. The trigger of "enhanced" minimal scrutiny is elusive, leading some justices—notably Thurgood Marshall and John Paul Stevens—to charge that traditional tiered review

> simply [does] not describe the inquiry the Court has undertaken—or should undertake—in equal protection cases. [T]he inquiry has been much more sophisticated and the Court should admit as much. It has focused on the character of the classification in question, the relative importance to individuals in the class discriminated against of the governmental benefits that they do not receive, and the state interests asserted in support of the classification.

Massachusetts Board of Retirement v. Murgia, 427 U.S. 307 (1976) (Marshall, J., dissenting). In the cases that follow, the Court says it does *not* adopt Justice Marshall's flexible, multi-factor approach, but is that really true? What explains the results that follow?

≡≡≡ *City of Cleburne, Texas v. Cleburne Living*
≡≡≡ *Center, Inc.*
≡≡≡ *473 U.S. 432 (1985)*

JUSTICE WHITE delivered the opinion of the Court.

A Texas city denied a special use permit for the operation of a group home for the mentally retarded, acting pursuant to a municipal zoning ordinance requiring permits for such homes. The Court of Appeals [held] that mental retardation is a "quasi-suspect" classification and that the ordinance violated [equal protection] because it did not substantially further an important governmental purpose. We hold that a lesser standard of scrutiny is appropriate, but conclude that under that standard the ordinance is invalid as applied in this case. . . .

II. [The] general rule [of equal protection] is that legislation is presumed to be valid and will be sustained if the classification drawn by the statute is rationally related to a legitimate state interest. When social or economic legislation is at issue [equal protection] allows the States wide latitude, and the Constitution presumes that even improvident decisions will eventually be rectified by the democratic processes. The general rule gives way, however, when a statute classifies by race, alienage, or national origin. These factors are so seldom relevant to the achievement of any legitimate state interest that laws grounded in such considerations are deemed to reflect prejudice and antipathy — a view that those in the burdened class are not as worthy or deserving as others. For these reasons and because such discrimination is unlikely to be soon rectified by legislative means, these laws are subjected to strict [scrutiny]. Similar oversight by the courts is due when state laws impinge on personal rights protected by the Constitution. Legislative classifications based on gender also call for a heightened standard of review. That factor generally provides no sensible ground for differential treatment. . . . [But] where individuals in the group affected by a law have distinguishing characteristics relevant to interests the State has the authority to implement, the courts have been very reluctant [to scrutinize closely] legislative choices as to whether, how, and to what extent those interests should be pursued. In such cases, [equal protection] requires only a rational means to serve a legitimate end.

III. Against this background, we conclude [that] the Court of Appeals erred in holding mental retardation a quasi-suspect classification calling for a more exacting standard of judicial review than is normally accorded economic and social legislation. First, it is undeniable [that the] mentally retarded have a reduced ability to cope with and function in the everyday world [and they are not] all cut from the same pattern. . . . How this large and diversified group is to be treated under the law is a difficult and often a technical matter, very much a task for legislators guided by qualified professionals and not by the perhaps ill-informed opinions of the judiciary. . . . Second, . . . lawmakers have been addressing their difficulties in a manner that belies a continuing antipathy or prejudice and a corresponding need for more intrusive oversight by the judiciary. [The] Federal Government has not only outlawed discrimination against the mentally retarded in federally funded programs, but it has also provided the retarded with the right to receive "appropriate treatment, services, and habilitation" in a setting that is "least restrictive of [their] personal liberty," [and has aided schooling and employment of the mentally retarded]. Texas has [enacted similar] legislation. . . . Third, the legislative response, which could hardly have occurred and survived without public support, negates any claim that the mentally retarded are politically [powerless]. Fourth, if the large and amorphous class of the mentally retarded were deemed quasi-suspect, [it] would be difficult to find a principled way to distinguish a variety of other groups who have perhaps immutable disabilities, [who] cannot themselves mandate the desired legislative responses, and who can claim some degree of prejudice from at least part of the public at large. One need mention [only] the aging, the disabled, the mentally ill, and the infirm. We are reluctant to set out on that course, and we decline to do [so]. . . .

[M]ental retardation is a characteristic that the government may legitimately take into account. [To] withstand equal protection review, legislation that distinguishes between the mentally retarded and others must be rationally related to a legitimate governmental purpose. . . .

IV. [The] constitutional issue is clearly posed. The city does not require a special use permit in an R-3 zone for apartment houses, multiple dwellings, boarding and lodging houses, fraternity or sorority houses, dormitories, apartment hotels, hospitals, sanitariums, nursing homes for convalescents or the aged (other than for the insane or feebleminded or alcoholics or drug addicts), private clubs or fraternal orders, and other specified uses. It does, however, insist on a special permit for the [Cleburne Living Center's proposed group] home, and it does so [because] it would be a facility for the mentally retarded. May the city require the permit for this facility when other care and multiple-dwelling facilities are freely permitted? [In] our view the record does not reveal any rational basis for believing that the [proposed] home would pose any special threat to the city's legitimate [interests].

The District Court found that the City Council's insistence on the permit rested on several factors. First, the Council was concerned with the negative attitude of the majority of property owners located within 200 feet of the [proposed home], as well as with the fears of elderly residents of the neighborhood. But mere negative attitudes, or fear, unsubstantiated by factors which are properly cognizable in a zoning proceeding, are not permissible bases for treating a home for the mentally retarded differently from apartment houses, multiple dwellings, and the like. [Second,] the Council [was] concerned that the [home] was across the street from a junior high school, and it feared that the students might harass the occupants of [the] home. But the school itself is attended by about 30 mentally retarded students, and denying a permit based on such vague, undifferentiated fears is again permitting some portion of the community to validate what would otherwise be an equal protection violation. The other objection to the home's location was that it was located on "a five hundred year flood plain." This concern with the possibility of a flood, however, can hardly be based on a distinction between the [proposed] home and, for example, nursing homes, homes for convalescents or the aged, or sanitariums or hospitals, any of which could be located on the [site] without obtaining a special use permit. [Fourth], the Council was concerned with the size of the home and the number of people that would occupy it. [There] would be no restrictions on the number of people who could occupy this home as a boarding house, nursing home, family dwelling, fraternity house, or dormitory. The question is whether it is rational to treat the mentally retarded differently. [This] record does not clarify [how] the characteristics of the intended occupants of the [group] home rationally justify denying to those occupants what would be permitted to groups occupying the same site for different purposes. [The] short of it is that requiring the permit in this case appears to us to rest on an irrational prejudice against the mentally retarded. . . .

JUSTICE STEVENS, joined by CHIEF JUSTICE BURGER, concurring.

[Our] cases reflect a continuum of judgmental responses to differing classifications which have been explained in opinions by terms ranging from "strict scrutiny" at one extreme to "rational basis" at the other. I have never been persuaded that these so-called "standards" adequately explain the decisional process. [In] every equal protection case, we have to ask certain basic questions. What class is harmed by the legislation, and has it been subjected to a "tradition of disfavor" by our laws? What is the public purpose that is being served by the law? What is the characteristic of the disadvantaged class that justifies the disparate treatment? [The] answers will result in the virtually automatic invalidation of racial classifications and in the validation of most economic classifications, but they will provide differing results in cases involving classifications based on alienage, gender, or illegitimacy [because] the characteristics of these groups are sometimes relevant and sometimes irrelevant to . . . the purpose that the challenged laws purportedly intended to serve. Every law that places the mentally retarded in a special class is not presumptively irrational. The differences between mentally retarded persons and those with greater mental capacity are obviously relevant to certain legislative decisions. [But the] record convinces me that this permit was required because of the irrational fears of neighboring property owners, rather than for the protection of the mentally retarded persons who would reside in respondent's home.

JUSTICE MARSHALL, joined by JUSTICES BRENNAN and BLACKMUN, concurring in the judgment in part and dissenting in part.

[The] Court holds the ordinance invalid on rational-basis grounds and disclaims that anything special, in the form of heightened scrutiny, is taking place. Yet Cleburne's ordinance surely would be valid under the traditional rational-basis test applicable to economic and commercial regulation. . . .

I. [The] rational-basis test invoked today is most assuredly not the rational-basis test of Williamson v. Lee Optical. [The] Court [implicitly] concludes that legitimate concerns for fire hazards or the serenity of the neighborhood do not justify singling out respondents to bear the burdens of these concerns, for analogous permitted uses appear to pose similar threats. Yet under the traditional and most minimal version of the rational-basis test, "reform may take one step at a [time]." Williamson v. Lee Optical. The "record" is said not to support the ordinance's classifications, but under the traditional standard we do not sift through the record to determine whether policy decisions are squarely supported by a firm factual foundation. Finally, the Court further finds it "difficult to believe" that the retarded present different or special hazards inapplicable to other groups. In normal circumstances, the burden is not on the legislature to convince the Court that the lines it has drawn are [sensible]. The refusal to acknowledge that something more than minimum rationality review is at work here is [unfortunate] in at least two respects. The suggestion that the traditional rational-basis test allows this sort of searching inquiry creates precedent for this Court and lower courts to subject economic and commercial classifications to similar and searching "ordinary" rational-basis review. . . . [Moreover], by failing to articulate the factors that justify today's [version of] rational-basis review, the Court provides no principled foundation for determining when more searching inquiry is to be invoked.

II. I have long believed the level of scrutiny employed in an equal protection case should vary with "the constitutional and societal importance of the interest adversely affected and the recognized invidiousness of the basis upon which the particular classification is drawn." When a zoning ordinance works to exclude the retarded from all residential districts in a community, these two considerations require that the ordinance be convincingly justified as substantially furthering legitimate and important purposes. First, the interest of the retarded in establishing group homes is substantial. [Second,] the mentally retarded have been subject to a "lengthy and tragic history" of segregation and discrimination that can only be called grotesque. [In] light of the importance of the interest at stake and the history of discrimination the retarded have suffered, [equal protection] requires us to do more than [apply minimal scrutiny]. . . . Cleburne's vague generalizations for classifying the "feeble-minded" with drug addicts, alcoholics, and the insane, and excluding them where the elderly, the ill, the boarder, and the transient are allowed, are not substantial or important enough to overcome the suspicion that the ordinance rests on impermissible assumptions or outmoded and perhaps invidious stereotypes. . . .

NOTES

1. Irrational or Illegitimate? Was *Cleburne's* treatment of the mentally retarded less rational than New York's treatment of ad-bearing trucks (in *Railway Express*) or Oklahoma's treatment of opticians (in *Lee Optical*)? Why? The Court accepted as legitimate the city's objectives of reducing overcrowding in group homes and minimizing flood hazards, yet it did not permit Cleburne to proceed to reach these objectives "one step at a time." Cleburne excluded *only* group homes for the retarded. Was this irrational because of its extreme under-inclusion? Or was this extraordinary under-inclusion circumstantial evidence that the city's purported objectives were bogus, leading the Court to conclude (without actually saying so) that *Cleburne's* true objective was to pander to the irrational fears and prejudices of local residents? In *Romer*, the Court rejected as pretextual Colorado's asserted legitimate objectives. Perhaps this is also true of *Cleburne*. If so, what triggered the Court to reject the government's asserted legitimate objectives as pretextual and, instead, to focus on hidden illegitimate objectives as the actual governmental objectives? Recall that in *Fritz* the Court said that under minimal scrutiny it will not search for a government's actual objectives, but will accept legitimate objectives that are purely conjectural. Perhaps this principle ends when conjectural objectives are not believable in light of the statutory effects. But what's plausible and what isn't? Why was it plausible in *Lee Optical* that Oklahoma was acting to protect the health and safety of its citizens and not to disadvantage opticians? Why was it implausible in *Romer* that Colorado was acting to protect associational freedom? If what is at work is an intuitively felt sense of the matter, is that a principled mode of adjudication?

2. De Facto Heightened Scrutiny? Was Justice Marshall correct to charge that the Court in *Cleburne* used a *sub rosa* form of heightened scrutiny? If so, what triggered heightened scrutiny? If so, why didn't the Court identify the factors that invoke heightened scrutiny? If this was disguised heightened scrutiny, why did the Court insist it was employing minimal scrutiny?

≡ *Plyler v. Doe*
≡ *457 U.S. 202 (1982)*

Justice Brennan delivered the opinion of the Court.

The question presented [is] whether, consistent with [equal protection], Texas may deny to undocumented school-age children the free public education that it provides to children who are citizens of the United States or legally admitted aliens.

I. . . . Unsanctioned entry into the United States is a crime, and those who have entered unlawfully are subject to deportation. [Yet] a substantial number of persons have succeeded in unlawfully entering the United States, and now live within various States, including [Texas]. In May 1975, the Texas Legislature [authorized] local school districts to deny enrollment in their public schools to children not "legally admitted" to the country [and denied state funds to those districts that did not exclude such children].

II. The Fourteenth Amendment provides that "[no] State shall [deny] to *any person within its jurisdiction* the equal protection of the laws." Appellants argue [that] undocumented aliens, because of their immigration status, are not "persons within the jurisdiction" of [Texas], and that they therefore have no right to the equal protection of Texas law. We reject this argument. [Aliens], even aliens whose presence in this country is unlawful, have long been recognized as "persons" [for other purposes of the] Fourteenth Amendment.

III. [In] applying [equal protection] to most forms of state action, we [seek] only the assurance that the classification at issue bears some fair relationship to a legitimate public purpose. But . . . certain forms of legislative classification, while not facially invidious, nonetheless give rise to recurring constitutional difficulties; in these limited circumstances we have sought the assurance that the classification reflects a reasoned judgment consistent with the ideal of equal protection by inquiring whether it may fairly be viewed as furthering a substantial interest of the State. . . . We turn to a consideration of the standard appropriate for the evaluation of [Texas's law].

A. [There exists] a substantial "shadow population" of illegal migrants—numbering in the millions—within our borders. [We] reject the claim that "illegal aliens" are a "suspect class." [Unlike] most of the classifi-cations that we have recognized as suspect, entry into this class, by virtue of entry into this country, is the product of voluntary action. Indeed, entry into the class is itself a crime. . . . Persuasive arguments support the view that a State may withhold its beneficence from those whose very presence within the United States is the product of their own unlawful conduct. These arguments do not apply with the same force to classifications imposing disabilities on the minor *children* of such illegal entrants. [The] children who are plaintiffs in these cases "can affect neither their parents' conduct nor their own status." Even if the State found it expedient to control the conduct of adults by acting against their children, legislation directing the onus of a parent's misconduct against his children does not comport with fundamental conceptions of jus-tice. [Of] course, undocumented status is not irrelevant to any proper legisla-tive goal. Nor is undocumented status an absolutely immutable characteristic since it is the product of conscious, indeed unlawful, action. But [the Texas law] is directed against children, and imposes its discriminatory burden on the basis of a legal characteristic over which children can have little control. It is thus difficult to conceive of a rational justification for penalizing these children for their presence within the United States. Yet that appears to be precisely the effect of [the law].

Public education is not a right granted to individuals by the Constitution. But neither is it merely some governmental benefit indistinguishable from other forms of social welfare legislation. Both the importance of education in maintaining our basic institutions, and the lasting impact of its deprivation on the life of the child, mark the distinction. [Education] provides the basic tools by which individuals might lead economically productive lives to the benefit of us all. In sum, education has a fundamental role in maintaining the fabric of our society. We cannot ignore the significant social costs borne by our Nation when select groups are denied the means to absorb the values and skills upon which our social order rests. In addition to the pivotal role of education in sus-taining our political and cultural heritage, denial of education to some isolated group of children poses an affront to one of the goals of [equal protection]: the abolition of governmental barriers presenting unreasonable obstacles to advancement on the basis of individual merit. Paradoxically, by depriving the children of any disfavored group of an education, we foreclose the means by which that group might raise the level of esteem in which it is held by the majority. [Illiteracy] is an enduring disability. . . . The inestimable toll of that deprivation on the social, economic, intellectual, and psychological well-being of the individual, and the obstacle it poses to individual achievement, make it most difficult to reconcile the cost or the principle of a status-based denial of basic education with the framework of equality embodied in [equal protection].

B. . . . [Texas] imposes a lifetime hardship on a discrete class of children not accountable for their disabling status. [In] determining the rationality of [Texas's law], we may appropriately take into account its costs to the Nation and to the innocent children who are its victims. In light of these countervailing costs, the discrimination contained in [this law] can hardly be considered rational unless it furthers some substantial goal of the State.

IV. [The] State's principal argument [is] that the undocumented status of these children *vel non* establishes a sufficient rational basis for denying them benefits that a State might choose to afford other residents. The State [contends that the illegal] presence of these children within the United States [provides] authority for its decision to impose upon them special disabilities. . . . [The] States enjoy no power with respect to the classification of aliens. [The] States do have some authority to act with respect to illegal aliens, at least where such action mirrors federal objectives and furthers a legitimate state goal, [but] there is no indication that the disability imposed by [Texas law] corresponds to any identifiable congressional policy. [Because] we perceive no national policy that supports [Texas] in denying these children an elementary education [we] therefore turn to the state objectives that are said to support [the Texas law].

V. Appellants argue that the classification at issue furthers an interest in the "preservation of the state's limited resources for the education of its lawful residents." The State must do more than justify its classification with a concise expression of an intention to discriminate. [But] we discern three colorable state interests that might support [the law].

First, . . . the State [seeks] to protect itself from an influx of illegal immigrants. While a State might have an interest in mitigating the potentially harsh economic effects of sudden shifts in population, [this law] hardly offers an effective method of dealing with an urgent demographic or economic problem. [The] dominant incentive for illegal entry into [Texas] is the availability of employment; few if any illegal immigrants come to [Texas] in order to avail themselves of a free education. Thus, [we] think it clear that "[charging] tuition to undocumented children constitutes a ludicrously ineffectual attempt to stem the tide of illegal immigration," at least when compared with the alternative of prohibiting the employment of illegal aliens.

Second, [appellants] suggest that undocumented children are appropriately singled out for exclusion because of the special burdens they impose on the State's ability to provide high-quality public education. But the record in no way supports the claim that exclusion of undocumented children is likely to improve the overall quality of education in the State. [Even] if improvement in the quality of education were a likely result of barring some *number* of children from [Texas's] schools, [Texas] must support its selection of *this* group as the appropriate target for exclusion. . . . Finally, appellants suggest that undocumented children are appropriately singled out because their unlawful presence within the United States renders them less likely than other children to remain within [Texas], and to put their education to productive social or political use within [Texas. But Texas] has no assurance that any child, citizen or not, will employ the education provided by the State within the confines of [its] borders. In any event, [many] of the undocumented children disabled by this classification will remain in this country indefinitely, and [some] will become lawful residents or citizens of the United States. It is difficult to understand precisely what the State hopes to achieve by promoting the creation and perpetuation of a subclass of illiterates within our boundaries, surely adding to the problems and costs of unemployment, welfare, and crime. It is thus clear that whatever savings might be achieved by denying these children an education, they are wholly insubstantial in light of the costs involved to these children, the State, and the Nation.

VI. If the State is to deny a discrete group of innocent children the free public education that it offers to other children residing within its borders, that denial must be justified by a showing that it furthers some substantial state interest. No such showing was made here. [Affirmed.]

JUSTICE MARSHALL, concurring.

While I join the Court opinion, [I] continue to believe that an individual's interest in education is [fundamental]. Furthermore, [this case] demonstrate[s] the wisdom of rejecting a rigidified approach to equal protection analysis, and of employing an approach that allows for varying levels of scrutiny depending upon "the constitutional and societal importance of the interest adversely affected and the recognized invidiousness of the basis upon which the particular classification is drawn." . . .

JUSTICE BLACKMUN, concurring.

[Classifications] involving the complete denial of education are in a sense unique, for they strike at the heart of equal protection values by involving the State in the creation of permanent class distinctions. [Denial] of an education . . . relegates the individual to second-class social status. . . . The State must offer something more than a rational basis for its classification. . . .

JUSTICE POWELL, concurring.

[Texas] effectively denies to the school-age children of illegal aliens the opportunity to attend the free public schools that the State makes available to all residents. They are excluded only because of a status resulting from the violation by parents or guardians of our immigration laws and the fact that they remain in our country unlawfully. The . . . children are innocent in this respect. [Our] review [is] properly heightened. . . . [The] State's denial of education to these children bears no substantial relation to any substantial state interest. . . .

CHIEF JUSTICE BURGER, joined by JUSTICES WHITE, REHNQUIST, and O'CONNOR, dissenting.

Were it our business to set the Nation's social policy, I would agree without hesitation that it is senseless for an enlightened society to deprive any children—including illegal aliens—of an elementary education. . . . We trespass on the assigned function of the political branches [when] we assume a policy-making role as the Court does today. . . . The Court [abuses] the Fourteenth Amendment in an effort to become an omnipotent and omniscient problem solver. [The] extent to which the Court departs from principled constitutional adjudication is . . . disturbing.

[The] Court . . . rejects any suggestion that illegal aliens are a suspect class or that education is a fundamental right. Yet by patching together bits and pieces of what might be termed quasi-suspect-class and quasi-fundamental-rights analysis, the Court spins out a theory custom-tailored to the facts. In the end, we are told little more than that the level of scrutiny employed to strike down the Texas law applies only when illegal alien children are deprived of a public education. If ever a court was guilty of an unabashedly result-oriented approach, this case is a prime example. [Equal protection] does not preclude legislators from classifying among persons on the basis of factors and characteristics over which individuals may be said to lack "control." [Equal protection] is not an all-encompassing "equalizer" designed to eradicate every distinction for which persons are not "responsible." . . .

[Once] it is conceded—as the Court does—that illegal aliens are not a suspect class, and that education is not a fundamental right, our inquiry should focus on and be limited to whether the legislative classification at issue bears a rational relationship to a legitimate state purpose. [It] simply is not "irrational" for a state to conclude that it does not have the same responsibility to provide benefits for persons whose very presence in the state and this country is illegal as it does to provide for persons lawfully present. By definition, illegal aliens have no right whatever to be here, and the state may reasonably, and constitutionally, elect not to provide them with governmental services at the expense of those who are lawfully in the state. . . . [Denying] a free education to illegal alien children is not a choice I would make were I a legislator. [But] the fact that there are sound *policy* arguments against the Texas Legislature's choice does not render that choice an unconstitutional one. . . .

NOTES

1. The Standard of Review. Note that the Court required the classification to be *rationally related* to a *substantial*, rather than simply a legitimate, state interest and effectively shifted to Texas the burden of proof on this issue. This was not intermediate scrutiny, which would have obliged Texas to prove that its statutory classification was *substantially related* to an *important* state interest. At the time some commentators regarded *Plyler* as an augury of a new, free-ranging equal protection. See Hutchinson, More Substantive Equal Protection?, 1982 Sup. Ct. Rev. 167. Did *Plyler* ignite the free-wheeling inquiry Justice Marshall repeatedly called for? Certainly not openly, but perhaps covertly. Consider the possibilities at the end of Note 2.

2. Unwise, Illegitimate, or Insubstantial? The Court acknowledged that the Texas classification was neither suspect nor infringing of a fundamental right. The Court did not find that Texas's desire to devote its scarce educational resources to those lawfully residing in the state was illegitimate; rather, the Court ruled that that goal was an insufficiently substantial state interest. But why? Was it because it was unwise—a punitive measure that would sow even greater social discord later? "In determining the rationality of [the Texas law], we [take] into account its costs to the Nation and to the innocent children who are its victims. In light of [these] costs," the Court found the Texas statute invalid. In Minnesota v. Clover Leaf Creamery, 449 U.S. 456 (1981), the Court upheld a Minnesota law banning the sale of milk in plastic containers, even though the challengers amassed empirical evidence that the ban was directly counterproductive to the state's objectives of promoting resource conservation, easing solid waste disposal problems, and conserving energy. Justice Brennan, speaking for the Court, declared that "[w]here there was evidence before the legislature reasonably supporting the classification" the law would be upheld regardless of the strength of the empirical evidence "that the legislature was mistaken. [States] are not required to convince the courts of the correctness of their legislative judgments" by empirical evidence. In *Plyler*, however, Justice Brennan insisted that Texas make precisely this showing. Why? Is the *Plyler* and *Cleburne* brand of "enhanced" minimal scrutiny a form of constitutional *gestalt*? If not, state the general principle that applies.

Consider the following alternative explanations of the cases in this and the previous section.

(1) *Moreno* and *Romer* are indeed cases in which the Court identified illegitimate actual purposes, spurred to do so by the poor fit between stated purposes and legislative classification, and, in *Moreno*, aided by unguarded statements of the proponents that revealed an illegitimate purpose. *Cleburne* is the rare case in which statutory under-inclusion was so bizarre that the classification was indeed irrational. *Plyler*'s "heightened," or just-a-bit-more-than-minimal, scrutiny remains one of a kind, as the dissent charged, but the case is the clearest instance in which the Court actually applied something like the multi-factor test Justice Thurgood Marshall advocated.

(2) All of the cases in this and the preceding section—*Moreno, Romer, Cleburne*, and *Plyler*—can be explained as applications of Marshall's multi-factor test. The cases are focused not so much on illegitimate purposes as on identifying classifications that arouse some suspicion of illegitimacy or that impinge on socially important values.

Queries: If the first explanation is the better one, why didn't the Court expressly identify the triggers that caused it to focus on actual purposes? If the second explanation is the better one, why didn't the Court expressly declare its methodology?

C. STRICT SCRUTINY AND SUSPECT CLASSIFICATIONS: RACE AND ETHNICITY

1. Overview

Suspect classifications are presumptively void and thus trigger strict scrutiny. There are three suspect classifications: race, ethnicity or national origin, and lawful resident alienage. All classifications by race or ethnicity trigger strict scrutiny, but only some classifications on the basis of status as a lawful resident alien do so; thus, alienage classifications are treated separately in Section D. This section deals with racial classifications, the problem that the equal protection clause was originally intended to address. Classifications by ethnicity or national origin, the close kin of racial classifications, are treated identically and are equally suspect. Castenada v. Partida, 430 U.S. 482 (1977).

Suspect classifications are classifications that immediately give rise to a presumption of invidious, or wrongful, discrimination. Discrimination per se is *not* suspect; it is simply making or perceiving differences and distinctions. We constantly discriminate—in buying shoes, selecting movies, purchasing books, choosing friends. Governments discriminate too—in limiting driving privileges to those above a certain age or denying insane people the right to own firearms. It is only *wrongful* or *invidious* discrimination by governments that is constitutionally significant.

The method of determining when a statutory classification is presumptively invidiously discriminatory (and thus suspect) was introduced in Section A, supra. Derived from Justice Stone's *Carolene Products* footnote 4, that method primarily focuses on the presence of the following factors:

Immutable traits. Classifications by an immutable trait—a fixed, unchangeable quality—are dubious. Sometimes the trait may be relevant to legitimate objectives, but more often it is not. When the immutable trait is irrelevant it becomes a more suspicious device for classification.

History of purposeful unequal treatment. By itself, this factor might not be significant. Perhaps Oklahoma opticians have been the victims of long-standing purposefully unequal treatment. But when a particular group sharing an immutable trait has received purposefully unequal treatment for a long period it is difficult to escape the conclusion that some prejudice is at the heart of that history. The combination of a history of purposeful unequal treatment and prejudice that blocks political redress of that treatment supports a powerful argument that such classifications are suspect.

Perennial lack of access to political power. Mere lack of political power is not the issue. Convicted felons lack political power in America, but that fact by itself does not render suspect a classification that treats convicted felons as different from other citizens. The issue is perennial lack of political power coupled with a lack of any *access* to that power. Persons barred from voting (e.g., lawful resident aliens) lack access to political power. By itself, this factor is not determinative, but when it is coupled with other factors the case for a suspect classification becomes stronger.

The principal category of suspect classifications is racial classifications, which clearly fit the above criteria. In Korematsu v. United States, 323 U.S. 214 (1944), the Court sustained Fred Korematsu's conviction for violating a 1942 military order excluding all persons of Japanese ancestry from certain portions of the Pacific Coast. Writing for the Court, Justice Black declared that all legal restrictions which curtail the civil rights of a single racial group are immediately suspect. That is not to say that all such restrictions are unconstitutional. It is to say that courts must subject them to the most rigid scrutiny. Pressing public necessity may sometimes justify the existence of such restrictions; racial antagonism never can.

Ironically, the Court concluded that the "pressing public necessity" of preventing espionage or sabotage by some unknown number of disloyal persons of Japanese ancestry justified deference to the military authorities' judgment that wholesale exclusion was necessary. Justices Murphy, Jackson, and Roberts dissented. Justice Murphy charged that the "forced exclusion was [unreasonable,] the result in good measure of [an] erroneous assumption of racial guilt rather than bona fide military necessity." Justice Jackson declared that the opinion sustaining

> this order is a far more subtle blow at liberty than the [order] itself. A military order, however unconstitutional, is not apt to last longer than the military emergency. [But] once a judicial opinion [rationalizes] the Constitution to show that the Constitution sanctions such an order, the Court for all time has validated the principle of racial [discrimination]. The principle then lies about like a loaded weapon ready for the hand of any authority that can bring forward a plausible claim of an urgent need.[1]

Nobody questions that racial classifications are suspect, but the meaning of equal protection with respect to race is contested. One view is that the essence of equal protection is government neutrality with respect to race. On this view, governments must be "color-blind," and can act in an explicitly race-based manner only when there is some exceedingly strong justification for doing so. This view commonly holds that equal protection, like other constitutional rights, protects individuals, not groups, from invidious discrimination by government. The other view is that equal protection commands governments to eradicate past official practices of racial subordination. According to this "anti-subordination" view, governments may (and sometimes must) act in an explicitly race-based manner when to do so would dismantle the decayed architecture of racial subordination. Adherents to this view typically assert that equal protection protects racial groups from invidious discrimination by government and that individual claims inconsistent with this principle are of lesser constitutional concern. These two views are not always in tension, but in some areas they are sharply opposed. In Brown v. Board of Education, for example, the two views are harmonious; in the affirmative action cases they are largely in opposition. Pay attention to this theme as you study the materials in this section.

1. Forty years later, Korematsu's conviction was vacated on grounds of government misconduct in presenting false information to the Supreme Court in *Korematsu* to justify the exclusion order. Korematsu v. United States, 584 F. Supp. 1406 (N.D. Cal. 1984). The evidence of government misconduct was largely uncovered by Peter Irons, a political scientist at U.C. San Diego, who published his findings in Irons, Justice at War (1983).

2. Purposeful Discrimination Required

For a legislative classification to be constitutionally suspect, the challenger must prove that the classification is *intentionally* discriminatory—it was adopted to use the suspect criterion (e.g., race) as the basis for classification. There are three ways to establish this:

Facially discriminatory classifications. If a classification directly employs the suspect criterion, intentional discrimination is revealed on the face of the statute, and no further inquiry is necessary to determine that the classification is suspect. An example is Strauder v. West Virginia, 100 U.S. 303 (1879). Strauder, a black man, was convicted of murder by a West Virginia jury limited by law to adult white males. The Court ruled that the facially discriminatory law violated equal protection.

A variation on the facially discriminatory classification is found in Loving v. Virginia, 388 U.S. 1 (1967). Virginia prohibited interracial marriage. The Lovings, a married couple consisting of a black woman and white man, were convicted of violating the statute. Virginia contended "that because its miscegenation statutes punish equally both the white and the Negro participants in an interracial marriage, these statutes, despite their reliance on racial classifications, do not constitute an invidious [racial] discrimination." The Court responded that

> the fact of equal application does not immunize the statute from the very heavy burden of justification which [equal protection requires] of state statutes drawn according to race. [Virginia's] miscegenation statutes rest solely upon distinctions drawn according to race. The statutes [have] no legitimate [purpose]. The fact that Virginia prohibits only interracial marriages involving white persons demonstrates that the racial classifications [are] designed to maintain White Supremacy. We have consistently denied the constitutionality of measures [that] restrict the rights of citizens on account of race. [Restricting] the freedom to marry solely because of racial classifications violates the central meaning of [equal protection].

Justice Stewart concurred on the ground that "it is simply not possible for a state law to be valid under our Constitution which makes the criminality of an act depend upon the race of the actor." See also McLaughlin v. Florida, 379 U.S. 184 (1964) (invalidating on equal protection grounds a state law making it a crime for interracial married couples to cohabit).

Neutral classifications applied in a discriminatory fashion. A facially neutral classification (one that classifies on a non-suspect basis) that is *actually applied* on a suspect basis is treated as a suspect classification, but the party challenging the classification has the burden of proving its suspect application. A classic example is Yick Wo v. Hopkins, 118 U.S. 356 (1886). To reduce the risk of fire, San Francisco prohibited operation of laundries in wooden buildings. All but 10 of San Francisco's 320 laundries were barred from further operations. Persons of Chinese ancestry operated 75 percent of the city's laundries, and virtually all of those were in wooden structures. Almost two-thirds of the 240 Chinese persons operating laundries were arrested for violation of the ordinance, while 80-odd laundries operated by European Americans in wooden buildings were "left unmolested." The Court invalidated the ordinance because San Francisco had no justification for its invidiously discriminatory application of a facially neutral law.

Neutral classifications motivated by discrimination that produce a discriminatory effect. A facially neutral classification that is adopted solely because of an invidiously discriminatory motive and that produces the intended effect is treated as a suspect classification. The classic example is Gomillion v. Lightfoot, 364 U.S. 339 (1960). Tuskegee, Alabama, redrew its boundaries from a square to an "uncouth twenty-eight sided figure." About 99 percent of the black voters were allegedly eliminated from Tuskegee, while not a single white voter was removed. The Court ruled that if the allegations were true, "the conclusion would be irresistible, tantamount for all practical purposes to mathematical demonstration, that the legislation is solely concerned with segregating white and [black] voters."

≡ **Washington v. Davis**
≡ *426 U.S. 229 (1976)*

JUSTICE WHITE delivered the opinion of the Court.

This case involves the validity of a qualifying test administered to applicants for positions as police officers in the District of Columbia Metropolitan Police Department. [Applicants were required to take and pass a qualifying examination that measured "verbal ability, vocabulary, reading and comprehension." Four times as many blacks than whites failed the test. Respondents, black applicants who had failed the test, made] no claim of "an intentional discrimination or purposeful discriminatory acts" but only a claim that [the test] "has a highly discriminatory impact in screening out black candidates." [The District Court granted summary judgment in favor of the city. The Court of Appeals applied the statutory standards of Title VII of the 1964 Civil Rights Act to resolve the equal protection issue. Those standards, as articulated by Griggs v. Duke Power Co., 401 U.S. 424 (1971), were that] disproportionate impact, standing alone and without regard to whether it indicated a discriminatory purpose, [was] sufficient to establish a constitutional violation, absent proof by petitioners that the test was an adequate measure of job performance [and] an indicator of probable [job] success, [a] burden which the court ruled [the city] had failed to [carry].

We have never held that the constitutional standard for adjudicating claims of invidious racial discrimination is identical to the standards applicable under Title VII, and we decline to do so today. The central purpose of [equal protection] is the prevention of official conduct discriminating on the basis of race. But our cases have not embraced the proposition that a law or other official act, without regard to whether it reflects a racially discriminatory purpose, is unconstitutional *solely* because it has a racially disproportionate impact. . . .

[For example, the] school desegregation cases [adhere] to the basic equal protection principle that the invidious quality of a law claimed to be racially discriminatory must ultimately be traced to a racially discriminatory purpose. That there are both predominantly black and predominantly white schools in a community is not alone violative of [equal protection. The] "differentiating factor between de jure segregation and so-called de facto segregation [is] *purpose* or *intent* to segregate." [Keyes v. Denver School District.]

This is not to say that the necessary discriminatory racial purpose must be express or appear on the face of the statute, or that a law's disproportionate impact is irrelevant in cases involving Constitution-based claims of racial discrimination. A statute, otherwise neutral on its face, must not be applied so as invidiously to discriminate on the basis of race. Yick Wo v. Hopkins. It is also clear from the cases dealing with racial discrimination in the selection of juries that [a] prima facie case of discriminatory purpose may be proved [by] the absence of Negroes on a particular jury combined with the failure of the jury commissioners to be informed of eligible Negro jurors in a community or with racially nonneutral selection procedures. With a prima facie case made out, "the burden of proof shifts to the State to rebut the presumption of unconstitutional action by showing that permissible racially neutral selection criteria and procedures have produced the monochromatic result."

Necessarily, an invidious discriminatory purpose may often be inferred from the totality of the relevant facts, including the fact, if it is true, that the law bears more heavily on one race than another. It is also not infrequently true that the discriminatory impact . . . may for all practical purposes demonstrate unconstitutionality because in various circumstances the discrimination is very difficult to explain on nonracial grounds. Nevertheless, we have not held that a law, neutral on its face and serving ends otherwise within the power of government to pursue, is invalid under [equal protection] simply because it may affect a greater proportion of one race than of another. Disproportionate impact is not irrelevant, but it is not the sole touchstone of an invidious racial discrimination forbidden by the Constitution. Standing alone, it does not trigger the rule that racial classifications are to be subjected to the strictest scrutiny and are justifiable only by the weightiest of considerations.

[We] have difficulty understanding how a law establishing a racially neutral qualification for employment is nevertheless racially discriminatory and denies "any person [equal protection]" simply because a greater proportion of Negroes fail to qualify than members of other racial or ethnic groups. . . . [The test], which is administered generally to prospective Government employees, concededly seeks to ascertain whether those who take it have acquired a particular level of verbal skill; and it is untenable that the Constitution prevents the Government from seeking modestly to upgrade the communicative abilities of its employees rather than to be satisfied with some lower level of competence, particularly where the job requires special ability to communicate orally and in writing. . . . Nor on the facts of the case before us would the disproportionate impact of [the test] warrant the conclusion that it is a purposeful device to discriminate against Negroes. [The] test is neutral on its face and rationally may be said to serve a purpose the Government is constitutionally empowered to pursue. [We] think the District Court correctly held that the affirmative efforts of the Metropolitan Police Department to recruit black officers, the changing racial composition of the recruit classes and of the force in general, and the relationship of the test to the training program negated any inference that the Department discriminated on the basis of [race].

. . . A rule that a statute designed to serve neutral ends is nevertheless invalid, absent compelling justification, if in practice it benefits or burdens one race more than another would be far reaching and would raise serious questions about, and perhaps invalidate, a whole range of tax, welfare, public service, regulatory, and licensing statutes that may be more burdensome to the poor and to the average black than to the more affluent white.[2] Given [such] consequences, [extension] of the rule beyond those areas where it is already applicable by reason of statute [should] await legislative prescription.

NOTES

1. Proving Discriminatory Intent. *Davis* established that proof of discriminatory intent is indispensable to shift a facially neutral classification into the suspect category. In Arlington Heights v. Metropolitan Housing Development Corp., 429 U.S. 252 (1977), the Court confronted the evidentiary issues. MHDC requested Arlington Heights, a mostly white Chicago suburb, to rezone property to permit construction of low-income housing, which would be occupied in part by racial minorities. Arlington Heights refused. MHDC and prospective occupants charged that the refusal was racially discriminatory and a violation of equal protection. The Court of Appeals concluded that Arlington Heights "was motivated by a concern for the integrity of the zoning plan, rather than by racial discrimination," but nevertheless subjected the zoning decision to strict scrutiny because the decision "had racially discriminatory effects." The Court of Appeals ruled that equal protection was violated because the village's legitimate concerns were not compelling interests. The Supreme Court reversed.

> [O]fficial action will not be held unconstitutional solely because it results in a racially disproportionate impact. [But] *Davis* does not require a plaintiff to prove that the challenged action rested solely on racially discriminatory purposes. Rarely can it be said that a legislature or administrative body operating

2. Goodman, De Facto School Segregation: A Constitutional and Empirical Analysis, 60 Cal. L. Rev. 275, 300 (1972), suggests that disproportionate-impact analysis might invalidate "tests and qualifications for voting, draft deferment, public employment, jury service, [sales] taxes, bail schedules, utility rates, bridge tolls, license fees, and other state-imposed charges." It has also been argued that minimum wage and usury laws as well as professional licensing requirements would require major modifications in light of the unequal-impact rule. Silverman, Equal Protection, Economic Legislation, and Racial Discrimination, 25 Vand. L. Rev. 1183 (1972). See also Demsetz, Minorities in the Market Place, 43 N.C. L. Rev. 271 (1965).

under a broad mandate made a decision motivated solely by a single concern, or even that a particular purpose was the "dominant" or "primary" one. [But when] there is proof that a discriminatory purpose has been a motivating factor in the decision, [judicial] deference is no longer justified.

[Determining] whether invidious discriminatory purpose was a motivating factor demands a sensitive inquiry into such circumstantial and direct evidence of intent as may be available. The [racial] impact of the official action [may] provide an important starting point. Sometimes a clear pattern, unexplainable on grounds other than race, emerges from the effect of the state action even when the governing legislation appears neutral on its face. The evidentiary inquiry is then relatively easy. But such cases are rare. Absent a pattern as stark as that in *Gomillion* or *Yick Wo*, impact alone is not determinative, and the Court must look to other evidence. The historical background of the decision is one evidentiary source, particularly if it reveals a series of official actions taken for invidious purposes. Griffin v. School Board, 377 U.S. 218 (1964). The specific sequence of events leading up to the challenged decision also may shed some light on the decisionmaker's purposes. For example, if the property involved here always had been zoned [to permit low-income housing] but suddenly was changed to [single-family residential] when the town learned of MHDC's plans to erect integrated housing, we would have a far different case. Departures from the normal procedural sequence also might afford evidence that improper purposes are playing a role. Substantive departures too may be relevant, particularly if the factors usually considered important by the decision-maker strongly favor a decision contrary to the one reached. The legislative or administrative history may be highly relevant, especially where there are contemporary statements by members of the decisionmaking body, minutes of its meetings, or reports.

[But none of these factors established intentional racial discrimination here.] Respondents simply failed to carry their burden of proving that discriminatory purpose was a motivating factor in the Village's decision. This conclusion ends the constitutional inquiry. [Even proof] that the decision by the Village was motivated in part by a racially discriminatory purpose would not necessarily have required invalidation of the challenged decision. Such proof would, however, have shifted to the Village the burden of establishing that the same decision would have resulted even had the impermissible purpose not been considered. If this were established, the complaining party [no] longer fairly could attribute the injury complained of to improper consideration of a discriminatory purpose. In such circumstances, there would be no justification for judicial interference with the challenged decision. But in this case respondents failed to make the required threshold showing. See Mt. Healthy v. Doyle, [429 U.S. 274 (1977)]. The Court of Appeals' further finding that the Village's decision carried a discriminatory "ultimate effect" is without independent constitutional significance.

2. Working with the *Arlington* Factors. The *Arlington* factors are highly contextual, as the following examples illustrate. A municipality could validly close its public schools, as the Constitution does not obligate states to provide public education. But when Prince Edward County, Virginia, did so after a court ruled that its racially segregated school system was unconstitutional, and coupled the closure with a public subsidy for private education that disproportionately benefited whites, the Court unhesitatingly applied strict scrutiny and invalidated the closure because it was "for one reason [only]: to ensure [that] white and colored children [would] not, under any circumstances, go to the same school." Griffin v. County School Board, 377 U.S. 218 (1964).

In 1911, Burke County, Georgia, created a five-person board of commissioners to govern the county, with each commissioner elected at large. The at-large system was "racially neutral when adopted," but in 1976 was challenged as being maintained for racially discriminatory purposes. In Rogers v. Lodge, 458 U.S. 613 (1982), the Court upheld a trial court determination that Burke County's history of past racial discrimination in voter registration and voting was enough to draw an inference of a present racially discriminatory purpose in maintaining the at-large electoral system. When coupled with evidence of (1) the lingering effects of past discrimination in education and voting (only 38 percent of blacks eligible to vote were registered voters), (2) a board of commissioners that was "unresponsive and insensitive to the needs of the black community," and (3) racial bloc voting, the Court was satisfied that the trial court's determination was not clearly erroneous.

Query: Suppose the D.C. Police Department had never used a written qualifying test for police applicants until significant numbers of blacks began to apply. Would that alone establish discriminatory intent? Suppose that, once MHDC's intentions became known but before it had requested rezoning, Arlington Heights adopted a rule that all rezoning applications are subject to final approval in a voter referendum. Would that alone establish discriminatory intent?

3. Burdens of Proof.   The challenger of legislative or executive action has the burden of proving discriminatory intent. The effect of discharging that burden is to shift to the state the burden of proving, "by a preponderance of the evidence, [that] it would have reached the same decision" without any intentionally discriminatory motive. If the government carries this burden of proof and thereby rebuts the challenger's proof of intentional discrimination, the government action is subjected to minimal scrutiny. Thus strict scrutiny applies only if the challenger proves that facially neutral action was intended to deliver invidiously discriminatory effects and the government is unable to rebut that proof by showing that the action would have been taken anyway. In Mount Healthy City School District Board of Education v. Doyle, 429 U.S. 274 (1977), the Court ruled that proof that a schoolteacher had been fired for exercising his free speech rights could be rebutted by proof that he would have been fired anyway for poor job performance.

Queries: Why permit governments found to have been motivated in part by racial discrimination the opportunity to escape strict scrutiny (and probable invalidation) of their actions? Is it because it is futile to do otherwise, as the government could take the same action so long as its motives were legitimate? Or should the presence of an improper motive, even when coupled with legitimate reasons, fatally infect the government action? If the latter is the better approach, what should the standard of proof be on the question of discriminatory intent? Preponderance of the evidence? Clear and convincing evidence? Your answer may depend on your view of the ease with which courts can accurately assess legislative or executive motive.

4. Applications Beyond Race. The discriminatory intent requirement applies whenever a litigant contends that a facially neutral classification is subject to heightened scrutiny because of its constitutionally suspicious disparate impact. In Personnel Administrator v. Feeney, 442 U.S. 256 (1979), the Court upheld a Massachusetts law that preferred military veterans to nonveterans in civil service hiring. Over 98 percent of Massachusetts veterans were male. Despite that stark disparate impact, the Court ruled that the classification was not the product of invidiously discriminatory intent. Writing for the Court, Justice Stewart noted that the law served

> legitimate and worthy purposes [and was] not a law that can plausibly be explained only as a gender-based classification. [Although] few women benefit from the preference, the nonveteran class is not substantially all-female. [Significant] numbers of nonveterans are men, and all nonveterans—male as well as female—are placed at a disadvantage. Too many men are affected by [the law] to permit the inference that the statute is but a pretext for preferring men over women. [While it would be] disingenuous to say that the adverse consequences of this [law] for women were unintended, in the sense that they were not volitional or in the sense that they were not foreseeable, "[d]iscriminatory purpose" [implies] more than intent as volition or intent as awareness of consequences. It implies that the decisionmaker, in this case a state legislature, selected or reaffirmed a particular course of action at least in part "because of," not merely "in spite of," its adverse effects upon an identifiable group. [The] inevitability or foreseeability of consequences of a neutral rule [permits] a strong inference that the adverse effects were desired. [But this] inference is a working tool, not a synonym for proof. When, as here, the impact is [an] unavoidable consequence of a legislative policy that has itself always been deemed to be legitimate, [and there is no other proof of discriminatory intent,] the inference simply fails to ripen into proof.

5. Criminal Jury Selection. A well-established feature of American law is to permit both prosecution and defense to excuse a limited number of prospective jurors for no reason at all. These peremptory challenges can collide with equal protection concerns when prosecutors surreptitiously use their peremptory challenges in a racially biased manner. Batson v. Kentucky, 476 U.S. 79 (1986), looked to "the totality of the relevant facts" about the prosecutor's conduct to decide whether a prima facie case of racial discrimination existed. A later case, Johnson v. California, 545 U.S. 162 (2005), held that a prima facie case is established if the defendant produces "evidence sufficient to permit the trial judge to draw an inference that discrimination has occurred." Once a prima facie case is established, *Batson* required prosecutors to articulate a race-neutral explanation for their peremptory challenges. Finally, the trial court must determine whether purposeful discrimination had been proven.

Some sense of the Supreme Court's view on this process of proof by circumstantial evidence can be found in Miller-El v. Dretke, 545 U.S. 231 (2005), in which the African American defendant, convicted of capital murder, successfully raised a *Batson* challenge in a habeas corpus petition. The prosecution had used peremptory challenges to excuse 10 of the 11 eligible black jurors, but had not objected to white jurors who provided the same answers in *voir dire* that purportedly triggered the prosecution's peremptory challenges on black prospective jurors. The prosecution also described the death penalty, which it sought in the case, in strikingly different terms when addressing black versus white prospective jurors, and had engaged in quite different lines of inquiry when confronted with black versus white prospective jurors who expressed the same views about the death penalty. Finally, the prosecution had used a "jury shuffle" to change the order in which prospective jurors were questioned only when blacks were at the top of the list of prospective jurors.

6. Government Response to Private Bias. When governments take into account private biases in formulating policy, are their acts the product of intentional invidious discrimination? Consider the following cases.

Palmer v. Thompson, 403 U.S. 217 (1971). Jackson, Mississippi closed its public swimming pools after a federal judge had ordered them to be desegregated. The closure, said the Court, affected all races equally and had been motivated by the city council's determination that operation of racially integrated swimming pools would be uneconomical, not because of "ideological opposition to racial integration." Assume that the city council was correct in concluding that integrated pools could not be operated economically. Was that the result of private bias?

Palmore v. Sidoti, 466 U.S. 429 (1984). A white divorced father sought custody of his three-year-old daughter from his white ex-wife after her marriage to a black man. A Florida judge ruled that the best interests of the child warranted the custody change, because "despite the strides that have been made in bettering [race] relations [it] is inevitable that [the girl will] suffer [from] social stigmatization." However right or wrong the trial judge was in his assessment of American society, the Court ruled that it was impermissible to take private racial bias into account in deciding what was in the best interests of the child: "The Constitution cannot control such prejudices but neither can it tolerate them. Private biases may be outside the reach of the law, but the law cannot, directly or indirectly, give them effect."

Queries: Can *Palmer* and *Palmore* be reconciled? Is the difference between the two the fact that the Florida judge openly adopted private racial bias as the basis of his decision, while Jackson's city council merely reacted to the economic effects produced by such bias? Note that the *Palmore* Court observed in dictum that governments "cannot, [even] *indirectly*, [give] effect" to private biases. Was the Florida judge's use of private bias as the determining factor *itself* intentionally discriminatory? By contrast, was Jackson's decision racially neutral, placing the burden of proof on the challengers to show more evidence of intentional discrimination?

3.   Official Racial Segregation

The application of equal protection to American practices of officially approved and enforced racial segregation is a tale of the evolution of the law on equal protection and race. When studying these materials, pay particular attention to the cases implementing Brown v. Board of Education. Did those cases simply provide remedies for the constitutional right articulated in Brown v. Board of Education, or did they revise and alter that right even as they sought to implement it? The point at which remediation turns into substantive alteration becomes sharply contentious in the context of affirmative action. As a prelude to that inquiry, try to identify the principles driving both the right identified in *Brown* and its implementation. Is the Court's vision of equal protection strict government neutrality on race or is it anti-subordination? Does equal protection protect individual rights or collective rights here?

a.   *The Road to* Brown

The road to Brown v. Board of Education begins in the early 1600s, when the first captive Africans were brought to Virginia to languish in slavery. Nearly two and a half centuries of white enslavement of black Africans hardened racial attitudes to the point that in Dred Scott v. Sandford, 60 U.S. (19 How.) 393 (1857), the Court ruled that "persons who are descendants of Africans [brought unwillingly] into this country, and sold as slaves" are not, and could not become, U.S. citizens. To add further insult, the Court observed that Americans of African ancestry "had no rights which the white man was bound to respect." Although the Civil War buried *Dred Scott*, along with anywhere from about 650,000 to 850,000 Americans,[3] and produced the Thirteenth, Fourteenth, and Fifteenth Amendments, the subordination of African Americans did not end. Once federal troops left the former Confederate states in the wake of the election of 1876, white Southerners quickly resumed governance and imposed draconian race-based laws that were designed to ensure the continued economic and social subjugation of black Americans.

The post-Reconstruction, Jim Crow era was given its legal blessing by Plessy v. Ferguson, 163 U.S. 537 (1896). Louisiana required railroads to provide "equal but separate accommodations for the white and colored races"

---

3. To put this number in perspective, if the United States were to suffer today the same proportion of deaths to total population, the death toll would be in the range of 6.2 to 8.6 million people.

and subjected passengers who used the wrong accommodations to criminal liability. Plessy refused to leave the "whites only" coach and was subsequently convicted under the law. The Court upheld his conviction. Justice Brown wrote that even though

> [t]he object of [equal protection] was undoubtedly to enforce the absolute equality of the two races before the law, [this did not] abolish distinctions based on color, [or operate] to enforce social, as distinguished from political, equality, [nor did it require] commingling of the two races upon terms unsatisfactory to either. [Louisiana was] at liberty to act with reference to the established usages, customs, and traditions of the people, and with a view to the promotion of their comfort, and the preservation of the public peace and good order. [It was a mere] assumption that the enforced separation of the two races stamps the colored race with a badge of inferiority. If this be so, it [is] solely because the colored race chooses to put that construction upon it.

In dissent, Justice Harlan declared:

> In respect of civil rights, common to all citizens, the Constitution [does not] permit any public authority to know the race of those entitled to be protected in the enjoyment of such rights. [The Civil War Amendments] removed the race line from our governmental systems. [In] view of the Constitution . . . there is in this country no superior, dominant, ruling class of citizens. There is no caste here. Our Constitution is color-blind, and neither knows nor tolerates classes among citizens. In respect of civil rights, all citizens are equal before the law.

The equality prong of "separate but equal" was repeatedly attacked in the years following *Plessy*. Among the high points were the following cases.

Missouri ex rel. Gaines v. Canada, 305 U.S. 337 (1938). Missouri required racially separate education. The white university system included a law school; the black system did not, but Missouri would pay reasonable tuition at out-of-state law schools to enable black students to attend law school. The Court found Missouri's scheme to be a violation of equal protection. "The basic consideration is not [what] sort of opportunities other states provide, or whether they are as good as those in Missouri, [but] opportunities Missouri itself furnishes to white students and denies to negroes solely upon the ground of color."

Sweatt v. Painter, 339 U.S. 629 (1950). The University of Texas refused to admit Sweatt, an African American, to its law school on the ground that a public "blacks only" law school was available. The Court found Texas's refusal a denial of equal protection because the black institution was quantitatively and qualitatively inferior.

McLaurin v. Oklahoma State Regents, 339 U.S. 637 (1950). The University of Oklahoma admitted McLaurin, an African American, to its education school but made him sit in a "blacks only" section in each classroom, gave him a special table in the library, and barred him from eating with white students in the cafeteria. Although McLaurin enjoyed the same physical facilities as whites, the Court found the arrangement unequal because it impaired and inhibited "his ability to study, to engage in discussions and exchange views with other students, and, in general, to learn his profession."

These cases were but a part of the attack on "separate but equal" that was systematically mounted by the National Association for the Advancement of Colored People, led by such lawyers as Charles Houston and Thurgood Marshall. A riveting account of the legal assault on Jim Crow is contained in Kluger, Simple Justice (1975). See also Klarman, From Jim Crow to Civil Rights: The Supreme Court and the Struggle for Racial Equality (2004).

b.   The End of "Separate but Equal"

Brown v. Board of Education of Topeka (Brown I)
347 U.S. 483 (1954)

CHIEF JUSTICE WARREN delivered the opinion of the Court.

In [these] cases, [black children] seek the aid of the courts in obtaining admission to the public schools of their community on a nonsegregated basis. In each instance, they had been denied admission to schools attended by white children under laws requiring or permitting segregation according to race. [The lower courts sustained the validity of the segregation under] the so-called "separate but equal" doctrine announced by this Court in Plessy v. Ferguson. [The] plaintiffs contend that segregated public schools are not "equal" and cannot be made "equal," and that hence they are deprived of the equal protection of the laws.

[The history of] the adoption of the Fourteenth Amendment in 1868 [is] inconclusive. [In] the South, the movement toward free common schools, supported by general taxation, had not yet taken hold. . . . [In] the North the conditions of public education did not approximate those existing today. [As] a consequence, it is not surprising that there should be so little in the history of the Fourteenth Amendment relating to its intended effect on public education.

In approaching this problem, we cannot turn the clock back to 1868, when the Amendment was adopted, or even to 1896, when Plessy v. Ferguson was written. We must consider public education in the light of its full development and its present place in American life throughout the Nation. [Today], education is perhaps the most important function of state and local governments. . . . It is the very foundation of good citizenship, [the] principal instrument in awakening the child to cultural values, in preparing him for later professional training, and in helping him to adjust normally to his environment. In these days, it is doubtful that any child may reasonably be expected to succeed in life if he is denied the opportunity of an education. Such an opportunity, where the state has undertaken to provide it, is a right which must be made available to all on equal terms.

We come then to the question presented: Does segregation of children in public schools solely on the basis of race, even though the physical facilities and other "tangible" factors may be equal, deprive the children of the minority group of equal educational opportunities? We believe that it does. In [deciding *Sweatt* and *McLaurin*, this Court] resorted to intangible considerations [as the basis for decision]. Such considerations apply with added force to children in grade and high schools. To separate them from others of similar age and qualifications solely because of their race generates a feeling of inferiority as to their status in the community that may affect their hearts and minds in a way unlikely ever to be undone. The effect of this separation . . . was well stated . . . in the Kansas case by a court which nevertheless felt compelled to rule against the Negro plaintiffs: "Segregation of white and colored children in public schools has a detrimental effect upon the colored children. The impact is greater when it has the sanction of the law; for the policy of separating the races is usually interpreted as denoting the inferiority of the negro group. A sense of inferiority affects the motivation of a child to learn. Segregation with the sanction of law, therefore, has a tendency to [retard] the educational and mental development of negro children and to deprive them of some of the benefits they would receive in a racial[ly] integrated school system." Whatever may have been the extent of psychological knowledge at the time of Plessy v. Ferguson, this finding is amply supported by modern authority. Any language in Plessy v. Ferguson contrary to this finding is rejected.

We conclude that in the field of public education the doctrine of "separate but equal" has no place. Separate educational facilities are inherently unequal. Therefore, we hold that the plaintiffs and others similarly situated for whom the actions have been brought are, by reason of the segregation complained of, deprived of [equal protection]. Because these are class actions, because of the wide applicability of this decision, and because of the great variety of local conditions, the formulation of decrees in these cases presents problems of considerable complexity. [In] order that we may have the full assistance of the parties in formulating decrees, the cases will be restored to the docket [for reargument on the question of appropriate remedies].

NOTES

1. Equal Protection and the Federal Government. In a companion case, Bolling v. Sharpe, 347 U.S. 497 (1954), the Court struck down laws that segregated public schools in the District of Columbia, ruling that such segregation was an impermissible infringement of the substantive liberty protected by the due process clause of the Fifth Amendment. The Court admitted that equal protection was "a more explicit safeguard of prohibited unfairness than [due process]," but did not expressly import equal protection *in toto* into the Fifth Amendment's due process clause. Nevertheless, it is now well settled that equal protection applies with equal force to the federal government.

2. *Brown II*: The Remedial Decree.   A year after *Brown I*, the Court decided Brown v. Board of Education of Topeka (*Brown II*), 349 U.S. 294 (1955), in which it reaffirmed "the fundamental principle that racial discrimination in public education is unconstitutional" and declared that "[all] provisions of federal, state, or local law requiring or permitting such discrimination must yield to this principle." But the Court remanded the cases to "the courts which originally heard these cases" for implementation of this principle. The Court noted that

> [each of those] courts will be guided by equitable principles [requiring] practical flexibility in shaping its remedies and [a] facility for adjusting and reconciling public and private needs. [At] stake is the personal interest of the plaintiffs in admission to public schools as soon as practicable on a nondiscriminatory basis. To effectuate this interest may call for elimination of a variety of obstacles in making the transition to school systems operated in accordance with the constitutional principles set forth in [*Brown I*]. Courts of equity may . . . take into account the public interest in the elimination of such obstacles in a systematic and effective manner. But . . . the vitality of these constitutional principles cannot be allowed to yield simply because of disagreement with them.
>
> While giving weight to these public and private considerations, the courts will require that the defendants make a prompt and reasonable start toward full compliance with [*Brown I*]. Once such a start has been made, the courts may find that additional time is necessary to carry out the ruling in an effective manner. The burden rests upon the defendants to establish that such time is necessary in the public interest and is consistent with good faith compliance at the earliest practicable date. To that end, the courts may consider problems related to administration, arising from the physical condition of the school plant, the school transportation system, personnel, revision of school districts and attendance areas into compact units to achieve a system of determining admission to the public schools on a nonracial basis, and revision of local laws and regulations which may be necessary in solving the foregoing problems. They will also consider the adequacy of any plans the defendants may propose to meet these problems and to effectuate a transition to a racially nondiscriminatory school system. During this period of transition, the courts will retain jurisdiction of these cases.
>
> The [cases] are remanded to the [trial courts] to take such proceedings and enter such orders and decrees consistent with this opinion as are necessary and proper to admit to public schools on a racially nondiscriminatory basis with all deliberate speed the parties to these cases.

3. The Constitutional Right Protected by *Brown*.   Was the right recognized in *Brown* a right to be free from official segregation or a right to racial integration? A government could comply with the first view simply by ending official segregation. So long as it was officially color-blind and engaged in no intentional racial discrimination, the government would conform to equal protection. To comply with the second view, however, a government might be compelled to take some affirmative steps to make racial integration a reality. For example, a government might be required to make race-conscious decisions about such things as pupil and teacher placement and teacher hiring. Ultimately, the choice between these two views is presented when one is forced to decide whether equal protection is violated when a government, though not intending to discriminate racially, fails to produce meaningful racial integration in public education.

4. Implementing *Brown.* The Court has consistently stated that *Brown* is violated only by acts of intentional racial discrimination, and thus courts lack *any* remedial power in this area in the absence of the unjustifiable intentional discrimination that amounts to a constitutional violation. Consider the following cases and then state the constitutional violation that was being remedied by each case.

Green v. County School Board, 391 U.S. 430 (1968). To remedy its prior deliberate racial segregation, a school district with two schools, approximately equal numbers of black and white students, and little residential racial segregation adopted a freedom-of-choice plan that permitted students to choose the school they wished to attend upon entering the system. After three years, the formerly all-black school was still all black and the formerly all-white school was about 85 percent white. The Court invalidated the plan in an opinion by Justice Brennan:

> [T]he transition to a unitary, nonracial system of public education was and is the ultimate end to be brought about [by *Brown I*]. It is against this [standard that] we must measure the effectiveness of [the] "freedom-of-choice" plan. [The] School Board contends that it has fully discharged its obligation by adopting a plan by which every student, regardless of race, may "freely" choose the school he will attend. The Board [argues] that its "freedom-of-choice" plan may be faulted only by reading [equal protection] as universally requiring "compulsory integration." [School boards] operating state-compelled dual systems [were] charged [by *Brown I*] with the affirmative duty to take whatever steps might be necessary to convert to a unitary system in which racial discrimination would be eliminated root and branch. [The] burden on a school board . . . is to come forward with a plan that promises realistically to work, [and] to work *now*.

Swann v. Charlotte-Mecklenburg Board of Education, 402 U.S. 1 (1971). Charlotte, North Carolina, initially desegregated its officially segregated schools by adopting a court-approved geographic zoning plan coupled with "freedom of choice" transfers. This left over half the black students attending schools that were nearly 100 percent black. After *Green*, the federal district court adopted a new plan involving racially gerrymandered districts and race-based busing of students. The Court, in an opinion by Chief Justice Burger, upheld the trial court's order:

> Once a right and violation have been shown, the scope of a district court's equitable powers to remedy past wrongs is broad. [But] it is important to remember that judicial powers may be exercised only on the basis of a constitutional violation. . . . The constitutional command to desegregate schools does not mean that every school in every community must always reflect the racial composition of the school system as a whole. [But here] the use made of mathematical ratios was no more than a starting point in the process of shaping a remedy, rather

than an inflexible requirement. [As] we said in *Green*, a school authority's remedial plan [is] to be judged by its effectiveness. Awareness of the racial composition of the whole school system is likely to be a useful starting point in shaping a remedy to correct past constitutional violations.

[The] existence of some small number of one-race, or virtually one-race, schools within a district is not in and of itself the mark of a system that still practices segregation by law. [But] in a system with a history of segregation the need for remedial criteria of sufficient specificity to assure a school authority's compliance with its constitutional duty warrants a presumption against schools that are substantially disproportionate in their racial composition. [As] an interim corrective measure, [pupil assignments by race] cannot be said to be beyond the broad remedial powers of a court.

Absent a constitutional violation there would be no basis for judicially ordering assignment of students on a racial basis. [But this school system was] deliberately constructed and maintained to enforce racial segregation. [Busing of pupils is also a legitimate] tool of school desegregation. . . . An objection to [busing] may have validity when the time or distance of travel is so great as to either risk the health of the children or significantly impinge on the educational process.

[At] some point, these school authorities and others like them should have achieved full compliance with this Court's decision in *Brown I*. The systems would then be "unitary." . . . Neither school authorities nor district courts are constitutionally required to make . . . adjustments of the racial composition of student bodies once the affirmative duty to desegregate has been accomplished and racial discrimination through official action is eliminated from the system. This does not mean that federal courts are without power to deal with future problems; but in the absence of a showing that either the school authorities or some other agency of the State has deliberately attempted to fix or alter demographic patterns to affect the racial composition of the schools, further intervention by a district court should not be necessary.

Keyes v. School District No. 1, 413 U.S. 189 (1973). Denver had never engaged in official racial segregation in public education. Nevertheless, a federal district court concluded that the city had deliberately maintained segregated schools in the Park Hill section through gerrymandered school zones. The district judge limited relief to the Park Hill section (where the deliberate violations had occurred) rather than ordering it system-wide. The Court reversed and remanded to the district court. Although de facto segregation violates the equal protection clause only when it was produced by intentionally invidious discrimination, "where no statutory dual system [of segregated schools] has ever existed, plaintiffs must prove not only that segregated schooling exists but also that it was brought about or maintained by intentional state action." Proof of this deliberate wrongdoing as to any part of a school system "creates a presumption that other segregated schooling within the system is not adventitious." The school system then has the "burden of proving that other segregated schools within the system are not also the result of intentionally segregative actions." To sustain that burden of proof, school officials must show either (1) that "segregative intent was not among the factors that motivated their actions" or (2) "that its past segregative acts did not create or contribute to the current segregated condition of the core city schools." In practice, proof of intentional "segregation affecting a substantial portion of the students, schools, teachers and facilities" should be enough to support system-wide remedies.

A good examination of the effect of *Brown II* is found in Michael Klarman, From Jim Crow to Civil Rights: The Supreme Court and the Struggle for Racial Equality 312-343 (2004).

5. The Limits of Judicial Remedial Power in School Desegregation. After a federal district judge had found that the Detroit schools had been unconstitutionally racially segregated, the district judge ordered 53 suburban school districts to participate in the desegregation of the Detroit public schools through interdistrict busing and other pupil assignment methods. In Milliken v. Bradley, 418 U.S. 717 (1974), the Court reversed the order:

> [T]he scope of the remedy is determined by the nature and extent of the constitutional violation. Before the boundaries of separate and autonomous school districts may be set aside [for] remedial purposes, [it] must first be shown that there has been a constitutional violation within one district that produces a significant segregative effect in another district. Specifically, it must be shown that racially discriminatory acts of the state or local school districts, or of a single school district have been a substantial cause of interdistrict segregation. Thus an interdistrict remedy might be in order where the racially discriminatory acts of one or more school districts caused racial segregation in an adjacent district, or where district lines have been deliberately drawn on the basis of race. In such circumstances an interdistrict remedy would be appropriate to eliminate the interdistrict segregation directly caused by the constitutional violation. Conversely, without an interdistrict violation and interdistrict effect, there is no constitutional wrong calling for an interdistrict remedy.

Query: Suppose that after the Detroit schools began to integrate, whites fled en masse to the suburbs but blacks were economically unable to do so. Suppose further that the suburbs constructed new schools to accommodate their new residents. Would (should) these facts be enough to support an interdistrict remedy? Why?

6. Achieving Unitary Status: The End of Judicial Supervision. A corollary to the *Milliken* principle that "the scope of the remedy is determined by the nature and extent of the constitutional violation" is that once the constitutional violation has been completely cured, judicial power to monitor the defendant should cease. Chief Justice Burger said as much in *Swann*. In the 1990s, the Court began to decide the first cases raising the issue of determining when sufficient "unitary status" has been achieved to warrant the end of judicial supervision.

Board of Education of Oklahoma City Public Schools v. Dowell, 498 U.S. 237 (1991). Oklahoma City maintained an officially racially segregated school system that since 1963 had been subject to judicial supervision. In 1977, satisfied that the city had achieved a unitary school system, the district court terminated the case. In 1984, responding to arguments that the pupil assignment scheme placed "greater burdens on young black children," the school board introduced a neighborhood school plan for grades K through 4, coupled with an option to transfer from any school in which the student was in the racial majority to any school in which the student would be part of a racial minority. The district court's denial of a motion to reopen the case was upheld by the Court. Chief Justice Rehnquist wrote for the Court:

> From the very first, federal supervision of local school systems was intended as a temporary measure to remedy past discrimination. [I]njunctions entered in school desegregation cases [are] not intended to operate in perpetuity. [The] legal justification for displacement of local authority by an injunctive decree in a school desegregation case is a violation of the Constitution by the local authorities. [A] federal court's regulatory control of [school] systems [may] not extend beyond the time required to remedy the effects of past intentional discrimination.

Unitary status is achieved and judicial control should cease when (1) all "vestiges of past discrimination" have been removed and (2) the schools are in "good faith compliance" with any existing court orders.

> A school district [that] has been released from an injunction imposing a desegregation plan no longer requires court authorization for the promulgation of policies and rules regulating matters such as assignment of students and the like, but of course remains subject to the mandates of [equal protection]. [The] Board's decision to implement [its neighborhood schools program should be evaluated] under appropriate equal protection principles [e.g., *Davis, Arlington Heights*].

Freeman v. Pitts, 503 U.S. 467 (1992). The Court applied *Dowell* in affirming a district court's partial termination of judicial supervision of the De Kalb County, Georgia, schools. Because the schools were unitary insofar as pupil assignment and physical facilities were concerned, the district court terminated its jurisdiction over those areas. The Court clarified the meaning of *Dowell*'s insistence on removal of all vestiges of past discrimination as a precondition to unitary status.

> The vestiges of segregation that are the concern of the law in a school case [must] have a causal link to the de jure violation being remedied. [But] resegregation [that] is a product not of state action but of private choices [does] not have constitutional implications. [Demographic] forces causing population change [do not necessarily] bear any real and substantial relation to a de jure violation.

Recall Palmer v. Thompson and Palmore v. Sidoti, which raised the problem of government decisions that react to or adopt private racial bias. Suppose that the De Kalb County public schools became resegregated because of private racial bias, manifested through private housing choices. Would the failure of school administrators to take action to ameliorate this resegregation be more akin to *Palmer* or to *Palmore*? Or does it fall into an entirely different category because the government has simply failed to act? Would *Green* be inapplicable because the De Kalb schools had achieved unitary status?

4. Affirmative Action

a. First Views: Bakke

≡ **Regents of the University of California v. Bakke**
≡ *438 U.S. 265 (1978)*

JUSTICE POWELL announced the judgment of the Court.

This case presents a challenge to the special admissions program of [the] Medical School of the University of California at Davis, which is designed to assure the admission of a specified number of students from certain minority groups. [The California Supreme Court upheld a lower court ruling that the special admissions program was unlawful, enjoined the U.C. Davis medical school from considering the race of any applicant, and ordered the admission of Alan Bakke, a white man.] For the reasons stated in the following opinion, I believe that so much of the judgment of the California court as holds petitioner's special admissions program unlawful and directs that respondent be admitted to the Medical School must be affirmed. For the reasons expressed in a separate opinion, [Chief Justice Burger and Justices Stewart, Rehnquist, and Stevens] concur in this judgment. I also conclude for the reasons stated in the following opinion that the portion of the court's judgment enjoining petitioner from according any consideration to race in its admissions process must be reversed. For reasons expressed in separate opinions, [Justices Brennan, White, Marshall, and Blackmun] concur in this judgment.

Affirmed in part and reversed in part.

I. [OPINION OF THE COURT].[4] The Medical School [set aside 16 places in each 100-person entering class for] "Blacks," "Chicanos," "Asians," and "American Indians," [and established a separate admissions process for those 16 spaces. Bakke applied and was rejected in 1973 and 1974.] In both years, applicants were admitted under the special program with grade point averages, MCAT scores, and benchmark scores significantly lower than Bakke's. [Because] the special admissions program involved a racial classification, the [California] Supreme Court [applied] strict scrutiny. . . . Although the court agreed that the goals of integrating the medical profession and increasing the number of physicians willing to serve members of minority groups were compelling state interests, it concluded that the

---

4. Justices Brennan, White, Marshall, and Blackmun joined Parts I and V.C of Justice Powell's opinion. Justice White also joined Part III.A. — ED.

special admissions program was not the least intrusive means of achieving those goals. . . .

III. A. [Opinion of JUSTICES POWELL and WHITE.] The parties [disagree] as to the level of judicial scrutiny to be applied to the special admissions program. [The] special admissions program is undeniably a classification based on race and ethnic background. [White] applicants could compete only for 84 seats in the entering class, rather than the 100 open to minority applicants. Whether this limitation is described as a quota or a goal, it is a line drawn on the basis of race and ethnic status. [Equal protection] extend[s] to all persons. [Nevertheless], petitioner argues that the court below erred in applying strict scrutiny [because] white males [are] not a "discrete and insular minority" requiring extraordinary protection from the majoritarian political process. . . . Racial and ethnic distinctions of any sort are inherently suspect and thus call for the most exacting judicial examination.

B. [Opinion of JUSTICE POWELL.] . . . Petitioner urges us to adopt for the first time a more restrictive view of [equal protection] and hold that discrimination against members of the white "majority" cannot be suspect if its purpose can be characterized as "benign."[5] [It] is far too late to argue that the guarantee of equal protection to *all* persons permits the recognition of special wards entitled to a degree of protection greater than that accorded others.

[The] difficulties entailed in varying the level of judicial review according to a perceived "preferred" status of a particular racial or ethnic minority are intractable. [The] white "majority" itself is composed of various minority groups, most of which can lay claim to a history of prior discrimination at the hands of the State and private individuals. [There] is no principled basis for deciding which groups would merit "heightened judicial solicitude" and which would not.

[Moreover], there are serious problems of justice connected with the idea of preference itself. First, it may not always be clear that a so-called preference is in fact benign. Courts may be asked to validate burdens imposed upon individual members of a particular group in order to advance the group's

5. In the view of [Justices Brennan, White, Marshall, and Blackmun], the pliable notion of "stigma" is the crucial element in analyzing racial classifications. The Equal Protection Clause is not framed in terms of "stigma." Certainly the word has no clearly defined constitutional meaning. It reflects a subjective judgment that is standardless. All state-imposed classifications that rearrange burdens and benefits on the basis of race are likely to be viewed with deep resentment by the individuals burdened. The denial to innocent persons of equal rights and opportunities may outrage those so deprived and therefore may be perceived as invidious. These individuals are likely to find little comfort in the notion that the deprivation they are asked to endure is merely the price of membership in the dominant majority and that its imposition is inspired by the supposedly benign purpose of aiding others. One should not lightly dismiss the inherent unfairness of, and the perception of mistreatment that accompanies, a system of allocating benefits and privileges on the basis of skin color and ethnic origin. Moreover, [the Brennan group] offer[s] no principle for deciding whether preferential classifications reflect a benign remedial purpose or a malevolent stigmatic classification, since they are willing in this case to accept mere post hoc declarations by an isolated state entity—a medical school faculty—unadorned by particularized findings of past discrimination, to establish such a remedial purpose.

general interest. Nothing in the Constitution supports the notion that individuals may be asked to suffer otherwise impermissible burdens in order to enhance the societal standing of their ethnic groups. Second, preferential programs may only reinforce common stereotypes holding that certain groups are unable to achieve success without special protection based on a factor having no relationship to individual worth. Third, [it is inequitable to force] innocent persons . . . to bear the burdens of redressing grievances not of their making. [When government classifications] touch upon an individual's race or ethnic background, he is entitled to a judicial determination that the burden he is asked to bear on that basis is precisely tailored to serve a compelling governmental interest. The Constitution guarantees that right to every person regardless of his background.

C. . . . [Here] there was no judicial determination of constitutional violation as a predicate for the formulation of a remedial classification. [We] have never approved preferential classifications in the absence of proved constitutional or statutory violations. . . . When a classification denies an individual opportunities or benefits enjoyed by others solely because of his race or ethnic background, it must be regarded as suspect.

IV. . . . The special admissions program purports to serve the purposes of (i) "reducing the historic deficit of traditionally disfavored minorities in medical schools and in the medical profession"; (ii) countering the effects of societal discrimination; (iii) increasing the number of physicians who will practice in communities currently underserved; and (iv) obtaining the educational benefits that flow from an ethnically diverse student body. It is necessary to decide which, if any, of these purposes is substantial enough to support the use of a suspect classification.

A. If petitioner's purpose is to assure within its student body some specified percentage of a particular group merely because of its race or ethnic origin, such a preferential purpose must be rejected not as insubstantial but as facially invalid. Preferring members of any one group for no reason other than race or ethnic origin is discrimination for its own sake. This the Constitution forbids.

B. The State certainly has a legitimate and substantial interest in ameliorating, or eliminating where feasible, the disabling effects of identified discrimination. [T]his state goal [is] far more focused than the remedying of the effects of "societal discrimination," an amorphous concept of injury that may be ageless in its reach into the past. We have never approved a classification that aids persons perceived as members of relatively victimized groups at the expense of other innocent individuals in the absence of judicial, legislative, or administrative findings of constitutional or statutory violations. [But without] such findings of constitutional or statutory violations, [the] government has no compelling justification for inflicting such harm. Petitioner does not purport to have made, and is in no position to make, such findings. . . . Hence, the purpose of helping certain groups whom the faculty of the Davis Medical School perceived as victims of "societal discrimination" does not justify a classification that imposes disadvantages upon persons like [Bakke]. . . .

C. [There] is virtually no evidence in the record indicating that petitioner's special admissions program is either needed or geared to promote [its claimed goal of "improving the delivery of health-care services to [underserved] communities"]. Petitioner simply has not carried its burden of demonstrating that it must prefer members of particular ethnic groups over all other individuals in order to promote better health-care delivery to deprived citizens. Indeed, petitioner has not shown that its preferential classification is likely to have any significant effect on the problem.

D. The fourth goal asserted by petitioner, [attainment] of a diverse student body, . . . is a constitutionally permissible goal for an institution of higher education. . . . [In] arguing that its universities must be accorded the right to select those students who will contribute the most to the "robust exchange of ideas," petitioner [must] be viewed as seeking to achieve a goal that is of paramount importance in the fulfillment of its mission. [As] the interest of diversity is compelling in the context of a university's admissions program, the question remains whether the program's racial classification is necessary to promote this interest.

V. A. [Petitioner's] argument that [its ethnic set-aside] is the only effective means of serving the interest of [ethnic] diversity is seriously flawed. [The] state interest . . . is not an interest in simple ethnic diversity, in which a specified percentage of the student body is in effect guaranteed to be members of selected ethnic groups. [The] diversity that furthers a compelling state interest encompasses a far broader array of qualifications and characteristics of which racial or ethnic origin is but a single though important element. Petitioner's special admissions program, focused *solely* on ethnic diversity, would hinder rather than further attainment of genuine diversity.

[The] experience of other university admissions programs [that] take race into account in achieving . . . educational diversity . . . demonstrates that the assignment of a fixed number of places to a minority group is not a necessary means toward that end. . . . Harvard College . . . "has expanded the concept of diversity to include students from disadvantaged economic, racial and ethnic groups. [In] practice, this new definition of diversity has meant that race has been a factor in some admission decisions. . . ." [Brief for Columbia, Harvard, Stanford, and the University of Pennsylvania as *amici curiae*.] In such an admissions program, race or ethnic background may be deemed a "plus" in a particular applicant's file, yet it does not insulate the individual from comparison with all other candidates for the available seats. [Race would not be the decisive factor but would become a quality considered along with such things as] exceptional personal talents, unique work or service experience, leadership potential, maturity, demonstrated compassion, a history of overcoming disadvantage, ability to communicate with the poor, or other qualifications deemed important. In short, an admissions program operated in this way is flexible enough to consider all pertinent elements of diversity in light of the particular qualifications of each applicant, and to place them on the same footing for consideration, although not necessarily according them the same weight. [This] kind of program treats each applicant as an individual in the admissions process.

[It] has been suggested that an admissions program which considers race only as one factor is simply a subtle and more sophisticated—but no less effective—means of according racial preference than the Davis program. A facial intent to discriminate, however, is evident in petitioner's preference program. . . . No such facial infirmity exists in an admissions program where race or ethnic background is simply one element—to be weighed fairly against other elements—in the selection process. [A] court would not assume that a university, professing to employ a facially nondiscriminatory admissions policy, would operate it as a cover for the functional equivalent of a quota system. In short, good faith would be presumed in the absence of a showing to the contrary in the manner permitted by our cases.[6]

B. [The] Davis special admissions program involves the use of an explicit racial classification never before countenanced by this Court. . . . The fatal flaw in petitioner's preferential program is its disregard of individual rights . . . . When a State's distribution of benefits or imposition of burdens hinges on ancestry or the color of a person's skin, that individual is entitled to a demonstration that the challenged classification is necessary to promote a substantial state interest. Petitioner has failed to carry this burden. For this reason, that portion of the California court's judgment holding petitioner's special admissions program invalid under [equal protection] must be affirmed.

C. [OPINION OF THE COURT.] In enjoining petitioner from ever considering the race of any applicant, however, the courts below failed to recognize that the State has a substantial interest that legitimately may be served by a properly devised admissions program involving the competitive consideration of race and ethnic origin. For this reason, so much of the California court's judgment as enjoins petitioner from any consideration of the race of any applicant must be reversed.

VI. [Petitioner] has conceded that it could not carry its burden of proving that, but for the existence of its unlawful special admissions program, respondent still would not have been admitted. Hence, respondent is entitled to the injunction [directing his admission to the Medical School], and that portion of the judgment must be affirmed.

---

6. Universities [may] make individualized decisions, in which ethnic background plays a part, under a presumption of legality and legitimate educational purpose. So long as the university proceeds on an individualized, case-by-case basis, there is no warrant for judicial interference in the academic process. If an applicant can establish that the institution does not adhere to a policy of individual comparisons, or can show that a systematic exclusion of certain groups results, the presumption of legality might be overcome, creating the necessity of proving legitimate educational [purpose].

JUSTICE BRENNAN, joined by JUSTICES WHITE, MARSHALL, and BLACKMUN, concurring in the judgment in part and dissenting in part.

[Government] may take race into account when it acts not to demean or insult any racial group, but to remedy disadvantages cast on minorities by past racial prejudice, at least when appropriate findings have been made by judicial, legislative, or administrative bodies with competence to act in this area. . . . Against [a] background [of racial inequality], claims that law must be "color-blind" [must] must be seen as aspiration rather than as description of reality.

[Unquestionably a] government practice or statute which [contains] "suspect classifications" is to be subjected to "strict scrutiny." [But] whites, as a class, [do not] have any of the "traditional indicia of suspectness. Nor has anyone suggested that the University's purposes contravene the cardinal principle that racial classifications that stigmatize—because they are drawn on the presumption that one race is inferior to another or because they put the weight of government behind racial hatred and separatism—are invalid without more. [A] number of considerations . . . lead us to conclude that racial classifications designed to further remedial purposes " 'must serve important governmental objectives and must be substantially related to achievement of those objectives.' " . . .

Davis's articulated purpose of remedying the effects of past societal discrimination [is] sufficiently important to justify the use of race-conscious admissions programs where there is a sound basis for concluding that minority underrepresentation is substantial and chronic, and that the handicap of past discrimination is impeding access of minorities to the Medical School. [Such] relief does not require as a predicate proof that recipients of preferential advancement have been individually discriminated against; it is enough that the recipient is within a general class of persons likely to have been the victims of discrimination. [States] also may adopt race-conscious programs designed to overcome substantial, chronic minority underrepresentation where there is reason to believe that the evil addressed is a product of past racial discrimination. [Thus,] Davis's goal of admitting minority students disadvantaged by the effects of past discrimination is sufficiently important to justify use of race-conscious admissions criteria. . . .

[The] second prong of our test—whether the Davis program stigmatizes any discrete group or individual and whether race is reasonably used in light of the program's objectives—is clearly satisfied by the Davis program. [True], whites are excluded from participation in the special admissions program [but the] use of racial preferences for remedial purposes does not inflict a pervasive injury upon individual whites in the sense that wherever they go or whatever they do there is a significant likelihood that they will be treated as second-class citizens because of their color. . . . The program does not establish a quota in the invidious sense of a ceiling on the number of minority applicants to be admitted. Nor can the program reasonably be regarded as stigmatizing the program's beneficiaries or their race as inferior. The Davis program . . . compensates applicants, who it is uncontested are fully qualified to study medicine, for educational disadvantages which it was reasonable to conclude were a product of state-fostered discrimination. . . .

JUSTICE MARSHALL.

[During] most of the past 200 years, the Constitution as interpreted by this Court did not prohibit the most ingenious and pervasive forms of discrimination against the Negro. Now, when a State acts to remedy the effects of that legacy of discrimination, I cannot believe that this same Constitution stands as a barrier. [The] legacy of years of slavery and of years of second-class citizenship in the wake of emancipation [are not] easily eliminated. The position of the Negro today in America is the tragic but inevitable consequence of centuries of unequal treatment.

[It] is more than a little ironic that, after several hundred years of class-based discrimination against Negroes, the Court is unwilling to hold that a class-based remedy for that discrimination is permissible. [The] dream of America as the great melting pot has not been realized for the Negro; because of his skin color he never even made it into the pot. These differences in the experience of the Negro make it difficult for me to accept that Negroes cannot be afforded greater protection under the Fourteenth Amendment where it is necessary to remedy the effects of past [societal discrimination].

JUSTICE BLACKMUN.

[In] order to get beyond racism, we must first take account of race. There is no other way. And in order to treat some persons equally, we must treat them differently. . . .

JUSTICE STEVENS, joined by CHIEF JUSTICE BURGER and JUSTICES STEWART and REHNQUIST, concurring in the judgment in part and dissenting in part.

[Our] settled practice [is] to avoid the decision of a constitutional issue if a case can be fairly decided on a statutory ground. [Only if U.C. Davis] should prevail on the statutory [Title VI] issue would it be necessary to decide whether the University's admissions program violated [equal protection]. [The] meaning of [Title VI] is crystal clear: Race cannot be the basis of excluding anyone from participation in a federally funded program. [The] University's special admissions program violated Title VI of the Civil Rights Act of 1964 by excluding Bakke from the Medical School because of his race. It is therefore our duty to affirm the judgment ordering Bakke admitted to the University. . . .

Note on the Meaning of *Bakke*

Even though Justice Powell wrote mostly for himself, his was the opinion that mattered most. According to Marks v. United States, 430 U.S. 188, 193 (1977): "When a fragmented Court decides a case and no single rationale explaining the result enjoys the assent of five Justices, 'the holding of the Court may be viewed as that position taken by those Members who concurred in the judgments on the narrowest grounds. . . .'"

The Stevens group never reached the constitutional issue, and the Brennan group would have adopted a relaxed form of intermediate scrutiny to test the validity of "benign" racial classifications—those adopted to remedy the present effects of societal racial discrimination. The Powell opinion presented the narrowest rationale that would command five votes, even if not all five of those justices actually joined in the rationale. Thus, in succeeding years the content of remedial affirmative action programs was driven by the Powell opinion.

Wygant v. Jackson Board of Education, 476 U.S. 297 (1986), reflects this influence. The Jackson, Michigan, public school district settled a racial discrimination suit by agreeing to take "affirmative steps" to hire minority teachers. When adverse economic conditions mandated layoffs of some teachers, the school board and the teachers' union agreed that teachers would be dismissed in inverse order of seniority, except that the proportion of minority teachers dismissed would not exceed the total proportion of minority teachers in the work force prior to the layoffs. This racial criterion resulted in the dismissal of some white teachers who had greater seniority than retained minority teachers. The Court held that the racially preferential layoffs violated equal protection but could not form a majority as to the reasons. The plurality opinion, authored by Justice Powell, applied strict scrutiny and concluded that "societal discrimination alone is [not] sufficient to justify a racial classification." Powell noted that "the Court has insisted upon some showing of prior discrimination by the governmental unit involved before allowing limited use of racial classifications in order to remedy such discrimination." When such race-conscious remedies are attacked, the challenger must prove that the government lacked "a strong basis in evidence for its conclusion that remedial action was necessary." In any case, said Powell, the layoff plan was "not sufficiently narrowly tailored" to the compelling objective of remedying past unlawful discrimination by the Jackson schools: "While hiring goals impose a diffuse burden, [layoffs] impose the entire burden of achieving racial equity on particular individuals" who are not themselves guilty of unlawful action. This "burden is too intrusive," especially since "[o]ther, less intrusive means [are] available."

b. General Principles

≡ *City of Richmond v. J.A. Croson Co.*
488 U.S. 469 (1989)

JUSTICE O'CONNOR announced the judgment of the Court and delivered the opinion of the Court with respect to Parts I, III.B, and IV, an opinion with respect to Part II, in which CHIEF JUSTICE REHNQUIST and JUSTICE WHITE joined, and an opinion with respect to Parts III.A and V, in which CHIEF JUSTICE REHNQUIST and JUSTICES WHITE and KENNEDY joined.

In this case, we confront once again the tension between the [constitutional] guarantee of equal treatment to all citizens, and the use of race-based measures to ameliorate the effects of past discrimination on the opportunities enjoyed by members of minority groups in our society. In Fullilove v. Klutznick, 448 U.S. 448 (1980), we held that a congressional program requiring that 10% of certain federal construction grants be awarded to minority contractors did not violate [equal protection, because Congress was entitled to deference concerning its conclusion that the federal government's "traditional procurement practices, when applied to minority businesses, could perpetuate the effects of past discrimination." But *Fullilove* did not say precisely what standard of review it was using to reach this conclusion and expressly disclaimed adoption of either the Powell or Brennan view in *Bakke*.] . . . We [now] consider . . . a minority set-aside program adopted by the city of Richmond, Virginia.

I. [OPINION OF THE COURT.] [Richmond's] Minority Business Utilization Plan (the Plan), [required] prime contractors to whom the city awarded construction contracts to subcontract at least 30% of the dollar amount of the contract to one or more Minority Business Enterprises (MBEs). The Plan defined an MBE as "[a] business at least fifty-one (51) percent of which is owned and controlled [by] minority group members," [defined] as "[c]itizens of the United States who are Blacks, Spanish-speaking, Orientals, Indians, Eskimos, or Aleuts." There was no geographic limit to the Plan; an otherwise qualified MBE from anywhere in the United States could avail itself of the 30% set-aside.

[The] Plan was adopted by the Richmond City Council, [relying] on a study which indicated that, while the general population of Richmond was 50% black, only 0.67% of the city's prime construction contracts had been awarded to minority businesses in the 5-year period from 1978 to 1983. It was also established that a variety of contractors' associations [had] virtually no minority businesses within their membership. . . . There was no direct evidence of race discrimination on the part of the city in letting contracts or any evidence that the city's prime contractors had discriminated against minority-owned subcontractors.

[Croson Co., a general plumbing contractor, brought suit after its winning bid on a city project was rejected for lack of an MBE subcontractor. A federal District Court upheld the Plan, and the Court of Appeals reversed, ruling that the Plan failed] both prongs of strict scrutiny under [equal protection. We] now affirm.

II. [Opinion of JUSTICE O'CONNOR, joined by CHIEF JUSTICE REHNQUIST and JUSTICE WHITE.] [Richmond relies] heavily on *Fullilove* for the proposition that a city council, like Congress, need not make specific findings of discrimination to engage in race-conscious relief. [That] Congress may identify and redress the effects of society-wide discrimination does not mean that, a fortiori, the States and their political subdivisions are free to decide that such remedies are appropriate. Section 1 of the Fourteenth Amendment is an explicit *constraint* on state power, and the States must undertake any remedial efforts in accordance with that provision. . . . [Richmond] has legislative authority over its procurement policies, and can use its spending powers to remedy private discrimination, if it identifies that discrimination with the particularity required by the Fourteenth Amendment. [Thus], if the city could show that it had essentially become a "passive participant" in a system of racial exclusion practiced by elements of the local construction industry, we think it clear that the city could take affirmative steps to dismantle such a system. It is beyond dispute that any public entity, state or federal, has a compelling interest in assuring that public dollars, drawn from the tax contributions of all citizens, do not serve to finance the evil of private prejudice.

III. A. [Opinion of Justice O'Connor, joined by Chief Justice Rehnquist and Justices White and Kennedy.] . . . [The equal protection] "rights created by the first section of the Fourteenth Amendment are, by its terms, guaranteed to the individual. The rights established are personal rights." Shelley v. Kraemer, 334 U.S. 1, 22 (1948). The Richmond Plan denies certain citizens the opportunity to compete for a fixed percentage of public contracts based solely upon their race. To whatever racial group these citizens belong, their "personal rights" to be treated with equal dignity and respect are implicated by a rigid rule erecting race as the sole criterion in an aspect of public decisionmaking. . . .

[T]he purpose of strict scrutiny is to "smoke out" illegitimate uses of race by assuring that the legislative body is pursuing a goal important enough to warrant use of a highly suspect tool. The test also ensures that the means chosen "fit" this compelling goal so closely that there is little or no possibility that the motive for the classification was illegitimate racial prejudice or stereotype. We thus reaffirm the view expressed by the plurality in *Wygant* that the standard of review under [equal protection] is not dependent on the race of those burdened or benefited by a particular classification. . . . [The] dissent's watered-down version of equal protection review effectively assures that race will always be relevant in American [life]. . . .

B. [Opinion of the Court.] [The] District Court found the city council's "findings sufficient to ensure that, in adopting the Plan, it was remedying the present effects of past discrimination in the *construction industry.*" [A] generalized assertion that there has been past discrimination in an entire industry provides no guidance for a legislative body to determine the precise scope of the injury it seeks to remedy. It "has no logical stopping point." "Relief" for such an ill-defined wrong could extend until the percentage of public contracts awarded to MBEs in Richmond mirrored the percentage of minorities in the population as a whole. . . . While there is no doubt that the sorry history of both private and public discrimination in this country has contributed to a lack of opportunities for black entrepreneurs, this observation, standing alone, cannot justify a rigid racial quota in the awarding of public contracts in Richmond, Virginia. Like the claim that discrimination in primary and secondary schooling justifies a rigid racial preference in medical school admissions, an amorphous claim that there has been past discrimination in a particular industry cannot justify the use of an unyielding racial quota.

It is sheer speculation how many minority firms there would be in Richmond absent past societal discrimination, just as it was sheer speculation how many minority medical students would have been admitted to the medical school at Davis absent past discrimination in educational opportunities. Defining these sorts of injuries as "identified discrimination" would give local governments license to create a patchwork of racial preferences based on statistical generalizations about any particular field of endeavor.

These defects are readily apparent in this case. The 30% quota cannot in any realistic sense be tied to any injury suffered by anyone. . . . There is nothing approaching a prima facie case of a constitutional or statutory violation by *anyone* in the Richmond construction industry.

The District Court accorded great weight to the fact that the city council designated the Plan as "remedial." But the mere recitation of a "benign" or legitimate purpose for a racial classification is entitled to little or no weight. Racial classifications are suspect, and that means that simple legislative assurances of good intention cannot suffice.

The District Court also relied on the highly conclusionary statement of a proponent of the Plan that there was racial discrimination in the construction industry "in this area, and the State, and around the nation." . . . [When] a legislative body chooses to employ a suspect classification, it cannot rest upon a generalized assertion as to the classification's relevance to its goals. [The] history of racial classifications in this country suggests that blind judicial deference to legislative or executive pronouncements of necessity has no place in equal protection analysis. Reliance on the disparity between the number of prime contracts awarded to minority firms and the minority population of the city of Richmond is similarly misplaced. [Where] special qualifications are necessary, the relevant statistical pool for purposes of demonstrating discriminatory exclusion must be the number of minorities qualified to undertake the particular task. In this case, the city does not even know how many MBEs in the relevant market are qualified to undertake prime or subcontracting work in public construction projects. Nor does the city know what percentage of total city construction dollars minority firms now receive as subcontractors on prime contracts let by the city. [Without] any information on minority participation in subcontracting, it is quite simply impossible to evaluate overall minority representation in the city's construction expenditures.

The city and the District Court also relied on evidence that MBE membership in local contractors' associations was extremely low. [Standing] alone this evidence is not probative of any discrimination in the local construction industry. . . . [For] low minority membership in these associations to be relevant, the city would have to link it to the number of local MBEs eligible for membership. If the statistical disparity between eligible MBEs and MBE membership were great enough, an inference of discriminatory exclusion could arise.

Finally, the city and the District Court relied on [a congressional] finding [that] there had been nationwide discrimination in the construction industry. The probative value of these findings for demonstrating the existence of discrimination in Richmond is extremely limited. [While] the States and their subdivisions may take remedial action when they possess evidence that their own spending practices are exacerbating a pattern of prior discrimination, they must identify that discrimination, public or private, with some specificity before they may use race conscious relief. . . . [N]one of the evidence presented by the city points to any identified discrimination in the Richmond construction industry. We, therefore, hold that the city has failed to demonstrate a compelling interest in apportioning public contracting opportunities on the basis of race. . . .

The foregoing analysis applies only to the inclusion of blacks within the Richmond set-aside program. There is *absolutely no evidence* of past discrimination against Spanish-speaking, Oriental, Indian, Eskimo, or Aleut persons in any aspect of the Richmond construction industry. [It] may well be that Richmond has never had an Aleut or Eskimo citizen. The random inclusion of racial groups that, as a practical matter, may never have suffered from discrimination in the construction industry in Richmond suggests that perhaps the city's purpose was not in fact to remedy past discrimination. If a 30% set-aside was "narrowly tailored" to compensate black contractors for past discrimination, one may legitimately ask why they are forced to share this "remedial relief" with an Aleut citizen who moves to Richmond tomorrow[.] The gross overinclusiveness of Richmond's racial preference strongly impugns the city's claim of remedial motivation.

IV. [OPINION OF THE COURT.] [It] is almost impossible to assess whether the Richmond Plan is narrowly tailored to remedy prior discrimination since it is not linked to identified discrimination in any way. We limit ourselves to two observations in this regard. First, there does not appear to have been any consideration of the use of race-neutral means to increase minority business participation in city contracting. [There] is no evidence [that] the Richmond City Council [considered] any alternatives to a race-based quota.

Second, the 30% quota cannot be said to be narrowly tailored to any goal, except perhaps outright racial balancing. It rests upon the "completely unrealistic" assumption that minorities will choose a particular trade in lock-step proportion to their representation in the local population. [T]here is no inquiry into whether or not the particular MBE seeking a racial preference has suffered from the effects of past discrimination by the city or prime contractors. . . . Under Richmond's scheme, a successful black, Hispanic, or Oriental entrepreneur from anywhere in the country enjoys an absolute preference over other citizens based solely on their race. We think it obvious that such a program is not narrowly tailored to remedy the effects of prior discrimination.

V. [Opinion of JUSTICE O'CONNOR, joined by CHIEF JUSTICE REHNQUIST and JUSTICES WHITE and KENNEDY.] [The] city has at its disposal a whole array of race-neutral devices to increase the accessibility of city contracting opportunities to small entrepreneurs of all races. . . . [But here the] city points to no evidence that qualified minority contractors have been passed over for city contracts or subcontracts, either as a group or in any individual case. Under such circumstances, it is simply impossible to say that the city has demonstrated "a strong basis in evidence for its conclusion that remedial action was necessary." Proper findings . . . are necessary to define both the scope of the injury and the extent of the remedy necessary to cure its effects . . . . Absent such findings, there is a danger that a racial classification is merely the product of unthinking stereotypes or a form of racial politics. Because [Richmond] has failed to identify the need for remedial action in the awarding of its public construction contracts, its treatment of its citizens on a racial basis violates [equal protection].

JUSTICE STEVENS, concurring in part and concurring in the judgment.
. . . [T]his litigation involves an attempt by a legislative body, rather than a court, to fashion a remedy for a past wrong. Legislatures are primarily policy-making bodies that promulgate rules to govern future conduct. [It] is the judicial system, rather than the legislative process, that is best equipped to identify past wrongdoers and to fashion remedies that will create the conditions that presumably would have existed had no wrong been committed. . . .

JUSTICE SCALIA, concurring in the judgment.
I agree with [the] conclusion that strict scrutiny must be applied to all governmental classification by race, whether or not its asserted purpose is "remedial" or "benign." I do not agree, however, with [the dicta] suggesting [that] state and local governments may in some circumstances discriminate on the basis of race in order (in a broad sense) "to ameliorate the effects of past discrimination." The benign purpose of compensating for social disadvantages, whether they have been acquired by reason of prior discrimination or otherwise, can[not] be pursued by the illegitimate means of racial discrimination. . . . The difficulty of overcoming the effects of past discrimination is as nothing compared with the difficulty of eradicating from our society the source of those effects, which is the tendency—fatal to a Nation such as ours—to classify and judge men and women on the basis of their country of origin or the color of their skin. A solution to the first problem that aggravates the second is no solution at all. I share the view expressed by Alexander Bickel that "[discrimination] on the basis of race is illegal, immoral, unconstitutional, inherently wrong, and destructive of democratic society." A. Bickel, The Morality of Consent 133 (1975). At least where state or local action is at issue, only a social emergency rising to the level of imminent danger to life and limb—for example, a prison race riot, requiring temporary segregation of inmates—can justify an exception to the principle [that] "[o]ur Constitution is [color-blind]."

In my view there is only one circumstance in which the States may act by race to "undo the effects of past discrimination": where that is necessary to eliminate their own maintenance of a system of unlawful racial classification. . . . [But] we have also made it clear that the remedial power extends no further than the scope of the continuing constitutional violation. And it is implicit in our cases that after the dual school system has been completely disestablished, the States may no longer assign students by race. . . .

It is plainly true that in our society blacks have suffered discrimination immeasurably greater than any directed at other racial groups. But those who

believe that racial preferences can help to "even the score" display, and reinforce, a manner of thinking by race that was the source of the injustice and that
will, if it endures within our society, be the source of more injustice still. The
relevant proposition is not that it was blacks, or Jews, or Irish who were discriminated against, but that it was individual men and women, "created equal,"
who were discriminated against. And the relevant resolve is that that should
never happen again. . . . Since blacks have been disproportionately disadvantaged by racial discrimination, any race-neutral remedial program aimed at the
disadvantaged *as such* will have a disproportionately beneficial impact on blacks.
Only such a program, and not one that operates on the basis of race, is in accord
with the letter and the spirit of our Constitution. Since I believe that [Croson]
had a constitutional right to have its bid succeed or fail under a decisionmaking
process uninfected with racial bias, I concur in the judgment of the Court.

JUSTICE MARSHALL, joined by JUSTICES BRENNAN and BLACKMUN, dissenting.
. . . [My] view has long been that race-conscious classifications designed
to further remedial goals "must serve important governmental objectives and
must be substantially related to achievement of those objectives" in order to
withstand constitutional scrutiny. Analyzed in terms of this two-pronged standard, Richmond's set-aside [is] "plainly constitutional." . . .

NOTE

A year later the Court, by a 5-4 vote, decided Metro Broadcasting v.
FCC, 497 U.S. 547 (1990), in which it upheld the validity of a racial preference system in the award or transfer of federal broadcast licenses. Justice
Brennan's majority opinion stated that "benign" racial preferences used by
the federal government would be subjected to intermediate scrutiny:

> We hold that benign race-conscious measures mandated by Congress—even if
> those measures are not "remedial" in the sense of being designed to compensate
> victims of past governmental or societal discrimination—are constitutionally
> permissible to the extent they serve important governmental objectives within
> the power of Congress and are substantially related to the accomplishment of
> those objectives.

That ruling produced an odd standard: Identical conduct would be evaluated differently, depending on whether a state or the federal government
engaged in it. For all practical purposes the federal government was able to
engage in "benign" racial discrimination and states were not. The Court's justification for this rule was that Congress was entitled to more deference than
the states, even though it had previously stated that the scope of equal protection was the same whether applied to the federal or to state governments. But
Metro Broadcasting's life was short.

≣ *Adarand Constructors, Inc. v. Pena*
515 U.S. 200 (1995)

JUSTICE O'CONNOR announced the judgment of the Court and delivered an opinion with respect to Parts I, II, III.A, III.B, III.D, and IV, which was for the Court except insofar as it might be inconsistent with the views expressed in JUSTICE SCALIA's concurrence, and an opinion with respect to Part III.C, in which JUSTICE KENNEDY joined.

[OPINION OF THE COURT.] [Adarand] claims that the Federal Government's practice of giving general contractors on government projects a financial incentive to hire subcontractors controlled by "socially and economically disadvantaged individuals," and in particular, the Government's use of race-based presumptions in identifying such individuals, violates the equal protection component of the Fifth Amendment's Due Process Clause. The Court of Appeals rejected Adarand's claim. We conclude . . . that courts should analyze cases of this kind under a different standard of review than the one the Court of Appeals applied. We therefore vacate the Court of Appeals' judgment and remand the case for further proceedings.

I. In 1989, [the federal government] awarded the prime contract for a highway construction project in Colorado to Mountain Gravel, [which] then solicited bids from subcontractors for the guardrail portion of the contract. Adarand, a [company] specializing in guardrail work, submitted the low bid. Gonzales Construction Company also submitted a bid. The prime contract's terms provide that Mountain Gravel would receive additional compensation if it hired subcontractors certified as small businesses controlled by "socially and economically disadvantaged individuals." Gonzales is certified as such a business; Adarand is not. Mountain Gravel awarded the subcontract to Gonzales, despite Adarand's low bid, [but] has submitted an affidavit stating that Mountain Gravel would have accepted Adarand's bid[ ] had it not been for the additional payment it received by hiring Gonzales instead. Federal law requires that a subcontracting clause similar to the one used here must appear in most federal agency contracts, and it also requires the clause to state that "the contractor shall presume that socially and economically disadvantaged individuals include Black Americans, Hispanic Americans, Native Americans, Asian Pacific Americans, and other [racial minorities]." Adarand claims that the presumption set forth in that statute discriminates on the basis of race in violation of the Federal Government's Fifth Amendment obligation not to deny anyone equal protection of the laws. . . .

III. The Government [concedes] that "the race-based rebuttable presumption . . ." is subject to some heightened level of scrutiny. The parties disagree as to what that level should be. . . .

A. [Our prior cases] did not distinguish between the duties of the States and the Federal Government to avoid racial classifications, [but have treated] the equal protection obligations imposed by the Fifth and the Fourteenth

Amendments as indistinguishable. [See] Karst, The Fifth Amendment's Guarantee of Equal Protection, 55 N.C. L. Rev. 541, 554 (1977).

B. . . . [In] *Croson*, the Court finally agreed that the Fourteenth Amendment requires strict scrutiny of all race-based action by state and local governments. But *Croson* of course had no occasion to declare what standard of review the Fifth Amendment requires for such action taken by the Federal Government. [H]owever, the Court's cases through *Croson* had established three general propositions with respect to governmental racial classifications. First, skepticism: "'any preference based on racial or ethnic criteria must necessarily receive a most searching examination,'" *Wygant*. Second, consistency: "the standard of review under the Equal Protection Clause is not dependent on the race of those burdened or benefited by a particular classification," *Croson*. [All] racial classifications reviewable under the Equal Protection Clause must be strictly scrutinized. And third, congruence: "equal protection analysis in the Fifth Amendment area is the same as that under the Fourteenth Amendment." Taken together, these three propositions lead to the conclusion that any person, of whatever race, has the right to demand that any governmental actor subject to the Constitution justify any racial classification subjecting that person to unequal treatment under the strictest judicial scrutiny.

[The] basic principle [of equal protection is that it] protect[s] persons, not groups. It follows from that principle that all governmental action based on race [should] be subjected to detailed judicial inquiry to ensure that the personal right to equal protection [has] not been infringed. These ideas have long been central to this Court's understanding of equal protection, and holding "benign" state and federal racial classifications to different standards does not square with [them]. Accordingly, we hold today that all racial classifications, imposed by whatever federal, state, or local governmental actor, must be analyzed by a reviewing court under strict scrutiny. [To] the extent that *Metro Broadcasting* is inconsistent with that holding, it is overruled.

. . . The principle of consistency simply means that whenever the government treats any person unequally because of his or her race, that person has suffered an injury that falls squarely within the language and spirit of the Constitution's guarantee of equal protection. It says nothing about the ultimate validity of any particular law; that determination is the job of the court applying strict scrutiny. The principle of consistency explains the circumstances in which the injury requiring strict scrutiny occurs. The application of strict scrutiny, in turn, determines whether a compelling governmental interest justifies the infliction of that injury. . . .

D. Our action today makes explicit [that] federal racial classifications, like those of a State, must serve a compelling governmental interest, and must be narrowly tailored to further that interest. [To] the extent (if any) that *Fullilove* held federal racial classifications to be subject to a less rigorous standard, it is no longer controlling. . . . Finally, we wish to dispel the notion that strict scrutiny is "strict in theory, but fatal in fact." [When] race-based action is necessary to further a compelling interest, such action is within constitutional constraints if it satisfies the "narrow tailoring" test this Court has set out in previous cases.

IV. Because our decision today alters the playing field in some important respects, we think it best to remand the case to the lower courts for further consideration in light of the principles we have announced.

JUSTICE SCALIA, concurring in part and concurring in the judgment.

In my view, government can never have a "compelling interest" in discriminating on the basis of race in order to "make up" for past racial discrimination in the opposite direction. Individuals who have been wronged by unlawful racial discrimination should be made whole; but under our Constitution there can be no such thing as either a creditor or a debtor race. That concept is alien to the Constitution's focus upon the individual, and its rejection of dispositions based on race. [To] pursue the concept of racial entitlement—even for the most admirable and benign of purposes—is to reinforce and preserve for future mischief the way of thinking that produced race slavery, race privilege, and race hatred. In the eyes of government, we are just one race here. It is American. . . .

JUSTICE THOMAS, concurring in part and concurring in the judgment.

I agree . . . that strict scrutiny applies to all government classifications based on race. I write separately . . . to express my disagreement with the premise . . . that there is a racial paternalism exception to the principle of equal protection. I believe that there is a "moral [and] constitutional equivalence" between laws designed to subjugate a race and those that distribute benefits on the basis of race in order to foster some current notion of equality. Government cannot make us equal; it can only recognize, respect, and protect us as equal before the law. That these programs may have been motivated . . . by good intentions cannot provide refuge from the principle that under our Constitution, the government may not make distinctions on the basis of race. As far as the Constitution is concerned, it is irrelevant whether a government's racial classifications are drawn by those who wish to oppress a race or by those who have a sincere desire to help those thought to be disadvantaged. There can be no doubt that the paternalism that appears to lie at the heart of this program is at war with the principle of inherent equality that underlies and infuses our Constitution.

[R]acial paternalism and its unintended consequences can be as poisonous and pernicious as any other form of discrimination. So-called "benign" discrimination teaches many that . . . minorities cannot compete with them without their patronizing indulgence. Inevitably, such programs engender attitudes of superiority or, alternatively, provoke resentment among those who believe that they have been wronged by the government's use of race. These programs stamp minorities with a badge of inferiority and may cause them to develop dependencies or to adopt an attitude that they are "entitled" to preferences. [In] my mind, government-sponsored racial discrimination based on benign prejudice is just as noxious as discrimination inspired by malicious prejudice. In each instance, it is racial discrimination, plain and simple.

JUSTICE STEVENS, joined by JUSTICE GINSBURG, dissenting.

. . . The Court. . . . assumes that there is no significant difference between a decision by the majority to impose a special burden on the members of a minority race and a decision by the majority to provide a benefit to certain members of that minority notwithstanding its incidental burden on some members of the majority. . . . There is no moral or constitutional equivalence between a policy that is designed to perpetuate a caste system and one that seeks to eradicate racial subordination. Invidious discrimination is an engine of oppression, subjugating a disfavored group to enhance or maintain the power of the majority. Remedial race-based preferences reflect the opposite impulse: a desire to foster equality in society. [The] consistency that the Court espouses would disregard the difference between a "No Trespassing" sign and a welcome mat. [The] Court's explanation for treating dissimilar race-based decisions as though they were equally objectionable is a supposed inability to differentiate between "invidious" and "benign" discrimination. But . . . people understand the difference between good intentions and bad. . . .

JUSTICE GINSBURG, joined by JUSTICE BREYER, dissenting.

[T]he persistence of racial inequality [is] evident in our workplaces, markets, and neighborhoods. Job applicants with identical resumes, qualifications, and interview styles still experience different receptions, depending on their race. White and African-American consumers still encounter different deals. People of color looking for housing still face discriminatory treatment by landlords, real estate agents, and mortgage lenders. Minority entrepreneurs sometimes fail to gain contracts though they are the low bidders, and they are sometimes refused work even after winning contracts. Bias both conscious and unconscious, reflecting traditional and unexamined habits of thought, keeps up barriers that must come down if equal opportunity and nondiscrimination are ever genuinely to become this country's law and practice. Given this history and its practical consequences, Congress surely can conclude that a carefully designed affirmative-action program may help to realize, finally, the "equal protection of the laws" the Fourteenth Amendment has promised since [1868].

NOTES AND PROBLEMS

1. Conflicting Visions. The essential conflict in *Croson* and *Adarand* is between two visions of how to reach a common goal: a society in which race is as irrelevant as eye color. One vision is that "to get beyond [race], we must first take account of race." To adherents of this vision, the cost of perpetuating racial consciousness in government decisions is less than the benefits of structural alterations in the name of racial justice. Once outcomes are more equal, this camp argues, racial consciousness will subside and fade away. So, too, will the need for race-conscious remedial measures.

The opposite vision is that racial consciousness is itself a cancer, a malignancy that inevitably promotes racism. The goal of a society free of racial consciousness will be frustrated so long as racially conscious government decisions are employed for anything other than to remedy specific, identifiable wrongdoing. To redress three centuries of racial wrongs by a new, compensatory scheme of racial entitlements is a cure that is worse than the disease. It perpetuates racial division, ignores the fact that the equal protection guarantee protects individuals, and is rooted in the concept, alien to the Constitution, that there is "such [a] thing as either a creditor or a debtor race."

A secondary conflict is the somewhat more technical issue of whether equal protection imposes identical limits on the states and the federal government. State governments were surely intended to be bound by the equal protection guarantee, and on the matter of race there is ample reason to believe that states have been particularly prone to abuse of the guarantee. But is there adequate reason to think that the federal government is much less likely to deny equal protection? The sorry history of the forcible exclusion of Japanese Americans from the West Coast in World War II and its constitutional ratification in *Korematsu* is not much cause for comfort.

The case for added deference to Congress cannot be made simply because Congress is the national legislature. The question is whether there is some institutional reason Congress is less likely than state legislatures to deny equal protection. Congressional judgments about interstate commerce are surely to be preferred to the inherently more parochial judgments of the states on such matters. But can the same be said of racial classifications?

2. Further Questions.   How much government involvement in private racial discrimination is needed to demonstrate that its race-based remedial measures are narrowly tailored to achieve the compelling objective of remedying government complicity in unlawful racial discrimination? Does "passive involvement" include unwitting government participation in private racial discrimination, or does it imply some government knowledge? What standard of proof is necessary to establish the requisite level of government involvement? Who should be entitled to make the remedial decision—courts only, courts and state legislatures, courts and any legislative body, or any government actor wielding significant and broad authority?

3. Problems: *Reparations for Slavery.*   Suppose that Congress appropriated a large sum of money to be expended in cash grants to Americans who can prove that they had an ancestor enslaved in America.

African History and Culture.   Suppose that a state appropriates money to fund the teaching in public schools the distinct subject of African history and culture, including the impact of Africa and its people on American history and culture, but stipulates that only people of African ancestry may teach the subject.

What level of scrutiny would apply to an equal protection challenge to either program? Is either program constitutionally valid?

4. Problem: *Avoiding Statutory Liability.* Title VII of the 1964 Civil Rights Act forbids any "employment practice that causes a disparate impact on the basis of race" unless the employer can show that the practice is job-related and consistent with business necessity. Suppose a City uses a reasonably necessary job-related test to make promotion decisions, but the test delivers racially disparate outcomes. Because it fears disparate impact liability under Title VII, the City refuses to use the test results and denies promotion to those who qualified under the test. Did the City violate the equal protection clause? See Ricci v. DeStefano, 557 U.S. 557 (2009).

c. Public Universities and Public Schools

Grutter v. Bollinger
539 U.S. 306 (2003)

JUSTICE O'CONNOR delivered the opinion of the Court.

This case requires us to decide whether the use of race as a factor in student admissions by the University of Michigan Law School (Law School) is unlawful.

I. The Law School . . . receives more than 3,500 applications each year for a class of around 350 students. Seeking to "admit a group of students who individually and collectively are among the most capable," the Law School . . . seeks "a mix of students with varying backgrounds and experiences who will respect and learn from each other." [The] written admissions policy to implement these goals [focuses] on academic ability coupled with a flexible assessment of applicants' talents, experiences, and potential "to contribute to the learning of those around them." . . . [The] policy requires admissions officials to look beyond grades and test scores to other criteria that are important to the Law School's educational objectives. So-called "'soft' variables" such as "the enthusiasm of recommenders, the quality of the undergraduate institution, the quality of the applicant's essay, and the areas and difficulty of undergraduate course selection" are all brought to bear in assessing an "applicant's likely contributions to the intellectual and social life of the institution." The policy aspires to "achieve that diversity which has the potential to enrich everyone's education and thus make a law school class stronger than the sum of its parts." The policy . . . recognizes "many possible bases for diversity admissions" [but] reaffirm[s] the Law School's longstanding commitment to "one particular type of diversity," that is, "racial and ethnic diversity with special reference to the inclusion of students from groups which have been historically discriminated against, like African-Americans, Hispanics and Native Americans, who without this commitment might not be represented in our student body in meaningful numbers." By enrolling a "'critical mass' of [underrepresented] minority students," the Law School seeks to "ensure their ability to make unique contributions to the character of the Law School." . . .

Petitioner Barbara Grutter is a white Michigan resident who applied to the Law School in 1996 with a 3.8 grade point average and 161 LSAT score. [After the Law School rejected her, Grutter filed suit in federal district court, alleging that the Law School had] discriminated against her on the basis of race in violation of the Fourteenth Amendment. . . . [Grutter] alleged that her application was rejected because the Law School uses race as a "predominant" factor, giving applicants who belong to certain minority groups "a significantly greater chance of admission than students with similar credentials from disfavored racial groups," [and that the Law School] "had no compelling interest to justify [its] use of race in the admissions process." . . .

[Following a court trial, the district judge ruled that "the Law School's use of race as a factor in admissions decisions was unlawful" because the Law School's "asserted interest in assembling a diverse student body was not compelling" and that, even if it was a compelling interest, "the Law School had not narrowly tailored its use of race to further that interest." The trial record indicated that (1) the admissions director consulted a daily report of "the racial and ethnic composition of the class" . . . to ensure that the Law School enrolled a critical mass of underrepresented minority students; (2) a "critical mass" means "meaningful numbers," sufficient to encourage minority students to participate in the classroom and not feel isolated; (3) a "critical mass of underrepresented minority students could not be enrolled if admissions decisions were based primarily on undergraduate GPAs and LSAT scores"; (4) in some cases the race of an applicant was a "determinative" factor in the admissions decision; (5) the admissions policy did not include Asians and Jews because they "were already being admitted to the Law School in significant numbers"; (6) the educational benefit of a "critical mass" of minority students is that "racial stereotypes lose their force because nonminority students learn there is no 'minority viewpoint' but rather a variety of viewpoints among minority students"; (7) race " 'is an extremely strong factor in the decision for acceptance' "; and (8) "if race were not considered . . . 'underrepresented minority students would have comprised 4 percent of the entering class in 2000 instead of the actual figure of 14.5 percent.' "]

Sitting en banc, the Court of Appeals reversed the District Court's judgment. . . . We granted certiorari to resolve . . . [w]hether diversity is a compelling interest that can justify the narrowly tailored use of race in selecting applicants for admission to public universities.

II. . . . Because the Fourteenth Amendment "protects *persons*, not *groups*," all . . . racial classifications imposed by government "must be analyzed by a reviewing court under strict scrutiny." This means that such classifications are constitutional only if they are narrowly tailored to further compelling governmental interests. . . . Context matters when reviewing race-based governmental action. . . . Not every decision influenced by race is equally objectionable and strict scrutiny is designed to provide a framework for carefully examining the importance and the sincerity of the reasons advanced by the governmental decisionmaker for the use of race in that particular context.

III. . . . [T]he Law School has a compelling interest in attaining a diverse student body. The Law School's educational judgment that such diversity is essential to its educational mission is one to which we defer. . . . We have long recognized that, given the important purpose of public education and the expansive freedoms of speech and thought associated with the university environment, universities occupy a special niche in our constitutional tradition. . . . Our conclusion that the Law School has a compelling interest in a diverse student body is informed by our view that attaining a diverse student body is at the heart of the Law School's proper institutional mission, and that "good faith" on the part of a university is "presumed" absent "a showing to the contrary."

. . . The Law School's interest is not simply "to assure within its student body some specified percentage of a particular group merely because of its race or ethnic origin." That would amount to outright racial balancing, which is patently unconstitutional. Rather, the Law School's concept of critical mass is defined by reference to the educational benefits that diversity is designed to produce. These benefits are substantial. [The] Law School's admissions policy promotes "cross-racial understanding," helps to break down racial stereotypes, and "enables [students] to better understand persons of different races." These benefits are "important and laudable," because "classroom discussion is livelier, more spirited, and simply more enlightening and interesting" when the students have "the greatest possible variety of backgrounds."

[Numerous] studies show that student body diversity promotes learning outcomes, and "better prepares students for an increasingly diverse workforce and society, and better prepares them as professionals." These benefits are not theoretical but real, as major American businesses have made clear that the skills needed in today's increasingly global marketplace can only be developed through exposure to widely diverse people, cultures, ideas, and viewpoints. . . .

Even in the limited circumstance when drawing racial distinctions is permissible to further a compelling state interest, [the] means chosen to accomplish the [government's] asserted purpose must be specifically and narrowly framed to accomplish that purpose. The purpose of the narrow tailoring requirement is to ensure that "the means chosen 'fit' . . . the compelling goal so closely that there is little or no possibility that the motive for the classification was illegitimate racial prejudice or stereotype." . . . To be narrowly tailored, a race-conscious admissions program cannot use a quota system. . . . Instead, a university may consider race or ethnicity only as a " 'plus' in a particular applicant's file," without "insulating the individual from comparison with all other candidates for the available seats." In other words, an admissions program must be "flexible enough to consider all pertinent elements of diversity in light of the particular qualifications of each applicant, and to place them on the same footing for consideration, although not necessarily according them the same weight."

We find that the Law School's admissions program bears the hallmarks of a narrowly tailored plan. . . . We are satisfied that the Law School's admissions program . . . does not operate as a quota. [A] "quota" is a program in which a certain fixed number or proportion of opportunities are "reserved exclusively for certain minority groups." . . . The Law School's goal of attaining a critical mass of underrepresented minority students does not transform its program into a quota. [There] is of course "some relationship between numbers and achieving the benefits to be derived from a diverse student body, and between numbers and providing a reasonable environment for those students admitted." [But "some] attention to numbers," without more, does not transform a flexible admissions system into a rigid quota. . . .

That a race-conscious admissions program does not operate as a quota does not, by itself, satisfy the requirement of individualized consideration. When using race as a "plus" factor in university admissions, [the] admissions program must . . . ensure that each applicant is evaluated as an individual and not in a way that makes an applicant's race or ethnicity the defining feature of his or her application. [T]his individualized consideration in the context of a race-conscious admissions program is paramount. [T]he Law School engages in a highly individualized, holistic review of each applicant's file, giving serious consideration to all the ways an applicant might contribute to a diverse educational environment. . . . Unlike the program at issue in Gratz v. Bollinger, the Law School awards no mechanical, predetermined diversity "bonuses" based on race or ethnicity. . . .

[T]he Law School's race-conscious admissions program adequately ensures that all factors that may contribute to student body diversity are meaningfully considered alongside race in admissions decisions. . . . [The] Law School actually gives substantial weight to diversity factors besides race. [It] frequently accepts nonminority applicants with grades and test scores lower than underrepresented minority applicants (and other nonminority applicants) who are rejected. This shows that the Law School seriously weighs many other diversity factors besides race that can make a real and dispositive difference for nonminority applicants as well. . . .

Narrow tailoring does not require exhaustion of every conceivable race-neutral alternative. Nor does it require a university to choose between maintaining a reputation for excellence [and] fulfilling a commitment to provide educational opportunities to members of all racial groups. Narrow tailoring does, however, require serious, good faith consideration of workable race-neutral alternatives that will achieve the diversity the university seeks. [The] Law School sufficiently considered workable race-neutral alternatives. . . .

We acknowledge that "there are serious problems of justice connected with the idea of preference itself." Narrow tailoring, therefore, requires that a race-conscious admissions program not unduly harm members of any racial group. . . . To be narrowly tailored, a race-conscious admissions program must not "unduly burden individuals who are not members of the favored racial and ethnic groups." We are satisfied that the Law School's . . . race-conscious admissions program does not unduly harm non-minority applicants.

. . . [R]ace-conscious admissions policies must be limited in time [because] racial classifications, however compelling their goals, are potentially so dangerous that they may be employed no more broadly than the interest demands. Enshrining a permanent justification for racial preferences would offend this fundamental equal protection principle. [All] governmental use of race must have a logical end point. . . . In the context of higher education, [this] requirement can be met by sunset provisions in race-conscious admissions policies and periodic reviews to determine whether racial preferences are still necessary to achieve student body diversity. . . . We take the Law School at its word that it would "like nothing better than to find a race-neutral admissions formula" and will terminate its race-conscious admissions program as soon as practicable. It has been 25 years since Justice Powell first approved the use of race to further an interest in student body diversity in the context of public higher education. Since that time, the number of minority applicants with high grades and test scores has indeed increased. We expect that 25 years from now, the use of racial preferences will no longer be necessary to further the interest approved today. . . .

CHIEF JUSTICE REHNQUIST, with whom JUSTICE SCALIA, JUSTICE KENNEDY, and JUSTICE THOMAS join, dissenting.

. . . I do not believe . . . that the University of Michigan Law School's . . . means are narrowly tailored to the interest it asserts. The Law School claims it must take the steps it does to achieve a " 'critical mass' " of underrepresented minority students. But its actual program bears no relation to this asserted goal. Stripped of its "critical mass" veil, the Law School's program is revealed as a naked effort to achieve racial balancing. . . . Although the Court recites the language of our strict scrutiny analysis, its application of that review is unprecedented in its deference.

. . . In practice, the Law School's program bears little or no relation to its asserted goal of achieving [a] "critical mass" . . . of *each* underrepresented minority group, [because] the record demonstrates that the Law School's admissions practices with respect to these groups differ dramatically and cannot be defended under any consistent use of the term "critical mass." From 1995 through 2000, the Law School admitted between 1,130 and 1,310 students. Of those, between 13 and 19 were Native American, between 91 and 108 were African-Americans, and between 47 and 56 were Hispanic. If the Law School is admitting between 91 and 108 African-Americans in order to achieve "critical mass," thereby preventing African-American students from feeling "isolated or like spokespersons for their race," one would think that a number of the same order of magnitude would be necessary to accomplish the same purpose for Hispanics and Native Americans. . . . In order for this pattern of admission to be consistent with the Law School's explanation of "critical mass," one would have to believe that the objectives of "critical mass" offered by respondents are achieved with only half the number of Hispanics and one-sixth the number of Native Americans as compared to African-Americans. But respondents offer no race-specific reasons for such disparities. Instead, they simply emphasize the importance of achieving "critical mass," without any explanation of why that concept is applied differently among the three underrepresented minority groups.

These different numbers, moreover, come only as a result of substantially different treatment among the three underrepresented minority groups. . . . For example, in 2000, 12 Hispanics who scored between a 159-160 on the LSAT and earned a GPA of 3.00 or higher applied for admission and only 2 were admitted. Meanwhile, 12 African-Americans in the same range of qualifications applied for admission and all 12 were admitted. Likewise, that same year, 16 Hispanics who scored . . . 151-153 on the LSAT and earned a 3.00 or higher applied for admission and only 1 of those applicants was admitted. Twenty-three similarly qualified African-Americans applied for admission and 14 were admitted.

These statistics have a significant bearing on petitioner's case. Respondents have *never* offered any race-specific arguments explaining why significantly more individuals from one underrepresented minority group are needed in order to achieve "critical mass" or further student body diversity. They certainly have not explained why Hispanics, who they have said are among "the groups most isolated by racial barriers in our country," should have their admission capped out in this manner. [The] Law School's disparate admissions practices with respect to these minority groups demonstrate that its alleged goal of "critical mass" is simply a sham. . . .

Only when the "critical mass" label is discarded does a likely explanation for these numbers emerge. The Court [says] that the Law School's use of race in admissions . . . only pays " 'some attention to numbers.' " But the correlation between the percentage of the Law School's pool of applicants who are members of the three minority groups and the percentage of the admitted applicants who are members of these same groups is far too precise to be dismissed as merely the result of the school paying "some attention to [the] numbers." As the tables below show, from 1995 through 2000 the percentage of admitted applicants who were members of these minority groups closely tracked the percentage of individuals in the school's applicant pool who were from the same groups.

TABLE 1

Year	Number of law school applicants	Number of African-American applicants	Percentage of applicants who were African-American	Number of applicants admitted by the Law School	Number of African-American applicants admitted	Percentage of admitted applicants who were African-American
1995	4147	404	9.7%	1130	106	9.4%
1996	3677	342	9.3%	1170	108	9.2%
1997	3429	320	9.3%	1218	101	8.3%
1998	3537	304	8.6%	1310	103	7.9%
1999	3400	247	7.3%	1280	91	7.1%
2000	3432	259	7.5%	1249	91	7.3%

TABLE 2

Year	Number of law school applicants	Number of Hispanic applicants	Percentage of applicants who were Hispanic	Number of applicants admitted by the Law School	Number of Hispanic applicants admitted	Percentage of admitted applicants who were Hispanic
1995	4147	213	5.1%	1130	56	5.0%
1996	3677	186	5.1%	1170	54	4.6%
1997	3429	163	4.8%	1218	47	3.9%
1998	3537	150	4.2%	1310	55	4.2%
1999	3400	152	4.5%	1280	48	3.8%
2000	3432	168	4.9%	1249	53	4.2%

TABLE 3

Years	Number of law school applicants	Number of Native American applicants	Percentage of applicants who were Native American	Number of applicants admitted by the Law School	Number of Native American applicants admitted	Percentage of admitted applicants who were Native American
1995	4147	45	1.1%	1130	14	1.2%
1996	3677	31	0.8%	1170	13	1.1%
1997	3429	37	1.1%	1218	19	1.6%
1998	3537	40	1.1%	1310	18	1.4%
1999	3400	25	0.7%	1280	13	1.0%
2000	3432	35	1.0%	1249	14	1.1%

For example, in 1995, when 9.7% of the applicant pool was African-American, 9.4% of the admitted class was African-American. By 2000, only 7.5% of the applicant pool was African-American, and 7.3% of the admitted class was African-American. This correlation is striking. . . . The tight correlation between the percentage of applicants and admittees of a given race . . . must result from careful race based planning by the Law School. It suggests a formula for admission . . . [such] that the proportion of each group admitted should be the same as the proportion of that group in the applicant pool.

[The] Law School cannot precisely control which of its admitted applicants decide to attend the university. But it can and . . . clearly does employ racial preferences in extending offers of admission. Indeed, the ostensibly flexible nature of the Law School's admissions program that the Court finds appealing appears to be, in practice, a carefully managed program designed to ensure proportionate representation of applicants from selected minority groups. . . . But this is precisely the type of racial balancing that the Court itself calls "patently unconstitutional."

Finally, I believe that the Law School's program fails strict scrutiny because it is devoid of any reasonably precise time limit on the Law School's use of race in admissions. . . . Our previous cases have required some limit on the duration of programs such as this because discrimination on the basis of race is invidious. The Court suggests a possible 25-year limitation on the Law School's current program. Respondents, on the other hand, remain more ambiguous, [identifying] "such a limit in the Law School's resolve to cease considering race when genuine race-neutral alternatives become available." These discussions of a time limit are the vaguest of assurances. In truth, they permit the Law School's use of racial preferences on a seemingly permanent basis. Thus, an important component of strict scrutiny—that a program be limited in time—is casually subverted. The Court, in an unprecedented display of deference under our strict scrutiny analysis, upholds the Law School's program despite its obvious flaws. We have said that when it comes to the use of race, the connection between the ends and the means used to attain them must be precise. But here the flaw is deeper than that; it is not merely a question of "fit" between ends and means. Here the means actually used are forbidden by the Equal Protection Clause of the Constitution.

JUSTICE KENNEDY, dissenting.

. . . The Court . . . does not apply strict scrutiny. By trying to say otherwise, it undermines both the test and its own controlling precedents. . . . Having approved the use of race as a factor in the admissions process, the majority proceeds to nullify the essential safeguard Justice Powell insisted upon as the precondition of the approval[:] . . . rigorous judicial review, with strict scrutiny as the controlling standard. . . . The Court confuses deference to a university's definition of its educational objective with deference to the implementation of this goal. In the context of university admissions the objective of racial diversity can be accepted . . . , but deference is not to be given with respect to the methods by which it is pursued. . . . The Court, in a review that is nothing short of perfunctory, . . . fails to confront the reality of how the Law School's admissions policy is implemented. . . . About 80 to 85[%] of the places in the entering class are given to applicants in the upper range of Law School Admissions Test scores and grades. An applicant with these credentials likely will be admitted without consideration of race or ethnicity. With respect to the remaining 15 to 20[%] of the seats, race is likely outcome determinative for many members of minority groups. . . .

The Law School has not demonstrated how individual consideration is, or can be, preserved at this stage of the application process given the instruction to attain what it calls critical mass. In fact the evidence shows otherwise. There was little deviation among admitted minority students during the years from 1995 to 1998. The percentage of enrolled minorities fluctuated only by 0.3%, from 13.5% to 13.8%. . . .

The narrow fluctuation band raises an inference that the Law School subverted individual determination, and strict scrutiny requires the Law School to overcome the inference. . . . The Law School has the burden of proving [under] strict scrutiny that it did not utilize race in an unconstitutional way. At the very least, [the statistical data] require the Law School either to produce a convincing explanation or to show it has taken adequate steps to ensure individual assessment. The Law School does neither.

The obvious tension between the pursuit of critical mass and the requirement of individual review increased by the end of the admissions season. Most of the decisions where race may decide the outcome are made during this period. The admissions officers consulted the daily reports which indicated the composition of the incoming class along racial lines. As [the admissions director] stated, "the further [he] went into the [admissions] season the more frequently [he] would want to look at these [reports] and see the change from day-to-day." These reports would "track exactly where [the Law School] stood at any given time in assembling the class," and so would tell the admissions personnel whether they were short of assembling a critical mass of minority students. . . . The consultation of daily reports during the last stages in the admissions process suggests there was no further attempt at individual review save for race itself. The admissions officers could use the reports to recalibrate the plus factor given to race depending on how close they were to achieving the Law School's goal of critical mass. The bonus factor of race would then become divorced from individual review; it would be premised instead on the numerical objective set by the Law School.

The Law School made no effort to guard against this danger. It provided no guidelines to its admissions personnel on how to reconcile individual assessment with the directive to admit a critical mass of minority students. . . . To be constitutional, a university's compelling interest in a diverse student body must be achieved by a system where individual assessment is safeguarded through the entire process. . . . The Law School failed to comply with this requirement, and [has not] carried its burden to show otherwise [under] strict scrutiny. . . .

JUSTICE SCALIA, with whom JUSTICE THOMAS joins, concurring in part and dissenting in part.

[The] University of Michigan Law School's mystical "critical mass" justification for its discrimination by race challenges even the most gullible mind. The admissions statistics show it to be a sham to cover a scheme of racially proportionate admissions.

I also join Parts I through VII of Justice Thomas's opinion. I find particularly unanswerable his central point: that the allegedly "compelling state interest" at issue here is not the incremental "educational benefit" that emanates from the fabled "critical mass" of minority students, but rather Michigan's interest in maintaining a "prestige" law school whose normal admissions standards disproportionately exclude blacks and other minorities. If that is a compelling state interest, everything is.

I add the following: The "educational benefit" that the University of Michigan seeks to achieve by racial discrimination consists, according to the Court, of " 'cross-racial understanding,' " and " 'better prepar[ation of] students for an increasingly diverse workforce and society,' " all of which is necessary not only for work, but also for good "citizenship." . . . If it is appropriate for the University of Michigan Law School to use racial discrimination for the purpose of putting together a "critical mass" that will convey generic lessons in socialization and good citizenship, surely it is no less appropriate—indeed, *particularly* appropriate—for the civil service system of the State of Michigan to do so. There, also, those exposed to "critical masses" of certain races will presumably become better Americans, better Michiganders, better civil servants. And surely private employers cannot be criticized—indeed, should be praised—if they also "teach" good citizenship to their adult employees through a patriotic, all-American system of racial discrimination in hiring. The nonminority individuals who are deprived of a legal education, a civil service job, or any job at all by reason of their skin color will surely understand.

Unlike a clear constitutional holding that racial preferences in state educational institutions are impermissible, or even a clear anti-constitutional holding that racial preferences in state educational institutions are OK, today's *Grutter-Gratz* split double header seems perversely designed to prolong the controversy and the litigation. Some future lawsuits will presumably focus on whether the discriminatory scheme in question contains enough evaluation of the applicant "as an individual," and sufficiently avoids "separate admissions tracks" to fall under *Grutter* rather than *Gratz*. Some will focus on whether a university has gone beyond the bounds of a " 'good faith effort' " and has so zealously pursued its "critical mass" as to make it an unconstitutional *de facto* quota system, rather than merely " 'a permissible goal.' " Other lawsuits may focus on whether, in the particular setting at issue, any educational benefits flow from racial diversity. . . . Still other suits may challenge the bona fides of the institution's expressed commitment to the educational benefits of diversity that immunize the discriminatory scheme in *Grutter*. (Tempting targets, one would suppose, will be those universities that talk the talk of multiculturalism and racial diversity in the courts but walk the walk of tribalism and racial segregation on their campuses—through minority-only student organizations, separate minority housing opportunities, separate minority student centers, even separate minority-only graduation ceremonies.) . . . Finally, litigation can be expected on behalf of minority groups intentionally short changed in the institution's composition of its generic minority "critical mass." I do not look forward to any of these cases. The Constitution proscribes government discrimination on the basis of race, and state-provided education is no exception.

JUSTICE THOMAS, with whom JUSTICE SCALIA joins as to Parts I-VII, concurring in part and dissenting in part.

Frederick Douglass, speaking to a group of abolitionists almost 140 years ago, delivered a message lost on today's majority:

> . . . What I ask for the negro is not benevolence, not pity, not sympathy, but simply *justice*. The American people have always been anxious to know what they shall do with us. . . . I have had but one answer from the beginning. Do nothing with us! Your doing with us has already played the mischief with us. Do nothing with us! . . . All I ask is, give him a chance to stand on his own legs! Let him alone! . . . Your interference is doing him positive injury.

What the Black Man Wants: An Address Delivered in Boston, Massachusetts, on 26 January 1865, reprinted in 4 The Frederick Douglass Papers 59, 68 (J. Blassingame & J. McKivigan eds., 1991) (emphasis in original).

Like Douglass, I believe blacks can achieve in every avenue of American life without the meddling of university administrators. Because I wish to see all students succeed whatever their color, I share, in some respect, the sympathies of those who sponsor the type of discrimination advanced by the . . . Law School. The Constitution does not, however, tolerate . . . racial discrimination. Nor does the Constitution countenance the unprecedented deference the Court gives to the Law School, an approach inconsistent with the very concept of "strict scrutiny."

No one would argue that a university could set up a lower general admission standard and then impose heightened requirements only on black applicants. Similarly, a university may not maintain a high admission standard and grant exemptions to favored races. The Law School, of its own choosing, and for its own purposes, maintains an exclusionary admissions system that it knows produces racially disproportionate results. Racial discrimination is not a permissible solution to the self-inflicted wounds of this elitist admissions policy. . . .

IV. . . . The Court . . . bases its unprecedented deference to the Law School—a deference antithetical to strict scrutiny—on an idea of "educational autonomy" grounded in the First Amendment. In my view, there is no basis for a right of public universities to do what would otherwise violate the Equal Protection Clause. . . .

The Court relies heavily on social science evidence to justify its deference [to the Law School but] never acknowledges . . . the growing evidence that racial (and other sorts) of heterogeneity actually impairs learning among black students. See, e.g., Flowers & Pascarella, Cognitive Effects of College Racial Composition on African American Students After 3 Years of College, 40 J. of College Student Development 669, 674 (1999) (concluding that black students experience superior cognitive development at Historically Black Colleges (HBCs). . . . The majority [defers] to the Law School's "assessment that diversity will, in fact, yield educational benefits." It follows, therefore, that an HBC's assessment that racial homogeneity will yield educational benefits would similarly be given deference. An HBC's rejection of white applicants in order to maintain racial homogeneity seems permissible, therefore, under the majority's view of the Equal Protection Clause. Contained within today's majority opinion is the seed of a new constitutional justification for a concept I thought long and rightly rejected—racial segregation. . . .

V. . . . [No] modern law school can claim ignorance of the poor performance of blacks, relatively speaking, on the Law School Admissions Test (LSAT). Nevertheless, law schools continue to use the test and then attempt to "correct" for black underperformance by using racial discrimination in admissions so as to obtain their aesthetic student body. The Law School's continued adherence to measures it knows produce racially skewed results is not entitled to deference by this Court. . . . The Court will not even deign to make the Law School try other methods, however, preferring instead to grant a 25-year license to violate the Constitution. . . .

VI. . . . I believe what lies beneath the Court's decision today are the benighted notions that one can tell when racial discrimination benefits (rather than hurts) minority groups, and that racial discrimination is necessary to remedy general societal ills. . . . I . . . contest the notion that the Law School's discrimination benefits those admitted as a result of it. . . . The Law School is not looking for those students who, despite a lower LSAT score or undergraduate grade point average, will succeed in the study of law. The Law School seeks only a facade—it is sufficient that the class looks right, even if it does not perform right. The Law School tantalizes unprepared students with the promise of a University of Michigan degree and all of the opportunities that it offers. These overmatched students take the bait, only to find that they cannot succeed in the cauldron of competition. . . .

It is uncontested that each year, the Law School admits a handful of blacks who would be admitted in the absence of racial discrimination. Who can differentiate between those who belong and those who do not? The majority of blacks are admitted to the Law School because of discrimination, and because of this policy all are tarred as undeserving. . . . When blacks take positions in the highest places of government, industry, or academia, it is an open question today whether their skin color played a part in their advancement. The question itself is the stigma—because either racial discrimination did play a role, in which case the person may be deemed "otherwise unqualified," or it did not, in which case asking the question itself unfairly marks those blacks who would succeed without discrimination. Is this what the Court means by "visibly open"?

VII. . . . It has been nearly 140 years since Frederick Douglass asked the intellectual ancestors of the Law School to "do nothing with us!" and the Nation adopted the Fourteenth Amendment. Now we must wait another 25 years to see this principle of equality vindicated. . . .

≡≡≡ **Gratz v. Bollinger**
≡≡≡ *539 U.S. 244 (2003)*

CHIEF JUSTICE REHNQUIST delivered the opinion of the Court.

We granted certiorari in this case to decide whether "the University of Michigan's use of racial preferences in undergraduate admissions violates the Equal Protection Clause of the Fourteenth Amendment, Title VI of the Civil Rights Act of 1964 (42 U.S.C. §2000d), or 42 U.S.C. §1981." Because we find that the manner in which the University considers the race of applicants in its undergraduate admissions guidelines violates these constitutional and statutory provisions, we reverse that portion of the District Court's decision upholding the guidelines.

I. Petitioners Jennifer Gratz and Patrick Hamacher both applied for admission to the University of Michigan's . . . College of Literature, Science, and the Arts (LSA) as residents of the State of Michigan. Both petitioners are Caucasian. Gratz [was denied admission to the LSA and] enrolled in the University of Michigan at Dearborn, from which she graduated in the spring of 1999. Hamacher applied for admission to the LSA for the fall of 1997, [he was denied,] and he enrolled at Michigan State University. . . .

Gratz and Hamacher filed a lawsuit in [federal court against the University and its officers, on behalf of a class] of "those individuals who applied for and were not granted admission to the College of Literature, Science and the Arts of the University of Michigan for all academic years from 1995 forward and who are members of those racial or ethnic groups, including Caucasian, that defendants treated less favorably on the basis of race in considering their application for admission." . . .

The University's Office of Undergraduate Admissions (OUA) oversees the LSA admissions process. . . . Beginning with the 1998 academic year, the OUA [used] a "selection index," on which an applicant could score a maximum of 150 points. This index was divided linearly into ranges generally calling for admissions dispositions as follows: 100-150 (admit); 95-99 (admit or postpone); 90-94 (postpone or admit); 75-89 (delay or postpone); 74 and below (delay or reject).

Each application received points based on high school grade point average, standardized test scores, academic quality of an applicant's high school, strength or weakness of high school curriculum, in-state residency, alumni relationship, personal essay, and personal achievement or leadership. Of particular significance here, . . . an applicant was entitled to 20 points based upon his or her membership in an underrepresented racial or ethnic minority group. . . .

Starting in 1999 . . . the University established an Admissions Review Committee (ARC), to provide an additional level of consideration for some applications. Under the new system, counselors may, in their discretion, "flag" an application for the ARC to review after determining that the applicant (1) is academically prepared to succeed at the University, (2) has achieved a minimum selection index score, and (3) possesses a quality or characteristic important to the University's composition of its freshman class, such as high class rank, unique life experiences, challenges, circumstances, interests or talents, socioeconomic disadvantage, and underrepresented race, ethnicity, or geography. After reviewing "flagged" applications, the ARC determines whether to admit, defer, or deny each applicant. . . .

II. . . . [Petitioners] argue that even if the University's interest in diversity can constitute a compelling state interest, the District Court erroneously concluded that the University's use of race in its current freshman admissions policy is narrowly tailored to achieve such an interest. . . . We find that the University's policy, which automatically distributes 20 points, or one-fifth of the points needed to guarantee admission, to every single "underrepresented minority" applicant solely because of race, is not narrowly tailored to achieve the interest in educational diversity that respondents claim justifies their program. . . .

Justice Powell's opinion in *Bakke* emphasized the importance of considering each particular applicant as an individual [and] did not contemplate that any single characteristic automatically ensured a specific and identifiable contribution to a university's diversity. . . . The current LSA policy does not provide such individualized consideration [because] it automatically distributes 20 points to every single applicant from an "underrepresented minority" group, as defined by the University. . . . [T]he LSA's automatic distribution of 20 points has the effect of making "the factor of race . . . decisive" for virtually every minimally qualified underrepresented minority applicant. . . .

Respondents contend that "the volume of applications and the presentation of applicant information make it impractical for [LSA] to use the . . . admissions system" upheld by the Court today in *Grutter*. But the fact that the implementation of a program capable of providing individualized consideration might present administrative challenges does not render constitutional an otherwise problematic system. Nothing in Justice Powell's opinion in *Bakke* signaled that a university may employ whatever means it desires to achieve the stated goal of diversity without regard to the limits imposed by our strict scrutiny analysis.

[B]ecause the University's use of race in its current freshman admissions policy is not narrowly tailored to achieve respondents' asserted compelling interest in diversity, the admissions policy violates the Equal Protection Clause of the Fourteenth Amendment.[7] We further find that the admissions policy also violates Title VI and 42 U.S.C. §1981. Accordingly, we reverse that portion of the District Court's decision granting respondents summary judgment with respect to liability and remand the case for proceedings consistent with this opinion.

JUSTICE SOUTER, with whom JUSTICE GINSBURG joins, dissenting.
. . . [T]he freshman admissions system here is . . . closer to what *Grutter* approves than to what *Bakke* condemns. . . . The very nature of a college's permissible practice of awarding value to racial diversity means that race must be considered in a way that increases some applicants' chances for admission. . . . The college simply does by a numbered scale what the law school accomplishes in its "holistic review." . . . Nor is it possible to say that the 20 points convert race into a decisive factor comparable to reserving minority places as in *Bakke*. . . . [N]onminority applicants may achieve higher selection point totals than minority applicants owing to characteristics other than race,

---

7. Justice Ginsburg in her dissent observes that "one can reasonably anticipate . . . that colleges and universities will seek to maintain their minority enrollment . . . whether or not they can do so in full candor through adoption of affirmative action plans of the kind here at issue." She goes on to say that "if honesty is the best policy, surely Michigan's accurately described, fully disclosed College affirmative-action program is preferable to achieving similar numbers through winks, nods, and disguises." These observations are remarkable for two reasons. First, they suggest that universities—to whose academic judgment we are told in Grutter v. Bollinger we should defer—will pursue their affirmative-action programs whether or not they violate the United States Constitution. Second, they recommend that these violations should be dealt with, not by requiring the universities to obey the Constitution, but by changing the Constitution so that it conforms to the conduct of the universities.

and the fact that the university admits "virtually every qualified underrepresented minority applicant" may reflect nothing more than the likelihood that very few qualified minority applicants apply, as well as the possibility that self-selection results in a strong minority applicant pool. . . .

JUSTICE GINSBURG, with whom JUSTICE SOUTER joins, and with whom JUSTICE BREYER joins as to Part I, dissenting.

I. . . . In implementing [the equal protection guarantee] government[s] may properly distinguish between policies of exclusion and inclusion. Actions designed to burden groups long denied full citizenship stature are not sensibly ranked with measures taken to hasten the day when entrenched discrimination and its after effects have been extirpated. . . . For . . . "the Constitution is both color blind and color conscious. To avoid conflict with the equal protection clause, a classification that denies a benefit, causes harm, or imposes a burden must not be based on race. In that sense, the Constitution is color blind. But the Constitution is color conscious to prevent discrimination being perpetuated and to undo the effects of past discrimination." . . .

II. . . . The stain of generations of racial oppression is still visible in our society, and the determination to hasten its removal remains vital. One can reasonably anticipate, therefore, that colleges and universities will seek to maintain their minority enrollment—and the networks and opportunities thereby opened to minority graduates—whether or not they can do so in full candor through adoption of affirmative action plans of the kind here at issue. Without recourse to such plans, institutions of higher education may resort to camouflage. For example, schools may encourage applicants to write of their cultural traditions in the essays they submit, or to indicate whether English is their second language. Seeking to improve their chances for admission, applicants may highlight the minority group associations to which they belong, or the Hispanic surnames of their mothers or grandparents. In turn, teachers' recommendations may emphasize who a student is as much as what he or she has accomplished. If honesty is the best policy, surely Michigan's accurately described, fully disclosed College affirmative action program is preferable to achieving similar numbers through winks, nods, and disguises.[8]

NOTES AND PROBLEM

1. The Meaning of Diversity as a Compelling Interest. What kind of diversity qualifies as a compelling interest? Is it a variety of socioeconomic backgrounds, interests, life experiences, ethnicity, and viewpoints? Is it simply

---

8. Contrary to the Court's contention, I do not suggest "changing the Constitution so that it conforms to the conduct of the universities." [T]he Constitution, properly interpreted, permits government officials to respond openly to the continuing importance of race. Among constitutionally permissible options, those that candidly disclose their consideration of race seem to me preferable to those that conceal it.

racial diversity? Is it limited to inclusion of specific historically disadvantaged racial minorities? If diversity means racial diversity, whether broadly or narrowly conceived, what is the essence of *Grutter* and *Gratz*? Do these cases stand for the proposition that the use of race in public university admissions is presumptively void, but the presence of multiple racial groups in the student body is a compelling interest that can be achieved only by using race; thus, racial discrimination in public university admissions is justified and constitutionally valid so long as such discrimination is practiced subjectively (and thus obscured from view) rather than objectively (and thus open to public scrutiny)? Or do they mean that while the use of race is presumptively void, the presence of multiple racial groups in the student body is a compelling interest that can be achieved only by using race, and courts will defer to university administrators regarding the method of racial discrimination that is needed to achieve that objective unless the chosen method permits admissions officers to avoid individualized assessment of the importance of race to the particular admission decision?

2. The Primacy of Strict Scrutiny of Racial Classifications. California's prison population is dominated by violent gangs organized along racial lines. To prevent racial violence while it determined where a prisoner should ultimately reside, California racially segregates prisoners placed in double cells for the first 60 days of their confinement. The state maintained that its practice should be upheld because it was reasonably related to its legitimate penological interests of protecting the safety of prisoners and guards alike. The Ninth Circuit agreed with California, but in Johnson v. California, 543 U.S. 499 (2005), the Supreme Court reversed.

> [We] apply strict scrutiny to *all* racial classifications. . . . We have . . . applied [the] reasonable-relationship test *only* to rights that are "inconsistent with proper incarceration." . . . The right not to be discriminated against based on one's race is not . . . a right that need necessarily be compromised for the sake of proper prison administration. [C]ompliance with the Fourteenth Amendment's ban on racial discrimination is not only consistent with proper prison administration, but also bolsters the legitimacy of the entire criminal justice system. . . . Prisons are dangerous places, and the special circumstances they present may justify racial classifications in some contexts. Such circumstances can be considered in applying strict scrutiny, which is designed to take relevant differences into account. . . . We hold only that strict scrutiny is the proper standard of review and remand the case to allow the Court of Appeals for the Ninth Circuit, or the District Court, to apply it. . . .

Surely California has a compelling interest in preserving the life and safety of prisoners and guards, so what must California prove to establish that its practice is narrowly tailored to that end? Is it sufficient for California to prove that its prison system is rife with racially based violent gangs? Must California also show that there are no effective race-neutral alternatives available? Will (should) the courts defer to the good-faith judgments of prison administrators about the necessity of using race as a factor in determining prison housing? If not, why is more deference due to the good-faith judgments of public university admissions officers?

3. Problem. You are the admissions director of a selective public university. Your university receives about 30,000 applications per year for 3,000 spaces in the entering freshman class. Your budget does not permit hiring enough staff to conduct detailed individualized reading and appraisal of every application, and the university president has told you that there is a "less than zero" chance that your budget will be increased. Nevertheless, the president has informed you that a racially diverse student body is "absolutely critical." The president has also told you that she is "not interested in litigation" and has instructed you to devise an admissions policy that will comply with current standards of constitutional law. Do so.

In the following case, the Court elaborated on the meaning of the "narrowly tailored" requirement.

Fisher v. University of Texas at Austin
133 S. Ct. 2411 (2013)

[In pursuit of its goal of educational diversity, the University of Texas at Austin concluded that racial minorities were largely absent from its many small enrollment classes, and thus decided to increase enrollment of racial minorities to achieve a "critical mass" of those minorities. To do so, race was explicitly considered in admissions decisions. Fisher, a white woman, sued UT Austin after she was denied admission. The Court of Appeals upheld a district court's grant of summary judgment to the University. The Supreme Court reversed, concluding that the Court of Appeals had failed to apply strict scrutiny, and remanded for consideration of Fisher's claim under the correct standard.]

JUSTICE KENNEDY delivered the opinion of the Court.

. . . Once the University has established that its goal of diversity is consistent with strict scrutiny, however, there must still be a further judicial determination that the admissions process meets strict scrutiny in its implementation. The University must prove that the means chosen by the University to attain diversity are narrowly tailored to that goal. On this point, the University receives no deference. *Grutter* made clear that it is for the courts, not for university administrators, to ensure that "[t]he means chosen to accomplish the [government's] asserted purpose must be specifically and narrowly framed to accomplish that purpose." . . . Narrow tailoring also requires that the reviewing court verify that it is "necessary" for a university to use race to achieve the educational benefits of diversity. This involves a careful judicial inquiry into whether a university could achieve sufficient diversity without using racial classifications. . . . The reviewing court must ultimately be satisfied that no workable race-neutral alternatives would produce the educational benefits of diversity. [S]trict scrutiny imposes on the university the ultimate burden of demonstrating, before turning to racial classifications, that available, workable race-neutral alternatives do not suffice.

Rather than perform this searching examination, however, the Court of Appeals held petitioner could challenge only "whether [the University's] decision to reintroduce race as a factor in admissions was made in good faith." And in considering such a challenge, the court would "presume the University acted in good faith" and place on petitioner the burden of rebutting that presumption. The Court of Appeals thus concluded that "the narrow-tailoring inquiry—like the compelling-interest inquiry—is undertaken with a degree of deference to the Universit[y]." These expressions of the controlling standard are at odds with *Grutter's* command that "all racial classifications imposed by government 'must be analyzed by a reviewing court under strict scrutiny.'" . . . *Grutter* did not hold that good faith would forgive an impermissible consideration of race. . . . Strict scrutiny does not permit a court to accept a school's assertion that its admissions process uses race in a permissible way without a court giving close analysis to the evidence of how the process works in practice. The higher education dynamic does not change the narrow tailoring analysis of strict scrutiny applicable in other contexts. . . .

The District Court and Court of Appeals confined the strict scrutiny inquiry in too narrow a way by deferring to the University's good faith in its use of racial classifications and affirming the grant of summary judgment on that basis. The Court vacates that judgment, but fairness to the litigants and the courts that heard the case requires that it be remanded so that the admissions process can be considered and judged under a correct analysis.

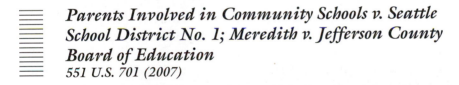

Parents Involved in Community Schools v. Seattle School District No. 1; Meredith v. Jefferson County Board of Education
551 U.S. 701 (2007)

CHIEF JUSTICE ROBERTS announced the judgment of the Court, and delivered the opinion of the Court with respect to Parts I, II, III.A, and III.C, and an opinion with respect to Parts III.B and IV, in which JUSTICES SCALIA, THOMAS, and ALITO joined.

[OPINION OF THE COURT.] The school districts in these cases voluntarily adopted student assignment plans that rely upon race to determine which public schools certain children may attend. The Seattle school district classifies children as white or nonwhite; the Jefferson County school district as black or "other." In Seattle, this racial classification is used to allocate slots in oversubscribed high schools. In Jefferson County, it is used to make certain elementary school assignments and to rule on transfer requests. In each case, the school district relies upon an individual student's race in assigning that student to a particular school, so that the racial balance at the school falls within a predetermined range based on the racial composition of the school district as a whole. Parents of students denied assignment to particular schools under these plans solely because of their race brought suit, contending that allocating children to different public schools on the basis of race violated the Fourteenth Amendment guarantee of equal protection. The Courts of Appeals below upheld the plans. We granted certiorari, and now reverse.

I. Both cases present the same underlying legal question—whether a public school that had not operated legally segregated schools or has been found to be unitary may choose to classify students by race and rely upon that classification in making school assignments. Although we examine the plans under the same legal framework, the specifics of the two plans, and the circumstances surrounding their adoption, are in some respects quite different.

A. [Seattle operates ten public high schools and permits prospective ninth-graders to rank order their preferred schools, but if too many students prefer the same school, the Seattle school district employs a series of "tiebreakers" to determine who gets in. The second] tiebreaker depends upon the racial composition of the particular school and the race of the individual student. [If a given high school fails to reflect the racial composition of the district student population as a whole—41 percent "white," 59 percent "non-white"[9]—race is used to bring the school into racial proportionality.]

B. Jefferson County Public Schools operates the public school system in metropolitan Louisville, Kentucky. [Although] Jefferson County had maintained a segregated school system, [in 2000 a federal District Court found] that the district had achieved unitary status. . . . [Jefferson County then adopted a pupil assignment plan that required schools to maintain a minimum black enrollment of 15 percent and a maximum black enrollment of 50 percent. A pupil entering the system is assigned to a cluster of schools determined by the student's residence, and may indicate a preference for a school within the cluster, but that preference is honored only to the extent that it would not upset the racial quota system. The same principles apply to transfer applications.]

III. A. It is well established that when the government distributes burdens or benefits on the basis of individual racial classifications, that action is reviewed under strict scrutiny. [T]he school districts must demonstrate that the use of individual racial classifications in the assignment plans here under review is "narrowly tailored" to achieve a "compelling" government interest.

[In] evaluating the use of racial classifications in the school context, [we] have recognized two interests that qualify as compelling. The first is the compelling interest of remedying the effects of past intentional discrimination. Yet the Seattle public schools have not shown that they were ever segregated by law, and were not subject to court-ordered desegregation decrees. . . . Jefferson County . . . does not rely upon an interest in remedying the effects of past intentional discrimination in defending its present use of race in assigning students. Nor could it. . . . Once Jefferson County achieved unitary status, it had remedied the constitutional wrong that allowed race-based assignments. Any continued use of race must be justified on some other basis.

---

9. "Non-white" included, as a percentage of the total population, 24 percent of Asian ethnicity, 23 percent of African ethnicity, 10 percent "Latino," and 3 percent aboriginal.—ED.

The second government interest we have recognized as compelling for purposes of strict scrutiny is the interest in diversity in higher education upheld in *Grutter*, [an interest that] was not focused on race alone but encompassed "all factors that may contribute to student body diversity." . . . The entire gist of the analysis in *Grutter* was . . . to ensure that the use of racial classifications was . . . not simply an effort to achieve racial balance, which the Court explained would be "patently unconstitutional." In the present cases, by contrast, race is not considered as part of a broader effort to achieve "exposure to widely diverse people, cultures, ideas, and viewpoints"; race, for some students, is determinative standing alone. . . . Even when it comes to race, the plans here employ only a limited notion of diversity, viewing race exclusively in white/nonwhite terms in Seattle and black/"other" terms in Jefferson County. [Seattle] speaks of the "inherent educational value" in "providing students the opportunity to attend schools with diverse student enrollment," [but] under the Seattle plan, a school with 50 percent Asian-American students and 50 percent white students but no African-American, Native-American, or Latino students would qualify as balanced, while a school with 30 percent Asian-American, 25 percent African-American, 25 percent Latino, and 20 percent white students would not. It is hard to understand how a plan that could allow these results can be viewed as being concerned with achieving enrollment that is "broadly diverse." . . . In upholding the admissions plan in *Grutter* . . . this Court relied upon considerations unique to institutions of higher education, noting that in light of "the expansive freedoms of speech and thought associated with the university environment, universities occupy a special niche in our constitutional tradition." . . . The present cases are not governed by *Grutter*.

B. [CHIEF JUSTICE ROBERTS and JUSTICES SCALIA, THOMAS, and ALITO.] Perhaps recognizing that reliance on *Grutter* cannot sustain their plans, both school districts assert additional interests . . . to justify their race-based assignments. . . . Seattle contends that its use of race helps to reduce racial concentration in schools and to ensure that racially concentrated housing patterns do not prevent nonwhite students from having access to the most desirable schools. Jefferson County [phrases] its interest in terms of educating its students "in a racially integrated environment." Each school district argues that educational and broader socialization benefits flow from a racially diverse learning environment, and each contends that because the diversity they seek is racial diversity—not the broader diversity at issue in *Grutter*—it makes sense to promote that interest directly by relying on race alone. [But] it is clear that the racial classifications employed by the districts are not narrowly tailored to the goal of achieving the educational and social benefits asserted to flow from racial diversity. In design and operation, the plans are directed only to racial balance, pure and simple, an objective this Court has repeatedly condemned as illegitimate.

The plans are tied to each district's specific racial demographics, rather than to any pedagogic concept of the level of diversity needed to obtain the asserted educational benefits. . . . The districts offer no evidence that the level of racial diversity necessary to achieve the asserted educational benefits happens to coincide with the racial demographics of the respective school districts—or rather the white/nonwhite or black/"other" balance of the districts, since that is the only diversity addressed by the plans. . . . [Moreover,] relying on race in assignments is unnecessary to achieve the stated goals, even as defined by the districts. For example, at Franklin High School in Seattle, [application of] the racial tiebreaker . . . resulted in an incoming ninth-grade class in 2000-2001 that was 30.3 percent Asian-American, 21.9 percent African-American, 6.8 percent Latino, 0.5 percent Native-American, and 40.5 percent Caucasian. Without the racial tiebreaker, the class would have been 39.6 percent Asian-American, 30.2 percent African-American, 8.3 percent Latino, 1.1 percent Native-American, and 20.8 percent Caucasian. When the actual racial breakdown is considered, enrolling students without regard to their race yields a substantially diverse student body under any definition of diversity.

Accepting racial balancing as a compelling state interest would justify the imposition of racial proportionality throughout American society, contrary to our repeated recognition that "at the heart of the Constitution's guarantee of equal protection lies the simple command that the Government must treat citizens as individuals, not as simply components of a racial, religious, sexual or national class." . . . Seattle [also says its plan is] necessary to address the consequences of racially identifiable housing patterns [but this] is contrary to our rulings that remedying past societal discrimination does not justify race-conscious government action. . . .

The principle that racial balancing is not permitted is one of substance, not semantics. Racial balancing is not transformed from "patently unconstitutional" to a compelling state interest simply by relabeling it "racial diversity." While the school districts use various verbal formulations to describe the interest they seek to promote—racial diversity, avoidance of racial isolation, racial integration—they offer no definition of the interest that suggests it differs from racial balance. . . . Jefferson County phrases its interest as "racial integration," but integration certainly does not require the sort of racial proportionality reflected in its plan. . . .

C. [OPINION OF THE COURT.] The districts assert, as they must, that the way in which they have employed individual racial classifications is necessary to achieve their stated ends. The minimal effect these classifications have on student assignments, however, suggests that other means would be effective. Seattle's racial tiebreaker results . . . only in shifting a small number of students between schools. . . . Jefferson County's use of racial classifications has only a minimal effect on the assignment of students. . . . While we do not suggest that *greater* use of race would be preferable, the minimal impact of the districts' racial classifications on school enrollment casts doubt on the necessity of using racial classifications. . . . The districts have also failed to show that they considered methods other than explicit racial classifications to achieve their stated goals. Narrow tailoring requires "serious, good faith consideration of workable race-neutral alternatives," and yet in Seattle several alternative assignment plans—many of which would not have used . . . racial classifications—were rejected with little or no consideration. Jefferson County has failed to present any evidence that it considered alternatives. . . .

IV. [CHIEF JUSTICE ROBERTS and JUSTICES SCALIA, THOMAS, and ALITO.]

. . . The parties . . . debate which side is more faithful to the heritage of *Brown,* but the position of the plaintiffs in *Brown* was spelled out in their brief and could not have been clearer: "The Fourteenth Amendment prevents states from according differential treatment to American children on the basis of their color or race." What do the racial classifications at issue here do, if not accord differential treatment on the basis of race? As counsel who appeared before this Court for the plaintiffs in *Brown* put it: "We have one fundamental contention[:] no State has any authority under the equal-protection clause of the Fourteenth Amendment to use race as a factor in affording educational opportunities among its citizens." . . . Before *Brown,* schoolchildren were told where they could and could not go to school based on the color of their skin. The school districts in these cases have not carried the heavy burden of demonstrating that we should allow this once again—even for very different reasons. . . . The way to stop discrimination on the basis of race is to stop discriminating on the basis of race.

[Reversed and remanded.]

JUSTICE THOMAS, concurring.

. . . I wholly concur in The Chief Justice's opinion. . . . Disfavoring a color-blind interpretation of the Constitution, the dissent would give school boards a free hand to make decisions on the basis of race—an approach reminiscent of that advocated by the segregationists in [*Brown I*]. This approach is just as wrong today as it was a half-century ago. . . .

The dissent repeatedly claims that the school districts are threatened with resegregation and that they will succumb to that threat if these plans are declared unconstitutional. . . . Racial imbalance is not segregation. . . . Although presently observed racial imbalance might result from past *de jure* segregation, racial imbalance can also result from any number of innocent private decisions, including voluntary housing choices. Because racial imbalance is not inevitably linked to unconstitutional segregation, it is not unconstitutional in and of itself. . . . Neither of the programs before us today is compelled as a remedial measure, and no one makes such a claim. . . . [It] is wrong to place the remediation of segregation on the same plane as the remediation of racial imbalance. . . . Remediation of past *de jure* segregation is a one-time process involving the redress of a discrete legal injury inflicted by an identified entity, [but] there is no ultimate remedy for racial imbalance. . . .

The dissent [rejects] the notion of a color-blind Constitution. . . . My view of the Constitution is Justice Harlan's view in *Plessy*: "Our Constitution is color-blind, and neither knows nor tolerates classes among citizens." And my view was the rallying cry for the lawyers who litigated *Brown*[:] "That the Constitution is color blind is our dedicated belief. . . ."

The dissent appears to pin its interpretation of the Equal Protection Clause to current societal practice and expectations, deference to local officials, likely practical consequences, and reliance on previous statements from this and other courts. . . . [In] *Plessy,* . . . the Court asked whether a state law providing for segregated railway cars was "a reasonable regulation" [and] deferred to local authorities in making its determination. . . . The Court likewise paid heed to societal practices, local expectations, and practical consequences by looking to "the established usages, customs and traditions of the people, and with a view to the promotion of their comfort, and the preservation of the public peace and good order." . . .

The segregationists in *Brown* embraced the arguments the Court endorsed in *Plessy.* . . . [T]oday's dissent replicates them to a distressing extent. Thus, the dissent argues that "each plan embodies the results of local experience and community consultation." Similarly, the segregationists made repeated appeals to societal practice and expectation. The dissent argues that "weight [must be given] to a local school board's knowledge, expertise, and concerns," and with equal vigor, the segregationists argued for deference to local authorities. . . . Like the dissent, the segregationists repeatedly cautioned the Court to consider practicalities and not to embrace too theoretical a view of the Fourteenth Amendment. And just as the dissent argues that the need for these programs will lessen over time, the segregationists claimed that reliance on segregation was lessening and might eventually end. . . .

What was wrong in 1954 cannot be right today. . . . The fact that state and local governments had been discriminating on the basis of race for a long time was irrelevant to the *Brown* Court. The fact that racial discrimination was preferable to the relevant communities was irrelevant to the *Brown* Court. . . . The same principles guide today's decision. . . .

Justice Kennedy, concurring in part and concurring in the judgment.
. . . I join [Parts I, II, III.A and III.C] of the Court's opinion. . . . My views do not allow me to join [Parts III.B and IV] of the opinion by The Chief Justice. . . . Justice Breyer's dissenting opinion . . . rests on . . . a misuse and mistaken interpretation of our precedents [and] advance[s] propositions that, in my view, are both erroneous and in fundamental conflict with basic equal protection principles. . . .

[Jefferson County] fails to make clear . . . who makes the decisions; what if any oversight is employed; the precise circumstances in which an assignment decision will or will not be made on the basis of race; or how it is determined which of two similarly situated children will be subjected to a given race-based decision. . . . When a court subjects governmental action to strict scrutiny, it cannot construe ambiguities in favor of the State.

[Seattle] does not explain how, in the context of its diverse student population, a blunt distinction between "white" and "non-white" furthers [its] goals [of enhancing education by diversity, ending racial isolation, and ensuring equitable access to good schools]. Far from being narrowly tailored to its purposes, this system threatens to defeat its own ends, and the school district has provided no convincing explanation for its design. . . .

In the administration of public schools by the state and local authorities it is permissible to consider the racial makeup of schools and to adopt general policies to encourage a diverse student body, one aspect of which is its racial composition. [T]hey are free to devise race-conscious measures to address the problem in a general way and without treating each student in different fashion solely on the basis of a systematic, individual typing by race. School boards may pursue the goal of bringing together students of diverse backgrounds and races through other means, including strategic site selection of new schools; drawing attendance zones with general recognition of the demographics of neighborhoods; allocating resources for special programs; recruiting students and faculty in a targeted fashion; and tracking enrollments, performance, and other statistics by race. These mechanisms are race conscious but do not lead to different treatment based on a classification that tells each student he or she is to be defined by race. . . .

A compelling interest exists in avoiding racial isolation, an interest that a school district, in its discretion and expertise, may choose to pursue. Likewise, a district may consider it a compelling interest to achieve a diverse student population. Race may be one component of that diversity, but other demographic factors, plus special talents and needs, should also be considered. What the government is not permitted to do, absent a showing of necessity not made here, is to classify every student on the basis of race and to assign each of them to schools based on that classification. Crude measures of this sort threaten to reduce children to racial chits valued and traded according to one school's supply and another's demand. . . .

JUSTICE STEVENS, dissenting.

. . . It is my firm conviction that no Member of the Court that I joined in 1975 would have agreed with today's decision.

JUSTICE BREYER, with whom JUSTICE STEVENS, JUSTICE SOUTER, and JUSTICE GINSBURG join, dissenting.

. . . The plurality . . . announces legal rules that will obstruct efforts by state and local governments to deal effectively with the growing resegregation of public schools. . . . This cannot be justified in the name of the Equal Protection Clause. . . .

Today, more than one in six black children attend a school that is 99-100% minority. In light of the evident risk of a return to school systems that are in fact (though not in law) resegregated, many school districts have felt a need to maintain or to extend their integration efforts. . . . Seattle and Louisville are two such districts. . . .

First, the school districts' plans serve "compelling interests" and are "narrowly tailored" on any reasonable definition of those terms. Second, the distinction between *de jure* segregation . . . and *de facto* segregation . . . is meaningless in the present context. . . . Third, real-world efforts to substitute racially diverse for racially segregated schools (however caused) are complex, to the point where the Constitution cannot plausibly be interpreted to rule out categorically all local efforts to use means that are "conscious" of the race of individuals. . . .

[T]he Equal Protection Clause permits local school boards to use race-conscious criteria to achieve positive race-related goals, even when the Constitution does not compel it. . . . There is [a] legal and practical difference between the use of race-conscious criteria . . . to keep the races apart and the use of race-conscious criteria . . . to bring the races together. . . .

Context matters. . . . Not every decision influenced by race is equally objectionable. . . . Here, the context is one in which school districts seek to advance or to maintain racial integration in primary and secondary schools. . . . This context is *not* a context that involves the use of race to decide who will receive goods or services that are normally distributed on the basis of merit and which are in short supply. It is not one in which race-conscious limits stigmatize or exclude. . . . The context here is one of racial limits that seek, not to keep the races apart, but to bring them together. . . .

[When] school administrators [use] a racial classification to end racial isolation or to achieve a diverse student body in public schools . . . [courts should apply] a standard of review that is not "strict" in the traditional sense of that word, although it does require . . . careful review. . . .

Nonetheless, I conclude that the plans before us pass both parts of the strict scrutiny test. [The districts' compelling interest] goes by various names[: racial diversity, racial balancing, or] an interest in promoting or preserving greater racial "integration" of public schools. . . . [This] interest . . . possesses three essential elements. First, there is . . . an interest in setting right the consequences of prior conditions of segregation. . . . Second, there is an . . . interest in overcoming the adverse educational effects produced by and associated with highly segregated schools. . . . Third, there is . . . an interest in producing an educational environment that reflects the "pluralistic society" in which our children will live. . . . The compelling interest at issue here . . . includes an effort . . . to create school environments that provide better educational opportunities for all children [and] to help create citizens better prepared to know, . . . understand, and . . . work with people of all races and backgrounds. . . .

[The] plans are "narrowly tailored" to achieve these "compelling" objectives. . . . First, the race-conscious criteria . . . constitute but one part of plans that depend primarily upon other, nonracial elements. To use race in this way is not to set a forbidden "quota." . . . Second, broad-range limits on voluntary school choice plans are less burdensome, and hence more narrowly tailored than other race-conscious restrictions this Court has previously approved. . . . Third, [each] plan embodies the results of local experience and community consultation [and] is the product of a process that has sought to enhance student choice. . . . [Giving] some degree of weight to a local school board's knowledge, expertise, and concerns in these particular matters is not inconsistent with rigorous judicial scrutiny. It simply recognizes that judges are not well suited to act as school administrators. . . .

[It] is important to consider the potential consequences of the plurality's approach. . . . [De facto] resegregation is on the rise. It is reasonable to conclude that such resegregation can create serious educational, social, and civic problems. Given the conditions in which school boards work to set policy, they may need all of the means presently at their disposal to combat those problems. Yet the plurality would deprive them of at least one tool that some districts now consider vital—the limited use of broad race-conscious student [assignment]. . . .

The last half-century has witnessed great strides toward racial equality, but we have not yet realized the promise of *Brown*. To invalidate the plans under review is to threaten the promise of *Brown*. The plurality's position, I fear, would break that promise. This is a decision that the Court and the Nation will come to regret. I must dissent.

PROBLEM

Suppose that a city with a population that is 50 percent white, 20 percent Asian, 20 percent Hispanic, and 10 percent black and extensive voluntary residential segregation by race adopts a policy of assigning students to public elementary and secondary schools on the basis of residential districts, but deliberately draws the district boundaries to create, within each district, a racial and ethnic distribution that approximates that of the city as a whole. Assess the validity of this plan under the plurality opinion, under Justice Kennedy's opinion, and under the dissenting view.

5. Race and the Political Process

Government action that makes race relevant to the political process poses many of the same problems that we have previously encountered. The explicit use of race to alter the political process surely triggers strict scrutiny. In Anderson v. Martin, 375 U.S. 399 (1964), the Court applied strict scrutiny in voiding a Louisiana law requiring each candidate's race to be designated on the ballot. When the political process is altered in a manner that does not explicitly use race but has a racially disparate impact, the problem is essentially identical to other disparate-impact cases: Was the alteration intended to work an invidiously discriminatory change to the political process?

Arguably, the Court failed to recognize the nature of the problem when it was first presented. California voters added Article I, section 26 to the state constitution, which prohibited the state from interfering with "the right of any person [to] decline to sell, lease or rent [his real] property to such person or persons as he, in his absolute discretion, chooses." In Reitman v. Mulkey, 387 U.S. 369 (1967), the Court subjected section 26 to strict scrutiny and invalidated it because it "was intended to authorize, and does authorize, [private] racial discrimination in the housing market." Though equal protection does not require a state to ban *private* racial discrimination, the California amendment was seen to be a device by which the state adopted as its own the private racial discrimination it insulated with constitutional protection. Thus the state itself was deemed the actor responsible for the private discrimination—although, as you will see in Chapter 11, that is a debatable conclusion. The Court failed to make anything of the fact that California had altered the *process* by which the state formulated its policies on private racial discrimination. Prior to adoption of section 26, proponents and opponents of state neutrality toward private racial discrimination were both able to obtain their desired outcome through the legislative process. After the enactment of section 26, opponents of state neutrality were required to amend the state constitution to obtain their desired outcome. Alteration of that process *by itself* would not trigger strict scrutiny, but the process of alteration coupled with circumstantial evidence that the motive for doing so was to make "[t]he right to discriminate [one] of the basic policies of the State" arguably ought to have been sufficient to trigger strict scrutiny.

When the issue came up again two years later, the Court first articulated its view of the political-process alteration problem.

≡≡≡ ### Hunter v. Erickson
≡≡≡ *393 U.S. 385 (1969)*

[In 1964, the Akron, Ohio, City Council enacted an ordinance to "assure equal opportunity to all persons to live in decent housing facilities regardless of race, color, religion, ancestry or national origin." Before this ordinance could be implemented, Akron's voters approved a charter amendment (§137), placed on the ballot by popular initiative, stipulating that any ordinance regulating "the use, sale, advertisement, transfer, listing agreement, lease, sublease or financing of real property [on] the basis of race, color, religion, national origin or ancestry must first be approved by a majority of the electors voting on the question." Hunter sought to compel implementation and enforcement of the 1964 ordinance. An Ohio trial court ruled that the 1964 ordinance was nullified by §137. The Ohio Supreme Court upheld that ruling, adding that §137 did not violate the Fourteenth Amendment's equal protection clause. The U.S. Supreme Court reversed.]

JUSTICE WHITE delivered the opinion for the Court.

The question in this case is whether [Akron] has denied a Negro citizen, Nellie Hunter, the equal protection of its laws by amending the city charter to prevent the city council from implementing any ordinance dealing with racial, religious, or ancestral discrimination in housing without the approval of the majority of the voters of Akron. [Section 137] was an explicitly racial classification treating racial housing matters differently from other racial and housing matters. [Section 137] drew a distinction between those groups who sought the law's protection against racial, religious, or ancestral discrimination in the sale or rental of real estate and those who sought to regulate real property transactions in the pursuit of other ends. [Most] ordinances regulating the real property market remained subject to the general rule [that] passage by the [City] Council sufficed unless the electors themselves invoked the general referendum provisions of the city charter. But for those who sought protection against racial bias, the approval of the City Council was not enough. A [special] referendum was [required].

Only laws to end housing discrimination based on "race, color, religion, national origin or ancestry" must run §137's gauntlet. It is true that the section draws no distinctions among racial and religious groups. Negroes and whites, Jews and Catholics are all subject to the same requirements if there is housing discrimination against them they wish to end. But §137 nevertheless disadvantages those who would benefit from laws barring racial, religious, or ancestral discriminations as against those who would bar other discriminations or who would otherwise regulate the real estate market in their favor. [Although facially neutral], the reality is that the law's impact falls on the minority. The majority needs no protection against discrimination. [Like] the law requiring specification of candidates' race on the ballot, §137 places special burdens on racial minorities within the governmental process.

Because the core of the Fourteenth Amendment is the prevention of meaningful and unjustified official distinctions based on race, [racial] classifications are "constitutionally suspect" [and] subject to the "most rigid scrutiny." [Applying strict scrutiny, we] hold §137 discriminates against minorities, and constitutes a real, substantial, and invidious denial of the equal protection of the laws.

JUSTICE HARLAN, joined by JUSTICE STEWART, concurring.

For equal protection purposes, [laws] which define the powers of political institutions fall into two classes. First, a statute may have the clear purpose of making it more difficult for racial and religious minorities to further their political aims. [Such a law is subject to strict scrutiny.] Most laws which define the structure of political institutions [fall] into a second class. They are designed with the aim of providing a just framework within which the diverse political groups in our society may fairly compete and are not enacted with the purpose of assisting one particular group in its struggle with its political opponents. Consider [Akron's] procedure which requires that almost any ordinance be submitted to a general referendum if 10% of the electorate signs an appropriate petition. This rule obviously does not have the purpose of protecting one particular group to the detriment of all others. It will sometimes operate in favor of one faction; sometimes in favor of another. [Statutes] of this type, which are grounded upon general democratic principle, do not violate [equal protection] simply because they occasionally operate to disadvantage Negro political interests. If a governmental institution is to be fair, one group cannot always be expected to win. If the Council's fair housing legislation were defeated at a [general] referendum, Negroes would undoubtedly lose an important political battle, but they would not thereby be denied equal protection. [But] Akron has not attempted to allocate governmental power on the basis of any general principle. [Section 137] has the clear purpose of making it more difficult for certain racial and religious minorities to achieve legislation that is in their interest.

JUSTICE BLACK, dissenting.

[There] is no constitutional provision . . . which bars any State from repealing any law on any subject at any time it pleases. [The] result of what the Court does is precisely as though it had commanded the State [to] keep on its books and enforce what the Court favors as a fair housing law. [While] the Court [has] power to invalidate state laws that discriminate on account of race [it] does not have power [to] prevent States from repealing [laws prohibiting private racial discrimination].

≣ ### Washington v. Seattle School District
≣ *458 U.S. 457 (1982)*

JUSTICE BLACKMUN delivered the opinion of the Court.

Because segregated housing patterns in Seattle have created racially imbalanced schools, the [Seattle School] District historically has taken steps to alleviate the isolation of minority students. [Although the Seattle School District had never engaged in unconstitutional racial segregation, the District] concluded that mandatory reassignment of students was necessary [and] enacted the so-called "Seattle Plan" for desegregation. The [plan] makes extensive use of [racially conscious] busing and mandatory reassignments. [Shortly] before the Seattle Plan was formally adopted, [a] number of Seattle residents [opposed to it] formed an organization called the Citizens for Voluntary Integration Committee (CiVIC). [CiVIC] drafted a statewide initiative designed to terminate the use of mandatory busing for purposes of racial integration. This proposal, known as Initiative 350, provided that "no school board [shall] directly or indirectly require any student to attend a school other than the school which is geographically nearest or next nearest the student's place of residence [and] which offers the course of study pursued by such student." The initiative then set out, however, a number of broad exceptions to this requirement: a student may be assigned beyond his neighborhood school if he "requires special education, care or guidance," or if "there are health or safety hazards, either natural or man made, or physical barriers or obstacles [between] the student's place of residence and the nearest or next nearest school," or if "the school nearest or next nearest to his place of residence is unfit or inadequate because of overcrowding, unsafe conditions or lack of physical facilities." Initiative 350 [envisioned] busing for racial purposes in only one circumstance: it did not purport to "prevent any court of competent jurisdiction from adjudicating constitutional issues relating to the public schools."

Initiative 350 [was] on the Washington ballot for the November 1978 general election. During [the] campaign, [CiVIC] did not [appeal] to "the racial biases of the voters" [but] focused almost exclusively on the wisdom of "forced busing" for integration. [Initiative] 350 passed by a substantial margin, drawing almost 66% of the vote statewide [and] some 61% of the vote [in Seattle]. A federal District Court [held] Initiative 350 unconstitutional [as] an impermissible racial classification in violation of Hunter v. Erickson, "because it permits busing for non-racial reasons but forbids it for racial reasons." [The Court of Appeals affirmed.]

[Equal protection] guarantees racial minorities the right to full participation in the political life of the community, [and] reaches [any measure that] subtly distorts governmental processes in such a way as to place special burdens on the ability of minority groups to achieve beneficial legislation. This principle received its clearest expression in [*Hunter*].

[L]aws structuring political institutions or allocating political power according to "neutral principles"—such as the executive veto, or the typically burdensome requirements for amending state constitutions—are not subject to equal protection attack, though they may "make it more difficult for minorities to achieve favorable legislation." Because such laws make it more difficult for every group in the community to enact comparable laws, they "[provide] a just framework within which the diverse political groups in our society may fairly compete." Thus, the political majority may generally restructure the political process to place obstacles in the path of everyone seeking to secure the benefits of governmental action. But a different analysis is required when the State allocates governmental power nonneutrally, by explicitly using the racial nature of a decision to determine the decisionmaking [process]. Initiative 350 must fall because it does "not [attempt] to allocate governmental power on the basis of any general principle" [but] uses the racial nature of an issue to define the governmental decisionmaking structure, and thus imposes substantial and unique burdens on racial minorities.

[Despite] its facial neutrality there is little doubt that the initiative was effectively drawn for racial purposes. . . . It is beyond reasonable dispute [that] the initiative was enacted "'because of,' not merely 'in spite of,' its adverse effects upon" busing for integration.

We are also satisfied that the practical effect of Initiative 350 is to work a reallocation of power of the kind condemned in *Hunter*. The initiative removes the authority to address a racial problem—and only a racial problem—from the existing decisionmaking body, in such a way as to burden minority interests. Those favoring the elimination of de facto school segregation now must seek relief from the state legislature, or from the statewide electorate. Yet authority over all other student assignment decisions, as well as over most other areas of educational policy, remains vested in the local school board. Indeed, by specifically exempting from Initiative 350's proscriptions most non-racial reasons for assigning students away from their neighborhood schools, the initiative expressly requires those championing school integration to surmount a considerably higher hurdle than persons seeking comparable legislative action. As in *Hunter*, then, the community's political mechanisms are modified to place effective decisionmaking authority over a racial issue at a different level of government. . . .

[Initiative 350] works something more than the "mere repeal" of a desegregation law by the political entity that created it. It burdens all future attempts to integrate Washington schools in districts throughout the State, by lodging decisionmaking authority over the question at a new and remote level of government. . . .

[Appellants] unquestionably are correct when they suggest that "purposeful discrimination is 'the condition that offends the Constitution.'" . . . But when the political process or the decisionmaking mechanism used to address racially conscious legislation—and only such legislation—is singled out for peculiar and disadvantageous treatment, the governmental action plainly "rests on 'distinctions based on race.'" And when the State's allocation of power places unusual burdens on the ability of racial groups to enact legislation specifically designed to overcome the "special condition" of prejudice, the governmental action seriously "[curtails] the operation of those political processes ordinarily to be relied upon to protect minorities." [*Carolene Products* n.4.] [Affirmed.]

JUSTICE POWELL, joined by CHIEF JUSTICE BURGER and JUSTICES REHNQUIST and O'CONNOR, dissenting.

The people of the State of Washington, by a two-to-one vote, have adopted a neighborhood school policy. The policy is binding on local school districts but in no way affects the authority of state or federal courts to order school transportation to remedy violations of the Fourteenth Amendment. Nor does the policy affect the power of local school districts to establish voluntary transfer programs for racial integration or for any other purpose.

In the absence of a constitutional violation, no decision of this Court compels a school district to adopt or maintain a mandatory busing program for racial integration. Accordingly, the Court does not hold that the adoption of a neighborhood school policy by local school districts would be unconstitutional. Rather, it holds that the adoption of such a policy at the state level—rather than at the local level—violates [equal protection]. I dissent from the Court's unprecedented intrusion into the structure of a state government. The School Districts in this case were under no federal constitutional obligation to adopt mandatory busing programs. The State of Washington, the governmental body ultimately responsible for the provision of public education, has determined that certain mandatory busing programs are detrimental to the education of its children. . . .

The Court has never held that there is an affirmative duty to integrate the schools in the absence of a finding of unconstitutional segregation. Certainly there is no constitutional duty to adopt mandatory busing in the absence of such a violation. [It is an equally] well-established principle that the States have "extraordinarily wide latitude [in] creating various types of political subdivisions and conferring authority upon them." The Constitution does not [define] institutions of local government. [A] State may choose to run its schools from the state legislature or through local school boards just as it may choose to address the matter of race relations at the state or local level. . . .

[By] Initiative 350, the State has adopted a policy of racial neutrality in student assignments. The policy in no way interferes with the power of state or federal courts to remedy constitutional violations. And if [that] policy had been adopted by any of the School Districts in this litigation there could have been no question that the policy was constitutional. The issue [arises] only because the Seattle School District—in the absence of a then-established state policy—chose to adopt race-specific school assignments with extensive busing. It is not questioned that the District itself, at any time thereafter, could have changed its mind and canceled its integration program without violating the Federal Constitution. Yet this Court holds that neither the legislature nor the people of the State of Washington could alter what the District had decided. The Court argues that the people of Washington by Initiative 350 created a racial classification, and yet must agree that identical action by the Seattle School District itself would have created no such classification. This is not an easy argument to answer because it seems to make no sense.

[Under] today's decision this heretofore undoubted supreme authority of a State's electorate is to be curtailed whenever a [state agency] or local instrumentality adopts a race-specific program that arguably benefits racial minorities. Once such a program is adopted, only the local or subordinate entity that approved it will have authority to change it. [It] is a strange notion—alien to our system—that local governmental bodies can forever pre-empt the ability of a State—the sovereign power—to address a matter of compelling concern to the State. The Constitution of the United States does not require such a bizarre result.

[In] moving to change a locally adopted policy [Washington has not] established a racially discriminatory requirement. Initiative 350 does not impede enforcement of the Fourteenth Amendment. If a Washington school district should be found to have established a segregated school system, Initiative 350 will place no barrier in the way of a remedial busing order. Nor does Initiative 350 authorize or approve segregation in any form or degree. It is neutral on its face, and racially neutral as public policy. Children of all races benefit from neighborhood schooling, just as children of all races benefit from exposure to " 'ethnic and racial diversity in the classroom.' "

Finally, Initiative 350 places no "special burdens on racial minorities within the governmental process," such that interference with the State's distribution of authority is justified. Initiative 350 is simply a reflection of the State's political process at work. It does not alter that process in any respect. It does not require, for example, that all matters dealing with race—or with integration in the schools—must henceforth be submitted to a referendum of the people. The State has done no more than precisely what the Court has said that it should do: It has "resolved through the political process" the "desirability and efficacy of [mandatory] school desegregation" where there has been no unlawful segregation. The political process in Washington [permits] persons who are dissatisfied at a local level to appeal to the state legislature or the people of the State for redress. It permits the people of a State to pre-empt local policies, and to formulate new programs and regulations. Such a process is inherent in the continued sovereignty of the States. This is our system. Any time a State chooses to address a major issue some persons or groups may be disadvantaged. In a democratic system there are winners and losers. But there is no inherent unfairness in this and certainly no constitutional violation.

[Nothing] in *Hunter* supports the Court's extraordinary invasion into the State's distribution of authority. [In] this case, unlike in *Hunter*, the political system has not been redrawn or altered. The authority of the State over the public school system, acting through initiative or the legislature, is plenary. Thus, the State's political system is not altered when it adopts for the first time a policy, concededly within the area of its authority, for the regulation of local school districts. And certainly racial minorities are not uniquely or comparatively burdened by the State's adoption of a policy that would be lawful if adopted by any school district in the State. *Hunter*, therefore, is simply irrelevant. It is the Court that by its decision today disrupts the normal course of State government. Under its unprecedented theory of a vested constitutional right to local decisionmaking, the State apparently is now forever barred from addressing the perplexing problems of how best to educate fairly all children in a multi-racial society where, as in this case, the local school board has acted first.

NOTES

1. *Crawford.* The Court decided Crawford v. Board of Education, 458 U.S. 527 (1982), on the same day as Washington v. Seattle School District. California courts had interpreted the California constitution to require busing of students to achieve racial balance in public schools under circumstances where such busing was *not* compelled by the federal Constitution. California voters then amended the state constitution to provide that "state courts shall not order mandatory pupil assignment or transportation unless a federal court would do so to remedy a violation of the Equal Protection Clause." The Court, 8 to 1, found no violation of equal protection. Strict scrutiny was not applicable because the amendment did not "embody a racial classification, [distort] the political process for racial reasons, [or] allocate[] governmental or judicial power on the basis of a discriminatory principle." Rather, it changed the substantive law of California on a race-neutral basis and did not alter the political process. Prior to the amendment advocates of busing were free to seek judicial orders to that effect under the state constitution; after the amendment advocates of busing were still free to do so, although their ability to obtain such orders was restricted by the substantive change to the state constitution. The Court repeated its declaration that "the mere repeal of race related legislation is [not] unconstitutional."

2. Questions. In Romer v. Evans, the Court did not rely on "alteration of the political process" to invalidate Colorado's Amendment 2, which banned laws prohibiting discrimination against gays and lesbians and stripped municipalities of the power to enact such laws. Did the Court in *Romer* not rely on the *Hunter* line of cases because those cases are limited to suspect classifications? Would a state constitutional amendment barring rent control laws and stripping municipalities of the power to enact rent control ordinances violate equal protection? Would a state constitutional amendment that repealed laws prohibiting sex discrimination and requiring that all such laws be enacted only at the state level violate equal protection?

Schuette v. Coalition to Defend Affirmative Action
134 S. Ct. 1623 (2014)

JUSTICE KENNEDY announced the judgment of the Court and delivered an opinion, in which THE CHIEF JUSTICE and JUSTICE ALITO join.

The Court . . . must determine whether an amendment to the Constitution of the State of Michigan . . . is invalid under the Equal Protection Clause of the Fourteenth Amendment. . . . [Michigan] voters in 2006 adopted an amendment to the State Constitution prohibiting state and other governmental entities in Michigan from granting . . . race-based preferences in a wide range of actions and decisions, [including] the admissions process for state universities. . . . The ballot proposal was called Proposal 2 and, after it passed by a margin of 58 percent to 42 percent, the resulting enactment became Article I, §26, of the Michigan Constitution.[1]

Section 26 was challenged in two cases, [consolidated by the federal district court, which] granted summary judgment to Michigan, thus upholding Proposal 2. [A panel of the Court of Appeals reversed, and that decision was upheld by the court, sitting en banc. Each of the panel and court, en banc] held that Proposal 2 had violated the principles . . . in *Washington v. Seattle School Dist. No. 1,* and in the cases that *Seattle* relied upon. [We] granted certiorari. . . .

The question here concerns not the permissibility of race-conscious admissions policies under the Constitution but whether, and in what manner, voters in the States may choose to prohibit the consideration of racial preferences in governmental decisions, in particular with respect to school admissions. . . . [S]ome States have decided to prohibit race-conscious admissions policies

---

1. Article 1, §26 states, in relevant part:

(1) The University of Michigan, Michigan State University, Wayne State University, and any other public college or university, community college, or school district shall not discriminate against, or grant preferential treatment to, any individual or group on the basis of race, sex, color, ethnicity, or national origin in the operation of public employment, public education, or public contracting.

(2) The state shall not discriminate against, or grant preferential treatment to, any individual or group on the basis of race, sex, color, ethnicity, or national origin in the operation of public employment, public education, or public contracting.

(3) For the purposes of this section "state" includes, but is not necessarily limited to, the state itself, any city, county, any public college, university, or community college, school district, or other political subdivision or governmental instrumentality of or within the State of Michigan not included in sub-section 1.[—ED.]

[and universities in those States] are currently engaged in experimenting with a wide variety of alternative approaches. In Michigan, . . . independent boards of trustees [have] plenary authority over public universities, including admissions policies, [though there is evidence that] they delegated authority over admissions policy to the faculty. But whether the boards or the faculty set the specific policy, Michigan's public universities did consider race as a factor in admissions decisions before 2006.

In holding §26 invalid in the context of student admissions at state universities, the Court of Appeals relied in primary part on *Seattle*, which it deemed to control. . . . But that . . . conclusion is mistaken here. . . .

Seattle involved a state initiative that "was carefully tailored to interfere only with desegregative busing." The *Seattle* Court, accepting the validity of the school board's busing remedy as a predicate to its analysis of the constitutional question, found that the State's disapproval of the school board's busing remedy was an aggravation of the very racial injury in which the State itself was complicit. The broad language used in *Seattle*, however, went well beyond the analysis needed to resolve the case. . . . *Seattle* stated that where a government policy "inures primarily to the benefit of the minority" and "minorities . . . consider" the policy to be "in their interest," then any state action that "place[s] effective decisionmaking authority over" that policy "at a different level of government" must be reviewed under strict scrutiny. In essence . . . , any state action with a "racial focus" that makes it "more difficult for certain racial minorities than for other groups" to "achieve legislation that is in their interest" is subject to strict scrutiny. It is this reading of *Seattle* that the Court of Appeals found to be controlling here. And that reading must be rejected. . . .

The expansive reading of *Seattle* has no principled limitation and raises serious questions of compatibility with the Court's settled equal protection jurisprudence. To the extent *Seattle* is read to require the Court to determine and declare which political policies serve the "interest" of a group defined in racial terms that rationale was unnecessary to the decision in *Seattle*; it has no support in precedent; and it raises serious constitutional concerns. That expansive language does not provide a proper guide for decisions and should not be deemed authoritative or controlling. The rule that the Court of Appeals elaborated and respondents seek to establish here would contradict central equal protection principles. . . .

It cannot be entertained as a serious proposition that all individuals of the same race think alike. Yet that proposition would be a necessary beginning point were the *Seattle* formulation to control. . . . And . . . still another beginning point would be to define individuals according to race. But in a society in which those lines are becoming more blurred, the attempt to define race-based categories also raises serious questions of its own. Government action that classifies individuals on the basis of race is inherently suspect and carries the danger of perpetuating the very racial divisions the polity seeks to transcend. Were courts to embark upon this venture not only would it be undertaken with no clear legal standards or accepted sources to guide judicial decision but also it would result in, or at least impose a high risk of, inquiries and categories dependent upon demeaning stereotypes, classifications of questionable constitutionality on their own terms.

Even assuming these initial steps could be taken in a manner consistent with a sound analytic and judicial framework, the court would next be required to determine the policy realms in which certain groups—groups defined by race—have a political interest. That undertaking, again without guidance from any accepted legal standards, would risk, in turn, the creation of incentives for those who support or oppose certain policies to cast the debate in terms of racial advantage or disadvantage. Thus could racial antagonisms and conflict tend to arise in the context of judicial decisions as courts undertook to announce what particular issues of public policy should be classified as advantageous to some group defined by race. This risk is inherent in adopting the *Seattle* formulation.

There would be no apparent limiting standards defining what public policies should be included in what *Seattle* called policies that "inur[e] primarily to the benefit of the minority" and that "minorities . . . consider" to be "in their interest." Those who seek to represent the interests of particular racial groups could attempt to advance those aims by demanding an equal protection ruling that any number of matters be foreclosed from voter review or participation. In a nation in which governmental policies are wide ranging, those who seek to limit voter participation might be tempted, were this Court to adopt the *Seattle* formulation, to urge that a group they choose to define by race or racial stereotypes are advantaged or disadvantaged by any number of laws or decisions. Tax policy, housing subsidies, wage regulations, and even the naming of public schools, highways, and monuments are just a few examples of what could become a list of subjects that some organizations could insist should be beyond the power of voters to decide, or beyond the power of a legislature to decide when enacting limits on the power of local authorities or other governmental entities to address certain subjects. . . .

Perhaps, when enacting policies as an exercise of democratic self-government, voters will determine that race-based preferences should be adopted. The constitutional validity of some of those choices regarding racial preferences is not at issue here. The holding in the instant case is simply that the courts may not disempower the voters from choosing which path to follow. . . .

[In this case] there was no infliction of a specific injury of the kind at issue in *Mulkey* and *Hunter* and in the history of the Seattle schools. . . . [The] question is not how to address or prevent injury caused on account of race but whether voters may determine whether a policy of race-based preferences should be continued. By . . . adding §26 to their State Constitution, the Michigan voters exercised their privilege to enact laws as a basic exercise of their democratic power. . . . Michigan voters used the initiative system to bypass public officials who were deemed not responsive to the concerns of a majority of the voters with respect to a policy of granting race-based preferences that raises difficult and delicate issues.

The freedom secured by the Constitution consists, in one of its essential dimensions, of the right of the individual not to be injured by the unlawful exercise of governmental power. Yet freedom does not stop with individual rights. Our constitutional system embraces, too, the right of citizens to debate so they can learn and decide and then, through the political process, act in concert to try to shape the course of their own times and the course of a nation. . . . Here Michigan voters acted in concert and statewide to seek consensus and adopt a policy on a difficult subject against a historical background of race in America that has been a source of tragedy and persisting injustice. That history demands that we continue to learn, to listen, and to remain open to new approaches if we are to aspire always to a constitutional order in which all persons are treated with fairness and equal dignity. Were the Court to rule that the question addressed by Michigan voters is too sensitive or complex to be within the grasp of the electorate; or that the policies at issue remain too delicate to be resolved save by university officials or faculties, acting at some remove from immediate public scrutiny and control; or that these matters are so arcane that the electorate's power must be limited because the people cannot prudently exercise that power even after a full debate, that holding would be an unprecedented restriction on the exercise of a fundamental right held not just by one person but by all in common. It is the right to speak and debate and learn and then, as a matter of political will, to act through a lawful electoral process. . . .

This case is not about how the debate about racial preferences should be resolved. It is about who may resolve it. There is no authority in the Constitution of the United States or in this Court's precedents for the Judiciary to set aside Michigan laws that commit this policy determination to the voters. Deliberative debate on sensitive issues such as racial preferences all too often may shade into rancor. But that does not justify removing certain court-determined issues from the voters' reach. Democracy does not presume that some subjects are either too divisive or too profound for public debate.

[Reversed.]

CHIEF JUSTICE ROBERTS, concurring.

The dissent devotes 11 pages to expounding its own policy preferences in favor of taking race into account in college admissions, while nonetheless concluding that it "do[es] not mean to suggest that the virtues of adopting race-sensitive admissions policies should inform the legal question before the Court." . . . The dissent states that "[t]he way to stop discrimination on the basis of race is to speak openly and candidly on the subject of race." And it urges that "[r]ace matters because of the slights, the snickers, the silent judgments that reinforce that most crippling of thoughts: 'I do not belong here.'" But it is not "out of touch with reality" to conclude that racial preferences may themselves have the debilitating effect of reinforcing precisely that doubt, and—if so—that the preferences do more harm than good. To disagree with the dissent's views on the costs and benefits of racial preferences is not to "wish away, rather than confront" racial inequality. People can disagree in good faith on this issue, but it similarly does more harm than good to question the openness and candor of those on either side of the debate.

JUSTICE SCALIA, with whom JUSTICE THOMAS joins, concurring in the judgment.

It has come to this. Called upon to explore the jurisprudential twilight zone between two errant lines of precedent, we confront a frighteningly bizarre question: Does the Equal Protection Clause . . . *forbid* what its text plainly *requires*? Needless to say (except that this case obliges us to say it), the question answers itself. "The Constitution proscribes government discrimination on the basis of race, and state-provided education is no exception." [*Grutter.*] It is precisely this understanding — the correct understanding — of the federal Equal Protection Clause that the people of the State of Michigan have adopted for their own fundamental law. By adopting it, they did not simultaneously *offend* it. . . .

But the battleground for this case is not the constitutionality of race-based admissions. . . . Rather, it is the so-called political-process doctrine. . . . I agree with those parts of the plurality opinion that repudiate this doctrine. But I do not agree with its reinterpretation of *Seattle* and *Hunter*, which makes them stand in part for the cloudy and doctrinally anomalous proposition that whenever state action poses "the serious risk . . . of causing specific injuries on account of race," it denies equal protection. I would instead reaffirm that the "ordinary principles of our law [and] of our democratic heritage" require "plaintiffs alleging equal protection violations" stemming from facially neutral acts to "prove intent and causation and not merely the existence of racial disparity." I would further hold that a law directing state actors to provide equal protection is (to say the least) facially neutral, and cannot violate the Constitution. Section 26 of the Michigan Constitution . . . rightly stands. . . .

The plurality . . . disavows the political-process-doctrine basis on which *Hunter* and *Seattle* were decided, [but] it does not take the next step of overruling those cases. Rather, it reinterprets them beyond recognition. . . . Patently atextual, unadministrable, and contrary to our traditional equal protection jurisprudence, *Hunter* and *Seattle* should be overruled. The problems with the political-process doctrine begin with its triggering prong, which assigns to a court the task of determining whether a law that reallocates policymaking authority concerns a "racial issue." . . . No good can come of such random judicial musing. . . . For one thing, it involves judges in the dirty business of dividing the Nation "into racial blocs." That task is as difficult as it is unappealing. (Does a half-Latino, half-American Indian have Latino interests, American-Indian interests, both, half of both?) What is worse, the exercise promotes the noxious fiction that, knowing only a person's color or ethnicity, we can be sure that he has a predetermined set of policy "interests. . . ." Whether done by a judge or a school board, such "racial stereotyping [is] at odds with equal protection mandates."

But that is not the "racial issue" prong's only defect. More fundamentally, it misreads the Equal Protection Clause to protect "particular group[s]," a construction that we have tirelessly repudiated in a "long line of cases understanding equal protection as a personal right." It is a "basic principle that the Fifth and Fourteenth Amendments to the Constitution protect *persons*, not *groups*." . . .

I turn now to the second part of the *Hunter-Seattle* analysis. . . . This part of the inquiry directs a court to determine whether the challenged act "place[s] effective decisionmaking authority over [the] racial issue at a different level of government." *Seattle*. The laws in both *Hunter* and *Seattle* were thought to fail this test. . . . By contrast, in another line of cases, we have emphasized the near-limitless sovereignty of each State to design its governing structure as it sees fit. . . . *Holt Civic Club v. Tuscaloosa*, 439 U.S. 60, 71 (1978). Accordingly, States have "absolute discretion" to determine the "number, nature and duration of the powers conferred upon [municipal] corporations and the territory over which they shall be exercised." *Holt Civic Club*. So it would seem to go without saying that a State may give certain powers to cities, later assign the same powers to counties, and even reclaim them for itself. Taken to the limits of its logic, *Hunter-Seattle* is the gaping exception that nearly swallows the rule of structural state sovereignty. . . .

As Justice Harlan observed over a century ago, "[o]ur Constitution is color-blind, and neither knows nor tolerates classes among citizens." *Plessy v. Ferguson* (dissenting opinion). The people of Michigan wish the same for their governing charter. It would be shameful for us to stand in their way.

JUSTICE BREYER, concurring in the judgment.

. . . [The] Constitution permits, though it does not require, the use of the kind of race-conscious programs that are now barred by the Michigan Constitution. . . . But the Constitution foresees the ballot box, not the courts, as the normal instrument for resolving differences and debates about the merits of these programs. [N]either *Hunter* nor *Seattle* applies here. And the parties do not . . . suggest that the amendment violates the Equal Protection Clause if not under the *Hunter-Seattle* doctrine.

Hunter and *Seattle* involved . . . a restructuring of the political process that changed the political level at which policies were enacted. . . . This case, in contrast, does not involve a reordering of the *political* process; it does not in fact involve the movement of decisionmaking from one political level to another. Rather, here, Michigan law delegated broad policymaking authority to elected university boards, but those boards delegated admissions-related decisionmaking authority to unelected university faculty members and administrators. Although the boards unquestionably retained the *power* to set policy regarding race-conscious admissions, in *fact* faculty members and administrators set the race-conscious admissions policies in question. . . . Thus, unelected faculty members and administrators, not voters or their elected representatives, adopted the race-conscious admissions programs affected by Michigan's constitutional amendment. The amendment took decisionmaking authority away from these unelected actors and placed it in the hands of the voters.

Why does this matter? . . . [In] *Hunter* and *Seattle* . . . minorities had participated in the political process and they had won. The majority's subsequent reordering of the political process repealed the minority's successes and made it more difficult for the minority to succeed in the future. The majority thereby diminished the minority's ability to participate meaningfully in the electoral process. But one cannot . . . characterize the movement of the decisionmaking mechanism at issue here—from an administrative process to an electoral process—as diminishing the minority's ability to participate meaningfully in the *political* process. There is no prior electoral process in which the minority participated. . . .

JUSTICE SOTOMAYOR, with whom JUSTICE GINSBURG joins, dissenting.

. . . A majority of the Michigan electorate changed the basic rules of the political process in that State in a manner that uniquely disadvantaged racial minorities. Prior to the enactment of the constitutional initiative at issue here, all of the admissions policies of Michigan's public colleges and universities—including race-sensitive admissions policies—were in the hands of each institution's governing board. . . . [R]acial minorities in Michigan . . . succeeded in persuading the elected board representatives to adopt admissions policies that took into account the benefits of racial diversity. . . . In the wake of *Grutter*, some voters in Michigan set out to eliminate the use of race-sensitive admissions policies. Those voters . . . could have persuaded existing board members to change their minds through individual or grassroots lobbying efforts, or through general public awareness campaigns. Or they could have mobilized efforts to vote uncooperative board members out of office, replacing them with members who would share their desire to abolish race-sensitive admissions policies. When this Court holds that the Constitution permits a particular policy, nothing prevents a majority of a State's voters from choosing not to adopt that policy. . . . But instead, the majority of Michigan voters changed the rules in the middle of the game, reconfiguring the existing political process in Michigan in a manner that burdened racial minorities. They did so in the 2006 election by amending the Michigan Constitution to enact Art. I, §26, [as a result of which] there are now two very different processes through which a Michigan citizen is permitted to influence the admissions policies of the State's universities: one for persons interested in race-sensitive admissions policies and one for everyone else. A citizen who is a University of Michigan alumnus, for instance, can advocate for an admissions policy that considers an applicant's legacy status by meeting individually with members of the Board of Regents to convince them of her views, by joining with other legacy parents to lobby the Board, or by voting for and supporting Board candidates who share her position. The same options are available to a citizen who wants the Board to adopt admissions policies that consider athleticism, geography, area of study, and so on. The one and only policy a Michigan citizen may not seek through this long-established process is a race-sensitive admissions policy that considers race in an individualized manner when it is clear that race-neutral alternatives are not adequate to achieve diversity. For that policy alone, the citizens of Michigan must undertake the daunting task of amending the State Constitution.

Our precedents do not permit political restructurings that create one process for racial minorities and a separate, less burdensome process for everyone else. . . . When the majority reconfigures the political process in a manner that burdens only a racial minority, that alteration triggers strict judicial scrutiny. . . . This case is not . . . about "who may resolve" the debate over the use of race in higher education admissions. . . . Rather, this case is about *how* the debate over the use of race-sensitive admissions policies may be resolved. . . . While our Constitution does not guarantee minority groups victory in the political process, it does guarantee them meaningful and equal access to that process. . . . Today, by permitting a majority of the voters in Michigan to do what our Constitution forbids, the Court ends the debate over race-sensitive admissions policies in Michigan in a manner that contravenes constitutional protections long recognized in our precedents. . . .

[Under] *Hunter* and *Seattle* . . . governmental action deprives minority groups of equal protection when it (1) has a racial focus, targeting a policy or program that "inures primarily to the benefit of the minority," and (2) alters the political process in a manner that uniquely burdens racial minorities' ability to achieve their goals through that process. . . .

Section 26 has a "racial focus." That is clear from its text, which prohibits Michigan's public colleges and universities from "grant[ing] preferential treatment to any individual or group on the basis of race." [R]ace-sensitive admissions policies "inur[e] primarily to the benefit of the minority," as they are designed to increase minorities' access to institutions of higher education. . . . Section 26 restructures the political process in Michigan in a manner that places unique burdens on racial minorities. It establishes a distinct and more burdensome political process for the enactment of admissions plans that consider racial diversity. . . .

Race matters. Race matters in part because of the long history of racial minorities being denied access to the political process. . . . Race also matters because of persistent racial inequality in society—inequality that cannot be ignored and that has produced stark socioeconomic disparities. . . . Race matters to a young man's view of society when he spends his teenage years watching others tense up as he passes, no matter the neighborhood where he grew up. Race matters to a young woman's sense of self when she states her hometown, and then is pressed, "No, where are you *really* from?", regardless of how many generations her family has been in the country. Race matters to a young person addressed by a stranger in a foreign language, which he does not understand because only English was spoken at home. Race matters because of the slights, the snickers, the silent judgments that reinforce that most crippling of thoughts: "I do not belong here." In my colleagues' view, examining the racial impact of legislation only perpetuates racial discrimination. This refusal to accept the stark reality that race matters is regrettable. The way to stop discrimination on the basis of race is to speak openly and candidly on the subject of race, and to apply the Constitution with eyes open to the unfortunate effects of centuries of racial discrimination. . . .

. . . Today's decision eviscerates an important strand of our equal protection jurisprudence. For members of historically marginalized groups, which rely on the federal courts to protect their constitutional rights, the decision can hardly bolster hope for a vision of democracy that preserves for all the right to participate meaningfully and equally in self-government.

I respectfully dissent.

JUSTICE KAGAN took no part in the consideration or decision of this case.

D. STRICT SCRUTINY AND SUSPECT CLASSIFICATIONS: LAWFUL RESIDENT ALIENS

Classifications treating lawful resident aliens differently than citizens are said to be subject to strict scrutiny, but the Court has recognized so many exceptions to this principle that in practice it means that the only alienage classifications subject to strict scrutiny are those used by *states*, and then only with respect to matters that do not implicate a state's legitimate power "to preserve the basic conception of a political community." Dunn v. Blumstein, 405 U.S. 330, 344 (1972). For many years state classifications by alienage triggered only minimal equal protection scrutiny, though such state laws were frequently invalidated on the ground that they were preempted by Congress's exercise of its exclusive control over immigration and naturalization. But in Graham v. Richardson, 403 U.S. 365 (1971), the Court used equal protection to void a Pennsylvania law restricting public assistance to citizens and an Arizona law limiting such benefits to citizens and longtime lawful resident aliens. The Court concluded that strict scrutiny applied to alienage classifications employed by states, characterizing "[a]liens as a class [as] a prime example of a 'discrete and insular' minority for whom such heightened judicial solicitude is appropriate." But application of the rule has been anything but monolithic.

≡ **Sugarman v. Dougall**
≡ *413 U.S. 634 (1973)*

[New York's Civil Service Law permitted only American citizens to hold permanent civil service positions. A lower federal court ruled that the limitation violated the equal protection guarantee. The Court affirmed.]

JUSTICE BLACKMUN delivered the opinion of the Court.

The Court is faced only with the question whether New York's flat statutory prohibition against the employment of aliens in the competitive classified civil service is constitutionally valid. The Court is not asked to decide whether [a] legislative scheme that bars some or all aliens from closely defined and limited classes of public employment on a uniform and consistent basis [is valid].

Appellants argue [that the law] does not violate [equal protection] because the statute "[reflects] the special requirements of public employment in the career civil service." The distinction drawn between the citizen and the alien, it is said, "rests on the fundamental concept of identity between a government and the members, or citizens, of the state." The civil servant "participates directly in the formulation and execution of government policy," and thus must be free of competing obligations to another power. The State's interest in having an employee of undivided loyalty is substantial, for obligations attendant upon foreign citizenship "might impair the exercise of his judgment or jeopardize public confidence in his objectivity."

[But] appellants' asserted justification proves both too much and too little. [The] State's broad prohibition of the employment of aliens applies to many positions with respect to which the State's proffered justification has little, if any, relationship. At the same time, the prohibition has no application at all to positions that would seem naturally to fall within the State's asserted purpose. Our standard of review of statutes that treat aliens differently from citizens requires a greater degree of precision.

[The law] does not withstand the necessary close scrutiny. We recognize a State's interest in establishing its own form of government, and in limiting participation in that government to those who are within "the basic conception of a political community." We recognize, too, the State's broad power to define its political community. But in seeking to achieve this substantial purpose, with discrimination against aliens, the means the State employs must be precisely drawn in light of the acknowledged purpose. [The law] is neither narrowly confined nor precise in its application. Its imposed ineligibility may apply to the "sanitation man, class B," to the typist, and to the office worker, as well as to the person who directly participates in the formulation and execution of important state policy. [We] hold that [the law] which denies all aliens the right to hold positions in New York's classified competitive civil service violates [equal protection].

[But] we do not hold that [a] State may not, in an appropriately defined class of positions, require citizenship as a qualification for office. [Such] power inheres in the State by virtue of its obligation "to preserve the basic conception of a political community." And this power and responsibility of the State applies, not only to the qualifications of voters, but also to persons holding state elective or important nonelective executive, legislative, and judicial positions, for officers who participate directly in the formulation, execution, or review of broad public policy perform functions that go to the heart of representative government. [While] such state action [is] not wholly immune from [equal protection] scrutiny, [our] scrutiny will not be so demanding where we deal with matters resting firmly within a State's constitutional prerogatives.

This is no more than a recognition of a State's historical power to exclude aliens from participation in its democratic political institutions. [Affirmed.]

JUSTICE REHNQUIST, dissenting.

The Court [holds] that an alien is not really different from a citizen, and that any legislative classification on the basis of alienage is "inherently suspect." [There] is no language used in the [Fourteenth] Amendment, or any historical evidence as to the intent of the Framers, which would suggest to the slightest degree that it was intended to render alienage a "suspect" classification, that it was designed in any way to protect "discrete and insular minorities" other than racial minorities, or that it would in any way justify the result reached by the Court. [The] aliens [here] took no steps to obtain citizenship or indicate any affirmative desire to become citizens. [Their] "status" [was] not, therefore, one with which they were forever encumbered; they could take steps to alter it when and if they chose.

[The] Court, by holding [that] a citizen-alien classification is "suspect" in the eyes of our Constitution, fails to mention the fact that the Constitution itself recognizes a basic difference between citizens and aliens. That distinction is constitutionally important in no less than 11 instances in a political document noted for its brevity. [Moreover, the] first sentence of the Fourteenth Amendment [defines] who is a citizen of the United States. . . . [That] a "citizen" was considered . . . to be a rationally distinct subclass of all "persons" is obvious from the language of the Amendment.

[This] Court has held time and again that legislative classifications on the basis of citizenship were subject to the rational-basis test of equal protection. [The] paramount "decision" upon which the Court relied in *Graham* [to repudiate this settled law], and which is merely quoted in the instant decisions, is [footnote 4 in *Carolene Products*]. On the "authority" of this footnote, which only four Members of the Court in *Carolene Products* joined, the Court in *Graham* merely stated that "classifications based on alienage [are] inherently suspect" because "aliens as a class are a prime example of a 'discrete and insular' minority [for] whom such heightened judicial solicitude is appropriate." . . .

The approach taken in *Graham* . . . appears to be that whenever the Court feels that a societal group is "discrete and insular," it has the constitutional mandate to prohibit legislation that somehow treats the group differently from some other group. Our society, consisting of over 200 million individuals of multitudinous origins, customs, tongues, beliefs, and cultures, is, to say the least, diverse. It would hardly take extraordinary ingenuity for a lawyer to find "insular and discrete" minorities at every turn in the road. Yet, unless the Court can precisely define and constitutionally justify both the terms and analysis it uses, these decisions today stand for the proposition that the Court can choose a "minority" it "feels" deserves "solicitude" and thereafter prohibit the States from classifying that "minority" differently from the "majority." I cannot find, and the Court does not cite, any constitutional authority for such a "ward of the Court" approach to equal protection. [Moreover,] there is a marked difference between a status or condition such as illegitimacy, national origin, or race, which cannot be altered by an individual and the "status" of [lawfully resident aliens, whose] status as aliens [can] be changed by their affirmative acts.

In my view, the proper judicial inquiry is whether any rational justification exists for prohibiting aliens from employment in the competitive civil service and from admission to a state bar. [I] do not believe that it is irrational for New York to require this class of civil servants to be citizens. . . . The proliferation of public administration that our society has witnessed . . . has vested a great deal of de facto decisionmaking or policymaking authority in the hands of employees who would not be considered the textbook equivalent of policymakers of the legislative or "top" administrative variety. [As] far as the private individual who must seek approval or services is concerned, many of these "low level" civil servants are in fact policymakers. [Nor is it] irrational to assume that aliens as a class are not familiar with how we as individuals treat others and how we expect "government" to treat us.

NOTES

1. Scope of Strict Scrutiny. In a companion case, In re Griffiths, 413 U.S. 717 (1973), the Court applied strict scrutiny to void Connecticut's exclusion of lawfully resident aliens from the practice of law. In the wake of *Sugarman*, the Court applied strict scrutiny to state laws barring lawfully resident aliens from becoming a notary public, Bernal v. Fainter, 467 U.S. 216 (1984); the practice of engineering, Examining Board v. Flores de Otero, 426 U.S. 572 (1976); and receipt of college financial aid (unless the alien had declared his intention to become an American citizen when eligible to do so), Nyquist v. Mauclet, 432 U.S. 1 (1977).

By contrast the Court has ruled that the "political function" exception to strict scrutiny identified in *Sugarman* applies to police officers, Foley v. Connelie, 435 U.S. 291 (1978); public schoolteachers, Ambach v. Norwick, 441 U.S. 68 (1979); and probation officers, Cabell v. Chavez-Salido, 454 U.S. 432 (1982). In each case the discretionary authority wielded by the officeholder, coupled with the role of the job as either an instrument of sovereign power (police and probation officers) or to inculcate distinct cultural values (schoolteachers) were the persuasive factors in finding the "political function" exception to apply.

2. Alienage Classifications by the Federal Government. The federal government has exclusive control over immigration and naturalization and thus enjoys broad authority to employ alienage as a statutory criterion in ways that are forbidden to the states. In Mathews v. Diaz, 426 U.S. 67 (1976), the Court applied minimal scrutiny in upholding a federal statute that limited Medicare eligibility to citizens and lawfully admitted aliens who had resided in the United States for at least five years. The Court applied the most minimal scrutiny in upholding the law against an equal protection challenge. The Court relied heavily upon Congress's "broad power over naturalization and immigration. [The] reasons that preclude judicial review of political questions also dictate a narrow standard of review of decisions made by the Congress or the President in the area of immigration and naturalization."

Though Congress or the President may use alienage as a classification device without triggering strict scrutiny, such classifications by administrative agencies may offend the due process clause, rather than equal protection. In Hampton v. Mow Sun Wong, 426 U.S. 88 (1976), the Court struck down a Civil Service Commission regulation that barred aliens from most civil service jobs. The Court voided the broad exclusion:

> [D]ue process requires that there be a legitimate basis for presuming that [an alienage classification] was actually intended to serve [an] overriding national interest. [Since] these residents were admitted as a result of decisions made by the Congress and the President, [due process] requires that the decision to [deprive them] of an important liberty be made either at a comparable level of government or, if it is to be permitted to be made by the [Commission], that it be justified by reasons which are properly the concern of that agency.

Could Congress authorize the states to discriminate against lawful resident aliens in the provision of federally financed social welfare benefits? Could the federal Health and Human Services Department (assuming it had statutory authority to do so) issue regulations limiting social welfare benefits to citizens or aliens lawfully resident for at least five years?

E.   INTERMEDIATE SCRUTINY: SEX AND ILLEGITIMACY

While sex classifications have been used to stereotype and marginalize women, facts that argue for heightened scrutiny, the Court also thinks that sex, far more often than race, may be relevant to legitimate government objectives. The tension between these opposing forces has resolved itself into an uneasy equilibrium of intermediate scrutiny.

Sex classifications invited only minimal scrutiny and were uniformly upheld until Reed v. Reed, 404 U.S. 71 (1971). Idaho law stipulated that men should be preferred to women as court-appointed administrators of an intestate decedent's estate. The Court applied minimal scrutiny to the law but invalidated it as irrational—"the very kind of arbitrary legislative choice forbidden by the Equal Protection Clause." The result, if not anything said by the Court, hinted at a de facto higher level of scrutiny.

The argument over the level of scrutiny broke into the open in Frontiero v. Richardson, 411 U.S. 677 (1973). Federal law permitted a male member of the armed services automatically to claim his wife as a dependent, and thus acquire increased housing and medical benefits, but it did not permit a female service member to do so unless she could demonstrate that her husband was in fact dependent on her for over half of his support. The Court struck down the provision as a violation of equal protection but could not muster a majority around any one standard of review. Four justices, led by Justice Brennan, argued for treating sex as a suspect classification, thus triggering strict scrutiny. Justice Brennan relied on "a long and unfortunate history of sex discrimination" and the fact that "sex, like race and national origin, is an immutable characteristic [that] frequently bears no relationship to ability to perform or contribute to society." Four justices thought the provision violated equal protection but were unwilling to declare that sex was a suspect classification. They did not specify the standard of review they were employing but intimated that it was minimal scrutiny. Only Justice Rehnquist dissented.

Over the next few years the Court struck down sex classifications rooted in what the Court described as "archaic and overbroad" generalizations about sex roles. In Weinberger v. Wiesenfeld, 420 U.S. 636 (1975), the Court voided a Social Security Act provision that entitled a widow, but not a widower, to benefits based on the earnings of the deceased spouse. The archaic and overbroad premise of the provision was "that male workers' earnings are vital to the support of their families, while the earnings of [females] do not significantly contribute to their families' support." In Stanton v. Stanton, 421 U.S. 7 (1975), the Court applied similar reasoning to a Utah law that required parental support of male offspring to age 21 but of female children only to age 18. The Court said that there was "nothing rational" in the underlying premise that "the female [is] destined solely for the home and the rearing of the family, and only the male for the marketplace and the world of ideas."

But in Kahn v. Shevin, 416 U.S. 351 (1974), the Court upheld a property tax exemption for widows, but not widowers, on the ground that the distinction was rationally related to the greater financial problems of widows. In Schlesinger v. Ballard, 419 U.S. 498 (1975), the Court upheld a Navy promotion rule that required male officers to be promoted or discharged within a shorter period than that imposed on women officers, on the ground that the longer promotion period for women was a rational compensation for the fewer opportunities available to women to display their merit. Finally, in Geduldig v. Aiello, 417 U.S. 484 (1974), the Court ruled that California's exclusion of pregnancy from disability insurance coverage was not a sex classification; it merely removed "one physical condition—pregnancy—from the list of compensable disabilities."

A majority of the Court finally settled on a single standard of review in the next case.

≣≣≣ ### Craig v. Boren
429 U.S. 190 (1976)

JUSTICE BRENNAN delivered the opinion of the Court.

[Oklahoma law] prohibits the sale of . . . 3.2% beer to males under the age of 21 and to females under the age of 18. The question to be decided is whether such a gender-based differential constitutes a denial to males 18-20 years of age of [equal protection]. To withstand constitutional challenge, previous cases establish that classifications by gender must serve important governmental objectives and must be substantially related to achievement of those objectives. Thus, in *Reed*, the objectives of "reducing the workload on probate courts" and "avoiding intrafamily controversy" were deemed of insufficient importance to sustain use of an overt gender criterion in the appointment of administrators of intestate decedents' estates. Decisions following *Reed* similarly have rejected administrative ease and convenience as sufficiently important objectives to justify gender-based classifications.

[*Reed*] has also provided the underpinning for decisions that have invalidated statutes employing gender as an inaccurate proxy for other, more germane bases of classification. Hence, "archaic and overbroad" generalizations concerning the financial position of servicewomen and working women could not justify use of a gender line in determining eligibility for certain governmental entitlements. Similarly, increasingly outdated misconceptions concerning the role of females in the home rather than in the "marketplace and world of ideas" were rejected as loose-fitting characterizations incapable of supporting state statutory schemes that were premised upon their accuracy. [We] turn then to the question whether [the] difference between males and females with respect to the purchase of 3.2% beer warrants the differential in age drawn by the Oklahoma statute. We conclude that it does not.

[T]he objective underlying [the classification is] enhancement of traffic safety. Clearly, the protection of public health and safety represents an important function of state and local governments. However, appellees' statistics . . . cannot support the conclusion that the gender-based distinction closely serves to achieve that objective and therefore the distinction cannot . . . withstand equal protection challenge.

[The statistical evidence showed that] 18-20-year-old male arrests for "driving under the influence" and "drunkenness" substantially exceeded female arrests for that same age period, [that] youths aged 17-21 were found to be overrepresented among those killed or injured in traffic accidents, with males again numerically exceeding females in this regard, [that] young males were more inclined to drive and drink beer than were their female counterparts, [and that evidence from other states confirmed] the pervasiveness of youthful participation in motor vehicle accidents following the imbibing of alcohol. [But this evidence] offers only a weak answer to the equal protection [question]. The [data on] arrests of 18-20-year-olds for alcohol-related driving offenses exemplifies the ultimate unpersuasiveness of this evidentiary record. Viewed in terms of the correlation between sex and the actual activity that Oklahoma seeks to regulate—driving while under the influence of alcohol—the statistics broadly establish that .18% of females and 2% of males in that age group were arrested for that offense. While such a disparity is not trivial in a statistical sense, it hardly can form the basis for employment of a gender line as a classifying device. Certainly if maleness is to serve as a proxy for drinking and driving, a correlation of 2% must be considered an unduly tenuous "fit."[10] . . .

Moreover, the statistics exhibit a variety of other shortcomings that seriously impugn their value to equal protection analysis. Setting aside the obvious methodological problems,[11] the surveys do not adequately justify the salient features of Oklahoma's gender-based traffic-safety law. . . . [P]roving broad sociological propositions by statistics is a dubious business, and one that inevitably is in tension with the normative philosophy that underlies [equal protection]. Suffice to say that the showing offered by the appellees does not satisfy us that sex represents a legitimate, accurate proxy for the regulation of drinking and driving. In fact, when it is further recognized that Oklahoma's statute prohibits only the selling of 3.2% beer to young males and not their drinking the beverage once acquired (even after purchase by their 18-20-year-old female companions), the relationship between gender and traffic safety becomes far too tenuous to satisfy [the] requirement that the gender-based difference be substantially related to achievement of the statutory objective.

We hold [that] Oklahoma's 3.2% beer statute invidiously discriminates against males 18-20 years of age [and] constitutes a denial of [equal protection].

JUSTICE POWELL, concurring.

[Candor] compels the recognition that the relatively deferential "rational basis" standard of review normally applied takes on a sharper focus when we address a gender-based classification.

I view this as a relatively easy case. No one questions the legitimacy or importance of the asserted governmental objective: the promotion of highway safety. The decision [turns] on whether the [classification] bears a " 'fair and substantial relation' " to this objective. [The] statistics [tend] generally to support the view that young men drive more, possibly are inclined to drink more, and [are] involved in more accidents than young women. Even so, I am not persuaded that these facts and the inferences fairly drawn from them justify this classification, [especially since it] is so easily circumvented as to be virtually meaningless. Putting it differently, this gender-based classification does not bear a fair and substantial relation to the object of the legislation.

JUSTICE STEVENS, concurring.

There is only one Equal Protection Clause. [It] does not direct the courts to apply one standard of review in some cases and a different standard in other cases. [What] has become known as the two-tiered analysis of equal

10. Obviously, arrest statistics do not embrace all individuals who drink and drive [but we] know of no way of extrapolating these arrest statistics to take into account the driving and drinking population at large, including those who avoided arrest.

11. The very social stereotypes that find reflection in age-differential laws are likely substantially to distort the accuracy of these comparative statistics. Hence "reckless" young men who drink and drive are transformed into arrest statistics, whereas their female counterparts are chivalrously escorted home.

protection claims does not describe a completely logical method of deciding cases, but rather is a method the Court has employed to explain decisions that actually apply a single standard in a reasonably consistent fashion.

[In] this case, the classification [is] objectionable because it is based on an accident of birth, because it is a mere remnant of the now almost universally rejected tradition of discriminating against males in this age bracket, and because, to the extent it reflects any physical difference between males and females, it is actually perverse. (Because males are generally heavier than females, they have a greater capacity to consume alcohol without impairing their driving ability than do females.) The question then is whether the traffic safety justification put forward by the State is sufficient to make an otherwise offensive classification acceptable.

The classification is not totally irrational. For the evidence does indicate that there are more males than females in this age bracket who drive and also more who drink. Nevertheless, [it] is difficult to believe that the statute was actually intended to cope with the problem of traffic safety, since it has only a minimal effect on access to a not very intoxicating beverage and does not prohibit its consumption. Moreover, [the] legislation imposes a restraint on 100% of the males in the class allegedly because about 2% of them have probably violated one or more laws relating to the consumption of alcoholic beverages. It is unlikely that this law will have a significant deterrent effect either on that 2% or on the law-abiding 98%. But even assuming some such slight benefit, it does not seem to me that an insult to all of the young men of the State can be justified by visiting the sins of the 2% on the 98%.

JUSTICE REHNQUIST, dissenting.

The Court's disposition of this case is objectionable on two grounds. First is its conclusion that *men* challenging a gender-based statute which treats them less favorably than women may invoke a more stringent standard of judicial review than pertains to most other types of classifications. Second is the Court's enunciation of this standard, without citation to any source, as being that "classifications by gender must serve *important* governmental objectives and must be *substantially* related to achievement of those objectives." The only redeeming feature of the Court's opinion, to my mind, is that it apparently signals a retreat [from the] view that sex is a "suspect" classification for purposes of equal protection analysis. I think the Oklahoma statute challenged here need pass only the "rational basis" equal protection [analysis].

There is no suggestion in the Court's opinion that males in this age group are in any way peculiarly disadvantaged, subject to systematic discriminatory treatment, or otherwise in need of special solicitude from the courts. [There] being no plausible argument that this is a discrimination against females, the Court's reliance on our previous sex-discrimination cases is ill-founded. It treats gender classification as a talisman which—without regard to the rights involved or the persons affected—calls into effect a heavier burden of judicial review. The Court's conclusion that a law which treats males less favorably than females "must serve important governmental objectives and must be substantially related to achievement of those objectives" apparently comes out of thin air. The Equal Protection Clause contains no such language, and none of our previous cases adopt that standard. I would think we have had enough difficulty with the two standards of review which our cases have recognized—the norm of "rational basis," and the "compelling state interest" required where a "suspect classification" is involved—so as to counsel weightily against the insertion of still another "standard" between those two. How is this Court to divine what objectives are important? How is it to determine whether a particular law is "substantially" related to the achievement of such objective, rather than related in some other way to its achievement? Both of the phrases used are so diaphanous and elastic as to invite subjective judicial preferences or prejudices relating to particular types of legislation, masquerading as judgments whether such legislation is directed at "important" objectives or, whether the relationship to those objectives is "substantial" enough. . . .

One survey of arrest statistics assembled in 1973 indicated that males in the 18-20 age group were arrested for "driving under the influence" almost 18 times as often as their female counterparts, and for "drunkenness" in a ratio of almost 10 to 1. [This] survey indicates a 2% arrest rate among males in the age group, as compared to a .18% rate among females. [The Oklahoma legislature] could reasonably infer that the incidence of drunk driving is a good deal higher than the incidence of arrest. And while [such] statistics may be distorted as a result of stereotyping, the legislature is not required to prove before a court that its statistics are perfect. In any event, if stereotypes are as pervasive as the Court suggests, they may in turn influence the conduct of the men and women in question, and cause the young men conform to the wild and reckless image which is their stereotype. . . .

The rationality of a statutory classification for equal protection purposes does not depend upon the statistical "fit" between the class and the trait sought to be singled out. It turns on whether there may be a sufficiently higher incidence of the trait within the included class than in the excluded class to justify different treatment. Therefore the present equal protection challenge to this gender-based discrimination poses only the question whether the incidence of drunk driving among young men is sufficiently greater than among young women to justify differential treatment. [The] evidence suggests clear differences between the drinking and driving habits of young men and women. Those differences are grounds enough for the State reasonably to conclude that young males pose by far the greater drunk-driving hazard, both in terms of sheer numbers and in terms of hazard on a per-driver basis. The gender-based difference in treatment in this case is therefore not irrational.

NOTES

1. Intentional Discrimination.   As in cases that call for strict scrutiny, a plaintiff in a constitutional sex discrimination suit must prove that the sex classification is intentional. Disparate impact by itself is not sufficient. Personnel

Administrator v. Feeney, 442 U.S. 256 (1979). Proof of legislative awareness of a differential impact by sex is not enough to prove discriminatory intent; the challenger must prove that the facially neutral law was adopted *because* of its sexually discriminatory impact.

2. Actual Purpose.   In assessing whether a state's purpose is sufficiently important to withstand intermediate scrutiny, courts insist upon determining the actual purpose of the classification. The conjectural post hoc purposes that suffice for minimal scrutiny are not adequate in intermediate scrutiny. Mississippi University for Women v. Hogan, 458 U.S. 718 (1982), struck down a public university's practice of admitting only women to its nursing school. Although Mississippi asserted that its policy substantially served an important state goal of compensating for discrimination against women in public education, the Court held that "although the State recited a 'benign, compensatory purpose,' it failed to establish that the alleged objective is the *actual purpose* underlying the discriminatory classification."

But which actual purposes are sufficiently important to support sex classifications? Alas, that is not an easy question to answer. The Court frequently asserts that policies that perpetuate stereotyped views of sex roles and that rely on archaic generalizations about men and women are inadequate. But the Court has also found sex classifications not to be invidious when they reflect "real differences" between the sexes. Are the policies underlying the sex classifications in the next pair of cases based on real differences between men and women or "archaic generalizations" about sex?

Michael M. v. Superior Court of Sonoma County
450 U.S. 464 (1981)

JUSTICE REHNQUIST announced the judgment of the Court and delivered an opinion in which CHIEF JUSTICE BURGER and JUSTICES STEWART and POWELL joined.

The question presented [is] whether California's "statutory rape" law violates [equal protection. California law] defines unlawful sexual intercourse as "an act of sexual intercourse accomplished with a female not the wife of the perpetrator, where the female is under the age of 18 years." The statute thus makes men alone criminally liable for the act of sexual intercourse.

[The California Supreme Court held that the law] "discriminates on the basis of sex because only females may be victims, and only males may violate the section." The court then subjected the classification to "strict scrutiny" [and] found that the classification was "supported not by mere social convention but by the immutable physiological fact that it is the female exclusively who can become pregnant." [The California] court concluded that the State has a compelling interest in preventing such pregnancies. [We affirm.]

[Equal protection] does not "demand that a statute necessarily apply equally to all persons" or require " 'things which are different in fact [to] be treated in law as though they were the same,' " this Court has consistently upheld statutes where the gender classification is not invidious, but rather realistically reflects the fact that the sexes are not similarly situated in certain circumstances. [Schlesinger v. Ballard.]

[The California] legislature sought to prevent illegitimate teenage pregnancies, [and] the State has a strong interest in preventing such pregnancy. At the risk of stating the obvious, teenage pregnancies, which have increased dramatically over the last two decades, have significant social, medical, and economic consequences for both the mother and her child, and the State. Of particular concern to the State is that approximately half of all teenage pregnancies end in abortion. And of those children who are born, their illegitimacy makes them likely candidates to become wards of the State. [Young] men and young women are not similarly situated with respect to the problems and the risks of sexual intercourse. Only women may become pregnant, and they suffer disproportionately the profound physical, emotional and psychological consequences of sexual activity. The statute at issue here protects women from sexual intercourse at an age when those consequences are particularly severe. [The] question thus boils down to whether a State may attack the problem of sexual intercourse and teenage pregnancy directly by prohibiting a male from having sexual intercourse with a minor female. We hold that such a statute is sufficiently related to the State's objectives to pass constitutional muster.

Because virtually all of the significant harmful and inescapably identifiable consequences of teenage pregnancy fall on the young female, a legislature acts well within its authority when it elects to punish only the participant who, by nature, suffers few of the consequences of his conduct. Moreover, the risk of pregnancy itself constitutes a substantial deterrence to young females. No similar natural sanctions deter males. A criminal sanction imposed solely on males thus serves to roughly "equalize" the deterrents on the sexes. . . .

It is argued that this statute is not necessary to deter teenage pregnancy because a gender-neutral statute, where both male and female would be subject to prosecution, would serve that goal equally well. The relevant inquiry, however, is not whether the statute is drawn as precisely as it might have been, but whether the line chosen by the California Legislature is within constitutional limitations. In any event, we cannot say that a gender-neutral statute would be as effective as the statute California has chosen to enact. The State persuasively contends that a . . . female is surely less likely to report violations of the statute if she herself would be subject to criminal prosecution. . . .

[This] is not a case [where] the gender classification is made "solely [for] administrative convenience," or rests on "the baggage of sexual stereotypes." [The] statute instead reasonably reflects the fact that the consequences of sexual intercourse and pregnancy fall more heavily on the female than on the male.

[Affirmed.]

JUSTICE STEWART, concurring.

[Equal protection] does not mean that the physiological differences between men and women must be disregarded. While those differences must never be permitted to become a pretext for invidious discrimination, [the] Constitution surely does not require a State to pretend that demonstrable differences between men and women do not really exist.

JUSTICE BRENNAN, joined by JUSTICES WHITE and MARSHALL, dissenting.

California vigorously asserts that the "important governmental objective" to be served by [its law] is the prevention of teenage pregnancy. [California] has the burden of proving that there are fewer teenage pregnancies under its gender-based statutory rape law than there would be if the law were gender-neutral. To meet this burden, the State must show that because its statutory rape law punishes only males, and not females, it more effectively deters minor females from having sexual intercourse.

[The] State has not produced such evidence in this case. [There] are at least two serious flaws in the State's assertion that law enforcement problems created by a gender-neutral statutory rape law would make such a statute less effective than a gender-based statute in deterring sexual activity. First, [there] are now at least 37 States that have enacted gender-neutral statutory rape laws. [California] has introduced no evidence that those States have been handicapped by the enforcement problems the plurality finds so persuasive. Surely, if those States could provide such evidence, we might expect that California would have introduced it.

The second flaw in the State's assertion is that even assuming that a gender-neutral statute would be more difficult to enforce, the State has still not shown that those enforcement problems would make such a statute less effective than a gender-based statute in deterring minor females from engaging in sexual intercourse. Common sense, however, suggests that a gender-neutral statutory rape law is potentially a greater deterrent of sexual activity than a gender-based law, for the simple reason that a gender-neutral law subjects both men and women to criminal sanctions and thus arguably has a deterrent effect on twice as many potential violators. . . .

[T]he State has not shown that [its law] is any more effective than a gender-neutral law would be in deterring minor females from engaging in sexual intercourse. It has therefore not met its burden of proving that the statutory classification is substantially related to the achievement of its asserted goal.

JUSTICE STEVENS, dissenting.

[T]he plurality is quite correct in [assuming] that the joint act that this law seeks to prohibit creates a greater risk of harm for the female than for the male. But the plurality surely cannot believe that the risk of pregnancy confronted by the female — any more than the risk of venereal disease confronted by males as well as females — has provided an effective deterrent to voluntary female participation in the risk-creating conduct. Yet the plurality's decision seems to rest on the assumption that the California Legislature acted on the basis of that rather fanciful notion. . . . [Finally], even if . . . there actually is some speculative basis for treating equally guilty males and females differently, . . . any such speculative justification would be outweighed by the paramount interest in evenhanded enforcement of the law. A rule that authorizes punishment of only one of two equally guilty wrongdoers violates the essence of the constitutional requirement that the sovereign must govern impartially.

Rostker v. Goldberg
453 U.S. 57 (1981)

JUSTICE REHNQUIST delivered the opinion of the Court.

The question presented is whether the Military Selective Service Act violates [equal protection] in authorizing the President to require the registration of males and not females.

[This] case arises in the context of Congress'[s] authority over national defense and military affairs, and perhaps in no other area has the Court accorded Congress greater deference. [None] of this is to say that Congress is free to disregard the Constitution when it acts in the area of military affairs. . . . We . . . do not abdicate our ultimate responsibility to decide the constitutional question, but simply recognize that the Constitution itself requires such deference to congressional choice. [W]e must be particularly careful not to substitute our judgment of what is desirable for that of Congress, or our own evaluation of evidence for a reasonable evaluation by the Legislative Branch.

[No] one could deny that . . . the Government's interest in raising and supporting armies is an "important governmental interest." Congress . . . carefully considered and debated two alternative means of furthering that interest: the first was to register only males for potential conscription, and the other was to register both sexes. Congress chose the former alternative. [In] light of the [legislative history, it] is apparent that Congress was fully aware [of] the current thinking as to the place of women in the Armed Services. . . .

This case is quite different from [prior] gender-based discrimination cases [in that] Congress did not act "unthinkingly" or "reflexively and not for any considered reason." [The] decision to exempt women from registration was not the "'accidental by-product of a traditional way of thinking about females.'" [Congress] determined that any future draft, which would be facilitated by the registration scheme, would be characterized by a need for combat troops. [But women] as a group [are statutorily] not eligible for combat. [Since] women are excluded from combat, Congress concluded that they would not be needed in the event of a draft, and therefore decided not to register them.

This is not a case of Congress arbitrarily choosing to burden one of two similarly situated groups, such as would be the case with an all-black or all-white, or an all-Catholic or all-Lutheran, or an all-Republican or all-Democratic registration. Men and women, because of the combat restrictions on women, are simply not similarly situated for purposes of a draft or registration for a draft. [The] exemption of women from registration is not only sufficiently but also closely related to Congress'[s] purpose in authorizing registration. . . . [A]ssuming that a small number of women could be drafted for noncombat roles, Congress simply did not consider it worth the added burdens of including women in draft and registration plans. . . . [Reversed.]

JUSTICE MARSHALL, joined by JUSTICE BRENNAN, dissenting.

[The] relevant inquiry . . . is . . . whether the gender-based classification [is] substantially related to the achievement of the asserted governmental interest. Thus, the Government's task in this case is to demonstrate that excluding women from registration substantially furthers the goal of preparing for a draft of combat troops. Or to put it another way, the Government must show that registering women would substantially impede its efforts to prepare for such a draft. [The] Government cannot meet this burden without showing that a gender-neutral statute would be a less effective means of attaining this end. [The] Government makes no claim that preparing for a draft of combat troops cannot be accomplished just as effectively by *registering* both men and women but *drafting* only men if only men turn out to be needed. [Or] the Government could employ a classification that is related to the statutory objective but is not based on gender, for example, combat eligibility. Under the current scheme, large subgroups of the male population who are ineligible for combat because of physical handicaps or conscientious objector status are nonetheless required to register. . . .

[The Court's analysis] rests on a premise that is demonstrably false. [The] majority simply assumes that registration prepares for a draft in which every draftee must be available for assignment to combat. But [the Defense] Department indicated that conscripts would [be] needed to staff a variety of support positions having no prerequisite of combat eligibility, and which therefore could be filled by women. [Testimony] about personnel requirements in the event of a draft established that women could fill at least 80,000 of the 650,000 positions for which conscripts would be inducted. Thus, with respect to these 80,000 or more positions, the statutes and policies barring women from combat do not provide a reason for distinguishing between male and female potential conscripts; the two groups are, in the majority's parlance, "similarly situated." As such, the combat restrictions cannot by themselves supply the constitutionally required justification for [the] gender-based classification. . . .

NOTES

1. Real Differences. Is the risk of pregnancy a sufficiently real difference to support California's sex-specific crime of statutory rape? It is undeniable that only women become pregnant, but is that the difference the Court relies on in *Michael M.*, or is it the socially constituted consequences of pregnancy that is the difference relied upon? Does (should) it matter?

The "real" difference between men and women in *Rostker* was a sex-specific policy barring women from combat that was itself unchallenged. Assuming the validity of that combat ban, does the ban then become "real," even if rooted in social views of the proper roles of men and women? To put it another way, does the validity of the *Rostker* decision depend on the validity of the sex-specific combat ban? (Was that ban valid?) Or is *Rostker* explainable more by the extreme deference the Court displays to congressional judgments concerning the staffing and administration of the armed services? What are the "real" differences between men and women that matter for equal protection purposes?

Consider the following facts: Eighty-four percent of the people arrested for juvenile drunk driving are male, and boys commit 94 percent of juvenile murders. Would a juvenile curfew applicable only to males be rooted in sufficient "real" differences between the sexes to be constitutionally justified? (Ignore for the moment any other possible constitutional challenges to the curfew.) Or would such a curfew be based on differences induced by society? If the latter, does that make the differences not "real," even though the statistics are true?

Women continue to be officially barred from combat, but are temporarily attached to combat units to perform specific functions. Over 100 female members of the U.S. armed services have died in Iraq and Afghanistan. Should those facts change your evaluation of *Rostker*?

2. Sex-Based Juror Challenges.   In J.E.B. v. Alabama ex rel. T.B., 511 U.S. 127 (1994), the Court ruled that peremptory challenges of jurors on the basis of their sex were unconstitutional. In a proceeding brought by Alabama against J.E.B. to establish his paternity of T.B., the state used its peremptory challenges to strike male jurors, producing an all-female jury. For the Court, Justice Blackmun declared:

> [Alabama] maintains that its decision to strike virtually all males "[may] reasonably have been based upon the perception [that men] might be more sympathetic [to] a man alleged in a paternity action to be the father of an out-of-wedlock child, while women [might] be more sympathetic [to] the complaining witness who bore the child." We shall not accept as a defense to gender-based peremptory challenges "the very stereotype the law condemns." [Alabama] offers virtually no support for the conclusion that gender alone is an accurate predictor of jurors' [attitudes].

In dissent, Chief Justice Rehnquist observed that "[it] is not merely 'stereotyping' to say that [sex] differences may produce a difference in outlook which is brought into the jury room." Justice Scalia, joined by Chief Justice Rehnquist and Justice Thomas, also dissented:

> [For] every man struck by [Alabama], petitioner's own lawyer struck a woman. To say that men were singled out for discriminatory treatment in this process is preposterous. [The] pattern here displays not a systemic sex-based animus but each side's desire to get a jury favorably disposed to its case. . . . Women were categorically excluded from juries because of doubt that they were competent; women are stricken from juries by peremptory challenge because of doubt that they are well-disposed to the striking party's case. There is discrimination and dishonor in the former, and not in the [latter].

Are sex-based juror challenges of the type at issue in *J.E.B.* based on "real" differences or archaic generalizations? Is the Court's vision of equal protection here based on formal equality, and is the Court oblivious to "real" differences? Gilligan, In a Different Voice (1982), famously contended that women's worldview differs from men's in that women have a greater inclination to cooperate, value relationships more highly, and evidence higher concern for others. Are these real differences, and, if so, should they have been recognized in *J.E.B.*?

3. Standard of Review.   The dissents in *Michael M.* and *Rostker* charged that the lead opinions in both cases covertly applied a less-than-intermediate standard of review. Is that true, or does the division between majority and minority simply reveal the subjective nature of assessing the importance of government objectives and the substantiality of the connection between sex-based classifications and those important objectives? Put another way, does intermediate scrutiny inevitably require second-guessing of legislative objectives and chosen means? The majority and minority in *Rostker* disagreed over the proper inferences to be drawn from the evidence adduced by Congress. The Court deferred to the inferences drawn by Congress, embodied in the statute, and the dissent reviewed the evidence de novo to decide whether Congress drew the proper inferences. Which approach is more appropriate?

Does the following case alter the standard of review for sex-based classifications?

United States v. Virginia
518 U.S. 515 (1996)

JUSTICE GINSBURG delivered the opinion of the Court.

Virginia's public institutions of higher learning include an incomparable military college, Virginia Military Institute (VMI). The United States maintains that the Constitution's equal protection guarantee precludes Virginia from reserving exclusively to men the unique educational opportunities VMI affords. We agree.

I. Founded in 1839, VMI is today the sole single-sex school among Virginia's 15 public institutions of higher learning. VMI's distinctive mission is to produce "citizen-soldiers," men prepared for leadership in civilian life and in military service. VMI pursues this mission through pervasive training of a kind not available anywhere else in Virginia. Assigning prime place to character development, VMI . . . constantly endeavors to instill physical and mental discipline in its cadets and impart to them a strong moral code. The school's graduates leave VMI with heightened comprehension of their capacity to deal with duress and stress, and a large sense of accomplishment for completing the hazardous course. [Neither] the goal of producing citizen-soldiers nor VMI's implementing methodology is inherently unsuitable to women. And the school's impressive record in producing leaders has made admission desirable to some women. Nevertheless, Virginia has elected to preserve exclusively for men the advantages and opportunities a VMI education affords.

II. [VMI] enrolls about 1,300 men as cadets. [VMI] produces its "citizen-soldiers" through "an adversative, or doubting, model of education" which features "physical rigor, mental stress, absolute equality of treatment, absence of privacy, minute regulation of behavior, and indoctrination in desirable values." [VMI] cadets live in spartan barracks where surveillance is constant and privacy nonexistent; they wear uniforms, eat together in the mess hall, and regularly participate in drills. Entering students are incessantly exposed to the rat line, "an extreme form of the adversative model," comparable in intensity to Marine Corps boot camp. Tormenting and punishing, the rat line bonds new cadets to their fellow sufferers and, when they have completed the 7-month experience, to their former tormentors.

[In] 1990, prompted by a complaint [by] a female high-school student seeking admission to VMI, the United States [sued], alleging that VMI's exclusively male admission policy violated [equal protection]. The District Court ruled in favor of VMI, [but the Court of Appeals reversed and remanded, suggesting] these options for the State: Admit women to VMI; establish parallel institutions or programs; or abandon state support, leaving VMI free to pursue its policies as a private institution. [In response], Virginia proposed a parallel program for women: Virginia Women's Institute for Leadership (VWIL). The 4-year, state-sponsored undergraduate program would be located at Mary Baldwin College, a private liberal arts school for women, and would be open, initially, to about 25 to 30 students. Although VWIL would share VMI's mission—to produce "citizen-soldiers"—the VWIL program would differ, as does Mary Baldwin College, from VMI in academic offerings, methods of education, and financial resources. The average combined SAT score of entrants at Mary Baldwin is about 100 points lower than the score for VMI freshmen. Mary Baldwin's faculty holds "significantly fewer Ph.D.s than the faculty at VMI" and receives significantly lower salaries. While VMI offers degrees in liberal arts, the sciences, and engineering, Mary Baldwin, at the time of trial, offered only bachelor of arts degrees. A VWIL student seeking to earn an engineering degree could gain one, without public support, by attending Washington University in St. Louis, Missouri, for two years, paying the required private tuition. VWIL students would participate in ROTC programs and a newly established, "largely ceremonial" Virginia Corps of Cadets. [In] lieu of VMI's adversative method, the VWIL Task Force favored "a cooperative method which reinforces self-esteem." Virginia represented that it will provide equal financial support for in-state VWIL students and VMI cadets.

[The District Court decided] the plan met the requirements of [equal protection]. A divided Court of Appeals [affirmed].

III. . . . First, does Virginia's exclusion of women from the educational opportunities provided by VMI deny to women "capable of all of the individual activities required of VMI cadets" [equal protection]? Second, if VMI's "unique" situation—as Virginia's sole single-sex public institution of higher education—offends the Constitution's equal protection principle, what is the remedial requirement?

IV. [Parties] who seek to defend gender-based government action must demonstrate an "exceedingly persuasive justification" for that action. . . . [The burden of justification is demanding and it rests entirely on the State. The State must show "at least that the [challenged] classification serves 'important governmental objectives and that the discriminatory means employed' are 'substantially related to the achievement of those objectives.'" The justification must be genuine, not hypothesized or invented post hoc in response to litigation. And it must not rely on overbroad generalizations about the different talents, capacities, or preferences of males and females.

The heightened review standard our precedent establishes does not make sex a proscribed classification. Supposed "inherent differences" are no longer accepted as a ground for race or national origin classifications. Physical differences between men and women, however, are enduring. . . . "Inherent differences" between men and women, we have come to appreciate, remain cause for celebration, but not for denigration of the members of either sex or for artificial constraints on an individual's opportunity. Sex classifications may be used to compensate women "for particular economic disabilities [they have] suffered," to "promote equal employment opportunity," [and] to advance full development of the talent and capacities of our Nation's people.[12] But such classifications may not be used, as they once were, to create or perpetuate the legal, social, and economic inferiority of women.

Measuring the record in this case against the review standard just described, we conclude that Virginia has shown no "exceedingly persuasive justification" for excluding all women from the citizen-soldier training afforded by VMI. [Because] the Mary Baldwin VWIL program does not cure the constitutional violation, [we] reverse the Fourth Circuit's final judgment in this case.

V. [Virginia asserts] two justifications in defense of VMI's exclusion of women. First, "[single-sex] education provides important educational benefits" and the option of single-sex education contributes to "diversity in educational approaches." Second, "[the] unique VMI method of character development and leadership training" . . . would have to be modified were VMI to admit women. We consider these two justifications in turn.

A. Single-sex education affords pedagogical benefits to at least some students [and] that reality is uncontested in this litigation. Similarly, it is not disputed that diversity among public educational institutions can serve the public

---

12. Several amici have urged that diversity in educational opportunities is an altogether appropriate governmental pursuit and that single-sex schools can contribute importantly to such diversity. Indeed, it is the mission of some single-sex schools "to dissipate, rather than perpetuate, traditional gender classifications." See Brief for Twenty-six Private Women's [Colleges]. We do not question the State's prerogative evenhandedly to support diverse educational opportunities. We address specifically and only an educational opportunity recognized by the [lower courts] as "unique," an opportunity available only at Virginia's premier military institute, the State's sole single-sex public university or college.

good. But Virginia has not shown that VMI was established, or has been maintained, with a view to diversifying . . . educational opportunities within the State. . . . [A] tenable justification must describe actual state purposes, not rationalizations for actions in fact differently grounded. [Neither] recent nor distant history bears out Virginia's alleged pursuit of diversity through single-sex educational options. In 1839, when the State established VMI, a range of educational opportunities for men and women was scarcely contemplated. . . . [In] sum, we find no persuasive evidence in this record that VMI's male-only admission policy "is in furtherance of a state policy of 'diversity.'" [A] purpose genuinely to advance an array of educational options [is] not served by VMI's historic and constant plan—a plan to "afford a unique educational benefit only to males." However "liberally" this plan serves the State's sons, it makes no provision whatever for her daughters. That is not equal protection.

B. Virginia next argues that VMI's adversative method of training provides educational benefits that cannot be made available, unmodified, to women. Alterations to accommodate women would necessarily be "radical," so "drastic," Virginia asserts, as to transform, indeed "destroy," VMI's program. Neither sex would be favored by the transformation, Virginia maintains: Men would be deprived of the unique opportunity currently available to them; women would not gain that opportunity because their participation would "eliminate the very aspects of [the] program that distinguish [VMI] from [other] institutions of higher education in Virginia."

[It] is uncontested that women's admission would require accommodations, primarily in arranging housing assignments and physical training programs for female cadets. It is also undisputed, however, that "the VMI methodology could be used to educate women." [The parties agree] that "some women can meet the physical standards [VMI] now imposes on men." [Nevertheless, in] support of its initial judgment for Virginia, [the] District Court made "findings" on "gender-based developmental differences." [For] example, "males tend to need an atmosphere of adversativeness," while "females tend to thrive in a cooperative atmosphere." [We] have cautioned reviewing courts to take a "hard look" at generalizations or "tendencies" of the kind pressed by Virginia and relied upon by the District Court. State actors controlling gates to opportunity [may] not exclude qualified individuals based on "fixed notions concerning the roles and abilities of males and females."

It may be assumed [that] most women would not choose VMI's adversative method, [just as] it is also probable that "many men would not want to be educated in such an environment." [The] issue, however, [is] whether the State can constitutionally deny to women who have the will and capacity, the training and attendant opportunities that VMI uniquely affords. The notion that admission of women would downgrade VMI's stature, destroy the adversative system and, with it, even the school, is a judgment hardly proved, a prediction hardly different from other "self-fulfilling prophecies" once routinely used to deny rights or opportunities. [Virginia's goal of creating citizen-soldiers] is not substantially advanced by women's categorical exclusion, in total disregard of their individual merit, from the State's premier "citizen-soldier" corps. Virginia, in sum, "has fallen far short of establishing the 'exceedingly persuasive justification'" that must be the solid base for any gender-defined classification.

VI. [Virginia's] remedial plan—maintain VMI as a male-only college and create VWIL as a separate program for women [is challenged by the United States] as pervasively misguided.

A. A remedial decree [must] closely fit the constitutional violation; it must be shaped to place persons unconstitutionally denied an opportunity or advantage in "the position they would have occupied in the absence of [discrimination]." The constitutional violation [here] is the categorical exclusion of women from an extraordinary educational opportunity afforded men. . . . Virginia chose not to eliminate, but to leave untouched, VMI's exclusionary policy. For women only, however, Virginia proposed a separate program, different in kind from VMI and unequal in tangible and intangible facilities. . . . Kept away from the pressures, hazards, and psychological bonding characteristic of VMI's adversative training, VWIL students will not know the "feeling of tremendous accomplishment" commonly experienced by VMI's successful cadets.

Virginia maintains that these methodological differences are "justified pedagogically," based on "important differences between men and women in learning and developmental needs," "psychological and sociological differences" Virginia describes as "real" and "not stereotypes." [But] generalizations about "the way women are," estimates of what is appropriate for most women, no longer justify denying opportunity to women whose talent and capacity place them outside the average description. . . . It is on behalf of these women that the United States has instituted this suit, and it is for them that a remedy must be crafted, a remedy that will end their exclusion from a state-supplied educational opportunity for which they are [fit]. . . .

C. . . . Virginia's remedy affords no cure at all for the opportunities and advantages withheld from women who want a VMI education and can make the grade. . . . Virginia's remedy does not match the constitutional violation; the State has shown no "exceedingly persuasive justification" for withholding from women qualified for the experience premier training of the kind VMI affords.

[The] initial judgment of the Court of Appeals is affirmed, the final judgment of the Court of Appeals is reversed, and the case is remanded for further proceedings consistent with this opinion.

[Justice Thomas, whose son was a VMI cadet at the time, took no part in the consideration or decision of this case.]

CHIEF JUSTICE REHNQUIST, concurring in the judgment.

[While] I agree with [its] conclusions, I disagree with the Court's analysis and so I write separately.

I. Two decades ago in Craig v. Boren we announced that "to withstand constitutional challenge, [classifications] by gender must serve important governmental objectives and must be substantially related to achievement of those objectives." [While] the majority adheres to this test today, it also says that the State must demonstrate an " 'exceedingly persuasive justification' " to support a gender-based classification. It is unfortunate that the Court thereby introduces an element of uncertainty respecting the appropriate test. While terms like "important governmental objective" and "substantially related" are hardly models of precision, they have more content and specificity than does the phrase "exceedingly persuasive justification." That phrase is best confined, as it was first used, as an observation on the difficulty of meeting the applicable test, not as a formulation of the test itself. . . .

II. The Court defines the constitutional violation in this case as "the categorical exclusion of women from an extraordinary educational opportunity afforded to men." [The] Court necessarily implies that the only adequate remedy would be the admission of women to the all-male institution. [It] is not the "exclusion of women" that violates [equal protection], but the maintenance of an all-men school without providing any—much less a comparable—institution for women. Accordingly, the remedy should not necessarily require either the admission of women to VMI, or the creation of a VMI clone for women. An adequate remedy [might] be a demonstration by Virginia that its interest in educating men in a single-sex environment is matched by its interest in educating women in a single-sex institution. To demonstrate such, the State does not need to create two [identical] institutions; [it] would be a sufficient remedy [if] the two institutions offered the same quality of education and were of the same overall calibre. [But VWIL] fails as a remedy because it is distinctly inferior to the existing men's institution and will continue to be for the foreseeable future. [I] therefore [agree] that Virginia has not provided an adequate remedy.

Justice Scalia, dissenting.

Today the Court [rejects] the factual findings of two courts below, sweeps aside the precedents of this Court, and ignores the history of our people. As to facts: it explicitly rejects the finding that there exist "gender-based developmental differences" supporting Virginia's restriction of the "adversative" method to only a men's institution, and the finding that the all-male composition of [VMI] is essential to that institution's character. As to precedent: it drastically revises our established standards for reviewing sex-based classifications. And as to history: it counts for nothing the long tradition [of] men's military [colleges].

Much of the Court's opinion is devoted to deprecating the closed-mindedness of our forebears with regard to women's [education]. Closed-minded they were—as every age is, including our [own]. The virtue of a democratic system [is] that it readily enables the people, over time, to be persuaded that what they took for granted is not so, and to change their laws accordingly. That system is destroyed if the smug assurances of each age are removed from the democratic process and written into the Constitution. So to counterbalance the Court's criticism of our ancestors, let me say a word in their praise:

they left us free to change. The same cannot be said of this most illiberal Court, which has embarked on a course of inscribing one after another of the current preferences of the society (and in some cases only the counter-majoritarian preferences of the society's law-trained elite) into our Basic Law. Today it enshrines the notion that no substantial educational value is to be served by an all-men's military academy — so that the decision by the people of Virginia to maintain such an institution denies equal protection to women who cannot attend that institution but can attend others. Since it is entirely clear that the [Constitution] — the old one — takes no sides in this educational debate, I dissent.

I. [Our] current equal-protection jurisprudence [regards] this Court as free to evaluate everything under the sun by applying one of three tests: "rational basis" scrutiny, intermediate scrutiny, or strict scrutiny. These tests are no more scientific than their names suggest, and a further element of randomness is added by the fact that it is largely up to us which test will be applied in each case. [Strict] scrutiny will be applied to the deprivation of whatever sort of right we consider "fundamental." We have no established criterion for "intermediate scrutiny" either, but essentially apply it when it seems like a good idea to load the dice. So far it has been applied to content-neutral restrictions that place an incidental burden on speech, to disabilities attendant to illegitimacy, and to discrimination on the basis of sex. . . .

[T]he function of this Court is to preserve our society's values, [not] to revise them; to prevent backsliding from the degree of restriction the Constitution imposed upon democratic government, not to prescribe, on our own authority, progressively higher degrees. [Thus], whatever abstract tests we may choose to devise, they cannot supersede — and indeed ought to be crafted so as to reflect — those constant and unbroken national traditions that embody the people's understanding of ambiguous constitutional texts. More specifically, it is my view that "when a practice not expressly prohibited by the text of the Bill of Rights bears the endorsement of a long tradition of open, widespread, and unchallenged use that dates back to the beginning of the Republic, we have no proper basis for striking it down."

[The] tradition of having government-funded military schools for men is as well rooted in the traditions of this country as the tradition of sending only men into military combat. The people may decide to change the one tradition, like the other, through democratic processes; but the assertion that either tradition has been unconstitutional through the centuries is not law, but politics-smuggled-into-law. . . .

II. . . . Although the Court in two places recites the [intermediate scrutiny] test, [the] Court never answers the question presented in anything resembling that form. When it engages in analysis, the Court instead prefers the phrase "exceedingly persuasive justification" from *Hogan* [and] proceeds to interpret [that] phrase [in] a fashion that contradicts the reasoning of *Hogan* and our other precedents. That is essential to the Court's result, which can only be achieved by establishing that intermediate scrutiny is not survived if there . . . exist several women (or, one would have to conclude under the Court's reasoning, a single woman) willing and able to undertake VMI's program. Intermediate scrutiny has never required a least-restrictive-means analysis, but only a "substantial relation" between the classification and the state interests that it serves. [There] is simply no support in our cases for the notion that a sex-based classification is invalid unless it relates to characteristics that hold true in every instance. . . .

[T]he Court purports to reserve the question whether . . . a higher standard (i.e., strict scrutiny) should apply. [The Court is] misleading, insofar as [it] suggest[s] that we have not already categorically *held* strict scrutiny to be inapplicable to sex-based classifications. [And] the [Court's] statements are irresponsible, insofar as they are calculated to destabilize current law. . . .

The Court's intimations are particularly out of place because it is perfectly clear that, if the question of the applicable standard of review for sex-based classifications were to be regarded as an appropriate subject for reconsideration, the stronger argument would be not for elevating the standard to strict scrutiny, but for reducing it to rational-basis review. . . . [It] is hard to consider women a "discrete and insular minority" unable to employ the "political processes ordinarily to be relied upon," when they constitute a majority of the electorate. And the suggestion that they are incapable of exerting that political power smacks of the same paternalism that the Court so roundly condemns. Moreover, a long list of legislation proves the proposition false.

III. . . . The question to be answered [is] whether the exclusion of women from VMI is "substantially related to an important governmental objective."

A. It is beyond question that Virginia has an important state interest in providing effective college education for its citizens. That single-sex instruction is an approach substantially related to that interest should be evident enough from the long and continuing history in this country of men's and women's colleges. . . .

B. . . . " 'The Court simply dispenses with the evidence submitted at trial—it never says that a single finding of the District Court is clearly erroneous—in favor of the Justices' own view of the [world]. It is not too much to say that this approach to the case has rendered the trial a sham. But treating the evidence as irrelevant is absolutely necessary for the Court to reach its conclusion. Not a single witness contested [Virginia's] "substantial body of 'exceedingly persuasive' evidence [that] some students, both male and female, benefit from attending a single-sex college" and "[that] for those students, the opportunity to attend a single-sex college is a valuable one, likely to lead to better academic and professional achievement."

[The] Court's analysis at least has the benefit of producing foreseeable results. Applied generally, it means that whenever a State's ultimate objective is "great enough to accommodate women" (as it always will be), then the State will be held to have violated [equal protection] if it restricts to men even one means by which it pursues that objective—no matter how few women are interested in pursuing the objective by that means, no matter how much the single-sex program will have to be changed if both sexes are admitted, and no matter how beneficial that program has theretofore been to its participants. . . .

IV. As is frequently true, the Court's decision today will have consequences that extend far beyond the parties to the case. . . . Under the constitutional principles announced and applied today, single-sex public education is unconstitutional. By going through the motions of applying a balancing test . . . the Court creates the illusion that government officials in some future case will have a clear shot at justifying some sort of single-sex public education. . . . [T]he rationale of today's decision is sweeping: for sex-based classifications, a redefinition of intermediate scrutiny that makes it indistinguishable from strict scrutiny. Indeed, the Court indicates that if any program restricted to one sex is "unique," it must be opened to members of the opposite sex "who have the will and capacity" to participate in it. [The] single-sex program that will not be capable of being characterized as "unique" is not only unique but nonexistent. In any event, . . . the Court's rationale . . . ensures that single-sex public education is functionally dead. The costs of litigating the constitutionality of a single-sex education program, and the risks of ultimately losing that litigation, are simply too high to be embraced by public officials. [The] enemies of single-sex education have won; by persuading only seven Justices [that] their view of the world is enshrined in the Constitution, they have effectively imposed that view on all 50 States. . . .

This is especially regrettable because . . . educational experts in recent years have increasingly come to "support [the] view that substantial educational benefits flow from a single-gender environment, be it male or female, that cannot be replicated in a coeducational setting." There are few extant single-sex public educational programs. The potential of today's decision for widespread disruption of existing institutions lies in its application to *private* single-sex education. Government support is immensely important to private educational institutions. [Charitable] status under the tax laws is also highly significant for private educational institutions, and it is certainly not beyond the Court that rendered today's decision to hold that a donation to a single-sex college should be deemed contrary to public policy and therefore not deductible if the college discriminates on the basis of sex. [The] issue will be not whether government assistance turns private colleges into state actors, but whether the government itself would be violating the Constitution by providing state support to single-sex colleges. . . .

NOTES

1. The Scope of the *VMI* Case. Does the *VMI* case doom public single-sex education? Suppose a public school district offers, in addition to mixed-sex schools, the choice of a girls' school and a boys' school. Would that program violate equal protection? What about single-sex athletic programs in the public schools?

Did the *VMI* case effectively ratchet up the standard of review to strict scrutiny, or was the case merely an application of intermediate scrutiny to "unique" facts? Does the phrase "exceedingly persuasive justification" imply that a state must prove the elements of its justification by more than a preponderance of the evidence?

2. "Real" Differences, Stereotypes, and the Standard of Review After VMI. In Nguyen v. Immigration and Naturalization Service, 533 U.S. 53 (2001), the Supreme Court upheld 8 U.S.C. §1409, which provides that a child born abroad and out of wedlock acquires at birth the nationality status of an American citizen mother who meets a residency requirement, but when the father is the citizen parent, §1409(a)(4) makes American citizenship dependent on the father taking one of three actions before the child turns 18: legitimization, a declaration of paternity under oath by the father, or a court order of paternity.

The Court applied intermediate scrutiny due to the differential treatment based on the sex of the parent and cited *VMI* for this standard of review. The Court concluded that the sex classification at issue was substantially related to two important government objectives:

> The first governmental interest . . . is the importance of assuring that a biological parent-child relationship exists. [Fathers] and mothers are not similarly situated with regard to the proof of biological parenthood. . . . Here, the use of gender specific terms takes into account a biological difference between the parents. . . .
>
> The second important governmental interest furthered in a substantial manner by [the scheme is ensuring] that the child and the citizen parent have some demonstrated opportunity or potential to develop [a] relationship that . . . consists of the real, everyday ties that provide a connection between child and citizen parent and, in turn, the United States. In the case of a citizen mother . . . the opportunity for a meaningful relationship between citizen parent and child inheres in the very event of birth. . . . The same opportunity does not result from the event of birth, as a matter of biological inevitability, in the case of the unwed father. [It] is not always certain that a father will know that a child was conceived, nor is it always clear that even the mother will be sure of the father's identity. . . . Principles of equal protection do not require Congress to ignore this reality. . . .
>
> [Section] 1409 addresses an undeniable difference in the circumstance of the parents at the time a child is born, [and that] difference does not result from some stereotype, defined as a frame of mind resulting from irrational or uncritical analysis. . . . [T]he means adopted by Congress are in substantial furtherance of important governmental objectives. The fit between the means and the important end is "exceedingly persuasive."

Justice O'Connor, joined by Justices Souter, Ginsburg, and Breyer, dissented, noting that the majority "casually dismisses the relevance of available sex-neutral alternatives" and arguing that the government's asserted ends could be adequately achieved by reliance on modern DNA testing. The dissenters thought that the relationship between the statute and the government's goal was grounded "not in biological differences but instead in a stereotype—i.e., 'the generalization that mothers are significantly more likely than fathers . . . to develop caring relationships with their children. . . .'" The dissenters argued that the "hallmark" of a sex stereotype was reliance upon a "simplistic, outdated assumption" that sex is an adequate "proxy for other, more germane bases of classification."

A Note on Illegitimate Children

Prior to 1968, statutes that discriminated on the basis of illegitimate birth were subjected to minimal scrutiny and were upheld. Between 1968, when the Court first invalidated such a law under minimal scrutiny, and 1988, when the Court finally adopted intermediate scrutiny for such classifications, the Court wavered between minimal scrutiny and some unspecified "heightened" scrutiny. Today, statutes that classify on the basis of illegitimate birth are subjected to intermediate scrutiny. For such laws to be valid, the state must prove that the classification is "substantially related to an important governmental objective." See Clark v. Jeter, 486 U.S. 456 (1988).

The justification for intermediate review is that there is little if anything the illegitimate child can do to overcome that status. While parents may marry and fathers may formally acknowledge their paternity in order to legitimize their illicit offspring, the child is unable to make them do these things. From a child's perspective, illegitimacy is immutable. But the other attributes of suspicious classifications are largely missing. Illegitimate children are not a "discrete and insular" minority, visible to all and subject to the kind of prejudice that walls them off from meaningful participation in the political process. As traditional concepts of marriage and family relationships erode, there is less stigma attached to birth outside marriage. Do these factors warrant reconsideration of intermediate scrutiny? How, if at all, ought these factors be taken into account in applying intermediate scrutiny?

Suppose that a state provides welfare assistance to families "which consist of a household composed of two adults of the opposite sex ceremonially married to each other who have at least one minor child [of] both, [or] the natural child of one and adopted by the other, or a child adopted by both." Is this classification substantially related to the important state objectives of (1) encouraging the maintenance of legally and socially sanctioned family relationships, (2) protecting the traditional family unit "from dissolution due to the economic vicissitudes of modern life," and (3) refusing to subsidize a living unit that may lead to a state of anomie and that violates laws against fornication and adultery? In New Jersey Welfare Rights Organization v. Cahill, 411 U.S. 619 (1973), the Court ruled that this classification was "contrary to the basic concept . . . that legal burdens should bear some relationship to individual responsibility or wrongdoing."

F. FUNDAMENTAL RIGHTS: STRICT SCRUTINY REDUX

1. Introduction

Whenever government action significantly impinges upon a "fundamental right or interest," that action is presumptively void. For its action to be valid, the government must prove that the infringement is necessary to accomplish some compelling government interest. This trigger for strict scrutiny is independent of suspect classifications; a statute that does not classify on a suspect basis but that seriously burdens a fundamental right is as subject to strict scrutiny as the statute that classifies on a suspect basis. The term "fundamental right or interest" requires definition. For purposes of equal protection, a right or interest is "fundamental" if (1) it is an *independently protected constitutional liberty* (e.g., free speech), *or* (2) it has been identified as "fundamental" for equal protection purposes even though it is *not* independently protected by the Constitution.

The first type of fundamental right is unremarkable; any government action that seriously infringes upon another constitutional right is also a presumptive equal protection violation. In Police Department of Chicago v. Mosley, 408 U.S. 92 (1972), the Court ruled that a Chicago ordinance barring all picketing near schools except labor picketing violated equal protection. The infringement upon free speech, a fundamental constitutional right independent of equal protection, was severe; the selective line drawn between permitted and prohibited speech was unjustified under strict scrutiny and thus an equal protection violation. Of course, the Chicago ordinance also violated the free speech guarantee incorporated into the Fourteenth Amendment's due process clause.

The second type of fundamental right is quite different. The source of these fundamental rights is *equal protection itself*, which is surprising because the equal protection clause mandates "equal protection of the laws" but does not specify the substance of those laws. So far, our encounters with equal protection have been concerned with ensuring that differential treatment inherent in government classifications is justified. But now our focus turns to the far more amorphous and textually untethered objective of identifying substantive values that must be delivered equally. This bootstrap exercise originated in the Warren Court of the 1950s and 1960s and eventually produced three distinct types of "equal-protection-only fundamental rights": (1) the right to vote, (2) a limited right of access to the judicial process, and (3) the independently recognized but unwritten right of interstate migration. We shall consider each in turn. First, however, consider the following case, which purported to arrest the development of additional fundamental rights grounded solely in equal protection itself.

San Antonio Independent School District v. Rodriguez
411 U.S. 1 (1973)

[Public schools in Texas were financed through property taxes levied by local school districts. Because districts with an abundance of expensive property had greater property tax revenues than districts with inexpensive property, and because the number of pupils per district varied greatly, there were wide differences in per-pupil expenditures among school districts. The challengers contended that strict scrutiny should apply to these disparities because (1) education was said to be a fundamental right and (2) classifications by wealth were said to be suspect. A federal district court agreed, applied strict scrutiny, and invalidated the financing scheme. The Supreme Court reversed. It rejected both contentions, applied minimal scrutiny, and upheld the Texas school finance system.]

JUSTICE POWELL delivered the opinion of the Court.

I. [We] must decide, first, whether the Texas system of financing public education operates to the disadvantage of some suspect class or impinges upon a fundamental right explicitly or implicitly protected by the Constitution, thereby requiring strict judicial scrutiny. . . . If not, the Texas scheme must still be examined to determine whether it rationally furthers some legitimate, articulated state purpose and therefore does not constitute an invidious discrimination in violation of [equal protection].

II. [We] find neither the suspect-classification nor the fundamental-interest analysis persuasive.

A. The wealth discrimination [here] is quite unlike any of the forms of wealth discrimination heretofore reviewed by this Court. [The people] who constituted the class discriminated against in our prior cases shared two distinguishing characteristics: because of their impecunity they were completely unable to pay for some desired benefit, and as a consequence, they sustained an absolute deprivation of a meaningful opportunity to enjoy that benefit. [Justice Powell cited Griffin v. Illinois, 351 U.S. 12 (1956), and Douglas v. California, 372 U.S. 353 (1963), each of which involved financial barriers to an indigent's ability to appeal his criminal conviction.] [Neither] of the two distinguishing characteristics of wealth classifications can be found here. First, . . . the poorest families are not necessarily clustered in the poorest property districts. [Second], . . . lack of personal resources has not occasioned an absolute deprivation of the desired benefit. The argument here . . . is that they are receiving a poorer quality education than that available to children in districts having more assessable wealth. Apart from the unsettled and disputed question whether the quality of education may be determined by the amount of money expended for it, [equal protection] does not require absolute equality or precisely equal advantages.[13]

---

13. An educational financing system might be hypothesized, however, in which the analogy to the wealth discrimination cases would be considerably closer. If elementary and secondary education were made available by the State only to those able to pay a tuition assessed against

[There is a] third way in which the classification scheme might be defined — *district* wealth discrimination. [This] asks this Court to extend its most exacting scrutiny to review a system that allegedly discriminates against a large, diverse, and amorphous class, unified only by the common factor of residence in districts that happen to have less taxable wealth than other districts. [This has] none of the traditional indicia of suspectness: the class is not saddled with such disabilities, or subjected to such a history of purposeful unequal treatment, or relegated to such a position of political powerlessness as to command extraordinary protection from the majoritarian political process. We thus conclude that the Texas system does not operate to the peculiar disadvantage of any suspect class. But [appellees] also assert that the State's system impermissibly interferes with the exercise of a "fundamental" right, [education, thus requiring] the strict standard of judicial review.

B. In [*Brown I*], a unanimous Court recognized that "education is perhaps the most important function of state and local governments." [We agree] that "the grave significance of education both to the individual and to our society" cannot be doubted. But the importance of a service performed by the State does not determine whether it must be regarded as fundamental for purposes of [equal protection]. . . . Lindsey v. Normet, 405 U.S. 56 (1972), reiterates that social importance is not the critical determinant for subjecting state legislation to strict scrutiny. The complainants [challenged] procedural limitations imposed on tenants in suits brought by landlords under [Oregon law]. The tenants argued [for strict scrutiny because] the statutory limitations implicated "fundamental interests which are particularly important to the poor," such as the "'need for decent shelter'" and the "'right to retain peaceful possession of one's home,'" [but the Court concluded that] "the Constitution does not provide judicial remedies for every social and economic ill." [The Court held that there is no] "constitutional guarantee of access to dwellings of a particular quality or any recognition of the right of a tenant to occupy the real property of his landlord beyond the term of his lease, without the payment of rent."

[In] Dandridge v. Williams, 397 U.S. 471 (1970), the Court's explicit recognition of the fact that the "administration of public welfare assistance [involves] the most basic economic needs of impoverished human beings" provided no basis for departing from [minimal scrutiny]. As in the case of housing, the central importance of welfare benefits to the poor was not an adequate foundation for requiring the State to justify its law by showing some compelling state interest.

---

each pupil, there would be a clearly defined class of "poor" people — definable in terms of their inability to pay the prescribed sum — who would be absolutely precluded from receiving an education. That case would present a far more compelling set of circumstances for judicial assistance than the case before us today. [Here,] Texas has [provided] an adequate base education for all [children].

The lesson of these cases [is] plain. It is not the province of this Court to create substantive constitutional rights in the name of guaranteeing equal protection of the laws. Thus, the key to discovering whether education is "fundamental" is not to be found in comparisons of the relative societal significance of education as opposed to subsistence or housing. Nor is it to be found by weighing whether education is as important as the right to travel. Rather, the answer lies in assessing whether there is a right to education explicitly or implicitly guaranteed by the Constitution. Education, of course, is not among the rights afforded explicit protection under our Federal Constitution. Nor do we find any basis for saying it is implicitly so protected. [Appellees] insist that education is . . . a fundamental personal right because it is essential to the effective exercise of First Amendment freedoms and to intelligent utilization of the right to vote. . . . [W]e have never presumed to possess either the ability or the authority to guarantee to the citizenry the most *effective* speech or the most *informed* electoral choice. [These are] desirable goals of a system of freedom of expression and of a representative form of government [but] they are not values to be implemented by judicial intrusion into otherwise legitimate state activities. . . .

. . . C. [Equal protection] requires only that the State's system be shown to bear some rational relationship to legitimate state purposes. [We] are asked to condemn the State's judgment in conferring on political subdivisions the power to tax local property to supply revenues for local interests. [A]ppellees would have the Court intrude in an area in which it has traditionally deferred to state legislatures. [The] Justices of this Court lack both the expertise and the familiarity with local problems so necessary to the making of wise decisions with respect to the raising and disposition of public revenues. [In] such a complex arena in which no perfect alternatives exist, the Court does well not to impose too rigorous a standard of scrutiny lest all local fiscal schemes become subjects of criticism under [equal protection. This] case also involves the most persistent and difficult questions of educational policy, another area in which this Court's lack of specialized knowledge and experience counsels against premature interference with the informed judgments made at the state and local levels. [The] very complexity of the problems of financing and managing a statewide public school system suggests that "there will be more than one constitutionally permissible method of solving them," and that, within the limits of rationality, "the legislature's efforts to tackle the problems" should be entitled to respect.

III. [T]he existence of "some inequality" in the manner in which the State's rationale is achieved is not alone a sufficient basis for striking down the entire system. [Nor] must the financing system fail because [other] methods of satisfying the State's interest, which occasion "less drastic" disparities in expenditures, might be conceived. Only where state action impinges on the exercise of fundamental constitutional rights or liberties must it be found to have chosen the least restrictive alternative. . . .

[We] cannot say that such disparities are the product of a system that is so irrational as to be invidiously discriminatory. [The] constitutional standard

[is] whether the challenged state action rationally furthers a legitimate state purpose or interest. We hold that the Texas plan abundantly satisfies this standard.

IV. [A contrary result] would occasion in Texas and elsewhere an unprecedented upheaval in public education. [The] consideration and initiation of fundamental reforms with respect to state taxation and education are matters reserved for the legislative processes of the various [States]. [The] ultimate solutions must come from the lawmakers and from the democratic pressures of those who elect them. Reversed.

JUSTICE STEWART, concurring.

. . . Unlike other provisions of the Constitution, the Equal Protection Clause confers no substantive rights and creates no substantive liberties. The function of [equal protection] is simply to measure the validity of *classifications* created by state laws. [In] refusing to invalidate the Texas system of financing its public schools, the Court today applies with thoughtfulness and understanding the basic principles [of equal protection].

JUSTICE MARSHALL, joined by JUSTICE DOUGLAS, dissenting.

[Once more I] voice my disagreement with the Court's rigidified approach to equal protection analysis. [The] Court [divides] equal protection cases . . . into one of two neat categories[:] . . . strict scrutiny or mere rationality. But this Court's [decisions] defy such easy categorization. [Rather], this Court [has] applied a spectrum of standards in reviewing discrimination allegedly violative of [equal protection]. This spectrum clearly comprehends variations in the degree of care with which the Court will scrutinize particular classifications, depending, I believe, on the constitutional and societal importance of the interest adversely affected and the recognized invidiousness of the basis upon which the particular classification is drawn. . . . [Although] not all fundamental interests are constitutionally guaranteed, the determination of which interests are fundamental should be firmly rooted in the text of the Constitution. The task in every case should be to determine the extent to which constitutionally guaranteed rights are dependent on interests not mentioned in the Constitution. As the nexus between the specific constitutional guarantee and the nonconstitutional interest draws closer, the nonconstitutional interest becomes more fundamental and the degree of judicial scrutiny applied when the interest is infringed on a discriminatory basis must be adjusted accordingly. Thus, . . . interests such as procreation, the exercise of the state franchise, and access to criminal appellate processes [have] been afforded special judicial consideration in the face of discrimination because they are, to some extent, interrelated with constitutional guarantees. . . . Only if we closely protect the related interests from state discrimination do we ultimately ensure the integrity of the constitutional guarantee itself. . . .

[It] is true that this Court has never deemed the provision of free public education to be required by the Constitution. [But] the fundamental importance of education is amply indicated by [its] unique status [in] our society and by the close relationship between education and [basic] constitutional values. . . . [In] 48 of our 50 States the provision of public education is mandated by the state constitution. No other state function is so uniformly recognized as an essential element of our society's well-being. [Education] directly affects the ability of a child to exercise his First Amendment [rights]. Of particular importance is the relationship between education and the political process. [Education instills] an understanding [of] our governmental processes, [the] interest and [tools] necessary for political discourse, [and] is the dominant factor affecting political consciousness and participation. . . . [These] factors [compel] us to recognize the fundamentality of education and to scrutinize with appropriate care the bases for State discrimination affecting equality of educational opportunity in Texas'[s] school [districts].

[D]iscrimination on the basis of group wealth in this case likewise calls for careful judicial scrutiny [because local district wealth] bears no relationship whatsoever to the interest of Texas school children in the [public] educational opportunity afforded [them]. Given the importance of [education], we must be particularly sensitive to the invidious characteristics of any form of discrimination that is not clearly intended to serve [education], as opposed to some other distinct state interest. . . .

NOTES

1. The Effect of *Rodriguez*.   *Rodriguez* signaled a practical end to the possibility of finding new fundamental rights in equal protection itself. No longer could the societal importance of an interest, or even its practical nexus to a recognized constitutional right, support the conclusion that the interest is fundamental for equal protection purposes. As a result, the category of "derived-from-equal-protection-only" fundamental rights has remained confined to voting, a limited right of access to the courts, and the hybrid case of penalties imposed on the exercise of the constitutionally independent right of interstate migration. The only post-*Rodriguez* case in which the Court wavered on this point was Plyler v. Doe, in which the Court refused to find education to be a fundamental right but nevertheless applied enhanced minimal scrutiny to strike down Texas's exclusion of unlawful resident children from its public schools. The heightened scrutiny employed in *Plyler* was induced as much by the penalty levied on children for conduct over which they had no control as by the importance of education.

2. Justice Marshall's "Nexus" or "Multi-Factor" Approach.   One of the charges made against intermediate scrutiny is that it invites wholly subjective judicial second-guessing of legislative means and objectives. Would this problem be aggravated or ameliorated by Justice Marshall's method? Does Marshall's method accurately reflect what the Court does?

2. Voting: Denial

The Constitution originally left to the states the power to determine who could vote. It was not uncommon in early-nineteenth-century America for states to limit the franchise to free white adult male property owners. Even as states progressively liberalized their voting eligibility rules, the Constitution was amended five times to restrict state discretion in granting the franchise: The Fourteenth Amendment (1868) imposes penalties for most state limits on voting by adult male citizens, the Fifteenth (1870) removes race as a criterion for voting, the Nineteenth (1920) removes sex as a criterion, the Twenty-fourth (1964) eliminates the poll tax as a precondition for voting in federal elections, and the Twenty-sixth (1971) strikes age as a criterion with respect to those 18 or older.

The imposition of constitutional limits on state voter eligibility rules was not confined to the amendment process. By the 1960s the Court came to regard the right to vote as constitutionally fundamental and used the equal protection clause as the device for scrutinizing state laws that burdened exercise of the franchise.

Harper v. Virginia State Board of Elections
383 U.S. 663 (1966)

[At issue was the validity of Virginia's imposition of a $1.50 annual poll tax as a precondition to voting in state elections.]

JUSTICE DOUGLAS delivered the opinion of the Court.

[The] right to vote in state elections is nowhere expressly mentioned [in the Constitution]. It is argued that the right to vote in state elections is implicit, particularly by reason of the First [Amendment]. We do not stop to canvass the relation between voting and political expression. For it is enough to say that once the franchise is granted to the electorate, lines may not be drawn which are inconsistent with [equal protection. A] State violates [equal protection] whenever it makes the affluence of the voter or payment of any fee an electoral standard. Voter qualifications have no relation to wealth nor to [taxpaying]. [Equal protection] restrains the States from fixing voter qualifications which invidiously discriminate. [Wealth], like race, [is] not germane to one's ability to participate intelligently in the electoral process. [The] right to vote is too precious, too fundamental to be so burdened or conditioned.

JUSTICE BLACK, dissenting.

[The Court] seems to be using the old "natural-law-due-process formula" to justify striking down state laws as violations of [equal protection. There is no] constitutional support for this Court to use the Equal Protection Clause, as it has today, to write into the Constitution its notions of what it thinks is good governmental policy.

JUSTICE HARLAN, joined by JUSTICE STEWART, dissenting.

[The] Court's analysis of the equal protection issue goes no further than to say that the electoral franchise is "precious" and "fundamental," and to conclude that "to introduce wealth or payment of a fee as a measure of a voter's qualifications is to introduce a capricious or irrelevant factor." [These] captivating phrases [are] wholly inadequate to satisfy the [equal protection] standard: [Is] there a rational basis for Virginia's poll tax as a voting qualification? I think the answer to that question is undoubtedly "yes." [Property] qualifications and poll taxes have been a traditional part of our political structure. [It] is certainly a rational argument that payment of some minimal poll tax promotes civic responsibility, weeding out those who do not care enough about public affairs to pay $1.50 or thereabouts a year for the exercise of the franchise. It [was] probably accepted as sound political theory by a large percentage of Americans through most of our history that people with some property have a deeper stake in community affairs, and are consequently more responsible, more educated, more knowledgeable, more worthy of confidence, than those without means, and that the community and Nation would be better managed if the franchise were restricted to such citizens. [While] property and poll-tax qualifications [are] not in accord with current egalitarian notions of how a modern democracy should be organized [it] is all wrong [for] the Court to adopt the political doctrines popularly accepted at a particular moment of our history and to declare all others to be irrational and invidious, barring them from the range of choice by reasonably minded people acting through the political process. It was not too long ago that Mr. Justice Holmes felt impelled to remind the Court that [due process] does not enact the laissez-faire theory of society. [*Lochner.*] The times have changed, and perhaps it is appropriate to observe that neither does [equal protection] rigidly impose upon America an ideology of unrestrained egalitarianism.

NOTES

1. Source of the Fundamental Right. Does *Harper* adequately explain the source of voting as a fundamental right? Can the right legitimately be found in the equal protection clause alone? Or is it another "penumbral" right, akin to the right of marital access to contraceptives located by the Court in *Griswold*? According to *Rodriguez*, equal-protection fundamental rights are those that are explicit or implicit in the Constitution, but given the Constitution's recognition of plenary state authority to determine who may vote, what makes the voting right implicit in the Constitution?

2. Selective Denial of the Right to Vote. Based on *Harper*, one would expect that any selective denial of the right to vote would be subject to strict scrutiny, but that is not the case.

a. Special-purpose elections. In Kramer v. Union Free School District, 395 U.S. 621 (1969), the Court applied strict scrutiny to void a New York law limiting the franchise in school district elections to (1) parents or guardians of children enrolled in the public schools, or (2) owners or lessees of taxable real property within the district. Writing for the Court, Chief Justice Warren observed that while "reasonable citizenship, age, and residency requirements" are not subject to strict scrutiny, selective restriction of the franchise within that group does trigger strict scrutiny.

> Statutes granting the franchise to residents on a selective basis always pose the danger of denying some citizens any effective voice in the governmental affairs which substantially affect their lives. [If] a challenged [law] grants the right to vote to some bona fide residents of requisite age and citizenship and denies the franchise to others, the Court must determine whether the exclusions are necessary to promote a compelling state interest. [The] presumption of constitutionality [is] based on an assumption that the institutions of state government are structured so as to represent fairly all the people. However, when the challenge to the statute is in effect a challenge of this basic assumption, the assumption can no longer serve as the basis for presuming constitutionality.

The Court conceded, arguendo, that New York's goal of limiting the franchise in school district elections to those people "primarily interested [in or] affected" by school board decisions might be a compelling one but struck down the law because it was not proven that "the exclusion of [Kramer and others like him] is necessary to achieve the articulated state goal."

Justices Stewart, Black, and Harlan dissented:

> [A] State may exclude nonresidents from participation in its elections. [Clearly] a State may reasonably assume that its residents have a greater stake in the outcome of elections held within its boundaries than do other persons [and] that residents, being generally better informed regarding state affairs than are nonresidents, will be more likely [to] vote responsibly. And the same may be said of legislative assumptions regarding the electoral competence of adults and literate persons on the one hand, and of minors and illiterates on the other. [So] long as the classification is rationally related to a permissible legislative end, [there] is no denial of equal protection. Thus judged, the statutory classification involved here seems to me clearly to be valid [and] the Court does not really argue the contrary. [The Court's] justification for applying [strict scrutiny] cannot withstand analysis. The voting qualifications at issue have been promulgated [by] the New York State Legislature and the appellant [is] fully able to participate in the election of representatives in that body. There is simply no claim whatever . . . that the state government is not "structured so as to represent fairly all the people," including the appellant. Nor is there any other justification for [strict scrutiny]. [The] "Constitution [does] not confer the right of suffrage upon any one." [Under] *any* equal protection standard, short of a doctrinaire insistence that universal suffrage is somehow mandated by the Constitution, the appellant's claim must be rejected.

Kramer was followed in Cipriano v. Houma, 395 U.S. 701 (1969), in which the Court struck down a Louisiana law limiting the vote to property owners in elections for the purpose of deciding whether to issue municipal utility revenue bonds; and in Phoenix v. Kolodziejski, 399 U.S. 204 (1970), which voided an Arizona law permitting only property-owning taxpayers to vote in elections considering issuance of general obligation bonds to be paid mostly from property tax revenues.

But the Court has applied minimal scrutiny in upholding property qualifications for voting in special-purpose elections for limited-purpose government units whose functions primarily affect the property-qualified electors. In Salyer Land Co. v. Tulare Lake Basin Water Storage District, 410 U.S. 719 (1973), the Court sustained a California law permitting only landowners within a water storage district to vote in district elections in proportion to the assessed value of the owner's land. Water storage districts maintain reservoirs and canals to provide water for farming and charge landowners for the costs of that effort in proportion to the benefits received. The Court said strict scrutiny was inapplicable because of the district's "special limited purpose [and] the disproportionate effect of its activities on landowners as a group." The voting scheme was rationally related to its legitimate objective of storing and distributing water for farming and passing on those costs to water users.

In Ball v. James, 451 U.S. 355 (1981), the Court extended *Salyer* to uphold a "one acre–one vote" voting scheme for directors of a large water storage district in Arizona that sold hydroelectric power to several hundred thousand residents. Minimal scrutiny was appropriate because the district was unable to "enact any laws governing the conduct of citizens, nor [administer] normal functions of government."

This "special purpose" exemption does not apply where the voter eligibility line is drawn along racial or ethnic lines. In Rice v. Cayetano, 528 U.S. 495 (2000), the Court struck down a Hawaii law limiting to ethnic Hawaiians the right to vote for trustees of the Office of Hawaiian Affairs, a state agency that administers programs designed to benefit descendants of the original inhabitants of Hawaii. Such openly racial limits on the franchise were treated as a per se violation of the Fifteenth Amendment.

b. Durational residency requirements. In Dunn v. Blumstein, 405 U.S. 330 (1972), the Court applied strict scrutiny to void Tennessee's one-year durational residency requirement for voting. While the Court conceded that Tennessee had a compelling interest in limiting the franchise to bona fide residents, preventing fraud, and ensuring that only "knowledgeable voters" would vote, it found the durational residency requirement unnecessary to accomplish these goals.

c. Convicted felons and prisoners. In Richardson v. Ramirez, 418 U.S. 24 (1974), the Court applied minimal scrutiny and upheld a California law barring convicted felons from voting, even after serving their sentences and completing parole. Minimal scrutiny was appropriate, said the Court, because section 2 of the Fourteenth Amendment explicitly contemplates state action barring convicted criminals from voting. Minimal scrutiny also applies to denials of absentee ballots to prisoners awaiting trial. See McDonald v. Board of Election Commissioners, 394 U.S. 802 (1969); O'Brien v. Skinner, 414 U.S. 524 (1974).

d. Limits on ballot access by parties and candidates. States have broad authority to regulate elections in the interest of obtaining an orderly and effective canvass of the public will. Thus they may restrict access to the ballot by imposing reasonable nondiscriminatory regulations on political parties and candidates. But when such regulations unduly or severely interfere with the fundamental rights of individuals to associate together in a political party or to cast their votes effectively, the Court applies strict scrutiny. Because democracy can function only when those out of power have a fair opportunity to convince the people to give them power, ballot access regulations that "stack the deck" in favor of certain interests are inimical to democracy. Strict scrutiny has a unique meaning here: While the state's objective must be *compelling*, the fit between the challenged electoral regulation and the compelling objective usually need not be the least restrictive, or most narrowly tailored, option open to the state. So long as the fit is *reasonable* and the result does not *effectively exclude from the ballot parties with significant support*, strict scrutiny is satisfied.

Williams v. Rhodes, 393 U.S. 23 (1968). The Court applied strict scrutiny to void an Ohio law providing that any political party receiving at least 10 percent of the vote in a gubernatorial election automatically qualified for the next presidential election ballot, but that denied other parties ballot access unless they had created a complicated party structure, held a primary election in conformity with "detailed and rigorous standards," and filed a petition signed by voters "totalling 15 percent of the number of ballots cast in the last preceding gubernatorial election." Ohio lacked any compelling reason to create this de facto two-party monopoly.

Jenness v. Fortson, 403 U.S. 431 (1971). The Court implicitly applied minimal scrutiny to uphold a Georgia law denying ballot access to independent candidates unless they paid a concededly valid filing fee and filed a nominating petition signed by voters representing at least 5 percent of the total registered voters at the last election. Unlike the Ohio law at issue in Williams v. Rhodes, Georgia's system did not substantially interfere with associational or voting rights because it had not attempted to "[freeze] the status quo"—independent voters with a modest amount of support could qualify for the ballot.

Munro v. Socialist Workers Party, 479 U.S. 189 (1986). The Court applied minimal scrutiny in upholding Washington's requirement that denied ballot access to political parties receiving less than 1 percent of the vote in a primary election open to all voters, regardless of party affiliation.

Storer v. Brown, 415 U.S. 724 (1974). Under strict scrutiny, the Court upheld a California requirement that barred independent candidates from the ballot if they had a registered party affiliation within the preceding year. The provision furthered California's compelling "interest in the stability of its political system" by preventing disgruntled losers in party primaries from running as spoilers in the general election.

Anderson v. Celebrezze, 460 U.S. 780 (1983). The Court voided an Ohio law requiring an independent presidential candidate to file nominating signatures of 5,000 voters by March 20 in order to appear on the November ballot. Justice Stevens, for the Court, declared that [a court] must first consider the character and magnitude of the asserted injury to [First and Fourteenth Amendment rights, then identify] and evaluate the precise interests put forward by the State as justifications for the burden imposed by its rule, [determine] the legitimacy and strength of each of those interests, [and] consider the extent to which those interests make it necessary to burden the plaintiff's rights. Only after weighing all these factors is the reviewing court in a position to decide whether the challenged provision is unconstitutional.

This "flexible" standard was criticized by Justice Rehnquist, dissenting, who pointed out that

the Ohio filing deadline prevents [a] candidate [from] seeking a party nomination and then, finding that he is rejected by the party, bolting from the party to form an independent candidacy. This is precisely the same behavior that California sought to prevent by the disaffiliation statute this Court upheld in *Storer*.

The "flexible" standard was applied in Burdick v. Takushi, 504 U.S. 428 (1992), which upheld Hawaii's prohibition of write-in voting, and in Timmons v. Twin Cities Area New Party, 520 U.S. 351 (1997), in which the Court upheld Minnesota's ban on "fusion" candidacies (in which a person appears on the ballot as the candidate of more than one party) after concluding that the ban was not a severe restriction. Minnesota's "interests in avoiding voter confusion, promoting candidate competition . . . , preventing electoral distortions and ballot manipulations, and discouraging party splintering" were sufficient.

≡ ### *Crawford v. Marion County Election Board*
553 U.S. 181 (2008)

[Indiana enacted a Voter ID law that required voters to produce government-issued photo identification in order to vote. About 99 percent of eligible voters possessed such identification, and a photo ID was available without charge to those who did not already have one. Indigent voters and voters with religious objections to being photographed were permitted to cast a provisional ballot that would be counted if they filed a required affidavit within ten days after the election. Voters who forgot their photo ID could cast a provisional ballot that would be counted if they presented their photo ID to a county clerk within ten days after the election. The statute was challenged as facially invalid. A federal District Court granted summary judgment to Indiana, which was upheld by the Court of Appeals. The Supreme Court affirmed.]

JUSTICE STEVENS announced the judgment of the Court and delivered an opinion in which CHIEF JUSTICE ROBERTS and JUSTICE KENNEDY joined.

[Under] *Harper*, even rational restrictions on the right to vote are invidious if they are unrelated to voter qualifications. In Anderson v. Celebrezze, however, we confirmed the general rule that "evenhanded restrictions that protect the integrity and reliability of the electoral process itself" are not invidious and satisfy the standard set forth in *Harper*. [Under *Anderson*,] a court must identify and evaluate the interests put forward by the State as justifications for the burden imposed by its rule. . . . [We] have followed *Anderson*'s balancing approach. [In] Burdick v. Takushi we applied *Anderson*'s standard for "reasonable, nondiscriminatory restrictions" and upheld Hawaii's prohibition on write-in voting despite the fact that it prevented a significant number of "voters from participating in Hawaii elections in a meaningful manner." We reaffirmed *Anderson*'s requirement that a court evaluating a constitutional challenge to an election regulation weigh the asserted injury to the right to vote against the "precise interests put forward by the State as justifications for the burden imposed by its rule." . . .

The State has identified several state interests. . . . The first is the interest in deterring and detecting voter fraud. The State . . . argues that it has a particular interest in preventing voter fraud [produced by the fact] that Indiana's voter registration rolls include a large number of names of persons who are either deceased or no longer live in Indiana. Finally, the State relies on its interest in safeguarding voter confidence. . . .

The only kind of voter fraud that [the statute] addresses is in-person voter impersonation at polling places. The record contains no evidence of any such fraud actually occurring in Indiana at any time in its history[, but] flagrant examples of such fraud in other parts of the country have been documented throughout this Nation's history[14] . . . , occasional examples have surfaced in recent years,[15] and . . . Indiana's own experience with fraudulent voting in the 2003 Democratic primary for East Chicago Mayor[16] . . . demonstrate that not only is the risk of voter fraud real but that it could affect the outcome of a close election. There is no question about the legitimacy or importance of the State's interest in counting only the votes of eligible voters. Moreover, the interest in orderly administration and

---

14. One infamous example is the New York City elections of 1868. William (Boss) Tweed set about solidifying and consolidating his control of the city. One local tough who worked for Boss Tweed, "Big Tim" Sullivan, insisted that his "repeaters" (individuals paid to vote multiple times) have whiskers: "'When you've voted 'em with their whiskers on, you take 'em to a barber and scrape off the chin fringe. Then you vote 'em again with the side lilacs and a mustache. Then to a barber again, off comes the sides and you vote 'em a third time with the mustache. If that ain't enough and the box can stand a few more ballots, clean off the mustache and vote 'em plain face. That makes every one of 'em good for four votes.'" A. Callow, The Tweed Ring 210 (1966) (quoting M. Werner, Tammany Hall 439 (1928)).

15. [The District Judge] cited record evidence containing examples from California, Washington, Maryland, Wisconsin, Georgia, Illinois, Pennsylvania, Missouri, Miami, and St. Louis. [Although] the record evidence of in-person fraud was overstated because much of the fraud was actually absentee ballot fraud or voter registration fraud, there remain scattered instances of in-person voter fraud. . . .

16. That incident involved absentee ballot fraud rather than in-person voter impersonation. — ED.

accurate recordkeeping provides a sufficient justification for carefully identifying all voters participating in the election process. [Moreover,] Indiana has an unusually inflated list of registered voters[, a fact that] provide[s] a neutral and nondiscriminatory reason supporting the State's decision to require photo identification. [Finally, while Indiana's] interest in protecting public confidence "in the integrity and legitimacy of representative government" . . . is closely related to the State's interest in preventing voter fraud, public confidence in the integrity of the electoral process has independent significance, because it encourages citizen participation in the democratic process. . . .

A photo identification requirement imposes some burdens on voters that other methods of identification do not share. For example, a voter may lose his photo identification, may have his wallet stolen on the way to the polls, or may not resemble the photo in the identification because he recently grew a beard. Burdens of that sort arising from life's vagaries, however, are neither so serious nor so frequent as to raise any question about the constitutionality of [the law]; the availability of the right to cast a provisional ballot provides an adequate remedy for problems of that character. The burdens that are relevant . . . are those imposed on persons who are eligible to vote but do not possess a current photo identification. . . . The fact that most voters already possess . . . some . . . form of acceptable identification would not save the statute under our reasoning in *Harper*, if the State required voters to pay a tax or a fee to obtain a new photo identification. But . . . the photo identification cards issued by Indiana's BMV are also free. For most voters who need them, the inconvenience of making a trip to the BMV, gathering the required documents, and posing for a photograph surely does not qualify as a substantial burden on the right to vote, or even represent a significant increase over the usual burdens of voting. [A] somewhat heavier burden may be placed on . . . elderly persons born out-of-state, who may have difficulty obtaining a birth certificate; persons who because of economic or other personal limitations may find it difficult either to secure a copy of their birth certificate or to assemble the other required documentation to obtain a state-issued identification; homeless persons; and persons with a religious objection to being photographed. . . . The severity of that burden is . . . mitigated by the fact that . . . voters without photo identification may cast provisional ballots that will ultimately be counted [if they] travel to the circuit court clerk's office within 10 days to execute the required affidavit. . . .

[Because] petitioners [seek] relief that would invalidate the statute in all its applications, they bear a heavy burden of persuasion. . . . A facial challenge must fail where the statute has a "plainly legitimate sweep." When we consider only the statute's broad application to all Indiana voters we conclude that it "imposes only a limited burden on voters' rights." *Burdick*. The "precise interests" advanced by the State are therefore sufficient to defeat petitioners' facial challenge. . . .

[A]ffirmed.

JUSTICE SCALIA, joined by JUSTICE THOMAS and JUSTICE ALITO, concurring in the judgment.

. . . *Burdick* . . . calls for application of a deferential "important regulatory interests" standard for non-severe, nondiscriminatory restrictions, reserving strict scrutiny for laws that severely restrict the right to vote. The lead opinion resists the import of *Burdick* by characterizing it as simply adopting "the balancing approach" of *Anderson*. Although *Burdick* liberally quoted *Anderson*, *Burdick* forged *Anderson*'s amorphous "flexible standard" into something resembling an administrable rule. . . .

To vote in person in Indiana, *everyone* must have and present a photo identification that can be obtained for free. . . . The Indiana photo-identification law is a generally applicable, nondiscriminatory voting regulation, and our precedents refute the view that individual impacts are relevant to determining the severity of the burden it imposes. In . . . *Burdick* . . . we considered the laws and their reasonably foreseeable effect on *voters generally*. We did not discuss whether the laws had a severe effect on Mr. Burdick's own right to vote, given his particular circumstances. . . . What mattered was the general assessment of the burden. . . .

This is an area where the dos and don'ts need to be known in advance of the election, and voter-by-voter examination of the burdens of voting regulations would prove especially disruptive. A case-by-case approach naturally encourages constant litigation. Very few new election regulations improve everyone's lot, so the potential allegations of severe burden are endless. . . . The lead opinion . . . neither rejects nor embraces the rule of our precedents, provides no certainty, and will embolden litigants who surmise that our precedents have been abandoned. . . .

The universally applicable requirements of Indiana's voter-identification law are eminently reasonable. The burden of acquiring, possessing, and showing a free photo identification is simply not severe, because it does not "even represent a significant increase over the usual burdens of voting." And the State's interests are sufficient to sustain that minimal burden. That should end the matter. That the State accommodates some voters by permitting (not requiring) the casting of absentee or provisional ballots, is an indulgence — not a constitutional imperative that falls short of what is required.

JUSTICE SOUTER, joined by JUSTICE GINSBURG, dissenting.

Indiana's "Voter ID Law" threatens to impose nontrivial burdens on the voting right of tens of thousands of the State's citizens, and a significant percentage of those individuals are likely to be deterred from voting. [A] State may not burden the right to vote merely by invoking abstract interests, be they legitimate or even compelling, but must make a particular, factual showing that threats to its interests outweigh the particular impediments it has imposed. The State has made no such justification here. . . .

[Judicial] scrutiny varies with the effect of the regulation at issue. . . . The first set of burdens . . . is the travel costs and fees necessary to get one of the limited variety of federal or state photo identifications needed to cast a regular ballot. . . . [A] a second financial hurdle [is the] need to present "a birth certificate, a certificate of naturalization, U.S. veterans photo identification, U.S. military photo identification, or a U.S. passport" [to obtain a photo ID. The] two most common of these documents come at a price[:] anywhere from $3 to $12 for a birth certificate [and] about $100 [for a passport]. . . .

Indiana's Voter ID Law . . . threatens to impose serious burdens on the voting right, even if not "severe" ones, and . . . the number of individuals likely to be affected is significant as well. . . . Petitioners, to be sure, failed to nail down precisely how great the cohort of discouraged and totally deterred voters will be. . . . While of course it would greatly aid a plaintiff to establish his claims beyond mathematical doubt, he does enough to show that serious burdens are likely. . . .

[H]aving found the Voter ID Law burdens far from trivial, I have to make a rigorous assessment of "the precise interests put forward by the State as justifications for the burden imposed by its rule. . . ." There is no denying the . . . compelling[nature of combating voter fraud[, but the Indiana law] addresses only one form of voter fraud: in-person voter impersonation. [That interest must] be discounted for the fact that the State has not come across a single instance of in-person voter impersonation fraud in all of Indiana's history. . . . The State responds to the want of evidence with the assertion that in-person voter impersonation fraud is hard to detect. But this is like saying the "man who wasn't there" is hard to spot. . . .[17] Without a shred of evidence that in-person voter impersonation is a problem in the State, much less a crisis, Indiana has adopted one of the most restrictive photo identification requirements in the country. . . . Like [the poll tax in *Harper*], the onus of the Indiana law is illegitimate just because it correlates with no state interest so well as it does with the object of deterring poorer residents from exercising the franchise. . . .

NOTE AND PROBLEM

1. The Operative Standard. The lead opinion says that *Anderson* controls, and interprets *Anderson* to mean that a state need only have some plausible nondiscriminatory interest relevant to voter qualifications to justify restrictions on the right to vote, no matter how lean the evidence supporting that interest. The Scalia group interprets *Anderson* and its progeny to mean that strict scrutiny applies only to severe voter restrictions, but any facially neutral restriction that does not impose a severe burden on the franchise is presumed to be valid. The Stevens group left open the possibility of as-applied challenges to the Voter ID law; the Scalia group's approach obviates that possibility. Under Marks v. United States, 430 U.S. 188 (1977), when "a fragmented Court decides a case and no single rationale explaining the result

---

17. "As I was going up the stair / I met a man who wasn't there." H. Mearns, Antigonish, reprinted in Best Remembered Poems 107 (M. Gardner ed. 1992).

enjoys the assent of five Justices, 'the holding of the Court may be viewed as that position taken by those Members who concurred in the judgment on the narrowest grounds. . . .'" What is the holding of *Crawford*?

2. Problem. In order to prevent non-citizens from voting illegally, suppose a state with a large population of non-citizens enacts a Voter ID law that requires each voter to prove his or her U.S. citizenship at the polling place, and to do so by providing either a passport or a birth certificate showing birth in the United States. Assume the absence of any federal law on the subject. Analyze the validity of the law under each of the three principal opinions in *Crawford*.

3. Voting: Dilution

Once the Court in Baker v. Carr ruled that equal protection challenges to state legislative apportionment schemes were justiciable, a flood of such challenges ensued. The essential argument was that legislative apportionment by any means other than population diluted the votes of some citizens by making the votes in sparsely populated legislative districts count more than the votes in populous districts. In *Reynolds*, which follows, the plaintiffs alleged that equal protection required that the Alabama legislature be apportioned strictly by population. In Bush v. Gore, the contention was that the failure to follow a uniform standard of ascertaining voter intent on ambiguously marked ballots diluted the votes of unambiguously marked ballots.

≡ *Reynolds v. Sims*
≡ *377 U.S. 533 (1964)*

CHIEF JUSTICE WARREN delivered the opinion of the Court.

[The] right of suffrage is a fundamental matter in a free and democratic society. Especially since the right to exercise the franchise in a free and unimpaired manner is preservative of other basic civil and political rights, any alleged infringement of the right of citizens to vote must be carefully and meticulously scrutinized. . . . Legislators represent people, not trees or acres. Legislators are elected by voters, not farms or cities or economic interests. As long as ours is a representative form of government, and our legislatures are those instruments of government elected directly by and directly representative of the people, the right to elect legislators in a free and unimpaired fashion is a bedrock of our political system. It could hardly be gainsaid that a constitutional claim had been asserted by an allegation that certain otherwise qualified voters had been entirely prohibited from voting for members of their state legislature. And, if a State should provide that the votes of citizens in one part of the State should be given two times, or five times, or 10 times the weight of votes of citizens in another part of the State, it could hardly be contended that the right to vote of those residing in the disfavored areas had not been effectively diluted. [Of] course, the effect of state legislative districting schemes which give the same number of representatives to unequal numbers of constituents is identical. [Weighting] the votes of citizens differently, by any method or means, merely because of where they happen to reside, hardly seems justifiable.

[Equal] protection has been traditionally viewed as requiring the uniform treatment of persons standing in the same relation to the governmental action questioned or challenged. With respect to the allocation of legislative representation, all voters, as citizens of a State, stand in the same relation regardless of where they live. [Equal protection] guarantees the opportunity for equal participation by all voters in the election of state legislators. Diluting the weight of votes because of place of residence impairs basic constitutional rights under the Fourteenth Amendment just as much as invidious discriminations based upon factors such as [race]. . . . Population is, of necessity, the starting point for consideration and the controlling criterion for judgment in legislative apportionment controversies. . . . [Equal protection] demands no less than substantially equal state legislative representation for all citizens, of all places as well as of all races. [We] hold that, as a basic constitutional standard, [equal protection] requires that the seats in both houses of a bicameral state legislature must be apportioned on a population basis. Simply stated, an individual's right to vote for state legislators is unconstitutionally impaired when its weight is in a substantial fashion diluted when compared with votes of citizens living in other parts of the State. . . .

[Equal] protection requires that a State make an honest and good faith effort to construct districts, in both houses of its legislature, as nearly of equal population as is practicable. . . . Mathematical exactness or precision is hardly a workable constitutional requirement. [So] long as the divergences from a strict population standard are based on legitimate considerations incident to the effectuation of a rational state policy, some deviations from the equal population principle are constitutionally permissible, [but] neither history alone, nor economic or other sorts of group interests, are permissible factors in attempting to justify disparities from population-based representation. [But] a State can rationally consider according political subdivisions some independent representation in at least one body of the state legislature, as long as the basic standard of equality of population among districts is maintained.

JUSTICE HARLAN, dissenting.

Stripped of aphorisms, the Court's argument boils down to the assertion that appellees' right to vote has been invidiously "debased" or "diluted" by systems of apportionment which entitle them to vote for fewer legislators than other voters, an assertion which is tied to the Equal Protection Clause only by the constitutionally frail tautology that "equal" means "equal." Had the Court paused to probe more deeply into the matter, it would have found that the Equal Protection Clause was never intended to inhibit the States in choosing any democratic method they pleased for the apportionment of their legislatures. This is shown by the language of the Fourteenth Amendment taken as a whole, by the understanding of those who proposed and ratified it, and by the political practices of the States at the time the Amendment was adopted. [The] failure of the Court to consider any of these matters cannot be [excused]. . . . Since [state] legislative apportionments, as such, are wholly free of constitutional limitations, save such as may be imposed by the Republican Form of Government Clause, the Court's action now bringing them within the purview of [equal protection] amounts to nothing less than an exercise of the amending power by this Court. . . .

[The Court] declares it unconstitutional for a State to give effective consideration to any of the following in establishing legislative districts: (1) history; (2) "economic or other sorts of group interests"; (3) area; (4) geographical considerations; (5) a desire "to insure effective representation for sparsely settled areas"; (6) "availability of access of citizens to their representatives"; (7) theories of bicameralism (except those approved by the Court); (8) occupation; (9) "an attempt to balance urban and rural power"; [and] (10) the preference of a majority of voters in the State.[18] [I] know of no principle of logic or practical or theoretical politics, still less any constitutional principle, which establishes all or any of these exclusions. [The Court] says only that "legislators represent people, not trees or acres." [While] this may be conceded [it] is surely equally obvious, and, in the context of elections, more meaningful to note that people are not ciphers and that legislators can represent their electors only by speaking for their interests—economic, social, political—many of which do reflect the place where the electors live. The Court does not establish, or indeed even attempt to make a case for the proposition that conflicting interests within a State can only be adjusted by disregarding them when voters are grouped for purposes of representation.

≡≡≡ ### *Bush v. Gore*
531 U.S. 98 (2000)

PER CURIAM. [The Court held that the Florida Supreme Court's ordered manual recount of only ballots cast in the Florida 2000 presidential election that failed to register a choice for President in the machine tally (so-called undervotes) violated equal protection.]

The individual citizen has no federal constitutional right to vote for electors for the President of the United States unless and until the state legislature chooses a statewide election as the means to implement its power to appoint

---

18. In Lucas v. Forty-fourth General Assembly, 377 U.S. 713 (1964), decided as a companion case, the Court voided a Colorado scheme, approved by voters in a state-wide referendum, that apportioned one house by population and the other by geography. The Court declared that an "individual's constitutionally protected right to cast an equally weighted vote cannot be denied even by a majority of a State's electorate, if the apportionment scheme adopted by the voters fails to measure up to the requirements of" equal protection. Justice Stewart, joined by Justice Clark, dissented, noting that the plan was rational and did not involve "the systematic frustration of the will of a majority of the electorate of the State."—ED.

members of the Electoral College. U.S. Const., Art. II, §1. This is the source for the statement in McPherson v. Blacker, 146 U.S. 1 (1892), that the State legislature's power to select the manner for appointing electors is plenary; it may, if it so chooses, select the electors itself, which indeed was the manner used by State legislatures in several States for many years after the Framing of our Constitution. History has now favored the voter, and in each of the several States the citizens themselves vote for Presidential electors. When the state legislature vests the right to vote for President in its people, the right to vote as the legislature has prescribed is fundamental; and one source of its fundamental nature lies in the equal weight accorded to each vote and the equal dignity owed to each voter. [The] right to vote is protected in more than the initial allocation of the franchise. Equal protection applies as well to the manner of its exercise. Having once granted the right to vote on equal terms, the State may not, by later arbitrary and disparate treatment, value one person's vote over that of another. . . . The question before us . . . is whether the recount procedures the Florida Supreme Court has adopted are consistent with its obligation to avoid arbitrary and disparate treatment of the members of its electorate. Much of the controversy seems to revolve around ballot cards designed to be perforated by a stylus but which, either through error or deliberate omission, have not been perforated with sufficient precision for a machine to count them. In some cases a piece of the card—a chad—is hanging, say by two corners. In other cases there is no separation at all, just an indentation. The Florida Supreme Court has ordered that the intent of the voter be discerned from such ballots, [but the] recount mechanisms implemented in response to [its] decisions [do] not satisfy the minimum requirement for non-arbitrary treatment of voters necessary to secure the fundamental right. Florida's basic command for the count of legally cast votes is to consider the "intent of the voter." This is unobjectionable as an abstract proposition and a starting principle. The problem inheres in the absence of specific standards to ensure its equal application. The formulation of uniform rules to determine intent based on these recurring circumstances is practicable and, we conclude, necessary.

The law does not refrain from searching for the intent of the actor in a multitude of circumstances; and in some cases the general command to ascertain intent is not susceptible to much further refinement. In this instance, however, the question is not whether to believe a witness but how to interpret the marks or holes or scratches on an inanimate object, a piece of cardboard or paper which, it is said, might not have registered as a vote during the machine count. The fact-finder confronts a thing, not a person. The search for intent can be confined by specific rules designed to ensure uniform treatment.

The want of those rules here has led to unequal evaluation of ballots in various respects. [The] standards for accepting or rejecting contested ballots might vary not only from county to county but indeed within a single county from one recount team to another. The record provides some examples. A monitor in Miami-Dade County testified at trial that he observed that three members of the county canvassing board applied different standards in defining a legal vote. And testimony at trial also revealed that at least one county changed its evaluative standards during the counting process. Palm Beach County, for example, began the process with a 1990 guideline which precluded counting completely attached chads, switched to a rule that considered a vote to be legal if any light could be seen through a chad, changed back to the 1990 rule, and then abandoned any pretense of a *per se* rule, only to have a court order that the county consider dimpled chads legal. This is not a process with sufficient guarantees of equal treatment. . . .

The recount process, in its features here described, is inconsistent with the minimum procedures necessary to protect the fundamental right of each voter in the special instance of a statewide recount under the authority of a single state judicial officer. Our consideration is limited to the present circumstances, for the problem of equal protection in election processes generally presents many complexities. The question before the Court is not whether local entities, in the exercise of their expertise, may develop different systems for implementing elections. Instead, we are presented with a situation where a state court with the power to assure uniformity has ordered a statewide recount with minimal procedural safeguards. When a court orders a statewide remedy, there must be at least some assurance that the rudimentary requirements of equal treatment and fundamental fairness are satisfied. . . .

JUSTICE SOUTER, joined by JUSTICE BREYER, dissenting.

I can conceive of no legitimate state interest served by these differing treatments of the expressions of voters' fundamental rights. The differences appear wholly arbitrary. . . . I would therefore remand the case to the courts of Florida with instructions to establish uniform standards for evaluating the several types of ballots that have prompted differing treatments, to be applied within and among counties when passing on such identical ballots in any further recounting (or successive recounting) that the courts might order.

NOTES

1. The Nature and Source of the Right. Nobody was denied the right to vote in *Reynolds*, so what made Alabama's scheme a violation of equal protection? Is the fundamental right to vote grounded in some other part of the Constitution, such as Article IV, section 4 (the guarantee of a republican form of government)? Is it proper to ground the right in the principle that the representative democracy envisioned by the Constitution requires equality of voting power? That was plainly not the intent of the Framers, in either 1789 or 1868, and it has been our historical practice to change voting eligibility by legislation or constitutional amendment. Should that have been given more consideration than it was?

2. The Scope of Bush v. Gore's Equal Protection. The Court expressly indicated that its ruling was confined to "the present circumstances, . . . where a state court with the power to assure uniformity has ordered a statewide recount with minimal procedural safeguards" and disclaimed any applicability of the decision to the question of "whether local entities, in the exercise of their expertise, may develop different systems for implementing elections." But can it be so neatly cabined? *Harper* and its kin dealt with formal obstacles to voting (e.g., the poll tax), *Reynolds* and its progeny dealt with structural defects in voting (e.g., ill-apportioned electoral districts), and Bush v. Gore deals with the actual mechanism of counting the ballots. Is this latest extension of equal protection workable? What standard can be used to detect when various methods of ascertaining the electorate's preferences are sufficiently disparate to violate equal protection? What differences in such methods are relevant to that inquiry? Are differences in accuracy enough? What if one method produces significantly more spoiled ballots than another method? What does it mean in this context to have "equally weighted" votes?

Is there a meaningful difference between disparities produced by differing mechanical or electronic methods of tabulation and disparities produced by human judgment in recounts, especially when those human actors know in advance the consequences of their judgments? Is it fair to say that there is less reason to be troubled about disparate machine counts than disparate human counts?

4. Voting: Gerrymanders

While Reynolds v. Sims and its progeny require apportionment by population, the question of what limits equal protection imposes on gerrymanders motivated by other reasons has proven to be controversial. In a sense, all gerrymanders are political, and that truism led the Court, in Gaffney v. Cummings, 412 U.S. 735 (1973), to signal that political gerrymanders might largely escape equal protection scrutiny. "Politics [is] inseparable from districting and apportionment. [While] judicial scrutiny under [equal protection is appropriate] if racial or political groups have been fenced out of the political process [we] have not [attempted] the impossible task of extirpating politics from what are the essentially political processes of the sovereign States." But the Court reversed direction.

≡≡≡ *Davis v. Bandemer*
≡≡≡ *478 U.S. 109 (1986)*

[Indiana Democrats claimed that state legislative apportionment unconstitutionally diluted their votes by a deliberate gerrymander to understate Democratic voting strength. The Court held that the claim was justiciable but rejected it on the merits.]

JUSTICE WHITE, joined by JUSTICES BRENNAN, MARSHALL and BLACKMUN, delivered a plurality opinion.

[In] order to succeed [on the equal protection claim, the] plaintiffs were required to prove both intentional discrimination against an identifiable political group and an actual discriminatory effect on that group. . . . District lines are rarely neutral phenomena. [The] reality is that districting inevitably has and is intended to have substantial political consequences. [As] long as redistricting is done by a legislature, it should not be very difficult to prove that the likely political consequences of the reapportionment were intended.

We do not accept, however, the [conclusion] that the [reapportionment] visited a sufficiently adverse effect on the appellees' constitutionally protected rights to make out [an equal protection] violation. [Our cases] foreclose any claim that the Constitution requires proportional representation or that legislatures in reapportioning must draw district lines to come as near as possible to allocating seats to the contending parties in proportion to what their anticipated statewide vote will be. The typical election for legislative seats in the United States is conducted in described geographical districts, with the candidate receiving the most votes in each district winning the seat allocated to that district. [Even] a narrow statewide preference for either party [can] produce an overwhelming majority for the winning party in the state legislature. This consequence, however, is inherent in winner-take-all, district-based elections, and we cannot hold that such a reapportionment law would violate [equal protection] because the voters in the losing party do not have representation in the legislature in proportion to the statewide vote received by their party candidates. [This] is true of a racial as well as a political group.

[The] mere fact that a particular apportionment scheme makes it more difficult for a particular group in a particular district to elect the representatives of its choice does not render that scheme constitutionally infirm. [A] group's electoral power is not unconstitutionally diminished by the simple fact of an apportionment scheme that makes winning elections more difficult, and a failure of proportional representation alone does not constitute impermissible discrimination under [equal protection. Unconstitutional] discrimination occurs only when the electoral system is arranged in a manner that will consistently degrade a voter's or a group of voters' influence on the political process as a whole. [An] equal protection violation may be found only where the electoral system substantially disadvantages certain voters in their opportunity to influence the political process effectively. [Such] a finding of unconstitutionality must be supported by evidence of continued frustration of the will of a majority of the voters or effective denial to a minority of voters of a fair chance to influence the political process.

Justice O'Connor, joined by Chief Justice Burger and Justice Rehnquist, concurring in the judgment.

[The] partisan gerrymandering claims of major political parties raise a nonjusticiable political question that the judiciary should leave to the legislative [branch]. This enterprise is flawed from its inception. The Equal Protection Clause does not supply judicially manageable standards for resolving purely political gerrymandering claims, and no group right to an equal share of political power was ever intended by the Framers of the Fourteenth Amendment. [There] is good reason to think that political gerrymandering is a self-limiting enterprise. In order to gerrymander, the legislative majority must weaken some of its safe seats, thus exposing its own incumbents to greater risks of defeat. [An] over-ambitious gerrymander can lead to disaster for the legislative majority: because it has created more seats in which it hopes to win relatively narrow victories, the same swing in overall voting strength will tend to cost the legislative majority more and more seats as the gerrymander becomes more ambitious. [There] is no proof [that] political gerrymandering is an evil that cannot be checked or cured by the people or by the parties themselves. Absent such proof, I see no basis for concluding that there is a need, let alone a constitutional basis, for judicial intervention. . . .

NOTES

1. The Uncertain Future of *Bandemer*.   In Vieth v. Jubelirer, 541 U.S. 267 (2004), a plurality of four justices would have overturned *Bandemer* and declared the question of the validity of political gerrymanders to be a nonjusticiable political question. Following the 2000 census, Pennsylvania's legislature, dominated by Republicans, adopted a congressional redistricting plan, which was attacked as a violation of equal protection because the plan "ignored all traditional redistricting criteria . . . solely for the sake of partisan advantage." Justice Scalia, joined by Chief Justice Rehnquist and Justices O'Connor and Thomas, concluded that there are "no judicially discernible and manageable standards for adjudicating political gerrymandering claims."

Although "intentional discrimination against an identifiable political group" is easy enough to prove, the plurality thought that judicial assessment of proof of "an actual discriminatory effect on that group" was well-nigh impossible. Next, the plurality rejected a proposed test focusing on "predominant intent" and specific effect. The problem with the "predominant intent" prong of the test was the near impossibility of proving that "partisan advantage was the predominant motivation" for the district boundaries. The "effects prong" of the proposed test would have required proof of (1) systematic "packing"[19] and "cracking"[20] of "the rival party's voters," and (2) a totality of circumstances establishing that the gerrymander " 'thwart[s] the plaintiffs' ability to translate a majority of votes into a majority of seats.' " The plurality thought this prong was neither discernible nor manageable. First, because "[p]olitical affiliation" is not an immutable characteristic, [it is] impossible to assess the effects of partisan gerrymandering, to fashion a

---

19. "Packing" is the practice of drawing district boundaries to include supermajorities of a given party's voters.

20. "Cracking" is the practice of drawing district boundaries to split a party's voters among a number of districts, in order to leave that party's voters in the minority in all the districts to which they have been distributed.

standard for evaluating a violation, and finally to craft a remedy."[21] Second, the proposed effects standard was not "judicially discernible in the sense of being relevant to some constitutional violation" because it "rests upon the principle that [political] groups have a right to proportional representation, [and] the Constitution contains no such principle." Finally, the proposed standard was "not judicially manageable" because it is virtually impossible to "identify a majority party" with certainty,[22] and even more difficult to ensure that the "majority" party wins a majority of seats, if only because voters remain maddeningly independent of party affiliation when it comes time to cast ballots.

Justices Stevens and Kennedy concurred in the judgment. Justice Kennedy concluded that the claim presented in *Vieth* was nonjusticiable, but was unwilling to conclude that all such claims are nonjusticiable: "I would not foreclose all possibility of judicial relief if some limited and precise rationale were found to correct an established violation of the Constitution in some redistricting cases." Justice Stevens contended that political gerrymandering claims at the individual district level are justiciable. He likened political gerrymanders to racial gerrymanders, an analogy disputed by the plurality: "[S]etting out to segregate voters by race is unlawful[;] setting out to segregate them by political affiliation is lawful. . . . A purpose to discriminate on the basis of race receives the strictest scrutiny under the Equal Protection Clause, while a similar purpose to discriminate on the basis of politics does not."

Justice Souter, joined by Justice Ginsburg, dissented, concluding that the case was justiciable and proposing a new, complicated, multi-factor test to identify such an "extremity of unfairness" in gerrymandering that equal protection is violated, a goal that the plurality derided as "utterly unhelpful" because it does not illuminate "the precise constitutional deprivation [the] test is designed to identify and prevent." Justice Breyer also dissented, contending that statewide political gerrymanders are justiciable when "the *unjustified* use of political factors . . . entrench a minority in power." The plurality tartly dismissed this approach by noting that it requires the judiciary to "assess whether a group (somehow defined) has achieved a level of political power (somehow defined) commensurate with that to which they would be entitled absent *unjustified* political machinations (whatever that means)."

2. The Elusive Quest for a Standard. After the 2000 census, Texas gained two House seats, but because the legislature could not agree on a

---

21. The plurality cited, as a "delicious illustration" of its conclusion, a case in which a trial judge had concluded that North Carolina's system of electing judges "had resulted in Republican candidates experiencing a consistent and pervasive lack of success and exclusion from the electoral process as a whole and that these effects were likely to continue unabated into the future." Five days later, every Republican candidate for superior court judge in North Carolina was victorious.

22. In Pennsylvania, in 2000, Democratic candidates received more votes for President and auditor general and Republicans garnered more votes for United States senator, attorney general, and treasurer. Or consider Massachusetts, in which a succession of Republican governors have presided along with a solidly Democratic legislature and a monolithically Democratic congressional delegation.

redistricting plan, a federal court devised a plan that did not disturb the disproportionate hold of Democrats on its House delegation (17 D, 15 R), even though Republicans garnered 59 percent of the statewide vote. By 2003, however, Republicans controlled both houses of the Texas legislature as well as the governorship, and they used their political muscle to enact a new redistricting plan that, in 2004, resulted in 58 percent of the statewide vote favoring Republicans, and a Texas House delegation of 21 Republicans and 11 Democrats.

Various groups and voters allied with Democratic interests brought suit, contending that the 2003 plan was an unconstitutional political gerrymander. In League of United Latin American Citizens v. Perry, 548 U.S. 399 (2006), the Court rejected the political gerrymander claim. The Court did not revisit the justiciability issue debated in *Vieth*, but confined itself to examination of whether the "claims offer the Court a manageable, reliable measure of fairness for determining whether a partisan gerrymander violates the Constitution." A plurality consisting of Justice Kennedy, Chief Justice Roberts, and Justice Alito concluded that a mid-decade redistricting was valid even though there was evidence that the Texas legislature was motivated primarily but not exclusively by the desire to obtain partisan advantage. However, it was uncontested that some Democratic desires for district lines were honored.

> . . . The text and structure of the Constitution and our case law indicate there is nothing inherently suspect about a legislature's decision to replace mid-decade a court-ordered plan with one of its own. [Appellants] would leave untouched the 1991 Texas redistricting, which entrenched [the Democratic Party,] a party on the verge of minority status, while striking down the 2003 redistricting plan, which resulted in the majority Republican Party capturing a larger share of the seats. [While] there is no constitutional requirement of proportional representation, . . . a congressional plan that more closely reflects the distribution of state party power seems a less likely vehicle for partisan discrimination than one that entrenches an electoral minority. . . .

Justice Stevens, joined by Justice Breyer, dissented:

> Because a desire to minimize the strength of Texas Democrats was the sole motivation for the adoption of [the challenged plan, it] cannot withstand constitutional scrutiny. . . . [A]lthough the Constitution places no *per se* ban on midcycle redistricting, a legislature's decision to redistrict in the middle of the census cycle, when the legislature is under no legal obligation to do so, . . . raises a fair inference that partisan machinations played a major role in the map-drawing process.

Chief Justice Roberts, joined by Justice Alito, took no position on the question of whether a political gerrymander constitutes a justiciable controversy because that issue had not been argued to the Court. Justice Scalia and Justice Thomas concurred in the judgment with respect to the mid-decade redistricting but dissented as to the justiciability of the claim. They reiterated their view, expressed in *Vieth*, that political gerrymanders present nonjusticiable political questions.

Two justices (Scalia and Thomas) think that political gerrymanders are not justiciable, four justices (Roberts, Alito, Sotomayor, and Kagan) have not declared their views on this point, and the remaining three believe that such claims are justiciable but cannot articulate—much less agree on—what ascertainable standard governs the substance of such claims.

3. Race and Politics in Gerrymanders. Long before *Bandemer*, the Court had embraced the idea that the intentional use of district boundaries to dilute the voting strength of racial minorities was a presumptive violation of equal protection. See, e.g., White v. Regester, 412 U.S. 755 (1973). The controversial aspect of *Bandemer* was its willingness to treat ordinary political gerrymanders as justiciable and to accept the principle that heightened scrutiny applied. The issue of racial gerrymanders returned to the Court in the 1990s. Section 5 of the Voting Rights Act, as amended, requires that certain "covered jurisdictions" (essentially those that used a test for voter eligibility and in which less than 50 percent of eligible persons voted in the 1972 presidential election) obtain the approval of the Justice Department before making any changes to election laws that have either the purpose or effect of diluting minority voting strength.[23] Section 2 of the Voting Rights Act prohibits electoral devices that have the effect of diluting racial minority voting power. Invoking sections 2 and 5 of the federal Voting Rights Act, the U.S. Department of Justice pressured states to create "majority-minority" districts—districts in which a majority of the voters were members of a racial minority. The following case, first in a line of similar cases, established the framework for examining the validity of these districts under equal protection.

≡≡≡ **Shaw v. Reno**
≡≡≡ *509 U.S. 630 (1993)*

JUSTICE O'CONNOR delivered the opinion of the Court.

This case involves two of the most complex and sensitive issues this Court has faced in recent years: the meaning of the constitutional "right" to vote, and the propriety of race-based state legislation designed to benefit members of historically disadvantaged racial minority groups. As a result of the 1990 census, North Carolina became entitled to a twelfth seat in the United States House of Representatives. The General Assembly enacted a reapportionment plan that included one majority-black congressional district. After the Attorney General of the United States objected to the plan pursuant to §5 of the Voting Rights Act, [the] General Assembly passed new legislation creating

---

23. Section 5 depends upon a coverage formula set forth in section 4. After the cases discussed here, the Supreme Court found the section 4 coverage formula to be invalid. See Shelby County v. Holder, Chapter 11. Congress has not addressed the coverage formula, so section 5 is effectively unenforceable after *Shelby County*.

a second majority-black district. Appellants allege that the revised plan, which contains district boundary lines of dramatically irregular shape, constitutes an unconstitutional racial gerrymander. The question before us is whether appellants have stated a cognizable claim.

The voting age population of North Carolina is approximately 78% white, 20% black, and 1% Native American; the remaining 1% is predominantly Asian. The black population is relatively dispersed; blacks constitute a majority of the general population in only 5 of the State's 100 counties. [The] first of the two majority-black districts [is] somewhat hook shaped. Centered in the northeast portion of the State, it moves southward until it tapers to a narrow band; then, with finger-like extensions, it reaches far into the southern-most part of the State near the South Carolina border. District 1 has been compared to a "Rorschach ink-blot test" and a "bug splattered on a windshield." The second majority-black district, District 12, is even more unusually shaped. It is approximately 160 miles long and, for much of its length, no wider than the I-85 corridor. It winds in snake-like fashion through tobacco country, financial centers, and manufacturing areas "until it gobbles in enough enclaves of black neighborhoods." Northbound and southbound drivers on I-85 sometimes find themselves in separate districts in one county, only to "trade" districts when they enter the next county. Of the 10 counties through which District 12 passes, five are cut into three different districts; even towns are divided. At one point the district remains contiguous only because it intersects at a single point with two other districts before crossing over them. One state legislator has remarked that "if you drove down the interstate with both car doors open, you'd kill most of the people in the district."

[Appellants] concede that race-conscious redistricting is not always unconstitutional. [What] appellants object to is redistricting legislation that is so extremely irregular on its face that it rationally can be viewed only as an effort to segregate the races for purposes of voting, without regard for traditional districting principles and without sufficiently compelling justification. [We] conclude that appellants have stated a claim upon which relief can be granted under the Equal Protection Clause.

The [central] purpose [of equal protection] is to prevent the States from purposefully discriminating between individuals on the basis of race. [Appellants] contend that redistricting legislation that is so bizarre on its face that it is "unexplainable on grounds other than race," demands the same close scrutiny that we give other state laws that classify citizens by race. Our voting rights precedents support that conclusion. [Redistricting] differs from other kinds of state decisionmaking in that the legislature always is aware of race when it draws district lines, just as it is aware of age, economic status, religious and political persuasion, and a variety of other demographic factors. That sort of race consciousness does not lead inevitably to impermissible race discrimination. [When] members of a racial group live together in one community, a reapportionment plan that concentrates members of the group in one district and excludes them from others may reflect wholly legitimate purposes. The district lines may be drawn, for example, to provide for compact districts of contiguous territory, or to maintain the integrity of political subdivisions.

[But a] reapportionment plan may be so highly irregular that, on its face, it rationally cannot be understood as anything other than an effort to "segregate [voters]" on the basis of race. *Gomillion*, in which a tortured municipal boundary line was drawn to exclude black voters, was such a case. So, too, would be a case in which a State concentrated a dispersed minority population in a single district by disregarding traditional districting principles such as compactness, contiguity, and respect for political subdivisions. We emphasize that these criteria are important not because they are constitutionally required—they are not—but because they are objective factors that may serve to defeat a claim that a district has been gerrymandered on racial lines.

Put differently, we believe that reapportionment is one area in which appearances do matter. A reapportionment plan that includes in one district individuals who belong to the same race, but who are otherwise widely separated by geographical and political boundaries, and who may have little in common with one another but the color of their skin, bears an uncomfortable resemblance to political apartheid. It reinforces the perception that members of the same racial group—regardless of their age, education, economic status, or the community in which the live—think alike, share the same political interests, and will prefer the same candidates at the polls. We have rejected such perceptions elsewhere as impermissible racial stereotypes. [By] perpetuating such notions, a racial gerrymander may exacerbate the very patterns of racial bloc voting that majority-minority districting is sometimes said to counteract. The message that such districting sends to elected representatives is equally pernicious. When a district [is] created solely to effectuate the perceived common interests of one racial group, elected officials are more likely to believe that their primary obligation is to represent only the members of that group, rather than their constituency as a whole. This is altogether antithetical to our system of representative democracy. For these reasons, we conclude that a plaintiff challenging a reapportionment statute under [equal protection] may state a claim by alleging that the legislation, though race-neutral on its face, rationally cannot be understood as anything other than an effort to separate voters into different districts on the basis of race, and that the separation lacks sufficient [justification]. . . .

Racial classifications of any sort pose the risk of lasting harm to our society. They reinforce the belief, held by too many for too much of our history, that individuals should be judged by the color of their skin. Racial classifications with respect to voting carry particular dangers. Racial gerrymandering, even for remedial purposes, may balkanize us into competing racial factions; it threatens to carry us further from the goal of a political system in which race no longer matters.

[Appellants] have stated a claim under [equal protection] by alleging that the North Carolina General Assembly adopted a reapportionment scheme so irrational on its face that it can be understood only as an effort to segregate voters into separate voting districts because of their race, and that the separation lacks sufficient justification.

JUSTICE WHITE, joined by JUSTICES BLACKMUN and STEVENS, dissenting.

[A] complaint stating that a plan has carved out districts on the basis of race can [state] a claim under [equal protection, but] there must be an allegation of discriminatory purpose and [effect]. . . . [W]e have put the plaintiff challenging the district lines to the burden of demonstrating that the plan was meant to, and did in fact, exclude an identifiable racial group from participation in the political process. Not so, apparently, when the districting "segregates" by drawing odd-shaped lines. In that case, we are told, . . . it is the State that must rebut the allegation that race was taken into [account]. A plan that "segregates" being functionally indistinguishable from any of the other varieties of gerrymandering, we should be consistent in what we require from a claimant: proof of discriminatory purpose and effect. . . .

JUSTICE SOUTER, dissenting.

[A] distinction between districting and most other governmental decisions in which race has figured is that those other decisions using racial criteria characteristically occur in circumstances in which the use of race to the advantage of one person is necessarily at the obvious expense of a member of a different race. [*Wygant.*] [But] the mere placement of an individual in one district instead of another denies no one a right or benefit provided to others. [In] whatever district, the individual voter has a right to vote in each election, and the election will result in the voter's representation.

[If] a cognizable harm like dilution or the abridgment of the right to participate in the electoral process is shown, the districting plan violates [equal protection]. If not, it does not. [In] the absence of an allegation of such cognizable harm, there is no need for further scrutiny because a gerrymandering claim cannot be proven without the element of harm.

NOTES

1. Subsequent Developments.   In Miller v. Johnson, 515 U.S. 900 (1995), the Court noted that the

> plaintiff's burden is to show, either through circumstantial evidence of a district's shape and demographics or more direct evidence going to legislative purpose, that race was the predominant factor motivating the legislature's decision to place a significant number of voters within or without a particular district. To make this showing, a plaintiff must prove that the legislature subordinated traditional race-neutral districting principles, including but not limited to compactness, contiguity, respect for political subdivisions or communities defined by actual shared interests, to racial considerations.

In Shaw v. Hunt (*Shaw II*), 517 U.S. 899 (1996), the Court ruled that because neither the district shape nor race-based districting was required to conform to the Voting Rights Act, the state lacked a compelling interest for its use of race. In Bush v. Vera, 517 U.S. 952 (1996), the Court ruled that Texas's race-based districting failed strict scrutiny because it was not necessary to cure past discrimination in voting.

2. The Nature of the Harm. Was anybody denied the *right* to vote in these cases? Was anybody's voted *diluted* in these cases? Was the harm the reinforcement of racial consciousness and stereotypical thinking about race? On that point, should it matter that racial minorities do (or do not) tend to vote as a bloc? Should the Court consider as relevant the question of whether it is "better" for racial minorities to have some influence over many representatives (by virtue of the presence of racial minorities, as a minority, in many districts) or a controlling influence over a few representatives (by virtue of concentration of bloc-voting racial minorities into a few majority-minority districts)?

3. A Change in Direction? Following Shaw v. Hunt, North Carolina again redrew the boundaries of its Twelfth Congressional District and a federal district court concluded, in a summary judgment, that the new boundaries had again been created with racial considerations dominating all others. In Hunt v. Cromartie (*Hunt I*), 526 U.S. 541 (1999), the Court reversed, finding that there was a genuine issue of material fact whether the boundaries were drawn with an impermissible race-based objective or to accomplish the constitutionally acceptable objective of a political gerrymander. On remand, the district court ruled that the boundaries were drawn with racial considerations foremost, relying on four findings: the district's shape, its splitting of towns and counties, its heavily African American voting population, and the legislative intention to draw the boundaries by collecting precincts with a high racial, rather than political, identification. In Hunt v. Cromartie (*Hunt II*), 532 U.S. 234 (2001), the Court reversed, ruling that these findings were clearly erroneous.

> [The] evidence taken together [does] not show that racial considerations predominated in the drawing of District 12's boundaries . . . because race in this case correlates closely with political behavior. . . . [Where] racial identification correlates highly with political affiliation, the party attacking the legislatively drawn boundaries must show at the least that the legislature could have achieved its legitimate political objectives in alternative ways that are comparably consistent with traditional districting principles. That party must also show that those districting alternatives would have brought about significantly greater racial balance. Appellees failed to make any such showing here.

Justice Thomas, joined by Chief Justice Rehnquist and Justices Scalia and Kennedy, dissented. They argued that the standard of review employed by the Court was in fact stricter than "clear error" review and that such strict review was warranted neither by precedent nor by the circumstances of the case. Applying a "clear error" standard, the dissenters said: "[R]acial gerrymandering offends the Constitution whether the motivation is malicious or benign. It is not a defense that the legislature merely may have drawn the district based on the stereotype that blacks are reliable Democratic voters."

Does *Hunt II* suggest that although the underlying constitutional standards have not changed, their application in terms of evidentiary burdens of proof may prove to be more lenient toward the creation of majority-minority districts? On the other hand, if the dissenters are correct to say that the Constitution is offended when legislatures indulge in the assumption that race is a proxy for political preferences, must legislatures as a practical matter do more than lump black voters together and claim that the reason was to create a Democratic district?

5.   Access to Courts

There is no independent constitutionally fundamental right of general access to every aspect of the judicial process. Nevertheless, the Court has subjected some state laws inhibiting access to the courts to heightened scrutiny. The common thread in these decisions is the presence of a state-imposed economic barrier to court access under circumstances where personal liberty or some other constitutionally fundamental liberty interest is at stake. These cases present both equal protection and due process issues. Any given state-imposed barrier to access may be thought of as applying with differential impact upon some people (raising an equal protection issue) or may be conceived as a denial of a procedural due process right of the "opportunity to be heard." The Court continues to debate which provision is the more relevant, though most cases seem to be primarily grounded in equal protection. After reading these cases, reconsider whether they properly raise due process or equal protection issues.

a.   *Criminal Litigation*

Griffin v. Illinois, 351 U.S. 12 (1956). The state charged all convicted criminals for the cost of a trial transcript, which was required for an appeal. The Court thought that charging indigents for necessary trial transcripts was a denial of equal protection and due process. Justice Black wrote for a plurality of four:

> [Due] process and equal protection both call for procedures in criminal trials which allow no invidious discriminations. . . . Plainly the ability to pay [for a transcript] bears no rational relationship [to] guilt or innocence. [It] is true that a State is not [constitutionally required to] provide appellate courts or a right to appellate review at all. . . . [There] can be no equal justice where the kind of trial a man gets depends on the amount of money he has.

Justice Harlan dissented, asserting that equal protection was irrelevant and due process not violated:

> All that Illinois has done is fail to alleviate the consequences of differences in economic circumstances that exist wholly apart from any state action. The Court['s] holding produces the anomalous result that a constitutional [requirement] to treat all persons equally means [that] Illinois must give to some what it requires others to pay for. [The] real issue [is] not whether Illinois has discriminated but whether it has a duty to discriminate. [T]he basis [for the Court's ruling] is simply an unarticulated conclusion that it violates "fundamental fairness" for a State which provides for appellate review [effectively to deny it to indigents]. That of course is the traditional language of due process.

Because a State could validly deny *any* appeal Harlan thought that it could condition appeal for reasons neither "arbitrary [n]or capricious."

Douglas v. California, 372 U.S. 353 (1963). [T]he Court extended *Griffin* by ruling that states that provide for appeal of criminal convictions must provide appellate counsel to convicted indigents only with respect to the "*first appeal*, granted as a matter of [statutory right], from a criminal conviction." The Court voided California's practice of appointing appellate counsel to indigent convicts only after an appeals court had concluded after a review of the record that a lawyer "would be helpful to the defendant or the court." Without much explanation the Court held that this procedure violated both equal protection and due process. Justice Harlan, joined by Justice Stewart, dissented, noting that equal protection does not

> prevent the State from adopting a law of general applicability that may affect the poor more harshly than the [rich]. Every financial exaction which the State imposes on a uniform basis is more easily satisfied by the well-to-do than by the indigent. . . . [Equal protection] does not impose on the States "an affirmative duty to lift the handicaps flowing from economic circumstances."

As in *Griffin*, Harlan argued that the real issue was whether California's procedure complied with due process. California denied "to no one the right to appeal," and ensured that "the indigent appellant receives [expert] and conscientious legal appraisal of the merits of his case [and] whether or not he is assigned counsel, is guaranteed full consideration of his appeal."

Ross v. Moffitt, 417 U.S. 600 (1974). The Court held that states need not provide appellate counsel to indigents for *discretionary* appeals. Due process, which does not require any appeal at all, was not offended by a state's refusal "to provide counsel to indigent defendants at every stage of the way." Equal protection would be violated if "indigents are singled out by the State and denied meaningful access to the appellate system because of their poverty." But that was not the case where the state had already provided counsel for one appeal as of right. "The duty of the State [is] not to duplicate the legal arsenal that may be privately retained by a criminal defendant, [but] only to assure the indigent defendant an adequate opportunity to present his claims fairly in the context of the State's appellate process."

b.   Civil Litigation

The Court has been less willing to find that state-imposed economic obstacles to the civil justice system violate equal protection. In those cases in which the Court has found equal protection to be violated, the interest at stake was a constitutionally independent fundamental liberty interest.

Boddie v. Connecticut, 401 U.S. 371 (1971). The Court struck down, as applied to indigents, Connecticut's requirement that persons seeking a divorce pay filing fees of about $60 in order to commence the civil process of divorce. The Court relied entirely on due process. Justice Harlan wrote for the Court:

> [G]iven the basic position of [marriage] in this society's hierarchy of values and the concomitant state monopolization of the means for legally dissolving this relationship, due process [prohibits] a State from denying, solely because of inability to pay, access to its courts to individuals who seek judicial dissolution of their marriages.

Little v. Streater, 452 U.S. 1 (1981). The Court held, on due process grounds, that an indigent defendant in a paternity action was entitled to free blood-grouping tests. The Court stressed the unique "exculpatory" power of such tests, "the State's prominent role in [the] litigation," and the "quasi-criminal" nature of the paternity proceeding.

United States v. Kras, 409 U.S. 434 (1973). The Court upheld the federal Bankruptcy Act's requirement of a $50 filing fee to institute bankruptcy proceedings. Unlike *Boddie,* where the fundamental interest of marriage was implicated by the access barrier of a filing fee, the Bankruptcy Act provision infringed no independently protected constitutional fundamental right.

Ortwein v. Schwab, 410 U.S. 656 (1973). The Court upheld a $25 filing fee to obtain appellate review of an administrative decision to reduce welfare benefits. Because the right to receive any welfare benefits, much less any particular level of benefits, is not an independently protected constitutional fundamental right, the Court applied minimal scrutiny.

≡≡≡
M.L.B. v. S.L.J.
519 U.S. 102 (1996)

JUSTICE GINSBURG delivered the opinion of the Court.

By order of a Mississippi Chancery Court, petitioner M.L.B.'s parental rights to her two minor children were forever terminated. M.L.B. sought to appeal from the termination decree, but Mississippi required that she pay in advance record preparation fees estimated at $2,352.36. Because M.L.B.

lacked funds to pay the fees, her appeal was dismissed. [May] a State, consistent with [due process] and [equal protection], condition appeals from trial court decrees terminating parental rights on the affected parent's ability to pay record preparation fees? We hold that [it] may not. . . . [We have] recognized a narrow category of civil cases in which the State must provide access to its judicial processes without regard to a party's ability to pay court fees. [*Boddie, Little.*] [In] United States v. Kras the Court clarified that a constitutional requirement to waive court fees in civil cases is the exception, not the general rule. . . . Absent a fundamental interest or classification attracting heightened scrutiny, we said [in *Ortwein*], the applicable equal protection standard "is that of rational justification." [While] this Court has not extended *Griffin* to the broad array of civil cases, [it] has consistently set apart from the mine run of cases those involving state controls or intrusions on family relationships. In that domain, to guard against undue official intrusion, the Court has examined closely and contextually the importance of the governmental interest advanced in defense of the intrusion. Choices about marriage, family life, and the upbringing of children are among associational rights this Court has ranked as "of basic importance in our society," rights sheltered by the Fourteenth Amendment against the State's unwarranted usurpation, disregard, or disrespect.

[We think] that the accusatory state action [M.L.B.] is trying to fend off is barely distinguishable from criminal condemnation in view of the magnitude and permanence of the loss she faces. [We] observe first that the Court's decisions concerning access to judicial processes [reflect] both equal protection and due process concerns. [The] equal protection concern relates to the legitimacy of fencing out would-be appellants based solely on their inability to pay court costs. The due process concern homes in on the essential fairness of the state-ordered proceedings anterior to adverse state action. . . . "Most decisions in this area," we have recognized, "rest on an equal protection framework" [because] due process does not independently require that the State provide a right to appeal. [In] line with those decisions, we inspect the character and intensity of the individual interest at stake [and] the State's justification for its [economic] exaction.

[The] stakes for [M.L.B.]—forced dissolution of her parental rights—are large, "'more substantial than mere loss of money.'" [Parental] status termination is "irretrievabl[y] destructi[ve]" of the most fundamental family relationship. And the risk of error [is] considerable. [The] countervailing government interest [is] financial. Mississippi urges, as the justification for its appeal cost prepayment requirement, the State's legitimate interest in offsetting the costs of its court system. But in the tightly circumscribed category of parental status termination cases, appeals are few, and not likely to impose an undue burden on the State. [We] do not question the general rule [that] fee requirements ordinarily are examined only for rationality. The State's need for revenue to offset costs, in the mine run of cases, satisfies the rationality requirement. States are not forced by the Constitution to adjust all tolls to account for "disparity in material circumstances." But our cases solidly establish [that] access to judicial processes in cases criminal or "quasi criminal in nature" [may not] turn on ability to pay. [We] place decrees forever terminating parental rights in the category of cases in which the State may not "bolt the door to equal justice." . . .

[M.L.B.] is endeavoring to defend against the State's destruction of her family bonds, and to resist the brand associated with a parental unfitness adjudication. Like a defendant resisting criminal conviction, she seeks to be spared from the State's devastatingly adverse action. [Parental termination] decrees "wor[k] a unique kind of deprivation," [involving] the awesome authority of the State "to destroy permanently all legal recognition of the parental relationship." [The] label "civil" should not entice us to leave undisturbed the Mississippi courts' disposition of this case, [and so] we hold that Mississippi may not withhold from M.L.B. "a 'record of sufficient completeness' to permit proper [appellate] consideration of [her] claims."

JUSTICE KENNEDY, concurring in the judgment.
In my view . . . , due process is quite a sufficient basis for our holding.

JUSTICE THOMAS, joined by JUSTICE SCALIA and (in part) CHIEF JUSTICE REHNQUIST, dissenting.
. . . The cases on which the majority relies, primarily cases requiring appellate assistance for indigent criminal defendants, were questionable when decided, and have, in my view, been undermined since. Even accepting those cases, however, I am of the view that the majority takes them too far. I therefore dissent.

Petitioner requests relief under both the Due Process and Equal Protection Clauses, though she does not specify how either clause affords it. The majority, [carrying] forward the ambiguity in the cases on which it relies, [does] not specify the source of the relief it grants. [If] neither Clause affords petitioner the right to a free, civil-appeal transcript, I assume that no amalgam of the two does.

[I] do not think that the Due Process Clause requires the result the majority reaches. [Petitioner] received not merely a hearing, but in fact enjoyed procedural protections above and beyond what our parental termination cases have required. She received both notice and a hearing before a neutral, legally trained decisionmaker [and] was represented by counsel—even though due process does not in every case require the appointment of counsel. Through her attorney, petitioner was able to confront the evidence and witnesses against her. And [the] Chancery Court was required to find that petitioner's parental unfitness was proved by clear and convincing evidence. [There] seems, then, no place in the Due Process Clause [for] the constitutional "right" crafted by the majority today.

[I] do not think that the equal protection theory underlying the *Griffin* line of cases remains viable. [The Equal Protection] Clause is not a panacea for perceived social or economic inequity; it seeks to "guarante[e] equal laws, not equal results." [Petitioner] desires "state aid to subsidize [her] privately initiated" appeal—an appeal that neither petitioner nor the majority claims Mississippi is required to provide—to overturn the determination that resulted from that hearing. I see no principled difference between a facially neutral rule that serves in some cases to prevent persons from availing themselves of state employment, or a state-funded education, or a state-funded abortion—each of which the State may, but is not required to, provide—and a facially neutral rule that prevents a person from taking an appeal that is available only because the State chooses to provide it. [Mississippi's] requirement of prepaid transcripts in civil appeals . . . is facially neutral; it creates no classification. . . . Any adverse impact that the transcript requirement has on any person seeking to appeal arises not out of the State's action, but out of factors entirely unrelated to it. . . .

NOTE

The Effect of *M.L.B.* Is *M.L.B.* a due process or an equal protection case? Which should it be? If it is an equal protection case, how far does *M.L.B.* expand the scope of equal protection in securing access to the judicial process? Is it limited to the principle that, whenever a state proposes to take away someone's constitutionally fundamental rights, the state may not erect economic barriers that prevent a full opportunity to vindicate those rights?

6. Penalties on the Right of Interstate Migration

This category of fundamental rights is unique. Unlike voting and access to courts, the right to interstate migration is a constitutional right independent of equal protection, albeit implicitly guaranteed by the Constitution. But in developing this strand of equal protection's fundamental rights doctrine, the Court has strictly scrutinized only those classifications that *penalize* the exercise of the right of migration. To identify such penal classifications, the Court has relied upon factors that are textually unconnected to the Constitution.

a. Origins

Shapiro v. Thompson, 394 U.S. 618 (1969). The Court struck down state and federal laws denying welfare assistance to residents who had not resided within their jurisdictions for at least one year immediately before seeking welfare assistance. Justice Brennan wrote for the Court:

[The] effect of the waiting-period requirement [is] to create two classes of needy resident families indistinguishable from each other except that one is composed of residents who have resided a year or more, and the second of residents who have resided less than a year, in the jurisdiction. [The] first class is granted and the second class is denied welfare aid upon which may depend the very means to subsist—food, shelter, and other necessities of life. [The] classification [constitutes] an invidious discrimination denying [equal protection]. The interests which appellants assert are promoted by the classification either may not constitutionally be promoted by government or are not compelling governmental interests.

[A]ppellants justify the waiting-period requirement as a protective device to preserve the fiscal integrity of state public assistance programs, [because] people who require welfare assistance during their first year of residence [are] likely to become continuing burdens on state welfare programs. [We] do not doubt that the one-year waiting-period device is well suited to discourage the influx of poor families in need of assistance. [But] the purpose of inhibiting migration by needy persons into the State is constitutionally impermissible. [All] citizens [are] free to travel throughout the length and breadth of our land uninhibited by statutes, rules, or regulations which unreasonably burden or restrict this movement. [We] have no occasion to ascribe the source of this right to travel interstate to a particular constitutional provision. It suffices that "[the] constitutional right to travel from one State to another [is] fundamental to the concept of our Federal Union. [The] right finds no explicit mention in the Constitution, [probably because it is] so elementary [that it] was conceived from the beginning to be a necessary concomitant of [Union]."

[Appellants] argue that . . . the challenged classification may be justified as a permissible state attempt to discourage those indigents who would enter the State solely to obtain larger benefits. [A] State may no more try to fence out those indigents who seek higher welfare benefits than it may try to fence out indigents generally. . . . [In] moving from State to State . . . appellees were exercising a constitutional right, and any classification which serves to penalize the exercise of that right, unless shown to be necessary to promote a compelling governmental interest, is unconstitutional.

b. Two Versions of a Single Right

Shapiro seems to rely on two versions of fundamental rights: (1) the idea that classifications that "penalize" exercise of the independent fundamental right of migration are subject to strict scrutiny, and (2) the idea that classifications that deny people important rights (or at least the basic necessities of life) are subject to strict scrutiny. The first idea endures today; the second has apparently been repudiated by *Rodriguez*. Would this second strand impose upon governments some unspecified obligation to transfer wealth from richer to poorer people? Compare Michelman, Foreword: On Protecting the Poor Through the Fourteenth Amendment, 83 Harv. L. Rev. 7 (1969), with Bork, The Impossibility of Finding Welfare Rights in the Constitution, 1979 Wash. U. L.Q. 695.

But what constitutes a "penalty"? Might a "penalty" be defined as occurring when "important" interests are adversely affected? The cases after *Shapiro* diverged in their appraisal of when durational residency requirements penalize interstate migration.

Memorial Hospital v. Maricopa County, 415 U.S. 250 (1974). Arizona law denied free nonemergency health care to indigents who had resided in the state for less than a year. Justice Marshall wrote for the Court:

> Whatever the ultimate parameters of the *Shapiro* penalty analysis, it is at least clear that medical care is as much "a basic necessity of life" to an indigent as welfare assistance. And, governmental privileges or benefits necessary to basic sustenance have often been viewed as being of greater constitutional significance than less essential forms of governmental entitlements. [Thus], Arizona's durational residence requirement for free medical care penalizes indigents for exercising their right to migrate to and settle in that State. Accordingly, the classification created by the residence requirement, "unless shown to be necessary to promote a compelling governmental interest, is unconstitutional."

Sosna v. Iowa, 419 U.S. 393 (1975). The Court upheld Iowa's one-year residency requirement for instituting divorce proceedings against a nonresident. Justice Rehnquist wrote for the Court:

> [What *Shapiro, Dunn,* and *Maricopa County*] had in common was that the durational residency requirements they struck down were justified on the basis of budgetary or record-keeping considerations [that] were held insufficient to outweigh the constitutional claims of the individuals. But Iowa's divorce residency requirement is of a different stripe. Appellant was not irretrievably foreclosed from obtaining some part of what she sought, as was the case with the welfare recipients in *Shapiro,* the voters in *Dunn,* or the indigent patient in *Maricopa County.* [Iowa's] requirement delayed her access to the courts, but, by fulfilling it, she could ultimately have obtained the same opportunity for adjudication which she asserts ought to have been hers at an earlier point in time. Iowa's residency requirement may reasonably be justified on grounds other than purely budgetary considerations or administrative convenience. A decree of divorce [typically provides for child] custody and support, [thus Iowa] may insist that one seeking to initiate such a proceeding have the modicum of attachment to the State required here. Such a requirement additionally furthers the State's parallel interests both in avoiding officious intermeddling in matters in which another State has a paramount interest, and in minimizing the susceptibility of its own divorce decrees to collateral attack. [Iowa] may quite reasonably decide that it does not wish to become a divorce mill.

Justice Marshall, joined by Justice Brennan, dissented. "The Court omits altogether what should be the first inquiry: whether the right to obtain a divorce is of sufficient importance that its denial to recent immigrants constitutes a penalty on interstate travel. In my view, it clearly meets that standard."

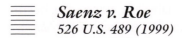

Saenz v. Roe
526 U.S. 489 (1999)

[In 1992, California enacted Cal. Welfare & Inst. Code §11450.03 to limit new residents, during their first year of residency in California, to the amount of welfare benefits for dependent children they would have received in their prior state of residency. In 1996, Congress enacted a welfare reform measure that expressly authorized states to do what California had sought to do by its 1992 amendment. This class action challenged the validity of California's welfare limits on new residents and the federal statutory approval of that scheme. A federal district court enjoined the program, and the Court of Appeals upheld the injunction. The Supreme Court affirmed.]

JUSTICE STEVENS delivered the opinion of the Court.

The word "travel" is not found in the text of the Constitution. Yet the "constitutional right to travel from one State to another" is firmly embedded in our jurisprudence. . . .

In this case California argues that §11450.03 was not enacted for the impermissible purpose of inhibiting migration by needy persons and that, unlike the legislation reviewed in *Shapiro*, it does not penalize the right to travel because new arrivals are not ineligible for benefits during their first year of residence. California submits that, instead of being subjected to the strictest scrutiny, the statute should be upheld if it is supported by a rational basis and that the State's legitimate interest in saving over $10 million a year satisfies that test.

The "right to travel" [embraces] at least three different components. It protects the right of a citizen of one State to enter and to leave another State, the right to be treated as a welcome visitor rather than an unfriendly alien when temporarily present in the second State, and, for those travelers who elect to become permanent residents, the right to be treated like other citizens of that State.

It was the right to go from one place to another, including the right to cross state borders while en route, that was vindicated in Edwards v. California, 314 U.S. 160 (1941), which invalidated a state law that impeded the free interstate passage of the indigent. [Given] that §11450.03 imposed no obstacle to respondents' entry into California, we think [the] statute does not directly impair the exercise of the right to free interstate movement. [Therefore], we need not identify the source of that particular right in the text of the Constitution, [which] may simply have been "conceived from the beginning to be a necessary concomitant of the stronger Union the Constitution created."

The second component of the right to travel is, however, expressly protected by the text of the Constitution, [the privileges and immunities clause of] Article IV, §2. [The] protections [of Article IV, §2] are not "absolute," but the [permissible] justifications for discrimination between residents and nonresidents are simply inapplicable to a nonresident's exercise of the right to move into another State and become a resident of that State.

What is at issue in this case [is] this third aspect of the right to travel—the right of the newly arrived citizen to the same privileges and immunities enjoyed by other citizens of the same State. That right is protected not only by the new arrival's status as a state citizen, but also by her status as a citizen of the United States. That additional source of protection is plainly identified in the

. . . Fourteenth Amendment: "All persons born or naturalized in the United States, and subject to the jurisdiction thereof, are citizens of the United States and of the State wherein they reside. No State shall make or enforce any law which shall abridge the privileges or immunities of citizens of the United States. . . ." Despite fundamentally differing views concerning the coverage of the Privileges or Immunities Clause of the Fourteenth Amendment, most notably expressed in the majority and dissenting opinions in the *Slaughter-House Cases*, it has always been common ground that this Clause protects the third component of the right to travel. [Neither] mere rationality nor some intermediate standard of review should be used to judge the constitutionality of a state rule that discriminates against some of its citizens because they have been domiciled in the State for less than a year.

[Because] this case involves discrimination against citizens who have completed their interstate travel, the State's argument that its welfare scheme affects the right to travel only "incidentally" is beside the point. Were we concerned solely with actual deterrence to migration, we might be persuaded that a partial withholding of benefits constitutes a lesser incursion on the right to travel than an outright denial of all benefits. But since the right to travel embraces the citizen's right to be treated equally in her new State of residence, the discriminatory classification is itself a penalty.

It is undisputed that respondents [are] citizens of California. [We] thus have no occasion to consider what weight might be given to a citizen's length of residence if the bona fides of her claim to state citizenship were questioned. Moreover, because whatever benefits they receive will be consumed while they remain in California, there is no danger that recognition of their claim will encourage citizens of other States to establish residency for just long enough to acquire some readily portable benefit, such as a divorce or a college education, that will be enjoyed after they return to their original domicile.

The classifications challenged in this case [are] defined entirely by (a) the period of residency in California and (b) the location of the prior residences of the disfavored class members. These classifications may not be justified by a purpose to deter welfare applicants from migrating to California. [Such] a purpose would be unequivocally impermissible. [California] has instead advanced an entirely fiscal justification. [The] enforcement of §11450.03 will save the State approximately $10.9 million a year. The question is not whether such saving is a legitimate purpose but whether the State may accomplish that end by the discriminatory means it has chosen. . . . [O]ur negative answer to the question does not rest on the weakness of the State's purported fiscal justification. It rests on the fact that the Citizenship Clause of the Fourteenth Amendment expressly equates citizenship with residence: "That Clause does not provide for, and does not allow for, degrees of citizenship based on length of residence." *Zobel.* It is equally clear that the Clause does not tolerate [classification] of similarly situated citizens based on the location of their prior residence. Thus §11450.03 is doubly vulnerable: Neither the duration of respondents' California residence, nor the identity of their prior States of residence, has any relevance to their need for benefits. [The] State's legitimate interest in saving money provides no justification for its decision to discriminate among equally eligible citizens.

The question that remains is whether congressional approval of durational residency requirements in the 1996 amendment to the Social Security Act somehow resuscitates the constitutionality of §11450.03. That question is readily answered, for we have consistently held that Congress may not authorize the States to violate the Fourteenth Amendment. . . . [Congress] has no affirmative power to authorize the States to violate the Fourteenth Amendment and is implicitly prohibited from passing legislation that purports to validate any such violation.

[Affirmed.]

Chief Justice Rehnquist, joined by Justice Thomas, dissenting.

The Court today breathes new life into the previously dormant Privileges or Immunities Clause of the Fourteenth Amendment — a Clause relied upon by this Court in only one other decision, [which was] overruled five years later. It uses this Clause to strike down what I believe is a reasonable measure falling under the head of a "good-faith residency requirement." Because I do not think any provision of the Constitution — and surely not a provision relied upon for only the second time since its enactment 130 years ago — requires this result, I dissent. . . .

I cannot see how the right to become a citizen of another State is a necessary "component" of the right to travel, or why the Court tries to marry these separate and distinct rights. A person is no longer "traveling" in any sense of the word when he finishes his journey to a State which he plans to make his home. Indeed, under the Court's logic, the protections of the Privileges or Immunities Clause recognized in this case come into play only when an individual stops traveling with the intent to remain and become a citizen of a new State. The right to travel and the right to become a citizen are distinct, their relationship is not reciprocal, and one is not a "component" of the other. [At] most, restrictions on an individual's right to become a citizen indirectly affect his calculus in deciding whether to exercise his right to travel in the first place, but such an attenuated and uncertain relationship is no ground for folding one right into the other.

No doubt the Court has, in the past 30 years, essentially conflated the right to travel with the right to equal state citizenship in striking down durational residence requirements similar to the one challenged here. [*Shapiro, Dunn, Maricopa County.*] These cases . . . held that restricting the provision of welfare benefits, votes, or certain medical benefits to new citizens for a limited time impermissibly "penalized" them under the Equal Protection Clause of the Fourteenth Amendment for having exercised their right to travel. . . . In other cases, the Court recognized that laws dividing new and old residents had little to do with the right to travel and merely triggered an inquiry into whether the resulting classification rationally furthered a legitimate government purpose. [*Zobel*, Hooper v. Bernalillo County Assessor.] While *Zobel* and *Hooper* reached the wrong result in my view, they at least put the Court on the proper track in identifying exactly what interests it was protecting[—] namely, the right of individuals not to be subject to unjustifiable classifications as opposed to infringements on the right to travel.

The Court today tries to clear much of the underbrush created by these prior right-to-travel cases, abandoning its effort to define what residence requirements deprive individuals of "important rights and benefits" or "penalize" the right to travel. Under its new analytical framework, a State, outside certain ill-defined circumstances, cannot classify its citizens by the length of their residence in the State without offending the Privileges or Immunities Clause of the Fourteenth Amendment. The Court thus departs from *Shapiro* and its progeny, and, while paying lip service to the right to travel, the Court does little to explain how the right to travel is involved at all. Instead, as the Court's analysis clearly demonstrates, this case is only about respondents' right to immediately enjoy all the privileges of being a California citizen in relation to that State's ability to test the good-faith assertion of this right.

[The] Court ignores a State's need to assure that only persons who establish a bona fide residence receive the benefits provided to current residents of the State. [States] retain the ability to use bona fide residence requirements to ferret out those who intend to take the privileges and run. As this Court explained in Martinez v. Bynum, 461 U.S. 321 (1983): "A bona fide residence requirement simply requires that the person does establish residence before demanding the services that are restricted to residents." The *Martinez* Court explained that "residence" requires "both physical presence and an intention to remain," and approved a Texas law that restricted eligibility for tuition-free education to families who met this minimum definition of residence.

While the physical presence element of a bona fide residence is easy to police, the subjective intent element is not. It is simply unworkable and futile to require States to inquire into each new resident's subjective intent to remain. Hence, States employ objective criteria such as durational residence requirements to test a new resident's resolve to remain before these new citizens can enjoy certain in-state benefits. Recognizing the practical appeal of such criteria, this Court has repeatedly sanctioned the State's use of durational residence requirements before new residents receive in-state tuition rates at state universities. Starns v. Malkerson, 401 U.S. 985 (1971), *summarily aff'g* 326 F. Supp. 234 (Minn. 1970) (upholding one-year residence requirement for in-state tuition); Sturgis v. Washington, 414 U.S. 1057, *summarily aff'g* 368 F. Supp. 38 (W.D. Wash. 1973) (same). [The] Court has done the same in upholding a 1-year residence requirement for eligibility to obtain a divorce in state courts[, *Sosna*,] and in upholding political party registration restrictions that amounted to a durational residency requirement for voting in primary elections, see Rosario v. Rockefeller, 410 U.S. 752 (1973).

If States can require individuals to reside in-state for a year before exercising the right to educational benefits, the right to terminate a marriage, or the right to vote in primary elections that all other state citizens enjoy, then States may surely do the same for welfare benefits. Indeed, there is no material difference between a 1-year residence requirement applied to the level of welfare benefits given out by a State, and the same requirement applied to the level of tuition subsidies at a state university. The welfare payment here and in-state tuition rates are cash subsidies provided to a limited class of people. . . . Durational residence requirements were upheld when used to regulate the provision of higher education subsidies, and the same deference should be given in the case of welfare payments. . . .

I therefore believe that the durational residence requirement challenged here is a permissible exercise of the State's power to "assure that services provided for its residents are enjoyed only by residents." The 1-year period established in §11450.03 is the same period this Court approved in *Starns* and *Sosna*. The requirement does not deprive welfare recipients of all benefits; indeed, the limitation has no effect whatsoever on a recipient's ability to enjoy the full 5-year period of welfare eligibility; to enjoy the full range of employment, training, and accompanying supportive services; or to take full advantage of health care benefits under Medicaid. This waiting period does not preclude new residents from all cash payments, but merely limits them to what they received in their prior State of residence. . . .

PROBLEMS

After *Saenz*, what role, if any, is left for the equal protection clause with respect to discrimination by states against newly arrived permanent residents? Does *Saenz* moot such cases as *Zobel* and *Hooper*, which used the equal protection clause to invalidate fixed, permanent distinctions drawn by states with respect to newcomers and old-timers?

Under the *Saenz* analysis, could a state impose durational residency requirements on newcomers as an objective method of assuring their bona fide residence and citizenship in any of the following cases?

a. A state requires one-year residence as proof of bona fide residence for purposes of limiting court-approved adoption procedures to its residents.

b. A state (e.g., Alaska) establishes a rigorous certification requirement for outdoor guides, so demanding compared with others elsewhere that Alaska-certified guides command premium rates and are much sought after throughout the world. Alaska acts to stem the surplus demand for its certification program by limiting enrollment to permanent Alaska residents and by defining "permanent residence" for this purpose to be continuous residence of at least one year.

c. To reduce the chances of losing portions of its library collection, a city limits borrowing privileges at its public library to bona fide permanent residents, and defines such residents as those people continuously resident in the city for one year.

9

Free Expression of Ideas

A. OVERVIEW OF FREE EXPRESSION

The First Amendment never mentions "free expression of ideas," but that is its central focus. Aside from the two religion clauses, which are considered in the next chapter, the Amendment provides: "Congress shall make no law . . . abridging the freedom of speech, or of the press, or the right of the people peaceably to assemble, and to petition the government for a redress of grievances." From this text the Court has inferred a necessary corollary: the right to associate freely with others. All of these rights are connected based on the perception that they involve the freedom to express ideas.

But why? What is the purpose of such a guarantee? Of what importance is it to understand its purpose? Before we can answer these questions, a sense of the doctrinal architecture is necessary.

1. Rationales for Free Expression

The basic divide in free speech is between government regulations that regulate speech on the basis of its *content* and those that regulate speech on a *content-neutral* basis. A law prohibiting all political speech in the public streets regulates the speech on the basis of its content. A law prohibiting all speech in the public streets that is amplified by bullhorns is a content-neutral regulation—what matters under the law is not *what* is said but *how* the speech is delivered.

Content-based regulations are generally presumed to be void. These regulations are subject to strict scrutiny, which, of course, places on the government the burden of proving that the law is necessary to achieve some compelling government interest. By contrast, content-neutral regulations—those that do not aim at the suppression of ideas—are generally subject to intermediate scrutiny. Such regulations are generally valid if they are reasonable, well suited to the achievement of a significant government interest, and leave open ample alternative channels of communication. There are enough exceptions to and permutations of this scheme, however, that free speech law is a complicated labyrinth.

An important exception is the doctrine that some categories of speech—*defined by the content of the speech*—are treated as unprotected by the free speech guarantee. This seeming paradox comes about because the Court has concluded that the societal interest in suppressing such speech outweighs the value of the speech. To make that comparison, however, the Court measures the value of speech in terms of its connection to the purposes of the free expression guarantee. The more closely speech is connected to the purposes of the free speech guarantee, the more valuable it is.

Obviously, such a calculus is heavily dependent on the breadth with which the purposes of free expression are conceived. The broader the purpose, the more easily speech will be seen to be closely connected to that purpose. Thus arises the necessity of understanding the purposes of free speech. Alas, there is no single purpose, nor is there much agreement on which purpose is the most central.

(1) *Self-Governance.* Democracy assumes that we govern ourselves. Free expression is indispensable to the unfettered exchange of ideas necessary for self-governance. The ultimate sovereigns, the people, must be free to choose among all conceivable ideas in formulating public policy. See Meiklejohn, Free Speech and Its Relation to Self-Government (1948). The self-governance rationale has several additional facets, which are sometimes asserted as independent purposes for free expression. First, free expression helps prevent entrenchment of interests in government. Democracy presumes that government power will be wielded by different hands over time. When that is no longer the case, democracy ceases. Second, free expression buys political stability. Losers in politics are less likely to contest their loss by violence if they have had a fair chance to be heard. See Emerson, The System of Freedom of Expression (1970). Third, free speech serves to "check the abuse of power by public officials" by providing to the citizenry the information needed to exercise their "veto power [when] the decisions of [public] officials pass certain bounds." Blasi, The Checking Value in First Amendment Theory, 1977 Am. B. Found. Res. J. 527, 540.

(2) *The Search for Truth.* Free speech is necessary to determine the truth. But a postmodern skeptic might wonder what is truth. "[T]he theory of our Constitution [is] that the best test of truth is the power of the thought to get itself accepted in the competition of the market." Abrams v. United States, 250 U.S. 616, 630 (1919) (Holmes, J., dissenting). On this view, truth is whatever most people say it is. While the marketplace of ideas may not always accurately filter that which is empirically verifiable as true from the false, "[t]he critical question is not how well truth will advance absolutely in conditions of freedom but how well it will advance in conditions of freedom as

compared with some alternative set of conditions." Greenawalt, Free Speech Justifications, 89 Colum. L. Rev. 119, 135 (1989). Those who hold to the idea that truth is knowable if not always verifiable are even more robust in their claim that free expression is critical to finding truth. "Let [Truth] and Falsehood grapple; who ever knew Truth put to the worst, in a free and open encounter?" Milton, Areopagitica—A Speech for the Liberty of Unlicensed Printing (1644). Mill, On Liberty (1859), argued that it was futile to suppress truth, for "truth always triumphs over persecution," no matter how long it takes for truth "to withstand [all] attempts to suppress it." Moreover, said Mill, free expression of false ideas is necessary, since "conflict [with] error is essential to a clear apprehension [of] truth." Finally, said Mill, "the conflicting doctrines, instead of being one true and the other false, [may] share the truth between them; and the nonconforming opinion [may be] needed to supply the remainder of the truth."

Related to truth is the idea that free expression is necessary to develop moral virtue. In a world of extreme moral relativism this may be but a facet of the "marketplace of ideas" metaphor, but however our moral compass is calibrated, our ability to make moral choices—to opt for good and to reject evil—requires that we be free to choose. The process of moral deliberation often involves the expression of views, which are then open to reconsideration when others reply or react to the expressed sentiments.

(3) *Societal Tolerance and Self-Restraint.* The practice of free expression cultivates the virtues of tolerance and self-restraint. Justice Holmes noted that free expression does not mean "free thought for those who agree with us but freedom for the thought we hate." United States v. Schwimmer, 279 U.S. 644, 655 (1929). See Bollinger, The Tolerant Society (1986). In an increasingly culturally diverse society, these virtues may be necessary for societal self-preservation. If so, this purpose is not unrelated to self-governance.

(4) *Autonomy.* Some contend that the purpose of free expression "derives from the widely accepted premise [that] the proper end of man is the realization of his character and potentialities as a human being." Emerson, Toward a General Theory of the First Amendment, 72 Yale L.J. 877, 879 (1963). Free "expression is an integral part of the development of ideas, of mental exploration and of the affirmation of self." Richards, Free Speech and Obscenity Law: Toward a Moral Theory of the First Amendment, 123 U. Pa. L. Rev. 45, 62 (1974). But individual self-realization does not end with verbal or symbolic expression. This rationale for free speech requires an explanation of why expression deserves special protection, while many other self-fulfilling activities do not receive protection.

With a sense of the possible purposes for a free expression guarantee in place, we can consider the various categories of speech, defined by content, that receive little or no free expression protection. That is the topic of Section B. In Section C, we consider content-neutral regulation of speech. Section D introduces the problem of the government as the regulator of speech in its "proprietary" capacity—when it performs functions not easily distinguishable from ordinary private behavior. Section E represents a departure; we will consider three limitations on the procedures used to regulate speech, focusing on impermissible *methods* of speech regulation rather than on the substance of the regulations. Section F examines freedom of association and its mirror twin, freedom from compelled association or speech. Section G takes up the issue of free expression and the political process, with a focus on government regulation of political contributions, expenditures, and political parties. Section H looks at freedom of the press, particularly the differences between the free expression and free speech guarantees.

2. The Distinction Between Content-Based Regulation and Content-Neutral Regulation

Content-based regulations are those that are aimed at the subject matter of the speech (e.g., "no political speech"). Viewpoint-based regulations—laws that discriminate on the basis of a specific viewpoint (e.g., "no libertarian speech")—are merely a more sharply focused subset of content-based regulations. On the other hand, content-neutral regulations are indifferent to the subject matter or viewpoint expressed. They typically regulate speech based on the "time, place, or manner" in which it occurs (e.g., "no amplified speech in the park between 10 P.M. and 7 A.M.").

In general, content-based regulations are presumed to be void; the government bears the burden of justifying them by proving that they are necessary to achieve a compelling public objective.

For example, a provision in the 1996 federal Telecommunications Act required cable television operators offering channels "primarily dedicated to sexually-oriented programming" either to "fully scramble" these channels or limit their transmission to the hours between 10 P.M. and 6 A.M. The reason for the requirement was to protect children from this material when their parents object to its viewing by children. In United States v. Playboy Entertainment Group, Inc., 529 U.S. 803 (2000), the Court invalidated this provision.

> The speech in question is defined by its content; and the statute which seeks to restrict it is content based. . . . If a statute regulates speech based on its content, it must be narrowly tailored to promote a compelling Government interest. If a less restrictive alternative would serve the Government's purpose, the legislature must use that alternative. . . . Cable systems have the capacity to block unwanted channels on a household-by-household basis. The option to block reduces the likelihood [that] traditional First Amendment scrutiny would deprive the Government of all authority to address this sort of problem. The corollary, of course, is that targeted blocking enables the Government to support parental authority without affecting the First Amendment interests of speakers and willing listeners—listeners for whom, if the speech is unpopular or indecent, the privacy of their own homes may be the optimal place of receipt. Simply put, targeted blocking is less restrictive than banning, and the Government cannot ban speech if targeted blocking is a feasible and effective means of furthering its compelling interests.

[When] a plausible, less restrictive alternative is offered to a content-based speech restriction, it is the Government's obligation to prove that the alternative will be ineffective to achieve its goals. The Government has not met that burden here. [When] the Government seeks to restrict speech based on its content, the usual presumption of constitutionality afforded congressional enactments is reversed. "Content-based regulations are presumptively invalid," and the Government bears the burden to rebut that presumption.

This is for good reason. [It] is through speech that our convictions and beliefs are influenced, expressed, and tested. It is through speech that we bring those beliefs to bear on Government and on society. It is through speech that our personalities are formed and expressed. The citizen is entitled to seek out or reject certain ideas or influences without Government interference or control. When a student first encounters our free speech jurisprudence, he or she might think it is influenced by the philosophy that one idea is as good as any other, and that in art and literature objective standards of style, taste, decorum, beauty, and esthetics are deemed by the Constitution to be inappropriate, indeed unattainable. Quite the opposite is true. The Constitution no more enforces a relativistic philosophy or moral nihilism than it does any other point of view. The Constitution exists precisely so that opinions and judgments, including esthetic and moral judgments about art and literature, can be formed, tested, and expressed. What the Constitution says is that these judgments are for the individual to make, not for the Government to decree, even with the mandate or approval of a majority. Technology expands the capacity to choose; and it denies the potential of this revolution if we assume the Government [may choose] for us.

It is rare that a regulation restricting speech because of its content will ever be permissible. . . . When First Amendment compliance is the point to be proved, the risk of non-persuasion—operative in all trials—must rest with the Government, not with the citizen. [The government did not prove that targeted blocking would be ineffective if cable subscribers were aware of the option.]

Basic speech principles are at stake in this case. . . . We cannot be influenced . . . by the perception that the regulation in question is not a major one because the speech is not very important. The history of the law of free expression is one of vindication in cases involving speech that many citizens may find shabby, offensive, or even ugly. . . . If television broadcasts can expose children to the real risk of harmful exposure to indecent materials, even in their own home and without parental consent, there is a problem the Government can address. It must do so, however, in a way consistent with First Amendment principles. Here the Government has not met the burden the First Amendment imposes.

Reed v. Town of Gilbert. 2015 U.S. LEXIS 4061. Gilbert, Arizona adopted a Sign Code that prohibited signs unless a permit was obtained, but exempted from the Code 23 categories of signs. Among the exemptions were "ideological signs," "political signs," and "temporary directional signs." Ideological signs were those that communicated a message or idea not covered by any other category, and could be as large as 20 square feet with no limit on placement or duration. Political signs those "designed to influence the outcome of an election," could be no larger than 32 square feet and displayed only during the election season. Temporary directional signs, those directing the public to a church or other "qualifying event," could be no larger than six square feet, may be displayed no earlier than 12 hours before the event and must be removed no later than one hour after the event. No more than four such signs could be on a single property at the same time.

Clyde Reed, the pastor of the Good News Community Church, whose services were held in various temporary locations, posted directional signs early Saturday for each Sunday service. Some of the signs were not removed within the one hour window after the service, and the town cited him for these infractions. Accommodation being impossible, Reed sued in federal court, claiming a violation of the free speech guarantee. A district court denied Reed's motion for a preliminary injunction on the ground that the Sign Code was content neutral and was adequately justified under the standards applicable to content-neutral regulations. The Ninth Circuit affirmed. The Supreme Court was unanimous in its reversal, although a variety of rationales were expressed.

The majority declared:

> Government regulation of speech is content based if a law applies to particular speech because of the topic discussed or the idea or message expressed. . . . [A] court [must] consider whether a regulation of speech "on its face" draws distinctions based on the message a speaker conveys. . . . [F]acial distinctions . . . defining regulated speech by particular subject matter [and those] defining regulated speech by its function or purpose [are each] based on the message a speaker conveys, and, therefore, are subject to strict scrutiny. . . . The Town's Sign Code is content based on its face. [T]he Church's signs inviting people to attend its worship services are treated differently from signs conveying other types of ideas.

The fact that Gilbert did not adopt the Code to disagree with the Church's message was irrelevant because the Code facially discriminated on the basis of content. A "government's purpose is [not] relevant . . . when a law is content based on its face." Nor did it matter that Gilbert had not singled out any viewpoint for disadvantageous treatment. A "speech regulation targeted at specific subject matter is content based even if it does not discriminate among viewpoints within that subject matter." To no avail was the town's contention that it sought to regulate speakers, not the content of their speech. "Speech restrictions based on the identity of the speaker are all too often simply a means to control content. . . . Thus, a law limiting the content of newspapers, but only newspapers, could not evade strict scrutiny simply because it could be characterized as speaker based." Applying strict scrutiny the Court concluded that the Code was not narrowly tailored to achieve any compelling objective. The Court assumed that the town's interest in aesthetics and traffic safety were compelling but found the regulation to be "hopelessly underinclusive."

In a concurrence Justices Alito, Kennedy, and Sotomayor noted a variety of sign regulations that would not be content-based: size, location, lighted or unlighted signs, among others. Justice Breyer concurred in the judgment, arguing that content discrimination should not always trigger strict scrutiny, but be treated as a "rule of thumb." Justice Kagan, joined by Justices Ginsburg and Breyer, concurred in the judgment, contending that sign ordinances that do not endanger the robust marketplace of ideas or are not directed at squelching viewpoints ought to be subject to a less rigid level of review than strict scrutiny.

B.   CONTENT-BASED REGULATION OF SPEECH

Existing side by side with the rule that content-based regulations are generally presumed to be void is the fact that a variety of categories of speech—defined by their content—are given either little or no protection from government suppression. The principal categories of unprotected speech are obscenity, child pornography, speech that incites the immediate commission of a crime, and fighting words. The principal category of speech that receives limited constitutional protection is commercial speech—advertising. Content-based regulation is generally permissible within a category of unprotected (or limited-protection) speech, so long as the basis for such regulation is consistent with the reason the category of speech receives no (or limited) constitutional protection. For example, it would be permissible to restrict only the most salaciously obscene speech, as obscenity goes unprotected because of its lascivious quality, but it would not be permissible to restrict only obscene speech that casts the President in an unfavorable light, because that content-based regulation has nothing to do with why obscenity lacks constitutional protection.

The rationale denying free speech protection to some categories of speech is that they are so far removed from the "core purposes" of free expression, and simultaneously present such a significant danger to the community, that these categories can safely be considered outside the purview of free expression altogether or deserving of only limited protection. This "categorical balancing" proceeds abstractly—the value of a *type* of speech is assessed, rather than the value of a *specific speech*. By contrast, if the value of speech in relation to the purposes of free speech is assessed with respect to each particular utterance, the temptation is far stronger to succumb to censorship because the unpopularity of a specific message may skew judgment. Consider how well "categorical balancing" works as you study the categories that follow.

1.   Incitement of Immediate Crime

The modern development of free speech law began with this category. Surprisingly, the Court had very few occasions to consider free speech until the twentieth century, so this vast corpus of constitutional law is almost all about a century old. The specific problem of speech that incites crime developed in roughly three phases, each of which is considered in the following subsections.

a. *"Clear and Present Danger"*

In reaction to World War I, the federal Espionage Act of 1917 made it a crime during war (1) to "make or convey false [statements] with intent to interfere" with the military success of the United States or "to promote the success of its enemies"; (2) intentionally to "cause or attempt to cause insubordination, disloyalty, mutiny, or refusal of duty, in the military or naval forces of the United States"; or (3) intentionally to "obstruct the recruiting or enlistment service of the United States." In 1918, the Act was amended to prohibit statements intended to hinder the production of materials necessary to wage war against Germany.

Schenck v. United States
249 U.S. 47 (1919)

JUSTICE HOLMES delivered the opinion of the Court.

This [indictment] charges a conspiracy to violate the Espionage Act [by] causing and attempting to cause insubordination [in] the military and naval forces of the United States, and to obstruct the recruiting and enlistment service of the United States, when the United States was at war with the German Empire. [Schenck was] general secretary of the Socialist party. [He and his co-defendants] circulated to men who had been called and accepted for military service [a] document [allegedly] calculated to [cause] insubordination and obstruction. [They were found guilty.] The document [recited] the Thirteenth Amendment, said that the idea embodied in it was violated by the Conscription Act. . . . In impassioned language it intimated that conscription was despotism in its worst form and a monstrous wrong against humanity in the interest of Wall Street's chosen few. It said "Do not submit to intimidation," but in form at least confined itself to peaceful measures such as a petition for the repeal of the act. The other and later printed side of the sheet was headed "Assert Your Rights." It stated reasons for alleging that any one violated the Constitution when he refused to recognize "your right to assert your opposition to the draft," and went on "If you do not assert and support your rights, you are helping to deny or disparage rights which it is the solemn duty of all citizens and residents of the United States to retain." It described the arguments on the other side as coming from cunning politicians and a mercenary capitalist press, and even silent consent to the conscription law as helping to support an infamous conspiracy. It denied the power to send our citizens away to foreign shores to shoot up the people of other lands, . . . winding up "You must do your share to maintain, support and uphold the rights of the people of this country." Of course the documents would not have been sent unless it had been intended to have some effect, and we do not see what effect it could be expected to have upon persons subject to the draft except to influence them to obstruct the carrying of it out.

[In] many places and in ordinary times the defendants in saying all that was said in the circular would have been within their constitutional rights. But the character of every act depends upon the circumstances in which it is done. The most stringent protection of free speech would not protect a man in falsely shouting fire in a theatre and causing a panic. [The] question in every case is whether the words used are used in such circumstances and are of such a nature as to create a clear and present danger that they will bring about the substantive evils that Congress has a right to prevent. It is a question of proximity and degree.

NOTE

In Frohwerk v. United States, 249 U.S. 204 (1919), the Court upheld an Espionage Act conviction for conspiracy to cause insubordination, disloyalty, mutiny, or refusal of duty in the armed services. The conspiracy consisted of publication of a series of articles in a German-language newspaper that were sharply critical of the American war effort in Europe, praised the spirit and strength of Germany, and asserted that illegal draft resistance was morally justified. The paper's circulation was tiny but "it was in quarters where a little breath would be enough to kindle a flame." Justice Holmes wrote the opinion.

In Debs v. United States, 249 U.S. 211 (1919), a companion case to *Frohwerk*, the Court sustained the Espionage Act conviction of Eugene Debs, the Socialist leader and frequent presidential candidate, for a speech made at a Socialist convention in Canton, Ohio. The speech was full of high praise for socialism and predictions of its ultimate success. Debs also intimated that three local Socialists jailed for aiding and abetting draft resistance were heroes to be admired and, perhaps, emulated. Justice Holmes, for the Court:

> [Debs] said that he had to be prudent and might not be able to say all that he thought, thus intimating to his hearers that they might infer that he meant more, but he did say "You need to know that you are fit for something better than slavery and cannon fodder." [If Debs's opposition to war] was so expressed that its natural and intended effect would be to obstruct recruiting [it] would not be protected [by the free speech clause]. [The] words used had as their natural tendency and reasonably probable effect [obstruction of] the recruiting service [and Debs] had the specific intent to do so in his mind.

Abrams v. United States
250 U.S. 616 (1919)

[In 1917, following the October Revolution, the Bolshevik government of Russia made peace with Germany. The United States, then at war with Germany, sent armed forces into northern Russia. Abrams and four other self-styled revolutionary anarchists were convicted of violating the Espionage

Act, as amended in 1918, by reason of their distribution of a leaflet urging a general strike in order to frustrate the American expedition in Russia, which they charged was designed to "crush the Russian revolution." On the strength of *Schenck* and *Frohwerk*, the Court affirmed the convictions.]

JUSTICE CLARKE delivered the opinion of the Court.

[The defendants printed and distributed circulars appealing] to the "workers" of this country to arise and put down by force the Government [and] to persuade the persons to whom it was addressed to turn a deaf ear to patriotic appeals in behalf of the Government of the United States, and to cease to render it assistance in the prosecution of the war. It will not do to say [that] the only intent of these defendants was to prevent injury to the Russian cause. Men must be held to have intended, and to be accountable for, the effects which their acts were likely to produce. Even if their primary purpose and intent was to aid the cause of the Russian Revolution, the plan of action which they adopted necessarily involved [defeat] of the war program of the United States. [W]hile the . . . defendant alien anarchists may have . . . resent[ed] our Government sending troops into Russia as a strategic operation against the Germans on the eastern battle front, yet the plain purpose of their propaganda was to excite, at the supreme crisis of the war, disaffection, sedition, riots, and, as they hoped, revolution, in this country for the purpose of embarrassing and if possible defeating the military plans of the Government in Europe. [Affirmed.]

JUSTICE HOLMES, joined by JUSTICE BRANDEIS, dissenting.

This indictment is founded wholly upon the publication of two [leaflets, stating:] "Workers in the ammunition factories, you are producing bullets, bayonets, cannon, to murder not only the Germans, but also your dearest, best, who are in Russia and are fighting for freedom." . . . "Workers, our reply to this barbaric intervention has to be a general strike!," and after a few words on the spirit of revolution, exhortations not to be afraid, and some usual tall talk ends "Woe unto those who will be in the way of progress. Let solidarity live! The Rebels."

[It] seems too plain to be denied that the [leaflets] urge curtailment of production of things necessary to the prosecution of the war within the meaning of the [amended Espionage Act]. But to make the conduct criminal that statute requires that it should be "with intent by such curtailment to cripple or hinder the United States in the prosecution of the war." It seems to me that no such intent is proved. [A] deed is not done with intent to produce a consequence unless that consequence is the aim of the deed. . . . [He] does not do the act with intent to produce it unless the aim to produce it is the proximate motive of the specific act. [A] patriot might think that we were wasting money on aeroplanes, or making more cannons of a certain kind than we needed, and might advocate curtailment with success, yet even if it turned out that the curtailment hindered and was thought by other minds to have been obviously likely to hinder the United States in the prosecution of the war, no one would hold such conduct a crime. . . . [The] United

States constitutionally may punish speech that produces or is intended to produce a clear and imminent danger that it will bring about forthwith certain substantive evils that the United States constitutionally may seek to prevent. The power undoubtedly is greater in time of war than in time of peace because war opens dangers that do not exist at other times. But [the] principle of the right to free speech is always the same. It is only the present danger of immediate evil or an intent to bring it about that warrants Congress in setting a limit to the expression of opinion where private rights are not concerned. Congress certainly cannot forbid all effort to change the mind of the country. . . . [In] this case sentences of twenty years imprisonment have been imposed . . . . Even if I am technically wrong and enough can be squeezed from these poor and puny anonymities to turn the color of legal litmus paper [the] most nominal punishment seems to me all that possibly could be inflicted, unless the defendants are to be made to suffer not for what the indictment alleges but for the creed that they [avow]. Persecution for the expression of opinions seems to me perfectly logical. If you have no doubt of your premises or your power and want a certain result with all your heart you naturally express your wishes in law and sweep away all opposition. . . . [But] when men have realized that time has upset many fighting faiths, they may come to believe [that] the ultimate good desired is better reached by free trade in ideas — that the best test of truth is the power of the thought to get itself accepted in the competition of the market, and that truth is the only ground upon which their wishes safely can be carried out. That at any rate is the theory of our Constitution. It is an experiment, as all life is an experiment. [While] that experiment is part of our system I think that we should be eternally vigilant against attempts to check the expression of opinions that we loathe and believe to be fraught with death, unless they so imminently threaten immediate interference with the lawful and pressing purposes of the law that an immediate check is required to save the country. . . .

NOTE

Clear and Present Danger. Was the application of the "clear and present danger" approach as clear as its rhetoric? How immediate must the danger be to constitute a "present" danger? What identifies a "clear" danger? Did specific intent matter, or was speech that posed a "clear and present" danger, regardless of the speaker's intent, outside the protective umbrella of the First Amendment?

Judge Learned Hand, as a federal district judge, declared that for speech inciting lawless conduct to lose constitutional protection it must constitute "direct advocacy" of illegal behavior; the speaker must expressly incite lawbreaking rather than simply advocating "dangerous ideas."

Holmes focused more on the probable effects of speech and Hand on the specific intent of the speaker. Would Eugene Debs's speech have been protected under the Hand formula? What about a speaker who indirectly but deliberately incites violence? What about a speaker who deliberately and directly urges violence to a group of committed pacifists?

b. Criminal Anarchy and Communists: Clear and Not So Present Danger

As World War I faded and the United States succumbed to the "Red Scare"—the fear that Bolshevik revolutionaries would foment a violent over-turning of American democracy—states began to enforce "criminal anarchy" or "criminal syndicalism" statutes, which typically punished the advocacy of violent overthrow of government.

Gitlow v. New York
268 U.S. 652 (1925)

[New York's criminal anarchy law punished "advocacy . . . of the doctrine that organized government should be overthrown by force or violence, or by assassination . . . or any unlawful means"; advocating, advising, or teaching "the duty, necessity or propriety . . . of overturning organized government by force or violence"; and printing, publishing, or distributing "written or printed matter in any form, containing . . . the doctrine that organized government should be overthrown by force, violence or any unlawful means."]

JUSTICE SANFORD delivered the opinion of the Court.

Benjamin Gitlow was [convicted of] criminal anarchy. . . . The indict-ment was in two counts. The first charged that the defendant had advocated, advised and taught the duty, necessity and propriety of overthrowing and overturning organized government by force, violence and unlawful means, by certain writings [titled] "The Left Wing Manifesto"; the second that he had printed, published and knowingly circulated and distributed a certain paper called "The Revolutionary Age," containing [writings] advocating, advising and teaching the doctrine that organized government should be overthrown by force, violence and unlawful means.

. . . There was no evidence of any effect resulting from the publication and circulation of the Manifesto.

Extracts from the Manifesto are set forth[:] "Revolutionary Socialism [insists] that it is necessary to destroy the parliamentary state, and construct a new state of the organized producers, which will deprive the bourgeoisie of political power, and function as a revolutionary dictatorship of the proletar-iat. [The] direct objective is the conquest by the proletariat of the power of the state. Revolutionary Socialism does not propose to 'capture' the bour-geois parliamentary state, but to conquer and destroy it." The sole conten-tion here [is] that as there was no evidence of any concrete result flowing from the publication of the Manifesto or of circumstances showing the likeli-hood of such result, the statute as construed and [applied] penalizes the mere utterance [of] "doctrine" having no quality of incitement, [and thus violates the free speech guarantee]. The statute . . . prohibits . . . language advocating, advising or teaching the overthrow of organized government by unlawful means. These words imply urging to action. [The] Manifesto . . . advocates and urges in fervent language mass action which shall progressively foment industrial disturbances and through political mass strikes and revolutionary mass action overthrow and destroy organized parliamentary government. It concludes with a call to [action]. This is not the expression of philosophical abstraction, the mere prediction of future events; it is the language of direct incitement. The means advocated for bringing about the destruction of organized parliamentary government, namely, mass industrial revolts usurping the functions of municipal government, political mass strikes directed against the parliamentary state, and revolutionary mass action for its final destruction, necessarily imply the use of force and violence, and in their essential nature are inherently unlawful in a constitutional government of law and order. That the jury were warranted in finding that the Manifesto advocated not merely the abstract doctrine of overthrowing organized government by force, violence and unlawful means, but action to that end, is clear.

[A] State may punish utterances endangering the foundations of organized government and threatening its overthrow by unlawful means. [Free speech] does not deprive a State of the primary and essential right of self preservation. [New York] has determined, through its legislative body, that utterances advocating the overthrow of organized government by force, violence and unlawful means, are so inimical to the general welfare and involve such danger of substantive evil that they may be penalized in the exercise of its police power. That determination must be given great weight. Every presumption is to be indulged in favor of the validity of the statute. [Utterances] inciting to the overthrow of organized government by unlawful means present a sufficient danger of substantive evil to bring their punishment within the range of legislative [discretion]. Such utterances . . . threaten breaches of the peace and ultimate revolution. And the immediate danger is none the less real and substantial, because the effect of a given utterance cannot be accurately foreseen. The State cannot reasonably be required to measure the danger from every such utterance in the nice balance of a jeweler's scale. A single revolutionary spark may kindle a fire that, smouldering for a time, may burst into a sweeping and destructive conflagration. It cannot be said that the State is acting [unreasonably when it] seeks to extinguish the spark without waiting until it has enkindled the flame or blazed into the conflagration. It cannot reasonably be required to defer the adoption of measures for its own peace and safety until the revolutionary utterances lead to actual disturbances of the public peace or imminent and immediate danger of its own destruction; but it may, in the exercise of its judgment, suppress the threatened danger in its incipiency. [We] sustain its constitutionality.

[When] the legislative body has determined generally, in the constitutional exercise of its discretion, that utterances of a certain kind involve such danger of substantive evil that they may be punished, the question whether any specific utterance coming within the prohibited class is likely . . . to bring about the substantive evil is not open to consideration. . . . [But] where the statute merely prohibits certain acts involving the danger of substantive evil, without any reference to language itself, and it is sought to apply its provisions to language used [for] the purpose of bringing about the prohibited results, [the] specific language used [must involve] such likelihood of bringing about the substantive evil as to deprive it of the constitutional protection. [The] general provisions of [such a] statute may be constitutionally applied to the specific utterance of the defendant if its natural tendency and probable effect was to bring about the substantive evil which the legislative body might prevent. [The] "clear and present danger" [test] was manifestly intended [to] apply only in cases of this class, and has no application [where, as here, the legislature] has previously determined the danger of substantive evil arising from utterances of a specified character. [Affirmed.]

JUSTICE HOLMES, dissenting.

Mr. Justice Brandeis and I are of opinion that this judgment should be reversed. [The *Schenck* "clear and present danger" test applies and it] is manifest that there was no present danger of an attempt to overthrow the government by force on the part of the admittedly small minority who shared the defendant's views. It is said that this manifesto was more than a theory, that it was an incitement. Every idea is an incitement. It offers itself for belief and if believed it is acted on unless some other belief outweighs it or some failure of energy stifles the movement at its birth. The only difference between the expression of an opinion and an incitement in the narrower sense is the speaker's enthusiasm for the result. Eloquence may set fire to reason. But whatever may be thought of the redundant discourse before us it had no chance of starting a present conflagration. If in the long run the beliefs expressed in proletarian dictatorship are destined to be accepted by the dominant forces of the community, the only meaning of free speech is that they should be given their chance and have their way. If the publication of this document had been [an] attempt to induce an uprising against government at once and not at some indefinite time in the future it would have presented a different question. The object would have been one with which the law might deal, subject to the doubt whether there was any danger that the publication could produce any result, or in other words, whether it was not futile and too remote from possible consequences. But the indictment alleges the publication and nothing more.

NOTES

1. The Substance of "Clear and Present Danger." In *Gitlow*, Holmes emphasized that subversive speech must pose an immediate harm for it to be validly punished. In a later case, Whitney v. California, 274 U.S. 357 (1927), Justice Brandeis added as a requirement that there "must be the probability of serious injury" resulting from the speech. The Brandeis formulation requires a showing that the danger from speech is (1) "clear"; (2) "imminent"; and (3) "substantial" or "serious." How might Brandeis treat a law banning Internet publication of precise instructions for making bombs? Would it make any difference if the bombs were nuclear? How might Brandeis view a law punishing incitement of crime as applied to a speaker urging pedestrians to jaywalk at a busy intersection that is notorious for such illegal behavior? Formulate the Brandeis view of the same incitement law as applied to a merchant who informs a customer that a certain lawful weapon is ideally suited for use in a political assassination.

2. Later Developments.   In De Jonge v. Oregon, 299 U.S. 353 (1937), the Court ruled that mere participation in an organization devoted to advocating criminal syndicalism could not be made a crime. In Herndon v. Lowry, 301 U.S. 242 (1937), the Court overturned the conviction of Herndon, a black Communist Party organizer, under Georgia's "insurrection" law, which prohibited "resistance to the lawful authority of the State [by intended] acts of violence." Herndon's conviction had been based on his advocacy of equal rights for blacks and for urging blacks to seek self-determination. Without proof of some incitement to immediate insurrection, Herndon's conviction violated free speech; mere membership in the Communist Party was insufficient. The Court also thought the law was unconstitutionally vague.

3. The Cold War Communists and the Smith Act.   In Dennis v. United States, 341 U.S. 494 (1951), the Court upheld the convictions of the chief leaders of the American Communist Party for violating the Smith Act, which prohibited the knowing advocacy, or attempted advocacy, of the "duty, necessity, desirability, or propriety of overthrowing [any] government in the United States by force or violence." A four-justice plurality led by Chief Justice Vinson concluded that speech could be prohibited as posing a clear and present danger of producing a substantive evil whenever "the gravity of the 'evil,' discounted by its improbability, justifies such invasion of free speech as is necessary to avoid the danger." Vinson stated that the government need not "wait until the putsch is about to be executed" before acting.

Justices Black and Douglas dissented. Justice Black charged that the Court had repudiated the "'clear and present danger' rule," and that the defendants were punished because "they agreed to assemble and to talk and publish certain ideas at a later date." Justice Douglas dissented because there was no proof that the defendants had advocated anything but ideas—they merely "preached the creed with the hope that some day it would be acted upon. [There] must be some immediate injury to society that is likely" to occur for speech validly to be curbed.

But six years after *Dennis*, the Court in Yates v. United States, 354 U.S. 298 (1957), overturned the Smith Act convictions of several lesser Communists because there was no proof that the defendants advocated "action for the overthrow of government by force and violence. [Those] to whom the advocacy is addressed must be urged to *do* something, now or in the future, rather than merely to *believe* in something."

The Smith Act also prohibited knowing membership in an "organization which advocates the overthrow of the Government of the United States by force or violence." In Scales v. United States, 367 U.S. 203 (1961), the Court interpreted this provision to require "clear proof that a defendant 'specifically intend[s] to accomplish [the organization's revolutionary objectives] by resort to violence.' [The] member for whom the organization is a vehicle for the advancement of legitimate aims and policies does not fall within the ban of the statute: he lacks the requisite specific intent 'to bring about the overthrow of the government as speedily as circumstances would permit.'"

But the convictions were upheld because there was adequate proof of "present advocacy of *future* action for violent overthrow." The Court treated *Dennis* as having eliminated any constitutional requirement that punishment be limited to "advocacy of *immediate* action to that end."

c. *The Contemporary Standard for Incitement*

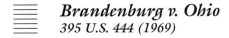

Brandenburg v. Ohio
395 U.S. 444 (1969)

PER CURIAM.

The appellant, a leader of a Ku Klux Klan group, was convicted under the Ohio Criminal Syndicalism statute for "advocat[ing] the duty, necessity, or propriety of crime, sabotage, violence, or unlawful methods of terrorism as a means of accomplishing industrial or political reform" and for "voluntarily assembl[ing] with any society, group, or assemblage of persons formed to teach or advocate the doctrines of criminal syndicalism." He was fined $1,000 and sentenced to one to 10 years' imprisonment.

The [appellant] telephoned an announcer-reporter on the staff of a Cincinnati television station and invited him to come to a Ku Klux Klan "rally" to be held at a [nearby farm]. With the cooperation of the organizers, the reporter and a cameraman attended the meeting and filmed the events. Portions of the films were later broadcast on the local station and on a national network. The prosecution's case rested on the films and on testimony identifying the appellant as the person [who] spoke at the rally. [One] film showed 12 hooded figures, some of whom carried firearms. They were gathered around a large wooden cross, which they burned. No one was present other than the participants and the newsmen who made the film. Most of the words uttered during the scene were incomprehensible when the film was projected, but scattered phrases could be understood that were derogatory of Negroes and, in one instance, of Jews.[1] Another scene on the same film showed the

---

1. The significant portions that could be understood were:
"How far is the nigger going to—yeah."
"This is what we are going to do to the niggers."
"A dirty nigger."

appellant, in Klan regalia, making a speech. The speech, in full, was as follows: "This is an organizers' meeting. We have had quite a few members here today which are—we have hundreds, hundreds of members throughout the State of Ohio. I can quote from a newspaper clipping from the Columbus, Ohio Dispatch, five weeks ago Sunday morning. The Klan has more members in the State of Ohio than does any other organization. We're not a revengent organization, but if our President, our Congress, our Supreme Court, continues to suppress the white, Caucasian race, it's possible that there might have to be some revengeance taken. We are marching on Congress July the Fourth, four hundred thousand strong. From there we are dividing into two groups, one group to march on St. Augustine, Florida, the other group to march into Mississippi. Thank you." The second film showed six hooded figures one of whom, later identified as the appellant, repeated a speech very similar to that recorded on the first film. The reference to the possibility of "revengeance" was omitted, and one sentence was added: "Personally, I believe the nigger should be returned to Africa, the Jew returned to Israel." Though some of the figures in the films carried weapons, the speaker did not.

[In *Whitney,*] this Court sustained the constitutionality of California's Criminal Syndicalism Act, the text of which is quite similar to that of the [Ohio law at issue here]. . . . But *Whitney* has been thoroughly discredited by later decisions [that] have fashioned the principle that the constitutional guarantees of free speech and free press do not permit a State to forbid or proscribe advocacy of the use of force or of law violation except where such advocacy is directed to inciting or producing imminent lawless action and is likely to incite or produce such action.[2] "[T]he mere abstract teaching [of] the moral propriety or even moral necessity for a resort to force and violence is not the same as preparing a group for violent action and steeling it to such action."

Measured by this test, Ohio's Criminal Syndicalism Act cannot be sustained. . . . Neither the indictment nor the [jury] instructions [in] any way refined the statute's bald definition of the crime in terms of mere advocacy not distinguished from incitement to imminent lawless action. [This] statute which, by its own words and as applied, purports to punish mere advocacy

---

"Send the Jews back to Israel."
"Let's give them back to the dark garden."
"Save America."
"Let's go back to constitutional betterment."
"Bury the niggers."
"We intend to do our part."
"Give us our state rights."
"Freedom for the whites."
"Nigger will have to fight for every inch he gets from now on."

2. It was on the theory that the Smith Act embodied such a principle and that it had been applied only in conformity with it that this Court sustained the Act's constitutionality [in *Dennis*]. That this was the basis for *Dennis* was emphasized in [*Yates*], in which the Court overturned convictions for advocacy of the forcible overthrow of the Government under the Smith Act, because the trial judge's instructions had allowed conviction for mere advocacy, unrelated to its tendency to produce forcible action.

and to forbid, on pain of criminal punishment, assembly with others merely to advocate the described type of action, [falls] within the condemnation of the First and Fourteenth Amendments. The contrary teaching of [*Whitney*] cannot be supported, and that decision is therefore overruled. Reversed.

JUSTICE BLACK, concurring.

[The] "clear and present danger" doctrine should have no place in the interpretation of the First Amendment.

JUSTICE DOUGLAS, concurring.

I see no place in the regime of the First Amendment for any "clear and present danger" test, whether strict and tight as some would make it, or freewheeling as the Court in *Dennis* rephrased it. When one reads the opinions closely and sees when and how the "clear and present danger" test has been applied, great misgivings are aroused. First, the threats were often loud but always puny and made serious only by judges so wedded to the status quo that critical analysis made them nervous. Second, the test was so twisted and perverted in *Dennis* as to make the trial of those teachers of Marxism an all-out political trial which was part and parcel of the cold war that has eroded substantial parts of the First Amendment. [The] line between what is permissible and not subject to control and subject to regulation is the line between ideas and overt acts. The example usually given by those who would punish speech is the case of one who falsely shouts fire in a crowded theatre, [but that is] a classic case where speech is brigaded with action.

NOTES AND PROBLEM

1. Applications of *Brandenburg*. In Hess v. Indiana, 414 U.S. 105 (1973), the Court applied *Brandenburg* to overturn a disorderly conduct conviction stemming from a campus anti-war demonstration. After some arrests had been made, over 100 demonstrators blocking a street were pushed onto the curb and sidewalk by police. Hess then said "We'll take the fucking street later [or again]." The Indiana courts treated this statement as intentional incitement that was likely to provoke further lawlessness. The Court disagreed, finding the imminence requirement unsatisfied. "At best, [the] statement could be taken as counsel for present moderation; at worst, it amounted to nothing more than advocacy of illegal action at some indefinite future time."

In NAACP v. Claiborne Hardware Co., 458 U.S. 886 (1982), the Court invoked free speech to strike a Mississippi judgment awarding damages against black participants in an economic boycott of white merchants. One of the grounds for imposing liability had been the conclusion that an NAACP official's "public speeches were likely to incite lawless action" and that such "unlawful conduct [in] fact followed within a reasonable period." For the Court, Justice Stevens wrote:

While many of the comments in [the] speeches might have contemplated "discipline" in the permissible form of social ostracism, it cannot be denied that references to the possibility that necks would be [broken] implicitly conveyed a sterner message [that] might have been understood as inviting an unlawful form of discipline [or creating] a fear of violence. [But] mere *advocacy* of the use of force or violence does not remove speech from the protection of [the free speech clause. This] emotionally charged rhetoric [did] not transcend the bounds of protected speech set forth in *Brandenburg*. Strong language was used [and if] that language had been followed by acts of violence, a substantial question would be presented whether [the speaker] could be held liable for the consequences of that unlawful conduct. [But here the] acts of violence occurred weeks or months after [the] speech. [When] appeals do not incite lawless action, they must be regarded as protected speech.

2. The Scope of *Brandenburg*.   Does *Brandenburg* prevent prosecution of solicitation of crime? Most jurisdictions make it a criminal offense purposely to request another person to engage in specific conduct that would itself be a crime. Suppose that a person intends to kill his partner and, filled with that intent, unwittingly requests an undercover police officer to perform the killing in exchange for money. Does (should) *Brandenburg* apply? Compare Rice v. Paladin Enterprises, Inc., 128 F.3d 233 (4th Cir. 1997).

3. *Gitlow* Redux?   In Holder v. Humanitarian Law Project, 561 U.S. 1 (2010), the Court upheld a ban on speech to a terrorist organization that constituted specific "training," "expert advice or assistance," or "service," as applied to the respondent's intended speech. The Court ruled that the ban was not unconstitutionally vague and then proceeded to apply strict scrutiny because the statutory prohibition singled out speech on the basis of its content. The Court deferred to congressional findings that "foreign organizations that engage in terrorist activity are so tainted by their criminal conduct that any contribution to such an organization facilitates that conduct." The Court said it did not defer because national security was at stake; rather, deference was warranted because "when it comes to collecting evidence and drawing factual inferences in this area, 'the lack of competence on the part of the courts is marked,' and respect for the Government's conclusions is appropriate [because] national security and foreign policy concerns arise in connection with efforts to confront evolving threats in an area where information can be difficult to obtain and the impact of certain conduct difficult [for courts] to assess."

Did the Court revert to the *Gitlow* standard, or is the deference in *Holder* both more limited and more warranted than in *Gitlow*?

4. Problem.   18 U.S.C. §2339A makes it a crime to provide "material support or resources" in furtherance of various specified crimes. Section 2339B imposes criminal punishment on anyone who "knowingly provides material support or resources to a foreign terrorist organization, or attempts or conspires to do so." Under §2339B, a foreign terrorist organization is any group designated as such by the Secretary of State after he or she finds that the organization (1) is foreign, (2) engages in terrorism as defined in other statutes, and (3) threatens the security of the United States or its citizens. Al Qaeda is such a designated foreign terrorist organization. Both sections define "material support" to include the provision of "personnel," specifically including "oneself." John Walker Lindh, the so-called American Taliban, was charged under §2339B. See United States v. Lindh, 212 F. Supp. 2d 541 (E.D. Va. 2002). Radical lawyer Lynne Stewart was convicted under §2339A, in connection with her legal representation of an Islamic terrorist cleric. See United States v. Sattar, 395 F. Supp. 2d 79 (S.D.N.Y. 2005).

Suppose that an American attends an Al Qaeda training camp, becomes well versed in explosives and weaponry, and returns to the United States, where he lives quietly and otherwise lawfully. Suppose further that this person swears fealty to Al Qaeda and its objectives. May the United States validly prosecute and convict him under §2339B for providing material support to Al Qaeda in the form of his person? What issues are presented? What cases are most relevant to disposition of the issue?

2. True Threats

The problem of a true threat, in which the speaker threatens to commit criminal harm to another, is a variant of incitement of others to commit criminal acts.

≡≡≡ *Virginia v. Black*
≡≡≡ *538 U.S. 343 (2003)*

JUSTICE O'CONNOR announced the judgment of the Court and delivered the opinion of the Court with respect to Parts I, II, and III, and an opinion with respect to Parts IV and V in which CHIEF JUSTICE REHNQUIST, JUSTICE STEVENS, and JUSTICE BREYER joined.

[We] consider whether . . . Virginia's statute banning cross burning with "an intent to intimidate a person or group of persons" violates the First Amendment. We conclude that while a State . . . may ban cross burning carried out with the intent to intimidate, the provision in the Virginia statute treating any cross burning as prima facie evidence of intent to intimidate renders the statute unconstitutional in its current form.

I. [OPINION OF THE COURT.] Respondents Barry Black, Richard Elliott, and Jonathan O'Mara were convicted separately of violating Virginia's cross-burning statute. . . . Black led a Ku Klux Klan rally which occurred on private property with the permission of the owner. . . . [The rally culminated in the ignition of a 25- to 30-foot-high cross, located about 300 to 350 yards from the public road.] Black was charged [and convicted of] burning a cross with the intent of intimidating a person or group of persons. . . . [T]he jury was instructed that . . . "the burning of a cross by itself is sufficient evidence from which you may infer the required intent." . . .

Richard Elliott and Jonathan O'Mara . . . attempted to burn a cross on the yard of James Jubilee, . . . an African-American, [who] was Elliott's next-door neighbor. . . . Before the cross burning, Jubilee spoke to Elliott's mother to inquire about shots being fired from behind the Elliott home. Elliott's mother explained to Jubilee that her son shot firearms as a hobby, and that he used the backyard as a firing range. [Elliott and O'Mara, who "were not affiliated with the Klan,"] drove a truck onto Jubilee's property, planted a cross, and set it on fire, [apparently] to "get back" at Jubilee for complaining about the shooting in the backyard. . . . Elliott and O'Mara were charged with attempted cross burning and conspiracy to commit cross burning. O'Mara pleaded guilty to both counts, reserving the right to challenge the constitutionality of the cross-burning statute. . . . At Elliott's trial, the judge . . . did not instruct the jury on the meaning of the word "intimidate," nor on the prima facie evidence provision. . . . The jury found Elliott guilty of attempted cross burning and acquitted him of conspiracy to commit cross burning. . . . The Supreme Court of Virginia consolidated all three cases, and held that the statute is unconstitutional on its face. . . . We granted certiorari.

II. Cross burning originated in the 14th century as a means for Scottish tribes to signal each other. . . . Cross burning in this country, however, long ago became unmoored from its Scottish ancestry. Burning a cross in the United States is inextricably intertwined with the history of the Ku Klux Klan. . . . [C]ross burnings have been used to communicate both threats of violence and messages of shared ideology. . . . Often, the Klan used cross burnings as a tool of intimidation and a threat of impending violence. . . .

The . . . civil rights movement of the 1950s and 1960s sparked another outbreak of Klan violence. These acts of violence included bombings, beatings, shootings, stabbings, and mutilations. Members of the Klan burned crosses on the lawns of those associated with the civil rights movement, assaulted the Freedom Riders, bombed churches, and murdered blacks as well as whites whom the Klan viewed as sympathetic toward the civil rights movement.

Throughout the history of the Klan, cross burnings have also remained potent symbols of shared group identity and ideology. The burning cross became a symbol of the Klan itself and a central feature of Klan gatherings. According to the Klan . . . , the "fiery cross" was the "emblem of that sincere, unselfish devotedness of all klansmen to the sacred purpose and principles we have espoused." . . . [A] burning cross has remained a symbol of Klan ideology and of Klan unity.

To this day, regardless of whether the message is a political one or whether the message is also meant to intimidate, the burning of a cross is a "symbol of hate." And while cross burning sometimes carries no intimidating message, at other times the intimidating message is the *only* message conveyed. . . . In sum, while a burning cross does not inevitably convey a message of intimidation, often the cross burner intends that the recipients of the message fear for their lives. And when a cross burning is used to intimidate, few if any messages are more powerful.

III. A. . . . The hallmark of the protection of free speech is to allow "free trade in ideas"—even ideas that the overwhelming majority of people might find distasteful or discomforting. . . . The First Amendment affords protection to symbolic or expressive conduct as well as to actual speech. The protections afforded by the First Amendment, however, are not absolute, [and] permit[] a State to ban a "true threat." "True threats" encompass those statements where the speaker means to communicate a serious expression of an intent to commit an act of unlawful violence to a particular individual or group of individuals. The speaker need not actually intend to carry out the threat. Rather, a prohibition on true threats "protects individuals from the fear of violence" and "from the disruption that fear engenders," in addition to protecting people "from the possibility that the threatened violence will occur." Intimidation in the constitutionally proscribable sense of the word is a type of true threat, where a speaker directs a threat to a person or group of persons with the intent of placing the victim in fear of bodily harm or death. [The] history of cross burning in this country shows that cross burning is often intimidating, intended to create a pervasive fear in victims that they are a target of violence.

B. . . . Virginia's statute does not run afoul of the First Amendment insofar as it bans cross burning with intent to intimidate. . . . [However,] in the case of Elliott and O'Mara, it is at least unclear whether the respondents burned a cross due to racial animus [or] "because they were angry that their neighbor had complained about the presence of a firearm shooting range in . . . Elliott's yard." The First Amendment permits Virginia to outlaw cross burnings done with the intent to intimidate because burning a cross is a particularly virulent form of intimidation. Instead of prohibiting all intimidating messages, Virginia may choose to regulate this subset of intimidating messages in light of cross burning's long and pernicious history as a signal of impending violence. . . .

IV. [JUSTICE O'CONNOR, joined by CHIEF JUSTICE REHNQUIST and JUSTICES STEVENS and BREYER.] . . . The prima facie evidence provision . . . renders the statute unconstitutional. . . . The act of burning a cross may mean that a person is engaging in constitutionally proscribable intimidation. But that same act may mean only that the person is engaged in core political speech. The prima facie evidence provision . . . chills constitutionally protected political speech because of the possibility that a State will prosecute—and potentially convict—somebody engaging only in lawful political speech at the core of what the First Amendment is designed to protect. . . .

V. [JUSTICE O'CONNOR, joined by CHIEF JUSTICE REHNQUIST and JUSTICES STEVENS and BREYER.] With respect to Barry Black, we agree with the Supreme Court of Virginia that his conviction cannot stand, and we affirm the judgment of the Supreme Court of Virginia. With respect to Elliott and O'Mara, we vacate the judgment of the Supreme Court of Virginia, and remand the case for further proceedings.

JUSTICES SOUTER, KENNEDY, and GINSBURG concurred in the judgment with respect to Black; JUSTICE SCALIA concurred in the judgment with respect to Elliott and O'Mara.

NOTES AND PROBLEM

1. Hyperbole: *Watts.*   During the Vietnam War, Watts was convicted of willfully threatening to kill or injure the President after he had addressed a small group of people during a public anti-war rally as follows: "I have got to go for my [draft] physical this Monday coming. I am not going. If they ever make me carry a rifle the first man I want to get in my sights is LBJ. [Nobody is] going to make me kill my black brothers." In Watts v. United States, 394 U.S. 705 (1969), the Court ruled that the law was facially valid, but held that Watts's remark was protected "political hyperbole." Was it protected hyperbole because Watts lacked the intent to place LBJ in fear of bodily harm, or did not intend to carry out the threat, or the context suggested it was nothing more than exaggeration?

2. Imminence?   During the boycott at issue in NAACP v. Claiborne Hardware Co., 458 U.S. 886 (1982), Charles Evers had warned those who did not adhere to the boycott: "If we catch any of you going in any of them racist stores, we're gonna break your damn neck." Weeks later, shots were fired into the homes of boycott violators. The Court viewed this "strong language" through the lens of incitement, and concluded that because the "acts of violence occurred weeks . . . after [the] speech" it was protected. What should be the result under true threat analysis?

3. Problem: After a series of well-publicized murders of abortion providers, a hypothetical anti-abortion advocacy group, Crusaders for Life, creates and distributes "Wanted" posters displaying the names, addresses, and photos of physicians who perform abortions, and proclaiming that the persons on the posters are "wanted for crimes against humanity." Neither Crusaders for Life nor any of its members had anything to do with the prior murders. The named physicians file suit under the Freedom of Access to Clinic Entrances Act (FACE), 18 U.S.C. §248, which gives aggrieved persons a right of action against anyone who by "threat of force . . . intentionally . . . intimidates . . . any person because that person is or has been . . . providing reproductive health services." May Crusaders' speech be punished by an award of damages or an injunction? Cf. Planned Parenthood of the Columbia/Willamette, Inc. v. American Coalition of Life Activists, 290 F. 3d 1058 (9th Cir. 2002), decided a year before Virginia v. Black.

Should it matter that the posters are "political speech in a public arena [rather than] purely private speech directed at an individual"? If so, does that mean that all public political speech is protected, no matter how clearly and specifically "the speech directly threatens actual injury to identifiable individuals"?

If fear of harm is the reason true threats are unprotected, why should it matter what the speaker's intent may be, so long as "a reasonable person would foresee that the statement would be interpreted by those to whom the maker communicates the statement as a serious expression of intent to harm or assault"?

4. More Questions; Few Answers.   Federal law, 18 U.S.C. §875(c), makes it a crime to transmit in interstate commerce "any communication containing any threat . . . to injure the person of another." After Elonis posted a series of violent messages on Facebook, describing murder and mayhem of his estranged wife, co-workers, and kindergarten classes, he was convicted of violating the statute. Because the statute contains no *mens rea* requirement the jury was instructed that it could convict if it found that a "reasonable person" could consider the communication a threat. The Third Circuit affirmed. Although his posts contained numerous disclaimers that he was exercising his First Amendment rights by adopting the persona of a rap artist—"Tone Dougie"—the Court 8-1, in *Elonis v. United States*, 2015 U.S. LEXIS 3719, grounded its decision on the statute. Something more than the reasonable person standard was necessary, but the Court did not specify what standard applied. Was it actual intent to harm? Was it intent to put the recipient in fear of harm, even if no harm was actually intended? Was it sufficient if the sender knew that his communication would regarded as a threat? All of these questions were left for consideration on remand.

Problems: Should the standard vary with context or the form of communication? Assume a state has enacted a version of 18 U.S.C. §875 that contains no requirement of interstate commerce but is otherwise identical.

a. Arnold, a hulking and menacing figure, approaches Jane, a waitress, and says "I'm going to kill you as soon as you leave work." Apart from whether these are fighting words, is it a true threat? Suppose Arnold scribbled the same message on a napkin as he left Jane's coffee shop? Suppose Arnold told Bill, the cook, to tell Jane that Arnold said he would kill her, and Bill did so? Any difference? If Arnold's communication is a true threat, is Bill also culpable?

b. Suppose Nitwitt, a vicious anti-Semite, posts a notice on the door of a synagogue stating "My mission is to kill Jews. I will succeed." Suppose Nitwitt operates a blog on which he daily repeats his intent to kill as many Jews as possible? True threats?

3. Obscenity, Pornography, and Putative Analogs

Not all sex-laden speech is outside the First Amendment. The Court has exiled obscenity, though it has had great difficulty defining what constitutes the genre, and has stripped child pornography, whether or not obscene, of any constitutional protection. But non-obscene pornography remains protected, though the level of its protection sometimes seems much reduced from that accorded political speech.

Throughout this section, consider the reasons for refusing to protect obscenity and child pornography while affording limited protection to non-obscene pornography. Is obscenity morally corrupting? Does obscenity or child pornography pose an unacceptable danger of inciting substantive evils (e.g., incitement to crime or abuse of children)? Are obscenity and child pornography unprotected in order to preserve community decency and prevailing sensibilities? Should the law take into account the fact that non-obscene pornography harms women by promoting cultural subordination and harassment, or are those harms (assuming their existence) simply the price of unfettered freedom of speech?

a. Obscenity

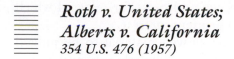

Roth v. United States;
Alberts v. California
354 U.S. 476 (1957)

JUSTICE BRENNAN delivered the opinion of the Court.

The constitutionality of a criminal obscenity statute is the question in each of these cases. In *Roth*, [the] question is whether the federal obscenity statute[3] violates the [free speech clause] of the First Amendment. In *Alberts*, [the] question is whether [California's criminal] obscenity provisions[4] invade the freedoms of speech and press [as] incorporated in the liberty protected from state action by the Due Process Clause of the Fourteenth Amendment. [Roth was convicted of mailing obscene advertising and an obscene book. Alberts was convicted of keeping for sale obscene and indecent books, and publishing an obscene advertisement of them.]

The dispositive question is whether obscenity is utterance within the area of protected speech and press. Although this is the first time the question has been squarely presented to this Court, [we have] always assumed that obscenity is not protected by the freedoms of speech and press. [There] is sufficiently contemporaneous evidence to show that obscenity [was] outside the protection intended for speech and press. [Free speech] was fashioned to assure unfettered interchange of ideas for the bringing about of political and social changes desired by the people. [All] ideas having even the slightest redeeming social importance—unorthodox ideas, controversial ideas, even ideas hateful to the prevailing climate of opinion—[have full constitutional] protection, unless excludable because they encroach upon the limited area of more important interests. But implicit in the history of the First Amendment is the rejection of obscenity as utterly without redeeming social importance. [We] hold that obscenity is not within the area of constitutionally protected speech or press. . . .

However, sex and obscenity are not synonymous. Obscene material is material which deals with sex in a manner appealing to prurient interest.[5]

3. The federal obscenity statute [prohibited mailing of] "obscene, lewd, lascivious, or filthy" [materials].

4. The California Penal Code [prohibits the willful and lewd creation, distribution, or advertising of] "any obscene or indecent writing, paper, book, picture, print or figure." . . .

5. That is, material having a tendency to excite lustful thoughts. *Webster's New International Dictionary* (Unabridged, 2d ed., 1949) defines *prurient*, in pertinent part, as follows: "Itching; longing; uneasy with desire or longing; of persons, having itching, morbid, or lascivious longings; of desire, curiosity, or propensity, lewd." [We] perceive no significant difference between the meaning of obscenity developed in the case law and the definition of the

The portrayal of sex, e.g., in art, literature and scientific works, is not itself sufficient reason to deny material the constitutional protection of freedom of speech and press. Sex, a great and mysterious motive force in human life, has indisputably been a subject of absorbing interest to mankind through the ages . . . . [The] fundamental freedoms of speech and press [are] indispensable to [a free society]. It is therefore vital that the standards for judging obscenity safeguard the protection of freedom of speech and press for material which does not treat sex in a manner appealing to prurient interest.

The early leading standard of obscenity allowed material to be judged merely by the effect of an isolated excerpt upon particularly susceptible persons. Regina v. Hicklin, [1868] L.R. 3 Q.B. 360 [defined obscenity as material that tends "to deprave and corrupt those whose minds are open to such immoral influences"]. Some American courts adopted this standard but later decisions have rejected it and substituted this test: whether to the average person, applying contemporary community standards, the dominant theme of the material taken as a whole appeals to prurient interest. The *Hicklin* test . . . must be rejected as unconstitutionally restrictive of the freedoms of speech and press. On the other hand, the substituted standard provides safeguards adequate to withstand the charge of constitutional infirmity. Both trial courts below [used] the proper definition of obscenity. [Affirmed.]

JUSTICE HARLAN, concurring in the result in *Alberts* and dissenting in *Roth*.

[The] Court seems to assume that "obscenity" is a peculiar genus of "speech . . ." which is as distinct, recognizable, and classifiable as poison ivy is among other plants. On this basis the constitutional question [becomes] whether "obscenity," as an abstraction, is [constitutionally protected, and] the question whether a particular book may be suppressed becomes a mere matter of classification, of "fact." [But] surely the problem cannot be solved in such a generalized fashion. Every communication has an individuality and "value" of its own. [Many] juries might find that Joyce's "Ulysses" or Boccaccio's "Decameron" was obscene, and yet the conviction of a defendant for selling either book would raise, for me, the gravest constitutional [problems].

I concur in [*Alberts* because] our function in reviewing state judgments under the Fourteenth Amendment is [to decide] whether the state action so subverts the fundamental liberties implicit in the Due Process Clause that it cannot be sustained as a rational exercise of power. [It] seems to me clear that it is not irrational . . . to consider that pornography can induce a type of sexual conduct which a State may deem obnoxious to the moral fabric of society. . . .

I dissent in [*Roth* because] I do not think it follows that state and federal powers in this area are the same, and that just because the State may suppress a particular utterance, it is automatically permissible for the Federal

---

[proposed] Model Penal Code: "A thing is obscene if, considered as a whole, its predominant appeal is to prurient interest, i.e., a shameful or morbid interest in nudity, sex, or excretion, and if it goes substantially beyond customary limits of candor in description or representation of such matters."

Government to do [so]. Congress has no substantive power over sexual morality. Such powers as the Federal Government has in this field are but incidental to its other powers, here the postal power, and are not of the same nature as those possessed by the States, which bear direct responsibility for the protection of the local moral fabric. [Not] only is the federal interest in protecting the Nation against pornography attenuated, but the dangers of federal censorship in this field are far greater than anything the States may do. [The] fact that the people of one State cannot read some of the works of D. H. Lawrence seems to me, if not wise or desirable, at least acceptable. But that no person in the United States should be allowed to do so seems to me to be intolerable, and violative of both the letter and spirit of the First Amendment.

JUSTICE DOUGLAS, joined by JUSTICE BLACK, dissenting.

When we sustain these convictions, we make the legality of a publication turn on the purity of thought which a book or tract instills in the mind of the reader. I do not think we can approve that standard and be faithful to the command of the First Amendment. [I] reject too the implication that problems of freedom of speech and of the press are to be resolved by weighing against the values of free expression, the judgment of the Court that a particular form of that expression has "no redeeming social importance." The First Amendment, its prohibition in terms absolute, was designed to preclude courts as well as legislatures from weighing the values of [speech]. Freedom of expression can be suppressed if, and to the extent that, it is so closely brigaded with illegal action as to be an inseparable part of it.

NOTES

1. Application of *Roth*. *Roth* proved to be unworkable. Nine years later, in Memoirs v. Massachusetts, 383 U.S. 413 (1966), a plurality of three (Warren, Brennan, and Fortas) restated *Roth* as follows:

> [T]hree elements must coalesce: it must be established that (a) the dominant theme of the material taken as a whole appeals to a prurient interest in sex; (b) the material is patently offensive because it affronts contemporary community standards relating to the description or representation of sexual matters; and (c) the material is utterly without redeeming social value.

As Chief Justice Burger later noted in *Miller*, "While *Roth* presumed 'obscenity' to be 'utterly without redeeming social importance,' *Memoirs* required that to prove obscenity it must be affirmatively established that the material is 'utterly without redeeming social value,' [a] burden virtually impossible to discharge under our criminal standards of proof." Nevertheless, this formulation was the most widely applied, even though no majority of the Court could agree on a standard to determine what constituted obscenity. Warren, Brennan, and Fortas subscribed to the *Memoirs* variation; Black and Douglas asserted that obscenity was constitutionally protected; Harlan held to his *Roth* view; and Stewart thought that both federal and state governments could suppress "hard-core" pornography. Justice Stewart's famous epigram in his concurrence in Jacobellis v. Ohio, 378 U.S. 184 (1964), dramatized the problem of defining "obscenity." Speaking of hard-core pornography, Stewart said: "I know it when I see it."

In the absence of a majority view, the Court adopted the practice of summarily reversing obscenity convictions when at least five members of the Court, applying their separate tests, found the material in question protected. Redrup v. New York, 386 U.S. 767 (1967). As Justice Brennan said in his dissent in *Paris Adult Theatre*, "[This approach] resolves cases [but] offers only the most obscure guidance to legislation, adjudication by other courts, and primary conduct."

2. Private Possession of Obscene Materials. In Stanley v. Georgia, 394 U.S. 557 (1969), the Court held that the free expression guarantee barred a state from "making the private possession of obscene material a crime." The Court reasoned that governments have no "right to control the moral content of a person's thoughts. [Whatever] may be the power of the state to control public dissemination of ideas inimical to public morality, it cannot constitutionally premise legislation on the desirability of controlling a person's private thoughts." The Court invoked Kingsley Pictures International Corp. v. Regents, 360 U.S. 684 (1959), which had struck down a New York law banning films displaying "sexual immorality" as applied to "Lady Chatterley's Lover." New York could not ban films because they "advocate an idea—that adultery [may] be proper. [The] First Amendment's basic guarantee is of freedom to advocate ideas." *Stanley* endorsed the notion that people had a limited right—in the privacy of their home—to absorb the ideas embodied in obscenity. What are those ideas? Is sexual stimulation an idea?

Any thought that *Stanley* might undercut laws prohibiting the distribution of obscene materials was soon squelched. In United States v. Reidel, 402 U.S. 351 (1971), the Court reversed dismissal of an indictment for mailing obscene material in violation of federal law. The notion that the right to possess obscene materials recognized in *Stanley* implied a right to obtain obscene materials "would effectively scuttle *Roth*." *Stanley* protected only "freedom of mind and thought [and] the privacy of one's home." In United States v. Orito, 413 U.S. 139 (1973), the Court upheld the federal prohibition of interstate transport of obscene materials as applied to transportation *purely for private use*, and in United States v. Twelve 200-Foot Reels, 413 U.S. 123 (1973), the Court sustained the application of federal law to prevent the importation of obscene material for personal use. The clearest indication that *Stanley* has been marooned is Osborne v. Ohio, 495 U.S. 103 (1990), where the Court ruled that *Stanley* did not protect the private possession of child pornography. The result of these post-*Stanley* cases is that child pornography is contraband, and obscenity depicting adults is semi-contraband—unprotected except for personal use in the narrow sanctuary of one's home.

3. Dissatisfaction with *Roth*. Not only was *Roth* unworkable, as evidenced by the *Redrup* practice of summary per curiam decisions, but it was undermined by the 1970 report of a presidential commission on obscenity and pornography, which called for repeal of most laws banning the distribution of sexually explicit materials, except with respect to juveniles or to the public display of such materials. But the Court's solution was not to abandon the field so much as to turn it over to the states for independent regulation.

Miller v. California
413 U.S. 15 (1973)

CHIEF JUSTICE BURGER delivered the opinion of the Court.

This is one of a group of "obscenity-pornography" cases being reviewed [in] a re-examination of standards enunciated in earlier cases involving what Mr. Justice Harlan called "the intractable obscenity problem." [Miller] conducted a mass mailing campaign to advertise the sale of illustrated books, euphemistically called "adult" material. [He] was convicted [of] knowingly distributing obscene matter [by] causing five unsolicited advertising brochures to be sent through the [mail. The brochures primarily] consist of pictures and drawings very explicitly depicting men and women in groups of two or more engaging in a variety of sexual activities, with genitals often prominently displayed. This case involves the application of a State's criminal obscenity statute to a situation in which sexually explicit materials have been thrust by aggressive sales action upon unwilling recipients who had in no way indicated any desire to receive such materials. [States] have a legitimate interest in prohibiting dissemination or exhibition of obscene material when the mode of dissemination carries with it a significant danger of offending the sensibilities of unwilling recipients or of exposure to juveniles. It is in this context that we are called on to define the standards which must be used to identify obscene material that a State may [regulate].

[Obscene] material is unprotected by the First Amendment, [but due to] the inherent dangers of undertaking to regulate any form of expression, [state] statutes designed to regulate obscene materials must be carefully limited. [Thus,] we now confine the permissible scope of such regulation to works which depict or describe sexual conduct. That conduct must be specifically defined by the applicable state law, as written or authoritatively construed. [The] basic guidelines for the trier of fact must be: (a) whether "the average person, applying contemporary community standards" would find that the work, taken as a whole, appeals to the prurient interest; (b) whether the work depicts or describes, in a patently offensive way, sexual conduct specifically defined by the applicable state law; and (c) whether the work, taken as a whole, lacks serious literary, artistic, political, or scientific value. We do not adopt as a constitutional standard the "*utterly* without redeeming social value" test of [*Memoirs*].

We emphasize that it is not our function to propose regulatory schemes for the States, [but it is possible to] give a few plain examples of what a state statute could define for regulation under part (b) of the standard announced in this opinion: (a) Patently offensive representations or descriptions of ultimate sexual acts, normal or perverted, actual or simulated. (b) Patently offensive representations or descriptions of masturbation, excretory functions, and lewd exhibition of the genitals.

Sex and nudity may not be exploited without limit by films or pictures exhibited or sold in places of public accommodation any more than live sex and nudity can be exhibited or sold without limit in such public places. . . . In resolving the inevitably sensitive questions of fact and law, we must continue to rely on the jury system, accompanied by [its legal] safeguards. . . .

[Under] a National Constitution, fundamental First Amendment limitations on the powers of the States do not vary from community to community, but this does not mean that there are, or should or can be, fixed, uniform national standards of precisely what appeals to the "prurient interest" or is "patently offensive." These are essentially questions of fact, and our Nation is simply too big and too diverse for this Court to reasonably expect that such standards could be articulated for all 50 States in a single formulation, even assuming the prerequisite consensus exists. [To] require a State to structure obscenity proceedings around evidence of a national "community standard" would be an exercise in futility. [It] is neither realistic nor constitutionally sound to read the First Amendment as requiring that the people of Maine or Mississippi accept public depiction of conduct found tolerable in Las Vegas or New York City. People in different States vary in their tastes and attitudes, and this diversity is not to be strangled by the absolutism of imposed uniformity. [The] requirement that the jury evaluate the materials with reference to "contemporary standards of the State of California" [is] constitutionally adequate. . . .

[In] sum, we (a) reaffirm [that] obscene material is not protected by the First Amendment; (b) hold that such material can be regulated by the States, subject to the specific safeguards enunciated above, without a showing that the material is "*utterly* without redeeming social value"; and (c) hold that obscenity is to be determined by applying "contemporary community standards," not "national standards." [Vacated] and remanded.

JUSTICE DOUGLAS, dissenting.

[There] are no constitutional guidelines for deciding what is and what is not "obscene." [What] shocks me may be sustenance for my neighbor. What causes one person to boil up in rage [may] reflect only his neurosis, not shared by others. [Obscenity]—which even we cannot define with precision—is a hodge-podge. To send men to jail for violating standards they cannot understand, construe, and apply is a monstrous thing to do in a Nation dedicated to fair trials and due process.

JUSTICE BRENNAN, joined by JUSTICES STEWART and MARSHALL, dissenting.

[It] is clear that under my dissent in *Paris Adult Theatre I*, the statute under which the prosecution was brought is unconstitutionally overbroad, and therefore invalid on its face.

≡ *Paris Adult Theatre I v. Slaton*
≡ *413 U.S. 49 (1973)*

CHIEF JUSTICE BURGER delivered the opinion of the Court.

Petitioners are two Atlanta [adult] movie theaters. [The] local state district attorney [sought a judicial declaration that two films were] obscene and that petitioners be enjoined from exhibiting the films. [The evidence at a court trial consisted of the films at issue and photographs that portrayed] the single entrance to both Paris Adult Theatre I and Paris Adult Theatre II. [These] photographs show a conventional, inoffensive theater entrance, without any pictures, but with signs indicating that the theaters exhibit "Atlanta's Finest Mature Feature Films." On the door . . . is a sign saying: "Adult Theatre—You must be 21 and able to prove it. If viewing the nude body offends you, Please Do Not Enter." [The state's criminal investigators testified] that they had paid admission to see the films and that nothing on the outside of the theater indicated . . . that the films depicted—as they did—scenes of simulated fellatio, cunnilingus, and group sex intercourse. [The] trial judge dismissed [the complaint, ruling that although] "obscenity is established" [the Constitution protected] "display of these films in a commercial theatre, when surrounded by requisite notice to the public of their nature and by reasonable protection against the exposure of these films to minors." [The] Georgia Supreme Court [reversed; we] vacate and remand this case for reconsideration in light of *Miller*.

[We] categorically disapprove the theory [that] obscene, pornographic films acquire constitutional immunity from state regulation simply because they are exhibited for consenting adults only. [There] are legitimate state interests at stake in stemming the tide of commercialized obscenity, even assuming it is feasible to enforce effective safeguards against exposure to juveniles and to passersby. These include the interest of the public in the quality of life and the total community environment, the tone of commerce in the great city centers, and, possibly, the public safety itself. The Hill-Link Minority Report of the Commission on Obscenity and Pornography indicates that there is at least an arguable correlation between obscene material and crime. Quite apart from sex crimes, however, there remains one problem of large proportions aptly described by Professor Bickel: "It concerns the tone of the society, the mode, [. . .] the style and quality of life, now and in the future. A man may be entitled to read an obscene book in his room, or expose himself indecently there. [We] should protect his privacy. But if he demands a right to obtain the books and pictures he wants in the market, and to foregather in public places—discreet, if you will, but accessible to all—with others who share his tastes, *then to grant him his right is to affect the world about the rest of us, and to impinge on other privacies*. Even supposing that each of us can, if he wishes, effectively avert the eye and stop the ear (which, in truth, we cannot), what is commonly read and seen and heard and done intrudes upon us all, want it or not." 22 The Public Interest 25-26 (Winter 1971). (Emphasis added.) As [Chief Justice] Warren stated, there is a "right of the Nation and of the States to maintain a decent society."

[Although] there is no conclusive proof of a connection between anti-social behavior and obscene material, the legislature of Georgia could quite reasonably determine that such a connection does or might exist. In deciding *Roth*, this Court implicitly accepted that a legislature could legitimately act on such a conclusion to protect "*the social interest in order and morality.*" . . .

It is argued that [state] regulation of access by consenting adults to obscene material violates the constitutionally protected right to privacy enjoyed by petitioners' customers. [But] it is unavailing to compare a theater open to the public for a fee with the private home of [*Stanley*]. . . . [Nor is Georgia] attempting to control the minds or thoughts of those who patronize theaters. Preventing [display] of obscene material [is] distinct from a control of reason and the intellect. Where communication of ideas [is] not involved [the] mere fact that [some] "thoughts" may be incidentally affected does not bar the State from acting to protect legitimate state interests. The fantasies of a drug addict are his own and beyond the reach of government, but government regulation of drug sales is not prohibited by the Constitution. . . .

Vacated and remanded.

JUSTICE BRENNAN, joined by JUSTICES STEWART and MARSHALL, dissenting.

[The] time has come to make a significant departure from [the *Roth*] approach. The essence of [the obscenity problem is] that we have been unable to . . . separate obscenity from other sexually oriented but constitutionally protected speech, so that efforts to suppress the former do not spill over into the suppression of the latter. [None] of the available formulas, including the one announced today, can reduce the vagueness [of obscenity] to a tolerable [level]. Although we have assumed that obscenity does exist and that we "know it when [we] see it," we are manifestly unable to describe it in advance except by reference to concepts so elusive that they fail to distinguish clearly between protected and unprotected speech. [The] vagueness of [obscenity] standards [produces] a number of separate problems: [a] lack of fair notice, [a] chill on protected expression, and [unusual] stress imposed on [the] judicial [system. A] significant change in direction is urgently required. . . . [I] am forced to conclude [that] "obscenity" cannot be defined with sufficient specificity and clarity to provide fair notice, [to] prevent substantial erosion of protected speech as a byproduct of the attempt to suppress unprotected speech, and to avoid very costly institutional harms. Given these inevitable side effects [of] efforts to suppress [obscenity], we must scrutinize with care the state interest that is asserted to justify the suppression. For in the absence of some very substantial interest in suppressing such speech, we can hardly condone the ill effects that seem to flow inevitably from the effort. [The] state interests in protecting children and in protecting unconsenting adults may [be great. A sexually explicit communication], "imposed upon a person contrary to his wishes, has all the characteristics of a physical assault [and it] constitutes an invasion of his privacy." Similarly, if children are "not possessed of that full capacity for individual choice which is the presupposition of the

First Amendment guarantees," then the State may have a substantial interest in precluding the flow of obscene materials even to consenting juveniles.

But, whatever the strength of the state interests in protecting juveniles and unconsenting adults from exposure to sexually oriented materials, those interests cannot be asserted [here]. The justification for the suppression must be found [in] some independent interest in regulating the reading and viewing habits of consenting adults. [While] a State [need not] remain utterly indifferent to [the] morality of the community, [the] State's interest in regulating morality by suppressing obscenity [remains] essentially unfocused and ill defined. And, since the attempt to curtail unprotected speech necessarily spills over into the area of protected speech, the effort to serve this speculative interest through the suppression of obscene material must tread heavily on rights protected by the First Amendment. . . . I would hold, therefore, that at least in the absence of distribution to juveniles or obtrusive exposure to unconsenting adults, the [free expression guarantee prohibits governments] from attempting wholly to suppress sexually oriented materials on the basis of their allegedly "obscene" contents.

NOTES AND PROBLEM

1. Why Oust Sexually Explicit Material from the First Amendment's Protection?   What is the strongest justification for suppression of obscenity? Among the possibilities are the following.

a. Avoiding offense.   The Court in *Miller* and *Paris Adult Theatre I* agreed that governments could regulate obscenity to avoid offense to unconsenting adults and to children. But that rationale is inadequate to explain why consenting adults cannot have access to pornography. Is the knowledge that obscenity is available to those who want it sufficient offense to merit its exclusion from First Amendment protections?

b. Incitement of crime.   Some argue that sexually explicit materials stimulate some people to commit criminal acts. Justice Harlan, in *Alberts*, would have deferred to California's rational judgment that this was so. In *Paris Adult Theatre I*, the Court thought it was plausible that obscenity could be linked to sex crimes. Should this rationale be held unsupportable unless the intended incitement and imminence requirements of *Brandenburg* are met? In *Brandenburg*, the intended incitement and imminence tests were devised to draw the line between protected and unprotected speech, while in the Court's discussions of obscenity the incitement rationale is offered as a justification for such a line, rather than as the dividing line itself.

c. Preservation of morals.   The Court's opinions in *Miller* and in *Paris Adult Theatre I* relied in part on the legitimacy of government attempts to preserve public morality by suppressing obscenity. Even Justice Brennan, dissenting, conceded that many laws are rooted in a legitimate "concern with the morality of the community," citing "compulsory education laws, civil rights laws, [and] abolition of capital punishment." Are laws against obscenity any different? What effect, if any, does Lawrence v. Texas have on this issue? If governments may ban obscenity because it is deemed immoral, may they also suppress other kinds of offensive speech that the legislature deems a threat to public morality, such as profanity, vulgarity, hate speech, non-obscene pornography, or praise for Nazi genocide?

Another moral issue is the notion, endorsed by the Court in *Paris Adult Theatre I*, that obscenity harms the quality of everyone's life, whether or not one views the obscene material. Its very existence has effects on the entire community. But isn't that true of all speech? Advocacy of fascism or communism has effects on the entire community, yet the message of *Brandenburg* is that such speech must be tolerated. Holmes's metaphor of the marketplace of ideas holds that it is the community's job to sort out these messages. Is obscenity different because it is not cognitive, but rather an irrational stimulant to sexual impulses? See Schauer, Speech and "Speech"—Obscenity and "Obscenity": An Exercise in the Interpretation of Constitutional Language, 67 Geo. L.J. 899 (1979); Sunstein, Words, Conduct, Caste, 60 U. Chi. L. Rev. 795 (1993). Would embracing the view that obscenity is a mere "sex aid" conflict with the Court's recognition in Cohen v. California, infra, that "words are often chosen as much for their emotive as their cognitive force" and that free speech protects the "emotive function which, practically speaking, may often be the more important element of the overall message"? What the Court said in *Cohen* of the emotive content of "words" is surely amplified when it comes to images.

d. Remote connection to the core purposes of free speech. Is obscenity exiled from free speech protection because it is only remotely connected to the central purposes of free speech? If so, what makes it the Neptune (or Pluto, if you prefer) of the free speech solar system? Is it the fact that obscenity is a long way from political speech? But even if political speech is the Mercury to the Sun of free speech, what does that mean for music, art, poetry, novels, sculpture, dance, and drama? Certainly Picasso's Guernica or Steinbeck's The Grapes of Wrath are overtly political, but what of Jackson Pollock's works or Jane Austen's Pride and Prejudice? Are they "political" because they shape attitudes and perceptions about the world around us? If so, why isn't obscenity equally "political"?

Is obscenity on the periphery of free speech because it delivers a message to which there is no response? The rationale of truth and Holmes's marketplace of ideas metaphor presume the possibility of rational debate. What reply can one give to a lurid depiction of sexual lust in action? Can there ever be an adequate cognate response to emotional speech? According to *Cohen*, emotive speech is equally entitled to constitutional protection. Advertising is designed to appeal to emotion, yet political advertising enjoys full constitutional protection, and commercial advertising has far more First Amendment protection than does obscenity.

2. Application of *Miller*. In Hamling v. United States, 418 U.S. 87 (1974), the Court ruled that local community standards, rather than state or national ones, were dispositive in applying the *Miller* test. But though local community standards govern the questions of "appeal to the prurient interest" and "patent offensiveness," the Court, in Jenkins v. Georgia, 418 U.S 153 (1974), made it clear that jury verdicts on these issues are subject to judicial review to determine whether a jury's view of local standards is constitutionally aberrant. In *Jenkins*, a Georgia jury had concluded that the widely praised film *Carnal Knowledge* was obscene. The film explored the evolution of sexual attitudes of two men from their youth through middle age, using occasional nudity but no graphic depictions of sexual acts or the human genitalia. The Court declared that, Georgia mores notwithstanding, "nudity alone is not enough to make material legally obscene under the *Miller* standards." The result is an uneasy paradox: Local standards govern on prurient appeal and patent offensiveness so long as those standards are not more prudish than some minimum constitutional threshold of prurience and offensiveness. Smith v. United States, 431 U.S. 291 (1977), and Pope v. Illinois, 481 U.S. 497 (1987), held that the final prong of *Miller*—the presence of serious content—is *not* to be governed by local community standards but by "whether a reasonable person would find such value in the material, taken as a whole."

b. Pornography

≡≡≡ **New York v. Ferber**
≡≡ *458 U.S. 747 (1982)*

JUSTICE WHITE delivered the opinion of the Court.

At issue in this case is the constitutionality of a New York criminal statute which prohibits persons from knowingly promoting sexual performances by children under the age of 16 by distributing material which depicts such performances.

I. [T]he exploitive use of children in the production of pornography has become a serious national problem. The Federal Government and 47 States have sought to combat the problem with statutes specifically directed at the production of child pornography. At least half of such statutes do not require that the materials produced be legally obscene. Thirty-five States and [Congress] have also passed legislation prohibiting the distribution of such materials; 20 States prohibit the distribution of material depicting children engaged in sexual conduct without requiring that the material be legally obscene. New York is one of the 20.[6] This case arose when Paul Ferber, the

---

6. The New York law made it a felony knowingly to

use [a] child in a sexual performance [by] employ[ing], authoriz[ing], or induc[ing] a child less than sixteen years of age to engage in a sexual performance or being a parent, legal guardian or custodian of such child, [consenting] to the participation by such child in a sexual performance. ["Sexual performance" was defined as] any performance [that] includes sexual conduct, [defined as] actual or simulated sexual intercourse, deviate sexual intercourse, sexual bestiality, masturbation, sadomasochistic abuse, or lewd exhibition of the genitals. [The New York statute proprietor of a Manhattan bookstore specializing in sexually oriented products, sold two films to an undercover police officer. The films are devoted almost exclusively to depicting young boys masturbating. Ferber was [convicted under the New York law, but the] New York Court of Appeals reversed [on] First Amendment [grounds]. We granted [certiorari to decide whether New York could], "consistent with the First Amendment, prohibit the dissemination of material which shows children engaged in sexual conduct, regardless of whether such material is obscene."

II. The Court of Appeals proceeded on the assumption that the [*Miller*] standard of obscenity [constitutes] the appropriate line dividing protected from unprotected expression by which to measure a regulation directed at child pornography. . . . [For] the following reasons [we] are persuaded that the States are entitled to greater leeway in the regulation of pornographic depictions of children.

First. It is evident [that] a State's interest in "safeguarding the physical and psychological well-being of a minor" is "compelling." [The] prevention of sexual exploitation and abuse of children constitutes a government objective of surpassing importance. [We] shall not second-guess [the] legislative judgment [that] the use of children as subjects of pornographic materials is harmful to the physiological, emotional, and mental health of the child.

Second. The distribution of photographs and films depicting sexual activity by juveniles is intrinsically related to the sexual abuse of children in at least two ways. First, the materials produced are a permanent record of the children's participation and the harm to the child is exacerbated by their circulation. Second, the distribution network for child pornography must be closed if the production of material which requires the sexual exploitation of children is to be effectively controlled. [There] is no serious contention that the legislature was unjustified in believing that [the] most expeditious if not the only practical method of law enforcement may be to dry up the market for this material by imposing severe criminal penalties on persons selling, advertising, or otherwise promoting the product. [Instead, Ferber] argues that it is enough for the State to prohibit the distribution of materials that are legally obscene under the *Miller* test. While some States may find that this approach properly accommodates its interests, it does not follow that the First Amendment prohibits a State from going further. The *Miller* standard [does] not reflect the State's particular and more compelling interest in prosecuting those who promote the sexual exploitation of children. [The *Miller* test] bears no connection to the issue of whether a child has been physically or psychologically harmed in the production of the work. "It is irrelevant to the child [who has been abused] whether or not the material [has] a literary, artistic, political or social value."

---

also made it a felony knowingly to] produce[ ], direct[ ] or promote[ ] any performance which includes sexual conduct by a child less than sixteen years of age [or to distribute any such material].—ED.

Third.   The advertising and selling of child pornography provide an economic motive for and are thus an integral part of the production of such materials, an activity illegal throughout the Nation. "It rarely has been suggested that the constitutional freedom for speech and press extends its immunity to speech or writing used as an integral part of conduct in violation of a valid criminal statute."

Fourth.   The value of permitting live performances and photographic reproductions of children engaged in lewd sexual conduct is exceedingly modest, if not de minimis. We consider it unlikely that visual depictions of children performing sexual acts or lewdly exhibiting their genitals would often constitute an important and necessary part of a literary performance or scientific or educational work. [If] it were necessary for literary or artistic value, a person over the statutory age who perhaps looked younger could be utilized. . . .

Fifth.   Recognizing and classifying child pornography as a category of material outside the protection of the First Amendment is not incompatible with our earlier decisions. [We have approved] a content-based classification of speech [when] it may be appropriately generalized that within the confines of the given classification, the evil to be restricted so overwhelmingly outweighs the expressive interests, if any, at stake, that no process of case-by-case adjudication is required.

[There] are, of course, limits on the category of child pornography which, like obscenity, is unprotected by the First Amendment. [The] conduct to be prohibited must be adequately defined by the applicable state law, as written or authoritatively construed. Here the nature of the harm to be combated requires that the state offense be limited to works that visually depict sexual conduct by children below a specified age. [The] test for child pornography is separate from the [*Miller*] obscenity standard, [but] may be compared to it for the purpose of clarity. The *Miller* formulation is adjusted in the following respects: A trier of fact need not find that the material appeals to the prurient interest of the average person; it is not required that sexual conduct portrayed be done so in a patently offensive manner; and the material at issue need not be considered as a whole. [The law's] definition of sexual conduct [comports] with the above-stated principles.

[We] hold that [the law] sufficiently describes a category of material the production and distribution of which is not entitled to First Amendment protection. [As] applied to Paul Ferber [the] statute does not violate the First Amendment as applied to the States. [Reversed.]

Justice Brennan, joined by Justice Marshall, concurring in the judgment.

[In] my view application of [the New York law] or any similar statute to depictions of children that in themselves do have serious literary, artistic, scientific, or medical value, would violate the First Amendment. [The] harm to the child [argument] lacks much of its force where the depiction is a serious contribution to art or science.

NOTES

1. Legislative Deference. The majority said it would not "second-guess" the legislative judgment that sexually explicit child pornography harms the child depicted. Yet the Court no longer defers to legislative judgments that advocacy of the violent overthrow of democratic government harms democracy. What accounts for this difference in deference? Is it because the Court shares the legislative judgment about child pornography but does not agree that advocacy of violent political change poses harm to society? Is that an adequate reason? Is the relevant difference between *Ferber* and *Gitlow* that the Court continued in *Ferber* to make its own examination of the reasons for creating a categorical exclusion of child pornography from the First Amendment, while the Court in *Gitlow* did not do so? How much should the Court defer to legislative judgments that entire categories of speech should be exiled from free speech protection?

2. Pornography as Subordination of Women. At about the same time *Ferber* was decided, some people began to argue that adult pornography, overwhelmingly aimed at a market of male heterosexuals, posed unique dangers to women. The argument, most closely associated with Catharine MacKinnon and Andrea Dworkin, is that pornography is a form of sex discrimination, a graphic method of subordinating women. It "eroticizes dominance and submission [and] makes hierarchy sexy." MacKinnon, Pornography, Civil Rights, and Speech, 20 Harv. C.R.-C.L. L. Rev. 1 (1985). "Pornography [is a] system of sexual exploitation that hurts women as a class by creating inequality and abuse." Dworkin, Against the Male Flood: Censorship, Pornography, and Equality, 8 Harv. Women's L.J. 1 (1985). The MacKinnon-Dworkin view was adopted in an Indianapolis city ordinance that was struck down by a federal district judge, whose order was affirmed by the Court of Appeals for the Seventh Circuit in the following case. The Supreme Court summarily affirmed.

≡ *American Booksellers Association v. Hudnut*
≡ *771 F.2d 323 (7th Cir. 1985), aff'd mem., 475 U.S. 1001 (1986)*

Easterbrook, Circuit Judge.

Indianapolis enacted an ordinance defining "pornography" as a practice that discriminates against women. [The] City's definition of "pornography" is considerably different from "obscenity," which [is] not protected by the First Amendment.

"Pornography" under the ordinance is "the graphic sexually explicit subordination of women, whether in pictures or in words, that also includes one or more of the following: (1) Women are presented as sexual objects who enjoy pain or humiliation; or (2) Women are presented as sexual objects who experience sexual pleasure in being raped; or (3) Women are presented as sexual objects tied up or cut up or mutilated or bruised or physically hurt, or as dismembered or truncated or fragmented or severed into body parts; or (4) Women are presented as being penetrated by objects or animals; or (5) Women are presented in scenarios of degradation, injury abasement, torture, shown as filthy or inferior, bleeding, bruised, or hurt in a context that makes these conditions sexual; or (6) Women are presented as sexual objects for domination, conquest, violation, exploitation, possession, or use, or through postures or positions of servility or submission or display." The statute provides that the "use of men, children, or transsexuals in the place of women [shall] also constitute pornography under this section." [The ordinance, as later amended, did not define the term "sexually explicit."]

The Indianapolis ordinance does not refer to the [*Miller* test of prurient interest], offensiveness, or to the standards of the community. It demands attention to particular depictions, not to the work judged as a whole. It is irrelevant under the ordinance whether the work has literary, artistic, political, or scientific value. The City and many amici point to these omissions as virtues. They maintain that pornography influences attitudes, and the statute is a way to alter the socialization of men and women rather than to vindicate community standards of offensiveness. And as one of the principal drafters of the ordinance has asserted, "if a woman is subjected, why should it matter that the work has other value?" [MacKinnon, 20 Harv. C.R.-C.L. L. Rev. 1, 21.] [Those] supporting the ordinance say that it will play an important role in reducing the tendency of men to view women as sexual objects, a tendency that leads to both unacceptable attitudes and discrimination in the workplace and violence away from it. Those opposing the ordinance point out that much radical feminist literature is explicit and depicts women in ways forbidden by the [ordinance]. It is unclear how Indianapolis would treat works from James Joyce's Ulysses to Homer's Iliad; both depict women as submissive objects for conquest and domination.

We do not try to balance [these arguments]. The ordinance discriminates on the ground of the content of the speech. Speech treating women in the approved way—in sexual encounters "premised on equality"—is lawful no matter how sexually explicit. Speech treating women in the disapproved way—as submissive in matters sexual or as enjoying humiliation—is unlawful no matter how significant the literary, artistic, or political qualities of the work taken as a whole. The state may not ordain preferred viewpoints in this way. The Constitution forbids the state to declare one perspective right and silence opponents.

"If there is any fixed star in our constitutional constellation, it is that no official [can] prescribe what shall be orthodox [in] matters of opinion." [Under] the First Amendment the government must leave to the people the evaluation of ideas. Bald or subtle, an idea is as powerful as the audience allows it to be. A belief may be pernicious—the beliefs of Nazis led to the death of millions, those of the Klan to the repression of millions. A pernicious belief may prevail. Totalitarian governments today rule much of the planet, practicing suppression of billions and spreading dogma that may enslave others. One of the things that separates our society from theirs is our absolute right to propagate opinions that the government finds wrong or even hateful. The ideas of the Klan may be propagated. Communists may speak freely and run for office. The Nazi Party may march through a city with a large Jewish population. [People] may seek to repeal laws guaranteeing equal opportunity in employment or to revoke the constitutional amendments granting the vote to blacks and women. They may do this because "above all else, the First Amendment means that government has no power to restrict expression because of its message [or] its ideas."

Under the ordinance graphic sexually explicit speech is "pornography" or not depending on the perspective the author adopts. Speech that "subordinates" women [or] even simply presents women in "positions of servility or submission or display" is forbidden, no matter how great the literary or political value of the work taken as a whole. Speech that portrays women in positions of equality is lawful, no matter how graphic the sexual content. This is thought control. It establishes an "approved" view of women, of how they may react to sexual encounters, of how the sexes may relate to each other. Those who espouse the approved view may use sexual images; those who do not, may not.

Indianapolis justifies the ordinance on the ground that pornography affects thoughts. Men who see women depicted as subordinate are more likely to treat them so. Pornography is an aspect of dominance. It does not persuade people so much as change them. It works by socializing, by establishing the expected and the permissible. In this view pornography is not an idea; pornography is the injury. There is much to this perspective. Beliefs are also facts. People often act in accordance with the images and patterns they find around them. . . . Words and images act at the level of the subconscious before they persuade at the level of the conscious.

Therefore we accept the premises of this legislation. Depictions of subordination tend to perpetuate subordination. The subordinate status of women in turn leads to affront and lower pay at work, insult and injury at home, battery and rape on the streets. In the language of the legislature, "pornography is central in creating and maintaining sex as a basis of discrimination. Pornography is a systematic practice of exploitation and subordination based on sex which differentially harms women. The bigotry and contempt it produces, with the acts of aggression it fosters, harm women's opportunities for equality and rights [of all kinds]." [We] mean only that there is evidence to this effect, that this evidence is consistent with much human experience, and that as judges we must accept the legislative resolution of such disputed empirical questions.

Yet this simply demonstrates the power of pornography as speech. All of these unhappy effects depend on mental intermediation. Pornography affects how people see the world, their fellows, and social relations. If pornography is what pornography does, so is other speech. Hitler's orations affected how some Germans saw Jews. Communism is a world view, not simply a Manifesto by Marx and Engels or a set of speeches. Religions affect socialization in the most pervasive way, [by dominating] an entire approach to life, governing much more than the relation between the sexes. Many people believe that the existence of television, apart from the content of specific programs, leads to intellectual laziness, to a penchant for violence, to many other ills. [Racial] bigotry, anti-semitism, violence on television, reporters' biases—these and many more influence the culture and shape our socialization. None is directly answerable by more speech, unless that speech too finds its place in the popular culture. Yet all is protected as speech, however insidious. Any other answer leaves the government in control of all of the institutions of culture, the great censor and director of which thoughts are good for us. Sexual responses often are unthinking responses, and the association of sexual arousal with the subordination of women therefore may have a substantial effect. But almost all cultural stimuli provoke unconscious responses. Religious ceremonies condition their participants. Teachers convey messages by selecting what not to [cover]. If the fact that speech plays a role in a process of conditioning were enough to permit governmental regulation, that would be the end of freedom of speech. . . .

Much of Indianapolis's argument rests on the belief that when speech is "unanswerable," and the metaphor that there is a "marketplace of ideas" does not apply, the First Amendment does not apply either. [A] power to limit speech on the ground that truth has not yet prevailed and is not likely to prevail implies the power to declare truth. . . . Under the First Amendment, however, there is no such thing as a false idea, so the government may not restrict speech on the ground that in a free exchange truth is not yet dominant. . . .

[We] come, finally, to the argument that pornography is "low value" speech, that it is enough like obscenity that Indianapolis may prohibit it. Some cases hold that speech far removed from politics and other subjects at the core of the Framers' concerns may be subjected to special regulation. [But these] cases do not sustain statutes that select among viewpoints; [thus], "pornography" is not low value speech within the meaning of these cases. . . . Indianapolis has created an approved point of view and so loses the support of these cases. [The] definition of "pornography" is unconstitutional. [Affirmed.]

NOTE

Reconciling *Ferber* and *Hudnut*. What, if anything, justifies the different outcomes of *Ferber* and *Hudnut*? Is the collateral harm of child pornography substantially greater than that of adult pornography? Was the New York statute at issue in *Ferber* content-based but viewpoint-neutral and the Indianapolis ordinance content- and viewpoint-based? If so, is this because the New York statute was aimed at preventing harm extrinsic to the message of the pornography, while the Indianapolis ordinance conceived of the harm as the message conveyed by pornography? The Canadian Supreme Court, in Regina v. Butler, [1992] 1 S.C.R. 452, held that prohibition of material depicting "women [in] positions of subordination, servile submission, or humiliation" was a justified infringement of the free expression guarantee contained in Canada's Charter of Rights and Freedoms because such material "is harmful to society, particularly women."

≡ **Ashcroft v. The Free Speech Coalition**
≡ *535 U.S. 234 (2002)*

JUSTICE KENNEDY delivered the opinion of the Court.

[The] Child Pornography Prevention Act of 1996 (CPPA) . . . extends the federal prohibition against child pornography to sexually explicit images that appear to depict minors but were produced without using any real children. The statute prohibits, in specific circumstances, possessing or distributing these images, which may be created by using adults who look like minors or by using computer imaging. The new technology . . . makes it possible to create realistic images of children who do not exist. . . .

The principal question to be resolved . . . is whether the CPPA is constitutional where it proscribes a significant universe of speech that is neither obscene under *Miller* nor child pornography under *Ferber*.

I. Before 1996, Congress defined child pornography as the type of depictions at issue in *Ferber*, images made using actual minors. The CPPA retains that prohibition [and adds §2256(8)(B), which] prohibits "any visual depiction, including any photograph, film, video, picture, or computer or computer-generated image or picture" that "is, or appears to be, of a minor engaging in sexually explicit conduct." The prohibition on "any visual depiction" . . . captures a range of depictions, sometimes called "virtual child pornography," which include computer-generated images, as well as images produced by more traditional means. . . .

[Free Speech Coalition], a California trade association for the adult entertainment industry, [together with a publisher, a painter, and a photographer, challenged the facial validity of these provisions. A federal district court] granted summary judgment to the Government [and, on appeal, the] Court of Appeals for the Ninth Circuit reversed, [finding] the CPPA invalid on its face. We granted certiorari.

II. [A] law imposing criminal penalties on protected speech is a stark example of speech suppression. The CPPA's penalties are indeed severe. A first offender may be imprisoned for 15 years [and a] repeat offender faces a prison sentence of [5 to] 30 years in prison. [This] case provides a textbook example of why we permit facial challenges to statutes that burden expression. With these severe penalties in force, few legitimate movie producers or book publishers, or few other speakers in any capacity, would risk distributing images in or near the uncertain reach of this law. The Constitution gives significant protection from overbroad laws that chill [constitutionally protected] speech; . . . the CPPA is unconstitutional on its face if it prohibits a substantial amount of protected expression. [Broadrick v. Oklahoma, excerpted in Section E.1, infra.]

. . . The CPPA . . . prohibits speech despite its serious literary, artistic, political, or scientific value. The statute proscribes the visual depiction of an idea—that of teenagers engaging in sexual activity—that is a fact of modern society and has been a theme in art and literature throughout the ages. Under the CPPA, images are prohibited so long as the persons appear to be under 18 years of age. . . . [T]eenage sexual activity and the sexual abuse of children have inspired countless literary works. William Shakespeare created the most famous pair of teenage lovers, one of whom is just 13 years of age. See Romeo and Juliet, act I, sc. 2, 1.9 ("She hath not seen the change of fourteen years"). . . . Last year's Academy Awards featured the movie, Traffic, which was nominated for Best Picture, [and which] portrays a teenager, identified as a 16-year-old, who becomes addicted to drugs. The viewer sees the degradation of her addiction, which in the end leads her to a filthy room to trade sex for drugs. The year before, American Beauty won the Academy Award for Best Picture. In the course of the movie, a teenage girl engages in sexual relations with her teenage boyfriend, and another yields herself to the gratification of a middle-aged man. . . .

The Government [argues] that speech prohibited by the CPPA is virtually indistinguishable from child pornography, which may be banned without regard to whether it depicts works of value. [*Ferber.*] Where the images are themselves the product of child sexual abuse, *Ferber* recognized that the State had an interest in stamping it out without regard to any judgment about its content. The production of the work, not its content, was the target of the statute. . . . In contrast to the speech in *Ferber*, . . . the CPPA prohibits speech that records no crime and creates no victims by its production. Virtual child pornography is not "intrinsically related" to the sexual abuse of children, as were the materials in *Ferber*. While the Government asserts that the images can lead to actual instances of child abuse, the causal link is contingent and indirect. The harm does not necessarily follow from the speech, but depends upon some unquantified potential for subsequent criminal acts.

III. . . . The Government . . . says that the possibility of producing images by using computer imaging makes it very difficult for it to prosecute those who produce pornography by using real children. Experts, we are told, may have difficulty in saying whether the pictures were made by using real children or by using computer imaging. The necessary solution, the argument runs, is to prohibit both kinds of images. The argument, in essence, is that protected speech may be banned as a means to ban unprotected speech. This analysis turns the First Amendment upside down. The Government may not suppress lawful speech as the means to suppress unlawful speech. Protected speech does not become unprotected merely because it resembles the latter. The Constitution requires the reverse. . . . The overbreadth doctrine prohibits the Government from banning unprotected speech if a substantial amount of protected speech is prohibited or chilled in the process. . . .

In sum, §2256(8)(B) covers materials beyond the categories recognized in *Ferber* and *Miller*, and the reasons the Government offers in support of limiting the freedom of speech have no justification. . . . The provision abridges the freedom to engage in a substantial amount of lawful speech [and] is overbroad and unconstitutional. . . . [Affirmed.]

PROBLEMS

1. Problem: Altered Images I.   Suppose a video of a real child engaged in innocent, nonsexual activity is altered by computer technology to depict that child engaged in sexual activity. Is this constitutionally protected? Would it be within the scope of the statute as construed by the dissent? Does it make a difference if the child in the computer-altered video can be identified as a real person?

2. Problem: Altered Images II.   Suppose a video of real adults engaged in real sexual activity is altered by computer technology to depict the actors as children. Is this constitutionally protected? Would it be within the scope of the statute as construed by the dissent?

c.   Analogs: Depictions of Cruelty and Violence

Miller confined obscenity to "works which depict or describe sexual conduct." Why? "Obscene" is defined as "offensive to taste; foul; loathsome; disgusting." Webster's New International Dictionary (2d ed. 1944). Suppose that Congress enacted a law banning depictions of unlawful animal cruelty, with an exception for depictions that are of serious literary, artistic, political, or scientific value? Or, suppose that a state enacted a statute that specifically defined depictions of violent conduct and then prohibited any such depictions when (1) the average person, applying contemporary community standards, would find that the depiction, taken as a whole, (a) appeals to the morbid interest and (b) depicts in a patently offensive way the defined violent conduct; and (2) the reasonable person would conclude that the work, taken a whole, lacks serious literary, artistic, political, or scientific value. The question of whether these analogs to obscenity can be categorically proscribed is central to the following cases.

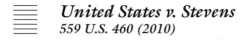

United States v. Stevens
559 U.S. 460 (2010)

CHIEF JUSTICE ROBERTS delivered the opinion of the Court.

Congress enacted 18 U.S.C. §48 to criminalize the commercial creation, sale, or possession of certain depictions of animal cruelty. The statute does not address underlying acts harmful to animals, but only portrayals of such conduct. The question presented is whether the prohibition in the statute is consistent with the freedom of speech guaranteed by the First Amendment.

I. Section 48 establishes a criminal penalty of up to five years in prison for anyone who knowingly "creates, sells, or possesses a depiction of animal cruelty," if done "for commercial gain" in interstate or foreign commerce. A depiction of "animal cruelty" is defined as one "in which a living animal is intentionally maimed, mutilated, tortured, wounded, or killed," if that conduct violates federal or state law where "the creation, sale, or possession takes place." In . . . the "exceptions clause," the law exempts from prohibition any depiction "that has serious religious, political, scientific, educational, journalistic, historical, or artistic value."

[Congress enacted §48 to eradicate the interstate market for "crush videos," which] feature the intentional torture and killing of helpless animals, including cats, dogs, monkeys, mice, and hamsters. Crush videos often depict women slowly crushing animals to death "with their bare feet or while wearing high heeled shoes," sometimes while "talking to the animals in a kind of dominatrix patter" over "[t]he cries and squeals of the animals, obviously in great pain." Apparently these depictions "appeal to persons with a very specific sexual fetish who find them sexually arousing or otherwise exciting." The acts depicted in crush videos are typically prohibited by the animal cruelty laws enacted by all 50 States and the District of Columbia. . . .

This case, however, involves an application of §48 to depictions of animal fighting. Dogfighting, for example, is unlawful in all 50 States and the District of Columbia . . . and has been restricted by federal law since 1976. Respondent Robert J. Stevens ran a business through which he sold videos of pit bulls engaging in dogfights and attacking other animals. Among these videos were [one showing] contemporary footage of dogfights in Japan (where such conduct is allegedly legal) [and a second one] of American dogfights from the 1960s and 1970s. A third video . . . depicts the use of pit bulls to hunt wild boar, as well as a "gruesome" scene of a pit bull attacking a domestic farm pig. On the basis of these videos, Stevens was indicted on three counts of violating §48.

[A] jury convicted Stevens on all counts, and the District Court sentenced him to . . . 37 months' imprisonment, followed by three years of supervised release.

The en banc Third Circuit . . . declared §48 facially unconstitutional and vacated Stevens's conviction. . . . We granted certiorari.

II. The Government's primary submission is that §48 necessarily complies with the Constitution because the banned depictions of animal cruelty, as a class, are categorically unprotected by the First Amendment. We disagree. . . .

[T]he prohibition of animal cruelty itself has a long history in American law, starting with the early settlement of the Colonies. But we are unaware of any similar tradition excluding *depictions* of animal cruelty from "the freedom of speech" codified in the First Amendment, and the Government points us to none. The Government contends that "historical evidence" about the reach of the First Amendment is not "a necessary prerequisite for regulation today," and that categories of speech may be exempted from the First Amendment's protection without any long-settled tradition of subjecting that speech to regulation. Instead, the Government points to Congress's "'legislative judgment that . . . depictions of animals being intentionally tortured and killed [are] of such minimal redeeming value as to render [them] unworthy of First Amendment protection,'" and . . . proposes that a claim of categorical exclusion should be considered under a simple balancing test: "Whether a given category of speech enjoys First Amendment protection depends upon a categorical balancing of the value of the speech against its societal costs."

As a free-floating test for First Amendment coverage, that sentence is startling and dangerous. The First Amendment's guarantee of free speech does not extend only to categories of speech that survive an ad hoc balancing of relative social costs and benefits. The First Amendment itself reflects a judgment by the American people that the benefits of its restrictions on the Government outweigh the costs. Our Constitution forecloses any attempt to revise that judgment simply on the basis that some speech is not worth it. . . .

As the Government correctly notes, this Court has often *described* historically unprotected categories of speech as being "of such slight social value as a step to truth that any benefit that may be derived from them is clearly outweighed by the social interest in order and morality." [*Chaplinsky.*] But such descriptions . . . do not set forth a test that may be applied as a general matter to permit the Government to imprison any speaker so long as his speech is deemed valueless or unnecessary, or so long as an ad hoc calculus of costs and benefits tilts in a statute's favor.

When we have identified categories of speech as fully outside the protection of the First Amendment, it has not been on the basis of a simple cost-benefit analysis. In *Ferber*, for example, [when] we classified child pornography as such a category, [w]e noted that the State of New York had a compelling interest in protecting children from abuse, and that the value of using children in these works (as opposed to simulated conduct or adult actors) was *de minimis.* . . . We made clear that *Ferber* presented a special case: The market for child pornography was "intrinsically related" to the underlying abuse, and was therefore "an integral part of the production of such materials, an activity illegal throughout the Nation." . . .

Our decisions in *Ferber* and other cases cannot be taken as establishing a freewheeling authority to declare new categories of speech outside the scope of the First Amendment. Maybe there are some categories of speech that have been historically unprotected, but have not yet been specifically identified or discussed as such in our case law. But if so, there is no evidence that "depictions of animal cruelty" is among them. We need not foreclose the future recognition of such additional categories to reject the Government's highly manipulable balancing test as a means of identifying them.

[The Court then concluded that the law was facially invalid. The law was "of alarming breadth" because it applied to any killing of an animal, no matter the reason, if the killing is illegal in the jurisdiction where the depiction is possessed. That meant that hunting videos would be included because hunting, while legal in all states, is illegal in the District of Columbia. The exceptions clause did not sufficiently limit the law's potential application to so-called crush videos, as the Government argued the law should be construed. Thus, §48 was found to be substantially overbroad and void on its face.]

NOTES AND QUESTIONS

1. History as the Guide to Categorically Excluded Speech. The majority says that the categories of speech that do not receive First Amendment protection are those that have been "historically unprotected." Note that several of the historically unprotected categories of speech in 1791 now receive either complete or limited constitutional protection. Blasphemy, for example, was unprotected in 1791 but is surely protected now. Defamation, vulgarity, and commercial speech, each unprotected in 1791, now receive limited protection. Obscenity, while still unprotected, is defined more narrowly than would have been the case in 1791. Much pornography that is protected today would have been unprotected in 1791. Does this suggest that a historically based approach to categorical exclusion is a one-way street, permitting extension of protection to historically unprotected categories but restricting the creation of new unprotected categories? Perhaps a tradition of no protection is a necessary but insufficient condition for denying protection to a category of speech.

2. Speech Integral to Criminal Conduct. The majority says that there has not been any historical protection for "speech integral to criminal conduct." What is included within the category of speech that is integral to criminal conduct? Are any of the following forms of speech exiled from First Amendment protection under this category? Should they be so exiled?

a. A book that details specifically how to commit murder for hire. See Rice v. Paladin Enterprises, 128 F.3d 233 (4th Cir. 1997).

b. A physician advises his patient to use marijuana, although such use is illegal. See, e.g., Pearson v. McCaffrey, 139 F. Supp. 2d 113, 121 (D.D.C. 2001). But see Conant v. Walters, 309 F.3d 629, 637-638 (9th Cir. 2002).

c. Employees of a business use racially and sexually offensive words to create a hostile work environment. See, e.g., Jarman v. City of Northlake, 950 F. Supp. 1375, 1379 (N.D. Ill. 1997); Robinson v. Jacksonville Shipyards, Inc., 760 F. Supp. 1486, 1535 (M.D. Fla. 1991).

For more on this topic, see Greenawalt, Speech, Crime, and the Uses of Language (1989); Volokh, Speech as Conduct: Generally Applicable Laws, Course of Conduct, "Situation-Altering Utterances," and the Uncharted Zones, 90 Cornell L. Rev. 1277 (2005).

≡≡≡ *Brown v. Entertainment Merchants Association*
≡≡ *131 S. Ct. 2729 (2011)*

JUSTICE SCALIA delivered the opinion of the Court.

We consider whether a California law imposing restrictions on violent video games comports with the First Amendment.

I. California [law] prohibits the sale or rental of "violent video games" to minors. . . . The Act covers games "in which the range of options available to a player includes killing, maiming, dismembering, or sexually assaulting an image of a human being, if those acts are depicted" in a manner that "[a] reasonable person, considering the game as a whole, would find appeals to a deviant or morbid interest of minors," that is "patently offensive to prevailing standards in the community as to what is suitable for minors," and that "causes the game, as a whole, to lack serious literary, artistic, political, or scientific value for minors." Violation of the Act is punishable by a civil fine of up to $1,000.

Respondents, representing the video-game and software industries, brought a pre-enforcement challenge to the Act in the United States District Court for the Northern District of California. That court concluded that the Act violated the First Amendment and permanently enjoined its enforcement. The Court of Appeals affirmed, and we granted certiorari.

II. California correctly acknowledges that video games qualify for First Amendment protection. . . . Like the protected books, plays, and movies that preceded them, video games communicate ideas—and even social messages—through many familiar literary devices (such as characters, dialogue, plot, and music) and through features distinctive to the medium (such as the player's interaction with the virtual world). That suffices to confer First Amendment protection. . . .

[*Stevens*] controls this case. As in *Stevens*, California has tried to make violent-speech regulation look like obscenity regulation by appending a saving clause required for the latter. That does not suffice. Our cases have been clear that the obscenity exception to the First Amendment does not cover whatever a legislature finds shocking, but only depictions of "sexual conduct." . . .

The California Act . . . does not adjust the boundaries of an existing category of unprotected speech to ensure that a definition designed for adults is not uncritically applied to children. California . . . wishes to create a wholly new category of content-based regulation that is permissible only for speech directed at children. That is unprecedented and mistaken. . . . No doubt a State possesses legitimate power to protect children from harm, but that does not include a free-floating power to restrict the ideas to which children may be exposed. . . .

California's argument would fare better if there were a longstanding tradition in this country of specially restricting children's access to depictions of violence, but there is none. Certainly the *books* we give children to read—or read to them when they are younger—contain no shortage of gore. Grimm's Fairy Tales, for example, are grim indeed. As her just deserts for trying to poison Snow White, the wicked queen is made to dance in red hot slippers "till she fell dead on the floor, a sad example of envy and jealousy." The Complete Brothers Grimm Fairy Tales 198 (2006 ed.). Cinderella's evil stepsisters have their eyes pecked out by doves. *Id.*, at 95. And Hansel and Gretel (children!) kill their captor by baking her in an oven. *Id.*, at 54.

High-school reading lists are full of similar fare. Homer's Odysseus blinds Polyphemus the Cyclops by grinding out his eye with a heated stake. The

Odyssey of Homer, Book IX, p. 125 (S. Butcher & A. Lang transls. 1909) ("Even so did we seize the fiery-pointed brand and whirled it round in his eye, and the blood flowed about the heated bar. And the breath of the flame singed his eyelids and brows all about, as the ball of the eye burnt away, and the roots thereof crackled in the flame"). In the Inferno, Dante and Virgil watch corrupt politicians struggle to stay submerged beneath a lake of boiling pitch, lest they be skewered by devils above the surface. Canto XXI, pp. 187-189 (A. Mandelbaum transl. Bantam Classic ed. 1982). And Golding's Lord of the Flies recounts how a schoolboy called Piggy is savagely murdered *by other children* while marooned on an island. W. Golding, Lord of the Flies 208-209 (1997 ed.). . . .

California claims that video games present special problems because they are "interactive," in that the player participates in the violent action on screen and determines its outcome. . . . As Judge Posner has observed, all literature is interactive. "[T]he better it is, the more interactive. Literature when it is successful draws the reader into the story, makes him identify with the characters, invites him to judge them and quarrel with them, to experience their joys and sufferings as the reader's own." American Amusement Machine Assn. v. Kendrick, 244 F.3d 572, 577 (CA7 2001) (striking down a similar restriction on violent video games).

Justice Alito has done considerable independent research to identify video games in which "the violence is astounding. Victims are dismembered, decapitated, disemboweled, set on fire, and chopped into little pieces. . . . Blood gushes, splatters, and pools." Justice Alito recounts all these disgusting video games in order to disgust us—but disgust is not a valid basis for restricting expression. And the same is true of Justice Alito's description of those video games he has discovered that have a racial or ethnic motive for their violence—"'ethnic cleansing' [of] . . . African Americans, Latinos, or Jews." [I]ronically, Justice Alito's argument highlights the precise danger posed by the California Act: that the *ideas* expressed by speech—whether it be violence, or gore, or racism—and not its objective effects, may be the real reason for governmental proscription.

III. Because the Act imposes a restriction on the content of protected speech, it is invalid unless California can demonstrate that it passes strict scrutiny—that is, unless it is justified by a compelling government interest and is narrowly drawn to serve that interest. The State must specifically identify an "actual problem" in need of solving, and the curtailment of free speech must be actually necessary to the solution. . . .

California cannot meet that standard. At the outset, it acknowledges that it cannot show a direct causal link between violent video games and harm to minors. . . . The State's evidence is not compelling. California relies primarily on the research of . . . a few . . . research psychologists whose studies purport to show a connection between exposure to violent video games and harmful effects on children. These studies have been rejected by every court to consider them, and with good reason: They do not prove that violent video games *cause* minors to *act* aggressively (which would at least be a beginning).

Instead, [they] show at best some correlation between exposure to violent entertainment and minuscule real-world effects, such as children's feeling more aggressive or making louder noises in the few minutes after playing a violent game than after playing a nonviolent game.

[California's expert psychologist] admitted that the . . . *same* effects have been found when children watch cartoons starring Bugs Bunny or the Road Runner. . . . The consequence is that its regulation is wildly underinclusive when judged against its asserted justification, which in our view is alone enough to defeat it. Underinclusiveness raises serious doubts about whether the government is in fact pursuing the interest it invokes, rather than disfavoring a particular speaker or viewpoint. Here, California has singled out the purveyors of video games for disfavored treatment—at least when compared to booksellers, cartoonists, and movie producers—and has given no persuasive reason why.

The Act is also seriously underinclusive in another respect. . . . The California Legislature is perfectly willing to leave this dangerous, mind-altering material in the hands of children so long as one parent (or even an aunt or uncle) says it's OK. And there are not even any requirements as to how this parental or avuncular relationship is to be verified; apparently the child's or putative parent's, aunt's, or uncle's say-so suffices. That is not how one addresses a serious social problem. . . .

And finally, the Act's purported aid to parental authority is vastly overinclusive. Not all of the children who are forbidden to purchase violent video games on their own have parents who *care* whether they purchase violent video games. While some of the legislation's effect may indeed be in support of what some parents of the restricted children actually want, its entire effect is only in support of what the State thinks parents *ought* to want. This is not the narrow tailoring to "assisting parents" that restriction of First Amendment rights requires. . . .

We affirm the judgment below.

JUSTICE ALITO, with whom THE CHIEF JUSTICE joins, concurring in the judgment.

. . . Although the California statute is well intentioned, its terms are not framed with the precision that the Constitution demands, and I therefore agree with the Court that this particular law cannot be sustained [because it is vague].

I disagree, however, with the approach taken in the Court's opinion. . . . [The] Court is far too quick to dismiss the possibility that the experience of playing video games (and the effects on minors of playing violent video games) may be very different from anything that we have seen before. . . . Today's most advanced video games create realistic alternative worlds in which millions of players immerse themselves for hours on end. These games feature visual imagery and sounds that are strikingly realistic, and in the near future video-game graphics may be virtually indistinguishable from actual video footage. Many of the games already on the market can produce high definition images, and it is predicted that it will not be long before video-game images will be seen in three dimensions. It is also forecast that video games will soon provide sensory feedback. By wearing a special vest or other device, a player will be able to experience physical sensations supposedly felt by a character on the screen. Some *amici* who support respondents foresee the day when " 'virtual-reality shoot-'em-ups' " will allow children to " 'actually feel the splatting blood from the blown-off head' " of a victim.

Persons who play video games also have an unprecedented ability to participate in the events that take place in the virtual worlds that these games create. Players can create their own video-game characters and can use photos to produce characters that closely resemble actual people. . . . [T]he means by which players control the action in video games now bear a closer relationship to the means by which people control action in the real world. . . . For example, a player who wants a video-game character to swing a baseball bat—either to hit a ball or smash a skull—could bring that about by simulating the motion of actually swinging a bat.

These present-day and emerging characteristics of video games must be considered together with characteristics of the violent games that have already been marketed. In some of these games, the violence is astounding. Victims by the dozens are killed with every imaginable implement, including machine guns, shotguns, clubs, hammers, axes, swords, and chainsaws. Victims are dismembered, decapitated, disemboweled, set on fire, and chopped into little pieces. They cry out in agony and beg for mercy. Blood gushes, splatters, and pools. Severed body parts and gobs of human remains are graphically shown. In some games, points are awarded based, not only on the number of victims killed, but on the killing technique employed. It also appears that there is no antisocial theme too base for some in the video-game industry to exploit. There are games in which a player can take on the identity and reenact the killings carried out by the perpetrators of the murders at Columbine High School and Virginia Tech. The objective of one game is to rape a mother and her daughters; in another, the goal is to rape Native American women. There is a game in which players engage in "ethnic cleansing" and can choose to gun down African-Americans, Latinos, or Jews. In still another game, players attempt to fire a rifle shot into the head of President Kennedy as his motorcade passes by the Texas School Book Depository.

If the technological characteristics of the sophisticated games that are likely to be available in the near future are combined with the characteristics of the most violent games already marketed, the result will be games that allow troubled teens to experience in an extraordinarily personal and vivid way what it would be like to carry out unspeakable acts of violence.

The Court is untroubled by this possibility. According to the Court, the "interactive" nature of video games is "nothing new" because "all literature is interactive." . . . But only an extraordinarily imaginative reader who reads a description of a killing in a literary work will experience that event as vividly as he might if he played the role of the killer in a video game. To take an example, think of a person who reads the passage in Crime and Punishment in which Raskolnikov kills the old pawn broker with an axe. See F. Dostoyevsky, Crime and Punishment 78 (Modern Library ed. 1950). Compare that reader with a video-game player who creates an avatar that bears his own image; who sees a realistic image of the victim and the scene of the killing in high definition and in three dimensions; who is forced to decide whether or not to kill the victim and decides to do so; who then pretends to grasp an axe, to raise it above the head of the victim, and then to bring it down; who hears the thud of the axe hitting her head and her cry of pain; who sees her split skull and feels the sensation of blood on his face and hands. For most people, the two experiences will not be the same.

When all of the characteristics of video games are taken into account, there is certainly a reasonable basis for thinking that the experience of playing a video game may be quite different from the experience of reading a book, listening to a radio broadcast, or viewing a movie. And if this is so, then for at least some minors, the effects of playing violent video games may also be quite different. The Court acts prematurely in dismissing this possibility out of hand. . . .

JUSTICE THOMAS, dissenting.

The Court's decision today does not comport with the original public understanding of the First Amendment. . . . The practices and beliefs of the founding generation establish that "the freedom of speech," as originally understood, does not include a right to speak to minors (or a right of minors to access speech) without going through the minors' parents or guardians. I would hold that the law at issue is not facially unconstitutional under the First Amendment, and reverse and remand for further proceedings. . . .

The historical evidence shows that the founding generation believed parents had absolute authority over their minor children and expected parents to use that authority to direct the proper development of their children. . . . In light of this history, the Framers could not possibly have understood "the freedom of speech" to include an unqualified right to speak to minors . . . without going through their parents. As a consequence, I do not believe that laws limiting such speech—for example, by requiring parental consent to speak to a minor—"abridg[e] the freedom of speech" within the original meaning of the First Amendment. . . .

I respectfully dissent.

JUSTICE BREYER, dissenting.

. . . California's statute provides "fair notice of what is prohibited," and consequently it is not impermissibly vague. . . .

California's law imposes no more than a modest restriction on expression. The statute prevents no one from playing a video game, it prevents no adult from buying a video game, and it prevents no child or adolescent from obtaining a game provided a parent is willing to help. All it prevents is a child or adolescent from buying, without a parent's assistance, a gruesomely violent video game of a kind that the industry *itself* tells us it wants to keep out of the hands of those under the age of 17. Nor is the statute, if upheld, likely to create a precedent that would adversely affect other media, say films, or videos, or books. . . .

The interest that California advances in support of the statute is compelling. [It] consists of both (1) the "basic" parental claim "to authority in their own household to direct the rearing of their children," which makes it proper to enact "laws designed to aid discharge of [parental] responsibility," and (2) the State's "independent interest in the well-being of its youth." . . . And where these interests work in tandem, it is not fatally "underinclusive" for a State to advance its interests in protecting children against the special harms present in an interactive video game medium through a default rule that still allows parents to provide their children with what their parents wish. . . .

At the same time, there is considerable evidence that California's statute significantly furthers this compelling interest. . . . Video games can help develop habits, accustom the player to performance of the task, and reward the player for performing that task well. Why else would the Armed Forces incorporate video games into its training? . . .

California argues that . . . extremely violent games can harm children by rewarding them for being violently aggressive in play, and thereby often teaching them to be violently aggressive in life. . . . There are many scientific studies that support California's views. . . . Experts debate the conclusions of all these studies. . . . I, like most judges, lack the social science expertise to say definitively who is right. . . . Unlike the majority, I would find sufficient grounds in these studies and expert opinions for this Court to defer to an elected legislature's conclusion that the video games in question are particularly likely to harm children. . . .

4.   Fighting Words

Chaplinsky v. New Hampshire
315 U.S. 568 (1942)

JUSTICE MURPHY delivered the opinion of the Court.

[Chaplinsky was convicted in state court for violation of this New Hampshire law]: "No person shall address any offensive, derisive or annoying word to any other person who is lawfully in any street or other public place, nor call him by any offensive or derisive name." [The New Hampshire Supreme Court, in affirming the conviction, construed the statute to prohibit only] "words likely to cause an average addressee to fight. [These] 'fighting words' [are] face-to-face words plainly likely to cause a breach of the peace by the addressee, words whose speaking constitutes a breach of the peace by the speaker."

There is no substantial dispute over the facts. Chaplinsky, [a Jehovah's Witness], was distributing the literature of his sect on the streets of Rochester on a busy Saturday afternoon. Members of the local citizenry complained to the City Marshal, Bowering, that Chaplinsky was denouncing all religion as a "racket." Bowering told them that Chaplinsky was lawfully engaged, and then warned Chaplinsky that the crowd was getting restless. Some time later, a disturbance occurred and the traffic officer on duty at the busy intersection started with Chaplinsky for the police station, but did not inform him that he was under arrest or that he was going to be arrested. On the way, they encountered Marshal Bowering, who had been advised that a riot was under way and was therefore hurrying to the scene. Bowering repeated his earlier warning to Chaplinsky, who then addressed to Bowering the words set forth in the complaint[:] " 'You are a God damned racketeer' and 'a damned Fascist and the whole government of Rochester are Fascists or agents of Fascists.' " Chaplinsky's version of the affair was slightly different. He testified that, when he met Bowering, he asked him to arrest the ones responsible for the disturbance. In reply, Bowering cursed him and told him to come along. Appellant admitted that he said the words charged in the complaint, with the exception of the name of the Deity.

[Chaplinsky] assails the statute as a violation [of] free speech. [It] is well understood that the right of free speech is not [absolute]. There are certain well-defined and narrowly limited classes of speech, the prevention and punishment of which have never been thought to raise any Constitutional problem. These include the lewd and obscene, the profane, the libelous, and the insulting or "fighting" words—those which by their very utterance inflict injury or tend to incite an immediate breach of the peace. It has been well observed that such utterances are no essential part of any exposition of ideas, and are of such slight social value as a step to truth that any benefit that may be derived from them is clearly outweighed by the social interest in order and morality. "Resort to epithets or personal abuse is not in any proper sense communication of information or opinion safeguarded by the [Constitution]." Cantwell v. Connecticut.

[The statute as authoritatively construed defines] and punish[es] specific conduct lying within the domain of state power, the use in a public place of words likely to cause a breach of the peace. [Argument] is unnecessary to demonstrate that the appellations "damned racketeer" and "damned Fascist" are epithets likely to provoke the average person to retaliation, and thereby cause a breach of the peace. [Affirmed.]

NOTES

1. The Scope of "Fighting Words." In a prior case, Cantwell v. Connecticut, 310 U.S. 296 (1940), the Court had overturned Jesse Cantwell's conviction of inciting a breach of the peace. On the public sidewalks, Cantwell, a Jehovah's Witness, had asked and received permission from two men to play a phonograph record that attacked Roman Catholicism. The men, who were Catholics, were sufficiently "incensed" that they "were tempted to strike Cantwell." But Cantwell departed peacefully when told to do so. Although the recording "embodie[d] a general attack on all organized religious systems as instruments of Satan and injurious to man [and] single[d] out the Roman Catholic Church for strictures couched in terms which naturally would offend not only persons of that persuasion, but all others who respect the honestly held religious faith of their fellows," the encounter did not involve any threat of "bodily harm, . . . truculent bearing, . . . intentional discourtesy, [or] personal abuse."

Chaplinsky defined the unprotected category of fighting words as words "which by their very utterance inflict injury or tend to incite an immediate breach of the peace." But in *Cantwell* the Court refused to permit punishment of words that inflicted psychic or emotional injury. *Chaplinsky* was not concerned with words that only "inflict injury"—the Court thought that Chaplinsky's curses were "epithets likely to provoke the average person to retaliation, and thereby cause a breach of the peace." Are words that do no more than inflict emotional injury (but which pose no immediate threat of breach of the peace) excluded from constitutional protection?

2. Subsequent Cases.   Assess the constitutional protection afforded words that inflict injury only to the hearer after considering the following cases.

Gooding v. Wilson, 405 U.S. 518 (1972).   Wilson was convicted under a Georgia law making it a misdemeanor to direct to another person "without [provocation], opprobrious words or abusive language, tending to cause a breach of the peace." Along with other Vietnam War protesters, Wilson had been blocking access to an Army induction center and refused to move. The police started to force them to move, and Wilson said to a police officer: "White son of a bitch, I'll kill you. You son of a bitch, I'll choke you to death." To another policeman, he said: "You son of a bitch, if you ever put your hands on me again, I'll cut you all to pieces." The Court reversed the conviction, finding the Georgia statute overbroad and void on its face. Writing for the Court, Justice Brennan said the statute was overbroad because it was not "limited in application, as in *Chaplinsky*, to words that 'have a direct tendency to cause acts of violence by the person to whom, individually, the remark is addressed.'" Note that while the *statute* was overbroad, in the sense that it punished substantial protected speech as well as unprotected speech, the actual application of the statute to Wilson's speech would be valid. On the overbreadth doctrine, see Section E.1, infra.

In the same term *Gooding* was decided, the Court vacated three convictions for use of offensive and vulgar language, and remanded the cases for reconsideration in light of *Gooding*. In Rosenfeld v. New Jersey, 408 U.S. 901 (1972), Rosenfeld had been convicted of uttering "indecent [and] offensive" language in a public place that was "likely to incite the hearer to an immediate breach of the peace [or] affect the sensibilities of a hearer." During the course of a public school board meeting with perhaps 110 adults and 40 children in attendance, Rosenfeld used various permutations of "mother fucker" to describe the "teachers, the school board, the town, and his own country." In Lewis v. New Orleans, 408 U.S. 913 (1972), Lewis had been convicted of using "obscene or opprobrious language" toward a police officer on duty. While the police were arresting her son, Lewis had cursed them as "god damn mother fuckers." In Brown v. Oklahoma, 408 U.S. 914 (1972), Brown, a Black Panther, had referred to police officers as "mother fucking fascist pig cops" and one particular officer as "that 'black mother fucking pig.'" That resulted in his conviction for uttering "obscene or lascivious language [in] any public place, or in the presence of females."

Finally, in Texas v. Johnson, 491 U.S. 397 (1989), the Court struck down Johnson's conviction for burning an American flag under circumstances he knew would "seriously offend" onlookers. Johnson had torched the flag in the midst of his participation in a strident anti-American rally in Dallas. Texas had argued that Johnson's conduct was unprotected fighting words. In rejecting that argument, Justice Brennan, writing for the Court, declared: "No reasonable onlooker would have regarded Johnson's [political protest by burning the flag] as a direct personal insult or an invitation to exchange fisticuffs."

Do these cases confirm John Ely's view that the category of fighting words is limited to words constituting "a quite unambiguous invitation to a brawl"? See Ely, Democracy and Distrust 114 (1980). If fighting words do or should extend to words that merely "inflict injury," how is the line to be drawn between unprotected words that inflict injury alone and protected words that offend, such as Jesse Cantwell's anti-Catholic recording?

5. Offensive Speech

Speech can offend others for a great many reasons and can thus produce a wide variety of reactions. Listeners can be annoyed, outraged, or moved to violence. The central question is, when, if ever, should speech lose its constitutional protection because it offends the hearer? The "fighting words" doctrine addresses the problem of speech that is likely to provoke violence against the speaker. But what if the speech inflicts deep emotional injury on the listener, though no violence is likely to result? What if the speech does not inflict any injury but simply offends listeners who cannot escape from it?

a. The General Rule

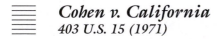

Cohen v. California
403 U.S. 15 (1971)

JUSTICE HARLAN delivered the opinion of the Court.

This case may seem at first blush too inconsequential to find its way into our books, but the issue it presents is of no small constitutional significance. [Paul] Cohen was convicted [of violating a California penal law that] prohibits "maliciously and willfully disturb[ing] the peace or quiet of any neighborhood or person [by] offensive conduct." He was given 30 days' imprisonment. The facts upon which his conviction rests are detailed in the opinion of the [California] Court of Appeal: "On April 26, 1968, the defendant was observed in the Los Angeles County Courthouse in the corridor outside of [the] municipal court wearing a jacket bearing the words 'Fuck the Draft.' [There] were women and children [present]. The defendant was arrested. The defendant testified that he wore the jacket [as] a means of informing the public of the depth of his feelings against the Vietnam War and the draft. The defendant did not engage in, nor threaten to engage in, nor did anyone as the result of his conduct in fact commit or threaten to commit any act of violence." [In] affirming the conviction the Court of Appeal held that "offensive conduct" means "behavior which has a tendency to provoke *others* to acts of violence or to in turn disturb the peace," and that the State had proved this element because, on the facts of this case, "it was certainly reasonably foreseeable that such conduct might cause others to rise up to commit a violent act against the person of the defendant or attempt to [forcibly] remove his jacket." [We] now reverse.

I. In order to lay hands on the precise issue which this case involves, it is useful first to canvass various matters which this record does *not* present. The conviction quite clearly rests upon the asserted offensiveness of the *words* Cohen used to convey his message to the public. The only "conduct" which the State sought to punish is the fact of communication. Thus, we deal here with a conviction resting solely upon "speech." [Further], the State certainly lacks power to punish Cohen for the underlying content of the message the inscription conveyed. At least so long as there is no showing of an intent to incite disobedience to or disruption of the draft, Cohen could not be punished for asserting the evident position on the inutility or immorality of the draft his jacket reflected. [Cohen's] conviction, then, rests squarely upon his exercise of the "freedom of speech" [and] can be justified, if at all, only as a valid regulation of the manner in which he exercised that freedom, not as a permissible prohibition on the substantive message it conveys. This does not end the inquiry, of course, for the [First Amendment has] never been thought to give absolute protection to every individual to speak whenever or wherever he pleases, or to use any form of address in any circumstances that he chooses. [However], we think it important to note that several issues typically associated with such problems are not presented here.

In the first place, [any] attempt to support this conviction on the ground that the statute seeks to preserve an appropriately decorous atmosphere in the courthouse where Cohen was arrested must fail in the absence of any language in the statute that would have put appellant on notice that certain kinds of otherwise permissible speech or conduct would nevertheless [not] be tolerated in certain places. No fair reading of the phrase "offensive conduct" can be said sufficiently to inform the ordinary person that distinctions between certain locations are thereby created.

In the second place, [this] case cannot be said to fall within those relatively few categories of [unprotected speech]. This is not, for example, an obscenity case. Whatever else may be necessary to give rise to the States' broader power to prohibit obscene expression, such expression must be, in some significant way, erotic. It cannot plausibly be maintained that this vulgar allusion to the [military draft] would conjure up such psychic stimulation in anyone likely to be confronted with Cohen's crudely defaced jacket.

This Court has also held that the States are free to ban the simple use [of] so-called "fighting words," those personally abusive epithets which, when addressed to the ordinary citizen, are, as a matter of common knowledge, inherently likely to provoke violent reaction. [*Chaplinsky.*] While the four-letter word displayed by Cohen in relation to the draft is not uncommonly employed in a personally provocative fashion, in this instance it was clearly not "directed to the person of the hearer." No individual actually or likely to be present could reasonably have regarded the words on appellant's jacket as a direct personal insult. Nor do we have here an instance of the exercise of the State's police power to prevent a speaker from intentionally provoking a given group to hostile reaction. Compare with *Feiner* [Section B.5.c, infra]. There [is] no showing that anyone who saw Cohen was in fact violently aroused or that [Cohen] intended such a result.

Finally, [much] has been made of the claim that Cohen's distasteful mode of expression was thrust upon unwilling or unsuspecting viewers, and that the State might therefore legitimately act as it did in order to protect the sensitive from otherwise unavoidable exposure to [Cohen's] crude form of protest. Of course, the mere presumed presence of unwitting listeners or viewers does not serve automatically to justify curtailing all speech capable of giving offense. While this Court has recognized that government may properly act in many situations to prohibit intrusion into the privacy of the home of unwelcome views and ideas which cannot be totally banned from the public dialogue, we have at the same time consistently stressed that "we are often 'captives' outside the sanctuary of the home and subject to objectionable speech." The ability of government, consonant with the Constitution, to shut off discourse solely to protect others from hearing it [is] dependent upon a showing that substantial privacy interests are being invaded in an essentially intolerable manner. Any broader view of this authority would effectively empower a majority to silence dissidents simply as a matter of personal predilections.

[Persons] confronted with Cohen's jacket were in a quite different posture than, say, those subjected to the raucous emissions of sound trucks blaring outside their residences. Those in the Los Angeles courthouse could effectively avoid further bombardment of their sensibilities simply by averting their eyes. And, while it may be that one has a more substantial claim to a recognizable privacy interest when walking through a courthouse corridor than, for example, strolling through Central Park, surely it is nothing like the interest in being free from unwanted expression in the confines of one's own home. [If] Cohen's "speech" was otherwise entitled to constitutional protection, we do not think the fact that some unwilling "listeners" in a public building may have been briefly exposed to it can serve to justify this breach of the peace conviction where, as here, there was no evidence that persons powerless to avoid appellant's conduct did in fact object to it, and where [the statute] evinces no concern [with] the special plight of the captive auditor, but, instead, indiscriminately sweeps within its prohibitions all "offensive conduct" that disturbs "any neighborhood or person."

II. Against this background, the issue flushed by this case stands out in bold relief. It is whether California can excise, as "offensive conduct," one particular scurrilous epithet from the public discourse, either upon the theory of the court below that its use is inherently likely to cause violent reaction or upon a more general assertion that the States, acting as guardians of public morality, may properly remove this offensive word from the public vocabulary. The rationale of the California court is plainly untenable. At most it reflects an "undifferentiated fear or apprehension of disturbance [which] is not enough to overcome the right to freedom of expression." We have been shown no evidence that substantial numbers of citizens are standing ready to strike out physically at whoever may assault their sensibilities with execrations like that uttered by Cohen. There may be some persons about with such lawless and violent proclivities, but that is an insufficient base upon which to erect, consistently with constitutional values, a governmental power to force persons who wish to ventilate their dissident views into avoiding particular forms of expression. The argument amounts to little more than the self-defeating proposition that to avoid physical censorship of one who has not sought to provoke such a response by a hypothetical coterie of the violent and lawless, the States may more appropriately effectuate that censorship themselves.

Admittedly, it is not so obvious that the [First Amendment] must be taken to disable the States from punishing public utterance of this unseemly expletive in order to maintain what they regard as a suitable level of discourse within the body politic. [But] examination and reflection will reveal the shortcomings of a contrary viewpoint. [First], most situations where the State has a justifiable interest in regulating speech will fall within one or more of the various established [categories of unprotected speech, none of which is] applicable here. [Second, the] constitutional right of free expression is powerful medicine in a society as diverse and populous as ours. It is designed and intended to remove governmental restraints from the arena of public discussion, putting the decision as to what views shall be voiced largely into the hands of each of us, in the hope that use of such freedom will ultimately produce a more capable citizenry and more perfect polity and in the belief that no other approach would comport with the premise of individual dignity and choice upon which our political system rests. See Whitney v. California, (Brandeis, J., concurring). To many, the immediate consequence of this freedom may often appear to be only verbal tumult, discord, and even offensive utterance. These are, however, within established limits, in truth necessary side effects of the broader enduring values which the process of open debate permits us to achieve. That the air may at times seem filled with verbal cacophony [is] not a sign of weakness but of strength. . . .

Against this perception of the constitutional policies involved, we discern certain more particularized considerations that peculiarly call for reversal of this conviction. First, the principle contended for by the State seems inherently boundless. How is one to distinguish this from any other offensive word? Surely the State has no right to cleanse public debate to the point where it is grammatically palatable to the most squeamish among us. Yet no readily ascertainable general principle exists for stopping short of that result were we to affirm the judgment below. For, while the particular four-letter word being litigated here is perhaps more distasteful than most others of its genre, it is nevertheless often true that one man's vulgarity is another's lyric. Indeed, we think it is largely because governmental officials cannot make principled distinctions in this area that the Constitution leaves matters of taste and style so largely to the individual.

Additionally, [much] linguistic expression serves a dual communicative function: it conveys not only ideas capable of relatively precise, detached explication, but otherwise inexpressible emotions as well. In fact, words are often chosen as much for their emotive as their cognitive force. We cannot sanction the view that the Constitution, while solicitous of the cognitive content of individual speech, has little or no regard for that emotive function which, practically speaking, may often be the more important element of the overall message sought to be communicated. [Finally], we cannot indulge the facile assumption that one can forbid particular words without also running a substantial risk of suppressing ideas in the process. Indeed, governments might soon seize upon the censorship of particular words as a convenient guise for banning the expression of unpopular views. [Absent] a more particularized and compelling reason for its actions, the State may not [make] the simple public display here involved of this single four-letter expletive a criminal offense. [Reversed.]

Justice Blackmun, joined by Chief Justice Burger and Justice Black, dissenting.

I dissent. [Cohen's] absurd and immature antic, in my view, was mainly conduct and little speech. Further, the case appears to me to be well within the sphere of [*Chaplinsky*]. This agonizing over First Amendment values seems misplaced and unnecessary.

NOTES AND PROBLEMS

1. *Cohen*'s Balancing: Categorical or Contextual? Did *Cohen* reject categorical balancing and employ contextual balancing by comparing the government's interest in punishing speech with the value of the speech at issue? Or was *Cohen* very much a categorical balancing case, in that its method was to decide whether the category of offensive speech is unprotected by assessing the governmental interests in suppressing such speech and the free speech values implicated by such suppression?

Which of the above two approaches is the more speech-protective? Why?

2. Problems in Applying *Cohen*. Consider Erznoznik v. Jacksonville, 422 U.S. 205 (1975), in which the Court voided a Jacksonville ban on the exhibition of nudity on movie screens visible from public streets. The ban, which included non-obscene material, was justified by Jacksonville as a way to "protect its citizens against unwilling exposure to materials that may be offensive." The Court, per Justice Powell, responded that

> when the government, acting as censor, undertakes selectively to shield the public from some kinds of speech on the ground that they are more offensive than others, the First Amendment strictly limits its power. [Such] selective restrictions have been upheld only when the speaker intrudes on the privacy of the home or the degree of captivity makes it impractical for the unwilling viewer or auditor to avoid exposure. [Much] that we encounter offends [our] sensibilities. Nevertheless, the Constitution does not permit government to decide which types of otherwise protected speech are sufficiently offensive to require protection for the unwilling listener or viewer. [The] ordinance discriminates among movies solely on the basis of content. [This] discrimination cannot be justified as a means of preventing significant intrusions on privacy. [The] limited privacy interest of persons on the public streets cannot justify this [content-based] censorship of otherwise protected speech.

Suppose a state prohibits the use of profanity or vulgarity in public under a statute that avoids vagueness problems by itemizing the familiar words (or root words) that cannot lawfully be used in public speech. Would prosecution and conviction of a person for using such speech be valid under the following circumstances?

a. A person who has narrowly avoided being struck by a car while lawfully crossing a street screams a string of profanities at the driver of the car.

b. A person who has inadvertently struck his finger with a hammer while repairing his front door, immediately adjacent to a vacant public sidewalk, screams several variations on Cohen's vulgarity in reaction the shock of the pain.

c. The person with the poorly aimed hammer screams the same vulgarities at the same place, except that a mother with two small children happens to be passing by within earshot.

d. The same errant carpenter with the wounded finger screams the same vulgarities in the same place, except that the only hearers are his neighbors, quietly reading in their own homes.

b. Hate Speech

Hate speech is an elusive concept. Surely it includes speech that is offensive, but given *Cohen*, there must be more than that the speech offends. Is it limited to speech that denigrates racial, ethnic, or religious minorities? Must it be directed personally, or can abstract expressions of hatred suffice?

In Beauharnais v. Illinois, 343 U.S. 250 (1952), the Court upheld the validity of an Illinois law that banned speech "which portrays depravity, criminality, unchastity, or lack of virtue of a class of citizens, of any race, color, creed or religion, [or] which exposes the citizens of any race, color, creed or religion to contempt, derision, or obloquy" and which had a "strong tendency [to] cause violence and disorder." Beauharnais was convicted under this law for distributing a leaflet that, among other things, asserted: "If persuasion and the need to prevent the white race from becoming mongrelized by the negro will not unite us, then the . . . rapes, robberies, knives, guns and marijuana of the negro, surely will." The Court upheld the conviction:

> [No] one will gainsay that it is libelous falsely to charge another with being a rapist, robber, carrier of knives and guns, and user of marijuana. The precise question [is] whether the [free speech guarantee] prevents a State from punishing such libels [directed] at designated collectivities and flagrantly disseminated. [If] an utterance directed at an individual may be the object of criminal sanctions, we cannot deny to a State power to punish the same utterance directed at a defined group, unless we can say that this is a willful and purposeless restriction unrelated to the peace and well-being of the State. . . . [Libelous] utterances not being within the area of constitutionally protected speech, it is unnecessary to consider the issues behind the phrase "clear and present danger." [We] find no warrant in the Constitution for denying to Illinois the power to pass the law here under attack.

Justices Black and Douglas dissented: "[The 'group libel'] label may make the Court's holding more palatable for those who sustain it, but the sugar-coating does not make the censorship less deadly. . . . [This] Act sets up a system of state censorship which is at war with the kind of free government envisioned by those who forced adoption of our Bill of Rights. [If] there be minority groups who hail this holding as their victory, they might consider the possible relevancy of this ancient remark: 'Another such victory and I am undone.'"

In Collin v. Smith, 578 F.2d 1197 (7th Cir. 1978), the Court of Appeals upheld a district court decision invalidating on free speech grounds a series of ordinances adopted by Skokie, Illinois, to prevent a planned march by the American Nazi Party. Skokie, home to many Jews, including some who had survived Nazi Germany's genocide, had prohibited the distribution or display of material within Skokie that intentionally "promotes hatred against persons by reason of their race, national origin, or religion." Although the wording of this ordinance was very similar to the "group libel law" upheld in *Beauharnais*, the Court of Appeals concluded that *Beauharnais* was a dubious precedent. "It may be questioned, after [*Cohen, Gooding*, and *Brandenburg*], whether the *tendency to induce violence* approach sanctioned implicitly in *Beauharnais* would pass constitutional muster today." The Supreme Court denied review of the Seventh Circuit's decision. Smith v. Collin, 439 U.S. 916 (1978).

There are three main reasons *Beauharnais* may have been eclipsed as good law, although the Court has never said so. First, the *Beauharnais* Court assumed that defamation of individuals was entirely unprotected by the Constitution. That is no longer true (see Section B.6, infra). Because "group defamation" involves claims about entire categories of people, such claims are likely to be treated as comments upon "public categories," akin to comments about "public figures," thus triggering some protection under the First Amendment. Also, claims made about individuals may be verified, but claims made about groups are evaluative opinions, thus taking them outside defamation. Claims made about an entire group raise the question of whether the claims "can appropriately be used to characterize the group. The fundamental issue is the nature of the group's identity, an issue that almost certainly ought to be characterized as one of evaluative opinion." Post, Racist Speech, Democracy, and the First Amendment, 32 Wm. & Mary L. Rev. 267, 298 (1991). Second, the Illinois courts construed the statute under which *Beauharnais* was convicted to prohibit only speech that had a "strong tendency [to] cause violence and disorder." That standard would not meet the present-day *Brandenburg* test. Third, to the extent the *Beauharnais* Court implicitly relied on *Chaplinsky*'s broad definition of "fighting words," that doctrine has been curtailed to reach only hostile speech delivered face to face and likely to trigger a violent reaction.

Arguments for Regulating Hate Speech. The arguments in favor of regulating hate speech—the denigration of identifiable groups—can be grouped into several categories. First, hate speech is a form of fighting words—the verbal equivalent of a slap in the face. This argument relies heavily on the "inflict injury" prong of *Chaplinsky*'s fighting-words formula, but that prong might not have any life in it.

Second, hate speech has such little connection to the core purposes of free speech and is sufficiently pernicious that it should be recognized as a new category of unprotected speech. A major problem with this approach is the necessity of defining the category with sufficient precision that it is neither vague nor overly broad. If hate speech is defined as the face-to-face utterance of racial epithets, it becomes a subcategory of fighting words. If hate speech is speech that tends to promote dislike of an identifiable group, it is hopelessly overbroad, for much of America's political rhetoric would be included. Nor has hate speech been historically regarded as unprotected, as *Stevens* appears to demand.

Finally, hate speech might violate equal protection. The argument is rooted in the premise that equal protection is grounded in anti-subordination, so any message that reinforces subordination of a historically disadvantaged group is constitutionally unprotected. The problem with this is twofold: (1) equal protection applies only to governments, and (2) equal protection and free speech are pitted against one another.

There is vast academic commentary on the subject. See, e.g., Matsuda, Public Response to Racist Speech: Considering the Victim's Story, 87 Mich. L. Rev. 2320 (1989); Delgado, Words That Wound: A Tort Action for Racial Insults, Epithets, and Name-Calling, 17 Harv. C.R.-C.L. L. Rev. 133 (1982); Lawrence, If He Hollers Let Him Go: Regulating Racist Speech on Campus, 1990 Duke L.J. 431.

Arguments Against Regulation of Hate Speech. The principal constitutional argument against hate speech regulation is that such regulation is nakedly content-based and is incapable of being bounded sufficiently to avoid serious overbreadth problems. If it is adequately bounded, nothing is added beyond what is already supplied by such existing categories as fighting words or the "civility torts." See, e.g., Strossen, Regulating Hate Speech on Campus: A Modest Proposal?, 1990 Duke L.J. 484; Fried, A New First Amendment Jurisprudence: A Threat to Liberty, 59 U. Chi. L. Rev. 225 (1992). The principal non-constitutional arguments are that hate speech regulation is either (1) unhelpful or (2) downright harmful to the interests of the minorities it seeks to benefit. It is unhelpful because, to avoid fatal overbreadth problems, such regulation would be limited to the crude epithet. Crude epithets are usually shunned by most people; it is the articulate, epithet-free form of racism that is most damaging to racial minorities.

Hate speech regulation is claimed to be harmful for several reasons. First, as the legacy of Martin Luther King, Jr., demonstrates, a prime method of escaping from social subordination is through speech. Anything that shrinks the circulation of ideas is a danger to subordinated groups. See Karst, Boundaries and Reasons: Freedom of Expression and the Subordination of Groups, 1990 Ill. L. Rev. 95. A second reason is grounded in psychological theory. The dark side to every personality is the "shadow," an unconscious collection of loathsome primitive impulses and emotions. Humans "project" their shadows onto others, with the result that the fear and loathing we have of others is often that of our own unrecognized dark side. The person who acknowledges this and faces the evil within himself

> has begun the process of transforming and transcending his inner demon. From a societal perspective, toleration of [hate speech] may be the avenue to recognition of our collective shadow. [Banning hate speech] enables the society to tell itself (smugly and falsely) that *it* has no problem; the problem lies within those horrid offenders whom we have righteously muzzled.

Massey, Pure Symbols and the First Amendment, 17 Hastings Const. L.Q. 369 (1990).

R.A.V. v. City of St. Paul
505 U.S. 377 (1992)

JUSTICE SCALIA delivered the opinion of the Court.

In the predawn hours of June 21, 1990, petitioner and several other teenagers allegedly assembled a crudely-made cross by taping together broken chair legs [and] burned the cross inside the fenced yard of a black family that lived across the street from the house where petitioner was staying. Although this conduct could have been punished under [laws prohibiting arson, terroristic threats, or criminal damage to property, St. Paul] chose to charge petitioner [under] the St. Paul Bias-Motivated Crime Ordinance, which provides: "Whoever places on public or private property a symbol, object, appellation, characterization or graffiti, including, but not limited to, a burning cross or

Nazi swastika, which one knows or has reasonable grounds to know arouses anger, alarm or resentment in others on the basis of race, color, creed, religion or gender commits disorderly conduct and shall be guilty of a misdemeanor." Petitioner moved to dismiss [on] the ground that the St. Paul ordinance was substantially overbroad and impermissibly content-based and therefore facially invalid under the First Amendment. The trial court granted this motion, but the Minnesota Supreme Court reversed, [finding that the phrase "arouses anger, alarm or resentment in others" in the ordinance only reached "fighting words" as defined by *Chaplinsky*].

I. [Assuming], arguendo, that all of the expression reached by the ordinance is proscribable under the "fighting words" doctrine, we nonetheless conclude that the ordinance is facially unconstitutional in that it prohibits otherwise permitted speech solely on the basis of the subjects the speech addresses. The First Amendment generally prevents government from proscribing speech, or even expressive conduct, because of disapproval of the ideas expressed. Content-based regulations are presumptively invalid. [But we have] permitted restrictions upon the content of speech in a few limited areas, which are "of such slight social value as a step to truth that any benefit that may be derived from them is clearly outweighed by the social interest in order and morality." *Chaplinsky*. . . .

We have sometimes said that these categories of expression are "not within the area of constitutionally protected speech," or that the "protection of the First Amendment does not extend" to them. [What these statements] mean is that these areas of speech can, consistently with the First Amendment, be regulated because of their constitutionally proscribable content (obscenity, defamation, etc.)—not that they are categories of speech entirely invisible to the Constitution, so that they may be made the vehicles for content discrimination unrelated to their distinctively proscribable content. Thus, the government may proscribe libel; but it may not make the further content discrimination of proscribing only libel critical of the government. [A] city council could [not] enact an ordinance prohibiting only those legally obscene works that contain criticism of the city government [or] that do not include endorsement of the city government. Such a simplistic, all-or-nothing-at-all approach to First Amendment protection is at odds with common sense and with our jurisprudence as well.

[The] proposition that a particular instance of speech can be proscribable on the basis of one feature (e.g., obscenity) but not on the basis of another (e.g., opposition to the city government) is commonplace, and has found application in many contexts. We have long held, for example, that nonverbal expressive activity can be banned because of the action it entails, but not because of the ideas it expresses—so that burning a flag in violation of an ordinance against outdoor fires could be punishable, whereas burning a flag in violation of an ordinance against dishonoring the flag is not.

[The] exclusion of "fighting words" from the scope of the First Amendment simply means that, for purposes of that Amendment, the unprotected features of the words are, despite their verbal character, essentially a "non-speech" element of communication. Fighting words are thus analogous to a noisy sound truck: [both] can be used to convey an idea; but neither has, in and of itself, a claim upon the First Amendment. As with the sound truck, however, so also with fighting words: The government may not regulate use based on hostility — or favoritism — towards the underlying message expressed.

The concurrences describe us as setting forth a new First Amendment principle that prohibition of constitutionally proscribable speech cannot be "underinclusive," [meaning that] "within a particular proscribable category of expression [a] government must either proscribe all speech or no speech at all." That easy target is of the concurrences' own invention. In our view, the First Amendment imposes not an "underinclusiveness" limitation but a "content discrimination" limitation upon a State's prohibition of proscribable speech. There is no problem whatever, for example, with a State's prohibiting obscenity (and other forms of proscribable expression) only in certain media or markets, for although that prohibition would be "underinclusive," it would not discriminate on the basis of content.

Even the prohibition against content discrimination that we assert the First Amendment requires is not absolute. It applies differently in the context of proscribable speech than in the area of fully protected speech. [Content discrimination with respect to protected speech] "raises the specter that the Government may effectively drive certain ideas or viewpoints from the marketplace," [but] content discrimination among various instances of a class of proscribable speech often does not pose this threat. When the basis for the content discrimination consists entirely of the very reason the entire class of speech at issue is proscribable, no significant danger of idea or viewpoint discrimination exists. [To] illustrate: A State might choose to prohibit only that obscenity which is the most patently offensive in its prurience — i.e., that which involves the most lascivious displays of sexual activity. But it may not prohibit, for example, only that obscenity which includes offensive political messages. And the Federal Government can criminalize only those threats of violence that are directed against the President — since the reasons why threats of violence are outside the First Amendment (protecting individuals from the fear of violence, from the disruption that fear engenders, and from the possibility that the threatened violence will occur) have special force when applied to the person of the President. But the Federal Government may not criminalize only those threats against the President that mention his policy on aid to inner cities. . . .

Another valid basis for according differential treatment to even a content-defined subclass of proscribable speech is that the subclass happens to be associated with particular "secondary effects" of the speech, so that the regulation is "justified without reference to the content of [the] speech." [Renton v. Playtime Theatres; see Section C.3, infra.] Moreover, since words can in some circumstances violate laws directed not against speech but against conduct (a law against treason, for example, is violated by telling the enemy the nation's defense secrets), a particular content-based subcategory of a proscribable class of speech can be swept up incidentally within the reach of a statute directed at conduct rather than speech. Thus, for example, sexually derogatory "fighting words," among other words, may produce a violation of Title VII's general prohibition against sexual discrimination in employment practices. Where the government does not target conduct on the basis of its expressive content, acts are not shielded from regulation merely because they express a discriminatory idea or philosophy. [Indeed], where totally proscribable speech is at issue it may [be that content-based discrimination is permissible], so long as the nature of the content discrimination is such that there is no realistic possibility that official suppression of ideas is afoot. (We cannot think of any First Amendment interest that would stand in the way of a State's prohibiting only those obscene motion pictures with blue-eyed actresses.)

II. Applying these principles to the St. Paul ordinance, we conclude that, even as narrowly construed by the Minnesota Supreme Court, the ordinance is facially unconstitutional. Although the phrase in the ordinance, "arouses anger, alarm or resentment in others," has been [construed] to reach only those symbols or displays that amount to "fighting words," the remaining, unmodified terms make clear that the ordinance applies only to "fighting words" that insult, or provoke violence, "on the basis of race, color, creed, religion or gender." Displays containing abusive invective, no matter how vicious or severe, are permissible unless they are addressed to one of the specified disfavored topics. Those who wish to use "fighting words" in connection with other ideas—to express hostility, for example, on the basis of political affiliation, union membership, or homosexuality—are not covered. The First Amendment does not permit St. Paul to impose special prohibitions on those speakers who express views on disfavored subjects.

In its practical operation, moreover, the ordinance goes even beyond mere content discrimination, to actual viewpoint discrimination. Displays containing some words—odious racial epithets, for example—would be prohibited to proponents of all views. But "fighting words" that do not themselves invoke race, color, creed, religion, or gender—aspersions upon a person's mother, for example—would seemingly be usable ad libitum in the placards of those arguing in favor of racial, color, etc. tolerance and equality, but could not be used by that speaker's opponents. One could hold up a sign saying, for example, that all "anti-Catholic bigots" are misbegotten; but not that all "papists" are, for that would insult and provoke violence "on the basis of religion." St. Paul has no such authority to license one side of a debate to fight freestyle, while requiring the other to follow Marquis of Queensbury Rules. [One] must wholeheartedly agree with the Minnesota Supreme Court that "it is the responsibility, even the obligation, of diverse communities to confront such notions in whatever form they appear," but the manner of that confrontation cannot consist [of] silencing speech on the basis of its content.

[Justice] Stevens suggests that [the] ordinance [is directed] not to speech of a particular content, but to particular "injuries" that are "qualitatively different" from other injuries. This is word-play. What makes the anger, fear, [or] sense of dishonor produced by violation of this ordinance distinct from the anger, fear, [or] sense of dishonor produced by other fighting words is nothing other than the fact that it is caused by a distinctive idea, conveyed by a distinctive message.

[The] reason why fighting words are categorically excluded from the protection of the First Amendment is not that their content communicates any particular idea, but that their content embodies a particularly intolerable (and socially unnecessary) mode of expressing whatever idea the speaker wishes to convey. St. Paul has not singled out an especially offensive mode of expression—it has not, for example, selected for prohibition only those fighting words that communicate ideas in a threatening (as opposed to a merely obnoxious) manner. Rather, it has proscribed fighting words of whatever manner that communicate messages of racial, gender, or religious intolerance. Selectivity of this sort creates the possibility that the city is seeking to handicap the expression of particular ideas. . . .

[Finally, St. Paul contends] that, even if the ordinance regulates expression based on hostility towards its protected ideological content, this discrimination is nonetheless justified because it is narrowly tailored to serve compelling state interests [of fostering the] rights of members of groups that have historically been subjected to discrimination [to] live in peace where they wish. We do not doubt that these interests are compelling, and that the ordinance can be said to promote them. But [the] dispositive question [is] whether content discrimination is reasonably necessary to achieve St. Paul's compelling interests; it plainly is not. An ordinance not limited to the favored topics . . . would have precisely the same beneficial effect. In fact the only interest distinctively served by the content limitation is that of displaying the city council's special hostility towards the particular biases thus singled out. That is precisely what the First Amendment forbids. The politicians of St. Paul are entitled to express that hostility—but not through the means of imposing unique limitations upon speakers who (however benightedly) disagree.

Let there be no mistake about our belief that burning a cross in someone's front yard is reprehensible. But St. Paul has sufficient means at its disposal to prevent such behavior without adding the First Amendment to the fire. [Reversed.]

JUSTICE WHITE, joined by JUSTICES BLACKMUN, O'CONNOR, and STEVENS, concurring in the judgment.

I agree with the majority that the judgment of the Minnesota Supreme Court should be reversed. However, our agreement ends there. This case could easily be decided [by] holding [that] the St. Paul ordinance is fatally overbroad because it criminalizes not only unprotected expression but expression protected by the First Amendment.

I . . . . C. The Court [says that] "[c]ontent-based distinctions may be drawn within an unprotected category of speech if the basis for the distinctions is the very reason the entire class of speech at issue is proscribable." [The] exception swallows the majority's rule. Certainly, it should apply to the St. Paul ordinance, since "the reasons why [fighting words] are outside the

First Amendment [have] special force when applied to [historically disfavored minorities]." A prohibition on fighting words [is] a ban on a class of speech that conveys an overriding message of personal injury and imminent violence, a message that is at its ugliest when directed against groups that have long been the targets of discrimination. . . .

II. Although I disagree with the Court's analysis, I do agree with its conclusion: The St. Paul ordinance is unconstitutional. However, I would decide the case on overbreadth grounds. [Although] the ordinance as construed reaches categories of speech that are constitutionally unprotected, it also criminalizes a substantial amount of expression that—however repugnant—is shielded by the First Amendment. [In] construing the St. Paul ordinance, the Minnesota Supreme Court [ruled] that St. Paul may constitutionally prohibit expression that "by its very utterance" causes "anger, alarm or resentment." Our fighting words cases have made clear, however, that such generalized reactions are not sufficient to strip expression of its constitutional protection. The mere fact that expressive activity causes hurt feelings, offense, or resentment does not render the expression unprotected. [The] ordinance is therefore fatally overbroad and invalid on its face.

JUSTICE STEVENS, concurring in the judgment.

. . . [The] St. Paul ordinance regulates speech not on the basis of its subject matter or the viewpoint expressed [but] on the basis of the harm the speech causes. [The] ordinance regulates only a subcategory of expression that causes injuries based on "race, color, creed, religion or gender," not a subcategory that involves discussions that concern those characteristics. [A] statute prohibiting race-based threats is justifiable because of the place of race in our social and political order. Although it is regrettable that race occupies such a place and is so incendiary an issue, until the Nation matures beyond that condition, laws such as St. Paul's ordinance will remain reasonable and justifiable. . . .

[W]ere the ordinance not overbroad, I would vote to uphold it.

Wisconsin v. Mitchell
508 U.S. 476 (1993)

[Wisconsin law increased the penalties for crimes where the defendant "intentionally selects the person against whom the crime [is] committed [because] of the race, religion, color, disability, sexual orientation, national origin or ancestry of that person."]

CHIEF JUSTICE REHNQUIST delivered the opinion of the Court.

On the evening of October 7, 1989, a group of young black men and boys, including Mitchell, gathered at an apartment complex in Kenosha, Wisconsin. Several members of the group discussed a scene from the motion picture " 'Mississippi Burning,' " in which a white man beat a young black boy who was praying. The group moved outside and Mitchell asked them:

" 'Do you all feel hyped up to move on some white people?' " Shortly thereafter, a young white boy approached the group on the opposite side of the street where they were standing. As the boy walked by, Mitchell said: " 'You all want to fuck somebody up? There goes a white boy; go get him.' " Mitchell counted to three and pointed in the boy's direction. The group ran toward the boy, beat him severely, and stole his tennis shoes. The boy was rendered unconscious and remained in a coma for four days.

[After] Mitchell was convicted of aggravated battery [the] maximum sentence for Mitchell's offense was increased [from two] to seven years [because the jury had found that Mitchell had intentionally selected his victim by race]. The [Wisconsin] Court sentenced Mitchell to four years' imprisonment for the aggravated battery. Mitchell [appealed and] the Wisconsin Supreme Court reversed, ruling that the statute "violates the First Amendment directly by punishing what the legislature has deemed to be offensive thought." [We] reverse.

[Because] the only reason for the enhancement is the defendant's discriminatory motive for selecting his victim, Mitchell argues [that] the statute violates the First Amendment by punishing offenders' bigoted beliefs. [It is true] that a defendant's abstract beliefs, however obnoxious to most people, may not be taken into consideration by a sentencing judge. Dawson v. Delaware, 503 U.S. 159 (1992). [But we have] allowed the sentencing judge to take into account the defendant's racial animus towards his victim [in] determining whether he should be sentenced to death, surely the most severe [penalty] "enhancement" of all. [Moreover, a defendant's motive is a traditional and important sentencing factor, and] motive plays the same role under the Wisconsin statute as it does under federal and state anti-discrimination laws which we have previously upheld against constitutional challenge.

Nothing [in] *R.A.V.* compels a different result here. [The] ordinance struck down in *R.A.V.* was explicitly directed at expression [but this statute is] aimed at conduct unprotected by the First Amendment. Moreover, the Wisconsin statute singles out for enhancement bias-inspired conduct because [bias-motivated] crimes are more likely to provoke retaliatory crimes, inflict distinct emotional harms on their victims, and incite community unrest. The State's desire to redress these perceived harms provides an adequate explanation for its penalty-enhancement provision over and above mere disagreement with offenders' beliefs or biases. As Blackstone said long ago, "it is but reasonable that among crimes of different natures those should be most severely punished, which are the most destructive of the public safety and happiness." 4 W. Blackstone, Commentaries *16. [Reversed.]

NOTES

1. Implications of *R.A.V.* and *Mitchell*. Assess the validity of the following government actions.

a. A town that has experienced severe racially motivated violence culminating in a race riot enacts an ordinance that prohibits anyone from "directly addressing another person with a racial epithet or any other term of racial abuse or scorn."

b. A state enacts a law prohibiting anyone from engaging in sexual harassment, defined as including "unwelcome sexual advances, requests for sexual favors, and other verbal or physical conduct of a sexual nature which is hostile, intimidating, or offensive."

c. Wisconsin amends its penalty enhancement statute upheld in *Mitchell* to permit enhancement for crimes "involving the communication of a message of racial hatred."

d. Wisconsin amends its penalty enhancement statute upheld in *Mitchell* to permit enhancement for crimes "motivated by the defendant's racial beliefs."

e. Wisconsin amends its penalty enhancement statute upheld in *Mitchell* to permit enhancement for crimes "motivated by the defendant's belief in white supremacy."

2. Cross Burning with Intent to Intimidate.   In Virginia v. Black, 538 U.S. 343 (2003), the Court upheld Virginia's statute banning cross burning with "an intent to intimidate a person or group of persons."

"Virginia's statute does not run afoul of the First Amendment insofar as it bans cross burning with intent to intimidate. Unlike the statute at issue in *R.A.V.*, the Virginia statute does not single out for opprobrium only that speech directed toward "one of the specified disfavored topics." It does not matter whether an individual burns a cross with intent to intimidate because of the victim's race, gender, or religion, or because of the victim's "political affiliation, union membership, or homosexuality." . . . The First Amendment permits Virginia to outlaw cross burnings done with the intent to intimidate because burning a cross is a particularly virulent form of intimidation. Instead of prohibiting all intimidating messages, Virginia may choose to regulate this subset of intimidating messages in light of cross burning's long and pernicious history as a signal of impending violence. Thus, just as a State may regulate only that obscenity which is the most obscene due to its prurient content, so too may a State choose to prohibit only those forms of intimidation that are most likely to inspire fear of bodily harm. A ban on cross burning carried out with the intent to intimidate is fully consistent with our holding in *R.A.V.* and is proscribable under the First Amendment. . . ."

Three justices dissented: "[The statute's] specific prohibition of cross burning with intent to intimidate selects a symbol with particular content from the field of all proscribable expression meant to intimidate. . . . [Even] when the symbolic act is meant to terrify, a burning cross may carry a further, ideological message of white Protestant supremacy. [The] burning cross can broadcast threat and ideology together, ideology alone, or threat alone. [Virginia has rejected a general prohibition of intimidation . . . in favor of a distinct proscription of intimidation by cross burning. The cross may have been selected because of its special power to threaten, but it may also have been singled out because of disapproval of its message of white supremacy, either because a legislature thought white supremacy was a pernicious doctrine or because it found that dramatic, public espousal of it was a civic embarrassment. Thus, there is no kinship between the cross-burning statute and the [kind of content-based regulation of proscribable speech that *R.A.V.* indicated was valid]."

NOTES

1. Are Categorical Differences Significant? Can *R.A.V.* and *Black* be harmonized by noting that *R.A.V.* involved St. Paul's attempt selectively to ban *fighting words* on the basis of their content, and that *Black* involved Virginia's attempt selectively to ban *true threats* on the basis of their content? Is it plausible to say that the St. Paul ban at issue in *R.A.V.* was not for the purpose of preventing immediate breach of the peace (the reason that fighting words are exiled from the First Amendment), and that Virginia's ban on intentionally intimidating cross burning was for the purpose of preventing the fear and anxiety experienced by the recipient of any true threat (the reason that true threats are constitutionally unprotected)?

2. The Peculiar Potency of Symbolic Expression. What, if anything, should be made of the fact that a burning cross, like the American flag, the Nazi swastika, the hammer and sickle, the Latin cross, and the star of David, among other possibilities, is a particularly powerful symbol? No matter how such symbols are used, they each necessarily convey a message. Does the fact that a burning cross conveys a message of white supremacy mean that the dissenters are correct in contending that the Virginia law is viewpoint discriminatory?

3. Workplace Harassment. Severe or pervasive harassment on the basis of religion, race, or national origin constitutes "employment discrimination" under Title VII of the Civil Rights Act of 1964, as amended. Meritor Savings Bank v. Vinson, 477 U.S. 57, 65-67 (1986); Harris v. Forklift Systems, 510 U.S. 17, 21-22 (1993). But under what circumstances does the free expression guarantee shield from such liability workplace speech that some people find offensive?

Rodriguez v. Maricopa County Community College District, 605 F.3d 703 (9th Cir. 2010). The college was sued by a class of Hispanic employees, claiming that the college's failure to squelch mathematics Professor Walter Kehowski's "racially-charged emails" sent over a college distribution list to each employee with an e-mail address constituted a "hostile work environment in violation of Title VII and the Equal Protection Clause." The district court denied the college's motion for summary judgment and the Ninth Circuit reversed. Kehowski's e-mails derided "La Raza" as racist, celebrated western civilization, voiced opposition to illegal immigration, and criticized as "shallow and self-contradictory" any ideology in which "[r]ace must be held meaningless only by whites." The Ninth Circuit said that "objection to Kehowski's speech is based entirely on his point of view, and it is axiomatic that the government may not silence speech because the ideas it promotes are thought to be offensive. . . . We therefore doubt that a college professor's expression on a matter of public concern, directed to the college community, could ever constitute unlawful harassment and justify the judicial intervention that plaintiffs seek. . . . Harassment law generally targets conduct, and it sweeps in speech as harassment only when consistent with the First Amendment. . . . But Kehowski's . . . emails were pure speech; they were the effective equivalent of standing on a soap box in a campus quadrangle and speaking to all within earshot. Their offensive quality was based entirely on their meaning, and not on any conduct or implicit threat of conduct that they contained. . . . We therefore conclude that defendants did not violate plaintiffs' right to be free of workplace harassment. . . . Those offended by Kehowski's ideas should engage him in debate or hit the "delete" button when they receive his emails. They may not invoke the power of the government to shut him up."

c.   Hostile Audiences

When, if at all, should the listeners' adverse reaction to speech trump the speaker's First Amendment rights? Listeners can be offended by both style and content. Should it matter which is the source of the offense? What is the extent of the government's obligation, if any, to protect the abrasive speaker from an angry audience? The Court has shied away from treating these cases categorically, preferring instead to reconcile these competing interests on a more piecemeal basis. Are these cases susceptible to a categorical approach?

≡≡≡ **Terminiello v. Chicago**
≡≡≡ *337 U.S. 1 (1949)*

[Arthur Terminiello, a former Roman Catholic priest who had once been a minister to poor tenant farmers in the South, delivered a well-publicized address sponsored by the Christian Veterans of America in a Chicago auditorium to an overflow crowd of over 800 people. Because Terminiello held right-wing views, and had been accused of being racist and anti-Semitic, a violent crowd of about 1,500 gathered outside. The crowd, described by the trial judge as "a surging, howling mob hurling epithets," assaulted people attempting to enter the auditorium, tearing the coat off one young woman, and denouncing all those inside as "fascists," "God damned fascists," "Nazis," and "Hitlers." "The street was black with people on both sides for at least a block either way; bottles, stink bombs and brickbats were thrown. Police were unable to control the mob, which kept breaking the windows at the meeting hall, drowning out the speaker's voice at times and breaking in through the back door of the auditorium. About 17 of the group outside were arrested by the police." Terminiello exhorted the crowd inside to defy the "communists," "snakes," and "scum" outside by showing no tolerance for them and "to stand up to them."]

JUSTICE DOUGLAS delivered the opinion of the Court.

Petitioner after jury trial was found guilty of disorderly conduct in violation of a city ordinance of Chicago [that defined "disorderly conduct" to include "breach of the peace"] and fined. [The] trial court charged [the jury] that "breach of the peace" consists of any "misbehavior" [that] "stirs the public to anger, invites dispute, brings about a condition of unrest, or creates a disturbance." [The conviction was affirmed by the Illinois Supreme Court.]

A function of free speech under our system of government is to invite dispute. It may indeed best serve its high purpose when it induces a condition of unrest, creates dissatisfaction with conditions as they are, or even stirs people to anger. Speech is often provocative and challenging. It may strike at prejudices and preconceptions and have profound unsettling effects as it presses for acceptance of an idea. That is why freedom of speech, though not absolute, is nevertheless protected against censorship or punishment, unless shown likely to produce a clear and present danger of a serious substantive evil that rises far above public inconvenience, annoyance, or unrest.

The ordinance as construed by the trial court seriously invaded this province. It permitted conviction of petitioner if his speech stirred people to anger, invited public dispute, or brought about a condition of unrest. A conviction resting on any of those grounds may not stand.

Feiner v. New York
340 U.S. 315 (1951)

CHIEF JUSTICE VINSON delivered the opinion of the Court.

Petitioner was convicted [of] disorderly conduct [and] sentenced to thirty days in the county penitentiary. The conviction was affirmed [by] the New York Court of Appeals.

[On] the evening of March 8, 1949, petitioner Irving Feiner, [a young college student], was addressing an open-air meeting [in] Syracuse. [Police responding to] a telephone complaint concerning the meeting [found] a crowd of about seventy-five or eighty people, both Negro and white, filling the sidewalk and spreading out into the street. [Feiner], standing on a large wooden box on the sidewalk, was addressing the crowd through a loud-speaker system, [urging] his listeners to attend a meeting [to] be held that night in the Syracuse Hotel. [He] was making derogatory remarks concerning President Truman [a "bum"], the American Legion ["a Nazi Gestapo"], the Mayor of Syracuse [a "champagne sipping bum"], and other local political officials. The police [made] no effort to interfere with petitioner's speech, [but] attempted to get the people listening to petitioner back on the sidewalk. The crowd was restless and there was some pushing, shoving and milling around. [Feiner], speaking in a "loud, high-pitched voice," gave the impression that he was endeavoring to arouse the Negro people against the whites, urging that they rise up in arms and fight for equal rights. [The statements] "stirred up a little excitement." [At least one onlooker said to a policeman:] "If you don't get that son of a bitch off, I will go over there and get him off there myself." There were others who appeared to be favoring petitioner's arguments. Because of the [strong feeling in] the crowd both for and against the speaker the officers finally "stepped in to prevent it from resulting in a fight." One of the officers approached the petitioner, not for the purpose of arresting him, but to get him to break up the crowd. He asked petitioner to get down off the box, but [Feiner] refused to accede to his request and continued talking. The officer waited for a minute and then demanded that he cease talking. [Feiner] continued talking. [As] the crowd was pressing closer around [Feiner] and the officer, the officer told petitioner he was under [arrest]. Petitioner stepped down, announcing over the microphone that "the law has arrived, and I suppose they will take over now." [Feiner's disorderly conduct conviction was specifically premised upon his] "ignoring and refusing to heed and obey reasonable police orders issued [to] regulate and control [the] crowd and to prevent a breach [of] the peace and to prevent injury to pedestrians [and] the public generally."

[The New York courts] found that the officers in making the arrest were motivated solely by a proper concern for the preservation of order and protection of the general welfare, and that there was no evidence [that] the acts of the police were a cover for suppression of petitioner's views and opinions. Petitioner was thus neither arrested nor convicted for the making or the content of his speech. Rather, it was the reaction which it actually engendered. . . .

"When clear and present danger of riot, disorder, [or] other immediate threat to public safety, peace, or order, appears, the power of the State to prevent or punish is obvious." [We] are well aware that the ordinary murmurings and objections of a hostile audience cannot be allowed to silence a speaker, and are also mindful of the possible danger of giving overzealous police officials complete discretion to break up otherwise lawful public meetings. [But] we are not faced here with such a situation. It is one thing to say that the police cannot be used as an instrument for the suppression of unpopular views, and another to say that, when as here the speaker passes the bounds of argument or persuasion and undertakes incitement to riot, they are powerless to prevent a breach of the peace. [The] imminence of greater disorder coupled with petitioner's deliberate defiance of the police officers convince us that we should not reverse this conviction in the name of free speech. Affirmed.

JUSTICE BLACK, dissenting.

[Feiner] has been sentenced to the penitentiary for the unpopular views he expressed on matters of public interest while lawfully making a street-corner [speech]. One isolated threat to assault the speaker [does not prove] imminent threat of riot or uncontrollable disorder. [Even if it was] a critical situation, I reject the implication of the Court's opinion that the police had no obligation to protect petitioner's constitutional right to talk. The police of course have power to prevent breaches of the peace. But if, in the name of preserving order, they ever can interfere with a lawful public speaker, they first must make all reasonable efforts to protect him. Here the policemen did not even try to protect petitioner. [No] attempt to quiet [the crowd was made]. The officers did nothing to discourage [threatened assault on the speaker] when even a word might have sufficed. Their duty was to protect [Feiner's] right to talk, even to the extent of arresting the man who threatened to inter-fere. Instead they shirked that duty and acted only to suppress the right to speak. [Today's] holding means that as a practical matter, minority speakers can be silenced in any city.

NOTE

Subsequent Cases. In a series of cases involving civil rights demonstra-tions in the 1960s, the Court revisited the "heckler's veto" problem.

Edwards v. South Carolina, 372 U.S. 229 (1963). About 200 protesters against racial discrimination paraded peacefully on the public grounds of the South Carolina State House in front of about 30 police officers and several hundred onlookers. Although the crowd was not threatening, after about 40 minutes the police announced that the demonstrators would be arrested if they did not disperse within 15 minutes. The demonstrators responded with patriotic songs, hand-clapping, and foot-stamping, resulting in their arrest and conviction for breach of the peace. The Court reversed, finding that "there was no violence or threat of violence" on the part of the demonstrators or "any member of the crowd watching them."

Cox v. Louisiana, 379 U.S. 536 (1965). Cox led about 2,000 black stu-dents protesting racial segregation and the previous arrest of 23 black stu-dents who had picketed stores maintaining segregated lunch counters. Cox complied with a police request to demonstrate on a specific street facing the courthouse and a crowd of several hundred whites across the street. About 75 police officers stood between the two groups. Cox denounced the "illegal arrest" of the 23 jailed students and urged the demonstrators to eat lunch at the store lunch counters closed to blacks. Because the white onlookers were hostile to these sentiments, the sheriff ordered the demonstrators to disperse. When they did not, the police broke up the demonstration with tear gas. Cox was convicted of breach of the peace. The Court unanimously reversed. As in *Edwards,* the Court concluded that the facts were "a far cry from the situa-tion in [*Feiner*]"; there was no evidence of threatened violence by either the demonstrators or the onlookers.

Gregory v. Chicago, 394 U.S. 111 (1969). Gregory led a group of 85 people to Chicago Mayor Daley's home to protest alleged segregation in the Chicago public schools. The demonstration began quietly, but as a hostile crowd gathered the mood turned ugly. Rocks, eggs, and racial insults were hurled at the marchers. Gregory ignored police requests to leave and was arrested and convicted of disorderly conduct, consisting of "any improper noise, riot, disturbance, breach of the peace, or diversion tending to a breach of the peace." The Court overturned the conviction, calling it "a simple case." The Court disregarded the Illinois Supreme Court's narrowing construction of the disorderly conduct ordinance because the jury had not been instructed in accordance with it. That construction had limited disorderly conduct pre-mised on speech arousing a hostile reaction to situations where there was "an imminent threat of violence[; the] police have made all reasonable efforts to protect the demonstrators, [have] requested that the demonstration be stopped and [have] explained the request if [time permits;] and [there] is a refusal of the police request." Is the Chicago disorderly conduct ordinance, as construed by the Illinois Supreme Court, consistent with the free speech guarantee?

d. Indecent Speech, Broadcasting, and Captive Audiences

Recall Justice Harlan's observation in *Cohen* that the constitutional ability of government "to shut off discourse solely to protect others from hearing it [is] dependent upon a showing that substantial privacy interests are being invaded in an essentially intolerable manner." Does (or should) this suggest that when an audience is held captive to offensive speech, the constitutional ability of governments to control such speech is augmented? Does (or should) the same hold true for audiences that are especially vulnerable to the effects of offensive speech?

≡ ## FCC v. Pacifica Foundation
438 U.S. 726 (1978)

[On a weekday afternoon Pacifica's New York radio station broadcast a 12-minute monologue by George Carlin, a satirist, titled "Filthy Words." Carlin expressed his feelings about the social taboos concerning the "seven words [you] couldn't say on the public [airwaves], ever." The seven words—"shit," "piss," "fuck," "cunt," "cocksucker," "motherfucker," and "tits"—were repeated in various familiar colloquial ways, to the amusement of Carlin's recorded audience but not to a man who had his radio tuned to the broadcast while driving with his young son. In response to the man's complaint, the FCC issued a reprimand to the station and informed it that patently offensive but non-obscene material should be confined "to times of day when children most likely would not be exposed." The Court upheld the FCC reprimand.]

JUSTICE STEVENS delivered the opinion of the Court in Parts I, II, III, and IV.C, and, in Parts IV.A and IV.B, an opinion joined by CHIEF JUSTICE BURGER and JUSTICE REHNQUIST.

This case requires that we decide whether the Federal Communications Commission has any power to regulate a radio broadcast that is indecent but not obscene. [In Parts I, II, and III the Court concluded that the FCC had statutory "authority to impose sanctions on licensees who engage in obscene, indecent, or profane broadcasting," that Carlin's monologue was "indecent" (defined as being in "nonconformance with accepted standards of morality"), and that the FCC's statutory power to sanction "indecent" broadcasts was independent of and broader than its power to sanction obscene broadcasts.]

IV. B. [JUSTICE STEVENS, joined by CHIEF JUSTICE BURGER and JUSTICE REHNQUIST.] The question is whether the First Amendment denies government any power to restrict the public broadcast of indecent language in any circumstances. For if the government has any such power, this was an appropriate occasion for its exercise. [The] question in this case is whether a broadcast of patently offensive words dealing with sex and excretion may be regulated because of its content. [The] fact that society may find speech offensive is not a sufficient reason for suppressing it. Indeed, if it is the speaker's opinion that gives offense, that consequence is a reason for according it constitutional protection. [The] government must remain neutral in the marketplace of ideas. If there were any reason to believe that the Commission's characterization of the Carlin monologue as offensive could be traced to its political content—or even to the fact that it satirized contemporary attitudes about four-letter words[7]—First Amendment protection might be required. But that is simply not this case. These words offend for the same reasons that obscenity offends. Their place in the hierarchy of First Amendment values was aptly sketched [in *Chaplinsky*]: "[Such] utterances are no essential part of any exposition of ideas, and are of such slight social value as a step to truth that any benefit that may be derived from them is clearly outweighed by the social interest in order and morality."

Although these words ordinarily lack literary, political, or scientific value, they are not entirely outside the protection of the First Amendment. Some uses of even the most offensive words are unquestionably protected. [*Hess, Cohen.*] Indeed, we may assume, arguendo, that this monologue would be protected in other contexts. Nonetheless, the constitutional protection accorded to a communication containing such patently offensive sexual and excretory language need not be the same in every context. It is a characteristic of speech such as this that both its capacity to offend and its "social value" [vary] with the circumstances. Words that are commonplace in one setting are shocking in another. To paraphrase [Justice] Harlan, one occasion's lyric is another's vulgarity. [It] is undisputed that the content of Pacifica's broadcast was "vulgar," "offensive," and "shocking." Because content of that character is not entitled to absolute constitutional protection under all circumstances, we must consider its context in order to determine whether the Commission's action was constitutionally permissible.

IV. C. [OPINION OF THE COURT.] We have long recognized that each medium of expression presents special First Amendment problems. And of all forms of communication, it is broadcasting that has received the most limited First Amendment protection. [The reasons are] complex, but two have relevance [here]. First, the broadcast media have established a uniquely pervasive

7. The monologue does present a point of view; it attempts to show that the words it uses are "harmless" and that our attitudes toward them are "essentially silly." The Commission objects, not to this point of view, but to the way in which it is expressed. The belief that these words are harmless does not necessarily confer a First Amendment privilege to use them while proselytizing, just as the conviction that obscenity is harmless does not license one to communicate that conviction by the indiscriminate distribution of an obscene leaflet.

presence in the lives of all Americans. Patently offensive, indecent material presented over the airwaves confronts the citizen, not only in public, but also in the privacy of the home, where the individual's right to be left alone plainly outweighs the First Amendment rights of an intruder. Because the broadcast audience is constantly tuning in and out, prior warnings cannot completely protect the listener or viewer from unexpected program content. To say that one may avoid further offense by turning off the radio when he hears indecent language is like saying that the remedy for an assault is to run away after the first blow. One may hang up on an indecent phone call, but that option does not give the caller a constitutional immunity or avoid a harm that has already taken place. Outside the home, the balance between the offensive speaker and the unwilling audience may sometimes tip in favor of the speaker, requiring the offended listener to turn away. [*Erznoznik, Cohen.*]

Second, broadcasting is uniquely accessible to children, even those too young to read. Although Cohen's written message might have been incomprehensible to a first grader, Pacifica's broadcast could have enlarged a child's vocabulary in an instant. Other forms of offensive expression may be withheld from the young without restricting the expression at its source. Bookstores and motion picture theaters, for example, may be prohibited from making indecent material available to children. [But the] ease with which children may obtain access to broadcast material [amply justifies] special treatment of indecent broadcasting.

[We] emphasize the narrowness of our holding. This case does not involve a two-way radio conversation between a cab driver and a dispatcher, or a telecast of an Elizabethan comedy. We have not decided that an occasional expletive in either setting would justify any sanction [or] that this broadcast would justify a criminal prosecution. The Commission's decision rested entirely on a nuisance rationale under which context is all-important. [The] time of day was emphasized by the Commission. The content of the program in which the language is used will also affect the composition of the audience, and differences between radio, television, and perhaps closed-circuit transmissions, may also be relevant. As [Justice] Sutherland wrote, a "nuisance may be merely a right thing in the wrong place,—like a pig in the parlor instead of the barnyard." We simply hold that when the Commission finds that a pig has entered the parlor, the exercise of its regulatory power does not depend on proof that the pig is obscene.

JUSTICE POWELL, joined by JUSTICE BLACKMUN, concurring in all of the Court's opinion except Part IV.B.

The Court today reviews only the Commission's holding that Carlin's monologue was indecent "as broadcast" at two o'clock in the [afternoon]. . . . [The FCC] sought to "channel" the monologue to hours when the fewest unsupervised children would be exposed to it. [This] consideration provides strong support for the Commission's holding. [In] most instances, the dissemination of this kind of speech to children may be limited without also limiting willing adults' access to it. [But] such a physical separation of the audience cannot be accomplished in the broadcast media. During most of the broadcast hours [the] broadcaster cannot reach willing adults without also reaching children. This [justifies] a different treatment of the broadcast media for First Amendment purposes. [The FCC] was entitled to give substantial weight to this [difference].

. . . [I] do not join Part IV.B [because] I do not subscribe to the theory that [we] are free generally to decide on the basis of its content which speech protected by the First Amendment is most "valuable" and hence deserving of the most protection, and which is less "valuable" and hence deserving of less protection. [This] case does not turn on whether Carlin's monologue [has] more or less "value" than a candidate's campaign speech. [The] result turns instead on the unique characteristics of the broadcast media, combined with society's right to protect its children from speech generally agreed to be inappropriate for their years, and with the interest of unwilling adults in not being assaulted by such offensive speech in their homes.

JUSTICE BRENNAN, joined by JUSTICE MARSHALL, dissenting.

[An] individual's actions in switching on and listening to communications transmitted over the public airways and directed to the public at large do not implicate fundamental privacy interests, even when engaged in within the home. [Because] the radio is undeniably a public medium these actions are more properly viewed as a decision to take part [in] an ongoing public discourse [by allowing] public radio communications into his home. [And] unlike other intrusive modes of communication, such as sound trucks, "[the] radio can be turned off"—and with a minimum of effort. [Whatever] the minimal discomfort suffered by a listener who inadvertently tunes into a program he finds offensive during the brief interval before he can simply extend his arm and switch stations or flick the "off" button, it is surely worth the candle to preserve the broadcaster's right to send, and the right of those interested to receive, a message entitled to full First Amendment protection. To reach a contrary balance [is], to follow [Justice] Stevens'[s] reliance on animal metaphors, "to burn the house to roast the pig."

NOTES AND PROBLEMS

1. Which Rationale?   Several different rationales might explain the *Pacifica* decision: (a) a captive audience—Carlin's monologue might be forced upon an audience of unwilling listeners; (b) a vulnerable audience—impressionable children might hear Carlin's vulgarities; (c) low-value speech—Carlin's monologue was so distant from the core purposes of free speech that it was of low value and thus deserving of only limited protection; or (d) broadcasting as a special medium—it is clothed with a public trust such that it may be subject to greater government control than other forms of speech. Which rationale was crucial?

a. Captive audience.   In Rowan v. United States Post Office Department, 397 U.S. 728 (1970), the Court upheld a federal law permitting recipients of

Cher's acceptance of a Billboard Music award, where she said of her critics, "Fuck 'em"; and various episodes of the television series NYPD Blue that included use of the terms "bullshit" and "dickhead." Is the FCC's ban of fleeting expletives valid? In Federal Communications Commission v. Fox Television Stations, 132 S. Ct. 2307 (2012), the Supreme Court ruled that the application of the FCC's rule banning "obscene, indecent, or profane language" to fleeting expletives and momentary nudity was void for vagueness because the rule provided insufficient notice of what might be prohibited indecency.

c. Fairness Doctrine Revived. In Red Lion Broadcasting Co. v. Federal Communications Commission, 395 U.S. 367 (1969), the Court ruled that the FCC's "fairness doctrine," which required broadcasters to provide equal time for rebuttals of editorial commentary, did not violate the free speech guarantee. The Court relied primarily on the scarcity of the broadcast spectrum, and thought that licensing a broadcaster carried with it a public trust to air both sides of any opinion expressed. The fairness doctrine was repealed in the late 1980s. Given the advent of satellite radio, cable television, and the Internet, if the fairness doctrine were reinstated today, would it violate the First Amendment?

e.   Indecency, Cable Television, and the Internet

With the explosive growth of new communications technology that characterized the last two decades of the twentieth century, the Court began to deal with attempted regulation of indecent speech in those media.

In Denver Area Educational Telecommunications Consortium v. FCC, 518 U.S. 727 (1996), the Court upheld section 10(a) of the Cable Television Consumer Protection and Competition Act of 1992, which authorized cable television operators to refuse to carry "programming that the cable operator reasonably believes describes or depicts sexual or excretory activities or organs in a patently offensive manner as measured by contemporary community standards," but struck down sections 10(b) and (c) of the same law. Section 10(b) required a cable operator to place on a single channel all indecent programs that it elected to carry and to block viewer access to that channel unless the viewer requested access in writing. Section 10(c) permitted cable operators to ban obscenities, "sexually explicit conduct," and "material soliciting or promoting unlawful conduct" from public access programs that the operator was required to carry. No single rationale captured a majority of the Court.

On section 10(a), a plurality of four relied on *Pacifica*: The "importance of . . . protecting children from exposure to patently offensive depictions of sex . . . lead[s] us to conclude that §10(a) is a sufficiently tailored response to an extraordinarily important problem." They perceived cable channels as akin to radio broadcasts—easily accessible by children and with content that strikes without warning into the home. Nor did section 10(a) mandate an absolute ban. Adults could obtain access to indecent programming via satellite or videotape, and "the permissive nature of 10(a) means that it will likely restrict less speech than [in] *Pacifica*."

Three justices thought that section 10(a) simply gave back to cable operators what was always theirs: Just as an "author [has] no right to have [his] book sold in a particular bookstore without the storeowner's consent, [a] programmer [has] no freestanding First Amendment right to have [his] programming transmitted" by an unwilling cable operator.

Two dissenters argued that because section 10(a) was a presumptively void content-based regulation of protected speech the government had failed to prove that it was narrowly tailored to fit the compelling objective of preventing children from access to indecent programming. Because section 10(a) left it up to cable operators whether to carry indecent materials, children would be only sporadically protected, and an operator's refusal to carry indecent but protected speech would reduce adults to watching only what was fit for children.

Five justices invalidated section 10(b). The section was not necessary to accomplish the compelling objective of shielding children from televised indecency because it forced viewers to opt in rather than out of access to protected indecency and ignored other, less restrictive alternatives to accomplish the objective.

Another five justices voided section 10(c). The Court thought that the interest of cable operators in refusing to air indecent public access programming was weak: Because regulation of such programming would originate with local governments, those governments were adequately accountable for their indecent programs through normal political channels. The dissenters maintained that nobody, including governments, has a freestanding right of access to a cable operator's distribution network.

≡
≡ *Reno v. American Civil Liberties Union*
521 U.S. 844 (1997)

JUSTICE STEVENS delivered the opinion of the Court.

At issue is the constitutionality of two statutory provisions enacted to protect minors from "indecent" and "patently offensive" communications on the Internet. Notwithstanding the legitimacy and importance of the congressional goal of protecting children from harmful materials, we agree with [the] District Court that the statute abridges "the freedom of speech" protected by the First Amendment. . . .

[The] two statutory provisions [of the] "Communications Decency Act of 1996" (CDA) challenged in this case [are] the "indecent transmission" provision and the "patently offensive display" provision. The ["indecent transmission" provision] prohibits the knowing transmission of obscene or indecent messages to any recipient under 18 years of age. [The "patently offensive display" provision] prohibits the knowing sending or displaying of patently offensive messages in a manner that is available to a person under 18 years of age. It [covers any communication via an interactive computer service that] "depicts or describes, in terms patently offensive as measured by contemporary community standards, sexual or excretory activities or organs." . . . [There] are significant differences between the order upheld in *Pacifica* and the CDA. First, the order in *Pacifica* [targeted] a specific broadcast that represented a rather dramatic departure from traditional program content in order to designate when—rather than whether—it would be permissible to air such a program in that particular medium. . . . Second, unlike the CDA, the [FCC's] declaratory order was not punitive; we expressly refused to decide whether the indecent broadcast "would justify a criminal prosecution." Finally, the [FCC's] order applied to a medium which as a matter of history had "received the most limited First Amendment protection," in large part because warnings could not adequately protect the listener from unexpected program content. The Internet, however, has no comparable history [and] the risk of encountering indecent material by accident is remote because a series of affirmative steps is required to access specific material. . . .

[The] CDA is a content-based blanket restriction on speech. . . . [Some] of our cases have recognized special justifications for regulation of the broadcast media [but those] factors are not present in cyberspace. Neither before nor after the enactment of the CDA have the vast democratic fora of the Internet been subject to the type of government supervision and regulation that has attended the broadcast industry. [The] Internet is not as "invasive" as radio or television. . . . [Finally], the Internet can hardly be considered a "scarce" expressive commodity. It provides relatively unlimited, low-cost capacity for communication of all kinds. [There is] no basis for qualifying the level of First Amendment scrutiny that should be applied to this medium. . . .

[The CDA] unquestionably silences some speakers whose messages would be entitled to constitutional protection. . . . In order to deny minors access to potentially harmful speech, the CDA effectively suppresses a large amount of speech that adults have a constitutional right to receive and to address to one another. [While it] is true that we have repeatedly recognized the governmental interest in protecting children from harmful materials, [that] interest does not justify an unnecessarily broad suppression of speech addressed to adults. . . . Given the size of the potential audience for most messages, in the absence of a viable age verification process, the sender must be charged with knowing that one or more minors will likely view it, [a fact that will] surely burden communication among adults. . . . The breadth of the CDA's coverage is wholly unprecedented. . . . [The general, undefined terms "indecent" and "patently offensive" cover large amounts of non-pornographic material with serious educational or other value. Moreover, the "community standards" criterion as applied to the Internet means that any communication available to a nation-wide audience will be judged by the standards of the community most likely to be offended by the message. [A] parent who sent his 17-year-old college freshman information on birth control via e-mail could be incarcerated even though neither he, his child, nor anyone in their home community, found the material "indecent" or "patently offensive," if the college town's community thought otherwise. The breadth of this content-based restriction of speech imposes an especially heavy burden on the Government to explain why a less restrictive provision would not be as effective as the CDA. It has not done so. [We] are persuaded that the CDA is not narrowly tailored. . . .

[Affirmed.]

NOTES

1. *Playboy Entertainment Group.* In United States v. Playboy Entertainment Group, 529 U.S. 803 (2000), the Court voided section 505 of the Telecommunications Act of 1996, which requires cable television operators providing channels "primarily dedicated to sexually-oriented programming" either to "fully scramble or otherwise fully block" those channels or to limit their transmission to hours when children are unlikely to be viewing, declared to be between 10 P.M. and 6 A.M. Because scrambling does not always work, most cable operators adopted the "time channeling" approach so that, for two-thirds of each day, no viewers in the service area could receive sexually oriented programming. The Court ruled that this content-based speech restriction was void because the government might further its interests in less restrictive ways, such as "targeted blocking," which requires a cable operator, "upon request by a cable service subscriber . . . without charge, [to] fully scramble or otherwise fully block" any channel the subscriber does not wish to receive.

2. **Regulating Computer Code.** The technology of the Internet is not fixed. The Court assumes that changes will come about through the private actions of those who write computer code. Is free speech implicated if governments require computer code to be written in such a way that nobody can access indecent material without revealing facts sufficient to verify that the user is an adult or a minor?

6. False Statements of Fact

The Court has declared that "[t]here is no constitutional value in false statements of fact," yet it has also said that "[u]nder the First Amendment there is no such thing as a false idea." Because false statements of fact are "inevitable in free debate, [the free speech guarantee] requires that we protect some falsehood in order to protect speech that matters." But which falsehoods should be protected and how much protection should they receive?

a. Defamation

≡ *New York Times Co. v. Sullivan*
≡ *376 U.S. 254 (1964)*

JUSTICE BRENNAN delivered the opinion of the Court.

We are required in this case to determine for the first time the extent to which the constitutional protections for speech and press limit a State's power to award damages in a libel action brought by a public official against critics of his official conduct. [Sullivan, the police commissioner of Montgomery, Alabama, successfully prosecuted a libel action in the Alabama courts against the New York Times and four black clergymen. A jury awarded $500,000 damages] and the Supreme Court of Alabama affirmed. [Sullivan] alleged that he had been libeled by [a] full-page advertisement [in] the New York Times on March 29, 1960, [entitled] "Heed Their Rising Voices." [The crux of the libel claim was based on a statement in the advertisement that in Montgomery, Alabama,] "the Southern violators have answered Dr. King's peaceful protests with intimidation and violence. They have bombed his home [and] assaulted his person. They have arrested him seven times — for 'speeding,' 'loitering' and similar 'offenses.'"

Although [Sullivan was not mentioned] by name, he contended that the word "police" [referred] to him as the Montgomery [Police Commissioner, and] that since arrests are ordinarily made by the police, the statement "They have arrested [Dr. King] seven times" would be read as referring to [him]. It is uncontroverted that . . . Dr. King had not been arrested seven times, but only [four].

[Under Alabama law the advertisement was libel per se, and the defendant's only defense is to prove the absolute truth of the statements. General damages could be awarded without proof of any pecuniary loss.] We reverse [because] the rule of law applied by the Alabama courts is constitutionally deficient for failure to provide the safeguards for freedom of speech and of the press that are required by the [First Amendment] in a libel action brought by a public official against critics of his official conduct. . . .

[Sullivan] relies heavily, as did the Alabama courts, on statements of this Court to the effect that the Constitution does not protect libelous publications. . . . None of the cases sustained the use of libel laws to impose sanctions upon expression critical of the official conduct of public officials. [Libel] can claim no talismanic immunity from constitutional limitations. It must be measured by standards that satisfy the First Amendment.

[We] consider this case against the background of a profound national commitment to the principle that debate on public issues should be uninhibited, robust, and wide-open, and that it may well include vehement, caustic, and sometimes unpleasantly sharp attacks on government and public officials. The present advertisement, as an expression of grievance and protest on one of the major public issues of our time, would seem clearly to qualify for the constitutional protection. The question is whether it forfeits that protection by the falsity of some of its factual statements and by its alleged defamation of respondent. [The] constitutional protection [afforded speech] does not turn upon "the truth [of] the ideas and beliefs which are offered." [Erroneous statement] is inevitable in free debate, and [it] must be protected if the freedoms of expression are to have the "breathing space" that they "need [to] survive." [Injury] to official reputation affords no more warrant for repressing speech that would otherwise be free than does factual error. [Criticism of] official conduct does not lose its constitutional protection merely because it is effective criticism and hence diminishes [official] reputations.

If neither factual error nor defamatory content suffices to remove the constitutional shield from criticism of official conduct, the combination of the two elements is no less inadequate. This is the lesson to be drawn from the great controversy over the Sedition Act of 1798, which first crystallized a national awareness of the central meaning of the First Amendment. See Levy, Legacy of Suppression (1960); Smith, Freedom's Fetters (1956). That statute made it a crime [to make] "any false, scandalous and malicious writing [against] the government, [or] Congress, [or] the President, [with] intent to defame, [bring into] contempt or disrepute; or to excite against them [the] hatred of the good people of the United States." [Although] the Sedition Act was never tested in this Court, the attack upon its validity has carried the day in the court of history. Fines levied in its prosecution were repaid by Act of Congress on the ground that it was unconstitutional. Jefferson, as President, pardoned those who had been convicted and sentenced under the Act and remitted their [fines]. Its invalidity [has] been assumed by Justices of this Court. . . . [What] a State may not constitutionally bring about by means of a criminal statute is likewise beyond the reach of its civil law of libel. The fear of damage awards . . . may be markedly more inhibiting than the fear of prosecution under a criminal statute. [Multiple judgments] may be awarded against petitioners for the same publication. Whether or not a newspaper can survive a succession of such judgments, the pall of fear and timidity imposed upon those who would give voice to public criticism is an atmosphere in which the First Amendment freedoms cannot survive.

[Alabama's] rule of law is not saved by its allowance of the defense of truth. [A] rule compelling the critic of official conduct to guarantee the truth of all his factual assertions—and to do so on pain of libel judgments virtually unlimited in amount—leads [to] "self-censorship." Allowance of the defense of truth, with the burden of proving it on the defendant, does not mean that only false speech will be deterred. Even a false statement may be deemed to make a valuable contribution to public debate, since it brings about "the clearer perception and livelier impression of truth, produced by its collision with error." Mill, On Liberty; Milton, Areopagitica. Under [the Alabama] rule, would-be critics of official conduct may be deterred from voicing their criticism, even though it is believed to be true and even though it is in fact true, because of doubt whether it can be proved in court or fear of the expense of having to do so. [The] rule thus dampens the vigor and limits the variety of public debate. It is inconsistent with the First [Amendment].

[Free expression requires] a federal rule that prohibits a public official from recovering damages for a defamatory falsehood relating to his official conduct unless he proves that the statement was made with "actual malice"—that is, with knowledge that it was false or with reckless disregard of whether it was false or not. [We] conclude that such a privilege is required by the First Amendment. [Applying this standard], we consider that the proof presented to show actual malice lacks the convincing clarity which the constitutional standard demands, and hence that it would not constitutionally sustain the judgment for [Sullivan]. There was no evidence whatever that [the individual defendants] were aware of any erroneous statements or were in any way [reckless]. As to the Times, [the evidence] supports at most a finding of negligence in failing to discover the misstatements, and is constitutionally insufficient to show the recklessness that is required for a finding of actual malice. . . . Reversed and remanded.

JUSTICE BLACK, joined by JUSTICE DOUGLAS, concurring in the judgment.

I base my vote to reverse on the belief that the [free expression guarantee does] not merely "delimit" a State's power to award damages to "public officials against critics of their official conduct" but completely prohibit[s] a State from exercising such a power. [The] requirement that malice be proved provides at best an evanescent protection for the right critically to discuss public [affairs]. I vote to reverse exclusively on the ground that the Times and the individual defendants had an absolute, unconditional constitutional right to publish [their] criticisms of the Montgomery agencies and officials.

JUSTICE GOLDBERG, joined by JUSTICE DOUGLAS, concurring in the judgment.

In my view, [the] Constitution afford[s] to the citizen and to the press an absolute, unconditional privilege to criticize official conduct despite the harm which may flow from excesses and abuses. [This] is not to say that the Constitution protects defamatory statements directed against the private conduct of a public official or private citizen. [Purely] private defamation has little to do with the political ends of a self-governing society.

NOTES

1. Why Protect Falsity? After *Sullivan*, a public official plaintiff has the burden of proving that the defendant made the defamatory statement with actual malice. But what is the value of protecting false statements? Is it, as Milton and Mill argued, that falsity helps clarify the truth? Or is there a more pragmatic reason—that false statements (although of no value) must be given some protection in order to foster and protect speech that does matter? *Sullivan* draws the line at the known or reckless lie about public officials, implying that honestly mistaken criticisms of public officials are of constitutional value but that the deliberate lie is of no value. Would the deliberate lie be of value to Milton or Mill? Does *Sullivan* inadequately protect the reputation interest of public figures? Would the free speech interests *Sullivan* sought to protect be adequately protected if public figures were able to establish liability for defamation under common law principles but were barred from receiving damages unless actual malice was proven? See, e.g., Epstein, Was New York Times v. Sullivan Wrong?, 53 U. Chi. L. Rev. 782 (1986); Franklin, A Declaratory Judgment Alternative to Current Libel Law, 74 Cal. L. Rev. 809 (1986).

2. The Extension of *Sullivan* to Public Figures. Two 1967 cases, Curtis Publishing Co. v. Butts and Associated Press v. Walker, decided together at 388 U.S. 130 (1967), extended the *Sullivan* rule to include defamation of public figures as well as of public officials. Wally Butts, a well-known former football coach at the University of Georgia, claimed he was defamed by an article in the Saturday Evening Post that asserted he had fixed a game. Edwin Walker, a prominent retired general, claimed that the Associated Press had defamed him by reporting that he had led a violent crowd in opposition to desegregation of the University of Mississippi. Walker and Butts were found to be public figures. Chief Justice Warren explained for the Court that

> "public figures," like "public officials," often play an influential role in ordering society [and have] as ready access as "public officials" to mass media, [both] to influence policy and counter criticism of [them]. Our citizenry has a legitimate and substantial interest in the conduct of such persons; [uninhibited] debate about their involvement in public issues and events is as crucial as [with] "public officials."

But who is a "public figure"? The Court in *Butts* and *Walker* suggested that public figures were those people who are "intimately involved in the resolution of important public questions or who, by reason of their fame, shape events in areas of concern to society at large." In Gertz v. Robert Welch, Inc., 418 U.S. 323 (1974), the Court opined that public figures were people

> [who] have assumed roles of special prominence in the affairs of society. Some occupy positions of such persuasive power and influence that they are deemed public figures for all purposes. More commonly, those classed as public figures have thrust themselves to the forefront of particular public controversies in order to influence the resolution of the issues involved.

As the *Gertz* quote suggests, an "unlimited" public figure—a public figure for all times and purposes—is a person who has achieved pervasive fame by reason of his or her involvement in public affairs. Is Al Gore an unlimited public figure? Is Rush Limbaugh? Oprah Winfrey? Jesse Jackson? George Clooney? The *Gertz* Court also noted an alternative way to become a public figure: "More commonly, an individual voluntarily injects himself or is drawn into a particular public controversy and thereby becomes a public figure for a limited range of issues." To become a "limited-purpose" public figure a person must either "thrust himself into the vortex of the public issue, [or] engage the public's attention in an attempt to influence its outcome." In Time, Inc. v. Firestone, 424 U.S. 448 (1976), the Court ruled that a Palm Beach socialite was not a public figure for purposes of her defamation suit against Time magazine, which had falsely reported that she had been divorced by her husband for adultery. She had no "especial prominence" in public affairs, nor had she "thrust herself to the forefront of any particular public controversy in order to influence the resolution of issues involved in it." Is a labor union leader who achieves local prominence in a strike a limited purpose public figure?

The Court has suggested that a person may, on "exceedingly rare" occasions, involuntarily become a public figure but has never so held. In Wolston v. Reader's Digest Association, 443 U.S. 157 (1979), the Court ruled that Wolston, who had been convicted of contempt some 20 years earlier for refusing to appear before a grand jury investigating Soviet espionage, was not a limited-purpose public figure for purposes of his defamation suit against the publisher of a book falsely identifying him as a Soviet agent. Despite the fact that the falsity involved "comment on a limited range of issues relating to his [contempt] conviction," Wolston had not sought "public [attention] in an attempt to influence the resolutions of the issues involved." Hutchinson v. Proxmire, 443 U.S. 111 (1979), held that a previously obscure professor studying monkeys at federal expense was not catapulted into public-figure status by Senator Proxmire's bestowal upon him of the senator's highly publicized "Golden Fleece Award," which dramatized receipt of federal money for purposes that Proxmire thought epitomized wasteful government spending. Is Monica Lewinsky a limited-purpose public figure?

3. Defamation of Private Figures.   In Rosenbloom v. Metromedia, Inc., 403 U.S. 29 (1971), a plurality of the Court argued that the subject matter of the alleged defamation ought to be the deciding factor for application of the *Sullivan* rule: "If a matter is a subject of general or public interest, it cannot suddenly become less so merely because a private individual is [involved]. The public's primary interest is in the event." But in *Gertz* the Court altered course.

≡≡≡ *Gertz v. Robert Welch, Inc.*
      418 U.S. 323 (1974)

[After Nuccio, a Chicago policeman, was convicted of murdering Nelson, Elmer Gertz, an active and modestly well-known Chicago lawyer, represented Nelson's family in a civil suit against Nuccio. American Opinion, the monthly magazine of the John Birch Society (published by Welch), ran an article that claimed Gertz had "framed" Nuccio and had a criminal record and long Communist affiliations. Gertz sued for defamation and received a damage award of $50,000. The trial court set the judgment aside, ruling that the *Sullivan* standard applied. The Supreme Court reversed, concluding that Gertz was not a public figure because he had no public role in the Nuccio prosecution and never discussed either the civil or criminal litigation with the press.]

JUSTICE POWELL delivered the opinion of the Court.

[We] reconsider the extent of a publisher's constitutional privilege against liability for defamation of a private citizen.

[Under] the First Amendment there is no such thing as a false idea. However pernicious an opinion may seem, we depend for its correction [on] the competition of other ideas. But there is no constitutional value in false statements of fact. Neither the intentional lie nor the careless error materially advances society's interest in "uninhibited, robust, and wide-open" debate on public issues. They belong to that category of utterances which "are no essential part of any exposition of ideas, and are of such slight social value as a step to truth that any benefit that may be derived from them is clearly outweighed by the social interest in order and morality."Although the erroneous statement of fact is not worthy of constitutional protection, it is nevertheless inevitable in free debate. And punishment of error runs the risk of inducing a cautious and restrictive exercise of the constitutionally guaranteed freedoms of speech and press. [A] rule of strict liability that compels a publisher or broadcaster to guarantee the accuracy of his factual assertions may lead to intolerable self-censorship. Allowing the media to avoid liability only by proving the truth of all injurious statements does not accord adequate protection to First Amendment liberties. [But the] need to avoid self-censorship by the news media [is] not the only societal value at issue. If it were, this Court would have embraced long ago the view that publishers and broadcasters enjoy an unconditional and indefeasible immunity from liability for defamation. [The] legitimate state interest underlying the law of libel is the compensation of individuals for the harm inflicted on them by defamatory falsehood. [In] our continuing effort to define the proper accommodation between these competing concerns, we have been especially anxious to assure to the freedoms of speech and press that "breathing space" essential to their fruitful exercise. [But redress for] injury to the reputation of private individuals requires that a different rule should obtain with respect to them.

[Public] officials and public figures usually enjoy significantly greater access to the channels of effective communication and hence have a more realistic opportunity to counteract false statements than private individuals normally enjoy. Private individuals are therefore more vulnerable to injury, and the state interest in protecting them is correspondingly greater. [There is also] a compelling normative consideration underlying the distinction between public and private defamation plaintiffs. An individual who decides to seek governmental office [runs] the risk of closer public scrutiny than might otherwise be the case. And society's interest in the officers of government is not strictly limited to the formal discharge of official duties. [Public] figures are in a similar position. [They] have thrust themselves to the forefront of particular public controversies in order to influence the resolution of the issues involved [and thus] invite attention and comment. [For] these reasons we conclude that the States should retain substantial latitude in their efforts to enforce a legal remedy for defamatory falsehood injurious to the reputation of a private individual.

We hold that, so long as they do not impose liability without fault, the States may define for themselves the appropriate standard of liability for a publisher or broadcaster of defamatory falsehood injurious to a private individual. This approach [recognizes] the strength of the legitimate state interest in compensating private individuals for wrongful injury to reputation, yet shields the press and broadcast media from the rigors of strict liability for defamation. At least this conclusion obtains where, as here, the substance of the defamatory statement "makes substantial danger to reputation apparent." [Our] inquiry would involve considerations somewhat different [if] a State purported to condition civil liability on a factual misstatement whose content did not warn a reasonably prudent editor or broadcaster of its defamatory potential. [In any case, liability premised on negligence] in defamation suits by private individuals [extends] no further than compensation for actual injury. [We] hold that the States may not permit recovery of presumed or punitive damages [when] liability is not based on a showing of knowledge of falsity or reckless disregard for the truth.

The common law of defamation is an oddity of tort law, for it allows [juries to] award substantial sums as compensation for supposed damage to reputation without any proof that such harm actually occurred. The largely uncontrolled discretion of juries to award damages where there is no loss unnecessarily compounds the potential of any system of liability for defamatory falsehood to inhibit the vigorous exercise of First Amendment freedoms. Additionally, the doctrine of presumed damages invites juries to punish unpopular opinion rather than to compensate individuals for injury sustained by the publication of a false fact. [States] have no substantial interest in securing for [private figure plaintiffs] gratuitous awards of money damages far in excess of any actual injury. [To] reconcile state [tort law with the] constitutional command of the First Amendment [it] is necessary to restrict defamation plaintiffs who do not prove knowledge of falsity or reckless disregard for the truth to compensation for actual injury. We need not define "actual injury," [but it] is not limited to out-of-pocket loss [and may] include impairment of reputation and standing in the community, personal humiliation, and mental anguish and suffering. [Reversed and remanded.]

JUSTICE DOUGLAS, dissenting.

Like Congress, States are without power "to use a civil libel law or any other law to impose damages for merely discussing public affairs."

JUSTICE BRENNAN, dissenting.

I cannot agree [that] free and robust debate [is] permitted adequate "breathing space" when, as the Court holds, the States may impose all but strict liability for defamation if the defamed party is a private person and "the substance of the defamatory statement 'makes substantial danger to reputation apparent.'" I adhere to my view expressed in [*Rosenbloom*] that we strike the proper accommodation between avoidance of media self-censorship and protection of individual reputations only when we require States to apply the [*Sullivan* actual malice] standard in civil libel actions concerning media reports of the involvement of private individuals in events of public or general interest.

JUSTICE WHITE, dissenting.

The impact of today's decision on the traditional law of libel is immediately obvious and indisputable. No longer will the plaintiff be able to rest his case with proof of a libel defamatory on its [face]. In addition, he must prove some further degree of culpable conduct on the part of the publisher, such as intentional or reckless falsehood or negligence. And if he succeeds in this respect, [his] recovery for loss of reputation will be conditioned upon "competent" proof of actual injury to his standing in the community. . . . The Court rejects the judgment of experience that some publications are so inherently capable of injury, and actual injury so difficult to prove, that the risk of falsehood should be borne by the publisher, not the victim. [These] are radical [changes]. They should at least be shown to be required by the First Amendment or necessitated by our present circumstances. Neither has been demonstrated.

[Scant], if any, evidence exists that the First Amendment was intended to abolish the common law of libel, at least to the extent of depriving ordinary citizens of meaningful redress against their defamers. [The] central meaning of *New York Times* . . . is that seditious libel—criticism of government and public officials—falls beyond the police power of the State. [But] neither *New York Times* nor its progeny suggest that the First Amendment intended [to] deprive the private citizen of his historic recourse to redress published false-hoods damaging to [reputation]. . . .

NOTES

1. **Defamatory Speech of Purely Private Concern.** Although *Gertz* scrapped the *Rosenbloom* plurality's "speech of public concern" test, the speech at issue in *Gertz* was in fact of public concern. That element was cru-cial in Dun & Bradstreet v. Greenmoss Builders, 472 U.S. 749 (1985). Dun & Bradstreet (D&B) provides confidential reports to its subscribers concern-ing the creditworthiness of individuals and businesses. D&B issued a false report that Greenmoss Builders had filed for bankruptcy. In a Vermont defa-mation action, the Vermont courts refused to apply either *Sullivan* or *Gertz*. Greenmoss prevailed at trial, receiving an award of $50,000 for compensatory damages and $300,000 in punitive damages. The Vermont Supreme Court upheld the award, and the Supreme Court agreed. Justice Powell, writing for himself and Justices Rehnquist and O'Connor, declared:

> The question presented [is] whether [*Gertz*] applies when the false and de-famatory statements [about a private figure] do not involve matters of public concern. [To determine this, we] balance the State's interest in compensating private individuals for injury to their reputation against the First Amendment in-terest in protecting this type of expression. This ["strong and legitimate"] state interest is [securing] "the individual's right to the protection of his own good name." [The] First Amendment interest, on the other hand, is less important than the one weighed in *Gertz*. . . . It is speech on "matters of public concern" that is "at the heart of the First Amendment's protection." [S]peech on mat-ters of purely private concern is of less First Amendment concern. [The] credit report concerns no public issue. It was speech solely in the individual interest of the speaker and its specific business audience. . . . [We] conclude that per-mitting recovery of presumed and punitive damages in defamation cases absent a showing of "actual malice" does not violate the First Amendment when the defamatory statements do not involve matters of public concern.

2. Burden of Proof of Defamation. In Philadelphia Newspapers, Inc. v. Hepps, 475 U.S. 767 (1986), the Court held that plaintiffs in cases governed by either the *Sullivan* or *Gertz* rules must prove the defamatory character of the speech, including its falsity. This reversed the common law rule, which placed on defendants the burden of proving the truth of defamatory statements.

3. No Special Protection for Opinions. In Milkovich v. Lorain Journal Co., 497 U.S. 1 (1990), the Court rejected the idea that a separate constitutional privilege must be created for opinions. Because actual malice must be proved in actions governed by *Sullivan* and *Gertz*, a defamation plaintiff must prove that the statement is actually false. When statements contain an inference of falsity, merely shrouding them in the language of opinion confers no constitutional immunity. "If a speaker says, 'In my opinion John Jones is a liar,' he implies a knowledge of facts which lead to the conclusion that Jones told an untruth [and] can cause as much damage to reputation as the statement, 'Jones is a liar.'"

4. Commercial Defamation. False disparagement of a product or service is an actionable tort in many jurisdictions. The Court has never ruled on the question of whether such speech is entitled to any constitutional protection and, if so, whether the *Sullivan* or *Gertz* standards apply. In Bose Corp. v. Consumers Union, 466 U.S. 485 (1984), the Court accepted the lower court's use of the actual malice standard in a product disparagement case but expressly reserved decision on whether actual malice was constitutionally required.

About a dozen states have enacted laws that create a cause of action in favor of farmers or ranchers whose food products are falsely disparaged. An example is Texas's Perishable Food Products Act, Tex. Civ. Prac. & Rem. Code §§96.001-004, which subjects to civil liability any person who publicizes information known to him to be false that "states or implies that [a] perishable food product is not safe for [public] consumption."

Query: Suppose Texas dropped the scienter requirement from its law, thus imposing civil liability on negligent product disparagement. If a person unwittingly makes false claims about the safety of irradiated food, or milk produced from cattle fed growth hormones, or genetically altered fruits, or food treated with herbicides or pesticides, should the *Sullivan* standard apply? Should *Gertz* apply? For a report claiming that the existence of these statutes has chilled public discussion of these issues, see N.Y. Times, June 1, 1999, at A1.

5. A Summary. The constitutional law of libel can be schematically outlined as follows. If the plaintiff is a public official or public figure, *Sullivan*'s actual malice rule applies. If the plaintiff is a private figure and the defamation is of public concern, recovery of actual damages requires proof of negligence, and recovery of punitive damages requires proof of actual malice. If the plaintiff is a private figure and the defamation is of purely private concern, actual and punitive damages can be recovered upon proof of negligence.

b. *"False Light" Invasion of Privacy*

Tortious invasions of legally protected privacy interests can occur in a variety of ways. This subsection is concerned with statements that cast a person in a "false light. The emergence of privacy as an interest capable of vindication by tort law came about in the latter part of the nineteenth century; the earliest recognition of the concept is generally credited to Warren and Brandeis, The Right to Privacy, 4 Harv. L. Rev. 193 (1890).

Time, Inc. v. Hill, 385 U.S. 374 (1967). The Court applied the *Sullivan* standard to suits brought under a New York statute that created a cause of action for materially false but non-defamatory statements about newsworthy events concerning the plaintiff. In 1952, the Hill family had been held hostage by criminals, who had not harmed them. Three years later, Life magazine published a story about a play, "The Desperate Hours," derived from a novel that was based on the experience of the Hill family. Scenes from the play depicting violent treatment of the hostages were photographed and published in Life, together with text that implied that the scenes depicted the actual treatment of the Hills. A judgment in favor of Hill was reversed by the Court. The Court said that "the constitutional protections for speech and press preclude the application of the New York statute to redress false reports of matters of public interest in the absence of proof that the defendant published the report with knowledge of its falsity or in reckless disregard of the truth."

Queries: Is *Hill* still good law after *Gertz?* Are the reasons for dispensing with actual malice in connection with defamation of private figures equally applicable to "false light" invasion of privacy of private figures? In Wood v. Hustler Magazine, 736 F.2d 1084 (5th Cir. 1984), the Court of Appeals applied a negligence standard to a suit against Hustler, which had published stolen nude photos of Wood accompanied by offensive statements. The Court of Appeals concluded that "false light" invasion of privacy claims were governed by the same constitutional standards applicable to defamation actions, but held that, after *Gertz,* liability for actual damages could be founded on Hustler's negligence in failing to investigate whether the forged consent accompanying the photos was genuine.

c. *Lies About Oneself*

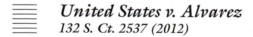

United States v. Alvarez
132 S. Ct. 2537 (2012)

JUSTICE KENNEDY delivered an opinion in which CHIEF JUSTICE ROBERTS and JUSTICES GINSBURG and SOTOMAYOR joined.

Lying was his habit. Xavier Alvarez . . . lied when he said that he played hockey for the Detroit Red Wings and that he once married a starlet from Mexico. But when he lied in announcing he held the Congressional Medal of

Honor [he violated] a federal criminal statute, the Stolen Valor Act of 2005. 18 U.S.C. §704.

In 2007, respondent attended his first public meeting as a board member of the Three Valley Water District Board. The board is a governmental entity with headquarters in Claremont, California. He introduced himself as follows: "I'm a retired marine of 25 years. I retired in the year 2001. Back in 1987, I was awarded the Congressional Medal of Honor. I got wounded many times by the same guy." None of this was true. For all the record shows, respondent's statements were but a pathetic attempt to gain respect that eluded him. The statements do not seem to have been made to secure employment or financial benefits or admission to privileges reserved for those who had earned the Medal.

Respondent was indicted [and convicted] under the Stolen Valor Act for lying about the Congressional Medal of Honor at the meeting. . . . The United States Court of Appeals for the Ninth Circuit . . . found the Act invalid under the First Amendment and reversed the conviction. . . . This Court granted certiorari. . . .

It is right and proper that Congress, over a century ago, established an award so the Nation can hold in its highest respect and esteem those who, in the course of carrying out the "supreme and noble duty of contributing to the defense of the rights and honor of the nation," have acted with extraordinary honor. And it should be uncontested that this is a legitimate Government objective, indeed a most valued national aspiration and purpose. [But] laws enacted to honor the brave must be consistent with the precepts of the Constitution for which they fought. . . . When content-based speech regulation is in question, . . . exacting scrutiny is required. . . . By this measure, the statutory provisions under which respondent was convicted must be held invalid, and his conviction must be set aside.

I. . . . [B]ecause [Alvarez's] lie concerned the Congressional Medal of Honor, he was subject to an enhanced penalty. . . .[8]

Respondent challenges the statute as a content-based suppression of pure speech, speech not falling within any of the few categories of expression where content-based regulation is permissible. The Government . . . argues that false statements "have no First Amendment value in themselves," and thus "are protected only to the extent needed to avoid chilling fully protected speech." . . . [T]he Government argues that [the Act] leaves breathing room for protected speech, for example speech which might criticize the idea of the Medal or the importance of the military. The Government's arguments cannot suffice to save the statute.

8. 18 U.S.C. §704 provides in part: "(b) Whoever falsely represents himself or herself, verbally or in writing, to have been awarded any decoration or medal authorized by Congress for the Armed Forces of the United States . . . shall be fined under this title, imprisoned not more than six months, or both. (c) If a decoration or medal involved in an offense under subsection (a) or (b) is a Congressional Medal of Honor, in lieu of the punishment provided in that subsection, the offender shall be fined under this title, imprisoned not more than 1 year, or both. — Ed.

lies can serve to reawaken and reinforce the public's respect for the Medal, its recipients, and its high purpose. . . .

The remedy for speech that is false is speech that is true. This is the ordinary course in a free society. The response to the unreasoned is the rational; to the uninformed, the enlightened; to the straight-out lie, the simple truth. . . . In addition, when the Government seeks to regulate protected speech, the restriction must be the "least restrictive means among available, effective alternatives." There is . . . at least one less speech-restrictive means by which the Government could likely protect the integrity of the military awards system. A Government-created database could list Congressional Medal of Honor winners. Were a database accessible through the Internet, it would be easy to verify and expose false claims. It appears some private individuals have already created databases similar to this, and at least one database of past winners is online and fully searchable. . . . The judgment of the Court of Appeals is affirmed.

JUSTICE BREYER, with whom JUSTICE KAGAN joins, concurring in the judgment.

I agree with the plurality that the Stolen Valor Act of 2005 violates the First Amendment . . . . In determining whether a statute violates the First Amendment, this Court has often found it appropriate to examine the fit between statutory ends and means. In doing so, it has examined speech-related harms, justifications, and potential alternatives. In particular, it has taken account of the seriousness of the speech-related harm the provision will likely cause, the nature and importance of the provision's countervailing objectives, the extent to which the provision will tend to achieve those objectives, and whether there are other, less restrictive ways of doing so. Ultimately the Court has had to determine whether the statute works speech-related harm that is out of proportion to its justifications. Sometimes the Court has referred to this approach as "intermediate scrutiny," sometimes as "proportionality" review, sometimes as an examination of "fit," and sometimes it has avoided the application of any label at all. Regardless of the label, some such approach is necessary if the First Amendment is to offer proper protection in the many instances in which a statute adversely affects constitutionally protected interests but warrants neither near-automatic condemnation (as "strict scrutiny" implies) nor near-automatic approval (as is implicit in "rational basis" review). But in this case, . . . "intermediate scrutiny" describes what I think we should do. . . .

False factual statements can serve useful human objectives, for example: in social contexts, where they may prevent embarrassment, protect privacy, shield a person from prejudice, provide the sick with comfort, or preserve a child's innocence; in public contexts, where they may stop a panic or otherwise preserve calm in the face of danger; and even in technical, philosophical, and scientific contexts, where (as Socrates' methods suggest) examination of a false statement (even if made deliberately to mislead) can promote a form of thought that ultimately helps realize the truth. . . .

[F]ew statutes, if any, simply prohibit without limitation the telling of a lie, even a lie about one particular matter. Instead, . . . limitations of context, requirements of proof of injury, and the like, narrow the statute to a subset of lies where specific harm is more likely to occur. . . . The statute before us lacks any such limiting features. . . . [T]hat breadth means that it creates a significant risk of First Amendment harm. . . .

[But] the statute nonetheless has substantial justification. It seeks to protect the interests of those who have sacrificed their health and life for their country. The statute . . . risks harming protected interests but only in order to achieve a substantial countervailing objective. . . . We must therefore ask whether it is possible substantially to achieve the Government's objective in less burdensome ways. In my view, the answer to this question is "yes." . . . [A] more finely tailored statute might, as other kinds of statutes prohibiting false factual statements have done, insist upon a showing that the false statement caused specific harm or at least was material, or focus its coverage on lies most likely to be harmful or on contexts where such lies are most likely to cause harm. . . . The Government has provided no convincing explanation as to why a more finely tailored statute would not work. . . . That being so, I find the statute as presently drafted works disproportionate constitutional harm. It consequently fails intermediate scrutiny, and so violates the First Amendment.

JUSTICE ALITO, with whom JUSTICE SCALIA and JUSTICE THOMAS join, dissenting.

. . . The statute reaches only knowingly false statements about hard facts directly within a speaker's personal knowledge. These lies have no value in and of themselves, and proscribing them does not chill any valuable speech. By holding that the First Amendment nevertheless shields these lies, the Court breaks sharply from a long line of cases recognizing that the right to free speech does not protect false factual statements that inflict real harm and serve no legitimate interest. I would adhere to that principle and would thus uphold the constitutionality of this valuable law. . . .

[T]his statute is limited in five significant respects. First, the Act applies to only a narrow category of false representations about objective facts that can almost always be proved or disproved with near certainty. Second, the Act concerns facts that are squarely within the speaker's personal knowledge. Third, . . . a conviction under the Act requires proof beyond a reasonable doubt that the speaker actually knew that the representation was false. Fourth, the Act applies only to statements that could reasonably be interpreted as communicating actual facts; it does not reach dramatic performances, satire, parody, hyperbole, or the like. Finally, the Act is strictly viewpoint neutral. The false statements proscribed by the Act are highly unlikely to be tied to any particular political or ideological message. . . .

It is well recognized in trademark law that the proliferation of cheap imitations of luxury goods blurs the " 'signal' given out by the purchasers of the originals." Landes & Posner, Trademark Law: An Economic Perspective, 30 J. Law & Econ. 265, 308 (1987). In much the same way, the proliferation of false claims about military awards blurs the signal given out by the actual awards by making them seem more common than they really are, and this diluting effect harms the military by hampering its efforts to foster morale and esprit de corps. Surely it was reasonable for Congress to conclude that the goal of preserving the integrity of our country's top military honors is at least as worthy as that of protecting the prestige associated with fancy watches and designer handbags. Cf. San Francisco Arts & Athletics, Inc. v. United States Olympic Comm., 483 U.S. 522, 539-541 (1987) (rejecting First Amendment challenge to law prohibiting certain unauthorized uses of the word "Olympic" and recognizing that such uses harm the U.S. Olympic Committee by "lessening the distinctiveness" of the term). . . .

[T]here are broad areas in which any attempt by the state to penalize purportedly false speech would present a grave and unacceptable danger of suppressing truthful speech. Laws restricting false statements about philosophy, religion, history, the social sciences, the arts, and other matters of public concern would present such a threat. The point is not that there is no such thing as truth or falsity in these areas or that the truth is always impossible to ascertain, but rather that it is perilous to permit the state to be the arbiter of truth. Even where there is a wide scholarly consensus concerning a particular matter, the truth is served by allowing that consensus to be challenged without fear of reprisal. Today's accepted wisdom sometimes turns out to be mistaken. And in these contexts, "[e]ven a false statement may be deemed to make a valuable contribution to public debate, since it brings about 'the clearer perception and livelier impression of truth, produced by its collision with error.'" Allowing the state to proscribe false statements in these areas also opens the door for the state to use its power for political ends. Statements about history illustrate this point. If some false statements about historical events may be banned, how certain must it be that a statement is false before the ban may be upheld? And who should make that calculation? . . .

In stark contrast to hypothetical laws prohibiting false statements about history, science, and similar matters, the Stolen Valor Act presents no risk at all that valuable speech will be suppressed. The speech punished by the Act is not only verifiably false and entirely lacking in intrinsic value, but it also fails to serve any instrumental purpose that the First Amendment might protect. Tellingly, when asked at oral argument what truthful speech the Stolen Valor Act might chill, even respondent's counsel conceded that the answer is none. . . .

The Stolen Valor Act is a narrow law enacted to address an important problem, and it presents no threat to freedom of expression. I would sustain the constitutionality of the Act, and I therefore respectfully dissent.

NOTES AND QUESTION

1. Lying and Harm. If it is necessary to prove harm resulting from a lie in order validly to forbid its utterance, what sort of harm qualifies? How much harm is needed?

2. Categories or Balancing. Is it better to deal with false statements of fact by refining the categories of such statements that do not receive constitutional protection, or by engaging in a balancing of the harm to free expression and the strength of the governmental interest in prohibiting lies?

3. Lies About Political Candidates. Fourteen states have statutes that prohibit making a "false statement of fact concerning a candidate for elective office, with knowledge of its falsity or in reckless disregard of its truth or falsity." Are such statutes valid? Consider Brown v. Hartlage, 456 U.S. 46 (1982) (see Section G.2, infra). Compare Pestrak v. Ohio Elections Commission, 926 F.2d 573 (6th Cir. 1991), 281 Care Committee v. Arneson, 638 F.3d 621 (8th Cir. 2011), and Rickert v. Public Disclosure Commission, 161 Wash. 2d 843 (2007).

7. Tortious Invasion of Emotional and Economic Interests

This section deals with the problem of speech that may not constitute defamation but that inflicts emotional injury or misappropriates expression belonging to other people.

a. *Intentional Infliction of Emotional Distress*

Because words can inflict emotional injury, the tort of intentional infliction of emotional distress may in some jurisdictions be premised on speech alone and in other jurisdictions, on speech coupled with physical injury. The First Amendment, however, limits this tort.

Hustler Magazine v. Falwell
485 U.S. 46 (1988)

CHIEF JUSTICE REHNQUIST delivered the opinion of the Court.

Petitioner Hustler Magazine [is a pornographic] magazine of nationwide circulation. Respondent Jerry Falwell, a nationally known minister who has been active as a commentator on politics and public affairs, sued petitioner and its publisher, petitioner Larry Flynt, to recover damages [for] intentional infliction of emotional distress. The [jury] found for respondent on the claim for intentional infliction of emotional distress and awarded [compensatory damages of $100,000 and punitive damages of $100,000]. We now consider whether this award is consistent with the [First Amendment].

The inside front cover of the November 1983 issue of Hustler Magazine featured a "parody" of an advertisement for Campari Liqueur that contained the name and picture of respondent and was entitled "Jerry Falwell talks about his first time." This parody was modeled after actual Campari ads that included interviews with various celebrities about their "first times." Although it was apparent by the end of each interview that this meant the first time they sampled Campari, the ads clearly played on the sexual double entendre of the general subject of "first times." Copying the form and lay-out of these Campari ads, Hustler's editors chose respondent as the featured celebrity and drafted an alleged "interview" with him in which he states that his "first time" was during a drunken incestuous rendezvous with his mother in an outhouse. The Hustler parody portrays respondent and his mother as drunk and immoral, and suggests that respondent is a hypocrite who preaches only when he is drunk. In small print at the bottom of the page, the ad contains the disclaimer, "ad parody—not to be taken seriously." The magazine's table of contents also lists the ad as "Fiction; Ad and Personality Parody."

[We] must decide whether a public figure may recover damages for emotional harm caused by the publication of an ad parody offensive to him, and doubtless gross and repugnant in the eyes of most. Respondent would have us find that a State's interest in protecting public figures from emotional distress is sufficient to deny First Amendment protection to speech that is patently offensive and is intended to inflict emotional injury, even when that speech could not reasonably have been interpreted as stating actual facts about the public figure involved. This we decline to do. [The] robust political debate encouraged by the First Amendment is bound to produce speech that is critical of [public officials or public figures]. Such criticism, inevitably, will not always be reasoned or moderate; public figures as well as public officials will be subject to "vehement, caustic, and sometimes unpleasantly sharp attacks."

[Falwell argues that] so long as the utterance was intended to inflict emotional distress, was outrageous, and did in fact inflict serious emotional distress, it is of no constitutional import whether the statement was a fact or an opinion, or whether it was true or false. It is the intent to cause injury that is the gravamen of the tort, and the State's interest in preventing emotional harm simply outweighs whatever interest a speaker may have in speech of this type. Generally speaking the law does not regard the intent to inflict emotional distress as one which should receive much solicitude, and it is quite understandable that most if not all jurisdictions have chosen to make it civilly culpable where the conduct in question is sufficiently "outrageous." But in the world of debate about public affairs, many things done with motives that are less than admirable are protected by the First Amendment. In Garrison v. Louisiana, 379 U.S. 64 (1964), we held that even when a speaker or writer is motivated by hatred or ill-will his expression was protected by the First Amendment. [While] such a bad motive may be deemed controlling for purposes of tort liability in other areas of the law, we think the First Amendment prohibits such a result in the area of public debate about public figures.

Were we to hold otherwise, there can be little doubt that political cartoonists and satirists would be subjected to damages awards without any showing that their work falsely defamed its subject. [The] appeal of the political cartoon or caricature is often based on exploration of unfortunate physical traits or politically embarrassing events—an exploration often calculated to injure the feelings of the subject of the portrayal. The art of the cartoonist is often not reasoned or evenhanded, but slashing and one-sided. [Despite] their sometimes caustic nature, from the early cartoon portraying George Washington as an ass down to the present day, graphic depictions and satirical cartoons have played a prominent role in public and political debate. Nast's castigation of the Tweed Ring, Walt McDougall's characterization of presidential candidate James G. Blaine's banquet with the millionaires at Delmonico's as "The Royal Feast of Belshazzar," and numerous other efforts have undoubtedly had an effect on the course and outcome of contemporaneous debate. [From] the viewpoint of history it is clear that our political discourse would have been considerably poorer without them.

[Falwell] contends, however, that the caricature in question here was so "outrageous" as to distinguish it from more traditional political cartoons. There is no doubt that the caricature of respondent and his mother published in Hustler is at best a distant cousin of the political cartoons described above, and a rather poor relation at that. If it were possible by laying down a principled standard to separate the one from the other, public discourse would probably suffer little or no harm. But we doubt that there is any such standard, and we are quite sure that the pejorative description "outrageous" does not supply one. "Outrageousness" in the area of political and social discourse has an inherent subjectiveness about it which would allow a jury to impose liability on the basis of the jurors' tastes or views, or perhaps on the basis of their dislike of a particular expression. An "outrageousness" standard thus runs afoul of our longstanding refusal to allow damages to be awarded because the speech in question may have an adverse emotional impact on the audience. . . . We conclude that public figures and public officials may not recover for the tort of intentional infliction of emotional distress by reason of publications such as the one here at issue without showing in addition that the publication contains a false statement of fact which was made with "actual malice," i.e., with knowledge that the statement was false or with reckless disregard as to whether or not it was true. This is not merely a "blind application" of the *New York Times* standard; it reflects our considered judgment that such a standard is necessary to give adequate "breathing space" to the freedoms protected by the First Amendment.

NOTES

1. What Limiting Standard Is Appropriate? The Court rejects "outrageousness" as a standard because of its inherent subjectivity. Robert Post rejected outrageousness "because it would enable a single community [to] confine speech within its own notions of propriety." The First Amendment "requires the state to remain neutral in the 'marketplace of communities.'" Post, The Constitutional Concept of Public Discourse: Outrageous Opinion, Democratic Deliberation and *Hustler Magazine v. Falwell*, 103 Harv. L. Rev. 603 (1990). But is "actual malice" all that much better? As the Court concedes, parody is necessarily false and exaggerated. Does the holding in *Hustler* mean that parody of public figures enjoys an absolute constitutional immunity from emotional distress claims? Are there any circumstances where a public figure can recover emotional distress damages as a result of statements that do not include a falsehood? The television commentator Bill Maher publicly referred to Sarah Palin as a "c**t" and "dumb twat." Does (should) actual malice apply to such comments?

2. Private Figures. Does the Constitution provide any protection to those who intentionally inflict emotional distress on private figures? Does it matter whether the substance of the communication is of public interest or concern? Consider these questions in the context of a claim against Hustler by Jerry Falwell's mother for intentional infliction of emotional distress.

Snyder v. Phelps
562 U.S. 443 (2011)

CHIEF JUSTICE ROBERTS delivered the opinion of the Court.

A jury held members of the Westboro Baptist Church liable for millions of dollars in damages for picketing near a soldier's funeral service. The picket signs reflected the church's view that the United States is overly tolerant of sin and that God kills American soldiers as punishment. The question presented is whether the First Amendment shields the church members from tort liability for their speech in this case.

I. A. Fred Phelps founded the Westboro Baptist Church in Topeka, Kansas, in 1955. The church's congregation believes that God hates and punishes the United States for its tolerance of homosexuality, particularly in America's military. The church frequently communicates its views by picketing, often at military funerals. In the more than 20 years that the members of Westboro Baptist have publicized their message, they have picketed nearly 600 funerals.

Marine Lance Corporal Matthew Snyder was killed in Iraq in the line of duty. Lance Corporal Snyder's father selected the Catholic church in the Snyders' hometown of Westminster, Maryland, as the site for his son's funeral. Local newspapers provided notice of the time and location of the service. Phelps became aware of Matthew Snyder's funeral and decided to travel to Maryland with six other Westboro Baptist parishioners (two of his daughters and four of his grandchildren) to picket. On the day of the memorial service, the Westboro congregation members picketed on public land adjacent to public streets near . . . Matthew Snyder's funeral. The Westboro picketers carried signs that . . . stated, for instance: "God Hates the USA/Thank God for 9/11," "America is Doomed," "Don't Pray for the USA," "Thank God for IEDs," "Thank God for Dead Soldiers," "Pope in Hell," "Priests Rape Boys," "God Hates Fags," "You're Going to Hell," and "God Hates You."

[T]he picketers complied with police instructions in staging their demonstration. The picketing took place within a 10- by 25-foot plot of public land adjacent to a public street, behind a temporary fence [that] was approximately 1,000 feet from the church where the funeral was held. . . . The Westboro picketers displayed their signs for about 30 minutes before the funeral began and sang hymns and recited Bible verses. None of the picketers entered church property or went to the cemetery. They did not yell or use profanity, and there was no violence associated with the picketing.

The funeral procession passed within 200 to 300 feet of the picket site. Although Snyder testified that he could see the tops of the picket signs as he drove to the funeral, he did not see what was written on the signs until later that night, while watching a news broadcast covering the event.[9]

B. Snyder filed suit against Phelps, Phelps's daughters, and the Westboro Baptist Church (collectively Westboro or the church) in [federal District Court. After trial, a jury found for Snyder on state tort law claims of intentional infliction of emotional distress, intrusion upon seclusion, and civil conspiracy. The jury] held Westboro liable for $2.9 million in compensatory damages and $8 million in punitive damages, [later reduced to $2.1 million. The Court of Appeals] reviewed the picket signs and concluded that Westboro's statements were entitled to First Amendment protection because those statements were on matters of public concern, were not provably false, and were expressed solely through hyperbolic rhetoric.

We granted certiorari.

II. To succeed on a claim for intentional infliction of emotional distress in Maryland, a plaintiff must demonstrate that the defendant intentionally or recklessly engaged in extreme and outrageous conduct that caused the plaintiff to suffer severe emotional distress. . . .

Whether the First Amendment prohibits holding Westboro liable for its speech in this case turns largely on whether that speech is of public or private concern, as determined by all the circumstances of the case. . . . "[S]peech on public issues occupies the highest rung of the hierarchy of First Amendment values, and is entitled to special protection."

[W]here matters of purely private significance are at issue, First Amendment protections are often less rigorous. That is because . . . "there is no threat to the free and robust debate of public issues; there is no potential interference with a meaningful dialogue of ideas"; and the "threat of liability" does not pose the risk of "a reaction of self-censorship" on matters of public import. *Dun & Bradstreet.* . . .

Speech deals with matters of public concern when it can "be fairly considered as relating to any matter of political, social, or other concern to the community," or when it "is a subject of legitimate news interest; that is, a subject of general interest and of value and concern to the public." The arguably "inappropriate or controversial character of a statement is irrelevant to the question whether it deals with a matter of public concern." . . .

---

9. A few weeks after the funeral, one of the picketers posted a message on Westboro's Web site discussing the picketing and containing religiously oriented denunciations of the Snyders, interspersed among lengthy Bible quotations. Snyder discovered the posting, referred to by the parties as the "epic," during an Internet search for his son's name. The epic is not properly before us and does not factor in our analysis. . . .

Deciding whether speech is of public or private concern requires us to examine the " 'content, form, and context' " of that speech, " 'as revealed by the whole record.' " . . . In considering content, form, and context, no factor is dispositive, and it is necessary to evaluate all the circumstances of the speech, including what was said, where it was said, and how it was said.

The "content" of Westboro's signs plainly relates to broad issues of interest to society at large, rather than matters of "purely private concern." . . . .

Apart from the content of Westboro's signs, Snyder contends that the "context" of the speech—its connection with his son's funeral—makes the speech a matter of private rather than public concern. The fact that Westboro spoke in connection with a funeral, however, cannot by itself transform the nature of Westboro's speech. Westboro's signs, displayed on public land next to a public street, reflect the fact that the church finds much to condemn in modern society . . . and the funeral setting does not alter [the] conclusion [that their speech is on matters of public concern].

Snyder argues that the church members in fact mounted a personal attack on Snyder and his family, and then attempted to "immunize their conduct by claiming that they were actually protesting the United States' tolerance of homosexuality or the supposed evils of the Catholic Church." We are not concerned in this case that Westboro's speech on public matters was in any way contrived to insulate speech on a private matter from liability. Westboro had been actively engaged in speaking on the subjects addressed in its picketing long before it became aware of Matthew Snyder, and there can be no serious claim that Westboro's picketing did not represent its "honestly believed" views on public issues. There was no pre-existing relationship or conflict between Westboro and Snyder that might suggest Westboro's speech on public matters was intended to mask an attack on Snyder over a private matter. . . .

Westboro conducted its picketing peacefully on matters of public concern at a public place adjacent to a public street. Such space occupies a "special position in terms of First Amendment protection." "[W]e have repeatedly referred to public streets as the archetype of a traditional public forum," noting that " '[t]ime out of mind' public streets and sidewalks have been used for public assembly and debate."

That said, . . . Westboro's choice of where and when to conduct its picketing is not beyond the Government's regulatory reach—it is "subject to reasonable time, place, or manner restrictions." . . . Maryland now has a law imposing restrictions on funeral picketing, . . . as do 43 other States and the Federal Government. To the extent these laws are content neutral, they raise very different questions from the tort verdict at issue in this case. Maryland's law, however, was not in effect at the time of the events at issue here, so we have no occasion to consider how it might apply to facts such as those before us, or whether it or other similar regulations are constitutional.[10] . . .

10. The Maryland law prohibits picketing within 100 feet of a funeral service or funeral procession; Westboro's picketing would have complied with that restriction.

III. The jury also found Westboro liable for the state law torts of intrusion upon seclusion and civil conspiracy. . . . Snyder argues that even assuming Westboro's speech is entitled to First Amendment protection generally, the church is not immunized from liability for intrusion upon seclusion because Snyder was a member of a captive audience at his son's funeral. We do not agree. . . .

As a general matter, we have applied the captive audience doctrine only sparingly to protect unwilling listeners from protected speech. [*Rowan;* Frisby v. Schultz] Here, Westboro stayed well away from the memorial service. Snyder could see no more than the tops of the signs when driving to the funeral. And there is no indication that the picketing in any way interfered with the funeral service itself. We decline to expand the captive audience doctrine to the circumstances presented here. . . .

IV. Our holding today is narrow. . . . Westboro believes that America is morally flawed; many Americans might feel the same about Westboro. Westboro's funeral picketing is certainly hurtful and its contribution to public discourse may be negligible. But Westboro addressed matters of public import on public property, in a peaceful manner, in full compliance with the guidance of local officials. The speech was indeed planned to coincide with Matthew Snyder's funeral, but did not itself disrupt that funeral. . . . [Affirmed.]

JUSTICE ALITO, dissenting.

Our profound national commitment to free and open debate is not a license for the vicious verbal assault that occurred in this case.

Petitioner Albert Snyder is not a public figure. . . . Mr. Snyder wanted [only] to bury his son in peace. But respondents, members of the Westboro Baptist Church, deprived him of that elementary right. They first issued a press release and thus turned Matthew's funeral into a tumultuous media event. They then appeared at the church, approached as closely as they could without trespassing, and launched a malevolent verbal attack on Matthew and his family at a time of acute emotional vulnerability. As a result, Albert Snyder suffered severe and lasting emotional injury. The Court now holds that the First Amendment protected respondents' right to brutalize Mr. Snyder. I cannot agree. . . .

After the funeral, the Westboro picketers . . . posted an online account entitled "The Burden of Marine Lance Cpl. Matthew A. Snyder. The Visit of Westboro Baptist Church to Help the Inhabitants of Maryland Connect the Dots!"[11] Belying any suggestion that they had simply made general comments about homosexuality, the Catholic Church, and the United States military, the "epic" addressed the Snyder family directly:

---

11. The Court refuses to consider the epic because it was not discussed in Snyder's petition for certiorari. The epic, however, is not a distinct claim but a piece of evidence that the jury considered in imposing liability for the claims now before this Court. The protest and the epic are parts of a single course of conduct that the jury found to constitute intentional infliction of emotional distress. . . .

God blessed you, Mr. and Mrs. Snyder, with a resource and his name was Matthew. He was an arrow in your quiver! In thanks to God for the comfort the child could bring you, you had a DUTY to prepare that child to serve the LORD his GOD—PERIOD! You did JUST THE OPPOSITE—you raised him for the devil. . . . Albert and Julie RIPPED that body apart and taught Matthew to defy his Creator, to divorce, and to commit adultery. They taught him how to support the largest pedophile machine in the history of the entire world, the Roman Catholic monstrosity. Every dime they gave the Roman Catholic monster they condemned their own souls. They also, in supporting satanic Catholicism, taught Matthew to be an idolater. . . .

Then after all that they sent him to fight for the United States of Sodom, a filthy country that is in lock step with his evil, wicked, and sinful manner of life, putting him in the cross hairs of a God that is so mad He has smoke coming from his nostrils and fire from his mouth! How dumb was that?

In light of this evidence, it is abundantly clear that respondents, going far beyond commentary on matters of public concern, specifically attacked Matthew Snyder because (1) he was a Catholic and (2) he was a member of the United States military. Both Matthew and petitioner were private figures, and this attack was not speech on a matter of public concern. While commentary on the Catholic Church or the United States military constitutes speech on matters of public concern, speech regarding Matthew Snyder's purely private conduct does not.

. . . In order to have a society in which public issues can be openly and vigorously debated, it is not necessary to allow the brutalization of innocent victims like petitioner. I therefore respectfully dissent.

b. *Public Disclosure of Private Facts*

In the interest of preserving various personal privacy interests, states typically impose civil liability on some public disclosures of true but private facts. The Restatement (Second) of Torts §625D states that a person who publicly discloses "a matter concerning the private life of another is subject to liability to the other for invasion of his privacy, if the matter publicized . . . would be highly offensive to a reasonable person, and is not of legitimate concern to the public." Does the Constitution impose limits on this tort?

The Court has reached this issue only in the context of disclosure of true and *newsworthy* private facts lawfully obtained from public sources. It has also provided a partial answer to the question of whether constitutional protection attaches to newsworthy private facts that are not lawfully obtained. The Court has never addressed the question of whether there is any constitutional protection for disclosure of true but non-newsworthy private information.

Cox Broadcasting Corp. v. Cohn, 420 U.S. 469 (1975). The Court held that civil liability could not be imposed on a broadcaster who had released the name of a deceased rape victim. The Court declared that "once true information is disclosed in public court documents open to public inspection, the press cannot be sanctioned for publishing it." But the opinion noted that it was an open question "whether truthful publication of very private matters unrelated to public affairs could be constitutionally proscribed."

Florida Star v. B.J.F., 491 U.S. 524 (1989). The Court held that Florida could not make a newspaper civilly liable for publishing the name of a rape victim that the newspaper had lawfully obtained from a police report that was accessible due to police negligence. Justice Marshall, for the Court, refused "to hold broadly that truthful publication may never be punished consistent with the First Amendment," but concluded that disclosure of truthful information lawfully obtained may be punished, "if at all, only when narrowly tailored to a state interest of the highest order." Justice White, joined by Chief Justice Rehnquist and Justice O'Connor, dissented:

> [As a result of publication of her name], B.J.F. received harassing phone calls, required mental health counseling, was forced to move from her home, and was even threatened with being raped again. . . . [By] holding that protecting a rape victim's right to privacy is not [a state interest] of the highest order, the Court [obliterates] the tort of the publication of private facts. [There] is no public interest in publishing the names, addresses, and phone numbers of persons who are the victims of crime—and no public interest in immunizing the press from liability in the rare cases where a State's efforts to protect a victim's privacy have failed.

Bartnicki v. Vopper, 532 U.S. 514 (2001). A federal law, 18 U.S.C. §2511(1)(c), imposes criminal penalties on anyone who discloses an illegally intercepted communication if that person knew or had reason to know of the illegal nature of the interception. Another statute imposes civil liability for such disclosures. During "contentious" labor negotiations between a teachers' union and a public school board, Bartnicki, the union's chief negotiator, called Kane, the union's president, using a cellular telephone. In the course of the conversation, which focused on the negotiations, Kane suggested that the union might need to "blow off their front porches" to induce the school board to accede to the teachers' demands. An unknown person illegally recorded the conversation and left a tape of it in the mailbox of Yocum, the head of a local taxpayers' organization. Yocum provided the tape to Vopper, a radio commentator, who broadcast the tape as part of his critical commentary on the union.

The Court struck down the two federal statutes as applied to Vopper, Yocum, and various media defendants who had participated in the disclosure. Even though the laws were "content-neutral law[s] of general applicability," the government failed to justify them under the applicable intermediate level of scrutiny. See Section C.1, infra. While "[p]rivacy of communication is an important interest" and the statutes served that interest by diminishing "the fear of public disclosure of private conversations [that] might well have a chilling effect on private speech," the statutes, as applied, implicated "the core purposes of the First Amendment" because they imposed "sanctions on the publication of truthful information of public concern."

Problems: *Revealed Intimacies.* Pete and Mary, who are each married (but not to each other) are fond of using a video camera to record their adulterous sexual passion. Each of them keeps DVDs of their liaisons. Once the relationship sours and Pete's marriage founders, Pete uploads the videos to his blog, causing extreme emotional distress to Mary, who is still married to her husband. Does the First Amendment impose any limits on Mary's suit against Pete for invasion of privacy?

Hypocritical Vegan. Jane is president of a local chapter of the Vegan Society, an organization devoted to publicizing the health, environmental, and ethical benefits of being vegan, and that seeks to persuade people to become vegans. Unknown to anyone, Jane has thick steaks shipped to her and she happily consumes them in the privacy of her home. One day a neighbor, Norma, observes the delivery to Jane of a package marked "Prime Steaks." Later, Norma stands on a public street and uses a telephoto lens to photograph Jane eating a steak in her kitchen. Norma mails copies of the photo to the local newspaper and to the members of the Vegan Society. Does the First Amendment impose any limits on Jane's suit against Norma for invasion of privacy?

c. Misappropriation of Expression

There are a number of federal and state laws that protect owners of intellectual property from the misappropriation of their work. These laws, such as copyright and trademark laws, prohibit speech that is identical to or substantially similar to the protected words, sounds, or images. Most states have laws that grant to a person the exclusive right to profit from the use of their name, image, or voice. Some statutes protect performers by barring others from publicizing the performance without the performer's consent.

Harper & Row v. Nation Enterprises, 471 U.S. 539 (1985). Without authorization, The Nation magazine published substantial portions of President Ford's copyrighted but not-yet-published memoir. The Court upheld an award of damages to Harper & Row, the publisher of Ford's memoir, for copyright infringement. Because copyright protection extends only to "an author's expression," but not to "the ideas or the facts he narrates," the Court concluded that the First Amendment imposed no limit on liability for copyright infringement that involved verbatim quotes from Ford's memoir. It did not matter that the material was of considerable public interest.

Zacchini v. Scripps-Howard Broadcasting Co., 433 U.S. 562 (1977). The Court held that there was no constitutional protection for violations of the right of publicity with respect to a performer's act. A television station filmed Hugo Zacchini's entire "human cannonball" act, in which he was blasted from a cannon into a net some 60 meters away, and showed the act in its entirety on the station's newscast. The Court drew a parallel to patent and copyright law and concluded that the state had a strong interest in protecting such proprietary matter from non-consensual publication. "We would have a very different case," said the Court, if the station "had merely reported that [Zacchini] was performing at the fair and described or commented on his act, with or without showing his picture," but not his entire act.

Problems: *Disheveled Detective.* Suppose an artist creates a series of comic books that feature the character Peter Palumbo, a disheveled detective depicted wearing a trench coat and chewing a cigar. Palumbo is a bumbler who always botches the job, and on those rare occasions when a problem is solved it turns out to be despite his efforts. There are a number of other daffy characters, including a corrupt police chief, a woman who believes herself to be Sherlock Holmes, and a surfboard-toting coroner who is fond of saying, "Death bores me" and "He's dead; you figure out why." Peter Falk, the actor who starred in the television series *Columbo* as Lieut. Columbo, the apparently addled detective who always got the culprit through the guile of appearing dumb, sues the comic book artist for violation of the right of publicity. What limits, if any, does the First Amendment impose? Compare Winters v. D.C. Comics, 30 Cal. 4th 881 (Cal. 2003), and Doe v. TCI Cablevision, 110 S.W.3d 363 (Mo. 2003).

Fantasy Football. Suppose that a corporation creates and sells a fantasy football computer game in which players can create their own teams using the actual names of NFL players and their performance statistics. The NFL players sue, alleging violation of their right of publicity. What limits, if any, does the First Amendment impose? See C.B.C. Distribution & Marketing, Inc. v. Major League Baseball Advanced Media, L.P., 505 F.3d 818 (8th Cir. 2007).

8. Commercial Speech

Advertising—speech that invites a commercial transaction—receives second-class constitutional protection. At one time the Court was of the view that such speech was wholly unprotected, but since 1976 it has received limited protection. There is a body of opinion that commercial advertising ought to receive full constitutional protection, save in those instances where the content of the speech poses some significant commercial harm, such as fraudulent advertising (e.g., a false securities prospectus) or advertising that solicits an independently illegal act (e.g., sale of an assault rifle to a child). This section charts the development of this constitutional doctrine.

The now discarded view asserting a lack of constitutional protection of commercial speech is exemplified by Valentine v. Chrestensen, 316 U.S. 52 (1942), in which the Court upheld a prohibition against advertising that solicited tours of a privately owned submarine. The free speech guarantee, said the Court, places no "restraint on government as respects purely commercial advertising." The *Valentine* approach required courts to distinguish between "purely" commercial advertising and advertising that focused on political or noncommercial ends. Thus, in New York Times v. Sullivan the allegedly defamatory advertisement was not denied constitutional protection simply because it was a "paid 'commercial' advertisement." Indeed, the advertisement, though purchased, was hardly commercial. The only commercial transaction it solicited was financial support for the civil rights movement.

In Pittsburgh Press Co. v. Pittsburgh Commission on Human Relations, 413 U.S. 376 (1973), the Court upheld a city ordinance banning employment advertisements limited to one sex. The forbidden advertisements were "no more than a proposal of possible employment" and did not address issues of public concern, such as "whether, as a matter of social policy, certain positions ought to be filled by members of one or the other sex." By contrast, in Bigelow v. Virginia, 421 U.S. 809 (1975), the Court struck down a Virginia law forbidding advertisement of legal abortions available in New York. While the advertising solicited a commercial transaction, the subject of the transaction involved an independently protected constitutional right.

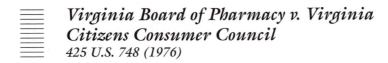

Virginia Board of Pharmacy v. Virginia Citizens Consumer Council
425 U.S. 748 (1976)

[Under Virginia law, only pharmacists could dispense prescription drugs, and they were guilty of unprofessional conduct if they advertised the price of any prescription drug. A three-judge district court declared the Virginia ban on price advertising of prescription drugs "void and of no effect" and enjoined its enforcement.]

JUSTICE BLACKMUN delivered the opinion of the Court.

[This] attack on the statute [is made by] prescription drug consumers who claim that they would greatly benefit if the prohibition were lifted and advertising freely allowed. [They] claim that the First Amendment entitles the user of prescription drugs to receive information that pharmacists wish to communicate to them through advertising [concerning] the prices of such drugs. Certainly that information may be of value. Drug prices in Virginia [strikingly] vary from outlet to outlet even within the same locality.

[Freedom] of speech presupposes a willing speaker, [but the] protection afforded is to the communication, to its source and to its recipients both. [This] Court has referred to a First Amendment right to "receive information and ideas." [Freedom] of speech "'necessarily protects the right to receive.'" If there is a right to advertise, there is a reciprocal right to receive the advertising. . . .

[Virginia contends] that the advertisement of prescription drug prices is outside the protection of the First Amendment because it is "commercial speech." There can be no question that in past decisions the Court has given some indication that commercial speech is unprotected. [*Valentine.*] [But last] Term, in *Bigelow,* [we] . . . rejected the contention that the publication was unprotected because it was commercial [because] the advertisement "did more than simply propose a commercial transaction. It contained factual material of clear 'public interest.'" [Here,] in contrast, the question . . . is whether speech which does "no more than propose a commercial transaction" is so removed from any "exposition of ideas" . . . that it lacks all protection. Our answer is that it is not.

[We] may assume that the advertiser's interest is a purely economic one. That hardly disqualifies him from protection under the First Amendment. The interests of the contestants in a labor dispute are primarily economic, but it has long been settled that both the employee and the employer are protected by the First Amendment when they express themselves on the merits of the dispute in order to influence its outcome. [As] to the particular consumer's interest in the free flow of commercial information, that interest may be as keen, if not keener by far, than his interest in the day's most urgent political debate. [Those] whom the suppression of prescription drug price information hits the hardest are the poor, the sick, and particularly the aged. A disproportionate amount of their income tends to be spent on prescription drugs; yet they are the least able to learn, by shopping from pharmacist to pharmacist, where their scarce dollars are best spent. When drug prices vary as strikingly as they do, information as to who is charging what becomes more than a convenience. It could mean the alleviation of physical pain or the enjoyment of basic necessities.

[Society] also may have a strong interest in the free flow of commercial information. Even an individual advertisement, though entirely "commercial," may be of general public interest. [While] not all commercial messages contain [a] public interest element [there] are few to which such an element [could] not be added. [A] pharmacist, for example, could cast himself as a commentator on store-to-store disparities in drug prices, giving his own and those of a competitor as proof. We see little point in requiring him to do so, and little difference if he does not.

Moreover, there is another consideration that suggests that no line between publicly "interesting" or "important" commercial advertising and the opposite kind could ever be drawn. Advertising, however tasteless and excessive it sometimes may seem, is nonetheless dissemination of information as to who is producing and selling what product, for what reason, and at what price. So long as we preserve a predominantly free enterprise economy, the allocation of our resources in large measure will be made through numerous private economic decisions. It is a matter of public interest that those decisions, in the aggregate, be intelligent and well informed. To this end, the free flow of commercial information is indispensable. And if it is indispensable to the proper allocation of resources in a free enterprise system, it is also indispensable to the formation of intelligent opinions as to how that system ought to be regulated or altered. Therefore, even if the First Amendment were thought to be primarily an instrument to enlighten public decision-making in a democracy we could not say that the free flow of information does not serve that goal.

Arrayed against these substantial individual and societal interests are a number of justifications for the advertising ban. . . . It is claimed that the aggressive price competition that will result from unlimited advertising will make it impossible for the pharmacist to supply professional services in the compounding, handling, and dispensing of prescription drugs. . . . The strength of these proffered justifications is greatly undermined by the fact that high professional standards [are] guaranteed by the close regulation to which pharmacists in Virginia are subject. . . .

[The] State's protectiveness of its citizens rests in large measure on the advantages of their being kept in ignorance. The advertising ban does not directly affect professional standards one way or the other. It affects them only through the reactions it is assumed people will have to the free flow of drug price information. [It] appears to be feared that if the pharmacist who wishes to provide low cost, and assertedly low quality, services is permitted to advertise, he will be taken up on his offer by too many unwitting customers. They will choose the low-cost, low-quality service and drive the "professional" pharmacist out of business. [All] this is not in their best interests, and all this can be avoided if they are not permitted to know who is charging what. . . . [The] alternative is to assume that this information is not in itself harmful, that people will perceive their own best interests if only they are well enough informed, and that the best means to that end is to open the channels of communication rather than to close them. . . . But the choice among these alternative approaches is not ours to make or [Virginia's]. It is precisely this kind of choice . . . that the First Amendment makes for us. Virginia is free to require whatever professional standards it wishes of its pharmacists; [but] it may not do so by keeping the public in ignorance of the entirely lawful terms that competing pharmacists are offering.

In concluding that commercial speech, like other varieties, is protected, we . . . do not hold that it can never be regulated in any way. Some forms of commercial speech regulation are surely permissible. We mention a few only to make clear that they are not before us and therefore are not foreclosed by this case. There is no claim, for example, that the prohibition on prescription drug price advertising is a mere time, place, and manner restriction. We have often approved [such] restrictions [provided] that they are justified without reference to the content of the regulated speech, that they serve a significant governmental interest, and that in so doing they leave open ample alternative channels for communication of the information. [But] this Virginia [law] singles out speech of a particular content and seeks to prevent its dissemination completely. Nor is there any claim that prescription drug price advertisements are forbidden because they are false or misleading in any way. Untruthful speech, commercial or otherwise, has never been protected for its own sake. [*Gertz.*] . . . Also, there is no claim that the transactions proposed in the forbidden advertisements are themselves illegal in any way. Finally, the special problems of the electronic broadcast media are likewise not in this case. What is at issue is whether a State may completely suppress the dissemination of concededly truthful information about entirely lawful activity, fearful of that information's effect upon its disseminators and its recipients. Reserving other questions, we conclude that the answer to this one is in the negative. [Affirmed.]

CHIEF JUSTICE BURGER, concurring.

[Quite] different factors would govern were we faced with a law regulating or even prohibiting advertising by the traditional learned professions of medicine or law.

JUSTICE REHNQUIST, dissenting.

The logical consequences of [elevating] commercial intercourse between a seller hawking his wares and a buyer seeking to strike a bargain to the same plane as has been previously reserved for the free marketplace of ideas are far reaching indeed. [The] way will be open not only for dissemination of price information but for active promotion of prescription drugs, liquor, cigarettes, and other products the use of which it has previously been thought desirable to discourage. Now, however, such promotion is protected by the First Amendment so long as it is not misleading or does not promote an illegal product or enterprise. . . .

[A pharmacist] may now presumably advertise not only the prices of prescription drugs, but may attempt to energetically promote their sale so long as he does so truthfully. But [this] simply makes no allowance whatever for what appears to have been a considered legislative judgment [that] while prescription drugs are a necessary and vital part of medical care and treatment, there are sufficient dangers attending their widespread use that they simply may not be promoted in the same manner as hair creams, deodorants, and toothpaste. The very real dangers that general advertising for such drugs might create in terms of encouraging, even though not sanctioning, illicit use of them by individuals for whom they have not been prescribed, or by generating patient pressure upon physicians to prescribe them, are simply not dealt with in the Court's opinion. . . .

NOTES

1. Commercial Advertising and the Purposes of Free Speech. Is advertising part of self-governance, or is there a fundamental difference between political and economic choices? Governments may regulate most private economic choices. Why should advertising be different? Is it because it is traffic in ideas, and self-governance requires a presumption in favor of unregulated traffic in all ideas?

Justice Blackmun asserted that advertisers, like other speakers, may offer competing visions of "truth": cheap drugs sold impersonally or expensive drugs sold with a pharmacist's personal care. Are political assertions of truth different from economic assertions? If free speech protects those who advocate the supremacy of one race over others, does it follow that it must protect those who advocate purchasing life insurance? Is it true that protecting advertising amounts to a revival of economic substantive due process in free speech garb? See, e.g., Jackson and Jeffries, Commercial Speech: Economic

Due Process and the First Amendment, 65 Va. L. Rev. 1 (1979). Consider that governments retain the power to regulate or even prohibit the ultimate private economic choices that advertising might induce.

2. The Standard of Review. While *Virginia Pharmacy* held that commercial advertising is constitutionally protected, the opinion also indicated that some content-based regulations of commercial speech are valid. Not until *Central Hudson*, however, did the Court articulate a precise standard of review—a form of intermediate scrutiny: Governments may regulate truthful, non-misleading advertising of lawful activities if the regulation "directly advances" a "substantial" government objective by means that are "not more extensive than necessary."

≡≡≡ ### *Central Hudson Gas & Electric Corp. v. Public Service Commission*
447 U.S. 557 (1980)

JUSTICE POWELL delivered the opinion of the Court.

This case presents the question whether a regulation of the [New York] Public Service Commission [violates free speech] because it completely bans promotional advertising by an electrical utility. [In order to conserve energy, the Commission in 1973] ordered electric utilities in New York State to cease all advertising that "[promotes] the use of electricity." [Three] years later, when the fuel shortage had eased, the Commission [extended the ban to all promotional advertising by utilities]—advertising intended to stimulate the purchase of utility services. [The] Commission's order was upheld by [the] New York Court of Appeals. [We] now reverse.

The Commission's order restricts only commercial speech, that is, expression related solely to the economic interests of the speaker and its audience. [Our] decisions have recognized "the 'commonsense' distinction between speech proposing a commercial transaction, which occurs in an area traditionally subject to government regulation, and other varieties of speech." The Constitution therefore accords a lesser protection to commercial speech than to other constitutionally guaranteed expression. [A] four-part analysis has developed. At the outset, we must determine whether the expression is protected by the First Amendment. For commercial speech to come within that provision, it at least must concern lawful activity and not be misleading. Next, we ask whether the asserted governmental interest is substantial. If both inquiries yield positive answers, we must determine whether the regulation directly advances the governmental interest asserted, and whether it is not more extensive than is necessary to serve that interest.

[The] Commission does not claim that the expression at issue either is inaccurate or relates to unlawful activity, [but argues that] the State's interest in conserving energy is sufficient to support suppression of advertising designed to increase consumption of electricity. . . . [N]o one can doubt the importance of energy conservation. Plainly, therefore, the state interest asserted is substantial. [The] State's interest in energy conservation is directly advanced by the [order]. There is an immediate connection between advertising and demand for electricity. Central Hudson would not contest the advertising ban unless it believed that promotion would increase its sales. Thus, we find a direct link between the state interest in conservation and the Commission's order.

We come finally to the critical inquiry in this case: whether the Commission's complete suppression of speech ordinarily protected by the First Amendment is no more extensive than necessary to further the State's interest in energy conservation. The Commission's order reaches all promotional advertising, regardless of the impact of the touted service on overall energy use. But the energy conservation rationale, as important as it is, cannot justify suppressing information about electric devices or services that would cause no net increase in total energy use. In addition, no showing has been made that a more limited restriction on the content of promotional advertising would not serve adequately the State's interests. [The] Commission's order prevents appellant from promoting electric services that would reduce energy use by diverting demand from less efficient sources, or that would consume roughly the same amount of energy as do alternative sources. In neither situation would the utility's advertising endanger conservation or mislead the public. To the extent that the Commission's order suppresses speech that in no way impairs the State's interest in energy conservation, the Commission's order violates the [free speech guarantee] and must be invalidated. . . .

In the absence of a showing that more limited speech regulation would be ineffective, we cannot approve the complete suppression of Central Hudson's advertising. [Reversed.]

JUSTICE BLACKMUN, joined by JUSTICE BRENNAN, concurring in the judgment.

[I] concur only in the Court's judgment [because] I believe the test now evolved and applied by the Court . . . does not provide adequate protection for truthful, nonmisleading, noncoercive commercial speech. [I agree that] intermediate scrutiny is appropriate for a restraint on commercial speech designed to protect consumers from misleading or coercive speech, or a regulation related to the time, place, or manner of commercial speech. I do not agree, however, that the Court's four-part test is the proper one to be applied when a State seeks to suppress information about a product in order to manipulate a private economic decision that the State cannot or has not regulated or outlawed directly. . . . [Such] a regulatory measure strikes at the heart of the First Amendment [because] it is a covert attempt by the State to manipulate the choices of its citizens, not by persuasion or direct regulation, but by depriving the public of the information needed to make a free choice. . . .

JUSTICE STEVENS, joined by JUSTICE BRENNAN, concurring in the judgment.

Because "commercial speech" is afforded less constitutional protection than other forms of speech, it is important that the commercial speech concept not be defined too broadly lest speech deserving of greater constitutional protection be inadvertently suppressed. [The Court describes] commercial speech as "expression related solely to the economic interests of the speaker and its audience." Although it is not entirely clear whether this definition uses the subject matter of the speech or the motivation of the speaker as the limiting factor, it seems clear to me that it encompasses speech that is entitled to the maximum protection afforded by the First Amendment. Neither a labor leader's exhortation to strike, nor an economist's dissertation on the money supply, should receive any lesser protection because the subject matter concerns only the economic interests of the audience. Nor should the economic motivation of a speaker qualify his constitutional protection; even Shakespeare may have been motivated by the prospect of pecuniary reward. [This] definition of commercial speech is unquestionably too broad. . . .

[I] concur in the result because I do not consider this to be a "commercial speech" case. Accordingly, I see no need to decide whether the Court's four-part analysis adequately protects commercial speech—as properly defined—in the face of a blanket ban of the sort involved in this case.

JUSTICE REHNQUIST, dissenting.

[The Court's test] elevates the protection accorded commercial speech [to] a level that is virtually indistinguishable from that of noncommercial speech. . . . New York's order here [is] more akin to an economic regulation to which virtually complete deference should be accorded by this Court. I doubt there would be any question as to the constitutionality of New York's conservation effort if the Public Service Commission had chosen to raise the price of electricity [or] to restrict its production. In terms of constitutional values, [such] controls are virtually indistinguishable from the State's ban on promotional advertising. . . .

NOTES

1. The "Least Restrictive Alternative" Prong. Any suggestion that the "no more than necessary" prong of *Central Hudson* meant that the regulation must be the "least restrictive alternative" sufficient to accomplish the regulatory objective was apparently obliterated in Board of Trustees, SUNY v. Fox, 492 U.S. 469 (1989). The Court upheld a public university regulation barring commercial enterprises on campus, as applied to Tupperware parties in dormitories. The Court applied *Central Hudson*. The commercial speech involved in sales of housewares was not misleading and promoted a lawful transaction. The university's interests—maintaining an educational environment on campus and protecting students—were found to be substantial. The Court's critical conclusion was that the restriction need not be the "least restrictive" way of achieving its objectives:

[What] our decisions require is a "'fit' between the legislature's ends and the means chosen to accomplish those ends" [that] is not necessarily perfect, but reasonable; that represents not necessarily the single best disposition but one whose scope is "in proportion to the interest served"; that employs not necessarily the least restrictive means but, as we have put it in the other contexts discussed above, a means narrowly tailored to achieve the desired objective. . . . [Here] we require the government goal to be substantial, and the cost to be carefully calculated. Moreover, since the State bears the burden of justifying its restrictions it must affirmatively establish the reasonable fit we require.

But in Thompson v. Western States Medical Center, 535 U.S. 357 (2002), the Court appeared to backtrack. At issue was a federal regulation banning the advertisement or promotion of compounded drugs. Drug compounding is a process by which pharmacists mix, combine, or alter the ingredients to produce medicines tailored to individual needs. Compounded drugs are exempt from the onerous approval requirements normally applicable to new drugs. The government asserted that the advertising ban was reasonably necessary to promote its objective of protecting public health by (1) preventing widespread subversion of the drug approval process through large-scale sales of compounded drugs, and (2) simultaneously making compounded drugs available to those who have a legitimate medical need for them. The Court agreed that these objectives were substantial and assumed that the advertising ban was directly related to these objectives, but struck down the ban because it was more extensive than necessary to serve those interests.

[We] have made clear that if the Government could achieve its interests in a manner that does not restrict speech, or that restricts less speech, the Government must do so. Several non-speech-related means of drawing a line between compounding and large-scale manufacturing might be possible here. [The] Government could ban the use of "commercial scale manufacturing or testing equipment for compounding drug products," [or] prohibit pharmacists from compounding more drugs in anticipation of receiving prescriptions than in response to prescriptions already received, [or] prohibit pharmacists from "offering compounded drugs at wholesale to other state licensed persons or commercial entities for resale." Alternately, it could limit the amount of compounded drugs, either by volume or by numbers of prescriptions, that a given pharmacist or pharmacy sells out of State. Another possibility . . . would be capping the amount of any particular compounded drug, either by drug volume, number of prescriptions, gross revenue, or profit that a pharmacist or pharmacy may make or sell in a given period of time. . . . The Government has not offered any reason why these possibilities, alone or in combination, would be insufficient to prevent compounding from occurring on such a scale as to undermine the new drug approval process. Indeed, there is no hint that the Government even considered these or any other alternatives. . . . If the First Amendment means anything, it means that regulating speech must be a last—not first—resort. Yet here it seems to have been the first strategy the Government thought to try.

2. Lawyer Advertising.   Bates v. State Bar of Arizona, 433 U.S. 350 (1977), held that lawyer advertising was constitutionally protected commercial speech. The case rejected arguments that prohibitions on lawyer advertising were justified to protect the quality of legal services, prevent unnecessary litigation, and keep fees down. But in Ohralik v. Ohio State Bar, 436 U.S. 447 (1978), the Court upheld Ohralik's suspension from law practice for his direct solicitation of "two young accident victims at a time when they were especially incapable of making informed judgments or of assessing and protecting their own interests." Ohralik "solicited Carol McClintock in a hospital room where she lay in traction and sought out Wanda Lou Holbert on the day she came home from the hospital." He used "a concealed tape recorder [to] insure [evidence of] oral assent to the representation" and then "refused to withdraw" when requested to do so. The Court concluded that Ohio could "proscribe in-person solicitation for pecuniary gain under circumstances likely to result in adverse consequences" without any showing of actual harm, but did not rule that states could bar all in-person solicitation. A companion case to *Ohralik*, In re Primus, 436 U.S. 412 (1978), voided discipline of an ACLU lawyer who had sought to represent a woman who had been sterilized in order to receive public medical assistance. Because the solicitation was not for private financial gain and was on behalf of an organization that uses litigation as a form of political expression, the Court ruled that the state must prove actual harm before it could impose discipline. Justice Rehnquist dissented, charging that there was "no principled distinction" between *Primus* and *Ohralik*, but merely reliance on "epithets and slogans" to ensure that " 'ambulance chasers' suffer one fate and 'civil liberties lawyers' another."

Later cases generally have struck down state limits on truthful, non-misleading advertising by lawyers and accountants. See, e.g., Ibanez v. Florida Department of Business and Professional Regulation, 512 U.S. 136 (1994); Edenfield v. Fane, 507 U.S. 761 (1993); Peel v. Attorney Registration and Disciplinary Commission of Illinois, 496 U.S. 91 (1990); Shapero v. Kentucky Bar Association, 486 U.S. 466 (1988) (striking down a ban on truthful, non-deceptive, direct mail solicitation of targeted clients); Zauderer v. Office of Disciplinary Counsel, 471 U.S. 626 (1985); and In re RMJ, 455 U.S. 191 (1982).

Yet, in Florida Bar v. Went For It, Inc., 515 U.S. 618 (1995), the Court limited the scope of *Shapero* in upholding, 5-4, a Florida bar rule banning direct mail solicitation of personal injury victims or their families within 30 days after the injury. The Court found the state's interests—protecting "the privacy and tranquility of personal injury victims" and protecting the "flagging reputations of Florida lawyers"—to be substantial. The ban directly advanced the goal because there was ample evidence of the erosion of client privacy and lawyers' reputations produced by such solicitations. The rule was narrowly tailored to the objective since it was limited in time and did not foreclose other advertising methods. Four justices dissented, charging that the Florida scheme was asymmetrical because it permitted sophisticated clients (typically insurers) to amass evidence immediately after an incident and even to contact injured parties to offer settlement. Moreover, the rule prohibited "far more speech than necessary to serve the purported state interest."

3. Treating Commercial Speech Differently from Similarly Situated Noncommercial Speech.   In Metromedia Inc. v. San Diego, 453 U.S. 490 (1981), the Court, without a majority rationale, voided portions of a San Diego ordinance regulating noncommercial billboards but upheld those portions that applied to commercial billboards. Only a plurality agreed that it was permissible for San Diego to distinguish between commercial and noncommercial billboards. The judgment was formed because three justices thought that the regulations were valid as to all billboards.

Cincinnati v. Discovery Network, Inc., 507 U.S. 410 (1993).   The Court held that commercial speech may not be treated differently from similar noncommercial speech in the absence of some clear and peculiarly commercial harm stemming from the commercial speech. Cincinnati had barred street-corner news racks containing purely advertising publications (e.g., real estate brochures) but permitted the same news racks if they contained newspapers of general circulation. The Court ruled that Cincinnati must prove a reasonable fit between the city's objective in barring advertising news racks—aesthetics—and the *differences* between advertising news racks and newspaper news racks. Cincinnati was unable to prove that news racks housing real estate flyers were any more an aesthetic blight than news racks containing newspapers. Justice Blackmun concurred on the ground that truthful, non-misleading advertisement of lawful transactions ought to be fully protected by the First Amendment.

Query: The federal Do Not Call Registry bars commercial telemarketers from calling telephone numbers on the registry but does not bar such calls by noncommercial telemarketers. The stated objective of the ban is to ensure tranquility in the home by eliminating annoying telephone solicitations. Is the prohibition valid? See Mainstream Marketing Services, Inc. v. Federal Trade Commission, 283 F. Supp. 2d 1151 (D. Colo. 2003), *reversed*, 358 F.3d 1228 (10th Cir. 2004).

4. The "Greater-Includes-the-Lesser" Principle.   In Posadas de Puerto Rico v. Tourism Co. of Puerto Rico, 478 U.S. 328 (1986), the Court upheld a Puerto Rico law prohibiting legal gambling casinos from advertising to Puerto Rico residents. For the Court, Justice Rehnquist declared:

> [T]he greater power to completely ban casino gambling necessarily includes the lesser power to ban advertising of casino gambling. [It] is precisely because the government could have enacted a wholesale prohibition of the underlying conduct that it is permissible for the government to take the less intrusive step of allowing the conduct, but reducing the demand through restrictions on advertising.

This theme was repeated in United States v. Edge Broadcasting Co., 509 U.S. 418 (1993), in which the Court upheld a federal law barring broadcasters from airing lottery advertising in states that prohibit lotteries. Edge operated a radio station in North Carolina, a state with no lottery, but which drew over 90 percent of its audience and advertisers from neighboring Virginia, a lottery state. The Court concluded that the federal government had a substantial interest in fostering state gambling policies, and that the restriction directly served this interest and was narrowly tailored to its accomplishment. The Court noted that Congress could "ban all radio or television lottery advertisements, even by stations in States that have legalized lotteries."

But the continued vitality of the principle was eroded, if not eliminated, by the following case.

44 Liquormart, Inc. v. Rhode Island
517 U.S. 484 (1996)

[Rhode Island prohibited advertising of the price of alcoholic beverages except by signs or tags within a liquor store. The state's objective was to promote "temperance." Two large liquor stores challenged the ban as a free speech violation. A federal district court voided the ban after finding that it produced no significant effect on alcohol consumption. The Court of Appeals reversed, reasoning that advertising would lead to lower prices, which would stimulate consumption of alcohol. The Supreme Court unanimously reversed the Court of Appeals but could not agree on a single rationale. Justice Stevens announced the judgment of the Court and delivered a plurality opinion joined at various points by two or three of Justices Kennedy, Souter, Thomas, and Ginsburg. The remaining justices authored or joined in separate concurrences in the judgment.]

JUSTICE STEVENS, joined by JUSTICES KENNEDY and GINSBURG.

. . . When a State regulates commercial messages to protect consumers from misleading, deceptive, or aggressive sales practices, or requires the disclosure of beneficial consumer information, the purpose of its regulation is consistent with the reasons for according constitutional protection to commercial speech and therefore justifies less than strict review. However, when a State entirely prohibits the dissemination of truthful, nonmisleading commercial messages for reasons unrelated to the preservation of a fair bargaining process, there is far less reason to depart from the rigorous review that the First Amendment generally demands. [Most] obviously, complete speech bans, unlike content-neutral restrictions on the time, place, or manner of expression, are particularly dangerous because they all but foreclose alternative means of disseminating certain information. . . .

JUSTICE STEVENS, joined by JUSTICES KENNEDY, SOUTER, and GINSBURG.

[There] is no question that Rhode Island's price advertising ban constitutes a blanket prohibition against truthful, nonmisleading speech about a lawful product. There is also no question that the ban serves an end unrelated to consumer protection. Accordingly, we must review the price advertising ban with "special care." [The] State argues that the price advertising prohibition should nevertheless be upheld because it directly advances the State's substantial interest in promoting temperance, and because it is no more extensive than necessary. . . . [We] assume that the State asserts an interest in reducing alcohol consumption.

[The] State bears the burden of showing not merely that its regulation will advance its interest, but also that it will do so "to a material degree." [A] prohibition against price advertising [will] tend to mitigate competition and maintain prices at a higher level than would prevail in a completely free market, [and it is] reasonable to assume that demand, and hence consumption . . . is somewhat lower whenever a higher, noncompetitive price level prevails. However, [we] cannot agree [that] the price advertising ban will significantly advance the State's interest in promoting temperance. [The] State has presented no evidence to suggest that its speech prohibition will significantly reduce . . . consumption. . . . [Any] connection between the ban and a significant change in alcohol consumption would be purely fortuitous. [A] conclusion that elimination of the ban would significantly increase alcohol consumption would require us to engage in the sort of "speculation or conjecture" that is an unacceptable means of demonstrating that a restriction on commercial speech directly advances the State's asserted interest.

[The] State also cannot satisfy the requirement that its restriction on speech be no more extensive than necessary. It is perfectly obvious that alternative forms of regulation that would not involve any restriction on speech would be more likely to achieve the State's goal of promoting temperance. [Higher] prices can be maintained either by direct regulation or by increased taxation. Per capita purchases could be limited as is the case with prescription drugs. Even educational campaigns focused on the problems of excessive, or even moderate, drinking might prove to be more effective. As a result, even under the less than strict standard that generally applies in commercial speech cases, the State has failed to establish a "reasonable fit" between its abridgment of speech and its temperance goal. It necessarily follows that the price advertising ban cannot survive the more stringent constitutional review that *Central Hudson* [applied to] the complete suppression of truthful, nonmisleading commercial speech.

JUSTICE STEVENS, joined by JUSTICES KENNEDY, THOMAS, and GINSBURG.

[Rhode Island contends that *Posadas*] requires us to give particular deference to [the] legislative choice because the State could, if it chose, ban the sale of alcoholic beverages outright. Finally, the State argues that deference is appropriate because alcoholic beverages are so-called "vice" products.

[We] are now persuaded [that] *Posadas* clearly erred in concluding that it was "up to the legislature" to choose suppression over a less speech-restrictive policy. The *Posadas* majority's conclusion on that point cannot be reconciled with the unbroken line of prior cases striking down similarly broad regulations on truthful, nonmisleading advertising when non-speech-related alternatives were available.

[We] also cannot accept the . . . "greater-includes-the-lesser" reasoning endorsed toward the end of the majority's opinion in *Posadas*. [Further] consideration persuades us that the "greater-includes-the-lesser" argument should be rejected for the additional and more important reason that it is inconsistent with both logic and well-settled doctrine. [Contrary] to the assumption made in *Posadas*, we think it quite clear that banning speech may sometimes prove far more intrusive than banning conduct. As a venerable proverb teaches, it may prove more injurious to prevent people from teaching others how to fish than to prevent fish from being sold.[12]

[Finally], we find unpersuasive the State's contention that, under *Posadas* and *Edge*, the price advertising ban should be upheld because it targets commercial speech that pertains to a "vice" activity. [Our decision in Rubin v. Coors Brewing Co., 514 U.S. 476 (1995)] striking down an alcohol-related advertising restriction effectively rejected the very contention respondents now make. . . .

JUSTICE SCALIA, concurring in part and concurring in the judgment.

I share Justice Thomas's discomfort with the *Central Hudson* test, which seems to me to have nothing more than policy intuition to support it. [But since] I do not believe we have before us the wherewithal to declare *Central Hudson* wrong—or at least the wherewithal to say what ought to replace it—I must resolve this case in accord with our existing jurisprudence. [I] merely concur in the judgment of the Court.

JUSTICE THOMAS, concurring in part, and concurring in the judgment.

In cases such as this, in which the government's asserted interest is to keep legal users of a product or service ignorant in order to manipulate their choices in the marketplace, the balancing test adopted in *Central Hudson* should not be applied. [Such] an "interest" is per se illegitimate and can no more justify regulation of "commercial" speech than it can justify regulation of "noncommercial" speech. . . .

JUSTICE O'CONNOR, joined by CHIEF JUSTICE REHNQUIST and JUSTICES SOUTER and BREYER, concurring in the judgment.

I agree with the Court that Rhode Island's price-advertising ban is invalid. I would resolve this case more narrowly, however, by applying our established *Central Hudson* test. . . . Under that test, [Rhode Island's] regulation fails First Amendment scrutiny. [While] the first two prongs of the *Central Hudson* test are met, [and even] if we assume arguendo that Rhode Island's regulation also satisfies the requirement that it directly advance the governmental interest, [the] ban is more extensive than necessary to serve the State's interest. . . .

---

12. "Give a man a fish, and you feed him for a day. Teach a man to fish, and you feed him for a lifetime." The International Thesaurus of Quotations 646 (compiled by R. Tripp 1970).

NOTES

1. The Meaning of *44 Liquormart*. Only four justices in *44 Liquormart*—Stevens, Kennedy, Thomas, and Ginsburg—took the position that commercial speech regulations should be subjected to strict scrutiny. As a result, *Central Hudson* remains the operative doctrine, but was its meaning altered? Does *44 Liquormart* change the fourth prong of *Central Hudson* by essentially repudiating *Fox* and endorsing *Thompson*? Does the *Posadas* "greater-includes-the-lesser" argument survive?

2. Tobacco Advertising. In Lorillard Tobacco Co. v. Reilly, 533 U.S. 525 (2001), the Court applied *Central Hudson* to invalidate Massachusetts's outdoor advertising regulations prohibiting smokeless tobacco or cigar advertising within 1,000 feet of a school or playground. Only the third and fourth prongs of *Central Hudson* were implicated. The regulations directly advanced the governmental interests asserted to justify them because there was ample evidence that (1) there was a problem with underage use of smokeless tobacco and cigars and (2) limiting such tobacco advertising would decrease minors' use of these tobacco products. But the regulations did not satisfy the fourth prong of *Central Hudson*. First, they were exceedingly broad in that they would prohibit tobacco advertising in a substantial portion of Massachusetts's major metropolitan areas and would constitute a near-complete ban on the communication of truthful information. Moreover, the ban applied to indoor advertising if visible from outside and to oral statements. Second, because the purchase and use of tobacco by adults is legal, a speech regulation cannot unduly impinge on the speaker's ability to propose a legal commercial transaction and the adult listener's opportunity to obtain information about legal products. Because the broad sweep of these regulations suggested that Massachusetts did not "carefully calculate the costs and benefits associated with the burden on speech imposed," Massachusetts failed its burden of proving that the regulations were not more extensive than necessary.

The Court concluded that the regulations prohibiting indoor, point-of-sale advertising of smokeless tobacco and cigars lower than 5 feet from the floor of a retail establishment located within 1,000 feet of a school or playground failed both the third and fourth prongs of *Central Hudson*. . . .

The Court upheld Massachusetts's regulations requiring retailers to place tobacco products behind counters and requiring customers to have contact with a salesperson before handling them. The Court assumed that tobacco vendors have a cognizable speech interest in a particular means of displaying their products, but thought that because unattended displays of tobacco enable access by minors, Massachusetts had demonstrated a substantial interest in preventing access to tobacco products by minors and had adopted an appropriately narrow means of advancing that interest. The regulations left ample alternative means of display to retailers and did not significantly impede adult access to tobacco products.

3. Regulation of Prescription Drug Information. Vermont requires that pharmacies keep a record of prescriptions authored by each physician.

The records do not disclose the patient's identity but do reveal each prescribing physician's choices. A Vermont law forbade the sale or use of this information for marketing purposes but permitted it to be sold, used, or given away for many other uses. Before the law was enacted, so-called data miners acquired this information and sold it to pharmaceutical manufacturers, who used it in their sales calls on physicians to explain why a branded drug offered by the representative's firm was superior to competing drugs that the physician had prescribed in the past. A federal district court upheld the law against a free speech challenge; the Second Circuit reversed and in Sorrell v. IMS Health, Inc., 131 S. Ct. 2653 (2011), the Supreme Court affirmed.

The Court concluded that the law was both content-based (it only applied to information used for marketing purposes) and speaker-based (it only applied to those speakers using the prescriber data for marketing purposes), and that in its application it was also viewpoint-based, because it banned the use of the information only to advance the view that branded drugs were better than generic drugs. Thus, heightened scrutiny was warranted, and the Court applied the *Central Hudson* test.

Vermont said its reasons for the ban were to preserve physician privacy and to lower health care costs. While Vermont's objectives were substantial the law did not directly advance the objectives and the fit between the means and ends was so poor that the Court concluded that the law was designed to suppress a disfavored message. The law did almost nothing to protect physician privacy—the data could be shared with just about anyone except pharmaceutical marketers. Vermont also claimed that doctors were harassed and pressured by pharmaceutical salespersons; the Court's reply was that doctors could refuse to see such salespersons. The means selected by Vermont to lower health care costs were impermissible:

> The State seeks to achieve its policy objectives through the indirect means of restraining certain speech by certain speakers—that is, by diminishing detailers' ability to influence prescription decisions. Those who seek to censor or burden free expression often assert that disfavored speech has adverse effects. But the "fear that people would make bad decisions if given truthful information" cannot justify content-based burdens on speech. . . . The State has burdened a form of protected expression that it found too persuasive. At the same time, the State has left unburdened those speakers whose messages are in accord with its own views. This the State cannot do.

Three dissenters thought that the question was "whether Vermont's regulatory provisions work harm to First Amendment interests that is disproportionate to their furtherance of legitimate regulatory objectives." How would a judge measure the "harm to free speech," on the one hand, against the efficacy of regulation, on the other hand? Is there a good reason to use such an open-ended balancing test for commercial speech, but not other forms of speech?

In any case, the dissent thought that *Central Hudson* was satisfied because it directly advanced the goal of reducing health care costs by making it more difficult to sell more expensive branded drugs, and the ban was well tailored to that end. In *Thompson*, however, the Court observed that "[w]e have previously rejected the notion that the Government has an interest in preventing the dissemination of truthful commercial information in order to prevent members of the public from making bad decisions with the information." Are there any circumstances in which the government may restrict truthful, non-misleading commercial speech because the speech may cause people to make bad decisions?

4. The Future of Commercial Speech Regulation: Queries. Should all commercial speech enjoy the same protections as noncommercial speech? Should full protection extend only to truthful, non-misleading commercial advertising?

C. CONTENT-NEUTRAL REGULATIONS OF SPEECH

The focus so far has been on the categories of speech that are not entitled to much, if any, constitutional protection. Our focus now shifts to the form of government regulation of speech. Regulation based on the *content* of speech is, of course, subject to strict scrutiny (unless the speech selected for regulation happens to be a category of unprotected speech and the regulation is viewpoint-neutral). But when governments regulate speech without reference to its content (typically by imposing limits on the time, place, or manner of any speech) a form of intermediate scrutiny generally applies.

The threat, if not the actual reality, of government censorship of ideas is the strongest argument for strict scrutiny of content-based regulation. This rationale is even more pointed when governments engage in viewpoint-based regulation. But content-neutral regulations can also foreclose a great deal of speech, though whether the regulation is motivated by censorship or something else is harder to detect. Consider the following possible laws banning

1. Auto bumper stickers critical of the government
2. Auto bumper stickers containing political messages
3. All auto bumper stickers
4. Auto bumper stickers visible to other drivers
5. All auto bumper stickers for the 60-day period prior to any general election

The first is viewpoint-based; the second is content-based; the third, fourth, and fifth are content-neutral. Each regulation would bar a motorist from affixing a bumper sticker reading "Vote the Rascals Out!" on the rear of her auto during an election campaign. Despite this effect, the first two regulations would be subjected to strict scrutiny, and the last three would be subjected to intermediate scrutiny. Why?

The intermediate scrutiny approach has developed in a variety of contexts where the purpose and effect of government regulation are not related to the content of speech. In Section C.1, we take a brief look at the general principle that content-neutral regulation of the time, place, or manner of speaking is subject to intermediate scrutiny. In Section C.2, we examine the related problem of "symbolic speech" or "expressive conduct," which involves conduct that may validly be regulated but can also communicate an idea and is readily understood to do so. If a political protester pelts the mayor with eggs, he is likely to be perceived as expressing extreme dissatisfaction with the mayor, but the assault itself is surely legitimately subject to punishment. Section C.3 deals with the "secondary effects" doctrine, which holds that facially content-based restrictions on speech will be treated as content-neutral and subject to less than strict scrutiny when such content-based restrictions are adequately founded upon a government purpose to regulate non-speech conduct that is produced not by the communicative impact of the speech, but as its adventitious by-product.

1. Time, Place, and Manner of Speech

≡≡≡ ***Ward v. Rock Against Racism***
≡≡≡ *491 U.S. 781 (1989)*

JUSTICE KENNEDY delivered the opinion of the Court.

This case arises from [New York City's] attempt to regulate the volume of amplified music at the [Central Park] band-shell so the performances are satisfactory to the audience without intruding upon those who use the Sheep Meadow or live on Central Park West and in its vicinity. The city's regulation requires band-shell performers to use sound-amplification equipment and a sound technician provided by the city. The challenge to this volume control technique comes from the sponsor of a rock concert. The trial court sustained the noise control measures, but the Court of Appeals [reversed].

Over the years, the city received numerous complaints about excessive sound amplification at respondent's concerts [and] RAR was less than cooperative when city officials asked that the volume be [reduced. After a series of such problems, the] city undertook to develop comprehensive [use guidelines for the band-shell]. A principal problem to be addressed by the guidelines was controlling the volume of amplified sound at band-shell events.[13] The city considered various solutions. [A] fixed decibel limit [was] rejected

13. The amplified sound heard at a rock concert consists of two components, volume and mix. Sound produced by the various instruments and performers on stage is picked up by microphones and fed into a central mixing board, where it is combined into one signal and then amplified through speakers to the audience. A sound technician is at the mixing board to select the appropriate mix, or balance, of the various sounds produced on stage, and to [control] the overall volume of sound reaching the audience. During the course of a performance, the sound technician is continually manipulating various controls on the mixing board to provide the desired sound mix and volume. [Relocated—ED.]

because the impact on listeners of a single decibel level is not constant. [A city] sound technician [operating] equipment provided by the various sponsors of band-shell events [was rejected] because the city's technician might have had difficulty satisfying the needs of sponsors while operating unfamiliar, and perhaps inadequate, sound equipment. Instead, the city concluded that the most effective way to achieve adequate but not excessive sound amplification would be for the city to furnish high quality sound equipment and retain an independent, experienced sound technician for all performances at the band-shell.

[Rather than] comply with the guidelines [RAR sought] a declaratory judgment striking down the guidelines as facially invalid. [The District Court] found the city's regulation valid. The Court of Appeals reversed. [We] now reverse.

[Music], as a form of expression and communication, is protected under the First Amendment. [The] band-shell was open [to] all performers and we decide the case as one in which the band-shell is a public forum for [musical performances] [see Section D.1, infra]. Our cases make clear, however, that even in a public forum the government may impose reasonable restrictions on the time, place, or manner of protected speech, provided the restrictions "are justified without reference to the content of the regulated speech, that they are narrowly tailored to serve a significant governmental interest, and that they leave open ample alternative channels for communication of the information." Clark v. Community for Creative Non-Violence, 468 U.S. 288, 293 (1984). We consider these requirements in turn.

The principal inquiry in determining content neutrality [is] whether the government has adopted a regulation of speech because of disagreement with the message it conveys. The government's purpose is the controlling consideration. A regulation that serves purposes unrelated to the content of expression is deemed neutral, even if it has an incidental effect on some speakers or messages but not others. See Renton v. Playtime Theatres [excerpted in Section C.3, infra]. The principal justification for the sound-amplification guideline is the city's desire to control noise levels at band-shell events, in order to retain the character of the Sheep Meadow and its more sedate activities, and to avoid undue intrusion into residential areas and other areas of the park. This justification "[has] nothing to do with content" and it satisfies the requirement that time, place, or manner regulations be content neutral.

[The] city's regulation [is] "narrowly tailored to serve a significant governmental interest [because government has] a substantial interest in protecting its citizens from unwelcome noise." This interest is perhaps at its greatest when government seeks to protect " 'the well-being, tranquility, and privacy of the home,' " [but] the government may act to protect even such traditional public forums as city streets and parks from excessive noise. We think it also apparent that the city's interest in ensuring the sufficiency of sound amplification at band-shell events is a substantial one. The record indicates that inadequate sound amplification has had an adverse effect on the ability of some audiences to hear and enjoy performances at the band-shell. The city enjoys a substantial interest in ensuring the ability of its citizens to enjoy whatever benefits the city parks have to offer, from amplified music to silent meditation.

[The] Court of Appeals erred in sifting through all the available or imagined alternative means of regulating sound volume in order to determine whether the city's solution was "the least intrusive means" of achieving the desired end. This "less-restrictive-alternative analysis [has] never been a part of the inquiry into the validity of a time, place, and manner regulation." Instead, our cases quite clearly hold that restrictions on the time, place, or manner of protected speech are not invalid "simply because there is some imaginable alternative that might be less burdensome on speech." The Court of Appeals apparently drew its least-intrusive-means requirement from [United States v. O'Brien, 391 U.S. 367 (1968), but] we have held that the *O'Brien* test "[is] little, if any, different from the standard applied to time, place, or manner restrictions." Indeed, in [Clark v. Community for Creative Non-Violence, involving a government ban on camping in Lafayette Park and the Mall as applied to demonstrators wishing to dramatize the plight of the homeless], we squarely rejected reasoning identical to that of the court [below]. Lest any confusion on the point remain, we reaffirm today that a regulation of the time, place, or manner of protected speech must be narrowly tailored to serve the government's legitimate, content-neutral interests but that it need not be the least restrictive or least intrusive means of doing so. Rather, the requirement of narrow tailoring is satisfied "so long as [the] regulation promotes a substantial government interest that would be achieved less effectively absent the regulation." To be sure, this standard does not mean that a time, place, or manner regulation may burden substantially more speech than is necessary to further the government's legitimate interests. Government may not regulate expression in such a manner that a substantial portion of the burden on speech does not serve to advance its goals. So long as the means chosen are not substantially broader than necessary to achieve the government's interest, however, the regulation will not be invalid simply because a court concludes that the government's interest could be adequately served by some less-speech-restrictive alternative.

It is undeniable that the city's substantial interest in limiting sound volume is served in a direct and effective way by the requirement that the city's sound technician control the mixing board during performances. Absent this requirement, the city's interest would have been served less well, as is evidenced by the complaints about excessive volume generated by respondent's past concerts. . . . .

The city's second content-neutral justification for the guideline, that of ensuring "that the sound amplification [is] sufficient to reach all listeners within the defined concert-ground," also supports the city's choice of regulatory methods. By providing competent sound technicians and adequate amplification equipment, the city eliminated the problems of inexperienced technicians and insufficient sound volume that had plagued some band-shell performers in the past. No doubt this concern is not applicable to respondent's concerts, which apparently were characterized by more-than-adequate sound amplification. But that fact is beside the point, for the validity of the regulation depends on the relation it bears to the overall problem the government seeks to correct, not on the extent to which it furthers the government's interests in an individual case. Here, [the regulation] is valid so long as the city could reasonably have determined that its interests overall would be served less effectively without the sound amplification guideline than with it. Considering these proffered justifications together, therefore, it is apparent that the guideline directly furthers the city's legitimate governmental interests and that those interests would have been less well served in the absence of the sound-amplification guideline.

Respondent nonetheless argues that the sound-amplification guideline is not narrowly tailored because, by placing control of sound mix in the hands of the city's technician, the guideline sweeps far more broadly than is necessary to further the city's legitimate concern with sound volume. [But because] the guideline allows the city to control volume without interfering with the performer's desired sound mix, it is not "substantially broader than necessary" to achieve the city's legitimate ends, and thus it satisfies the requirement of narrow tailoring.

The final requirement, that the guideline leave open ample alternative channels of communication, is easily met. [The] guideline . . . does not attempt to ban any particular manner or type of expression at a given place or time. Rather, the guideline [has] no effect on the quantity or content [of] expression beyond regulating the extent of amplification. That the city's limitations on volume may reduce to some degree the potential audience for respondent's speech is of no consequence, for there has been no showing that the remaining avenues of communication are inadequate. [Reversed.]

JUSTICE MARSHALL, joined by JUSTICES BRENNAN and STEVENS, dissenting.

[Until] today, a key safeguard of free speech has been government's obligation to adopt the least intrusive restriction necessary to achieve its goals. . . . My complaint is with the majority's serious distortion of the narrow tailoring requirement. Our cases have not, as the majority asserts, "clearly" rejected a less-restrictive-alternative test. [In] practice, the Court has interpreted the narrow tailoring requirement to mandate an examination of alternative methods of serving the asserted governmental interest and a determination whether the greater efficacy of the challenged regulation outweighs the increased burden it places on protected speech. See, e.g., Martin v. Struthers, 319 U.S. 141 (1943); Schneider v. State, 308 U.S. 147 (1939). In *Schneider*, for example, the Court invalidated a ban on handbill distribution on public streets, notwithstanding that it was the most effective means of serving government's legitimate interest in minimizing litter, noise, and traffic congestion, and in preventing fraud. The Court concluded that punishing those who actually litter or perpetrate frauds was a much less intrusive, albeit not quite as effective, means to serve those significant interests. [In *Martin*, the Court invalidated a] ban on door-to-door distribution of handbills because directly punishing fraudulent solicitation was a less intrusive, yet still effective, means of serving government's interest in preventing fraud. . . .

NOTES AND PROBLEMS

1. Total Medium Bans. The *Ward* Court discusses Martin v. Struthers and Schneider v. State, where total medium bans were invalidated. Yet in Kovacs v. Cooper, 336 U.S. 77 (1949), the Court upheld a ban on "sound trucks," vehicles equipped with a speaker and amplification devices to enable broadcasting while moving through public streets. A three-justice plurality thought the ordinance valid because the state courts had construed it to apply only to "loud and raucous" sound trucks, but doubted that a total ban on sound trucks would be valid. Justices Jackson and Frankfurter concurred in the result, reasoning that the ordinance was a flat ban on sound trucks but was nevertheless valid because it was both content- and viewpoint-neutral.

Schad v. Mount Ephraim, 452 U.S. 61 (1981). A local zoning law banned all "live entertainment," thus precluding nude dancing before a "peep-show" audience. The Court voided the law, as applied to a nude dancing establishment:

> Entertainment [is] protected. . . . [T]he Borough totally excludes all live entertainment, including nonobscene nude dancing. . . . The Borough . . . contends that live entertainment in general and nude dancing in particular are amply available in close-by areas outside the limits of the Borough, [but] there is no evidence . . . to support the proposition that the kind of entertainment appellants wish to provide is available in reasonably nearby areas. . . . "[One] is not to have the exercise of his liberty of expression in appropriate places abridged on the plea that it may be exercised in some other place." *Schneider.*

City of Ladue v. Gilleo, 512 U.S. 43 (1994). The Court voided a near-total ban on signs displayed on or in residences. Even though the ordinance was content-neutral,

> Ladue has almost completely foreclosed a venerable means of communication that is both unique and important. [Although] prohibitions foreclosing entire media may be completely free of content or viewpoint discrimination, the danger they pose to the freedom of speech is readily apparent—by eliminating a common means of speaking, such measures can suppress too much speech.

Is a total medium ban invalid per se? Even if a medium is closed, could other media provide an ample alternative channel of communication?

2. Focused Protests. Opponents of abortion engaged in peaceful but persistent picketing of the residence of a physician who performed abortions. In response, the town enacted an ordinance banning "picketing before or about the residence . . . of any individual." In Frisby v. Schultz, 487 U.S. 474 (1988), the Supreme Court upheld the ordinance. The ban was content-neutral. It left open ample alternatives: door-to-door solicitation, marches, and mail and telephonic communication. It served the significant purpose of preserving the home as a sanctuary from unwanted speech, and it was narrowly tailored to that interest because it banned only picketing that focused on a residence.

Colorado made it unlawful for a person within 100 feet of a health care facility to "knowingly approach" within 8 feet of another person—without the consent of the other person—to tender "a leaflet or handbill to, display a sign to, or engage in oral protest, education, or counseling with [the other] person." The statute was intended to limit harassment and intimidation of women seeking abortions and medical personnel providing abortions. In Hill v. Colorado, 530 U.S. 703 (2000), the Court upheld the law, finding it to be content-neutral and narrowly tailored to accomplish the state's significant interests of protecting access to medical services, preserving its citizens from unwanted speech, and leaving open ample alternative channels of communication. The majority said the regulation was content-neutral because it regulated the place of speech, the state's interests were unrelated to the content of the speech, and the law was viewpoint-neutral.

The dissenters (Scalia, Kennedy, and Thomas) charged that the law was content-based and likened it to a prohibition on reciting poetry in certain public places, or to a law prohibiting all but "happy" speech in certain public places. The three justices noted that the purpose of the statute was to control anti-abortion speakers even though the law was facially neutral as to the speaker's viewpoint. Moreover, the dissenters claimed that the majority's willingness to find a significant and legitimate state interest in protecting people from unwanted speech in public ran counter to cases such as *Erznoznik* and *Cohen*, which protected offensive speech in public.

≡≡≡ ## *McCullen v. Coakley*
134 S. Ct. 2518 (2014)

CHIEF JUSTICE ROBERTS delivered the opinion of the Court.

A Massachusetts statute makes it a crime to knowingly stand on a "public way or sidewalk" within 35 feet of an entrance or driveway to any place, other than a hospital, where abortions are performed. Petitioners are individuals who approach and talk to women outside such facilities, attempting to dissuade them from having abortions. The statute prevents petitioners from doing so near the facilities' entrances. The question presented is whether the statute violates the First Amendment. . . .

The statute . . . provides:

> No person shall knowingly enter or remain on a public way or sidewalk adjacent to a reproductive health care facility within a radius of 35 feet of any portion of an entrance, exit or driveway of a reproductive health care facility or within the area within a rectangle created by extending the outside boundaries of any entrance, exit or driveway of a reproductive health care facility in straight lines to the point where such lines intersect the sideline of the street in front of such entrance, exit or driveway.

A "reproductive health care facility," . . . is defined as "a place, other than within or upon the grounds of a hospital, where abortions are offered or performed."

The 35-foot buffer zone applies only "during a facility's business hours," and the area must be "clearly marked and posted." In practice, facilities typically mark the zones with painted arcs and posted signs on adjacent sidewalks and streets. A first violation of the statute is punishable by a fine of up to $500, up to three months in prison, or both, while a subsequent offense is punishable by a fine of between $500 and $5,000, up to two and a half years in prison, or both.

The Act exempts four classes of individuals: (1) "persons entering or leaving such facility"; (2) "employees or agents of such facility acting within the scope of their employment"; (3) "law enforcement, ambulance, firefighting, construction, utilities, public works and other municipal agents acting within the scope of their employment"; and (4) "persons using the public sidewalk or street right-of-way adjacent to such facility solely for the purpose of reaching a destination other than such facility." . . .

Petitioners . . . attempt to engage women approaching the clinics in what they call "sidewalk counseling," which involves offering information about alternatives to abortion and help pursuing those options. . . . McCullen and the other petitioners consider it essential to maintain a caring demeanor, a calm tone of voice, and direct eye contact during these exchanges. . . .

The buffer zones have displaced petitioners from their previous positions outside the clinics. . . . Petitioners at all three clinics claim that the buffer zones have considerably hampered their counseling efforts. . . .

The second statutory exemption allows clinic employees and agents acting within the scope of their employment to enter the buffer zones. Relying on this exemption, the Boston clinic uses "escorts" to greet women as they approach the clinic, accompanying them through the zones to the clinic entrance. Petitioners claim that the escorts sometimes thwart petitioners' attempts to communicate with patients by blocking petitioners from handing literature to patients, telling patients not to "pay any attention" or "listen to" petitioners, and disparaging petitioners as "crazy."

[In federal District Court, Petitioners] sought to enjoin enforcement of the Act, . . . both on its face and as applied to them. The District Court denied petitioners' facial challenge after a bench trial based on a stipulated record. The . . . First Circuit affirmed . . . as a reasonable "time, place, and manner" regulation under the test set forth in Ward v. Rock Against Racism. . . . The case then returned to the District Court, which held that the First Circuit's decision foreclosed all but one of petitioners' as-applied challenges. After another bench trial, it denied the remaining as-applied challenge, finding that the Act left petitioners ample alternative channels of communication. The Court of Appeals once again affirmed. We granted certiorari.

II. By its very terms, the Massachusetts Act regulates access to "public way[s]" and "sidewalk[s]." . . . These places . . .—"traditional public fora"—"have immemorially been held in trust for the use of the public and, time out of mind, have been used for purposes of assembly, communicating thoughts between citizens, and discussing public questions." . . . [Even] though the Act says nothing about speech on its face, there is no doubt . . .

that it restricts access to traditional public fora and is therefore subject to First Amendment scrutiny. [A]lthough "[b]y its terms, the Act regulates only conduct," it "incidentally regulates the place and time of protected speech." [The principle that the] "government has no power to restrict expression because of its message, its ideas, its subject matter, or its content" applies with full force in a traditional public forum. . . . [But] "in a public forum the government may impose reasonable restrictions on the time, place, or manner of protected speech, provided the restrictions 'are justified without reference to the content of the regulated speech, that they are narrowly tailored to serve a significant governmental interest, and that they leave open ample alternative channels for communication of the information.'" . . .

III. Petitioners contend that the Act is not content neutral. . . . First, they argue that it discriminates against abortion-related speech because it establishes buffer zones only at clinics that perform abortions. Second, [they] contend that the Act, by exempting clinic employees and agents, favors one viewpoint about abortion over the other. If either of these arguments is correct, then the Act must satisfy strict scrutiny—that is, it must be the least restrictive means of achieving a compelling state interest. . . .

A. [The] Act does not draw content-based distinctions on its face. . . . The Act would be content based if it required "enforcement authorities" to "examine the content of the message that is conveyed to determine whether" a violation has occurred. But it does not. Whether petitioners violate the Act "depends" not "on what they say," but simply on where they say it. . . . It is true [that] the Act has the "inevitable effect" of restricting abortion-related speech more than speech on other subjects. But a facially neutral law does not become content based simply because it may disproportionately affect speech on certain topics. . . . [But by] choosing to pursue these interests only at abortion clinics, petitioners argue, the Massachusetts Legislature evinced a purpose to "single[ ] out for regulation speech about one particular topic: abortion." We cannot infer such a purpose from the Act's limited scope. . . . "States adopt laws to address the problems that confront them." The Massachusetts Legislature [responded] to a problem that was, in its experience, limited to abortion clinics. There was a record of crowding, obstruction, and even violence outside such clinics. There were apparently no similar recurring problems associated with other kinds of healthcare facilities. . . . In light of the limited nature of the problem, it was reasonable for the Massachusetts Legislature to enact a limited solution. When selecting among various options for combating a particular problem, legislatures should be encouraged to choose the one that restricts less speech, not more.

B. Petitioners also argue that the Act is content based because it exempts . . . "employees or agents of [a reproductive healthcare] facility acting within the scope of their employment." This exemption, petitioners say, favors one side in the abortion debate and thus constitutes viewpoint discrimination—an "egregious form of content discrimination." [P]etitioners argue that the exemption allows clinic employees and agents—including the volunteers who "escort" patients arriving at the Boston clinic—to speak inside the buffer zones. An "exemption from an otherwise permissible regulation of speech may represent a governmental 'attempt to give one side of a debatable public question an advantage in expressing its views to the people,'" [but this] does not appear to be such an attempt. [The] exemption cannot be regarded as simply a carve-out for the clinic escorts; it also covers employees such as the maintenance worker shoveling a snowy sidewalk or the security guard patrolling a clinic entrance. Given the need for an exemption for clinic employees, the "scope of their employment" qualification simply ensures that the exemption is limited to its purpose of allowing the employees to do their jobs. . . .

We thus conclude that the Act is neither content nor viewpoint based and therefore need not be analyzed under strict scrutiny.

IV. Even though the Act is content neutral, it still must be "narrowly tailored to serve a significant governmental interest." . . . For a content-neutral time, place, or manner regulation to be narrowly tailored, it must not "burden substantially more speech than is necessary to further the government's legitimate interests." . . .

A. [While the] buffer zones clearly serve [the] interests of "ensuring public safety and order, promoting the free flow of traffic on streets and sidewalks, protecting property rights, and protecting a woman's freedom to seek pregnancy-related services," [they] impose serious burdens on petitioners' speech. . . . The zones . . . compromise petitioners' ability to initiate the close, personal conversations that they view as essential to "sidewalk counseling." . . .

[W]hile the First Amendment does not guarantee a speaker the right to any particular form of expression, some forms—such as normal conversation and leafletting on a public sidewalk—have historically been more closely associated with the transmission of ideas than others. When the government makes it more difficult to engage in these modes of communication, it imposes an especially significant First Amendment burden. . . .

B. The buffer zones burden substantially more speech than necessary to achieve the Commonwealth's asserted interests. [The] Commonwealth has too readily forgone options that could serve its interests just as well, without substantially burdening the kind of speech in which petitioners wish to engage. . . . The Commonwealth's interests include ensuring public safety outside abortion clinics, preventing harassment and intimidation of patients and clinic staff, and combating deliberate obstruction of clinic entrances. The Act itself contains a separate provision . . . that prohibits much of this conduct. . . . The Act, . . . categorically excludes non-exempt individuals from the buffer zones, unnecessarily sweeping in innocent individuals and their speech. . . .

Petitioners wish to converse with their fellow citizens about an important subject on the public streets and sidewalks—sites that have hosted discussions about the issues of the day throughout history. Respondents assert undeniably significant interests in maintaining public safety on those same streets and sidewalks, as well as in preserving access to adjacent healthcare facilities. But here the Commonwealth has pursued those interests by the extreme step of closing a substantial portion of a traditional public forum to all speakers. It has done so without seriously addressing the problem through alternatives that leave the forum open for its time-honored purposes. The Commonwealth may not do that consistent with the First Amendment.

[Reversed and remanded.]

JUSTICE SCALIA, with whom JUSTICE KENNEDY and JUSTICE THOMAS join, concurring in the judgment.

. . . Inasmuch as Part IV holds that the Act is unconstitutional because it does not survive the lesser level of scrutiny associated with content-neutral "time, place, and manner" regulations, there is no principled reason for the majority to decide whether the statute is subject to strict scrutiny. . . . The Court invites Massachusetts, as a means of satisfying the tailoring requirement, to "consider an ordinance" [that] "makes it a crime 'to follow and harass another person within 15 feet of the premises of a reproductive health care facility.'" Is it harassment, one wonders, for Eleanor McCullen to ask a woman, quietly and politely, two times, whether she will take literature or whether she has any questions? Three times? Four times? . . .

It blinks reality to say, as the majority does, that a blanket prohibition on the use of streets and sidewalks where speech on only one politically controversial topic is likely to occur—and where that speech can most effectively be communicated—is not content based. Would the Court exempt from strict scrutiny a law banning access to the streets and sidewalks surrounding the site of the Republican National Convention? Or those used annually to commemorate the 1965 Selma-to-Montgomery civil rights marches? Or those outside the Internal Revenue Service? Surely not.

. . . [The] Act burdens only the public spaces outside abortion clinics. One might have expected the majority to defend the statute's peculiar targeting by arguing that those locations regularly face the safety and access problems that it says the Act was designed to solve. But the majority does not make that argument because it would be untrue. [Although] the statute applies to all abortion clinics in Massachusetts, only one is known to have been beset by the problems that the statute supposedly addresses. The Court uses this striking fact . . . as a basis for concluding that the law is insufficiently "tailored" to safety and access concerns rather than as a basis for concluding that it is not *directed* to those concerns at all, but to the suppression of antiabortion speech. That is rather like invoking the eight missed human targets of a shooter who has killed one victim to prove, not that he is guilty of attempted mass murder, but that *he has bad aim*.

. . . Showing that a law that suppresses speech on a specific subject is so far-reaching that it applies even when the asserted non-speech-related problems are not present is persuasive evidence that the law is content based. . . . The structure of the Act also indicates that it rests on content-based concerns. The goals of "public safety, patient access to healthcare, and the unobstructed use of public sidewalks and roadways," are already achieved by an earlier-enacted subsection of the statute. . . . Thus, the speech-free zones carved out by [the 2007 amendment] add nothing to safety and access; what they achieve, and what they were obviously designed to achieve, is the suppression of speech opposing abortion. . . .

In concluding that the statute is content based and therefore subject to strict scrutiny, I necessarily conclude that *Hill* should be overruled. . . . Protecting people from speech they do not want to hear is not a function that the First Amendment allows the government to undertake in the public streets and sidewalks. . . .

[By] stating that "the Act would not be content neutral if it were concerned with undesirable effects that arise from . . . '[l]isteners' reactions to speech," and then holding the Act unconstitutional for being insufficiently tailored to safety and access concerns, the Court itself has *sub silentio* . . . overruled *Hill*. The unavoidable implication . . . is that protection against unwelcome speech cannot justify restrictions on the use of public streets and sidewalks. . . .

Petitioners contend that the Act['s exemption for abortion clinic employees or agents] constitutes a presumptively invalid viewpoint-discriminatory restriction. . . . Is there any serious doubt that *abortion-clinic employees or agents* "acting within the scope of their employment" near clinic entrances may—indeed, often will—speak in favor of abortion . . . ? Or speak in opposition to the message of abortion opponents . . . ? The Court's contrary assumption is simply incredible. . . . [So] long as the statute permits speech favorable to abortion rights while excluding antiabortion speech, it discriminates on the basis of viewpoint. . . .

[The] Act should be reviewed under the strict-scrutiny standard applicable to content-based legislation. That standard requires that a regulation represent "the least restrictive means" of furthering "a compelling Government interest." . . . "Suffice it to say that if protecting people from unwelcome communications"—the actual purpose of the provision—"is a compelling state interest, the First Amendment is a dead letter." . . .

JUSTICE ALITO, concurring in the judgment.

. . . [If] the Massachusetts law discriminates on the basis of viewpoint, it is unconstitutional, and I believe the law clearly discriminates on this ground. . . . Consider this entirely realistic situation. A woman enters a buffer zone and heads haltingly toward the entrance. A sidewalk counselor, such as petitioners, enters the buffer zone, approaches the woman and says, "If you have doubts about an abortion, let me try to answer any questions you may have. The clinic will not give you good information." At the same time, a clinic employee . . . approaches the same woman and says, "Come inside and we will give you honest answers to all your questions." The sidewalk counselor and the clinic employee expressed opposing viewpoints, but only the first violated the statute. . . . It is clear on the face of the Massachusetts law that it discriminates based on viewpoint. Speech in favor of the clinic and its work by employees and agents is permitted; speech criticizing the clinic and its work is a crime. This is blatant viewpoint discrimination. . . .

NOTES AND PROBLEMS

1. Problems: *Tobacco Protesters.* Suppose Colorado or Massachusetts made it unlawful for any person to "knowingly approach" within 8 feet of a person who is "using or displaying tobacco products or paraphernalia," without that person's consent, to tender "a leaflet or handbill to, display a sign to, or engage in oral protest, education, or counseling with [the other] person." Would this be content-neutral regulation? Would it be valid under Hill v. Colorado? Under *McCullen*?

Funeral Protesters. As noted in *Snyder*, members of the Westboro Baptist Church frequently picket the funerals of soldiers killed in combat because church leaders assert that God is killing them to punish America for condoning homosexuality. In response, a state enacts a law that forbids "picketing activity within 100 feet of a funeral, burial, memorial service, or funeral procession." Does this law violate the free speech guarantee? If it does, what changes are necessary for the law to comply with the First Amendment?

2. Content-Neutral Prohibitions on Disclosure of Private Communications of Matters of Public Concern. Vast amounts of information are communicated daily by wireless communications devices and through the porous web of computers that constitutes the Internet, all of which is susceptible to interception by unauthorized persons. To protect the privacy of these communications, governments have enacted content-neutral prohibitions on disclosure of intercepted communications, thus producing a tension between preserving privacy and fostering public knowledge of matters of public concern. In Bartnicki v. Vopper, 532 U.S. 514 (2001), the Court struck down two federal statutes that, as applied, imposed criminal and civil penalties on the disclosure of a private communication intercepted illegally by an unknown party but that was obtained lawfully by the person making the disclosure. The facts at issue in *Bartnicki* are discussed in Section B.7.b, supra.

The Court concluded that the laws were content-neutral, but found their application to be an unjustified means of accomplishing the government's objectives. The first objective, "removing an incentive . . . to intercept private conversations," was "plainly insufficient" because the "normal method of deterring unlawful conduct is to [to punish] the person who engages in it" rather than suppress speech "by a law-abiding possessor of information . . . in order to deter conduct by a non-law-abiding third party." The second objective, "minimizing the harm to persons whose conversations have been illegally intercepted," was "considerably stronger" because it was intended to promote "the uninhibited exchange of ideas and information among private parties" and to reduce "fear of public disclosure of private conversations [that] might well have a chilling effect on private speech." But because the statutes imposed "sanctions on the publication of truthful information of public concern," they implicated "core purposes" of free speech. The Court noted: "In this case, privacy concerns give way when balanced against the interest in publishing matters of public importance. [One] of the costs associated with participation in public affairs is an attendant loss of privacy." The Court never explained exactly what level of review it was applying and disclaimed any opinion on whether sanctions might validly apply to "disclosures of trade secrets or domestic gossip or other information of purely private concern."

Chief Justice Rehnquist, in a dissent joined by Justices Scalia and Thomas, charged that the Court had subjected a content-neutral speech restriction that was conceded to serve "interests of the 'highest order' . . . to the strict scrutiny normally reserved for governmental attempts to censor different viewpoints or ideas."

Queries: What was the flaw in the federal statutes struck down in *Bartnicki*? Did the laws burden substantially more speech than was necessary to achieve the important government interest in maintaining privacy of communications? If so, explain why. Was the government interest—communications privacy—unimportant? Or was this a case where two important objectives—securing privacy and vindicating free speech by ensuring robust, wide-open debate on matters of public concern—collided? Does *Bartnicki* stand for the proposition that some content-neutral speech regulations that serve important objectives well are still subject to strict scrutiny? If so, what factors identify the speech regulations that will receive this higher scrutiny? Is it limited to all content-neutral regulations that choke off disclosure of matters of public concern?

2.   Expressive Conduct

Expressive conduct cases are merely a variety of content-neutral regulation of speech. In every case the government regulates conduct and, by doing so, burdens expression that is clearly communicated by that conduct.

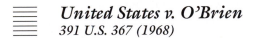

United States v. O'Brien
391 U.S. 367 (1968)

CHIEF JUSTICE WARREN delivered the opinion of the Court.

On the morning of March 31, 1966, David Paul O'Brien and three companions burned their Selective Service registration certificates on the steps of the South Boston Courthouse. A sizable crowd, including several agents of the Federal Bureau of Investigation, witnessed the event. [O'Brien] stated to FBI agents that he had burned his registration certificate because of his beliefs, knowing that he was violating federal law. [For] this act, O'Brien was indicted, tried, convicted, and sentenced in the [federal] District Court. [He] stated in argument to the jury that he burned the certificate publicly to influence others to adopt his antiwar beliefs, as he put it, "so that other people would reevaluate their positions with Selective Service, with the armed forces, and reevaluate their place in the culture of today, to hopefully consider my position."

The indictment . . . charged that he "willfully and knowingly did mutilate, destroy, and [burn his] Registration Certificate" [in] violation of [section

462(b)(3)] of the Universal Military Training and Service Act of 1948, [amended] by Congress in 1965 (adding the words italicized below), so that at the time O'Brien burned his certificate an offense was committed by any person, "who forges, alters, *knowingly destroys, knowingly mutilates,* or in any manner changes any such certificate." (Italics supplied.)

[The] Court of Appeals [held] the 1965 Amendment unconstitutional as a law abridging freedom of speech. At the time the Amendment was enacted, a regulation of the Selective Service System required registrants to keep their registration certificates in their "personal possession at all times." Willful violations [were] made criminal by statute. The Court of Appeals, therefore, was of the opinion that conduct punishable under the 1965 Amendment was already punishable under the nonpossession regulation, [that] the Amendment [thus] served no valid purpose, [and that] the Amendment must have been "directed at public as distinguished from private destruction." On this basis, the court concluded that the 1965 Amendment ran afoul of the First Amendment by singling out persons engaged in protests for special treatment. [We] hold that the 1965 Amendment is constitutional both as enacted and as applied.

When a male reaches the age of 18, he is required by [law] to register with a local draft board [and] is issued a registration certificate. [He is then] assigned a classification denoting his eligibility for induction and [issued] a Notice of Classification, [subject to reclassification if] the registrant's status changes in some relevant way. Both the registration and classification certificates are small white cards, approximately 2 by 3 inches [bearing information relevant to the registrant and his draft status]. Both the registration and classification certificates bear notices that the registrant must notify his local board in writing of every change in address, physical condition, and [of] any other fact which might change his classification. [The] 1965 Amendment plainly does not abridge free speech on its face, [but] deals with conduct having no connection with speech. It prohibits the knowing destruction of certificates issued by the Selective Service System, and there is nothing necessarily expressive about such conduct. The Amendment does not . . . punish only destruction engaged in for the purpose of expressing views. A law prohibiting destruction of Selective Service certificates no more abridges free speech on its face than a motor vehicle law prohibiting the destruction of drivers' licenses, or a tax law prohibiting the destruction of books and records. . . .

O'Brien first argues that the 1965 Amendment is unconstitutional as applied to him because his act of burning his registration certificate was protected "symbolic speech" within the First Amendment. His argument is that the freedom of expression which the First Amendment guarantees includes all modes of "communication of ideas by conduct," and that his conduct is within this definition because he did it in "demonstration against the war and against the draft." We cannot accept the view that an apparently limitless variety of conduct can be labeled "speech" whenever the person engaging in the conduct intends thereby to express an idea. However, even on the assumption that the alleged communicative element in O'Brien's conduct is sufficient to bring into play the First Amendment, it does not necessarily follow that the destruction of a registration certificate is constitutionally protected activity. This Court has held that when "speech" and "nonspeech" elements are combined in the same course of conduct, a sufficiently important governmental interest in regulating the nonspeech element can justify incidental limitations on First Amendment freedoms. [We] think it clear that a government regulation is sufficiently justified if it is within the constitutional power of the Government; if it furthers an important or substantial governmental interest; if the governmental interest is unrelated to the suppression of free expression; and if the incidental restriction on alleged First Amendment freedoms is no greater than is essential to the furtherance of that interest. We find that the 1965 Amendment [meets] all of these requirements, and consequently that O'Brien can be constitutionally convicted for violating it. . . . The power of Congress to classify and conscript manpower for military service is "beyond question." . . . Congress may establish a system of registration for individuals liable for training and service, and may require such individuals within reason to cooperate in the registration system. The issuance of certificates indicating the registration and eligibility classification of individuals is a legitimate and substantial administrative aid in the functioning of this system. And legislation to insure the continuing availability of issued certificates serves a legitimate and substantial purpose in the system's administration.

[Draft registration certificates serve purposes that] would be defeated by the certificates' destruction or mutilation. Among these are [proof of registration for the draft, facilitation of communication between the registrant and his draft board, providing a constant reminder to the registrant to notify his draft board of any change of status, and providing clear, simple evidence of draft status in times of dire emergency]. The many functions performed by Selective Service certificates establish beyond doubt that Congress has a legitimate and substantial interest in preventing their wanton and unrestrained destruction and assuring their continuing availability by punishing people who knowingly and willfully destroy or mutilate them. And we are unpersuaded that the pre-existence of the nonpossession regulations in any way negates this interest. In the absence of a question as to multiple punishment, it has never been suggested that there is anything improper in Congress's providing alternative statutory avenues of prosecution to assure the effective protection of one and the same interest. . . . We think it apparent that the continuing availability to each registrant of his Selective Service certificates substantially furthers the smooth and proper functioning of the system that Congress has established to raise armies.

[It] is equally clear that the 1965 Amendment specifically protects this substantial governmental interest. We perceive no alternative means that would more precisely and narrowly assure the continuing availability of issued Selective Service certificates than a law which prohibits their willful mutilation or destruction. The 1965 Amendment prohibits such conduct and does nothing more; [both] the governmental interest and the operation of the 1965 Amendment are limited to the noncommunicative aspect of O'Brien's conduct[:] preventing harm to the smooth and efficient functioning of the

Selective Service System. When O'Brien deliberately rendered unavailable his registration certificate, he willfully frustrated this governmental interest. For this noncommunicative impact of his conduct, and for nothing else, he was convicted.

[This case] is therefore unlike one where the alleged governmental interest in regulating conduct arises in some measure because the communication allegedly integral to the conduct is itself thought to be harmful. In Stromberg v. California, 283 U.S. 359 (1931), for example, this Court struck down a [statute] which punished people who expressed their "opposition to organized government" by displaying "any flag, badge, banner, or device." Since the statute there was aimed at suppressing communication it could not be sustained as a regulation of noncommunicative conduct [when applied to people brandishing a red flag]. In conclusion, we find that because of the Government's substantial interest in assuring the continuing availability of issued Selective Service certificates, because [the 1965 Amendment] is an appropriately narrow means of protecting this interest and condemns only the independent noncommunicative impact of conduct within its reach, and because the noncommunicative impact of O'Brien's act of burning his registration certificate frustrated the Government's interest, a sufficient governmental interest has been shown to justify O'Brien's conviction.

O'Brien finally argues that the 1965 Amendment is unconstitutional as enacted because what he calls the "purpose" of Congress was "to suppress freedom of speech." . . . It is a familiar principle of constitutional law that this Court will not strike down an otherwise constitutional statute on the basis of an alleged illicit legislative motive. [Inquiries] into congressional motives or purposes are a hazardous matter. When the issue is simply the interpretation of legislation, the Court will look to statements by legislators for guidance as to the purpose of the legislature, because the benefit to sound decision-making in this circumstance is thought sufficient to risk the possibility of misreading Congress's purpose. It is entirely a different matter when we are asked to void a statute that [is] constitutional on its face, on the basis of what fewer than a handful of Congressmen said about it. What motivates one legislator to make a speech about a statute is not necessarily what motivates scores of others to enact it, and the stakes are sufficiently high for us to eschew guesswork. [In any case, while the] reports of the Senate and House Armed Services Committees [make] clear a concern with the "defiant" destruction of so-called "draft cards" and with "open" encouragement to others to destroy their cards, both reports also indicate that this concern stemmed from an apprehension that unrestrained destruction of cards would disrupt the smooth functioning of the Selective Service System. [The] 1965 Amendment [is] constitutional as enacted and as applied.

JUSTICE HARLAN, concurring.

I wish to make explicit my understanding that [the Court's test] does not foreclose consideration of First Amendment claims in those rare instances when an "incidental" restriction upon expression, imposed by a regulation which furthers an "important or substantial" governmental interest and satisfies the Court's other criteria, in practice has the effect of entirely preventing a "speaker" from reaching a significant audience with whom he could not otherwise lawfully communicate. This is not such a case, since O'Brien manifestly could have conveyed his message in many ways other than by burning his draft card.

NOTES AND PROBLEMS

1. **"Unrelated to the Suppression of Free Expression."** A pivotal prong of the *O'Brien* test is the requirement that the government's regulatory interest be "unrelated to the suppression of free expression." If it is not, strict scrutiny applies unless the suppressed speech is unprotected and the regulation is viewpoint-neutral. If it is, the more relaxed intermediate scrutiny of *O'Brien* applies. This makes critical the question of how one determines whether the government's interest is related to the suppression of ideas. Sometimes this is evident from the statute (as in *Stromberg*, the "red flag" case discussed in *O'Brien*).

Schacht v. United States, 398 U.S. 58 (1970), is an example. As a result of his performance in a skit protesting the Vietnam War, Schacht was convicted of the federal crime of wearing an American military uniform without authorization. The Court reversed the conviction because another federal law authorized the wearing of military uniforms in dramatic productions so long as "the portrayal does not tend to discredit" the American military.

Usually, however, the statute will not provide the answer. The government will always advance an objective that is unrelated to the suppression of ideas; the question is whether that objective is implicated on the facts of the case. For example, if the government banned the exhibition of "rainbow-striped flags" in order to preserve public tranquility, the question would be why public tranquility is advanced. The plausible, and fatal, answer must be that the exhibition of a symbol celebrating cultural diversity is thought to provoke possibly violent reactions.

2. **The Limits of *O'Brien*.** Not every incidental restriction on speech produced by some other regulation is subject to the *O'Brien* test. In Arcara v. Cloud Books, 478 U.S. 697 (1986), the Court upheld the closure of a pornographic bookstore as a public nuisance because it was a site for prostitution. The bookstore claimed that the closure, even for reasons unrelated to speech suppression, amounted to an incidental restriction on speech that required justification under *O'Brien*. The Court disagreed, concluding that the burden on speech was so incidental that *O'Brien* did not apply. There was no symbolic expression in the prostitution, the closure law did not single out bookstores or other speech for differential treatment, and the burden on speech was slight—the proprietor remained "free to sell the same materials at another location." In any case, the Court stated, "we have [applied heightened scrutiny] only where it was conduct with a significant expressive element

that drew the remedy in the first place, [or] where a statute based on a nonexpressive activity has the inevitable effect of singling out . . . expressive activity."

According to the Court in Rumsfeld v. FAIR, 547 U.S. 47 (2006), only conduct that is "inherently expressive" is protected expressive conduct. At issue in *FAIR* was a federal requirement that universities provide equal access to military recruiters or else lose substantial federal funds. Law schools contended that they expressed their disagreement with the military's policy of discriminating on the basis of sexual orientation by giving military recruiters inferior treatment. But this was not inherently expressive, said the Court. The only way an observer would divine expression in the practice of exiling a military recruiter to some obscure office far away from the law school would be by overt speech explaining the reason for the differential treatment: "The expressive component of a law school's actions is not created by the conduct itself but by the speech that accompanies it."

3. Problems. Which, if any, of the following are subject to *O'Brien* analysis?

1. Application of a murder statute to a political assassination.
2. Application of a "no trailers on city streets" ordinance to a person towing a trailer on which is mounted a billboard urging citizens to vote Democratic in an imminent election.
3. IRS seizure of a newspaper printing plant for the owner's failure to pay an admitted tax liability.
4. A law banning open flames in public after dark, as applied to the candlelight vigil of an anti-war group.

══ *Texas v. Johnson*
══ *491 U.S. 397 (1989)*

JUSTICE BRENNAN delivered the opinion of the Court.

After publicly burning an American flag as a means of political protest, Gregory Lee Johnson was convicted of desecrating a flag in violation of Texas law. This case presents the question whether his conviction is consistent with the First Amendment. We hold that it is not.

I. While the Republican National Convention was taking place in Dallas in 1984, [Johnson] participated in a political demonstration [protesting] the policies of the Reagan administration. [The] demonstrators marched through the Dallas streets, chanting political slogans and stopping at several corporate locations to stage "die-ins" intended to dramatize the consequences of nuclear war. On several occasions they spray-painted the walls of buildings and overturned potted plants, but Johnson himself took no part in such activities. He did, however, accept an American flag handed to him by a fellow protestor who had taken it from a flagpole outside one of the targeted buildings. [In] front of Dallas City Hall [Johnson] unfurled the American flag, doused it with kerosene, and set it on fire. While the flag burned, the protestors chanted:

"America, the red, white, and blue, we spit on you." After the demonstrators dispersed, a witness to the flag burning collected the flag's remains and buried them in his backyard. No one was physically injured or threatened with injury, though several witnesses testified that they had been seriously offended by the flag burning. [Johnson was charged with] desecration of a venerated object.[14] [He] was convicted, sentenced to one year in prison, and fined $2,000. [The] Texas Court of Criminal Appeals reversed, holding that the State could not, consistent with the First Amendment, punish Johnson for burning the flag in these circumstances. [We] now affirm.

II. [Because] Johnson was convicted of flag desecration for burning the flag rather than for uttering insulting words, [we] must first determine whether Johnson's burning of the flag constituted expressive conduct, permitting him to invoke the First Amendment in challenging his conviction. If his conduct was expressive, we next decide whether the State's regulation is related to the suppression of free expression. If the State's regulation is not related to expression, then the less stringent standard we announced in [*O'Brien*] for regulations of noncommunicative conduct controls. If it is, then we are outside of *O'Brien*'s test, and we must ask whether this interest justifies Johnson's conviction under a more demanding standard.

[The] First Amendment literally forbids the abridgment only of "speech," but we have long recognized that its protection does not end at the spoken or written word. [In] deciding whether particular conduct possesses sufficient communicative elements to bring the First Amendment into play, we have asked whether "[a]n intent to convey a particularized message was present, and [whether] the likelihood was great that the message would be understood by those who viewed it." [Texas conceded that] Johnson's conduct was expressive conduct and this concession seems [prudent]. Johnson burned an American flag as part—indeed, as the culmination—of a political [demonstration]. The expressive, overtly political nature of this conduct was both intentional and overwhelmingly [apparent].

III. The government generally has a freer hand in restricting expressive conduct than it has in restricting the written or spoken word. It may not, however, proscribe particular conduct because it has expressive elements. Thus, [we] have limited the applicability of *O'Brien*'s relatively lenient standard to those cases in which "the governmental interest is unrelated to the suppression of free expression."

In order to decide whether *O'Brien*'s test applies here [we] must decide whether Texas has asserted an interest in support of Johnson's conviction that is unrelated to the suppression of expression. If we find that an interest asserted by the State is simply not implicated on the facts before us, we need

---

14. Texas Penal Code §42.09 (1989): "(a) A person commits an offense if he intentionally or knowingly desecrates: (1) a public monument; (2) a place of worship or burial; or (3) a state or national flag. (b) For purposes of this section, 'desecrate' means deface, damage, or otherwise physically mistreat in a way that the actor knows will seriously offend one or more persons likely to observe or discover his action."

not ask whether *O'Brien*'s test applies. The State offers two separate interests to justify this conviction: preventing breaches of the peace and preserving the flag as a symbol of nationhood and national unity. We hold that the first interest is not implicated on this record and that the second is related to the suppression of expression.

A. Texas claims that its interest in preventing breaches of the peace justifies Johnson's conviction for flag desecration. However, no disturbance of the peace actually occurred or threatened to occur because of Johnson's burning of the flag. [The] State's position [amounts] to a claim that an audience that takes serious offense at particular expression is necessarily likely to disturb the peace and that the expression may be prohibited on this basis. Our precedents do not countenance such a presumption. On the contrary, they recognize that a principal "function of free speech under our system of government is to invite dispute." [*Terminiello.*] Thus, we have [asked] whether the expression "is directed to inciting or producing imminent lawless action and is likely to incite or produce such action." [*Brandenburg.*] To accept Texas'[s] arguments that it need only demonstrate "the potential for a breach of the peace," and that every flag burning necessarily possesses that potential, would be to eviscerate our holding in *Brandenburg.* . . .

Nor does Johnson's expressive conduct fall within that small class of "fighting words" that are "likely to provoke the average person to retaliation, and thereby cause a breach of the peace." [*Chaplinsky.*] No reasonable onlooker would have regarded Johnson's generalized expression of dissatisfaction with the policies of the Federal Government as a direct personal insult or an invitation to exchange fisticuffs. [The] State's interest in maintaining order is not implicated on these [facts].

B. The State also asserts an interest in preserving the flag as a symbol of nationhood and national unity. [But] the government's interest in preserving the flag's special symbolic value "is directly related to expression in the context of activity" such as [Johnson's] burning of the flag. The State, apparently, is concerned that such conduct will lead people to believe either that the flag does not stand for nationhood and national unity, but instead reflects other, less positive concepts, or that the concepts reflected in the flag do not in fact exist, that is, that we do not enjoy unity as a Nation. These concerns blossom only when a person's treatment of the flag communicates some message, and thus are related "to the suppression of free expression" within the meaning of *O'Brien*. We are thus outside of *O'Brien*'s test altogether.

IV. It remains to consider whether the State's interest in preserving the flag as a symbol of nationhood and national unity justifies Johnson's conviction. [Johnson] was prosecuted because he knew that his politically charged expression would cause "serious offense." If he had burned the flag as a means of disposing of it because it was dirty or torn, he would not have been convicted of flag desecration under this Texas law: federal law designates burning as the preferred means of disposing of a flag "when it is in such condition that it is no longer a fitting emblem for display" and Texas has no quarrel with this means of disposal. The Texas law is thus not aimed at protecting the physical integrity of the flag in all circumstances, but is designed instead to protect it only against impairments that would cause serious offense to others. Texas concedes as [much]. Whether Johnson's treatment of the flag violated Texas law thus depended on the likely communicative impact of his expressive conduct. [This] restriction on Johnson's expression is content based. [We] must therefore subject [Texas's] asserted interest in preserving the special symbolic character of the flag to "the most exacting scrutiny."

Texas argues that its interest in preserving the flag as a symbol of nationhood and national unity survives this close analysis. . . . According to Texas, if one physically treats the flag in a way that would tend to cast doubt on either the idea that nationhood and national unity are the flag's referents or that national unity actually exists, the message conveyed thereby is a harmful one and therefore may be prohibited. If there is a bedrock principle underlying the First Amendment, it is that the government may not prohibit the expression of an idea simply because society finds the idea itself offensive or disagreeable. We have not recognized an exception to this principle even where our flag has been involved. . . . [The] government [may not] compel conduct that would evince respect for the flag. [West Virginia State Bd. of Educ. v. Barnette, 319 U.S. 624 (1943).] In holding in *Barnette* that the Constitution did not leave this course open to the government, Justice Jackson described one of our society's defining principles in words deserving of their frequent repetition: "If there is any fixed star in our constitutional constellation, it is that no official, high or petty, can prescribe what shall be orthodox in politics, nationalism, religion, or other matters of opinion or force citizens to confess by word or act their faith therein."

In [Spence v. Washington, 418 U.S. 405 (1974)], we held that the same interest asserted by Texas here was insufficient to support a criminal conviction under a flag-misuse statute for the taping of a peace sign to an American flag. See also [Smith v. Goguen, 415 U.S. 566 (1974), where Justice White, concurring in the judgment, declared that] to convict [a] person who had sewn a flag onto the seat of his pants for "contemptuous" treatment of the flag would be . . . "to punish for communicating ideas unacceptable to the controlling majority in the legislature."

In short, nothing in our precedents suggests that a State may foster its own view of the flag by prohibiting expressive conduct relating to it. . . . [To] conclude that the government may permit designated symbols to be used to communicate only a limited set of messages would be to enter territory having no discernible or defensible boundaries. Could the government, on this theory, prohibit the burning of state flags? Of copies of the Presidential seal? Of the Constitution? In evaluating these choices under the First Amendment, how would we decide which symbols were sufficiently special to warrant this unique status? To do so, we would be forced to consult our own political preferences, and impose them on the citizenry, in the very way that the First Amendment forbids us to do. . . .

It is not the State's ends, but its means, to which we object. [To] say that the government has an interest in encouraging proper treatment of the flag, however, is not to say that it may criminally punish a person for burning a flag as a means of political protest. . . .

Our decision is a reaffirmation of the principles of freedom and inclusiveness that the flag best reflects, and of the conviction that our toleration of criticism such as Johnson's is a sign and source of our strength. . . . We do not consecrate the flag by punishing its desecration, for in doing so we dilute the freedom that this cherished emblem represents. [Affirmed.]

JUSTICE KENNEDY, concurring.

I join [the Court's] opinion without reservation, but with a keen sense that this [case] exacts its personal toll. [The] hard fact is that sometimes we must make decisions we do not like. We make them because they are right, right in the sense that the law and the Constitution [compel] the result. [It] is poignant but fundamental that the flag protects those who hold it in contempt.

CHIEF JUSTICE REHNQUIST, joined by JUSTICES WHITE and O'CONNOR, dissenting.

[The] Court ignores Justice Holmes's familiar aphorism that "a page of history is worth a volume of logic." For more than 200 years, the American flag has occupied a unique position as the symbol of our Nation, a uniqueness that justifies a governmental prohibition against flag burning in the way [Johnson] did here. . . .

[As in *Chaplinsky*], the public burning of the American flag by Johnson was no essential part of any exposition of ideas and at the same time [had] a tendency to incite a breach of the peace. Johnson was free to make any verbal denunciation of the flag that he wished; indeed, [he] shouted out various slogans, [including] "red, white and blue, we spit on you, you stand for plunder, you will go under." For none of these acts was he arrested or prosecuted; it was only when he proceeded to burn publicly an American flag stolen from its rightful owner that he violated the Texas statute. [Johnson's] act, like Chaplinsky's provocative words, conveyed nothing that could not have been conveyed and was not conveyed just as forcefully in a dozen different ways. As with "fighting words," so with flag burning, for purposes of the First Amendment.

[Flag] burning is the equivalent of an inarticulate grunt or roar that [is] most likely to be indulged in not to express any particular idea, but to antagonize others. [The] Texas statute deprived Johnson of only one rather inarticulate symbolic form of protest—a form of protest that was profoundly offensive to many—and left him with a full panoply of other symbols and every conceivable form of verbal expression to express his deep disapproval of national policy. [It] was Johnson's use of this particular symbol, and not the idea that he sought to convey by it or by his many other expressions, for which he was punished. . . .

But the Court today will have none of this. . . . [The] Court decides that the American flag is just another symbol, about which not only must opinions pro and con be tolerated, but for which the most minimal public respect may not be enjoined. The government may conscript men into the Armed Forces where they must fight and perhaps die for the flag, but the government may not prohibit the public burning of the banner under which they fight. I would uphold the Texas statute as applied in this case.

JUSTICE STEVENS, dissenting.

[This] case has nothing to do with "disagreeable ideas." It involves disagreeable conduct [that] diminishes the value of an important national asset.... [Johnson] was prosecuted because of the method he chose to express his dissatisfaction with [the nation's] policies. Had he chosen to spray-paint [his] message of dissatisfaction on the facade of the Lincoln Memorial, there would be no question about the power of the Government to prohibit his means of expression. The prohibition would be supported by the legitimate interest in preserving the quality of an important national asset. Though the asset at stake in this case is intangible, . . . the same interest supports a prohibition on the desecration of the American flag.

NOTE AND PROBLEMS

1. The Politics of Flag Desecration. Texas v. Johnson sparked calls for a constitutional amendment to overturn the ruling. Other opponents of the decision argued that a carefully drawn statute would be upheld. In the end, the statutory approach prevailed in the form of the Flag Protection Act of 1989, which provided in pertinent part:

> Whoever knowingly mutilates, defaces, physically defiles, burns, maintains on the floor or ground, or tramples upon any flag of the United States shall be [fined] or imprisoned [or] both. This subsection does not prohibit any conduct consisting of the disposal of the flag when it has become worn or soiled.

Almost immediately the law was publicly violated by people eager to test its validity. In United States v. Eichman, 496 U.S. 310 (1990), the Court upheld district court rulings that the Flag Protection Act of 1989 violated the First Amendment. For the Court, Justice Brennan wrote:

> The Government contends that the Flag Protection Act is constitutional because, unlike the statute addressed in Johnson, the Act does not target expressive conduct on the basis of the content of its message. . . . [Although] the Flag Protection Act contains no explicit contest-based limitation on the scope of prohibited conduct, it is nevertheless clear that the Government's asserted *interest* is "related 'to the suppression of free expression'" and concerned with the content of such expression. The Government's interest in protecting the "physical integrity" of a privately owned flag rests upon a perceived need to preserve the flag's status as a symbol of our Nation and certain national ideals. [Because] the secret destruction of a flag in one's own basement would not threaten the flag's recognized meaning, [the] Government's desire to preserve the flag as a symbol

for certain national ideals is implicated "only when a person's treatment of the flag communicates [a] message" to others that is inconsistent with those ideals. Moreover, [the] explicit exemption [for] disposal of "worn or soiled" flags protects certain acts traditionally associated with patriotic respect for the flag. [The Act] suppresses expression out of concern for its likely communicative impact. [Its] restriction on expression cannot be " 'justified without reference to the content of the regulated speech.' " The Act therefore must be subjected to "the most exacting scrutiny," and for the reasons stated in *Johnson* the Government's interest cannot justify its infringement on First Amendment rights.

Justice Stevens, joined by Chief Justice Rehnquist and Justices White and O'Connor, dissented.

Eichman revived interest in a constitutional amendment to permit bans on flag desecration, but those proposals have failed in Congress.

2. Problems: *Banning Public Fires.* Could a state validly enact a law forbidding fires in public places (except for public campgrounds) and apply that law to public flag burning?

Comprehensive Flag Burning Bans. Could a state validly enact a law forbidding the public burning of an American flag for any reason? What if the law prohibited burning an American flag *anywhere*?

Ban on Unauthorized Wearing of Military Uniforms. Suppose Congress were to prohibit anyone except military personnel on active duty from wearing an American military uniform, and did not provide the exception at issue in *Schacht*. Would this law be valid?

3. The "Secondary Effects" Doctrine

The essence of the "secondary effects" doctrine is that governments may regulate speech by its content if its purpose for doing so is wholly unrelated to that content, but is instead designed to ameliorate some phenomenon closely associated with but not produced by the content of the speech. When that occurs, the Court declares that the regulation is content-neutral. The secondary-effects doctrine began with Young v. American Mini Theatres, 427 U.S. 50 (1976), in which the Court upheld a Detroit zoning ordinance designed to force the dispersal of pornographic businesses throughout the city. The Court reasoned that the law was viewpoint-neutral and did not materially restrict either the creation of or access to pornography. After *American Mini Theatres*, a government could regulate the location of businesses dealing in non-obscene sexually explicit expression in order to address the problem—frequently associated with the areas surrounding such businesses—of public drunkenness, drug dealing, and petty theft, as those problems are not produced by the sexually explicit speech. A government could not regulate those same businesses to address the problem of patrons of those businesses committing sex crimes, because the sex crimes are arguably induced in some part by the sexually explicit speech. In reading these materials, ask whether the doctrine is (or should be) limited to government attempts to control the crime and social pathology associated with businesses purveying pornographic expression.

≡≡≡ ### *City of Renton v. Playtime Theatres, Inc.*
475 U.S. 41 (1986)

[Renton, Washington, a Seattle suburb, adopted a zoning ordinance that prohibited "adult motion picture theaters from locating within 1,000 feet of any [residence], church, park, or school." This effectively forced such theaters to concentrate in an extremely limited portion of Renton. The Court upheld the validity of the ordinance.]

JUSTICE REHNQUIST delivered the opinion of the Court.

[Resolution] of this case is largely dictated by [*American Mini Theatres*]. The Renton ordinance, like the one in *American Mini Theatres*, does not ban adult theaters altogether, but merely [regulates their location]. The ordinance is therefore properly analyzed as a form of time, place, and manner regulation. [While] regulations enacted for the purpose of restraining speech on the basis of its content presumptively violate the First Amendment, [so-called] "content-neutral" time, place, and manner regulations are acceptable so long as they are designed to serve a substantial governmental interest and do not unreasonably limit alternative avenues of communication.

At first glance, the Renton ordinance, like the ordinance in *American Mini Theatres*, does not appear to fit neatly into either the "content-based" or the "content-neutral" category. To be sure, the ordinance treats theaters that specialize in adult films differently from other kinds of theaters. Nevertheless, [the] Renton ordinance is aimed not at the content of the films shown at "adult motion picture theatres," but rather at the *secondary effects* of such theaters on the surrounding community. The District [Court's findings that Renton's predominant concerns] were with the secondary effects of adult theaters, and not with the content of adult films themselves, [is] more than adequate to establish that the city's pursuit of its zoning interests here was unrelated to the suppression of free expression. The ordinance by its terms is designed to prevent crime, protect the city's retail trade, maintain property values, and generally "[protect and preserve] the quality of [the city's] neighborhoods, commercial districts, and the quality of urban life," not to suppress the expression of unpopular views.

[The] appropriate inquiry [is] whether the Renton ordinance is designed to serve a substantial governmental interest and allows for reasonable alternative avenues of communication. It is clear that the ordinance meets such a standard. [As] in *American Mini Theatres*, [Renton's] "interest in attempting to preserve the quality of urban life is one that must be accorded high respect." [We find] no constitutional defect in the method chosen by Renton to further its substantial interests. Cities may regulate adult theaters by dispersing them, as in Detroit, or by effectively concentrating them, as in Renton. [Moreover], the Renton ordinance is "narrowly tailored" to affect only that category of theaters shown to produce the unwanted secondary effects. . . .

[Finally], turning to the question whether the Renton ordinance allows for reasonable alternative avenues of communication, we note that the ordinance leaves some 520 acres, or more than five percent of the entire land area of Renton, open to use as adult theater sites. [Respondents] argue, however, that some of the land in question is already occupied by existing businesses, that "practically none" of the undeveloped land is currently for sale or lease, and that in general there are no "commercially viable" adult theater sites within the 520 acres left open by the Renton ordinance. [That] respondents must fend for themselves in the real estate market, on an equal footing with other prospective purchasers and lessees, does not give rise to a First Amendment violation. And although we have cautioned against the enactment of zoning regulations that have "the effect of suppressing, or greatly restricting access to, lawful speech," we have never suggested that the First Amendment compels the Government to ensure that adult theaters, or any other kinds of speech-related businesses for that matter, will be able to obtain sites at bargain prices. [The] First Amendment requires only that Renton refrain from effectively denying respondents a reasonable opportunity to open and operate an adult theater within the city, and the ordinance before us easily meets this requirement.

JUSTICE BRENNAN, joined by JUSTICE MARSHALL, dissenting.

Renton's zoning ordinance selectively imposes limitations on the location of a movie theater based exclusively on the content of the films shown there. The constitutionality of the ordinance is therefore not correctly analyzed under standards applied to content-neutral time, place, and manner restrictions. But even assuming that the ordinance [is] content-neutral, it is plainly unconstitutional under the standards [that apply to content-neutral speech restrictions.]

[The] ordinance discriminates on its face against certain forms of speech based on content. [This] selective treatment strongly suggests that Renton was interested not in controlling the "secondary effects" associated with adult businesses, but in discriminating against adult theaters based on the content of the films they exhibit. . . .

Even assuming that the ordinance should be treated like a content-neutral time, place, and manner restriction, I would still find it unconstitutional. "[Restrictions] of this kind are valid provided [that] they are narrowly tailored to serve a significant governmental interest, and that they leave open ample alternative channels for communication of the information." [First,] the city made no showing as to how [the ordinance would] further Renton's substantial interest in "[preserving] the quality of urban life." [Second], the ordinance is invalid because it does not provide for reasonable alternative avenues of communication. [The fact that much of the] 520 acres in Renton available for adult theater sites [was] already occupied [or] largely unsuited for use by movie theaters [serves] to distinguish this case from *American Mini Theatres*, where there was no indication that the Detroit zoning ordinance seriously limited the locations available for adult businesses. . . .

NOTES AND PROBLEMS

1. The Scope of the Secondary-Effects Doctrine. Is the secondary-effects doctrine confined to sexually explicit speech? If so, is that because such speech is "low value"? If not, what limits, if any, are there to the secondary-effects doctrine? In Boos v. Barry, 485 U.S. 312 (1988), the Court voided a D.C. law barring display within 500 feet of any foreign embassy of any sign that might bring the foreign government into "public odium" or "public disrepute." D.C. claimed that the law was content-neutral because it was intended to address a secondary effect of such speech—the increased likelihood of crime or public disorder. The Court rejected the argument, with a plurality explaining why: "Listeners' reactions to speech are [not] 'secondary effects' [of speech]." Speech regulations "that focus on the direct impact of speech on its audience" are content-based. Since *Boos*, this distinction has been endorsed by a majority of the Court.

2. Nude Dancing. In City of Erie v. Pap's A.M., 529 U.S. 277 (2000), the Court upheld an Erie, Pennsylvania, ban on public nudity as applied to Kandyland, a nude dancing establishment. A plurality of four (O'Connor, Rehnquist, Kennedy, and Breyer) first concluded that nude dancing was expressive conduct, "although . . . it falls only within the outer ambit" of expression. The plurality then determined that the ban was unrelated to the suppression of free expression because "it bans all public nudity, . . . is aimed at combating crime and other negative secondary effects caused by the presence of adult entertainment establishments like Kandyland and not at suppressing the erotic message conveyed by this type of nude dancing." Erie's law did not "regulate the primary effects of the expression, i.e., the effect on the audience of watching nude erotic dancing, but rather the secondary effects, such as the impacts on public health, safety, and welfare . . . 'caused by the presence of even one such' establishment," and that interest was not related to suppression of expression. Accordingly, the plurality applied *O'Brien*. The interest in combating crime and other secondary effects was deemed important, and the restriction was "no greater than is essential to the furtherance of the government interest. Because dancers "are free to perform wearing pasties and G-strings [a]ny effect on the overall expression is de minimis" and "leaves ample capacity to convey the dancer's erotic message." Moreover, because "this is a content-neutral restriction, least restrictive means analysis is not required."

Justices Scalia and Thomas concurred in the judgment because the Erie ordinance was "a general law regulating conduct and not specifically directed at expression," and thus was "not subject to First Amendment scrutiny at all." The city's interest in addressing the secondary effects of nude dancing was irrelevant, they said. "The traditional power of government to foster good morals, . . . and the acceptability of the traditional judgment . . . that nude public dancing *itself* is immoral, have not been repealed by the First Amendment."

Justices Stevens and Ginsburg dissented, arguing that the law amounted to a total ban on a form of expression, and thus offended the no-greater-restriction-than-essential prong of *O'Brien*.

Queries: Did the Erie ordinance totally foreclose a medium of expression, as the dissenters charged? What if a government's non-speech-related interest can be achieved only by an absolute ban of a particular mode of expression? Is *Erie* that case?

In Barnes v. Glen Theatre, Inc., 501 U.S. 560 (1991), five justices agreed that Indiana's interest in banning public nudity was to preserve a moral sense that human genitalia should remain covered in public. Is that good law after Lawrence v. Texas?

3. *O'Brien* or *Arcara*? Is Justice Scalia correct in *Erie* that the public nudity ban is so incidental to expression that *O'Brien* is irrelevant (as in *Arcara*, Section C.2, supra), or does that interest merely satisfy *O'Brien*'s criterion that it be "unrelated to the suppression of free expression"? In *Arcara*, the Court said that heightened scrutiny applies only to regulations of "conduct with a significant expressive element [or] where a statute based on a nonexpressive activity has the inevitable effect of singling out those engaged in expressive activity." Is Scalia's approach—making *O'Brien* irrelevant to "general law[s] regulating conduct and not specifically directed at expression"—an improvement on *Arcara* because of its greater clarity, or is it an abandonment of the effort to protect expressive conduct?

4. The Evidentiary Standard. In City of Los Angeles v. Alameda Books, 535 U.S. 425 (2002), a four-justice plurality ruled that the "substantial government interest" prong of the *Renton* test for secondary effects is satisfied if the evidence "fairly support[s]" the rationale for the law. To overcome such "fairly supportive" evidence, a plaintiff must establish either that the government's evidence does not support the law's rationale or that the government's evidence is factually in dispute, in which case the burden of proving the "substantial government interest" by additional relevant evidence shifts back to the government. Justice Kennedy, concurring in the judgment, argued that the secondary-effects doctrine is a narrow exception to the ordinary rule that content-based speech regulations are subject to strict scrutiny. Therefore, to invoke the doctrine successfully it is necessary for a government to establish that its "substantial interest" is to reduce the costs of identified secondary effects of speech *without* suppressing speech. In Kennedy's view, a law that seeks to reduce the secondary effects of, say, pornography by reducing the amount of pornography available would not adequately state a substantial government interest.

Can a government ever have a substantial interest in reducing speech? What if the government's interest is genuinely something other than suppressing speech, but the only avenue for accomplishment of the non-speech objective is reducing the volume of speech? How would Renton's ordinance fare under Justice Kennedy's approach in *Alameda Books*?

5. The Effect of *Reed*. In *Reed v. Town of Gilbert*, 2015 U.S. LEXIS 4061, the Court held that strict scrutiny applied to any regulation that, on its face, was content-discriminatory. The Town of Gilbert, Arizona, regulated sign displays and distinguished between ideological, political, and directional signs. The first category was treated favorably, the second category somewhat less so, and the third category was subject to much greater limits. Although Gilbert's motivation was to preserve community aesthetics and increase traffic safety, the Court applied strict scrutiny to invalidate the regulation as applied to a church which used directional signs to guide its parishioners to the worship site of the week,

Does *Reed* cast doubt on the continued viability of the secondary effects doctrine? The rationale for intermediate scrutiny under the secondary effects doctrine is that the government is not trying squelch viewpoints or strangle the free marketplace of ideas. That was also true in *Reed*. Or does the secondary effect doctrine remain untarnished because it applies to particularly "low value" smutty speech? If so, why is protected smut not entitled to the same degree of constitutional protection as a sign guiding guests to a party?

6. Problems. Which, if any, of the following laws would be properly analyzed under the secondary-effects doctrine? If subject to the secondary-effects doctrine, is the law valid?

a. A ban on advertising circulars inserted under the windshield wipers of parked cars to curb littering.
b. A ban on depictions of graphic violence in computer video games to reduce violence in children and young adults.
c. A ban on profanity uttered in public places to preserve municipal tranquility.
d. A ban on televised sporting events during evenings and weekends to reduce illegal gambling.

D. REGULATION OF SPEECH WHEN THE GOVERNMENT IS BOTH SOVEREIGN AND PROPRIETOR

We examine here the question of whether speech regulations should receive lesser scrutiny when governments regulate in a capacity that mimics private entities: as property owner, educator, employer, or sponsor of speech.

1. Public Forum

Governments, as the agents of the people, control public property that is theoretically "owned" by the people. The problem is that some of that public property is devoted to "proprietary" uses incompatible with public use for speech (e.g., a missile launch site), and other property is open for such public use (e.g., streets, highways, parks, plazas, and public squares). Some property fluctuates in its use—it is both proprietary and public (e.g., a public library, or a school building opened after hours for community meetings). The difficulty lies in formulating a rule for deciding when the public may speak on "its" property and when it may not. The Court's method for deciding is to characterize the nature of the property.

At one time, the Court agreed with the view expressed by Justice Holmes when he was a member of the Massachusetts Supreme Judicial Court: "For the legislature [to] forbid public speaking in a highway or public park is no more an infringement of the rights of a member of the public than for the owner of a private house to forbid it in his house." Massachusetts v. Davis, 162 Mass. 510 (1895), *aff'd*, 167 U.S. 43 (1897). That view was repudiated by dicta by Justice Roberts in Hague v. CIO, 307 U.S. 496 (1939), a case that spawned the public forum doctrine:

> Wherever the title to streets and parks may rest they have immemorially been held in trust for the use of the public and, time out of mind, have been used for purposes of assembly, communicating thoughts between citizens, and discussing public questions. Such use of the streets and public places has, from ancient times, been a part of the privileges, immunities, rights and liberties of citizens.

The result, said Professor Harry Kalven, who is generally credited with inventing the term "public forum," is that "a . . . First-Amendment easement" for speech was created by prescription. See Kalven, The Concept of the Public Forum: Cox v. Louisiana, 1965 Sup. Ct. Rev. 1, 13.

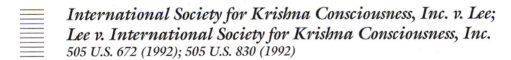

International Society for Krishna Consciousness, Inc. v. Lee; Lee v. International Society for Krishna Consciousness, Inc.
505 U.S. 672 (1992); 505 U.S. 830 (1992)

[The Port Authority of New York and New Jersey, a public entity, banned solicitation of money and the distribution of leaflets in La Guardia, Kennedy, and Newark Airports. ISKCON asserted that the bans violated the free speech guarantee. The first case involved the solicitation ban; the second case addressed the handbill ban. The opinions in the two cases have been consolidated here. The Court's opinion on the solicitation ban is presented first, followed by the Court's per curiam judgment on the leafleting ban, and the various remaining opinions.]

CHIEF JUSTICE REHNQUIST delivered the opinion of the Court.

[We] consider whether an airport terminal operated by a public authority is a public forum and whether a regulation prohibiting solicitation in the interior of an airport terminal violates the First Amendment. [ISKCON] is a not-for-profit religious corporation whose members perform a ritual known as *sankirtan*, [which] consists of "'going into public places, disseminating religious literature and soliciting funds to support the religion.'" [Lee] was the police superintendent of the Port Authority of New York and New Jersey . . . [, which] owns and operates . . . John F. Kennedy International Airport

(Kennedy), La Guardia Airport (La Guardia), and Newark International Airport (Newark). The three airports . . . serve [over 100] million passengers annually. The airports are funded by user fees and operated to make a regulated profit. . . .

The terminals are generally accessible to the general public and contain various commercial establishments such as restaurants, snack stands, bars, newsstands, and stores of various types. Virtually all who visit the terminals do so for purposes related to air travel. These visitors principally include passengers, those meeting or seeing off passengers, flight crews, and terminal employees.

The Port Authority has adopted a regulation forbidding within the terminals the repetitive solicitation of money or distribution of literature. The regulation states:

> The following conduct is prohibited within the interior areas of buildings or structures at an air terminal if conducted by a person to or with passers-by in a continuous or repetitive manner:
>   (a) The sale or distribution of any merchandise, including but not limited to jewelry, food stuffs, candles, flowers, badges and clothing.
>   (b) The sale or distribution of flyers, brochures, pamphlets, books or any other printed or written material.
>   (c) The solicitation and receipt of funds.

The regulation . . . effectively prohibits ISKCON from performing *sankirtan* in the terminals. . . .

[Charitable] solicitation . . . is a form of speech protected under the First Amendment. But it is also well settled that the government need not permit all forms of speech on property that it owns and controls. Where the government is acting as a proprietor, managing its internal operations, rather than acting as lawmaker with the power to regulate or license, its action will not be subjected to the heightened review to which its actions as a lawmaker may be subject. Thus, we have upheld a ban on political advertisements in city-operated transit vehicles, Lehman v. Shaker Heights, 418 U.S. 298 (1974), even though the city permitted other types of advertising on those vehicles. Similarly, we have permitted a school district to limit access to an internal mail system used to communicate with teachers employed by the district. Perry Education Ass'n v. Perry Local Educators' Ass'n, 460 U.S. 37 (1983).

These cases reflect . . . a "forum based" approach for assessing restrictions that the government seeks to place on the use of its property. Under this approach, regulation of speech on government property that has traditionally been available for public expression is subject to the highest scrutiny. Such regulations survive only if they are narrowly drawn to achieve a compelling state interest. The second category of public property is the designated public forum, whether of a limited or unlimited character—property that the State has opened for expressive activity by part or all of the public. Regulation of such property is subject to the same limitations as that governing a traditional public forum. Finally, there is all remaining public property. Limitations on expressive activity conducted on this last category of property . . . need only be reasonable, as long as the regulation is not an effort to suppress the speaker's activity due to disagreement with the speaker's view. . . .

[T]he government has a high burden in justifying speech restrictions relating to traditional public fora [because] "streets and parks . . . have immemorially been held in trust for the use of the public and, time out of mind, have been used for purposes of assembly, communicating thoughts between citizens, and discussing public questions." [A] traditional public forum is property that has as "a principal purpose . . . the free exchange of ideas." Moreover, consistent with the notion that the government—like other property owners—"has power to preserve the property under its control for the use to which it is lawfully dedicated," the government does not create a public forum by inaction. Nor is a public forum created "whenever members of the public are permitted freely to visit a place owned or operated by the Government." The decision to create a public forum must instead be made "by intentionally opening a nontraditional forum for public discourse." . . .

. . . These precedents foreclose the conclusion that airport terminals are public fora. Reflecting the general growth of the air travel industry, airport terminals have only recently achieved their contemporary size and character. But given the lateness with which the modern air terminal has made its appearance, it hardly qualifies for the description of having "immemorially . . . time out of mind" been held in the public trust and used for purposes of expressive activity. Moreover, even within the rather short history of air transport, it is only "in recent years [that] it has become a common practice for various religious and nonprofit organizations to use commercial airports as a forum for the distribution of literature, the solicitation of funds, the proselytizing of new members, and other, similar activities." Thus, the tradition of airport activity does not demonstrate that airports have historically been made available for speech activity. Nor can we say that these particular terminals, or airport terminals generally, have been intentionally opened by their operators to such activity; the frequent and continuing litigation evidencing the operators' objections belies any such claim. In short, there can be no argument that society's time-tested judgment, expressed through acquiescence in a continuing practice, has resolved the issue in petitioners' favor.

Petitioners attempt to circumvent the history and practice governing airport activity by pointing our attention to the variety of speech activity that they claim historically occurred at various "transportation nodes" such as rail stations, bus stations, wharves, and Ellis Island. Even if we were inclined to accept petitioners' historical account describing speech activity at these locations, an account respondent contests, we think that such evidence is of little import for two reasons.

First, much of the evidence is irrelevant to *public* fora analysis, because sites such as bus and rail terminals traditionally have had *private* ownership. The development of privately owned parks that ban speech activity would not change the public fora status of publicly held parks. But the reverse is also true. The practices of privately held transportation centers do not bear on the government's regulatory authority over a publicly owned airport.

Second, the relevant unit for our inquiry is an airport, not "transportation nodes" generally. When new methods of transportation develop, new methods for accommodating that transportation are also likely to be needed. And with each new step, it therefore will be a new inquiry whether the transportation necessities are compatible with various kinds of expressive activity. To make a category of "transportation nodes," therefore, would unjustifiably elide what may prove to be critical differences of which we should rightfully take account. . . . "[S]ecurity [screening]," for example, is an airport commonplace that lacks a counterpart in bus terminals and train stations. And public access to air terminals is also not infrequently restricted. . . . To blithely equate airports with other transportation centers, therefore, would be a mistake.

[A]irports are commercial establishments funded by user fees and designed to make a regulated profit, and [thus] must provide services attractive to the marketplace. In light of this, it cannot fairly be said that an airport terminal has as a principal purpose promoting "the free exchange of ideas." To the contrary, the record demonstrates that Port Authority management considers the purpose of the terminals to be the facilitation of passenger air travel, not the promotion of expression. Even if we look beyond the intent of the Port Authority to the manner in which the terminals have been operated, the terminals have never been dedicated (except under the threat of court order) to expression in the form [of] the solicitation of contributions and the distribution of literature. . . . Thus, we think that neither by tradition nor purpose can the terminals be described as satisfying the standards we have previously set out for identifying a public forum.

The restrictions here challenged, therefore, need only satisfy a requirement of reasonableness[:] The restriction " 'need only be *reasonable*; it need not be the most reasonable or the only reasonable limitation.' " We have no doubt that under this standard the prohibition on solicitation passes muster.

We have on many prior occasions noted the disruptive effect that solicitation may have on business. "Solicitation requires action by those who would respond: The individual solicited must decide whether or not to contribute (which itself might involve reading the solicitor's literature or hearing his pitch), and then, having decided to do so, reach for a wallet, search it for money, write a check, or produce a credit card." Passengers who wish to avoid the solicitor may have to alter their paths, slowing both themselves and those around them. The result is that the normal flow of traffic is impeded. This is especially so in an airport, where "air travelers, who are often weighted down by cumbersome baggage . . . may be hurrying to catch a plane or to arrange ground transportation." Delays may be particularly costly in this setting, as a flight missed by only a few minutes can result in hours worth of subsequent inconvenience.

In addition, face-to-face solicitation presents risks of duress that are an appropriate target of regulation. The skillful, and unprincipled, solicitor can target the most vulnerable, including those accompanying children or those suffering physical impairment and who cannot easily avoid the solicitation. The unsavory solicitor can also commit fraud through concealment of his affiliation or through deliberate efforts to shortchange those who agree to purchase. Compounding this problem is the fact that, in an airport, the targets of such activity frequently are on tight schedules. This in turn makes such visitors unlikely to stop and formally complain to airport authorities. As a result, the airport faces considerable difficulty in achieving its legitimate interest in monitoring solicitation activity to assure that travelers are not interfered with unduly.

The Port Authority has concluded that its interest in monitoring the activities can best be accomplished by limiting solicitation and distribution to the sidewalk areas outside the terminals. This sidewalk area is frequented by an overwhelming percentage of airport users. Thus the resulting access of those who would solicit the general public is quite complete. [W]e think it would be odd to conclude that the Port Authority's terminal regulation is unreasonable despite the Port Authority having otherwise assured access to an area universally traveled.

The inconveniences to passengers and the burdens on Port Authority officials flowing from solicitation activity may seem small, but viewed against the fact that "pedestrian congestion is one of the greatest problems facing the three terminals," the Port Authority could reasonably worry that even such incremental effects would prove quite disruptive. Moreover, "the justification for the Rule should not be measured by the disorder that would result from granting an exemption solely to ISKCON." For if ISKCON is given access, so too must other groups. "Obviously, there would be a much larger threat to the State's interest in crowd control if all other religious, nonreligious, and noncommercial organizations could likewise move freely." As a result, we conclude that the solicitation ban is reasonable.

PER CURIAM.

For the reasons expressed in the opinions of Justice O'Connor, Justice Kennedy, and Justice Souter, the judgment of the Court of Appeals holding that the ban on distribution of literature in the Port Authority airport terminals is invalid under the First Amendment is affirmed.

JUSTICE O'CONNOR, concurring [in the Court's opinion on the solicitation ban and concurring in the judgment on the literature distribution ban].

[I] agree that publicly owned airports are not public fora. . . . [R]estrictions on speech in nonpublic fora are valid only if they are "reasonable" and "not an effort to suppress expression merely because public officials oppose the speaker's view." . . . "The reasonableness of the Government's restriction . . . must be assessed in light of the purpose of the forum and all the surrounding circumstances." . . . [A] restriction on speech in a nonpublic forum is "reasonable" when it is "consistent with the [government's] legitimate interest in 'preserving the property . . . for the use to which it is lawfully dedicated.'"

Ordinarily, this inquiry is relatively straightforward, because we have almost always been confronted with . . . fora [that] were discrete, single-purpose facilities. . . . But . . . the Port Authority is operating a shopping mall as well as an airport. The reasonableness inquiry, therefore, is not whether the restrictions on speech are "consistent with . . . preserving the property" for air travel, but whether they are reasonably related to maintaining the multipurpose environment that the Port Authority has deliberately created.

Applying that standard, I agree . . . that the ban on solicitation is reasonable . . . [, but] the regulation banning leafletting [is not] reasonable. . . . [L]eafletting does not entail the same kinds of problems presented by face-to-face solicitation. . . . With the possible exception of avoiding litter, it is difficult to point to any problems intrinsic to the act of leafletting that would make it naturally incompatible with a large, multipurpose forum such as [these airports]. Although we do not "require . . . proof . . . to justify the denial of access to a nonpublic forum on grounds that the proposed use may disrupt the property's intended function," we have required some explanation as to why certain speech is inconsistent with the intended use of the forum. . . . Because I cannot see how peaceful pamphleteering is incompatible with the multipurpose environment of the Port Authority airports, I cannot accept that a total ban on that activity is reasonable without an explanation as to why such a restriction "preserves the property" for the several uses to which it has been put.

JUSTICE KENNEDY, with whom JUSTICE BLACKMUN, JUSTICE STEVENS, and JUSTICE SOUTER join as to Part I, concurring in the judgments.

. . . In my view the airport corridors and shopping areas outside of the passenger security zones . . . are public forums. . . . The [ban] on the distribution or sale of literature cannot [be justified under the] stringent standards [that apply to public forums]. The . . . rule disallowing in-person solicitation of money . . . , however, is in my view a narrow and valid regulation of the time, place, and manner of protected speech in this forum, or else is a valid regulation of the non-speech element of expressive conduct.

I. . . . The Court's approach is contrary to the underlying purposes of the public forum doctrine. The liberties protected by our doctrine . . . are essential to a functioning democracy. Public places are of necessity the locus for discussion of public issues, as well as protest against arbitrary government action. At the heart of our jurisprudence lies the principle that in a free nation citizens must have the right to gather and speak with other persons in public places. The recognition that certain government-owned property is a public forum provides open notice to citizens that their freedoms may be exercised there without fear of a censorial government, adding tangible reinforcement to the idea that we are a free people. . . .

The types of property that we have recognized as the quintessential public forums are streets, parks, and sidewalks, [but] the principal purpose of streets and sidewalks, like airports, is to facilitate transportation, not public discourse. . . . Similarly, the purpose for the creation of public parks may be as much for beauty and open space as for discourse. Thus under the Court's analysis, even the quintessential public forums would appear to lack the necessary elements of what the Court defines as a public forum. . . .

[T]he purpose of the public forum doctrine is to . . . protect speech from governmental interference, [but this cannot occur] unless we recognize that open, public spaces and thoroughfares that are suitable for discourse may be public forums, whatever their historical pedigree and without concern for a precise classification of the property. . . . Without this recognition our forum doctrine retains no relevance in times of fast-changing technology and increasing insularity. In a country where most citizens travel by automobile, and parks all too often become locales for crime rather than social intercourse, our failure to recognize the possibility that new types of government property may be appropriate forums for speech will lead to a serious curtailment of our expressive activity. One of the places left in our mobile society that is suitable for discourse is a metropolitan airport. [An] airport is one of the few government-owned spaces where many persons have extensive contact with other members of the public. . . . [O]ur public forum doctrine must recognize this reality, and allow the creation of public forums that do not fit within the narrow tradition of streets, sidewalks, and parks.

If the objective, physical characteristics of the property at issue and the actual public access and uses that have been permitted by the government indicate that expressive activity would be appropriate and compatible with those uses, the property is a public forum. The most important considerations in this analysis are whether the property shares physical similarities with more traditional public forums, whether the government has permitted or acquiesced in broad public access to the property, and whether expressive activity would tend to interfere in a significant way with the uses to which the government has as a factual matter dedicated the property. In conducting the last inquiry, courts must consider the consistency of those uses with expressive activities in general, rather than the specific sort of speech at issue in the case before it; otherwise the analysis would be one not of classification but rather of case-by-case balancing, and would provide little guidance to the State regarding its discretion to regulate speech. Courts must also consider the availability of reasonable time, place, and manner restrictions in undertaking this compatibility analysis. The possibility of some theoretical inconsistency between expressive activities and the property's uses should not bar a finding of a public forum, if those inconsistencies can be avoided through simple and permitted regulations.

Under this analysis, . . . the public spaces of the . . . airports are public forums. First, . . . the public spaces in the airports are broad, public thoroughfares full of people and lined with stores and other commercial activities. . . . Second, the airport areas involved here are open to the public without restriction. . . . Third, and perhaps most important, . . . when adequate time, place, and manner regulations are in place, expressive activity is quite compatible with the uses of major airports. . . .

II. [JUSTICE KENNEDY, concurring in the judgment upholding the validity of the solicitation ban.]

[T]he Port Authority's [solicitation ban] should be upheld under the standards applicable to speech regulations in public forums. . . . "[I]n a public forum the government may impose reasonable restrictions on the time, place, or manner of protected speech, provided the restrictions 'are justified without reference to the content of the regulated speech, that they are narrowly tailored to serve a significant governmental interest, and that they leave open ample alternative channels for communication of the information.'" [*Ward.*] And . . . we have recognized that the standards for assessing time, place, and manner restrictions are little, if any, different from the standards applicable to regulations of conduct with an expressive component. [T]he government regulation at issue [here] can be described with equal accuracy as a regulation of the manner of expression, or as a regulation of conduct with an expressive component. . . .

If the [solicitation ban] prohibited all speech that requested the contribution of funds, I would conclude that it was a direct, content-based restriction of speech in clear violation of the First Amendment, [but the] regulation does not prohibit all solicitation[;] it prohibits [only] the physical exchange of money, which is an element of conduct interwoven with otherwise expressive solicitation. . . . In-person solicitation of funds, when combined with immediate receipt of that money, creates a risk of fraud and duress that is well recognized, and that is different in kind from other forms of expression or conduct. Travelers who are unfamiliar with the airport, perhaps even unfamiliar with this country, its customs, and its language, are an easy prey for the money solicitor. . . . The [ban] recognizes that the risk of fraud and duress is intensified by particular conduct, the immediate exchange of money; and it addresses only that conduct. . . .

The regulation does not burden any broader category of speech or expressive conduct than is the source of the evil sought to be avoided. . . . [T]he Port Authority has left open ample alternative channels for the communication of the message which is an aspect of solicitation. [Its] rule . . . restricts only the manner of the solicitation, or the conduct associated with solicitation, to prohibit immediate receipt of the solicited money. Requests for money continue to be permitted, and in the course of requesting money solicitors may explain their cause, or the purposes of their organization, without violating the regulation.

JUSTICE SOUTER, with whom JUSTICE BLACKMUN and JUSTICE STEVENS join, concurring in the judgment in [the literature distribution ban] and dissenting in [the solicitation ban].

. . . "[T]he solicitation of money by charities [is as] fully protected as the dissemination of ideas." . . . Even if I assume, *arguendo*, that the ban on the . . . activity at issue here is both content neutral and merely a restriction on the manner of communication, the regulation must be struck down for its failure to satisfy the requirements of narrow tailoring to further a significant state interest. . . . The claim to be preventing coercion is weak. . . . While a solicitor can be insistent, a pedestrian on the street or airport concourse can simply walk away or walk on. . . . As for fraud, our cases do not provide government with plenary authority to ban solicitation just because it could be fraudulent. . . . The evidence of fraudulent conduct here is virtually nonexistent. [By] the Port Authority's own calculation, there has not been a single claim of fraud or misrepresentation since 1981. . . .

Even assuming a governmental interest adequate to justify some regulation, the present ban would fall when subjected to the requirement of narrow tailoring [because fraud] "can be prohibited and the penal laws used to punish such conduct directly." . . . Finally, [the] solicitation ban [does not] leave[] open the "ample" channels of communication required of a valid content-neutral time, place, and manner restriction. A distribution of pre-addressed envelopes is unlikely to be much of an alternative. The practical reality of the regulation . . . is that it shuts off a uniquely powerful avenue of communication for organizations like the International Society for Krishna Consciousness, and may, in effect, completely prohibit unpopular and poorly funded groups from receiving funds in response to protected solicitation.

CHIEF JUSTICE REHNQUIST, with whom JUSTICE WHITE, JUSTICE SCALIA, and JUSTICE THOMAS join, dissenting [as to the literature distribution ban].

Leafletting presents risks of congestion similar to those posed by solicitation, [which] must be evaluated . . . with an eye to the cumulative impact that will result if all groups are permitted terminal access. . . . [T]he distribution ban, no less than the solicitation ban, is reasonable. . . . The weary, harried, or hurried traveler may have no less desire and need to avoid the delays generated by having literature foisted upon him than he does to avoid delays from a financial solicitation. And while a busy passenger perhaps may succeed in fending off a leafletter with minimal disruption to himself by agreeing simply to take the proffered material, this does not completely ameliorate the dangers of congestion flowing from such leafletting. Others may choose not simply to accept the material but also to stop and engage the leafletter in debate, obstructing those who follow. Moreover, those who accept material may often simply drop it on the floor once out of the leafletter's range, creating an eyesore, a safety hazard, and additional cleanup work for airport staff.

NOTES

1. Classification of Public Property: Practice. The Court divides public property into three basic categories: (1) the unlimited or traditional public forum, open to all subjects and speakers to the fullest degree protected by the First Amendment; (2) the designated public forum, public property that is not traditionally open to speech but has been so opened by deliberate act of the government; and (3) the "nonpublic forum," which is not a public forum at all and may be closed to all or some speech so long as the closure is reasonable. The designated public forum can be unlimited or limited to some speakers or topics, provided that the limiting criteria are not viewpoint-based or otherwise offensive to some other constitutional guarantee (e.g., a public forum limited only to those of a given race). The "designated unlimited public forum" is a very small subset. There are few public places that are open to all speech but are not "traditional" public fora. However created—by tradition or designation—speech in the unlimited public forum receives the full protection of the First Amendment. The limited public forum is always created by government act and is thus always a designated public forum. The principal difficulty with the limited designated public forum is to determine whether the limiting criteria are viewpoint-based rather than content-based.

Public property that is not a public forum may be closed selectively or absolutely to speech so long as the closure is reasonable in light of the non-speech purposes to which the property is devoted. The Oval Office is closed to all speech save that which the President invites to occur within. The President's selection of permitted speech may well be viewpoint-based, but that does not matter so long as the exclusion is reasonable in light of the governance purposes to which the Oval Office is devoted.

a. Public property but not public fora.   *Adderley v. Florida, 385 U.S. 39 (1966).*   The Court sustained trespass convictions of demonstrators blocking a jail entrance normally used only by sheriff's deputies: "The State, no less than a private owner of property, has power to preserve the property under its control for the use to which it is lawfully dedicated." The "part of the jail grounds" on which the demonstration occurred was "reserved for jail uses" and was not open to large public gatherings. It was neither a traditional nor a designated public forum.

Lehman v. City of Shaker Heights, 418 U.S. 298 (1974).   A public transit system that offered advertising space on its vehicles refused to accept paid political advertising by a candidate for public office. A plurality ruled that the advertising space was not a public forum. The offer of advertising space was a purely commercial venture and, like a private advertiser, the transit authority was free to refuse advertising so long as it acted in a viewpoint-neutral fashion. Closing of all political speech in a nonpublic forum was permissible; denying advertising space to only some political speakers would not be valid.

Greer v. Spock, 424 U.S. 828 (1976).   The Court upheld the Fort Dix military reservation's policy permitting civilian access to the unrestricted portions of the base, but prohibiting "political speeches." The Court sustained the prohibition: "[T]he business [of] Fort Dix [is] to train soldiers, not to provide a public forum."

Cornelius v. NAACP Legal Defense and Educational Fund, 473 U.S. 788 (1985).   An executive order permitted tax-exempt charitable organizations to participate in a coordinated charity drive directed at federal employees during working hours, but barred legal and political advocacy groups. The Court upheld the order. The charity drive was a nonpublic forum because there was no traditional access right and the government had opened its workplace to limited charitable solicitation not "to provide an open forum" but "to minimize the disruption to the workplace [by] *lessening* the amount of expressive activity." The government's intention was critical; it did not intend to dedicate its property to speech purposes.

United States v. Kokinda, 493 U.S. 807 (1990). The Court upheld a postal regulation barring solicitations on postal property as applied to a political advocacy group soliciting contributions on a post office sidewalk that ran from a postal parking lot to the post office and was used solely by postal customers. It was not a public thoroughfare and thus was not a traditional public forum even though it was open to the public. As in *Cornelius*, a plurality of the Court relied on the lack of proof of any government intent to open its sidewalk to speech purposes; indeed, there was strong proof to the contrary. Because the regulation was a reasonable content-neutral regulation of speech, it was valid.

United States v. American Library Association, 539 U.S. 194 (2003). The Children's Internet Protection Act (CIPA) denies federal money for Internet access to public libraries unless they install software to block obscene or pornographic images and to prevent minors from accessing material harmful to them. A plurality of the Court rejected the argument that Internet access in public libraries is a public forum. Such access, said the plurality

> is neither a "traditional" nor a "designated" public forum. First, this resource — which did not exist until quite recently — has not "immemorially been held in trust for the use of the public and, time out of mind, . . . used for purposes of assembly, communication of thoughts between citizens, and discussing public questions." . . . Nor does Internet access in a public library satisfy our definition of a "designated public forum." To create such a forum, the government must make an affirmative choice to open up its property for use as a public forum. . . . A public library does not acquire Internet terminals in order to create a public forum for Web publishers to express themselves, any more than it collects books in order to provide a public forum for the authors of books to speak.

Pleasant Grove v. Summum, 555 U.S. 460 (2009). A Utah city refused a donation of a stone monument containing the "Seven Aphorisms" of the Summum faith, to be displayed in a public park. The Summum sect contended that Pleasant Grove's refusal was an unjustified content-based restriction on speech in a traditional public forum. The Supreme Court disagreed. Public forum

> doctrine has been applied in situations in which government-owned property or a government program was capable of accommodating a large number of public speakers without defeating the essential function of the land or the program. [While] a park can accommodate many speakers and, over time, many parades and demonstrations, [they] can accommodate only a limited number of permanent monuments. . . . Speakers, no matter how long-winded, eventually come to the end of their remarks; persons distributing leaflets and carrying signs at some point tire and go home; monuments, however, endure. They monopolize the use of the land on which they stand and interfere permanently with other uses of public space. . . . As a general matter, forum analysis simply does not apply to the installation of permanent monuments on public property.

Walker v. Texas Division, Sons of Confederate Veterans, 2015 U.S. LEXIS 4063. Texas issues specialty license plates that advertise a wide variety of sentiments, ranging from the trivial ("I'd Rather Be Golfing"), to the commercial ("Mighty Fine Burgers"), to the associational ("4-H"), to the political ("Choose Life"). Over 350 varieties have been issued upon request of private groups and approval by the state. Texas refused to issue a plate honoring the Sons of Confederate Veterans because it bore the Confederate battle flag, a symbol offensive to many people. The Supreme Court, 5-4, first concluded that the slogans on such plates were government speech and thus immune from free speech analysis. The Court regarded this case as the mirror image of *Summum* and relied heavily on *Summum* to support its conclusion. Second, the specialty plates were neither a traditional, designated, or limited public forum. Rather, because license plates are government property and motorists are required to display them for identification purposes their entire content was deemed to be government speech. Because Texas controlled the entire process of issuing license plates and retained final authority over approval of specialty plates it had not created any kind of public forum.

The dissenters charged that this was nonsense, as no reasonable observer would conclude that Texas, as a state, had officially endorsed golfing, or the University of Oklahoma, or any particular race car driver. The slogans expressed were those of the motorist, and Texas' willingness to open its property to private speech made it a public forum, to which principles of viewpoint discrimination were applicable. The dissent wondered whether the majority's rationale would permit such blatant viewpoint discrimination as a public university denying access to a student list server for messages containing views disliked by the university.

b. Limited public fora. *Heffron v. International Society for Krishna Consciousness, 452 U.S. 640 (1981).* The Court upheld a Minnesota State Fair rule prohibiting the sale or distribution of merchandise or literature except from booths available for rent on a nondiscriminatory basis. The rule was challenged by Krishna adherents, who wished to solicit donations and sell literature in public spaces by walking among the crowds of fairgoers on the streets and sidewalks of the 125-acre fairgrounds. The Court ruled that the State Fair "is a limited public forum in that it exists to provide a means for a great number of exhibitors temporarily to present their products or views [to] a large number of people in an efficient fashion." It was not voluntarily opened to general speech. The Court found the rule content-neutral and concluded that it served the State Fair's significant interest of protecting the safety and convenience of the over 100,000 fairgoers. The rule was well suited to the end, as an exemption for the Krishnas would mean that all other groups would be entitled to freedom from the booth rule, thus posing a "much larger threat to the State's interest in crowd control," and because it was "quite improbable [that] alternative means" of accomplishing the state's goal would "deal adequately with the [problem]."

In a series of cases involving public property made available to some users (but not religious users) the Court emphasized that the limitations of the limited public forum may not be drawn on viewpoint-based lines.

Widmar v. Vincent, 454 U.S. 263 (1981). A public university made its facilities available to student groups except those who wished to engage in "religious worship or religious teaching." Although the university had thereby created a limited public forum, its device for doing so was viewpoint-based, thus subject to strict scrutiny, and ultimately voided. See also Rosenberger v. Rector and Visitors of the University of Virginia, 515 U.S. 819 (1995); Lamb's Chapel v. Center Moriches Union Free School District, 508 U.S. 384 (1993).

Good News Club v. Milford Central School, 533 U.S. 98 (2001). The Court extended its viewpoint discrimination approach to the case of a public school that created a limited public forum by opening its facilities after school hours to virtually all community uses, but excluding religious use. The school denied access to the Good News Club, a private Christian organization for children ages 6 to 12 that engaged in Bible lessons, prayer, memorization of Bible passages, and singing of religious songs, on the ground that the Good News Club was engaged in religious worship. The Court held that the denial of access to the Good News Club was viewpoint discrimination that was not justified on the theory that access must be denied to avoid creation of a forbidden establishment of religion. On the establishment of religion aspects of the case, see Chapter 10, Section C.2.a. Justice Stevens dissented on the ground that it should be permissible for a public entity to create a limited public forum open to speech "from a religious point of view" but closed to religious worship or speech "that is aimed principally at proselytizing or inculcating belief in a particular religious faith."

Christian Legal Society v. Martinez, 561 U.S. 661 (2010). As a condition of access to school facilities and modest funding, a public law school required student groups to accept any student as a member. The "all-comers" policy was challenged by the Christian Legal Society, a group that required its members to adhere to a statement of faith that included the pledge that they abstain from sexual intimacies outside of a traditional marriage. The Court (5-4) upheld the policy, reasoning that the law school had created a limited public forum and concluded that the "all-comers" access condition was reasonable and viewpoint-neutral. It was reasonable, said the majority, because it furthered the school's desire to (1) make available to all students the leadership, educational, and social opportunities afforded by student organizations, (2) bring together individuals with diverse backgrounds and beliefs in the hope of encouraging tolerance, cooperation, and learning among students, and (3) signal the school's support of state nondiscrimination mandates. The Court thought that the "all-comers" policy was viewpoint-neutral because it made no distinction between groups based on their message or perspective. The dissent charged that the "all-comers" policy was devised as a pretext to mask the school's selective enforcement of the policy, with the effect of targeting the Christian Legal Society's viewpoint.

2. Classification of Public Property: Theory. The idea of a traditional public forum—public property to which is attached an ancient prescriptive easement for speech—suggests that the First Amendment requires some minimal level of access to public property for speech. This is sometimes described as an "affirmative" theory of free speech: The First Amendment functions to expand opportunities for speech. Applied to public forum issues, it suggests that governments must open some public property to speech. But the concept of the limited public forum is inconsistent with this notion and suggests that, instead, the First Amendment merely requires that government be neutral, or evenhanded, in regulating speech access to public property. This is sometimes described as the "negative" theory of free speech. Applied to public forum issues, it requires that governments not bias public discourse by opening its property only to speakers of a favored viewpoint. It is apparent that both theories exist in the public forum area, and this fact helps to explain some of the tension in the doctrine. Confirmed affirmative theorists will have an expansive notion of the traditional public forum and a restrictive notion of the limits that may be imposed on the limited public forum. Devoted negative theorists are likely to have a narrower conception of the traditional public forum and will tolerate many more limitations on speakers and subjects in the limited public forum, so long as the limitations are viewpoint-neutral.

3. The Importance of Context. In Grayned v. Rockford, 408 U.S. 104 (1972), the Court sustained an ordinance that made it illegal during school sessions to "willfully make [any] noise [which] disturbs or tends to disturb the peace or good order of such school session," as applied to demonstrators outside a school. The Court declared that

> [it is the] nature of a place, "the pattern of its normal activities, [that] dictate the kinds of regulations of time, place, and manner that are reasonable." [The] crucial question is whether the manner of expression is basically incompatible with the normal activity of a particular place at a particular time. [Though] the regulation must be narrowly tailored to further the State's legitimate interest, [this] ordinance is narrowly tailored to further [the city's] compelling interest in having an undisrupted school session conducive to the students' learning.

At the time, some saw in *Grayned* a general principle that would make characterization of public property unnecessary. Stone, Fora Americana: Speech in Public Places, 1974 Sup. Ct. Rev. 233:

> No longer does the right to effective freedom of expression turn on [the forum status of public property. Instead], publicly owned places are all brought under the same roof. In each case, the "crucial question is whether the manner of expression is basically incompatible with the normal activity of a particular place at a particular time."

Now that you have reviewed the current state of public forum doctrine, was Stone correct? If not, should the Court have heeded Stone?

2. Public Education

Much of the speech that occurs in public education is highly regulated. Some is content-based. A biology teacher who teaches nothing but Mozart is likely to be disciplined for his speech. A student who answers a physics exam with a love sonnet is likely to be punished in the form of a low grade.

Other regulations are viewpoint-based. A history student who declares that the American Civil War was caused by the demise of the Japanese shogunate will likely receive a low grade for his viewpoint. But not all student and teacher speech is curriculum-related. What of the student who urges her classmates, during the break between classes, to boycott class? Or the student who wears to school a shirt bearing a large Nazi swastika? Or the student who uses the school newspaper to call for the dismissal of the principal?

≣ *Tinker v. Des Moines School District*
393 U.S. 503 (1969)

[Petitioners, three adolescent public school students, were suspended from school because they wore black armbands to school in December 1965 to protest the Vietnam War. The Des Moines schools had adopted a policy against armbands upon becoming aware of the plan to wear them. Petitioners sought and were denied an injunction restraining school officials from disciplining the students. The Court of Appeals affirmed.]

JUSTICE FORTAS delivered the opinion of the Court.

[Wearing] an armband for the purpose of expressing certain views is the type of symbolic act, [closely] akin to "pure speech." [It] can hardly be argued that either students or teachers shed their constitutional rights to freedom of speech or expression at the schoolhouse gate. [Our] problem lies in the area where students in the exercise of First Amendment rights collide with the rules of the school authorities. [This] case does not relate [to] deportment [or] aggressive, disruptive action or even group demonstrations. [The] school officials . . . sought to punish petitioners for a silent, passive expression of opinion, unaccompanied by any disorder or disturbance on the part of petitioners. There is here no evidence whatever of petitioners' interference, actual or nascent, with the schools' work or of collision with the rights of other students to be secure and to be let alone. Accordingly, this case does not concern speech or action that intrudes upon the work of the schools or the rights of other students.

[The] District Court concluded that the action of the school authorities was reasonable because it was based upon their fear of a disturbance from the wearing of the armbands. But, in our system, undifferentiated fear or apprehension of disturbance is not enough to overcome the right to freedom of expression. [In] order for the State [to] justify prohibition of a particular expression of opinion, it must [show] that its action was caused by something more than a mere desire to avoid the discomfort and unpleasantness that always accompany an unpopular viewpoint. Certainly where there is no [evidence] that engaging in the forbidden conduct would "materially and substantially interfere with the requirements of appropriate discipline in the operation of the school," the prohibition cannot be sustained. [Here], school authorities had [no] reason to anticipate that the wearing of the armbands would substantially interfere with the work of the school or impinge upon the rights of other students. [On] the contrary, the action of the school authorities appears to have been based upon an urgent wish to avoid the controversy which might result from the expression, even by the silent symbol of arm-bands, of opposition to this Nation's part in the conflagration in Vietnam.

[S]chool authorities did not purport to prohibit the wearing of all symbols of political or controversial significance. [Students] wore buttons relating to national political campaigns, and some even wore the Iron Cross. [The] order prohibiting the wearing of armbands did not extend to these. Instead, [this] particular symbol [was] singled out for prohibition. [Public] schools may not be enclaves of totalitarianism. . . . Students . . . may not be . . . confined to the expression of those sentiments that are officially approved.

[A student] may express his opinions . . . if he does so without "materially and substantially interfer[ing] with the requirements of appropriate discipline in the operation of the school" and without colliding with the rights of others. But conduct by the student, in class or out of it, which for any reason — whether it stems from time, place, or type of behavior — materially disrupts classwork or involves substantial disorder or invasion of the rights of others is, of course, not immunized by the constitutional guarantee of freedom of speech. [Reversed] and remanded.

JUSTICE STEWART, concurring.

[I] cannot share the Court's uncritical assumption that, school discipline aside, the First Amendment rights of children are co-extensive with those of adults. [A] "State may permissibly determine that, at least in some precisely delineated areas, a child [is] not possessed of that full capacity for individual choice which is the presupposition of First Amendment guarantees."

JUSTICE BLACK, dissenting.

The Court's holding [transfers] the power to control pupils [from school officials] to the Supreme Court. [The record shows] that the armbands [took] the students' minds off their classwork and diverted them to thoughts about the highly emotional subject of the Vietnam war. [School] discipline, like parental discipline, is an integral and important part of training our children to be good [citizens]. Here a very small number of students have crisply and summarily refused to obey a school order designed to give pupils who want to learn the opportunity to do so. One does not need to be a prophet [to] know that after the Court's holding today some students [will] be ready, able, and willing to defy their teachers on practically all orders. This is the more unfortunate for the schools since groups of students all over the land are already running loose, conducting break-ins, sit-ins, lie-ins, and smash-ins.

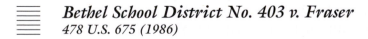

Bethel School District No. 403 v. Fraser
478 U.S. 675 (1986)

CHIEF JUSTICE BURGER delivered the opinion of the Court.

We granted certiorari to decide whether the First Amendment prevents a school district from disciplining a high school student for giving a lewd speech at a school assembly. [Fraser], a student at Bethel High School, [delivered] a speech nominating a fellow student for student elective office. Approximately 600 high school students, many of whom were 14-year-olds, attended the assembly. [During] the entire speech, Fraser referred to his candidate in terms of an elaborate, graphic, and explicit sexual metaphor. [Some] students hooted and yelled; some by gestures graphically simulated the sexual activities pointedly alluded to in respondent's speech. Other students appeared to be bewildered and embarrassed by the speech. One teacher reported that on the day following the speech, she found it necessary to forgo a portion of the scheduled class lesson in order to discuss the speech with the class.

[Bethel High School prohibits conduct, including speech], "which materially and substantially interferes with the educational process." [Fraser was] suspended for three days, and [he was] removed from the list of candidates for graduation speaker at the school's commencement exercises. [In federal court, Fraser sought and obtained] both injunctive relief and monetary [damages]. The Court of Appeals [affirmed]. We reverse.

[The] undoubted freedom to advocate unpopular and controversial views in schools . . . must be balanced against the society's countervailing interest in teaching students the boundaries of socially appropriate behavior. [The] First Amendment guarantees wide freedom in matters of adult public discourse, [but it] does not follow . . . that simply because the use of an offensive form of expression may not be prohibited to adults . . . , the same latitude must be permitted to children in a public school. "[The] First Amendment gives a high school student the classroom right to wear Tinker's armband, but not Cohen's jacket." [It] is a highly appropriate function of public school education to prohibit the use of vulgar and offensive terms in public discourse.

Unlike the sanctions imposed [in] *Tinker*, the penalties imposed in this case were unrelated to any political viewpoint. The First Amendment does not prevent [school] officials from determining that to permit a vulgar and lewd speech [would] undermine the school's basic educational mission. A high school assembly or classroom is no place for a sexually explicit monologue directed towards an unsuspecting audience of teenage students. Accordingly, it was perfectly appropriate for the school to . . . make the point to the pupils that vulgar speech and lewd conduct is wholly inconsistent with the "fundamental values" of public school education.

Justice Brennan, concurring in the judgment.

Respondent gave the following speech at a high school assembly in support of a candidate for student government office: " 'I know a man who is firm—he's firm in his pants, he's firm in his shirt, his character is firm—but most [of] all, his belief in you, the students of Bethel, is firm. Jeff Kuhlman is a man who takes his point and pounds it in. If necessary, he'll take an issue and nail it to the wall. He doesn't attack things in spurts—he drives hard, pushing and pushing until finally—he succeeds. Jeff is a man who will go to the very end—even the climax, for each and every one of you. So vote for Jeff for A.S.B. vice-president—he'll never come between you and the best our high school can be.' " [I] find it difficult to believe that [this] is the same speech the Court describes. [The] most that can be said about respondent's speech—and all that need be said—is that in light of the discretion school officials have to teach high school students how to conduct civil and effective public discourse, and to prevent disruption of school educational activities, it was not unconstitutional for school officials to conclude, under the circumstances of this case, that respondent's remarks exceeded permissible limits.

[If] respondent had given the same speech outside of the school environment, he could not have been penalized simply because government officials considered his language to be inappropriate. [*Cohen.*] Respondent's speech may well have been protected had he given it in school but under different circumstances, where the school's legitimate interests in teaching and maintaining civil public discourse were less weighty. [I concur because] school officials did not violate the First Amendment [by punishing] respondent . . . for the disruptive language he used while addressing a high school assembly.

JUSTICE MARSHALL, dissenting.

[T]he School District failed to demonstrate that respondent's remarks were indeed disruptive.

≡ *Hazelwood School District v. Kuhlmeier*
≡ *484 U.S. 260 (1988)*

JUSTICE WHITE delivered the opinion of the Court.

This case concerns the extent to which educators may exercise editorial control over the contents of a high school newspaper produced as part of the school's journalism curriculum. [Respondents] are three former Hazelwood East students who were staff members of Spectrum, the school newspaper. They contend that school officials violated their First Amendment rights by deleting two pages of articles from the May 13, 1983, issue of Spectrum. Spectrum was written and edited by the Journalism II class at Hazelwood East. The newspaper was published every three weeks or so during the 1982-1983 school year. More than 4,500 copies of the newspaper were distributed during that year to students, school personnel, and members of the community. [Over 80 percent of the costs of the newspaper were borne by the School District; the remainder was from sales of the paper.]

One of the [deleted] stories described three Hazelwood East students' experiences with pregnancy; the other discussed the impact of divorce on students at the school. [The school principal] was concerned that, although the pregnancy story used false names "to keep the identity of these girls a secret," the pregnant students still might be identifiable from the text. He also believed that the article's references to sexual activity and birth control were inappropriate for some of the younger students at the school. [The divorce story contained unflattering remarks made by a student about her father. The principal] believed that the student's parents should have been given an opportunity to respond to these remarks or to consent to their publication.

[We] deal first with the question whether Spectrum may appropriately be characterized as a forum for public expression. . . . School officials did not evince either "by policy or by practice" any intent to open the pages of Spectrum to "indiscriminate use" by its student reporters and editors, or by the student body generally. Instead, they "reserve[d] the forum for its intended purpos[e]" as a supervised learning experience for journalism students. Accordingly, school officials were entitled to regulate the contents of Spectrum in any reasonable manner. It is this standard, rather than our decision in *Tinker*, that governs this case.

The question whether the First Amendment requires a school to tolerate particular student speech—the question that we addressed in *Tinker*—is different from the question whether the First Amendment requires a school affirmatively to promote particular student speech. The former question addresses educators' ability to silence a student's personal expression that happens to occur on the school premises. The latter question concerns educators' authority over school-sponsored publications, theatrical productions, and other expressive activities that students, parents, and members of the public might reasonably perceive to bear the imprimatur of the school. These activities [are] part of the school curriculum, whether or not they occur in a traditional classroom setting, so long as they are supervised by faculty members and designed to impart particular knowledge or skills to student participants and audiences.

Educators are entitled to exercise greater control over this second form of student expression to assure that participants learn whatever lessons the activity is designed to teach, that readers or listeners are not exposed to material that may be inappropriate for their level of maturity, and that the views of the individual speaker are not erroneously attributed to the school. Hence, a school may in its capacity as publisher of a school newspaper or producer of a school play "disassociate itself" not only from speech that would "substantially interfere with [its] work [or] impinge upon the rights of other students," but also from speech that is, for example, ungrammatical, poorly written, inadequately researched, biased or prejudiced, vulgar or profane, or unsuitable for immature audiences. A school must be able to set high standards for the student speech that is disseminated under its auspices [and] may refuse to disseminate student speech that does not meet those standards. In addition, a school must be able to take into account the emotional maturity of the intended audience in determining whether to disseminate student speech on potentially sensitive [topics].

[We] hold that educators do not offend the First Amendment by exercising editorial control over the style and content of student speech in school-sponsored expressive activities so long as their actions are reasonably related to legitimate pedagogical concerns. This standard is consistent with our oft-expressed view that the education of the Nation's youth is primarily the responsibility of parents, teachers, and state and local school officials, and not of federal judges. It is only when the decision to censor a school-sponsored publication, theatrical production, or other vehicle of student expression has no valid educational purpose that the First Amendment [requires] judicial intervention to protect students' constitutional rights.

[The school principal] acted reasonably. . . . The principal could reasonably have feared that the [pregnancy] article violated whatever pledge of anonymity had been given to the pregnant students [and] that the article was not sufficiently sensitive to the privacy interests of the students' boyfriends and parents, who were discussed in the article but who were given no opportunity to consent to its publication or to offer a response. [While the] article did not contain graphic accounts of sexual activity, [the] girls did comment [on] their sexual histories and their use or nonuse of birth control. It was not unreasonable for the principal to have concluded that such frank talk was inappropriate in a school-sponsored publication distributed to 14-year-old freshmen and presumably taken home to be read by students' even younger brothers and sisters. The student who was quoted by name in [the divorce article] made comments sharply critical of her father. The principal could reasonably have concluded that an individual publicly identified as an inattentive parent—indeed, as one who chose "playing cards with the guys" over home and family—was entitled to an opportunity to defend himself as a matter of journalistic fairness. [Accordingly], no violation of First Amendment rights occurred.

JUSTICE BRENNAN, joined by JUSTICES MARSHALL and BLACKMUN, dissenting.

[The] Court today . . . erects a taxonomy of school censorship, concluding that *Tinker* applies to one category and not another. On the one hand is censorship "to silence a student's personal expression that happens to occur on the school premises." On the other hand is censorship of expression that arises in the context of "school-sponsored [expressive] activities that students, parents, and members of the public might reasonably perceive to bear the imprimatur of the school."

[The] Court offers . . . three excuses to afford educators "greater control" over school-sponsored speech than the *Tinker* test would permit: the public educator's prerogative to control curriculum; the pedagogical interest in shielding the high school audience from objectionable viewpoints and sensitive topics; and the school's need to dissociate itself from student expression. [*Tinker*] fully addresses the first concern; the second is illegitimate; and the third is readily achievable through less oppressive means. [The] censorship . . . cannot . . . have been designed to prevent "materia[l] disrup[tion of] classwork." Nor [was] the censorship . . . necessary to prevent student expression from "inva[ding] the rights of others."

NOTES AND PROBLEMS

1. The Scope of School Regulations of Speech. In Morse v. Frederick, 551 U.S. 393 (2007), the Court confronted the scope of public school speech regulations that banned speech that was not disruptive of the usual pedagogical business of the school. To observe the passing of the Olympic Torch through Juneau, Alaska, the local public school decided to permit students to move outside and watch the procession as "an approved social event." This recess was monitored by teachers and confined to the sidewalks immediately adjacent to the school. In the presence of his fellow students, Frederick unfurled a banner reading "Bong Hits 4 Jesus." Morse, the school principal, ordered Frederick to cease the display. When Frederick refused, Morse confiscated the banner and suspended Frederick for ten days because its message either advocated or celebrated illegal drug use, which was a clear violation of school regulations governing student speech.

The Court upheld the suspension and confiscation. First, the Court concluded that the banner was exhibited at a school event, and thus there was no occasion to consider the ability of schools to regulate student speech occurring outside of school. Next, the Court concluded that while "[t]he message on Frederick's banner is cryptic, . . . Morse thought the banner would be interpreted by those viewing it as promoting illegal drug use, and that interpretation is plainly a reasonable one." The Court then noted that *Fraser* established that schools may validly regulate student speech at school without proof that the speech was materially disruptive, as had been required by *Tinker*. Although *Kuhlmeier* did not apply "because no one would reasonably believe that Frederick's banner bore the school's imprimatur," *Kuhlmeier* "confirms that the rule of *Tinker* is not the only basis for restricting student speech." Because "deterring drug use by schoolchildren is an 'important—indeed, perhaps compelling' interest, . . . [t]he 'special characteristics of the school environment' and the governmental interest in stopping student drug abuse . . . allow schools to restrict student expression that they reasonably regard as promoting illegal drug use." The Court said the school could not suppress Frederick's speech simply because it was "offensive."

Justice Thomas concurred, declaring that he would overrule *Tinker* because "the history of public education suggests that the First Amendment, as originally understood, does not protect student speech in public schools." Justices Alito and Kennedy also concurred, "on the understanding that [while] a public school may restrict speech that a reasonable observer would interpret as advocating illegal drug use [it may not restrict] speech that can plausibly be interpreted as commenting on any political or social issue, including speech on issues such as 'the wisdom of the war on drugs or of legalizing marijuana for medicinal use.'"

2. Universities. Do university students enjoy greater speech rights than their younger counterparts? Student speech in connection with the curriculum is subject to reasonable control; discrimination on the basis of the content and viewpoint of student speech is the basic method of assessment of student academic performance. But what about noncurricular speech? *Healy v. James*, 408 U.S. 169 (1972), involved the validity of a public university's refusal to recognize Students for a Democratic Society as a campus organization because it was a radical group advocating "violence and disruption." The Court remanded the case, instructing the lower courts that "the mere expression of [such] repugnant [views] would not justify the denial of First Amendment rights." In Papish v. Board of Curators of the University of Missouri, 410 U.S. 667 (1973), the Court voided a public university's expulsion of a student for distributing on campus a newspaper depicting a policeman raping the Statue of Liberty and employing vulgar language. The Court reasoned that the university had expelled the student because of the content of the speech and invoked *Tinker* for the proposition that the university could not prohibit expression "in the absence of any disruption of campus order or interference with the rights of others."

3. Book Banning. In Board of Education, Island Trees Union Free School District v. Pico, 457 U.S. 853 (1982), a plurality of the Court led by Justice Brennan ruled that the validity of book banning in public school libraries turns on the motivation for the ban. If the decisive motivation was the desire "to deny [students] access to ideas with which [the school board] disagreed, [then the school board has exercised its] discretion in violation of the Constitution." But a school board acts validly if it removes books because of a good faith belief that they are vulgar or otherwise educationally unsuitable. Suppression of ideas violates free speech, but limiting the school library to educationally suitable materials does not.

In dissent, Justice Rehnquist, joined by Chief Justice Burger and Justice Powell, argued that when government

> acts as an educator, at least in the elementary and secondary school level, the government is engaged in inculcating social values and knowledge in relatively impressionable young people. . . . The failure of a [school] library to acquire a book denies access to its contents just as effectively as does the removal of the book from the library's shelf. [And] yet only the latter action would violate the First Amendment under [the Brennan plurality's analysis]. Bad motives and good motives alike deny access to the books removed; [it] is difficult to see why the reason for the denial makes any difference.

Has Justice Rehnquist's view effectively been adopted by the Court?

4. Problems. Assess the validity of the following public high school actions.

a. *Confederate Battle Flag.* Multiethnic High School bans the "wearing or display of symbols or words likely to disturb the learning environment." Joe, a white male, wears to school a shirt displaying a Confederate battle flag. Joe is suspended. See Castorina v. Madison County School Board, 246 F.3d 536 (6th Cir. 2001); West v. Derby Unified School District, 206 F.3d 1358 (10th Cir. 2000).

b. *Vulgar Jacket.* Under the same rule as in the prior problem, Multiethnic High suspends Paul Cohen, Jr., for wearing a jacket with "Fuck Barack Obama" inscribed on the back.

c. *Sexual Orientation Commentary.* (i) On the day after a "Day of Silence," sponsored by the student Gay-Straight Alliance to promote tolerance for homosexuals, Dan wears a shirt to Multiethnic High bearing the inscription "Homosexuality is Shameful. Romans 1:27." Dan is suspended. See Harper v. Poway Unified School District, 445 F.3d 1166 (9th Cir. 2006).

(ii) On the day after a "Day of Silence," sponsored by the student Gay-Straight Alliance to promote tolerance for homosexuals, Bill wears a shirt to Cosmopolitan High School bearing the inscription "Be Happy, Not Gay." Bill is suspended under Cosmopolitan High's regulation banning "derogatory comments that refer to race, religion, sex, sexual orientation, or disability." See Nuxoll v. Indian Prairie School District #204, 523 F.3d 668 (7th Cir. 2008).

d. *School Uniforms.*   Multiethnic High requires all students to wear a prescribed uniform.

e. *Athletic Gag Order.*   Cosmopolitan High bars its athletes from talking to the press.

f. *Underground Press Ban.*   Judy, a student at Cosmopolitan High, dislikes her journalism class sufficiently that she organizes, writes for, and prints, at her expense and using her own off-campus facilities, an underground newspaper, the *Cosmo Sewer*, which she distributes to Cosmopolitan High students on the public street adjacent to the school. Cosmopolitan High bans the paper and confiscates all copies that appear on school premises.

g. *Off-Campus Slurs.*   Eleanor, a student at Cosmopolitan High, posts comments on her blog, which she maintains via her home computer, that refer to certain Cosmopolitan High teachers as "bitches," "fags," and "weird cripples." Eleanor is suspended.

Special Deference to Prison and Military Administrators

When governments incarcerate convicted criminals they are, of course, acting in a purely sovereign capacity. Nevertheless, the courts exhibit considerable deference to the judgment of prison administrators. In Turner v. Safley, 482 U.S. 78 (1987), the Supreme Court articulated the general standard for review of prison regulations and policies that impinge upon constitutionally protected liberties enjoyed by free persons. Such rules must be "reasonably related to legitimate penological interests" and must not be an "exaggerated response" to those legitimate objectives. In *Turner*, the Court held that a prison rule that allowed inmates to marry only when the warden agreed that there were compelling reasons for the marriage violated substantive due process. In Overton v. Bazzetta, 539 U.S. 126 (2003), the Court upheld Michigan's practice of denying inmates visits by former inmates or unrelated children. The Court concluded that an "inmate does not retain rights inconsistent with proper incarceration. [F]reedom of association is among the rights least compatible with incarceration." See also Jones v. North Carolina Prisoners' Labor Union, Inc. 433 U.S. 119 (1977).

In Pell v. Procunier, 417 U.S. 817 (1974), the Court upheld California's refusal to permit media interviews of certain high-profile prisoners. The Court conceded that "a prison inmate retains those First Amendment rights that are not inconsistent with his status as a prisoner or with the legitimate penological objectives of the corrections system" but stated that "challenges to prison restrictions that are asserted to inhibit First Amendment interests must be analyzed in terms of the legitimate policies and goals of the corrections system, to whose custody and care the prisoner has been committed in accordance with due process of law."

To determine whether prison regulations are reasonably related to legitimate penological objectives, the Court in *Turner* identified four relevant factors bearing on the matter: (1) a valid, rational connection between the regulation and the legitimate penological objective; (2) the availability to prison inmates of "alternative means of exercising the right" at issue; (3) the impact upon guards, other inmates, and "the allocation of prison resources" that would result from "accommodation of the asserted constitutional right"; and (4) the presence of "ready alternatives" for accomplishing the legitimate penological objective supporting the regulation. Similar judicial deference is displayed to the decisions of military officials. In Goldman v. Weinberger, 475 U.S. 503 (1986), the Court upheld a military uniform regulation that, as applied to Goldman, prohibited his wearing of a yarmulke. Though the regulation impinged upon Goldman's religious practice, the Court concluded that "great deference" must be afforded "to the professional judgment of military authorities" in determining what constitutes military necessity sufficient to justify burdens on otherwise constitutionally protected conduct. In Rumsfeld v. Forum for Academic and Institutional Rights, 547 U.S. 47 (2006), in the course of upholding a bar of federal funding to universities that restrict unequally the access of military recruiters to campus, the Court noted that "'judicial deference . . . is at its apogee' when Congress legislates under its authority to raise and support armies." The theme of deference to the military percolates through all areas of constitutional law, not just free expression. In Rostker v. Goldberg, 453 U.S. 57 (1981), the Court ruled that male-only military draft registration did not constitute sex discrimination in violation of the equal protection guarantee, relying in part upon the Court's extreme deference to congressional judgments about military affairs and national defense. Such deference is based on the breadth of congressional authority over military matters and "the lack of competence on the part of courts." While there is some room for judicial review of military affairs, the rigor of that review appears to be much diminished, approaching the default level of minimal scrutiny.

3. Public Employment

Private employers are constitutionally free to impose speech restrictions on their employees as a condition of employment. A private law firm may discharge a lawyer employee who disparages the firm to a news reporter.

Should the Constitution prevent a district attorney from discharging a lawyer employee who disparages the district attorney to a news reporter? More generally, under what circumstances is the public employer the sovereign (and subject to the full measure of constitutional restraints) and under what circumstances is the public employer a mere proprietor (and less restrained by the Constitution)?

The old, and now rejected, position was that because there was no constitutionally protected right to public employment, there was no constitutional limit on the speech-inhibiting terms of employment that the government could impose. This position is exemplified by a famous quote from Justice Holmes, made when he was serving on the Massachusetts Supreme Judicial Court: "The petitioner may have a constitutional right to talk politics, but he has no constitutional right to be a policeman. [He] cannot complain, as he takes the employment on the terms which are offered him." McAuliffe v. Mayor of New Bedford, 155 Mass. 216 (1892).

The current position is that a public employee's speech made in the course of performing official duties is constitutionally unprotected, as is non-official employee speech that is not of public concern. A government may limit a public employee's non-official speech on issues of public concern when the limitation is reasonably necessary to maintain efficiency in the performance of the public task for which the employee is engaged. The balancing approach used when public employees speak out on matters of public concern is another application of the unconstitutional conditions doctrine—the idea that while a person may have no right to a government benefit, and that benefit can be denied for many reasons, the government cannot deny the benefit simply because the person exercises a constitutional right. The twist in this area is that the employee's free speech rights are determined by balancing the government employer's legitimate need for employee control against the degree to which the employee's speech implicates the core concerns of the First Amendment.

The Court's initial decision of the current era was Pickering v. Board of Education, 391 U.S. 563 (1968), in which the Court ruled that a public school board violated the First Amendment by dismissing a teacher for writing a letter to a local newspaper criticizing the way school officials had spent money raised from prior bond issues. The Court stated that

> teachers may [not] constitutionally be compelled to relinquish the First Amendment rights they would otherwise enjoy as citizens to comment on matters of public interest in connection with the operation of the public schools in which they work. [But] the State has interests as an employer in regulating the speech of its employees that differ significantly from those it possesses in connection with regulation of the speech of the citizenry in general. The problem [is] to arrive at a balance between the interests of the teacher, as a citizen, in commenting upon matters of public concern and the interest of the State, as an employer, in promoting the efficiency of the public services it performs through its employees.

[Here], a teacher [made] public statements upon issues then currently the subject of public attention which [were] critical of his ultimate employer but which [were not proven] to have in any way either impeded the teacher's proper performance of his daily duties in the classroom or to have interfered with the regular operation of the schools generally. In these circumstances . . . the interest of the school administration in limiting teachers' opportunities to contribute to public debate is not significantly greater than its interest in limiting a similar contribution by any member of the general public.

≡≡≡ *Connick v. Myers*
461 U.S. 138 (1983)

JUSTICE WHITE delivered the opinion of the Court.

[Respondent,] Sheila Myers, was employed as an Assistant District Attorney in New Orleans, [serving] at the pleasure of petitioner Harry Connick, the District Attorney for Orleans Parish. [Myers] was informed that she would be transferred to prosecute cases in a different section of the criminal court. Myers was strongly opposed to the proposed transfer and expressed her view to several of her supervisors, including Connick. [Waldron, one of her supervisors, suggested] that her concerns were not shared by others in the office [and Myers replied] that she would do some research on the matter. [Myers] prepared a questionnaire soliciting the views of her fellow staff members concerning office transfer policy, office morale, the need for a grievance committee, the level of confidence in supervisors, and whether employees felt pressured to work in political campaigns. [She] distributed the questionnaire to 15 Assistant District Attorneys. [Waldron informed Connick] that Myers was creating a "mini-insurrection" within the office. [Connick then fired Myers] because of her refusal to accept the transfer [and for] distribution of the questionnaire, [which Connick] considered an act of insubordination. [Myers] filed suit, [contending] that her employment was wrongfully terminated because she had exercised her constitutionally protected right of free speech. The District Court agreed. [The Court of Appeals affirmed.]

[A] State cannot condition public employment on a basis that infringes the employee's constitutionally protected interest in freedom of expression. Our task . . . is to seek "a balance between the interests of the [employee], as a citizen, in commenting upon matters of public concern and the interest of the State, as an employer, in promoting the efficiency of the public services it performs through its employees." The [lower courts] misapplied *Pickering*.

[Connick contends that] no balancing of interests is required in this case because [Myers's] questionnaire concerned only internal office matters and that such speech is not upon a matter of "public concern." [The] repeated emphasis in *Pickering* on the right of a public employee "as a citizen, in commenting upon matters of public concern," was not accidental. This language [reflects] both the historical . . . rights of public employees and the common-sense realization that government offices could not function if every employment decision became a constitutional matter. [If Myers's] questionnaire cannot be fairly characterized as constituting speech on a matter of public concern, it is unnecessary for us to scrutinize the reasons for her discharge. [We hold] that when a public employee speaks not as a citizen upon matters of public concern, but instead as an employee upon matters only of personal interest, absent the most unusual circumstances, a federal court is not the appropriate forum in which to review the wisdom of a personnel decision taken by a public agency allegedly in reaction to the employee's behavior. . . .

Whether an employee's speech addresses a matter of public concern must be determined by the content, form, and context of a given statement, as revealed by the whole record. In this case, with but one exception, the questions posed by Myers to her co-workers do not fall under the rubric of matters of "public concern." We view the questions pertaining to the confidence and trust that [Myers's] co-workers possess in various supervisors, the level of office morale, and the need for a grievance committee as mere extensions of [Myers's] dispute over her transfer to another section of the criminal court. Unlike the dissent, we do not believe these questions are of public import in evaluating the performance of the District Attorney as an elected official. Myers did not seek to inform the public that the District Attorney's Office was not discharging its governmental responsibilities in the investigation and prosecution of criminal cases. Nor did Myers seek to bring to light actual or potential wrongdoing or breach of public trust on the part of Connick and others. Indeed, the questionnaire, if released to the public, would convey no information at all other than the fact that a single employee is upset with the status quo. While discipline and morale in the workplace are related to an agency's efficient performance of its duties, the focus of [Myers's] questions is not to evaluate the performance of the office but rather to gather ammunition for another round of controversy with her superiors. . . . To presume that all matters which transpire within a government office are of public concern would mean that virtually every remark—and certainly every criticism directed at a public official—would plant the seed of a constitutional case.

[One question in Myers's] questionnaire, however, does touch upon a matter of public concern. Question 11 inquires if assistant district attorneys "ever feel pressured to work in political campaigns on behalf of office supported candidates." We have recently noted that official pressure upon employees to work for political candidates not of the worker's own choice constitutes a coercion of belief in violation of fundamental constitutional rights. [Branti v. Finkel, Elrod v. Burns, infra.] In addition, there is a demonstrated interest in this country that government service should depend upon meritorious performance rather than political service. [Thus], the issue of whether assistant district attorneys are pressured to work in political campaigns is a matter of interest to the community upon which it is essential that public employees be able to speak out freely without fear of retaliatory dismissal.

Because one of the questions in [Myers's] survey touched upon a matter of public concern and contributed to her discharge, we must determine whether Connick was justified in discharging Myers. . . . [The] State's burden in justifying a particular discharge varies depending upon the nature of the employee's expression. . . .

The *Pickering* balance requires full consideration of the government's interest in the effective and efficient fulfillment of its responsibilities to the public. [Connick's judgment was that Myers's] questionnaire was an act of insubordination which interfered with working relationships. When close working relationships are essential to fulfilling public responsibilities, a wide degree of deference to the employer's judgment is appropriate. Furthermore, we do not see the necessity for an employer to allow events to unfold to the extent that the disruption of the office and the destruction of working relationships is manifest before taking action. We caution that a stronger showing may be necessary if the employee's speech more substantially involved matters of public concern. [Also] relevant is the manner, time, and place in which the questionnaire was distributed. [The] fact that Myers, unlike Pickering, exercised her rights to speech at the office supports Connick's fears that the functioning of his office was endangered.

Finally, the context in which the dispute arose is also significant. This is not a case where an employee, out of purely academic interest, circulated a questionnaire so as to obtain useful research. [When] employee speech concerning office policy arises from an employment dispute concerning the very application of that policy to the speaker, additional weight must be given to the supervisor's view that the employee has threatened the authority of the employer to run the office. [The] questionnaire emerged after a persistent dispute between Myers and Connick and his deputies over office transfer policy.

[Myers's] questionnaire touched upon matters of public concern in only a most limited sense; her survey, in our view, is most accurately characterized as an employee grievance concerning internal office policy. The limited First Amendment interest involved here does not require that Connick tolerate action which he reasonably believed would disrupt the office, undermine his authority, and destroy close working relationships. [Myers's] discharge therefore did not offend the First Amendment. [Reversed.]

JUSTICE BRENNAN, joined by JUSTICES MARSHALL, BLACKMUN, and STEVENS, dissenting.

. . . The First Amendment affords special protection to speech that may inform public debate about how our society is to be governed—regardless of whether it actually becomes the subject of a public controversy. [Myers's] questionnaire addressed matters of public concern because it discussed subjects that could reasonably be expected to be of interest to persons seeking to develop informed opinions about the manner in which the Orleans Parish District Attorney, an elected official charged with managing a vital governmental agency, discharges his responsibilities. . . .

NOTES

1. The Scope of Public Concern.   Shortly after the assassination attempt on President Reagan, a clerical worker in a Texas county constable's office remarked to her coworker and boyfriend, "If they go for him again, I hope they get him." Her remark was overheard and she was discharged. In *Rankin v. McPherson*, 483 U.S. 378 (1987), the Court held that her discharge violated the free speech guarantee. The remark involved a matter of public concern, no matter how "inappropriate or controversial" it may have been. The burden was thus on the government to establish that the remark impeded the "effective functioning" of the constable's office. The Court stated that the State interest in punishing employees for the content of their speech was much diminished when employees serve "no confidential, policy-making, or public contact role."

Justice Scalia, joined by Chief Justice Rehnquist and Justices White and O'Connor, dissented: "No law enforcement agency is required by the First Amendment to permit one of its employees to 'ride with the cops and cheer for the robbers.'" Not only was the remark not of public concern, the Court's distinction between policy-making and non-policy-making employees was untenable. Each can "hurt working relationships and undermine public confidence in an organization."

In United States v. National Treasury Employees Union, 513 U.S. 454 (1995), the Court voided a federal law that forbade federal employees from receiving monetary honoraria for speeches or articles. The ban was challenged by an aerospace engineer who spoke on black history, a postal worker who wrote about the Quaker religion, and a scientist who reviewed dance performances. The Court concluded that their speech was of public concern, that the ban on monetary honoraria imposed a "significant burden" on speech, and that the government's interest in preventing actual and apparent misuse of official power was insufficiently supported with respect to the class of challengers, relatively low-level executive branch employees.

San Diego discharged a policeman for producing and offering for sale via the Internet indecent videos in which he stripped off his police uniform and engaged in sexual acts. In *City of San Diego v. Roe*, 543 U.S. 77 (2004), the officer contended that his speech was protected under *National Treasury Employees Union* and was of public concern. The Court rejected both contentions. While the speech at issue in *National Treasury Employees Union* was unrelated to employment and had no effect on the mission and purpose of the employer, "Roe took deliberate steps to link his videos . . . to his police work, all in a way injurious to his employer." Nor was Roe's speech of public concern. Speech of public concern . . . "is something that is a subject of legitimate news interest; that is, a subject of general interest and of value and concern to the public at the time of publication." Because the officer's . . . expression "did nothing to inform the public about any aspect of the SDPD's functioning or operation," and was hardly a commentary "on an item of political news," the speech was not of public concern.

2. Independent Contractors. In Board of Commissioners v. Umbehr, 518 U.S. 668 (1996), the Court extended *Pickering* to independent contractors. Umbehr, under contract to haul trash for Wabaunsee County, Kansas, was a strident and insistent critic of county government. As a result, his contract was terminated. Although independent contractors have greater financial independence from government than do government employees, the risk of government use of its purse to mandate political conformity among those who do business with the government was sufficiently great to require application of *Pickering*. The Court cautioned that this extension of *Pickering* applied only to terminations of contracts, not "bidders or applicants for new government contracts."

3. Party Affiliation. Conditioning public employment on affiliation with the winning political party is a venerable tradition that has produced both legislative attempts to curb the practice and First Amendment challenges to its validity. The legislative response has taken many forms, most notably the creation of a merit-based Civil Service. To keep the Civil Service nonpolitical, Congress and various states have enacted laws that forbid such employees from engaging in active political campaigning. The federal version of these laws, the Hatch Act, which forbids certain executive branch employees from "any active part in political management or in political campaigns," has been upheld against two challenges. In United Public Workers v. Mitchell, 330 U.S. 75 (1947), the Court upheld the application of the Hatch Act prohibition to a production worker in the U.S. Mint who "was a ward executive [of] a political party and was politically active on election day as a worker at the polls." Within "reasonable limits," said the Court, Congress could proscribe the political activities of its employees. In United States Civil Service Commission v. National Association of Letter Carriers, 413 U.S. 548 (1973), the Court upheld the same prohibition against a facial challenge and reaffirmed *Mitchell*. The Court said that "the problem [is to] balance" the speech interests of the employee and the "obviously important [government] interests sought to be served by [the] Hatch Act." Through the Hatch Act, the government sought to achieve three different, but equally important, objectives: (1) unbiased administration of the law, both in actual fact and in appearance; (2) preventing recruitment of government workers into "a powerful, invincible, and perhaps corrupt political machine"; and (3) ensuring "that Government employees [are] free from pressure [to] vote in a certain way or perform political chores in order to curry favor with their superiors rather than to act out of their own beliefs."

First Amendment challenges to patronage employment have resulted in doctrine that permits political party affiliation to be used as the criterion for hiring, dismissal, or promotion decisions only where party affiliation appropriately ensures effective job performance. The government has the burden of proving that party affiliation is appropriate for any particular job. It must show that the patronage practice at issue is "narrowly tailored to further vital governmental interests."

Elrod v. Burns, 427 U.S. 347 (1976). Once Elrod, a Democrat, became sheriff of Cook County, Illinois, he promptly discharged Burns, a process server, solely because Burns was a Republican. The Court concluded that patronage dismissals may be justified by "the need for political loyalty of employees" in order to implement the policies resulting from the electorate's decision, but "[l]imiting patronage dismissals to policymaking positions is sufficient to achieve this governmental end." The Court suggested that patronage dismissals must be shown to be "the least restrictive alternative" to accomplishment of the legitimate government end.

Branti v. Finkel, 445 U.S. 507 (1980). The Court ruled that the discharge of two assistant public defenders solely because of their Republican Party affiliation violated free expression. "[T]he ultimate inquiry is not whether the label 'policymaker' or 'confidential' fits a particular position; rather, the question is whether the hiring authority can demonstrate that party affiliation is an appropriate requirement for the effective performance of the public office involved."

Rutan v. Republican Party of Illinois, 497 U.S. 62 (1990). The Court extended its patronage doctrine to sanctions other than dismissal, including refusal to promote. For governments to justify patronage practices as appropriate to job performance they must prove that the practice at issue is "narrowly tailored to further vital governmental interests." Justice Scalia, joined by Chief Justice Rehnquist and Justices O'Connor and Kennedy, dissented, arguing that *Elrod* and *Branti* should be overruled and condemning the majority's use of the "strict-scrutiny standard" as without "support in our cases." The dissent noted that patronage is deeply rooted in our tradition, is important to the health of political parties, poses no real threat of coercion, involves no "significant impairment of free speech or free association," and can be remedied by the ordinary political process.

The *Elrod-Branti* doctrine was extended to independent contractors in O'Hare Truck Services, Inc. v. City of Northlake, 518 U.S. 712 (1996). A tow truck operator was removed from the city's "rotation list" of tow trucks to summon for traffic purposes after he refused to support the incumbent mayor and backed the opponent. The Court perceived no difference between employees and contractors for purposes of patronage dismissals and specifically rejected the idea that contractors were less susceptible to coercion than employees. In dissent, Justices Scalia and Thomas rejected the entire doctrine because it was the nature of government to "favor[] those who agree with its political views and disfavor[] those who disagree. . . ."

Queries: Could Harry Connick have dismissed Sheila Myers because she was not a member of his political party? The *Elrod-Branti* test requires that the government prove that party-based dismissal is narrowly tailored to accomplish a vital state interest.

Suppose Harry Connick had discharged Myers because her questionnaire revealed that she preferred Connick's political opponent for district attorney. Should *Pickering-Connick* or *Elrod-Branti* apply? Could Connick have discharged Myers if she belonged to a political party espousing racial hatred? See, e.g., State v. Henderson, 277 Neb. 240 (2009).

Garcetti v. Ceballos
547 U.S. 410 (2006)

[Richard Ceballos, a deputy district attorney for Los Angeles County, was asked by a defendant's lawyer to review an affidavit used to obtain a critical search warrant. The defendant's lawyer contended that the affidavit was false and intended to challenge the validity of the search based on the warrant. Before doing so, he asked Ceballos to review the case, a common request. Ceballos concluded that the affidavit made serious misrepresentations, and recommended by memo to his supervisors, Carol Najera and Frank Sundstedt, that the case be dismissed. After investigation and a meeting, Sundstedt decided to continue the prosecution. Ceballos testified as a witness for the defense in the hearing to challenge the search warrant, but the trial court upheld the warrant. Ceballos was reassigned, transferred, and denied a promotion by Gil Garcetti, the District Attorney. Ceballos claimed that these actions constituted retaliation against him for his speech, and filed suit under 42 U.S.C. §1983. The District Court granted summary judgment for Garcetti on the ground that the memorandum was not protected speech because Ceballos wrote it pursuant to his employment duties. The Ninth Circuit reversed.]

JUSTICE KENNEDY delivered the opinion of the Court.

. . . The question presented . . . is whether the First Amendment protects a government employee from discipline based on speech made pursuant to the employee's official duties. . . .

II. [The] First Amendment protects a public employee's right, in certain circumstances, to speak as a citizen addressing matters of public concern. . . . So long as employees are speaking as citizens about matters of public concern, they must face only those speech restrictions that are necessary for their employers to operate efficiently and effectively. . . . The Court has [also] acknowledged the importance of promoting the public's interest in receiving the well-informed views of government employees engaging in civic discussion. . . .

III . . . The controlling factor is that [Ceballos's] expressions were made pursuant to his duties as a calendar deputy. . . . We hold that when public employees make statements pursuant to their official duties, the employees are not speaking as citizens for First Amendment purposes, and the Constitution does not insulate their communications from employer discipline. . . . Restricting speech that owes its existence to a public employee's professional responsibilities does not infringe any liberties the employee might have enjoyed as a private citizen. It simply reflects the exercise of employer control over what the employer itself has commissioned or created. Contrast, for example, the expressions made by the speaker in *Pickering*, whose letter to the newspaper had no official significance and bore similarities to letters submitted by numerous citizens every day. Ceballos did not . . . speak as a citizen by writing a memo that addressed the proper disposition of a pending criminal case. . . . The fact that his duties sometimes required him to speak or write does not mean his supervisors were prohibited from evaluating his performance.

... Refusing to recognize First Amendment claims based on government employees' work product does not prevent them from participating in public debate. The employees retain the prospect of constitutional protection for their contributions to the civic discourse, [but this] does not invest them with a right to perform their jobs however they see fit. ... Employers have heightened interests in controlling speech made by an employee in his or her professional capacity. Official communications have official consequences, creating a need for substantive consistency and clarity. Supervisors must ensure that their employees' official communications are accurate, demonstrate sound judgment, and promote the employer's mission. Ceballos's memo ... demanded the attention of his supervisors and led to a heated meeting with employees from the sheriff's department. If Ceballos's superiors thought his memo was inflammatory or misguided, they had the authority to take proper corrective action.

[The] contrary rule ... would commit state and federal courts to a new, permanent, and intrusive role, mandating judicial oversight of communications between and among government employees and their superiors in the course of official business. This displacement of managerial discretion by judicial supervision finds no support in our precedents. When an employee speaks as a citizen addressing a matter of public concern, the First Amendment requires a delicate balancing of the competing interests surrounding the speech and its consequences. When, however, the employee is simply performing his or her job duties, there is no warrant for a similar degree of scrutiny. To hold otherwise would be to demand permanent judicial intervention in the conduct of governmental operations to a degree inconsistent with sound principles of federalism and the separation of powers. ...

Two final points warrant mentioning. First, [because] Ceballos wrote his ... memo pursuant to his employment duties [we] have no occasion to articulate a comprehensive framework for defining the scope of an employee's duties in cases where there is room for serious debate. [When that occurs, the] proper inquiry is a practical one. Formal job descriptions often bear little resemblance to the duties an employee actually is expected to perform. ... Second, [because] expression related to academic scholarship or classroom instruction implicates additional constitutional interests [we] need not ... decide whether the analysis we conduct today would apply in the same manner to a case involving speech related to scholarship or teaching.

IV. [While exposing] governmental inefficiency and misconduct is a matter of considerable significance [there is a] powerful network of legislative enactments—such as whistle-blower protection laws and labor codes—available to those who seek to expose wrongdoing. These imperatives, as well as obligations arising from any other applicable constitutional provisions and mandates of the criminal and civil laws, protect employees and provide checks on supervisors who would order unlawful or otherwise inappropriate actions.

JUSTICE STEVENS, dissenting.

The proper answer to the question "whether the First Amendment protects a government employee from discipline based on speech made pursuant to the employee's official duties," is "Sometimes," not "Never." Of course a supervisor may take corrective action when such speech is "inflammatory or misguided," [but] what if it is just unwelcome speech because it reveals facts that the supervisor would rather not have anyone else discover?

. . . The notion that there is a categorical difference between speaking as a citizen and speaking in the course of one's employment is quite wrong. Over a quarter of a century has passed since . . . a unanimous Court rejected "the conclusion that a public employee forfeits his protection against governmental abridgment of freedom of speech if he decides to express his views privately rather than publicly." Givhan v. Western Line Consol. School Dist., 439 U.S. 410, 414 (1979). We had no difficulty recognizing that the First Amendment applied when Bessie Givhan, an English teacher, raised concerns about the school's racist employment practices to the principal. Our silence as to whether or not her speech was made pursuant to her job duties demonstrates that the point was immaterial. That is equally true today, for it is senseless to let constitutional protection for exactly the same words hinge on whether they fall within a job description. Moreover, it seems perverse to fashion a new rule that provides employees with an incentive to voice their concerns publicly before talking frankly to their superiors.

JUSTICE SOUTER, with whom JUSTICE STEVENS and JUSTICE GINSBURG join, dissenting.

. . . In [*Givhan*] we followed *Pickering* when a teacher was fired for complaining to a superior about the racial composition of the school's administrative, cafeteria, and library staffs. . . . The difference between a case like *Givhan* and this one is that the subject of Ceballos's speech fell within the scope of his job responsibilities, whereas choosing personnel was not what the teacher was hired to do. The effect of the majority's constitutional line between these two cases . . . is that a *Givhan* schoolteacher is protected when complaining to the principal about hiring policy, but a school personnel officer would not be if he protested that the principal disapproved of hiring minority job applicants. This is an odd place to draw a distinction. . . .

[The] qualified speech protection embodied in *Pickering* balancing . . . hardly disappears when an employee speaks on matters his job requires him to address; rather, . . . the individual and public value of such speech is no less, and may well be greater, when the employee speaks pursuant to his duties in addressing a subject he knows intimately for the very reason that it falls within his duties. As for the importance of such speech to the individual, . . . a citizen may well place a very high value on a right to speak on the public issues he decides to make the subject of his work day after day. . . . Nor is there any reason to [think that] the public interest in hearing informed employees evaporates when they speak as required on some subject at the core of their jobs. . . . The majority is rightly concerned that the employee who speaks out . . . in doing his own work [may] create office uproars and fracture the government's authority to set policy to be carried out coherently through the ranks. . . . But [the] basic *Pickering* balancing scheme is perfectly feasible here. [An] employee commenting on subjects in the course of duties should not prevail . . . unless he speaks on a matter of unusual importance and satisfies high standards of responsibility in the way he does it. [O]nly comment on official dishonesty, deliberately unconstitutional action, other serious wrongdoing, or threats to health and safety can weigh out in an employee's favor. . . .

NOTE AND PROBLEMS

1. Sworn Testimony Relating to Official Duties. Lane v. Franks, 134 S. Ct. (2014), involved Lane, a public employee who, in the course of his duties, audited a public agency and discovered financial misconduct by another employee, who was prosecuted for her conduct. In the prosecution Lane provided sworn testimony of the circumstances of his investigation. Later, Franks, Lane's supervisor, fired him, ostensibly for budgetary reasons. Lane claimed that he was fired for his speech. The Supreme Court held that Lane spoke as a citizen on a matter of public concern in giving sworn testimony, not in the course of his official duties. His duty was to audit and report his findings, but his testimony in the subsequent prosecution was part of his duty as a citizen. Unlike *Garcetti*, where the speech itself was within the scope of the speaker's job duties, this speech arose from an independent civic obligation. Because Lane's testimony pertained to public corruption and misuse of government funds it "obviously involve[d] matters of significant public concern." However, Franks was entitled to qualified immunity because the question of whether sworn testimony stemming from job duties was protected by the First Amendment was not clearly resolved at the time Franks fired Lane.

Query: In a footnote the Court said it was not deciding whether a police officer's speech pursuant to a subpoena to testify is entitled to constitutional protection. Part of a police officer's official duties is the duty to testify regarding events he encounters in the course of his job. Assuming that such speech is of public concern should the police officer's testimony be treated as unprotected, pursuant to *Garcetti*, or protected, as an extension of *Lane?*

2. Problems: *Controversial Professor.* Suppose an untenured public university law professor publishes an academic article contending that torture is entirely justified when national security is at stake. After the article's publication, students protest the professor's views by disrupting his classes and noisily picketing in the hallway outside his office. The law school disciplines the students engaged in the disruptive activity, which results in a general boycott of classes and a precipitous decline in applications. The law school then discharges the professor, who sues the university for violation of his free speech rights. Analyze the merits of the claim.

Avian Influenza. Suppose that the head of the Centers for Disease Control and Prevention (CDC), a public agency, is asked to appear on PBS's News Hour, to speak about avian influenza and she does so. In the course of the interview, she voices her sincerely held opinion that the United States would suffer millions of deaths from avian influenza, should that form of influenza become capable of human-to-human transmission. She states that public health agencies are "woefully unprepared" for such an epidemic. The result of the appearance is a political firestorm, in which members of Congress demand her resignation for "recklessly inflammatory" remarks. For months, the head of the CDC and her staff devote nearly 75 percent of their time to the political fallout from the appearance. The CDC then discharges her for her comments on the News Hour and she sues, contending that her free speech rights have been violated. Analyze the merits of the claim.

University Human Resources Official. A public university voluntarily adopts a policy providing parity of benefits for same-sex partners and heterosexual married couples. A human resources manager employed by the university and charged with the responsibility for administering those benefits writes a column for the local newspaper in which she expresses her opposition to treating same-sex couples the same as heterosexual married couples. She states: "As a Black woman, I take great umbrage at the notion that those choosing the homosexual lifestyle are civil rights victims. Here's why. I cannot wake up tomorrow and not be a Black woman. I am genetically and biologically a Black woman, but every day thousands of homosexuals make a life decision to leave the gay lifestyle." The manager is discharged because she holds values that "are not in accord with the university's values." She sues, contending that her free speech rights have been violated. Analyze the merits of the claim. See Dixon v. University of Toledo, 842 F. Supp. 2d 1044 (N.D. Ohio 2012).

Drug Enforcement Administration Agent. A DEA agent publicly proclaims that drug enforcement is a mistake and that all drugs should be legal. He's fired. Is the discharge valid?

Food and Drug Administration Scientist. An FDA scientist is overheard commenting to a coworker that the FDA's desire to regulate nicotine is motivated by political ambition on the part of FDA administrators. She's fired. Is the discharge valid?

Garbage Collector. A municipal garbage collector states in a letter to the editor of the local newspaper that "much of the garbage I pick up is good, usable stuff but the city won't let us keep it; off it goes to the dump." He's fired. Is the discharge valid?

4. Public Sponsorship of Speech

The unconstitutional conditions doctrine—the idea that, while government need not confer a benefit, it may not condition the receipt of a benefit upon the relinquishment of an independent constitutional right—defines the line between government-sponsored speech and private speech. A government is free to pay for speech it agrees with and to refuse to pay for speech with which it disagrees, but a government cannot withhold some unrelated benefit from private speakers who use their own resources to say things the government dislikes. The former is a permissible government subsidy of speech; the latter is a penalty imposed on those who utter disfavored speech. An early recognition of this principle occurred in Speiser v. Randall, 357 U.S. 513 (1958), in which the Court held that California's denial of a property tax exemption to veterans who refused to state that they did not favor the forcible overthrow of government was an unconstitutional penalty imposed on free expression. A pair of more recent cases illustrates the subtleties of the distinction between unconstitutional penalty and constitutional subsidy.

Regan v. Taxation with Representation of Washington (TWR), 461 U.S. 540 (1983). The Court upheld provisions of federal tax law that permit donors to charitable organizations that do not engage in political lobbying to deduct the amount of their donations from income, but forbid such deductibility with respect to donations to charities that engage in lobbying. Tax deductibility amounts to a subsidy because it reduces the cost of the donation to the donor, thus encouraging donations. In the Court's view, these deductibility rules represented a choice by Congress "not to subsidize lobbying [but] to subsidize other activities that nonprofit organizations undertake to promote the public welfare." But this was no penalty:

> The [tax] Code does not deny TWR the right to receive deductible contributions to support its nonlobbying activity, nor does it deny TWR any independent benefit on account of its intention to lobby. Congress has merely refused to pay for the lobbying out of public moneys. [Congress] is not required . . . to subsidize lobbying.

The Court noted that the deductibility scheme did not involve viewpoint discrimination and observed that it "would be different if Congress were to discriminate invidiously in its subsidies in such a way as to [seek to suppress] 'dangerous ideas.'"

FCC v. League of Women Voters, 468 U.S. 364 (1984). The Court struck down a portion of a federal law forbidding any public radio or television station receiving federal grants from engaging in "editorializing." Unlike *Regan*, this case involved a penalty because a public broadcaster "that receives only 1% of its overall income from [government] grants is barred absolutely from editorializing." Unlike the nonprofit organization in *Regan*, "such a station is not able to segregate its activities according to the source of its funding. The station [is] barred from using even wholly private funds to finance its editorial activity." Justice Rehnquist, joined by Chief Justice Burger and Justice White, dissented, arguing that

> Congress [has] simply determined that public funds shall not be used to subsidize [public broadcasters] which engage in "editorializing." [When] the government is simply exercising its power to allocate its own public funds, we need only find that the condition imposed has a rational relationship to Congress'[s] purpose in providing the subsidy and that it is not primarily "aimed at the suppression of dangerous ideas."

Rust v. Sullivan
500 U.S. 173 (1991)

CHIEF JUSTICE REHNQUIST delivered the opinion of the Court.

These cases concern a facial challenge to Department of Health and Human Services (HHS) regulations which limit the ability of Title X fund recipients to engage in abortion related activities. [The regulations forbade health projects receiving federal money for family planning under Title X of the Public Health Service Act from counseling or referring women for abortion and from encouraging, advocating, or promoting abortion. Title X projects were permitted to supply information about childbirth and prenatal care. Any organization receiving Title X funds that engaged in the prohibited abortion activities was required to maintain a physical and financial separation between itself and its Title X project. The Court of Appeals] upheld the regulations, finding them to be a permissible construction of the statute as well as consistent with the First [Amendment]. We affirm.

[The] broad language of Title X plainly allows the [HHS] Secretary's construction of the statute. [Petitioners] contend that the regulations violate the First Amendment by impermissibly discriminating based on viewpoint because they prohibit "all discussion about abortion as a lawful option [while] compelling the clinic or counselor to provide information that promotes continuing a pregnancy to term, [thus penalizing] speech funded with non-Title X monies." [The] Government is exercising [its] authority [to] subsidize family planning services which will lead to conception and childbirth, and declining to "promote or encourage abortion." The Government can, without violating the Constitution, selectively fund a program to encourage certain activities it believes to be in the public interest, without at the same time funding an alternative program which seeks to deal with the problem in another way. In so doing, the Government has not discriminated on the basis of viewpoint; it has merely chosen to fund one activity to the exclusion of the other. . . . To hold that the Government unconstitutionally discriminates on the basis of viewpoint when it chooses to fund a program dedicated to advance certain permissible goals, because the program in advancing those goals necessarily discourages alternative goals, would render numerous Government programs constitutionally suspect. When Congress established a National Endowment for Democracy to encourage other countries to adopt democratic principles, it was not constitutionally required to fund a program to encourage competing lines of political philosophy such as communism and fascism. [When] the government appropriates public funds to establish a program it is entitled to define the limits of that program.

[Petitioners] also contend that the restrictions on the subsidization of abortion-related speech contained in the regulations are impermissible because they condition the receipt of a benefit, in these cases Title X funding, on the relinquishment of a constitutional right, the right to engage in abortion advocacy and counseling. [H]ere the Government is not denying a benefit to anyone, but is instead simply insisting that public funds be spent for the purposes for which they were authorized. The [HHS] Secretary's regulations do not force the Title X grantee to give up abortion-related speech; they merely require that the grantee keep such activities separate and distinct from Title X activities. . . . In contrast, our "unconstitutional conditions" cases involve situations in which the Government has placed a condition on the recipient of the subsidy, [thus] effectively prohibiting the recipient from engaging in the protected conduct. [Affirmed.]

JUSTICE BLACKMUN, joined by JUSTICES MARSHALL and STEVENS, dissenting.
. . . Remarkably, the majority concludes that "the Government has not discriminated on the basis of viewpoint; it has merely chosen to fund one activity to the exclusion of the other." [By] refusing to fund those family-planning projects that advocate abortion because they advocate abortion, the Government plainly has targeted a particular viewpoint.

NOTES AND PROBLEMS

1. Suppression of Dangerous Ideas. A consistent caveat voiced by the Court throughout the cases concerning government-sponsored speech is that government subsidies of speech may not be delivered with the aim of suppressing "dangerous ideas." That theme was acted upon in Rosenberger v. Rector and Visitors of the University of Virginia, 515 U.S. 819 (1995). The University of Virginia, a public institution, used mandatory student fees to pay the "printing costs of a variety of student publications" but refused to pay those costs for Wide Awake, a student-edited paper with a "Christian viewpoint," because it refused to fund any student "religious activity." The University argued that (1) its refusal to pay Wide Awake's printing costs was no penalty on speech but a permissible refusal to subsidize speech, and (2) the refusal was justified as necessary to avoid violation of the First Amendment's establishment of religion clause.

The Court rejected both arguments, holding that the refusal to fund violated free expression. With respect to the first issue, Justice Kennedy, writing for the Court, declared:

[We] have observed a distinction between . . . content discrimination, which may be permissible if it preserves the purposes of [a limited public] forum, and . . . viewpoint discrimination, which is presumed impermissible when directed against speech otherwise within the forum's limitations. [The fund for printing costs] is a forum more in a metaphysical than in a spatial or geographic sense, but the same principles are applicable. . . . [The] University does not exclude religion as a subject matter but selects for disfavored treatment those student journalistic efforts with religious editorial viewpoints. Religion may be a vast area of inquiry, but it also provides, as it did here, a specific premise, a perspective, a standpoint from which a variety of subjects may be discussed and considered. The prohibited perspective, not the general subject matter, resulted in the refusal to [pay printing costs], for the subjects discussed were otherwise within the approved category of publications. . . .

[When] the University determines the content of the education it provides, it is the University speaking, and we have permitted the government to regulate the content of what is or is not expressed when it is the speaker or when it enlists private entities to convey its own message. . . . When the government disburses public funds to private entities to convey a governmental message, it may take legitimate and appropriate steps to ensure that its message is neither garbled nor distorted by the grantee. It does not follow, however, [that] viewpoint-based restrictions are proper when the University does not itself speak or subsidize transmittal of a message it favors but instead expends funds to encourage a diversity of views from private speakers. . . . The University declares that the student groups [it funds] are not the University's agents, are not subject to its control, and are not its responsibility. Having offered to pay the [printing costs] on behalf of private speakers who convey their own messages, the University may not silence the expression of selected viewpoints.

Justice Kennedy distinguished *Rust* as a case concerning government speech, not as a case in which viewpoint discrimination was absent.

Query: Could the government pay all the costs of a private television broadcast network, provided that the network agreed not to air any material critical of the government? What if the government owns the network?

2. Subsequent Developments: *Finley.* In National Endowment for the Arts v. Finley, 524 U.S. 569 (1998), the Court upheld the facial validity of an amendment to the funding act for the NEA that directed the agency to ensure that "artistic excellence [and] merit are the criteria by which [grant] applications are judged, taking into consideration general standards of decency and respect for the diverse beliefs and values of the American public." The Court concluded that "the Government may allocate competitive funding according to criteria that would be impermissible were direct regulation of speech or a criminal penalty at stake. [Congress] has wide latitude to set spending priorities." Justice Scalia, joined by Justice Thomas, concurred in the judgment on the ground that, although the statute was viewpoint and content discriminatory, it did not abridge anyone's freedom of speech.

Those who wish to create indecent and disrespectful art are as unconstrained now as they were before the enactment of this statute. Avant-garde artistes . . . remain entirely free to *epater les bourgeois;* they are merely deprived of the additional satisfaction of having the bourgeoisie taxed to pay for it. It is preposterous to equate the denial of taxpayer subsidy with measures "aimed at the *suppression* of dangerous ideas."

Justice Souter was the sole dissenter, arguing that the law constituted viewpoint-based discrimination like that voided in *Rosenberger*.

3. Problems: *Climate Change Research.* Suppose Congress conditioned the awarding of federal grants to scientists studying the global climate upon their promise that they will not speak or write in support of the proposition that the Earth is experiencing global warming. Valid? Suppose Congress conditioned such grants on the scientists' agreement that they would not use the results of their funded research in support of any public commentary they may make in support of the proposition that global warming is occurring. Valid?

Cancer Research.   Suppose Congress required, as a condition of federal funding for cancer research, that researchers refrain from stating any view on the relationship between cancer and environmental toxins that is based, even in part, on their federally funded research. Valid?

▦▦▦ *Legal Services Corp. v. Velasquez*
▦▦▦ *531 U.S. 533 (2001)*

JUSTICE KENNEDY delivered the opinion of the Court.

[Congress established the Legal Services Corporation (LSC)] to distribute funds appropriated by Congress to eligible local grantee organizations "for the purpose of providing financial support for legal assistance in noncriminal proceedings or matters to persons financially unable to afford legal assistance." . . . LSC grantees consist of hundreds of local organizations . . . funded by a combination of LSC funds and other public or private sources. The grantee organizations hire and supervise lawyers to provide free legal assistance to indigent clients . . . seeking welfare benefits.

This suit requires us to decide whether one of the conditions imposed by Congress on the use of LSC funds violates the First Amendment rights of LSC grantees and their clients. [Congress barred LSC-funded] legal representation . . . if the representation involves an effort to amend or otherwise challenge existing welfare law. [The] restriction prevents an attorney from arguing to a court that a state statute conflicts with a federal statute or that either a state or federal statute by its terms or in its application [violates] the United States Constitution. [The] restriction violates the First Amendment. . . .

II. . . . We have said that viewpoint-based funding decisions can be sustained in instances in which the government is itself the speaker, see Board of Regents of Univ. of Wis. System v. Southworth, 529 U.S. 217 (2000), or instances, like *Rust*, in which the government "used private speakers to transmit information pertaining to its own program." . . . [But] "it does not follow . . . that viewpoint-based restrictions are proper when the [government] does not itself speak or subsidize transmittal of a message it favors but instead expends funds to encourage a diversity of views from private speakers." [*Rosenberger*.]

Although the LSC program['s] purpose is not to "encourage a diversity of views," the salient point is that, like the program in *Rosenberger*, the LSC program was designed to facilitate private speech, not to promote a governmental message. Congress funded LSC grantees to provide attorneys to represent the interests of indigent clients. [An] LSC-funded attorney speaks on the behalf of the client in a claim against the government for welfare benefits. The lawyer is not the government's speaker. The attorney defending the decision to deny benefits will deliver the government's message in the litigation. . . . The Government has designed this program . . . to accomplish its end of assisting welfare claimants in determination or receipt of their benefits.

[The] Government seeks to use an existing medium of expression and to control it [in] ways which distort its usual functioning. . . . Restricting LSC attorneys in advising their clients and in presenting arguments and analyses to the courts distorts the legal system by altering the traditional role of the attorneys. . . . An informed, independent judiciary presumes an informed, independent bar. . . . [H]owever, cases would be presented by LSC attorneys who could not advise the courts of serious questions of statutory validity. The disability is inconsistent with the proposition that attorneys should present all the reasonable and well-grounded arguments necessary for proper resolution of the case. By seeking to prohibit the analysis of certain legal issues and to truncate presentation to the courts, the enactment under review prohibits speech and expression upon which courts must depend for the proper exercise of the judicial power. . . . The statute is an attempt to draw lines around the LSC program to exclude from litigation those arguments and theories Congress finds unacceptable but which by their nature are within the province of the courts to consider. . . .

The attempted restriction is designed to insulate the Government's interpretation of the Constitution from judicial challenge. The Constitution does not permit the Government to confine litigants and their attorneys in this manner. We must be vigilant when Congress imposes rules and conditions which in effect insulate its own laws from legitimate judicial challenge. . . . Affirmed.

Justice Scalia, joined by Chief Justice Rehnquist and Justices O'Connor and Thomas, dissenting.

[The statute] defines the scope of a federal spending program. It does not directly regulate speech, and it neither establishes a public forum nor discriminates on the basis of viewpoint. The Court agrees with all this, yet applies a novel and unsupportable interpretation of our public-forum precedents to declare [the statute] facially unconstitutional. This holding not only has no foundation in our jurisprudence; it is flatly contradicted by [*Rust*].

I. [When Congress created the Legal Services Corporation it recognized] that the program could not serve its purpose unless it was "kept free from the influence of or use by it of political pressures." [Thus], from the program's inception [Congress has] tightly regulated the use of its funds. No [LSC] funds may be used, for example, for "encouraging . . . labor or antilabor activities," for "litigation relating to the desegregation of any elementary or secondary school or school system," or for "litigation which seeks to procure a nontherapeutic abortion." Congress discovered through experience, however, that these restrictions did not exhaust the politically controversial uses to which LSC funds could be put, [so] Congress added new restrictions, [including] the one at issue here.

[The] LSC can sponsor neither challenges to *nor* defenses of existing welfare reform law. . . . If a suit for benefits raises a claim outside the scope of the LSC program, the LSC-funded lawyer may not participate in the suit, [but the lawyers] *must* explain to the client why they cannot represent him. They are also free to express their views of the legality of the welfare law to the client, and they may refer the client to another attorney who can accept the representation.

II. The LSC Act is a federal subsidy program, not a federal regulatory program. . . . Regulations directly restrict speech; subsidies do not. Subsidies, it is true, may *indirectly* abridge speech, but only if the funding scheme is [coercive. When a] spending program has universal coverage and excludes only certain speech [it is] unconstitutional only when the exclusion [is] "aimed at the suppression of dangerous ideas." . . . When the limited spending program does not create a public forum, proving coercion is virtually impossible, because simply denying a subsidy "does not 'coerce' belief," and because the criterion of unconstitutionality is whether denial of the subsidy threatens "to drive certain ideas or viewpoints from the marketplace." Absent such a threat, "the Government may allocate . . . funding according to criteria that would be impermissible were direct regulation of speech . . . at stake." [*Finley.*] . . .

The LSC Act . . . simply declines to subsidize a certain class of litigation, and under *Rust* that decision "does not infringe the right" to bring such litigation. . . . The Court contends that *Rust* is different because the program at issue subsidized government speech, while the LSC funds private speech. This is so unpersuasive it hardly needs response. If the private doctors' confidential advice to their patients at issue in *Rust* constituted "government speech," it is hard to imagine what subsidized speech would *not* be government speech. Moreover, the majority's contention that the subsidized speech in these cases is not government speech because the lawyers have a professional obligation to represent the interests of their clients founders on the reality that the doctors in *Rust* had a professional obligation to serve the interests of their patients. . . .

The Court further asserts that . . . the welfare funding restriction "seeks to use an existing medium of expression and to control it . . . in ways which distort its usual functioning." This is wrong on both the facts and the law. It is wrong on the law because there is utterly no precedent for the novel and facially implausible proposition that the First Amendment has anything to do with government funding that—though it does not actually abridge anyone's speech—"distorts an existing medium of expression." . . . The Court's "nondistortion" principle is also wrong on the facts, since there is no basis for believing that [the law], by causing "cases [to] be presented by LSC attorneys who cannot advise the courts of serious questions of statutory validity," will distort the operation of the courts. It may well be that the bar . . . will cause LSC-funded attorneys to decline or to withdraw from cases that involve statutory validity. But that means at most that fewer statutory challenges to welfare laws will be presented to the courts because of the unavailability of free legal services for that purpose. So what? The same result would ensue from excluding LSC-funded lawyers from welfare litigation entirely. . . .

The LSC subsidy neither prevents anyone from speaking nor coerces anyone to change speech, and is indistinguishable in all relevant respects from the subsidy upheld in Rust v. Sullivan. There is no legitimate basis for declaring [the law] facially unconstitutional. . . .

NOTES AND PROBLEMS

1. The Distinction Between Government Speech and Private Speech. Why was the physicians' speech at issue in *Rust* the government's speech, but the lawyers' speech at issue in *Velasquez* private speech? Both speakers were speaking in the course of delivering a government aid program. Is the difference rooted in the nature of lawyers' speech—that lawyers are employed to speak *for* their clients through advocacy, and physicians are employed to speak *to* their patients about medical diagnosis and treatment?

2. The Role of Coercion and Distortion. In *Rust*, the Court thought that the abortion counseling restriction was not coercive because indigent women remained free to seek other advice. Was the restriction at issue in *Velasquez* coercive or was coercion simply irrelevant to the Court's analysis in *Velasquez*?

What is the meaning of distortion? Doesn't any speech restriction—even permissible ones that are inextricably connected to legitimate government subsidies—distort speech? Justice Kennedy saw distortion in LSC lawyers' speech and its effect on the judicial process. If the problem posed by distortion is the effect on the judicial process of the LSC restrictions, should the problem be resolved by assessing whether the LSC restrictions prevent the judiciary from hearing those arguments from anyone? If the problem posed by distortion is the effect on LSC lawyers' speech, why did the Court distinguish *Rust* rather than overrule it? Would it be an unconstitutional distortion of speech if Congress simply terminated the LSC?

3. Subsequent Developments: *United States v. American Library Association, 539 U.S. 194 (2003).* The Court found facially valid two federal programs that made funds available to public libraries to assist them in providing Internet access to their patrons, but that conditioned such aid on installation of software filters that block obscenity and child pornography, and to prevent minors from accessing material deemed harmful to them. The condition permitted the libraries to disable the filters at the request of adult patrons. Relying in part on *Finley*, a four-justice plurality first concluded that in a library context "the government has broad discretion to make content-based judgments in deciding what private speech to make available to the public. . . . Public library staffs necessarily consider content in making collection decisions and enjoy broad discretion in making them." The plurality then rejected the contention that the condition was an unconstitutional abridgment of free speech:

In *Rust*, [we recognized] that "the Government [was] not denying a benefit to anyone, but [was] instead simply insisting that public funds be spent for the purposes for which they were authorized." The same is true here. [These] programs were intended to help public libraries fulfill their traditional role of obtaining material of requisite and appropriate quality for educational and informational purposes. . . .

Appellees mistakenly contend, in reliance on [*Velazquez*], that [the] filtering conditions "distor[t] the usual functioning of public libraries." [The] role of lawyers who represent clients in welfare disputes is to advocate *against* the Government, and there was thus an assumption that counsel would be free of state control. . . . Public libraries, by contrast, have no comparable role that pits them against the Government, and there is no comparable assumption that they must be free of any conditions that their benefactors might attach the use of donated funds or other assistance.

Pleasant Grove. Pioneer Park in Pleasant Grove, Utah is a public park that has at least 15 permanent displays, 11 of which were donated by private entities. Among the displays are "an historic granary, a wishing well, the City's first fire station, a September 11 monument, and a Ten Commandments monument donated by the Fraternal Order of Eagles in 1971." The Summum Church requested that the city accept its donation of a stone monument, similar in size and shape to the Ten Commandments monument, on which would be inscribed the Seven Aphorisms of Summum.[15] The City refused. After the Summum Church sued, the Tenth Circuit concluded that the proposed display was speech of the Summum sect, that the park was a traditional public forum, and that the City had failed to justify its content-based exclusion of the Summum Church's speech. In Pleasant Grove v. Summum, 555 U.S. 460 (2009), the Supreme Court reversed.

The Court concluded that Pleasant Grove was not affording a public forum for private speech by displaying monuments in its park. Rather, the city was delivering its own message by accepting donated monuments for display in Pioneer Park. Citing Johanns v. Livestock Marketing Association, 544 U.S. 550 (2005), the Court repeated that "the Government's own speech . . . is exempt from First Amendment scrutiny." While government speech is limited by the establishment clause, the question of whether the City's display of the Ten Commandments violated the establishment clause had not been briefed or argued, and thus the Court did not rule on this issue. The Court

---

15. Summum is a religion that incorporates elements of Gnostic Christianity, specifically the belief "that spiritual knowledge is experiential and that through devotion comes revelation, which 'modifies human perception, and transfigures the individual.'" Summum holds that the Seven Aphorisms, or Seven Principles of Creation, were inscribed on the original stone tablets given to Moses by God. The Biblical account is that when Moses brought the first set of tablets down from Mount Sinai and witnessed his people worshipping a golden calf, "his anger burned and he threw the tablets out of his hands, breaking them to pieces at the foot of the mountain." Exodus 32:19 (New International Version). After the Israelites repented, God wrote the Ten Commandments on a second set of tablets, which Moses brought to his people. Exodus 34. Summum adherents believe that the Seven Aphorisms were on the first tablets, but because the people were not ready to receive them, the Aphorisms, though shared with a few believers, were destroyed. See also http://www.summum.us/philosophy/tencommandments.shtml.

ruled that "[p]ermanent monuments displayed on public property typically represent government speech," reasoning that "[g]overnments have long used monuments to speak to the public," and that there was no distinction between governmentally funded monuments and those accepted from private donors. "[P]ersons who observe donated monuments . . . interpret them as conveying some message on the property owner's behalf. . . ." The conclusion that such monuments constitute governmental speech was reinforced by the fact that "throughout our Nation's history, the general government practice with respect to donated monuments has been one of selective receptivity." By accepting or rejecting donations, governments choose what they wish to say.

Walker v. Texas Division, Sons of Confederate Veterans, 2015 U.S. LEXIS 4063. The Court followed *Pleasant Grove* in Walker v. Texas Division, Sons of Confederate Veterans, 2015 U.S. LEXIS 4063. Texas issued hundreds of varieties of specialty license plates upon application by private groups and state approval. Those plates bore all sorts of slogans, from "Choose Life" to "I'd Rather Be Golfing" but Texas refused to issue a plate proposed by the Sons of Confederate Veterans because it bore a Confederate battle flag emblem. The Court said that all of these slogans were government speech and thus immune from free speech doctrine that presumes viewpoint discrimination to be unlawful. It was government speech because Texas owned the plates, required motorists to display some authorized Texas plate, and retained control over the issuance of specialty plates. Does the fact that a reasonable observer would surely think a slogan like "NASCAR 24 Jeff Gordon" is the sentiment of the motorist rather than the state cast any doubt on this conclusion? The dissent characterized Texas' program as renting space on state-owned mobile bill-boards. What result after Walker if Texas erected electronic billboards along its highways, bearing state messages (e.g. "Construction Ahead") but also rented time and space on these billboards for private messages? Could Texas permit slogans urging the University of Texas athletic teams to victory but deny such slogans supporting the University of Oklahoma?

Agency for International Development v. Alliance for Open Society International, 133 S. Ct. 2321 (2013). To combat the spread of the HIV virus, Congress enacted the "Leadership Act," which appropriated federal funds to be given to private recipients, but stipulates that "no funds may be used by an organization 'that does not have a policy explicitly opposing prostitution and sex trafficking.'" This Policy Requirement was attacked as a violation of the recipient's free speech rights. The Court agreed:

"The Policy Requirement mandates that recipients of Leadership Act funds explicitly agree with the Government's policy to oppose prostitution and sex trafficking. It is, however, a basic First Amendment principle that "freedom of speech prohibits the government from telling people what they must say." . . . Were it enacted as a direct regulation of speech, the Policy Requirement would plainly violate the First Amendment. The question is whether the Government may nonetheless impose that requirement as a condition on the receipt of federal funds. . . . [The] relevant distinction that has emerged from our cases is between conditions that define the limits of the government spending program—those that specify the activities Congress wants to subsidize—and conditions that seek to leverage funding to regulate speech outside the contours of the program itself . . . . [The] Policy Requirement falls on the unconstitutional side of the line. [The] Leadership Act has two conditions relevant here. The first—unchallenged in this litigation—prohibits Leadership Act funds from being used "to promote or advocate the legalization or practice of prostitution or sex trafficking." The Government concedes that [this] by itself ensures that federal funds will not be used for the prohibited purposes. The Policy Requirement therefore must be doing something more—and it is. . . . The Policy Requirement is an ongoing condition on recipients' speech and activities, a ground for terminating a grant after selection is complete. This case is not about the Government's ability to enlist the assistance of those with whom it already agrees. It is about compelling a grant recipient to adopt a particular belief as a condition of funding."

4. Problems: *Pacifist Chaplains.* Suppose the federal government adopts a regulation that bars military chaplains from advocating pacifism, including within their liturgical celebration. Assess the validity of the regulation. Are chaplains private speakers or government speakers?

Subsidies to History Teachers. Suppose Congress appropriates substantial salary supplements to teachers of history in public and private nonsectarian schools, but stipulates that any recipient must refrain from criticizing the Framers of the Constitution for their tolerance of slavery. Assess the constitutional validity of the subsidy.

E.   OVERBREADTH, VAGUENESS, AND PRIOR RESTRAINTS

The doctrines of overbreadth, vagueness, and prior restraint involve impermissible modes or procedures of regulating speech. The problem is not so much the substance of a regulation as it is the way in which it is implemented.

1.   Overbreadth

An overbroad statute regulates constitutionally unprotected conduct by also regulating much constitutionally protected conduct. Governments may not use "means which sweep unnecessarily broadly and thereby invade the area of protected freedoms" in order to control behavior legitimately susceptible to government control. NAACP v. Alabama, 357 U.S. 449 (1958). But only statutes that are *substantially* overbroad are voided for overbreadth. Broadrick v. Oklahoma, 413 U.S. 601 (1973).

In the context of free expression, overbreadth doctrine examines all possible applications of a speech regulation rather than its application just to the litigant challenging the regulation. Thus a statute claimed to be overbroad is tested *on its face* rather than as actually applied to the litigant before the court, as overbreadth is concerned with the *possible* applications of a statute. That means that speakers of constitutionally unprotected speech are permitted to challenge the validity of the law under which they are prosecuted on the ground that the law is too sweeping rather than on the ground that their own speech is constitutionally protected. As a result, a successful overbreadth challenge may permit the speaker of unprotected speech to go unpunished for speech for which he could validly be punished under a more narrowly drafted law. By permitting a party to assert another's claims, this seems to operate as a de facto exception to the normal standing rules. This is true if the right at issue is perceived to be the substantive right of free expression, but not if what is at issue is the right to be free of prosecution under a law that is inherently invalid. In that view, the unprotected speaker is asserting his own right to have his behavior judged by a constitutionally valid rule of law. See Monaghan, Overbreadth, 1981 Sup. Ct. Rev. 1.

Facial review is exceptional. The usual analysis in constitutional law is to examine the validity of a law as it is actually applied to the challenger. If it is struck down, it is only that application that is voided, thus effectively narrowing the scope of the statute. But when a statute is found to be overbroad and thus invalid on its face, the statute is void *in toto*—it is wiped out with respect to all possible applications. When the Court voids a statute as applied, it is using the judicial equivalent of the surgeon's scalpel; when it voids a statute on its face, it is using the judicial equivalent of the butcher's cleaver. What, then, accounts for judicial embrace of this exceptional and crude tool?

There are several answers. First, because the overbroad statute controls constitutionally unprotected speech by also regulating protected speech, courts assume it has the effect of deterring law-abiding citizens from speaking in a manner prohibited by the law but protected by the First Amendment. If this assumption is universally true, there would never be an occasion for the courts to rule upon an invalid application of the law because the overbroad law would deter all protected speech within its scope. A law-abiding person is not likely to violate the statute in order to assert his constitutionally guaranteed free speech right. A combination of respect for the law—even an invalid law—and a rational fear of prosecution combine to deter protected speech. Thus, even if governments do not enforce the overbroad law against protected speech, the very presence of the law intimidates some unknown number of speakers from uttering some unknown amount of protected speech. It is much more likely that the reckless, non-law-abiding citizen who has spoken out in a way that offends the law but is not within the protection of the First Amendment will challenge the law in court.

Second, an overbroad law invites selective enforcement against certain speakers or certain viewpoints. Free speech is most threatened and of the most value when unpopular speech is at issue. Voiding overbroad statutes on their face reduces the opportunity of governments to engage in this sort of selective enforcement.

There are two principal criticisms of overbreadth. First, it is said that in effect the doctrine permits advisory opinions, because the statute's validity is resolved in its entirety in the absence of the concrete, adversarial facts that are supposed to characterize a "case or controversy." Second, because overbreadth permits speakers of unprotected speech to go unpunished because the law might impede someone else's free expression rights, public safety might be imperiled. A speaker who urges the angry armed mob to lynch the suspect surrounded by the mob will go free if prosecuted under a statute forbidding all speech that "tends to promote public disorder."

Broadrick v. Oklahoma
413 U.S. 601 (1973)

JUSTICE WHITE delivered the opinion of the Court.

[Oklahoma law prohibits] the State's classified civil servants [from soliciting for political contributions and "'tak[ing] part in the management or affairs of any political party or in any political campaign, except to exercise his right as a citizen privately to express his opinion and to cast his vote.'" Appellants, three public employees subject to the law, sought a judicial declaration of its unconstitutionality and injunction against its enforcement on grounds] of asserted vagueness and overbreadth. [The] District Court upheld the [law]. We affirm.

[Section 818 is] not so vague that "men of common intelligence must necessarily guess at its meaning." . . . [Appellants] are charged with actively engaging in partisan political activities—including the solicitation of money—among their coworkers for the benefit of their superior, [who was campaigning for reelection]. Appellants concede [that] §818 would be constitutional as applied to this type of conduct. They nevertheless maintain that the statute is overbroad and purports to reach protected, as well as unprotected conduct, and must therefore be struck down on its face and held to be incapable of any constitutional application. We do not believe that the overbreadth doctrine may appropriately be invoked in this manner here.

Embedded in the traditional rules governing constitutional adjudication is the principle that a person to whom a statute may constitutionally be applied will not be heard to challenge that statute on the ground that it may conceivably be applied unconstitutionally to others, in other situations not before the Court. A closely related principle is that constitutional rights are personal and may not be asserted vicariously. These principles [reflect] the conviction that under our constitutional system courts are not roving commissions assigned to pass judgment on the validity of the Nation's laws. [In] the past, the Court has recognized some limited exceptions to these principles. . . . One such exception [has] been carved out in the area of the First Amendment. It has long been recognized that the First Amendment needs breathing space and that statutes attempting to restrict or burden the exercise of First Amendment rights must be narrowly drawn and represent a considered legislative judgment that a particular mode of expression has to give way to other compelling needs of society. As a corollary, the Court has altered its traditional rules of standing to permit [litigants] in the First Amendment area [to] challenge a statute not because their own rights of free expression are violated, but because [we assume] that the statute's very existence may cause others not before the court to refrain from constitutionally protected speech or expression.

[The consequence] is that any enforcement of [an overbroad statute] is totally forbidden until and unless a limiting construction or partial invalidation so narrows it as to remove the seeming threat or deterrence to constitutionally protected expression. Application of the overbreadth doctrine [is] strong medicine. It has been employed by the Court sparingly and only as a last resort. Facial overbreadth has not been invoked when a limiting construction has been or could be placed on the challenged statute. . . .

[Because] overbreadth adjudication is an exception to our traditional rules of practice . . . its function . . . attenuates as the otherwise unprotected behavior that it forbids the State to sanction moves from "pure speech" toward conduct and that conduct—even if expressive—falls within the scope of otherwise valid criminal [laws]. Although such laws, if too broadly worded, may deter protected speech to some unknown extent, there comes a point where that effect—at best a prediction—cannot, with confidence, justify invalidating a statute on its face and so prohibiting a State from enforcing the statute against conduct that is admittedly within its power to proscribe. To put the matter another way, particularly where conduct and not merely speech is involved, we believe that the overbreadth of a statute must not only be real, but substantial as well, judged in relation to the statute's plainly legitimate sweep. It is our view that §818 is not substantially overbroad and that whatever overbreadth may exist should be cured through case-by-case analysis of the fact situations.

[Section 818] is not a censorial statute, directed at particular groups or viewpoints, [but] seeks to regulate political activity in an even-handed and neutral manner. [Such] statutes have in the past been subject to a less exacting overbreadth scrutiny. Moreover, [section 818] regulates a substantial spectrum of conduct that is as manifestly subject to state regulation. . . . [Appellants assert that section 818 restricts] such allegedly protected activities as the wearing of political buttons or the use of bumper stickers. It may be that such restrictions are impermissible and that §818 may be susceptible of some other improper applications. But, as presently construed, [section 818] is not substantially overbroad and is not, therefore, unconstitutional on its face.

JUSTICE BRENNAN, joined by JUSTICES STEWART and MARSHALL, dissenting.

[The] Court makes no effort to define what it means by "substantial overbreadth."

NOTES

1. Substantial Overbreadth. How much overbreadth is substantial? Is it merely a matter of estimating the ratio between valid and invalid applications? If so, what proportion of invalid applications qualifies as substantial overbreadth? Or is the relevant inquiry more qualitative? If a statute is viewpoint-based, would a smaller proportion of invalid applications qualify as substantial overbreadth? The law at issue in *Broadrick* was content-based but viewpoint-neutral. Would a content-neutral statute be subject to even more relaxed overbreadth scrutiny, or does this apparent spectrum of overbreadth scrutiny merely reflect the fact that a content-neutral law likely has a broader range of valid applications than a content-based law, which in turn likely has more valid applications than a viewpoint-based law?

Note also the Court's view that overbreadth has less applicability to expressive conduct. How much overbreadth is necessary to void a conduct regulation that impedes symbolic expression? Would a law barring fires on public streets be overbroad, as the law would ban flag burning? Would a law banning the public burning of all flags for any reason be overbroad? A law banning the public burning of the American flag? A law banning the disrespectful public burning of the American flag?

2. Overbreadth Claims by Speakers of Protected Speech. May the person whose speech was constitutionally protected assert an overbreadth claim, or is such a person limited to an "as applied" challenge? The answer appears to depend on whether the law is capable of being narrowed by judicial construction to avoid overbreadth. If a court with authority to do so can prune the overbroad limbs from the statutory trunk by construction, the speaker of protected speech should be limited to an "as applied" challenge.

Schaumberg v. Citizens for a Better Environment, 444 U.S. 620 (1980). The Court voided an ordinance that banned public in-person solicitation of money by charitable organizations that did not use at least 75 percent of their contributions for their charitable purpose. Although there was no showing that the law was valid as applied to CBE, an overbreadth challenge by CBE was accepted by the Court. The ordinance had a content-based effect on speech, said the Court, as it would apply mostly to bar advocacy groups (who rely upon paid solicitors and thus typically exceed the 25 percent overhead limit). The justifications for the law (preventing fraud, crime, and "undue annoyance") were substantial but only "peripherally promoted" by the 25 percent overhead limit. Because the statute was founded "on a fundamentally mistaken premise that high solicitation costs are an accurate measure of fraud" there was no way the statute could be construed to narrow its scope to valid applications, and it was voided on its face. See also Secretary of State v. Joseph H. Munson, Inc., 467 U.S. 947 (1984).

Brockett v. Spokane Arcades, Inc., 472 U.S. 491 (1985). A Washington law prohibited obscenity, defined to include material that "incites lasciviousness or lust," a definition that swept within "obscenity" material that did not appeal to the "prurient interest" in sex. The Court voided the law only as applied to Spokane Arcades, even though Spokane Arcades had challenged the law as facially overbroad. The "normal rule [is] that partial, rather than facial invalidation, is the required course." The Washington law could be narrowed, and thus its overbroad branches trimmed to valid scope, by a proper judicial construction.

Consider the possibility that *Schaumberg* involved a law that was invalid in every application, much like a law barring "any speech critical of the government." If so, *Schaumberg* is not an overbreadth case at all, and *Spokane Arcades* states the general rule for true overbreadth cases.

3. Overbreadth After *Broadrick*. In Board of Airport Commissioners of Los Angeles v. Jews for Jesus, Inc., 482 U.S. 569 (1987), the Court held that a regulation adopted by the Los Angeles Airport Commission that forbade "First Amendment activities within the Central Terminal Area at Los Angeles International Airport" was overbroad and thus facially invalid. That is perhaps the easiest overbreadth judgment imaginable, given that the regulation "prohibits even talking or reading." A more difficult case was Houston v. Hill, 482 U.S. 451 (1987). A Houston ordinance made it a crime to "assault, strike, or in any manner oppose, molest, abuse, or interrupt any policeman in the execution of his duty." Hill was convicted of violating the ordinance by shouting "Why don't you pick on somebody your own size?" at a policeman questioning Hill's friend. The Court decided that the ordinance was substantially overbroad, and thus facially invalid, because the law granted "unfettered discretion" to the police "to arrest individuals for words or conduct that annoy or offend them." The risk of selective enforcement was high and the law implicitly gave to police officers the power to exercise a censorship function by arresting the speaker who dares criticize perceived police misconduct. By striking the law as overbroad the Court avoided deciding the much harder question of whether Hill's speech could constitutionally be punished.

4. The Scope and Limits of Overbreadth. Although overbreadth analysis has particular applicability to free speech, it is not confined to expression cases. The Court has recognized that overbreadth challenges may be made with respect to laws that inhibit the right to travel, Aptheker v. Secretary of State, 378 U.S. 500 (1964); infringe the right to an abortion, Stenberg v. Carhart, 530 U.S. 914, 938-946 (2000); and exceed Congress's power to enforce the substantive provisions of the Fourteenth Amendment, City of Boerne v. Flores, 521 U.S. 507, 532-535 (1997). In Sabri v. United States, 541 U.S. 600 (2004), the Court rejected a challenge to the facial validity of a federal statute that makes bribery of officials of state and local governments that receive at least $10,000 in federal funds a federal crime. Sabri asserted that the law was void because it failed to predicate criminal liability upon "proof of a connection between the federal funds and the alleged bribe." As the statute was applied, it was

> obvious that the acts charged against Sabri himself were well within the limits of legitimate congressional concern. [Sabri's] substantive constitutional claim [was] an overbreadth challenge; the most he could say was that the statute could not be enforced against him, because it could not be enforced against someone else whose behavior would be outside the scope of Congress's Article I authority to legislate. Facial challenges of this sort are especially to be discouraged. . . . [We] have recognized the validity of facial attacks alleging overbreadth (though not necessarily using that term) in relatively few settings, and, generally, on

the strength of specific reasons weighty enough to overcome our well-founded reticence.

Gonzales v. Carhart, 550 U.S. 124 (2007), cast doubt on the continued vitality of overbreadth challenges of abortion regulations. In United States v. Salerno, 481 U.S. 739, 745 (1987), the Court rejected a facial challenge to the federal Bail Reform Act, noting that for a facial challenge to succeed, "the challenger must establish that no set of circumstances exists under which the Act would be valid." Despite this seemingly absolute command, exceptions to this rule exist. The exceptions that warrant judicial receptivity to facial challenges are canvassed and discussed in Gans, Strategic Facial Challenges, 85 B.U. L. Rev. 1333 (2005). Professor David Gans suggests that facial challenges operate as a constitutional prophylaxis and are desirable in three broad circumstances: (1) whenever a chilling effect on constitutional rights would exist without entertaining a facial challenge; (2) when statutes confer excessive discretion upon officials, raising the risk that invalid exercises of discretion might go undetected in as-applied challenges; and (3) when statutes inflict severe stigmatic injury that cannot be readily eradicated by the glacial pace of as-applied challenges.

2.   Vagueness

A law is unconstitutionally vague if persons "of common intelligence must necessarily guess at its meaning and differ as to its application." Connally v. General Construction Co., 269 U.S. 385, 391 (1926). If a law does not provide "sufficiently definite warning as to the proscribed conduct when measured by common understanding and practices," it is unconstitutionally vague and its enforcement is a denial of due process. Jordan v. De George, 341 U.S. 223 (1951). In Smith v. Goguen, 415 U.S. 566 (1974), the Court invalidated as vague a Massachusetts law that made it a crime to treat the U.S. flag contemptuously in public. The ban did not "draw reasonably clear lines between the kinds of nonceremonial treatment that are criminal and those that are not." Moreover, the Court stated that when statutes impinge upon expression, they will be held to "a greater degree of specificity" in order to avoid their invalidation as vague.

Unconstitutionally vague laws burdening expression are usually, but not invariably, facially invalid because such laws chill speech and permit covert viewpoint-based enforcement. But vagueness and overbreadth are not congruent. A statute may be precise but overbroad. In Shelton v. Tucker, 364 U.S. 479 (1960), the Court voided as overbroad an Arkansas requirement that public school teachers declare annually every organization to which the teacher either belonged or contributed. Though precise, the law had a sweeping and chilling effect on schoolteachers' association rights protected by the free expression guarantee. Conversely, a statute may be vague but not overbroad. A law that prohibits "any public speech that is not protected by the federal or state constitutions" is not overbroad—it does not prohibit any protected speech—but may be vague. The ordinary person must guess about the boundaries of constitutionally protected speech.

Typically, however, vagueness and overbreadth are linked. In Coates v. Cincinnati, 402 U.S. 611 (1971), the Court struck down as facially invalid a Cincinnati ordinance that made it unlawful for three or more persons to assemble on public sidewalks and "conduct themselves in a manner annoying to persons passing by." The law was "unconstitutionally vague" because what constitutes "annoyance" is an inherently subjective and variable standard. It was overbroad because, to paraphrase Justice Harlan in *Cohen*, one person's annoyance is another's delight, and the First Amendment prohibits muzzling expression merely because it might offend a passerby.

Note that if a precise overbroad statute is not invalidated on its face but only as applied, it may become vague by reason of the limiting judicial construction. Consider a law that bans all outdoor speaking. While it is not vague, it is terribly overbroad. If courts invalidate it only as it is applied to protected speech, the law might become vague because it is in effect altered by judicial construction into a law that bans all outdoor speaking "that is not protected by the Constitution." Does this suggest that the rule of Brockett v. Spokane Arcades should be subject to an exception to address this problem?

3. Prior Restraints

Prior restraints of speech are among the most disfavored of speech restrictions and are presumptively void. Stifling speech before it occurs may be void even though the speech suppressed might be subject to criminal punishment or civil liability after the fact. But if a prior restraint suppresses only speech that can be validly punished after the fact, why should this prophylactic means of regulating speech be presumptively void?

A prior restraint is an administrative or judicial order that prohibits speech before it occurs on the basis of the speech's content. A content-neutral ban on speech before the fact is permissible if its purpose and effect are not to suppress ideas but to advance legitimate state interests unrelated to the suppression of speech. In Madsen v. Women's Health Center, Inc., 512 U.S. 753 (1994), the Court held that a Florida court's injunction barring anti-abortion protesters from intruding upon a 36-foot zone extending outward from the property line of an abortion clinic into a public street and sidewalk was not a prior restraint. The injunction was content-neutral and was not issued to control expression but to control "prior unlawful conduct" on the part of the defendants. Had the injunction been issued "because of the content of petitioners' expression," it would have been treated as a prior restraint.

Punishments after the fact of speech are not prior restraints. In Alexander v. United States, 509 U.S. 544 (1993), Alexander was convicted of violating federal obscenity and racketeering laws, with the result that his entire business (consisting of more than a dozen stores and theaters selling sexually explicit but non-obscene material) was forfeited. The Court upheld the validity of the forfeiture, rejecting Alexander's contention that the seizure of the non-obscene books and films was a prior restraint on speech. The Court reasoned that the forfeiture did not forbid Alexander "from engaging in any expressive activities in the future, nor does it require him to obtain prior approval for any expressive activities."

There are two principal types of prior restraints: licensing and injunctions. Licensing of speech before its utterance or publication raises the concern that government officials can exercise licensing authority in a manner that discriminates on the basis of content or viewpoint. Injunctions restraining speech from occurring at all raise the question of whether it is better "to punish the few who abuse rights of speech *after* they break the law than to throttle [them] beforehand. It is always difficult to know in advance what an individual will say." Southeastern Promotions, Ltd. v. Conrad, 420 U.S. 546, 559 (1975).

a.   Licensing

Licensing requires speakers to obtain the permission of the government before they speak. English law prior to 1695 required publishers of written materials to obtain the permission of the Crown and the Church before publishing. One of the central purposes of the First Amendment was to reject this legacy of suppression and censorship. Licensing can be coupled with censorship but does not necessarily involve it. The validity of licensing schemes depends upon the purpose for requiring speakers to obtain a pre-speech permit to speak and upon the criteria established to determine when licenses will be issued or denied. If the criteria and procedures employed allow licenses for protected speech and deny them only for unprotected speech, much of the reason for disfavoring prior restraints is eliminated. When there are no criteria for issuance of a required license the danger to free speech is much higher.

Standardless licensing.   In Lovell v. Griffin, 303 U.S. 444 (1938), the Court overturned a conviction for distributing religious tracts in violation of a city ordinance that prohibited anyone from distributing "literature of any kind" within the city "without first obtaining written permission from the City Manager." The Court found that "the ordinance [was] void on its face" because of the broad discretion vested in the City Manager to curb speech of any kind and for any reason. The ordinance struck "at the very foundation of the freedom of the press by subjecting it to license and censorship." See also Kunz v. New York, 340 U.S. 290 (1951), in which the Court struck down a New York City ordinance that prohibited religious street meetings without a permit and also banned any such meetings that involved "ridicule [of] religious belief" because the ordinance gives "an administrative official discretionary power to control in advance the right of citizens to speak on religious matters on the [public streets]. As such, the ordinance is clearly invalid as a prior restraint. . . .”

The Court elaborated in City of Lakewood v. Plain Dealer Publishing Co., 486 U.S. 750 (1988). A city ordinance prohibited unlicensed news racks on city sidewalks and gave the mayor discretion to grant news rack licenses on terms and conditions that he “deemed necessary and reasonable.” The Court found the ordinance facially invalid and explained why standardless licensing is always facially invalid. The “licensor’s unfettered discretion [coerces] parties into censoring their own speech,” and self-censorship cannot be challenged as applied because “it derives from the individual’s own actions, not an abuse of government power.” While governments may use “licensing procedures for conduct commonly associated with expression . . . the Constitution requires that [a government] establish neutral criteria to insure that [its] licensing decision is not based on the content or viewpoint of the speech.” Thus, laws “of general application that are not aimed at [expression] carry with them little danger of censorship. [A] law requiring building permits is rarely effective as a means of censorship.”

A three-justice dissent argued that facial challenges should be entertained only where the license scheme forecloses protected speech altogether:

> [*Lovell*] would be applicable [if the City] sought to license the distribution of all newspapers in the City, or if it required licenses for all stores which sold newspapers. . . . But [the City] has sought to license only the placement of newsracks [on] City property, [and] the Plain Dealer has [no] constitutional right to distribute its papers by means of [news racks] affixed to the public sidewalks. [Where] an activity that could be forbidden altogether (without running afoul of the First Amendment) is subjected to [a] licensing requirement, the mere presence of administrative discretion will not render it invalid per se. In such a case . . . the [*Lovell*] doctrine does not apply.

The Court applied *Lakewood* in Forsyth County v. The Nationalist Movement, 505 U.S. 123 (1992), where it found facially invalid a Forsyth County, Georgia, ordinance that gave a county administrator discretion to base the fee for a parade permit on the expected expense of preserving the public peace in connection with the parade or demonstration. The administrator’s discretion was so great that it was predictable that the size of the permit fee might well turn on the “listeners’ reaction to speech,” which “is not a content-neutral basis for regulation.” The Court stated that speech “cannot be financially burdened, any more than it can be punished or banned, simply because it might offend a hostile mob.”

Licensing with standards. Licensing schemes that contain clear standards limiting the denial of licenses to circumstances where the speech could validly be punished after the fact are facially valid but remain susceptible to constitutional challenges to the way they are applied. In Cox v. New Hampshire, 312 U.S. 569 (1941), the Court upheld the convictions of people who marched in a religious parade without first obtaining a permit. Under New Hampshire law, a permit could be conditioned only for "considerations of time, place and manner so as to conserve the public convenience." The Court concluded that because permits could be denied only when the speech could be constitutionally regulated or prohibited, there was no facial infirmity to the licensing scheme. "[T]he licensing board was not vested with arbitrary power or an unfettered discretion."

Licensing schemes designed to prevent publication of obscene materials are a recurring issue. Although obscenity is not a protected category of speech, there is a chronic problem in defining "obscenity" with sufficient precision to avoid overbreadth or vagueness problems. Licensing schemes to prevent obscenity must confront the same definitional problem and are valid only if they incorporate certain procedural safeguards. In Freedman v. Maryland, 380 U.S. 51 (1965), in the course of striking down a Maryland statute designed to prevent exhibition of obscene films, the Court identified the "procedural safeguards" necessary to "avoid constitutional infirmit[ies]" with a licensing scheme: "[The] burden of proving that the film is unprotected expression must rest on the [censor]. While the State may require advance submission of all films, [only a] judicial determination in an adversary proceeding [suffices] to impose a valid final restraint." The government must, "within a specified brief period, either issue a license or go to court to restrain showing the film." A licensing "procedure must also assure a prompt final judicial decision, to minimize the deterrent effect of an interim and possibly erroneous denial of a license."

Content-neutral licensing. In Thomas v. Chicago Park District, 534 U.S. 316 (2002), a unanimous Court held that the *Freedman* standards were not applicable to a content-neutral permit ordinance directed "to *all* activity conducted in a public park [in order] to coordinate multiple uses of limited space; to assure preservation of the park facilities; to prevent uses that are dangerous, unlawful, or impermissible under the Park District's rules; and to assure financial accountability for damage caused by the event. . . . Regulations of the use of a public forum that ensure the safety and convenience of the people [do] not raise the censorship concerns that prompted us to impose the extraordinary procedural safeguards on the film licensing process in *Freedman*."

The Court in *Thomas* reemphasized the principle that content-neutral licensing may be done only with clear and definite standards: "We have . . . required that a time, place, and manner regulation contain adequate standards to guide the official's decision and render it subject to effective judicial review."

b. Injunctions

An injunction of speech before it occurs is a powerful weapon. Only the most compelling reasons will support the issuance of an injunction restraining speech in advance.

Near v. Minnesota
283 U.S. 697 (1931)

CHIEF JUSTICE HUGHES delivered the opinion of the Court.

[Minnesota law] provides for the abatement, as a public nuisance, of a "malicious, scandalous and defamatory newspaper, magazine or other periodical." [A Minneapolis prosecutor invoked the law] to enjoin the publication [of] "The Saturday Press," [which had published articles charging] in substance that a Jewish gangster was in control of gambling, bootlegging and racketeering in Minneapolis, and that law enforcing officers and agencies were not energetically performing their duties. [There] is no question but that the articles made serious accusations against the public officers named and others in connection with the prevalence of crimes and the failure to expose and punish them. [After trial, the state court judge ordered that the Press be] "abated" and he perpetually enjoined the defendants "from producing, editing, publishing, circulating, having in their possession, selling or giving away any publication whatsoever which is a malicious, scandalous or defamatory newspaper" [and] also "from further conducting [The] Saturday Press [under that] or any other name." [The Minnesota Supreme Court affirmed.]

[The] object of the statute is not punishment [but] suppression of the offending newspaper. [The] operation and effect of the statute [is] that public authorities may bring the owner or publisher of a newspaper . . . before a judge upon a charge [of] publishing scandalous [allegations] against public officers of official dereliction[, and] unless the owner or publisher is able [to prove] that the charges are true and are published with good motives and for justifiable ends, his newspaper . . . is suppressed and further publication is made punishable as a contempt. This is of the essence of censorship.

The question is whether [such] a statute [is] consistent with the conception of the liberty of the press as historically conceived and guaranteed. [It] has been generally, if not universally, considered that it is the chief purpose of the guaranty to prevent previous restraints upon publication. . . . [The] protection even as to previous restraint is not absolutely unlimited. But the limitation has been recognized only in exceptional [cases]. No one would question but that a government might prevent actual obstruction to its recruiting service or the publication of the sailing dates of transports or the number and location of troops. On similar grounds, the primary requirements of decency may be enforced against obscene publications. The security of the community life may be protected against incitements to acts of violence and the overthrow by force of orderly government. [These] limitations are not applicable here. . . .

[Reckless] assaults upon public men, and efforts to bring obloquy upon those who are endeavoring faithfully to discharge official duties, exert a baleful influence and deserve the severest condemnation in public opinion. [But] the fact that the liberty of the press may be abused by miscreant purveyors of scandal does not make any the less necessary the immunity of the press from previous restraint in dealing with official misconduct. Subsequent punishment for such abuses as may exist is the appropriate remedy, consistent with constitutional privilege.

[The] statute [infringes] the liberty of the press. [Judgment] reversed.

NOTES

1. The Vice of Injunctions. Content-based injunctions of speech bear a heavy presumption of invalidity. Unless the government can prove that the restraint is no broader than is absolutely necessary to achieve a state objective of the very first magnitude, the injunction is invalid. Yet, unlike licensing, injunctions do not present the problem of stifling speech before a court can determine whether the speech is protected. Assuming that a court has reached a preliminary determination that the speech in question may be punished after the fact, what harm is there in preventing its occurrence?

Chilled speech. Injunctions chill speech, but if the only speech deterred is speech that may validly be punished after the fact, why should we care? Is it because injunctions may not be this precise and might proscribe some protected speech in order to enjoin the unprotected speech? Or is it because speakers will not utter constitutionally protected speech that does not violate a precisely drawn injunction out of fear of violating the injunction?

The collateral bar rule. The collateral bar rule has a strongly intimidating effect in providing that a person who violates an injunction may be punished for the violation even if it turns out later that the injunction was invalid. The rule is generally applicable to all injunctions and has been upheld by the Court as applied to injunctions of speech. Walker v. Birmingham, 388 U.S. 307 (1967). Even if the injunction is in error, protected speech may not be uttered without triggering the collateral penalty of punishment for contempt of the injunction.

2. Interests Adequate to Justify Prior Restraint. What sort of showing of necessity suffices to justify an injunction of speech based on its content? National security? Imminent catastrophic injury to the people?

National security. The issue of national security produced a variety of opinions in New York Times v. United States (*The Pentagon Papers*), 403 U.S. 713 (1971). Over several days in June 1971, the New York Times and the Washington Post published excerpts from a secret Defense Department study of the Vietnam War. The study, which quickly became known as the "Pentagon Papers," reviewed in great detail military operations and secret diplomatic initiatives concerning the Vietnam War. The study was given to the newspapers by a former Pentagon official who had illegally copied and disclosed it. On June 15, the federal government filed suit and obtained a temporary restraining order preventing further publication of the papers. Eleven days later, the Supreme Court heard argument, and it issued its decision on June 30, 1971. The Court ruled 6 to 3 in a per curiam opinion that the government had not overcome the "heavy presumption against [the] constitutional validity" of a prior restraint upon expression.

In their individual opinions the justices could not agree on when national security reasons justified a prior restraint. Justice Black, joined by Justice Douglas, thought that national security reasons were never sufficient to justify a prior restraint of the press. Justice Douglas, joined by Justice Black, thought that in the absence of statutory authority to suppress publication of military and diplomatic secrets the government lacked any "inherent power" to enjoin speech in the name of national security. Justice Brennan thought a prior restraint predicated upon national security concerns was justified only during war or equivalent emergency, and then only if the government has "clearly" proven that "publication must inevitably, directly, and immediately cause the occurrence of an event kindred to imperiling the safety of a transport already at sea." Justice Stewart, joined by Justice White, thought that in the absence of specific statutes prohibiting disclosure of "government secrets," a prior restraint could be founded only on proof that disclosure of such secrets would "surely result in direct, immediate, and irreparable damage to our Nation or its people." Justice White, joined by Justice Stewart, thought that Congress might have power to authorize injunctions preventing disclosures of government secrets that would produce "substantial damage to public interests," but in the absence of such statutory authority, the executive lacked any power to enjoin publication of such materials. Justice Marshall thought that because Congress had specifically not given the President the power to enjoin speech, it would violate separation of powers to issue such an injunction.

Justice Harlan, joined by Chief Justice Burger and Justice Blackmun, dissented. Justice Harlan argued that so long as the material the government seeks to suppress is "within the proper compass of the President's foreign relations power" and "the determination that disclosure would irreparably impair the national security" is made at the highest levels of the executive branch, it was improper for the judiciary to "redetermine for itself the probable impact of disclosure on the national security." Justice Blackmun and Chief Justice Burger were unwilling to reach the merits. Justice Blackmun urged remand of the case for a fuller development of the standards by which to evaluate the propriety of a prior restraint. Chief Justice Burger decried the "unseemly haste" with which the issue had been hustled before the Court, declaring that "we literally do not know what we are acting on."

Catastrophic injury. In United States v. Progressive, Inc., 467 F. Supp. 990 (W.D. Wis. 1979), a district judge, relying in part on provisions of the Atomic Energy Act authorizing injunctions to prevent communication of restricted atomic information where disclosure would "injure the United States," enjoined the Progressive magazine from publishing an article disclosing the technical details of manufacture of a thermonuclear weapon. The district judge contended that the Pentagon Papers study was different because the information there was historical, there was inadequate proof of the damage to national security, and there was no statutory authority for issuance of an injunction. The proceedings were abandoned before appeal because the same information was independently published by nonparties to the *Progressive* case.

Queries: Was the district judge correct? Is publication of the "recipe" for a nuclear bomb akin to *Near*'s reference to disclosure of location of army units or troopship sailings? Is the catastrophic nature of a nuclear detonation a sufficiently large risk to warrant a prior restraint? What about publication of the method of constructing the type of bomb Timothy McVeigh used to destroy the Oklahoma City federal building or that the Tsarnaev brothers used to kill and maim people at the 2013 Boston Marathon? Or publication of an article detailing various methods of poisoning food?

3. Injunctive Restraints in the Interest of a Fair Trial.   May a trial judge forbid publication of details of an ongoing criminal prosecution in order to protect the criminal defendant's right to a fair trial? In Nebraska Press Association v. Stuart, 427 U.S. 539 (1976), the Court unanimously held unconstitutional a Nebraska trial judge's order restraining the press from reporting confessions, incriminating statements, or other facts "strongly implicative" of a man accused of mass murder in a small Nebraska town. In dicta, the Court suggested that three factors were useful in helping a trial judge determine when the harm attendant to publicity was so probable as to justify restraints on the press: (1) the likelihood of an unfair trial, (2) the lack of adequate alternatives, and (3) the probable efficacy of the prior restraint in securing a fair trial. The Court conceded that the trial judge "was justified in concluding [that] intense and pervasive pre-trial publicity [might] impair the defendant's right to a fair trial," but suggested that a prior restraint was permissible only if there were no other alternatives. Among the alternatives mentioned by the Court were change of venue, trial postponement, juror sequestration, and gag orders on selected trial participants. Finally, if a prior restraint is not likely to make the difference in allowing the accused a fair trial, the restraint is surely unjustified. In *Stuart*, the Court thought that the prior restraint would not likely have much effect on information that was already well known in the Nebraska town of 850 people where the trial would be held and from whom the jury would be selected.

F.   EXPRESSION RIGHTS IMPLICIT IN THE FREE SPEECH GUARANTEE

The First Amendment guarantees "free speech," but the Court has read that guarantee to include more general rights of expression: the right to associate with others to express ideas, the corollary right *not* to associate, the related right *not* to speak, and the right to fund political speech through the expenditure of money.

1. Freedom of Association

People associate for different reasons and in different contexts. The First Amendment's freedom of association extends only to associational choices that directly express ideas or are for the purpose of expressing ideas.

NAACP v. Alabama, 357 U.S. 449 (1958). The Court held that Alabama could not compel the NAACP to disclose its membership list because forced disclosure would produce "a substantial restraint upon the exercise by [NAACP] members of their right to freedom of association," due to "economic reprisal, loss of employment, threat of physical coercion, and other manifestations of public hostility" that "may induce members to withdraw from the Association and dissuade others from joining it because of fear of exposure of their beliefs shown through their associations and of the consequences of this exposure." The Court thought

> [it was] beyond debate that freedom to engage in association for the advancement of beliefs and ideas is an inseparable aspect [of] freedom of speech. [It] is immaterial whether the beliefs sought to be advanced by association pertain to political, economic, religious or cultural matters, and state action which may have the effect of curtailing the freedom to associate is subject to the closest scrutiny.

Alabama's interest in obtaining the membership list—"to determine whether [the NAACP] was conducting intrastate business in violation of the Alabama foreign corporation registration statute"—was insufficiently compelling, and production of the membership list had no "substantial bearing" on the vindication of that interest.

Buckley v. Valeo, 424 U.S. 1 (1976). The Federal Election Campaign Act, enacted in 1974 to curb perceived abuses of the electoral process, required every political candidate or committee to maintain records of contributors and to disclose to federal regulators the name, address, and, in the case of larger contributors, the occupation of each contributor. The Court treated the contribution and expenditure of money for political purposes as a form of protected association, but upheld these requirements: "[S]ignificant encroachments on First Amendment rights of the sort that compelled disclosure imposes" must be justified by "exacting scrutiny" that involves proof of a "'substantial relation' between the governmental interest [asserted] and the information required to be disclosed" and more than a "mere showing of some legitimate governmental interest" in forced disclosure. The Court identified three government interests that were "sufficiently important" to meet this standard: (1) "disclosure provides the electorate with information [about the source of campaign funding] in order to aid the voters in [their choice], (2) disclosure deter[s] actual corruption and avoid[s] the appearance of corruption by [public exposure], and (3) disclosure is an essential means of gathering the data necessary to detect violations of the contribution [limits]," which the Court upheld. Did Buckley v. Valeo alter the standard of review established by NAACP v. Alabama?

After California voters amended the state constitution to prohibit same-sex marriage, the constitutional validity of the amendment was challenged in federal court, and the challengers sought discovery of internal campaign strategy memoranda of the proponents. In Perry v. Schwarzenegger, 591 F.3d 1147 (9th Cir. 2010), the Ninth Circuit ruled that such disclosure, including the identity of campaign strategists and volunteers, would chill protected political association. There was no compelling interest in disclosure. The Supreme Court denied certiorari. Hollingsworth v. Perry, 559 U.S. 1118 (2010).

Consider two Supreme Court precedents that bear on this issue. In EEOC v. University of Pennsylvania, 493 U.S. 182 (1990), the Court rejected a claim of academic freedom to shield from discovery peer review materials in a tenure denial case. In Herbert v. Lando, 441 U.S. 153 (1979), the Court denied a claim that the free press guarantee exempted discovery of editorial communications in a defamation case. Are these cases distinguishable from *Perry* on the grounds that neither involved an inquiry into the effect of disclosure on *political* association?

Query: Suppose a group of friends play poker together every week under an agreement by which the winners donate their winnings to their favorite charity. Are they associating for expressive purposes? Could the government ban such poker games without violating the First Amendment?

≡≡≡ **Roberts v. United States Jaycees**
≡≡≡ *468 U.S. 609 (1984)*

JUSTICE BRENNAN delivered the opinion of the Court.

This case requires us to address a conflict between [Minnesota's] efforts to eliminate gender-based discrimination against its citizens and the constitutional freedom of association asserted by members of a private organization. [The] Jaycees, a national nonprofit membership corporation devoted to promoting "personal development," "achievement," and "intelligent participation by young men in the affairs of their community," limits regular membership to men between 18 and 35. The Minnesota Human Rights Act prohibits discrimination in any "place of public accommodation" because of sex. [T]he Minnesota Human Rights Department concluded that the Jaycees is a "place of public accommodation" and that it had engaged in an unfair discriminatory practice by excluding women from regular membership. [T]he "public accommodation" status of the Jaycees was confirmed by the Minnesota Supreme Court. The Jaycees brought suit in federal court and, on appeal, the Court of Appeals concluded that, by requiring the United States Jaycees to admit women as full voting members, the Minnesota Human Rights Act violates the [freedom of association] rights of the organization's members. We [now] reverse.

[Our] decisions have referred to constitutionally protected "freedom of association" in two distinct senses. In one line of decisions, the Court has concluded that choices to enter into and maintain certain intimate human relationships must be secured against undue intrusion by the State because [it is a fundamental] personal liberty. In another set of decisions, the Court has recognized a right to associate for the purpose of engaging in those activities protected by the First Amendment—speech, assembly, petition for the redress of grievances, and the exercise of religion. The Constitution guarantees freedom of association of this kind as an indispensable means of preserving other individual liberties.

[The] nature and degree of constitutional protection afforded freedom of association may vary depending on the extent to which one or the other aspect of the constitutionally protected liberty is at stake in a given case. We therefore [consider] separately the effect of applying the Minnesota statute to the Jaycees on what could be called its members' freedom of intimate association and their freedom of expressive association.

The Court has long recognized that, because the Bill of Rights is designed to secure individual liberty, it must afford the formation and preservation of certain kinds of highly personal relationships a substantial measure of sanctuary from unjustified interference by the State. [*Pierce, Meyer, Griswold, Zablocki, Moore.*] The constitutional shelter afforded such relationships reflects the realization that individuals draw much of their emotional enrichment from close ties with others. Protecting these relationships from unwarranted state interference therefore safeguards the ability independently to define one's identity that is central to any concept of liberty. [These] personal affiliations [are] distinguished by such attributes as relative smallness, a high degree of selectivity in decisions to begin and maintain the affiliation, and seclusion from others in critical aspects of the relationship. [Conversely], an association lacking these qualities—such as a large business enterprise—seems remote from the concerns giving rise to this constitutional protection. Accordingly, the Constitution undoubtedly imposes constraints on the State's power to control the selection of one's spouse that would not apply to regulations affecting the choice of one's fellow employees. Between these poles [lies] a broad range of human relationships that may make greater or lesser claims to constitutional protection from particular incursions by the State. [In this case, several] features of the Jaycees clearly [place it] outside of the category of relationships worthy of this kind of constitutional protection. [Local] chapters of the Jaycees are large and basically unselective groups [and] much of the activity central to the formation and maintenance of the association involves the participation of strangers to that relationship. [We] turn therefore to consider the extent to which application of the Minnesota statute to compel the Jaycees to accept women infringes the group's freedom of expressive association.

An individual's freedom to speak, to worship, and to petition the government for the redress of grievances could not be vigorously protected from interference by the State unless a correlative freedom to engage in group effort toward those ends were not also guaranteed. Consequently, we have long understood as implicit in the right to engage in activities protected by the First Amendment a corresponding right to associate with others in pursuit of a wide variety of political, social, economic, educational, religious, and cultural ends. In view of the various protected activities in which the Jaycees engages, that right is plainly implicated in this case.

Government actions that may unconstitutionally infringe upon this freedom can take a number of forms. Among other things, government may seek to impose penalties or withhold benefits from individuals because of their membership in a disfavored group; it may attempt to require disclosure of the fact of membership in a group seeking anonymity; and it may try to interfere with the internal organization or affairs of the group. By requiring the Jaycees to admit women as full voting members, the Minnesota Act works an infringement of the last type. There can be no clearer example of an intrusion into the internal structure or affairs of an association than a regulation that forces the group to accept members it does not desire. Such a regulation may impair the ability of the original members to express only those views that brought them together. Freedom of association therefore plainly presupposes a freedom not to associate.

The right to associate for expressive purposes is not, however, absolute. Infringements on that right may be justified by regulations adopted to serve compelling state interests, unrelated to the suppression of ideas, that cannot be achieved through means significantly less restrictive of associational freedoms. We are persuaded that Minnesota's compelling interest in eradicating discrimination against its female citizens justifies the impact that application of the statute to the Jaycees may have on the male members' associational freedoms. On its face [and as applied here], the Minnesota Act does not aim at the suppression of speech, does not distinguish between prohibited and permitted activity on the basis of viewpoint, and does not license enforcement authorities to administer the statute on the basis of such constitutionally impermissible criteria. [Instead], the Act reflects [Minnesota's] strong historical commitment to eliminating discrimination and assuring its citizens equal access to publicly available goods and services. . . . [In] applying the Act to the Jaycees, the State has advanced those interests through the least restrictive means of achieving its ends. Indeed, the Jaycees has failed to demonstrate that the Act imposes any serious burdens on the male members' freedom of expressive association. To be sure, [a] "not insubstantial part" of the Jaycees' activities constitutes protected expression on political, economic, cultural, and social affairs. [There] is, however, no basis in the record for concluding that admission of women as full voting members will impede the organization's ability to engage in these protected activities or to disseminate its preferred views. The Act requires no change in the Jaycees' creed of promoting the interests of young men, and it imposes no restrictions on the organization's ability to exclude individuals with ideologies or philosophies different from those of its existing members. Moreover, the Jaycees already invites women to share the group's views and philosophy and to participate in much of its training and community activities. Accordingly, any claim that admission of women as full voting members will impair a symbolic message conveyed by the very fact that women are not permitted to vote is attenuated at best. [In] any event, even if enforcement of the Act causes some incidental abridgment of the Jaycees' protected speech, that effect is no greater than is necessary to accomplish the State's legitimate purposes. [Acts] of invidious discrimination in the distribution of publicly available goods [cause] unique evils that government has a compelling interest to prevent—wholly apart from the point of view such conduct may transmit. [Like] violence or other types of potentially expressive activities that produce special harms distinct from their communicative impact, such practices are entitled to no constitutional protection.

Justice O'Connor, concurring in part and concurring in the judgment.

I agree with the Court that application of the Minnesota law to the Jaycees does not contravene the First Amendment, but I reach that conclusion for [different] reasons. [The Court uses] a test that I find both overprotective of activities undeserving of constitutional shelter and underprotective of important First Amendment concerns. The Court declares that the Jaycees' right of association depends on the organization's making a "substantial" showing that the admission of unwelcome members "will change the message communicated by the group's speech." [Focus] on such a connection is objectionable. [Whether] an association is or is not constitutionally protected in the selection of its membership should not depend on what the association says or why its members say it. [Moreover, the] Court entirely neglects to establish at the threshold that the Jaycees is an association whose activities or purposes should engage the strong protections that the First Amendment extends to expressive associations.

On the one hand, an association engaged exclusively in protected expression enjoys First Amendment protection of both the content of its message and the choice of its members. [Protection] of the association's right to define its membership derives from the recognition that the formation of an expressive association is the creation of a voice, and the selection of members is the definition of that voice. [On] the other hand, there is only minimal constitutional protection of the freedom of commercial association. [The] Constitution does not guarantee a right to choose employees, customers, suppliers, or those with whom one engages in simple commercial transactions, without restraint from the State. A shopkeeper has no constitutional right to deal only with persons of one sex. . . . [In] my view, an association should be characterized as commercial, and therefore subject to rationally related state regulation of its membership and other associational activities, when, and only when, the association's activities are not predominantly of the type protected by the First Amendment. It is only when the association is predominantly engaged in protected expression that state regulation of its membership will necessarily affect, change, dilute, or silence one collective voice that would otherwise be heard. An association must choose its market. Once it enters the marketplace of commerce in any substantial degree it loses the complete control over its membership that it would otherwise enjoy if it confined its affairs to the marketplace of ideas.

[Minnesota's] attempt to regulate the membership of the Jaycees chapters operating in that State presents a relatively easy case for application of the expressive-commercial dichotomy. [The Jaycees is], first and foremost, an organization that, at both the national and local levels, promotes and practices the art of solicitation and management. [The] Jaycees itself refers to its members as customers and membership as a product it is selling. [Minnesota] has a legitimate interest in ensuring nondiscriminatory access to the commercial opportunity presented by membership in the Jaycees. The members of the Jaycees may not claim constitutional immunity from Minnesota's antidiscrimination law by seeking to exercise their First Amendment rights through this commercial organization.

NOTES

1. **The Scope of *Roberts*.** In Board of Directors of Rotary International v. Rotary Club of Duarte, 481 U.S. 537 (1987), the Court upheld the application of California's Unruh Act, which forbids discrimination on the basis of sex, to the Rotary Club. The Rotary Club is devoted to civic and humanitarian goals, and insists that local clubs admit only men as members, but insures that each local club includes a representative of every business, professional, and institutional activity in the community. In New York State Club Association v. City of New York, 487 U.S. 1 (1988), the Court unanimously upheld a New York City ordinance that barred discrimination by race, sex, or creed in any club with more than 400 members that provides regular meal service and regularly receives payment from non-members for the furtherance of trade or business activities. Could a city or state validly enact a law requiring all private clubs to select members without discrimination on the basis of race, sex, or creed?

Is Justice O'Connor's distinction between expressive associations and commercial associations viable, given the increasing protection the Court provides to commercial speech?

2. **The Future of *Roberts*: Boy Scouts of America v. Dale.** After the Boy Scouts revoked James Dale's membership as an assistant scoutmaster, the New Jersey Supreme Court concluded that the Boy Scouts had violated New Jersey law prohibiting discrimination on the basis of sexual orientation in places of public accommodations. In Boy Scouts of America v. Dale, 530 U.S. 640 (2000), the Supreme Court, 5-4, reversed, finding that New Jersey had unjustifiably infringed the Boy Scouts' right of expressive association. The majority ruled that an association is "expressive" whenever it *engages* in expressive activity, not just when the association is for the *purpose* of expressing a particular message. The majority concluded that the Boy Scouts' practice of using adults to inculcate its value system to youngsters was expressive activity sufficient to make the Scouts an expressive association. The expressive association right is infringed, said the majority, whenever the state's forcible inclusion of an unwanted member significantly affects the group's ability to advocate its viewpoints. The Boy Scouts asserted that homosexuality was inconsistent with its

inculcation of moral purity (the Scouts teach their members to be "morally straight" and "clean"), and the Court accepted the idea that forced inclusion of a homosexual member would significantly undercut the Scouts' ability to convey its message that homosexuality and moral purity were incompatible.

The Court accepted the Scouts' assertion as to its creed at face value, applied strict scrutiny because "New Jersey's public accommodations law directly and immediately affects associational rights," and found that, although New Jersey had a compelling interest in eliminating discrimination against sexual minorities, the method of accomplishing that objective—forcible inclusion of gay Scouts and scoutmasters—was, unlike the situation in *Roberts,* a severe burden on the Scouts' freedom of expressive association. Four dissenters argued that the moral values the Scouts seek to inculcate did not include antipathy to homosexuals, and that thus the New Jersey law did not pose any significant obstacle to the Scouts' ability to inculcate their proclaimed moral values.

> [N]either one of these principles—"morally straight" and "clean"—says the slightest thing about homosexuality. . . . We have [rejected] assertions of this right by expressive organizations with discriminatory membership policies, such as private schools. [In] Runyon v. McCrary, 427 U.S. 160 (1976), [we] "assumed that parents have a First Amendment right to send their children to educational institutions that promote the belief that racial segregation is desirable, and that the children have an equal right to attend such institutions. But it does not follow that the *practice* of excluding racial minorities from such institutions is also protected by the same principle."
>
> [It] is not sufficient merely to articulate some connection between the group's expressive activities and its exclusionary policy. [In *Roberts*], we asked whether . . . the admission of women "imposed any *serious burdens*" on the group's "collective effort on behalf of [its] *shared goals.*" . . . The [Scouts have], at most, simply adopted an exclusionary membership policy and [have] no shared goal of disapproving of homosexuality. [The Scouts'] mission statement and federal charter say nothing on the matter; its official membership policy is silent; its Scout Oath and Law—and accompanying definitions—are devoid of any view on the topic; its guidance for Scouts and Scoutmasters on sexuality declare that such matters are "not construed to be Scouting's proper area," but are the province of a Scout's parents and pastor; and [the Scouts'] posture respecting religion tolerates a wide variety of views on the issue of homosexuality. . . . [The Scouts] are simply silent on homosexuality. There is no shared goal or collective effort to foster a belief about homosexuality at all—let alone one that is significantly burdened by admitting homosexuals.

The dissent did not mention that the Boy Scout Handbook contains a section entitled "Sexual Responsibility," that discusses a Scout's responsibilities to the girls and women with whom he has relationships, including sexual relationships. What is the significance of the fact that the Handbook deals with sexuality in an exclusively heterosexual manner?

Rumsfeld v. Forum for Academic and Institutional Rights, Inc.
547 U.S. 47 (2006)

CHIEF JUSTICE ROBERTS delivered the opinion of the Court.

When law schools began restricting the access of military recruiters to their students because of disagreement with the Government's policy on homosexuals in the military, Congress responded by enacting the Solomon Amendment, [which] specifies that if any part of an institution of higher education denies military recruiters access equal to that provided other recruiters, the entire institution would lose certain federal funds. The law schools [alleged] that the Solomon Amendment infringed their First Amendment freedoms of speech and association . . . .

I. Respondent Forum for Academic and Institutional Rights, Inc. (FAIR), is an association of law schools and law faculties [that] have adopted policies expressing their opposition to discrimination based on . . . sexual orientation. They would like to restrict military recruiting on their campuses because they object to the policy Congress has adopted with respect to homosexuals in the military.[16] The Solomon Amendment, however, forces institutions to choose between enforcing their nondiscrimination policy against military recruiters in this way and continuing to receive specified federal funding. . . .

II. The Solomon Amendment denies federal funding to an institution of higher education that "has a policy or practice . . . that either prohibits, or in effect prevents" the military "from gaining access to campuses, or access to students . . . on campuses, for purposes of military recruiting in a manner that is at least equal in quality and scope to the access to campuses and to students that is provided to any other employer." 10 U.S.C. §983(b) (Supp. 2005). . . . The Government and FAIR agree on what this statute requires: In order for a law school and its university to receive federal funding, the law school must offer military recruiters the same access to its campus and students that it provides to the nonmilitary recruiter receiving the most favorable access. . . .

III. . . . A. The Solomon Amendment neither limits what law schools may say nor requires them to say anything. Law schools remain free under the statute to express whatever views they may have on the military's congressionally mandated employment policy, all the while retaining eligibility for federal funds. . . . As a general matter, the Solomon Amendment regulates conduct, not speech. It affects what law schools must *do*—afford equal access to military recruiters—not what they may or may not *say*. . . .

B. . . . FAIR argues that the Solomon Amendment violates law schools' freedom of expressive association [because the] law schools' ability to express

---

16. Under this policy, a person generally may not serve in the Armed Forces if he has engaged in homosexual acts, stated that he is a homosexual, or married a person of the same sex. [See 10 U.S.C. §654.] Respondents do not challenge that policy in this litigation.

their message that discrimination on the basis of sexual orientation is wrong is significantly affected by the presence of military recruiters on campus and the schools' obligation to assist them. . . .

[Unlike *Dale*, the] Solomon Amendment . . . does not . . . affect a law school's associational rights. To comply with the statute, law schools must allow military recruiters on campus and assist them in whatever way the school chooses to assist other employers. Law schools therefore "associate" with military recruiters in the sense that they interact with them. But recruiters are not part of the law school. Recruiters are, by definition, outsiders who come onto campus for the limited purpose of trying to hire students — not to become members of the school's expressive association. This distinction is critical. Unlike the public accommodations law in *Dale*, the Solomon Amendment does not force a law school " 'to accept members it does not desire.' " . . . Students and faculty are free to associate to voice their disapproval of the military's message; nothing about the statute affects the composition of the group by making group membership less desirable. The Solomon Amendment therefore does not violate a law school's First Amendment rights. A military recruiter's mere presence on campus does not violate a law school's right to associate, regardless of how repugnant the law school considers the recruiter's message. . . .

NOTES AND PROBLEMS

1. Problems: *Overtly Sexist Jaycees.* Would the outcome of *Roberts* have been different if the Jaycees had maintained as its central tenet that "the world of commerce belongs to men, and a woman's place is in the home," but was otherwise the same?

National Organization for Preservation of Traditional Sex Roles. Assume that this group is a large nonprofit organization open to any man (and only men) and devoted to the message that "a woman's place is in the home." What result under *Roberts*? Under Justice O'Connor's approach?

Islamic Law Students. The Islamic Law Students, an organization at Public University Law School, limits membership to students who are profess to be Muslims and who sign a pledge that "Allah is the one God, and Mohammed was his Prophet." The law school bars student groups from discriminating on the basis of sex, race, religion, or sexual orientation. As a result, the Islamic Law Students are barred from using school facilities. Does the law school's regulation violate the Islamic Law Students' right of expressive association?

See Volokh, Freedom of Expressive Association and Governmental Subsidies, 58 Stan. L. Rev. 1919 (2006).

2. Unprotected Association. Consider Dallas v. Stanglin, 490 U.S. 19 (1989), in which the Court unanimously upheld a Dallas ordinance that limited the use of certain dance halls to persons between the ages of 14 and 18. The Court said the "hundreds of teenagers who congregate each night at [this] dance hall [are simply] patrons of the same business establishment. Most are strangers to one another, and the dance hall admits all who are willing to pay the admission fee. [R]ecreational dancing . . . is not protected by the First Amendment." In Erie v. Pap's A.M. and Barnes v. Glen Theatre, the Court conceded that nude dancing was expressive. Did Dallas teenagers lack expressive associational rights because they were dancing clothed? Because they were minors? For some other reason?

3. Freedom Not to Associate.   *Roberts* involves the freedom not to associate just as much as the freedom to associate. The claimed freedom of the Jaycees to choose men as their associates is inseparable from the claimed freedom of the Jaycees not to associate with women in the context of the organization. But not every case of the freedom not to associate is a mirror image of the freedom to associate.

Abood v. Detroit Board of Education, 431 U.S. 209 (1977).   A Michigan law authorized "agency shop" collective bargaining for public employees. In an agency shop, a union representing all workers in a workplace is entitled to withhold a "service charge" from the paychecks of nonunion members equal to the union dues collected from union members. Abood, a nonunion public schoolteacher, asserted that the agency shop practice violated his First Amendment rights because he did not believe in collective bargaining and because the union used his money to advocate political positions with which he disagreed. The Court rejected his first contention but accepted the second one. The Court reasoned that the agency shop arrangement was justified by the interests of (1) effective maintenance of collective bargaining, (2) ensuring labor peace, and (3) preventing "free-riders" by distributing the cost of collective bargaining among all who benefit, even those who prefer to do without those benefits. However, forced support for repugnant ideological causes is just another form of compelled speech, said the Court. See also Lehnert v. Ferris Faculty Association, 500 U.S. 507 (1991). The distinction between valid forced contributions toward non-ideological objectives and invalid forced contributions to ideological speech extends to bar dues. See Keller v. State Bar of California, 496 U.S. 1 (1990).

Davenport v. Washington Education Association, 551 U.S. 177 (2007).   The state of Washington also permits public-sector labor unions to operate "agency shops" and thus collect an "agency fee," equal to union dues, from nonunion employees. The Court concluded that Washington could validly impose upon public-sector labor unions a requirement that, before expending "agency fees" for election-related purposes, the unions obtain the affirmative consent of its nonmembers for such expenditures. The Court noted that Washington need not have permitted agency fees at all, and that "it is undeniably unusual for a government agency to give a private entity the power, in essence, to tax government employees." The affirmative consent requirement, said the Court, "is simply a condition on the union's exercise of this extraordinary power." . . . The constitutional floor for unions' collection and spending of agency fees is not also a constitutional ceiling for state-imposed restrictions." In Knox v. Service Employees International Union, 132 S. Ct. 2156 (2012), the Court extended *Davenport,* holding that the First Amendment requires unions representing all workers in an "agency shop" to obtain the affirmative consent of nonunion members to collection of fees used for political purposes. After *Knox,* the First Amendment requires an "opt-in" rule rather than an "opt-out" rule for agency shop fees devoted to political purposes.

Harris v. Quinn, 134 S. Ct. 2618 (2014). Illinois permitted Medicaid recipients to hire "personal assistants" to care for them in their home, using Medicaid funds provided by the state to pay the personal assistants. The patient was deemed to be the employer of the assistants and the patient had control over the terms and length of the employment relationship. Then Illinois enacted legislation that made the state the employer of the personal assistants "solely for the purposes of coverage under the Illinois Public Labor Relations Act," under which public employees were given the right to join labor unions and to bargain collectively on the terms and conditions of employment. Once a bargaining unit is recognized Illinois law requires employees who do not join the union to pay an "agency fee" to the union, usually in the amount of union dues.

The Court refused to extend *Abood* to such "partial public employees" as the personal assistants. First, the Court questioned the foundation of *Abood.* It noted that in the case of public sector unions the line between spending on collective bargaining and for political purposes is blurry. Wages and pension benefits of public employees are both matters for collective bargaining and raise controversial political issues. But the Court did not overrule *Abood,* although it reiterated "the bedrock principle that, except perhaps in the rarest of circumstances, no person in this country may be compelled to subsidize speech by a third party that he or she does not wish to support." Second, the Court questioned the assumption in *Abood* that "labor peace" can only be purchased at the price of an agency fee from non-union employees. Third, the Court noted that *Abood*'s rationale for the agency fee was rooted in the notion that a union is obligated to represent all the members of the bargaining unit, including non-union employees, but that rationale was not applicable where personal assistants must be paid at identical rates and the union was barred from asserting grievances on behalf of the assistants. Because *Abood* did not apply, generally applicable First Amendment principles applied. The agency fee imposed by Illinois did not serve "a compelling state interest that cannot be achieved through means significantly less restrictive of associational freedoms." The "labor peace" argument failed because there was no inextricable link between exclusive union representation and the agency fee and because the assistants did not work together "in a common state facility." The argument that the agency fee was vital to providing benefits to personal assistants because there was no proof that the benefits could not have been obtained without the agency fee.

Queries: When public sector unions bargain for higher wages, enhanced pension benefits, and favorable work rules, are their demands divorced from political or ideological positions? If so, what is the difference? If not, is *Abood* wrong? Can agency fees ever be imposed in the public employee context?

Note that in the context of private unions, the contest between management and labor is a zero-sum game. Management's gains are labor's losses, and vice versa. But in the public context, management (in the form of elected politicians) tends to reap rewards from labor's gains (in the coin of political support), albeit at the expense of the taxpaying public.

How solid is the "bedrock principle"? We pay taxes and those funds are used in part to pay for government speech with which we may disagree. Should the bedrock principle be limited to governmental compulsion of contributions to private third parties to support speech with which we may disagree?

Is the issue really about forced association rather than forced contributions to support speech with which we disagree?

4. Forced Contributions for Commercial Speech. *United States v. United Foods, Inc., 533 U.S. 405 (2001).* *Keller* and *Abood* applied to invalidate a provision of federal law that required mushroom producers to pay assessments used primarily to fund advertisements promoting generic mushroom sales. United Foods wanted to convey the message that its brand of mushrooms is superior to those grown by other producers, and so objected to being charged for a contrary message. The Court said:

> First Amendment concerns apply here because of the requirement that producers subsidize speech with which they disagree. [The compelled] message is that mushrooms are worth consuming whether or not they are branded. First Amendment values are at serious risk if the government can compel a particular citizen, or a discrete group of citizens, to pay special subsidies for speech on the side that it favors; and there is no apparent principle which distinguishes out of hand minor debates about whether a branded mushroom is better than just any mushroom.

In a prior case, Glickman v. Wileman Brothers & Elliott, Inc., 521 U.S. 457 (1997), the Court had upheld a federal requirement that producers of California tree fruits pay assessments for product advertising. The *United Foods* Court distinguished *Glickman* by noting that there

> the mandated assessments for speech were ancillary to a more comprehensive program restricting marketing autonomy. Here, . . . the advertising itself . . . is the principal object of the regulatory scheme. [*Glickman*] proceeded upon the premise that the producers were bound together and required by the statute to market their products according to cooperative rules. To that extent, their mandated participation in an advertising program with a particular message was the logical concomitant of a valid scheme of economic regulation.

Glickman was thus roughly analogous to the portion of *Abood* in which the Court upheld mandatory union dues for collective bargaining purposes. But the "features of the marketing scheme found important in *Glickman*" were not present in *United Foods*: "[A]lmost all of the funds collected under the mandatory assessments are for . . . generic advertising. [There] are no marketing orders that regulate how mushrooms may be produced and sold [and nothing prevents] individual producers from making their own market-ing decisions." The speech that United Foods "is required to support is not germane to a purpose related to an association independent from the speech itself; and the rationale of *Abood*" dictates that the "assessments are not per-mitted under the First Amendment."

Johanns v. Livestock Marketing Association, 544 U.S. 550 (2005). The Beef Promotion and Research Act of 1985 established a federal policy of pro-moting the sale and consumption of beef, using funds raised by a tax on cattle sales and importation. While this program appeared to be a virtual clone of the mushroom promotion at issue in *United Foods*, the federal government prescribed and controlled the message of beef promotion; as a result, it was the government that was speaking: "When, as here, the government sets the overall message to be communicated and approves every word that is dissem-inated, it is not precluded from relying on the government-speech doctrine merely because it solicits assistance from nongovernmental sources in devel-oping specific messages." Thus, the First Amendment was inapplicable when governments force people to fund the *government's* speech.

Queries. Suppose that in an effort to mitigate the secondary effects of non-obscene pornography a city requires all vendors of non-obscene pornography to contribute to a fund that is used for advertisements that seek to discourage demand for pornography. Would such a program be valid after *United Foods?* Would it make any difference if the fund were used only to provide additional police protection in neighborhoods with a disproportionately large number of vendors of pornography? Some states levy taxes on the purchase of cigarettes and earmark those funds for advertising campaigns to discourage smoking. If those taxes were levied on the producers of cigarettes instead of the consumer, would *United Foods* or *Johanns* apply?

5. Litigation as an Associational Right. Litigation for political or constitutional purposes possesses a sufficiently expressive dimension to come within the protection of the First Amendment. In NAACP v. Button, 371 U.S. 415 (1963), the Court voided a Virginia regulation that prohib-ited "improper solicitation of [legal] business" as applied to the NAACP's practice of explaining to parents and children the legal steps necessary to accomplish school desegregation in the wake of *Brown*, and then distribut-ing forms authorizing the NAACP to represent the signer in desegregation suits. The Court held that the NAACP's actions were protected "modes of expression and association." Because the litigation was intended to achieve "equality of treatment for the members of the Negro community," it was deemed by the Court to be "a form of political expression. [Litigation] may well be the sole practicable avenue open to a minority to petition for redress of grievances."

The Court has also recognized that some nonpolitical litigation involves expressive association. In a series of cases the Court has struck down state restrictions on labor union assistance to union members designed to ensure members' awareness of their legal rights and to ensure competent legal rep-resentation. See United Transportation Union v. State Bar of Michigan,

401 U.S. 576 (1971); United Mine Workers v. Illinois Bar Association, 389 U.S. 217 (1967); Brotherhood of Railroad Trainmen v. Virginia, 377 U.S. 1 (1964).

6. Political Boycotts as an Associational Right.   Boycotts undertaken for purposes of political expression rather than for economic coercion are a protected form of expression. In NAACP v. Claiborne Hardware Co., 458 U.S. 886 (1982), the Court overturned a civil damages award based on tortious interference with economic advantage. The case stemmed from a boycott organized by the NAACP against white businesses to dramatize claims of racial discrimination. Because the boycott was intended to express political views and a boycott necessarily involves association to achieve its ends, the state could "not award compensation for the consequences of nonviolent, protected activity." But in International Longshoremen's Association v. Allied International, 456 U.S. 212 (1982), the Court ruled that the union's refusal to handle cargoes coming from or going to the Soviet Union in order to protest the Soviet Union's invasion of Afghanistan was not a form of protected expression, despite its apparent political nature, because it was "conduct designed not to communicate but to coerce." Why was it not a form of protected expression?

2.   The Freedom Not to Speak

The mirror image of the right of free expression is the right *not* to express ideas. Just as government control of the content of expression is presumptively invalid, so is government compulsion of specified expression. Like other content-based speech regulation, government compulsion to speak or associate may be justified if the government can prove that the compulsion is the least restrictive means of accomplishing a compelling government interest that is unrelated to the forced expression of ideas.

≡≡≡ *West Virginia State Board of Education v. Barnette*
≡≡≡ *319 U.S. 624 (1943)*

[In Minersville School District v. Gobitis, 310 U.S. 586 (1940), the Court upheld the validity of a flag salute required of schoolchildren. Pursuant to statutory authority, the West Virginia State Board of Education adopted a regulation that required all teachers and pupils to deliver a "stiff-arm" flag salute: keeping the right hand raised with palm turned up while the pledge of allegiance was recited. Failure to conform resulted in expulsion, the expelled child being deemed "unlawfully absent" and subject to delinquency proceedings, while his parents or guardians were liable to prosecution, fine, and imprisonment. Appellees, Jehovah's Witnesses, alleged that these laws and regulations denied religious freedom and freedom of speech because they believe that the law of God is superior to human laws, construe God's law to forbid obeisance to any "graven image," consider the flag to be such an "image," and so refused to salute it. Children of this faith were expelled from school and threatened with confinement in reformatories maintained for criminally inclined juveniles. Parents of such children were prosecuted for causing delinquency. A federal district court enjoined enforcement of the flag salute, and a direct appeal was taken to the Supreme Court.]

JUSTICE JACKSON delivered the opinion of the Court.

The compulsory flag salute and pledge requires affirmation of a belief and an attitude of mind. [To] sustain the compulsory flag salute we are required to say that a Bill of Rights which guards the individual's right to speak his own mind, left it open to public authorities to compel him to utter what is not in his mind. [The Court in *Gobitis* assumed] that power exists in the State to impose the flag salute discipline upon school children in general [and] only examined and rejected a claim based on religious beliefs of immunity from an unquestioned general rule. The question [here is whether a flag salute, which touches] matters of opinion and political attitude, may be imposed upon the individual by official [authority]. We examine rather than assume existence of this [power].

The very purpose of a Bill of Rights was to withdraw certain subjects from the vicissitudes of political controversy, to place them beyond the reach of majorities and officials and to establish them as legal principles to be applied by the courts. One's right [to] free speech [may] not be submitted to vote. [While the flag salute is said to foster national unity, the] problem is whether under our Constitution compulsion as here employed is a permissible means for its achievement. [Those] who begin coercive elimination of dissent soon find themselves exterminating dissenters. Compulsory unification of opinion achieves only the unanimity of the graveyard. It seems trite but necessary to say that the First Amendment [was] designed to avoid these ends by avoiding these beginnings. [We] set up government by consent of the governed, and the Bill of Rights denies those in power any legal opportunity to coerce that consent. [To] believe that patriotism will not flourish if patriotic ceremonies are voluntary and spontaneous instead of a compulsory routine is to make an unflattering estimate of the appeal of our institutions to free minds.

[Freedom] to differ is not limited to things that do not matter much. That would be a mere shadow of freedom. The test of its substance is the right to differ as to things that touch the heart of the existing order. If there is any fixed star in our constitutional constellation, it is that no official, high or petty, can prescribe what shall be orthodox in politics, nationalism, religion, or other matters of opinion or force citizens to confess by word or act their faith therein. If there are any circumstances which permit an exception, they do not now occur to us.

We think the action of the local authorities in compelling the flag salute and pledge transcends constitutional limitations on their power and invades the sphere of intellect and spirit which it is the purpose of the First Amendment to our Constitution to reserve from all official control. [*Gobitis* is] overruled. [Affirmed.]

Wooley v. Maynard
430 U.S. 705 (1977)

CHIEF JUSTICE BURGER delivered the opinion of the Court.

The issue [is whether] New Hampshire may constitutionally enforce criminal sanctions against persons who cover the motto "Live Free or Die" on passenger vehicle license plates because that motto is repugnant to their moral and religious beliefs. [New Hampshire law requires] that noncommercial vehicles bear license plates embossed with the state motto, "Live Free or Die," [and makes] it a misdemeanor "knowingly [to obscure]" the state motto. The Maynards consider the New Hampshire State motto to be repugnant to their moral, religious, and political beliefs [and covered] up the motto on their license plates. [George Maynard was thrice convicted of obscuring the motto by covering it up with tape, and served a 15-day jail sentence. Upon the Maynards' suit, a federal court enjoined] the State "from arresting and prosecuting [the Maynards] at any time in the future for covering over that portion of their license plates that contains the motto 'Live Free or Die.'"

[We are] faced with the question of whether the State may constitutionally require an individual to participate in the dissemination of an ideological message by displaying it on his private property in a manner and for the express purpose that it be observed and read by the public. We hold that the State may not do so.

[The] right of freedom of thought protected by the First Amendment against state action includes both the right to speak freely and the right to refrain from speaking at all. [*Barnette.*] The right to speak and the right to refrain from speaking are complementary components of the broader concept of "individual freedom of mind." New Hampshire's statute in effect requires that appellees use their private property as a "mobile billboard" for the State's ideological message—or suffer a penalty, as Maynard already has. As a condition to driving an automobile—a virtual necessity for most Americans—the Maynards must display "Live Free or Die" to hundreds of people each day. . . . The First Amendment protects the right of individuals to hold a point of view different from the majority and to refuse to foster, in the way New Hampshire commands, an idea they find morally objectionable.

[We] must also determine whether the State's countervailing interest is sufficiently compelling to justify requiring appellees to display the state motto on their license plates. The two interests advanced by the State are that display of the motto (1) facilitates the identification of passenger vehicles, and (2) promotes appreciation of history, individualism, and state pride. [But] New Hampshire passenger license plates normally consist of a specific configuration of letters and numbers which makes them readily distinguishable from other types of plates, even without reference to the state motto. Even were we to credit the State's reasons and "even though the governmental purpose be legitimate and substantial, that purpose cannot be pursued by means that broadly stifle fundamental personal liberties when the end can be more narrowly achieved." The State's second claimed interest is not ideologically neutral. The State is seeking to communicate to others an official view as to proper appreciation of history, state pride, and individualism.[17] [While] the State may legitimately pursue such interests in any number of ways, [it may not override] an individual's First Amendment right to avoid becoming the courier for such message. We conclude [that] New Hampshire may not require appellees to display the state motto upon their vehicle license plates. [Affirmed.]

JUSTICE REHNQUIST, joined by JUSTICE BLACKMUN, dissenting.

The State has not forced appellees to "say" anything; and it has not forced them to communicate ideas with nonverbal actions reasonably likened to "speech," such as wearing a lapel button promoting a political candidate or waving a flag as a symbolic gesture. The State has simply required [that] non-commercial automobiles bear license tags with the state motto. [Appellees] have not been forced to affirm or reject that motto; they are simply required by the State, under its police power, to carry a state auto license tag for identification and registration purposes. [The] Court cites *Barnette* for the proposition that there is a constitutional right [to] "refrain from speaking." What the Court does not demonstrate is that there is any "speech" or "speaking" in the context of this case. The Court [treats] the state law in this case as if it were forcing appellees [to] advocate an ideological point of view. But this begs the question. The issue [is] whether appellees, in displaying, as they are required to do, state license tags, the format of which is known to all as having been prescribed by the State, would be considered to be advocating political or ideological views.

The Court recognizes [that] this case substantially differs from *Barnette*, [but] the Court states "the difference is essentially one of degree." [The] Court suggests that the test is whether the individual is forced "to be an instrument for fostering public adherence to an ideological point of view he finds unacceptable." But [these] are merely conclusory words, barren of analysis. For example, were New Hampshire to erect a multitude of billboards, each proclaiming "Live Free or Die," and tax all citizens for the cost of erection and maintenance, clearly the message would be "fostered" by the individual citizen-taxpayers and just as clearly those individuals would be "instruments" in that communication. Certainly, however, that case would not fall within the ambit of *Barnette*. In that case, as in this case, there is no affirmation of belief. For First Amendment principles to be implicated, the State must place the citizen in the position of either apparently or actually "asserting as true" the message . . .

The logic of the Court's opinion leads to startling, and I believe totally unacceptable, results. For example, the mottoes "In God We Trust" and "E Pluribus Unum" appear on the coin and currency of the United States. I

---

17. Appellants do not explain why advocacy of these values is enhanced by display on private citizens' cars but not on the cars of officials such as the Governor, Supreme Court Justices, Members of Congress, and sheriffs.

cannot imagine that the statutes proscribing defacement of United States currency impinge upon the First Amendment rights of an atheist. The fact that an atheist carries and uses United States currency does not, in any meaningful sense, convey any affirmation of belief on his part in the motto "In God We Trust." Similarly, there is no affirmation of belief involved in the display of state license tags upon the private automobiles involved here.

NOTES

1. The Right at Issue.   Did *Wooley* involve forced speech, a restriction on Maynard's speech, or no speech at all? If Justice Rehnquist was correct in contending that nobody would think Maynard was endorsing the motto by driving a car with New Hampshire license plates, was the thrust of the New Hampshire law to prevent Maynard from communicating his own message of disapproval of the motto? And if that was the case, should the issue have been seen as whether Maynard had a First Amendment right to deliver his message of disapproval in the manner he preferred? What would have been the result under that analysis?

Was the majority correct that New Hampshire was forcing Maynard to profess a sentiment that he did not believe? Suppose that Maynard had been issued license plate "666" and that he objected because he was being forced to display what he regarded as the "Mark of the Beast," a figure of evil in apocalyptic Christianity. Same result?

Was the law infirm because New Hampshire appropriated Maynard's personal property (his auto) to display the state's ideological message?

2. The Scope of *Wooley*.   Justice Rehnquist noted that 18 U.S.C. §§331 and 333 prohibit defacing U.S. currency. Suppose that those statutes were applied to a person who alters the national motto on the currency he holds to read "In US We Trust" instead of "In God We Trust." Would Wooley v. Maynard operate to invalidate that application of the hypothesized law?

≣≣≣ *Pacific Gas & Electric Co. v. Public Utilities Commission*
475 U.S. 1 (1986)

JUSTICE POWELL announced the judgment of the Court and delivered an opinion in which CHIEF JUSTICE BURGER and JUSTICES BRENNAN and O'CONNOR joined.

The question in this case is whether the California Public Utilities Commission may require a privately owned utility company to include in its billing envelopes speech of a third party with which the utility disagrees. [PG&E had long made a practice of including in its billing envelopes an informational flyer of its own creation. At the instigation of TURN, an organization devoted to criticizing utility rates and practices, the PUC concluded that] "the space remaining in the billing envelope, after inclusion of the monthly bill and any required legal notices, [up] to such total envelope weight as would not result in any additional postage cost" [was the property of utility ratepayers].[18] [In] an effort to apportion this "extra space" between appellant and its customers, the Commission permitted TURN to use the "extra space" four times a year for the next two years. During these months, appellant may use any space not used by TURN, and it may include additional materials if it pays any extra postage. [The] Commission placed no limitations on what TURN or appellant could say in the envelope, except that TURN is required to state that its messages are not those of appellant. Appellant [argues] that it has a First Amendment right not to help spread a message with which it disagrees. . . .

[Compelled] access like that ordered in this case both penalizes the expression of particular points of view and forces speakers to alter their speech to conform with an agenda they do not set. . . . This Court has previously considered the question whether compelling a private corporation to provide a forum for views other than its own may infringe the corporation's freedom of speech. Miami Herald Publishing Co. v. Tornillo, 418 U.S. 241 (1974). *Tornillo* involved a challenge to Florida's right-of-reply statute [that] provided that, if a newspaper assailed a candidate's character or record, the candidate could demand that the newspaper print a reply of equal prominence and space. We found that the right-of-reply statute directly interfered with the newspaper's right to speak in two ways. First, the newspaper's expression of a particular viewpoint triggered an obligation to permit other speakers, with whom the newspaper disagreed, to use the newspaper's facilities to spread their own message. The statute purported to advance free discussion, but its effect was to deter newspapers from speaking out in the first instance: by forcing the newspaper to disseminate opponents' views, the statute penalized the newspaper's own expression. We therefore concluded that a "[government]-enforced right of access inescapably 'dampens the vigor and limits the variety of public debate.'"[19] Second, we noted that the newspaper's "treatment of public issues and public officials—whether fair or unfair—[constitutes] the exercise of editorial control and judgment." Florida's statute interfered with this "editorial

---

18. The Commission summarized its reasoning as follows: "[Envelope] and postage costs and any other costs of mailing bills are a necessary part of providing utility service to the customer [but], due to the nature of postal rates [extra] space exists in these billing envelopes. [Mindful] that the extra space is an artifact generated with ratepayer funds [and] that the only alternative treatment would unjustly enrich PG&E and simultaneously deprive the ratepayers of the value of that space, we concluded that the extra space in the billing envelope 'is properly considered as ratepayer property.'"

19. This Court has sustained a limited government-enforced right of access to broadcast media, [the FCC's so-called fairness doctrine]. Red Lion Broadcasting Co. v. FCC, 395 U.S. 367 (1969). Appellant's billing envelopes do not [present] the same constraints that justify the result in *Red Lion:* "[A] broadcaster communicates through use of a scarce, publicly owned resource. No person can broadcast without a license, whereas all persons are free to send correspondence to private homes through the mails." [The fairness doctrine has since been repealed.—ED.]

control and judgment" by forcing the newspaper to tailor its speech to an opponent's agenda, and to respond to candidates' arguments where the newspaper might prefer to be silent. Since all speech inherently involves choices of what to say and what to leave unsaid, this effect was impermissible. . . .

The Commission's order [discriminates] on the basis of the viewpoints of the selected speakers. [Access] to the envelopes thus is not content neutral. [Access] is limited to persons or groups — such as TURN — who disagree with appellant's views [and] who oppose appellant in Commission proceedings. Such one-sidedness impermissibly burdens appellant's own expression. [Because] access is awarded only to those who disagree with appellant's views and who are hostile to appellant's interests, appellant must contend with the fact that whenever it speaks out on a given issue, it may be forced — at TURN'S discretion — to help disseminate hostile views. Appellant "might well conclude" that, under these circumstances, "the safe course is to avoid controversy," thereby reducing the free flow of information and ideas that the First Amendment seeks to promote. [*Tornillo.*]

Appellant does not, of course, have the right to be free from vigorous debate. But it does have the right to be free from government restrictions that abridge its own rights in order to "enhance the relative voice" of its opponents. The Commission's order requires appellant to assist in disseminating TURN's views; it does not equally constrain both sides of the debate about utility regulation. [The] Commission's order identifies a favored speaker "based on the identity of the interests that [the speaker] may represent" and forces the speaker's opponent [to] assist in disseminating the speaker's message. Such a requirement necessarily burdens the expression of the disfavored speaker.

The Commission's access order also impermissibly requires appellant to associate with speech with which appellant may disagree. [Should] TURN choose . . . to urge appellant's customers to vote for a particular slate of legislative candidates, or to argue in favor of legislation that could seriously affect the utility business, appellant may be forced either to appear to agree with TURN'S views or to respond. [That] forced response is antithetical to the free discussion that the First Amendment seeks to foster. For corporations as for individuals, the choice to speak includes within it the choice of what not to say. And we have held that speech does not lose its protection because of the corporate identity of the speaker. [First National Bank of Boston v. Bellotti, 435 U.S. 765 (1978).] Were the government freely able to compel corporate speakers to propound political messages with which they disagree, this protection would be empty, for the government could require speakers to affirm in one breath that which they deny in the next.

[Notwithstanding] that it burdens protected speech, the Commission's order could be valid if it were a narrowly tailored means of serving a compelling state interest. Appellees identify two assertedly compelling state interests that the access order is said to advance. First, [the] State's interest in fair and effective utility regulation may be compelling, [but] the State can serve that interest through means that would not violate appellant's First Amendments rights, such as awarding costs and fees [to TURN for its assistance in rate-making proceedings]. Second, [the] State's interest in promoting speech by making a variety of views available to appellant's customers . . . is not furthered by an order that is not content neutral. Moreover, the means chosen to advance variety tend to inhibit expression of appellant's views in order to promote TURN's. [The] State cannot advance some points of view by burdening the expression of others. It follows that the Commission's order is not a narrowly tailored means of furthering this interest.

[We] conclude that the Commission's order impermissibly burdens appellant's First Amendment rights because it forces appellant to associate with the views of other speakers, and because it selects the other speakers on the basis of their viewpoints. The order is not a narrowly tailored means of furthering a compelling state [interest].

JUSTICE REHNQUIST, joined by JUSTICE WHITE and, as to Part I, JUSTICE STEVENS, dissenting.

I believe that the right of access here is constitutionally indistinguishable from the right of access approved in [PruneYard Shopping Center v. Robins, 447 U.S. 74 (1980),] and therefore I dissent.

I. [Our] cases cannot be squared [with] the view that the First Amendment prohibits governmental action that only indirectly and remotely affects a speaker's contribution to the overall mix of information available to society. [*PruneYard* illustrates the point.] California interpreted its own Constitution to afford a right of access to private shopping centers for the reasonable exercise of speech and petitioning. While acknowledging that the First Amendment does not itself grant a right of access to private forums, the Court upheld the state-created right against a First Amendment challenge. It reasoned that Wooley v. Maynard does not prohibit such a right of access because the views of those taking advantage of the right would not likely be identified with those of the owners, the State was not dictating any specific message, and the owners were free to disavow any connection to the message by posting disclaimers. . . .

II. The plurality argues [that] the right of access also implicates PG&E's right not to speak or to associate with the speech of others, thereby triggering heightened scrutiny. [But] because PG&E retains complete editorial freedom over the content of its inserts, the effect of the right of access is likely to be qualitatively different from a direct prescription by the government of "what shall be orthodox [in] matters of opinion." [*Barnette.*]

NOTES

1. Speech Access Rights to Private Property. Should *PG&E* have been perceived as a case involving the question of whether the Constitution compels public access for speech to private property and, if so, under what circumstances?

In Marsh v. Alabama, 326 U.S. 501 (1946), the Court overturned a criminal trespass conviction of a Jehovah's Witness who had distributed literature without a license on a sidewalk in Chickasaw, Alabama, a wholly owned company town described by the Court as having

> all the characteristics of any other American town. [The] town and its shopping district are accessible to and freely used by the public in general and there is nothing to distinguish them from any other town and shopping center except the fact that the title to the property belongs to a private corporation.

Because the company that owned the town had assumed the public functions of a municipality, it was treated like the state and was subject to the First Amendment.

But *Marsh* is the exception. In general, the Court has rejected the idea that the Constitution commands private owners to make their property accessible to the public for speech purposes. In Lloyd Corp. v. Tanner, 407 U.S. 551 (1972), the Court held that a privately owned shopping center could validly exclude people wishing to distribute handbills protesting the Vietnam War. Unlike *Marsh*, there was "no comparable assumption or exercise of municipal functions or power." Since there was "no such dedication of [the] privately owned and operated shopping center to public use," there was no occasion to apply the First Amendment. See also Hudgens v. NLRB, 424 U.S. 507 (1976), in which the Court ruled that a privately owned shopping center could validly exclude labor picketers from entering the center for the purpose of picketing a business within the center.

In *PG&E*, the Court cited both Miami Herald Publishing Co. v. Tornillo, 418 U.S. 241 (1974), and Red Lion Broadcasting Co. v. FCC, 395 U.S. 367 (1969). The right-of-reply law in *Tornillo* forced private newspapers to print views that were inimical to the newspaper. The fairness doctrine, upheld in *Red Lion*, required broadcasters to give a right of reply to points of view different from the editorial voice of the broadcaster. The Court thought that the scarcity of the public resource of the broadcast spectrum justified the fairness doctrine, a fact not present in *Tornillo*. Alternatives to broadcast spectrum are now legion; does that suggest that *Red Lion* is no longer good law?

In Turner Broadcasting System v. FCC (*Turner I*), 512 U.S. 622 (1994), and Turner Broadcasting System v. FCC (*Turner II*), 520 U.S. 180 (1997), the Court upheld a federal law requiring privately owned cable transmission systems to carry, free of charge, local broadcast television signals. The Court concluded that the "must carry" provisions were content-neutral and no more burdensome than necessary to accomplish the government's significant objective, unrelated to the suppression of ideas, of protecting the economic viability of over-the-air television broadcasters.

2. The Relevance of *PruneYard*. In PruneYard Shopping Center v. Robins, 447 U.S. 74 (1980), the Court ruled that California had not violated the free speech rights of the owner of a shopping center by requiring him to permit access to persons soliciting signatures on a political petition. *PruneYard* justified this by noting the absence of government dictation of a message, the improbability that the unwanted speakers' views would be attributed to the shopping center owner, and the ability of the owner to dissociate himself from the unwanted speech by posting disclaimers. However, *PruneYard* did not pose the problem of whether the forced access might burden or hamper the shopping center owner's independent right to speak. Is that problem presented in *PG&E*? Did the California PUC's appropriation of the "extra space" for TURN's benefit constitute a burden on PG&E's ability to speak independently?

Hurley v. Irish-American Gay, Lesbian and Bisexual Group of Boston
515 U.S. 557 (1995)

JUSTICE SOUTER delivered the opinion of the Court.

The issue in this case is whether Massachusetts may require private citizens who organize a parade to include among the marchers a group imparting a message the organizers do not wish to convey. [The St. Patrick's Day parade in Boston is organized and conducted by the South Boston Allied War Veterans Council pursuant to an annual permit issued by the City of Boston. The Council refused to allow GLIB to march under its banner advertising the group's pride in their sexual orientation and Irish heritage. GLIB brought suit under a Massachusetts law barring discrimination on account of sexual orientation in places of public accommodation. The state courts ruled in GLIB's favor, ordering the Council to include GLIB.] We hold that such a mandate violates the [free expression guarantee].

Parades are [a] form of expression, not just motion, and [the] protected expression that inheres in a parade is not limited to its banners and songs. [The] First Amendment shields [symbolic expression and] a narrow, succinctly articulable message is not a condition of constitutional protection, which if confined to expressions conveying a "particularized message" would never reach the unquestionably shielded painting of Jackson Pollock, music of Arnold Schönberg, or Jabberwocky verse of Lewis Carroll.

[A] private speaker does not forfeit constitutional protection simply by combining multifarious voices, or by failing to edit their themes to isolate an exact message as the exclusive subject matter of the speech. Nor [does] First Amendment protection require a speaker to generate, as an original matter, each item featured in the communication. Cable operators, for example, are engaged in protected speech activities even when they only select programming originally produced by others. [*Turner I.*] The selection of contingents to make a parade is entitled to similar protection.

[GLIB's] participation as a unit in the parade was equally expressive. GLIB was formed for the very purpose of marching in it [in] order to celebrate its members' identity as openly gay, lesbian, and bisexual descendants of the Irish immigrants, to show that there are such individuals in the community, and to support the like men and women who sought to march in the New York parade. [GLIB] understandably seeks to communicate its ideas as part of the existing parade, rather than staging one of its own.

[The] petitioners disclaim any intent to exclude homosexuals as such, and no individual member of GLIB claims to have been excluded from parading as a member of any group that the Council has approved to march. Instead, the disagreement goes to the admission of GLIB as its own parade unit carrying its own banner. Since every participating unit affects the message conveyed by the private organizers, the state courts' application of the [anti-discrimination] statute produced an order essentially requiring petitioners to alter the expressive content of their parade. Although the state courts spoke of the parade as a place of public accommodation, [the] state courts' application of the statute had the effect of declaring the sponsors' speech itself to be the public accommodation. Under this approach any contingent of protected individuals with a message would have the right to participate in petitioners' speech, so that the communication produced by the private organizers would be shaped by all those . . . who wished to join in with some expressive demonstration of their own. But this use of the State's power violated the fundamental rule of protection under the First Amendment, that a speaker has the autonomy to choose the content of his own message.

"Since all speech inherently involves choices of what to *say* and what to leave *unsaid*," one important manifestation of the principle of free speech is that one who chooses to speak may also decide "what not to say." [It] boils down to the choice of a speaker not to propound a particular point of view, and that choice is presumed to lie beyond the government's power to control. . . . [Reversed and remanded.]

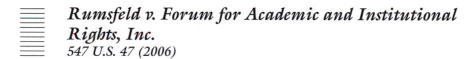

Rumsfeld v. Forum for Academic and Institutional Rights, Inc.
547 U.S. 47 (2006)

[A portion of this case is included in Section F.1, supra. The federal Solomon Amendment "specifies that if any part of an institution of higher education denies military recruiters access equal to that provided other recruiters, the entire institution would lose certain federal funds." Certain law schools sought to restrict "the access of military recruiters to their students because of disagreement with the Government's policy on homosexuals in the military." They contended that the Solomon Amendment compelled them to deliver an unwanted message.]

CHIEF JUSTICE ROBERTS delivered the opinion of the Court.

. . . [F]reedom of speech prohibits the government from telling people what they must say. The Solomon Amendment does not require any similar expression by law schools. Nonetheless, recruiting assistance provided by the schools often includes elements of speech. For example, schools may send e-mails or post notices on bulletin boards on an employer's behalf. Law schools offering such services to other recruiters must also send e-mails and post notices on behalf of the military to comply with the Solomon Amendment. . . .

This sort of recruiting assistance, however, is a far cry from the compelled speech in *Barnette* and *Wooley*. The Solomon Amendment, unlike the laws at issue in those cases, does not dictate the content of the speech at all, which is only "compelled" if, and to the extent, the school provides such speech for other recruiters. There is nothing in this case approaching a Government-mandated pledge or motto that the school must endorse. . . . Compelling a law school that sends scheduling e-mails for other recruiters to send one for a military recruiter is simply not the same as forcing a student to pledge allegiance, or forcing a Jehovah's Witness to display the motto "Live Free or Die," and it trivializes the freedom protected in *Barnette* and *Wooley* to suggest that it is.

Our compelled-speech cases are not limited to the situation in which an individual must personally speak the government's message. We have also . . . limited the government's ability to force one speaker to host or accommodate another speaker's message. [*Hurley; PG&E; Tornillo.*] The compelled-speech violation in each of [these] cases . . . resulted from the fact that the complaining speaker's own message was affected by the speech it was forced to accommodate. . . .

In this case, accommodating the military's message does not affect the law schools' speech, because the schools are not speaking when they host interviews and recruiting receptions. Unlike a parade organizer's choice of parade contingents, a law school's decision to allow recruiters on campus is not inherently expressive. Law schools facilitate recruiting to assist their students in obtaining jobs. A law school's . . . accommodation of a military recruiter's message is not compelled speech because the accommodation does not sufficiently interfere with any message of the school.

The schools respond that if they treat military and nonmilitary recruiters alike in order to comply with the Solomon Amendment, they could be viewed as sending the message that they see nothing wrong with the military's policies, when they do. [In *PruneYard*], . . . we upheld a state law requiring a shopping center owner to allow certain expressive activities by others on its property[, explaining] that there was little likelihood that the views of those engaging in the expressive activities would be identified with the owner, who remained free to disassociate himself from those views and who was "not . . . being compelled to affirm [a] belief in any governmentally prescribed position or view." The same is true here. Nothing about recruiting suggests that law schools agree with any speech by recruiters, and nothing in the Solomon Amendment restricts what the law schools may say about the military's policies. We have held that high school students can appreciate the difference between speech a school sponsors and speech the school permits because legally required to do so, pursuant to an equal access policy. Surely students have not lost that ability by the time they get to law school.

PROBLEMS

Forced Disclaimer.   Suppose Public University adopts a rule that any of its professors who comment publicly on issues (such as speeches or op-ed articles) include in their comment the statement that the "opinions expressed are not necessarily endorsed by Public University." Is the requirement valid?

Forced Disclosure.   Federal law prohibits homeowners' associations from enforcing any covenant or restriction that bars association members from display of the American flag. Could Congress validly require homeowners' associations to disclose, in writing, to association members that they have the right to display the American flag?

"I'm Donald Trump, and I approved this message."   In political advertising paid for by a candidate, 2 U.S.C. §441d(d)(1) compels the candidate to state that he or she has approved the ad and, if it is a television ad, requires that it include either "an unobscured, full-screen view of the candidate making the statement" or the candidate's voice delivering the required statement along with "a clearly identifiable . . . image of the candidate." Is §441d(d)(1) valid?

Anonymous Speech

May a government compel a speaker to reveal his identity? Anonymous political pamphlets have a long and honorable tradition in American life, the Federalist Papers being perhaps the most notable example.

Talley v. California, 362 U.S. 60 (1960).   A Los Angeles ordinance prohibited the distribution of a handbill unless the name and address of the sponsor appeared on its face. The Court invalidated it, reasoning "that identification and fear of reprisal might deter perfectly peaceful discussions of public matters of importance." Los Angeles said it desired to identify "those responsible for fraud, false advertising, and libel," but that justification was insufficient because there are less speech-restrictive ways of addressing fraud and libel.

McIntyre v. Ohio Elections Commission, 514 U.S. 334 (1995).   The Court voided an Ohio law that prohibited the distribution of anonymous literature "designed to influence voters in an election." Because the law burdened "core political speech," the Court applied "exacting scrutiny"—the law could be upheld only if Ohio proved it was "narrowly tailored to serve an overriding state interest." The Court concluded that neither interest advanced by Ohio—ensuring that the electorate possesses all "relevant information" and "preventing fraud and libel"—was sufficiently "overriding" to justify the restriction. In Buckley v. American Constitutional Law Foundation, Inc., 525 U.S. 182 (1999), the Court relied on *McIntyre* to strike down Colorado's requirement that initiative petition circulators wear a name badge that identified them.

Doe v. Reed, 561 U.S. 186 (2010). Washington law required disclosure of the names and addresses of signatories to initiative or referendum petitions. Because signing such a petition expresses either the view that the subject of the petition should be adopted or that the public ought to vote on the matter, disclosure implicates free expression. For mandated disclosure to be valid the state must prove that there is a substantial relationship between disclosure and a "sufficiently important" governmental interest. In making this assessment courts must consider the strength of the interest asserted in light of the seriousness of the burden on expression imposed by disclosure. The Court rejected a facial challenge; the government's interest in detecting fraudulent signatories was sufficiently important and substantially related to the disclosure requirement. However, the plaintiffs objecting to disclosure remained free to prove that, as applied to them, disclosure would lead to threats, harassment, and reprisals. The Court noted that evidence of a reasonable probability that disclosure will produce these harms is enough to establish that disclosure would violate free expression rights. Does the right to anonymous speech extend beyond political speech?

PROBLEMS

Required Name Badges. The City of Seattle requires a "street artist" performing in the Seattle Center, a traditional public forum, to wear a name badge while performing. Is this regulation valid? See Berger v. City of Seattle, 569 F.3d 1069 (9th Cir. 2009).

Banning Pseudonymous Publication. Suppose Congress prohibits the publication of books, articles, or other literature under pseudonymous pen names. Is this valid? What if the ban is limited to non-political writings?

G. FREE EXPRESSION AND THE POLITICAL PROCESS

In a broad sense, the entire body of free expression law is essential to and pervades the political process. More narrowly, the free expression guarantee plays two significant roles in the political process: (1) limiting government regulation of political contributions and expenditures, the fuel of campaign speech; and (2) checking government regulation of political parties.

1. Money as Speech: Political Contributions and Expenditures

In our populous and technologically advanced society it is virtually impossible to communicate political messages without using money. Speech may be free, but it is not cheap.

≣ *Buckley v. Valeo*
≣ *424 U.S. 1 (1976)*

PER CURIAM.

These appeals present constitutional challenges to the key provisions of the Federal Election Campaign Act [Act]. [The Act limits individual political contributions, independent expenditures by individuals and groups "relative to a clearly identified candidate," campaign spending by candidates for various federal offices, and spending for national conventions by political parties. The Act requires that contributions and expenditures above certain threshold levels be reported and publicly disclosed, creates a system for public funding of Presidential campaign activities, and establishes a Federal Election Commission to administer and enforce the legislation. The Court upheld the individual contribution limits, the disclosure and reporting provisions, and the public financing scheme. The Court voided the limits on campaign and independent expenditures, and on expenditures by a candidate from his or her personal funds.]

Contribution and Expenditure Limits. . . . The major contribution and expenditure limitations in the Act prohibit individuals from contributing more than $25,000 in a single year or more than $1,000 to any single candidate for an election campaign and from spending more than $1,000 a year "relative to a clearly identified candidate." Other provisions restrict a candidate's use of personal and family resources in his campaign and limit the overall amount that can be spent by a candidate in campaigning for federal office.

The Act's contribution and expenditure limitations operate in an area of the most fundamental First Amendment activities. Discussion of public issues and debate on the qualifications of candidates are integral to the operation of [our] system of government. [This] Court has never suggested that the dependence of a communication on the expenditure of money operates . . . to reduce the exacting scrutiny required by the First Amendment.

[T]he . . . expenditure . . . limitations challenged here would [fail] because the governmental interests advanced in support of the Act involve "suppressing communication." The interests served by the Act include restricting the voices of people and interest groups who have money to spend and reducing the overall scope of federal election campaigns. Although the Act does not focus on the ideas expressed by persons or groups subjected to its regulations, it is aimed in part at equalizing the relative ability of all voters to affect electoral outcomes by placing a ceiling on expenditures for political expression by citizens and groups. . . . [The] present Act's contribution and expenditure limitations impose direct quantity restrictions on political communication and association by persons, groups, candidates, and political parties in addition to any reasonable time, place, and manner regulations otherwise imposed.[20]

---

20. [Appellees] argue that just as the decibels emitted by a sound truck can be regulated consistently with the First Amendment, Kovacs v. Cooper, the Act may restrict the volume of dollars in political campaigns without impermissibly restricting freedom of speech. This comparison underscores a fundamental misconception. The decibel restriction upheld in *Kovacs*

A restriction on the amount of money a person or group can spend on political communication during a campaign necessarily reduces the quantity of expression by restricting the number of issues discussed, the depth of their exploration, and the size of the audience reached.[21] This is because virtually every means of communicating ideas in today's mass society requires the expenditure of money. [The Act's] expenditure limitations [represent] substantial rather than merely theoretical restraints on the quantity and diversity of political speech. . . .

By contrast, [a] limitation upon the amount that any one person or group may contribute to a candidate or political committee entails only a marginal restriction upon the contributor's ability to engage in free communication. A contribution serves as a general expression of support for the candidate and his views, but does not communicate the underlying basis for the support. [Expression] rests solely on the . . . symbolic act of contributing. [A] limitation on the amount of money a person may give to a candidate or campaign organization [involves] little direct restraint on his political communication, for it permits the symbolic expression of support evidenced by a contribution but does not in any way infringe the contributor's freedom to discuss candidates and issues. While contributions may result in political expression if spent by a candidate or an association to present views to the voters, the transformation of contributions into political debate involves speech by someone other than the contributor.

Given the important role of contributions in financing political campaigns, contribution restrictions could have a severe impact on political dialogue if the limitations prevented candidates and political committees from amassing the resources necessary for effective advocacy. There is no indication, however, that the contribution limitations imposed by the Act would have any dramatic adverse effect on the funding of campaigns and political associations. [Only] approximately 5.1% of the [total amount] raised by [all] candidates for Congress in 1974 was obtained in amounts in excess of $1,000. The overall effect of the Act's contribution ceilings is merely to require candidates and political committees to raise funds from a greater number of persons and to compel people who would otherwise contribute amounts greater than the statutory limits to expend such funds on direct political expression, rather than to reduce the total amount of money potentially available to promote political expression.

The Act's contribution and expenditure limitations also impinge on protected associational freedoms. Making a contribution [serves] to affiliate a person with a candidate [and] enables like-minded persons to pool their resources in furtherance of common political goals. The Act's contribution

---

limited the *manner* of operating a soundtrack, but not the *extent* of its proper use. By contrast, the Act's dollar ceilings restrict the extent of the reasonable use of virtually every means of communicating information.

21. Being free to engage in unlimited political expression subject to a ceiling on expenditures is like being free to drive an automobile as far and as often as one desires on a single tank of gasoline.

ceilings thus limit one [means of association], but leave the contributor free to become a member of any political association and to assist personally in the association's efforts on behalf of candidates. And the Act's contribution limitations permit associations and candidates to aggregate large sums of money to promote effective advocacy. By contrast, the Act's $1,000 limitation on independent expenditures "relative to a clearly identified candidate" precludes most associations from effectively amplifying the voice of their adherents.

[While] governmental "action which may have the effect of curtailing the freedom to associate is subject to the closest scrutiny, [even a] 'significant interference' with protected rights of political association" may be sustained if the State demonstrates a sufficiently important interest and employs means closely drawn to avoid unnecessary abridgment of associational freedoms.

[The] Act's primary purpose—to limit the actuality and appearance of corruption resulting from large individual financial contributions—[is] a constitutionally sufficient justification for the $1,000 contribution limitation. [To] the extent that large contributions are given to secure political quid pro quos from current and potential office holders, the integrity of our system of representative democracy is undermined. [Of] almost equal concern . . . is the impact of the appearance of corruption stemming from public awareness of the opportunities for abuse inherent in a regime of large individual financial contributions. [The] Act's $1,000 contribution limitation focuses precisely on the problem of large campaign contributions—the narrow aspect of political association where the actuality and potential for corruption have been identified—while leaving persons free to engage in independent political expression. . . .

The Act's expenditure ceilings impose direct and substantial restraints on the quantity of political speech. . . . The restrictions, while neutral as to the ideas expressed, limit political expression "at the core of our electoral process and of the First Amendment freedoms."

Section 608(e)(1) provides that "[n]o person may make any expenditure [relative] to a clearly identified candidate during a calendar year [that] exceeds $1,000." [The] governmental interest in preventing corruption and the appearance of corruption is inadequate to justify [this] ceiling on independent expenditures. First, [so] long as persons and groups eschew expenditures that in express terms advocate the election or defeat of a clearly identified candidate, they are free to spend as much as they want to promote the candidate and his views. [Second], the independent advocacy restricted by the provision does not . . . pose dangers of real or apparent corruption comparable to those [posed by] large campaign contributions. [Section] 608(e)(1) limits expenditures for express advocacy of candidates made totally independently of the candidate and his campaign. [The] absence of prearrangement and coordination . . . with the candidate [alleviates] the danger that expenditures will be given as a quid pro quo for improper commitments from the candidate. [The] independent expenditure ceiling thus fails to serve any substantial governmental interest in stemming the reality or appearance of corruption in the electoral process [and] it heavily burdens core First Amendment expression.

[It] is argued, however, that the ancillary governmental interest in equalizing the relative ability of individuals and groups to influence the outcome of elections serves to justify the [independent expenditure limitation. But] the concept that government may restrict the speech of some elements of our society in order to enhance the relative voice of others is wholly foreign to the First Amendment, which was designed "to secure 'the widest possible dissemination of information from diverse and antagonistic sources,'" and "'to assure unfettered interchange of ideas for the bringing about of political and social changes desired by the people.'" . . . [Section] 608(e)(1)'s independent expenditure limitation is unconstitutional under the First Amendment.

The Act also sets limits on expenditures by a candidate "from his personal funds, or the personal funds of his immediate family, in connection with his campaigns during any calendar year."[22] [The] ceiling on personal expenditures by candidates on their own behalf [imposes] a substantial restraint on the ability of persons to engage in protected First Amendment expression. [It] is of particular importance that candidates have the unfettered opportunity to make their views known so that the electorate may intelligently evaluate the candidates' personal qualities and their positions on vital public issues before choosing among them on election day. [The] ceiling on personal expenditures by a candidate in furtherance of his own candidacy . . . directly interferes with constitutionally protected freedoms. The . . . interest [of] prevention of actual and apparent corruption . . . does not support [limiting] the candidate's expenditure of his own personal funds. [The] interest in equalizing the relative financial resources of candidates competing for elective office [is] not sufficient to justify the provision's infringement of fundamental First Amendment rights. [The] First Amendment simply cannot tolerate [this] restriction upon the freedom of a candidate to speak . . . on behalf of his own candidacy. [The restriction] is unconstitutional. Section 608(c) places limitations on overall campaign expenditures by candidates seeking nomination for election and election to federal office. [No] governmental interest that has been suggested is sufficient to justify [these restrictions] on the quantity of political expression. The major evil associated with rapidly increasing campaign expenditures is the danger of candidate dependence on large contributions. The interest in alleviating the corrupting influence of large contributions is served by the Act's contribution limitations and disclosure provisions rather than [by] campaign expenditure ceilings. [The] interest in equalizing the financial resources of candidates competing for federal office is no more convincing a justification for restricting the scope of federal election campaigns. [There] is nothing invidious, improper, or unhealthy in permitting [funds] to be spent to carry the candidate's message to the electorate. . . . [The] First Amendment denies government the power to determine that spending to promote one's political views is wasteful, excessive, or unwise. [It] is not the government but the

---

22. These ceilings vary from $50,000 for Presidential or Vice Presidential candidates to $35,000 for senatorial candidates, and $25,000 for most candidates for the House of Representatives.

people—individually as citizens and candidates and collectively as associations and political committees—who must retain control over the quantity and range of debate on public issues in a political campaign. [Section] 608(c) is constitutionally invalid.

A series of statutes [created a presidential election campaign fund funded by taxpayer election on tax returns. As a condition of receiving such funds, candidates were required to limit their campaign expenditures to the amount of the public subsidy and to forgo private contributions except to the extent the fund was insufficient to provide the full amount of the statutory subsidy. This scheme did not] abridge, restrict, or censor speech, [but merely enlarged] public discussion and participation in the electoral process, goals vital to a self-governing people. . . . Just as a candidate may voluntarily limit the size of the contributions he chooses to accept, he may decide to forgo private fundraising and accept public funding.

CHIEF JUSTICE BURGER, concurring in part and dissenting in part.

[C]ontributions and expenditures are two sides of the same First Amendment coin. . . . [C]andidates and contributors . . . spend money on political activity because they wish to communicate ideas, and their constitutional interest in doing so is precisely the same whether they or someone else utters the words. . . .

JUSTICE WHITE, concurring in part and dissenting in part.

I dissent [from] the Court's view that the expenditure [limitations] violate the First Amendment. [Because] the contribution and expenditure limitations are [content-neutral and] are not motivated by fear of the consequences [of] political speech, [this] case depends on whether the non-speech interests of the Federal Government in regulating the use of money in political campaigns are sufficiently urgent to justify the incidental effects that the limitations visit upon the First Amendment interests of candidates and their supporters. [The] Court . . . accepts the congressional judgment that the evils of unlimited contributions are sufficiently threatening to warrant [contribution restrictions]. . . . It would make little sense to me, and apparently made none to Congress, to limit the amounts an individual may give to a candidate or spend with his approval but fail to limit the amounts that could be spent on his behalf. [I] would take the word of those who know—that limiting independent expenditures is essential to prevent transparent and widespread evasion of the contribution limits. . . .

[Expenditure] ceilings reinforce the contribution limits and help eradicate the hazard of corruption. [The] expenditure limit imposed on candidates [lessens] the chance that the contribution ceiling will be violated. Without limits on total expenditures, campaign costs will inevitably and endlessly escalate, [pressure] to raise funds will constantly build and with it the temptation to resort [to] those sources of large sums, who, history shows, are sufficiently confident of not being caught to risk flouting contribution limits. . . . [It] is also important to restore and maintain public confidence in federal elections.

It is critical to obviate or dispel the impression that federal elections are purely and simply a function of money, that federal offices are bought and sold or that political races are reserved for those who have the facility—and the stomach—for doing whatever it takes to bring together those interests, groups, and individuals that can raise or contribute large fortunes in order to prevail at the polls. . . .

[I] also disagree with the Court's judgment that [the limit on] the amount of money that a candidate or his family may spend on his campaign violates the Constitution. Although it [does] not promote any interest in preventing the corruption of candidates, [it does] serve salutary purposes related to the integrity of federal campaigns. By limiting the importance of personal wealth, [it] helps to assure that only individuals with a modicum of support from others will be viable candidates. This in turn would tend to discourage any notion that the outcome of elections is primarily a function of money. . . .

NOTES

1. Developments Since *Buckley*: Contributions. While *Buckley* upheld contribution limits to or on behalf of political candidates, it did not deal with contributions to independent political action committees or in connection with ballot measures. In California Medical Association v. FEC, 453 U.S. 182 (1981), the Court upheld a federal limitation on contributions by individuals or associations to "multi-candidate" political action committees. But in Citizens Against Rent Control v. Berkeley, 454 U.S. 290 (1981), the Court voided a Berkeley, California, ordinance that limited contributions to committees supporting or opposing ballot measures. The ordinance posed a "significant restraint" upon free association and free speech, and the goal of limiting contributions to curb corruption was totally inapplicable to ballot measures. In Nixon v. Shrink Missouri Government PAC, 528 U.S. 377 (2000), the Court extended *Buckley* to uphold state limits on contributions.

2. Developments Since *Buckley*: Independent Expenditures. In FEC v. NCPAC, 470 U.S. 480 (1985), the Court voided a federal law barring independent political action committees from spending more than $1,000 in support of any presidential candidate. The Court reasoned that, as in the case of expenditures by individuals or the candidate from personal funds, there was an insufficient risk of corruption to justify the limitation. In Colorado Republican Federal Campaign Committee v. FEC ("*Colorado I*"), 518 U.S. 604 (1996), the Court struck down federal limits on expenditures of a political party that were made independently of the party's candidate.

In Meyer v. Grant, 486 U.S. 414 (1988), the Court struck down a Colorado law barring the use of paid workers to gather citizen signatures necessary to qualify proposed state constitutional amendments for the ballot. Speech was substantially burdened because the law restricted "access to the most effective, fundamental, and perhaps economical avenue of political discourse, direct one-on-one communication." The Court rejected Colorado's argument that the statute was "justified by its interest in making sure that an initiative has sufficient grass roots support to be placed on the ballot, or by its interest in protecting the integrity of the initiative process."

3. Developments Since *Buckley*: Coordinated Expenditures. In FEC v. Colorado Republican Federal Campaign Committee ("*Colorado II*"), 533 U.S. 431 (2001), the Court upheld limits imposed on a political party's expenditures made in coordination with a candidate. The Court reasoned that coordinated party expenditures posed a risk of corruption similar to direct contributions to candidates. Political parties are "necessarily the instruments of some contributors whose object is . . . to support a specific candidate . . . who will be obliged to the contributors. [Whether] they like it or not, [parties] act as agents for spending on behalf of those who seek to produce obligated officeholders."

4. Analytical Problems with *Buckley*.   What standard of review did the Court employ? Did the Court employ a more lenient standard for contribution limits than for expenditure limits?

The Court declared that "the concept that government may restrict the speech of some elements of our society in order to enhance the relative voice of others is wholly foreign to the First Amendment." Would expenditure limits really equalize speech? If candidates were not permitted to air their message to the fullest degree of their capabilities and desires, what alternative voices would fill that void? The media? The accumulated fame of candidates, derived from prominence in other activities or from incumbency? What about other forms of inequality? Should the most linguistically skilled and persuasive speakers be muted by government because they possess a more powerful voice?

≡ *McConnell v. Federal Election Commission*
≡ *540 U.S. 93 (2003)*

[Prior to enactment of the Bipartisan Campaign Reform Act of 2002 (the BCRA), contributions unlimited in amount could be made to influence state or local elections, to register voters and get them to vote, to promote political parties, and to advocate legislation. This "soft money" could be used to purchase advertising for such purposes, and could mention a candidate's name so long as the advertising did not explicitly urge the election or defeat of a candidate (so-called issue ads).]

JUSTICE STEVENS and JUSTICE O'CONNOR delivered the opinion of the Court with respect to BCRA Titles I and II.

II. . . . Title I regulates the use of soft money by political parties, officeholders, and candidates. Title II . . . prohibits corporations and labor unions from using general treasury funds for [speech] that [is] intended to, or [has] the effect of, influencing the outcome of federal elections. . . .

III. . . . The cornerstone of Title I is new FECA §323(a), which prohibits national party committees and their agents from soliciting, receiving, directing, or spending any soft money. . . . New FECA §323(b) prevents the wholesale shift of soft-money influence from national to state party committees by prohibiting state and local party committees from using such funds for activities that affect federal elections. . . . New FECA §323(d) reinforces these soft-money restrictions by prohibiting political parties from soliciting and donating funds to tax-exempt organizations that engage in electioneering activities. New FECA §323(e) restricts federal candidates and officeholders from receiving, spending, or soliciting soft money in connection with federal elections and limits their ability to do so in connection with state and local elections. [N]ew FECA §323(f) prevents circumvention of the restrictions on national, state, and local party committees by prohibiting state and local candidates from raising and spending soft money to fund advertisements and other public communications that promote or attack federal candidates.

Plaintiffs mount a facial First Amendment challenge to new FECA §323. . . . [When] reviewing . . . contribution limits, "there is no place for a strong presumption against constitutionality, of the sort often thought to accompany the words 'strict scrutiny.'" The less rigorous standard of review we have applied to contribution limits (*Buckley*'s "closely drawn" scrutiny) shows proper deference to Congress's ability to weigh competing constitutional interests in an area in which it enjoys particular expertise. . . .

Like the contribution limits we upheld in *Buckley*, §323's restrictions have only a marginal impact on the ability of contributors, candidates, officeholders, and parties to engage in effective political speech. [Section] 323, in the main, does little more than regulate the ability of wealthy individuals, corporations, and unions to contribute large sums of money to influence federal elections, federal candidates, and federal officeholders. . . .

The] relevant inquiry is whether the mechanism adopted to implement the contribution limit, or to prevent circumvention of that limit, burdens speech in a way that a direct restriction on the contribution itself would not. That is not the case here. . . . [These provisions] simply limit the source and individual amount of donations. That they do so by prohibiting the spending of soft money does not render them expenditure limitations. . . . As with direct limits on contributions, therefore, §323's spending and solicitation restrictions have only a marginal impact on political speech. . . .

Congress enacted §323 as an integrated whole to vindicate the Government's important interest in preventing corruption and the appearance of corruption.

. . . Our cases have made clear that the prevention of corruption or its appearance constitutes a sufficiently important interest to justify political contribution limits. . . . The question . . . is whether large *soft-money* contributions to national party committees have a corrupting influence or give rise to the appearance of corruption . . . . [P]laintiffs conceive of corruption too narrowly. . . . Congress's legitimate interest extends beyond preventing simple cash-for-votes corruption to curbing "undue influence on an officeholder's judgment, and the appearance of such influence." . . . [We] reject the plaintiffs' First Amendment challenge to new FECA §323(a).

. . . Congress recognized that, given the close ties between federal candidates and state party committees, BCRA's restrictions on national committee activity would rapidly become ineffective if state and local committees remained available as a conduit for soft-money donations. Section 323(b) is designed to foreclose wholesale evasion of §323(a)'s anticorruption measures by sharply curbing state committees' ability to use large soft-money contributions to influence federal elections. . . .

[In] addressing the problem of soft-money contributions to state committees, Congress both drew a conclusion and made a prediction. Its conclusion . . . was that the corrupting influence of soft money does not insinuate itself into the political process solely through national party committees. Rather, state committees function as an alternate avenue for precisely the same corrupting forces. . . . Congress also made a prediction. . . . Congress knew that soft-money donors would react to §323(a) by scrambling to find another way to purchase influence. It was "neither novel nor implausible" for Congress to conclude that political parties would react to §323(a) by directing soft-money contributors to the state committees, and that federal candidates would be just as indebted to these contributors as they had been to those who had formerly contributed to the national parties. . . . Preventing corrupting activity from shifting wholesale to state committees and thereby eviscerating FECA clearly qualifies as an important governmental interest.

. . . We conclude that §323(b) is a closely drawn means of countering both corruption and the appearance of corruption. . . .

[Section] 323(d)'s ban on solicitations to tax-exempt organizations engaged in political activity [prevents] circumvention of Title I's limits on contributions of soft money to national, state, and local party committees. . . . Absent the solicitation provision, national, state, and local party committees would have significant incentives to mobilize their formidable fund-raising apparatuses, including the peddling of access to federal office-holders, into the service of like-minded tax-exempt organizations that conduct activities benefiting their candidates. . . . Section 323(d)'s solicitation restriction is closely drawn to prevent political parties from using tax-exempt organizations as soft-money surrogates. Though phrased as an absolute prohibition, the restriction does nothing more than subject contributions solicited by parties to FECA's regulatory regime, leaving open substantial opportunities for solicitation and other expressive activity in support of these organizations. . . .

New FECA §323(e) . . . prohibits federal candidates and officeholders from "soliciting, receiving, directing, [transferring], or spending" any soft money in connection with federal elections [and] limits the ability of federal candidates and officeholders to solicit, receive, direct, transfer, or spend soft money in connection with state and local elections. . . . Section 323(e)'s restrictions on solicitations are . . . valid anti-circumvention measures. Large soft-money donations at a candidate's or officeholder's behest give rise to all of the same corruption concerns posed by contributions made directly to the candidate or officeholder. Though the candidate may not ultimately control how the funds are spent, the value of the donation to the candidate or office-holder is evident from the fact of the solicitation itself. . . .

[N]ew FECA §323(f) generally prohibits candidates for state or local office, or state or local officeholders, from spending soft money to fund "public communications" . . . i.e., a communication that "refers to a clearly identified candidate for Federal office . . . and that promotes or supports a candidate for that office, or attacks or opposes a candidate for that office." . . . Section 323(f) . . . limits only the source and amount of contributions that state and local candidates can draw on to fund expenditures that [have a direct impact upon] federal elections. And, by regulating only contributions used to fund "public communications," §323(f) focuses narrowly on those soft-money donations with the greatest potential to corrupt or give rise to the appearance of corruption of federal candidates and officeholders. . . . The proliferation of sham issue ads has driven the soft-money explosion. Parties have sought out every possible way to fund and produce these ads with soft money. . . . We . . . uphold §323(f) against plaintiffs' First Amendment challenge. . . .

IV. Title II of BCRA, entitled "Noncandidate Campaign Expenditures," is divided into two subtitles: "Electioneering Communications" and "Independent and Coordinated Expenditures." . . . The first section of Title II, §201, . . . coins a new term, "electioneering communication," to replace the narrowing construction of FECA's disclosure provisions adopted by this Court in *Buckley*. [That] construction limited the coverage of FECA's disclosure requirement to communications expressly advocating the election or defeat of particular candidates. By contrast, the term "electioneering communication" . . . is defined to encompass any "broadcast, cable, or satellite communication" that . . . "refers to a clearly identified candidate for Federal office; is made within 60 days before a general, special, or runoff election for the office sought by the candidate; or 30 days before a primary or preference election, or a convention or caucus of a political party that has authority to nominate a candidate, for the office sought by the candidate; and in the case of a communication which refers to a candidate other than President or Vice President, is targeted to the relevant electorate." . . . Section 203 of BCRA [provides that] corporations and unions may not use their general treasury funds to finance electioneering communications, but they remain free to organize and administer segregated funds, or PACs, for that purpose. . . . [We] examine the degree to which BCRA burdens First Amendment expression and evaluate whether a compelling governmental interest justifies that burden. The latter question—whether the state interest is compelling—is easily answered by [Austin v. Michigan Chamber of Commerce, 494 U.S. 652 (1990), in which we] sustained legislation aimed at "the corrosive and distorting effects of immense aggregations of wealth that are accumulated with the help of the corporate form and that have little or no correlation to the public's support for the corporation's political ideas." [We uphold] the constitutionality of BCRA §203. Ever since our decision in *Buckley*, it has been settled that expenditures by a non-candidate that are "controlled by or coordinated with the candidate and his campaign" may be treated as indirect contributions subject to FECA's source and amount limitations. . . . Section 214(a) of BCRA . . . applies the same rule to expenditures coordinated with "a national, State, or local committee of a political party" [and is upheld].

CHIEF JUSTICE REHNQUIST, joined by JUSTICES SCALIA and KENNEDY, dissenting with respect to BCRA Titles I and V.

. . . The [linchpin] of Title I, new FECA §323(a), . . . regulates *all donations* to national political committees, no matter the use to which the funds are put. . . . [A] close association with others, especially in the realm of political speech, is not a surrogate for corruption; it is one of our most treasured First Amendment rights. . . . The Court fails to recognize that the national political parties are exemplars of political speech. . . . [Political] parties often foster speech crucial to a healthy democracy and fulfill the need for like-minded individuals to band together and promote a political philosophy. When political parties engage in pure political speech that has little or no potential to corrupt their federal candidates and officeholders, the government cannot constitutionally burden their speech any more than, it could burden the speech of individuals engaging in these same activities. . . .

[T]he Court concludes that because [Congress sought to regulate activities that either] *benefit* federal candidates and officeholders or prevent the circumvention of preexisting or contemporaneously enacted restrictions it must defer to the "predictive judgments of Congress." Yet the Court cannot truly mean what it says. Newspaper editorials and political talk shows *benefit* federal candidates and officeholders every bit as much as a generic voter registration drive conducted by a state party; there is little doubt that the endorsement of a major newspaper *affects* federal elections, and federal candidates and officeholders are surely "grateful" for positive media coverage. I doubt . . . the Court would seriously contend that we must defer to Congress's judgment if it chose to reduce the influence of political endorsements in federal elections. [*Tornillo.*]

It is also true that any circumvention rationale ultimately must rest on the circumvention itself leading to the corruption of federal candidates and officeholders. All political speech that is not sifted through federal regulation circumvents the regulatory scheme to some degree or another, and thus by the Court's standard would be a "loophole" in the current system. Unless the Court would uphold federal regulation of all funding of political speech, a rationale dependent on circumvention alone will not do. By untethering its inquiry from corruption or the appearance of corruption, the Court has removed the touchstone of our campaign finance precedent and has failed to replace it with any logical limiting principle.

But such an untethering is necessary to the Court's analysis. . . . Any campaign finance law aimed at reducing corruption will . . . , if broad enough, . . . reduce some appearance of corruption. [It] is precisely because broad laws are likely to nominally further a legitimate interest that we require Congress to tailor its restrictions. . . . In allowing Congress to rely on general principles such as affecting a federal election or prohibiting the circumvention of existing law, the Court all but eliminates the "closely drawn" tailoring requirement and meaningful judicial review. . . .

JUSTICE SCALIA, concurring with respect to BCRA Titles III and IV, dissenting with respect to BCRA Titles I and V, and concurring in the judgment in part and dissenting in part with respect to BCRA Title II.

. . . This is a sad day for freedom of speech. . . . We are governed by Congress, and this legislation prohibits the criticism of Members of Congress by those entities most capable of giving such criticism loud voice: national political parties and corporations, both of the commercial and the not-for-profit sort. . . . To be sure, the legislation is evenhanded: It similarly prohibits criticism of the candidates who oppose Members of Congress in their reelection bids. But as everyone knows, this is an area in which evenhandedness is not fairness. If *all* electioneering were evenhandedly prohibited, incumbents would have an enormous advantage. . . .

Beyond that, however, the present legislation *targets* for prohibition certain categories of campaign speech that are particularly harmful to incumbents. Is it accidental, do you think, that incumbents raise about three times as much "hard money"—the sort of funding generally *not* restricted by this legislation—as do their challengers? Or that lobbyists (who seek the favor of incumbents) give 92 percent of their money in "hard" contributions? Is it an oversight, do you suppose, that the so-called millionaire provisions raise the contribution limit for a candidate running against an individual who devotes to the campaign (as challengers often do) great personal wealth, but do not raise the limit for a candidate running against an individual who devotes to the campaign (as incumbents often do) a massive election "war chest"? And is it mere happenstance, do you estimate, that national-party funding, which is severely limited by the Act, is more likely to assist cash-strapped challengers than flush-with-hard-money incumbents? Was it unintended, by any chance, that incumbents are free personally to receive some soft money and even to solicit it for other organizations, while national parties are not?

I wish to address [some] fallacious propositions that might be thought to justify some or all of the provisions of this legislation—only the last of which is explicitly embraced by the principal opinion for the Court, but all of which underlie, I think, its approach to these cases.

(a) Money Is Not Speech

. . . In any economy operated on even the most rudimentary principles of division of labor, effective public communication requires the speaker to make use of the services of others. An author may write a novel, but he will seldom publish and distribute it himself. A freelance reporter may write a story, but he will rarely edit, print, and deliver it to subscribers. . . . Division of labor requires a means of mediating exchange, and in a commercial society, that means is supplied by money. The publisher pays the author for the right to sell his book; it pays its staff who print and assemble the book; it demands payments from booksellers who bring the book to market. This . . . presents opportunities for repression: Instead of regulating the various parties to the enterprise individually, the government can suppress their ability to coordinate by regulating their use of money. What good is the right to print books without a right to buy works from authors? Or the right to publish newspapers without the right to pay deliverymen? The right to speak would be largely ineffective if it did not include the right to engage in financial transactions that are the incidents of its exercise. . . .

[W]here the government singles out money used to fund speech as its legislative object, it is acting against speech as such, no less than if it had targeted the paper on which a book was printed or the trucks that deliver it to the bookstore. . . . It should be obvious, then, that a law limiting the amount a person can spend to broadcast his political views is a direct restriction on speech. . . .

(b)   Pooling Money Is Not Speech

Another proposition which could explain at least some of the results of today's opinion is that the First Amendment right to spend money for speech does not include the right to combine with others in spending money for speech. Such a proposition fits uncomfortably with the concluding words of our Declaration of Independence: "And for the support of this Declaration, . . . we mutually pledge to each other our Lives, *our Fortunes and* our sacred Honor." (Emphasis added.) The freedom to associate with others for the dissemination of ideas—not just by singing or speaking in unison, but by pooling financial resources for expressive purposes—is part of the freedom of speech. . . . The principle that such financial association does not enjoy full First Amendment protection threatens the existence of all political parties. . . .

Another theme prominent in the legislative debates was the notion that there is too much money spent on elections. . . . And what exactly are these outrageous sums frittered away in determining who will govern us? [The] total amount, in hard and soft money, spent on the 2000 federal elections was between $2.4 and $2.5 billion. *All* campaign spending in the United States including state elections, ballot initiatives, and judicial elections, has been estimated at $3.9 billion for 2000. Even taking this last, larger figure as the benchmark, it means that Americans spent about half as much electing all their Nation's officials, state and federal, as they spent on movie tickets ($7.8 billion); about a fifth as much as they spent on cosmetics and perfume ($18.8 billion); and about a sixth as much as they spent on pork (the nongovernmental sort) ($22.8 billion). If our democracy is drowning from this much spending, it cannot swim. . . .

This litigation is about preventing criticism of the government. . . .

Justice Kennedy, joined by Chief Justice Rehnquist and, in part, by Justice Scalia and Justice Thomas.
. . . I. . . . In *Buckley*, the Court held that one, and only one, interest justified the significant burden on the right of association involved there: eliminating, or preventing, actual corruption or the appearance of corruption stemming from contributions to candidates. . . . *Buckley* made clear . . . that campaign finance regulation that restricts speech . . . withstands constitutional challenge only if it regulates conduct posing a demonstrable *quid pro*

quo danger. . . . The Court ignores these constitutional bounds and in effect interprets the anticorruption rationale to allow regulation not just of "actual or apparent *quid pro quo* arrangements," but of any conduct that wins good-will from or influences a Member of Congress. . . . This new definition of corruption sweeps away all protections for speech that lie in its path. . . . Access in itself . . . shows only that in a general sense an officeholder favors someone or that someone has influence on the officeholder. There is no basis, in law or in fact, to say favoritism or influence in general is the same as corrupt favoritism or influence in particular. . . .

The generic favoritism or influence theory articulated by the Court is . . . unbounded and susceptible to no limiting principle. . . . Favoritism and influence are not . . . avoidable in representative politics. It is in the nature of an elected representative to favor certain policies, and, by necessary corollary, to favor the voters and contributors who support those policies. It is well understood that a substantial and legitimate reason, if not the only reason, to cast a vote for, or to make a contribution to, [a] candidate . . . is that the candidate will respond by producing those political outcomes the supporter favors. Democracy is premised on responsiveness. . . .

NOTES

1. Randall v. Sorrell: Whither *McConnell?* Whither *Buckley?* The validity of Vermont's Act 64 was at issue in Randall v. Sorrell, 548 U.S. 230 (2006). Act 64 limited contributions by individuals and political parties to candidates for state office to $200 (for state representatives) and to $400 (for statewide offices such as governor) in any two-year election cycle period. Included in the definition of contribution were the expenses (such as travel) incurred by uncompensated volunteers working on behalf of a candidate. Act 64 also limited the amount that candidates for Vermont offices could spend. Candidates for Governor could spend up to $300,000 in any two-year election cycle period, and the expenditure limits became progressively tighter for candidates for lesser offices, reaching a low of $2,000 in any two-year election cycle period for candidates for state representative. By a 6-3 margin, the Supreme Court struck down each of the contribution and expenditure limits, but no majority could be mustered for the rationale. Justice Breyer, joined by Chief Justice Roberts and, for the most part, Justice Alito, reaffirmed that *Buckley* controlled as to the expenditure limits. There was no evidence of any increase in corruption in Vermont, nor were expenditure limits were the only way to attack such a perceived problem. As to the latter argument, Vermont's interest was simply insufficient to overcome the burden of justification required by *Buckley* with respect to expenditure limits. The low contribution limits posed a significant negative

> effect on political parties and on volunteer activity in Vermont elections. . . .
> [T]he Act is not closely drawn to meet its objectives. . . . First, [the] contribution

limits will significantly restrict the amount of funding available for challengers to run competitive campaigns. . . . Second, [the Act] threatens harm to a
particularly important political right, the right to associate in a political party.
[The] Act's contribution limits "would reduce the voice of political parties" in
Vermont to a "whisper." . . . Third, the Act's treatment of volunteer services
aggravates the problem [because its] contribution limits are so low, and its definition of "contribution" so broad, that the Act may well impede a campaign's
ability effectively to use volunteers, thereby making it more difficult for individuals to associate in this way. . . . Fourth, [because] Act 64's contribution
limits are not adjusted for inflation [its] limits decline in real value each year. . . .
Fifth, [there is no] special justification that might warrant a contribution limit
so low or so restrictive as to bring about the serious associational and expressive
problems that we have described.

Justice Thomas, joined by Justice Scalia, concurred only in the judgment.
They contended that *Buckley* should be overruled because it "provides insufficient protection to political speech, the core of the First Amendment [and
cannot be applied] in a coherent and principled fashion." Justice Thomas
declared that he would subject both contribution and expenditure limits to
strict scrutiny. Justice Kennedy also concurred only in the judgment, expressing his continued "skepticism regarding [the] system [of campaign finance
regulation] and its operation."

Justice Stevens, joined by Justice Souter, dissented, arguing that *Buckley*'s
"holding on expenditure limits is wrong, and that the time has come to
overrule it." Expenditure limits "are far more akin to time, place, and manner restrictions than to restrictions on the content of speech. . . . I would
uphold them so long as the purposes they serve are legitimate and sufficiently
substantial."

Lost in the torrent of opinions was much discussion of *McConnell*, which
may suggest that the Court as a whole views *McConnell* as a mere application
of *Buckley*.

2. Asymmetrical Contribution Limits. *Davis v. Federal Election
Commission, 554 U.S. 724 (2008).* Section 319(a) of the BCRA triples the
contribution limits applicable to a candidate for federal office who is opposed
by a candidate who spends over $350,000 of his or her own money for elec-
toral purposes, while retaining the original contribution limits for the self-
funded candidate. Section 319(a) also lifted the ban on coordinated party
expenditures for the candidate opposed by a wealthy self-funded candidate.
The Court struck down this scheme, reasoning that the asymmetry of §319(a)
imposed a "substantial burden on the exercise of the First Amendment right
to use personal funds for campaign speech." Accordingly, the government was
required to justify the scheme under strict scrutiny, a burden that could not
be overcome. The asymmetrical contribution limits did nothing to prevent
corruption or the appearance of corruption. The desire to "level electoral
opportunities for candidates of different personal wealth" was not a legitimate
governmental objective. The objective of reducing the advantage enjoyed
by wealthy candidates due to statutory restrictions on contributions and

coordinated party expenditures was not only insufficiently compelling, but was "fundamentally at war with the analysis of expenditure and contributions limits that this Court adopted in *Buckley* and has [since] applied." The Court also invalidated the disclosure requirements imposed on the self-funded candidate that were related to §319(a).

Arizona Free Enterprise Club's Freedom Club PAC v. Bennett, 131 S. Ct. 2806 (2011). Arizona law provided that candidates for state office who accept public financing receive roughly one additional dollar of public money for every dollar over a set level spent by either a privately funded candidate or an independent group supporting the privately funded candidate. Because there can be multiple candidates in any election, a privately funded candidate who expends his funds above the limit would face rivals who have each received public matching funds. Thus, in a four-person race, three public candidates could receive an aggregate of three dollars for each dollar above the limit spent by the private candidate. The Court voided this asymmetrical device because its substantial burdens on speech were even worse than in *Davis*:

> First, the penalty in *Davis* consisted of raising the contribution limits for one of the candidates. The candidate who benefited from the increased limits still had to go out and raise the funds. He may or may not have been able to do so. The other candidate, therefore, faced merely the possibility that his opponent would be able to raise additional funds. . . . Second, . . . the matching funds provision can create a multiplier effect. [In a multi-party race,] privately funded candidates [must] fight a political hydra of sorts. Each dollar they spend generates [multiple] adversarial dollars in response. . . .

The Arizona law lacked any compelling interest: Avoiding corruption or the appearance of corruption was not implicated by the law, and the state's interest in "leveling the playing field" was illegitimate. That interest amounted to the state's desire to make " 'judgments about which strengths should be permitted to contribute to the outcome of an election'—a dangerous enterprise that cannot justify burdening protected speech."

Four justices, led by Justice Kagan, dissented. They argued that the law imposed no substantial burden on speech because "all the law does is fund more speech."

≡≡ ## *Citizens United v. Federal Election Commission*
≡≡ *558 U.S. 310 (2010)*

JUSTICE KENNEDY delivered the opinion of the Court.

Federal law prohibits corporations and unions from using their general treasury funds to make independent expenditures for speech defined as an "electioneering communication" or for speech expressly advocating the election or defeat of a candidate. 2 U.S.C. §441b. Limits on electioneering communications were upheld in *McConnell*. . . . The holding of *McConnell* rested to a large extent on . . . Austin v. Michigan Chamber of Commerce, 494 U.S.

652 (1990). *Austin* had held that political speech may be banned based on the speaker's corporate identity.

In this case we are asked to reconsider *Austin* and, in effect, *McConnell*. [Because] "*Austin* was a significant departure from ancient First Amendment principles," [we] hold that *stare decisis* does not compel the continued acceptance of *Austin*. The Government may regulate corporate political speech through disclaimer and disclosure requirements, but it may not suppress that speech altogether. . . .

I. A. Citizens United is a nonprofit corporation [which] has an annual budget of about $12 million. Most of its funds are from donations by individuals; but, in addition, it accepts a small portion of its funds from for-profit corporations. In January 2008, Citizens United released a film entitled *Hillary: The Movie*. We refer to the film as *Hillary*. It is a 90-minute documentary about then-Senator Hillary Clinton, who was a candidate in the Democratic Party's 2008 Presidential primary elections. *Hillary* mentions Senator Clinton by name and depicts interviews with political commentators and other persons, most of them quite critical of Senator Clinton. *Hillary* was released in theaters and on DVD, but Citizens United wanted . . . to make *Hillary* available on a video-on-demand channel called "Elections '08." [To] promote the film [Citizens United] produced two 10-second ads and one 30-second ad for *Hillary*. Each ad includes a short (and, in our view, pejorative) statement about Senator Clinton, followed by the name of the movie and the movie's Website address. Citizens United desired to promote the video-on-demand offering by running advertisements on broadcast and cable television. . . .

C. Citizens United . . . feared . . . that both the film and the ads would be covered by §441b's ban on corporate-funded independent expenditures, thus subjecting the corporation to civil and criminal penalties. . . . Citizens United sought declaratory and injunctive relief against the FEC. It argued that (1) §441b is unconstitutional as applied to *Hillary;* and (2) BCRA's disclaimer and disclosure requirements, BCRA §§201 and 311, are unconstitutional as applied to *Hillary* and to the three ads for the movie. [A three-judge] District Court denied Citizens United's motion for a preliminary injunction, and then granted the FEC's motion for summary judgment. . . . We noted probable jurisdiction. . . .

III. . . . . Laws enacted to control or suppress speech may operate at different points in the speech process. . . . The law before us is an outright ban, backed by criminal sanctions. Section 441b makes it a felony for all corporations—including nonprofit advocacy corporations—either to expressly advocate the election or defeat of candidates or to broadcast electioneering communications within 30 days of a primary election and 60 days of a general election. Thus, the following acts would all be felonies under §441b: The Sierra Club runs an ad, within the crucial phase of 60 days before the general election, that exhorts the public to disapprove of a Congressman who favors logging in national forests; the National Rifle Association publishes a book urging the public to vote for the challenger because the incumbent U.S. Senator supports a handgun ban; and the American Civil Liberties Union creates a Web site telling the public to vote for a Presidential candidate in light of that candidate's defense of free speech. These prohibitions are classic examples of censorship. . . .

Section 441b's prohibition on corporate independent expenditures is thus a ban on speech. As a "restriction on the amount of money a person or group can spend on political communication during a campaign," that statute "necessarily reduces the quantity of expression by restricting the number of issues discussed, the depth of their exploration, and the size of the audience reached." *Buckley.* Were the Court to uphold these restrictions, the Government could repress speech by silencing certain voices at any of the various points in the speech process. . . . If §441b applied to individuals, no one would believe that it is merely a time, place, or manner restriction on speech. Its purpose and effect are to silence entities whose voices the Government deems to be suspect.

Speech is an essential mechanism of democracy, for it is the means to hold officials accountable to the people. . . . The right of citizens to inquire, to hear, to speak, and to use information to reach consensus is a precondition to enlightened self-government and a necessary means to protect it. The First Amendment " 'has its fullest and most urgent application' to speech uttered during a campaign for political office." Eu v. San Francisco County Democratic Central Comm., 489 U.S. 214, 223 (1989) (quoting Monitor Patriot Co. v. Roy, 401 U.S. 265, 272 (1971)). . . . For these reasons, political speech must prevail against laws that would suppress it, whether by design or inadvertence. Laws that burden political speech are "subject to strict scrutiny," which requires the Government to prove that the restriction "furthers a compelling interest and is narrowly tailored to achieve that interest." . . .

Premised on mistrust of governmental power, the First Amendment stands against attempts to disfavor certain subjects or viewpoints. Prohibited, too, are restrictions distinguishing among different speakers, allowing speech by some but not others. See First Nat. Bank of Boston v. Bellotti, 435 U.S. 765, 784 (1978). As instruments to censor, these categories are interrelated: Speech restrictions based on the identity of the speaker are all too often simply a means to control content.

Quite apart from the purpose or effect of regulating content, moreover, the Government may commit a constitutional wrong when by law it identifies certain preferred speakers. By taking the right to speak from some and giving it to others, the Government deprives the disadvantaged person or class of the right to use speech to strive to establish worth, standing, and respect for the speaker's voice. The Government may not by these means deprive the public of the right and privilege to determine for itself what speech and speakers are worthy of consideration. The First Amendment protects speech and speaker, and the ideas that flow from each.

The Court has upheld a narrow class of speech restrictions that operate to the disadvantage of certain persons, but these rulings were based on an interest in allowing governmental entities to perform their functions. [The Court cited cases dealing with public education, prisoners, the military, and public employees.] The corporate independent expenditures at issue in this case, however, would not interfere with governmental functions, so these cases are inapposite. These precedents stand only for the proposition that there are certain governmental functions that cannot operate without some restrictions on particular kinds of speech. By contrast, it is inherent in the nature of the political process that voters must be free to obtain information from diverse sources in order to determine how to cast their votes. At least before *Austin*, the Court had not allowed the exclusion of a class of speakers from the general public dialogue.

We find no basis for the proposition that, in the context of political speech, the Government may impose restrictions on certain disfavored speakers. Both history and logic lead us to this conclusion.

A. The Court has recognized that First Amendment protection extends to corporations [and] to the context of political speech. [P]olitical speech does not lose First Amendment protection "simply because its source is a corporation." . . . "The identity of the speaker is not decisive in determining whether speech is protected. Corporations and other associations, like individuals, contribute to the 'discussion, debate, and the dissemination of information and ideas' that the First Amendment seeks to foster." The Court has thus rejected the argument that political speech of corporations or other associations should be treated differently under the First Amendment simply because such associations are not "natural persons." . . .

[N]ot until 1947 did Congress first prohibit independent expenditures by corporations and labor unions in §304 of the Labor Management Relations Act 1947. In passing this Act Congress overrode the veto of President Truman, who warned that the expenditure ban was a "dangerous intrusion on free speech." . . .

Buckley did not consider [the] ban on corporate and union independent expenditures. . . . Less than two years after *Buckley*, [the Court in] *Bellotti* reaffirmed the First Amendment principle that the Government cannot restrict political speech based on the speaker's corporate identity. *Bellotti* could not have been clearer when it struck down a state-law prohibition on corporate independent expenditures related to referenda issues:

> We thus find no support in the First . . . Amendment, or in the decisions of this Court, for the proposition that speech that otherwise would be within the protection of the First Amendment loses that protection simply because its source is a corporation that cannot prove, to the satisfaction of a court, a material effect on its business or property. . . . [That proposition] amounts to an impermissible legislative prohibition of speech based on the identity of the interests that spokesmen may represent in public debate over controversial issues and a requirement that the speaker have a sufficiently great interest in the subject to justify communication. . . . In the realm of protected speech, the legislature is constitutionally disqualified from dictating the subjects about which persons may speak and the speakers who may address a public issue.

. . . *Bellotti* did not address the constitutionality of the State's ban on corporate independent expenditures to support candidates [but] that restriction would have been unconstitutional under *Bellotti*'s central principle: that the First Amendment does not allow political speech restrictions based on a speaker's corporate identity.

Thus the law stood until *Austin*. . . . [The] Michigan Chamber of Commerce sought to use general treasury funds to run a newspaper ad supporting a specific candidate. Michigan law, however, prohibited corporate independent expenditures that supported or opposed any candidate for state office. A violation of the law was punishable as a felony. The Court sustained the speech prohibition. To bypass *Buckley* and *Bellotti*, the *Austin* Court identified a new governmental interest in limiting political speech: an anti-distortion interest. *Austin* found a compelling governmental interest in preventing "the corrosive and distorting effects of immense aggregations of wealth that are accumulated with the help of the corporate form and that have little or no correlation to the public's support for the corporation's political ideas."

B. The Court is thus confronted with conflicting lines of precedent: a pre-*Austin* line that forbids restrictions on political speech based on the speaker's corporate identity and a post-*Austin* line that permits them. No case before *Austin* had held that Congress could prohibit independent expenditures for political speech based on the speaker's corporate identity. . . . In its defense of the corporate-speech restrictions in §441b, the Government notes the anti-distortion rationale on which *Austin* [rests], yet it all but abandons reliance upon it. It argues instead that two other compelling interests support *Austin*'s holding that corporate expenditure restrictions are constitutional: an anti-corruption interest and a shareholder-protection interest. We consider the three points in turn.

1. As for *Austin*'s anti-distortion rationale, the Government does little to defend it. And with good reason, for the rationale cannot support §441b. If the First Amendment has any force, it prohibits Congress from fining or jailing citizens, or associations of citizens, for simply engaging in political speech. . . .

Political speech is "indispensable to decision-making in a democracy, and this is no less true because the speech comes from a corporation rather than an individual." . . . "[T]he concept that government may restrict the speech of some elements of our society in order to enhance the relative voice of others is wholly foreign to the First Amendment." . . . *Austin* sought to defend the anti-distortion rationale as a means to prevent corporations from obtaining "an unfair advantage in the political marketplace" by using "resources amassed in the economic marketplace." But *Buckley* rejected the premise that the Government has an interest "in equalizing the relative ability of individuals and groups to influence the outcome of elections." . . .

[*Austin*] distinguish[ed] wealthy individuals from corporations on the ground that "[s]tate law grants corporations special advantages—such as limited liability, perpetual life, and favorable treatment of the accumulation and distribution of assets," [but it] "is rudimentary that the State cannot exact as the price of those special advantages the forfeiture of First Amendment rights."

It is irrelevant for purposes of the First Amendment that corporate funds may "have little or no correlation to the public's support for the corporation's political ideas." All speakers, including individuals and the media, use money amassed from the economic marketplace to fund their speech. The First Amendment protects the resulting speech, even if it was enabled by economic transactions with persons or entities who disagree with the speaker's ideas. . . .

Austin interferes with the "open marketplace" of ideas protected by the First Amendment. It permits the Government to ban the political speech of millions of associations of citizens. [About 5.8 million for-profit corporations filed 2006 tax returns.] Most of these are small corporations without large amounts of wealth. This fact belies the Government's argument that the statute is justified on the ground that it prevents the "distorting effects of immense aggregations of wealth." It is not even aimed at amassed wealth.

The censorship we now confront is vast in its reach. . . . By suppressing the speech of manifold corporations, both for-profit and nonprofit, the Government prevents their voices and viewpoints from reaching the public and advising voters on which persons or entities are hostile to their interests. Factions will necessarily form in our Republic, but the remedy of "destroying the liberty" of some factions is "worse than the disease." The Federalist No. 10 (J. Madison). Factions should be checked by permitting them all to speak, and by entrusting the people to judge what is true and what is false. . . .

When Government seeks to use its full power, including the criminal law, to command where a person may get his or her information or what distrusted source he or she may not hear, it uses censorship to control thought. This is unlawful. The First Amendment confirms the freedom to think for ourselves.

2. [The Government argues] that corporate political speech can be banned in order to prevent corruption or its appearance. . . . Limits on independent expenditures, such as §441b, have a chilling effect extending well beyond the Government's interest in preventing *quid pro quo* corruption. . . . Indeed, 26 States do not restrict independent expenditures by for-profit corporations. The Government does not claim that these expenditures have corrupted the political process in those States. . . .

When *Buckley* identified a sufficiently important governmental interest in preventing corruption or the appearance of corruption, that interest was limited to *quid pro quo* corruption. The fact that speakers may have influence over or access to elected officials does not mean that these officials are corrupt: "It is in the nature of an elected representative to favor certain policies, and, by necessary corollary, to favor the voters and contributors who support those policies. It is well understood that a substantial and legitimate reason, if not the only reason, to cast a vote for, or to make a contribution to, one candidate over another is that the candidate will respond by producing those political outcomes the supporter favors." . . .

3. The Government contends further that corporate independent expenditures can be limited because of its interest in protecting dissenting shareholders from being compelled to fund corporate political speech. . . . There is . . . little evidence of abuse that cannot be corrected by shareholders "through the procedures of corporate democracy."

Those reasons are sufficient to reject this shareholder-protection interest; and, moreover, the statute is both underinclusive and overinclusive. As to the first, if Congress had been seeking to protect dissenting shareholders, it would not have banned corporate speech in only certain media within 30 or 60 days before an election. A dissenting shareholder's interests would be implicated by speech in any media at any time. As to the second, the statute is overinclusive because it covers all corporations, including nonprofit corporations and for-profit corporations with only single shareholders. . . .

Austin should be and now is overruled. We return to the principle established in *Buckley* and *Bellotti* that the Government may not suppress political speech on the basis of the speaker's corporate identity. No sufficient governmental interest justifies limits on the political speech of nonprofit or for-profit corporations.

D. [Because *Austin* is overruled,] Section 441b's restrictions on corporate independent expenditures are therefore invalid and cannot be applied to *Hillary*. [We] are further required to overrule the part of *McConnell* that upheld BCRA §203's extension of §441b's restrictions on corporate independent expenditures. . . .

IV. [The Court upheld] BCRA's disclaimer and disclosure provisions as applied to *Hillary* and the three advertisements for the movie. . . . Disclaimer and disclosure requirements may burden the ability to speak, but they "impose no ceiling on campaign-related activities" and "do not prevent anyone from speaking." . . . [The facial validity of forced disclosure is] justified [by the] governmental interest in "provid[ing] the electorate with information" about the sources of election-related spending, [but] as-applied challenges would be available if a group could show a " 'reasonable probability' " that disclosure of its contributors' names " 'will subject them to threats, harassment, or reprisals from either Government officials or private parties.' " [W]e find the statute valid as applied to the ads for the movie and to the movie itself. . . .

V. . . . The judgment of the District Court is reversed with respect to the constitutionality of 2 U.S.C. §441b's restrictions on corporate independent expenditures. The judgment is affirmed with respect to BCRA's disclaimer and disclosure requirements. The case is remanded for further proceedings consistent with this opinion.

JUSTICE STEVENS, with whom JUSTICE GINSBURG, JUSTICE BREYER, and JUSTICE SOTOMAYOR join, concurring in part and dissenting in part.

The real issue in this case concerns how, not if, the appellant may finance its electioneering. . . . Neither Citizens United's nor any other corporation's speech has been "banned." All that the parties dispute is whether Citizens United had a right to use the funds in its general treasury to pay for broadcasts during the 30-day period. The notion that the First Amendment dictates an affirmative answer to that question is, in my judgment, profoundly misguided. . . .

The basic premise underlying the Court's ruling is . . . the proposition that the First Amendment bars regulatory distinctions based on a speaker's identity, including its "identity" as a corporation. . . . The conceit that corporations must be treated identically to natural persons in the political sphere is not only inaccurate but also inadequate to justify the Court's disposition of this case. In the context of election to public office, the distinction between corporate and human speakers is significant. Although they make enormous contributions to our society, corporations are not actually members of it. They cannot vote or run for office. Because they may be managed and controlled by nonresidents, their interests may conflict in fundamental respects with the interests of eligible voters. The financial resources, legal structure, and instrumental orientation of corporations raise legitimate concerns about their role in the electoral process. . . .

Although I concur in the Court's decision to sustain BCRA's disclosure provisions and join Part IV of its opinion, I emphatically dissent from its principal holding. . . .

The So-Called "Ban." [The law at issue here] functions as a source restriction or a time, place, and manner restriction. It applies in a viewpoint-neutral fashion to a narrow subset of advocacy messages about clearly identified candidates for federal office, made during discrete time periods through discrete channels. . . .

Identity-Based Distinctions. [In] a variety of contexts, we have held that speech can be regulated differentially on account of the speaker's identity, when identity is understood in categorical or institutional terms. The Government routinely places special restrictions on the speech rights of students, prisoners, members of the Armed Forces, foreigners, and its own employees. When such restrictions are justified by a legitimate governmental interest, they do not necessarily raise constitutional problems. . . . It is fair to say that our First Amendment doctrine has "frowned on" certain identity-based distinctions, particularly those that may reflect invidious discrimination or preferential treatment of a politically powerful group.

The election context is distinctive in many ways, and the Court . . . is right that the First Amendment closely guards political speech. But in this context, too, the authority of legislatures to enact viewpoint-neutral regulations based on content and identity is well settled. We have, for example, allowed state-run broadcasters to exclude independent candidates from televised debates. Arkansas Ed. Television Comm'n v. Forbes, 523 U.S. 666 (1998). We have upheld statutes that prohibit the distribution or display of campaign materials near a polling place. Burson v. Freeman, 504 U.S. 191 (1992). . . . And we have consistently approved laws that bar Government employees, but not others, from contributing to or participating in political activities. . . .

Not only has the distinctive potential of corporations to corrupt the electoral process long been recognized, but . . . campaign finance . . . distinctions based on corporate identity tend to be less worrisome . . . because the "speakers" are not natural persons, much less members of our political community, and the governmental interests are of the highest order. . . .

[The majority's view is] that the only "sufficiently important governmental interest in preventing corruption or the appearance of corruption" is one that is "limited to *quid pro quo* corruption." . . . Corruption can take many forms. Bribery may be the paradigm case. But the difference between selling a vote and selling access is a matter of degree, not kind. And selling access is not qualitatively different from giving special preference to those who spent money on one's behalf. Corruption operates along a spectrum, and the majority's apparent belief that *quid pro quo* arrangements can be neatly demarcated from other improper influences does not accord with the theory or reality of politics. . . . Yet the majority's understanding of corruption would leave lawmakers impotent to address all but the most discrete abuses. . . . At stake in the legislative efforts to address this threat is . . . not only the legitimacy and quality of Government but also the public's faith therein. . . . A democracy cannot function effectively when its constituent members believe laws are being bought and sold. . . .

[T]he consequences of today's holding will not be limited to the legislative or executive context. The majority of the States select their judges through popular elections. At a time when concerns about the conduct of judicial elections have reached a fever pitch, the Court today unleashes the floodgates of corporate and union general treasury spending in these races. . . .

Unlike natural persons, corporations have "limited liability" for their owners and managers, "perpetual life," separation of ownership and control, "and favorable treatment of the accumulation and distribution of assets . . . that enhance their ability to attract capital and to deploy their resources in ways that maximize the return on their shareholders' investments." . . . It might also be added that corporations have no consciences, no beliefs, no feelings, no thoughts, no desires. Corporations help structure and facilitate the activities of human beings, to be sure, and their "personhood" often serves as a useful legal fiction. But they are not themselves members of "We the People" by whom and for whom our Constitution was established. . . . It is an interesting question "who" is even speaking when a business corporation places an advertisement that endorses or attacks a particular candidate. Presumably it is not the customers or employees, who typically have no say in such matters. It cannot realistically be said to be the shareholders, who tend to be far removed from the day-to-day decisions of the firm and whose political preferences may be opaque to management. Perhaps the officers or directors of the corporation have the best claim to be the ones speaking, except their fiduciary duties generally prohibit them from using corporate funds for personal ends. . . .

While American democracy is imperfect, few outside the majority of this Court would have thought its flaws included a dearth of corporate money in politics.

NOTES

1. Bans or Limits on Speech? The majority says that corporate and union speech was banned. The dissent says that such speech was simply limited in time and place—no electioneering communications in the period immediately prior to an election. Such speech is forbidden in that period—is that ban more constitutionally significant than the fact that corporate and union speech might be permitted at other times and in other forms? On this distinction hangs the Court's division over the applicable standard of review.

2. Is Speech About Judicial Elections Different?   Prior to Caperton v. A.T. Massey Coal Co., 556 U.S. 868 (2009), due process required judicial recusal only when a judge has a "direct, personal, substantial, pecuniary interest" in a case. Tumey v. Ohio, 273 U.S. 510 (1927). *Caperton* broadened the constitutional requirement for recusal:

> We conclude that there is a serious risk of actual bias—based on objective and reasonable perceptions—when a person with a personal stake in a particular case had a significant and disproportionate influence in placing the judge on the case by raising funds or directing the judge's election campaign when the case was pending or imminent. The inquiry centers on the contribution's relative size in comparison to the total amount of money contributed to the campaign, the total amount spent in the election, and the apparent effect such contribution had on the outcome of the election.

What implications, if any, does *Caperton* have with respect to campaign finance issues? If independent expenditures can create a probability of bias on the part of a judicial candidate who is the beneficiary of such expenditures, do such expenditures create a similar probability of bias on the part of legislative or executive candidates who are benefitted by such expenditures? If so, does this bolster the argument that such expenditures may be limited to prevent the appearance of corruption? Or does *Caperton* suggest only that the probability of bias is more constitutionally significant in the case of judicial elections?

3. *McCutcheon*: Aggregate Limits on Contributions.   *McCutcheon v. Federal Election Commission, 134 S. Ct. 1434 (2014).* Federal law imposes "base limits" on contributions made to a single candidate and also "aggregate limits" on the total amount any donor may contribute to many different candidates. McCutcheon challenged the aggregate limits only, as the base limits were upheld in *Buckley.* The government argued that the aggregate limits were necessary to prevent circumvention of the base limits. Because "the aggregate limits do little, if anything, to address that concern, while seriously restricting participation in the democratic process," the Court held that they were invalid under the First Amendment:

> Congress may regulate campaign contributions to protect against corruption or the appearance of corruption. . . . [But] Congress may not regulate contributions simply to reduce the amount of money in politics, or to restrict the political participation of some in order to enhance the relative influence of others. . . . [T]o draw the constitutional line between the permissible goal of avoiding corruption in the political process and the impermissible desire simply to limit political speech [we] have said that government regulation may not target the general gratitude a candidate may feel toward those who support him or his allies, or the political access such support may afford. "Ingratiation and access

. . . are not corruption." They embody a central feature of democracy—that constituents support candidates who share their beliefs and interests, and candidates who are elected can be expected to be responsive to those concerns. Any regulation must instead target what we have called "*quid pro quo*" corruption or its appearance. . . . An aggregate limit on *how many* candidates and committees an individual may support through contributions is not a "modest restraint" at all. The Government may no more restrict how many candidates or causes a donor may support than it may tell a newspaper how many candidates it may endorse.

Because the connection between avoiding *quid pro quo* corruption and limiting the total amount a donor may give to many candidates, with each contribution within the base limits, was so tenuous the aggregate limits failed the requisite "close scrutiny" applicable to contribution limits. Justices Breyer, Ginsburg, Sotomayor, and Kagan dissented.

2. Government Regulation of Elections

The function of a political party is to create and articulate a vision of public policy. The point of political candidacy is to present a policy vision in seeking public office. A proper function of government is the regulation of elections to ensure a fair method of aggregating citizen preferences. These postulates collide when the state seeks to regulate party primaries, in which the electoral process is used to select the nominees of the political parties for public office, or when the government seeks to regulate campaign speech.

Many states conduct "closed" primary elections—in which voters may vote only in the primary of the party in which they are registered. To conduct closed primaries it is necessary to impose some "cutoff" or "record" date in advance of the primary election for voters to establish party affiliation for purposes of the primary election. These schemes are subject to strict scrutiny to the extent they *substantially* interfere with a voter's or political party's First Amendment rights of speech or free association.

Voter's associational rights. In Rosario v. Rockefeller, 410 U.S. 752 (1973), the Court applied minimal scrutiny and upheld a New York requirement that voters register in a party 8 to 11 months prior to the primary election in order to participate in the primary. This did not absolutely foreclose voting; it simply foreclosed switching parties in order to vote in a primary election. The rule furthered the legitimate purpose of preventing voters of one party from "poaching" on another's party primary, with detrimental effects on the second party's integrity. But in Kusper v. Pontikes, 414 U.S. 51 (1973), the Court applied strict scrutiny to strike down an Illinois law barring voters from a party primary election if they had voted in a primary election of any other party during the preceding 23 months. The rule "substantially [restricted] freedom to change [political] party affiliation" and thus materially interfered with a voter's First Amendment right of free association. Though Illinois had a compelling interest in preventing "poaching," this lengthy forced political marriage was unnecessary to furtherance of that end. In New York State Board of Elections v. Lopez Torres, 552 U.S. 196 (2008), the Supreme Court rejected a claim that the associational rights of voters and candidates were violated by a New York law that required political parties to select their nominees for trial judgeships at a convention of delegates chosen by party members in a primary election.

Political parties' associational rights. In Tashjian v. Republican Party, 479 U.S. 208 (1986), the Court applied strict scrutiny to void a Connecticut law requiring that all voters in a party primary be registered voters of that party. As applied to Connecticut's Republican Party, which had adopted a party rule opening the Republican primary to independent voters, the law substantially interfered with the First Amendment associational rights of Republicans to decide for themselves who should vote in their primary. In Eu v. San Francisco Democratic Central Committee, 489 U.S. 214 (1989), the Court applied strict scrutiny to void a California law barring political parties from endorsing, supporting, or opposing any candidate for nomination by that party for a partisan elective office.

California Democratic Party v. Jones
530 U.S. 567 (2000)

JUSTICE SCALIA delivered the opinion of the Court.

This case presents the question whether the State of California may, consistent with the First Amendment, [use] a so-called "blanket" primary to determine a political party's nominee for the general election. . . . In 1996 the citizens of California adopted by initiative Proposition 198. Promoted largely as a measure that would "weaken" party "hard-liners" and ease the way for "moderate problem-solvers," Proposition 198 changed California's partisan primary from a closed primary to a blanket primary. Under the new system, "all persons entitled to vote, including those not affiliated with any political party, shall have the right to vote . . . for any candidate regardless of the candidate's political affiliation." Whereas under the closed primary each voter received a ballot limited to candidates of his own party, as a result of Proposition 198 each voter's primary ballot now lists every candidate regardless of party affiliation and allows the voter to choose freely among them. It remains the case, however, that the candidate of each party who wins the greatest number of votes "is the nominee of that party at the ensuing general election."

Petitioners [are] four political parties—the California Democratic Party, the California Republican Party, the Libertarian Party of California, and the Peace and Freedom Party—each of which has a rule prohibiting persons not members of the party from voting in the party's primary. Petitioners brought suit in [federal district court] against respondent California Secretary of State, alleging that California's blanket primary violated their First Amendment rights of association, and seeking declaratory and injunctive relief. [The]

District Court recognized that the new law would inject into each party's primary substantial numbers of voters unaffiliated with the party [and] that this might result in selection of a nominee different from the one party members would select, or at the least cause the same nominee to commit himself to different positions. Nevertheless, the District Court held that the burden on petitioners' rights of association was not a severe one, and was justified by state interests ultimately reducing to this: "enhancing the democratic nature of the election process and the representativeness of elected officials." The Ninth Circuit, adopting the District Court's opinion as its own, affirmed.

Respondents rest their defense of the blanket primary upon the proposition that primaries play an integral role in citizens' selection of public officials, [that] primaries are public rather than private proceedings, and the States may and must play a role in ensuring that they serve the public interest. . . . [We] have recognized, of course, that States have a major role to play in structuring and monitoring the election process, including primaries. We have considered it "too plain for argument" [that] a State may require parties to use the primary format for selecting their nominees, in order to assure that intraparty competition is resolved in a democratic fashion. American Party of Texas v. White, 415 U.S. 767 (1974). Similarly, in order to avoid burdening the general election ballot with frivolous candidacies, a State may require parties to demonstrate "a significant modicum of support" before allowing their candidates a place on that ballot. See Jenness v. Fortson, 403 U.S. 431 (1971). Finally, in order to prevent "party raiding"—a process in which dedicated members of one party formally switch to another party, to alter the outcome of that party's primary—a State may require party registration a reasonable period of time before a primary election. [*Rosario.*] What we have not held, however, is that the processes by which political parties select their nominees are . . . wholly public affairs that States may regulate freely. To the contrary, we have continually stressed that when States regulate parties' internal processes they must act within limits imposed by the Constitution.

Representative democracy in any populous unit of governance is unimaginable without the ability of citizens to band together in promoting among the electorate candidates who espouse their political views. . . .

[In] no area is the political association's right to exclude more important than in the process of selecting its nominee. That process often determines the party's positions on the most significant public policy issues of the day, and even when those positions are predetermined it is the nominee who becomes the party's ambassador to the general electorate in winning it over to the party's views. Unsurprisingly, our cases vigorously affirm the special place the First Amendment reserves for, and the special protection it accords, the process by which a political party "selects a standard bearer who best represents the party's ideologies and preferences." . . . California's blanket primary violates [these] principles. Proposition 198 forces political parties to associate with—to have their nominees, and hence their positions, determined by—those who, at best, have refused to affiliate with the party, and, at worst, have expressly affiliated with a rival. In this respect, it is qualitatively different from a closed primary. Under that system, even when it is made quite easy for a voter to change his party affiliation the day of the primary, and thus, in some sense, to "cross over," at least he must formally *become a member of the party;* and once he does so, he is limited to voting for candidates of that party.[23]

The evidence in this case demonstrates that under California's blanket primary system, the prospect of having a party's nominee determined by adherents of an opposing party is far from remote — indeed, it is a clear and present danger. For example, in one 1997 survey of California voters 37 percent of Republicans said that they planned to vote in the 1998 Democratic gubernatorial primary, and 20 percent of Democrats said they planned to vote in the 1998 Republican United States Senate primary. . . . [The] impact of voting by non-party members is much greater upon minor parties, such as the Libertarian Party and the Peace and Freedom Party. In the first primaries these parties conducted following California's implementation of Proposition 198, the total votes cast for party candidates in some races was more than *double* the total number of *registered party members.* . . .

Nor can we accept [the] contention that the burden imposed by Proposition 198 is minor because petitioners are free to endorse and financially support the candidate of their choice in the primary. The ability of the party leadership to endorse a candidate is simply no substitute for the party members' ability to choose their own nominee. . . .

In sum, Proposition 198 forces petitioners to adulterate their candidate-selection process — the "basic function of a political party" — by opening it up to persons wholly unaffiliated with the party. Such forced association has the likely outcome — indeed, [the] *intended* outcome — of changing the parties' message. We can think of no heavier burden on a political party's associational freedom. Proposition 198 is therefore unconstitutional unless it is narrowly tailored to serve a compelling state interest.

Respondents proffer seven state interests they claim are compelling. Two of them — producing elected officials who better represent the electorate and expanding candidate debate beyond the scope of partisan concerns — are simply circumlocution for producing nominees and nominee positions other than those the parties would choose if left to their own devices. Indeed, respondents admit as much. [Both] of these supposed interests, therefore, reduce to nothing more than a stark repudiation of freedom of political association: Parties should not be free to select their own nominees because those nominees . . . will not be congenial to the majority. We have recognized the inadmissibility of this sort of "interest" before. [*Hurley.*]

Respondents' third asserted compelling interest is that the blanket primary is the only way to ensure [that] independents and members of the minority party in "safe" districts [have] an "effective" vote. . . . [But] a "nonmember's desire to participate in the party's affairs is overborne by the countervailing

---

23. In this sense, the blanket primary also may be constitutionally distinct from the open primary, in which the voter is limited to one party's ballot. [This] case does not require us to determine the constitutionality of open primaries.

and legitimate right of the party to determine its own membership qualifications." [*Tashjian.*] [The] voter who feels himself disenfranchised should simply join the party. That may put him to a hard choice, but it is not a state-imposed restriction upon *his* freedom of association, whereas compelling party members to accept his selection of their nominee *is* a state-imposed restriction upon theirs.

Respondents' remaining four asserted state interests—promoting fairness, affording voters greater choice, increasing voter participation, and protecting privacy—are not, like the others, automatically out of the running; but neither are they, *in the circumstances of this case,* compelling. That determination is not to be made in the abstract, by asking whether fairness, privacy, etc., are highly significant values; but rather by asking whether the *aspect* of fairness, privacy, etc., addressed by the law at issue is highly significant. And for all four of these asserted interests, we find it not to be. The aspect of fairness addressed by Proposition 198 is presumably the supposed inequity of not permitting non-party members in "safe" districts to determine the party nominee. If that is unfair at all . . . , it seems to us less unfair than permitting non-party members to hijack the party. As for affording voters greater choice, it is obvious that the net effect of this scheme—indeed, its avowed purpose—is to *reduce* the scope of choice, by assuring a range of candidates who are all more "centrist." This . . . is hardly a compelling state interest, if indeed it is even a legitimate one. The interest in increasing voter participation is just a variation on the same theme (more choices favored by the majority will produce more voters), and suffers from the same defect. As for the protection of privacy: The specific privacy interest at issue [is the] confidentiality of one's party affiliation. Even if (as seems unlikely) a scheme for administering a closed primary could not be devised in which the voter's declaration of party affiliation would not be public information, we do not think that the State's interest in assuring the privacy of this piece of information in all cases can conceivably be considered a "compelling" one. . . .

Finally, we may observe that even if all these state interests were compelling ones, Proposition 198 is not a narrowly tailored means of furthering them. Respondents could protect them all by resorting to a *nonpartisan* blanket primary. . . . [The] State of California has [forced] political parties to associate with those who do not share their beliefs. And it has done this at the "crucial juncture" at which party members traditionally find their collective voice and select their spokesman. The burden Proposition 198 places on petitioners' rights of political association is both severe and unnecessary. [Reversed.]

JUSTICE STEVENS, joined by JUSTICE GINSBURG, dissenting.

. . . [An] election, unlike a convention or caucus, is a public affair. . . . In my view, while state rules abridging participation in its elections should be closely scrutinized, the First Amendment does not inhibit the State from acting to broaden voter access to state-run, state-financed elections. When a State acts not to limit democratic participation but to expand the ability of individuals to participate in the democratic process, it is acting not as a foe of the First Amendment but as a friend and ally. . . .

Even if the "right not to associate" did authorize the Court to review the State's policy choice, its evaluation of the competing interests at stake is seriously flawed. [California's] interest in fostering democratic government by "increasing the representativeness of elected officials, giving voters greater choice, and increasing voter turnout and participation" [is compelling]. In an era of dramatically declining voter participation, States should be free to experiment with reforms designed to make the democratic process more robust by involving the entire electorate in the process of selecting those who will serve as government officials.

NOTES

1. The Scope of *Jones*.   Does *Jones* stand for the proposition that, aside from voter criteria specifically forbidden by the Constitution (e.g., race and sex), a state may not force a political party to accept any voters it does not want? If so, does this mean that "open" primaries are also void? In an open primary any person, regardless of party affiliation, may vote for a party's nominee, but his choice is limited to that party's nominees *for all offices*. He may not, for example, support a Republican nominee for governor and a Democratic nominee for attorney general. What if a political party (rather than the state) sought by party rule to close its primary to all voters save those registered in the party for a continuous period of two years prior to the primary election? Such a rule would conflict with the voters' associational rights upheld in Rosario v. Rockefeller. Which associational right should prevail? Why?

2. Clingman v. Beaver: The "Semi-Closed Primary."   Under Oklahoma law, a political party may invite its own members and unaffiliated independent voters to vote in its party primary, but may not allow voters registered in another party to vote in the party primary. Oklahoma's Libertarian Party, joined by individual Democrats and Republicans who wished to vote in the Libertarian primary, challenged these restrictions. In Clingman v. Beaver, 544 U.S. 581 (2005), the Supreme Court upheld the validity of the semi-closed primary. A four-justice plurality reiterated that state primary election "[r]egulations that impose severe burdens on associational rights must be narrowly tailored to serve a compelling state interest," but noted that "when regulations impose lesser burdens, 'a State's important regulatory interests will usually be enough to justify reasonable, nondiscriminatory restrictions.'" Oklahoma's associational burdens were "minor and justified by legitimate state interests." The plurality thought that, unlike California in *Jones*, Oklahoma did not compel "association with unwanted members or voters," nor did Oklahoma make it difficult for voters to change their party registration status in order to vote in the Libertarian primary: "Oklahoma merely prohibits the [Libertarians] from leaving the selection of its candidates to people who are members of another political party." The associational interest of voters registered in other parties was simply to cast "a vote for a Libertarian candidate in a particular primary election, rather than in banding together with fellow citizens committed to the [Libertarians'] political goals and ideas." The plurality considered the associational burdens imposed by Oklahoma as of even lesser magnitude than those at issue in Timmons v. Twin Cities Area New Party, 520 U.S. 351 (1997), in which the Court upheld a Minnesota election law prohibiting a candidate from appearing on the ballot as the nominee of more than one party. As in *Timmons*, Oklahoma had not compelled unwanted association, nor had it interfered with the Libertarians' ability "to govern themselves internally and to communicate with the public as they wished." Thus, the associational burdens were "not severe."

Justices O'Connor and Breyer concurred with the plurality on the standard of review: "Regulations imposing severe burdens on associational rights must be narrowly tailored to advance a compelling government interest. Regulations imposing lesser burdens are subject to less intensive scrutiny, and reasonable, nondiscriminatory restrictions ordinarily will be sustained if they serve important regulatory interests." They also agreed that the specific disaffiliation requirement at issue was not severe, but they left open the question of whether that requirement, when taken together with other Oklahoma election laws pertaining to ballot access and voter registration, might combine to impose a severe associational burden.

3. Washington's Artful Dodge of *Jones*. In Washington State Grange v. Washington State Republican Party, 552 U.S. 442 (2008), the Court upheld the facial validity of a Washington primary election law that required candidates to self-identify their party preference, permitted voters to vote for any candidate, and restricted the general election ballot to the top two candidates (regardless of party preference). The majority reasoned that the scheme did not impose a severe burden on political parties' associational rights because parties remained free to nominate their candidates (although the fact of party nomination could not appear on the primary ballot). The gravamen of the complaint, said the Court, was that "voters will be confused as to the meaning of the party-preference designation," and this was "sheer speculation." The Court left open the possibility that, once the scheme was implemented, an as-applied challenge based on proof of such confusion might succeed.

Justice Scalia, joined by Justice Kennedy, dissented, arguing that the self-identified party preference permitted candidates to distort the message of political parties because there was no vehicle to ensure that a candidate who claims to prefer a party actually believes in the principles that the party seeks to profess. The whole point of the scheme, said the dissenters, was to express "dislike for bright-colors partisanship, and . . . blunt the ability of political parties with noncentrist views to endorse and advocate their own candidates." Washington sought "to use its monopoly power over the ballot to undermine the expressive activities of the political parties. . . . Washington's electoral system permits individuals to appropriate the parties' trademarks, so to speak, at the most crucial stage of election, thereby distorting the parties' messages and impairing their endorsement of candidates. [This is] a system which . . .

does not merely refuse to assist, but positively impairs, the legitimate role of political parties."

Regulating Campaign Speech

Campaign finance limits are grounded on the interest of avoiding actual or apparent corruption. May a government prohibit other corrupt practices that can influence electoral outcomes—such as vote buying or lying to the electorate? Candidate Brown promised the voters that, if elected, he would reduce the salary of the office that he sought to occupy. After he won, a Kentucky judge ruled the election void on the ground that Brown had violated the Kentucky Corrupt Practices Act, which prohibited a political candidate from "giving, or promising to give, anything of value to a voter in exchange for his vote or support." In Brown v. Hartlage, 456 U.S. 46 (1982), the Court reversed, stating that the law might validly be applied to secret vote buying but not to promises "made openly, subject to the comment and criticism [of] political opponent[s] and to the scrutiny of the voters."

Queries: Should governments be able to prohibit intentionally false or deceptive campaign speech? Deliberately false political speech undermines the integrity of the political process and saps voter confidence in the statements of any candidate. Is that an adequate interest to justify penalties on false or misleading political speech? Or is it necessary to protect some political lies to ensure that legitimate political speech is not chilled? Some 14 states have laws that prohibit some form of false campaign speech. Compare Rickert v. Public Disclosure Commission, 161 Wash. 2d 843 (2007), with Pestrak v. Ohio Elections Commission, 926 F.2d 573 (6th Cir. 1991), and 281 Care Committee v. Arneson, 638 F.3d 621 (8th Cir. 2011).

Republican Party of Minnesota v. White
536 U.S. 765 (2002)

JUSTICE SCALIA delivered the opinion of the Court.

The question . . . is whether the First Amendment permits the Minnesota Supreme Court to prohibit candidates for judicial election in that State from announcing their views on disputed legal and political issues.

I. Since Minnesota's admission to the Union in 1858, the State's Constitution has provided for the selection of all state judges by popular election. . . . Since 1974, they have been subject to a legal restriction which states that a "candidate for a judicial office, including an incumbent judge," shall not "announce his or her views on disputed legal or political issues." This prohibition, . . . known as the "announce clause," [subjects] judges who violate it . . . to discipline, including removal, censure, civil penalties, and suspension without pay. Lawyers who run for judicial office also must comply with the announce clause [and those] who violate it are subject to . . . disbarment, suspension, and probation.

[A lawyer candidate for election to the Minnesota Supreme Court who] distributed literature criticizing several Minnesota Supreme Court decisions on issues such as crime, welfare, and abortion [became the subject of a complaint that he violated the "announce rule." In federal court he sought] a declaration that the announce clause violates the First Amendment and an injunction against its enforcement. [The District Court, on summary judgment, upheld the validity of the "announce rule," and the Eighth Circuit affirmed.]

II. . . . The prohibition [of the announce clause] extends to the candidate's mere statement of his current position, even if he does not bind himself to maintain that position after election. [The announce clause, as interpreted by the Minnesota courts, reaches only "disputed issues that are likely to come before the candidate if he is elected judge." But this] is not much of a limitation at all. One would hardly expect the "disputed legal or political issues" raised in the course of a state judicial election to include such matters as whether the Federal Government should end the embargo of Cuba. Quite obviously, they will be those legal or political disputes that are the proper (or by past decisions have been made the improper) business of the state courts. [It] is clear that the announce clause prohibits a judicial candidate from stating his views on any specific non-fanciful legal question within the province of the court for which he is running. . . .

Respondents contend that this still leaves plenty of topics for discussion on the campaign trail. These include a candidate's "character," "education," "work habits," and "how [he] would handle administrative duties if elected." . . . Whether this list . . . , and other topics not prohibited by the announce clause, adequately fulfill the First Amendment's guarantee of freedom of speech is the question to which we now turn.

III. [The] announce clause both prohibits speech on the basis of its content and burdens a category of speech that is "at the core of our First Amendment freedoms"—speech about the qualifications of candidates for public office. . . . The Court of Appeals concluded that respondents had established two interests as sufficiently compelling to justify the announce clause: preserving the impartiality of the state judiciary and preserving the appearance of the impartiality of the state judiciary. Respondents [argue] that the first is compelling because it protects the due process rights of litigants, and that the second is compelling because it preserves public confidence in the judiciary. Respondents are rather vague, however, about what they mean by "impartiality." . . . Clarity on this point is essential [to] decide whether impartiality is indeed a compelling state interest, and, if so, whether the announce clause is narrowly tailored to achieve it.

A. One meaning of "impartiality" in the judicial context—and of course its root meaning—is the lack of bias for or against either *party* to the proceeding. Impartiality in this sense . . . guarantees a party that the judge who hears his case will apply the law to him in the same way he applies it to any other party. This is the traditional sense in which the term is used. [The] announce clause is not narrowly tailored to serve impartiality (or the appearance of impartiality) in this sense. Indeed, the clause is barely tailored to serve that interest *at all*, inasmuch as it does not restrict speech for or against particular *parties*, but rather speech for or against particular *issues*. To be sure, when a case arises that turns on a legal issue on which the judge (as a candidate) had taken a particular stand, the party taking the opposite stand is likely to lose. But not because of any bias against that party, or favoritism toward the other party. *Any* party taking that position is just as likely to lose. The judge is applying the law (as he sees it) evenhandedly.

B. It is perhaps possible to use the term "impartiality" in the judicial context (though this is certainly not a common usage) to mean lack of preconception in favor of or against a particular *legal view*. This sort of impartiality would be concerned, not with guaranteeing litigants equal application of the law, but rather with guaranteeing them an equal chance to persuade the court on the legal points in their case. Impartiality in this sense may well be an interest served by the announce clause, but it is not a *compelling* state interest, as strict scrutiny requires. A judge's lack of predisposition regarding the relevant legal issues in a case has never been thought a necessary component of equal justice, and with good reason. For one thing, it is virtually impossible to find a judge who does not have preconceptions about the law. . . . Indeed, even if it were possible to select judges who did not have preconceived views on legal issues, it would hardly be desirable to do so. "Proof that a Justice's mind at the time he joined the Court was a complete *tabula rasa* in the area of constitutional adjudication would be evidence of lack of qualification, not lack of bias." [Laird v. Tatum, 409 U.S. 824, 835 (1972).] The Minnesota Constitution positively forbids the selection to courts of general jurisdiction of judges who are impartial in the sense of having no views on the law. Minn. Const., Art. VI, §5 ("Judges of the supreme court, the court of appeals and the district court shall be learned in the law"). And since avoiding judicial preconceptions on legal issues is neither possible nor desirable, pretending otherwise by attempting to preserve the "appearance" of that type of impartiality can hardly be a compelling state interest either.

C. A third possible meaning of "impartiality" (again not a common one) might be described as openmindedness. This quality in a judge demands, not that he have no preconceptions on legal issues, but that he be willing to consider views that oppose his preconceptions, and remain open to persuasion, when the issues arise in a pending case. This sort of impartiality seeks to guarantee each litigant, not an *equal* chance to win the legal points in the case, but at least *some* chance of doing so. It may well be that impartiality in this sense, and the appearance of it, are desirable in the judiciary, but we need not pursue that inquiry, since we do not believe the Minnesota Supreme Court adopted the announce clause for that purpose. [Minnesota, in fact, encourages judges to] state their views on disputed legal issues outside the context of adjudication—in classes that they conduct, and in books and speeches. . . . That is quite incompatible with the notion that the need for openmindedness (or for the appearance of openmindedness) lies behind the prohibition at issue here. . . .

[The] notion that the special context of electioneering justifies an *abridgment* of the right to speak out on disputed issues sets our First Amendment jurisprudence on its head. "Debate on the qualifications of candidates" is "at the core of our electoral process and of the First Amendment freedoms," not at the edges. "The role that elected officials play in our society makes it . . . imperative that they be allowed freely to express themselves on matters of current public importance." "It is . . . not the function of government to select which issues are worth discussing or debating in the course of a political campaign." We have never allowed the government to prohibit candidates from communicating relevant information to voters during an election.

Justice Ginsburg would do so—and much of her dissent confirms rather than refutes our conclusion that the purpose behind the announce clause is not openmindedness in the judiciary, but the undermining of judicial elections. . . .

IV. . . .

There is an obvious tension between . . . Minnesota's [constitutional requirement that] judges shall be elected, and the Minnesota Supreme Court's announce clause which places most subjects of interest to the voters off limits. . . . This disparity is perhaps unsurprising, since the ABA, which originated the announce clause, has long been an opponent of judicial elections. . . . [The] First Amendment does not permit it to achieve its goal by leaving the principle of elections in place while preventing candidates from discussing what the elections are about.

The Minnesota Supreme Court's canon of judicial conduct prohibiting candidates for judicial election from announcing their views on disputed legal and political issues violates the First Amendment.

JUSTICE O'CONNOR, concurring.

I join the opinion of the Court but write separately to express my concerns about judicial elections generally. . . .

We of course want judges to be impartial, in the sense of being free from any personal stake in the outcome of the cases to which they are assigned. But if judges are subject to regular elections they are likely to feel that they have at least some personal stake in the outcome of every publicized case. Elected judges cannot help being aware that if the public is not satisfied with the outcome of a particular case, it could hurt their reelection prospects. See Eule, Crocodiles in the Bathtub: State Courts, Voter Initiatives and the Threat of Electoral Reprisal, 65 U. Colo. L. Rev. 733, 739 (1994) (quoting former California Supreme Court Justice Otto Kaus's statement that ignoring the political consequences of visible decisions is " 'like ignoring a crocodile in your bathtub' "). . . . Even if judges were able to suppress their awareness of the potential electoral consequences of their decisions and refrain from acting on it, the public's confidence in the judiciary could be undermined simply by the possibility that judges would be unable to do so.

Moreover, contested elections generally entail campaigning. And campaigning for a judicial post today can require substantial funds. . . . [T]he cost of campaigning requires judicial candidates to engage in fundraising. Yet relying on campaign donations may leave judges feeling indebted to certain parties or interest groups. . . . [The] mere possibility that judges' decisions may be motivated by the desire to repay campaign contributors is likely to undermine the public's confidence in the judiciary.

Despite these significant problems, . . . Minnesota has chosen to select its judges through contested popular elections; [in] doing so the State has voluntarily taken on the risks to judicial bias described above. As a result, the State's claim that it needs to significantly restrict judges' speech in order to protect judicial impartiality is particularly troubling. If the State has a problem with judicial impartiality, it is largely one the State brought upon itself by continuing the practice of popularly electing judges.

JUSTICE KENNEDY, concurring.

I agree with the Court [and] I join its opinion. I adhere to my view, however, that content-based speech restrictions that do not fall within any traditional exception should be invalidated without inquiry into narrow tailoring or compelling government interests. . . . The political speech of candidates is at the heart of the First Amendment, and direct restrictions on the content of candidate speech are simply beyond the power of government to impose. . . .

JUSTICE GINSBURG, with whom JUSTICE STEVENS, JUSTICE SOUTER, and JUSTICE BREYER join, dissenting.

. . . Legislative and executive officials act on behalf of the voters who placed them in office; "judges represent the Law." . . . I would differentiate elections for political offices, in which the First Amendment holds full sway, from elections designed to select those whose office it is to administer justice without respect to persons. Minnesota's choice to elect its judges . . . does not preclude the State from installing an election process geared to the judicial office.

Judges . . . are not political actors. They do not sit as representatives of particular persons, communities, or parties; they serve no faction or constituency. . . . They must strive to do what is legally right. . . . Even when they develop common law or give concrete meaning to constitutional text, judges act only in the context of individual cases, the outcome of which cannot depend on the will of the public. . . . Thus, the rationale underlying unconstrained speech in elections for political office—that representative government depends on the public's ability to choose agents who will act at its behest—does not carry over to campaigns for the bench. . . .

NOTES

1. Are All Elections Equal?   Consider, in this context, the views of Robert Rantoul, a prominent nineteenth-century lawyer and politician, on the discretion afforded judges by the common law:

Judge-made law is ex post facto law, and therefore unjust. . . . Judge-made law is special legislation. The judge is human, and feels the bias which the coloring of the particular case gives. If he wishes to decide the next case differently, he has only to distinguish, and thereby make a new law. . . . The Common Law is the perfection of human reason—just as alcohol is the perfection of sugar. The subtle spirit of the Common Law is reason double distilled, till what was wholesome and nutritive becomes rank poison. . . . The judge makes law, by extorting from precedents something which they do not contain [and thus creates] a whole system of law . . . built up without the authority or interference of the legislator.

Robert Rantoul, Oration at Scituate, July 7, 1836, in Kermit L. Hall et al., American Legal History 317-318 (1991).

Rantoul was speaking in favor of the codification movement later associated with the Field Codes promoted by David Dudley Field and his brother, Stephen Field. Suppose that his remarks, however colorful, capture the essence of the freedom of adjudication afforded the common law judge. Does this argue in favor of the majority or the dissent? If elected judges can make the law whatever they want it to be, should they be as accountable as all other elected lawmakers? Or does the freedom of decision possessed by judges require that elected judges be selected in a speech-proscribed process?

Perhaps Rantoul was wrong. Do these opinions assume that judges do, or do not, exercise the discretionary law-making power that Rantoul accuses them of possessing?

2. More Implications of *Caperton*. After *White* voided Minnesota's "announce clause" the case was remanded for consideration of the validity of Minnesota's rules forbidding judicial candidates from political activities or soliciting campaign contributions. The political activities ban prohibited judicial candidates from identifying themselves as part of a political organization; attending "political gatherings"; or seeking, accepting, or using endorsements from a "political organization." In Republican Party v. White (*White II*), 416 F.3d 738 (8th Cir. 2005), both rules failed strict scrutiny. In Weaver v. Bonner, 309 F.3d 1312 (11th Cir. 2002), a Georgia ban on the solicitation of campaign contributions by judicial candidates was voided. Recall that *Caperton* holds that judicial recusal is constitutionally required when a judge seeking election has been the beneficiary of "significant and disproportionate" campaign expenditures or contributions by a person or entity with a personal stake in a case that is pending or imminent before the successfully elected judge. The obvious result is that judicial candidates may solicit funds at the cost of recusal in any case in which a "disproportionate" supporter has a personal interest. How much, if any, support does *Caperton* lend to the claim that prohibitions upon the solicitation of campaign funds or public support by judicial candidates should be valid?

3. Williams-Yulee v. The Florida Bar. In Florida voters elect judges. The state Supreme Court adopted a rule prohibiting judicial candidates from personally soliciting campaign funds but permitted judicial candidates to establish committees to raise money for them. Williams-Yulee, a judicial candidate, was disciplined for violating this rule. The Florida Supreme Court upheld the sanctions and the U.S. Supreme Court, 5-4, affirmed. Williams-Yulee v. The Florida Bar, 2015 U.S. LEXIS 2983. A plurality of four applied strict scrutiny to evaluate the validity of the rule. Justice Ginsburg concurred in the judgment but contended that strict scrutiny should not apply to judicial elections. The plurality reasoned that Florida's objective, preserving public confidence in the judiciary's integrity, was compelling. Because most donors are lawyers or litigants who may appear before the judge, the risk of undermining judicial integrity was especially acute. Personal solicitation aggravates that risk in a way that solicitation by a campaign committee does not. The rule was narrowly tailored to the objective: It was neither under- nor over-inclusive. It focused on the gravest risk—personal solicitation—and left open all manner of communications that a candidate may wish to make to the electorate or to an individual, with the sole exception of asking for campaign cash. The Court expressed no opinion on the wisdom of electing judges.

Four justices dissented, led by Justice Scalia, who contended that the rule was content-based and that the justifications offered by Florida were sufficiently imprecise as to fail to establish a compelling interest and that there was no proof that the rule advanced the state's objective to any material degree.

Queries: Was this strict scrutiny? Is "preserving public confidence in judicial integrity" a compelling interest? Even if it is, was the rule narrowly tailored to achieve this objective? In thinking about this question, consider the following actions that are not covered by the Florida Bar rule: (1) personalized thank-you notes from judicial candidates to donors, (2) formation of campaign committees to raise money for the candidate, (3) personal conversations between candidates and donors (so long as there is never a request for money), (4) disclosure of the identity of donors to the candidate, and (5) a candidate silently present while his or her campaign manager asks the donor for money. On this last point, is there any difference between the supplication of an eight-year-old Girl Scout to buy her cookies and the same request made by her mother while the Girl Scout silently looks beseechingly at you?

Are judicial elections sufficiently different from other elections to warrant reduced scrutiny? The Court thought otherwise in Republican Party v. White. Does *Williams-Yulee* suggest that *White* is on thin ice? Or can *White* and *Williams-Yulee* be harmonized on the basis that campaign contributions are different from other electoral speech? If so, does this cast doubt on *Citizens United* and related cases? Or is there a developing exception to the campaign finance cases when judicial elections are the subject?

H. FREEDOM OF THE PRESS

What, if anything, does the explicit guarantee of freedom of the press add to the free speech clause? Does the unique role played by the press in investigation, criticism, and reporting upon public affairs—functions critical to democratic self-governance—imply some degree of enhanced protection? If so, what is the scope of that protection? Are prior restraints of the press especially suspect? Does the press have the right to shield its sources from government inquiry to facilitate complete reporting of the news? Does the press enjoy constitutional protection from the consequences of breaching its promise of confidentiality given to a source when the press thinks the public need to know justifies the breach? May the press demand access to government information and proceedings in order to expose government actions to the light of public accountability? If so, may any government operations be concealed from the press? These questions are considered below.

1. Special Privileges for the Press?

Does the press play such an important role in self-governance and societal communication that it deserves special privileges not generally available to ordinary citizens?

a. A "Reporter's Privilege"?

In general, the press may not refuse to respond to legitimate government demands for information.

Branzburg v. Hayes, 408 U.S. 665 (1972). Branzburg had written several news articles about drug activities and was subpoenaed to testify before a grand jury about the drug transactions he had witnessed. He refused to testify. The Court stated that "the Constitution does [not] exempt the newsman from performing the citizen's normal duty of appearing and furnishing information relevant to the grand jury's task." While the Court conceded there might be some circumstances where the Constitution provides such a privilege, it concluded that the strong public interest in investigating crime outweighs the press interest in protecting its sources. The Court left open the question of whether there might be some constitutional shield with respect to administrative or legislative investigations.

Herbert v. Lando, 441 U.S. 153 (1979). The Court refused to fashion a constitutional shield to protect publishers from inquiry into their editorial processes in the context of civil defamation actions, although it did not squarely reject all claims to a reporter's privilege in civil cases. Some lower courts have found such a privilege, which can be overcome by a showing both that the matter sought to be discovered is central to the claim and that all alternative sources of information have been exhausted. See, e.g., Democratic National Committee v. McCord, 356 F. Supp. 1394 (D.D.C. 1973).

Some states have enacted so-called shield laws that provide a statutory reporter's privilege. One issue raised by such laws is who counts as a reporter. Oregon's shield law, for example, protects any "person connected with, employed by or engaged in any medium of communication to the public" from forced disclosure of sources. In Obsidian Finance Group, LLC v. Cox, 2011 U.S. Dist. LEXIS 137548, 40 Media L. Rep. 1084 (2011), a blogger was denied the protections of this law. As of April 2012, the case is on appeal.

When a shield law would operate to deprive a criminal defendant of access to potentially exculpatory evidence, some courts have ruled that the shield law must yield to the constitutional guarantee of a fair trial. See, e.g., In re Farber, 78 N.J. 259, 394 A.2d 330 (1978). This outcome has been criticized on the ground that many other evidentiary privileges have long been regarded as enforceable without violating a criminal defendant's fair trial right.

b. Immunity from Search?

Zurcher v. Stanford Daily, 436 U.S. 547 (1978). The Stanford Daily, a student newspaper at Stanford University, published photos of a violent encounter on campus between student demonstrators and the police. The police obtained a warrant to search the Daily for photo evidence that might aid in identifying the demonstrators who had assaulted the police. The Daily sought damages for what it contended was a search that violated the First Amendment, but the Supreme Court rejected the contention, reasoning that so long as a search complies with the Fourth Amendment, the First Amendment does not impose any requirement that law enforcement officials proceed by subpoena instead of by search warrant. The Privacy Protection Act, a federal statute enacted in response to *Zurcher*, limits the power of federal or state officials to obtain evidence from the news media by search warrant unless the medium itself is believed to be the criminal or there is a reasonable basis to believe that the evidence would be destroyed if sought by subpoena. See 42 U.S.C. §2000aa.

c. A Right of Access to Government Information and Proceedings?

In general, the press may not be excluded from criminal trials or preliminary hearings in criminal cases. Only if there is some overriding public interest (such as preserving a defendant's fair-trial right) may the press be excluded. However, the press enjoys no general right of access to government information and nonjudicial government proceedings.

▃▃
▃▃ **Richmond Newspapers, Inc. v. Virginia**
▃▃ *448 U.S. 555 (1980)*

CHIEF JUSTICE BURGER announced the judgment of the Court and delivered an opinion, in which JUSTICES WHITE and STEVENS joined.

The narrow question presented in this case is whether the right of the public and press to attend criminal trials is guaranteed under the United States Constitution.

[Stevenson had been tried three times for murder. His initial conviction was reversed, and the two subsequent trials ended in mistrials. The second mistrial was apparently due to a juror's knowledge of the prior trials, derived from newspaper accounts, and communication of that knowledge to other jurors. At the beginning of Stevenson's fourth trial, his lawyer asked that the trial be closed to the public. The trial judge granted the request, relying on a Virginia statute giving judges "discretion [to] exclude from the trial any persons whose presence would impair the conduct of a fair trial, provided that the right of the accused to a public trial shall not be violated." The Virginia Supreme Court upheld the closure order.]

For the first time the Court is asked to decide whether a criminal trial [may] be closed to the public upon the unopposed request of a defendant, without any demonstration that closure is required to protect the defendant's [right] to a fair trial, or that some other overriding consideration requires closure. [Throughout its evolution in England and in America the criminal] trial has been open to all who cared to observe. . . . This is no quirk of history; rather, it has long been recognized as an indispensable attribute of an Anglo-American trial: [It] gave assurance that the proceedings were conducted fairly to all concerned, and it discouraged perjury, the misconduct of participants, and decisions based on secret bias or partiality. [The] early history of open trials [also] reflects the widespread acknowledgment [that] public trials had significant community therapeutic value. [People] sensed from experience and observation that, especially in the administration of criminal justice, the means used to achieve justice must have the support derived from public acceptance of both the process and its results. [Thus], we . . . conclude that a presumption of openness inheres in the very nature of a criminal trial under our system of justice.

[The First Amendment's guarantees of free expression] share a common core purpose of assuring freedom of communication on matters relating to the functioning of government. Plainly it would be difficult to single out any aspect of government of higher concern and importance to the people than the manner in which criminal trials are conducted. . . . [In] guaranteeing freedoms such as those of speech and press, the First Amendment can be read as protecting the right of everyone to attend trials so as to give meaning to those explicit guarantees. [The] "First Amendment goes beyond protection of the press and the self-expression of individuals to prohibit government from limiting the stock of information from which members of the public may draw." Free speech carries with it some freedom to listen. [What] this means in the context of trials is that the First Amendment guarantees of speech and press, standing alone, prohibit government from summarily closing courtroom doors. . . . [It] is not crucial whether we describe this right to attend criminal trials to hear, see, and communicate observations concerning them as a "right of access," or a "right to gather information," for we have recognized that "without some protection for seeking out the news, freedom of the press could be eviscerated." The explicit, guaranteed rights to speak and to publish concerning what takes place at a trial would lose much meaning if access to observe the trial could, as it was here, be foreclosed arbitrarily.

[Virginia] argues that the Constitution nowhere spells out a guarantee for the right of the public to attend trials, and that accordingly no such right is protected. The possibility that such a contention could be made did not escape the notice of the Constitution's draftsmen; they were concerned that some important rights might be thought disparaged because not specifically guaranteed. It was even argued that because of this danger no Bill of Rights should be adopted. See, e.g., The Federalist No. 84 (A. Hamilton). In a letter to Thomas Jefferson in October 1788, James Madison explained why he, although "in favor of a bill of rights," [thought] "that in a certain degree [the] rights in question are reserved by the manner in which the federal powers are granted," [and] "there is great reason to fear that a positive declaration of some of the most essential rights could not be obtained in the requisite latitude."[24]

But arguments such as [Virginia] makes have not precluded recognition of important rights not enumerated. [The] Court has acknowledged that certain unarticulated rights are implicit in enumerated guarantees. For example, the rights of association and of privacy, the right to be presumed innocent, and the right to be judged by a standard of proof beyond a reasonable doubt in a criminal trial, as well as the right to travel, appear nowhere in the Constitution or Bill of Rights. Yet these important but unarticulated rights have nonetheless been found to share constitutional protection in common with explicit guarantees. The concerns expressed by Madison and others have thus been resolved; fundamental rights, even though not expressly guaranteed, have been recognized by the Court as indispensable to the enjoyment of rights explicitly defined. We hold that the right to attend criminal trials is implicit in the guarantees of the First Amendment; without the freedom to attend such trials, which people have exercised for centuries, important aspects of freedom of speech and "of the press could be eviscerated."

[There was inadequate justification for] the closure order. . . . [The] trial judge made no findings to support closure; no inquiry was made as to whether alternative solutions would have met the need to ensure fairness; there was no recognition of any right under the Constitution for the public or press to attend the trial. [Moreover], there exist [various] tested alternatives to satisfy the constitutional demands of fairness. [Any] problems with witnesses could [have] been dealt with by their exclusion from the courtroom or their sequestration during the trial. [Sequestration] of the jurors would [have] guarded

---

24. Madison's comments in Congress also reveal the perceived need for some sort of constitutional "saving clause," which, among other things, would serve to foreclose application to the Bill of Rights of the maxim that the affirmation of particular rights implies a negation of those not expressly defined. Madison's efforts, culminating in the Ninth Amendment, served to allay the fears of those who were concerned that expressing certain guarantees could be read as excluding others.

against their being subjected to any improper information. [Absent] an over-riding interest articulated in findings, the trial of a criminal case must be open to the public. [Reversed.]

JUSTICE BRENNAN, joined by JUSTICE MARSHALL, concurring in the judgment.

[The] Court's approach in right-of-access cases . . . reflects the special nature of a claim of First Amendment right to gather information. [The] First Amendment embodies more than a commitment to free expression and communicative interchange for their own sakes; it has a structural role to play in securing and fostering our republican system of self-government. Implicit in this structural role is not only "the principle that debate on public issues should be uninhibited, robust, and wide-open," but also the anteced-ent assumption that valuable public debate—as well as other civic behav-ior—must be informed. . . .

JUSTICE REHNQUIST, dissenting.

[The] issue here is not whether the "right" to freedom of the press con-ferred by the First Amendment to the Constitution overrides the defendant's "right" to a fair trial conferred by other Amendments to the Constitution; it is instead whether any provision in the Constitution may fairly be read to pro-hibit what the trial judge in the Virginia state-court system did in this case. Being unable to find any such prohibition in the First, Sixth, Ninth, or any other Amendment to the United States Constitution, or in the Constitution itself, I dissent.

NOTES

1. Scope of the *Richmond Newspapers* Access Right. In Globe Newspaper Co. v. Superior Court, 457 U.S. 596 (1982), the Court voided a Massachusetts law requiring exclusion of the press and public from a court-room during testimony by a minor allegedly the victim of a sex crime. The Court ruled that the state's inflexible closure rule was not narrowly tailored to achieving the state's compelling interest of protecting the minor victims of sex crimes from further trauma. In Press-Enterprise Co. v. Superior Court (*Press-Enterprise I*), 464 U.S. 501 (1984), the Court extended *Richmond Newspapers* to voir dire of the jury pool in a criminal trial involving the rape and murder of a teenager. In Press-Enterprise Co. v. Superior Court (*Press-Enterprise II*), 478 U.S. 1 (1986), the Court further extended *Richmond Newspapers* to transcripts of a preliminary hearing in a criminal case, over the objections of the judge, prosecutor, and the defendant, all of whom thought that public access to the transcripts would endanger a fair trial. The Court treated a preliminary hearing, at which the court decides whether there is sufficient evidence against the accused to warrant a trial, as the constitutional equivalent of a criminal trial.

2. Rights of Access to Other Government Proceedings. *Richmond Newspapers* did not decide whether the right of access to criminal trials extends to civil courtroom proceedings or to other aspects of government operations. The issue has been litigated with respect to a claimed press right of access to prisons. In Pell v. Procunier, 417 U.S. 817 (1974), the Court upheld a California regulation that barred the press from face-to-face interviews with prison inmates. The Court reasoned that the regulation did not abridge free expression because it did "not deny the press access to sources of information available to members of the general public." The Court rejected the contention "that the Constitution imposes upon government the affirmative duty to make available to journalists sources of information not available to members of the public generally." Even though this was a pre–*Richmond Newspapers* case, this principle has not been disturbed since. The access rights of the press recognized in *Richmond Newspapers, Globe*, and the *Press-Enterprise* cases are coextensive with the access rights of the general public. Saxbe v. Washington Post, 417 U.S. 843 (1974), upheld a federal prison regulation virtually identical to California's policy at issue in *Pell*. See also Houchins v. KQED, Inc., 438 U.S. 1 (1978).

2.   Singling Out the Press for Unfavorable Treatment

Governments may impose generally applicable regulations upon the press, in common with other citizens, that may be burdensome (e.g., OSHA, labor laws, antitrust laws), but when governments subject the press to unique treatment that is based on the content of speech or that "threatens to suppress the expression of particular ideas or viewpoints," the regulations are "constitutionally suspect." Such regulations are valid only when the government proves that they are "necessary to achieve an overriding governmental interest."

Minneapolis Star & Tribune Co. v. Minnesota Commissioner of Revenue
460 U.S. 575 (1983)

JUSTICE O'CONNOR delivered the opinion of the Court.

This case presents the question of a State's power to impose a special tax on the press and, by enacting exemptions, to limit its effect to only a few newspapers. Since 1967, Minnesota has imposed a sales tax on most [retail sales of goods and a use tax] on the "privilege of using, storing or consuming in Minnesota tangible personal property" [on which no] sales tax was paid. [This] use tax protects the State's sales tax by eliminating the residents' incentive to travel to States with lower sales taxes to buy goods rather than buying them in Minnesota. . . .

Minneapolis Star & Tribune Co., "Star Tribune," is the publisher of a . . . newspaper . . . in Minneapolis. From 1967 until 1971, it enjoyed an exemption from the sales and use tax provided by Minnesota for periodic publications. In 1971, however, while leaving the exemption from the sales tax in place, the legislature . . . impose[d] a "use tax" on the cost of paper and ink products consumed in the production of a publication. [In] 1974, the legislature again amended the statute, this time to exempt the first $100,000 worth of ink and paper consumed by a publication in any calendar year. . . . Publications remained exempt from the sales tax. After the enactment of the $100,000 exemption, 11 publishers, producing 14 of the 388 paid circulation newspapers in the State, incurred a tax liability in 1974. Star Tribune was one of the 11, and, of the $893,355 collected, it paid $608,634, or roughly two-thirds of the total revenue raised by the tax. In 1975, 13 publishers, producing 16 out of 374 paid circulation papers, paid a tax. That year, Star Tribune again bore roughly two-thirds of the total receipts from the use tax on ink and paper. Star Tribune instituted this action to seek a refund of the use taxes it paid [on the ground that] imposition of the use tax on ink and paper used in publications [violated the guarantee] of freedom of the press. [The] Minnesota Supreme Court upheld the tax. [We] now reverse. . . .

It is beyond dispute that [governments] can subject newspapers to generally applicable economic regulations without creating constitutional problems. Minnesota, however, [has] created a special tax that applies only to certain publications protected by the First Amendment. Although the State argues now that the tax on paper and ink is part of the general scheme of taxation, the use tax provision is facially discriminatory, singling out publications for treatment that [is] unique in Minnesota tax law.

Minnesota's treatment of publications differs from that of other enterprises in at least two important respects: it imposes a use tax that does not serve the function of protecting the sales tax, and it taxes an intermediate transaction rather than the ultimate retail sale. [By] creating this special use tax, [Minnesota] has singled out the press for special treatment. We then must determine whether the First Amendment permits such special taxation. A tax that burdens rights protected by the First Amendment cannot stand unless the burden is necessary to achieve an overriding governmental interest.

[There] is substantial evidence that differential taxation of the press would have troubled the Framers of the First Amendment, [and those fears] were well founded. A power to tax differentially, as opposed to a power to tax generally, gives a government a powerful weapon against the taxpayer selected. When the State imposes a generally applicable tax, there is little cause for concern. We need not fear that a government will destroy a selected group of taxpayers by burdensome taxation if it must impose the same burden on the rest of its constituency. When the State singles out the press, though, the political constraints that prevent a legislature from passing crippling taxes of general applicability are weakened, and the threat of burdensome taxes becomes acute. That threat can operate as effectively as a censor to check critical comment by the press, undercutting the basic assumption of our political system that the press will often serve as an important restraint on government. [Differential] treatment, unless justified by some special characteristic of the press, suggests that the goal of the regulation is not unrelated to suppression of expression, and such a goal is presumptively unconstitutional. Differential taxation of the press, then, places such a burden on the interests protected by the First Amendment that we cannot countenance such treatment unless the State asserts a counterbalancing interest of compelling importance that it cannot achieve without differential taxation.

The main interest asserted by Minnesota in this case is the raising of revenue. [But that interest] cannot justify the special treatment of the press, for an alternative means of achieving the same interest without raising concerns under the First Amendment is clearly available: the State could raise the revenue by taxing businesses generally, avoiding the censorial threat implicit in a tax that singles out the press. [Minnesota says the tax is] merely a substitute for the sales tax, which, as a generally applicable tax, would be constitutional as applied to the press. There are two fatal flaws in this reasoning.

First, the State has offered no explanation of why it chose to use a substitute for the sales tax rather than the sales tax itself. [If] the real goal of this tax is to duplicate the sales tax, it is difficult to see why the State did not achieve that goal by the obvious and effective expedient of applying the sales tax. Further, even assuming that the legislature did have valid reasons for substituting another tax for the sales tax, [we] would be hesitant to fashion a rule that automatically allowed the State to single out the press for a different method of taxation as long as the effective burden was no different from that on other taxpayers or the burden on the press was lighter than that on other businesses. [The] very selection of the press for special treatment threatens the press not only with the current *differential* treatment, but also with the possibility of subsequent differentially *more burdensome* treatment. Thus, even without actually imposing an extra burden on the press, the government might be able to achieve censorial effects, for "[the] threat of sanctions may deter [the] exercise [of First Amendment rights] almost as potently as the actual application of sanctions."

A second reason to avoid the proposed rule is that courts as institutions are poorly equipped to evaluate with precision the relative burdens of various methods of taxation. The complexities of factual economic proof always present a certain potential for error, and courts have little familiarity with the process of evaluating the relative economic burden of taxes. In sum, the possibility of error inherent in the proposed rule poses too great a threat to concerns at the heart of the First Amendment, and we cannot tolerate that possibility.[25] Minnesota, therefore, has offered no adequate justification for the special treatment of newspapers.

---

25. If a State employed the same *method* of taxation but applied a lower *rate* to the press, so that there could be no doubt that the legislature was not singling out the press to bear a more burdensome tax, we would, of course, be in a position to evaluate the relative burdens. [Such] a lower tax rate for the press would not raise the threat that the legislature might later impose an extra burden that would escape detection by the courts. Thus, our decision does not, as the dissent suggests, require Minnesota to impose a greater tax burden on publications.

Minnesota's ink and paper tax violates the First Amendment not only because it singles out the press, but also because it targets a small group of newspapers. The effect of the [1974 exemption] is that only a handful of publishers pay any tax at all, and even fewer pay any significant amount of tax. The State explains this exemption as part of a policy favoring an "equitable" tax system, although there are no comparable exemptions for small enterprises outside the press. [Whatever] the motive of the legislature in this case, we think that recognizing a power in the State not only to single out the press but also to tailor the tax so that it singles out a few members of the press presents such a potential for abuse that no interest suggested by Minnesota can justify the scheme.

We need not and do not impugn the motives of the Minnesota Legislature in passing the ink and paper tax. [Even] regulations aimed at proper governmental concerns can restrict unduly the exercise of rights protected by the First Amendment. A tax that singles out the press, or that targets individual publications within the press, places a heavy burden on the State to justify its action. Since Minnesota has offered no satisfactory justification for its tax on the use of ink and paper, the tax violates the First Amendment. [Reversed.]

JUSTICE REHNQUIST, dissenting.

Today we learn from the Court that a State runs afoul of the First Amendment [where] the State structures its taxing system to the advantage of newspapers. This seems very much akin to protecting something so overzealously that in the end it is smothered. [The] Court recognizes [that] Minnesota could avoid constitutional problems by imposing on newspapers the 4% sales tax that it imposes on other retailers. Rather than impose such a tax, however, the Minnesota Legislature decided to provide newspapers with an exemption from the sales tax and impose a 4% use tax on ink and paper; thus, while both taxes are part of one "system of sales and use taxes," newspapers are classified differently within that system. The problem the Court finds too difficult to deal with is whether this difference in treatment results in a significant burden on newspapers. [Had] a 4% sales tax been imposed, the Minneapolis Star & Tribune would have been liable for $1,859,950 in 1974. The same "complexities of factual economic proof" can be analyzed for 1975. [Had] the sales tax been imposed, as the Court agrees would have been permissible, the [Star Tribune's] liability for 1974 and 1975 would have been $3,685,092. [But the Star Tribune] paid $608,634 in use taxes in 1974 and $636,113 in 1975 — a total liability of $1,244,747. We need no expert testimony [to] determine that the $1,224,747 paid in use taxes is significantly less burdensome than the $3,685,092 that could have been levied by a sales tax. A fortiori, the Minnesota taxing scheme which singles out newspapers for "differential treatment" has benefitted, not burdened, the "freedom of speech, [and] of the press." . . .

[But] "differential treatment" [alone is not enough to subject] governmental action to the most stringent constitutional review. [No] First Amendment issue is raised unless First Amendment rights have been infringed. [Of course,

Minnesota] is required to show that its taxing scheme is rational. But [that] showing can be made easily. [So] long as the State can find another way to collect revenue from the newspapers, imposing a sales tax on newspapers would be to no one's advantage[—]not the newspaper and its distributors[,] who would have to collect the tax[;] not the State[,] who would have to enforce collection[;] and not the consumer[,] who would have to pay for the paper in odd amounts. The reasonable alternative Minnesota chose was to impose the use tax on ink and paper.

[The] Court finds [that] the exemption newspapers receive for the first $100,000 of ink and paper used also violates the First Amendment because the result is that only a few of the newspapers actually pay a use tax. I cannot agree. [The] exemption is in effect a $4,000 credit which benefits all newspapers. [Absent] any improper motive on the part of the Minnesota Legislature in drawing the limits of this exemption, it cannot [violate] the First Amendment.

[To] collect from newspapers their fair share of taxes under the sales and use tax scheme and at the same time avoid abridging the freedoms of speech and press, the Court holds [that] Minnesota must subject newspapers to millions of additional dollars in sales tax liability. Certainly this is a hollow victory for the newspapers, and I seriously doubt [that] this result would have been intended by the [Framers].

NOTES

1. Developments Since *Star Tribune*. In Arkansas Writers' Project, Inc. v. Ragland, 481 U.S. 221 (1987), the Court struck down an Arkansas law that exempted from its sales tax all newspapers and "religious, professional, trade and sports journals" but no other magazines: A "magazine's tax status depends entirely on its content." In Simon & Schuster, Inc. v. New York State Crime Victims Board, 502 U.S. 105 (1991), the Court voided a New York statute calling for confiscation of any income earned by a person "accused or convicted of a crime" from any publications concerning the crime, and providing that such proceeds be held in trust to satisfy civil judgments obtained against the accused or convicted criminal by his victims. A "statute is presumptively inconsistent with the First Amendment if it imposes a financial burden on speakers because of the content of their speech." While New York's interest in facilitating compensation to crime victims was a compelling interest, the law was not sufficiently narrowly tailored to achieve New York's compelling interest in victim compensation. Not only did the law apply to "accused" persons, it also reached any book in which the author admitted to a crime, thus including such authors as Henry David Thoreau and Saint Augustine.

But in Leathers v. Medlock, 499 U.S. 439 (1991), the Court upheld an extension by Arkansas of its sales tax to cable television services, combined with a continued exemption for sales of newspapers, magazines, and satellite broadcast services. The Court reasoned that because the tax did not threaten "to suppress the expression of particular ideas or viewpoints," it did not discriminate on the basis of the content of particular publications within a general class of publications. Rather, the Arkansas tax system distinguished between two different media. Because the tax was on an entire medium the Court thought it posed no danger of censorship of content or viewpoint; it would not "distort the market for ideas."

2. Generally Applicable Laws.   In contrast to a law that singles out the press for differential treatment, the press enjoys no immunity from generally applicable laws. Cohen v. Cowles Media Co., 501 U.S. 663 (1991), raised this issue in connection with the application to a newspaper of common law principles that subject persons to liability for breach of explicit promises of confidentiality. Pursuant to such a promise, Cohen, a political campaign worker, provided reporters of the Minneapolis Star with information about the past criminal activities of a political candidate. The information was accurate but its significance was highly exaggerated. The Star then wrote stories that revealed Cohen's name, which resulted in his dismissal. Cohen sought and obtained damages on a promissory estoppel theory. Reasoning that Cohen's claim was founded on a content-neutral principle of contact law, the Court rejected the Star's claim that the First Amendment insulated it from liability.

10

The Religion Clauses

The First Amendment contains two clauses pertaining to religious freedom. The establishment clause provides that "Congress shall make no law respecting an establishment of religion," and the free exercise clause provides that "Congress shall make no [law] prohibiting the free exercise" of religion. As with free expression, although the clauses appear to be directed at congressional action only, they apply to *any* action of the federal government. These religion clauses have been incorporated into the Fourteenth Amendment's due process clause and thereby apply with equal force to both the states and the federal government. See Cantwell v. Connecticut, 310 U.S. 296 (1940) (free exercise clause); Everson v. Board of Education, 330 U.S. 1 (1947) (establishment clause).

Section A of this chapter provides a short introduction to the history and theory of the religion clauses. Section B examines the scope of the protection afforded by the free exercise clause: Section C probes the important issues raised by the establishment clause: (1) whether and to what extent governments may provide financial aid to religion, (2) to what extent governments may display or adopt the overt or symbolic messages of religions, and (3) to what extent governments may accommodate religious belief when not constitutionally required to do so.

A. A SUMMARY OF THE HISTORY AND THEORY OF THE RELIGION CLAUSES

The religion clauses were intended to work together to secure religious autonomy, but there has never been agreement on precisely how that was to be accomplished. There is nearly universal agreement that the Framers intended to bar the national government from establishing an official state religion and to prevent interference with individual religious beliefs. But agreement ends there.

1. Two Views of History

There are competing visions of the intended purpose of the establishment clause. One view (the "wall of separation" view) is that the establishment clause was designed to preserve a private space for individuals to make voluntary choices about religious belief and commitment, free of government influence. The establishment clause ensures this in two ways: by disabling the government from any meaningful support of religion and keeping government free of any substantial infusion of religious doctrine. The first way makes religion the product of purely private and voluntary support; the latter ensures that secular governance of a religiously diverse nation will be free of sectarian dogma.

The "wall of separation" view dates back to the 1785-1786 struggle in Virginia over whether to renew Virginia's tax that supported the state-established church. James Madison and Thomas Jefferson led a successful fight to kill the tax and succeeded in persuading the Virginia General Assembly to enact the "Bill for Religious Liberty," which ended state-compelled support of or attendance at the established church and provided that no person should "suffer on account of his religious opinions." This history is recounted at length in Justice Black's opinion for the Court in Everson v. Board of Education, 330 U.S. 1 (1947), which, as to the history, also garnered the support of the four dissenters in *Everson*. Justice Rutledge, for the dissenters, stated that to Madison "religion was a wholly private matter beyond the scope of civil power either to restrain or to support. [State] aid was no less obnoxious or destructive to freedom and to religion itself than other forms of state interference." The *Everson* opinions and the history upon which they were based have led to many commentators' assertions that this view has become the received wisdom of the religion clauses.

But there is another view of the history. On this view (the "non-preferential" view), the aim of the religion clauses (and, in particular, the establishment clause) was to bar the national government from preferring any religion over all others. See, e.g., Philip Hamburger, Separation of Church and State (2004); Feldman, The Intellectual Origins of the Establishment Clause, 77 N.Y.U. L. Rev. 346 (2002); Natelson, The Original Meaning of the Establishment Clause, 14 Wm. & Mary Bill Rts. J. 73 (2005). This view is supported by the facts that Madison's original draft of the establishment clause barred the establishment of a "*national* religion," that the Virginia taxation plan opposed so strenuously by Madison and Jefferson was designed to aid only the "Christian Religion," that Madison's objections to the Virginia plan were primarily rooted in its preference for a particular religion, and, finally, that the early historical practice of the nation was to provide non-preferential government support to religion (e.g., the first Congress's provision of finan-cial aid to sectarian schools in the Northwest Territory and creation of paid chaplains).

Justice Souter, in particular, took issue with this view, arguing that the fact that Congress rejected Madison's original establishment clause and substituted a broader prohibition suggests an implicit rejection of non-pref-erential interpretation of the clause, that it is unfair to characterize Madison's remonstrance in opposition to the Virginia tax as based primarily on non-preferential objections, and that the early history of non-preferential state aid to religion "prove[s] only that public officials, no matter when they serve, can turn a blind eye to constitutional principle."

No matter how finely the dross of the historical record is sifted, there are apt to be nuggets of wisdom falling to each side. If intentions and practices are ambiguous, how much weight should history have in our contemporary jurisprudence of the religion clauses? Should it matter that our society today is far more religiously diverse than it was in 1789? In any case, adopting the "wall of separation" view of history says nothing about where that wall should be located, how high it should be built, or how porous it should be.

2.   The Quest for a Unifying Theory

The common observation that the religion clauses are united in their pur-suit of religious liberty obscures the tension produced by the different ways each clause upholds that ideal. If the establishment clause is read as barring all government accommodation of or assistance to religion, no matter how slight and regardless of whether the assistance is provided to all members of soci-ety, religion is singled out for ill treatment, for such a rule would presumably bar a municipal fire department from rendering aid to a blazing church. And less extreme interpretations might be equally pernicious to religious liberty. Would the establishment clause forbid the armed services from employing chaplains? If so, would the absence of chaplains be an unconstitutional inter-ference with the conscript's right to exercise freely his religious belief?

On the other hand, a reading of the free exercise clause that requires government to accommodate every religious duty, no matter how much at odds with the general rules applicable to every member of civil society, would produce enormous government favoritism. In this view, governments would be forbidden to tax those who have religious objections to taxation or to pun-ish those whose religion requires human sacrifices. Less dramatically, govern-ments would be required to exempt religious adherents from any civic duty that conflicts with their religious beliefs. Given the multiplicity of religious beliefs in America, this would confer immense benefits upon religion, to the extent that the establishment clause could be offended.

There are two imperfect solutions to the problem of conflict between the two religion clauses. The first—strict separation—is skewed toward avoiding establishment of religion at the expense of free exercise. The second—recognizing a generous zone of permitted but not required accommodation of religion—allows government a relatively free hand in adjusting the tension between the two clauses.

The "strict separation" view, never adopted by the Court, holds that religion may never be used by government "as a basis for classification, [whether in] the conferring of rights [or] the imposition [of] obligations." Kurland, Of Church and State and the Supreme Court, 29 U. Chi. L. Rev. 1 (1961). This view would bar government accommodations of religion unless such accommodations were an accidental by-product of purely secular decisions.

However, the Court actually adheres to a more accommodating view. Stated generally, this view holds that some government accommodations of religion are permitted but not required, some are prohibited because of the establishment clause, and some are required because of the free exercise clause. The difficulty is deciding which accommodations fall into which classification. This view does not eliminate conflict between the clauses; instead, it requires the Court to mediate that conflict. Imagine a spectrum with the establishment clause at the left end and the free exercise clause at the right end. The establishment end marks a zone of prohibited accommodations and the free exercise end marks a region of required accommodations. In the middle lies a zone of permissible (but not required) accommodations. The Court has never agreed on the precise boundaries at the ends of the spectrum, and much of the doctrinal debate is an attempt to chart these frontiers.

There are four essential positions that can be taken in this debate: (1) The polar regions of required and prohibited accommodations are small, leaving to legislative discretion a vast middle ground of permissible accommodation. (2) The polar regions are large, leaving a narrow band of permissible accommodation for legislative discretion. (3) The establishment clause zone of prohibited accommodations is large and the free exercise zone of required accommodations is small, leaving a modest zone of permissible accommodations that is skewed to the right-hand side of the spectrum. (4) The establishment zone of prohibited accommodations is small and the free exercise zone of required accommodations is large, with the modest zone of permissible accommodations skewed to the left end of the spectrum. To be sure, the Court does not speak in this vernacular. Its doctrine is more piecemeal, addressing establishment clause and free exercise issues in seeming isolation, but lurking in the background is the broad issue of theoretical reconciliation of the two clauses.

3. A Threshold Problem: Defining Religion

The very nature of the religion clauses suggests the necessity of defining "religion," but any attempt to do so in terms of theological concepts risks the creation of a forbidden establishment of religion. Even a neutral definition—one free of religious values—raises the question of whether it is possible to distinguish between religious and philosophical beliefs. In a series of Vietnam War era cases in which the Court upheld the validity of a statutory exemption from military conscription that applied only to those who opposed all war "by reason of religious training and belief," the Court was forced to determine whether individual claims to the exemption were sincerely held or offered only for the expedient purpose of avoiding military service. The statutory exemption defined "religious training and belief" to mean a "belief in a relation to a Supreme Being involving duties superior to those arising from any human relation" and specifically excluded "political, sociological, or philosophical views or a purely personal moral code." In United States v. Seeger, 380 U.S. 163 (1965), the Court concluded that a person was entitled to the exemption even though he stated he had "a religious faith in a purely ethical creed" but had no "belief in God, except in the remotest sense." The Court declared that the "test of belief 'in a relation to a Supreme Being' is whether a given belief that is sincere and meaningful occupies a place in the life of its possessor parallel to that filled by the orthodox belief in God of one who clearly qualifies for the exemption."

This method — inquiry into whether a given set of beliefs are sincerely held, rather than into their substance — involves fine and difficult distinctions. An example is United States v. Ballard, 322 U.S. 78 (1944). Ballard was prosecuted for mail fraud in connection with his solicitation of money for the "I Am" movement, a cult that claimed to be divine messengers of a deity, "Saint Germain," and to be endowed by that deity with supernatural powers to cure disease. The Court ruled that the religion clauses barred a jury from determining the truth or falsity of Ballard's beliefs, but did permit the jury to determine whether Ballard and his fellow defendants sincerely believed in what they said.

> Men may believe what they cannot prove. They may not be put to the proof of their religious doctrines or beliefs. [If] one could be sent to jail because a jury found [belief in the miracles of the New Testament or life after death] false, little indeed would be left of religious freedom.

The dissent charged that it was not possible to "separate an issue as to what is believed from considerations as to what is believable."

Similar considerations have prompted the Court to refuse to "[resolve] church property disputes on the basis of religious doctrine or practice." Jones v. Wolf, 443 U.S. 595 (1979). In *Jones*, a church had acquired property in the name of the "Vineville Presbyterian Church." A majority of the congregation left the national Presbyterian Church, which body declared the local minority to be the "true congregation." In a suit to determine true ownership of the church property, the Court ruled that secular courts may apply secular, "neutral principles [of] trust and property law" to resolve such intra-church disputes. But even those "neutral principles" are of no help when their resolution depends on a construction of theological doctrine. Presbyterian Church v. Mary Elizabeth Blue Hull Church, 393 U.S. 440 (1969), involved a transfer in trust to the national church of the property owned by a local church until such time as the national church abandoned church doctrine existing at the time of the transfer. The Court held that secular courts could not determine whether the condition triggering termination of the trust had occurred because its resolution was dependent on construction of church dogma.

Jones complicated matters by holding that, as an alternative to secular principles of trust and property law, civil courts could defer to internal church governance rules in resolving church property disputes. Deference to the internal rules of religious organizations but not secular charities raises the question of whether this may constitute a religious preference that violates the establishment clause. See Greenawalt, Hands Off! Civil Court Involvement in Conflicts over Religious Property, 98 Colum. L. Rev. 1843 (1998).

Though the principle that the government may not interfere with a church's selection of its clergy arose in the context of church property disputes, in Hosanna-Tabor Evangelical Lutheran Church & School v. EEOC, 132 S. Ct. 694 (2012), the Court unanimously extended it to claims of employment discrimination made by a minister against her church. This ministerial exception prevents such laws from being applied to disputes involving the employment relationship between a religious institution and its ministers. To require a church to accept or keep an unwanted minister, or punishing a church for failing to do so, interferes with the church's internal governance of the church, thus preventing a church from selecting those persons who embody and present its beliefs. This would infringe the free exercise clause, which guarantees to religious institutions the right to profess their faith without government interference. It would also violate the establishment clause, which denies to governments the power to dictate ecclesiastical decisions. The Court eschewed any rigid formula for determining who is a minister, but noted that the complainant was commissioned as a "called teacher," held herself out as a minister, was so regarded by her church employer, and performed duties that required her to articulate and advance the church's message and mission. The fact that she performed many secular duties as well was not dispositive. Justices Alito and Kagan, concurring, thought that the definition of a minister should be functional: The ministerial exception should apply to any employee "who leads a religious organization, conducts worship services or important religious ceremonies or rituals, or serves as a messenger or teacher of its faith." Justice Thomas, concurring, argued that courts should defer to a church's determination of who counts as a minister.

B. THE FREE EXERCISE CLAUSE

The practice of religion is rarely a complete abstraction. Few people cling to religious *belief* without manifesting that belief through religiously inspired *conduct*. But religious conduct may clash with secular rules of conduct that are generally applicable to everyone. When that conflict occurs, does the free exercise clause insulate religious conduct from such secular laws? Is the free exercise clause more protective of religious conduct when the law that impinges upon religious conduct is not generally applicable or is intended simply to impede religious conduct?

1. Generally Applicable Laws That Impede Religious Conduct

The Court's initial view was that the free exercise clause never bars regulation of religious conduct.

Reynolds v. United States, 98 U.S. 145 (1879). The Court upheld Reynolds's conviction under a federal law barring polygamy despite his religious belief in the practice, because the free exercise clause does not bar generally applicable regulations that impede religious conduct. While laws "cannot interfere with mere religious belief and opinions, they may with practices." Permitting exemptions from general laws because of religiously inspired conduct would "make the professed doctrines of religious belief superior to the law of the land, and in effect to permit every citizen to become a law unto himself. Government could exist only in name under such circumstances."

To similar effect was Jacobson v. Massachusetts, 197 U.S. 11 (1905), upholding compulsory smallpox vaccinations of religious objectors.

Braunfeld v. Brown, 366 U.S. 599 (1961). An orthodox Jew challenged Pennsylvania's Sunday Closing law as a violation of his free exercise rights because he was compelled by law to close on Sunday and compelled by his religion to close on Saturday. The Court upheld the law, ruling that generally applicable laws that impose an "indirect burden on religious observance" are valid "unless the State may accomplish its purposes by means which do not impose such a burden." Pennsylvania's objective of a uniform "family day of rest" would be undermined by religious exemptions. In essence, from *Reynolds* to *Braunfeld* the Court moved from the position that general regulations that hinder religious conduct are always valid to the position that such regulations are valid unless there is a less burdensome means to achieve the state's objective.

≡≡≡ *Sherbert v. Verner*
≡≡≡ *374 U.S. 398 (1963)*

JUSTICE BRENNAN delivered the opinion of the Court.

Appellant, a [Seventh Day Adventist], was discharged by [her] employer because she would not work on Saturday, the Sabbath Day of her faith. When she was unable to obtain other employment because [she] would not take Saturday work, she filed a claim for unemployment compensation benefits, [but the claim was denied because her refusal to accept Saturday employment meant that she had failed], without good cause, to accept "suitable work when offered," [as required by the compensation law. The South Carolina

Supreme Court upheld the denial of benefits, rejecting] appellant's contention that, as applied to her, [the] South Carolina statute abridged her right to the free exercise of her religion. [We reverse and remand.]

[If] the decision of the South Carolina Supreme Court is to withstand appellant's constitutional challenge, it must be either because her disqualification as a beneficiary represents no infringement by the State of her constitutional rights of free exercise, or because any incidental burden on the free exercise of appellant's religion may be justified by a "compelling state interest in the regulation of a subject within the State's constitutional power to regulate." We turn first to the question whether the disqualification for benefits imposes any burden on the free exercise of appellant's religion. We think it is clear that it does. If "the purpose or effect of a law is to impede the observance of one or all religions or is to discriminate invidiously between religions, that law is constitutionally invalid even though the burden may be characterized as being only indirect." [*Braunfeld.*] Here not only is it apparent that appellant's declared ineligibility for benefits derives solely from the practice of her religion, but the . . . ruling forces her to choose between following the precepts of her religion and forfeiting benefits, on the one hand, and abandoning one of the precepts of her religion in order to accept work, on the other hand. Governmental imposition of such a choice puts the same kind of burden upon the free exercise of religion as would a fine imposed against appellant for her Saturday worship.

Nor may the [statute as applied] be saved from constitutional infirmity on the ground that unemployment compensation benefits are not appellant's "right" but merely a "privilege." [While] the State was surely under no obligation to afford [unemployment benefits], to condition the availability of benefits upon this appellant's willingness to violate a cardinal principle of her religious faith effectively penalizes the free exercise of her constitutional liberties.

[We] must next consider whether some compelling state interest [justifies] the substantial infringement of appellant's First Amendment right. [The] appellees suggest no more than a possibility that the filing of fraudulent claims by unscrupulous claimants feigning religious objections to Saturday work might not only dilute the unemployment compensation fund but also hinder the scheduling by employers of necessary Saturday work. But [there] is no proof whatever to warrant such fears of malingering or deceit. [Even if there were such proof], it would plainly be incumbent upon the appellees to demonstrate that no alternative forms of regulation would combat such abuses without infringing First Amendment rights. [The Sunday closing law upheld in *Braunfeld* was] saved by a countervailing factor which finds no equivalent in the instant case—a strong state interest in providing one uniform day of rest for all workers. That secular objective could be achieved, the Court found, only by declaring Sunday to be that day of rest. Requiring exemptions for Sabbatarians . . . appeared to present an administrative problem of such magnitude, or to afford the exempted class so great a competitive advantage, that such a requirement would have rendered the entire statutory scheme unworkable. [Here], no such justifications underlie the determination of the state court that appellant's religion makes her ineligible to receive benefits.

In holding as we do, plainly we are not fostering the "establishment" of the Seventh Day Adventist religion in South Carolina, for the extension of unemployment benefits to Sabbatarians in common with Sunday worshippers reflects nothing more than the governmental obligation of neutrality in the face of religious differences, and does not represent that involvement of religious with secular institutions which it is the object of the Establishment Clause to forestall. [Nor do we declare] the existence of a constitutional right to unemployment benefits on the part of all persons whose religious convictions are the cause of their unemployment. This is not a case in which an employee's religious convictions serve to make him a nonproductive member of society. [Our] holding today is only that South Carolina may not constitutionally apply the eligibility provisions so as to constrain a worker to abandon his religious convictions respecting the day of rest.

JUSTICE STEWART, concurring in the result.

[I] cannot agree that today's decision can stand consistently with [*Braunfeld*]. The Court says that there was a "less direct burden upon religious practices" in that case than in this. [The] Court is mistaken. . . . *Braunfeld* . . . involved a state *criminal* statute [that] "put an individual to a choice between his business and his religion." The impact upon the appellant's religious freedom [here] is considerably less onerous. [The] appellant at the worst would be denied a maximum of 22 weeks of compensation payments. I agree . . . that the possibility of that denial is enough to infringe upon the appellant's constitutional right to the free exercise of her religion. But it is clear to me that in order to reach this conclusion the Court must explicitly reject the reasoning of [*Braunfeld*]. I think the *Braunfeld* case was wrongly decided and should be overruled. . . .

JUSTICE HARLAN, joined by JUSTICE WHITE, dissenting.

[The] South Carolina Supreme Court [has] consistently held that one is not "available for work" if his unemployment has resulted not from the inability of industry to provide a job but rather from personal circumstances, no matter how compelling. [Here], all that the state court has done is to apply these accepted principles. [The] fact that these personal considerations sprang from her religious convictions was wholly without relevance to the state court's application of the law. Thus in no proper sense can it be said that the State discriminated against the appellant on the basis of her religious beliefs or that she was denied benefits because she was a Seventh Day Adventist. She was denied benefits just as any other claimant would be denied benefits who was not "available for work" for personal reasons.

[What the Court holds] is that if the State chooses to condition unemployment compensation on the applicant's availability for work, it is constitutionally compelled to *carve out an exception*—and to provide benefits—for those whose unavailability is due to their religious convictions. . . . First, despite the Court's protestations to the contrary, the decision necessarily overrules [*Braunfeld*]. Second, [the] meaning of today's holding [is] that the State [must] *single out* for financial assistance those whose behavior is religiously motivated, even though it denies such assistance to others whose identical behavior (in this case, inability to work on Saturdays) is not religiously motivated. It has been suggested that such singling out of religious conduct for special treatment may violate the [Constitution]. See Kurland, Of Church and State and The Supreme Court, 29 U. Chi. L. Rev. 1 [(1961)]. My own view, however, is that [it] would be a permissible accommodation of religion for the State, if it *chose* to do so, to create an exception to its eligibility requirements for persons like the appellant. . . . [There is] enough flexibility in the Constitution to permit a legislative judgment accommodating an unemployment compensation law to the exercise of religious beliefs such as appellant's. For very much the same reasons, however, I cannot subscribe to the conclusion that the State is constitutionally *compelled* to carve out an exception to its general rule of eligibility in the present case. Those situations in which the Constitution may require special treatment on account of religion are, in my view, few and far between. [Such] compulsion in the present case is particularly inappropriate in light of the indirect, remote, and insubstantial effect of the decision below on the exercise of appellant's religion and in light of the direct financial assistance to religion that today's decision requires.

NOTES

1. Burden or Refusal to Subsidize? Justice Brennan saw South Carolina's action as a penalty upon Sherbert's observance of her religious duties. Justice Harlan saw the same action as a constitutionally permissible refusal to subsidize Sherbert's religious faith. What is the source of these different perspectives? Is it the fact that Brennan assumed that Sherbert's unemployment was not voluntary, and Harlan assumed that it was? Who is correct?

Queries: Suppose that a state-operated toll road collects a toll from Sherbert while she is en route to church. Is that a burden on Sherbert's religion or a mere refusal to subsidize it? Suppose Saturdays are toll-free. Does Sherbert receive a special benefit to assist her religion? Suppose Saturdays are toll-free but Sherbert is charged a toll because the state knows she is on her way to church. Burden or mere refusal to subsidize?

2. Strict Scrutiny Under *Sherbert*. The era of strict scrutiny introduced by *Sherbert* was less sweeping in scope than it might have initially appeared. The Court applied the *Sherbert* test to a string of unemployment compensation cases, requiring states to afford religious exemptions from regulation that would otherwise deny unemployment compensation. In Thomas v. Review Board, 450 U.S. 707 (1981), the Court struck down Indiana's denial of unemployment benefits to a Jehovah's Witness who quit his job in a munitions factory for religious reasons. Accord, Hobbie v. Unemployment Appeals Commission of Florida, 480 U.S. 136 (1987). In Frazee v. Employment Security Department,

489 U.S. 829 (1989), the Court unanimously voided the state's denial of unemployment benefits to Frazee, who, though not a member of any church or sect, refused to work on Sundays because he was a generic Christian.

Wisconsin v. Yoder, 406 U.S. 205 (1972). Wisconsin law required children to attend school until age 16. The Old Order Amish believe education beyond age 14 to be contrary to their "fundamental belief that salvation requires life in a church community separate and apart from the world." The Court voided the law because it imposed a substantial burden on the Amish, and the state's goal—fostering an educated populace—was not substantially undercut by granting an exemption to the Amish.

United States v. Lee, 455 U.S. 252 (1982). The Court held that imposition of Social Security taxes on Lee, an Amish farmer and carpenter, was justified despite "the Amish [belief that it is] sinful not to provide for their own elderly." Mandatory participation in Social Security was "indispensable" to the "fiscal vitality" of Social Security; thus, denial of a religious exemption from Social Security taxation was "essential to accomplish an overriding governmental interest."

Bob Jones University v. United States, 461 U.S. 574 (1983). Based on religious belief, Bob Jones University practiced racial discrimination. On free exercise grounds, the university challenged the IRS's denial to it of tax-exempt status. The Court concluded that the government's interest in eliminating racial discrimination in education was compelling and that the religious burden imposed—denial of tax-exempt status—was essential to the achievement of this objective.

3. Minimal Scrutiny: A Parallel Track.   Despite *Sherbert*, the Court sometimes has applied minimal scrutiny when government action was not a substantial burden on religious conduct or when governments regulated religious conduct in special institutional contexts, such as prisons or the military.

Johnson v. Robison, 415 U.S. 361 (1974). The Court upheld a federal law that made veterans' benefits available to veterans of the armed forces but not to conscientious objectors who had performed mandatory service in lieu of military service. The law imposed only an "incidental burden" on religious conduct, and the government's "substantial interest in raising and supporting armies" was "clearly sufficient" to uphold the legislation.

Goldman v. Weinberger, 475 U.S. 503 (1986). The Court sustained military discipline administered to Goldman, an Air Force officer and orthodox Jew, for wearing a yarmulke in violation of military uniform regulations. The Court applied a version of minimal scrutiny—courts "must give great deference to the professional judgment of military authorities" in deciding whether "military needs" justify a burden on religious conduct.

O'Lone v. Estate of Shabazz, 482 U.S. 342 (1987). The Court, 5-4, upheld prison regulations that prevented Islamic prison inmates from observing a Friday midday religious service. The Court applied a "reasonableness" standard and specifically rejected the contention that prison officials were under a burden to prove the absence of less restrictive alternative means to achieve the prison's objectives.

Lyng v. Northwest Indian Cemetery Protective Association, 485 U.S. 439 *(1988)*. The Court applied minimal scrutiny in rejecting a free exercise challenge to the U.S. Forest Service's planned logging road through an area regarded as sacred by several Indian tribes. The government action imposed a substantial burden on religious conduct but was neither coercive nor a penalty.

Queries: What, if anything, makes South Carolina's denial of Sherbert's claim for unemployment compensation different? Do these cases suggest that the Court was unwilling to apply *Sherbert* or that *Sherbert* was premised on an especially pointed state interference with religious practice? If the latter, why was the interference in *Lyng* insufficiently pointed?

Employment Division, Department of Human Resources of Oregon v. Smith
494 U.S. 872 (1990)

JUSTICE SCALIA delivered the opinion of the Court.

This case requires us to decide whether the Free Exercise Clause [permits] Oregon to include religiously inspired peyote use within the reach of its general criminal prohibition on use of that drug, and thus permits the State to deny unemployment benefits to persons dismissed from their jobs because of such religiously inspired use.

I. Oregon law prohibits the knowing or intentional possession of a "controlled substance," [which includes] peyote, a hallucinogen derived from [a cactus] plant. [Respondents] Alfred Smith and Galen Black [were] fired from their jobs with a private drug rehabilitation organization because they ingested peyote for sacramental purposes at a ceremony of the Native American Church, of which both are members. When respondents applied [for] unemployment compensation, they were determined to be ineligible for benefits because they had been discharged for work-related "misconduct." [Their] religiously inspired use of peyote fell within the prohibition of the Oregon statute, which "makes no exception for the sacramental use" of the drug. . . .

II. Respondents' claim for relief rests on our decisions in [*Sherbert, Thomas,* and *Hobbie*], in which we held that a State could not condition the availability of unemployment insurance on an individual's willingness to forgo conduct required by his religion. [But] the conduct at issue in those cases was not prohibited by law. . . . Oregon does prohibit the religious use of peyote, [so] we proceed to consider whether that prohibition is permissible under the Free Exercise Clause.

A. [Free] exercise of religion means, first and foremost, the right to believe and profess whatever religious doctrine one desires. [But] the "exercise of religion" often involves not only belief and profession but the performance of (or abstention from) physical acts: assembling with others for a worship service, participating in sacramental use of bread and wine, proselytizing, abstaining from certain foods or certain modes of transportation. It would be true, we think (though no case of ours has involved the point), that a State would be "prohibiting the free exercise [of religion]" if it sought to ban such acts or abstentions only when they are engaged in for religious reasons, or only because of the religious belief that they display. It would doubtless be unconstitutional, for example, to ban the casting of "statues that are to be used for worship purposes," or to prohibit bowing down before a golden calf.

Respondents . . . seek to carry the meaning of "prohibiting the free exercise [of religion]" one large step further. They contend that their religious motivation for using peyote places them beyond the reach of a criminal law that is not specifically directed at their religious practice, and that is concededly constitutional as applied to those who use the drug for other reasons. They assert . . . that "prohibiting the free exercise [of religion]" includes requiring any individual to observe a generally applicable law that requires (or forbids) the performance of an act that his religious belief forbids (or requires). As a textual matter, we do not think the words must be given that meaning. It is no more necessary to regard the collection of a general tax, for example, as "prohibiting the free exercise [of religion]" by those citizens who believe support of organized government to be sinful, than it is to regard the same tax as "abridging the freedom [of] the press" of those publishing companies that must pay the tax as a condition of staying in business. It is a permissible reading of the text . . . to say that if prohibiting the exercise of religion (or burdening the activity of printing) is not the object of the tax but merely the incidental effect of a generally applicable and otherwise valid provision, the First Amendment has not been offended.

[The] latter reading is the correct one. We have never held that an individual's religious beliefs excuse him from compliance with an otherwise valid law prohibiting conduct that the State is free to regulate. On the contrary, the record of more than a century of our free exercise jurisprudence contradicts that proposition. . . . [We] first had occasion to assert that principle in [*Reynolds*], where we rejected the claim that criminal laws against polygamy could not be constitutionally applied to those whose religion commanded the practice. [Subsequent] decisions have consistently held that the right of free exercise does not relieve an individual of the obligation to comply with a "valid and neutral law of general applicability on the ground that the law proscribes (or prescribes) conduct that his religion prescribes (or proscribes)." United States v. Lee (Stevens, J., concurring in judgment).

[The] only decisions in which we have held that the First Amendment bars application of a neutral, generally applicable law to religiously motivated action have involved not the Free Exercise Clause alone, but the Free Exercise Clause in conjunction with other constitutional protections, such as freedom of speech and of the press, see Cantwell v. Connecticut; or the right of parents, acknowledged in Pierce v. Society of Sisters, to direct the education of their children, see Wisconsin v. Yoder. Some of our cases prohibiting compelled expression, decided exclusively upon free speech grounds, have also involved freedom of religion. [*Wooley, Barnette.*]

[This] case does not present such a hybrid situation, but a free exercise claim unconnected with any communicative activity or parental right.

Respondents urge us to hold, quite simply, that when otherwise prohibitable conduct is accompanied by religious convictions, . . . the conduct itself must be free from governmental regulation. We have never held that, and decline to do so now. There being no contention that Oregon's drug law represents an attempt to regulate religious beliefs, the communication of religious beliefs, or the raising of one's children in those beliefs, the rule to which we have adhered ever since *Reynolds* plainly controls.

B. [Respondents] argue that even though exemption from generally applicable criminal laws need not automatically be extended to religiously motivated actors, at least the claim for a religious exemption must be evaluated under . . . *Sherbert*[:] governmental actions that substantially burden a religious practice must be justified by a compelling governmental interest. [We] have never invalidated any governmental action on the basis of the *Sherbert* test except the denial of unemployment compensation. Although we have sometimes purported to apply the *Sherbert* test in contexts other than that, we have always found the test satisfied. In recent years we have abstained from applying the *Sherbert* test (outside the unemployment compensation field) at all. . . .

[Even] if we were inclined to breathe into *Sherbert* some life beyond the unemployment compensation field, we would not apply it to require exemptions from a generally applicable criminal law. The *Sherbert* test [was] developed in a context that lent itself to individualized governmental assessment of the reasons for the relevant conduct. [A] distinctive feature of unemployment compensation programs is that their eligibility criteria invite consideration of the particular circumstances behind an applicant's unemployment. [The] unemployment cases stand for the proposition that where the State has in place a system of individual exemptions, it may not refuse to extend that system to cases of "religious hardship" without compelling reason.

Whether or not the decisions are that limited, they at least have nothing to do with an across-the-board criminal prohibition on a particular form of conduct. . . . We conclude today that the sounder approach, and the approach in accord with the vast majority of our precedents, is to hold the [*Sherbert*] test inapplicable to such challenges. The government's ability to enforce generally applicable prohibitions of socially harmful conduct, like its ability to carry out other aspects of public policy, "cannot depend on measuring the effects of a governmental action on a religious objector's spiritual development." *Lyng.* To make an individual's obligation to obey such a law contingent upon the law's coincidence with his religious beliefs, except where the State's interest is "compelling"—permitting him, by virtue of his beliefs, "to become a law unto himself" [*Reynolds*]—contradicts both constitutional tradition and common sense. . . .

Nor is it possible to limit the impact of respondents' proposal by requiring a "compelling state interest" only when the conduct prohibited is "central" to the individual's religion. It is no more appropriate for judges to determine the "centrality" of religious beliefs before applying a "compelling interest" test in the free exercise field than it would be for them to determine the "importance" of ideas before applying the "compelling interest" test in the free speech field. . . .

If the "compelling interest" test is to be applied at all, then it must be applied across the board to all actions thought to be religiously commanded. Moreover, if "compelling interest" really means what it says (and watering it down here would subvert its rigor in the other fields where it is applied), many laws will not meet the test. Any society adopting such a system would be courting anarchy, but that danger increases in direct proportion to the society's diversity of religious beliefs, and its determination to coerce or suppress none of them. Precisely because "we are a cosmopolitan nation made up of people of almost every conceivable religious preference," and precisely because we value and protect that religious divergence, we cannot afford the luxury of deeming *presumptively invalid*, as applied to the religious objector, every regulation of conduct that does not protect an interest of the highest order. . . .

It may fairly be said that leaving accommodation to the political process will place at a relative disadvantage those religious practices that are not widely engaged in; but that unavoidable consequence of democratic government must be preferred to a system in which each conscience is a law unto itself or in which judges weigh the social importance of all laws against the centrality of all religious beliefs.

Justice O'Connor, concurring in the judgment [Justices Brennan, Marshall, and Blackmun joined Part II of Justice O'Connor's opinion, but did not concur in the judgment].

Although I agree with the result the Court reaches, [I] cannot join its opinion. . . .

II. A. [Because] the First Amendment does not distinguish between religious belief and religious conduct, conduct motivated by sincere religious belief, like the belief itself, must be at least presumptively protected by the Free Exercise clause. . . . A person who is barred from engaging in religiously motivated conduct is barred from freely exercising his religion, [regardless] of whether the law prohibits the conduct only when engaged in for religious reasons [or] by all persons. [The free exercise clause] does not distinguish between laws that are generally applicable and laws that target particular religious practices. Indeed, few States would be so naive as to enact a law directly prohibiting or burdening a religious practice as such.

[To] say that a person's right to free exercise has been burdened, of course, does not mean that he has an absolute right to engage in the conduct. [We] have recognized that the freedom to act, unlike the freedom to believe, cannot be absolute. Instead, we have . . . [required] the government to justify any substantial burden on religiously motivated conduct by a compelling state interest and by means narrowly tailored to achieve that interest. . . . [We] have never distinguished between cases in which a State conditions receipt of a benefit on conduct prohibited by religious beliefs and cases in which a State affirmatively prohibits such conduct. The *Sherbert* compelling interest test applies in both kinds of cases. . . . [There] is nothing talismanic about neutral laws of general applicability or general criminal prohibitions, for laws neutral toward religion can coerce a person to violate his religious conscience or intrude upon his religious duties just as effectively as laws aimed at religion. [A] law that makes criminal such an activity therefore triggers constitutional concern—and heightened judicial scrutiny—even if it does not target the particular religious conduct at issue. . . .

III. . . . I would reach the [Court's] result applying our established free exercise jurisprudence. [There is] no dispute that Oregon has a . . . compelling interest in prohibiting the possession of peyote by its citizens. [The] critical question [is] whether exempting respondents from the State's general criminal prohibition "will unduly interfere with fulfillment of the governmental interest." . . . [U]niform application of Oregon's criminal prohibition is "essential to accomplish" its overriding interest in preventing the physical harm caused by the use of [peyote and to prevent] trafficking in controlled substances. [The fact that other governments grant a religious exemption for peyote use does not mean that Oregon is] required to do so by the First Amendment. [Also, it is irrelevant] that the sacramental use of peyote is central to the tenets of the Native American Church. [Our] determination of the constitutionality of Oregon's general criminal prohibition cannot, and should not, turn on the centrality of the particular religious practice at issue.

JUSTICE BLACKMUN, joined by JUSTICES BRENNAN and MARSHALL, dissenting.

[Oregon's] asserted interest in enforcing its drug laws [is] not the State's broad interest in fighting the critical "war on drugs," [but the] narrow interest in refusing to make an exception for the religious, ceremonial use of peyote. Failure to reduce the competing interests to the same plane of generality tends to distort the weighing process in the State's favor. . . . [Oregon] does not claim that it has made significant enforcement efforts [against] religious users of peyote, [so its] interest . . . amounts only to the symbolic preservation of an unenforced prohibition. But a government interest in [symbolism] cannot suffice to abrogate the constitutional rights of individuals.

[Oregon] proclaims an interest in protecting the health and safety of its citizens from the dangers of unlawful drugs [but offers] no evidence that the religious use of peyote has ever harmed anyone. . . . [Oregon] also seeks to support its refusal to make an exception for religious use of peyote by invoking its interest in abolishing drug trafficking [but there is] practically no illegal traffic in peyote. . . . Finally, the State argues that granting an exception for religious peyote use would erode its interest in the uniform, fair, and certain enforcement of its drug laws. The State fears that, if it grants an exemption for religious peyote use, a flood of other claims to religious exemptions will follow. . . . [The] State's apprehension of a flood of other religious claims is purely speculative. Almost half the States, and the Federal Government, have maintained an exemption for religious peyote use for many years, and apparently have not found themselves overwhelmed by claims to other religious exemptions. . . .

NOTES

1. The Methodology of *Smith*. Writing for the Court, Justice Scalia employed a categorical approach: The category of generally applicable laws that incidentally burden religious conduct are valid, absent the presence of another constitutional claim (the "hybrid" cases) or a benefits statute that relies on specific, individualized inquiry as to eligibility (the unemployment compensation cases). Justice Scalia objected to the idea that the judiciary should "regularly balance against the importance of general laws the significance of religious practice." Are these two factors capable of commensurate valuation? Justice O'Connor and the three dissenters all employed a balancing approach. Justice O'Connor claimed that courts could compare the burden on religion imposed by any general law with the government's interest in enforcing that law without assessing the "centrality" of the burdened practice to religious belief. Is it possible to assess the burden on religious practice without taking into account the relation of the burdened practice to religious belief? Is it an unacceptable threat to free exercise to inquire into the relationship of religious practices and religious beliefs? Does such inquiry require courts to examine the legitimacy of religious beliefs? If so, how is "legitimacy" to be determined?

2. The Religious Freedom Restoration Act and the Religious Land Use and Institutionalized Persons Act. Congress reacted to *Smith* by enacting the Religious Freedom Restoration Act (RFRA), 42 U.S.C. §§2000bb *et seq.*, which provided that governments

> shall not substantially burden a person's exercise of religion even if the burden results from a rule of general applicability, except [that] Government may substantially burden a person's exercise of religion only if it demonstrates that application of the burden to the person (1) is in furtherance of a compelling governmental interest and (2) is the least restrictive means of furthering that compelling governmental interest.

In enacting RFRA, Congress relied on its power under section 5 of the Fourteenth Amendment "to enforce, by appropriate legislation, the provisions of [the Fourteenth Amendment]." Those provisions include the due process clause that incorporates the free exercise clause. But in City of Boerne v. Flores, 521 U.S. 507 (1997), the Court held that Congress exceeded its powers in making RFRA applicable to the states. Congress could not simply redefine the substantive meaning of free exercise via a purported exercise in enforcement of the free exercise clause. However, RFRA continues to apply to the federal government. In Gonzales v. O Centro Espírita Beneficente União do Vegetal, 546 U.S. 418 (2006), the Court concluded that the federal government lacked a compelling reason to ban the importation of hoasca, a tea containing banned hallucinogens that is used in sacramental rites of the tiny American branch of a Brazilian Christian Spiritist sect. Congress had never considered the harm that might be produced by this sacramental use, and the exemption afforded the sacramental use of peyote fatally undermined the government's argument that it had a compelling reason to ban hoasca.

Congress reacted to *City of Boerne* by using its spending and commerce powers to enact the Religious Land Use and Institutionalized Persons Act (RLUIPA), 42 U.S.C. §§2000cc *et seq.* RLUIPA applies to any government program that receives federal funds, a category that includes state prisons. RLUIPA states: "No government shall impose or implement a land use regulation in a manner that imposes a substantial burden on the religious exercise of a person, including a religious assembly or institution, [nor shall any government] impose a substantial burden on the religious exercise of a person residing in or confined to an institution" unless the burden "is in furtherance of a compelling government interest" and "is the least restrictive means" of furthering that interest. RLUIPA has been attacked as a violation of the establishment clause, an issue taken up in more detail in Section C.3.b, infra.

3. Mandates to Provide Contraceptives. *Burwell v. Hobby Lobby Stores, Inc.; Conestoga Wood Specialties Corporation v. Burwell, 134 S. Ct. 2751 (2014).* The federal Affordable Care Act ("ACA") and regulations promulgated thereunder require certain employers' group health insurance plans to provide a wide range of contraceptive devices, including four devices that act by preventing a fertilized egg from implantation in the uterus. Owners of three for-profit corporations who held sincere religious beliefs that life begins at conception objected to the mandate that they provide insurance coverage for the four abortifacients, invoking RFRA.

The Court held that Congress intended the term "person" in RFRA to include corporations. Because the cases involved only closely-held corporations it had no occasion to decide whether its analysis might be different in the case of a publicly held corporation. The contraceptive regulations substantially burdened the exercise of religion because the economic consequences of adhering to their religious scruples would be ruinous and because the regulations squarely precluded the parties from conducting their businesses in accord with their religious beliefs. The Court declared that the interest asserted by the Government must be particularly applicable to the religious objector, an inquiry that requires courts "to look to the marginal interest in enforcing the contraceptive mandate in these cases." The Court assumed, without deciding, that for purposes of RFRA, the Government had a compelling reason for the burden: "guaranteeing cost-free access to the four challenged contraceptive methods." But the Government failed to establish that it had employed the least restrictive means to achieve this end. It could have afforded the objectors the same accommodation it extended to non-profit organizations that hold sincere religious objections or it could directly subsidize an employee's desire to obtain one of the four devices. (The accommodation involved exempting the objecting employer's insurance plan from any obligation to provide the services to which religious objections were made while requiring the insurer to provide those services without any cost to the employer or employee. The compensation to the insurer came in the form of a reduced fee to participate in the federal insurance exchanges created under the ACA.)

The Court cautioned that its decision was "concerned solely with the contraceptive mandate [and] should not be understood to hold that an insurance-coverage mandate must necessarily fall if it conflicts with an employer's religious beliefs. Other coverage requirements, such as immunizations, may be supported by different interests (for example, the need to combat the spread of infectious diseases) and may involve different arguments about the least restrictive means of providing them. Our decision . . . provides no . . . shield [for] discrimination in hiring, for example on the basis of race, [which] might be cloaked as religious practice to escape legal sanction. . . . The Government has a compelling interest in providing an equal opportunity to participate in the workforce without regard to race, and prohibitions on racial discrimination are precisely tailored to achieve that critical goal."

Query: Suppose that the owners of a closely-held corporation that performs federal contracts hold sincere religious objections to same-sex marriage. Can the owners successfully invoke RFRA to obtain exemption from a federal mandate that businesses engaged in federal contracts provide the same benefits to same-sex spouses as provided to opposite-sex spouses?

2.   Legislation That Targets Religious Conduct or Belief

Laws that single out religious *belief* for unfavorable treatment are void per se. Laws that single out religious *conduct* for unfavorable treatment are presumptively void. In Torcaso v. Watkins, 367 U.S. 488 (1961), the Court invalidated a Maryland requirement that public officials swear that they believe in the existence of God. No government "can constitutionally force a person to profess a belief or disbelief in any religion [or prefer] those religions based on a belief in the existence of God as against those religions founded on different beliefs."

In McDaniel v. Paty, 435 U.S. 618 (1978), the Court struck down a Tennessee law that barred clergy from holding legislative office. A four-justice plurality ruled that the ban singled out religious conduct—ministerial status—for unfavorable treatment. Tennessee said that avoiding a forbidden establishment of religion was a compelling interest, but treating ministers equally to other citizens is not an establishment of religion. Three justices concurred on the ground that the ban interfered with freedom of belief and thus was void per se.

Smith did not disturb these conclusions. Indeed, the Court in *Smith* took pains to distinguish generally applicable laws interfering with religious conduct from laws that target religious conduct for unfavorable treatment.

Church of the Lukumi Babalu Aye, Inc. v. City of Hialeah
508 U.S. 520 (1993)

Justice Kennedy delivered the opinion of the Court, except as to Part II.A.2.

The principle that government may not enact laws that suppress religious belief or practice is so well understood that few violations are recorded in our

opinions. [But these] laws . . . were enacted by officials who did not understand, failed to perceive, or chose to ignore the fact that their official actions
violated the Nation's essential commitment to religious freedom. The challenged laws had an impermissible object; and . . . the principle of general
applicability was violated because the secular ends asserted in defense of the
laws were pursued only with respect to conduct motivated by religious beliefs.
We invalidate the challenged enactments.

[This] case involves practices of the Santeria religion, which originated
in the nineteenth century. When hundreds of thousands of members of the
Yoruba people were brought as slaves from . . . Africa to Cuba, their traditional African religion absorbed significant elements of Roman Catholicism.
The resulting . . . fusion is Santeria, "the way of the saints." The Cuban
Yoruba express their devotion to spirits, called *oris has*. [Santeria] teaches that
every individual has a destiny from God, a destiny fulfilled with the aid and
energy of the *oris has*. The basis of the Santeria religion is the nurture of a
personal relation with the *oris has*, and one of the principal forms of devotion
is an animal sacrifice. [According] to Santeria teaching, the *oris has* [depend]
for survival on the sacrifice. Sacrifices are performed at birth, marriage, and
death rites, for the cure of the sick, for the initiation of new members and
priests, and during an annual celebration. Animals sacrificed in Santeria rituals
include chickens, pigeons, doves, ducks, guinea pigs, goats, sheep, and turtles.
The animals are killed by the cutting of the carotid arteries in the neck. The
sacrificed animal is cooked and eaten, except after healing and death rituals.
Santeria adherents faced widespread persecution in Cuba, so the religion and
its rituals were practiced in secret. The open practice of Santeria and its rites
remains infrequent [although the] District Court estimated that there are at
least 50,000 practitioners in South Florida today.

[In] April 1987, the Church [planned] to establish a house of worship
[in Hialeah, Florida] to bring the [Santeria] ritual of animal sacrifice into
the open. [The announcement] prompted the city council to hold an emergency, public session [at which] the city council adopted Resolution 87-66,
which noted the "concern" expressed by residents of the city "that certain
religions may propose to engage in practices which are inconsistent with public morals, peace or safety," and declared that "the City reiterates its commitment to a prohibition against any and all acts of any and all religious groups
which are inconsistent with public morals, peace or safety." [The] city council
[unanimously] adopted three substantive ordinances addressing the issue of
religious animal sacrifice. Ordinance 87-52 defined "sacrifice" as "to unnecessarily kill, torment, torture, or mutilate an animal in a public or private
ritual or ceremony . . . regardless of whether or not the flesh or blood of
the animal is to be consumed" [and] contained an exemption for slaughtering by "licensed establishments" of animals "specifically raised for food
purposes." [Ordinance 87-71] defined sacrifice as had Ordinance 87-52, and
then provided that "it shall be unlawful for any person, persons, corporations
or associations to sacrifice any animal [within] Hialeah, Florida." The final
ordinance, 87-72, defined "slaughter" as "the killing of animals for food" and

prohibited slaughter outside of areas zoned for slaughterhouse use. The ordinance provided an exemption, however, for the slaughter or processing for sale of "small numbers of hogs and/or cattle per week in accordance with an exemption provided by state law." . . . Violations of each of the . . . ordinances were punishable by fines . . . or imprisonment . . . or both.

[The church then challenged the validity of the ordinances as violations of the free exercise clause. The federal district court and the Court of Appeals for the Eleventh Circuit upheld the validity of the ordinances.]

The protections of the Free Exercise Clause pertain if the law at issue discriminates against some or all religious beliefs or regulates or prohibits conduct because it is undertaken for religious reasons. [Although] a law targeting religious beliefs as such is never permissible, if the object of a law is to infringe upon or restrict practices because of their religious motivation, the law is not neutral; and it is invalid unless it is justified by a compelling interest and is narrowly tailored to advance that interest. [To] determine the object of a law, we must begin with its text, for the minimum requirement of neutrality is that a law not discriminate on its face. A law lacks facial neutrality if it refers to a religious practice without a secular meaning discernible from the language or context. [Although] three of the ordinances . . . use the words "sacrifice" and "ritual," words with strong religious connotations, [this] is not conclusive [because the] words "sacrifice" and "ritual" [also have] secular meanings. [But the] Free Exercise Clause protects against governmental hostility which is masked, as well as overt.

The record [compels] the conclusion that suppression of the central element of the Santeria worship service was the object of the ordinances. [Almost] the only conduct subject to [the ordinances] is the religious exercise of Santeria church members. [The ordinances] exclude[] almost all killings of animals except for religious sacrifice, and [their scope is narrowed] even further . . . by exempting Kosher slaughter. We need not discuss whether this differential treatment of two religions is itself an independent constitutional violation. It suffices to recite this feature of the law as support for our conclusion that Santeria alone was the exclusive legislative concern. The net result of the gerrymander is that few if any killings of animals are prohibited other than Santeria sacrifice, which is proscribed because it occurs during a ritual or ceremony and its primary purpose is to make an offering to the *oris has*, not food consumption. Indeed, careful drafting ensured that, although Santeria sacrifice is prohibited, killings that are no more necessary or humane in almost all other circumstances are unpunished. . . . Thus, religious practice is being singled out for discriminatory treatment.

We also find significant evidence of the ordinances' improper targeting of Santeria sacrifice in the fact that they proscribe more religious conduct than is necessary to achieve their stated ends. [The] legitimate governmental interests in protecting the public health and preventing cruelty to animals could be addressed by restrictions stopping far short of a flat prohibition of all Santeria sacrificial practice. [Indeed], these broad ordinances prohibit Santeria sacrifice even when it does not threaten the city's interest in the public health. . . .

[JUSTICE KENNEDY, joined by JUSTICES STEVENS, BLACKMUN, and O'CONNOR.]

[II.A.2.] In determining if the object of a law is a neutral one under the Free Exercise Clause, we can also find guidance in our equal protection cases. [Here], as in equal protection cases, we may determine the city council's object from both direct and circumstantial evidence. That the ordinances were enacted "'because of,' not merely 'in spite of,'" their suppression of Santeria religious practice is revealed by the events preceding enactment of the ordinances. [The] minutes and taped excerpts of the [city council] session . . . evidence significant hostility exhibited by residents, members of the city council, and other city officials toward the Santeria religion and its practice of animal sacrifice. The public crowd that attended the . . . meetings interrupted statements by council members critical of Santeria with cheers and the brief comments of [the church head cleric] with taunts. When [a council member] stated that in pre-revolution Cuba "people were put in jail for practicing this religion," the audience applauded. [Councilman] Cardoso said that Santeria [is] "in violation of everything this country stands for." Councilman Mejides indicated that he was "totally against the sacrificing of animals" and distinguished Kosher slaughter because it had a "real purpose." [The] president of the city council, Councilman Echevarria, asked, "What can we do to prevent the Church from opening?" Various Hialeah city officials made comparable comments. The chaplain of the Hialeah Police Department told the city council that Santeria was a sin, "foolishness," "an abomination to the Lord," and the worship of "demons." He advised the city council: "We need to be helping people and sharing with them the truth that is found in Jesus Christ." He concluded: "I would exhort [you] not to permit this Church to exist." [This] history discloses the object of the ordinances to target animal sacrifice by Santeria worshippers because of its religious motivation.

[JUSTICE KENNEDY, for the Court.]

[The] ordinances had as their object the suppression of religion. The pattern we have recited discloses animosity to Santeria adherents and their religious practices; the ordinances by their own terms target this religious exercise; the texts of the ordinances were gerrymandered with care to proscribe religious killings of animals but to exclude almost all secular killings; and the ordinances suppress much more religious conduct than is necessary in order to achieve the legitimate ends asserted in their defense. These ordinances are not neutral. A law burdening religious practice that is not neutral or not of general application must undergo the most rigorous of scrutiny. [A] law that targets religious conduct for distinctive treatment or advances legitimate governmental interests only against conduct with a religious motivation will survive strict scrutiny only in rare cases. [T]hese ordinances cannot withstand this scrutiny. First, even were the governmental interests compelling, the ordinances are not drawn in narrow terms to accomplish those interests. [They] are overbroad or underinclusive. [The] absence of narrow tailoring suffices to establish the invalidity of the ordinances. [Also, where] government restricts only conduct protected by the First Amendment and fails to enact feasible measures to restrict other conduct producing substantial harm or alleged harm of the same sort, the interest given in justification of the restriction is not compelling. [Reversed.]

JUSTICE SCALIA, joined by CHIEF JUSTICE REHNQUIST, concurring in part and concurring in the judgment.

[I] do not join [Part II.A.2] because it departs from the opinion's general focus on the object of the laws at issue to consider the subjective motivation of the lawmakers, i.e., whether the Hialeah City Council actually intended to disfavor the religion of Santeria. [It] is virtually impossible to determine the singular "motive" of a collective legislative body, and this Court has a long tradition of refraining from such inquiries. [The] First Amendment does not refer to the purposes for which legislators enact laws, but to the effects of the laws enacted. [Had] the Hialeah City Council set out resolutely to suppress the practices of Santeria, but ineptly adopted ordinances that failed to do so, I do not see how those laws could be said to "prohibit the free exercise" of religion. Nor . . . does it matter that a legislature consists entirely of the pure-hearted, if the law it enacts in fact singles out a religious practice for special burdens. Had the ordinances here been passed with no motive . . . except the ardent desire to prevent cruelty to animals (as might in fact have been the case), they would nonetheless be invalid.

NOTES AND PROBLEM

1. Purpose or Effect? The Court has encountered the problem of purpose or effect in two other contexts: disparate racial impact of racially neutral classifications and the problem of when state laws that are facially neutral toward interstate commerce should be treated as discriminatory. In this context, is strict scrutiny triggered by *either* effect or purpose, or the combination of a forbidden purpose and delivery of discriminatory effects?

2. The Constitutional Basis for Evaluating Discrimination Among Religions. The Court has treated some discriminatory laws as posing establishment clause problems rather than free exercise issues. Consider Larson v. Valente, 456 U.S. 228 (1982). Minnesota regulated charitable solicitations but exempted religious organizations that solicit at least half of their contributions from members. The Unification Church (the "Moonies") challenged the law, and the Court invalidated it as a forbidden establishment of religion. Although the law was facially neutral as to various religions, it had been carefully designed to apply only to the Unification Church. An earlier draft bill had been discarded because it would apply to the Roman Catholic Church as well, but the clincher was probably the incredibly revealing statement of one Minnesota legislator, who asked his colleagues during debate "why we're so hot to regulate the Moonies, anyway." The Court looked to these indicia of religious favoritism to conclude that the "express design" of the law was to "burden or favor selected religious denominations" in a manner that was "'religious gerrymandering.'"

Queries: What makes the Minnesota law an establishment of religion and the Hialeah city ordinances a breach of free exercise? Is it because charitable solicitation is not religiously inspired conduct and Santeria sacrifice is such conduct? Is it plausible to say that *Lukumi* involved intentionally discriminatory religious burdens and *Larson* involved intentionally discriminatory religious favoritism? Are these concepts distinguishable?

3. Problem: *Mortmain Statutes.* The first mortmain statute, enacted in the thirteenth century during the reign of Edward I, was designed to prevent land from being owned in perpetuity by religious orders. In modern times, the term is applied to statutes that void deathbed bequests or devises to religious entities or, more generally, to charities. Suppose you are an aide to a state legislator whose legislature is considering enactment of either of the following laws:

1. No bequest or devise to a religious entity or clergyman is valid if it is made within six months before the testator's death.
2. No bequest or devise to a charity is valid if it is made within six months before the testator's death.

Advise your employer as to the validity of either or both proposed statutes. Would it make any difference if the second proposal was motivated by bias against religious institutions?

≡≡≡ *Locke v. Davey*
    540 U.S. 712 (2004)

CHIEF JUSTICE REHNQUIST delivered the opinion of the Court.

The State of Washington established the Promise Scholarship Program to assist academically gifted students with postsecondary education expenses. In accordance with the State Constitution, students may not use the scholarship at an institution where they are pursuing a degree in devotional theology. We hold that such an exclusion from an otherwise inclusive aid program does not violate the Free Exercise Clause of the First Amendment.

[The] Promise Scholarship Program . . . provides a scholarship, renewable for one year, to eligible students for postsecondary education expenses. Students may spend their funds on any education-related expense. . . . The scholarships are funded through the State's general fund. . . . To be eligible for the scholarship, a student must . . . graduate from a Washington public or private high school and either graduate in the top 15% of his graduating class, or attain on the first attempt a cumulative score of 1,200 or better on the Scholastic Assessment Test I or a score of 27 or better on the American College Test. The student's family income must be less than 135% of the State's median. Finally, the student must enroll "at least half time in an eligible postsecondary institution in the state of Washington." . . . Private institutions, including those religiously affiliated, qualify as "eligible postsecondary institutions" if they are accredited. . . . A "degree in theology" is "not defined in the statute, but, as both parties concede, the statute simply codifies the State's constitutional prohibition on providing funds to students to pursue degrees that are "devotional in nature or designed to induce religious faith." . . .

Respondent, Joshua Davey, was awarded a Promise Scholarship, and chose to attend Northwest College . . . , a private, Christian college [that] is an eligible institution under the Promise Scholarship Program. [Davey] decided to pursue a double major in pastoral ministries and business management/administration. There is no dispute that the pastoral ministries degree is devotional and therefore excluded under the Promise Scholarship Program.

[After Davey was denied his scholarship because he intended to] pursue a devotional theology degree [he] brought an action . . . against various state officials (hereinafter State) in [federal] District Court . . . to enjoin the State from refusing to award the scholarship solely because a student is pursuing a devotional theology degree, and for damages. . . . The District Court . . . granted summary judgment in favor of the State. [The] Ninth Circuit reversed, [concluding] that the State had singled out religion for unfavorable treatment and thus under our decision in [*Lukumi*] the State's exclusion of theology majors must be narrowly tailored to achieve a compelling state interest. Finding that the State's own antiestablishment concerns were not compelling, the court declared Washington's Promise Scholarship Program unconstitutional. We . . . now reverse.

The Religion Clauses of the First Amendment . . . are frequently in tension. Yet we have long said that "there is room for play in the joints" between them. In other words, there are some state actions permitted by the Establishment Clause but not required by the Free Exercise Clause. This case involves that "play in the joints." [There] is no doubt that the State could, consistent with the [Establishment Clause], permit Promise Scholars to pursue a degree in devotional theology, and the State does not contend otherwise. [*Zelman, Zobrest, Witters, Mueller*; Section C.1, infra.] The question before us, however, is whether Washington, pursuant to its own constitution, which has been authoritatively interpreted as prohibiting even indirectly funding religious instruction that will prepare students for the ministry, can deny them such funding without violating the Free Exercise Clause.

Davey . . . contends that . . . the program is presumptively unconstitutional because it is not facially neutral with respect to religion. We reject his claim of presumptive unconstitutionality, however; to do otherwise would extend the *Lukumi* line of cases well beyond not only their facts but their reasoning. [Unlike *Lukumi*, here the State] imposes neither criminal nor civil sanctions on any type of religious service or rite. It does not deny to ministers the right to participate in the political affairs of the community. See McDaniel v. Paty. And it does not require students to choose between their religious beliefs and receiving a government benefit [because] Promise Scholars may still use their scholarship to pursue a secular degree at a different institution from where they are studying devotional theology. . . . The State has merely chosen not to fund a distinct category of instruction.

[Training] someone to lead a congregation is an essentially religious endeavor. Indeed, majoring in devotional theology is akin to a religious calling as well as an academic pursuit. And the subject of religion is one in which both the United States and state constitutions embody distinct views—in favor of free exercise, but opposed to establishment—that find no counterpart with respect to other callings or professions. That a State would deal differently with religious education for the ministry than with education for other callings is a product of these views, not evidence of hostility toward religion. Even though the . . . Washington Constitution draws a more stringent line than that drawn by the United States Constitution, the interest it seeks to further is scarcely novel. . . . Since the founding of our country, there have been popular uprisings against procuring taxpayer funds to support church leaders, which was one of the hallmarks of an "established" religion. . . . Far from evincing the hostility toward religion which was manifest in *Lukumi*, we believe that the entirety of the Promise Scholarship Program goes a long way toward including religion in its benefits. The program permits students to attend pervasively religious schools, so long as they are accredited. . . . And under the Promise Scholarship Program's current guidelines, students are still eligible to take devotional theology courses, [so long as they do not major in the subject]. In short, we find [nothing in] Article I, §11 of the Washington Constitution, nor in the operation of the Promise Scholarship Program, . . . that suggests animus toward religion. Given the historic and substantial state interest at issue, we therefore cannot conclude that the denial of funding for vocational religious instruction alone is inherently constitutionally suspect.

Without a presumption of unconstitutionality, Davey's claim must fail. The State's interest in not funding the pursuit of devotional degrees is substantial and the exclusion of such funding places a relatively minor burden on Promise Scholars. If any room exists between the two Religion Clauses, it must be here. We need not venture further into this difficult area in order to uphold the Promise Scholarship Program as currently operated by the State of Washington.

JUSTICE SCALIA, with whom JUSTICE THOMAS joins, dissenting.

In [*Lukumi*,] the majority opinion held that "[a] law burdening religious practice that is not neutral . . . must undergo the most rigorous of scrutiny," and that "the minimum requirement of neutrality is that a law not discriminate on its face." . . .

I. . . . When the State makes a public benefit generally available, that benefit becomes part of the baseline against which burdens on religion are measured; and when the State withholds that benefit from some individuals solely on the basis of religion, it violates the Free Exercise Clause no less than if it had imposed a special tax. That is precisely what the State of Washington has done here. It has created a generally available public benefit, whose receipt is conditioned only on academic performance, income, and attendance at an accredited school. It has then carved out a solitary course of study for exclusion: theology. No field of study but religion is singled out for disfavor in this fashion. Davey is not asking for a special benefit to which others are not entitled. He seeks only *equal* treatment—the right to direct his scholarship to his chosen course of study, a right every other Promise Scholar enjoys.

The Court's reference to historical "popular uprisings against procuring taxpayer funds to support church leaders" is therefore quite misplaced. That history involved not the inclusion of religious ministers in public benefits programs like the one at issue here, but laws that singled them out for financial aid. . . . One can concede the Framers' hostility to funding the clergy *specifically*, but that says nothing about whether the clergy had to be excluded from benefits the State made available to all. No one would seriously contend, for example, that the Framers would have barred ministers from using public roads on their way to church.

The Court does not dispute that the Free Exercise Clause places some constraints on public benefits programs, but finds none here, based on a principle of " 'play in the joints.' " . . . Even if "play in the joints" were a valid legal principle, surely it would apply only when it was a close call whether complying with one of the Religion Clauses would violate the other. But that is not the case here. . . . Perhaps some formally neutral public benefits programs are so gerrymandered and devoid of plausible secular purpose that they might raise specters of state aid to religion, but an evenhanded Promise Scholarship Program is not among them. In any case, the State already has all the play in the joints it needs. . . . It could make the scholarships redeemable only at public universities (where it sets the curriculum), or only for select courses of study. Either option would replace a program that facially discriminates against religion with one that just happens not to subsidize it. . . .

II. . . . [The] reason the Court thinks this particular facial discrimination less offensive is that the scholarship program was not motivated by animus toward religion. The Court does not explain why the legislature's motive matters, and I fail to see why it should. If a State deprives a citizen of trial by jury or passes an *ex post facto* law, we do not pause to investigate whether it was actually trying to accomplish the evil the Constitution prohibits. It is sufficient that the citizen's rights have been infringed. . . .

Let there be no doubt: This case is about discrimination against a religious minority. Most citizens of this country identify themselves as professing some religious belief, but the State's policy poses no obstacle to practitioners of only a tepid, civic version of faith. Those the statutory exclusion actually affects—those whose belief in their religion is so strong that they dedicate their study and their lives to its ministry—are a far narrower set. One need not delve too far into modern popular culture to perceive a trendy disdain for deep religious conviction. . . .

NOTE AND PROBLEM

1. "Play in the Joints": How Much Room for Government Accommodation of Religion or Refusal to Accommodate Religion? Chief Justice Rehnquist characterized the religion clauses as having "play in the joints" between them, meaning that there is some room for governmental discretion in deciding to accommodate religion or to refuse to accommodate religion. The establishment clause specifies when governments *may not accommodate* religion, whereas the free exercise clause specifies when governments *must accommodate* religion. *Smith* held that general laws that apply equally to everybody, including religious believers, are presumptively valid and are subject to minimal scrutiny. *Lukumi* held that laws that single out religious conduct are presumed to be void, and subject to strict scrutiny.

Queries: After *Locke*, does *Lukumi* stand for the proposition that laws that are focused on religion *and* that are purposefully hostile to religion are presumptive violations of the free exercise clause, which may be upheld only if the government can sustain its burden of justification under strict scrutiny? Does *Locke* establish that laws that focus on religion or have an effect on religious practice are presumptively valid *unless* they manifest hostility to religion? Are such laws subject to minimal scrutiny or to some other level of reduced scrutiny? What level of scrutiny applied in *Locke*?

2. Problem: *Property Tax Exemptions.* Assume that the Washington legislature enacts a law stripping churches of their exemption from property taxes while retaining that exemption for non-sectarian charities. The legislature declares that it acted to conform to the requirements of Art. I, §11, of the Washington Constitution; the Washington Supreme Court, in a case properly before it, agrees that the exclusion is required by the Washington Constitution. A church that has lost its property tax exemption contends that the law violates either or both of the religion clauses. What should be the result? Why?

C.   THE ESTABLISHMENT CLAUSE

The establishment clause was surely intended to prevent the federal government from creating an official state-supported church. The establishment clause, however, was not understood to bar *states* from creating officially established churches. Indeed, one function of the clause was to prevent Congress from disestablishing the state-supported official churches that existed in 1791. Nevertheless, the Court has incorporated the establishment clause into the Fourteenth Amendment's due process clause, thus preventing states from religious establishments. Everson v. Board of Education, 330 U.S. 1 (1947).

In a concurrence in Abington School District v. Schempp, 374 U.S. 203 (1963), Justice Brennan justified incorporation by noting that because "the last of the formal state establishments was dissolved more than three decades before the Fourteenth Amendment was ratified, . . . the problem of protecting official state churches from federal encroachments could hardly have been any concern of those who framed the post-Civil War Amendments." Because the incorporation doctrine is based on an expansive reading of "liberty," Justice Brennan also argued that the establishment clause was "a co-guarantor, with the Free Exercise Clause, of religious liberty. The Framers did not entrust the liberty of religious beliefs to either clause alone."

The incorporation issue having been settled, contemporary argument about the meaning of the establishment clause centers on how forbidden establishments of religion should be identified. The prevailing answer is found in a version of neutrality, derived from Lemon v. Kurtzman, 403 U.S. 602 (1971), in which the Court voided certain forms of government financial aid to religious schools. In *Lemon*, the Court declared that three things must be true of any law for it to survive an establishment clause challenge: "First, the statute must have a secular legislative purpose; second, its principal or primary effect must be one that neither advances nor inhibits religion; finally, the statute must not foster 'an excessive government entanglement with religion.'" There is significant dissatisfaction with the *Lemon* test, and two competing principles vie for supremacy in establishment clause interpretation.

The principal alternative is the idea that the establishment clause "prohibits government from making adherence to a religion relevant in any way to a person's standing in the political community." Lynch v. Donnelly, 465 U.S. 668 (1984) (O'Connor, J., concurring). What this means, according to Justice O'Connor, is that governments may not endorse religious belief or disbelief, since endorsement "sends a message to nonadherents that they are outsiders, not full members of the political community, and [to] adherents that they are insiders, favored members of the political community. Disapproval sends the opposite message." The "endorsement" approach has been used by the Court particularly in the area of government display of religious symbolism but has not displaced *Lemon* as an all-purpose establishment clause test. Indeed, the endorsement test may be seen as a way to implement *Lemon*: It serves to assess the principal effect of a law.

The other alternative to *Lemon* is the notion that only government practices that coerce religious belief or practice (or denial of religious belief or practice) offend the establishment clause. "The coercion that was a hallmark of historical establishments of religion was coercion of religious orthodoxy and of financial support [for a state church] by force of law or threat of penalty." Lee v. Weisman, 505 U.S. 577 (1992) (Scalia, J., dissenting). This approach accommodates much government assistance to religion, as many forms of government aid are unlikely to have coercive effect. Though the coercion test has had multiple adherents on the Court, it has never managed to garner a majority. For the moment, then, *Lemon* reigns as the doctrinal king of the establishment clause, but its reign has been uneasy and embattled.

1. Government Financial Aid to Religion

≡ *Everson v. Board of Education*
≡ *330 U.S. 1 (1947)*

[New Jersey authorized local school districts to pay the cost of transporting children to and from school, including private schools. A local school district agreed to reimburse parents for the cost of using public buses to transport their children to school. A local taxpayer brought suit, arguing that the Constitution forbade such payments to parents of children attending Roman Catholic religious schools. The New Jersey Court of Errors and Appeals refused to invalidate the plan.]

JUSTICE BLACK delivered the opinion of the Court.

[The] "establishment of religion" clause [means] at least this: Neither a state nor the Federal Government can set up a church. Neither can pass laws which aid one religion, aid all religions, or prefer one religion over another. Neither can force nor influence a person to go or to remain away from church against his will or force him to profess a belief or disbelief in any religion. No person can be punished for entertaining or professing religious beliefs, for church attendance or non-attendance. No tax in any amount, large or small, can be levied to support any religious activities or institutions, whatever they may be called, or whatever form they may adopt to teach or practice religion. Neither a state nor the Federal Government can, openly or secretly, participate in the affairs of any religious organizations or groups and vice versa. In the words of Jefferson, the clause against establishment of religion by law was intended to erect "a wall of separation between church and State."

[New Jersey] cannot consistently with the establishment clause [contribute] tax-raised funds to the support of an institution which teaches the tenets and faith of any church. On the other hand, [New Jersey] cannot hamper its citizens in the free exercise of their own religion. Consequently, it cannot exclude individual Catholics, Lutherans, Mohammedans, Baptists, Jews, Methodists, Non-believers, Presbyterians, or the members of any other faith, *because of their faith, or lack of it,* from receiving the benefits of public welfare legislation. While we do not intimate that a state could not provide transportation only to children attending public schools, we must be careful, in protecting the citizens of New Jersey against state-established churches, to be sure that we do not inadvertently prohibit New Jersey from extending its general state law benefits to all its citizens without regard to their religious belief.

Measured by these standards, we cannot say that the First Amendment prohibits New Jersey from spending tax-raised funds to pay the bus fares of parochial school pupils as a part of a general program under which it pays the fares of pupils attending other schools. It is undoubtedly true that children are helped to get to church schools. There is even a possibility that some of the children might not be sent to the church schools if the parents were compelled to pay their children's bus fares out of their own pockets when transportation to a public school would have been paid for by the State. [But it is also true that] parents might be reluctant to permit their children to attend schools which the state had cut off from such general government services as ordinary police and fire protection, connections for sewage disposal, public highways and sidewalks. Of course, cutting off church schools from these services . . . would make it far more difficult for the schools to operate. But such is obviously not the purpose of the First Amendment, [which] requires the state to be neutral in its relations with groups of religious believers and non-believers; it does not require the state to be their adversary. State power is no more to be used so as to handicap religions than it is to favor them.

[The] State contributes no money to the schools. It does not support them. Its legislation, as applied, does no more than provide a general program to help parents get their children, regardless of their religion, safely and expeditiously to and from accredited schools. The First Amendment has erected a wall between church and state. That wall must be kept high and impregnable. We could not approve the slightest breach. New Jersey has not breached it here.

JUSTICE JACKSON, joined by JUSTICE FRANKFURTER, dissenting.

[The] undertones of the [Court's] opinion, advocating complete and uncompromising separation of Church from State, seem utterly discordant with its conclusion yielding support to their commingling in [education].

JUSTICE RUTLEDGE, joined by JUSTICES FRANKFURTER, JACKSON, and BURTON, dissenting.

[The purpose of the establishment clause was to] create a complete and permanent separation of the spheres of religious activity and civil authority by comprehensively forbidding every form of public aid or support for religion. . . . New Jersey's action furnish[es] support for religion by use of the taxing power. [Money] taken by taxation [is] not to be used or given to [support] religious training or belief. [The] prohibition is absolute.

[Two] great drives are constantly in motion to abridge, in the name of education, the complete division of religion and civil authority which our forefathers made. One is to introduce religious education and observances into the public schools. The other [is] to obtain public funds for the aid and support of various private religious schools. [Both] avenues were closed by the Constitution. Neither should be opened by this Court. The matter is not one of quantity, to be measured by the amount of money expended. Now as in Madison's day it is one of principle.

NOTES

1. The "Wall of Separation" Metaphor. Is the wall of separation between church and state constructed on the basis of a categorical rule or a balancing test? If the former, state the rule. In *Lemon*, the Court said that "the line of separation, far from being a 'wall,' is a blurred, indistinct, and variable barrier depending on all the circumstances of a particular relationship." Is the *Lemon* three-part test—secular purpose, neutral effect, but no excessive entanglement—a better reflection of *Everson*'s conception of the "wall"?

2. Developments After *Everson*: Direct and Indirect Aid. *Everson* seemed to draw a line between aid delivered directly to religious institutions and aid delivered to individuals, even though the effect of the aid is to benefit religious institutions. In Board of Education v. Allen, 392 U.S. 236 (1968), the Court upheld New York's practice of lending secular textbooks to all students, finding that, like bus transport in *Everson*, the program both had a secular purpose and effect and lacked any involvement with religious institutions. But in Meek v. Pittenger, 421 U.S. 349 (1975), the Court struck down Pennsylvania's loan of secular instructional materials such as laboratory equipment and maps to religious schools on the ground that the primary effect of the aid was to advance religion. In Wolman v. Walter, 433 U.S. 229 (1977), the Court voided Ohio's loan of instructional materials other than textbooks to students on the theory that books primarily benefit students but other materials are more adaptable to teaching of religion and thus of providing primary aid to teachers who were employees of the religious institution.

≡≡≡ *Mueller v. Allen*
463 U.S. 388 (1983)

JUSTICE REHNQUIST delivered the opinion of the Court.

Minnesota allows taxpayers, in computing their state income tax, to deduct certain expenses incurred in providing for the education of their children. [Deductible expenses include actual expenses of up to $500 for each elementary school child and up to $700 for each secondary school child for tuition, textbooks (other than religious books designed to inculcate religious tenets, doctrines, or worship), and transportation costs of sending a child to a public or nonprofit private school.] The [Court] of Appeals [held] that the Establishment Clause [was] not offended by this arrangement. [We] now affirm.

Minnesota, like every other State, provides its citizens with free elementary and secondary schooling. [About] 820,000 students attended this school system in the most recent school year. During the same year, approximately 91,000 elementary and secondary students attended some 500 privately supported schools located in Minnesota, and about 95% of these students attended [religious schools].

One fixed principle in this field is our consistent rejection of the argument that "any program which in some manner aids an institution with a religious affiliation" violates the Establishment Clause. For example, it is now well established that a State may reimburse parents for expenses incurred in transporting their children to school, [*Everson*], and that it may loan secular textbooks to all schoolchildren within the State. [*Allen*.] [But we] also have struck down arrangements resembling, in many respects, these forms of assistance. See, e.g., [*Lemon, Meek,* and *Wolman*].

The general nature of our inquiry in this area has been guided . . . by the [*Lemon*] "three-part" test. . . . [O]ur cases have also emphasized that it provides "no more than [a] helpful [signpost]" in dealing with Establishment Clause challenges. . . . Little time need be spent on the question of whether the Minnesota tax deduction has a secular purpose. [G]overnmental assistance programs have consistently survived this inquiry even when they have run afoul of other aspects of the *Lemon* framework. This reflects, at least in part, our reluctance to attribute unconstitutional motives to the States, particularly when a plausible secular purpose for the State's program may be discerned from the face of the statute. [Minnesota's] decision to defray the cost of educational expenses incurred by parents — regardless of the type of schools their children attend — evidences a purpose that is both secular and understandable. An educated populace is essential to the political and economic health of any community, and a State's efforts to assist parents in meeting the rising cost of educational expenses plainly serves this secular purpose of ensuring that the State's citizenry is well educated. Similarly, Minnesota, like other States, could conclude that there is a strong public interest in assuring the continued financial health of private schools, both sectarian and nonsectarian. By educating a substantial number of students such schools relieve public schools of a correspondingly great burden — to the benefit of all taxpayers. In addition, private schools may serve as a benchmark for public schools. [Each of] these justifications [is] sufficient to satisfy the secular purpose inquiry of *Lemon*.

We turn therefore to the . . . question whether the Minnesota statute has "the primary effect of advancing the sectarian aims of the nonpublic schools." In concluding that it does not, we find several features of the Minnesota tax deduction particularly significant. First, an essential feature of Minnesota's arrangement is the fact that [the deduction] is only one among many deductions [available] under the Minnesota tax laws. . . . [The] Minnesota Legislature's judgment that a deduction for educational expenses fairly equalizes the tax burden of its citizens and encourages desirable expenditures for educational purposes is entitled to substantial deference. . . . [T]he deduction is available for educational expenses incurred by all parents, including those whose children attend public schools and those whose children attend nonsectarian private schools or sectarian private schools. [The] "provision of benefits to so broad a spectrum of groups is an important index of secular effect." In this respect, as well as others, this case is vitally different from the scheme struck down in [Committee for Public Education v. Nyquist, 413 U.S. 756 (1973)]. There, public assistance amounting to tuition grants was provided only to parents of children in *nonpublic* schools. . . . Unlike the assistance at issue in *Nyquist*, [the Minnesota tax deduction] permits all parents — whether their children attend public school or private — to deduct their children's educational expenses. [A program] that neutrally provides state assistance to a broad spectrum of citizens is not readily subject to challenge under the Establishment Clause.

[Moreover], by channeling whatever assistance it may provide to parochial schools through individual parents, Minnesota has reduced the Establishment Clause objections to which its action is subject. It is true, of course, that financial assistance provided to parents ultimately has an economic effect comparable to that of aid given directly to the schools attended by their children. It is also true, however, that under Minnesota's arrangement public funds become available only as a result of numerous private choices of individual parents of school-age children. [Where], as here, aid to parochial schools is available only as a result of decisions of individual parents no "imprimatur of state approval" can be deemed to have been conferred on any particular religion, or on religion generally. . . .

Petitioners argue that, notwithstanding [its] facial neutrality, [in] application the statute primarily benefits religious institutions. Petitioners . . . contend that most parents of public school children incur no tuition expenses, and that other expenses deductible [are] negligible in value; moreover, they claim that 96% of the children in private schools in 1978-1979 attended religiously affiliated institutions. Because of all this, they reason, the bulk of deductions [will] be claimed by parents of children in sectarian schools. Respondents reply that petitioners have failed to consider the impact of deductions for items such as transportation, summer school tuition, tuition paid by parents whose children attended schools outside the school districts in which they resided, rental or purchase costs for a variety of equipment, and tuition for certain types of instruction not ordinarily provided in public schools. We need not consider these contentions in detail.

We would be loath to adopt a rule grounding the constitutionality of a facially neutral law on annual reports reciting the extent to which various classes of private citizens claimed benefits under the law. Such an approach would scarcely [provide] certainty, [nor] can we perceive principled standards by which such statistical evidence might be evaluated. Moreover, the fact that private persons fail in a particularly year to claim the tax relief to which they are entitled—under a facially neutral statute—should be of little importance in determining the constitutionality of the statute permitting such relief.

Finally, private educational institutions, and parents paying for their children to attend these schools, make special contributions to the areas in which they operate. "Parochial schools [have] provided an educational alternative; [they] often afford wholesome competition with our public schools; and in some States they relieve substantially the tax burden incident to the operation of public schools." . . . [W]hatever unequal effect may be attributed to the statutory classification can fairly be regarded as a rough return for the benefits [provided] to the State and all taxpayers by parents sending their children to parochial schools. In the light of all this, we believe it wiser to decline to engage in the type of empirical inquiry into those persons benefited by state law which petitioners urge. Thus, we hold that the Minnesota tax deduction for educational expenses satisfies the primary effect inquiry of our Establishment Clause cases.

Turning to the third part of the *Lemon* inquiry, we have no difficulty in concluding that the Minnesota statute does not "excessively entangle" the State in religion. The only plausible source of the "comprehensive, discriminating, and continuing state surveillance" necessary to run afoul of this standard would lie in the fact that state officials must determine whether particular textbooks qualify for a deduction. In making this decision, state officials must disallow deductions taken for "instructional books and materials used in the teaching of religious tenets, doctrines or worship, the purpose of which is to inculcate such tenets, doctrines or worship." Making decisions such as this does not differ substantially from making the types of decisions approved in earlier opinions of this Court.

JUSTICE MARSHALL, joined by JUSTICES BRENNAN, BLACKMUN, and STEVENS, dissenting.

The Establishment Clause [prohibits] a State from subsidizing religious education, whether it does so directly or indirectly. In my view, this principle of neutrality forbids [any] tax benefit, including the tax deduction at issue here, which subsidizes tuition payments to sectarian schools [and] the cost of books and other instructional materials used for sectarian purposes.

[The] Minnesota tax statute violates the Establishment Clause for . . . the same reason as the statute struck down in *Nyquist*: it has a direct and immediate effect of advancing religion. . . . [Indirect] assistance in the form of financial aid to parents for tuition payments is . . . impermissible because it is not "subject [to] restrictions" which "guarantee the separation between secular and religious educational functions [and] ensure that State financial aid supports only the former." [*Lemon*.] . . .

[That] the Minnesota statute makes some small benefit available to all parents cannot alter the fact that the most substantial benefit provided by the statute is available only to those parents who send their children to schools that charge tuition. [That] this deduction has a primary effect of promoting religion [is established by the fact that] the deduction permitted for tuition expenses primarily benefits those who send their children to religious schools. . . .

NOTES

1. Incidental Aid as Part of a General Benefit Scheme. Even before *Mueller*, the Court found no fault with government aid to religion that was incidental to a general benefit scheme that did not target religious institutions for favorable treatment. For example, in Walz v. Tax Commission, 397 U.S. 664 (1970), the Court upheld a tax exemption for "property used exclusively for religious, educational or charitable purposes." Even though the exemption benefited churches, the benefit was part of a broader benefit conferred on "nonprofit, quasi-public corporations which include hospitals, libraries, playgrounds, scientific, professional, historical and patriotic groups."

The validity of government provision of non-instructional assistance (such as therapy or guidance counseling) directly to students in religious schools generally depends on how that assistance is delivered. *Meek* struck down a program by which public school employees delivered such services to students at their religious schools. By contrast, *Wolman* upheld the delivery of the same services to religious school students so long as the assistance did not occur at the religious school. The Court's rationale was that there was less danger of religious instruction infiltrating therapy for educational or health disabilities when it happened away from the religious institution. After *Mueller*, however, the Court became progressively more tolerant of such services delivered at religious institutions.

Witters v. Washington Department of Services for the Blind, 474 U.S. 481 (1986). The Court unanimously sustained a Washington law granting scholarships to handicapped students, as applied to a scholarship given a blind student who used the funds to pay tuition at a Christian college where he was preparing for the ministry. The majority applied *Lemon* and concluded that Washington had a secular purpose—helping handicapped students achieve self-sufficiency—and that the scholarship was neutral in its effect because the aid was given to the student rather than the college. Because the private person, rather than the state, made the choice of delivering it to a religious institution the law had a neutral effect.

Zobrest v. Catalina Foothills School District, 509 U.S. 1 (1993). Public school districts paid the cost of a sign-language interpreter for deaf students, no matter what school they attended. An Arizona school district hired a signer for Zobrest, a student at a Roman Catholic high school. The Court upheld this program because it provided benefits without reference to religion, and there was virtually no benefit received by the religious school itself.

2. Direct Aid for Secular Purposes. The Adolescent Family Life Act provided federal funds to a variety of public and private organizations, including religious institutions, to counsel adolescents concerning sexual relations and pregnancy. In Bowen v. Kendrick, 487 U.S. 589 (1988), the Court applied *Lemon* and found the Act to be facially valid. Congress's secular purpose was to eliminate or reduce the social and economic problems associated with teenage sexuality. The effect of grants to religious institutions to further that purpose was neutral because the services provided were "not religious in character" and did not involve the furtherance of sectarian dogma. Any overlap between the government's secular goals and religious principles concerning teenage sexuality was not enough to produce a conclusion that the "primary effect" of the Act was to advance religion. Government monitoring of the services provided under the Act by religious institutions was too insignificant to trigger the entanglement prong of *Lemon*.

Two post-*Mueller* cases sharply limited the ability of governments to supply aid to religious schools for secular purposes. In Grand Rapids School District v. Ball, 473 U.S. 373 (1985), the Court voided two separate programs. In one, public school teachers taught remedial reading in parochial school classrooms for part of the school day. In the other, parochial school teachers were paid by the public schools to teach wholly secular "community education" subjects after-hours in parochial school classrooms. The Court thought the program posed an unacceptable risk that public school teachers might "conform their instruction" to the religious environment of the school and that it created a "symbolic union of government and religion in one sectarian enterprise."

The background to Aguilar v. Felton, 473 U.S. 402 (1985), a companion case, was a federal law that provided financial aid to public and private schools meeting the educational needs of low-income children. New York's public schools did so by supplying public teachers to teach remedial reading and arithmetic in parochial schools. The teachers were prohibited from any religious instruction or participating in any religious activities as part of their teaching duties. Parochial school administrators were required to remove all religious symbols from classrooms in which this remedial instruction occurred. The requirements were enforced by unannounced visits to the classrooms by public officials. The Court invoked the excessive-entanglement prong of *Lemon* to void the program. But in Agostini v. Felton the Court reconsidered *Aguilar* and concluded that neither it nor the "shared time" aspect of *Ball* were good law.

≡ *Agostini v. Felton*
≡ *521 U.S. 203 (1997)*

JUSTICE O'CONNOR delivered the opinion of the Court.

Twelve years [after *Aguilar*, petitioners] ask that we explicitly recognize what our more recent cases already dictate: *Aguilar* is no longer good law. We agree. . . . Distilled to essentials, the Court's conclusion that the Shared Time program in *Ball* had the impermissible effect of advancing religion rested on three assumptions: (i) any public employee who works on the premises of a religious school is presumed to inculcate religion in her work; (ii) the presence of public employees on private school premises creates a symbolic union between church and state; and (iii) any and all public aid that directly aids the educational function of religious schools impermissibly finances religious indoctrination, even if the aid reaches such schools as a consequence of private decision-making. Additionally, in *Aguilar* there was a fourth assumption: that New York City's Title I program necessitated an excessive government entanglement with religion because public employees who teach on the premises of religious schools must be closely monitored to ensure that they do not inculcate religion. Our more recent cases have undermined the assumptions upon which *Ball* and *Aguilar* relied. [First], we have abandoned the presumption erected in *Meek* and *Ball* that the placement of public employees on parochial school grounds inevitably results in the impermissible effect of state-sponsored indoctrination or constitutes a symbolic union between government and religion. In [*Zobrest*, we] refused to presume that a publicly employed interpreter would be pressured by the pervasively sectarian surroundings to inculcate religion by "adding to [or] subtracting from" the lectures translated. [*Zobrest*] expressly rejected the notion—relied on in *Ball* and *Aguilar*—that, solely because of her presence on private school property, a public employee will be presumed to inculcate religion in the students. *Zobrest* also implicitly repudiated another assumption on which *Ball* and *Aguilar* turned: that the presence of a public employee on private school property creates an impermissible "symbolic link" between government and religion.

[Second], we have departed from the rule relied on in *Ball* that all government aid that directly aids the educational function of religious schools is invalid. In [*Witters*], we held that the Establishment Clause did not bar a State from issuing a vocational tuition grant to a blind person who wished to use the grant to attend a Christian college and become a pastor, missionary, or youth director. Even though the grant recipient clearly would use the money to obtain religious education, we observed that the tuition grants were "'made available generally without regard to the sectarian-nonsectarian, or public-nonpublic nature of the institution benefited.'" The grants were disbursed directly to students, who then used the money to pay for tuition at the educational institution of their choice. [This] transaction was no different from a State's issuing a paycheck to one of its employees, knowing that the employee would donate part or all of the check to a religious institution. In both situations, any money that ultimately went to religious institutions did so "only as a result of the genuinely independent and private choices of" individuals.

[*Zobrest*] and *Witters* make clear that [each] of the premises upon which we relied in *Ball* [is] no longer valid. [Where] aid is allocated on the basis of neutral, secular criteria that neither favor nor disfavor religion, and is made available to both religious and secular beneficiaries on a nondiscriminatory basis, [the] aid is less likely to have the effect of advancing religion. [In] *Ball* and *Aguilar*, the Court gave this consideration no weight. [Applying] this reasoning to New York City's Title I program, it is clear that Title I services are allocated on the basis of criteria that neither favor nor disfavor religion. The services are available to all children who meet the Act's eligibility requirements, no matter what their religious beliefs or where they go to school. . . .

We turn now to *Aguilar*'s conclusion that New York City's Title I program resulted in an excessive entanglement between church and state. . . . We have considered entanglement both in the course of assessing whether an aid program has an impermissible effect of advancing religion and as a factor separate and apart from "effect." [H]owever, the factors we use to assess whether an entanglement is "excessive" are similar to the factors we use to examine "effect." That is, to assess entanglement, we have looked to "the character and purposes of the institutions that are benefited, the nature of the aid that the State provides, and the resulting relationship between the government and religious authority." Similarly, we have assessed a law's "effect" by examining the character of the institutions benefited (e.g., whether the religious institutions were "predominantly religious") and the nature of the aid that the State provided (e.g., whether it was neutral and non-ideological). Not all entanglements, of course, have the effect of advancing or inhibiting religion. Interaction between church and state is inevitable, and we have always tolerated some level of involvement between the two. Entanglement must be "excessive" before it runs afoul of the Establishment Clause. [The] Court's finding of "excessive" entanglement in *Aguilar* rested on three grounds: (i) the program would require "pervasive monitoring by public authorities" to ensure that Title I employees did not inculcate religion; (ii) the program required "administrative cooperation" between the Board and parochial schools; and (iii) the program might increase the dangers of "political divisiveness." Under our current understanding of the Establishment Clause, the last two considerations are insufficient by themselves to create an "excessive" entanglement. [And because] we no longer presume that public employees will inculcate religion simply because they happen to be in a sectarian environment, [we] must also discard the assumption that pervasive monitoring of [such] teachers is required.

[To] summarize, New York City's Title I program does not run afoul of any of three primary criteria we currently use to evaluate whether government aid has the effect of advancing religion: it does not result in governmental indoctrination; define its recipients by reference to religion; or create an excessive entanglement. . . . *Aguilar*, as well as the portion of *Ball* addressing Grand Rapids' Shared Time program, are no longer good law.

NOTE AND PROBLEMS

1. Subsequent Developments. Does *Agostini* fold the "excessive entanglement" prong of *Lemon* into the "effect" prong?

Mitchell v. Helms, 530 U.S. 793 (2000). The Court upheld the validity of a federal program by which library and media materials and computer hardware and software were loaned to public and private schools (including religious schools) to implement "secular, neutral, and nonideological" programs. Prior to this decision, the validity of state loans of instructional materials to religious schools depended on whether the loan was to all school children (valid) or to the religious school itself (invalid). *Mitchell* eliminated this formalistic division. Four justices (Thomas, joined by Rehnquist, Scalia, and Kennedy) applied *Agostini*'s gloss on *Lemon*, but thought that the question of whether government indoctrination was present depended on whether any indoctrination that did occur was reasonably attributable to the government. The plurality thought that this issue, in turn, depended on whether the aid was broadly distributed to secular recipients as well or resulted from a private choice:

> If the government, seeking to further some legitimate secular purpose, offers aid on the same terms, without regard to religion, to all who adequately further that purpose, then it is fair to say that any aid going to a religious recipient only has the effect of furthering that secular purpose. The government, in crafting such an aid program, has had to conclude that a given level of aid is necessary

to further that purpose among secular recipients and has provided no more than that same level to religious recipients.

Justices O'Connor and Breyer concurred in the judgment. All six justices concurring in the result agreed that *Meek* and *Wolman*, to the extent inconsistent with *Helms*, were overruled.

2. Problems: *Biology Teachers.* In order to "further science education and to keep science and religion separated," a public school district offers to provide biology teachers to all private schools. A religious school agrees to participate in the plan, and a group of citizens object. Valid?

Mathematics Teachers. Under the same program as in the prior problem, the public school district provides mathematics teachers to religious schools. Is this valid?

≡≡≡ *Zelman v. Simmons-Harris*
≡≡≡ *536 U.S. 639 (2002)*

CHIEF JUSTICE REHNQUIST delivered the opinion of the Court.

The State of Ohio has established a pilot program designed to provide educational choices to families with children who reside in the Cleveland City School District. The question presented is whether this program offends the Establishment Clause of the United States Constitution. We hold that it does not.

There are more than 75,000 children enrolled in the Cleveland City School District. The majority of these children are from low-income and minority families. Few of these families enjoy the means to send their children to any school other than an inner-city public school. For more than a generation, however, Cleveland's public schools have been among the worst performing public schools in the Nation. In 1995, [a federal court placed] the entire Cleveland school district under state control. . . . The district had failed to meet any of the 18 state standards for minimal acceptable performance. . . . It is against this backdrop that Ohio enacted . . . its Pilot Project Scholarship Program, [which] provides financial assistance to families in any Ohio school district that is or has been "under federal court order requiring supervision and operational management of the district by the state superintendent." Cleveland is the only Ohio school district to fall within that category.

The program provides two basic kinds of assistance. . . . First, the program provides tuition aid for students in kindergarten through . . . eighth grade, to attend a participating public or private school of their parents' choosing. Second, the program provides tutorial aid for students who choose to remain enrolled in public school.

The tuition aid . . . is designed to provide educational choices to parents. . . . Any private school, whether religious or nonreligious, may participate in the program and accept program students so long as the school is located within the boundaries of a covered district and meets statewide educational standards. Participating private schools must agree not to discriminate on the basis of race, religion, or ethnic background . . . . Any public school located in a school district adjacent to the covered district may also participate in the program. Adjacent public schools are eligible to receive a $2,250 tuition grant for each program student accepted in addition to the full amount of per-pupil state funding attributable to each additional student. . . . Tuition aid is distributed to parents according to financial need. . . . Where tuition aid is spent depends solely upon where parents who receive tuition aid choose to enroll their child. If parents choose a private school, checks are made payable to the parents who then endorse the checks over to the chosen school.

The tutorial aid portion of the program provides tutorial assistance through grants to any student in a covered district who chooses to remain in public school. Parents arrange for registered tutors to provide assistance to their children and then submit bills for those services to the State for payment. . . . The number of tutorial assistance grants offered to students in a covered district must equal the number of tuition aid scholarships provided to students enrolled at participating private or adjacent public schools. . . .

In the 1999-2000 school year, 56 private schools participated in the program, 46 (or 82%) of which had a religious affiliation. None of the public schools in districts adjacent to Cleveland have elected to participate. More than 3,700 students participated in the scholarship program, most of whom (96%) enrolled in religiously affiliated schools. Sixty percent of these students were from families at or below the poverty line. In the 1998-1999 school year, approximately 1,400 Cleveland public school students received tutorial aid. This number was expected to double during the 1999-2000 school year.

The program is part of a broader undertaking by the State to enhance the educational options of Cleveland's schoolchildren in response to the 1995 takeover. That undertaking includes . . . community and magnet schools. Community schools are funded under state law but are run by their own school boards, not by local school districts. These schools enjoy academic independence to hire their own teachers and to determine their own curriculum. They can have no religious affiliation and are required to accept students by lottery. During the 1999-2000 school year, there were 10 start-up community schools in the Cleveland City School District with more than 1,900 students enrolled. For each child enrolled in a community school, the school receives state funding of $4,518, twice the funding a participating program school may receive.

Magnet schools are public schools operated by a local school board that emphasize a particular subject area, teaching method, or service to students. For each student enrolled in a magnet school, the school district receives $7,746, including state funding of $4,167, the same amount received per student enrolled at a traditional public school. As of 1999, parents in Cleveland were able to choose from among 23 magnet schools, which together enrolled more than 13,000 students in kindergarten through eighth grade. These schools provide specialized teaching methods, such as Montessori, or a particularized curriculum focus, such as foreign language, computers, or the arts.

[Respondents], a group of Ohio taxpayers, . . . filed this action in United States District Court, seeking to enjoin the . . . program on the ground that it violated the Establishment Clause. [The] District Court granted summary judgment for respondents. [A] divided panel of the Court of Appeals affirmed . . . , finding that the program had the "primary effect" of advancing religion in violation of the Establishment Clause. . . . We . . . now reverse the Court of Appeals. . . .

There is no dispute that the program . . . was enacted for the valid secular purpose of providing educational assistance to poor children in a demonstrably failing public school system. [The] question presented is whether the Ohio program . . . has the forbidden "effect" of advancing or inhibiting religion. To answer that question, our decisions have drawn a consistent distinction between government programs that provide aid directly to religious schools and programs of true private choice, in which government aid reaches religious schools only as a result of the genuine and independent choices of private individuals. [W]here a government aid program is neutral with respect to religion, and provides assistance directly to a broad class of citizens who, in turn, direct government aid to religious schools wholly as a result of their own genuine and independent private choice, the program is not readily subject to challenge under the Establishment Clause. A program that shares these features permits government aid to reach religious institutions only by way of the deliberate choices of numerous individual recipients. The incidental advancement of a religious mission, or the perceived endorsement of a religious message, is reasonably attributable to the individual recipient, not to the government, whose role ends with the disbursement of benefits. . . . It is precisely for these reasons that we have never found a program of true private choice to offend the Establishment Clause.

We believe that the program challenged here is a program of true private choice, consistent with *Mueller, Witters,* and *Zobrest,* and thus constitutional. [T]he Ohio program is neutral in all respects toward religion. It is part of a general and multifaceted undertaking by the State of Ohio to provide educational opportunities to the children of a failed school district. It confers educational assistance directly to a broad class of individuals defined without reference to religion, i.e., any parent of a school-age child who resides in the Cleveland City School District. The program permits the participation of *all* schools within the district, religious or nonreligious. Adjacent public schools also may participate and have a financial incentive to do so. Program benefits are available to participating families on neutral terms, with no reference to religion. The only preference stated anywhere in the program is a preference for low-income families, who receive greater assistance and are given priority for admission at participating schools. . . .

Respondents suggest that . . . the program creates a "public perception that the State is endorsing religious practices and beliefs." But we have repeatedly recognized that no reasonable observer would think a neutral program of private choice, where state aid reaches religious schools solely as a result of the numerous independent decisions of private individuals, carries with it the *imprimatur* of government endorsement . . . .

There also is no evidence that the program fails to provide genuine opportunities for Cleveland parents to select secular educational options for their school-age children. Cleveland schoolchildren enjoy a range of educational choices: They may remain in public school as before, remain in public school with publicly funded tutoring aid, obtain a scholarship and choose a religious school, obtain a scholarship and choose a nonreligious private school, enroll in a community school, or enroll in a magnet school. . . . The Establishment Clause question is whether Ohio is coercing parents into sending their children to religious schools, and that question must be answered by evaluating *all* options Ohio provides Cleveland schoolchildren, only one of which is to obtain a program scholarship and then choose a religious school. . . .

In sum, the Ohio program is entirely neutral with respect to religion. It provides benefits directly to a wide spectrum of individuals, defined only by financial need and residence in a particular school district. It permits such individuals to exercise genuine choice among options public and private, secular and religious. The program is therefore a program of true private choice. In keeping with an unbroken line of decisions rejecting challenges to similar programs, we hold that the program does not offend the Establishment Clause.

JUSTICE THOMAS, concurring.

. . . I agree with the Court that Ohio's program easily passes muster under our stringent [Establishment Clause] test, but, as a matter of first principles, I question whether this test should be applied to the States. . . . On its face, [the Establishment Clause] places no limit on the States with regard to religion. The Establishment Clause originally protected States, and by extension their citizens, from the imposition of an established religion by the Federal Government. . . . When rights are incorporated against the States through the Fourteenth Amendment they should advance, not constrain, individual liberty. Consequently, in the context of the Establishment Clause, it may well be that state action should be evaluated on different terms than similar action by the Federal Government. "States, while bound to observe strict neutrality, should be freer to experiment with involvement [in religion]—on a neutral basis—than the Federal Government." [*Walz* (Harlan, J., concurring).] Thus, while the Federal Government may "make no law respecting an establishment of religion," the States may pass laws that include or touch on religious matters so long as these laws do not impede free exercise rights or any other individual religious liberty interest. . . .

JUSTICE STEVENS, dissenting.

Is a law that authorizes the use of public funds to pay for the indoctrination of thousands of grammar school children in particular religious faiths a "law respecting an establishment of religion" within the meaning of the First Amendment? In answering that question, I think we should ignore three factual matters that are discussed at length by my colleagues.

First, the severe educational crisis that confronted the Cleveland City School District . . . is not a matter that should affect our appraisal of its constitutionality. . . . Second, the wide range of choices that have been made available to students *within the public school system* has no bearing on the question whether the State may pay the tuition for students who wish to reject public education entirely and attend private schools that will provide them with a sectarian education. . . . Third, the voluntary character of the private choice to prefer a parochial education over an education in the public school system seems to me quite irrelevant to the question whether the government's choice to pay for religious indoctrination is constitutionally permissible. . . .

I am convinced that the Court's decision is profoundly misguided. . . .

JUSTICE SOUTER, with whom JUSTICE STEVENS, JUSTICE GINSBURG, and JUSTICE BREYER join, dissenting.

. . . [The] majority's twin standards of neutrality and free choice . . . cannot convincingly legitimize the Ohio scheme. . . .

Neutrality . . . refers . . . to evenhandedness in setting eligibility as between potential religious and secular recipients of public money. . . . Here, one would ask whether the voucher provisions . . . were written in a way that skewed the scheme toward benefiting religious schools, [but] the majority looks not to the provisions for tuition vouchers but to every provision for educational opportunity. . . .

The majority [asks] whether . . . potential recipients of voucher aid have a choice of public schools among secular alternatives to religious schools, [but the] question is whether the private hand is genuinely free to send the money in either a secular direction or a religious one. . . . If "choice" is present whenever there is any educational alternative to the religious school to which vouchers can be endorsed, then there will always be a choice and the voucher can always be constitutional. . . . [However,] something is influencing choices in a way that aims the money in a religious direction: . . . 96.6% of all voucher recipients go to religious schools, only 3.4% to nonreligious ones. [There] is no explanation . . . that suggests the religious direction results simply from free choices by parents. One answer . . . might be that 96.6% of families choosing to avail themselves of vouchers choose to educate their children in schools of their own religion. [But] almost two out of three families using vouchers to send their children to religious schools did not embrace the religion of those schools. . . . [There is] no way to interpret the 96.6% of current voucher money going to religious schools as reflecting a free and genuine choice by the families that apply for vouchers. The 96.6% reflects, instead, the fact that too few nonreligious school desks are available and few but religious schools can afford to accept more than a handful of voucher students. And . . . public schools in adjacent districts hardly have a financial incentive to participate in the Ohio voucher program, and none has. For the overwhelming number of children in the voucher scheme, the only alternative to the public schools is religious. And it is entirely irrelevant that the State did not deliberately design the network of private schools for the sake of channeling money into religious institutions. The criterion is one of genuinely free choice on the part of the private individuals who choose, and a Hobson's choice is not a choice, whatever the reason for being Hobsonian. . . .

. . . The scale of the aid to religious schools . . . is unprecedented, both in the number of dollars and in the proportion of systemic school expenditure supported. [The] sheer quantity of aid [is] suspect on the theory that the greater the aid, the greater its proportion to a religious school's existing expenditures, and the greater the likelihood that public money [is] supporting religious as well as secular instruction. . . .

[Religion] "may be compromised . . . as government largesse brings government regulation." . . . When government aid goes up, so does reliance on it; the only thing likely to go down is independence. . . . A day will come when religious schools will learn what political leverage can do. . . .

As appropriations for religious subsidy rise, competition for the money will tap sectarian religion's capacity for discord. "Public money . . . brings the quest for more, [and] the struggle of sect against sect for the larger share or for any." [The] intensity of the expectable friction can be gauged by realizing that the scramble for money will energize not only contending sectarians, but taxpayers who take their liberty of conscience seriously. Religious teaching at taxpayer expense simply cannot be cordoned from taxpayer politics, and every major religion currently espouses social positions that provoke intense opposition. . . .

NOTES AND PROBLEM

1. The Meaning of Neutral Effect. Does *Zelman* mean that the only effects that count are those that are produced by governments without the intervening choice of private citizens? Assuming a secular purpose for a government program that funnels money to religious institutions through private choice, is neutral effect established by virtue of a theoretical private choice between religious and nonreligious alternatives? Must the choice be "meaningful"? If so, what constitutes meaningful choice?

2. The Death of Entanglement? After *Agostini*, the "excessive entanglement" prong of *Lemon* was largely subsumed into the "neutral effects" prong. Has it now disappeared altogether, as a practical matter? The dissents sound the warning of religious strife. Was that concern adequately addressed by the Court? The Court regarded the dissenters' concerns as speculative; if those concerns become concretely manifested, how will (should) the Court respond? Will (should) the response differ if the problem is (i) sectarian conflict over access to government money or (ii) government regulation of the religious institutions that ultimately receive public funds?

3. Problem: *Veterans' Education Benefit.* Under 38 U.S.C. §§3201 *et seq.*, the federal government contributes two dollars for every dollar contributed by a member of the armed services toward educational costs. The total fund may be used by the ex-service member at any qualified educational institution, a category that includes religious institutions. Valid?

2. Governmental Endorsement of Religious Belief or Non-belief and Governmental Coercion to Believe or Not Believe

The Court's approach to government acts that might symbolically endorse religion is similar to its approach to financial aid. Government actions that unequivocally endorse religious beliefs violate the establishment clause, but actions that merely facilitate or defer to private voluntary choices are far less likely to be perceived as establishment clause violations.

a. Religion and Public Schools

The early cases concerned the practice by public schools of releasing pupils from a portion of the required school day for the purpose of religious instruction. In McCollum v. Board of Education, 333 U.S. 203 (1948), the Court invalidated a public school practice of releasing students for religious education provided at the public school by sectarian teachers. The use of public school facilities for religious instruction was forbidden. The scheme also gave "invaluable aid" to the benefited religious institutions because the state compelled attendance at school, only to release those students desiring religious instruction.

Zorach v. Clauson, 343 U.S. 306 (1952). New York City released public school students early to attend religious instruction away from the school. For the Court, Justice Douglas stated:

> This "released time" program involves neither religious instruction in public school classrooms nor the expenditure of public funds. [The] case is therefore unlike [*McCollum*]. Appellants [argue that] the weight and influence of the school is put behind a program for religious instruction; public school teachers police it, keeping tab on students who are released; the classroom activities come to a halt while the students who are released for religious instruction are on leave; the school is a crutch on which the churches are leaning for support in their religious training; without the cooperation of the schools this "released time" program [would] be futile and ineffective. [No] one is forced to go to the religious classroom and no religious exercise or instruction is brought to the classrooms of the public schools. [There is no] coercion to get public school students into religious classrooms. . . .
>
> [The] First Amendment . . . does not say that in every and all respects there shall be a separation of Church and State. [Otherwise] the state and religion would be aliens to each other—hostile, suspicious, and even unfriendly. . . . [Prayers] in our legislative halls; the appeals to the Almighty in the messages of the Chief Executive; the proclamations making Thanksgiving Day a holiday; "so help me God" in our courtroom oaths—these and all other references to the Almighty that run through our laws, our public rituals, our ceremonies would be flouting the First Amendment. A fastidious atheist or agnostic could even object to the supplication with which the Court opens each session: "God save the

United States and this Honorable Court." We would have to press the concept of separation of Church and State to these extremes to condemn the present law on constitutional grounds. [We] are a religious people whose institutions pre-suppose a Supreme Being. [We] sponsor an attitude on the part of government that shows no partiality to any one group. . . . When the state encourages reli-gious instruction or cooperates with religious authorities by adjusting the sched-ule of public events to sectarian needs, [it] respects the religious nature of our people and accommodates the public service to their spiritual needs. To hold that it may not would be to find in the Constitution a requirement that the gov-ernment show a callous indifference to religious groups. That would [prefer] those who believe in no religion over those who do believe. [In *McCollum*,] the classrooms were used for religious instruction and the force of the public school was used to promote that instruction. [Here], the public schools do no more than accommodate their schedules to a program of outside religious instruction.

Justice Black dissented because he saw the case as virtually identical to *McCollum*. Justice Jackson, joined by Justice Frankfurter, dissented on the ground that

[the] program is founded upon a use of the State's power of coercion. . . . [The] State compel[s] each student to yield a large part of his time for public secular education and [then "releases" some of it] to him on condition that he devote it to sectarian religious purposes. . . .

A decade after the released-time cases, the Court confronted the issue of officially sponsored prayer in public schools.

Engel v. Vitale, 370 U.S. 421 (1962). New York recommended, but did not require, that students recite the following nondenominational prayer each morning: "Almighty God, we acknowledge our dependence upon Thee, and beg Thy blessings upon us, our parents, our teachers and our Country." Wherever implemented, objectors were excused from the daily recital. The Court struck it down; the prayer was "a religious activity" and

it is no part of the business of government to compose official prayers [for] the people to recite as part of a religious program carried on by government. [When] the power, prestige and financial support of government is placed be-hind a particular religious belief, the indirect coercive pressure upon religious minorities to conform to the prevailing officially approved religion is plain.

Abington School District v. Schempp, 374 U.S. 203 (1963). The Court invalidated a state requirement that ten verses of the Bible be read aloud at the beginning of each public school day. The law had a religious purpose and a distinctly religious effect: the Bible readings were "religious exercises, required by the State in violation of the command [that] the Government maintain strict neutrality." As in *Engel*, Justice Stewart was the sole dissenter.

Wallace v. Jaffree, 472 U.S. 38 (1985). Alabama authorized its public schools to devote one minute at the start of each day "for meditation or vol-untary prayer." Because Alabama's motive in enacting the law was "to return voluntary prayer" to the public schools, the Court voided the law. The evidence of this motive was that the law had amended an existing statute that authorized a one-minute period of silence "for meditation," and a legislator's forthright declaration that his purpose in sponsoring the amendment was to return prayer to schools. The permissible purpose of "protecting every student's right to engage in voluntary [silent] prayer" was fully secured by the preexisting law; the amendment served only to make the symbolic point that the state was endorsing and promoting silent prayer "as a favored practice. Such an endorsement is not consistent with the established principle that the Government must pursue a course of complete neutrality toward religion." Justice O'Connor concurred, opining that the critical issue was whether the "purpose and likely effect" of the law was "to endorse and sponsor voluntary prayer in the public schools." She thought that there was no endorsement of religion if a state were to authorize its schools merely to observe a moment of silence because an unadorned moment of silence is unaccompanied by any government suggestion that the silence be occupied by prayer.

Several threads wind through these cases. Two opposing strands are strict neutrality and accommodation of voluntary religious observance. Which of the following principles best define the boundaries of neutrality or the limits of accommodation: coercion, endorsement, or absolute neutrality? Which seems to best explain the cases? Which seems the most consistent with the purpose of the establishment clause? Does your selection depend on how you view the purposes of the establishment clause?

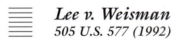

Lee v. Weisman
505 U.S. 577 (1992)

JUSTICE KENNEDY delivered the opinion of the Court.

School principals in the [Providence, R.I.,] public school system [are] permitted to invite members of the clergy to offer invocation and benediction prayers as part of the formal graduation ceremonies for middle schools and for high schools. The question . . . is whether including [such] prayers as part of the official school graduation ceremony is consistent with the Religion Clauses of the First Amendment. . . .

Deborah Weisman graduated from Nathan Bishop Middle School, a public school in Providence, at a formal ceremony in June 1989. She was about 14 years old. [Over the objections of] Deborah's father, Daniel Weisman, [the] school principal [invited] a rabbi to deliver prayers at the graduation exercises for Deborah's class. [The rabbi's invocation was] as follows: "God of the Free, Hope of the Brave: For the legacy of America where diversity is celebrated and the rights of minorities are protected, we thank You. May these young men and women grow up to enrich it. For the liberty of America, we thank You. May these new graduates grow up to guard it. For the political process of America in which all its citizens may participate, for its court system where all may seek justice we thank You. May those we honor this morning always turn to it in trust. For the destiny of America we thank You. May the graduates of Nathan Bishop Middle School so live that they might help to share it. May our aspirations for our country and for these young people, who are our hope for the future, be richly fulfilled. Amen." [The rabbi's benediction was as follows:] "O God, we are grateful to You for having endowed us with the capacity for learning which we have celebrated on this joyous commencement. Happy families give thanks for seeing their children achieve an important milestone. Send Your blessings upon the teachers and administrators who helped prepare them. The graduates now need strength and guidance for the future, help them to understand that we are not complete with academic knowledge alone. We must each strive to fulfill what You require of us all: To do justly, to love mercy, to walk humbly. We give thanks to You, Lord, for keeping us alive, sustaining us and allowing us to reach this special, happy occasion. Amen."

[A federal district court ruled that the prayers violated the establishment clause. The Court of Appeals affirmed. We] now affirm.

These dominant facts mark and control the confines of our decision: State officials direct the performance of a formal religious exercise at promotional and graduation ceremonies for secondary schools. Even for those students who object to the religious exercise, their attendance and participation in the state-sponsored religious activity are in a fair and real sense obligatory, though the school district does not require attendance as a condition for receipt of the diploma. . . . [It] is beyond dispute that, at a minimum, the Constitution guarantees that government may not coerce anyone to support or participate in religion or its exercise. [The] State's involvement in the school prayers challenged today violates these central principles.

[The] degree of school involvement here made it clear that the graduation prayers bore the imprint of the State and thus put school-age children who objected in an untenable position. [There] are heightened concerns with protecting freedom of conscience from subtle coercive pressure in the elementary and secondary public schools. [Prayer] exercises in public schools carry a particular risk of indirect coercion. [The] undeniable fact is that the school district's supervision and control of a high school graduation ceremony places public pressure, as well as peer pressure, on attending students to stand as a group or, at least, maintain respectful silence during the Invocation and Benediction. This pressure, though subtle and indirect, can be as real as any overt compulsion. Of course, in our culture, standing or remaining silent can signify adherence to a view or simple respect for the views of others. And no doubt some persons who have no desire to join a prayer have little objection to standing as a sign of respect for those who do. But for the dissenter of high school age, who has a reasonable perception that she is being forced by the State to pray in a manner her conscience will not allow, the injury is no less real. . . . It is of little comfort to a dissenter, then, to be told that for her the act of standing or remaining in silence signifies mere respect, rather than participation. What matters is that, given our social conventions, a reasonable dissenter in this milieu could believe that the group exercise signified her own participation or approval of it.

Finding no violation under these circumstances would place objectors in the dilemma of participating, with all that implies, or protesting. We do not address whether that choice is acceptable if the affected citizens are mature adults, but we think the State may not, consistent with the Establishment Clause, place primary and secondary school children in this position. . . .

[The argument] that the option of not attending the graduation excuses any inducement or coercion in the ceremony itself [lacks] persuasion. [Everyone] knows that in our society and in our culture high school graduation is one of life's most significant occasions. . . . Attendance may not be required by official decree, yet it is apparent that a student is not free to absent herself from the graduation exercise in any real sense of the term "voluntary." . . .

[No] holding by this Court suggests that a school can persuade or compel a student to participate in a religious exercise. That is being done here, and it is forbidden by the Establishment Clause. [Affirmed.]

JUSTICE BLACKMUN, joined by JUSTICES STEVENS and O'CONNOR, concurring.

[Although] proof of government coercion is not necessary to prove an Establishment Clause violation, it is sufficient. Government pressure to participate in a religious activity is an obvious indication that the government is endorsing or promoting religion. But it is not enough that the government restrain from compelling religious practices: it must not engage in them either. . . . When the government puts its imprimatur on a particular religion, it conveys a message of exclusion to all those who do not adhere to the favored beliefs.

JUSTICE SOUTER, joined by JUSTICES STEVENS and O'CONNOR, concurring.

[That] government must remain neutral in matters of religion does not foreclose it from ever taking religion into account. The State may "accommodate" the free exercise of religion by relieving people from generally applicable rules that interfere with their religious callings. [Such] accommodation does not necessarily signify an official endorsement of religious observance over disbelief. [Whatever] else may define the scope of accommodation permissible under the Establishment Clause, one requirement is clear: accommodation must lift a discernible burden on the free exercise of religion. . . .

Petitioners [argue] that graduation prayers are no different from presidential religious proclamations and similar official "acknowledgments" of religion in public life. But religious invocations in Thanksgiving Day addresses and the like, rarely noticed, ignored without effort, conveyed over an impersonal medium, and directed at no one in particular, inhabit a pallid zone worlds apart from official prayers delivered to a captive audience of public school students and their families. [When] public school officials . . . convey an endorsement of religion to their students, they strike near the core of the Establishment Clause. However "ceremonial" their messages may be, they are flatly unconstitutional.

JUSTICE SCALIA, joined by CHIEF JUSTICE REHNQUIST and JUSTICES WHITE and THOMAS, dissenting.

[The] Establishment Clause must be construed in light of the "government policies of accommodation, acknowledgment, and support for religion [that] are an accepted part of our political and cultural heritage." [Its meaning] "is to be determined by reference to historical practices and understandings." [Any test that] "would invalidate longstanding traditions cannot be a proper reading of the Clause." [In] holding that the Establishment Clause prohibits invocations and benedictions at public-school graduation ceremonies, the Court—with nary a mention that it is doing so—lays waste a tradition that is as old as public-school graduation ceremonies themselves, and that is a component of an even more longstanding American tradition of nonsectarian prayer to God at public celebrations generally. As its instrument of destruction, the bulldozer of its social engineering, the Court invents a boundless, and boundlessly manipulable, test of psychological [coercion]. . . .

Justice Holmes's aphorism that "a page of history is worth a volume of logic" applies with particular force to our Establishment Clause jurisprudence. [From] our Nation's origin, prayer has been a prominent part of governmental ceremonies and proclamations. And this Court's own sessions have opened with the invocation "God save the United States and this Honorable Court" since the days of Chief Justice Marshall.

In addition to this general tradition of prayer at public ceremonies, there exists a more specific tradition of invocations and benedictions at public-school graduation exercises. [The] Court presumably would separate graduation invocations and benedictions from other instances of public "preservation and transmission of religious beliefs" on the ground that they involve "psychological coercion." . . . [The] Court has gone beyond the realm where judges know what they are doing. The Court's argument that state officials have "coerced" students to take part in the invocation and benediction at graduation ceremonies is, not to put too fine a point on it, incoherent. [The] Court's notion that a student who simply sits in "respectful silence" during the invocation and benediction (when all others are standing) has somehow joined—or would somehow be perceived as having joined—in the prayers is nothing short of ludicrous. We indeed live in a vulgar age. But surely "our social conventions" have not coarsened to the point that anyone who does not stand on his chair and shout obscenities can reasonably be deemed to have assented to everything said in his presence. Since the Court does not dispute that students exposed to prayer at graduation ceremonies retain (despite "subtle coercive pressures") the free will to sit, there is absolutely no basis for the Court's decision. . . .

[I] find it odd that the Court concludes that high school graduates may not be subjected to this supposed psychological coercion, yet refrains from addressing whether "mature adults" may. I had thought that the reason graduation from high school is regarded as so significant an event is that it is generally associated with transition from adolescence to young adulthood. Many graduating seniors . . . are old enough to vote. Why, then, does the Court treat them as though they were first-graders? Will we soon have a jurisprudence that distinguishes between mature and immature adults? . . .

The deeper flaw in the Court's opinion does not lie in its wrong answer to the question whether there was state-induced "peer-pressure" coercion; it lies, rather, in the Court's making violation of the Establishment Clause hinge on such a precious question. The coercion that was a hallmark of historical establishments of religion was coercion of religious orthodoxy and of financial support by force of law and threat of penalty. Typically, attendance at the state church was required; only clergy of the official church could lawfully perform sacraments; and dissenters, if tolerated, faced an array of civil disabilities. . . . I see no warrant for expanding the concept of coercion beyond acts backed by threat of penalty—a brand of coercion that, happily, is readily discernible to those of us who have made a career of reading the disciples of Blackstone rather than of Freud. . . .

Our religion-clause jurisprudence has become bedeviled (so to speak) by reliance on formulaic abstractions that are not derived from, but positively conflict with, our long-accepted constitutional traditions. Foremost among these has been the so-called *Lemon* test. [The] Court today demonstrates the irrelevance of *Lemon* by essentially ignoring it, and the interment of that case may be the one happy byproduct of the Court's otherwise lamentable decision. Unfortunately, however, the Court has replaced *Lemon* with its psycho-coercion test, which suffers the double disability of having no roots whatever in our people's historic practice, and being as infinitely expandable as the reasons for psychotherapy itself. . . .

NOTES

1. Coercion, Endorsement, and *Lemon*. The Court did not apply the *Lemon* test, but was Justice Scalia's interment of *Lemon* premature? There was no majority for the proposition that coercion (even the "psycho-coercion" of Justice Kennedy's opinion) is a *necessary* element of an establishment clause violation. Did the majority coalesce on the principle that endorsement alone is the indicator of an establishment clause violation? *Lemon* was not *expressly* repudiated by Lee v. Weisman, and in *Agostini*, decided five years later, the Court analyzed and restated the meaning of *Lemon*. Under what circumstances will *Lemon* be applied now?

2. Student-Led Prayer. To what extent are student-led prayers that occur in a school context the private acts of the students, and thus beyond the scope of the establishment clause? In Santa Fe Independent School District v. Doe, 530 U.S. 290 (2000), the Court extended *Weisman* to strike down as facially invalid a school district policy, never implemented, that permitted students to vote on whether to have a student speaker "solemnize" high school football games and, if so, to select the student speaker. The Court, 6-3, regarded the policy as designed to perpetuate prayer at the opening of football games, thought the student vote and the football game forum made the speech officially sanctioned rather than private, and concluded that the policy would both constitute endorsement of religion and coercion of those students (such as band members) required to attend football games. Chief Justice Rehnquist, joined by Justices Scalia and Thomas, dissented, arguing that it was premature to rule on the facial validity of the policy.

Queries: Suppose the high school football team, as a whole and without prior knowledge or encouragement of school officials, kneeled in prayer on the sideline before the opening kickoff? Would it make any constitutional difference if the team captain told the coach before the prayer that the team intended to pray in public? What if the coach knelt in prayer too?

3. Religious Beliefs in the Public School Curriculum. Issues similar to voluntary prayer are raised by the injection of religious beliefs in the curriculum. Because the Kentucky legislature concluded that "the Ten Commandments have had a significant secular impact on the development of secular [law in] the Western World," Kentucky required that they be posted in every public school classroom. In Stone v. Graham, 449 U.S. 39 (1980), the Court summarily invalidated the law on the ground that it lacked any actual secular purpose, despite the Kentucky legislature's finding. The Court viewed the Ten Commandments as a "sacred text" and thus treated the purpose of the law as "plainly religious." In Epperson v. Arkansas, 393 U.S. 97 (1968), the Court struck down an Arkansas law that prohibited its public schools and universities from teaching "the theory that man evolved from other species of life." The Court reasoned that the law's purpose and effect was to conform "a particular segment" of the curriculum to "the religious views of some of its citizens." Although states have an "undoubted right to prescribe the curriculum for the public schools," they may not tailor the curriculum to the "fundamentalist sectarian conviction [that] was and is the law's reason for existence."

The issue of regulating the teaching of evolution in public schools returned to the Court in the following case, noteworthy for the controversy it produced concerning the propriety, utility, and method of applying the "purpose" prong of *Lemon*.

Edwards v. Aguillard
482 U.S. 578 (1987)

JUSTICE BRENNAN delivered the opinion of the Court.

The question [is] whether Louisiana's "Balanced Treatment for Creation-Science and Evolution-Science in Public School Instruction" Act [is] facially invalid as violative of the Establishment Clause. The [Act] forbids the teaching of the theory of evolution in public schools unless accompanied by instruction in "creation science." No school is required to teach evolution or creation science. If either is taught, however, the other must also be taught.

[The] Court has been particularly vigilant in monitoring compliance with the Establishment Clause in elementary and secondary schools. . . . [We evaluate] the Act under the *Lemon* test. [Appellants] have identified no clear secular purpose for the Louisiana Act. True, the Act's stated purpose is to protect academic freedom, [and even] if "academic freedom" [means] "teaching all of the evidence" with respect to the origin of human beings, the Act does not further this purpose. . . . While the Court is normally deferential to a State's articulation of a secular purpose, [the] statement of such purpose [must] be sincere and not a sham. [It is] clear that requiring schools to teach creation science with evolution does not advance academic freedom. The Act does not grant teachers a flexibility that they did not already possess. [Furthermore, the Act has a] discriminatory preference for the teaching of creation science and against the teaching of evolution. While requiring that curriculum guides be developed for creation science, the Act says nothing of comparable guides for evolution. . . . The Act forbids school boards to discriminate against anyone who "chooses to be a creation-scientist" or to teach "creationism," but fails to protect those who choose to teach evolution or any other non-creation science theory. . . . [The] Act does not serve to protect academic freedom, but has the distinctly different purpose of discrediting "evolution by counterbalancing its teaching at every turn with the teaching of creationism."

[We] need not be blind [to] the legislature's preeminent religious purpose in enacting this statute. There is a historic and contemporaneous link between the teachings of certain religious denominations and the teaching of evolution. It was this link that concerned the Court in [*Epperson*, where] the Court could not ignore that "the statute was a product of the upsurge of 'fundamentalist' religious fervor" that has long viewed this particular scientific theory as contradicting the literal interpretation of the Bible. [There] can be no legitimate state interest in protecting particular religions from scientific views "distasteful to them." [These] same historic and contemporaneous antagonisms between the teachings of certain religious denominations and the teaching of evolution are present [here]. The preeminent purpose of the Louisiana Legislature was clearly to advance the religious viewpoint that a supernatural being created humankind. [The] term "creation science" [embodies] the religious belief that a supernatural creator was responsible for the creation of humankind. . . . The legislation . . . sought to alter the science curriculum to reflect endorsement of a religious view that is antagonistic to the theory of evolution. [The] purpose of the Creationism Act was to restructure the science curriculum to conform with a particular religious viewpoint.

[We] do not imply that a legislature could never require that scientific critiques of prevailing scientific theories be taught. [Teaching] a variety of scientific theories about the origins of humankind to schoolchildren might be validly done with the clear secular intent of enhancing the effectiveness of science instruction. But because the primary purpose of the . . . Act is to endorse a particular religious doctrine, the Act furthers religion in violation of the Establishment Clause.

JUSTICE POWELL, joined by JUSTICE O'CONNOR, concurring.

[A] religious purpose alone is not enough to invalidate an act. [The] religious purpose must predominate.

JUSTICE SCALIA, joined by CHIEF JUSTICE REHNQUIST, dissenting.

Even if I agreed with the questionable premise that legislation can be invalidated under the Establishment Clause on the basis of its motivation alone, without regard to its effects, I would still find no justification for today's decision.

[For] the purpose of the *Lemon* test ["legislative purpose"] means the "actual" motives of those responsible for the challenged action. [Thus], if those legislators who supported the [Act] in fact acted with a "sincere" secular purpose, the Act survives the first component of the *Lemon* test, regardless of whether that purpose is likely to be achieved by the provisions they enacted. Our cases have also confirmed that when the *Lemon* Court referred to "a secular purpose," it meant "*a* secular purpose." [Thus], invalidation of the [Act] is defensible only if the record indicates that the Louisiana Legislature had no secular purpose.

[There] is ample evidence that the majority is wrong in holding that the [Act] is without secular purpose. [The legislative testimony was to the effect that] creation science is educationally valuable and strictly scientific, [but is] being censored from or misrepresented in the public schools, [with the effect that students are deprived] of knowledge of one of the two scientific explanations for the origin of life and [led] to believe that evolution is proven fact. [We] have no way of knowing, of course, how many legislators believed [this] testimony, [but] in the absence of evidence to the contrary, we have to assume that many of them did. Given that assumption, the Court today plainly errs in holding that the Louisiana Legislature passed the [Act] for exclusively religious purposes.

[Even] if the legislative history were silent or ambiguous about the existence of a secular purpose—and here it is not—the statute should survive *Lemon*'s purpose test. But [the] Louisiana Legislature explicitly set forth its secular purpose ("protecting academic freedom") in the very text of the Act. . . . The legislature wanted to ensure that students would be free to decide for themselves how life began, based upon a fair and balanced presentation of the scientific evidence. [If] one adopts the obviously intended meaning of the statutory term "academic freedom," there is no basis whatever for concluding that the purpose they express is a "sham." To the contrary, the Act . . . treats the teaching of [evolution and] creation the same way. It does not mandate instruction in creation science; forbids teachers to present creation science "as proven scientific fact"; and bans the teaching of creation science unless the theory is (to use the Court's terminology) "discredit[ed] '[at] every turn'" with the teaching of evolution. It surpasses understanding how the Court can see in this a purpose "to restructure the science curriculum to conform with a particular religious viewpoint," "to provide a persuasive advantage to a particular religious doctrine," "to promote the theory of creation science which embodies a particular religious tenet," and "to endorse a particular religious doctrine." . . .

I have to this point assumed the validity of the *Lemon* "purpose" test, [but it] is "a constitutional theory [that] has no basis in the history of the amendment it seeks to interpret, is difficult to apply and yields unprincipled results." [We] have said essentially the following: Government may not act with the purpose of advancing religion, except when forced to do so by the Free Exercise Clause (which is now and then); or when eliminating existing governmental hostility to religion (which exists sometimes); or even when merely accommodating governmentally uninhibited religious practices, except that at some point (it is unclear where) intentional accommodation results in the fostering of religion, which is of course unconstitutional.

But the difficulty of knowing what vitiating purpose one is looking for is as nothing compared with the difficulty of knowing how or where to find it. [Discerning] the subjective motivation of those enacting [a] statute [is] almost always an impossible task. The number of possible motivations, to begin with, is not binary, or indeed even finite. In the present case, for example, a particular legislator need not have voted for the Act either because he wanted to foster religion or because he wanted to improve education. He may have thought the bill would provide jobs for his district, or may have wanted to make amends with a faction of his party he had alienated on another vote, or he may have been a close friend of the bill's sponsor, or he may have been repaying a favor he owed the Majority Leader, or he may have hoped the Governor would appreciate his vote and make a fundraising appearance for him, or he may have been pressured to vote for a bill he disliked by a wealthy contributor or by a flood of constituent mail, or he may have been seeking favorable publicity, or he may have been reluctant to hurt the feelings of a loyal staff member who worked on the bill, or he may have been settling an old score with a legislator who opposed the bill, or he may have been mad at his wife who opposed the bill, or he may have been intoxicated and utterly unmotivated when the vote was called, or he may have accidentally voted "yes" instead of "no," or, of course, he may have had (and very likely did have) a combination of some of the above and many other motivations. To look for the sole purpose of even a single legislator is probably to look for something that does not exist. . . .

[We] must still confront the question (yet to be addressed in any of our cases) how many of them must have the invalidating intent. If a state senate approves a bill by vote of 26 to 25, and only one of the 26 intended solely to advance religion, is the law unconstitutional? What if 13 of the 26 had that intent? What if 3 of the 26 had the impermissible intent, but 3 of the 25 voting against the bill were motivated by religious hostility or were simply attempting to "balance" the votes of their impermissibly motivated colleagues? Or is it possible that the intent of the bill's sponsor is alone enough to invalidate it—on a theory, perhaps, that even though everyone else's intent was pure, what they produced was the fruit of a forbidden tree? Because there are no good answers to these questions, this Court has recognized from Chief Justice

Marshall to Chief Justice Warren, that determining the subjective intent of legislators is a perilous enterprise.

Given the many hazards involved in assessing the subjective intent of governmental decision makers, the first prong of *Lemon* is defensible [only] if the text of the Establishment Clause demands it. That is surely not the case. . . . [In] the past we have attempted to justify our embarrassing Establishment Clause jurisprudence on the ground that it "sacrifices clarity and predictability for flexibility," [a phrase that has been] aptly characterized as "a euphemism [for] the absence of any principled rationale." [Choper, The Religion Clauses of the First Amendment: Reconciling the Conflict, 41 U. Pitt. L. Rev. 673 (1980).] I think it time that we sacrifice some "flexibility" for "clarity and predictability." Abandoning *Lemon*'s purpose test—a test which exacerbates the tension between the Free Exercise and Establishment Clauses, has no basis in the language or history of the Amendment, and, as today's decision shows, has wonderfully flexible consequences—would be a good place to start.

NOTE

Intelligent Design. The intelligent design theory holds that some features of the cosmos and life are more explicable as a product of deliberate, intelligent cause rather than natural selection. A popular exposition of intelligent design is Davis and Kenyon, Of Pandas and People (1989), later reissued by Dembski and Wells as The Design of Life (2007). The Dover, Pennsylvania, public schools adopted a policy that ninth-grade biology students "be made aware of gaps/problems in Darwin's theory and of other theories of evolution including, but not limited to, intelligent design." To that end, students were told the following:

> The Pennsylvania Academic Standards require students to learn about Darwin's Theory of Evolution and eventually to take a standardized test of which evolution is a part. Because Darwin's Theory is a theory, it continues to be tested as new evidence is discovered. The Theory is not a fact. Gaps in the Theory exist for which there is no evidence. A theory is defined as a well-tested explanation that unifies a broad range of observations. Intelligent Design is an explanation of the origin of life that differs from Darwin's view. The reference book, *Of Pandas and People*, is available for students who might be interested in gaining an understanding of what Intelligent Design actually involves.

In Kitzmiller v. Dover Area School District, 400 F. Supp. 2d 707 (M.D. Pa. 2005), the court ruled that the purpose for adopting the policy was to promote religion, and that it amounted to an endorsement by the public schools of a religious view on the origins of life.

Queries: Suppose that to save money, the Dover schools stopped teaching evolution. Valid? What if the Dover schools abandoned biology instruction? Could Pennsylvania validly cease testing its students on evolution?

≡≡≡ ### Good News Club v. Milford Central School
≡≡≡ *533 U.S. 98 (2001)*

JUSTICE THOMAS delivered the opinion of the Court.

[The Milford Central School created a limited public forum when it opened its facilities to after-hours uses encompassing education, learning, the arts, and social, civic, recreational, and entertainment uses pertaining to community welfare, but not for religious purposes. The school denied access to the Good News Club, a private Christian organization for children ages 6 to 12, because the proposed use—Bible lessons, prayer, memorization of Bible passages, and singing of religious songs—was considered to be religious worship. The Court concluded that the school's denial of the Club's access to the forum was viewpoint-based, but then considered whether the viewpoint discrimination was] justified by Milford's concern that permitting the Club's activities would violate the Establishment Clause. We conclude that . . . no Establishment Clause concern justifies the [free speech] violation. . . .

According to Milford, children will perceive that the school is endorsing the Club and will feel coercive pressure to participate, because the Club's activities take place on school grounds, even though they occur during nonschool hours. This argument is unpersuasive.

First, . . . "a significant factor in upholding governmental programs in the face of Establishment Clause attack is their *neutrality* toward religion." [But] the "guarantee of neutrality is respected, not offended, when the government, following neutral criteria and evenhanded policies, extends benefits to recipients whose ideologies and viewpoints, including religious ones, are broad and diverse." The Good News Club seeks nothing more than to be treated neutrally and given access to speak about the same topics as are other groups.

Second, to the extent we consider whether the community would feel coercive pressure to engage in the Club's activities, the relevant community would be the parents, not the elementary school children. It is the parents who choose whether their children will attend the Good News Club meetings. Because the children cannot attend without their parents' permission, they cannot be coerced into engaging in the Good News Club's religious activities. Milford does not suggest that the parents of elementary school children would be confused about whether the school was endorsing religion. Nor do we believe that such an argument could be reasonably advanced.

Third, whatever significance we may have assigned in the Establishment Clause context to the suggestion that elementary school children are more impressionable than adults, we have never extended our Establishment Clause jurisprudence to foreclose private religious conduct during nonschool hours merely because it takes place on school premises where elementary school children may be present. . . . Here, where the school facilities are being used for a nonschool function and there is no government sponsorship of the Club's activities, [*Weisman*] is inapposite. . . .

Fourth, [there is no likelihood "that small children would perceive endorsement here" because the meetings were not held] in an elementary school classroom, [the] instructors are not schoolteachers, [and] the children in the group are not all the same age as in the normal classroom setting; their ages range from 6 to 12. . . . Finally, even if we were to inquire into the minds of schoolchildren in this case, we cannot say the danger that children would misperceive the endorsement of religion is any greater than the danger that they would perceive a hostility toward the religious viewpoint if the Club were excluded from the public forum. . . . We cannot operate [under] the assumption that any risk that small children would perceive endorsement should counsel in favor of excluding the Club's religious activity. We decline to employ Establishment Clause jurisprudence using a modified heckler's veto, in which a group's religious activity can be proscribed on the basis of what the youngest members of the audience might misperceive.

b. Other Government Adoption of Religious Symbols

Outside the public schools, the Court has been more deferential toward the government's adoption of religious symbols and messages as its own. In this area, the Court's focus is on whether the government has acted impermissibly to endorse religion (or hostility to religion) or whether it has merely accommodated religion in a manner that lacks endorsement. Moreover, it is not clear whether the Court's endorsement test is a device to assess the effects prong of *Lemon*, or a separate test.

In McGowan v. Maryland, 366 U.S. 420 (1961), the Court upheld Maryland's Sunday closing law against an establishment clause challenge. Notwithstanding the original religious motivations of the law, the Court concluded that

> as presently written and administered, most [such laws] are of a secular [character. They] provide a uniform day of rest for all citizens; the fact that this day is Sunday [does] not bar the State from achieving [this] secular [goal]. Sunday is a day apart from all others. The cause is irrelevant; the fact exists.

Two decades later the Court confronted the Nebraska legislature's practice of opening each daily session with a prayer by a Presbyterian chaplain employed by the state. In Marsh v. Chambers, 463 U.S. 783 (1983), the Court upheld the practice, relying mostly on a long history of analogous practices to justify the result: "In light of the unambiguous and unbroken history of more than 200 years, there can be no doubt that the practice of opening legislative sessions with a prayer has become part of the fabric of our society. [It] is simply a tolerable acknowledgement of beliefs widely held among the people of this country."

Justice Brennan, joined by Justice Marshall, dissented, charging that

> [the] prayer . . . It requires the State to commit itself [on] theological issues. [And] it injects religion into the political sphere by creating the potential that

[selection of a chaplain or] a particular prayer, or even reconsideration of the practice itself, will provoke a political battle along religious lines.

Justice Brennan concluded that the prayer failed all three prongs of *Lemon*. Justice Stevens also dissented, arguing that "the designation of a member of one religious faith to serve as the sole official chaplain of a state legislature for [sixteen] years constitutes the preference of one faith over another."

Lynch v. Donnelly
465 U.S. 668 (1984)

CHIEF JUSTICE BURGER delivered the opinion of the Court.

We granted certiorari to decide whether the Establishment Clause [prohibits] a municipality from including a crèche, or Nativity scene, in its annual Christmas display. Each year, . . . the city of Pawtucket, R.I., erects a Christmas display as part of its observance of the Christmas holiday season. The display is situated in a park owned by a nonprofit organization and located in the heart of the shopping district. The display is essentially like those to be found in hundreds of towns or cities across the Nation—often on public grounds—during the Christmas season. The Pawtucket display comprises many of the figures and decorations traditionally associated with Christmas, including, among other things, a Santa Claus house, reindeer pulling Santa's sleigh, candy-striped poles, a Christmas tree, carolers, cutout figures representing such characters as a clown, an elephant, and a teddy bear, hundreds of colored lights, a large banner that reads "SEASONS GREETINGS," and the crèche at issue here. All components of this display are owned by the city. The crèche, which has been included in the display for 40 or more years, consists of the traditional figures, including the Infant Jesus, Mary and Joseph, angels, shepherds, kings, and animals, all ranging in height from 5" to 5'. [A federal district court held that the crèche violated the establishment clause.] A divided panel of the Court of Appeals [affirmed] and we reverse.

[The] concept of a "wall" of separation [between church and state] is a useful figure of speech[, but] the metaphor itself is not a wholly accurate description of the practical aspects of the relationship that in fact exists between church and state. [The] Constitution [does not] require complete separation of church and state; it affirmatively mandates accommodation, not merely tolerance, of all religions, and forbids hostility toward any. [The] Court's interpretation of the Establishment Clause has comported with what history reveals was the contemporaneous understanding of its guarantees. [There] is an unbroken history of official acknowledgment by all three branches of government of the role of religion in American life from at least 1789. . . . [In] each case, the inquiry calls for line-drawing; no fixed, per se rule can be framed. [The Establishment] Clause erects a "blurred, indistinct, and variable barrier depending on all the circumstances of a particular relationship." *Lemon*. [While in] the line-drawing process we have often found it useful to [employ the *Lemon* test], we have repeatedly emphasized our unwillingness to be confined to any single test or criterion in this sensitive area.

[Here], the focus of our inquiry must be on the crèche in the context of the Christmas season. [When so viewed], there is insufficient evidence to establish that the inclusion of the crèche is a purposeful or surreptitious effort to express some kind of subtle governmental advocacy of a particular religious message. In a pluralistic society a variety of motives and purposes are implicated. The city [has] taken note of a significant historical religious event long celebrated in the Western World. The crèche [depicts] the historical origins of this traditional event long recognized as a National Holiday. [The] display is sponsored by the city to celebrate the Holiday and to depict the origins of that Holiday. These are legitimate secular purposes.

The District Court found that the primary effect of including the crèche is to confer a substantial and impermissible benefit on religion in general and on the Christian faith in particular. [We] are unable to discern a greater aid to religion deriving from inclusion of the crèche than from [the] benefits and endorsements previously held not violative of the Establishment Clause [in *Allen, Everson, Walz, McGowan, Zorach*, and *Marsh*]. [Even assuming] that the display advances religion [by displaying a Christian symbol], our precedents plainly contemplate that on occasion some advancement of religion will result from governmental action. [Here], whatever benefit there is to one faith or religion or to all religions, is indirect, remote, and incidental; display of the crèche is no more an advancement or endorsement of religion than the Congressional and Executive recognition of the origins of the Holiday itself as "Christ's Mass," or the exhibition of literally hundreds of religious paintings in governmentally supported museums. [We] are satisfied that the city has a secular purpose for including the crèche, that the city has not impermissibly advanced religion, and that including the crèche does not create excessive entanglement between religion and government. . . .

JUSTICE O'CONNOR, concurring.

I concur in the opinion of the Court. I write separately to suggest a clarification of our Establishment Clause doctrine.

[The] Establishment Clause prohibits government from making adherence to a religion relevant in any way to a person's standing in the political community. Government can run afoul of that prohibition in two principal ways. One is excessive entanglement with religious institutions, which may interfere with the independence of the institutions, give the institutions access to government or governmental powers not fully shared by non-adherents of the religion, and foster the creation of political constituencies defined along religious lines. The second and more direct infringement is government endorsement or disapproval of religion. Endorsement sends a message to non-adherents that they are outsiders, not full members of the political community, and an accompanying message to adherents that they are insiders, favored members of the political community. Disapproval sends the opposite message.

[The] central issue [is] whether Pawtucket has endorsed Christianity by its display of the crèche. To answer that question, we must examine both what Pawtucket intended to communicate in displaying the crèche and what message the city's display actually conveyed. The purpose and effect prongs of the *Lemon* test represent these two aspects of the meaning of the city's action. The meaning of a statement to its audience depends both on the intention of the speaker and on the "objective" meaning of the statement in the community. [The] purpose prong of the *Lemon* test asks whether government's actual purpose is to endorse or disapprove of religion. The effect prong asks whether, irrespective of government's actual purpose, the practice under review in fact conveys a message of endorsement or disapproval. An affirmative answer to either question should render the challenged practice invalid.

[Pawtucket] did not intend to convey any message of endorsement of Christianity or disapproval of non-Christian religions. The evident purpose of including the crèche in the larger display was not promotion of the religious content of the crèche but celebration of the public holiday through its traditional symbols. Celebration of public holidays, which have cultural significance even if they also have religious aspects, is a legitimate secular purpose.

[The] effect prong of the *Lemon* test [bars government practices that] have the effect of communicating a message of government endorsement or disapproval of religion. [Only] practices having that effect, whether intentionally or unintentionally, [make] religion relevant, in reality or public perception, to status in the political community. [Pawtucket's] display of its crèche [does] not communicate a message that the government intends to endorse the Christian beliefs represented by the crèche. [The] overall holiday setting changes what viewers may fairly understand to be the purpose of the display—as a typical museum setting, though not neutralizing the religious content of a religious painting, negates any message of endorsement of that content. The display celebrates a public holiday, [which] has very strong secular components and traditions. Government celebration of the holiday, which is extremely common, generally is not understood to endorse the religious content of the holiday, just as government celebration of Thanksgiving is not so understood. The crèche is a traditional symbol of the holiday that is very commonly displayed along with purely secular symbols, as it was in Pawtucket.

These features combine to make the government's display of the crèche in this particular physical setting no more an endorsement of religion than such governmental "acknowledgments" of religion as legislative prayers [*Marsh*], government declaration of Thanksgiving as a public holiday, printing of "In God We Trust" on coins, and opening court sessions with "God save the United States and this honorable court." Those government acknowledgments of religion serve, in the only ways reasonably possible in our culture, the legitimate secular purposes of solemnizing public occasions, expressing confidence in the future, and encouraging the recognition of what is worthy of appreciation in society. For that reason, and because of their history and ubiquity, those practices are not understood as conveying government approval of particular religious beliefs. The display of the crèche likewise [cannot] fairly be understood to convey a message of government endorsement of religion.

JUSTICE BRENNAN, joined by JUSTICES MARSHALL, BLACKMUN, and STEVENS, dissenting.

[Pawtucket's] action amounts to an impermissible governmental endorsement of a particular faith. [The] city's inclusion of the crèche in its Christmas display simply does not reflect a "clearly secular [purpose]." The nativity scene, unlike every other element of the [display], reflects a sectarian exclusivity that the avowed purposes of celebrating the holiday season and promoting retail commerce simply do not encompass. [The] inclusion of a distinctively religious element like the crèche [demonstrates] that a narrower sectarian purpose lay behind the decision to include a nativity scene. [The] "primary effect" of including a nativity scene in the city's display [is] to place the government's imprimatur of approval on the particular religious beliefs exemplified by the crèche. [Pawtucket] has singled out Christianity for special treatment. . . . [The] nativity scene is [the] chief symbol of the characteristically Christian belief that a divine Savior was brought into the world and that the purpose of this miraculous birth was to illuminate a path toward salvation and redemption. [For] those who do not share these beliefs, the symbolic reenactment of the birth of a divine being who has been miraculously incarnated as a man stands as a dramatic reminder of their differences with Christian faith. [To have] one's elected government [deliver this message of religious exclusion] is an insult and an injury that, until today, could not be countenanced by the Establishment Clause.

[The] Court . . . overlooks the fact that the Christmas holiday in our national culture contains both secular and sectarian elements. To say that government may recognize the holiday's traditional, secular elements [does] not mean that government may indiscriminately embrace the distinctively sectarian aspects of the holiday. When government decides to recognize Christmas Day as a public holiday, it does no more than accommodate the calendar of public activities to the plain fact that many Americans will expect on that day to spend time visiting with their families, attending religious services, and perhaps enjoying some respite from preholiday activities. [The] Establishment Clause [is not] offended by such a step. [But when public officials] participate in or appear to endorse the distinctively religious elements of this otherwise secular event, they [place] the prestige, power, and financial support of a civil authority in the service of a particular faith.

The inclusion of a crèche in Pawtucket's otherwise secular celebration of Christmas clearly violates these principles. Unlike such secular figures as Santa Claus, reindeer, and carolers, a nativity scene represents far more than a mere "traditional" symbol of Christmas. [It is] a mystical re-creation of an event that lies at the heart of Christian faith. To suggest [that] such a symbol is merely "traditional" and therefore no different from Santa's house or reindeer is not only offensive to those for whom the crèche has profound significance, but insulting to those who insist [that] the story of Christ is in [not] an unavoidable element of our national "heritage." . . .

[While] I do not presume to offer a comprehensive approach [to the problem of when government may acknowledge religion in public ceremonies and proclamations], at least three principles [may] be identified. [First], although the government may not be compelled to do so by the Free Exercise Clause, it may, consistently with the Establishment Clause, act to accommodate to some extent the opportunities of individuals to practice their religion. . . . [Second], while a particular governmental practice may have derived from religious motivations and retain certain religious connotations, it is nonetheless permissible for the government to pursue the practice when it is continued today solely for secular reasons. Thanksgiving Day [fits] easily within this principle. [Finally], government cannot be completely prohibited from recognizing in its public actions the religious beliefs and practices of the American people as an aspect of our national history and culture. [Such] practices as the designation of "In God We Trust" as our national motto, or the references to God contained in the Pledge of Allegiance to the flag can best be understood [as] a form a "ceremonial deism" protected from Establishment Clause scrutiny chiefly because they have lost through rote repetition any significant religious content.

The crèche fits none of these categories.

NOTES

1. Subsequent Developments. In Allegheny County v. Greater Pittsburgh ACLU, 492 U.S. 573 (1989), the Court used the endorsement test to evaluate government displays of religious imagery. Shifting majorities of a divided Court invalidated the display of a crèche by itself in the central public space of a county courthouse but upheld the display of a menorah accompanied by a Christmas tree and a sign saluting liberty. Four justices (Rehnquist, Scalia, Kennedy, and White) rejected the endorsement test and would have upheld both displays because the displays were not coercive. Three justices (Brennan, Marshall, and Stevens) would have voided both displays. Justices Blackmun and O'Connor, the pivotal votes, found the undiluted message of the crèche to be an endorsement of Christianity. The menorah was permissible because its religious symbolism was diluted by the Christmas tree and the sign saluting liberty to one of "pluralism and freedom to choose one's own beliefs."

2. Private Religious Speech on Government Property. *Capitol Square Review & Advisory Board v. Pinette, 515 U.S. 753 (1995).* An Ohio government agency denied the Ku Klux Klan permission to erect an unattended Latin cross in the public square in front of Ohio's capitol building. After Ohio was enjoined from refusing permission, the Klan displayed a cross with a sign disclaiming government involvement. Although Ohio conceded that the square was a public forum and that its denial was based on the content of the image (thus creating a presumptive free speech violation), it defended the denial by claiming that the establishment clause prohibited the display. For a four-justice plurality, Justice Scalia concluded that while the establishment clause prohibited *government* endorsements of religion, it did not forbid "the government's neutral treatment of *private* religious expression." The fact that "private speech can be mistaken for government speech" when it "is conducted too close to the symbols of government" was not controlling, "at least where, as here, the government has not fostered or encouraged the mistake." In short, "[r]eligious expression cannot violate the Establishment Clause where it (1) is purely private and (2) occurs in a traditional or designated public forum [open] to all on equal terms." Justice O'Connor, joined by Justices Souter and Breyer, concurred, opining that the establishment clause was not violated because a reasonable observer would not think the private message was the government's due to the sign declaring the Klan's authorship of the cross. Justices Stevens and Ginsburg dissented. Justice Stevens thought that private religious displays "in, on, or before a seat of government" were so likely to be seen as government endorsements of the religious sentiments that they were always invalid. Justice Ginsburg thought that the Klan's disclaimer was ineffective because of its small size.

Similar issues were raised in cases involving government denial of access to school facilities to religious users while making those facilities available to others. The cases are partly rooted in the public forum doctrine of free speech, but the Court concluded in each case that the establishment clause permits a public school to make its facilities available for religious purposes. See Widmar v. Vincent, 454 U.S. 263 (1981); Lamb's Chapel v. Center Moriches Union Free School District, 508 U.S. 384 (1993); Rosenberger v. Rector and Visitors of the University of Virginia, 515 U.S. 819 (1995).

In Board of Education of Westside Community Schools v. Mergens, 496 U.S. 226 (1990), the Court upheld the validity of the federal Equal Access Act, which prohibits public schools that receive federal financial aid and make their facilities available to student groups from denying access to those facilities on religious grounds. A four-justice plurality, led by Justice O'Connor, applied *Lemon.* Justices Brennan and Marshall concurred in the judgment, but opined that the establishment clause required the schools to dissociate themselves from the religious speech. Justices Scalia and Kennedy concurred because mandated equal access was neither coercive nor a preferment of any sect.

3. The State of the Doctrine.   Has *Lemon* been repudiated in this area? If so, what is the operative test? Consider the following possibility: Governments may neither coerce nor endorse religious belief or observance, but they are otherwise free to acknowledge the religious beliefs and practices of the people. How much government pressure constitutes coercion? When does acknowledgment turn to endorsement? One of the articles of faith of the separationists is that government involvement with religion will "degrade religion." Is that true with respect to the government practices at issue in *Lynch* and *Allegheny County*?

4. The Pledge of Allegiance: "One Nation, Under God."   Under a public school district regulation authorized by California law, each class day begins with a voluntary recitation of the Pledge of Allegiance. In Newdow v. U.S. Congress, 292 F.3d 597 (9th Cir. 2002), the Court of Appeals concluded that because the Pledge includes the phrase "one nation, under God," its recitation in a public school conveyed an impermissible endorsement of religion and constituted the same sort of coercion that was present in *Weisman*. The dissent viewed the words "under God" as a permissible "ceremonial deism." The decision touched a raw political nerve, as politicians of all persuasions rushed to condemn it. In Elk Grove Unified School District v. Newdow, 542 U.S. 1 (2004), the Supreme Court reversed, concluding that Newdow lacked standing because he was not the custodial parent of the public school pupil involved. Chief Justice Rehnquist concurred in the judgment, but on the merits rather than the standing issue. In short, "Reciting the Pledge, or listening to others recite it, is a patriotic exercise, not a religious one; participants promise fidelity to our flag and our Nation, not to any particular God, faith, or church." Justices O'Connor and Thomas also concurred on the merits. Justice O'Connor applied the endorsement test and concluded that the phrase was a "ceremonial deism." She based this conclusion on four factors: the history and ubiquity of including reference to God in official actions, the absence of any element of worship or prayer, the absence of any reference to a particular religion (it "acknowledges religion in a general way: a simple reference to a generic 'God'"), and its "minimal reference to religion." Justice Thomas thought that, under *Weisman*, the reference to God in the Pledge was unconstitutional, but he rejected *Weisman*. Because there was no "actual legal coercion" there was no prohibited establishment of religion. Justice Thomas repeated his view that "the Establishment Clause is best understood as a federalism provision—it protects state establishments [of religion] from federal interference but does not protect any individual right."

Queries: Which is it—forbidden endorsement and coercive as well, ceremonial deism, or noncoercive and thus a permissible endorsement of religion? What if the Pledge said, "one nation, under Allah"? What if the Pledge said, "one nation, under our respective Deities"? Or "one nation, part of Gaia"? What if the Pledge proclaimed, "one secular nation"?

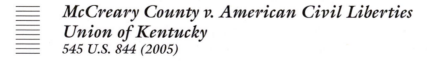

McCreary County v. American Civil Liberties Union of Kentucky
545 U.S. 844 (2005)

[Two Kentucky counties displayed the Ten Commandments in their courthouses. After the ACLU brought suit, claiming a violation of the establishment clause, the counties modified the displays by including "eight other documents in smaller frames, each either having a religious theme or excerpted to highlight a religious element." The expanded display included the Declaration of Independence, the preamble to the Kentucky Constitution, the national motto, several presidential proclamations and letters, and a portion of the Congressional Record. After a trial judge ordered removal of the modified display, the counties responded with a third display: the Ten Commandments, coupled with "framed copies of the Magna Carta, the Declaration of Independence, the Bill of Rights, the lyrics of the Star Spangled Banner, the Mayflower Compact, the National Motto, the Preamble to the Kentucky Constitution, and a picture of Lady Justice. The collection is entitled 'The Foundations of American Law and Government Display' and each document comes with a statement about its historical and legal significance." The counties said that the display was intended "to demonstrate that the Ten Commandments were part of the foundation of American Law and Government" and "to educate the citizens of the county regarding some of the documents that played a significant role in the foundation of our system of law and government." A federal district court found that it lacked a secular purpose, and the Sixth Circuit affirmed. The Supreme Court affirmed.]

JUSTICE SOUTER delivered the opinion of the Court.

. . . [W]e have found government action motivated by an illegitimate purpose only four times since *Lemon*. Though "the secular purpose requirement alone may rarely be determinative . . . , it nevertheless serves an important function." . . . The touchstone for our analysis is the principle that the "First Amendment mandates governmental neutrality between religion and religion, and between religion and nonreligion."

[The] Counties [argue that] "purpose" is unknowable, and its search merely an excuse for courts to act selectively and unpredictably in picking out evidence of subjective intent. . . . But scrutinizing purpose does make practical sense . . . where an understanding of official objective emerges from readily discoverable fact, without any judicial psychoanalysis of a drafter's heart of hearts. . . . *Lemon* said that government action must have "a secular . . . purpose," and . . . although a legislature's stated reasons will generally get deference, the secular purpose required has to be genuine, not a sham, and not merely secondary to a religious objective. [The] Counties . . . argue that purpose . . . should be inferred, if at all, only from the latest news about the last in a series of governmental actions, however close they may all be in time. . . . But the world is not made brand new every morning, and the Counties are simply asking us to ignore perfectly probative evidence; they want an absentminded objective observer, not one presumed to be familiar with the history of the government's actions and competent to learn what history has to show. . . . The Counties' position just bucks common sense: reasonable observers have reasonable memories, and our precedents sensibly forbid an observer "to turn a blind eye to the context in which [the] policy arose." [Because the] "question is what viewers may fairly understand to be the purpose of the display [and that] inquiry, of necessity, turns upon the context in which the contested object appears," we look to the record of evidence showing the progression leading up to the third display of the Commandments. . . .

[At the] ceremony for [the first] posting [of] the framed Commandments . . . , the county executive was accompanied by his pastor, who testified to the certainty of the existence of God. The reasonable observer could only think that the Counties meant to emphasize and celebrate the Commandments' religious message. [The second version displayed the Commandments along with] other documents with highlighted references to God as their sole common element. The display's unstinting focus was on religious passages, showing that the Counties were posting the Commandments precisely because of their sectarian content. That demonstration of the government's objective was enhanced by serial religious references and the accompanying resolution's claim about the embodiment of ethics in Christ. [The Counties'] refusal to defend the second display is understandable, but the reasonable observer could not forget it.

[The] Counties . . . third display . . . placed the Commandments in the company of other documents the Counties thought especially significant in the historical foundation of American government. . . . No reasonable observer could swallow the claim that the Counties had cast off the objective so unmistakable in the earlier displays. . . . [An observer] would be puzzled . . . when he read the Declaration of Independence seeking confirmation for the Counties' posted explanation that the "Ten Commandments' . . . influence is clearly seen in the Declaration"; in fact the observer would find that the Commandments are sanctioned as divine imperatives, while the Declaration of Independence holds that the authority of government to enforce the law derives "from the consent of the governed." [The observer] would probably suspect that the Counties were simply reaching for any way to keep a religious document on the walls of courthouses constitutionally required to embody religious neutrality.

[We] do not decide that the Counties' past actions forever taint any effort on their part to deal with the subject matter. We hold only that purpose needs to be . . . understood in light of context; an implausible claim that governmental purpose has changed should not carry the day in a court of law any more than in a head with common sense. . . .

JUSTICE O'CONNOR, concurring.

. . . Given the history of this particular display of the Ten Commandments, the Court correctly finds an Establishment Clause violation. The purpose behind the counties' display is relevant because it conveys an unmistakable message of endorsement to the reasonable observer.

JUSTICE SCALIA, joined by CHIEF JUSTICE REHNQUIST, JUSTICE THOMAS, and, as to Parts II and III, JUSTICE KENNEDY, dissenting.

. . . I shall discuss first, why the Court's oft repeated assertion that the government cannot favor religious practice is false; second, why today's opinion extends the scope of that falsehood even beyond prior cases; and third, why even on the basis of the Court's false assumptions the judgment here is wrong.

I. [One] model of the relationship between church and state [is that religion] is to be strictly excluded from the public forum. This is not, and never was, the model adopted by America. [Justice Scalia cited a series of invocations of God by all three branches of the federal government.] . . . These actions of our First President and Congress and the Marshall Court were not idiosyncratic; they reflected the beliefs of the period.

. . . Nor have the views of our people on this matter significantly changed. . . . As one of our Supreme Court opinions rightly observed, "We are a religious people whose institutions presuppose a Supreme Being."

With all of this reality (and much more) staring it in the face, how can the Court *possibly* assert that "the First Amendment mandates governmental neutrality between . . . religion and non-religion," and that "manifesting a purpose to favor . . . adherence to religion generally" is unconstitutional? Who says so? Surely not the words of the Constitution. Surely not the history and traditions that reflect our society's constant understanding of those words. Surely not even the current sense of our society, recently reflected in an Act of Congress adopted *unanimously* by the Senate and with only 5 nays in the House of Representatives, criticizing a Court of Appeals opinion that had held "under God" in the Pledge of Allegiance unconstitutional. Nothing stands behind the Court's assertion that governmental affirmation of the society's belief in God is unconstitutional except the Court's own say-so. . . .

[T]oday's opinion suggests that the posting of the Ten Commandments violates the principle that the government cannot favor one religion over another. That is indeed a valid principle where public aid or assistance to religion is concerned, or where the free exercise of religion is at issue, but it necessarily applies in a more limited sense to public acknowledgment of the Creator. If religion in the public forum had to be entirely nondenominational, there could be no religion in the public forum at all. . . . With respect to public acknowledgment of religious belief, it is entirely clear from our Nation's historical practices that the Establishment Clause permits this disregard of polytheists and believers in unconcerned deities, just as it permits the disregard of devout atheists. . . .

II. As bad as the *Lemon* test is, it is worse for the fact that, since its inception, [it has] been manipulated to fit whatever result the Court aimed to achieve. Today's opinion is no different. In two respects it modifies *Lemon* to ratchet up the Court's hostility to religion. First, the Court justifies inquiry into legislative purpose, not as an end itself, but as a means to ascertain the appearance of the government action to an "objective observer." Because in the Court's view the true danger to be guarded against is that the objective observer would feel like an "outsider" . . . , its inquiry focuses not on the *actual purpose* of government action, but the "purpose apparent from government action." Under this approach, even if a government could show that its actual purpose was not to advance religion, it would presumably violate the Constitution as long as the Court's objective observer would think otherwise. . . .

Second, the Court replaces *Lemon*'s requirement that the government have "*a* secular . . . purpose" (emphasis added), with the heightened requirement that the secular purpose "predominate" over any purpose to advance religion. The Court treats this extension as a natural outgrowth of the long-standing requirement that the government's secular purpose not be a sham, but simple logic shows the two to be unrelated. If the government's proffered secular purpose is not genuine, then the government has no secular purpose at all. The new demand that secular purpose predominate contradicts *Lemon*'s more limited requirement, and finds no support in our cases. . . . By shifting the focus of *Lemon*'s purpose prong from the search for a genuine, secular motivation to the hunt for a predominantly religious purpose, the Court converts what has in the past been a fairly limited inquiry into a rigorous review of the full record. . . .

III. Even accepting the Court's *Lemon*-based premises, the displays at issue here were constitutional. To any person who happened to walk down the hallway of the McCreary or Pulaski County Courthouse during the roughly nine months when the Foundations Displays were exhibited, the displays must have seemed unremarkable—if indeed they were noticed at all. The walls of both courthouses were already lined with historical documents and other assorted portraits; each Foundations Display was exhibited in the same format as these other displays and nothing in the record suggests that either County took steps to give it greater prominence. . . .

On its face, the Foundations Displays manifested the purely secular purpose [of displaying] "documents that played a significant role in the foundation of our system of law and government." That the Displays included the Ten Commandments did not transform their apparent secular purpose into one of impermissible advocacy for Judeo-Christian beliefs. [The] context communicates that the Ten Commandments are included, not to teach their . . . nature as a religious text, but to show their unique contribution to the development of the legal system. . . .

≡≡≡ *Van Orden v. Perry*
≡≡≡ *545 U.S. 677 (2005)*

[The 22-acre grounds of the Texas State Capitol contain 21 historical markers and 17 monuments, one of which is a 6-foot-high granite block on which is carved the text of the Ten Commandments. The markers and monuments commemorate the "people, ideals, and events that compose Texan identity." Texas accepted the monument as a gift from the Eagles, a fraternal organization devoted to social, patriotic, and civic causes. A federal district court ruled that Texas had a valid secular purpose—recognizing and commending the Eagles for their efforts to reduce juvenile delinquency—and that a reasonable observer, aware of the purpose, history, and context surrounding the display, would not conclude that it conveyed the message that Texas endorsed religion. The Fifth Circuit affirmed. The Supreme Court affirmed.]

CHIEF JUSTICE REHNQUIST announced the judgment of the Court and delivered an opinion, in which JUSTICE SCALIA, JUSTICE KENNEDY, and JUSTICE THOMAS join.

. . . Our cases, Januslike, point in two directions in applying the Establishment Clause. One face looks toward the strong role played by religion and religious traditions throughout our Nation's history. . . . The other face looks toward the principle that governmental intervention in religious matters can itself endanger religious freedom. . . . This case, like all Establishment Clause challenges, presents us with the difficulty of respecting both faces. . . .

Whatever may be the fate of the *Lemon* test in the larger scheme of Establishment Clause jurisprudence, we think it not useful in dealing with the sort of passive monument that Texas has erected on its Capitol grounds. Instead, our analysis is driven both by the nature of the monument and by our Nation's history. . . . In this case we are faced with a display of the Ten Commandments on government property outside the Texas State Capitol. Such acknowledgments of the role played by the Ten Commandments in our Nation's heritage are common throughout America. We need only look within our own Courtroom. Since 1935, Moses has stood, holding two tablets that reveal portions of the Ten Commandments written in Hebrew, among other lawgivers in the south frieze. Representations of the Ten Commandments adorn the metal gates lining the north and south sides of the Courtroom as well as the doors leading into the Courtroom. Moses also sits on the exterior east facade of the building holding the Ten Commandments tablets. Similar acknowledgments can be seen throughout a visitor's tour of our Nation's Capital. For example, a large statue of Moses holding the Ten Commandments, alongside a statue of the Apostle Paul, has overlooked the rotunda of the Library of Congress'[s] Jefferson Building since 1897. And the Jefferson Building's Great Reading Room contains a sculpture of a woman beside the Ten Commandments with a quote above her from the Old Testament (Micah 6:8). A medallion with two tablets depicting the Ten Commandments decorates the floor of the National Archives. Inside the Department of Justice, a statue entitled "The Spirit of Law" has two tablets representing the Ten Commandments lying at its feet. In front of the Ronald Reagan Building is another sculpture that includes a depiction of the Ten Commandments. [A] 24-foot-tall sculpture, depicting, among other things, the Ten Commandments and a cross, stands outside the federal courthouse . . . for the District of Columbia. Moses is also prominently featured in the Chamber of the United States House of Representatives. . . .

Of course, the Ten Commandments are religious. . . . According to Judeo-Christian belief, the Ten Commandments were given to Moses by God on Mt. Sinai. But Moses was a lawgiver as well as a religious leader. And the Ten Commandments have an undeniable historical meaning, as the foregoing examples demonstrate. Simply having religious content or promoting a message consistent with a religious doctrine does not run afoul of the Establishment Clause.

There are, of course, limits to the display of religious messages or symbols. [We] held unconstitutional [in Stone v. Graham, 449 U.S. 39 (1980),] a Kentucky statute requiring the posting of the Ten Commandments in every public schoolroom [because, in] the classroom context, . . . the Kentucky statute had an improper and plainly religious purpose. . . . Neither *Stone* itself nor subsequent opinions have indicated that *Stone*'s holding would extend to a legislative chamber or to capitol grounds.

The placement of the Ten Commandments monument on the Texas State Capitol grounds is a far more passive use of those texts than was the case in *Stone,* where the text confronted elementary school students every day. . . . Texas has treated her Capitol grounds monuments as representing the several strands in the State's political and legal history. The inclusion of the Ten Commandments monument in this group has a dual significance, partaking of both religion and government. We cannot say that Texas'[s] display of this monument violates the Establishment Clause of the First Amendment.

JUSTICE THOMAS, concurring.

. . . I join the Chief Justice's opinion in full. This case would be easy if the Court were willing to . . . return to the original meaning of the Clause. [The] Clause's text and history "resist incorporation" against the States. If the Establishment Clause does not restrain the States, then it has no application here, where only state action is at issue.

Even if the Clause is incorporated . . . [the] Framers understood an establishment "necessarily [to] involve actual legal coercion." . . . In no sense does Texas compel petitioner Van Orden to do anything. The only injury to him is that he takes offense at seeing the monument as he passes it on his way to the Texas Supreme Court Library. He need not stop to read it or even to look at it. . . . The mere presence of the monument along his path involves no coercion and thus does not violate the Establishment Clause.

JUSTICE BREYER, concurring in the judgment.

[T]he First Amendment's Religion Clauses . . . seek to avoid that divisiveness based upon religion that promotes social conflict, sapping the strength of government and religion alike. [G]overnment must "neither engage in nor compel religious practices," . . . it must "effect no favoritism among sects or between religion and nonreligion," and . . . it must "work deterrence of no religious belief." The government must avoid excessive interference with, or promotion of, religion. But the Establishment Clause does not compel the government to purge from the public sphere all that in any way partakes of the religious. Such absolutism is not only inconsistent with our national traditions but would also tend to promote the kind of social conflict the Establishment Clause seeks to avoid. . . .

If the relation between government and religion is one of separation, but not of mutual hostility and suspicion, one will inevitably find difficult borderline cases. . . . The case before us is a borderline case. [To] determine the message that the text here conveys, we must . . . consider the context of the display. In certain contexts, . . . the Ten Commandments can convey . . . a secular moral message, [or] a historical message. . . . Here the tablets have been used as part of a display that communicates not simply a religious message, but a secular message as well. The circumstances surrounding the display's placement on the capitol grounds and its physical setting suggest that the State . . . intended the . . . nonreligious aspects of the tablets' message to predominate. And the monument's 40-year history on the Texas state grounds indicates that that has been its effect. The group that donated the monument, . . . sought to highlight the Commandments' role in shaping civic morality, [and the] physical setting of the monument . . . suggests little or nothing of the sacred. The setting does not readily lend itself to . . . religious activity. But it does provide a context of history and moral ideals. It . . . suggests that the State intended the display's moral message—an illustrative message reflecting the historical "ideals" of Texans—to predominate.

[T]hese factors provide a strong, but not conclusive, indication that the . . . monument conveys a predominantly secular message, [but] a further factor is determinative here. As far as I can tell, 40 years passed in which the presence of this monument, legally speaking, went unchallenged. . . . [T]hose 40 years suggest more strongly than can any set of formulaic tests that few individuals, whatever their system of beliefs, are likely to have understood the monument as amounting . . . to a government effort to favor a particular religious sect, primarily to promote religion over nonreligion, to "engage in" any "religious practice," to "compel" any "religious practice," or to "work deterrence" of any "religious belief." . . . This case . . . differs from *McCreary County*, where the short (and stormy) history of the courthouse Commandments' displays demonstrates the substantially religious objectives of those who mounted them, and the effect of this readily apparent objective upon those who view them. . . .

Justice Stevens, joined by Justice Ginsburg, dissenting.

The sole function of the monument on the grounds of Texas'[s] State Capitol is to display the full text of one version of the Ten Commandments. . . . It is significant . . . only because it communicates [a religious] message. . . . Texas'[s] display [does not] provide the reasonable observer with any basis to guess that it was erected to honor any individual or organization. The message transmitted by Texas'[s] chosen display is quite plain: This State endorses the divine code of the "Judeo-Christian" God. . . .

The reason this message stands apart is that the Decalogue is a venerable religious text. . . . Moreover, . . . the Ten Commandments [monument] projects not just a religious, but an inherently sectarian message. There are many distinctive versions of the Decalogue, [sub]scribed to by different religions and even different denominations within a particular faith. . . . Given that the chosen text inscribed on the Ten Commandments monument invariably places the State at the center of a serious sectarian dispute, the display is unquestionably unconstitutional under our case law. . . . And, at the very least, the text of the Ten Commandments impermissibly commands a preference for religion over irreligion. . . .

Justice Souter, joined by Justice Stevens and Justice Ginsburg, dissenting.

. . . A governmental display of an obviously religious text cannot be squared with neutrality, except in a setting that plausibly indicates that the statement is not placed in view with a predominant purpose on the part of government either to adopt the religious message or to urge its acceptance by others. [The] Ten Commandments constitute a religious statement. . . . Nothing on the monument . . . detracts from its religious nature. . . . It would therefore be difficult to miss the point that . . . Texas is telling everyone who sees the monument to live up to a moral code because God requires it. . . .

NOTES AND PROBLEMS

1. *Lemon* **and Endorsement.**   Does the majority opinion in *McCreary* refine the endorsement test or modify *Lemon* by its assertion that the government's secular purpose must be readily divined by a reasonable and informed observer? Taken together with the contention by Justice Souter in *McCreary* that the secular purpose must predominate, is this a revised version of *Lemon*? If so, is it better configured than the endorsement test to assess the validity of government displays of religious imagery? Or will this new version degenerate into a debate about perception and misperception, as Justice Scalia charged?

2. The Role of "Judgment."   Justice Breyer, who alone among the Justices voted with the majority result in both cases, contended in his *Van Orden* concurrence that these cases are all fact-driven, contextual, and must be decided by "judgment" and not a personal predilection. Can this be so? Do the factors used by Justice Breyer persuade you that an objective judgment can be rendered in any given case?

3. Polytheists and Atheists.   Justice Scalia argued that the objections of atheists and polytheists to public acknowledgments of God are of little concern to establishment clause analysis because such acknowledgments pose an irreconcilable conflict between the portion of the polity for whom such acknowledgments are anathema and the portion of the polity who regard the deliberate excision of such acknowledgments as a message of hostility toward persons of faith. Justice Scalia argued, in part, that this Gordian knot should be cut in favor of acknowledgment of God because the overwhelming portion of the population are nominal or devout believers in a monotheistic God. Is Justice Scalia correct to view this issue as a "zero-sum" game, in which one side's gain inexorably produces a corresponding loss? If not, what mediating principle preserves the possibility of gains to both sides? If there is no such principle, is counting theological noses an acceptable way of resolving the conflict?

4. Problems: *Pledge of Allegiance.*   Assess the validity of the Pledge's inclusion of "under God" in light of *McCreary County* and *Van Orden*.

Mandala Community Logo. Suppose that a "New Age" community in Colorado were to adopt a mandala as its community logo, stating that it represents the cycle of life and the renewal of all things. Mandalas are of Hindu and Buddhist origin. In Hinduism, the mandala depicts the sacred texts of the Rig Veda. In Buddhism, the mandala, in general, is a microcosmic representation of divine power. Is the adoption of the mandala as a community logo permissible? See Weinbaum v. City of Las Cruces, 541 F.3d 1017 (2008).

Civic Prayer Tower. Suppose that a community erects a "prayer tower" in which bells are housed that signal the beginning of services in the local Christian churches, from which a mullah calls the Islamic faithful to prayer, and that is open to all other religious faiths for the purpose of calling their adherents to worship as well as to religious nonbelievers to denounce religion. The community says that it erected the tower to dampen sectarian division, increase public understanding of all religious viewpoints, and foster greater appreciation of the multicultural diversity of the community. Is this permissible?

Town of Greece v. Galloway
134 S. Ct. 1811 (2014)

JUSTICE KENNEDY delivered the opinion of the Court, except as to Part II-B.

The Court must decide whether the town of Greece, New York, imposes an impermissible establishment of religion by opening its monthly board meetings with a prayer. [C]onsistent with the Court's opinion in Marsh v. Chambers, . . . no violation of the Constitution has been shown.

I. Greece, a town with a population of 94,000, is in upstate New York. For some years, it began its monthly town board meetings with a moment of silence. In 1999, the newly elected town supervisor, John Auberger, decided to replicate the prayer practice he had found meaningful while serving in the county legislature. Following the roll call and recitation of the Pledge of Allegiance, Auberger would invite a local clergyman to the front of the room to deliver an invocation. After the prayer, Auberger would thank the minister for serving as the board's "chaplain for the month" and present him with a commemorative plaque. The prayer was intended to place town board members in a solemn and deliberative frame of mind, invoke divine guidance in town affairs, and follow a tradition practiced by Congress and dozens of state legislatures. The town followed an informal method for selecting prayer givers, all of whom were unpaid volunteers. A town employee would call the congregations listed in a local directory until she found a minister available for that month's meeting. The town eventually compiled a list of willing "board chaplains" who had accepted invitations and agreed to return in the future. The town at no point excluded or denied an opportunity to a would-be prayer giver. Its leaders maintained that a minister or layperson of any persuasion, including an atheist, could give the invocation. But nearly all of the congregations in town were Christian; and from 1999 to 2007, all of the participating ministers were too.

Greece neither reviewed the prayers in advance of the meetings nor provided guidance as to their tone or content, in the belief that exercising any degree of control over the prayers would infringe both the free exercise and speech rights of the ministers. . . . The resulting prayers often sounded both civic and religious themes. Typical were invocations that asked the divinity to abide at the meeting and bestow blessings on the community:

> "Lord we ask you to send your spirit of servanthood upon all of us gathered here this evening to do your work for the benefit of all in our community. We ask you to bless our elected and appointed officials so they may deliberate with wisdom and act with courage. Bless the members of our community who come here to speak before the board so they may state their cause with honesty and humility. . . . Lord we ask you to bless us all, that everything we do here tonight will move you to welcome us one day into your kingdom as good and faithful servants. We ask this in the name of our brother Jesus. Amen."

Some of the ministers spoke in a distinctly Christian idiom; and a minority invoked religious holidays, scripture, or doctrine, as in the following prayer:

> "Lord, God of all creation, we give you thanks and praise for your presence and action in the world. We look with anticipation to the celebration of Holy Week and Easter. It is in the solemn events of next week that we find the very heart and center of our Christian faith. We acknowledge the saving sacrifice of Jesus Christ on the cross. We draw strength, vitality, and confidence from his resurrection at Easter. . . . We pray for peace in the world, an end to terrorism, violence, conflict, and war. We pray for stability, democracy, and good government in those countries in which our armed forces are now serving, especially in Iraq and Afghanistan. . . . Praise and glory be yours, O Lord, now and forever more. Amen."

Respondents Susan Galloway and Linda Stephens attended town board meetings to speak about issues of local concern, and they objected that the prayers violated their religious or philosophical views. At one meeting, Galloway admonished board members that she found the prayers "offensive," "intolerable," and an affront to a "diverse community." After respondents complained that Christian themes pervaded the prayers, to the exclusion of citizens who did not share those beliefs, the town invited a Jewish layman and the chairman of the local Baha'i temple to deliver prayers. A Wiccan priestess who had read press reports about the prayer controversy requested, and was granted, an opportunity to give the invocation.

Galloway and Stephens brought suit in [federal] District Court, [alleging] that the town violated the . . . Establishment Clause by preferring Christians over other prayer givers and by sponsoring sectarian prayers, such as those given "in Jesus' name." They did not seek an end to the prayer practice, but rather requested an injunction that would limit the town to "inclusive and ecumenical" prayers that referred only to a "generic God" and would not associate the government with any one faith or belief. The District Court on summary judgment upheld the prayer practice. . . . The Court of Appeals for the Second Circuit reversed, [holding that] the prayer program, viewed in

[its] totality by a reasonable observer, conveyed the message that Greece was endorsing Christianity. . . . Having granted certiorari . . . , the Court now reverses the judgment of the Court of Appeals.

II. In Marsh v. Chambers the Court found no First Amendment violation in the Nebraska Legislature's practice of opening its sessions with a prayer delivered by a chaplain paid from state funds. The decision concluded that legislative prayer, while religious in nature, has long been understood as compatible with the Establishment Clause. As practiced by Congress since the framing of the Constitution, legislative prayer lends gravity to public business, reminds lawmakers to transcend petty differences in pursuit of a higher purpose, and expresses a common aspiration to a just and peaceful society. The Court has considered this symbolic expression to be a "tolerable acknowledgement of beliefs widely held," rather than a first, treacherous step towards establishment of a state church. . . .

. . . *Marsh* must not be understood as permitting a practice that would amount to a constitutional violation if not for its historical foundation. The case teaches instead that the Establishment Clause must be interpreted "by reference to historical practices and understandings." . . . The Court's inquiry, then, must be to determine whether the prayer practice in the town of Greece fits within the tradition long followed in Congress and the state legislatures.

Respondents assert that the town's prayer exercise falls outside that tradition. . . . First, they argue that *Marsh* did not approve prayers containing sectarian language or themes. . . . Second, they argue that the setting and conduct of the town board meetings create social pressures that force non-adherents to remain in the room or even feign participation in order to avoid offending the representatives who sponsor the prayer and will vote on matters citizens bring before the board. The sectarian content of the prayers compounds the subtle coercive pressures, they argue, because the nonbeliever who might tolerate ecumenical prayer is forced to do the same for prayer that might be inimical to his or her beliefs. . . .

The contention that legislative prayer must be generic or nonsectarian derives from dictum in *County of Allegheny* that was disputed when written and has been repudiated by later cases. . . . *Marsh* nowhere suggested that the constitutionality of legislative prayer turns on the neutrality of its content. . . . To the contrary, the Court instructed that the "content of the prayer is not of concern to judges," provided "there is no indication that the prayer opportunity has been exploited to proselytize or advance any one, or to disparage any other, faith or belief."

To hold that invocations must be nonsectarian would force the legislatures that sponsor prayers and the courts that are asked to decide these cases to act as supervisors and censors of religious speech, a rule that would involve government in religious matters to a far greater degree than is the case under the town's current practice of neither editing or approving prayers in advance nor criticizing their content after the fact. . . .

In rejecting the suggestion that legislative prayer must be nonsectarian, the Court does not imply that no constraints remain on its content. The relevant constraint derives from its place at the opening of legislative sessions, where it is meant to lend gravity to the occasion and reflect values long part of the Nation's heritage. Prayer that is solemn and respectful in tone, that invites lawmakers to reflect upon shared ideals and common ends before they embark on the fractious business of governing, serves that legitimate function. If . . . invocations denigrate nonbelievers or religious minorities, threaten damnation, or preach conversion, . . . the prayer [may] fall short of the desire to elevate the purpose of the occasion and to unite lawmakers in their common effort. That circumstance would present a different case than the one presently before the Court. . . .

The prayers delivered in the town of Greece do not fall outside the tradition this Court has recognized. A number of the prayers did invoke the name of Jesus, the Heavenly Father, or the Holy Spirit, but they also invoked universal themes, as by celebrating the changing of the seasons or calling for a "spirit of cooperation" among town leaders. Among numerous examples of such prayer in the record is the invocation given by the Rev. Richard Barbour at the September 2006 board meeting:

> "Gracious God, you have richly blessed our nation and this community. Help us to remember your generosity and give thanks for your goodness. Bless the elected leaders of the Greece Town Board as they conduct the business of our town this evening. Give them wisdom, courage, discernment and a single-minded desire to serve the common good. We ask your blessing on all public servants, and especially on our police force, firefighters, and emergency medical personnel. . . . Respectful of every religious tradition, I offer this prayer in the name of God's only son Jesus Christ, the Lord, Amen."

. . . Finally, . . . [so] long as the town maintains a policy of nondiscrimination, the Constitution does not require it to search beyond its borders for non-Christian prayer givers in an effort to achieve religious balancing. The quest to promote "a 'diversity' of religious views" would require the town "to make wholly inappropriate judgments about the number of religions [it] should sponsor and the relative frequency with which it should sponsor each," a form of government entanglement with religion that is far more troublesome than the current approach.

Respondents [contend that] the town's prayer practice . . . coerces participation by non-adherents. . . . Citizens attend town meetings . . . to accept awards; speak on matters of local importance, and petition the board for action that may affect their economic interests, such as the granting of permits, business licenses, and zoning variances. Respondents argue that the public may feel subtle pressure to participate in prayers that violate their beliefs in order to please the board members from whom they are about to seek a favorable ruling. . . . It is . . . elemental . . . that government may not coerce its citizens "to support or participate in any religion or its exercise." [But] the Court is not persuaded that the town of Greece, through the act of offering a brief, solemn, and respectful prayer to open its monthly meetings, compelled its citizens to engage in a religious observance. The inquiry remains a fact-sensitive one that considers both the setting in which the prayer arises and the audience to whom it is directed. The prayer . . . must be evaluated against the backdrop of historical practice. . . . [L]egislative prayer has become part of our heritage and tradition, part of our expressive idiom . . . . It is presumed that the reasonable observer is acquainted with this tradition and understands that its purposes are to lend gravity to public proceedings and to acknowledge the place religion holds in the lives of many private citizens, not to afford government an opportunity to proselytize or force truant constituents into the pews. [Those] who disagree are [not] compelled to join the expression or approve its content. West Virginia Bd. of Ed. v. Barnette. . . . [R]espondents stated that the prayers gave them offense and made them feel excluded and disrespected [but offense] does not equate to coercion. . . . This case can be distinguished from . . . Lee v. Weisman. [The] circumstances the Court confronted there are not present in this case and do not control its outcome. Nothing in the record suggests that members of the public are dissuaded from leaving the meeting room during the prayer, arriving late, or even, as happened here, making a later protest. In this case, as in *Marsh*, board members and constituents are "free to enter and leave with little comment and for any number of reasons." . . .

In the town of Greece, the prayer is delivered during the ceremonial portion of the town's meeting. Board members are not engaged in policymaking at this time, but in more general functions, such as swearing in new police officers, inducting high school athletes into the town hall of fame, and presenting proclamations to volunteers, civic groups, and senior citizens. It is a moment for town leaders to recognize the achievements of their constituents and the aspects of community life that are worth celebrating. By inviting ministers to serve as chaplain for the month, and welcoming them to the front of the room alongside civic leaders, the town is acknowledging the central place that religion, and religious institutions, hold in the lives of those present. [Reversed.]

JUSTICE THOMAS, with whom JUSTICE SCALIA joins as to Part II, concurring in part and concurring in the judgment.

Except for Part II-B, I join the opinion of the Court. . . . I write separately to reiterate my view that the Establishment Clause is "best understood as a federalism provision," and to state my understanding of the proper "coercion" analysis.

The . . . text and history of the [Establishment] Clause "resis[t] incorporation" against the States. If the Establishment Clause is not incorporated, then it has no application here, where only municipal action is at issue. . . .

Even if the Establishment Clause were properly incorporated against the States, the municipal prayers at issue in this case bear no resemblance to the coercive state establishments that existed at the founding. "The coercion that was a hallmark of historical establishments of religion was coercion of religious orthodoxy and of financial support *by force of law and threat of penalty.* [W]hatever non-establishment principles existed in 1868 [when the Fourteenth Amendment was adopted], they included no concern for the finer sensibilities of the "reasonable observer."

Thus, to the extent coercion is relevant to the Establishment Clause analysis, it is actual legal coercion that counts. . . . [An] "Establishment Clause violation is not made out any time a person experiences a sense of affront from the expression of contrary religious views in a legislative forum," [and] "[p]eer pressure, unpleasant as it may be, is not coercion" either.

JUSTICE BREYER, dissenting.

. . . The question in this case is whether the prayer practice of the town of Greece . . . promote[d] the "political division along religious lines" that "was one of the principal evils against which the First Amendment was intended to protect." In seeking an answer to that fact-sensitive question, "I see no test-related substitute for the exercise of legal judgment." Van Orden v. Perry (Breyer, J., concurring in judgment). Having applied my legal judgment to the relevant facts, I conclude . . . that the town of Greece failed to make reasonable efforts to include prayer givers of minority faiths, with the result that, although it is a community of several faiths, its prayer givers were almost exclusively persons of a single faith. Under these circumstances, . . . Greece's prayer practice violated the Establishment Clause.

JUSTICE KAGAN, with whom JUSTICE GINSBURG, JUSTICE BREYER, and JUSTICE SOTOMAYOR join, dissenting.

For centuries now, people have come to this country from every corner of the world to share in the blessing of religious freedom. Our Constitution promises that they may worship in their own way . . . and that in itself is a momentous offering. Yet our Constitution makes a commitment still more remarkable—that however those individuals worship, they will count as full and equal American citizens. . . . I respectfully dissent . . . because I think the Town of Greece's prayer practices violate that norm of religious equality—the breathtakingly generous constitutional idea that our public institutions belong no less to the Buddhist or Hindu than to the Methodist or Episcopalian. I do not contend that principle translates here into a bright separationist line. To the contrary, I agree with the Court's decision in *Marsh* [and] I believe that pluralism and inclusion in a town hall can satisfy the constitutional requirement of neutrality; such a forum need not become a religion-free zone. But still, the Town of Greece should lose this case. The practice at issue here differs from the one sustained in *Marsh* because Greece's town meetings involve participation by ordinary citizens, and the invocations given—directly to those citizens—were predominantly sectarian in content. Still more, Greece's Board did nothing to recognize religious diversity: In arranging for clergy members to open each meeting, the Town never sought (except briefly when this suit was filed) to involve, accommodate, or in any way reach out to adherents of non-Christian religions. So month in and month out for over a decade, prayers steeped in only one faith, addressed toward members of the public, commenced meetings to discuss local affairs and distribute government benefits. In my view, that practice does not square with the First Amendment's promise that every citizen, irrespective of her religion, owns an equal share in her government.

. . . The clearest command of the Establishment Clause . . . is that one religious denomination cannot be officially preferred over another." Larson v. Valente. . . . By authorizing and overseeing prayers associated with a single religion—to the exclusion of all others—. . . government officials [violate] that foundational principle. They have embarked on a course of religious favoritism anathema to the First Amendment.

And making matters still worse: They have done so in a place where individuals come to interact with, and participate in, the institutions and processes of their government. A person goes to court, to the polls, to a naturalization ceremony—and a government official or his hand-picked minister asks her, as the first order of official business, to stand and pray with others in a way conflicting with her own religious beliefs. Perhaps she feels sufficient pressure to go along—to rise, bow her head, and join in whatever others are saying: After all, she wants, very badly, what the judge or poll worker or immigration official has to offer. Or perhaps she is made of stronger mettle, and she opts not to participate in what she does not believe—indeed, what would, for her, be something like blasphemy. She then must make known her dissent from the common religious view, and place herself apart from other citizens, as well as from the officials responsible for the invocations. And so a civic function of some kind brings religious differences to the fore: That public proceeding becomes (whether intentionally or not) an instrument for dividing her from adherents to the community's majority religion, and for altering the very nature of her relationship with her government.

That is not . . . what our Constitution permits. Here, when a citizen stands before her government, whether to perform a service or request a benefit, her religious beliefs do not enter into the picture. . . . The government she faces favors no particular religion, either by word or by deed. And that government, in its various processes and proceedings, imposes no religious tests on its citizens, sorts none of them by faith, and permits no exclusion based on belief. . . .

None of this means that Greece's town hall must be religion or prayer-free. "[W]e are a religious people," *Marsh* observed, [but what] the circumstances here demand is the recognition that we are a pluralistic people too. When citizens of all faiths come to speak to each other and their elected representatives in a legislative session, the government must take especial care to ensure that the prayers they hear will seek to include, rather than serve to divide. [That] is not difficult to do. If the Town Board had let its chaplains know that they should speak in nonsectarian terms, common to diverse religious groups, then no one would have valid grounds for complaint. . . . But Greece could not . . . infuse a participatory government body with one (and only one) faith. . . . In this country, when citizens go before the government, they go not as Christians or Muslims or Jews (or what have you), but just as Americans. . . . That is what it means to be an equal citizen, irrespective of religion. And that is what the Town of Greece precluded by so identifying itself with a single faith. . . .

I therefore respectfully dissent from the Court's decision.

NOTES AND QUESTIONS

1. Endorsement, Coercion, *Lemon*, Ad Hoc "Legal Judgment"? Before *Town of Greece,* the constitutional decision rules for finding an Establishment Clause violation had fractured into a shifting kaleidoscope of tests, albeit with some possibility of identifying circumstances in which a particular test might apply. Roughly speaking, and with misleading simplicity, we might have said that *Lemon* applied to religion funding cases, the endorsement test was useful to assess government displays of religious messages or images, the coercion test was particularly apt for school prayer (especially in the younger grades), and Justice Breyer's frank reliance on the application of "legal judgment" to the specific facts was a recognition that the tests are impossibly malleable. What is the state of affairs after *Town of Greece?*

In the majority's view, does an ancient practice of sectarian legislative prayer trump endorsement? Coercion remains an element at least to the plurality that composed Part II-B, but the meaning of coercion to Justices Thomas and Scalia is the mailed fist to the nose. *Lemon* goes unmentioned, and Justice Breyer relies on the specific facts filtered through his "legal judgment."

2. Parsing the Facts to Find a Rule. The prayer in *Marsh* was in a state legislature before the day's political wrangling began, the *Greece* prayers were ceremonially delivered in a local government body before the public policy work began. Is prayer limited to moments before the official governance begins? The prayer in *Marsh* was drained of sectarian substance, the *Greece* prayers were frankly sectarian. Does this mean that all sectarian legislative prayer is constitutionally valid? If not, what limits exist? When is a sectarian prayer "proselytizing"? When does a sectarian prayer denigrate other faiths? The prayers in *Marsh* were delivered by a chaplain; those in *Greece* were delivered by volunteer clergy or laymen. Unlike *Marsh,* the *Greece* prayers were given by anybody the town invited. In *Marsh*, only the chaplain prayed; in *Greece*, town officials joined in the prayers and other displays of religious belief. While the government may not prescribe the content of prayer it also has no obligation to search diligently for religious diversity in prayer. In both *Marsh* and *Greece,* the audience was entirely (or almost entirely) adults. Is Lee v. Weisman still good law? Finally, and perhaps of most importance, in future cases challenging legislative prayer, the courts are confined to an examination of the pattern of prayer, and may not second-guess individual prayers. Given the Court's approval of overtly sectarian prayers, how will this be determined? Does it all boil down to *ad hoc* "legal judgment"?

3. Governmental Accommodation of Religion

Every justice thinks that there is some room between the free exercise clause and the establishment clause for accommodation of religious beliefs, but there is little agreement about the extent of that territory. This section focuses on accommodations that are not required by the free exercise clause, but that arguably violate the establishment clause.

a.   *Cession of Government Power to Religion*

At one extreme is government accommodation that amounts to cession of government power to religious institutions. Such delegation is plainly inconsistent with the establishment clause.

Larkin v. Grendel's Den, 459 U.S. 116 (1982). The Court voided a Massachusetts law that granted churches an absolute veto of liquor license applications for sites located within 500 feet of a religious institution. The law delegated public power to churches, thus advancing religion by vesting public power in a sectarian body and by sanctioning the symbolic union of church and state. The law also created an excessive entanglement between church and state due to the necessity of church approval of the conferral of state authority to dispense liquor. The delegation was also an endorsement by government of religious decision-making on issues of public policy.

Board of Education of Kiryas Joel Village v. Grumet, 512 U.S. 687 (1994). A Hasidic Jewish sect that vigorously rejects assimilation into the mainstream culture created a community, Kiryas Joel, consisting entirely of members of the sect. Adherents to the religion educate their children in parochial schools. Federal and state law requires public schools to provide special educational services to handicapped children. Hasidic residents of Kiryas Joel, however, preferred to do without such education rather than enroll their handicapped children in the public schools. New York responded by authorizing Kiryas Joel to create its own public school district. Kiryas Joel did so but confined its public schooling to the provision of special educational services to handicapped children. All the handicapped children enrolled in the Kiryas Joel system were members of the Hasidic sect. The Court regarded the New York legislation as "tantamount to an allocation of political power on a religious criterion." The boundaries of the district were carefully drawn to include all Hasidim and to exclude those who were not members of the sect. The benefit received by the Hasidim of Kiryas Joel was not provided equally to those of other religions. Justice Kennedy concurred in the judgment, specifying a three-part test for acceptable accommodations of religion: (1) the state seeks "to alleviate a specific and identifiable burden" on religious practices, (2) the accommodation does "not impose or increase any burden" on nonmembers of the accommodated religions, and (3) there is no evidence the state has denied other religions the same benefit "under analogous circumstances." In *Kiryas Joel*, the religious gerrymander was designed to deliver a specific benefit to a particular sect.

Justices Scalia, Rehnquist, and Thomas dissented. They argued that New York had a secular purpose—to spare children from the emotional trauma of education in an environment where they would likely be treated as objects of curiosity and ridicule. New York had simply accommodated the deeply held and unusual religious beliefs and practices of the Kiryas Joel Hasidim. Rather than favoring the Hasidic residents of Kiryas Joel, New York had responded to the cultural insularity of the sect by accommodating their desire to remain apart from the mainstream.

b. Religious Exemptions from General Requirements

At the other end of the extreme are religion-based exemptions from statutory requirements that, while constitutional, impinge upon religious conduct.

Gillette v. United States, 401 U.S. 437 (1971). The Court upheld an exemption from military conscription of persons who, because of their "religious training and belief," were opposed to "war in any form." Gillette claimed that, in accordance with Roman Catholic doctrine, he was opposed to "unjust" wars and that Congress's failure to exempt him from the draft constituted an impermissible establishment of religion in the form of a government preference for religions, such as the Quakers, that reject all war. Because the law was not discriminatory on its face, the burden fell on Gillette to prove that there was no "neutral, secular basis for the lines the government has drawn." The Court accepted the government's argument that extending the exemption to selective conscientious objectors would jeopardize the fairness of the exemption by injecting much subjectivity and uncertainty into its administration.

Corporation of Presiding Bishop v. Amos, 483 U.S. 327 (1987). The Court upheld a provision of Title VII of the Civil Rights Act that exempts churches from Title VII's ban on employment discrimination on the basis of religion. Mayson, a janitor at a Mormon church gymnasium, was discharged from his employment because he was a lapsed Mormon. The Court rejected Mayson's contention that the statutory exemption violated the establishment clause. Applying *Lemon*, the Court reasoned that a secular purpose need not be "unrelated to religion" and the government's purpose is valid so long as the government has not acted "with the intent of promoting a *particular* point of view in religious matters." The Court thought that the effects prong of *Lemon* was satisfied because the exemption merely permitted *churches* to advance religion; for "a law to have forbidden 'effects' [the] *government itself* [must have] advanced religion through its own activities and influence."

Estate of Thornton v. Caldor, Inc., 472 U.S. 703 (1985). The Court struck down a Connecticut law that prohibited employers from forcing an employee to work on the employee's Sabbath or dismissing the employee for refusal to do so. The law was adopted as part of Connecticut's revision of its Sunday closing law, permitting some businesses to open on Sunday. The Court regarded the law as lacking any purpose other than protecting religious observance and practice because (1) the Connecticut law focused exclusively on religion and was not simply one aspect of a state attempt to reach the broader, and secular, goal of limiting invidious discrimination in employment; (2) the law *mandated* observance of religious practice rather than simply *permitting* such observance unimpeded by the state; (3) the law absolutely preferred religious to secular interests; and (4) the burden of Sunday work was shifted to other employees who could not claim a religious reason for refusing to work on Sundays. In *Amos,* the Court distinguished *Caldor* on the ground that Connecticut had compelled private employers to make religious distinctions, but Title VII permitted only churches to do so.

Texas Monthly v. Bullock, 489 U.S. 1 (1989). Texas exempted religious periodicals and books from its otherwise applicable sales tax. In a plurality opinion by Justice Brennan, the Court struck down the exemption, relying primarily on the fact that the exemption was not available to any nonreligious publications. The benefits accorded religion were not part of a wider package of benefits aimed at furthering secular goals. By limiting the tax exemption to religious publications, Texas had sought to advance only religious purposes. Justice Scalia, joined by Chief Justice Rehnquist and Justice Kennedy, dissented, arguing that *Walz* controlled and that government may accommodate religion by affording non-preferential exemptions to all religions without broadening the scope of such exemptions to include secular institutions. The dissenters contended that the plurality's position would shrink the scope of religious accommodation to only that required by the free exercise clause.

Cutter v. Wilkinson, 544 U.S. 709 (2005). Section 3 of the federal Religious Land Use and Institutionalized Persons Act (RLUIPA) forbids the imposition of any "substantial burden" on religious exercise with respect to any person in a federally supported government institution, unless that burden can be justified under strict scrutiny. The Court unanimously agreed that §3 constituted "a permissible legislative accommodation of religion." The strict scrutiny standard mandated by RLUIPA did not, on its face, "elevate accommodation of religious observances over an institution's need to maintain order and safety, . . . override other significant interests" (whether of government or nonbelievers), and was intended by Congress to be applied with " 'due deference to the experience and expertise of prison and jail administrators in establishing necessary regulations and procedures to maintain good order, security and discipline. . . .' " Nor did §3 facially "differentiate among bona fide faiths. . . . It confers no privileged status on any particular religious sect, and singles out no bona fide faith for disadvantageous treatment." Finally, the fact that only religious believers were benefited by §3 was of no significance. Relying on *Amos,* the Court concluded that accommodations of religion "need not 'come packaged with benefits to secular entities.' " Any other conclusion, said the Court, would cause "all manner of religious accommodations [to] fall."

Queries: What is the key to harmonizing these cases? Is it the presence (or absence) of an advantage conferred upon religion and denied to analogous secular groups? Is it the difference between a law conferring such an advantage and a law removing a burden that was uniquely visited upon religion? Is a law providing a sectarian advantage especially suspect? If *Amos* rested on the ground that governments may create a religious exemption to avoid a unique burden visited on religion, does that rationale apply to RLUIPA? Why didn't §3 of RLUIPA violate the establishment clause because it provides benefits only to religious adherents and compels states, as in *Caldor*, to make religious distinctions that serve almost entirely to advance religion?

Problem: Suppose that a state prison confiscates any objects in a prisoner's possession that could be used to inflict injury on others. The warden confiscates a Catholic inmate's rosary beads and a Sikh inmate's turban, on the ground that each article could be used to garrote someone. Suppose that, under RLUIPA, the state is unable to justify these seizures. Is RLUIPA, as applied to these facts, a permissible accommodation of religion?

State Action and the Power to Enforce Constitutional Rights

This chapter deals with two overarching realities of constitutional law. First, nearly all of the Constitution's protections of individual liberty are restraints upon government. For example, the Fourteenth Amendment prevents *governments* from engaging in invidious racial discrimination; it does not prevent private individuals from doing so. Of course, the states and the federal government may use their legislative powers to prevent private citizens from engaging in such discrimination, but the Constitution does not compel them to do so. With few exceptions, as a *constitutional* matter, individual liberties are protected against government invasion, not against private abuse. The shorthand expression for this principle is the "state action" requirement: A person asserting a constitutional right must demonstrate that the injury to that right comes at the hands of government.

Second, the Constitution gives Congress specific power to enforce many constitutional rights. The most important such grant of power is in section 5 of the Fourteenth Amendment, which authorizes Congress "to enforce, by appropriate legislation, the provisions" of the Amendment, principally the equal protection and due process guarantees. Two major questions are presented by this grant of power: (1) To what extent, if any, may Congress use it to regulate private conduct? (2) To what extent, if any, may Congress use it to define the content of the guaranteed rights (e.g., equal protection) differently than the Court defines such rights?

Section A addresses the state action problem. Section B deals with the scope of the enforcement powers of Congress.

A. STATE ACTION

In most cases the state action requirement is fairly straightforward: The government acts through legislation, executive order, or judicial decision.

1205

When the power of the state is expressly invoked to infringe constitutional liberties, there is no argument about the presence or absence of state action. A much more difficult question is when, if at all, state *inaction*—failure to act—amounts to state action sufficient to trigger constitutional protections. Generally, governments are under no obligation to take affirmative action, and pure inaction by government will not be considered state action.

The tragic facts of DeShaney v. Winnebago County Department of Social Services, 489 U.S. 189 (1989), are illustrative. Joshua DeShaney, a small boy in the custody of his father following his parents' divorce, was so severely beaten by his father that he suffered permanent brain damage, which required him to be institutionalized for life. Through his mother, Joshua sought damages from a Wisconsin state agency for its alleged deprivation of Joshua's liberty in violation of the due process clause. The essence of the claim was that Wisconsin social workers, having received and investigated reports of child abuse prior to Joshua's disabling injuries, should have acted to remove Joshua from the custody of his father. The Court rejected the claim that Wisconsin's failure to act was a form of state action. Due process operates "as a limitation on the State's power to act, not as a guarantee of certain minimal levels of safety and security." The Wisconsin social services agency had not assumed a special duty "of care and protection," as it does when it "takes a person into its custody and holds him there against his will." The Court noted that even though Joshua had no constitutional claim, he was still entitled to pursue available tort remedies against the Wisconsin agency and, of course, his father.

But when state inaction is alloyed with private action in ways that unduly lend state power to the private action, the state action doctrine may be triggered. In general, state action is present when "there is a sufficiently close nexus between the State and the challenged action of the [private] entity so that the action of the latter may be fairly treated as that of the State itself." Jackson v. Metropolitan Edison Co., 419 U.S. 345 (1971). By itself, this statement is too general to be useful; it comes into focus upon a canvassing of the various circumstances that trigger this conclusion. There are three principal avenues by which the actions of a private individual may be attributed to the state. First, the government may delegate its power to perform a public function to a private person. Second, the government may become so inextricably entangled with the private person that their separate identities are lost. Third, the state may so coerce or extraordinarily encourage the private action that the private actor is seen to have lost its presumptive power of voluntary choice—its act is directed by the state. While these categories form the architecture for the remainder of our study of state action, note that even the Court has admitted that "formulating an infallible test" of state action is "an impossible task." Reitman v. Mulkey, 387 U.S. 369, 378 (1967).

1. The Public Function Doctrine

When states delegate to private persons the power to perform quintessential public functions, the actions of the private persons become attributable to the state. But this raises two important issues: (1) What constitutes a "delegation"? (2) What is a public function?

Some early answers are provided by the so-called white primary cases—the tangled history of litigation concerning the efforts of the Texas Democratic Party to exclude African Americans from its primary elections. In Nixon v. Herndon, 273 U.S. 536 (1927), the Court voided a Texas statute that expressly barred blacks from voting in the Democratic Party primary. The law was promptly revised to empower each party to prescribe the qualifications for voting in the party primary. When the Texas Democratic Party adopted racially exclusive qualifications, they were struck down in Nixon v. Condon, 286 U.S. 73 (1932), as violations of the equal protection clause. State action was present because the Democratic Party was wielding public power expressly delegated to it by law. The Democrats' next gambit was to adopt a party rule, entirely on their own, that forbade blacks from becoming members of the party. In Grovey v. Townsend, 295 U.S. 45 (1935), the Court found no state action because the Democratic Party was not a state instrumentality and the rules for party membership were something with which Texas "need have no concern."

Nine years later, however, in Smith v. Allwright, 321 U.S. 649 (1944), the Court overruled *Grovey*. While party membership may be "no concern of a State," when party membership "is also the essential qualification for voting in a primary to select nominees for a general election, the State makes the action of the party the action of the State." Texas's indirect but effective grant to the Democratic Party of the power to establish voter qualifications "is delegation of a state function that may make the party's action the action of the State." Because Texas limited its general elections to candidates picked by party primaries, it had involved itself sufficiently in the party primary process to make the Democratic Party's actions the actions of Texas.

Texas Democrats reacted to *Allwright* by creating a voluntary club, the Jaybird Democratic Association, which held "pre-primaries" for its members. There were no legal or formal links between the Jaybirds and the Democratic Party, but the winners of the Jaybird pre-primaries nearly always ran without opposition in the official Democratic primary. The Jaybirds frankly admitted that their raison d'être was to exclude blacks from voting. By an 8-1 vote, in Terry v. Adams, 345 U.S. 461 (1953), the Court found state action and invalidated this racially exclusionary process. However, the Court could not muster a majority opinion. Four justices, led by Justice Clark, thought that there was adequate proof that the Jaybirds were the Democrats under another name, making *Allwright* controlling. Three justices, led by Justice Black, found state action in Texas's regulating the electoral process from the general election back to the point of the Jaybirds, and then winking at the Jaybirds' racist selection process. Justice Frankfurter found state action because state election officials participated in the activities of the Jaybirds. Justice Minton dissented, arguing that the Jaybirds' "straw vote" was only the "concerted action" of private citizens and that "concerted action of individuals [does not] somehow become state action."

Marsh v. Alabama
326 U.S. 501 (1946)

[The town of Chickasaw, Alabama, a suburb of Mobile, was entirely owned by the Gulf Shipbuilding Corp. but otherwise had "all the characteristics of any other American town." Its streets, sidewalks, and shopping district were "accessible to and freely used by the public in general and there [was] nothing to distinguish them from any other town and shopping center except the fact that the title to the property [belonged] to a private corporation." Marsh was convicted of criminal trespass after she refused to stop distributing religious tracts on the streets of Chickasaw. The Alabama courts affirmed her conviction.]

JUSTICE BLACK delivered the opinion of the Court.

In this case we are asked to decide whether a State [can] impose criminal punishment on a person who undertakes to distribute religious literature on the premises of a company-owned town contrary to the wishes of the town's management. [Had] the title to Chickasaw belonged not to a private but to a municipal corporation and had appellant been arrested for violating a municipal ordinance rather than a [private rule,] it would have been clear that appellant's conviction must be reversed. [Lovell v. Griffin, Martin v. Struthers.] Our question then narrows down to this: Can those people who live in or come to Chickasaw be denied [constitutional liberties] simply because a single company has legal title to all the town?

[We] do not agree that the corporation's property interests settle the question. The State urges in effect that the corporation's right to control the inhabitants of Chickasaw is coextensive with the right of a homeowner to regulate the conduct of his guests. We cannot accept that contention. Ownership does not always mean absolute dominion. The more an owner, for his advantage, opens up his property for use by the public in general, the more do his rights become circumscribed by the statutory and constitutional rights of those who use it. [Whether] a corporation or a municipality owns or possesses the town the public in either case has an identical interest in the functioning of the community in such manner that the channels of communication remain free. [Chickasaw] does not function differently from any other town. [The] corporation cannot curtail the [constitutional liberties] of these people, [and] a state statute—as the one here involved, which enforces such action by criminally punishing those who attempt to distribute religious literature—clearly violates the First and Fourteenth Amendments to the Constitution.

JUSTICE FRANKFURTER, concurring.

[A] company-owned town is a town. In its community aspects it does not differ from other towns. These community aspects are decisive. [Title] to property as defined by State law controls property relations; it cannot control issues of civil liberties which arise precisely because a company town is a town as well as a congeries of property relations.

NOTES

1. The Limits of *Marsh*. In Amalgamated Food Employees Union v. Logan Valley Plaza, Inc., 391 U.S. 308 (1968), the Court held that a privately owned shopping center was "the functional equivalent" of the company town and that the actions of its owners in interfering with labor picketing were state action. But that conclusion has been repudiated, implicitly by Lloyd Corp. v. Tanner, 407 U.S. 551 (1972), and explicitly by Hudgens v. NLRB, 424 U.S. 507 (1976). In *Lloyd,* the Court concluded that the operators of a privately owned shopping center were not state actors when they excluded persons distributing anti-war literature from the center, distinguishing *Logan Valley* because, unlike the labor picketing in *Logan Valley*, the leaflet distribution in *Lloyd* "had no relation to any purpose [of] the center." In *Hudgens,* the Court expressly overruled *Logan Valley*. The Court adopted the position taken by Justice Black, the author of *Marsh*, who dissented in *Logan Valley*: Privately owned shopping centers could be treated as public only "when that property has taken on *all* the attributes of a town."

The highest courts in a handful of states, interpreting their state constitutions, have reached different results, finding that various guarantees of the relevant state constitution extend to privately owned shopping centers. See, e.g., Robins v. PruneYard Shopping Center, 23 Cal. 3d 899 (1979) (relying on California's free expression guarantee); Batchelder v. Allied Stores International, 388 Mass. 83 (1983) (relying on the Massachusetts right to petition and seek public office to confer a right to solicit signatures in a shopping center); State v. Schmid, 84 N.J. 535 (1980) (relying on New Jersey's free expression guarantee to confer a right to gather signatures on a private university campus); New Jersey Coalition Against War in the Middle East v. J.M.B. Realty Corp., 650 A.2d 757 (N.J. 1994) (extending *Schmid* to shopping centers and broadening the right beyond petition signature solicitation).

2. Evans v. Newton: Private Parks as Public "Function." The 1911 will of Senator Augustus Bacon devised to the city of Macon, Georgia, in trust, a parcel of real property, Baconsfield, so long as it was used as a park for whites only. The city was named trustee and administered Baconsfield. Once it became clear that Macon could not validly enforce the racial exclusion, the city began to admit blacks to the park. The park managers then brought suit to remove Macon as trustee, prompting the city to resign. A state court then appointed a private trustee, who continued the exclusion of nonwhites from the park. In Evans v. Newton, 382 U.S. 296 (1966), the Supreme Court ruled that state action was present and the constitutional requirement of equal protection applied for two independent reasons: (1) The record showed that the park continued to be operated and maintained by the city of Macon, despite the substitution of a private trustee; (2) "The service rendered even by a private park of this character is municipal in nature. [A park] traditionally serves the community. Mass recreation through the use of parks is plainly in the public domain. [Like] the streets of the company town in [Marsh v. Alabama,] the predominant character and purpose of this park are municipal."

Jackson v. Metropolitan Edison Co.
419 U.S. 345 (1974)

JUSTICE REHNQUIST delivered the opinion of the Court.

Respondent Metropolitan Edison Co. is a privately owned and operated [corporation authorized] by the Pennsylvania Public Utility Commission [to] deliver electricity to a service area which includes the city of York [and is] subject to extensive regulation by the Commission. Under a provision of its general tariff filed with the Commission, it has the right to discontinue service to any customer on reasonable notice of nonpayment of bills.

Petitioner Catherine Jackson, [a] resident of York, [received] electric service to her home [until] October 11, 1971, [when] Metropolitan employees disconnected her service [for nonpayment]. Petitioner then filed suit . . . , [seeking] an injunction requiring Metropolitan to continue providing power to her residence until she had been afforded notice, a hearing, and an opportunity to pay any amounts found due. She urged that under state law she had an entitlement to reasonably continuous electrical service to her home and that Metropolitan's termination of her service for alleged nonpayment, action allowed by a provision of its general tariff filed with the Commission, constituted "state action" depriving her of property in violation of the Fourteenth Amendment's guarantee of due process of law. The District Court [dismissed] petitioner's complaint on the ground that the termination did not constitute state action. [The Court of Appeals] affirmed, also finding an absence of state action.

[While] the principle that private action is immune from the restrictions of the Fourteenth Amendment is well established, [the] question whether particular conduct is "private" [or] "state action" [frequently] admits of no easy answer. [Metropolitan] is privately owned and operated, but [is] subject to extensive state regulation. The mere fact that a business is subject to state regulation does not by itself convert its action into that of the State for purposes of the Fourteenth Amendment. Nor does the fact that the regulation is extensive and detailed [do so, even when coupled] with at least something of a governmentally protected monopoly. [The] inquiry must be whether there is a sufficiently close nexus between the State and the challenged action of the regulated entity so that the action of the latter may be fairly treated as that of the State itself. The true nature of the State's involvement may not be immediately obvious, and detailed inquiry may be required in order to determine whether the test is met.

Petitioner advances a series of contentions. . . . We find none of them persuasive. Petitioner first argues that "state action" is present because of the monopoly status allegedly conferred upon Metropolitan by the State of Pennsylvania. As a factual matter, it may well be doubted that the State ever granted or guaranteed Metropolitan a monopoly. But assuming that it had, this fact is not determinative in considering whether Metropolitan's termination of service to petitioner was "state action." [In prior cases involving private monopolies created by government action] we expressly disclaimed reliance on the monopoly status [and concluded that] there was insufficient relationship between the challenged actions of the entities involved and their monopoly status. There is no indication of any greater connection here.

Petitioner next urges that state action is present because respondent provides an essential public service required to be supplied on a reasonably continuous basis by [state law] and hence performs a "public function." We have, of course, found state action present in the exercise by a private entity of powers traditionally exclusively reserved to the State. See, e.g., Nixon v. Condon; Terry v. Adams; Marsh v. Alabama; Evans v. Newton. If we were dealing with the exercise by Metropolitan of some power delegated to it by the State which is traditionally associated with sovereignty, such as eminent domain, our case would be quite a different one. But while the Pennsylvania statute imposes an obligation to furnish service on regulated utilities, it imposes no such obligation on the State. The Pennsylvania courts have rejected the contention that the furnishing of utility services is either a state function or a municipal duty.

Perhaps in recognition of the fact that the supplying of utility service is not traditionally the exclusive prerogative of the State, petitioner invites [creation of] a broad principle that all businesses "affected with the public interest" are state actors in all their actions. We decline the invitation[:] "The phrase 'affected with a public interest' can, in the nature of things, mean no more than that an industry, for adequate reason, is subject to control for the public good. [The phrase is] not susceptible of definition and form[s] an unsatisfactory test." Doctors, optometrists, lawyers, [and] Metropolitan [are] all in regulated businesses, providing arguably essential goods and services, "affected with a public interest." We do not believe that such a status converts their every action, absent more, into that of the State.

We also reject the notion that Metropolitan's termination is state action because the State "has specifically authorized and approved" the termination practice. In the instant case, Metropolitan filed with the Public Utility Commission a general tariff—a provision of which states Metropolitan's right to terminate service for nonpayment. This provision has appeared in Metropolitan's previously filed tariffs for many years and has never been the subject of a hearing or other scrutiny by the Commission. [As] a threshold matter, it is less than clear under state law that Metropolitan was even required to file this provision as part of its tariff or that the Commission would have had the power to disapprove it. [In any event, the] nature of governmental regulation of private utilities is such that a utility may frequently be required by the state regulatory scheme to obtain approval for practices a business regulated in less detail would be free to institute without any approval from a regulatory body. [Such approval], where the commission has not put its own weight on the side of the proposed practice by ordering it, does not transmute a practice initiated by the utility and approved by the commission into "state action." At most, the Commission's failure to overturn this practice amounted to no more than a determination that a Pennsylvania utility was authorized to employ such a practice if it so desired. Respondent's exercise of the choice allowed by state law where the initiative comes from it and not from the State, does not make its action in doing so "state action."

[All] of petitioner's arguments taken together show no more than that Metropolitan was a heavily regulated, privately owned utility, enjoying at least a partial monopoly in the providing of electrical service within its territory, and that it elected to terminate service to petitioner in a manner which the Pennsylvania Public Utility Commission found permissible under state law. [T]his is not sufficient to connect . . . Pennsylvania with respondent's action so as to make the latter's conduct attributable to the State for purposes of the Fourteenth Amendment.

JUSTICE DOUGLAS, dissenting.

[Metropolitan is] a monopolist providing essential public services as a licensee of the State and within a framework of extensive state supervision and control. The particular regulations . . . were authorized by state law and were made enforceable by the weight and authority of the State. Moreover, the State retains the power of oversight to review and amend the regulations if the public interest so requires. Respondent's actions are sufficiently intertwined with those of the State, and its termination-of-service provisions are sufficiently buttressed by state law to warrant a holding that respondent's actions in terminating this householder's service were "state action."

JUSTICE MARSHALL, dissenting.

[Our] state-action cases have repeatedly relied on several factors clearly presented by this case: a state-sanctioned monopoly; an extensive pattern of cooperation between the "private" entity and the State; and a service uniquely public in nature. [When] the State confers a monopoly on [an] organization, this Court has held that the organization assumes many of the obligations of the State [and] that the monopoly factor weighs heavily in determining whether constitutional obligations can be imposed on formally private entities. [The] pattern of cooperation between Metropolitan Edison and the State has led to significant state involvement in virtually every phase of the company's business. . . . [The] fact that [Metropolitan] supplies an essential public service that is in many communities supplied by the government weighs . . . heavily for me. . . . The whole point of the "public function" cases is to look behind the State's decision to provide public services through private parties. In my view, utility service is traditionally identified with the State through universal public regulation or ownership to a degree sufficient to render it a "public function." . . . [W]hen the activity in question is of such public importance that the State invariably either provides the service itself or permits private companies to act as state surrogates in providing it, much more is involved than just a matter of public interest.

NOTES

1. Powers Traditionally Exclusively Reserved to the State. *Jackson* limits the public function doctrine to instances where the private actor exercises powers "traditionally exclusively reserved" for governments.

Flagg Brothers v. Brooks, 436 U.S. 149 (1978). Brooks stored her possessions in Flagg's warehouse, then disputed the storage and moving charges and
refused to pay them. Flagg Brothers threatened to sell the goods to enforce its
warehouseman's lien in the stored goods. Brooks brought suit, claiming that
a sale without prior notice and hearing violated due process and arguing that
state action was present because New York, by creating the warehouseman's
lien, had delegated to Flagg Brothers a "traditional function of civil government, . . . the resolution of private disputes." The Court held that there was
no state action involved and thus no occasion to consider due process. Flagg
Brothers was not exercising a power *exclusively* reserved to the State. New
York had not "delegated to Flagg Brothers an exclusive prerogative of the sovereign" because its statutory "system of rights and remedies" simply recognized "the traditional place of private arrangements" in resolving commercial
disputes. The New York lien law acquiesced in a common private commercial
practice—the sale of stored goods when the owner fails to claim them or
refuses to pay for storage.

Rendell-Baker v. Kohn, 457 U.S. 830 (1982). A teacher fired by a private
school for "students who have experienced difficulty completing public high
schools" sued, claiming that it was in retaliation for her speech. The Court
held that there was no state action even though virtually all of the school's
students were referred to it by the state, almost all of the school's revenue was
from public sources, and the school was heavily regulated by the state. The
fact that the school was performing a public service by educating maladjusted
high school students was insufficient; the school was not exercising an exclusive prerogative of the State.

Blum v. Yaretsky, 457 U.S. 991 (1982). Patients at private nursing homes,
the cost of whose care was paid by Medicaid, claimed that they had due process rights to a hearing prior to their discharge or transfer to a new facility.
The Court held that the decisions of the private nursing home operators were
state action. No public function was performed by the nursing home operators because the decision to discharge or transfer a patient is not a function
traditionally and exclusively exercised by the sovereign.

2. Specific Approval by the State. The *Jackson* Court found no significance in the fact that Metropolitan had filed a tariff or rate application
with the Public Utility Commission (PUC) that included its termination procedure, and the PUC had approved the entire application. The termination
procedure had not been the focus of special state inquiry and approval. The
Court thus distinguished *Jackson* from Public Utilities Commission v. Pollak,
343 U.S. 451 (1952). Capital Transit, a private entity regulated by the PUC,
provided bus service in D.C. After Capital began playing amplified radio programs through loudspeakers in its vehicles, the PUC ordered an investigation
into the practice to determine whether it was "consistent with public convenience, comfort and safety." Following a thorough investigation, including
formal public hearings, the PUC concluded "that the public safety, comfort
and convenience were not impaired" by amplified radio programming in the
buses. Pollak and other passengers attacked the PUC's decision and Capital

Transit's practice as a violation of free speech and due process. The Court concluded that state action was present. While state action was not produced by the mere fact that Capital Transit was a publicly licensed and regulated monopoly, it was created by the PUC's in-depth inquiry into and approval of the very practice at issue.

2.   Inextricable Entanglement

When a government becomes so entangled or involved in the affairs of a private actor that it is difficult to separate their respective identities, the private actor will be deemed a state actor for purposes of constitutional claims made against the private actor. This happens rarely. For such state action to be present it is necessary to establish either an extraordinary degree of interdependence or some necessarily joint action by private and public actors. Mere regulation or provision of substantial funds to the private actor is not enough to create state action.

≡≡≡ *Burton v. Wilmington Parking Authority*
≡≡≡ *365 U.S. 715 (1961)*

JUSTICE CLARK delivered the opinion of the Court.

[Burton sued] the Eagle Coffee Shoppe, Inc., a restaurant located within an off-street automobile parking building in Wilmington, Delaware, [because it refused to serve him] solely because he is a Negro. The parking building is owned and operated by the Wilmington Parking Authority, an agency of the State of Delaware, and the restaurant is the Authority's lessee. [Burton] claims that such refusal abridges his rights under the Equal Protection Clause of the Fourteenth Amendment to the United States Constitution. The [Delaware] Supreme Court [held] that Eagle was acting in "a purely private capacity" under its lease; that its action was not that of the Authority and was not, therefore, state action. [We conclude] that the exclusion of appellant . . . was discriminatory state action in violation of the Equal Protection Clause.

[The Parking Authority undertook] the erection of a parking facility [in] downtown Wilmington. [Before] it began actual construction . . . , the Authority was advised by its retained experts that the anticipated revenue from the parking of cars and proceeds from sale of its bonds would not be sufficient to finance the construction costs of the facility. Moreover, the bonds were not expected to be marketable if payable solely out of parking revenues. To secure additional capital [and] make bond financing practicable, the Authority decided it was necessary to enter long-term leases with responsible tenants for commercial use of some of the space available in the projected "garage building." [The Authority entered into a 20-year lease] with Eagle Coffee Shoppe Inc., for use as a "restaurant, dining room, banquet hall, cocktail lounge and bar." [Eagle's restaurant], although "within the exterior walls of the structure, has no marked public entrance leading from the parking portion of the facility into the restaurant proper [whose main entrance] is located on Ninth Street." [Although] Eagle covenanted to "occupy and use the leased premises in accordance with all applicable laws, statutes, ordinances and rules and regulations of any federal, state or municipal authority," [the lease] contains no requirement that its restaurant services be made available to the general public on a nondiscriminatory basis, in spite of the fact that the Authority has power to adopt rules and regulations respecting the use of its facilities except any as would impair the security of its bondholders.

Other portions of the structure were leased to other tenants, including a bookstore, a retail jeweler, and a food store. Upon completion of the building, the Authority located at appropriate places thereon official signs indicating the public character of the building, and flew from mastheads on the roof both the state and national flags.

[The] land and building were publicly owned. [T]he building was dedicated to "public uses" in performance of the Authority's "essential governmental functions." [The] commercially leased areas [constituted an] indispensable part of the State's plan to operate its project as a self-sustaining unit. Upkeep and maintenance of the building, including necessary repairs, were responsibilities of the Authority and were payable out of public funds. It cannot be doubted that the peculiar relationship of the restaurant to the parking facility in which it is located confers on each an incidental variety of mutual benefits. Guests of the restaurant are afforded a convenient place to park their automobiles, even if they cannot enter the restaurant directly from the parking area. Similarly, its convenience for diners may well provide additional demand for the Authority's parking facilities. . . . Neither can it be ignored, especially in view of Eagle's affirmative allegation that for it to serve Negroes would injure its business, that profits earned by discrimination not only contribute to, but also are indispensable elements in, the financial success of a governmental agency.

Addition of all these activities, obligations and responsibilities of the Authority, the benefits mutually conferred, together with the obvious fact that the restaurant is operated as an integral part of a public building devoted to a public parking service, indicates that degree of state participation and involvement in discriminatory action which it was the design of the Fourteenth Amendment to condemn. [Moreover], in its lease with Eagle the Authority could have affirmatively required Eagle to discharge the responsibilities under the Fourteenth Amendment imposed upon the private enterprise as a consequence of state participation. [By] its inaction, the Authority [has] not only made itself a party to the refusal of service, but has elected to place its power, property and prestige behind the admitted discrimination. The State has so far insinuated itself into a position of interdependence with Eagle that it must be recognized as a joint participant in the challenged activity, which, on that account, cannot be considered to have been so "purely private" as to fall without the scope of the Fourteenth Amendment.

[This conclusion is] drawn from the facts and circumstances of this [case and is] by no means declared [as] universal. [While] a multitude of relationships might appear to some to fall within [state action, that] can be determined only in the framework of the peculiar facts or circumstances. [What] we hold today is that when a State leases public property in the manner and for the purpose shown to have been the case here, the proscriptions of the Fourteenth Amendment must be complied with by the lessee as certainly as though they were binding covenants written into the agreement itself. [Reversed and remanded.]

JUSTICE STEWART, concurring.

I agree that the judgment must be reversed, but I reach that conclusion by a route much more direct than the one traveled by the Court. In upholding Eagle's right to deny service to the appellant solely because of his race, the Supreme Court of Delaware relied upon a [state] statute . . . which permits the proprietor of a restaurant to refuse to serve "persons whose reception or entertainment by him would be offensive to the major part of his customers." [The] highest court of Delaware [has] construed this [statute] as authorizing discriminatory classification based exclusively on color. Such a law seems to me clearly violative of the Fourteenth Amendment.

NOTES

1. Financial Interdependence. If financial interdependence was the critical factor that led the Court to conclude that Eagle and the Parking Authority had a sufficiently interdependent relationship to make Eagle's actions attributable to the state, why did the Court reject the claim that state action was present in Blum v. Yaretsky, 457 U.S. 991 (1982), and Rendell-Baker v. Kohn, 457 U.S. 830 (1982)? In *Blum*, the decision of private nursing home operators to discharge or transfer certain Medicaid patients, the costs of whose care was borne entirely by the State, was not state action. Even though the state subsidized both operating and capital expenses of the homes, regulated their operations, and paid for the costs of care of over 90 percent of the patients, the court concluded that there had been an insufficient showing of the interdependence required by *Burton*.

In *Rendell-Baker*, the decision of a private school to discharge certain employees was not state action even though the school existed to educate "maladjusted" students who could not be accommodated in the public schools, almost all of its revenue came from the state, and it operated in conformity with state-imposed standards. The Court rejected the contention that this was a form of *Burton*'s financial interdependence; rather, the school was just another "contractor performing services for the government."

2. Actions That Require Joint Efforts of Private and Public Actors. When action can be taken only with the joint active participation of both private and public actors, state action is likely present. Lugar v. Edmondson Oil Co., 457 U.S. 922 (1982), is a prime example. Edmondson Oil sued Lugar in Virginia state court to collect a debt. In the course of that suit Edmondson

Oil filed an ex parte petition seeking a pre-judgment attachment of Lugar's assets. The court clerk issued the writ of attachment, which was executed by the sheriff. After the attachment was dismissed on the merits, Lugar brought suit in federal court against Edmondson Oil, contending that the wrongful attachment had deprived him of his property without due process. No one disputed that the Virginia sheriff and court clerk engaged in state action, but Lugar did not sue them. The question was entirely whether Edmondson Oil, a private litigant, had engaged in state action by enlisting the aid of the courts to collect a debt. The Court, 5-4, found Edmondson Oil to be a state actor because Virginia's procedure required "officers of the State [to] act jointly with a creditor in securing the property in dispute." The Court distinguished *Flagg Brothers* because the New York procedure invoked by the creditor required no state participation of any kind. The Court noted that "the procedural scheme created by the [Virginia] statute [is] the product of state action" because it worked only with the joint participation of public and private actors. The four dissenters argued that it was "implausible" and "unjust" to hold that "a private citizen who did no more than commence a legal action of a kind traditionally initiated by private parties, thereby engaged in 'state action.'" Compare with Tulsa Professional Collection Services v. Pope, 485 U.S. 478 (1988).

Brentwood Academy v. Tennessee Secondary School Athletic Association
531 U.S. 288 (2001)

JUSTICE SOUTER delivered the opinion of the Court.

The issue is whether a statewide association incorporated to regulate interscholastic athletic competition among public and private secondary schools may be regarded as engaging in state action when it enforces a rule against a member school. The association in question here includes most public schools located within the State, acts through their representatives, draws its officers from them, is largely funded by their dues and income received in their stead, and has historically been seen to regulate in lieu of the State Board of Education's exercise of its own authority. We hold that the association's regulatory activity may and should be treated as state action owing to the pervasive entwinement of state school officials in the structure of the association.

I. . . . Tennessee Secondary School Athletic Association (Association) is a not-for-profit membership corporation organized to regulate interscholastic sport among the public and private high schools in Tennessee that belong to it. No school is forced to join, but . . . almost all the State's public high schools (some 290 of them or 84% of the Association's voting membership) [are members], far outnumbering the 55 private schools that belong. A member school's team may play or scrimmage only against the team of another member, absent a dispensation.

The Association's rulemaking arm is its legislative council, [the] voting membership of [which] is limited under the Association's bylaws to high school principals, assistant principals, and superintendents elected by the member schools, and the public school administrators who so serve typically attend meetings during regular school hours. Although the Association's staff members are not paid by the State, they are eligible to join the State's public retirement system for its employees. Member schools pay dues to the Association, though the bulk of its revenue is gate receipts at member teams' football and basketball tournaments, many of them held in public arenas rented by the Association. The [Association] has the power "to suspend, to fine, or otherwise penalize any member school for the violation of any of the rules of the Association or for other just cause." Ever since the Association was incorporated in 1925, Tennessee's State Board of Education (State Board) has (to use its own words) acknowledged the corporation's functions "in providing standards, rules and regulations for interscholastic competition in the public schools of Tennessee." More recently, the State Board [in 1972 adopted] a rule expressly "designating" the Association as "the organization to supervise and regulate the athletic activities in which the public junior and senior high schools in Tennessee participate on an interscholastic basis. . . . " In 1996, however, the State Board dropped [its rule] expressly designating the Association as regulator; it substituted a statement . . . "authorizing the public schools of the state to voluntarily maintain membership in [the Association]." . . .

Brentwood Academy, a private parochial high school member of the Association [was found by the Association to have] violated a rule prohibiting "undue influence" in recruiting athletes, when it wrote to incoming students and their parents about spring football practice. The Association . . . placed Brentwood's athletic program on probation for four years, declared its football and boys' basketball teams ineligible to compete in playoffs for two years, and imposed a $3,000 fine. When these penalties were imposed, all the [Association's] voting members . . . were public school administrators. Brentwood sued the Association and its executive director in federal court, . . . claiming that enforcement of the Rule was state action and a violation of the First and Fourteenth Amendments. The District Court entered summary judgment for Brentwood and enjoined the Association from enforcing the Rule. In holding the Association to be a state actor [the] District Court found that the State had delegated authority over high school athletics to the Association, characterized the relationship between the Association and its public school members as symbiotic, and emphasized the predominantly public character of the Association's membership and leadership. . . . The . . . Sixth Circuit reversed. [We] now reverse.

II. A. . . . The judicial obligation is not only to "'preserve an area of individual freedom by limiting the reach of federal law' and avoid the imposition of responsibility on a State for conduct it could not control," but also to assure that constitutional standards are invoked "when it can be said that the State is *responsible* for the specific conduct of which the plaintiff complains."

. . . What is fairly attributable [to the state] is a matter of normative judgment, and the criteria lack rigid simplicity. [No] one fact can function as a necessary condition across the board for finding state action; nor is any set of circumstances absolutely sufficient, for there may be some countervailing reason against attributing activity to the government. Our cases have identified a host of facts that can bear on the fairness of such an attribution.

[National Collegiate Athletic Association v. Tarkanian, 488 U.S. 179 (1988),] arose when an undoubtedly state actor, the University of Nevada, suspended its basketball coach, Tarkanian, in order to comply with rules and recommendations of the National Collegiate Athletic Association (NCAA). The coach charged the NCAA with state action, arguing that the state university had delegated its own functions to the NCAA, clothing the latter with authority to make and apply the university's rules, the result being joint action making the NCAA a state actor. [We] found no state action on the part of the NCAA [because its] policies were shaped not by the University of Nevada alone, but by several hundred member institutions, most of them having no connection with Nevada, and exhibiting no color of Nevada law. But dictum in *Tarkanian* pointed to a contrary result on facts like ours[:] "The situation would, of course, be different if the [Association's] membership consisted entirely of institutions located within the same State, many of them public institutions created by the same sovereign."

B. Just as we foresaw in *Tarkanian* [there is] state action here. The nominally private character of the Association is overborne by the pervasive entwinement of public institutions and public officials in its composition and workings, and there is no substantial reason to claim unfairness in applying constitutional standards to it. The Association is not an organization of natural persons acting on their own, but [of] public schools to the extent of 84% of the total. Under the Association's bylaws, each member school is represented by its principal or a faculty member, who has a vote in selecting members of the governing legislative council and board of control from eligible principals, assistant principals and superintendents. [Public] school officials act within the scope of their duties when they represent their institutions. . . . In sum, to the extent of 84% of its membership, the Association is an organization of public schools represented by their officials acting in their official capacity to provide an integral element of secondary public schooling. There would be no recognizable Association, legal or tangible, without the public school officials, who do not merely control but overwhelmingly perform all but the purely ministerial acts by which the Association exists and functions in practical terms. . . .

To complement the entwinement of public school officials with the Association from the bottom up, the State of Tennessee has provided for entwinement from top down. State Board members are assigned ex officio to serve as members of the [Association's governing boards], and the Association's ministerial employees are treated as state employees to the extent of being eligible for membership in the state retirement system. [While the] State Board's Rule expressly designating the Association as regulator of interscholastic athletics in public schools was deleted in 1996, [this] affected nothing but words. . . . The . . . State Board once freely acknowledged the Association's official character but now does it by winks and nods. [The] entwinement down from the State Board is . . . unmistakable, just as the entwinement up from the member public schools is overwhelming. Entwinement will support a conclusion that an ostensibly private organization ought to be charged with a public character and judged by constitutional standards; entwinement to the degree shown here requires it. . . . [Reversed and remanded.]

JUSTICE THOMAS, joined by CHIEF JUSTICE REHNQUIST and JUSTICES SCALIA and KENNEDY, dissenting.

We have never found state action based upon mere "entwinement." . . . The majority's holding [not] only extends state-action doctrine beyond its permissible limits but also encroaches upon the realm of individual freedom that the doctrine was meant to protect. . . .

I. A. [No] public school need join the TSSAA. The TSSAA's rules are enforced not by a state agency but by its own board of control, . . . none of whom must work at a public school. . . . The State of Tennessee did not create [or fund] the TSSAA [and] does not pay its employees. [The] bulk of its operating budget is derived from gate receipts at tournaments it sponsors. . . . No Tennessee law authorizes the State to coordinate interscholastic athletics or empowers another entity to organize interscholastic athletics on behalf of the State. The only state pronouncement acknowledging the TSSAA's existence is a rule providing that the State Board of Education permits public schools to maintain membership in the TSSAA if they so choose. Moreover, the State of Tennessee has never had any involvement in the particular action taken by the TSSAA in this case [and there] is no indication that the State has ever had any interest in how schools choose to regulate recruiting. . . .

B. . . . The TSSAA has not performed a function that has been "traditionally exclusively reserved to the State." The organization of interscholastic sports is neither a traditional nor an exclusive public function of the States.

[The] State of Tennessee has not "exercised coercive power or . . . provided such significant encouragement [to the TSSAA], either overt or covert," that the TSSAA's regulatory activities must in law be deemed to be those of the State. The State has not promulgated any regulations of interscholastic sports, and nothing in the record suggests that the State has encouraged or coerced the TSSAA in enforcing its recruiting rule. . . . Furthermore, there is no evidence of "joint participation" between the State and the TSSAA in the TSSAA's enforcement of its recruiting rule. [Finally], there is no "symbiotic relationship" between the State and the TSSAA. . . . The TSSAA provides a service—the organization of athletic tournaments—in exchange for membership dues and gate fees, just as a vendor could contract with public schools to sell refreshments at school events. . . . Also, there is no suggestion in this case that, as was the case in *Burton*, the State profits from the TSSAA's decision to enforce its recruiting rule. . . .

II. Although the TSSAA's enforcement activities cannot be considered state action as a matter of common sense or under any of this Court's existing theories of state action, the majority presents a new theory. Under this theory, . . . "entwinement" of the State with the TSSAA . . . converts private action into state action. The majority does not define "entwinement," and the meaning of the term is not altogether clear. But whatever this new "entwinement" theory may entail, it lacks any support in our state-action jurisprudence. . . .

NOTES AND PROBLEMS

1. Entwinement as a Distinct Concept.   What is the difference between entwinement and the inextricable entanglement of government and private action that was at issue in *Burton*? What element(s) are present in *Brentwood Academy* that were absent in *Burton*? What element(s) were present in *Burton* that were absent in *Brentwood Academy*? If there is no difference, why did the Court insist on identifying entwinement as a separate, distinct approach to state action?

2. Formalism and Functionalism.   Does the difference between the majority and the dissent reflect fundamentally different approaches to state action? Consider the possibility that the majority treats state action as a question of discerning the functional relationship of the challenged action to the state and the dissent regards state action as turning on formal actions of the government. If the defect of formalism is that it allows states to escape constitutional scrutiny by enabling compliant private parties to do their bidding, is the defect of functionalism that it draws no detectable lines between the public and private spheres? Some commentators, especially those aligned with the Critical Legal Studies movement, criticize the entire distinction between public and private as a "false dichotomy." Is the Court in *Brentwood Academy* endorsing that view? If not, what factual elements constitute sufficient "entwinement" to constitute state action? Should it trouble us if it proves to be impossible to give a solid answer to that question?

3. The Value of State Action Doctrine.   Justice Souter said that state action should not be found when there is present "some value at odds with finding public accountability in the circumstances." What values might these be? Justice Thomas claimed that the state action doctrine "preserves . . . individual freedom by limiting the reach of federal law and federal judicial power," and "promotes important values of federalism [by] 'avoiding the imposition of responsibility on a State for conduct it could not control.'" Are these principles helpful in locating the outer edges of state action?

4. Problems: *Spring Prom.* The Municipal Brotherhood of Police, a voluntary private association whose members are limited to current and retired "peace officers," sponsors a dance at its hall for seniors at Public High School each spring and refuses admission to students whom it considers to be gay or lesbian. The term "peace officer" is defined by state law to include law enforcement officers and private security guards. The revenue of the

Brotherhood is derived from membership dues and profits from a concession granted the Brotherhood by the municipality at the annual municipal fair. Is the Brotherhood's refusal to admit gay or lesbian students to its dance, otherwise open to all high school seniors, state action?

People for the Ethical Treatment of Animals. Public High School's chapter of PETA is provided space in the high school for after-school meetings. The local chapter refuses to admit a student who is an enthusiastic carnivore. The state bars discrimination in public accommodations on the basis of ethical or political beliefs. Is the refusal state action? On what additional facts might resolution of this depend?

Free Taxis. A municipality enters into a contract with a private taxicab company by which the municipality agrees to pay to the company a fee, in return for which the taxi company agrees to provide free service from midnight until 5 A.M. Under the contract, the city and the company establish a five-person board of directors to oversee the nocturnal taxi service. Public officials occupy two of those director positions. Over the objection of the two public directors, the taxi company refuses to permit "punks" (which it describes as people with odd or unusual body piercing, hair styles, ragged clothing, or any combination of the above) to ride the cabs. Is state action present? Does it matter if the public directors do not object, or vote in favor of the idea?

3. Coercion and Encouragement

When governments coerce private action by law, the law itself is, of course, state action. When such coercion occurs by means short of the force of law, the coerced private action is treated as state action. But what constitutes coercion? When governments encourage rather than coerce private action, but that encouragement is extraordinary, unusual, or extreme, the nominal private action may well be treated as state action.

≡≡≡ *Shelley v. Kraemer*
≡≡≡ *334 U.S. 1 (1948)*

CHIEF JUSTICE VINSON delivered the opinion of the Court.

These cases present [questions] relating to the validity of court enforcement of [private] restrictive covenants, which have as their purpose the exclusion of persons of designated race or color from the ownership or occupancy of real property. [Petitioners] Shelley, who are Negroes, [purchased a residence in St. Louis that was burdened with a restrictive covenant barring occupancy "by any person not of the Caucasian race." Respondents], owners of other property subject to the terms of the restrictive covenant, brought suit in [Missouri state court] praying that petitioners Shelley be restrained from taking possession of the property. [The] Supreme Court of Missouri [concluded] that enforcement of [the restrictive covenant] violated no rights guaranteed to petitioners by the Federal Constitution. [The] circumstances presented [by the second case, from Michigan,] do not differ materially from the Missouri case.

[Petitioners] urge that they have been denied [equal protection]. Whether the equal protection clause [inhibits] judicial enforcement by state courts of restrictive covenants based on race or color is a question which this Court has not heretofore been called upon to consider. [It is] clear that restrictions on the right of occupancy of the sort sought to be created by the private agreements in these cases could not be squared with the requirements of the Fourteenth Amendment if imposed by state statute or local ordinance. [But] the present cases [do] not involve action by state legislatures or city councils. Here the [racial] discrimination and the [restrictive covenants are produced] by the terms of agreements among private individuals. Participation of the State consists in the enforcement of the restrictions.

Since [the] Civil Rights Cases, 109 U.S. 3 (1883), the principle has become firmly embedded in our constitutional law that the action inhibited by [the] Fourteenth Amendment is only such action as may fairly be said to be that of the States. That Amendment erects no shield against merely private conduct, however discriminatory or wrongful. [Therefore], the restrictive agreements standing alone cannot be regarded as violative of any rights guaranteed to petitioners by the Fourteenth Amendment. So long as the purposes of those agreements are effectuated by voluntary adherence to their terms, [there] has been no action by the State and the provisions of the Amendment have not been violated. But here there was more. [The] purposes of the agreements were secured only by judicial enforcement by state courts of the restrictive terms of the agreements. [Action] of state courts and judicial officers in their official capacities [has] long been established [as state action].

We have no doubt that there has been state action in these cases. [Petitioners] were willing purchasers of properties upon which they desired to establish homes. The owners of the properties were willing sellers; and contracts of sale were accordingly consummated. [But] for the active intervention of the state courts, supported by the full panoply of state power, petitioners would have been free to occupy the properties in question without restraint. These are not cases [in] which the States have merely abstained from action, leaving private individuals free to impose such discriminations as they see fit. Rather, these are cases in which the States have made available to such individuals the full coercive power of government to deny to petitioners, on the grounds of race or color, the enjoyment of property rights in premises which petitioners are willing and financially able to acquire and which the grantors are willing to sell. . . . [State] action [refers] to exertions of state power in all forms. [We] hold that in granting judicial enforcement of the restrictive agreements in these cases, the States have denied petitioners [equal protection] and that, therefore, the action of the state courts cannot stand. [Reversed.]

NOTES

1. Framing the Issue: What Is the State Action? Why did the Court discuss whether state action was present? Isn't the judicial act of issuing an injunction state action? To get a sense of what really may be at issue here, consider the following: A person summons the police on Hallowe'en night, complaining of revelers partying on his front lawn. His motivation for summoning the police is his dislike of the race of the revelers. May the revelers defend against the resulting criminal trespass charge by asserting that the state's prosecution violates equal protection? In other words, is the racially discriminatory motive of the homeowner attributable to the state or merely a private bias? Note that the state's trespass law is completely neutral on the substantive issue of race.

Bell v. Maryland, 378 U.S. 226 (1964). The Court was confronted by a challenge to the application of trespass laws to sit-in demonstrators protesting racial segregation in private businesses such as restaurants. Although the Court did not reach the state action issue (it reversed the convictions on unrelated grounds), the justices divided individually on the point. Justice Black argued that the reason there was state action in *Shelley* was that the state "had acted 'to deny to petitioners, on the grounds of race, [the] enjoyment of property [that] petitioners are willing [and] able to acquire and which the grantors are willing to sell.'" But, said Black, there is no state action "when one party is unwilling."

2. The Outer Boundaries of Coercion of Private Behavior. Was Justice Black correct in Bell v. Maryland to assert that state action was present in *Shelley* because the state, through the means of an injunction, frustrated private ordering? But for the state's coercion, the transaction in *Shelley* between willing parties would have occurred without interference. Missouri in effect said to the private parties, "You *must* obey the racially restrictive covenant." By contrast, had the seller declined to sell to Shelley in the first instance, there would have been no state action, according to Justice Black. The decision not to sell (even if motivated by racial prejudice) would be an entirely private act. Of course, state and federal statutes can and do prohibit such private racial discrimination, but those statutes do not raise issues of constitutional law. To help you assess whether that account of *Shelley* is accurate, consider the following cases.

Barrows v. Jackson, 346 U.S. 249 (1953). Jackson entered into a racially restrictive ("whites only") real covenant with respect to her property, then violated the covenant by permitting nonwhites to occupy the property. Barrows, a "beneficiary" of the covenant, sued Jackson for damages for breach of the covenant. The Court concluded that delivery of damages via the state's judicial machinery constituted state action because it operated

> to coerce [Jackson] to observe a restrictive covenant that [the state had no] right to enforce in equity. [If] the State may thus punish [Jackson] for her failure to carry out her covenant, she is coerced to continue to use her property in

a discriminatory manner. [It is no longer Jackson's] voluntary choice but the State's choice that she observe her covenant or suffer damages.

The Court further observed that the coercive effect of the damages remedy would also manifest itself in either a refusal of prospective sellers to sell to nonwhites or a sale at "a higher price to meet the damages which the seller may incur." As in *Shelley*, both private parties wished to transfer the property in violation of the covenant; only the coercive hand of the state's judicial system frustrated them.

Evans v. Abney, 396 U.S. 435 (1970).   Following the Court's decision in Evans v. Newton that the operation of Senator Bacon's racially restrictive park in nominally private hands was state action and constitutionally infirm, the case was remanded to the Georgia state courts. The Georgia courts ruled that Senator Bacon's trust had failed because it was no longer possible to achieve his racially biased intent. Accordingly, the possibility of reverter in Baconsfield held by Bacon's heirs became possessory. The Court, 6-2, affirmed this decision:

> [T]he Georgia courts did no more than apply well-settled general principles of Georgia law to determine the meaning and effect of a Georgia [will]. Senator Bacon's will [embodied] a preference for termination of the park rather than its integration. [The] Georgia court had no alternative under its relevant trust laws, which are long standing and neutral with regard to race, but to end the Baconsfield trust and return the property to the Senator's heirs.

Do these cases confine *Shelley* to only those instances when the state's judicial system operates to coerce willing private parties to refrain from their desired conduct? Is it fair to say that when private parties invoke facially valid rules of law to achieve ends impermissible to the state itself, there is no state action?

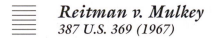

Reitman v. Mulkey
387 U.S. 369 (1967)

JUSTICE WHITE delivered the opinion of the Court.

[By an initiative, Proposition 14, California voters amended the California Constitution to provide in Article I, section 26, that

> [n]either the State nor any subdivision or agency thereof shall deny, limit or abridge, directly or indirectly, the right of any person, who is willing or desires to sell, lease or rent any part or all of his [residential] real property, to decline to sell, lease or rent such property to such person or persons as he, in his absolute discretion, chooses.]

The question here is whether Art. I, §26, of the California Constitution denies [equal protection].

[The Mulkeys brought suit under the Unruh Act, a California law that bars private racial discrimination in housing, alleging that Reitman] had refused to rent them an apartment solely on account of their race. [The trial court granted Reitman's motion for summary judgment on the ground that the Unruh Act] had been rendered null and void by the adoption of Proposition 14. [The California Supreme Court reversed.] We affirm.

[The] California Supreme Court [examined] the constitutionality of §26 in terms of its "immediate objective," its "ultimate effect" and its "historical context and the conditions existing prior to its enactment." [First, Proposition 14's] immediate design and intent . . . were "to overturn state laws that bore on the right of private sellers and lessors to discriminate," and "to forestall future state action that might circumscribe this right." This aim was successfully achieved: [Proposition 14] establishes "a purported constitutional right to privately discriminate on grounds which admittedly would be unavailable under the Fourteenth Amendment should state action be involved."

Second, the [California] court conceded that the State was permitted a neutral position with respect to private racial discriminations and that the State was not bound by the Federal Constitution to forbid them. But, because a significant state involvement in private discriminations could amount to unconstitutional state action, [*Burton*], the court deemed it necessary to determine whether Proposition 14 invalidly involved the State in racial discriminations in the housing market. Its conclusion was that it did. [The California court] concluded that [state action] could be found "even where the state can be charged with only encouraging," rather than commanding discrimination. [The] California court [found that] the State had taken affirmative action designed to make private discriminations legally possible. Section 26 was said to have changed the situation from one in which discrimination was restricted "to one wherein it is encouraged"; [section 26] was legislative action "which authorized private discrimination" and made the State "at least a partner in the [act] of discrimination." The [California] court could "conceive of no other purpose [for] section 26 aside from authorizing the perpetration of a purported private discrimination." The judgment of the California court was that §26 unconstitutionally involves the State in racial discriminations and is therefore invalid under the Fourteenth Amendment. There is no sound reason for rejecting this judgment.

[The] California court [did] not posit a constitutional violation on the mere repeal of the Unruh and Rumford Acts. It did not read either our cases or the Fourteenth Amendment as establishing an automatic constitutional barrier to the repeal of an existing law prohibiting racial discriminations in housing; nor did the court rule that a State may never put in statutory form an existing policy of neutrality with respect to private discriminations. What the court below did was [deal with §26] as though it expressly authorized . . . the private right to discriminate. [Thus], the court [concluded that] the ultimate impact of §26 [would] encourage and significantly involve the State in private racial discrimination contrary to the Fourteenth Amendment.

The California court could very reasonably conclude that §26 would and did have wider impact than a mere repeal of existing statutes. . . . But the section struck more deeply and more widely. Private discriminations in housing were now not only free from Rumford and Unruh but they also enjoyed a far different status than was true before the passage of those statutes. The right to discriminate, including the right to discriminate on racial grounds, was now embodied in the State's basic charter, immune from legislative, executive, or judicial regulation at any level of the state government. Those practicing racial discriminations need no longer rely solely on their personal choice. They could now invoke express constitutional authority, free from censure or interference of any kind from official sources.

This Court has never attempted the "impossible task" of formulating an infallible test for determining whether the State "in any of its manifestations" has become significantly involved in private discriminations. "Only by sifting facts and weighing circumstances" on a case-by-case basis can a "nonobvious involvement of the State in private conduct be attributed its true significance." [The] California court, armed [with] the knowledge of the facts and circumstances concerning the passage and potential impact of §26, and familiar with the milieu in which that provision would operate, . . . determined that the provision would involve the State in private racial discriminations to an unconstitutional degree. We accept this holding of the California court.

JUSTICE HARLAN, joined by JUSTICES BLACK, CLARK, and STEWART, dissenting.

[The] Equal Protection Clause [forbids] a State to use its authority to foster discrimination based on such factors as race [but] does not undertake to control purely personal prejudices and predilections, and individuals acting on their own are left free to discriminate on racial grounds if they are so minded. [By] the same token, the Fourteenth Amendment does not require of States the passage of laws preventing such private discrimination, although it does not of course disable them from enacting such legislation if they wish. [By section 26, California] has decided to remain "neutral" in the realm of private discrimination affecting the sale or rental of private residential property. . . . [All] that has happened is that California has effected a pro tanto repeal of its prior statutes forbidding private discrimination. This runs no more afoul of the Fourteenth Amendment than would have California's failure to pass any such antidiscrimination statutes in the first instance. . . . I do not think the Court's opinion . . . denies any of these fundamental constitutional propositions. Rather it attempts to escape them by resorting to arguments which appear to me to be entirely ill-founded.

[The] Court attempts to fit §26 within the coverage of the Equal Protection Clause by characterizing it as in effect an affirmative call to residents of California to discriminate. [But the] provision is neutral on its face, and it is only by in effect asserting that this requirement of passive official neutrality is camouflage that the Court is able to reach its conclusion. . . . [The] Fourteenth Amendment . . . only forbids a State to pass or keep in effect laws discriminating on account of race. California has not done this. A state enactment, particularly one that is simply permissive of private decision-making rather than coercive and one that has been adopted in this most democratic of processes, should not be struck down by the judiciary under the Equal Protection Clause without persuasive evidence of an invidious purpose or effect. . . .

The core of the Court's opinion is that §26 is offensive to the Fourteenth Amendment because it effectively encourages private discrimination. By focusing on "encouragement" the Court [is] forging a slippery and unfortunate criterion by which to measure the constitutionality of a statute simply permissive in purpose and effect, and inoffensive on its face. . . . Here . . . we have only the straightforward adoption of a neutral provision restoring to the sphere of free choice . . . private behavior within a limited area. The [Court concludes that this] has the effect of lending encouragement to those who wish to discriminate. . . . Every act of private discrimination is either forbidden by state law or permitted by it. There can be little doubt that such permissiveness—whether by express constitutional or statutory provision, or implicit in the common law—to some extent "encourages" those who wish to discriminate to do so. Under this theory "state action" in the form of laws that do nothing more than passively permit private discrimination could be said to tinge all private discrimination with the taint of unconstitutional state encouragement. [A state's] refusal to involve itself at all [is] very different from [*Evans* and *Burton*], where the Court found active involvement of state agencies and officials in specific acts of discrimination. [The] state action required to bring the Fourteenth Amendment into operation must be affirmative and purposeful, actively fostering discrimination. Only in such a case is ostensibly "private" action more properly labeled "official." I do not believe that the mere enactment of §26 [falls] within this class of cases.

NOTES

1. State Encouragement of Private Action. As *Reitman* indicates, the line between undue or unusual governmental encouragement of private action and ordinary public policy is thin indeed. All the justices agreed that California could validly repeal its fair housing laws, and the California constitutional amendment was facially neutral with respect to race. The provision surely had the effect of insulating private racial prejudice from attack and thus facilitated racial discrimination, but in what sense did it *encourage* such discrimination? Put another way, how much encouragement must the state lend to private action in order to transmute private action into state action? Recall *Flagg Brothers*, where the Court concluded that New York's statutorily created warehouseman's lien—legislation that insulated private action from private legal attack—was insufficient encouragement to constitute state action. New York, said the Court, had merely acquiesced in private action. New York had not acted; it had merely "refused to act": "New York has not compelled the sale [but] has merely announced the circumstances under which its courts will not interfere with a private sale." But both California and New York adopted laws that insulated private action from legal challenge. Why was private prejudice treated as California's act but private refusal to afford notice and hearing before sale not New York's act? Why wasn't California's constitutional amendment a mere announcement of "the circumstances under which its courts will not interfere with" private prejudice? Has *Reitman* been implicitly overruled, or confined to its facts?

2. *Reitman* as a Political Process Case. The obvious state action in *Reitman* was the adoption of the constitutional amendment. The nonobvious state action was Reitman's private racially biased refusal to rent to the Mulkeys. Consider the possibility that *Reitman* makes more sense as an example of a case like Hunter v. Erickson or Washington v. Seattle School District (Chapter 8, Section C.5), where the political process itself was restructured in a fashion that was designed to disadvantage racial minorities. In this view, while California did not have to enact laws against private racial discrimination and could repeal them if it wished, it could not alter the political process to place racial minorities at a political disadvantage on this issue. Once the state constitutional provision was in place, the only way racial minorities could secure passage of laws barring private racial discrimination in housing would be to go to the extraordinary effort of amending the state constitution to repeal the amendment.

But consider the flaws of this argument as well. In *Hunter*, the power to enact laws forbidding private racial discrimination in housing (and only such laws) was transferred from the city council to the people as a whole. In *Seattle School District*, the power of local school boards to institute pupil busing for racial diversity when not constitutionally required was barred by a state constitutional amendment; almost all other reasons for pupil busing were left within the authority of local schools. In both *Hunter* and *Seattle School District*, the political process was altered only with respect to an issue framed explicitly by race. By contrast, California's Proposition 14 was absolutely neutral on the issue of race. Implicit support for this contrary view might be derived from *Schuette* (Chapter 8, Section C.5).

3. State Action as a Shadow to Constitutional Substance. Does the revisionist view of *Reitman*—as a political process case—shed light on the nature of the state action inquiry? Note that the substance of the alleged equal protection violation changes as the nature of the alleged state action changes. In the Court's view of *Reitman*, the state action problem is difficult (does a facially neutral and otherwise permissible change of law constitute such encouragement to private bigotry that the private acts become those of the government?), but the underlying equal protection problem is simple (if private racism is deemed state action, it will clearly be unjustified and thus violate equal protection). In the revisionist view of *Reitman*, the state action problem is simple (the state amended its constitution), but the underlying equal protection problem is difficult: Is a racially neutral change of law that in practice disadvantages racial minorities an unjustifiable act of racial discrimination?

B. CONGRESSIONAL POWER TO ENFORCE CONSTITUTIONAL RIGHTS

The Reconstruction Amendments each grant to Congress power to enforce the substantive terms of the Amendment by "appropriate legislation." These grants of power are contained in section 2 of each of the Thirteenth and Fifteenth Amendments and in section 5 of the Fourteenth Amendment. What is the scope of these powers? More specifically, may Congress use these powers to regulate private conduct? Does Congress have any power to enforce a substantive vision of the amendments that differs from the Court's interpretations?

1. The Scope of Enforcement Power: Public or Private Conduct?

≣ *Civil Rights Cases*
≣ *109 U.S. 3 (1883)*

[The federal Civil Rights Act of 1875 prohibited private racial discrimination in public accommodations and subjected violators to civil liability and criminal penalties. By an 8-1 margin, the Court held that Congress lacked any source of authority to enact the legislation.]

JUSTICE BRADLEY delivered the opinion of the Court.

Has Congress constitutional power to make such a law? [No] one will contend that the power to pass it was contained in the Constitution before the adoption of the [Thirteenth, Fourteenth, and Fifteenth] amendments. [The Fourteenth Amendment prohibits] State action of a particular [character]. Individual invasion of individual rights is not the subject matter of the amendment. [It] nullifies and makes void all State legislation, and State action of every kind, which impairs the privileges and immunities of citizens of the United States, or which injures them in life, liberty or property without due process of law, or which denies to any of them the equal protection of the laws. It not only does this, [but section 5] of the amendment invests Congress with power to enforce it by appropriate legislation. To enforce what? To enforce the prohibition [by] correcting the effects of such prohibited State laws and State acts, and thus to render them effectually null, void, and innocuous. This is the legislative power conferred upon Congress, and this is the whole of it. [Such] legislation must necessarily be predicated [upon] State laws or State proceedings [that violate the Fourteenth Amendment], and be directed to the correction of their operation and effect. [Until] some State law has been passed, or some State action [taken], adverse to the rights of citizens sought to be protected by the Fourteenth Amendment, no legislation of the United States under said amendment [can] be called into activity: for the prohibitions of the amendment are against State laws and acts done under State authority.

[The Civil Rights Act] makes no reference whatever to any supposed or apprehended violation of the Fourteenth Amendment on the part of the States. [It] proceeds . . . to declare that certain acts committed by individuals shall be deemed offences, and shall be prosecuted and punished by proceedings in the courts of the United States. It does not profess to be corrective of any constitutional wrong committed by the States. . . . [It] lays down rules for the conduct of individuals in society towards each other, and imposes sanctions for the enforcement of those rules, without referring in any manner to any supposed action of the State or its authorities.

[Civil rights], guaranteed by the Constitution against State aggression, cannot be impaired by the wrongful acts of individuals, unsupported by State authority in the shape of laws, customs, or judicial or executive proceedings. The wrongful act of an individual, unsupported by any such authority, is simply a private wrong, or a crime of that individual. [Where] the Constitution seeks to protect the rights of the citizen against discriminative and unjust laws of the State by prohibiting such laws, it is not individual offences, but abrogation and denial of rights [by States], which it denounces, and for which it clothes the Congress with power to provide a remedy.

[Of] course, these remarks do not apply to those cases in which Congress is clothed with direct and plenary powers of legislation over the whole subject, [as] in the regulation of commerce with foreign nations, among the several States, and with the Indian tribes. [In] these cases Congress has power to pass laws for regulating the subjects specified in every detail, and the conduct and transactions of individuals in respect thereof.

[It] is clear that [the Act] cannot be sustained by any grant of legislative power made to Congress by the Fourteenth Amendment. [The Act], without any reference to adverse State legislation on the subject, [is] not corrective legislation; it is primary and direct; it takes immediate and absolute possession of the subject of the right of admission to inns, public conveyances, and places of amusement. [The] Thirteenth Amendment, which abolishes slavery, [is] not a mere prohibition of State laws establishing or upholding slavery, but an absolute declaration that slavery or involuntary servitude shall not exist in any part of the United States. [The] power vested in Congress to enforce the article by appropriate legislation clothes Congress with power to pass all laws necessary and proper for abolishing all badges and incidents of slavery in the United States. [But we conclude that private racial discrimination in public accommodations] has nothing to do with slavery or involuntary servitude. [It] would be running the slavery argument into the ground to make it apply to every act of discrimination which a person may see fit to make as to the guests he will entertain, or as to the people he will take into his coach or cab or car, or admit to his concert or theatre, or deal with in other matters of intercourse or business. Innkeepers and public carriers, by the laws of all the States, [are] bound [to] furnish proper accommodation to all unobjectionable persons who in good faith apply for them. If the laws themselves make any unjust discrimination, amenable to the prohibitions of the Fourteenth Amendment, Congress has full power to afford a remedy under that amendment and in accordance with it. When a man has emerged from slavery, and by the aid of beneficent legislation has shaken off the inseparable concomitants of that state, there must be some stage in the progress of his elevation when he takes the rank of a mere citizen, and ceases to be the special favorite of the laws, and when his rights as a citizen [are] to be protected in the ordinary modes by which other men's rights are protected. [The Civil Rights Act of 1875 is] unconstitutional and void.

JUSTICE HARLAN, dissenting.

[The Court errs in concluding] that Congress is without power, under either the Thirteenth or Fourteenth Amendment, to [enact the Civil Rights Act].

I do not contend that the Thirteenth Amendment invests Congress with authority [to] define and regulate the entire body of the civil rights which citizens enjoy, or may enjoy, in the several States. But I hold that since slavery [was] the moving or principal cause of the adoption of that amendment, and since that institution rested wholly upon the inferiority, as a race, of those held in bondage, their freedom necessarily involved immunity from, and protection against, all discrimination against them, because of their race, in respect of such civil rights as belong to freemen of other races. Congress, therefore, under its express power to enforce that amendment, by appropriate legislation, may enact laws to protect that people against the deprivation, because of their race, of any civil rights granted to other freemen in the same State; and such legislation may be of a direct and primary character, operating upon States [and] such individuals and corporations as exercise public functions and wield power and authority under the State. . . .

The first clause of the first section [of the Fourteenth Amendment]— "All persons born or naturalized in the United States, and subject to the jurisdiction thereof, are citizens of the United States, and of the State wherein they reside"—is of a distinctly affirmative character. [The] citizenship thus acquired by [American blacks], in virtue of an affirmative grant from the nation, may be protected [by] congressional legislation of a primary direct character; this, because the power of Congress is not restricted to the enforcement of prohibitions upon State laws or State action. It is, in terms distinct and positive, to enforce "*the provisions of this article*" of amendment; not simply those of a prohibitive character, but the provisions—*all* of the provisions—affirmative and prohibitive, of the amendment.

[It] is scarcely just to say that the colored race has been the special favorite of the laws. The [Act] is for the benefit of citizens of every race and color.

NOTES AND PROBLEMS

1. Congressional Power to Determine the "Badges and Incidents" of Slavery.   In the *Civil Rights Cases,* the Court concluded that section 2 of the Thirteenth Amendment granted Congress "power to pass all laws necessary and proper for abolishing all badges and incidents of slavery in the United States," but was of the opinion that private racial discrimination in public accommodations was not such a badge or incident of slavery. The Thirteenth Amendment, however, applies equally to private and state action. Congress enacted the Civil Rights Act of 1875 to secure equal dignity and treatment for blacks, a population that in 1875 was overwhelmingly composed of former slaves. Why did the Court defer not at all to the congressional judgment about what constituted a "badge or incident" of slavery?

Eighty-five years later, this aspect of the *Civil Rights Cases* was reversed in Jones v. Alfred H. Mayer Co., 392 U.S. 409 (1968). Jones brought suit under 42 U.S.C. §1982, claiming that Mayer, a private entity, had refused to sell him a home solely on account of his race. The statute provides that "[a]ll citizens [shall] have the same right [as] white citizens [to] purchase [real] property." The Court held that section 1982 "bars *all* racial discrimination, private as well as public, in the sale or rental of property, and that the statute, thus construed, is a valid exercise of the power of Congress to enforce the 13th Amendment." Congress had the power "rationally to determine what are the badges and the incidents of slavery," and it was rational for Congress to conclude that private racial discrimination in the sale or rental of property was such a badge or incident. But *Jones* does not mean that Congress has a free rein to regulate anything it might think is related to the defunct system of race-based slavery. The congressional enforcement power under the Thirteenth Amendment is effectively limited to addressing racial issues. This power has not been used much for this purpose, though, because the commerce power has proven to be the source of sufficient authority for Congress to enact legislation governing private acts of racial discrimination.

2. Problem: *Confederate Battle Flag.*   Suppose that Congress invoked section 2 of the Thirteenth Amendment to enact a law forbidding the states to exhibit the Confederate battle flag as part of an official display of symbolic state authority. Valid? Suppose that the law also prohibited individuals from displaying the Confederate battle flag under circumstances that constituted a true threat of violence to another person? Valid?

3. Congressional Power to Reach Private Acts That Interfere with Equal Access to Public Facilities.   In United States v. Guest, 383 U.S. 745 (1966), the Court reversed the dismissal of criminal indictments against six people for conspiracy to violate 18 U.S.C. §241, which makes it a crime for "two or more persons [to] conspire to injure, oppress, threaten, or intimidate any citizen in the free exercise or enjoyment of any right or privilege secured to him by the Constitution or laws of the United States." The defendants, private citizens, were alleged to have engaged in murder and other, lesser acts of violence and intimidation against African Americans seeking to exercise their rights as citizens. Two of the defendants had been tried and acquitted in the Georgia state courts for the murder of Lemuel Penn, a reserve Army officer who had been abducted and murdered while en route home from active military duty at Fort Benning, Georgia. Writing for the Court, Justice Stewart concluded that the indictment must be sustained because its allegations were "broad enough to cover a charge of active connivance by agents of the State in the making of the 'false reports' [of crimes committed by blacks] or other conduct amounting to official discrimination clearly sufficient to constitute denial of rights protected by the Equal Protection Clause."

Alternatively, Justice Stewart thought that the constitutional right to travel was applicable to private as well as state conduct that interferes with that right. Justice Harlan concurred in the majority's analysis of the Fourteenth Amendment but disagreed that Congress had power to reach purely private conspiracies to interfere with the right to travel. Justice Clark, joined by Justices Black and Fortas, concurred with the majority but noted "that there now can be no doubt [that] §5 empowers the Congress to enact laws punishing all conspiracies—with or without state action—that interfere with Fourteenth Amendment rights." Justice Brennan, joined by Chief Justice Warren and Justice Douglas, concurred as to the right of travel and the judgment with respect to the Fourteenth Amendment but argued that Congress had power under section 5 to prohibit private conspiracies to deny any person racially nondiscriminatory access to public facilities.

While six justices subscribed in dicta to some version of the view that Congress's Fourteenth Amendment enforcement power authorizes regulation of purely private behavior that interfered with a citizen's exercise of constitutional rights, the Court did not address the point, having found that state action was in fact alleged. Thus the holding of *Guest* did not reverse the *Civil Rights Cases* as to the scope of congressional enforcement power of Fourteenth Amendment rights and, indeed, did not even reach the question of whether Congress has power to regulate private behavior in the interest of protecting rights to equal protection. That question was reached and decided in United States v. Morrison, 529 U.S. 598 (2000). In striking down 42 U.S.C. §13981, a federal civil remedy for victims of gender-motivated violence, the Court reaffirmed the holding of the *Civil Rights Cases* that congressional power to enforce the Fourteenth Amendment is limited to regulation of government behavior, not private behavior, and explicitly disavowed the notion that *Guest* had overruled that rule: "[It] would take more than the naked dicta contained in Justice Clark's [*Guest*] opinion, when added to Justice Brennan's [*Guest*] opinion, to cast any doubt on the enduring vitality of the Civil Rights Cases." The fatal defect of the law was that it was "directed not at any State or state actor, but at individuals who have committed criminal acts motivated by gender bias."

Queries: May Congress prohibit private acts that keep public officials from discharging their Fourteenth Amendment obligations? May Congress prohibit private acts that prevent other private persons from enjoying rights with which governments could not interfere?

4. Problems: *Angry Mob.* Under 18 U.S.C. §241, a federal prosecutor indicts members of an angry mob of private persons who have forcibly prevented public school officials from implementing a school desegregation order. Will the indictments be dismissed?

Skinheads.   Under 18 U.S.C. §241, a federal prosecutor indicts a group of skinheads who have intimidated black children sufficiently to deter them from entering a public park. Will the indictments be dismissed?

Old Boys Club.   A group of affluent white males purchase 1,000 acres from the state government and convert it into the Old Boys Club, a private retreat limited to its members, who must be white and male. Some of the club members are state legislators, and many of the guests at the club are state officials. Congress invokes section 5 of the Fourteenth Amendment to enact a law forbidding discrimination on the basis of race or sex by private clubs that accept state officials as members or guests. Is the law within Congress's authority to enact?

2.   The Scope of Enforcement Power: Remedial or Substantive?

As you have no doubt realized from your study of equal protection and due process, the content of the important substantive rights guaranteed by the Fourteenth Amendment is not self-evident, but is largely the product of judicial interpretation. But because Congress has power to enforce these guarantees by appropriate legislation, does Congress have a power, independent of the Court, to enforce its own interpretation of these guarantees? Or, may Congress only implement the Court's interpretations? The province and the duty of the courts, said John Marshall in *Marbury*, is to say what the law is. Once the Court has done so, by identifying a constitutional violation, is Congress's enforcement power limited to providing remedies for past, present, or future violations of the Court-defined right? Or may Congress address any condition it reasonably believes involves a denial of rights protected by the Fourteenth Amendment, even if the congressional view of those rights is broader than that of the Court? With respect to the Thirteenth Amendment, Congress has the power to define the "badges and incidents" of slavery more broadly than might the Court. See Jones v. Alfred H. Mayer Co. But the answer is different with respect to the Fourteenth and Fifteenth Amendments: Congress's power to enforce those provisions is remedial only, but the power to remedy violations includes the power to prevent constitutional injury.

South Carolina v. Katzenbach, 383 U.S. 301 (1966).   The Voting Rights Act of 1965 forbade certain state practices with respect to voting, such as literacy tests, and subjected many changes in electoral systems to pre-clearance by the Department of Justice, but the Act applied only to counties that used a test for voter eligibility and in which less than 50 percent of eligible persons voted in the 1964 presidential election. The Court upheld the Act. Congress could rationally conclude that such jurisdictions (which typically have large numbers of racial minorities but few minority voters) were using racially neutral criteria (such as literacy) to produce racial discrimination in voting. In essence, the Court suggested that while it is the judiciary's job to determine the substance of Fifteenth Amendment rights, Congress is free to ascertain facts that establish substantive violations and then act to remedy those violations.

City of Rome v. United States, 446 U.S. 156 (1980). Rome, Georgia, held at-large elections for its legislative body. This was alleged to violate the federal Voting Rights Act, which prohibits electoral systems that have either the *purpose* or *effect* of diluting the voting strength of racial minorities. In a companion case, Mobile v. Bolden, 446 U.S. 55 (1980), the Court held that an at-large electoral system that effectively diluted racial minority voting strength but was not purposefully designed to do so did not violate the Fifteenth Amendment because it bars only intentional racial discrimination in voting. Given that conclusion, did Congress have the power under the Fifteenth Amendment to ban electoral systems that have only the *effect* of diluting the voting power of racial minorities? Yes, said the Court: "[B]ecause electoral changes by jurisdictions with a demonstrable history of intentional racial discrimination in voting create the risk of purposeful discrimination, [Congress could] prohibit changes that have a discriminatory impact." In other words, Congress could declare a prophylactic rule to head off future violations of the Fifteenth Amendment, so long as there was adequate reason to believe that the conduct barred was commonly motivated by racial animus.

The next case involves congressional enforcement power under both the Fourteenth and Fifteenth Amendments and charts the limits of that power as expansively as the Court has ever done. But the outer reaches of that power were repudiated, and the mechanisms for drawing the boundaries of congressional enforcement power were reformulated in the second case that follows, City of Boerne v. Flores.

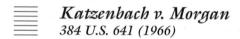

Katzenbach v. Morgan
384 U.S. 641 (1966)

JUSTICE BRENNAN delivered the opinion of the Court.

These cases concern the constitutionality of §4(e) of the Voting Rights Act of 1965. [Section 4(e) provided that persons who had completed the sixth grade in Puerto Rico, where Spanish is the language of instruction, could not be required to demonstrate English literacy in order to vote. In Lassiter v. Northampton Election Board, 360 U.S. 45 (1959), the Court had held that English literacy requirements did not violate either the Fourteenth or Fifteenth Amendment. A federal district court ruled that §4(e) was beyond Congress's power to enforce either of the amendments.] We reverse.

[New York argues] that §4(e) cannot be sustained as appropriate legislation to enforce the Equal Protection Clause unless the judiciary decides—even with the guidance of a congressional judgment—that the application of the English literacy requirement prohibited by §4(e) is forbidden by the Equal Protection Clause itself. We disagree. [A] construction of §5 [of the Fourteenth Amendment] that would require a judicial determination that the enforcement of the state law precluded by Congress violated the Amendment, as a condition of sustaining the congressional enactment, would depreciate both congressional resourcefulness and congressional responsibility for implementing the Amendment. It would confine the legislative power in this context to the insignificant role of abrogating only those state laws that the judicial branch was prepared to adjudge unconstitutional.

[Since] our task in this case is not to determine whether the New York English literacy requirement [violates] the Equal Protection Clause, [our] decision in Lassiter v. Northampton Election Bd. sustaining the North Carolina English literacy requirement [is] inapposite. *Lassiter* did not present the question before us here: Without regard to whether the judiciary would find that the Equal Protection Clause itself nullifies New York's English literacy requirement, [could] Congress prohibit the enforcement of the state law by legislating under §5 of the Fourteenth Amendment? . . .

[We] proceed to the consideration whether §4(e) is "appropriate legislation" to enforce the Equal Protection Clause, that is, [whether it] is "plainly adapted to that end" and whether it is not prohibited by but is consistent with "the letter and spirit of the constitution." [McCulloch v. Maryland].[1] There can be no doubt that §4(e) may be regarded as an enactment to enforce the Equal Protection Clause. Congress explicitly declared that it enacted §4(e) "to secure [Fourteenth Amendment] rights." [More] specifically, section 4(e) may be viewed as a measure to secure for the Puerto Rican community residing in New York nondiscriminatory treatment by government—both in the imposition of voting qualifications and the provision or administration of governmental services, such as public schools, public housing and law enforcement. Section 4(e) may be readily seen as "plainly adapted" to furthering these aims of the Equal Protection Clause. The practical effect of §4(e) is to prohibit New York from denying the right to vote to large segments of its Puerto Rican community. [This] enhanced political power will be helpful in gaining nondiscriminatory treatment in public services for the entire Puerto Rican community. Section 4(e) thereby enables the Puerto Rican minority better to obtain "perfect equality of civil rights and the equal protection of the laws." It was well within congressional authority to say that this need of the Puerto Rican minority for the vote warranted federal intrusion upon any state interests served by the English literacy requirement. It was for Congress [to] assess and weigh the various conflicting considerations—the risk or pervasiveness of the discrimination in governmental services, the effectiveness of eliminating the state restriction on the right to vote as a means of dealing with the evil, the adequacy or availability of alternative remedies, and the nature and significance of the state interests that would be affected by the nullification of the English literacy requirement as applied to residents who have successfully

---

1. Contrary to the suggestion of the dissent, §5 does not grant Congress power to exercise discretion in the other direction and to enact "statutes so as in effect to dilute equal protection and due process decisions of this Court." We emphasize that Congress'[s] power under §5 is limited to adopting measures to enforce the guarantees of the Amendment; §5 grants Congress no power to restrict, abrogate, or dilute these guarantees. Thus, for example, an enactment authorizing the States to establish racially segregated systems of education would not be—as required by §5—a measure "to enforce" the Equal Protection Clause since that clause of its own force prohibits such state laws.

completed the sixth grade in a Puerto Rican school. It is not for us to review the congressional resolution of these factors. It is enough that we be able to perceive a basis upon which the Congress might resolve the conflict as it did.

[The] result is no different if we confine our inquiry to the question whether §4(e) was merely legislation aimed at the elimination of an invidious discrimination in establishing voter qualifications. New York's English literacy requirement originated in the desire to provide an incentive for non-English speaking immigrants to learn the English language and in order to assure the intelligent exercise of the franchise. Yet Congress might well have questioned, in light of the many exemptions provided, and some evidence suggesting that prejudice played a prominent role in the enactment of the requirement, whether these were actually the interests being served. [Congress] might well have concluded that as a means of furthering the intelligent exercise of the franchise, an ability to read or understand Spanish is as effective as ability to read English for those to whom Spanish-language newspapers and Spanish-language radio and television programs are available to inform them of election issues and governmental affairs. [It] was Congress'[s] prerogative to weigh these competing considerations. Here again, it is enough that we perceive a basis upon which Congress might predicate a judgment that the application of New York's English literacy requirement to deny the right to vote to a person with a sixth grade education in Puerto Rican schools in which the language of instruction was other than English constituted an invidious discrimination in violation of the Equal Protection Clause. [Reversed.]

JUSTICE HARLAN, joined by JUSTICE STEWART, dissenting.

. . . I believe the Court has confused the issue of how much enforcement power Congress possesses under §5 with the distinct issue of what questions are appropriate for congressional determination and what questions are essentially judicial in nature. When recognized state violations of federal constitutional standards have occurred, Congress is of course empowered by §5 to take appropriate remedial measures to redress and prevent the wrongs. [But the] question here is not whether [§4(e)] is appropriate remedial legislation to cure an established violation of a constitutional command, but whether there has in fact been an infringement of that constitutional command, that is, whether a particular state [statute offends] the Equal Protection Clause. [That] question is one for the judicial branch ultimately to determine. Were the rule otherwise, Congress would be able to qualify [by ordinary legislation] this Court's constitutional decisions under the Fourteenth and Fifteenth Amendments. [In] effect the Court reads §5 of the Fourteenth Amendment as giving Congress the power to define the substantive scope of the Amendment.

NOTES

1. Alternative Holdings. Justice Brennan's majority opinion offers two independent rationales for its conclusion. The first is a remedial rationale:

With the removal of a state barrier to Puerto Rican voting the Puerto Rican minority in New York would be better able to prevent ethnic discrimination in the provision of public services. But note that the remedy Congress created (elimination of English literacy as a requirement for voting) had nothing to do with unconstitutional voting eligibility rules; indeed, *Lassiter* established that English literacy as a voting eligibility rule was valid. Rather, the statutory remedy was designed to remedy *other possible unconstitutional acts* (ethnic discrimination in public services) that were connected to voting only remotely at best.

The second rationale, however, is not remedial at all. Congress, said Justice Brennan, could reasonably have concluded that English literacy as a precondition to voting violated the equal protection clause, even though the Court had squarely declared that such a requirement did not violate equal protection. This "substantive" rationale conferred upon Congress wide discretion to define for itself the substance of the Fourteenth Amendment, regardless of what the Court's interpretation of those substantive rights might be.

2. Criticism of the Substantive Rationale.   In dissent, Justice Harlan criticized the substantive rationale as conferring upon Congress the power to perform judicial functions. In a later case, Oregon v. Mitchell, 400 U.S. 112 (1970), in which no clear majority could be mustered for the substantive rationale, Justice Harlan elaborated on this criticism:

> Congress's expression of [its view] cannot displace the duty of this Court to make an independent determination whether Congress has exceeded its powers. The reason for [this] inheres in the structure of the constitutional system itself. Congress is subject to none of the institutional restraints imposed on judicial decisionmaking; it is controlled only by the political process. In Article V, the Framers expressed the view that the political restraints on Congress alone were an insufficient control over the process of constitution making. The concurrence of two-thirds of each House and of three-fourths of the States was needed for the political check to be adequate. To allow a simple majority of Congress to have final say on matters of constitutional interpretation is therefore fundamentally out of keeping with the constitutional structure.

3. The "Ratchet" Footnote.   Justice Brennan's footnote in *Morgan* is often called the "ratchet" footnote because it would permit Congress to expand but not contract the substantive scope of the Fourteenth Amendment. Does it adequately answer Justice Harlan? How can one tell when a congressional initiative restricts, abrogates, or dilutes Fourteenth Amendment guarantees? Justice Brennan offered as an example a hypothetical federal law authorizing states to create racially segregated schools. But suppose that Congress makes well-supported findings of fact that the educational progress of teenage black males would be enhanced by education in an all-male, all-black school. Congress then enacts a law that authorizes states to offer to African American youngsters the choice of attending a single-sex, all-black public school. Is this a dilution of equal protection or an aid to enforcement of equal protection?

4. The Religious Freedom Restoration Act.   The "substantive" rationale of *Morgan* no doubt emboldened Congress to enact the Religious Freedom Restoration Act (RFRA) in the wake of the Court's decision in Employment Division v. Smith, Chapter 10, Section B.1. In *Smith,* the Court held that Oregon could, consistent with the free exercise clause, bar anyone from using peyote, thus making its use illegal in sacramental rites of the Native American Church. [A] generally applicable rule of conduct that impinges on religious practice is presumptively valid and does not merit any heightened scrutiny to test its compliance with the free exercise clause. Congress responded by enacting the RFRA, which forbade governments from engaging in significant interference with religious conduct unless they could prove that the interference was necessary to accomplish a compelling government objective. Because the free exercise clause is incorporated in the Fourteenth Amendment's due process clause, Congress relied on its section 5 enforcement powers to enact the RFRA.

≡≡≡ *City of Boerne v. Flores*
≡≡≡ *521 U.S. 507 (1997)*

JUSTICE KENNEDY delivered the opinion of the Court.

A decision by local zoning authorities to deny a church a building permit was challenged under the Religious Freedom Restoration Act of 1993 (RFRA). The case calls into question the authority of Congress to enact RFRA. We conclude the statute exceeds Congress's power.

[After Boerne, Texas, near San Antonio, declared St. Peter Catholic Church a historic landmark, it refused to issue a building permit to the church to increase its size to accommodate the worship needs of its growing congregation. Flores, the Roman Catholic archbishop, brought suit in federal court, invoking RFRA. The district court ruled that Congress lacked authority to enact RFRA. The Court of Appeals reversed. We] now reverse.

Congress enacted RFRA in direct response to the Court's decision in [Employment Division v. Smith, where] we declined to apply [Sherbert v. Verner], under which we would have asked whether Oregon's prohibition [of peyote use] substantially burdened a religious practice and, if it did, whether the burden was justified by a compelling government interest. [Members] of Congress [criticized] the Court's reasoning, and this disagreement resulted in the passage of RFRA. [RFRA prohibits any government] from "substantially burden[ing]" a person's exercise of religion even if the burden results from a rule of general applicability unless the government can demonstrate the burden "(1) is in furtherance of a compelling governmental interest; and (2) is the least restrictive means of furthering that compelling governmental interest."

[Congress] relied on its Fourteenth Amendment enforcement power in enacting the [portions of RFRA that] impose its requirements on the States. [Respondent Flores] contends . . . that RFRA is permissible enforcement legislation [because] Congress . . . is only protecting by legislation one of the liberties guaranteed by the Fourteenth Amendment's Due Process Clause, the free exercise of religion, beyond what is necessary under *Smith*. It is said the congressional decision to dispense with proof of deliberate or overt discrimination and instead concentrate on a law's effects accords with the settled understanding that §5 includes the power to enact legislation designed to prevent as well as remedy constitutional violations. It is further contended that Congress's §5 power is not limited to remedial or preventive legislation.

[Legislation] which deters or remedies constitutional violations can fall within the sweep of Congress's enforcement power even if in the process it prohibits conduct which is not itself unconstitutional and intrudes into "legislative spheres of autonomy previously reserved to the States." [South Carolina v. Katzenbach, Katzenbach v. Morgan.] It is also true, however, that "[a]s broad as the congressional enforcement power is, it is not unlimited." [We] begin with its text. Congress has been given the power "to enforce" the "provisions of this article."

Congress's power under §5, however, extends only to "enforc[ing]" the provisions of the Fourteenth Amendment. The Court has described this power as "remedial." The design of the Amendment and the text of §5 are inconsistent with the suggestion that Congress has the power to decree the substance of the Fourteenth Amendment's restrictions on the States. Legislation which alters the meaning of the Free Exercise Clause cannot be said to be enforcing the Clause. Congress does not enforce a constitutional right by changing what the right is. It has been given the power "to enforce," not the power to determine what constitutes a constitutional violation. Were it not so, what Congress would be enforcing would no longer be, in any meaningful sense, the "provisions of [the Fourteenth Amendment]."

While the line between measures that remedy or prevent unconstitutional actions and measures that make a substantive change in the governing law is not easy to discern, and Congress must have wide latitude in determining where it lies, the distinction exists and must be observed. There must be a congruence and proportionality between the injury to be prevented or remedied and the means adopted to that end. Lacking such a connection, legislation may become substantive in operation and effect. History and our case law support drawing the distinction, one apparent from the text of the Amendment. The Fourteenth Amendment's history confirms the remedial, rather than substantive, nature of the Enforcement Clause. [The Thirty-ninth Congress rejected an initial draft of the Fourteenth Amendment that would have given Congress plenary legislative authority in favor of a remedial power that became §5 of the Fourteenth Amendment.] The remedial and preventive nature of Congress's enforcement power, and the limitation inherent in the power, were confirmed in our earliest cases on the Fourteenth Amendment[, *Civil Rights Cases*, and] their treatment of Congress's §5 power as corrective or preventive, not definitional, has not been questioned.

Recent cases have continued to revolve around the question of whether §5 legislation can be considered remedial. In South Carolina v. Katzenbach we emphasized that "[t]he constitutional propriety of [legislation adopted under the Enforcement Clause] must be judged with reference to the historical experience [it] reflects." There we upheld various provisions of the Voting Rights Act of 1965, finding them to be "remedies aimed at areas where voting discrimination has been most flagrant," and necessary to "banish the blight of racial discrimination in voting, which has infected the electoral process in parts of our country for nearly a century." . . . [But any] suggestion that Congress has a substantive, non-remedial power under the Fourteenth Amendment is not supported by our case law. In Oregon v. Mitchell, a majority of the Court concluded Congress had exceeded its enforcement powers by enacting legislation lowering the minimum age of voters from 21 to 18 in state and local elections. [A plurality was] explicit in rejecting the position that §5 endowed Congress with the power to establish the meaning of constitutional provisions.

[While there] is language in our opinion in Katzenbach v. Morgan which could be interpreted as acknowledging a power in Congress to enact legislation that expands the rights contained in §1 of the Fourteenth Amendment, [this] is not a necessary interpretation, however, or even the best one. . . .

If Congress could define its own powers by altering the Fourteenth Amendment's meaning, no longer would the Constitution be "superior paramount law, unchangeable by ordinary means." It would be "on a level with ordinary legislative acts, and, like other [acts], alterable when the legislature shall please to alter it." Marbury v. Madison. Under this approach, it is difficult to conceive of a principle that would limit congressional power. Shifting legislative majorities could change the Constitution and effectively circumvent the difficult and detailed amendment process contained in Article V.

We now turn to consider whether RFRA can be considered enforcement legislation under §5 of the Fourteenth Amendment. Respondent contends that RFRA is a proper exercise of Congress's remedial or preventive power [because it] prevents and remedies laws which are enacted with the unconstitutional object of targeting religious beliefs and practices. To avoid the difficulty of proving such violations, it is said, Congress can simply invalidate any law which imposes a substantial burden on a religious practice unless it is justified by a compelling interest and is the least restrictive means of accomplishing that interest.

While preventive rules are sometimes appropriate remedial measures, there must be a congruence between the means used and the ends to be achieved. The appropriateness of remedial measures must be considered in light of the evil presented. Strong measures appropriate to address one harm may be an unwarranted response to another, lesser one. A comparison between RFRA and the Voting Rights Act is instructive. In contrast to the record which confronted Congress and the judiciary in the voting rights cases, RFRA's legislative record lacks examples of modern instances of generally applicable laws passed because of religious bigotry. . . . Rather, the emphasis of the hearings was on laws of general applicability which place incidental burdens on religion. [It] is difficult to maintain that [such] legislation [is] enacted or enforced due to animus or hostility to the burdened religious practices or that [it indicates] some widespread pattern of religious discrimination in this country. Congress's concern was with the incidental burdens imposed, not the object or purpose of the legislation. This lack of support in the legislative record, however, is not RFRA's most serious shortcoming.

[Regardless] of the state of the legislative record, RFRA cannot be considered remedial, preventive legislation, if those terms are to have any meaning. RFRA is so out of proportion to a supposed remedial or preventive object that it cannot be understood as responsive to, or designed to prevent, unconstitutional behavior. It appears, instead, to attempt a substantive change in constitutional protections. Preventive measures prohibiting certain types of laws may be appropriate when there is reason to believe that many of the laws affected by the congressional enactment have a significant likelihood of being unconstitutional. See *City of Rome*. Remedial legislation under §5 "should be adapted to the mischief and wrong which the [Fourteenth] [A]mendment was intended to provide against." RFRA is not so confined. Sweeping coverage ensures its intrusion at every level of government, displacing laws and prohibiting official actions of almost every description and regardless of subject matter. RFRA's restrictions apply to every agency and official of the Federal, State, and local Governments [and] to all federal and state law, statutory or otherwise, whether adopted before or after its enactment. RFRA has no termination date or termination mechanism. Any law is subject to challenge at any time by any individual who alleges a substantial burden on his or her free exercise of religion. . . .

[The] substantial costs RFRA exacts, both in practical terms of imposing a heavy litigation burden on the States and in terms of curtailing their traditional general regulatory power, far exceed any pattern or practice of unconstitutional conduct under the Free Exercise Clause as interpreted in *Smith*. Simply put, RFRA is not designed to identify and counteract state laws likely to be unconstitutional because of their treatment of religion. . . .

Broad as the power of Congress is under the Enforcement Clause of the Fourteenth Amendment, RFRA contradicts vital principles necessary to maintain separation of powers and the federal balance. [Reversed.]

NOTES AND PROBLEMS

1. Application of *Flores*. The Court suggested in *Flores* that there must be some empirical evidence of constitutional violations that Congress is seeking to remedy by using its section 5 enforcement power and that the remedial legislation must be both "congruent" with the violations and "proportional" to the injuries sought to be remedied. Does the congruence requirement mean that the remedial legislation must attack the violation precisely? If so, was the alternative holding of Katzenbach v. Morgan implicitly overruled? Or, does congruence mean that the remedy cannot be substantially broader than the constitutional violation?

Is proportionality in essence a "narrow tailoring" requirement that Congress must meet whenever it uses its section 5 enforcement power? The Court regarded the broad sweep of the RFRA—putting every law of every government to the burden of justification under strict scrutiny upon a claim of a substantial burden upon religious conduct—as a wildly overbroad response to the skimpy empirical evidence of intentional discrimination against religious conduct. If so, how good must the fit be? Does the precision of the fit depend on how strong the empirical evidence is of the constitutional violation that Congress seeks to remedy?

If congruence is a fit between the constitutional violation and the acts prohibited by Congress, what does proportionality add? If it is just another way to measure the fit between the violation and the remedy, it is duplicative, but proportionality is also a way to determine whether the feared constitutional violation is really occurring. If it is not a real problem, a broad prohibition is not proportional to the existence of the problem.

2. Subsequent Developments. *Florida Prepaid Postsecondary Education Expense Board v. College Savings Bank, 527 U.S. 627 (1999).* The Court ruled that Congress lacked power under section 5 to subject states to liability for damages in federal court for their patent infringements. Absent proof that there was a real and persistent problem of state patent infringement, the federal legislation was not proportional.

Kimel v. Florida Board of Regents, 528 U.S. 62 (2000). Congress was held to have exceeded its enforcement powers under section 5 of the Fourteenth Amendment by the Age Discrimination in Employment Act (ADEA) provisions that subjected states to damage suits in federal court for age discrimination with respect to their employees. The issue arose in the context of whether Congress had validly used its section 5 power to abrogate the states' Eleventh Amendment sovereign immunity. Because age discrimination does not violate the equal protection guarantee if it is rationally related to a legitimate government purpose, the Court concluded that the ADEA provisions in question were not remedial or preventive because they " 'cannot be understood as responsive to, or designed to prevent, unconstitutional behavior.' " The ADEA provisions, which made *all* age discrimination unlawful, prohibited "substantially more state employment decisions and practices than would likely be held unconstitutional under the applicable . . . rational basis standard." Moreover, there was no evidence of widespread and unconstitutional age discrimination by the States.

United States v. Morrison, 529 U.S. 598 (2000). The Court ruled that 42 U.S.C. §13981, a federal civil remedy for victims of gender-motivated violence, exceeded the scope of the section 5 enforcement power. Congress had enacted the law after concluding that "there is pervasive bias in various state justice systems against victims of gender-motivated violence," and that such bias "denies victims of gender-motivated violence the equal protection of the laws." The Court concluded that the law was "simply not 'corrective in its character' " because it lacked "congruence and proportionality between the injury to be prevented or remedied and the means adopted to that end." The incongruity and lack of proportionality was embodied in two facts. First, the law was "directed not at any State or state actor, but at individuals who have committed criminal acts motivated by gender bias. [The law] visits no consequence whatever on any Virginia public official involved in investigating or prosecuting" the rape that produced the civil claim at issue in *Morrison*. Second, the remedy adopted by Congress was national in scope but Congress had acted on evidence of unconstitutional sex-based discrimination in only 21 states.

In dissent, Justice Breyer wondered why Congress could "not take the evidence before it as evidence of a national problem," noting that the Court has never "held that Congress must document the existence of a problem in every State prior to proposing a national solution."

Query: Does *Morrison* suggest two new limits on "congruence and proportionality" — that the federal remedy must work directly on states or state actors and that the scope of the remedy must be geographically tailored to the scope of the unconstitutional conduct?

3. Problems: *Ban of Sexual Orientation Discrimination.* Suppose Congress invokes section 5 of the Fourteenth Amendment to enact the following law: "Based on congressional findings of fact that state and local governments have refused to employ homosexuals as schoolteachers, lawyers, or other public employees, and based on Congress's judgment that such refusal is utterly irrational, Congress hereby prohibits any state or local government from discriminating on the basis of sexual orientation in hiring, contracting, or the provision of any public service." Does Congress have authority under section 5 to enact this law? Note that under current law governmental discrimination on the basis of sexual orientation is valid so long as it is rationally related to a legitimate objective.

Civil Remedy for Sex-Motivated Violence. Suppose Congress invokes section 5 of the Fourteenth Amendment to enact the following law: "Based on congressional findings of fact that state governments have violated equal protection by failing to provide victims of sex-motivated violence with adequate remedies for that violence, Congress hereby provides that the failure of any state to (a) investigate and prosecute any such sex-motivated crime without sexual bias, or (b) provide an adequate civil remedy for such violence, shall subject any state actor found to have acted with sexual bias in connection with the investigation or civil or criminal prosecution of an act of sex-motivated violence to fine or imprisonment, and shall further subject the perpetrator of any act of sex-motivated violence to civil liability in an amount not greater than treble actual damages plus attorneys' fees." Does Congress have authority under section 5 to enact this law?

≡≡≡ **Board of Trustees of the University of Alabama v. Garrett**
531 U.S. 356 (2001)

CHIEF JUSTICE REHNQUIST delivered the opinion of the Court.

We decide here whether employees of the State of Alabama may recover money damages by reason of the State's failure to comply with the provision of Title I of the Americans with Disabilities Act of 1990 (ADA or Act). We hold that such suits are barred by the Eleventh Amendment. The ADA prohibits certain employers, including the States, from "discriminating against a qualified individual with a disability because of the disability of such individual in regard to [the] terms, conditions, and privileges of employment." [The] Act requires employers to "make reasonable accommodations to the known physical or mental limitations of an otherwise qualified individual with a disability who is an applicant or employee, unless [the employer] can demonstrate that the accommodation would impose an undue hardship on the operation of the [employer's] business." . . .

[Garrett and Ash were each employed by units of the state of Alabama. Garrett, a nurse whose cancer treatments necessitated substantial absence from work, was demoted upon her return to work. Ash, a security officer, was denied accommodations for his chronic asthma and sleep apnea.] Garrett and Ash filed separate lawsuits in [federal] District Court, both seeking money damages under the ADA. Petitioners moved for summary judgment, claiming that the ADA exceeds Congress's authority to abrogate the State's Eleventh Amendment immunity. In a single opinion disposing of both cases, the District Court agreed with petitioners' position and granted their motions for summary judgment. The cases were consolidated on appeal to the Eleventh Circuit, [which court] reversed, [ruling] that the ADA validly abrogates the States' Eleventh Amendment immunity. We granted certiorari. . . .

I. . . . Congress may abrogate the States' Eleventh Amendment immunity when it both unequivocally intends to do so and "acts pursuant to a valid grant of constitutional authority." The first of these requirements is not in dispute here. The question [is] whether Congress acted within its constitutional authority by subjecting the States to suits in federal court for money damages under the ADA. . . . [Congress may abrogate the States' Eleventh Amendment immunity by a valid exercise of its power under §5 of the Fourteenth Amendment.] Section 5 of the Fourteenth Amendment grants Congress the power to enforce the substantive guarantees contained in §1 by enacting "appropriate legislation." Congress is not limited to mere legislative repetition of this Court's constitutional jurisprudence. "Rather, Congress's power 'to enforce' the Amendment includes the authority both to remedy and to deter violation of rights guaranteed thereunder by prohibiting a somewhat broader swath of conduct, including that which is not itself forbidden by the Amendment's text." *Kimel. City of Boerne* also confirmed, however, the long-settled principle that it is the responsibility of this Court, not Congress, to define the substance of constitutional guarantees. Accordingly, §5 legislation reaching beyond the scope of §1's actual guarantees must exhibit "congruence and proportionality between the injury to be prevented or remedied and the means adopted to that end."

II. The first step in applying these now familiar principles is to identify with some precision the scope of the constitutional right at issue. Here, that inquiry requires us to examine the limitations §1 of the Fourteenth Amendment places upon States' treatment of the disabled. As we did last Term in *Kimel* we look to our prior decisions under the Equal Protection Clause dealing with this issue. . . . States are not required by the Fourteenth Amendment to make special accommodations for the disabled, so long as their actions towards such individuals are rational. They could quite hard headedly—and perhaps hardheartedly—hold to job-qualification requirements which do not make allowance for the disabled. If special accommodations for the disabled are to be required, they have to come from positive law and not through the Equal Protection Clause.

III. Once we have determined the metes and bounds of the constitutional right in question, we examine whether Congress identified a history and pattern of unconstitutional employment discrimination by the States against the disabled. . . . Congress's §5 authority is appropriately exercised only in response to state transgressions. The legislative record of the ADA, however, simply fails to show that Congress did in fact identify a pattern of irrational state discrimination in employment against the disabled. . . .

Even were it possible to squeeze out . . . a pattern of unconstitutional discrimination by the States, the rights and remedies created by the ADA against the States would raise the same . . . concerns as to congruence and proportionality as were found in _City of Boerne_. For example, whereas it would be entirely rational (and therefore constitutional) for a state employer to conserve scarce financial resources by hiring employees who are able to use existing facilities, the ADA requires employers to "make existing facilities used by employees readily accessible to and usable by individuals with disabilities" [except when such accommodation would impose an undue burden on employers]. The ADA accommodation duty far exceeds what is constitutionally required in that it makes unlawful a range of alternate responses that would be reasonable but would fall short of imposing an "undue burden" upon the employer. . . .

[For Congress] to authorize private individuals to recover money damages against the States, there must be a pattern of discrimination by the States which violates the Fourteenth Amendment, and the remedy imposed by Congress must be congruent and proportional to the targeted violation. Those requirements are not met here, and to uphold the Act's application to the States would allow Congress to rewrite the Fourteenth Amendment. . . .[2] Section 5 does not so broadly enlarge congressional authority. . . . Reversed.

JUSTICE KENNEDY, joined by JUSTICE O'CONNOR, concurring.
. . . If the States had been transgressing the Fourteenth Amendment by their mistreatment or lack of concern for those with impairments, one

---

2. Our holding here that Congress did not validly abrogate the States' sovereign immunity from suit by private individuals for money damages under Title I does not mean that persons with disabilities have no federal recourse against discrimination. Title I of the ADA still prescribes standards applicable to the States. Those standards can be enforced by the United States in actions for money damages, as well as by private individuals in actions for injunctive relief under Ex parte Young, 209 U.S. 123 (1908). In addition, state laws protecting the rights of persons with disabilities in employment and other aspects of life provide independent avenues of redress.

would have expected to find in decisions of the courts of the States and also the courts of the United States extensive litigation and discussion of the constitutional violations. This confirming judicial documentation does not exist. . . .

JUSTICE BREYER, joined by JUSTICES STEVENS, SOUTER, and GINSBURG, dissenting.

. . . As the Court recognizes, state discrimination in employment against persons with disabilities might "run afoul of the Equal Protection Clause" where there is no "rational relationship between the disparity of treatment and some legitimate governmental purpose." In my view, Congress reasonably could have concluded that the remedy before us constitutes an "appropriate" way to enforce this basic equal protection requirement. And that is all the Constitution requires.

I. . . . Congress compiled a vast legislative record documenting "massive, society wide discrimination" against persons with disabilities. [The] powerful evidence of discriminatory treatment throughout society in general . . . implicates state governments as well. [There] is no particular reason to believe that they are immune from the "stereotypic assumptions" and pattern of "purposeful unequal treatment" that Congress found prevalent. . . . [In] any event, there is no need to rest solely upon evidence [of] general societal discrimination. There are roughly 300 examples of discrimination by state governments themselves in the legislative record. . . . Congress, unlike courts, must, and does, routinely draw general conclusions [from] anecdotal and opinion-based evidence of this kind. . . .

II. [The] Court fails to find in the legislative record sufficient indication that Congress has [negated] the presumption that state action is rationally related to a legitimate objective. The problem with the Court's approach is that neither the "burden of proof" that favors States nor any other rule of restraint applicable to *judges* applies to *Congress* when it exercises its §5 power. Rational-basis review—with its presumptions favoring constitutionality—is "a paradigm of *judicial* restraint." And the Congress of the United States is not a lower court. . . . There is simply no reason to require Congress, seeking to determine facts relevant to the exercise of its §5 authority, to adopt rules or presumptions that reflect a court's institutional limitations. Unlike courts, Congress can readily gather facts from across the Nation, assess the magnitude of a problem, and more easily find an appropriate remedy. Unlike courts, Congress directly reflects public attitudes and beliefs, enabling Congress better to understand where, and to what extent, refusals to accommodate a disability amount to behavior that is callous or unreasonable to the point of lacking constitutional justification. Unlike judges, Members of Congress can directly obtain information from constituents who have first-hand experience with discrimination and related issues. . . . To apply a rule designed to restrict courts as if it restricted Congress's legislative power is to stand the underlying principle [of] judicial restraint on its head. . . .

NOTES AND PROBLEMS

1. Determining the Scope of the Enforcement Power. The Court tied the substance of the rights protected by the Fourteenth Amendment (in this case, equal protection) to the judicial standards for ascertaining equal protection violations. Because Congress sought to outlaw discrimination against the disabled, the Court applied the judicial standards for determination of when such discrimination is unconstitutional. That standard, of course, is minimal scrutiny. As with judicial application of minimal scrutiny, the Court placed the burden of proof on Congress to demonstrate that state employment discrimination against the disabled was irrational or illegitimate. Thus, the Court required Congress to make a convincing demonstration that (1) such discrimination actually exists and (2) it is an irrational means to accomplish legitimate government ends or an illegitimate end in itself.

a. Congressional determination of the existence of constitutional violations. How much should the Court defer to congressional judgment about the existence of constitutional violations? Is it true, as Justice Breyer argued, that Congress has more institutional competence to determine when constitutional violations are occurring? Or is that determination the special province of courts? Perhaps Congress is better situated than courts to assess when states are engaging in actions that, while not constitutional violations, are so close to the line that their continued tolerance will likely lead to constitutional violations. If so, Congress would simply be acting to *prevent* constitutional violations before they occur. Justice Kennedy responded to this argument by noting that if there was any realistic likelihood of constitutional violations, one would observe a few surfacing in the courts. Is it fair to say that without such evidence there is no reason to believe that there are any constitutional violations to be prevented?

b. Congruence and proportionality. Was Congress's remedy not congruent with the constitutional violation because the remedy—subjecting states to private suit for damages for their failure to provide "reasonable accommodations"—prohibited much more conduct than is constitutionally forbidden? Did Congress's remedy lack proportionality because Congress had not identified constitutional violations that were as extensive as the remedy it provided? May Congress validly invoke its enforcement power only if (1) it regulates conduct that Congress has established is a pretext for accomplishing constitutionally forbidden ends, (2) the scope of the forbidden conduct is limited to the actual likely occurrence of the constitutional violation, and (3) the geographic scope of the law is dovetailed to the extent of the violations?

2. The Role of the Eleventh Amendment and the Scope of *Garrett*. The majority was careful to point out that the case raised only the narrow issue of whether Congress could use its enforcement power to abrogate the states' Eleventh Amendment immunity. Does Congress have greater latitude to use its enforcement power when it prohibits state activities that it thinks violate the Constitution but do not subject the states to private suits for damages for those actions? See, e.g., Massey, Two Zones of Prophylaxis: The

Scope of the Fourteenth Amendment Enforcement Power, 76 Geo. Wash. L. Rev. 1 (2007). Perhaps the Eleventh Amendment's special solicitude for state treasuries dictates a narrow scope for the enforcement power, but otherwise Congress may act as broadly as in Katzenbach v. Morgan. But if there is nothing special about the Eleventh Amendment, does *Garrett* augur a diminished ability of Congress to prohibit state action that is not itself constitutionally improper but that implicates widely held societal notions of justice?

3. Problems: *Mandatory Coeducation.* Suppose Congress invokes its section 5 enforcement power to prohibit all single-sex public schools, and a girl who alleges that the presence of boys in her classroom hinders her ability to learn challenges the validity of Congress's action, introducing voluminous evidence supporting her contention, evidence that Congress ignored in enacting the bar. What should be the result? Recall that in United States v. Virginia, the Court ruled that Virginia's exclusion of women from its publicly funded Virginia Military Institute was a violation of equal protection, but left open the question of when, if ever, single-sex public schooling might be constitutionally valid.

Mandated Color-Blind University Admissions. Suppose Congress invokes its section 5 enforcement power to bar consideration of race by public universities in their admissions decisions. State University sues, claiming that Congress lacks authority to enact the law. What should be the result?

≡≡≡ *Nevada Department of Human Resources v. Hibbs*
538 U.S. 721 (2003)

[The "family leave" provision of the Family and Medical Leave Act of 1993 (FMLA or the Act) requires employers, including state governments, to grant up to 12 weeks of unpaid leave annually to permit an employee to care for a "serious health condition" in an employee's spouse, child, or parent. The Act creates a private right of action to seek both equitable relief and money damages. Hibbs, an employee of the Nevada Department of Human Resources, sued the state agency for money damages after his termination, allegedly in violation of the FMLA. A District Court granted summary judgment to the state agency on the grounds that the FMLA claim was barred by the Eleventh Amendment and that Hibbs's Fourteenth Amendment rights had not been violated. The Ninth Circuit reversed and the Supreme Court affirmed.]

CHIEF JUSTICE REHNQUIST delivered the opinion of the Court.

. . . This case turns . . . on whether Congress acted within its constitutional authority when it sought to abrogate the States' immunity for purposes of the FMLA's family-leave provision. . . . Congress may, in the exercise of its §5 power, do more than simply proscribe conduct that we have held unconstitutional. . . . Congress may enact . . . prophylactic legislation that proscribes facially constitutional conduct, in order to prevent and deter unconstitutional conduct. . . .

We distinguish appropriate prophylactic legislation from "substantive redefinition of the Fourteenth Amendment right at issue," by applying the test set forth in *City of Boerne*: Valid §5 legislation must exhibit "congruence and proportionality between the injury to be prevented or remedied and the means adopted to that end." . . . The FMLA aims to protect the right to be free from gender-based discrimination in the workplace. [C]lassifications that distinguish between males and females are [presumed to violate equal protection, and are valid only if "the discriminatory means employed" are "substantially related" to the achievement of actual "important governmental objectives" that do "not rely on overbroad generalizations about the different talents, capacities, or preferences of males and females"]. We now inquire whether Congress had evidence of a pattern of constitutional violations on the part of the States. . . .

According to evidence that was before Congress when it enacted the FMLA, States continue to rely on invalid gender stereotypes in the employment context, specifically in the administration of leave benefits. Reliance on such stereotypes cannot justify the States' gender discrimination in this area. [The] persistence of such unconstitutional discrimination by the States justifies Congress'[s] passage of prophylactic §5 legislation. [The] FMLA's legislative [record revealed] differential leave policies [that] were not attributable to any differential physical needs of men and women, but rather to the pervasive sex-role stereotype that caring for family members is women's work. . . . Congress had evidence that, even where state laws and policies were not facially discriminatory, they were applied in discriminatory ways. . . . In sum, the States' record of unconstitutional participation in, and fostering of, gender-based discrimination in the administration of leave benefits is weighty enough to justify the enactment of prophylactic §5 legislation.

We reached the opposite conclusion in *Garrett* and *Kimel*. . . . Here, however, Congress directed its attention to state gender discrimination, which triggers a heightened level of scrutiny. Because the standard for demonstrating the constitutionality of a gender-based classification is more difficult to meet than our rational-basis test . . . it was easier for Congress to show a pattern of state constitutional violations. . . . The impact of the discrimination targeted by the FMLA is significant. . . . Stereotypes about women's domestic roles are reinforced by parallel stereotypes presuming a lack of domestic responsibilities for men. Because employers continued to regard the family as the woman's domain, they often denied men similar accommodations or discouraged them from taking leave. These mutually reinforcing stereotypes created a self-fulfilling cycle of discrimination that forced women to continue to assume the role of primary family caregiver, and fostered employers' stereotypical views about women's commitment to work and their value as employees. Those perceptions, in turn, Congress reasoned, lead to subtle discrimination that may be difficult to detect on a case-by-case basis.

[Congress's] chosen remedy, the family-care leave provision of the FMLA, is "congruent and proportional to the targeted violation." Congress had already tried unsuccessfully to address this problem through Title VII and the amendment of Title VII by the Pregnancy Discrimination Act. Here, as in [South Carolina v. Katzenbach], Congress again confronted a "difficult and intractable problem," where previous legislative attempts had failed. Such problems may justify added prophylactic measures in response. By creating an across-the-board, routine employment benefit for all eligible employees, Congress sought to ensure that family-care leave would no longer be stigmatized as an inordinate drain on the workplace caused by female employees, and that employers could not evade leave obligations simply by hiring men. By setting a minimum standard of family leave for *all* eligible employees, irrespective of gender, the FMLA attacks the formerly state-sanctioned stereotype that only women are responsible for family caregiving, thereby reducing employers' incentives to engage in discrimination by basing hiring and promotion decisions on stereotypes. . . . Unlike the statutes at issue in *City of Boerne, Kimel,* and *Garrett,* which applied broadly to every aspect of state employers' operations, the FMLA is narrowly targeted at the fault line between work and family—precisely where sex-based overgeneralization has been and remains strongest—and affects only one aspect of the employment relationship. . . . Affirmed.

JUSTICE SCALIA, dissenting.
. . . The constitutional violation that is a prerequisite to "prophylactic" congressional action to "enforce" the Fourteenth Amendment is a violation *by the State against which the enforcement action is taken.* There is no guilt by association, enabling the sovereignty of one State to be abridged under §5 of the Fourteenth Amendment because of violations by another State, or by most other States, or even by 49 other States. . . . Today's opinion for the Court . . . treats "the States" as some sort of collective entity which is guilty or innocent as a body. . . . This will not do. Prophylaxis in the sense of extending the remedy beyond the violation is one thing; prophylaxis in the sense of extending the remedy beyond the violator is something else. . . .

JUSTICE KENNEDY, joined by JUSTICE SCALIA and JUSTICE THOMAS, dissenting.
. . . The Court is unable to show that States have engaged in a pattern of unlawful conduct which warrants the remedy of opening state treasuries to private suits. The inability to adduce evidence of alleged discrimination, coupled with the inescapable fact that the federal scheme is not a remedy but a benefit program, demonstrate the lack of the requisite link between any problem Congress has identified and the program it mandated.
[The] Court gives superficial treatment to the requirement that we "identify with some precision the scope of the constitutional right at issue." *Garrett.* . . . The relevant question . . . is whether . . . the States . . . engage in widespread discrimination on the basis of gender in the provision of family leave benefits. . . . The evidence to substantiate this charge must be far more specific . . . than a simple recitation of a general history of employment discrimination against women. . . . Respondents fail to make the requisite showing. [The] evidence considered by Congress concerned discriminatory practices of the private sector, not those of state employers. . . . The question is not whether the family leave provision is a congruent and proportional

response to general gender-based stereotypes in employment which "have historically produced discrimination in the hiring and promotion of women"; the question is whether it is a proper remedy to an alleged pattern of unconstitutional discrimination by States in the grant of family leave. The evidence of gender-based stereotypes is too remote to support the required showing. [Nor] does the Constitution require States to provide their employees with any family leave at all. A State's failure to devise a family leave program is not, then, evidence of unconstitutional behavior. Considered in its entirety, the evidence fails to document a pattern of unconstitutional conduct sufficient to justify the abrogation of States' sovereign immunity. . . .

Our concern with gender discrimination, which is subjected to heightened scrutiny, . . . does not alter this conclusion. . . . This consideration does not divest respondents of their burden to show that "Congress identified a history and pattern of unconstitutional employment discrimination by the States." . . . Congress was not responding with a congruent and proportional remedy to a perceived course of unconstitutional conduct. Instead, it enacted a substantive entitlement program of its own. If Congress had been concerned about different treatment of men and women with respect to family leave, a congruent remedy would have sought to ensure the benefits of any leave program enacted by a State are available to men and women on an equal basis. Instead, the Act imposes, across the board, a requirement that States grant a minimum of 12 weeks of leave per year. This requirement may represent Congress'[s] considered judgment as to the optimal balance between the family obligations of workers and the interests of employers. . . . It does not follow, however, that if the States choose to enact a different benefit scheme, they should be deemed to engage in unconstitutional conduct and forced to open their treasuries to private suits for damages. . . .

The Act on its face is not drawn as a remedy to gender-based discrimination in family leave. . . .

NOTES

1. What (If Anything) Changed from *Garrett*? Apart from the result, did anything change from *Garrett* to *Hibbs*? Did the Court in *Hibbs* alter the standard—congruence and proportionality? Did the Court in *Hibbs* apply the same standard in a different way? Does *Hibbs* suggest that the evidentiary burden that Congress must carry to invoke its section 5 power lessens as the presumptive invalidity of the problem attacked increases?

2. Later Developments. *Tennessee v. Lane*, 541 *U.S. 509 (2004).* Title II of the Americans with Disabilities Act of 1990 (ADA) provides that "no qualified individual with a disability shall, by reason of such disability, be excluded from participation in or be denied the benefits of the services, programs or activities of a public entity, or be subjected to discrimination by any such entity." 42 U.S.C. §12132. George Lane, a paraplegic confined to a wheelchair, was required to appear twice at a county courthouse to answer criminal charges against him. The first time he crawled up two flights of stairs because the courthouse lacked an elevator and the hearing room was on the second floor. The second time he refused the court's offer to carry him up the stairs or to move the hearing room to a wheel chair-accessible courtroom in a nearby town; as a result, he was arrested for his failure to appear. In federal court, Lane invoked Title II of the ADA to seek damages from and equitable relief against Tennessee.

The Court, 5-4, applied the congruence-and-proportionality test and upheld the validity of Title II as applied to the narrow issue raised by Lane: "Title II, as it applies to the class of cases implicating the fundamental right of access to the courts, constitutes a valid exercise of Congress's §5 authority to enforce the guarantees of the Fourteenth Amendment." Because access to courts is a fundamental constitutional right, its infringement is "subject to more searching judicial review." As in *Hibbs*, this fact made it easier for Congress to show a pattern of state constitutional violations sufficient to establish congruence between the statutory prohibition and the constitutional violation it sought to remedy.

Because Congress had adequately documented "pervasive unequal treatment in the administration of state services and programs, including systematic deprivations of [such] fundamental rights" as voting, jury service, and marriage,[3] the Court found Title II to be proportional to the asserted constitutional violation. Also, the Court found proportionality by declining to rule on the entire scope of Title II. Taken as a whole, Title II subjects states to monetary liability for denying disabled persons access to such things as "state-owned hockey rinks" as well as "voting-booth access." Tennessee argued that "the broad range of Title II's applications"—mandating access to constitutionally fundamental state services and programs as well as constitutionally trivial services and programs—fatally impeached its claim to proportionality. But the Court refused to consider Title II "as an undifferentiated whole. . . . [T]he question . . . is not whether Congress can validly subject the States to private suits for money damages for failing to provide reasonable access to hockey rinks, or even to voting booths, but whether Congress had the power under §5 to enforce the constitutional right of access to the courts. Because we find that Title II unquestionably is valid §5 legislation as it applies to the class of cases implicating the accessibility of judicial services, we need go no further."

In dissent, Chief Justice Rehnquist, joined by Justices Kennedy and Thomas, chided the majority for relying "on a wide-ranging account of societal discrimination against the disabled" to prove the much narrower claim that states have systematically deprived disabled people of access to courts. "Some of this evidence would be relevant if the Court were considering the constitutionality of the statute as a whole; but the Court rejects that approach in favor

---

3. The laws cited by the majority generally impose a categorical disqualification upon "idiots," "lunatics," or the mentally disabled, without any individualized assessment of mental competence to vote, serve on a jury, or marry.

of a narrower 'as-applied' inquiry." The dissent thought that "outdated, gen-eralized evidence" was "irrelevant to Title II's purported enforcement of Due Process access-to-the-courts rights. . . . [T]here is *nothing* in the legislative record or statutory findings to indicate that disabled persons were systemat-ically denied the right to be present at criminal trials, denied the meaningful opportunity to be heard in civil cases, unconstitutionally excluded from jury service, or denied the right to attend criminal trials." Finally, the dissent noted that "the congruence-and-proportionality test" is designed to determine

> whether Congress has attempted to statutorily redefine the constitutional rights protected by the Fourteenth Amendment. This question can only be answered by measuring the breadth of a statute's coverage against the scope of the consti-tutional rights it purports to enforce and the record of violations it purports to remedy. In conducting its as-applied analysis, however, the majority posits a hy-pothetical statute, never enacted by Congress, that applies only to courthouses. The effect is to rig the congruence-and-proportionality test by artificially con-stricting the scope of the statute to closely mirror a recognized constitutional right. But Title II is not susceptible of being carved up in this manner; it applies indiscriminately to all "services," "programs," or "activities" of any "public en-tity." [T]he majority's approach is not really an assessment of whether Title II is "appropriate *legislation*" at all, but a test of whether the Court can conceive of a hypothetical statute narrowly tailored enough to constitute valid prophylactic legislation.

Justice Scalia, dissenting separately, rejected the congruence-and-propor-tionality test entirely because it, "like all such flabby tests, is a standing invi-tation to judicial arbitrariness and policy-driven decision making. Worse still, it casts this Court in the role of Congress's taskmaster. Under it, the courts (and ultimately this Court) must regularly check Congress's homework to make sure that it has identified sufficient constitutional violations to make its remedy congruent and proportional." Justice Scalia would replace this test with one focusing on Congress's power, textually limited in section 5, to *enforce* the Fourteenth Amendment: "Nothing in §5 allows Congress to go *beyond* the provisions of the Fourteenth Amendment to proscribe, prevent, or 'remedy' conduct that does not *itself* violate any provision of the Fourteenth Amendment. So-called prophylactic legislation is reinforcement rather than enforcement. [P]rincipally for reasons of *stare decisis*," said Justice Scalia, the only exception is for "congressional measures designed to remedy racial dis-crimination by the States."

Coleman v. Court of Appeals of Maryland, 132 S. Ct. 1327 (2012). A four-justice plurality concluded that the "self-care leave" provision of the FMLA was not intended to address sex discrimination, so the constitutional right Congress sought to protect—equal protection—is violated only by the absence of a legitimate objective or an irrational means to obtain a legitimate end. Neither condition was present. As applied to a suit for money damages the provision was not congruent (it barred all denials of medical self-care leave, including those denials that are rationally related to legitimate ends) and was not proportional to the constitutional injury (there was no evidence of wholesale *irrational* denials of self-leave). Though the plurality did not mention *Lane*, it considered the self-care provision in isolation from the rest of the FMLA. Four justices dissented. Justice Scalia concurred in the judgment, adhering to his view expressed in *Lane*. He claimed that each of the plurality and dissent's opinions were "a faithful application of our 'congruence and proportionality' jurisprudence . . . because the varying outcomes we have arrived at under the 'congruence and proportionality' test make no sense."

3. The Fifteenth Amendment and the Voting Rights Act.   Under the Fifteenth Amendment neither the federal government nor the states may deny or abridge the vote on account of "race, color or previous condition of servitude." Section 5 of the Voting Rights Act prohibits "covered jurisdictions" from making any changes in their electoral laws without obtaining permission to do so from the Attorney General. "Covered jurisdictions" were initially defined to include only those states or political subdivisions that in 1964 used certain voter eligibility tests and had less than 50 percent voter registration or turnout in the 1964 presidential election. As originally enacted, the Act would expire in 1970, but its life was extended to 1975, then to 1982, then to 2007, and finally to 2032. The validity of the original Act was upheld in South Carolina v. Katzenbach, 383 U.S. 301 (1966), and each of the subsequent extensions was also upheld, on the ground that the factual circumstances justified the extension. Georgia v. United States, 411 U.S. 526 (1973); City of Rome v. United States, 446 U.S. 156 (1980); Lopez v. Monterey County, 525 U.S. 266 (1999). The 1970 extension moved the date for assessing the criteria for determining covered jurisdictions to 1968 and the 1975 extension moved that date to 1972. Significantly, however, neither the 1982 extension (to 2007) nor the 2006 extension (to 2032) advanced the date beyond 1972.

≡≡≡
≡≡≡ *Shelby County v. Holder*
≡≡≡ *133 S. Ct. 2612 (2013)*

CHIEF JUSTICE ROBERTS delivered the opinion of the Court.

The Voting Rights Act of 1965 employed extraordinary measures to address an extraordinary problem. Section 5 of the Act required States to obtain federal permission before enacting any law related to voting—a drastic departure from basic principles of federalism. And §4 of the Act applied that requirement only to some States—an equally dramatic departure from the principle that all States enjoy equal sovereignty. This was strong medicine, but Congress determined it was needed to address entrenched racial discrimination in voting, "an insidious and pervasive evil which had been perpetuated in certain parts of our country through unremitting and ingenious defiance of the Constitution." As we explained in upholding the law, "exceptional conditions can justify legislative measures not otherwise appropriate." Reflecting the unprecedented nature of these measures, they were scheduled to expire after five years.

Nearly 50 years later, they are still in effect; indeed, they have been made more stringent, and are now scheduled to last until 2031. There is no denying, however, that the conditions that originally justified these measures no longer characterize voting in the covered jurisdictions. By 2009, "the racial gap in voter registration and turnout [was] lower in the States originally covered by §5 than it [was] nationwide." Since that time, Census Bureau data indicate that African-American voter turnout has come to exceed white voter turnout in five of the six States originally covered by §5, with a gap in the sixth State of less than one half of one percent.

At the same time, voting discrimination still exists; no one doubts that. The question is whether the Act's extraordinary measures, including its disparate treatment of the States, continue to satisfy constitutional requirements. As we put it a short time ago, "the Act imposes current burdens and must be justified by current needs."

The Fifteenth Amendment was ratified in 1870, in the wake of the Civil War. It provides that "[t]he right of citizens of the United States to vote shall not be denied or abridged by the United States or by any State on account of race, color, or previous condition of servitude," and it gives Congress the "power to enforce this article by appropriate legislation."

"The first century of congressional enforcement of the Amendment, however, can only be regarded as a failure." In the 1890s, Alabama, Georgia, Louisiana, Mississippi, North Carolina, South Carolina, and Virginia began to enact literacy tests for voter registration and to employ other methods designed to prevent African-Americans from voting. Congress passed statutes outlawing some of these practices and facilitating litigation against them, but litigation remained slow and expensive, and the States came up with new ways to discriminate as soon as existing ones were struck down. Voter registration of African-Americans barely improved. . . . Congress responded in 1965 with the Voting Rights Act. . . . At the time of the Act's passage, [the] "covered" jurisdictions[, defined in Section 4,] were those States or political subdivisions that had maintained a test or device as a prerequisite to voting as of November 1, 1964, and had less than 50 percent voter registration or turnout in the 1964 Presidential election. Such tests or devices included literacy and knowledge tests, good moral character requirements, the need for vouchers from registered voters, and the like. In 1965, the covered States included Alabama, Georgia, Louisiana, Mississippi, South Carolina, and Virginia. The additional covered subdivisions included 39 counties in North Carolina and one in Arizona. . . .

Section 5 provided that no change in voting procedures [in covered jurisdictions] could take effect until it was approved by federal authorities in Washington, D.C.—either the Attorney General or a court of three judges. A jurisdiction could obtain such "preclearance" only by proving that the change had neither "the purpose [nor] the effect of denying or abridging the right to vote on account of race or color." Sections 4 and 5 were intended to be temporary; they were set to expire after five years. In *South Carolina v. Katzenbach*, we upheld the 1965 Act against constitutional challenge, explaining that it was justified to address "voting discrimination where it persists on a pervasive scale."

In 1970, Congress reauthorized the Act for another five years, and extended the coverage formula in §4(b) to jurisdictions that had a voting test and less than 50 percent voter registration or turnout as of 1968. That swept in several counties in California, New Hampshire, and New York. In 1975, Congress reauthorized the Act for seven more years, and extended its coverage to jurisdictions that had a voting test and less than 50 percent voter registration or turnout as of 1972. Congress also amended the definition of "test or device" to include the practice of providing English-only voting materials in places where over five percent of voting-age citizens spoke a single language other than English. As a result of these amendments, the States of Alaska, Arizona, and Texas, as well as several counties in California, Florida, Michigan, New York, North Carolina, and South Dakota, became covered jurisdictions. . . . In 1982, Congress reauthorized the Act for 25 years, but did not alter its coverage formula. . . . We upheld each of these reauthorizations against constitutional challenge.

In 2006, Congress again reauthorized the Voting Rights Act for 25 years, again without change to its coverage formula. Congress also amended §5 to prohibit more conduct than before. Section 5 now forbids voting changes with "any discriminatory purpose" as well as voting changes that diminish the ability of citizens, on account of race, color, or language minority status, "to elect their preferred candidates of choice." . . .

Shelby County is located in Alabama, a covered jurisdiction. [The] Attorney General has recently objected to voting changes proposed from within the county [and] the county sued the Attorney General in Federal District Court . . . , seeking a declaratory judgment that sections §4(b) and 5 of the Voting Rights Act are facially unconstitutional, as well as a permanent injunction against their enforcement. The District Court . . . upheld the Act. . . . The Court of Appeals for the D.C. Circuit affirmed. . . . We granted certiorari.

In *Northwest Austin Municipal Utility District No. 1 v. Holder*[, 557 U.S 193 (2009)], we stated that "the Act imposes current burdens and must be justified by current needs." And we concluded that "a departure from the fundamental principle of equal sovereignty requires a showing that a statute's disparate geographic coverage is sufficiently related to the problem that it targets." These basic principles guide our review of the question before us. . . .

The Federal Government does not . . . have a general right to review and veto state enactments before they go into effect. . . . Outside the strictures of the Supremacy Clause, States retain broad autonomy in structuring their governments and pursuing legislative objectives. Indeed, the Constitution provides that all powers not specifically granted to the Federal Government are reserved to the States or citizens. This "allocation of powers in our federal system preserves the integrity, dignity, and residual sovereignty of the States." But the federal balance "is not just an end in itself: Rather, federalism secures to citizens the liberties that derive from the diffusion of sovereign power."

More specifically, " 'the Framers of the Constitution intended the States to keep for themselves, as provided in the Tenth Amendment, the power to regulate elections.' " Of course, the Federal Government retains significant control over federal elections. For instance, the Constitution authorizes Congress to establish the time and manner for electing Senators and Representatives. Art. I, §4, cl. 1. But States have "broad powers to determine the conditions under which the right of suffrage may be exercised." . . .

Not only do States retain sovereignty under the Constitution, there is also a "fundamental principle of equal sovereignty" among the States. Indeed, "the constitutional equality of the States is essential to the harmonious operation of the scheme upon which the Republic was organized." [The] fundamental principle of equal sovereignty remains highly pertinent in assessing . . . disparate treatment of States. The Voting Rights Act sharply departs from these basic principles. It suspends "all changes to state election law—however innocuous—until they have been pre-cleared by federal authorities in Washington, D.C." States must beseech the Federal Government for permission to implement laws that they would otherwise have the right to enact and execute on their own. . . .

And despite the tradition of equal sovereignty, the Act applies to only nine States (and several additional counties). While one State waits months or years and expends funds to implement a validly enacted law, its neighbor can typically put the same law into effect immediately, through the normal legislative process. Even if a noncovered jurisdiction is sued, there are important differences between those proceedings and preclearance proceedings; the preclearance proceeding "not only switches the burden of proof to the supplicant jurisdiction, but also applies substantive standards quite different from those governing the rest of the nation."

All this explains why, when we first upheld the Act in 1966, we described it as "stringent" and "potent." We recognized that it "may have been an uncommon exercise of congressional power," but concluded that "legislative measures not otherwise appropriate" could be justified by "exceptional conditions." We have since noted that the Act . . . represents an "extraordinary departure from the traditional course of relations between the States and the Federal Government." As we reiterated in *Northwest Austin,* the Act constitutes "extraordinary legislation otherwise unfamiliar to our federal system."

In 1966, we found these departures from the basic features of our system of government justified. The "blight of racial discrimination in voting" had "infected the electoral process in parts of our country for nearly a century." Several States had enacted a variety of requirements and tests "specifically designed to prevent" African-Americans from voting. Case-by-case litigation had proved inadequate to prevent such racial discrimination in voting, in part because States "merely switched to discriminatory devices not covered by the federal decrees," "enacted difficult new tests," or simply "defied and evaded court orders." Shortly before enactment of the Voting Rights Act, only 19.4 percent of African-Americans of voting age were registered to vote in Alabama, only 31.8 percent in Louisiana, and only 6.4 percent in Mississippi.

Those figures were roughly 50 percentage points or more below the figures for whites. In short, we concluded that "[u]nder the compulsion of these unique circumstances, Congress responded in a permissibly decisive manner." At the time, the coverage formula—the means of linking the exercise of the unprecedented authority with the problem that warranted it—made sense. We found that "Congress chose to limit its attention to the geographic areas where immediate action seemed necessary." . . .

Nearly 50 years later, things have changed dramatically. Shelby County contends that the preclearance requirement, even without regard to its disparate coverage, is now unconstitutional. Its arguments have a good deal of force. In the covered jurisdictions, "[v]oter turnout and registration rates now approach parity. Blatantly discriminatory evasions of federal decrees are rare. And minority candidates hold office at unprecedented levels." The tests and devices that blocked access to the ballot have been forbidden nationwide for over 40 years. Those conclusions are not ours alone. Congress said the same when it reauthorized the Act in 2006. . . . [In 1965, the gap between white and black voter registration in six covered jurisdictions ranged from 23% to 63%. In 2004, when Congress considered the most recent extension, the gap had narrowed to 4% more whites and to 4% more blacks.]

There is no doubt that these improvements are in large part because of the Voting Rights Act. The Act has proved immensely successful at redressing racial discrimination and integrating the voting process. . . . Yet the Act has not eased the restrictions in §5 or narrowed the scope of the coverage formula in §4(b) along the way. Those extraordinary and unprecedented features were reauthorized—as if nothing had changed. In fact, the Act's unusual remedies have grown even stronger. When Congress reauthorized the Act in 2006, it did so for another 25 years on top of the previous 40—a far cry from the initial five-year period. . . . The provisions of §5 apply only to those jurisdictions singled out by §4. We now consider whether that coverage formula is constitutional in light of current conditions.

When upholding the constitutionality of the coverage formula in 1966, we concluded that it was "rational in both practice and theory." . . . By 2009, however, we concluded that the "coverage formula raise[d] serious constitutional questions." *Northwest Austin.* As we explained, a statute's "current burdens" must be justified by "current needs," and any "disparate geographic coverage" must be "sufficiently related to the problem that it targets." The coverage formula met that test in 1965, but no longer does so.

Coverage today is based on decades-old data and eradicated practices. . . . [V]oter registration and turnout numbers in the covered States have risen dramatically in the years since. Racial disparity in those numbers was compelling evidence justifying the preclearance remedy and the coverage formula. There is no longer such a disparity.

In 1965, the States could be divided into two groups: those with a recent history of voting tests and low voter registration and turnout, and those without those characteristics. Congress based its coverage formula on that distinction. Today the Nation is no longer divided along those lines, yet the Voting Rights Act continues to treat it as if it were. . . .

The Government falls back to the argument that because the formula was relevant in 1965, its continued use is permissible so long as any discrimination remains in the States Congress identified back then—regardless of how that discrimination compares to discrimination in States unburdened by coverage. This argument does not look to "current political conditions," but instead relies on a comparison between the States in 1965. . . .

But history did not end in 1965. By the time the Act was reauthorized in 2006, there had been 40 more years of it. In assessing the "current need[ ]" for a preclearance system that treats States differently from one another today, that history cannot be ignored. During that time, largely because of the Voting Rights Act, voting tests were abolished, disparities in voter registration and turnout due to race were erased, and African-Americans attained political office in record numbers. And yet the coverage formula that Congress reauthorized in 2006 ignores these developments, keeping the focus on decades-old data relevant to decades-old problems, rather than current data reflecting current needs. . . .

Congress—if it is to divide the States—must identify those jurisdictions to be singled out on a basis that makes sense in light of current conditions. It cannot rely simply on the past. We made that clear in *Northwest Austin*, and we make it clear again today. . . .

There is no valid reason to insulate the coverage formula from review merely because it was previously enacted 40 years ago. If Congress had started from scratch in 2006, it plainly could not have enacted the present coverage formula. It would have been irrational for Congress to distinguish between States in such a fundamental way based on 40-year-old data, when today's statistics tell an entirely different story. And it would have been irrational to base coverage on the use of voting tests 40 years ago, when such tests have been illegal since that time. But that is exactly what Congress has done. . . . Our country has changed, and while any racial discrimination in voting is too much, Congress must ensure that the legislation it passes to remedy that problem speaks to current conditions.

The judgment of the Court of Appeals is reversed.

JUSTICE THOMAS, concurring.

I join the Court's opinion in full but write separately to explain that I would find §5 of the Voting Rights Act unconstitutional as well. . . .

JUSTICE GINSBURG, with whom JUSTICE BREYER, JUSTICE SOTOMAYOR, and JUSTICE KAGAN join, dissenting.

In the Court's view, the very success of §5 of the Voting Rights Act demands its dormancy. . . . Congress determined . . . that the scourge of discrimination was not yet extirpated. The question this case presents is who decides whether, as currently operative, §5 remains justifiable, this Court, or a Congress charged with the obligation to enforce the post-Civil War

Amendments "by appropriate legislation." With overwhelming support in both Houses, Congress concluded that, for two prime reasons, §5 should continue in force, unabated. First, continuance would facilitate completion of the impressive gains thus far made; and second, continuance would guard against backsliding. Those assessments were well within Congress' province to make. . . .

Although the VRA wrought dramatic changes in the realization of minority voting rights, the Act, to date, surely has not eliminated all vestiges of discrimination against the exercise of the franchise by minority citizens. . . . Efforts to reduce the impact of minority votes, in contrast to direct attempts to block access to the ballot, are aptly described as "second-generation barriers" to minority voting. Second-generation barriers come in various forms[:] racial gerrymandering, the redrawing of legislative districts in an "effort to segregate the races for purposes of voting"; [and] at-large voting in lieu of district-by-district voting in a city with a sizable black minority. . . .

As the 1982 reauthorization approached its 2007 expiration date, Congress made the following findings: The VRA has directly caused significant progress in eliminating first-generation barriers to ballot access, leading to a marked increase in minority voter registration and turnout and the number of minority elected officials. But despite this progress, "second generation barriers constructed to prevent minority voters from fully participating in the electoral process" continued to exist, as well as racially polarized voting in the covered jurisdictions, which increased the political vulnerability of racial and language minorities in those jurisdictions. . . . Based on these findings, Congress reauthorized preclearance for another 25 years. . . . The question before the Court is whether Congress had the authority under the Constitution to act as it did. . . .

The question . . . for judicial review is whether the chosen means are "adapted to carry out the objects the amendments have in view." The Court's role, then, is not to substitute its judgment for that of Congress, but to determine whether the legislative record sufficed to show that "Congress could rationally have determined that [its chosen] provisions were appropriate methods." . . .

The sad irony of today's decision lies in its utter failure to grasp why the VRA has proven effective. The Court appears to believe that the VRA's success in eliminating the specific devices extant in 1965 means that preclearance is no longer needed. . . . [But] the VRA is grounded in Congress' recognition of the "variety and persistence" of measures designed to impair minority voting rights. . . . [T]he evolution of voting discrimination into more subtle second-generation barriers is powerful evidence that a remedy as effective as preclearance remains vital to protect minority voting rights and prevent backsliding. . . .

For the reasons stated, I would affirm the judgment of the Court of Appeals.

NOTE

The Court's decision permits Congress to amend the coverage formula of section 4(b) to align it with contemporary realities. In the event Congress fails to do so, the preclearance requirement of section 5 is effectively inoperative. However, section 3 of the VRA permits the federal government to impose preclearance on a defendant jurisdiction if the government can prove to a court that the jurisdiction has engaged in recent racially discriminatory voting practices. Section 2 permits the government and private parties to seek injunctions of voting practices that are racially discriminatory either in purpose or effect. Those sections were not at issue in *Shelby County*.

12 The Right to Keep and Bear Arms

The Second Amendment states: "A well regulated Militia, being necessary to the security of a free State, the right of the people to keep and bear Arms, shall not be infringed." This has been the subject of a flood of academic commentary but little judicial interpretation. The commentators divide into two camps. One view is that the Amendment protects only a collective right to bear arms in a military capacity. The other view is that the Amendment protects an individual's right to possess firearms. The "collective rights" view asserts that the Amendment secures to states the right to continue to organize and maintain an armed militia of citizens, which could be mobilized into a military force for the defense of the nation in time of need. The "individual rights" view asserts that the Amendment ensures an individual's right to possess firearms for any number of reasons. In the following case, the Supreme Court decided that the Second Amendment does guarantee an individual's right to possess firearms for self-defense, but left an enormous number of questions unanswered. The Court announced a "constitutionally operative rule," but did little to articulate any "constitutional decision rules"—the actual standards by which a court can determine whether any particular regulation of firearms is constitutionally valid. The indeterminate nature of these decision rules provides an unusual opportunity to speculate about what those rules should be with respect to an individual's constitutional right that has not yet developed a body of decisional law. In thinking through these problems, you will have an opportunity to apply many of the ideas and principles that have informed your study so far of individual constitutional liberties.

District of Columbia v. Heller
554 U.S. 570 (2008)

JUSTICE SCALIA delivered the opinion of the Court.

We consider whether a District of Columbia prohibition on the possession of usable handguns in the home violates the Second Amendment to the Constitution.

I. The District of Columbia generally prohibits the possession of handguns. It is a crime to carry an unregistered firearm, and the registration of handguns is prohibited. [D.C.] law also requires residents to keep their lawfully owned firearms, such as registered long guns, "unloaded and dissembled or bound by a trigger lock or similar device" unless they are located in a place of business or are being used for lawful recreational activities. . . . Dick Heller is a D.C. special police officer authorized to carry a handgun while on duty at the Federal Judicial Center. He applied for a registration certificate for a handgun that he wished to keep at home, but the District refused. [On] Second Amendment grounds, [he sought] to enjoin the city from enforcing the bar on the registration of handguns, the licensing requirement insofar as it prohibits the carrying of a firearm in the home without a license, and the trigger-lock requirement insofar as it prohibits the use of "functional firearms within the home." The District Court dismissed [Heller's] complaint. The Court of Appeals for the District of Columbia Circuit . . . reversed, [and] held that the Second Amendment protects an individual right to possess firearms and that the city's total ban on handguns, as well as its requirement that firearms in the home be kept nonfunctional even when necessary for self-defense, violated that right. . . . We granted certiorari.

II. We turn first to the meaning of the Second Amendment. . . . In interpreting [its] text, we are guided by the principle that "[t]he Constitution['s] words and phrases were used in their normal and ordinary as distinguished from technical meaning." Normal meaning may . . . include an idiomatic meaning, but it excludes secret or technical meanings that would not have been known to ordinary citizens in the founding generation. [D.C. and the] dissenting Justices believe that [the Amendment] protects only the right to possess and carry a firearm in connection with militia service. [Heller] argues that it protects an individual right to possess a firearm unconnected with service in a militia, and to use that arm for traditionally lawful purposes, such as self-defense within the home.

The Second Amendment is . . . divided into two parts: its prefatory clause and its operative clause. The former does not limit the latter grammatically, but rather announces a purpose. The Amendment could be rephrased, "Because a well regulated Militia is necessary to the security of a free State, the right of the people to keep and bear Arms shall not be infringed." Although this structure of the Second Amendment is unique in our Constitution, other legal documents of the founding era, particularly individual-rights provisions of state constitutions, commonly included a prefatory statement of purpose. Logic demands that there be a link between the stated purpose and the command. That requirement . . . may cause a prefatory clause to resolve an ambiguity in the operative clause ("The separation of church and state being an important objective, the teachings of canons shall have no place in our jurisprudence." The preface makes clear that the operative clause refers not to canons of interpretation but to clergymen.). But apart from [clarification], a prefatory clause does not limit or expand the scope of the operative clause. [Thus,] we will return to the prefatory clause to ensure that our reading of the operative clause is consistent with the announced purpose.

1. Operative Clause

a. "Right of the People"

The first salient feature of the operative clause is that it codifies a "right of the people." The unamended Constitution and the Bill of Rights use the phrase "right of the people" two other times, in the First Amendment's Assembly-and-Petition Clause and in the Fourth Amendment's Search-and-Seizure Clause. The Ninth Amendment uses very similar terminology. All three of these instances unambiguously refer to individual rights, not "collective" rights, or rights that may be exercised only through participation in some corporate body. Three provisions of the Constitution refer to "the people" in a context other than "rights"—the famous preamble ("We the people"), §2 of Article I (providing that "the people" will choose members of the House), and the Tenth Amendment (providing that those powers not given the Federal Government remain with "the States" or "the people"). Those provisions arguably refer to "the people" acting collectively—but they deal with the exercise or reservation of powers, not rights. Nowhere else in the Constitution does a "right" attributed to "the people" refer to anything other than an individual right. What is more, in all six other provisions of the Constitution that mention "the people," the term unambiguously refers to all members of the political community, not an unspecified subset. [But] the "militia" in colonial America consisted of a subset of "the people"—those who were male, able bodied, and within a certain age range. Reading the Second Amendment as protecting only the right to "keep and bear Arms" in an organized militia therefore fits poorly with the operative clause's description of the holder of that right as "the people." We start therefore with a strong presumption that the Second Amendment right is exercised individually and belongs to all Americans.

b. "Keep and Bear Arms"

We move now from the holder of the right—"the people"—to the substance of the right: "to keep and bear Arms." . . . Timothy Cunningham's important 1771 legal dictionary defined "arms" as "any thing that a man wears for his defence, or takes into his hands, or useth in wrath to cast at or strike another." 1 A New and Complete Law Dictionary (1771); see also N. Webster, American Dictionary of the English Language (1828) (reprinted 1989) (hereinafter Webster) (similar). The term was applied, then as now, to weapons that were not specifically designed for military use and were not employed in a military capacity. . . .

Some have made the argument, bordering on the frivolous, that only those arms in existence in the 18th century are protected by the Second Amendment. We do not interpret constitutional rights that way. Just as the First Amendment protects modern forms of communications and the Fourth Amendment applies to modern forms of search, the Second Amendment extends . . . to all instruments that constitute bearable arms, even those that were not in existence at the time of the founding.

We turn to the phrases "keep arms" and "bear arms." Johnson defined "keep" as, most relevantly, . . . "[t]o have in custody." Webster defined it as "[t]o hold; to retain in one's power or possession." No party has apprised us of an idiomatic meaning of "keep Arms." Thus, the most natural reading of "keep Arms" in the Second Amendment is to "have weapons." The phrase . . . was not prevalent in the written documents of the founding period . . . , but there are a few examples, all of which favor viewing the right to "keep Arms" as an individual right unconnected with militia service. William Blackstone, for example, wrote that Catholics convicted of not attending service in the Church of England suffered certain penalties, one of which was that they were not permitted to "keep arms in their houses." Petitioners point to militia laws of the founding period that required militia members to "keep" arms in connection with militia service, and they conclude from this that the phrase "keep Arms" has a militia-related connotation. This is rather like saying that, since there are many statutes that authorize aggrieved employees to "file complaints" with federal agencies, the phrase "file complaints" has an employment-related connotation. "Keep arms" was simply a common way of referring to possessing arms, for militiamen *and everyone else.* . . .

At the time of the founding, as now, to "bear" meant to "carry." When used with "arms," [it means] "being armed and ready for offensive or defensive action in a case of conflict with another person." . . . Although the phrase implies that the carrying of the weapon is for the purpose of "offensive or defensive action," it in no way connotes participation in a structured military organization. From our review of founding-era sources, we conclude that . . . "bear arms" was unambiguously used to refer to the carrying of weapons outside of an organized militia. The most prominent examples are [nine] state constitutional provisions written in the 18th century or the first two decades of the 19th, which enshrined a right of citizens to "bear arms in defense of themselves and the state" or "bear arms in defense of himself and the state."

The phrase "bear Arms" also had at the time of the founding an idiomatic meaning . . . : "to serve as a soldier, do military service, fight" or "to wage war." But it *unequivocally* bore that idiomatic meaning only when followed by the preposition "against," which was in turn followed by the target of the hostilities. (That is how, for example, our Declaration of Independence used the phrase: "He has constrained our fellow Citizens taken Captive on the high Seas to bear Arms against their Country . . .".) Petitioners justify their limitation of "bear arms" to the military context by pointing out the unremarkable fact that it was often used in that context—the same mistake they made with respect to "keep arms." . . . The common references to those "fit to bear arms" in congressional discussions about the militia are matched by use of the same phrase in the few nonmilitary federal contexts where the concept would be relevant. Other legal sources frequently used "bear arms" in nonmilitary contexts. . . . And if one looks beyond legal sources, "bear arms" was frequently used in nonmilitary contexts. . . .

c.   Meaning of the Operative Clause

Putting all of these textual elements together, we find that they guarantee the individual right to possess and carry weapons in case of confrontation. This meaning is strongly confirmed by the historical background of the Second Amendment. We look to this because it has always been widely understood that the Second Amendment, like the First and Fourth Amendments, codified a *pre-existing* right. The very text of the Second Amendment implicitly recognizes the pre-existence of the right and declares only that it "shall not be infringed." As we said in United States v. Cruikshank, 92 U.S. 542, 553 (1876), "[t]his is not a right granted by the Constitution. Neither is it in any manner dependent upon that instrument for its existence. . . ."

Between the Restoration and the Glorious Revolution, the Stuart Kings succeeded in using select militias loyal to them to suppress political dissidents, in part by disarming their opponents. These experiences caused Englishmen to be extremely wary of concentrated military forces run by the state and to be jealous of their arms. They accordingly obtained an assurance from William and Mary, in the Declaration of Right (which was codified as the English Bill of Rights), that Protestants would never be disarmed: "That the subjects which are Protestants may have arms for their defense suitable to their conditions and as allowed by law." This right has long been understood to be the predecessor to our Second Amendment. It was clearly an individual right, having nothing whatever to do with service in a militia. To be sure, it was an individual right not available to the whole population, given that it was restricted to Protestants, and like all written English rights it was held only against the Crown, not Parliament. But it was secured to them as individuals, . . . not as members of a fighting force.

By the time of the founding, the right to have arms had become fundamental for English subjects. Blackstone, whose works, we have said, "constituted the preeminent authority on English law for the founding generation," cited the arms provision of the Bill of Rights as one of the fundamental rights of Englishmen. His description of it cannot possibly be thought to tie it to militia or military service. It was, he said, "the natural right of resistance and self-preservation," and "the right of having and using arms for self-preservation and defence." Other contemporary authorities concurred. Thus, the right secured in 1689 as a result of the Stuarts' abuses was by the time of the founding understood to be an individual right protecting against both public and private violence. And, of course, what the Stuarts had tried to do to their political enemies, George III had tried to do to the colonists. In the tumultuous decades of the 1760s and 1770s, the Crown began to disarm the inhabitants of the most rebellious areas. That provoked polemical reactions by Americans invoking their rights as Englishmen to keep arms. . . . They understood the right to enable individuals to defend themselves. As the most important early American edition of Blackstone's Commentaries (by the law professor and former Antifederalist St. George Tucker) made clear in the notes to the description of the arms right, Americans understood the "right of self-preservation" as permitting a citizen to "repe[l] force by force" when "the intervention of society in his behalf, may be too late to prevent an injury."

There seems to us no doubt, on the basis of both text and history, that the Second Amendment conferred an individual right to keep and bear arms.

Of course the right was not unlimited, just as the First Amendment's right of free speech was not. Thus, we do not read the Second Amendment to protect the right of citizens to carry arms for *any sort* of confrontation, just as we do not read the First Amendment to protect the right of citizens to speak for *any purpose*. Before turning to limitations upon the individual right, however, we must determine whether the prefatory clause of the Second Amendment comports with our interpretation of the operative clause.

2. Prefatory Clause

The prefatory clause reads: "A well regulated Militia, being necessary to the security of a free State . . ."

a. "Well Regulated Militia"

In United States v. Miller, 307 U.S. 174, 179 (1939), we explained that "the Militia comprised all males physically capable of acting in concert for the common defense." That definition comports with founding-era sources. [This reading is supported by Congress's] power to "provide for calling forth the militia," and the power not to create, but to "organiz[e]" it—and not to organize "a" militia, which is what one would expect if the militia were to be a federal creation, but to organize "the" militia, connoting a body already in existence. . . . From that pool, Congress has plenary power to organize the units that will make up an effective fighting force. That is what Congress did in the first militia Act, which specified that "each and every free able-bodied white male citizen of the respective states, resident therein, who is or shall be of the age of eighteen years, and under the age of forty-five years (except as is herein after excepted) shall severally and respectively be enrolled in the militia." . . . Although the militia consists of all able-bodied men, the federally organized militia may consist of a subset of them. Finally, the adjective "well-regulated" implies nothing more than the imposition of proper discipline and training.

b. "Security of a Free State"

The phrase "security of a free state" meant "security of a free polity," not security of each of the several States. . . . It is true that the term "State" elsewhere in the Constitution refers to individual States, but the phrase "security of a free state" and close variations seem to have been terms of art in 18th-century political discourse, meaning a "free country" or free polity. Moreover, the other instances of "state" in the Constitution are typically accompanied by modifiers making clear that the reference is to the several States. . . . There are many reasons why the militia was thought to be "necessary to the security of a free state." First, . . . it is useful in repelling invasions and suppressing insurrections. Second, it renders large standing armies unnecessary—an argument that Alexander Hamilton made in favor of federal control over the militia. Third, when the able-bodied men of a nation are trained in arms and organized, they are better able to resist tyranny.

3.   Relationship Between Prefatory Clause and Operative Clause

We reach the question, then: Does the preface fit with an operative clause that creates an individual right to keep and bear arms? It fits perfectly, once one knows the history that the founding generation knew and that we have described above. That history showed that the way tyrants had eliminated a militia consisting of all the able-bodied men was not by banning the militia but simply by taking away the people's arms, enabling a select militia or standing army to suppress political opponents. This is what had occurred in England that prompted codification of the right to have arms in the English Bill of Rights. . . . During the 1788 ratification debates, the fear that the federal government would disarm the people in order to impose rule through a standing army or select militia was pervasive in Antifederalist rhetoric. . . . It is therefore entirely sensible that the Second Amendment's prefatory clause announces the purpose for which the right was codified: to prevent elimination of the militia. The prefatory clause does not suggest that preserving the militia was the only reason Americans valued the ancient right; most undoubtedly thought it even more important for self-defense and hunting. But the threat that the new Federal Government would destroy the citizens' militia by taking away their arms was the reason that right—unlike some other English rights—was codified in a written Constitution. . . .

Our interpretation is confirmed by analogous arms-bearing rights in state constitutions that preceded and immediately followed adoption of the Second Amendment. Four States adopted analogues to the Federal Second Amendment in the period between independence and the ratification of the Bill of Rights. Two of them—Pennsylvania and Vermont—clearly adopted individual rights unconnected to militia service. [The North Carolina and Massachusetts provisions protected the right to bear arms "for the defence of the State" and "for the common defence," but these provisions were interpreted by the courts of those states as not being limited to militia service.] We therefore believe that the most likely reading of all four of these pre–Second Amendment state constitutional provisions is that they secured an individual right to bear arms for defensive purposes.

Between 1789 and 1820, nine States adopted Second Amendment analogues. Four of them—Kentucky, Ohio, Indiana, and Missouri—referred to the right of the people to "bear arms in defence of themselves and the State." Another three States—Mississippi, Connecticut, and Alabama—used the even more individualistic phrasing that each citizen has the "right to bear arms in defence of himself and the State." Finally, two States—Tennessee and Maine—used the "common defence" language of Massachusetts. That of the nine state constitutional protections for the right to bear arms enacted immediately after 1789 at least seven unequivocally protected an individual citizen's right to self-defense is strong evidence that that is how the founding generation conceived of the right. And with one possible exception . . . , 19th-century courts and commentators interpreted these state constitutional provisions to protect an individual right to use arms for self-defense. . . .

We now address how the Second Amendment was interpreted from immediately after its ratification through the end of the 19th century.

1. Post-Ratification Commentary

Three important founding-era legal scholars interpreted the Second Amendment in published writings. All three understood it to protect an individual right unconnected with militia service. St. George Tucker's version of Blackstone's Commentaries . . . conceived of the Blackstonian arms right as necessary for self-defense. . . . William Rawle, a prominent lawyer who had been a member of the Pennsylvania Assembly that ratified the Bill of Rights . . . , analyzed the Second Amendment as [denying to any government any] "power to disarm the people." . . . Rawle clearly differentiated between the people's right to bear arms and their service in a militia: "In a people permitted and accustomed to bear arms, we have the rudiments of a militia. . . ." Joseph Story published his famous Commentaries on the Constitution of the United States in 1833. . . . Story explained that the English Bill of Rights had also included a "right to bear arms," a right that . . . had nothing to do with militia service. He then equated the English right with the Second Amendment. . . . As the Tennessee Supreme Court recognized 38 years after Story wrote his Commentaries, . . . "Story shows clearly that this right was intended . . . and was guaranteed to, and to be exercised and enjoyed by the citizen as such, and not by him as a soldier, or in defense solely of his political rights." Andrews v. State, 50 Tenn. 165, 183 (1871). Story's Commentaries also cite as support Tucker and Rawle, both of whom clearly viewed the right as unconnected to militia service. . . .

2. Pre–Civil War Case Law

The 19th-century cases that interpreted the Second Amendment universally support an individual right unconnected to militia service. . . . In the famous fugitive-slave case of Johnson v. Tompkins, 13 F. Cas. 840, 850, 852 (CC Pa. 1833), [Justice] Baldwin, sitting as a circuit judge, cited both the Second Amendment and the Pennsylvania analogue for his conclusion that a citizen has "a right to carry arms in defence of his property or person, and to use them, if either were assailed with such force, numbers or violence as made it necessary for the protection or safety of either."

Many early 19th-century state cases indicated that the Second Amendment right to bear arms was an individual right unconnected to militia service, though subject to certain restrictions. . . . An 1829 decision by the Supreme Court of Michigan said: "The constitution of the United States also grants to the citizen the right to keep and bear arms. But the grant of this privilege cannot be construed into the right in him who keeps a gun to destroy his neighbor. No rights are intended to be granted by the constitution for an unlawful or unjustifiable purpose." It is not possible to read this as discussing anything other than an individual right unconnected to militia service. If it did have to do with militia service, the limitation upon it would not be any "unlawful or unjustifiable purpose," but any nonmilitary purpose whatsoever. In Nunn v. State, 1 Ga. 243,

251 (1846), the Georgia Supreme Court construed the Second Amendment as protecting the "*natural* right of self-defence" and therefore struck down a ban on carrying pistols openly. Its opinion perfectly captured the way in which the operative clause of the Second Amendment furthers the purpose announced in the prefatory clause, in continuity with the English right:

> The right of the whole people, old and young, men, women and boys, and not militia only, to keep and bear *arms* of every description, and not *such* merely as are used by the *militia,* shall not be *infringed,* curtailed, or broken in upon, in the smallest degree; and all this for the important end to be attained: the rearing up and qualifying a well-regulated militia, so vitally necessary to the security of a free State.

Those who believe that the Second Amendment preserves only a militia-centered right place great reliance on the Tennessee Supreme Court's 1840 decision in Aymette v. State, 21 Tenn. 154. The case does not stand for that broad proposition; . . . *Aymette* held that the state constitutional guarantee of the right to "bear" arms did not prohibit the banning of concealed weapons. . . . More importantly, seven years earlier the Tennessee Supreme Court had treated the state constitutional provision as conferring a right "of all the free citizens of the State to keep and bear arms for their defence," and 21 years later the court held that the "keep" portion of the state constitutional right included the right to personal self-defense. . . .

3. Post–Civil War Legislation

In the aftermath of the Civil War, there was an outpouring of discussion of the Second Amendment in Congress and in public discourse, as people debated whether and how to secure constitutional rights for newly free slaves. Since those discussions took place 75 years after the ratification of the Second Amendment, they do not provide as much insight into its original meaning as earlier sources. Yet those born and educated in the early 19th century faced a widespread effort to limit arms ownership by a large number of citizens; their understanding of the origins and continuing significance of the Amendment is instructive.

Blacks were routinely disarmed by Southern States after the Civil War. Those who opposed these injustices frequently stated that they infringed blacks' constitutional right to keep and bear arms. Needless to say, the claim was not that blacks were being prohibited from carrying arms in an organized state militia. . . . The understanding that the Second Amendment gave freed blacks the right to keep and bear arms was reflected in congressional discussion of the [Freedmen's Bureau Act]. Similar discussion attended the passage of the Civil Rights Act of 1871 and the Fourteenth Amendment. For example, Representative Butler said [that the] Act "is intended to enforce the well-known constitutional provision guaranteeing the right of the citizen to 'keep and bear arms.' . . ." With respect to the proposed Amendment, Senator Pomeroy described as one of the three "indispensable" "safeguards of liberty . . . under the Constitution" a man's "right to bear arms for the defense of himself and family and his homestead."

Representative Nye thought the Fourteenth Amendment unnecessary because "[a]s citizens of the United States [blacks] have equal right to protection, and to keep and bear arms for self-defense."

It was plainly the understanding in the post–Civil War Congress that the Second Amendment protected an individual right to use arms for self-defense.

4. Post–Civil War Commentators

Every late-19th-century legal scholar that we have read interpreted the Second Amendment to secure an individual right unconnected with militia service. The most famous was the judge and professor Thomas Cooley. . . . The Second Amendment, he said, "was adopted with some modification and enlargement from the English Bill of Rights of 1688, where it stood as a protest against arbitrary action of the overturned dynasty in disarming the people. . . . It might be supposed . . . that the right to keep and bear arms was only guaranteed to the militia; but this would be an interpretation not warranted by the intent. . . . The meaning of the provision . . . is, that the people, from whom the militia must be taken, shall have the right to keep and bear arms; and they need no permission or regulation of law for the purpose. . . ." All other post–Civil War 19th-century sources we have found concurred with Cooley.

We now ask whether any of our precedents forecloses the conclusions we have reached about the meaning of the Second Amendment.

United States v. Cruikshank . . . held that the Second Amendment does not by its own force apply to anyone other than the Federal Government. . . . We described the right protected by the Second Amendment as " 'bearing arms for a lawful purpose.' "

Presser v. Illinois, 116 U.S. 252 (1886), held that the right to keep and bear arms was not violated by a law that forbade "bodies of men to associate together as military organizations, or to drill or parade with arms in cities and towns unless authorized by law." This does not refute the individual-rights interpretation of the Amendment; no one supporting that interpretation has contended that States may not ban such groups.

Justice Stevens places overwhelming reliance upon this Court's decision in United States v. Miller, 307 U.S. 174 (1939). [He contends that *Miller* held that] the Second Amendment "protects the right to keep and bear arms for certain military purposes, but that it does not curtail the legislature's power to regulate the nonmilitary use and ownership of weapons." . . . *Miller* did not hold that and cannot possibly be read to have held that. The judgment in the case upheld against a Second Amendment challenge two men's federal convictions for transporting an unregistered short-barreled shotgun in interstate commerce, in violation of the National Firearms Act. It is entirely clear that the Court's basis for saying that the Second Amendment did not apply was . . . that the *type of weapon at issue* was not eligible for Second Amendment protection: "In the absence of any evidence tending to show that the possession or use of a [short-barreled shotgun] at this time has some reasonable relationship to the preservation or efficiency of a well regulated militia, we cannot say that the Second Amendment guarantees the right to keep and bear *such an instrument*." . . . This holding is not only consistent with, but positively suggests, that the Second Amendment confers an individual right to keep and bear arms (though only arms that "have some reasonable relationship to the preservation or efficiency of a well regulated militia"). Had the Court believed that the Second Amendment protects only those serving in the militia, it would have been odd to examine the character of the weapon rather than simply note that the two crooks were not militiamen. . . . *Miller* stands only for the proposition that the Second Amendment right, whatever its nature, extends only to certain types of weapons.

It is particularly wrongheaded to read *Miller* for more than what it said, because the case did not even purport to be a thorough examination of the Second Amendment. . . . The respondent made no appearance in the case, neither filing a brief nor appearing at oral argument; the Court heard from no one but the Government (reason enough, one would think, not to make that case the beginning and the end of this Court's consideration of the Second Amendment). The Government's brief spent two pages discussing English legal sources, concluding "that at least the carrying of weapons without lawful occasion or excuse was always a crime." . . . It then went on to rely primarily on the discussion of the English right to bear arms in *Aymette* for the proposition that the only uses of arms protected by the Second Amendment are those that relate to the militia, not self-defense. The final section of the brief recognized that "some courts have said that the right to bear arms includes the right of the individual to have them for the protection of his person and property," and launched an alternative argument that "weapons which are commonly used by criminals," such as sawed-off shotguns, are not protected. The Government's *Miller* brief thus provided scant discussion of the history of the Second Amendment—and the Court was presented with no counterdiscussion. [The] Court's opinion . . . discusses *none* of the history of the Second Amendment. . . . Not a word (*not a word*) about the history of the Second Amendment. This is the mighty rock upon which the dissent rests its case.

We may as well consider at this point . . . *what* types of weapons *Miller* permits. [To permit] "ordinary military equipment" . . . would be a startling reading of the opinion, since it would mean that the National Firearms Act's restrictions on machineguns (not challenged in *Miller*) might be unconstitutional, machineguns being useful in warfare in 1939. We think that *Miller*'s "ordinary military equipment" language must be read in tandem with what comes after: "[When] called for [militia] service [able-bodied] men were expected to appear bearing arms supplied by themselves and of the kind in common use at the time." The traditional militia was formed from a pool of men bringing arms "in common use at the time" for lawful purposes like self-defense. . . . *Miller* [says] only that the Second Amendment does not protect those weapons not typically possessed by law-abiding citizens for lawful purposes, such as short-barreled shotguns. That accords with the historical understanding of the scope of the right.

We conclude that nothing in our precedents forecloses our adoption of the original understanding of the Second Amendment. It should be unsurprising that such a significant matter has been for so long judicially unresolved. For most of our history, the Bill of Rights was not thought applicable to the States, and the Federal Government did not significantly regulate the possession of firearms by law-abiding citizens. . . .

III. Like most rights, the right secured by the Second Amendment is not unlimited. . . . [N]othing in our opinion should be taken to cast doubt on longstanding prohibitions on the possession of firearms by felons and the mentally ill, or laws forbidding the carrying of firearms in sensitive places such as schools and government buildings, or laws imposing conditions and qualifications on the commercial sale of arms. We also recognize another important limitation on the right to keep and carry arms. *Miller* said . . . that the sorts of weapons protected were those "in common use at the time." We think that limitation is fairly supported by the historical tradition of prohibiting the carrying of "dangerous and unusual weapons." It may be objected that if weapons that are most useful in military service—M-16 rifles and the like—may be banned, then the Second Amendment right is completely detached from the prefatory clause. . . . It may well be true today that a militia, to be as effective as militias in the 18th century, would require sophisticated arms that are highly unusual in society at large. . . . But the fact that modern developments have limited the degree of fit between the prefatory clause and the protected right cannot change our interpretation of the right.

IV. We turn finally to the law at issue here. As we have said, the law totally bans handgun possession in the home. It also requires that any lawful firearm in the home be disassembled or bound by a trigger lock at all times, rendering it inoperable. [T]he inherent right of self-defense has been central to the Second Amendment right. The handgun ban amounts to a prohibition of an entire class of "arms" that is overwhelmingly chosen by American society for that lawful purpose. The prohibition extends, moreover, to the home, where the need for defense of self, family, and property is most acute. Under any of the standards of scrutiny that we have applied to enumerated constitutional rights,[1] banning from the home "the most preferred firearm in the nation to 'keep' and use for protection of one's home and family," would fail constitutional muster. . . . It is no answer to say . . . that it is permissible to ban the possession of handguns so long as the possession of other firearms (*i.e.*, long guns) is allowed. It is enough to note . . . that the American people have considered the handgun to be the quintessential self-defense weapon. There are many reasons that a citizen may prefer a handgun for home defense: It is easier to store in a location that is readily accessible in an emergency; it cannot easily be redirected or wrestled away by an attacker; it is easier to use for those

---

1. Justice Breyer correctly notes that this law, like almost all laws, would pass rational-basis scrutiny. But rational-basis scrutiny . . . could not be used to evaluate the extent to which a legislature may regulate a specific, enumerated right, be it the freedom of speech, the guarantee against double jeopardy, the right to counsel, or the right to keep and bear arms. See United States v. Carolene Products Co., 304 U.S. 144, 152, n.4 (1938) ("There may be narrower scope for operation of the presumption of constitutionality [i.e., narrower than that provided by rational-basis review] when legislation appears on its face to be within a specific prohibition of the Constitution, such as those of the first ten amendments . . ."). If all that was required to overcome the right to keep and bear arms was a rational basis, the Second Amendment would . . . have no effect.

without the upper-body strength to lift and aim a long gun; it can be pointed at a burglar with one hand while the other hand dials the police. Whatever the reason, handguns are the most popular weapon chosen by Americans for self-defense in the home, and a complete prohibition of their use is invalid. [T]he District's requirement . . . that firearms in the home be rendered and kept inoperable at all times . . . makes it impossible for citizens to use them for the core lawful purpose of self-defense and is hence unconstitutional. . . . We . . . assume that [the District's] issuance of a license [to possess a handgun] will satisfy [Heller's] prayer for relief and do not address the licensing requirement. . . .

Justice Breyer . . . proposes . . . a judge-empowering "interest-balancing inquiry" that "asks whether the statute burdens a protected interest in a way or to an extent that is out of proportion to the statute's salutary effects upon other important governmental interests." After an exhaustive discussion of the arguments for and against gun control, Justice Breyer arrives at his interest-balanced answer: because handgun violence is a problem, because the law is limited to an urban area, . . . the interest-balancing inquiry results in the constitutionality of the handgun ban. QED. We know of no other enumerated constitutional right whose core protection has been subjected to a freestanding "interest-balancing" approach. The very enumeration of the right takes out of the hands of government—even the Third Branch of Government—the power to decide on a case-by-case basis whether the right is *really worth* insisting upon. A constitutional guarantee subject to future judges' assessments of its usefulness is no constitutional guarantee at all. . . . We would not apply an "interest-balancing" approach to the prohibition of a peaceful neo-Nazi march through Skokie. See National Socialist Party of America v. Skokie, 432 U.S. 43 (1977). The First Amendment contains the freedom-of-speech guarantee that the people ratified, which included exceptions for obscenity, libel, and disclosure of state secrets, but not for the expression of extremely unpopular and wrongheaded views. The Second Amendment is no different. Like the First, it is the very *product* of an interest-balancing by the people—which Justice Breyer would now conduct for them anew.

[S]ince this case [is] this Court's first in-depth examination of the Second Amendment, one should not expect it to clarify the entire field. . . . [T]he District's ban on handgun possession in the home violates the Second Amendment, as does its prohibition against rendering any lawful firearm in the home operable for the purpose of immediate self-defense. Assuming that Heller is not disqualified from the exercise of Second Amendment rights, the District must permit him to register his handgun and must issue him a license to carry it in the home. . . .

We are aware of the problem of handgun violence in this country, and we take seriously the concerns raised by the many *amici* who believe that prohibition of handgun ownership is a solution. The Constitution leaves the District of Columbia a variety of tools for combating that problem, including some measures regulating handguns. But the enshrinement of constitutional rights necessarily takes certain policy choices off the table. These include the absolute prohibition of handguns held and used for self-defense in the home.

Undoubtedly some think that the Second Amendment is outmoded in a society where our standing army is the pride of our Nation, where well-trained police forces provide personal security, and where gun violence is a serious problem. That is perhaps debatable, but what is not debatable is that it is not the role of this Court to pronounce the Second Amendment extinct. We affirm the judgment of the Court of Appeals.

JUSTICE STEVENS, joined by JUSTICES SOUTER, GINSBURG, and BREYER, dissenting.

. . . Whether [the Second Amendment] protects the right to possess and use guns for nonmilitary purposes like hunting and personal self-defense is the question presented. . . . The Second Amendment was adopted to protect the right of the people of each of the several States to maintain a well-regulated militia. It was a response to concerns raised during the ratification of the Constitution that the power of Congress to disarm the state militias and create a national standing army posed an intolerable threat to the sovereignty of the several States. Neither the text of the Amendment nor the arguments advanced by its proponents evidenced the slightest interest in limiting any legislature's authority to regulate private civilian uses of firearms. Specifically, there is no indication that the Framers of the Amendment intended to enshrine the common-law right of self-defense in the Constitution. . . . The view of the Amendment we took in *Miller*—that it protects the right to keep and bear arms for certain military purposes, but that it does not curtail the Legislature's power to regulate the nonmilitary use and ownership of weapons—is both the most natural reading of the Amendment's text and the interpretation most faithful to the history of its adoption. Since our decision in *Miller*, hundreds of judges have relied on the view of the Amendment we endorsed there. . . .

[The words "keep and bear Arms"] describe a unitary right: to possess arms if needed for military purposes and to use them in conjunction with military activities. . . . The term "bear arms" is a familiar idiom; when used unadorned by any additional words, its meaning is "to serve as a soldier, do military service, fight." 1 Oxford English Dictionary 634 (2d ed. 1989). . . . Had the Framers wished to expand the meaning of the phrase "bear arms" to encompass civilian possession and use, they could have done so by the addition of phrases such as "for the defense of themselves," as was done in the Pennsylvania and Vermont Declarations of Rights. . . . The proper allocation of military power in the new Nation was an issue of central concern for the Framers. . . . "On the one hand, there was a widespread fear that a national standing Army posed an intolerable threat to individual liberty and to the sovereignty of the separate States." . . . On the other hand, the Framers recognized the dangers inherent in relying on inadequately trained militia members "as the primary means of providing for the common defense." In order to respond to those twin concerns, a compromise was reached: Congress would be authorized to raise and support a national Army and Navy, and also to organize, arm, discipline, and provide for the calling forth of "the Militia." . . . But [this] did not prove sufficient to allay fears about the dangers posed by a standing army. For it was perceived by some that [while] Article I . . . empowered Congress to organize, arm, and discipline the militia, it did not prevent Congress from providing for the militia's *dis*armament. As George Mason argued during the debates in Virginia on the ratification of the original Constitution: "The militia may be here destroyed by that method which has been practiced in other parts of the world before; that is, by rendering them useless—by disarming them. . . ."

Although it gives short shrift to the drafting history of the Second Amendment, the Court dwells at length on four other sources: the 17th-century English Bill of Rights; Blackstone's Commentaries on the Laws of England; postenactment commentary on the Second Amendment; and post–Civil War legislative history. All of these sources shed only indirect light on the question before us, and in any event offer little support for the Court's conclusion. . . . The Court's reliance on Article VII of the 1689 English Bill of Rights . . . is misguided both because Article VII was enacted in response to different concerns from those that motivated the Framers of the Second Amendment, and because the guarantees of the two provisions were by no means coextensive. . . . The English Bill of Rights . . . did not establish a general right of all persons, or even of all Protestants, to possess weapons. Rather, the right was qualified in two distinct ways: First, it was restricted to those of adequate social and economic status ("suitable to their Condition"); second, it was only available subject to regulation by Parliament ("as allowed by Law"). [T]hat right—adopted in a different historical and political context and framed in markedly different language—tells us little about the meaning of the Second Amendment. The Court's reliance on Blackstone's Commentaries . . . is unpersuasive for the same reason as its reliance on the English Bill of Rights. Blackstone's invocation of "the natural right of resistance and self-preservation," and "the right of having and using arms for self-preservation and defence" referred specifically to Article VII in the English Bill of Rights. . . .

The [first federal Militia Act] commanded every able-bodied white male citizen between the ages of 18 and 45 to be enrolled therein and to "provide himself with a good musket or firelock" and other specified weaponry. The statute is significant, for it confirmed the way those in the founding generation viewed firearm ownership: as a duty linked to military service. . . . The post-ratification history of the Second Amendment is strikingly similar. The Amendment played little role in any legislative debate about the civilian use of firearms for most of the 19th century, and it made few appearances in the decisions of this Court. . . . [T]he *Miller* Court unanimously concluded that the Second Amendment did not apply to the possession of a firearm that did not have "some reasonable relationship to the preservation or efficiency of a well regulated militia." [*Miller*] did not . . . turn on the difference between muskets and sawed-off shotguns; it turned, rather, on the basic difference between the military and nonmilitary use and possession of guns. . . . If use for self-defense were the relevant standard, why did the Court not inquire into the suitability of a particular weapon for self-defense purposes? . . .

Until today, it has been understood that legislatures may regulate the civilian use and misuse of firearms so long as they do not interfere with the preservation of a well-regulated militia. The Court's announcement of a new constitutional right to own and use firearms for private purposes upsets that settled understanding, but leaves for future cases the formidable task of defining the scope of permissible regulations. . . .

JUSTICE BREYER, joined by JUSTICES STEVENS, SOUTER, and GINSBURG, dissenting.

. . . The majority's conclusion is wrong [because] the Second Amendment protects militia-related, not self-defense-related, interests, [and because] the protection the Amendment provides is not absolute. [T]he District's law is consistent with the Second Amendment even if that Amendment is interpreted as protecting a wholly separate interest in individual self-defense . . . because the District's regulation, which focuses upon the presence of handguns in high-crime urban areas, represents a permissible legislative response to a serious, indeed life-threatening, problem. [A] legislature could reasonably conclude that the law will advance goals of great public importance, namely, saving lives, preventing injury, and reducing crime. The law is tailored to the urban crime problem in that it is local in scope and thus affects only a geographic area both limited in size and entirely urban; the law concerns handguns, which are specially linked to urban gun deaths and injuries, and which are the overwhelmingly favorite weapon of armed criminals; and at the same time, the law imposes a burden upon gun owners that seems proportionately no greater than restrictions in existence at the time the Second Amendment was adopted. In these circumstances, the District's law falls within the zone that the Second Amendment leaves open to regulation by legislatures. . . .

How is a court to determine whether a particular firearm regulation . . . is consistent with the Second Amendment? What kind of constitutional standard should the court use? How high a protective hurdle does the Amendment erect? The question matters. The . . . District's law . . . would not be unconstitutional under . . . a "rational basis" standard. . . . The law at issue here, which in part seeks to prevent gun-related accidents, at least bears a "rational relationship" to that "legitimate" life-saving objective. [Heller] proposes that the Court adopt a "strict scrutiny" test [but] the majority implicitly, and appropriately, rejects that suggestion by broadly approving a set of laws—prohibitions on concealed weapons, forfeiture by criminals of the Second Amendment right, prohibitions on firearms in certain locales, and governmental regulation of commercial firearm sales—whose constitutionality under a strict scrutiny standard would be far from clear. Indeed, adoption of a true strict-scrutiny standard for evaluating gun regulations would be impossible . . . because almost every gun-control regulation will seek to advance [the compelling interest of] "a concern for the safety and indeed the lives of its citizens." . . .

Thus, any attempt *in theory* to apply strict scrutiny to gun regulations will *in practice* turn into an interest-balancing inquiry, with the interests protected by the Second Amendment on one side and the governmental public-safety concerns on the other, the only question being whether the regulation at issue impermissibly burdens the former in the course of advancing the latter. I would simply adopt such an interest-balancing inquiry explicitly. The fact that important interests lie on both sides of the constitutional equation suggests that review of gun-control regulation is not a context in which a court should effectively presume either constitutionality (as in rational-basis review) or unconstitutionality (as in strict scrutiny). Rather, "where a law significantly implicates competing constitutionally protected interests in complex ways," the Court generally asks whether the statute burdens a protected interest in a way or to an extent that is out of proportion to the statute's salutary effects upon other important governmental interests. Any answer would take account both of the statute's effects upon the competing interests and the existence of any clearly superior less restrictive alternative. . . . In applying this kind of standard the Court normally defers to a legislature's empirical judgment in matters where a legislature is likely to have greater expertise and greater institutional factfinding capacity. . . .

I next assess the extent to which the District's law burdens the interests that the Second Amendment seeks to protect[:] (1) the preservation of a "well regulated Militia"; (2) safeguarding the use of firearms for sporting purposes, *e.g.*, hunting and marksmanship; and (3) assuring the use of firearms for self-defense. . . . The District's statute burdens the Amendment's first and primary objective hardly at all. [In] enacting the present provisions, the District sought "to take nothing away from sportsmen." [Any] inability of District residents to hunt near where they live has much to do with the jurisdiction's exclusively urban character and little to do with the District's firearm laws. . . . The District's law does prevent a resident from keeping a loaded handgun in his home[, which] makes it more difficult for the householder to use the handgun for self-defense in the home against intruders, such as burglars. . . .

In weighing needs and burdens, we must take account of the possibility that there are reasonable, but less restrictive alternatives. . . . The reason there is no clearly superior, less restrictive alternative to the District's handgun ban is that the ban's very objective is to reduce significantly the number of handguns in the District . . . by allowing a law enforcement officer immediately to assume that *any* handgun he sees is an *illegal* handgun. And there is no plausible way to achieve that objective other than to ban the guns. [T]he very attributes that make handguns particularly useful for self-defense are also what make them particularly dangerous. That they are easy to hold and control means that they are easier for children to use. That they are maneuverable and permit a free hand likely contributes to the fact that they are by far the firearm of choice for crimes such as rape and robbery. That they are small and light makes them easy to steal and concealable. This symmetry suggests that any measure less restrictive in respect to the use of handguns for self-defense will, to that same extent, prove less effective in preventing the use of handguns for illicit purposes. . . .

The upshot is that the District's objectives are compelling; its predictive judgments as to its law's tendency to achieve those objectives are adequately supported; the law does impose a burden upon any self-defense interest that the Amendment seeks to secure; and there is no clear less restrictive alternative. . . . Does the District's law *disproportionately* burden Amendment-protected interests? Several considerations, taken together, convince me that it does not. First, the District law is tailored to the life-threatening problems it attempts to address. The law concerns one class of weapons, handguns, [and the] area that falls within its scope is totally urban. . . . Second, the self-defense interest in maintaining loaded handguns in the home to shoot intruders is not the *primary* interest, but at most a subsidiary interest, that the Second Amendment seeks to serve. . . . Further, any self-defense interest at the time of the Framing could not have focused exclusively upon urban-crime related dangers. . . . Nor [were] *handguns* in particular . . . central to the Framers' conception of the Second Amendment. . . . Third, . . . colonial law[s existed] that could have impeded a homeowner's ability to shoot a burglar. . . . Fourth, . . . today's decision will have unfortunate consequences. [It] will encourage legal challenges to gun regulation throughout the Nation. Because it says little about the standards used to evaluate regulatory decisions, it will leave the Nation without clear standards for resolving those challenges. And litigation over the course of many years, or the mere specter of such litigation, threatens to leave cities without effective protection against gun violence and accidents during that time. . . . In the majority's view, the Amendment . . . protects an interest in armed personal self-defense, [but] the majority does not tell us precisely what that interest is. [T]he majority says [the Second Amendment] "guarantee[s] the individual right to possess and carry weapons in case of confrontation" [but also] says that "we do not read the Second Amendment to permit citizens to carry arms for *any sort* of confrontation." . . . Nor is it at all clear to me how the majority decides *which* loaded "arms" a homeowner may keep. The majority says that that Amendment protects those weapons "typically possessed by law-abiding citizens for lawful purposes." This definition conveniently excludes machineguns, but permits handguns, which the majority describes as "the most popular weapon chosen by Americans for self-defense in the home." But what sense does this approach make? According to the majority's reasoning, if Congress and the States lift restrictions on the possession and use of machineguns, and people buy machineguns to protect their homes, the Court will have to reverse course and find that the Second Amendment *does*, in fact, protect the individual self-defense-related right to possess a machinegun. . . . I am similarly puzzled by the majority's list . . . of provisions that in its view would survive Second Amendment scrutiny. . . . Why these? . . . At the same time the majority ignores a more important question: [H]ow should [the Second Amendment] be applied to modern-day circumstances that they could not have anticipated? Assume . . . that the Framers did intend the Amendment to offer a degree of self-defense protection. Does that mean that the Framers also intended to guarantee a right to possess a loaded gun near swimming pools, parks, and playgrounds? That they would not have cared about the children who might pick up a loaded gun on their parents' bedside table? [A]nswering questions such as the questions in this case requires judgment—judicial judgment exercised within a framework for constitutional analysis that guides that judgment and which makes its exercise transparent. One cannot answer those questions by combining inconclusive historical research with judicial *ipse dixit*. [T]here simply is no untouchable constitutional right guaranteed by the Second Amendment to keep loaded handguns in the house in crime-ridden urban areas. . . . I conclude that the District's measure is a proportionate, not a disproportionate, response to the compelling concerns that led the District to adopt it. . . . I dissent.

NOTES

1. Methodologies. What is the dominant interpretive method used by each opinion? Are they each driven by a search for original meaning? Do they combine various interpretive methods? If so, which ones? If original meaning is the lodestar of interpretation, what explains the starkly different readings of that meaning? Perhaps the Founders were concerned about private arms possession *and* preservation of state militias as a bulwark against the threat of a federal standing army. Justice Scalia emphasized the first concern; Justice Stevens emphasized the latter concern. Would a better reading of original meaning have synthesized the two concerns?

Justice Breyer's opinion seems to be the least tethered to original meaning. What method does he use? Does Justice Breyer's approach differ from the method that a conscientious legislator would employ in considering firearms regulations? If so, how does it differ? If not, is that a serious flaw in his approach, or is it merely an attempt to bring transparency to the process of adjudicating constitutional cases?

2. Constitutional "Decision Rules." The Court rejects minimal scrutiny, or rational-basis scrutiny, as the appropriate standard for sifting valid firearms regulations from unconstitutional ones, but what decision rule does it adopt? Which of the following possibilities *should* the Court employ? Are there other possibilities?

a. Categorical balancing. In free speech, certain categories of speech are exiled from the protections of the First Amendment. In a reverse manner, should entire categories of gun regulations be determined to be valid per se? The Court suggests that prohibitions on gun possession by felons or the mentally ill may be valid, as would bans on carrying concealed weapons or any weapons in "sensitive places" such as schools or government buildings, and regulations on the commercial sale of weapons. Is this a promising direction? Why? Categorical balancing in the free speech area combines an understanding of what free speech was thought to encompass at the founding moment with an inquiry into the purposes of the free speech guarantee. How would such an approach work with respect to gun rights? To test this approach, apply it to the Court's suggested categories.

b. Tiered scrutiny. The Court's rejection of minimal scrutiny necessarily implies some form of heightened scrutiny. What should it be? Justice

Breyer used a version of intermediate scrutiny borrowed from free speech, but applied it with great deference to the legislative judgment. How, if at all, is that different from rational-basis scrutiny? Justice Breyer suggested that gun regulations always serve the compelling interest of public safety, and (at least in *Heller* itself) thought that D.C. had no less restrictive alternatives available to achieve its objectives. Did the majority apply strict scrutiny without saying so? If so, was the D.C. handgun ban defective because it failed to serve a compelling interest, or because it suffered from a lack of narrow tailoring?

c. Interest balancing. Justice Breyer's approach requires judges to assess the public purposes of gun regulations and whether those purposes impose a *disproportionate* impact on the protected right to keep and bear arms. How does one identify the requisite proportionality, or lack thereof? Is this approach a form of judicial *gestalt*? Or is it an honest and transparent statement of the necessity of judicial balancing of public and private interests? Given that judges are human and that the calculus involved is likely to be subjective, would this method be stable, or would the results vary with the judge? Is the result of Justice Breyer's method any different from that which would result from rejecting a claimed individual right to firearms possession?

d. Bounded right. The Court found an individual right to firearms possession, but suggested a number of limitations upon the right. Some people (e.g., felons and lunatics) are presumably barred from exercising the right. Some weapons (e.g., those that are not ordinarily used for private self-defense) are ineligible for exercise of the right. Some conditions on the exercise of the right (e.g., licensing and registration) are presumably permitted. Can a constitutional decision rule be crafted entirely by incremental bounding of the right? At some point, however bounded the right may be, it will conflict with governmental regulation. Is the right absolute within its bounded sphere? The Court disclaimed any absolute right, yet a sane, law-abiding adult who wishes to possess in his home a loaded pistol for self-defense appears to have an absolute right to do so.

3. Incorporation into the Fourteenth Amendment's Due Process Clause. In McDonald v. City of Chicago, 561 U.S. 742 (2010), the Supreme Court ruled that the Second Amendment right to possession of a firearm for purposes of self-defense was "fundamental to *our* scheme of ordered liberty" and "deeply rooted in this Nation's history and tradition." Thus, the Fourteenth Amendment made the Second Amendment right applicable to the states. But the justices could not agree on the rationale. Justice Alito, joined by Chief Justice Roberts and Justices Scalia and Kennedy, concluded that the Second Amendment right is one of the fundamental rights that are made applicable to the states via the due process guarantee.

> Self-defense is a basic right [and] individual self-defense is the "*central component*" of the Second Amendment right. [By] 1765 Blackstone was able to assert that the right to keep and bear arms was "one of the fundamental rights of Englishmen," [and his] assessment was shared by the American colonists. King George III's attempt to disarm the colonists in the 1760s and 1770s "provoked

polemical reactions by Americans invoking their rights as Englishmen to keep arms." . . . The right to keep and bear arms was considered no less fundamental by those who drafted and ratified the Bill of Rights. . . . This understanding persisted in the years immediately following the ratification of the Bill of Rights. By the 1850s . . . the right to keep and bear arms was highly valued for purposes of self-defense. . . . The 1864 Democratic Party Platform complained that the confiscation of firearms by Union troops occupying parts of the South constituted "[a] denial of the right of the people to bear arms in their defense." . . . [In] debating the Civil Rights Act of 1871, Congress routinely referred to the right to keep and bear arms and decried the continued disarmament of blacks in the South. Finally, legal commentators from the period emphasized the fundamental nature of the right. The right to keep and bear arms was also widely protected by state constitutions at the time when the Fourteenth Amendment was ratified. [It] is clear that the Framers and ratifiers of the Fourteenth Amendment counted the right to keep and bear arms among those fundamental rights necessary to our system of ordered liberty. . . .

Under our precedents, if a Bill of Rights guarantee is fundamental from an American perspective, then . . . that guarantee is fully binding on the States and thus *limits* (but by no means eliminates) their ability to devise solutions to social problems that suit local needs and values. . . . We therefore hold that the Due Process Clause of the Fourteenth Amendment incorporates the Second Amendment right recognized in *Heller*.

4.   Incorporation via the Fourteenth Amendment's Privileges and Immunities Clause.   Justice Thomas concurred in the judgment in *McDonald*, but contended that the Second Amendment right was a privilege of national citizenship encompassed in the Fourteenth Amendment's command that no state may "abridge the privileges or immunities of citizens of the United States."

By the time of Reconstruction, it had long been established that both the States and the Federal Government existed to preserve their citizens' inalienable rights, and that these rights were considered "privileges" or "immunities" of citizenship. . . . As English subjects, the colonists considered themselves to be vested with the same fundamental rights as other Englishmen. They consistently claimed the rights of English citizenship in their founding documents, repeatedly referring to these rights as "privileges" and "immunities." . . . Consistent with their English heritage, the founding generation generally did not consider many of the rights identified in [the Bill of Rights] as new entitlements, but as inalienable rights of all men, given legal effect by their codification in the Constitution's text. . . . Section 1 [of the Fourteenth Amendment] protects the rights of citizens "of the United States" specifically. The evidence overwhelmingly demonstrates that the privileges and immunities of such citizens included individual rights enumerated in the Constitution, including the right to keep and bear arms. . . . Evidence from the political branches in the years leading to the Fourteenth Amendment's adoption demonstrates broad public understanding that the privileges and immunities of United States citizenship included rights set forth in the Constitution. . . . Records from the 39th Congress further support this understanding. . . . When interpreting constitutional text, the goal is to discern the most likely public understanding of a particular provision at the time it was adopted. . . . [T]his evidence is useful not because it demonstrates what the draftsmen of the text may have been thinking, but only insofar as it illuminates what the public understood the words chosen by the draftsmen to mean.

Representative John Bingham, the principal draftsman of §1 [of the Fourteenth Amendment] emphasized that §1 was designed "to arm the Congress of the United States . . . with the power to enforce the bill of rights as it stands in the Constitution today." . . . Senator Jacob Howard introduced the new draft on the floor of the Senate, [explaining] that the Constitution recognized "a mass of privileges, immunities, and rights, some of them secured by . . . the first eight amendments of the Constitution," and that "there is no power given in the Constitution to enforce and to carry out any of these guarantees" against the States. Howard then stated that "the great object" of §1 was to "restrain the power of the States and compel them at all times to respect these great fundamental guarantees." Section 1, he indicated, imposed "a general prohibition upon all the States, as such, from abridging the privileges and immunities of the citizens of the United States," [including] *the personal rights guaranteed by the first eight amendments of the Constitution*; such as freedom of speech . . . and *the right to keep and bear arms.*" News of Howard's speech was carried in major newspapers across the country, including the New York Herald, which was the best-selling paper in the Nation at that time. . . . As a whole, these well-circulated speeches indicate that §1 was understood to enforce constitutionally declared rights against the States, and they provide no suggestion that any language in the section other than the Privileges or Immunities Clause would accomplish that task. . . .

[T]he ratifying public understood the Privileges or Immunities Clause to protect constitutionally enumerated rights, including the right to keep and bear arms. As the Court demonstrates, there can be no doubt that §1 was understood to enforce the Second Amendment against the States. In my view, this is because the right to keep and bear arms was understood to be a privilege of American citizenship guaranteed by the Privileges or Immunities Clause.

Table of Cases

Italics indicate principal cases.

Index